RUSSIA

KAZAKHSTAN

Lake Ladoga

St. Petersburg

Tallinn

LATVIA

Minsk

BELARUS

Moscow

Volga R.

Volga R.

Astana

Aral Sea

UZBEKISTAN

Kiev

Kharkov

Dnieper R.

UKRAINE

Dnepropetrovsk

Donetsk

Don R.

Caspian Sea

TURKMENISTAN

MOLDOVA

Chisinau

Odessa

Ashgabat

MANIA

Bucharest

Black Sea

GEORGIA

Tbilisi

Baku

Danube R.

ARMENIA

AZERBAIJAN

BULGARIA

Yerevan

Sofia

Istanbul

AZER.

IRAN

Ankara

Tehran

TURKEY

Athens

SYRIA

Nicosia

Baghdad

CYPRUS

Beirut

IRAQ

LEBANON

Damascus

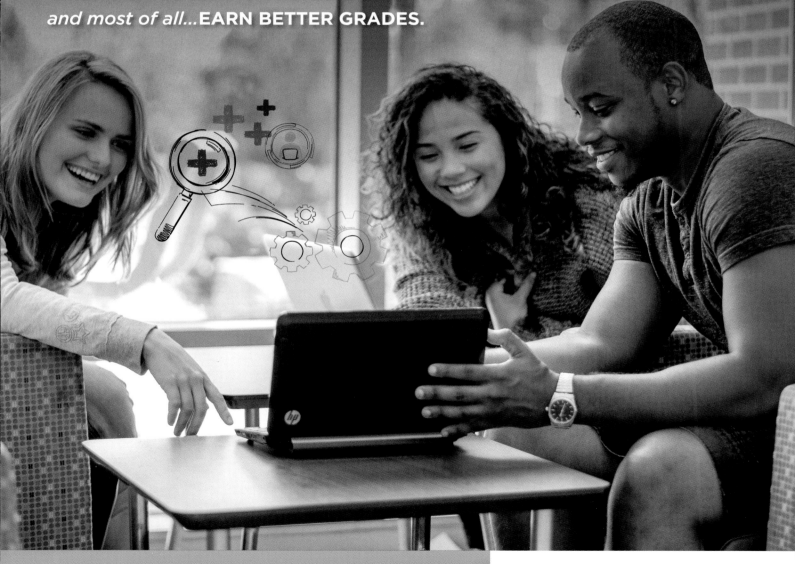

WESTERN CIVILIZATION

VOLUME II: SINCE 1500

Jackson J. Spielvogel

The Pennsylvania State University

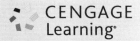

CENGAGE
Learning·

Australia • Brazil • Mexico • Singapore • United Kingdom • United States

**Western Civilization, Tenth Edition,
Volume II: Since 1500**
Jackson J. Spielvogel

Product Director: Paul Banks

Product Manager: Scott Greenan

Senior Content Developer: Margaret Beasley

Associate Content Developer: Andrew Newton

Product Assistant: Emma Guiton

Media Developer: Kate McLean

Senior Marketing Manager: Valerie Hartman

Senior Content Project Manager:
    Carol Newman

Senior Art Director: Cate Rickard Barr

Manufacturing Planner: Fola Orekoya

IP Analyst: Betsy Hathaway

IP Project Manager: Alex Ricciardi

Production Service/Compositor:
    Thistle Hill Publishing Services/
    Cenveo® Publisher Services

Text and Cover Designer: Deborah Dutton/
    Dutton & Sherman Design

Cover Image: Commoner writing while seated
    at kitchen table, 1840. DEA/G. Dagli Orti/
    Getty Images

For product information and technology assistance, contact us at
Cengage Learning Customer & Sales Support, 1-800-354-9706

For permission to use material from this text or product,
submit all requests online at **www.cengage.com/permissions**.
Further permissions questions can be emailed to
permissionrequest@cengage.com.

Library of Congress Control Number: 2016945331

Student Edition:
ISBN: 978-1-305-95280-5

Loose-leaf Edition:
ISBN: 978-1-305-95318-5

Cengage Learning
20 Channel Center Street
Boston, MA 02210
USA

Cengage Learning is a leading provider of customized learning solutions
with employees residing in nearly 40 different countries and sales in
more than 125 countries around the world. Find your local representative at
www.cengage.com.

Cengage Learning products are represented in Canada by Nelson
Education, Ltd.

To learn more about Cengage Learning Solutions, visit **www.cengage.com**.

Purchase any of our products at your local college store or at our preferred
online store **www.cengagebrain.com**.

Printed in the United States of America
Print Number: 01   Print Year: 2016

ABOUT THE AUTHOR

JACKSON J. SPIELVOGEL is associate professor emeritus of history at The Pennsylvania State University. He received his Ph.D. from The Ohio State University, where he specialized in Reformation history under Harold J. Grimm. His articles and reviews have appeared in such journals as *Moreana*, *Journal of General Education*, *Catholic Historical Review*, *Archiv für Reformationsgeschichte*, and *American Historical Review*. He has also contributed chapters or articles to *The Social History of the Reformation*, *The Holy Roman Empire: A Dictionary Handbook*, the *Simon Wiesenthal Center Annual of Holocaust Studies*, and *Utopian Studies*. His work has been supported by fellowships from the Fulbright Foundation and the Foundation for Reformation Research. At Penn State, he helped inaugurate the Western civilization courses as well as a popular course on Nazi Germany. His book *Hitler and Nazi Germany* was published in 1987 (seventh edition, 2014). He is the coauthor (with William Duiker) of *World History*, first published in 1998 (eighth edition, 2016), and *The Essential World History* (eighth edition, 2017). Professor Spielvogel has won five major university-wide teaching awards. In 1988–1989, he held the Penn State Teaching Fellowship, the university's most prestigious teaching award. He won the Dean Arthur Ray Warnock Award for Outstanding Faculty Member in 1996 and the Schreyer Honors College Excellence in Teaching Award in 2000.

TO DIANE,
WHOSE LOVE AND SUPPORT MADE IT ALL POSSIBLE
J.J.S.

BRIEF CONTENTS

Documents   xiv

Maps   xix

Features   xx

Preface   xxi

Acknowledgments   xxv

Introduction to Students of Western Civilization   xxix

Western Civilization to 1500   xxxi

13 REFORMATION AND RELIGIOUS WARFARE IN THE SIXTEENTH CENTURY   365

14 EUROPE AND THE WORLD: NEW ENCOUNTERS, 1500–1800   399

15 STATE BUILDING AND THE SEARCH FOR ORDER IN THE SEVENTEENTH CENTURY   432

16 TOWARD A NEW HEAVEN AND A NEW EARTH: THE SCIENTIFIC REVOLUTION AND THE EMERGENCE OF MODERN SCIENCE   472

17 THE EIGHTEENTH CENTURY: AN AGE OF ENLIGHTENMENT   499

18 THE EIGHTEENTH CENTURY: EUROPEAN STATES, INTERNATIONAL WARS, AND SOCIAL CHANGE   528

19 A REVOLUTION IN POLITICS: THE ERA OF THE FRENCH REVOLUTION AND NAPOLEON   559

20 THE INDUSTRIAL REVOLUTION AND ITS IMPACT ON EUROPEAN SOCIETY   592

21 REACTION, REVOLUTION, AND ROMANTICISM, 1815–1850   620

22 AN AGE OF NATIONALISM AND REALISM, 1850–1871   653

23 MASS SOCIETY IN AN "AGE OF PROGRESS," 1871–1894   686

24 AN AGE OF MODERNITY, ANXIETY, AND IMPERIALISM, 1894–1914   719

25 THE BEGINNING OF THE TWENTIETH-CENTURY CRISIS: WAR AND REVOLUTION   757

26 THE FUTILE SEARCH FOR STABILITY: EUROPE BETWEEN THE WARS, 1919–1939   792

27 THE DEEPENING OF THE EUROPEAN CRISIS: WORLD WAR II   827

28 COLD WAR AND A NEW WESTERN WORLD, 1945–1965   863

29 PROTEST AND STAGNATION: THE WESTERN WORLD, 1965–1985   896

30 AFTER THE FALL: THE WESTERN WORLD IN A GLOBAL AGE (SINCE 1985)   920

Glossary   G-1

Index   I-1

CONTENTS

Documents   xiv

Maps   xix

Features   xx

Preface   xxi

Acknowledgments   xxv

Introduction to Students of Western Civilization   xxix

Western Civilization to 1500   xxxi

13 REFORMATION AND RELIGIOUS WARFARE IN THE SIXTEENTH CENTURY   365

Prelude to Reformation   366
    Christian or Northern Renaissance Humanism   366
    Church and Religion on the Eve of the Reformation   368

Martin Luther and the Reformation in Germany   369
    The Early Luther   369
    FILM & HISTORY
    Luther (2003)   372
    The Rise of Lutheranism   372
    Organizing the Church   373
    Germany and the Reformation: Religion and Politics   374

The Spread of the Protestant Reformation   377
    Lutheranism in Scandinavia   377
    The Zwinglian Reformation   377
    OPPOSING VIEWPOINTS
    A Reformation Debate: Conflict at Marburg   379
    The Radical Reformation: The Anabaptists   379
    The Reformation in England   380
    John Calvin and Calvinism   382

The Social Impact of the Protestant Reformation   383
    The Family   383
    Education in the Reformation   385
    Religious Practices and Popular Culture   386

The Catholic Reformation   386
    Catholic Reformation or Counter-Reformation?   386
    The Society of Jesus   387
    A Revived Papacy   389
    The Council of Trent   389

Politics and the Wars of Religion in the Sixteenth Century   390
    The French Wars of Religion (1562–1598)   390
    Philip II and Militant Catholicism   392
    Revolt of the Netherlands   393
    The England of Elizabeth   394
    FILM & HISTORY
    Elizabeth (1998)   396

CHAPTER SUMMARY • CHAPTER TIMELINE • CHAPTER REVIEW • KEY TERMS • SUGGESTIONS FOR FURTHER READING • NOTES   396

14 EUROPE AND THE WORLD: NEW ENCOUNTERS, 1500–1800   399

On the Brink of a New World   400
    The Motives for Expansion   400
    The Means for Expansion   402

New Horizons: The Portuguese and Spanish Empires   403
    The Development of a Portuguese Maritime Empire   403
    IMAGES OF EVERYDAY LIFE
    Spices and World Trade   405
    Voyages to the New World   406
    The Spanish Empire in the New World   407
    Disease in the New World   410

New Rivals on the World Stage   412
    Africa: The Slave Trade   412
    The West in Southeast Asia   415
    GLOBAL PERSPECTIVES
    West Meets East: An Exchange of Royal Letters   417
    The French and British in India   418
    China   419
    Japan   420
    The Americas   421

The Impact of European Expansion   423
    The Conquered   423
    FILM & HISTORY
    The Mission   424
    The Conquerors   425

Toward a World Economy   427
    Economic Conditions in the Sixteenth Century   427
    The Growth of Commercial Capitalism   427
    Mercantilism   428
    Overseas Trade and Colonies: Movement Toward Globalization   428

CHAPTER SUMMARY • CHAPTER TIMELINE • CHAPTER REVIEW • KEY TERMS • SUGGESTIONS FOR FURTHER READING • NOTES   429

15 STATE BUILDING AND THE SEARCH FOR ORDER IN THE SEVENTEENTH CENTURY   432

Social Crises, War, and Rebellions   433
    The Witchcraft Craze   433
    The Thirty Years' War   435

Was There a Military Revolution? 438
Rebellions 439

The Practice of Absolutism: Western Europe 440
Absolute Monarchy in France 440
The Reign of Louis XIV (1643–1715) 441
GLOBAL PERSPECTIVES
Sun Kings, West and East 442
The Decline of Spain 447

Absolutism in Central, Eastern, and Northern Europe 448
The German States 448
Italy: From Spanish to Austrian Rule 449
Russia: From Fledgling Principality to Major Power 450
The Great Northern States 453
The Ottoman Empire 453
The Limits of Absolutism 455

Limited Monarchy and Republics 455
The Weakness of the Polish Monarchy 455
The Golden Age of the Dutch Republic 456
IMAGES OF EVERYDAY LIFE
Dutch Domesticity 457
England and the Emergence of Constitutional Monarchy 458
OPPOSING VIEWPOINTS
Oliver Cromwell: Three Perspectives 460

The Flourishing of European Culture 464
The Changing Faces of Art 464
A Wondrous Age of Theater 466

CHAPTER SUMMARY • CHAPTER TIMELINE •
CHAPTER REVIEW • KEY TERMS • SUGGESTIONS
FOR FURTHER READING • NOTES 469

16 TOWARD A NEW HEAVEN AND A NEW EARTH: THE SCIENTIFIC REVOLUTION AND THE EMERGENCE OF MODERN SCIENCE 472

Background to the Scientific Revolution 473
Ancient Authors and Renaissance Artists 473
Technological Innovations and Mathematics 473
Renaissance Magic 474

Toward a New Heaven: A Revolution in Astronomy 474
Copernicus 475
Brahe 477
Kepler 477
Galileo 478
OPPOSING VIEWPOINTS
A New Heaven? Faith Versus Reason 481
Newton 482

Advances in Medicine and Chemistry 484
Paracelsus 484
Vesalius 485
William Harvey 485
Chemistry 486

Women in the Origins of Modern Science 486
Margaret Cavendish 486
Maria Merian 487
Maria Winkelmann 487
Debates on the Nature of Women 488

Toward a New Earth: Descartes, Rationalism, and a New View of Humankind 488

The Scientific Method and the Spread of Scientific Knowledge 490
The Scientific Method 490
The Spread of Scientific Knowledge 491
IMAGES OF EVERYDAY LIFE
The Science of Collecting 492
Science and Religion 493

CHAPTER SUMMARY • CHAPTER TIMELINE •
CHAPTER REVIEW • KEY TERMS • SUGGESTIONS
FOR FURTHER READING • NOTES 496

17 THE EIGHTEENTH CENTURY: AN AGE OF ENLIGHTENMENT 499

The Enlightenment 500
The Paths to Enlightenment 500
The Philosophes and Their Ideas 502
The Social Environment of the Philosophes 510

Culture and Society in the Enlightenment 510
OPPOSING VIEWPOINTS
Women in the Age of the Enlightenment: Rousseau and Wollstonecraft 511
IMAGES OF EVERYDAY LIFE
Women and the Enlightenment Salon 512
Innovations in Art, Music, and Literature 513
FILM & HISTORY
Amadeus 515
The High Culture of the Eighteenth Century 516
Crime and Punishment 518
The World of Medicine 518
Popular Culture 519
GLOBAL PERSPECTIVES
Popular Culture in the West and East 520

Religion and the Churches 521
The Institutional Church 521
Popular Religion in the Eighteenth Century 523

CHAPTER SUMMARY • CHAPTER TIMELINE •
CHAPTER REVIEW • KEY TERMS • SUGGESTIONS
FOR FURTHER READING • NOTES 525

18 THE EIGHTEENTH CENTURY: EUROPEAN STATES, INTERNATIONAL WARS, AND SOCIAL CHANGE 528

The European States 529
Enlightened Absolutism? 529
The Atlantic Seaboard States 529

FILM & HISTORY
Marie Antoinette (2006) 530
Absolutism in Central and Eastern Europe 532
OPPOSING VIEWPOINTS
Enlightened Absolutism: Enlightened or Absolute? 536
The Mediterranean World 538
The Scandinavian States 539
Enlightened Absolutism Revisited 539

Wars and Diplomacy 539
The War of the Austrian Succession (1740–1748) 540
The Seven Years' War (1756–1763) 540
European Armies and Warfare 542

Economic Expansion and Social Change 543
Growth of the European Population 543
Family, Marriage, and Birthrate Patterns 543
Was There an Agricultural Revolution? 546
New Methods of Finance 548
European Industry 548
Mercantile Empires and Worldwide Trade 549

The Social Order of the Eighteenth Century 550
The Peasants 551
The Nobility 551
IMAGES OF EVERYDAY LIFE
The Aristocratic Way of Life 553
The Inhabitants of Towns and Cities 554

CHAPTER SUMMARY • CHAPTER TIMELINE •
CHAPTER REVIEW • KEY TERMS • SUGGESTIONS
FOR FURTHER READING • NOTES 556

**19 A REVOLUTION IN POLITICS: THE
ERA OF THE FRENCH REVOLUTION
AND NAPOLEON 559**

*The Beginning of the Revolutionary Era: The American
Revolution* 560
The War for Independence 560
Forming a New Nation 560
Impact of the American Revolution on Europe 563

Background to the French Revolution 563
Social Structure of the Old Regime 563
Other Problems Facing the French Monarchy 565

The French Revolution 566
From Estates-General to a National Assembly 566
Destruction of the Old Regime 567
GLOBAL PERSPECTIVES
Revolution and Revolt in France and China 569
OPPOSING VIEWPOINTS
The Natural Rights of the French People: Two Views 570
The Radical Revolution 573
Reaction and the Directory 581

The Age of Napoleon 582
The Rise of Napoleon 582
The Domestic Policies of Emperor Napoleon 584

Napoleon's Empire and the European Response 586
The Fall of Napoleon 589

CHAPTER SUMMARY • CHAPTER TIMELINE •
CHAPTER REVIEW • KEY TERMS • SUGGESTIONS
FOR FURTHER READING • NOTES 589

**20 THE INDUSTRIAL REVOLUTION
AND ITS IMPACT ON EUROPEAN
SOCIETY 592**

The Industrial Revolution in Great Britain 593
Origins 593
Technological Changes and New Forms of Industrial
Organization 594
Britain's Great Exhibition of 1851 599

The Spread of Industrialization 601
Industrialization on the Continent 601
The Industrial Revolution in the United States 603
Limiting the Spread of Industrialization in the
Nonindustrialized World 604

The Social Impact of the Industrial Revolution 605
Population Growth 605
The Growth of Cities 607
IMAGES OF EVERYDAY LIFE
Living Conditions of London's Poor 608
New Social Classes: The Industrial Middle Class 609
GLOBAL PERSPECTIVES
Attitudes of the Industrial Middle Class in Britain
and Japan 610
New Social Classes: Workers in the Industrial Age 611
Efforts at Change: The Workers 615
Efforts at Change: Reformers and Government 616

CHAPTER SUMMARY • CHAPTER TIMELINE •
CHAPTER REVIEW • KEY TERMS • SUGGESTIONS
FOR FURTHER READING • NOTES 617

**21 REACTION, REVOLUTION, AND
ROMANTICISM, 1815–1850 620**

The Conservative Order (1815–1830) 621
The Peace Settlement 621
The Ideology of Conservatism 622
Conservative Domination: The Concert of Europe 623
Conservative Domination: The European States 627

The Ideologies of Change 630
Liberalism 630
Nationalism 632
Early Socialism 632

Revolution and Reform (1830–1850) 634
Another French Revolution 634
Revolutionary Outbursts in Belgium, Poland, and Italy 635
Reform in Great Britain 635
OPPOSING VIEWPOINTS
Response to Revolution: Two Perspectives 636
The Revolutions of 1848 637

IMAGES OF EVERYDAY LIFE
Political Cartoons: Attacks on the King   639
The Maturing of the United States   641

The Emergence of an Ordered Society   642
New Police Forces   642
Prison Reform   644

Culture in an Age of Reaction and Revolution: The Mood of Romanticism   645
The Characteristics of Romanticism   645
Romantic Poets   645
Romanticism in Art   646
Romanticism in Music   648
The Revival of Religion in the Age of Romanticism   649

CHAPTER SUMMARY • CHAPTER TIMELINE •
CHAPTER REVIEW • KEY TERMS • SUGGESTIONS
FOR FURTHER READING • NOTES   650

22 AN AGE OF NATIONALISM AND REALISM, 1850–1871   653

The France of Napoleon III   654
Louis Napoleon: Toward the Second Empire   654
The Second Napoleonic Empire   654
OPPOSING VIEWPOINTS
The Practice of *Realpolitik*: Two Approaches   655
Foreign Policy: The Mexican Adventure   656
Foreign Policy: The Crimean War   656

National Unification: Italy and Germany   658
The Unification of Italy   659
The Unification of Germany   661

Nation Building and Reform: The National State in Midcentury   665
The Austrian Empire: Toward a Dual Monarchy   666
Imperial Russia   666
Great Britain: The Victorian Age   669
FILM & HISTORY
The Young Victoria (2009)   669
The United States: Slavery and War   670
The Emergence of a Canadian Nation   671

Industrialization and the Marxist Response   672
Industrialization on the Continent   672
Marx and Marxism   673

Science and Culture in an Age of Realism   675
A New Age of Science   675
Charles Darwin and the Theory of Organic Evolution   676
A Revolution in Health Care   677
Science and the Study of Society   680
Realism in Literature   680
Realism in Art   680
Music: The Twilight of Romanticism   682

CHAPTER SUMMARY • CHAPTER TIMELINE •
CHAPTER REVIEW • KEY TERMS • SUGGESTIONS
FOR FURTHER READING • NOTES   683

23 MASS SOCIETY IN AN "AGE OF PROGRESS," 1871–1894   686

The Growth of Industrial Prosperity   687
New Products   687
New Markets   688
New Patterns in an Industrial Economy   689
GLOBAL PERSPECTIVES
East and West: Textile Factory Work   692
Women and Work: New Job Opportunities   692
Organizing the Working Classes   693

The Emergence of a Mass Society   697
Population Growth   697
Emigration   698
Transformation of the Urban Environment   698
Social Structure of the Mass Society   702
"The Woman Question": The Role of Women   703
OPPOSING VIEWPOINTS
Advice to Women: Two Views   704
IMAGES OF EVERYDAY LIFE
The Middle-Class Family   706
Education in the Mass Society   708
Mass Leisure   709
Mass Consumption   711

The National State   712
Western Europe: The Growth of Political Democracy   712
Central and Eastern Europe: Persistence of the Old Order   713

CHAPTER SUMMARY • CHAPTER TIMELINE •
CHAPTER REVIEW • KEY TERMS • SUGGESTIONS
FOR FURTHER READING • NOTES   716

24 AN AGE OF MODERNITY, ANXIETY, AND IMPERIALISM, 1894–1914   719

Toward the Modern Consciousness: Intellectual and Cultural Developments   720
Developments in the Sciences: The Emergence of a New Physics   720
Toward a New Understanding of the Irrational   721
Sigmund Freud and Psychoanalysis   722
The Impact of Darwin   722
The Attack on Christianity   724
The Culture of Modernity: Literature   725
Modernism in the Arts   725
GLOBAL PERSPECTIVES
Impressionist Painting: West and East   728
Modernism in Music   729

Politics: New Directions and New Uncertainties   731
The Movement for Women's Rights   731
IMAGES OF EVERYDAY LIFE
The Struggle for the Right to Vote   733
FILM & HISTORY
Suffragette (2015)   734

Jews in the European Nation-State 734

The Transformation of Liberalism: Great Britain
and Italy 735

France: Travails of the Third Republic 737

Growing Tensions in Germany 737

Austria-Hungary: The Problem of the Nationalities 738

Industrialization and Revolution in Imperial Russia 738

The Rise of the United States 739

The Growth of Canada 741

The New Imperialism 741

Causes of the New Imperialism 741

The Scramble for Africa 742

OPPOSING VIEWPOINTS
White Man's Burden Versus Black Man's
Burden 743

Imperialism in Asia 747

Responses to Imperialism 749

Results of the New Imperialism 751

International Rivalry and the Coming of War 751

The Bismarckian System 751

New Directions and New Crises 752

**CHAPTER SUMMARY • CHAPTER TIMELINE •
CHAPTER REVIEW • KEY TERMS • SUGGESTIONS
FOR FURTHER READING • NOTES** 754

**25 THE BEGINNING OF THE
TWENTIETH-CENTURY CRISIS:
WAR AND REVOLUTION** 757

The Road to World War I 758

Nationalism 758

Internal Dissent 758

Militarism 759

The Outbreak of War: The Summer of 1914 759

The War 762

1914–1915: Illusions and Stalemate 762

1916–1917: The Great Slaughter 765

FILM & HISTORY
Paths of Glory (1957) 768

IMAGES OF EVERYDAY LIFE
Life in the Trenches 769

The Widening of the War 770

GLOBAL PERSPECTIVES
Soldiers from Around the World 771

A New Kind of Warfare 771

The Home Front: The Impact of Total War 772

War and Revolution 777

The Russian Revolution 777

The Last Year of the War 783

Revolutionary Upheavals in Germany and
Austria-Hungary 784

The Peace Settlement 785

Peace Aims 785

OPPOSING VIEWPOINTS
Three Voices of Peacemaking 786

The Treaty of Versailles 786

The Other Peace Treaties 787

**CHAPTER SUMMARY • CHAPTER TIMELINE •
CHAPTER REVIEW • KEY TERMS • SUGGESTIONS
FOR FURTHER READING • NOTES** 790

**26 THE FUTILE SEARCH FOR
STABILITY: EUROPE BETWEEN
THE WARS, 1919–1939** 792

An Uncertain Peace 793

The Impact of World War I 793

The Search for Security 793

The Hopeful Years (1924–1929) 795

The Great Depression 796

The Democratic States in the West 798

Great Britain 798

France 798

The Scandinavian States 799

The United States 799

European States and the World: The Colonial Empires 799

The Authoritarian and Totalitarian States 801

The Retreat from Democracy: Did Europe Have
Totalitarian States? 801

Fascist Italy 802

Hitler and Nazi Germany 805

The Soviet Union 812

Authoritarianism in Eastern Europe 814

Dictatorship in the Iberian Peninsula 815

The Expansion of Mass Culture and Mass Leisure 817

Radio and Movies 818

FILM AND HISTORY
Triumph of the Will (1934) 819

Mass Leisure 819

Cultural and Intellectual Trends in the Interwar Years 819

Nightmares and New Visions: Art and Music 820

The Search for the Unconscious in Literature 822

The Unconscious in Psychology: Carl Jung 823

The "Heroic Age of Physics" 823

**CHAPTER SUMMARY • CHAPTER TIMELINE •
CHAPTER REVIEW • KEY TERMS • SUGGESTIONS
FOR FURTHER READING • NOTES** 824

**27 THE DEEPENING OF THE
EUROPEAN CRISIS: WORLD
WAR II** 827

Prelude to War (1933–1939) 828

The Role of Hitler 828

The "Diplomatic Revolution" (1933–1936) 828

The Path to War in Europe (1937–1939) 830

OPPOSING VIEWPOINTS
The Munich Conference: Two Views 833

The Path to War in Asia 833

The Course of World War II   835
   Victory and Stalemate   835
   The War in Asia   838
   The Turning Point of the War (1942–1943)   839
   The Last Years of the War   842

The New Order   843
   The Nazi Empire   843
   Resistance Movements   845
   The Holocaust   845
   FILM & HISTORY
   Europa, Europa (1990)   846
   The New Order in Asia   848

The Home Front   850
   The Mobilization of Peoples   850
   Front-Line Civilians: The Bombing of Cities   853

Aftermath of the War   854
   GLOBAL PERSPECTIVES
   The Impact of Total War in West and East   855
   The Costs of World War II   856
   The Impact of Technology   856
   FILM & HISTORY
   The Imitation Game (2014)   856
   The Allied War Conferences   856
   Emergence of the Cold War   859

   **CHAPTER SUMMARY • CHAPTER TIMELINE •
   CHAPTER REVIEW • KEY TERMS • SUGGESTIONS
   FOR FURTHER READING • NOTES   860**

**28   COLD WAR AND A NEW WESTERN
     WORLD, 1945–1965   863**

Development of the Cold War   864
   Confrontation of the Superpowers: Who Started the
     Cold War?   864
   OPPOSING VIEWPOINTS
   Who Started the Cold War? American and Soviet
     Perspectives   865
   FILM & HISTORY
   The Third Man (1949)   866
   Globalization of the Cold War   867

Europe and the World: Decolonization   870
   Africa: The Struggle for Independence   871
   Conflict in the Middle East   872
   Asia: Nationalism and Communism   875
   Decolonization and Cold War Rivalries   877

Recovery and Renewal in Europe   877
   The Soviet Union: From Stalin to Khrushchev   877
   Eastern Europe: Behind the Iron Curtain   879
   Western Europe: The Revival of Democracy and
     the Economy   880
   Western Europe: The Move Toward Unity   884

The United States and Canada: A New Era   884
   American Politics and Society in the 1950s   885

Decade of Upheaval: America in the 1960s   885
   The Development of Canada   886

Postwar Society and Culture in the Western World   886
   The Structure of European Society   886
   GLOBAL PERSPECTIVES
   The Rise of the Supermarket in West and East   887
   Creation of the Welfare State   888
   Women in the Postwar Western World   889
   Postwar Art and Literature   889
   The Philosophical Dilemma: Existentialism   891
   The Attempt to Revive Religion   892
   The Explosion of Popular Culture   892

   **CHAPTER SUMMARY • CHAPTER TIMELINE •
   CHAPTER REVIEW • KEY TERMS • SUGGESTIONS
   FOR FURTHER READING • NOTES   893**

**29   PROTEST AND STAGNATION:
     THE WESTERN WORLD,
     1965–1985   896**

A Culture of Protest   897
   A Revolt in Sexual Mores   897
   Youth Protest and Student Revolt   897
   IMAGES OF EVERYDAY LIFE
   Youth Culture in the 1960s   898
   The Feminist Movement   900
   Antiwar Protests   901

A Divided Western World   901
   Stagnation in the Soviet Union   901
   Conformity in Eastern Europe   902
   Repression in East Germany and Romania   903
   OPPOSING VIEWPOINTS
   Czechoslovakia, 1968: Two Faces of
     Communism   904
   Western Europe: The Winds of Change   904
   FILM & HISTORY
   The Iron Lady (2011)   906
   The United States: Turmoil and Tranquility   908
   Canada   908

The Cold War: The Move to Détente   908
   The Second Vietnam War   909
   China and the Cold War   910
   The Practice of Détente   911
   The Limits of Détente   911

Society and Culture in the Western World   912
   The World of Science and Technology   912
   The Environment and the Green Movements   913
   Postmodern Thought   914
   Trends in Art, Literature, and Music   914
   Popular Culture: Image and Globalization   916
   The Growth of Mass Sports   917

   **CHAPTER SUMMARY • CHAPTER TIMELINE •
   CHAPTER REVIEW • KEY TERMS • SUGGESTIONS
   FOR FURTHER READING • NOTES   918**

30 AFTER THE FALL: THE WESTERN WORLD IN A GLOBAL AGE (SINCE 1985) 920

Toward a New Western Order   921
    The Revolutionary Era in the Soviet Union   921
    Eastern Europe: The Revolutions of 1989 and the Collapse of the Communist Order   925
    The Reunification of Germany   927
    The Disintegration of Yugoslavia   927
    Western Europe and the Search for Unity   929
    FILM & HISTORY
    Das Leben der Anderen (The Lives of Others) (2006)   930
    The Unification of Europe   932
    The United States: Move to the Center   933
    Contemporary Canada   934

After the Cold War: New World Order or Age of Terrorism?   934
    The End of the Cold War   935
    An Age of Terrorism?   936
    Terrorist Attack on the United States   936
    The West and Islam   937

New Directions and New Problems in Western Society   939
    Transformation in Women's Lives   939
    Guest Workers and Immigrants   940
    The New Urban Environment   941

Western Culture Today   941
    Varieties of Religious Life   942
    The Digital Age   942
    Art in the Contemporary World   943
    Music since 1985   945

Toward a Global Civilization: New Challenges and Hopes   945
    The Global Economy   945
    GLOBAL PERSPECTIVES
    The New Global Economy: Fast Fashion   946
    Globalization and the Environmental Crisis   948
    The Social Challenges of Globalization   950
    New Global Movements and New Hopes   950

    CHAPTER SUMMARY • CHAPTER TIMELINE •
    CHAPTER REVIEW • KEY TERMS • SUGGESTIONS
    FOR FURTHER READING • NOTES   951

    Glossary   G-1

    Index   I-1

DOCUMENTS

CHAPTER 13

ERASMUS: IN PRAISE OF FOLLY 368
(Erasmus, *The Praise of Folly*)

LUTHER AND THE NINETY-FIVE THESES 371
(Martin Luther, *Selections from the Ninety-Five Theses*)

LUTHER AND THE "ROBBING AND MURDERING HORDES OF PEASANTS" 374
(Martin Luther, *Against the Robbing and Murdering Hordes of Peasants*)

OPPOSING VIEWPOINTS: A REFORMATION DEBATE: CONFLICT AT MARBURG 379
(The Marburg Colloquy, 1529)

CALVIN'S RULES FOR THE CHURCH IN GENEVA 384
(Plan for the Elders and Consistory and Rules for the Church in Geneva)

A PROTESTANT WOMAN 385
(A Letter to the Whole Citizenship of the City of Strasbourg from Katharine Zell)

LOYOLA AND OBEDIENCE TO "OUR HOLY MOTHER, THE HIERARCHICAL CHURCH" 388
(Ignatius of Loyola, "Rules for Thinking with the Church")

QUEEN ELIZABETH I: "I HAVE THE HEART OF A KING" 395
(Queen Elizabeth I, Speech to the Troops at Tilbury)

CHAPTER 14

MARCO POLO'S *TRAVELS* 401
(Marco Polo, "Description of the Great City of Kinsay")

COLUMBUS LANDS IN THE NEW WORLD 407
(Letter to Raphael Sanchez, Treasurer to the King and Queen of Spain)

THE SPANISH CONQUISTADOR: CORTÉS AND THE CONQUEST OF MEXICO 409
(Cortés's Description of Tenochtitlán)

LAS CASAS AND THE SPANISH TREATMENT OF THE AMERICAN NATIVES 411
(Bartolomé de Las Casas, *The Tears of the Indians*)

THE ATLANTIC SLAVE TRADE 414
(Diary of a Citizen)

GLOBAL PERSPECTIVES: WEST MEETS EAST: AN EXCHANGE OF ROYAL LETTERS 417
(A Letter to the King of Tonkin from Louis XIV and Answer from the King of Tonkin to Louis XIV)

AN IMPERIAL EDICT TO THE KING OF ENGLAND 420
(An Imperial Edict to the King of England)

THE MISSION 424
(Félix de Azara, Description and History of Paraguay and Rio de la Plata)

CHAPTER 15

A WITCHCRAFT TRIAL IN FRANCE 434
(The Trial of Suzanne Gaudry)

THE DESTRUCTION OF MAGDEBURG IN THE THIRTY YEARS' WAR 439
(An Account of the Destruction of Magdeburg)

THE KING'S DAY BEGINS 445
(Duc de Saint-Simon, *Memoirs*)

PETER THE GREAT DEALS WITH A REBELLION 451
(Peter and the Streltsy)

OPPOSING VIEWPOINTS: OLIVER CROMWELL: THREE PERSPECTIVES 460
(Oliver Cromwell on the Victory at Naseby; Cromwell on the Massacre at Drogheda; Edmund Ludlow, *Memoirs*; and Lord Clarendon, *The History of the Rebellion and Civil Wars in England*)

THE BILL OF RIGHTS 462
(The Bill of Rights)

WILLIAM SHAKESPEARE: IN PRAISE OF ENGLAND 468
(William Shakespeare, *Richard II*)

CHAPTER 16

ON THE REVOLUTIONS OF THE HEAVENLY SPHERES 476
(Nicolaus Copernicus, *On the Revolutions of the Heavenly Spheres*)

KEPLER AND THE EMERGING SCIENTIFIC COMMUNITY 478
(Galileo to Kepler, Padua, August 4, 1597 and Kepler to Galileo, Graz, October 13, 1597)

THE STARRY MESSENGER 479
(Galileo Galilei, *The Starry Messenger*)

OPPOSING VIEWPOINTS: A NEW HEAVEN? FAITH VERSUS REASON 481–482
(Galileo, Letter to the Grand Duchess Christina, 1614 and Robert Bellarmine, Letter to Paolo Foscarini, 1615)

NEWTON'S RULES OF REASONING 483
(Isaac Newton, *Rules of Reasoning in Philosophy*)

MARGARET CAVENDISH: THE EDUCATION OF WOMEN 487
(Margaret Cavendish, "The Philosophical and Physical Opinions")

THE FATHER OF MODERN RATIONALISM   490
(Renè Descartes, *Discourse on Method*)

PASCAL: "WHAT IS A MAN IN THE INFINITE?"   495
(Blaise Pascal, *Pensées*)

CHAPTER 17

THE SEPARATION OF POWERS   504
(Montesquieu, "Of the Constitution of England")

THE ATTACK ON RELIGIOUS INTOLERANCE   505
(Voltaire, *The Ignorant Philosopher* and Voltaire, *Candide*)

DIDEROT QUESTIONS CHRISTIAN SEXUAL STANDARDS   506
(Denis Diderot, *Supplement to the Voyage of Bougainville*)

A SOCIAL CONTRACT   509
(Jean-Jacques Rousseau, *The Social Contract* Book 1, Chapter 6: "The Social Pact")

OPPOSING VIEWPOINTS: WOMEN IN THE AGE OF THE ENLIGHTENMENT: ROUSSEAU AND WOLLSTONECRAFT   511
(Rousseau, *Émile*, 1762 and Mary Wollstonecraft, *Vindication of the Rights of Woman*, 1792)

THE PUNISHMENT OF CRIME   518
(Restif de la Bretonne, "The Broken Man")

THE CONVERSION EXPERIENCE IN WESLEY'S METHODISM   524
(The Journal of the Reverend John Wesley)

CHAPTER 18

THE FRENCH KING'S BEDTIME   531
(Comtesse de Boigne, *Memoirs*)

FREDERICK THE GREAT AND HIS FATHER   534
(letters, Frederick to His Father, Frederick William I, September 11, 1728 and Frederick William to His Son Frederick)

OPPOSING VIEWPOINTS: ENLIGHTENED ABSOLUTISM: ENLIGHTENED OR ABSOLUTE?   536
(Letter of the Baron de Breteuil; Catherine II, Proposals for a New Law Code; and Catherine II, Decree on Serfs)

BRITISH VICTORY IN INDIA   542
(Robert Clive's Account of His Victory at Plassey)

MARITAL ARRANGEMENTS   544
(Richard Sheridan, *The Rivals*)

THE IMPACT OF AGRICULTURAL CHANGES   547
(David Davies, *The Case of Labourers in Husbandry Stated and Considered*)

THE BEGINNINGS OF MECHANIZED INDUSTRY: THE ATTACK ON NEW MACHINES   550
(The Leeds Woolen Workers' Petition, 1786)

POVERTY IN FRANCE   556
(M. de la Bourdonnaye, *Intendant* of Bordeaux, to the Controller General, September 30, 1708 and Marginal Comments by the Controller General)

CHAPTER 19

THE ARGUMENT FOR INDEPENDENCE   562
(The Declaration of Independence)

THE FALL OF THE BASTILLE   568
(A Parisian Newspaper Account of the Fall of the Bastille)

OPPOSING VIEWPOINTS: THE NATURAL RIGHTS OF THE FRENCH PEOPLE: TWO VIEWS   570–571
(Declaration of the Rights of Man and the Citizen and Declaration of the Rights of Woman and the Female Citizen)

RESPONSE TO THE KING'S FLIGHT TO VARENNES   572
(Response to the King's Flight to Varennes Louis-Marie Prudhomme, *Révolutions de Paris*, 1791)

JUSTICE IN THE REIGN OF TERROR   577
(J. G. Milligen, *The Revolutionary Tribunal*, Paris, October 1793)

ROBESPIERRE AND REVOLUTIONARY GOVERNMENT   578
(Robespierre, Speech on Revolutionary Government)

DE-CHRISTIANIZATION   580
(The Temple of Reason)

NAPOLEON AND PSYCHOLOGICAL WARFARE   584
(Napoleon Bonaparte, Proclamation to the French Troops in Italy, April 26, 1796)

CHAPTER 20

THE TRAITS OF THE BRITISH INDUSTRIAL ENTREPRENEUR   594
(Edward Baines, *The History of the Cotton Manufacture in Great Britain*)

THE STEAM ENGINE AND COTTON   595
(Richard Guest, *A Compendius History of the Cotton-Manufacture*)

DISCIPLINE IN THE NEW FACTORIES   599
(Factory Rules, Foundry and Engineering Works of the Royal Overseas Trading Company, Berlin)

THE GREAT IRISH POTATO FAMINE   606
(Nicholas Cummins, "The Famine in Skibbereen")

GLOBAL PERSPECTIVES: ATTITUDES OF THE INDUSTRIAL MIDDLE CLASS IN BRITAIN AND JAPAN   610
(Samuel Smiles, *Self-Help*; Shibusawa Eiichi, *Autobiography*; and Shibusawa Eiichi on Progress)

CHILD LABOR: DISCIPLINE IN THE TEXTILE MILLS   614
(Keeping the Children Awake and The Sadistic Overlooker)

CHILD LABOR: THE MINES   615
(The Black Holes of Worsley)

CHAPTER 21

THE VOICE OF CONSERVATISM: METTERNICH OF AUSTRIA 623
(Klemens von Metternich, *Memoirs*)

UNIVERSITY STUDENTS AND GERMAN UNITY 629
(Heinrich von Gagern, Letter to His Father)

THE VOICE OF LIBERALISM: JOHN STUART MILL ON LIBERTY 631
(John Stuart Mill, *On Liberty*)

OPPOSING VIEWPOINTS: RESPONSE TO REVOLUTION: TWO PERSPECTIVES 636–637
(Thomas Babington Macaulay, Speech of March 2, 1831 and Carl Schurz, *Reminiscences*)

THE VOICE OF ITALIAN NATIONALISM: GIUSEPPE MAZZINI AND YOUNG ITALY 641
(Giuseppe Mazzini, *The Young Italy Oath*)

THE NEW BRITISH POLICE: "WE ARE NOT TREATED AS MEN" 644
(Complaints from Constables of D Division of the London Metropolitan Police)

BEETHOVEN'S INSTRUMENTAL MUSIC 649
(Beethoven's Instrumental Music, 1813)

CHAPTER 22

OPPOSING VIEWPOINTS: THE PRACTICE OF *REALPOLITIK*: TWO APPROACHES 655
(Louis Napoleon, Proclamation to the People, 1851; Bismarck, Speech to the Prussian Reichstag, 1862; and Bismarck, Speech to the German Reichstag, 1888)

GARIBALDI AND ROMANTIC NATIONALISM 661
(*London Times*, June 13, 1860)

EMANCIPATION: SERFS AND SLAVES 668
(Tsar Alexander II, Imperial Decree, March 3, 1861 and President Abraham Lincoln, Emancipation Proclamation, January 1, 1863)

THE CLASSLESS SOCIETY 675
(Karl Marx and Friedrich Engels, *The Communist Manifesto*)

DARWIN AND THE DESCENT OF MAN 677
(Charles Darwin, *The Descent of Man*)

ANESTHESIA AND MODERN SURGERY 679
(The First Public Demonstration of Ether Anesthesia, October 16, 1846)

FLAUBERT AND AN IMAGE OF BOURGEOIS MARRIAGE 681
(Gustave Flaubert, *Madame Bovary*)

CHAPTER 23

THE DEPARTMENT STORE AND THE BEGINNINGS OF MASS CONSUMERISM 689
(E. Lavasseur, *On Parisian Department Stores*)

PROSTITUTION IN VICTORIAN *LONDON* 694
(Henry Mayhew, *London Labour and the London Poor*)

THE VOICE OF EVOLUTIONARY SOCIALISM: EDUARD BERNSTEIN 696
(Eduard Bernstein, *Evolutionary Socialism*)

THE HOUSING VENTURE OF OCTAVIA HILL 701
(Octavia Hill, *Homes of the London Poor*)

OPPOSING VIEWPOINTS: ADVICE TO WOMEN: TWO 704–705
(Elizabeth Poole Sanford, *Woman in Her Social and Domestic Character* and Henrik Ibsen, *A Doll's House*)

WOMEN'S SOCCER, 1881 711
(Ladies' International Match, Scotland V. England)

BISMARCK AND THE WELFARE OF THE WORKERS 715
(Bismarck, Address to the Reichstag)

CHAPTER 24

FREUD AND THE CONCEPT OF REPRESSION 723
(Sigmund Freud, *The Origin and Development of Psychoanalysis*)

DOSTOEVSKY: AN ATTACK ON REASON 726
(Fyodor Dostoevsky, *Notes from Underground*)

THE STRUGGLE FOR THE RIGHT TO VOTE 732
(Emmeline Pankhurst, *My Own Story*)

THE VOICE OF ZIONISM: THEODOR HERZL AND THE JEWISH STATE 736
(Theodor Herzl, *The Jewish State*)

BLOODY SUNDAY 740
(An Account of Bloody Sunday)

OPPOSING VIEWPOINTS: WHITE MAN'S BURDEN VERSUS BLACK MAN'S BURDEN 743–744
(Rudyard Kipling, "The White Man's Burden" and Edward Morel, *The Black Man's Burden*)

DOES GERMANY NEED COLONIES? 746
(Friedrich Fabri, *Does Germany Need Colonies?*)

CHAPTER 25

"YOU HAVE TO BEAR THE RESPONSIBILITY FOR WAR OR PEACE" 761
(Communications between Berlin and Saint Petersburg on the Eve of World War I)

THE EXCITEMENT OF WAR 763
(Stefan Zweig, *The World of Yesterday*; Robert Graves, *Goodbye to All That*; and Walter Limmer, "Letter to His Parents")

THE REALITY OF WAR: TRENCH WARFARE 767
(Erich Maria Remarque, *All Quiet on the Western Front*)

THE REALITY OF WAR: THE VIEWS OF BRITISH POETS 768
(Wilfred Owen, *Dulce et Decorum Est* and Siegfried Sassoon, *Suicide in the Trenches*)

WOMEN IN THE FACTORIES 775
(Naomi Loughnan, "Munition Work")

WAR AND LOVE 777
(*Letters from a Lost Generation*)

SOLDIER AND PEASANT VOICES   781
(Letter from a Soldier in Leningrad to Lenin, January 6, 1918 and Letter from a Peasant to the Bolshevik Leaders, January 10, 1918)

OPPOSING VIEWPOINTS: THREE VOICES OF PEACEMAKING   786–787
(Woodrow Wilson, Speeches; Georges Clemenceau, *Grandeur and Misery of Victory*; and Pan-African Congress)

CHAPTER 26

THE DECLINE OF EUROPEAN CIVILIZATION   794
(Johan Huizinga, *In the Shadow of Tomorrow*)

THE GREAT DEPRESSION: UNEMPLOYED AND HOMELESS IN GERMANY   797
(Heinrich Hauser, "With Germany's Unemployed")

THE VOICE OF ITALIAN FASCISM   804
(Benito Mussolini, "The Political and Social Doctrine of Fascism")

ADOLF HITLER'S HATRED OF THE JEWS   806
(Adolf Hitler, *Mein Kampf*)

PROPAGANDA AND MASS MEETINGS IN NAZI GERMANY   809
(Adolf Hitler, Speech at the Nuremberg Party Rally, 1936 and A Teacher's Impression of a Hitler Rally, 1932)

THE FORMATION OF COLLECTIVE FARMS   814
(Max Belov, *The History of a Collective Farm*)

SPAIN DIVIDED: A VIEW FROM BARCELONA   816
(George Orwell, Barcelona, 1936)

HESSE AND THE UNCONSCIOUS   823
(Hermann Hesse, *Demian*)

CHAPTER 27

HITLER'S FOREIGN POLICY GOALS   829
(Hitler's *Secret Book*, 1928)

OPPOSING VIEWPOINTS: THE MUNICH CONFERENCE: TWO VIEWS   833
(Winston Churchill, Speech to the House of Commons, October 5, 1938 and Neville Chamberlain, Speech to the House of Commons, October 6, 1938)

A GERMAN SOLDIER AT STALINGRAD   841
(Diary of a German Soldier)

HITLER'S PLANS FOR A NEW ORDER IN THE EAST   844
(Hitler's *Secret Conversations*, October 17, 1941)

HEINRICH HIMMLER: "WE HAD THE MORAL RIGHT"   849
(Heinrich Himmler, Speech to SS Leaders)

THE BOMBING OF CIVILIANS   853
(London, 1940; Hamburg, 1943; and Hiroshima, August 6, 1945)

EMERGENCE OF THE COLD WAR: CHURCHILL AND STALIN   859
(Churchill's Speech at Fulton, Missouri, March 5, 1946 and Stalin's Reply to Churchill, March 14, 1946)

CHAPTER 28

OPPOSING VIEWPOINTS: WHO STARTED THE COLD WAR? AMERICAN AND SOVIET PERSPECTIVES   865
(George Kennan, The Long Telegram, February 1946 and Nikolai Novikov, Telegram, September 27, 1946)

THE CUBAN MISSILE CRISIS FROM KHRUSHCHEV'S PERSPECTIVE   871
(Nikita Khrushchev, *Khrushchev Remembers*)

FRANTZ FANON AND THE WRETCHED OF THE EARTH   874
(*The Wretched of the Earth* : Colonial War and Mental Disorders, Series B)

KHRUSHCHEV DENOUNCES STALIN   878
(Nikita Khrushchev, Address to the Twentieth Party Congress, February 1956)

SOVIET REPRESSION IN EASTERN EUROPE: HUNGARY, 1956   880
(Statement of the Soviet Government, October 30, 1956 and The Last Message of Imry Nagy, November 4, 1956)

THE BURDEN OF GUILT   883
(Hannah Vogt, The *Burden of Guilt*)

THE VOICE OF THE WOMEN'S LIBERATION MOVEMENT   890
(Simone de Beauvoir, *The Second Sex*)

CHAPTER 29

"THE TIMES THEY ARE A-CHANGIN'": THE MUSIC OF YOUTHFUL PROTEST   899
(Bob Dylan, "The Times They Are A-Changin'")

1968: THE YEAR OF STUDENT REVOLTS   900
(A Student Manifesto in Search of a Real and Human Educational Alternative, University of British Columbia, June 1968)

BETTY FRIEDAN: THE PROBLEM THAT HAS NO NAME   902
(Betty Friedan, *The Feminine Mystique*)

OPPOSING VIEWPOINTS: CZECHOSLOVAKIA, 1968: TWO FACES OF COMMUNISM   904–905
(Two Thousand Words Manifesto and A Letter to Czechoslovakia)

MARGARET THATCHER: ENTERING A MAN'S WORLD   907
(Margaret Thatcher, The Renewal of Britain)

THE FURY OF THE RED GUARDS   911
(Nien Cheng, *Life and Death in Shanghai*)

THE LIMITS OF MODERN TECHNOLOGY   913
(E. F. Schumacher, *Small Is Beautiful*)

CHAPTER 30

GORBACHEV AND *PERESTROIKA*   923
(Mikhail Gorbachev, *Perestroika*)

VÁCLAV HAVEL: THE CALL FOR A NEW POLITICS   926
(Václav Havel, Address to the People of Czechoslovakia,
January 1, 1990)

**A CHILD'S ACCOUNT OF THE SHELLING OF
SARAJEVO**   929
(Zlata Filipović, *Zlata's Diary: A Child's Life in Sarajevo*)

THE WEST AND ISLAM   938
(Abbas Amanat, Empowered Through Violence:
The Reinvention of Islamic Extremism)

A WARNING TO HUMANITY   948–949
(World Scientists' Warning to Humanity, 1992;
Findings of the IPCC Fifth Assessment Report,
2013; and Additional IPCC Findings on Recent
Climate Change)

MAPS

MAP 13.1   The Empire of Charles V   375

SPOT MAP   The Swiss Cantons   377

MAP 13.2   Catholics and Protestants in Europe by 1560   387

MAP 13.3   The Height of Spanish Power Under Philip II   392

MAP 14.1   Discoveries and Possessions in the Fifteenth and Sixteenth Centuries   404

SPOT MAP   The Maya   408

SPOT MAP   The Aztecs   408

SPOT MAP   The Inca   408

MAP 14.2   Triangular Trade Route in the Atlantic Economy   413

SPOT MAP   Southeast Asia, ca. 1700   416

SPOT MAP   The Mughal Empire   418

SPOT MAP   The Qing Empire   419

SPOT MAP   The West Indies   421

MAP 14.3   The Columbian Exchange   426

MAP 15.1   The Thirty Years' War   436

MAP 15.2   The Wars of Louis XIV   446

MAP 15.3   The Growth of Brandenburg-Prussia   448

MAP 15.4   The Growth of the Austrian Empire   449

MAP 15.5   Russia: From Principality to Nation-State   452

SPOT MAP   Sweden in the Seventeenth Century   453

MAP 15.6   The Ottoman Empire   454

SPOT MAP   Poland in the Seventeenth Century   456

SPOT MAP   Civil War in England   459

MAP 17.1   The Enlightenment in Europe   503

MAP 17.2   Religious Populations of Eighteenth-Century Europe   522

MAP 18.1   Europe in 1763   533

SPOT MAP   Pugachev's Rebellion   537

MAP 18.2   The Partitioning of Poland   538

MAP 18.3   Battlefields of the Seven Years' War   540

MAP 19.1   North America, 1700–1803   561

SPOT MAP   Rebellion in France   574

MAP 19.2   French Expansion During the Revolutionary Wars, 1792–1799   576

SPOT MAP   Revolt in Saint-Domingue (Haiti)   580

MAP 19.3   Napoleon's Grand Empire in 1810   587

MAP 20.1   The Industrial Revolution in Britain by 1850   597

MAP 20.2   The Industrialization of Europe by 1850   602

MAP 21.1   Europe After the Congress of Vienna, 1815   622

MAP 21.2   Latin America in the First Half of the Nineteenth Century   626

SPOT MAP   The Balkans by 1830   627

SPOT MAP   Italy, 1815   628

MAP 21.3   The Distribution of Languages in Nineteenth-Century Europe   633

MAP 21.4   The Revolutions of 1848–1849   638

MAP 22.1   Decline of the Ottoman Empire   657

SPOT MAP   The Crimean War   657

MAP 22.2   The Unification of Italy   659

MAP 22.3   The Unification of Germany   663

MAP 22.4   Europe in 1871   665

MAP 22.5   Ethnic Groups in the Dual Monarchy, 1867   667

MAP 22.6   The United States: The West and the Civil War   671

MAP 23.1   The Industrial Regions of Europe at the End of the Nineteenth Century   691

MAP 23.2   Population Growth in Europe, 1820–1900   698

SPOT MAP   Palestine   735

MAP 24.1   Africa in 1914   744

SPOT MAP   The Struggle for South Africa   745

MAP 24.2   Asia in 1914   748

SPOT MAP   Japanese Expansion   750

SPOT MAP   The Balkans in 1878   752

MAP 24.3   The Balkans in 1913   753

MAP 25.1   Europe in 1914   759

MAP 25.2   The Western Front, 1914–1918   764

SPOT MAP   The Schlieffen Plan   764

MAP 25.3   The Eastern Front, 1914–1918   765

MAP 25.4   The Russian Revolution and Civil War   782

SPOT MAP   The Middle East in 1919   788

MAP 25.5   Europe in 1919   789

SPOT MAP   The Little Entente   794

SPOT MAP   Territory Gained by Italy   802

SPOT MAP   Eastern Europe After World War I   815

MAP 27.1   Changes in Central Europe, 1936–1939   832

MAP 27.2   World War II in Europe and North Africa   837

MAP 27.3   World War II in Asia and the Pacific   839

MAP 27.4   The Holocaust   848

MAP 27.5   Territorial Changes After World War II   858

SPOT MAP   The Berlin Air Lift   866

MAP 28.1   The New European Alliance Systems in the 1950s and 1960s   868

SPOT MAP   The Korean War   869

MAP 28.2   Decolonization in Africa   873

MAP 28.3   Decolonization in the Middle East   875

MAP 28.4   Decolonization in Asia   876

SPOT MAP   European Economic Community, 1957   884

SPOT MAP   The Vietnam War   909

MAP 30.1   The New Europe   922

SPOT MAP   Chechnya   924

MAP 30.2   The Lands of the Former Yugoslavia, 1995   930

MAP 30.3   European Union, 2013   933

SPOT MAP   Quebec   934

FEATURES

OPPOSING VIEWPOINTS

A Reformation Debate: Conflict at Marburg   379

Oliver Cromwell: Three Perspectives   460

A New Heaven? Faith Versus Reason   481

Women in the Age of the Enlightenment: Rousseau and Wollstonecraft   511

Enlightened Absolutism: Enlightened or Absolute?   536

The Natural Rights of the French People: Two Views   570

Response to Revolution: Two Perspectives   636

The Practice of *Realpolitik:* Two Approaches   655

Advice to Women: Two Views   704

White Man's Burden Versus Black Man's Burden   743

Three Voices of Peacemaking   786

The Munich Conference: Two Views   833

Who Started the Cold War? American and Soviet Perspectives   865

Czechoslovakia, 1968: Two Faces of Communism   904

IMAGES OF EVERYDAY LIFE

Spices and World Trade   405

Dutch Domesticity   457

The Science of Collecting   492

Women and the Enlightenment Salon   512

The Aristocratic Way of Life   553

Living Conditions of London's Poor   608

Political Cartoons: Attacks on the King   639

The Middle-Class Family   706

The Struggle for the Right to Vote   733

Life in the Trenches   769

Youth Culture in the 1960s   898

FILM & HISTORY

Luther (2003)   372

Elizabeth (1998)   396

The Mission   424

Amadeus   515

Marie Antoinette (2006)   530

The Young Victoria (2009)   669

Suffragette (2015)   734

Paths of Glory (1957)   768

Triumph of the Will (1934)   819

Europa, Europa (1990)   846

The Imitation Game (2014)   856

The Third Man (1949)   866

The Iron Lady (2011)   906

Das Leben der Anderen (The Lives of Others) (2006)   930

GLOBAL PERSPECTIVES

West Meets East: An Exchange of Royal Letters   417

Sun Kings, West and East   442

Popular Culture in the West and East   520

Revolution and Revolt in France and China   569

Attitudes of the Industrial Middle Class in Britain and Japan   610

East and West: Textile Factory Work   692

Impressionist Painting: West and East   728

Soldiers from Around the World   771

The Impact of Total War in West and East   855

The Rise of the Supermarket in West and East   887

The New Global Economy: Fast Fashion   946

DURING A VISIT to Great Britain, where he studied as a young man, Mohandas Gandhi, the leader of the effort to liberate India from British colonial rule, was asked what he thought of Western civilization. "I think it would be a good idea," he replied. Gandhi's response was as correct as it was clever. Western civilization has led to great problems as well as great accomplishments, but it remains a good idea. And any complete understanding of today's world must take into account the meaning of Western civilization and the role Western civilization has played in history. Despite modern progress, we still greatly reflect our religious traditions, our political systems and theories, our economic and social structures, and our cultural heritage. I have written this history of Western civilization to assist a new generation of students in learning more about the past that has helped create them and the world in which they live.

At the same time, for the tenth edition, as in the ninth, I have added new material on world history to show the impact other parts of the world have made on the West. Certainly, the ongoing struggle with terrorists since 2001 has made clear the intricate relationship between the West and the rest of the world. It is important then to show not only how Western civilization has affected the rest of the world but also how it has been influenced and even defined since its beginnings by contacts with other peoples around the world.

Another of my goals was to write a well-balanced work in which the political, economic, social, religious, intellectual, cultural, and military aspects of Western civilization have been integrated into a chronologically ordered synthesis. I have been especially aware of the need to integrate the latest research on social history and women's history into each chapter of the book rather than isolating it either in lengthy topical chapters, which confuse the student by interrupting the chronological narrative, or in separate sections that appear at periodic intervals between chapters.

Another purpose in writing this history of Western civilization has been to put the *story* back in history. That story is an exciting one, yet many textbooks fail to capture the imagination of their readers. Narrative history effectively transmits the knowledge of the past and is the form that best aids remembrance. At the same time, I have not overlooked the need for the kind of historical analysis that makes students aware that historians often disagree on their interpretations of the past.

Features of the Text

To enliven the past and to let readers see for themselves the materials that historians use to create their pictures of the past, I have included in each chapter **primary sources** (boxed documents) that are keyed to the discussion in the text. The documents include examples of the religious, artistic, intellectual, social, economic, and political aspects of Western life. Such varied sources as a Renaissance banquet menu, letters exchanged between a woman and her fiancé on the battle front in World War I, the Declaration of the Rights of Woman and the Female Citizen in the French Revolution, and a debate in the Reformation era all reveal in vivid fashion what Western civilization meant to the individual men and women who shaped it by their activities. I have added questions at the end of each source to help students in analyzing the documents.

To help students examine how and why historians differ in their interpretation of specific topics, new historiographical sections were introduced in the ninth edition. Examples include "Was There a United Kingdom of Israel?"; "Was There a Renaissance for Women?"; "Was There an Agricultural Revolution?"; "The Retreat from Democracy: Did Europe Have Totalitarian States?"; and "Why Did the Soviet Union Collapse?" Each of these sections is now preceded by the heading **Historians Debate** to make students more aware of the interpretive nature of history.

An additional feature that began in the seventh edition was **Images of Everyday Life**, which combines two or more illustrations with a lengthy caption to provide insight into various aspects of social life and includes such topics as "Children in the Roman World," "Family and Marriage in Renaissance Italy," "Women and the Enlightenment Salon," and "Political Cartoons: Attacks on the King." **Film & History**, which now appears in a new, brief format, can be found in eighteen chapters; the features reference twenty films, including the new additions of *Suffragette* and *The Imitation Game*.

Each chapter has an introduction and illustrated chapter summary to help maintain the continuity of the narrative and to provide a synthesis of important themes. Anecdotes in the chapter introductions dramatically convey the major theme or themes of each chapter. Detailed chronologies reinforce the events discussed in the text, and a **Chapter Timeline** at the end of each chapter enables students to review at a glance the chief developments of an era. Some of the timelines also show parallel developments in different cultures or nations. Beginning with the eighth edition, a new format was added at the end of each chapter. The **Chapter Summary** is illustrated with thumbnail images of chapter illustrations and combined with the **Chapter Timeline**. A **Chapter Review** assists students in studying the chapter. This review includes **Upon Reflection** essay questions and a list of **Key Terms** from the chapter. The **Suggestions for Further Reading** at the end of each chapter has been thoroughly updated and is organized under subheadings to make it more useful.

Updated maps and extensive illustrations serve to deepen the reader's understanding of the text. Detailed map captions are designed to enrich students' awareness of the importance of geography to history, and numerous spot maps enable readers to see at a glance the region or subject being discussed in the text. Map captions also include a map question to guide students' reading of the map. To facilitate understanding of cultural movements, illustrations of artistic works discussed in the text are placed near the discussions. Throughout the text, illustration captions have been revised and expanded to further students' understanding of the past. Chapter outlines and focus questions, including critical thinking questions, at the beginning of each chapter give students a useful overview and guide them to the main subjects of each chapter. The section **Connections to Today** is intended to help students appreciate the relevance of history by asking them to draw connections between the past and present.

The focus questions are then repeated at the beginning of each major section in the chapter. A glossary of important terms (boldfaced in the text when they are introduced and defined) is provided at the back of the book to maximize reader comprehension. A guide to pronunciation is provided in the text in parentheses following the first mention of a complex name or term, and **Chapter Notes** is now at the end of each chapter.

New to This Edition

While preparing the revision of *Western Civilization*, I reexamined the entire book and analyzed the comments and reviews of many colleagues who have found the book to be a useful instrument for introducing their students to the history of Western civilization. In making revisions to the tenth edition, I sought to build on the strengths of the first nine editions and, above all, to maintain the balance, synthesis, and narrative qualities that characterized those editions. To keep up with the ever-growing body of historical scholarship, new or revised material has been added throughout the book on the following topics:

Chapter 1 new Historians Debate feature, "Why Did Early Civilizations Develop?"; discovery of new hominids in Indonesia; Neanderthals and modern humans; the Lascaux cave; Enheduanna as chief priestess in Sumer; new feature, Global Perspectives: "The Stele in the Ancient World"; Hatshepsut.

Chapter 2 the Hebrew Bible, including the Documentary Hypothesis; the role of rabbis; the Ten Commandments; Assyrian society; Assyrian women; new document, "The Code of Assura"; new section, "Assyrian Culture."

Chapter 3 Minoan Crete; Mycenaean Greece; the so-called "Dark Age" in Greece; the polis; Greek cultural identity; new document, "The Teaching of Tyranny"; new feature, Global Perspectives: "The Influence of the East on the Greeks"; new Film & History format for *300*; the role of the Persian threat for a growing sense of Greek cultural identity; the decline of the Greek states and the Sacred Band of Thebes; Euripides and a new section, "The Themes of Greek Tragedies"; growing sense of Greek cultural identity due to athletic games.

Chapter 4 new Film & History format for *Alexander*; new document, "The Character of Alexander"; the Ptolemaic kingdom of Egypt; the Greco-Bactrian kingdom; the Indo-Greek

kingdom; political and military institutions; new feature, Global Perspectives: "The Influence of the Greeks on India"; new section, "The Appeal of Epicureanism and Stoicism"; the mystery religions; Judas Maccabeus.

Chapter 5 new Historians Debate feature, "Who Were the Etruscans?"; Aeneas and Romulus and Remus and the legendary founding of Rome; Brutus and the founding of the Roman Republic; citizenship policy and the Roman army; new feature, Global Perspectives: "Roman and Chinese Roads"; Roman imperialism; edited coverage of Roman slavery; new Film & History format for *Spartacus*.

Chapter 6 comparison of Augustus and Julius Caesar; revolts against Roman rule during the *Pax Romana*; new Historians Debate feature, "What Was Romanization?"; the provinces; contacts with Han China; trade with India; new Film & History format for *Gladiator*; revolts against Roman rule in Judaea; new feature, Global Perspectives: "Women in the Roman and Han Empires."

Chapter 7 Diocletian's religious policy and persecution of Christians; the emperor Constantine; the early Germans; the Ostrogothic Kingdom of Italy; the Visigothic Kingdom of Spain; Pope Leo I; new document, "Pope Leo I and Attila the Hun."

Chapter 8 new feature, Global Perspectives: "Lords, Vassals, and Samurai in Europe and Japan"; new document, "A Manor House"; Empress Irene; new section, "Women in the Islamic World"; Islamic women.

Chapter 9 the role of agriculture in the development of trade in the High Middle Ages; the Commercial Revolution of the High Middle Ages; new feature, Global Perspectives: "Medieval Cities in West and East"; universities and the introduction of Aristotle's works in the West.

Chapter 10 new Film & History format for *The Lion in Winter*; Bernard of Clairvaux; new Film & History format for *Vision*; monasticism; new feature, Global Perspectives: "Medieval Monastic Life in West and East"; new document, "The Miraculous Power of the Sacraments"; new Historians Debate feature, "What Motivated the Crusaders?"; the Fourth Crusade; the effects of the crusades.

Chapter 11 the longbow; the battles of the Hundred Years' War; new document, "The Hundred Years' War"; new Film & History format for *Joan of Arc* and *The Messenger*; the Babylonian Captivity of the church; the Great Schism and popular religion; new feature, Global Perspectives: "Religious Imagery in the Medieval World"; new directions in medicine.

Chapter 12 the Hanseatic League and the city of Lübeck; Florence in the Renaissance; the spiritual perspective of Italian Renaissance humanism; new document, "The Genius of Michelangelo"; Albrecht Dürer.

Chapter 13 Erasmus; new Film & History format for *Luther*; the spread of Luther's ideas; new document, "Calvin's Rules for the Church in Geneva"; Calvin's view of female rulers; new Film & History format for *Elizabeth*.

Chapter 14 the Aztecs; Spanish cities in the New World; new feature, "Global Perspectives: West Meets East: An Exchange of Royal Letters"; Mughal India; British India; new Film & History format for *The Mission*; the Columbian Exchange.

Chapter 15 new material on women and witchcraft; new document, "The Destruction of Magdeburg in the Thirty Years' War"; new feature, Global Perspectives: "Sun Kings: West and East"; Peter the Great.

Chapter 16 technological innovations; academic institutions; Hermetic magic and the Scientific Revolution; Tycho Brahe; medical practice; new Images of Everyday Life feature: "The Science of Collecting."

Chapter 17 John Locke; Rococo art; new Film & History format for *Amadeus*; popular culture and the coffee house; new feature, Global Perspectives: "Popular Culture in West and East"; toleration and religion.

Chapter 18 new Film & History format for *Marie Antoinette*; Frederick II of Prussia; Joseph II of Austria; Spain; Portugal; the agricultural revolution; the consumer revolution.

Chapter 19 the Three Estates; French finances; new feature, Global Perspectives: "Revolution and Revolt in France and China"; the formation of political factions; new document, "Response to the King's Flight to Varennes"; the flight to Varennes; the French émigrés; the Terror.

Chapter 20 new document, "The Steam Engine and Cotton"; early railroads; the Industrial Revolution on the continent; British policies in India; cheap cotton; new feature, Global Perspectives: "Attitudes of the Industrial Middle Class in Britain and Japan".

Chapter 21 the French Revolution of 1830; the Revolutions of 1848; Romanticism; new document, "Beethoven's Instrumental Music."

Chapter 22 the Ottoman Empire; the Crimean War; the Franco-Prussian War; reforms in Russia; political life in Russia; Realism in art.

Chapter 23 economic growth; new feature, Global Perspectives: "West and East: Textile Factory Work"; the social classes; mass tourism; new document, "Women's Soccer, 1881."

Chapter 24 new document, "Dostovesky: An Attack on Reason"; new feature, Global Perspectives: "Impressionist Painting: West and East"; modernism and the arts; new Film & History feature on *Suffragette*; the United States; imperialism.

Chapter 25 new material in the Introduction; new Film & History format for *Paths of Glory*; new document, "The Reality of War: The Views of British Poets"; life in the trenches; new feature, Global Perspectives, "Soldiers from Around the World"; the November armistice; the Treaty of Versailles.

Chapter 26 the colonial empires; new document, "Spain in Turmoil: A View from Barcelona"; arts, film, and culture; new Film & History format for *Triumph of the Will*; new section, "The Culture of Nazism."

Chapter 27 naval battles, including the Battle of North Atlantic and Battle of Leyte Gulf; resistance movements; new Film & History format for *Europa, Europa*; new feature, Global Perspectives: "The Impact of Total War in West and East"; new section, "The Impact of Technology"; new Film & History feature on *The Imitation Game*.

Chapter 28 new Film & History format for *The Third Man*; decolonization in Africa; decolonization in the Middle East; new feature, Global Perspectives: "The Rise of the Supermarket in West and East."

Chapter 29 the European economy; new Film & History format for *The Iron Lady*; new document, "Margaret Thatcher: 'Thatcherism' and the Free Market"; Italy; the United States economy.

Chapter 30 Russia; Eastern Europe; Germany; Great Britain; France; Italy; the United States; Canada; new Film & History format for *The Lives of Others*; new document, "The West and Islam"; new sections, "Terrorism as a Global War," "Migration Crisis," "The New Urban Environment," "The Digital Age," "Art in the Contemporary World," and "Music Since 1985"; technology; religion; new feature, Global Perspectives: "The New Global Economy: Fast Fashion."

The enthusiastic response to the primary sources (boxed documents) led me to evaluate the content of each document carefully and add new documents throughout the text. The feature **Opposing Viewpoints**, which was introduced in the seventh edition, presents a comparison of two or three primary sources in order to facilitate student analysis of historical documents. This feature now appears in almost every chapter and includes such topics as "The Great Flood: Two Versions," "The Black Death: Contemporary Views," "A New Heaven: Faith Versus Reason," "The Response to Revolution," and "Czechoslovakia, 1968: Two Faces of Communism." Focus questions are included to help students evaluate the documents.

New to the tenth edition is a feature entitled **Global Perspectives**, which reinforces the relationship between the West and other parts of the world. This new feature, which is found in twenty chapters, includes such topics as "The Stele in the Ancient World," "Women in the Roman and Han Empires," "Medieval Monastic Life in West and East," "Revolution and Revolt in France and China," "West and East: Textile Factory Work," and "The New Global Economy: Fast Fashion."

Because courses in Western civilization at American and Canadian colleges and universities follow different chronological divisions, a one-volume edition, two two-volume editions, a three-volume edition, and a volume covering events since 1300 are being made available to fit the needs of instructors. Teaching and learning ancillaries include the following.

Supplements

MindTap Instant Access Code (full volume): ISBN–9781305952362
MindTap Instant Access Code (Volume 1): ISBN–9781305953239
MindTap Instant Access Code (Volume 2): ISBN–9781305953369

MindTap Printed Access Card (Full Volume): ISBN–9781305952379
MindTap Printed Access Card (Volume 1): ISBN–9781305953246
MindTap Printed Access Card (Volume 2): ISBN–9781305953376

MindTap for *Western Civilization*, 10e, is a personalized online learning platform that provides students with an immersive learning experience to build and foster critical thinking skills. Through a carefully designed chapter-based learning path, MindTap allows students to easily identify learning objectives; draw connections and improve writing skills by completing unit-level essay assignments; read short, manageable sections from the e-book; and test their content knowledge with map- and timeline-based critical thinking questions.

MindTap allows instructors to customize their content, providing tools that seamlessly integrate YouTube clips, outside websites, and personal content directly into the learning path. Instructors can assign additional primary source content through the Instructor Resource Center and Questia primary and secondary source databases that house thousands of peer-reviewed journals, newspapers, magazines, and full-length books.

The additional content available in MindTap mirrors and complements the authors' narrative but also includes primary source content and assessments not found in the printed text. To learn more, ask your Cengage Learning sales representative to demo it for you—or go to *www.Cengage.com/MindTap*.

Instructor's Companion Website   The Instructor's Companion Website, accessed through the Instructor Resource Center (*login.cengage.com*), houses all of the supplemental materials you can use for your course. This includes a test bank, instructor's manual, and PowerPoint lecture presentations. The test bank, offered in Microsoft Word and Cognero formats, contains multiple-choice, identification, true or false, and essay questions for each chapter. Cognero is a flexible online system that allows you to author, edit, and manage test bank content for *Western Civilization*, 10e. Create multiple test versions instantly and deliver through your learning management system from your classroom or wherever you may be, with no special installs or downloads required. The instructor's resource manual includes chapter summaries, suggested lecture topics, map exercises, discussion questions for the primary sources, topics for student research, relevant websites, suggestions for additional videos, and online resources for information on historical sites. Finally, the PowerPoint Lectures are ADA-compliant slides that collate the key takeaways from the chapter in concise visual formats perfect for in-class presentations or for student review.

Cengagebrain.com   Save your students time and money. Direct them to *www.cengagebrain.com* for a choice in formats and savings and a better chance to succeed in your class. *Cengagebrain.com*, Cengage Learning's online store, is a single destination for more than 10,000 new textbooks, e-textbooks, e-chapters, study tools, and audio supplements. Students have the freedom to purchase à la carte exactly what they need and when they need it. Students can save 50 percent on the electronic textbook and can purchase an individual e-chapter for as little as $1.99.

Doing History: Research and Writing in the Digital Age, 2e ISBN: 9781133587880   Prepared by Michael J. Galgano, J. Chris Arndt, and Raymond M. Hyser of James Madison University. Whether you're starting down the path as a history major or simply looking for a straightforward, systematic guide to writing a successful paper, this text's "soup to nuts" approach to researching and writing about history addresses every step of the process: locating your sources, gathering information, writing and citing according to various style guides, and avoiding plagiarism.

Writing for College History, 1e ISBN: 9780618306039   Prepared by Robert M. Frakes of Clarion University. This brief handbook for survey courses in American, western, and world history guides students through the various types of writing assignments they may encounter in a history class. Providing examples of student writing and candid assessments of student work, this text focuses on the rules and conventions of writing for the college history course.

The Modern Researcher, 6e ISBN: 9780495318705   Prepared by Jacques Barzun and Henry F. Graff of Columbia University. This classic introduction to the techniques of research and the art of expression thoroughly covers every aspect of research, from the selection of a topic through the gathering of materials, analysis, writing, revision, and publication of findings. The authors present the process not as a set of rules but through actual cases that put the subtleties of research in a useful context. Part One covers the principles and methods of research; Part Two covers writing, speaking, and getting one's work published.

Reader Program   Cengage Learning publishes a number of readers. Some contain exclusively primary sources, others are devoted to essays and secondary sources, and still others provide a combination of primary and secondary sources. All of these readers are designed to guide students through the process of historical inquiry. Visit *www.cengage.com/history* for a complete list of readers.

Custom Options   Nobody knows your students like you, so why not give them a text that tailor-fits their needs? Cengage Learning offers custom solutions for your course—whether it's making a small modification to *Western Civilization*, 10e, to match your syllabus or combining multiple sources to create something truly unique. Contact your Cengage Learning representative to explore custom solutions for your course.

ACKNOWLEDGMENTS

I BEGAN TO TEACH at age five in my family's grape arbor. By the age of ten, I wanted to know and understand everything in the world, so I set out to memorize our entire set of encyclopedia volumes. At seventeen, as editor of the high school yearbook, I chose "patterns" as its theme. With that as my early history, followed by many rich years of teaching, writing, and family nurturing, it seemed quite natural to accept the challenge of writing a history of Western civilization as I approached that period in life often described as the age of wisdom. Although I see this writing adventure as part of the natural unfolding of my life, I gratefully acknowledge that without the generosity of many others, it would not have been possible.

David Redles gave generously of his time and ideas, especially for Chapters 28, 29, and 30. Chris Colin provided research on the history of music, while Laurie Batitto, Alex Spencer, Stephen Maloney, Shaun Mason, Peter Angelos, and Fred Schooley offered valuable editorial assistance. I deeply appreciate the valuable technical assistance provided by Dayton Coles. I am deeply grateful to John Soares for his assistance in preparing the map captions and to Charmarie Blaisdell of Northeastern University for her detailed suggestions on women's history. Daniel Haxall of Kutztown University provided valuable assistance with materials on postwar art, popular culture, postmodern art and thought, and the Digital Age. I am especially grateful to Kathryn Spielvogel for her work as editorial associate for Chapters 15–30. I am also thankful to the thousands of students whose questions and responses have caused me to see many aspects of Western civilization in new ways.

My ability to undertake a project of this magnitude was in part due to the outstanding European history teachers that I had as both an undergraduate and graduate student. These included Kent Forster (modern Europe) and Robert W. Green (early modern Europe) at The Pennsylvania State University and Franklin Pegues (medieval), Andreas Dorpalen (modern Germany), William MacDonald (ancient), and Harold J. Grimm (Renaissance and Reformation) at The Ohio State University. These teachers provided me with profound insights into Western civilization and also taught me by their examples that learning only becomes true understanding when it is accompanied by compassion, humility, and open-mindedness.

I would like to thank the many teachers and students who have used the first nine editions. Their enthusiastic response to a textbook that was intended to put the story back in history and capture the imagination of the reader has been very gratifying. I especially thank the many teachers and students who made the effort to contact me personally to share their enthusiasm. Thanks to Cengage's comprehensive review process, many historians were asked to evaluate my manuscript and review each edition. I am grateful to the following people for their innumerable suggestions over the course of the first nine editions, which have greatly improved my work:

Anne J. Aby
Minnesota West Community and Technical College, Worthington Campus

Paul Allen
University of Utah

Randall Allen
Bay de Noc Community College

Gerald Anderson
North Dakota State University

Susan L. H. Anderson
Campbell University

Letizia Argenteri
University of San Diego

Roy A. Austensen
Illinois State University

James A. Baer
Northern Virginia Community College—Alexandria

James T. Baker
Western Kentucky University

Patrick Bass
Morningside College

John F. Battick
University of Maine

Frederic J. Baumgartner
Virginia Polytechnic Institute

Phillip N. Bebb
Ohio University

Anthony Bedford
Modesto Junior College

F. E. Beemon
Middle Tennessee State University

Leonard R. Berlanstein
University of Virginia

Cyriaque Beurtheret
Salt Lake Community College

Douglas T. Bisson
Belmont University

Charmarie Blaisdell
Northeastern University

Benay Blend
Central New Mexico Community College

Stephen H. Blumm
Montgomery County Community College

John Bohstedt
University of Tennessee—Knoxville

Hugh S. Bonar
California State University

Werner Braatz
University of Wisconsin—Oshkosh

Alfred S. Bradford
University of Missouri

Owen Bradley
Columbia College at Coast Guard Island

Janet Brantley
Texarkana College

Maryann E. Brink
College of William & Mary

Jerry Brookshire
Middle Tennessee State University

Daniel Patrick Brown
Moorpark College

Gregory S. Brown
University of Nevada—Las Vegas

Blaine T. Browne
Broward Community College

Daniel Bubb
Gonzaga University

Kevin W. Caldwell
Blue Ridge Community College

J. Holden Camp Jr.
Hillyer College, University of Hartford

Jack Cargill
Rutgers University

Martha Carlin
University of Wisconsin—Milwaukee

Elizabeth Carney
Clemson University

Susan Carrafiello
Wright State University

Jane Laurel Carrington
St. Olaf College

Joseph J. Casino
St. Joseph's University

Eric H. Cline
Xavier University

Robert G. Clouse
Indiana State University

Robert Cole
Utah State University

Elizabeth Collins
Triton College

William J. Connell
Rutgers University

Nancy Conradt
College of DuPage

Marc Cooper
Southwest Missouri State

Richard A. Cosgrove
University of Arizona

David A. Crain
South Dakota State University

Michael A. Crane Jr. (student)
Everett Community College

Luanne Dagley
Pellissippi State Technical Community College

John Davies
University of Delaware

Michael Dolski
Ball State University

Michael F. Doyle
Ocean County College

Hugh Dubrulle
Saint Anselm College

Joseph J. Eble
Burlington County College

James W. Ermatinger
University of Nebraska—Kearney

Porter Ewing
Los Angeles City College

Carla Falkner
Northeast Mississippi Community College

Steven Fanning
University of Illinois—Chicago

Ellsworth Faris
California State University—Chico

Gary B. Ferngren
Oregon State University

Mary Helen Finnerty
Westchester Community College

Jennifer Foray
Purdue University

Amy Forbes
Millsaps College

Jennifer E. Forster
Lakeland Community College

Patricia Frank
St. Clair County Community College

A. Z. Freeman
Robinson College

Marsha Frey
Kansas State University

Frank J. Frost
University of California—Santa Barbara

Frank Garosi
California State University—Sacramento

Laura Gellott
University of Wisconsin—Parkside

Richard M. Golden
University of North Texas

Manuel G. Gonzales
Diablo Valley College

Amy G. Gordon
Denison University

Richard J. Grace
Providence College

Charlotte M. Gradie
Sacred Heart University

Candace Gregory
California State University—Sacramento

Katherine Gribble
Highline Community College

Hanns Gross
Loyola University

John F. Guilmartin
Ohio State University

Paul Hagenloh
The University of Alabama

Jeffrey S. Hamilton
Gustavus Adolphus College

J. Drew Harrington
Western Kentucky University

James Harrison
Siena College

Doina Pasca Harsanyi
Central Michigan University

Jay Hatheway
Edgewood College

A. J. Heisserer
University of Oklahoma

Carol Herringer
Wright State University

Betsey Hertzler
Mesa Community College

Robert Herzstein
University of South Carolina

Michael C. Hickey
Bloomsburg University

Shirley Hickson
North Greenville College

Martha L. Hildreth
University of Nevada

Boyd H. Hill Jr.
University of Colorado—Boulder

Michael Hofstetter
Bethany College

Donald C. Holsinger
Seattle Pacific University

Frank L. Holt
University of Houston

W. Robert Houston
University of South Alabama

Michael W. Howell
College of the Ozarks

Anne Huebel
Franklin Pierce University

David Hudson
California State University—Fresno

Paul J. L. Hughes
Sussex County Community College

Richard A. Jackson
University of Houston

Fred Jewell
Harding University

Nicole Jobin
University of Colorado

Jenny M. Jochens
Towson State University

William M. Johnston
University of Massachusetts

George Kaloudis
Rivier College

Jeffrey A. Kaufmann
Muscatine Community College

David O. Kieft
University of Minnesota

Patricia Killen
Pacific Lutheran University

Jay Kilroy
Mesa Community College

William E. Kinsella Jr.
Northern Virginia Community College—Annandale

James M. Kittelson
Ohio State University

Doug Klepper
Santa Fe Community College

Cynthia Kosso
Northern Arizona University

Ed Krzemienski
The Citadel

Paul E. Lambert
Nichols College

Clayton Miles Lehmann
University of South Dakota

Diana Chen Lin
Indiana University, Northwest

Paul Douglas Lockhart
Wright State University

Ursula W. MacAffer
Hudson Valley Community College

Harold Marcuse
University of California—Santa Barbara

Mike Markowski
Westminster College

Michael Martin
Fort Lewis College

Mavis Mate
University of Oregon

Derek Maxfield
Genesee Community College

Priscilla McArthur
Troy State University—Dothan

T. Ronald Melton
Brewton Parker College

Martin Menke
Rivier College

Jack Allen Meyer
University of South Carolina

Eugene W. Miller Jr.
*The Pennsylvania State University—
Hazleton*

David B. Mock
Tallahassee Community College

John Patrick Montano
University of Delaware

Rex Morrow
Trident Technical College

Wyatt S. Moulds
Jones County Junior College

Kenneth Mouré
University of California—Santa Barbara

Thomas M. Mulhern
University of North Dakota

Pierce Mullen
Montana State University

Cliona Murphy
California State University—Bakersfield

Frederick I. Murphy
Western Kentucky University

William M. Murray
University of South Florida

Otto M. Nelson
Texas Tech University

Sam Nelson
Willmar Community College

John A. Nichols
Slippery Rock University

Lisa Nofzinger
*Albuquerque Technical Vocational
Institute*

Chris Oldstone-Moore
Augustana College

Donald Ostrowski
Harvard University

James O. Overfield
University of Vermont

Matthew L. Panczyk
Bergen Community College

Kathleen A. Parrow
Black Hills State University

Kathleen Paul
University of South Florida

Jody Peterson
Centralia College

Ted Petro
New England College

Carla Rahn Phillips
University of Minnesota

Keith Pickus
Wichita State University

Linda J. Piper
University of Georgia

Jeff Plaks
University of Central Oklahoma

Marjorie Plummer
Western Kentucky University

Janet Polasky
University of New Hampshire

Ann Pond
Bishop State Community College

Thomas W. Porter
Randolph-Macon College

Charles A. Povlovich
California State University—Fullerton

Penne L. Prigge
Rockingham Community College

Timothy Pytell
*California State University—
San Bernardino*

Nancy Rachels
Hillsborough Community College

Norman G. Raiford
Greenville Technical College

Charles Rearick
University of Massachusetts—Amherst

Jerome V. Reel Jr.
Clemson University

Roger Reese
Texas A&M University

William Roba
Scott Community College

Kevin Robbins
*Indiana University Purdue University—
Indianapolis*

Eric C. Roberson
Wake Technical Community College

Joseph Robertson
Gadsden State Community College

Jonathan Roth
San Jose State University

Constance M. Rousseau
Providence College

Beverly J. Rowe
Texarkana College

Matthew Ruane
Florida Institute of Technology

Julius R. Ruff
Marquette University

Mark Edward Ruff
Saint Louis University

David L. Ruffley
Pikes Peak Community College

Geraldine Ryder
Ocean County College

Richard Saller
University of Chicago

Magdalena Sanchez
Texas Christian University

Thomas J. Schaeper
St. Bonaventure University

Jack Schanfield
Suffolk County Community College

Roger Schlesinger
Washington State University

Joanne Schneider
Rhode Island College

Thomas C. Schunk
University of Wisconsin—Oshkosh

Kyle C. Sessions
Illinois State University

Linda Simmons
*Northern Virginia Community College—
Manassas*

Donald V. Sippel
Rhode Island College

Stuart Smyth
University at SUNY—Albany

Glen Spann
Asbury College

Heath A. Spencer
Seattle University

John W. Steinberg
Georgia Southern University

Barbara Stengel
Yuba College

Robert P. Stephens
Virginia Tech

Paul W. Strait
Florida State University

James E. Straukamp
*California State University—
Sacramento*

Brian E. Strayer
Andrews University

Fred Suppe
Ball State University

Roger Tate
Somerset Community College

Tom Taylor
Seattle University

Emily Teipe
Fullerton College

David Tengewall
Anne Arundel Community College

Jack W. Thacker
Western Kentucky University

Thomas Turley
Santa Clara University

John G. Tuthill
University of Guam

Maarten Ultee
University of Alabama

Donna L. Van Raaphorst
Cuyahoga Community College

J. Barry Vaughn
University of Alabama

Allen M. Ward
University of Connecticut

Richard D. Weigel
Western Kentucky University

Michael Weiss
Linn-Benton Community College

Alison Williams
Saint Joseph's University

Arthur H. Williamson
California State University—Sacramento

Daniel Woods
Ferrum College

Katherine Workman
Wright State University

Judith T. Wozniak
Cleveland State University

Walter J. Wussow
University of Wisconsin—Eau Claire

Edwin M. Yamauchi
Miami University

Robert W. Young
Carroll Community College

Sergei Zhuk
Ball State University

The following individuals contributed suggestions for the tenth edition:

Betsy Anderson
East Central Community College

Patrick Brennan
Gulf Coast State College

Matt Brent
Rappahannock Community College

Robert Brown
SUNY—Finger Lakes Community College

Claire Cage
University of South Alabama

Christine Eubank
Bergen Community College

Eric Fournier
West Chester University of Pennsylvania

Stella Gomezdelcampo
Roane State Community College

Awad Halabi
Wright State University

Sarah Jurenka
Bishop State

Thomas Mockaitis
DePaul University

Steven J. Williams
New Mexico Highlands University

Julianna Wilson
Pima Community College

The editors at Cengage Wadsworth have been both helpful and congenial at all times. I especially wish to thank Clark Baxter, who originally asked me to do this project, and whose clever wit, wisdom, gentle prodding, and good friendship added great depth to our working relationship. Margaret Beasley thoughtfully, wisely, efficiently, and pleasantly guided the overall development of the tenth edition. I also thank Scott Greenan for his suggestions and valuable editorial assistance. I also want to express my gratitude to Angela Urquhart, whose well-advised suggestions and generous support made the production process easier. Above all, I thank my family for their support. The gifts of love, laughter, and patience from my daughters, Jennifer and Kathryn; my sons, Eric and Christian; my daughters-in-law, Liz and Laurie; and my sons-in-law, Daniel and Eddie, were enormously appreciated. I also wish to acknowledge my grandchildren, Devyn, Bryn, Drew, Elena, Sean, Emma, and Jackson, who bring great joy to my life. My wife and best friend, Diane, contributed editorial assistance, wise counsel, good humor, and the loving support that made it possible for me to accomplish a project of this magnitude. I could not have written the book without her.

CIVILIZATION, AS HISTORIANS define it, first emerged between five and six thousand years ago when people in different parts of the world began to live in organized communities with distinct political, military, economic, and social structures. Religious, intellectual, and artistic activities assumed important roles in these early societies. The focus of this book is on Western civilization, a civilization that many people identify with the continent of Europe.

Defining Western Civilization

Western civilization itself has evolved considerably over the centuries. Although the concept of the West did not yet exist at the time of the Mesopotamians and Egyptians, their development of writing, law codes, and different roles based on gender all eventually influenced what became Western civilization. Although the Greeks did not conceive of Western civilization as a cultural entity, their artistic, intellectual, and political contributions were crucial to the foundations of Western civilization. The Romans produced a remarkable series of accomplishments that were fundamental to the development of Western civilization, a civilization that came to consist largely of lands in Europe conquered by the Romans, in which Roman cultural and political ideals were gradually spread. Nevertheless, people in these early civilizations viewed themselves as subjects of states or empires, not as members of Western civilization.

With the rise of Christianity during the Late Roman Empire, however, peoples in Europe began to identify themselves as part of a civilization different from others, such as that of Islam, leading to a concept of a Western civilization different from other civilizations. In the fifteenth century, Renaissance intellectuals began to identify this civilization not only with Christianity but also with the intellectual and political achievements of the ancient Greeks and Romans.

Important to the development of the idea of a distinct Western civilization were encounters with other peoples. Between 700 and 1500, encounters with the world of Islam helped define the West. After 1500, however, as European ships began to move into other parts of the world, encounters with peoples in Asia, Africa, and the Americas not only had an impact on the civilizations found there but also affected how people in the West defined themselves. At the same time, as they set up colonies, Europeans began to transplant a sense of Western identity to other areas of the world, especially North America and parts of Latin America, that have come to be considered part of Western civilization.

As the concept of Western civilization has evolved over the centuries, so have the values and unique features associated with that civilization. Science played a crucial role in the development of modern Western civilization. The societies of the Greeks, Romans, and medieval Europeans were based largely on a belief in the existence of a spiritual order; a dramatic departure to a natural or material view of the universe occurred in the seventeenth-century Scientific Revolution. Science and technology have been important in the growth of today's modern and largely secular Western civilization, although antecedents to scientific development also existed in Greek and medieval thought and practice, and religion remains an important component of the Western world today.

Many historians have viewed the concept of political liberty, belief in the fundamental value of every individual, and a rational outlook based on a system of logical, analytical thought as unique aspects of Western civilization. Of course, the West has also witnessed horrendous negations of liberty, individualism, and reason. Racism, slavery, violence, world wars, totalitarian regimes—these too form part of the complex story of what constitutes Western civilization.

The Dating of Time

In our examination of Western civilization, we also need to be aware of the dating of time. In recording the past, historians try to determine the exact time when events occurred. World War II in Europe, for example, began on September 1, 1939, when Hitler sent German troops into Poland, and ended on May 7, 1945, when Germany surrendered. By using dates, historians can place events in order and try to determine the development of patterns over periods of time.

If someone asked you when you were born, you would reply with a number, such as 1999. In the United States, we would all accept that number without question because it is part of the dating system followed in the Western world (Europe and the Western Hemisphere). In this system, events are dated by counting backward or forward from the year 1. When the system was first devised, the year 1 was assumed to be the year of the birth of Jesus, and the abbreviations B.C. (before Christ) and A.D. (for the Latin *anno Domini,* meaning "in the year of the Lord") were used to refer to the periods before and after the birth of Jesus, respectively. Historians now generally prefer to refer to the year 1 in nonreligious terms as the beginning of the "common era." The abbreviations B.C.E. (before the common era) and C.E. (common era) are used instead of B.C. and A.D., although the years are the same. Thus, an event that took place four hundred years before the year 1 would be dated 400 B.C.E. (before the common era)—or the date could be expressed as 400 B.C. Dates after the year 1 are labeled C.E. Thus, an event that took place two hundred years after the year 1 would be dated 200 C.E. (common era), or the date could be written as A.D. 200. It can also be written simply as 200, just as you would not give your birth year as 1999 C.E., but simply as 1999. In keeping with the current usage by most historians, this book will use the abbreviations B.C.E. and C.E.

Historians also make use of other terms to refer to time. A *decade* is ten years, a *century* is one hundred years, and a *millennium* is one thousand years. Thus, "the fourth century B.C.E." refers to the fourth period of one hundred years counting backward from the year 1, the beginning of the common era. Since the first century B.C.E. would be the years 100 B.C.E. to 1 C.E., the fourth century B.C.E. would be the years 400 B.C.E. to 301 B.C.E. We could say, then, that an event in 350 B.C.E. took place in the fourth century B.C.E.

Similarly, "the fourth century C.E." refers to the fourth period of one hundred years after the beginning of the common era. Since the first period of one hundred years would be the years 1 to 100, the fourth period or fourth century would be the years 301 to 400. We could say, then, that an event in 350 took place in the fourth century. Likewise, the first millennium B.C.E. refers to the years 1000 B.C.E. to 1 C.E.; the second millennium C.E. refers to the years 1001 to 2000.

The dating of events can also vary from people to people. Most people in the Western world use the Western calendar, also known as the Gregorian calendar after Pope Gregory XIII, who refined it in 1582. The Hebrew calendar uses a different system in which the year 1 is the equivalent of the Western year 3760 B.C.E., considered to be the date of the creation of the world according to the Bible. Thus, the Western year 2017 is the year 5777 on the Hebrew calendar. The Islamic calendar begins year 1 on the day Muhammad fled Mecca, which is the year 622 on the Western calendar.

ALTHOUGH EARLY CIVILIZATIONS emerged in different parts of the world, we begin our story of Western civilization with the Mesopotamians and Egyptians, who developed cities and struggled with the problems of organized states. They developed writing to keep records and created literature. They  constructed monumental architecture to please their gods, symbolize their power, and preserve their culture. They developed political, military, social, and religious structures to deal with the basic problems of human existence and organization. These first literate civilizations left detailed records that allow us to view how they grappled with three of the fundamental problems that humans have pondered: the nature of human relationships, the nature of the universe, and the role of divine forces in the cosmos. Although later peoples in Western civilization would provide different answers from those of the Mesopotamians and Egyptians, it was they who first posed the questions, gave answers, and wrote them down. Human memory begins with these two civilizations.

By 1500 B.C.E., much of the creative impulse of the Mesopotamian and Egyptian civilizations was beginning to wane. The entry of new peoples known as Indo-Europeans who moved into Asia Minor and Anatolia (modern Turkey) led to the creation of a Hittite kingdom that entered into conflict with the Egyptians. The invasion of the Sea Peoples around 1200 B.C.E., however, destroyed the Hittites, severely weakened the Egyptians, and created a power vacuum that allowed a patchwork of petty kingdoms and city-states to emerge, especially in the area of Syria and Palestine. All of them were eventually overshadowed by the rise of the great empires of the Assyrians, Chaldeans, and Persians. The Assyrian Empire was the first to unite almost all of the ancient Near East. Far larger was the empire of the Great Kings of Persia. Although it owed much to the administrative organization developed by the Assyrians, the Persian Empire had its own peculiar strengths. Persian rule was tolerant as well as efficient. Conquered peoples were allowed to keep their own religions, customs, and methods of doing business. The many years of peace that the Persian Empire brought to the Near East facilitated trade and the general well-being of its peoples. Many Near Eastern peoples expressed gratitude for being subjects of the Great Kings of Persia.

The Israelites were one of these peoples. Never numerous, they created no empire and were dominated by the Assyrians,  Chaldeans, and Persians. Nevertheless, they left a spiritual legacy that influenced much of the later development of Western civilization. The evolution of Hebrew monotheism (belief in a single god) created in Judaism one of the world's great religions; it influenced the development of both Christianity and Islam. When we speak of the Judeo-Christian heritage of Western civilization, we refer not only to the concept of monotheism but also to ideas of law, morality, and social justice that have become important parts of Western culture.

On the western fringes of the Persian Empire, another relatively small group of people, the Greeks, were creating cultural and political ideals that would also have an important impact on Western civilization. The first Greek civilization, known as the Mycenaean, took shape around 1600 B.C.E. and fell to new Greek-speaking invaders five hundred years later. By the eighth century B.C.E., the polis or city-state had become the chief focus of Greek life. Loyalty to the polis created a close-knit community but also divided Greece into a host of independent states, two of which, Sparta and Athens, became the most important. They were very different, however. Sparta created a closed, highly disciplined society, whereas Athens moved toward an open, democratic civilization.

The classical age in Greece (ca. 500–338 B.C.E.) began with a mighty confrontation between the Greeks and the Persian Empire. After their victory over the Persians, the Greeks began to divide into two large alliances, one headed by Sparta and the other by Athens. Athens created a naval empire and flourished during the age of Pericles, but fear of Athens led to the Great Peloponnesian War between Sparta and Athens and their allies. For all of their brilliant accomplishments, the Greeks were unable to rise above the divisions and rivalries that caused them to fight each other and undermine their own civilization.

The accomplishments of the Greeks formed the fountainhead of Western culture. Socrates, Plato, and Aristotle established the foundations of Western philosophy. Our literary forms are largely derived from Greek poetry and drama. Greek notions of harmony, proportion, and beauty have remained the touchstones for all subsequent Western art. A rational method of inquiry, so important to modern science, was conceived in ancient Greece. Many of our political terms are Greek in origin, as are  our concepts of the rights and duties of citizenship, especially as they were conceived in Athens, the first great democracy. Especially during their classical period, the Greeks raised and debated fundamental questions about the purpose of human existence, the structure of human society, and the nature of the universe that have concerned Western thinkers ever since.

While the Greek city-states were pursuing their squabbles, to their north a new and powerful kingdom—Macedonia—emerged. Under King Philip II, the Macedonians defeated a Greek allied army in 338 B.C.E. and then consolidated their control over the Greek peninsula. Although the independent Greek city-states lost their freedom when they were conquered by the Macedonians, Greek culture did not die. Under the leadership of Alexander the Great, son of Philip II, both the Macedonians and Greeks invaded and conquered the Persian Empire. In the conquered lands, Greeks and non-Greeks established a series of kingdoms (known as the Hellenistic kingdoms) and inaugurated the Hellenistic era.

The Hellenistic period was, in its own way, a vibrant one. New cities arose and flourished. New philosophical ideas captured the minds of many. Significant achievements occurred in art, literature, and science. Greek culture spread throughout the Near East and made an impact wherever it was carried. In some areas of the Hellenistic world, queens played an active role in political life, and many upper-class women found new avenues for expressing themselves. Although the Hellenistic era achieved a degree of political stability, by the late third century B.C.E., signs of decline were beginning to multiply, and the growing power of Rome eventually endangered the Hellenistic world.

Sometime in the eighth century B.C.E., a group of Latin-speaking people built a small community called Rome on the Tiber River in Italy. Between 509 and 264 B.C.E., this city expanded and united almost all of Italy under its control. Even more dramatically, between 264 and 133 B.C.E., Rome expanded to the west and east and became master of the Mediterranean Sea.

After 133 B.C.E., however, Rome's republican institutions proved inadequate for the task of ruling an empire. In the breakdown that ensued, ambitious individuals saw opportunities for power unparalleled in Roman history and succumbed to the temptations. After a series of bloody civil wars, peace was finally achieved when Octavian defeated Antony and Cleopatra. Octavian, who came to be known by the title of Augustus, created a new system of government that seemed to preserve the Republic while establishing the basis for a new system that would rule the empire in an orderly fashion.

After a century of internal upheaval, Augustus established a new order that began the Roman Empire, which experienced peace and prosperity between 14 and 180. During this era trade flourished and the provinces were governed efficiently. In the course of the third century, however, the Roman Empire almost collapsed because of invasions, civil wars, and economic decline. Although the emperors Diocletian and Constantine brought new life to the so-called Late Empire at the beginning of the fourth century, their efforts shored up the empire only temporarily. In the course of the fifth century, the empire divided into western and eastern parts.

The Roman Empire was the largest empire in antiquity. Using their practical skills, the Romans produced achievements in language, law, engineering, and government that were bequeathed to the future. The Romance languages of today (French, Italian, Spanish, Portuguese, and Romanian) are based on Latin. Western practices of impartial justice and trial by jury owe much to Roman law. As great builders, the Romans left

monuments to their skills throughout Europe, some of which, such as aqueducts and roads, are still in use today. Aspects of Roman administrative practices survived in the Western world for centuries. The Romans also preserved the intellectual heritage of the ancient world.

During its last two hundred years, the Roman world underwent a slow transformation with the spread of Christianity. The rise of Christianity marked an important break with the dominant values of the Roman world. Christianity began as a small Jewish sect, but under the guidance of Paul of Tarsus it became a world religion that appealed to both Jews and non-Jews. Despite persecution by Roman authorities, Christianity grew and became widely accepted by the fourth century. At the end of that century, it was made the official state religion of the Roman Empire.

The period of late antiquity that saw the disintegration of the western part of the Roman Empire also witnessed the emergence of a new European civilization in the Early Middle Ages. This early medieval civilization was formed by the coalescence of three major elements: the Germanic peoples who moved into the western part of the empire and established new kingdoms, the continuing attraction of the Greco-Roman cultural legacy, and the Christian church.  Politically, a new series of Germanic kingdoms emerged in western Europe. Each fused Roman and Germanic elements to create a new society. The Christian church (or Roman Catholic Church, as it came to be called in the west) played a crucial role in the growth of the new European civilization. The church developed an organized government under the leadership of the pope. It also assimilated the classical tradition and through its clergy brought Christianized civilization to the Germanic tribes. Especially important were the monks and nuns who led the way in converting the Germanic peoples in Europe to Christianity.

At the end of the eighth century, a new kingdom—the Carolingian Empire—came to control much of western and central Europe, especially during the reign of Charlemagne. In the long run, the creation of a western empire fostered the idea of a distinct European identity and marked a shift of power from the south to the north. Italy and the Mediterranean had been the center of the Roman Empire. The lands north of the Alps now became the political center of Europe, and increasingly, Europe emerged as the focus and center of Western civilization.

Building on a fusion of Germanic, classical, and Christian elements, the Carolingian Empire was well governed but held together primarily by personal loyalty to the strong king. The economy of the eighth and ninth centuries was based almost entirely on farming, which proved inadequate for maintaining a large monarchical system. As a result, a new political and military order—known as

fief-holding—subsequently evolved to become an integral part of the political world of the Middle Ages. Fief-holding was characterized by a decentralization of political power, in which lords exercised legal, administrative, and military power. This transferred public power into many private hands and seemed to provide security that the weak central government could not provide.

The new European civilization that had emerged in the ninth and tenth centuries began to come into its own in the eleventh and twelfth centuries, and Europeans established new patterns that reached their high point in the thirteenth century. The High Middle Ages (1000–1300) was a period of recovery and growth for Western civilization, characterized by a greater sense of security and a burst of energy and enthusiasm. Climatic improvements that produced better growing conditions, an expansion of cultivated land, and technological changes combined to enable Europe's food supply to increase significantly after 1000. This increase in agricultural production helped sustain a dramatic rise in population that was physically apparent in the expansion of towns and cities.

The development of trade and the rise of cities added a dynamic new element to the civilization of the High Middle Ages. Trading activities flourished first in northern Italy and  Flanders and then spread outward from these centers. In the late tenth and eleventh centuries, this renewal of commercial life led to a revival of cities. Old Roman sites came back to life, and new towns arose at major crossroads or natural harbors favorable to trading activities. By the twelfth and thirteenth centuries, both the urban centers and the urban population of Europe were experiencing a dramatic expansion. The revival of trade, the expansion of towns and cities, and the development of a money economy did not mean the end of a predominantly rural European society, but they did open the door to new ways to make a living and new opportunities for people to expand and enrich their lives. Eventually, they created the foundations for the development of a predominantly urban industrial society.

During the High Middle Ages, a landed aristocracy whose primary function was to fight dominated European society. These nobles built innumerable castles that gave a distinctive look to the countryside. Although lords and vassals seemed forever mired in endless petty conflicts, over time medieval  kings began to exert a centralizing authority and inaugurated the process of developing new kinds of monarchical states. By the thirteenth century, European monarchs were solidifying their governmental institutions in pursuit of greater power. The nobles, who rationalized their warlike attitudes by calling themselves the defenders of Christian society, continued to dominate the medieval world politically, economically, and socially. But quietly and surely, within this world of castles and private

power, kings gradually began to extend their public powers and developed the machinery of government that would enable them to become the centers of political authority in Europe. The actions of these medieval monarchs laid the foundation for the European kingdoms that in one form or another have dominated the European political scene ever since.

During the High Middle Ages, the power of both nobles and kings was often overshadowed by the authority of the Catholic Church, perhaps the dominant institution of the High Middle Ages. In the Early Middle Ages, the Catholic Church had shared in the challenge of new growth by reforming itself and striking out on a path toward greater papal power, both within the church and over European society. The High Middle Ages witnessed a spiritual renewal that led to numerous and even divergent paths: revived papal leadership, the development of centralized administrative machinery that buttressed papal authority, and new dimensions to the religious life of the clergy and laity. A wave of religious enthusiasm in the twelfth and thirteenth centuries led to the formation of new religious orders that worked to provide for the needs of the people, especially their concern for achieving salvation.

The economic, political, and religious growth of the High Middle Ages also gave European society a new confidence that enabled it to look beyond its borders to the lands and empires of the east. Only a confident Europe could have undertaken the crusades, a concerted military effort to recover the Holy Land of the Near East from the Muslims.

Western assurance and energy, so crucial to the crusades, were also evident in a burst of intellectual and artistic activity. New educational institutions known as universities came into being in the twelfth century. New literature, written in the vernacular language, appealed to the growing number of people in cities or at courts who could read. The study of theology, "queen of the sciences," reached a high point in the work of Thomas Aquinas. At  the same time, a religious building spree—especially evident in the great Romanesque and Gothic cathedrals of the age—left the landscape bedecked with churches that were the visible symbols of Christian Europe's vitality.

Growth and optimism seemed to characterize the High Middle Ages, but underneath the calm exterior lay seeds of discontent and change. Dissent from church teaching and practices grew in the thirteenth century, leading to a climate of fear and intolerance as the church responded with inquisitorial instruments to enforce conformity to its teachings. The breakdown of the old agricultural system and the creation of new relationships between lords and peasants led to local peasant uprisings in the late thirteenth century. The crusades ended ignominiously with the fall of the last crusading foothold in the east in 1291. By that time, more and more signs of ominous troubles were appearing. The fourteenth century would prove to be a time of crisis for European civilization.

In the High Middle Ages, European civilization had developed many of its fundamental features. Monarchical states, capitalist trade and industry, banks, cities, and vernacular literature were all products of that fertile period. During the same time, the Catholic Church, under the direction of the papacy, reached its apogee. Fourteenth-century European society, however, was challenged by an overwhelming number of crises that led to the disintegration of medieval civilization. At midcentury, one of the most destructive natural disasters in history erupted— the Black Death, a devastating plague that wiped out at least one-third of the European population. Economic crises and social upheavals, including a decline in trade and industry, bank failures, and peasant revolts pitting the lower classes against the upper classes, followed in the wake of the Black Death. The Hundred Years' War, a long, drawn-out conflict between the English and French, undermined political stability. The Catholic Church, too, experienced a crisis with the absence of the popes from Rome and even the spectacle of two popes condemning each other as the anti-Christ.

The new European society proved remarkably resilient, however. Periods of disintegration are often fertile grounds for change and new developments. Out of the dissolution of medieval civilization came a rebirth of culture that historians have labeled the Renaissance. It was a period of transition that witnessed a continuation of the economic, political, and social trends that had begun in the High Middle Ages. It was also a movement in which artists and intellectuals proclaimed a new vision of humankind and raised fundamental questions about the value and importance of the individual.

The humanists or intellectuals of the age called their period (from the mid-fourteenth to the mid-sixteenth century) an age of rebirth, believing that they had restored arts and letters to new glory after they had been "neglected" or "dead" for centuries. Of course, intellectuals and artists existed only among the upper classes, and the brilliant intellectual, cultural, and artistic accomplishments of the Renaissance were therefore products of and for the elite. The ideas of the Renaissance did not have a broad base among the masses.

The Renaissance did, however, raise new questions about medieval traditions. In advocating a return to the early sources of Christianity and criticizing current religious practices, the humanists raised fundamental issues about the Catholic Church, which was still an important institution. In the sixteenth century, the intellectual revolution of the fifteenth century gave way to a religious renaissance that touched the lives of people, including the masses, in new and profound ways.

When the monk Martin Luther entered the public scene with an attack on the sale of indulgences, few people suspected that he would eventually divide Europe along religious lines. But the yearning to reform the church and for meaningful religious experience caused a seemingly simple dispute to escalate into a powerful movement.

REFORMATION AND RELIGIOUS WARFARE IN THE SIXTEENTH CENTURY

A nineteenth-century engraving showing Luther before the Diet of Worms

bpk, Berlin/Art Resource, NY

CHAPTER OUTLINE AND FOCUS QUESTIONS

Prelude to Reformation

Q What were the chief ideas of the Christian humanists, and how did they differ from the ideas of the Protestant reformers?

Martin Luther and the Reformation in Germany

Q What were Martin Luther's main disagreements with the Roman Catholic Church, and what political, economic, and social conditions help explain why the movement he began spread so quickly across Europe?

The Spread of the Protestant Reformation

Q What were the main tenets of Lutheranism, Zwinglianism, Anabaptism, and Calvinism, and how did they differ from each other and from Catholicism? What impact did political, economic, and social conditions have on the development of these four reform movements?

The Social Impact of the Protestant Reformation

Q What impact did the Protestant Reformation have on society in the sixteenth century?

The Catholic Reformation

Q What measures did the Roman Catholic Church take to reform itself and to combat Protestantism in the sixteenth century?

Politics and the Wars of Religion in the Sixteenth Century

Q What role did politics, economic and social conditions, and religion play in the European wars of the sixteenth century?

Critical Thinking

Q *Where and how did the reform movements take hold, and how did the emergence of these reform movements affect the political and social realms where they were adopted?*

Connections to Today

Q *How are the religious controversies of the sixteenth century related to religious and social conditions in the Western world today?*

ON APRIL 18, 1521, a lowly monk stood before the emperor and princes of Germany in the city of Worms. He had been called before this august gathering to answer charges of heresy, charges that could threaten his very life. The monk was confronted with a pile of his books and asked if he wished to defend them all or reject a part. Courageously, Martin Luther defended them all and asked to be shown where any part was in error on the basis of "Scripture and plain reason." The emperor was outraged by Luther's response and made his own position clear the next day: "Not only I, but you of this noble German nation, would be forever disgraced if by our negligence not only heresy but the very suspicion of heresy were to survive. After having heard yesterday the obstinate defense of Luther, I regret that I have so long delayed in proceeding against him and his false teaching. I will have no more to do with him."[1] Luther's appearance at Worms set the stage for a serious challenge to the authority of the Catholic Church. This was by no means the first crisis in the church's fifteen-hundred-year history, but its consequences were more far-reaching than anyone at Worms in 1521 could have imagined.

Throughout the Middle Ages, the Christian church had continued to assert its primacy of position. It had overcome defiance of its temporal authority by emperors and kings, and challenges to its doctrines had been crushed by the Inquisition and combated by new religious orders that carried its message of salvation to all the towns and villages of medieval Europe. The growth of the papacy had paralleled the growth of the church, but by the end of the Middle Ages, challenges to papal authority from the rising power of monarchical states had resulted in a loss of papal temporal authority. An even greater threat to papal authority and church unity arose in the sixteenth century when the Reformation shattered the unity of Christendom.

The movement begun by Martin Luther when he made his dramatic stand quickly spread across Europe, a clear indication of dissatisfaction with Catholic practices. Within a short time, new forms of religious practices, doctrines, and organizations, including Zwinglianism, Calvinism, Anabaptism, and Anglicanism, were attracting adherents all over Europe. Although seemingly helpless to stop the new Protestant churches, the Catholic Church also underwent a reformation and managed to revive its fortunes by the mid-sixteenth century. All too soon, the doctrinal divisions between Protestants and Catholics led to a series of religious wars that dominated the history of western Europe in the second half of the sixteenth century.

Prelude to Reformation

 FOCUS QUESTION: What were the chief ideas of the Christian humanists, and how did they differ from the ideas of the Protestant reformers?

Martin Luther's reform movement was by no means the first. During the second half of the fifteenth century, the new classical learning that was part of Italian Renaissance humanism spread to northern Europe and spawned a movement called **Christian (northern Renaissance) humanism** whose major goal was the reform of Christianity.

Christian or Northern Renaissance Humanism

Like their Italian counterparts, northern humanists cultivated knowledge of the classics, the bond that united all humanists into a kind of international fellowship. In returning to the writings of antiquity, northern humanists (also called Christian humanists because of their profound preoccupation with religion) focused on the sources of early Christianity, the Holy Scriptures and the writings of such church fathers as Augustine, Ambrose, and Jerome. In these early Christian writings, they discovered a simple religion that they came to feel had been distorted by the complicated theological arguments of the Middle Ages.

The most important characteristic of northern humanism was its reform program. Convinced of the ability of human beings to reason and improve themselves, the northern humanists felt that through education in the sources of classical, and especially Christian, antiquity, they could instill a true inner piety or an inward religious feeling that would bring about a reform of the church and society. For this reason, Christian humanists supported schools, brought out new editions of the classics, and prepared new editions of the Bible and writings of the church fathers. In the preface to his edition of the Greek New Testament, the famous humanist Erasmus wrote:

> I disagree very much with those who are unwilling that Holy Scripture, translated into the vulgar tongue, be read by the uneducated, as if Christ taught such intricate doctrines that they could scarcely be understood by very few theologians, or as if the strength of the Christian religion consisted in men's ignorance of it. . . . I would that even the lowliest women read the Gospels and the Pauline Epistles. And I would that they were translated into all languages so that they could be read and understood not only by Scots and Irish but also by Turks and Saracens. . . . Would that, as a result, the farmer sing some portion of them at the plow, the weaver hum some parts of them to the movement of his shuttle, the traveler lighten the weariness of the journey with stories of this kind![2]

This belief in the power of education would remain an important characteristic of European civilization. Like later intellectuals, Christian humanists believed that to change society, they must first change the human beings who compose it. Although some critics have called the Christian humanists naive, they were in fact merely optimistic. The turmoil of the Reformation, however, shattered much of this intellectual optimism, as the lives and careers of two of the most prominent Christian humanists, Desiderius Erasmus and Thomas More, illustrate.

ERASMUS The most influential of all the Christian humanists was Desiderius Erasmus (dez-ih-DEER-ee-uss ih-RAZZ-mus) (1466–1536), who formulated and popularized the reform program of Christian humanism. Born in Holland, Erasmus was educated at one of the schools of the Brothers of the Common Life (see Chapter 11). He wandered to France, England, Italy, Germany, and Switzerland, conversing everywhere in the classical Latin that might be called his mother tongue. The *Handbook of the Christian Knight*, printed in 1503, reflected his preoccupation with religion. He called his conception of religion "the philosophy of Christ," by which he meant that Christianity should be a guiding philosophy for the direction of daily life rather than the system of dogmatic beliefs and practices that the medieval church seemed to stress. In other words, he emphasized inner piety and de-emphasized the external forms of religion (such as the sacraments, pilgrimages, fasts, veneration of saints, and relics). To return to the simplicity

Erasmus. Desiderius Erasmus was the most influential of the northern Renaissance humanists. He sought to restore Christianity to the early simplicity found in the teachings of Jesus. This portrait of Erasmus was painted in 1523 by Hans Holbein the Younger, who had formed a friendship with the great humanist while they were both in Basel.

of the early church, people needed to understand the original meaning of the Scriptures and the writings of the early church fathers. Because Erasmus thought that the standard Latin edition of the Bible, known as the Vulgate, contained errors, he edited the Greek text of the New Testament from the earliest available manuscripts and published it, along with a new Latin translation, in 1516. Erasmus also wrote *Annotations*, a detailed commentary on the Vulgate Bible itself. In his day, Erasmus's work on the New Testament was considered his most outstanding achievement, and Martin Luther himself would use Erasmus's work as the basis for his German translation of the New Testament.

To Erasmus, the reform of the church meant spreading an understanding of the philosophy of Jesus, providing enlightened education in the sources of early Christianity, and making common-sense criticisms of the abuses in the church. This last is especially evident in *The Praise of Folly*, written in 1509, in which Erasmus engaged in humorous yet effective criticism of the most corrupt practices of his own society. He was especially harsh on the abuses within the ranks of the clergy (see the box on p. 368).

In another satirical work, *Julius Excluded from Heaven*, Erasmus pilloried the Renaissance papacy in the person of Julius II, the "warrior pope" (see Chapter 12). When Julius dies, he appears before the gates of heaven, expecting a quick entry.

When St. Peter denies him entrance because of Julius' misdeeds, Julius threatens to raise an army and storm heaven itself.

Erasmus's program did not achieve the reform of the church that he so desired. His moderation and his emphasis on education were quickly overwhelmed by the passions of the Reformation. Undoubtedly, though, his work helped prepare the way for the Reformation; as contemporaries proclaimed, "Erasmus laid the egg that Luther hatched." Yet Erasmus eventually disapproved of Luther and the Protestant reformers. He had no intention of destroying the unity of the medieval Christian church; rather, his whole program was based on reform within the church.

THOMAS MORE The son of a London lawyer, Thomas More (1478–1535) received the benefits of a good education. Although trained in the law, he took an avid interest in the new classical learning and became proficient in both Latin and Greek. Like the Italian humanists, who believed in putting their learning at the service of the state, More embarked on a public career that ultimately took him to the highest reaches of power as lord chancellor of England.

His career in government service, however, did not keep More from the intellectual and spiritual interests that were so dear to him. He was well acquainted with other English humanists and became an intimate friend of Erasmus. He made translations from Greek authors and wrote both prose and poetry in Latin. A devout man, he spent many hours in prayer and private devotions. Contemporaries praised his household as a shining model of Christian family life.

More's most famous work, and one of the most controversial of his age, was *Utopia*, written in 1516. This literary masterpiece is an account of the idealistic life and institutions of the community of Utopia (Greek for "nowhere"), an imaginary island in the vicinity of the recently discovered New World. It reflects More's own concerns with the economic, social, and political problems of his day. He presented a new social system in which cooperation and reason replaced power and fame as the proper motivating agents for human society. Utopian society, therefore, was based on communal ownership rather than private property. All residents of Utopia worked nine hours a day, regardless of occupation, and were rewarded according to their needs. Possessing abundant leisure time and relieved of competition and greed, Utopians were free to lead wholesome and enriching lives.

In serving King Henry VIII, More came face to face with the abuses and corruption he had criticized in *Utopia*. But he did not allow idealism to outweigh his own ultimate realism, and in *Utopia* itself he justified his service to the king:

> If you can't completely eradicate wrong ideas, or deal with
> inveterate vices as effectively as you could wish, that's no
> reason for turning your back on public life altogether. . . . On
> the other hand, it's no use attempting to put across entirely
> new ideas, which will obviously carry no weight with people
> who are prejudiced against them. You must go to work
> indirectly. You must handle everything as tactfully as you
> can, and what you can't put right you must try to make as
> little wrong as possible. For things will never be perfect, until
> human beings are perfect—which I don't expect them to be
> for quite a number of years.[3]

ERASMUS: IN PRAISE OF FOLLY

THE PRAISE OF FOLLY IS ONE OF THE MOST famous pieces of literature produced in the sixteenth century. Erasmus, who wrote it in a short time during a visit to the home of Thomas More, considered it a "little diversion" from his "serious work." Yet both contemporaries and later generations have appreciated "this laughing parody of every form and rank of human life." In this selection, Erasmus belittles one of his favorite objects of scorn, the monks. They were, however, merely one of the many groups he disparaged.

Erasmus, *The Praise of Folly*

Those who are the closest to these [the theologians] in happiness are generally called "the religious" or "monks," both of which are deceiving names, since for the most part they stay as far away from religion as possible and frequent every sort of place. I [Folly] cannot, however, see how any life could be more gloomy than the life of these monks if I did not assist them in many ways. Though most people detest these men so much that accidentally meeting one is considered to be bad luck, the monks themselves believe that they are magnificent creatures. One of their chief beliefs is that to be illiterate is to be of a high state of sanctity, and so they make sure that they are not able to read. Another is that when braying out their gospels in church they are making themselves very pleasing and satisfying to God, when in fact they are uttering these psalms as a matter of repetition rather than from their hearts. . . .

Moreover, it is amusing to find that they insist that everything be done in fastidious detail, as if employing the orderliness of mathematics, a small mistake in which would be a great crime. Just so many knots must be on each shoe and the shoelace may be of only one specified color; just so much lace is allowed on each habit; the girdle must be of just the right material and width; the hood of a certain shape and capacity; their hair of just so many fingers' length; and finally they can sleep only the specified number of hours per day. Can they not understand that, because of a variety of bodies and temperaments, all this equality of restrictions is in fact very unequal? Nevertheless, because of all this detail that they employ they think that they are superior to all other people. And what is more, amid all their pretense of Apostolic charity, the members of one order will denounce the members of another order clamorously because of the way in which the habit has been belted or the slightly darker color of it. . . .

Many of them work so hard at protocol and at traditional fastidiousness that they think one heaven hardly a suitable reward for their labors; never recalling, however, that the time will come when Christ will demand a reckoning of that which he had prescribed, namely charity, and that he will hold their deeds of little account. One monk will then exhibit his belly filled with every kind of fish; another will profess a knowledge of over a hundred hymns. Still another will reveal a countless number of fasts that he has made, and will account for his large belly by explaining that his fasts have always been broken by a single large meal. Another will show a list of church ceremonies over which he has officiated so large that it would fill seven ships.

 What are Erasmus's main criticisms of monks? What do you think he hoped to achieve by this satirical attack on monastic practices? How do you think the circulation of many printed copies of such attacks would have affected popular attitudes toward the Catholic Church?

Source: Erasmus, "The Praise of Folly," in *The Essential Erasmus*, trans. J. P. Dolan (New York: Dutton Signet, 1964).

More's religious devotion and belief in the universal Catholic Church ultimately proved even more important than his service to the king, however. While in office, More's intolerance of heresy led him to advocate persecution of those who would fundamentally change the Catholic Church. Moreover, always the man of conscience, More willingly gave up his life opposing England's break with the Roman Catholic Church over the divorce of King Henry VIII.

Church and Religion on the Eve of the Reformation

Corruption in the Catholic Church was another factor that spurred people to want reform. No doubt the failure of the Renaissance popes to provide spiritual leadership had affected the spiritual life of all Christendom. The papal court's preoccupation with finances had an especially strong impact on the clergy. So did the economic changes of the fourteenth and fifteenth centuries. Increasingly, nobles or wealthy members of the bourgeoisie held the highest positions among the clergy. Moreover, to increase their revenues, high church officials (bishops, archbishops, and cardinals) took over more than one church office. This so-called **pluralism** led in turn to absenteeism: church officeholders ignored their duties and hired underlings who sometimes lacked the proper qualifications. Complaints about the ignorance and ineptness of parish priests became widespread in the fifteenth century.

THE SEARCH FOR SALVATION While many of the leaders of the church were failing to meet their responsibilities, ordinary people were clamoring for meaningful religious expression and certainty of salvation. As a result, for some the salvation process became almost mechanical. As more and more people sought certainty of salvation through veneration of relics, collections of such objects grew. Frederick the Wise, elector of Saxony and Martin Luther's prince, had amassed more than 19,000 relics to which were attached indulgences that could reduce one's time in purgatory by nearly 2 million years. (An indulgence, you will recall, is a remission, after death, of all or part of the punishment for sin.) Other people sought certainty of salvation in the popular mystical movement known as the Modern Devotion, which downplayed religious dogma and stressed the need to follow the teachings of Jesus. Thomas à Kempis, author of *The Imitation of Christ*, wrote that "truly, at the day of judgment we shall not be examined by what we have read, but what we have done; not how well we have spoken, but how religiously we have lived."

What is striking about the revival of religious piety in the fifteenth century—whether expressed through such external forces as the veneration of relics and the buying of indulgences or the mystical path—was its adherence to the orthodox beliefs and practices of the Catholic Church. The agitation for certainty of salvation and spiritual peace occurred within the framework of the "holy mother Church." But disillusionment grew as the devout experienced the clergy's inability to live up to their expectations. The deepening of religious life, especially in the second half of the fifteenth century, found little echo among the worldly-wise clergy, and this environment helps explain the tremendous and immediate impact of Luther's ideas.

CALLS FOR REFORM At the same time, several sources of reform were already at work within the Catholic Church at the end of the fifteenth and the beginning of the sixteenth century. Especially noticeable were the calls for reform from the religious orders of the Franciscans, Dominicans, and Augustinians. Members of these groups put particular emphasis on preaching to laypeople. One of the popular preachers was Johannes Geiler of Kaisersberg (KY-zerz-bayrk), who denounced the corruption of the clergy.

The Oratory of Divine Love, first organized in Italy in 1497, was not a religious order but an informal group of clergy and laymen who worked to foster reform by emphasizing personal spiritual development and outward acts of charity. The "philosophy of Christ," advocated by the Christian humanist Erasmus, was especially appealing to many of them. The Oratory's members included a number of cardinals who favored church reform. A Spanish archbishop, Cardinal Ximenes, was especially active in using Christian humanism to reform the church. To foster spirituality among the people, he had a number of religious writings, including Thomas à Kempis's *The Imitation of Christ*, translated into Spanish.

Martin Luther and the Reformation in Germany

 FOCUS QUESTION: What were Martin Luther's main disagreements with the Roman Catholic Church, and what political, economic, and social conditions help explain why the movement he began spread so quickly across Europe?

The Protestant Reformation began with a typical medieval question: What must I do to be saved? Martin Luther, a deeply religious man, found an answer that did not fit within the

traditional teachings of the late medieval church. Ultimately, he split with that church, destroying the religious unity of western Christendom. That other people were concerned with the same question is evident in the rapid spread of the Reformation. But religion was so entangled in the social, economic, and political forces of the period that the Protestant reformers' hope of transforming the church quickly proved illusory.

The Early Luther

Martin Luther was born in Germany on November 10, 1483. His father wanted him to become a lawyer, so Luther enrolled at the University of Erfurt, where he received his bachelor's degree in 1502. Three years later, after becoming a master in the liberal arts, the young man began to study law. But Luther was not content, not in small part due to his long-standing religious inclinations. That summer, while returning to Erfurt after a brief visit home, he was caught in a ferocious thunderstorm and vowed that if he survived unscathed, he would become a monk. He then entered the monastic order of the Augustinian Hermits in Erfurt, much to his father's disgust. In the monastery, Luther focused on his major concern, the assurance of salvation. The traditional beliefs and practices of the church seemed unable to relieve his obsession with this question, especially evident in his struggle with the sacrament of penance or **confession**. The sacraments were a Catholic's chief means of receiving God's grace; confession offered the opportunity to have one's sins forgiven. Luther spent hours confessing his sins, but he was always doubtful. Had he remembered all of his sins? Even more, how could a hopeless sinner be acceptable to a totally just and all-powerful God? Luther threw himself into his monastic routine with a vengeance:

> I was indeed a good monk and kept my order so strictly that I could say that if ever a monk could get to heaven through monastic discipline, I was that monk. . . . And yet my conscience would not give me certainty, but I always doubted and said, "You didn't do that right. You weren't contrite enough. You left that out of your confession." The more I tried to remedy an uncertain, weak and troubled conscience with human traditions, the more I daily found it more uncertain, weaker and more troubled.[4]

Despite his strenuous efforts, Luther achieved no certainty.

To help overcome his difficulties, his superiors recommended that the monk study theology. He received his doctorate in 1512 and then became a professor in the theological faculty at the University of Wittenberg (VIT-ten-bayrk), lecturing on the Bible. Sometime between 1513 and 1516, through his study of the Bible, he arrived at an answer to his problem.

Catholic doctrine had emphasized that both faith and good works were required for a Christian to achieve personal salvation. In Luther's eyes, human beings, weak and powerless in the sight of an almighty God, could never do enough good works to merit salvation. Through his study of the Bible, especially his work on Paul's Epistle to the Romans, Luther rediscovered another way of viewing this problem. To Luther, humans are saved not through their good works but through faith in the promises of God, made possible by the sacrifice of Jesus on

Martin Luther and Katherina von Bora. This double portrait of Martin Luther and his wife was done by Lucas Cranach the Elder in 1529. By this time, Luther's reforms had begun to make an impact in many parts of Germany. Luther married Katherina von Bora in 1525, thus creating a new model of family life for Protestant ministers.

the cross. The doctrine of salvation or justification by grace through faith alone became the primary doctrine of the Protestant Reformation (**justification** is the act by which a person is made deserving of salvation). Because Luther had arrived at this doctrine from his study of the Bible, the Bible became for Luther, as for all other Protestants, the chief guide to religious truth. Justification by faith and the Bible as the sole authority in religious affairs were the twin pillars of the Protestant Reformation.

THE INDULGENCE CONTROVERSY Luther did not see himself as either a revolutionary innovator or a heretic, but his involvement in the indulgence controversy propelled him into an open confrontation with church officials and forced him to see the theological implications of justification by faith alone. In 1517, Pope Leo X had issued a special jubilee indulgence to finance the ongoing construction of Saint Peter's Basilica in Rome. Johann Tetzel, a rambunctious Dominican, hawked the indulgences in Germany with the slogan "As soon as the coin in the coffer rings, the soul from purgatory springs."

Greatly distressed by the sale of indulgences, Luther was certain that people who relied on these pieces of paper to assure themselves of salvation were guaranteeing their eternal damnation instead. Angered, he issued his Ninety-Five Theses, although scholars are unsure whether he nailed them to a church door in Wittenberg, as is traditionally alleged, or mailed them to his ecclesiastical superior. In either case, his theses were a stunning indictment of the abuses in the sale of indulgences (see the box on p. 371). It is doubtful that Luther intended any break with the church over the issue of indulgences. If the pope had clarified the use of indulgences, as Luther wished, he would probably have been satisfied, and the controversy would

have ended. But Pope Leo X did not take the issue seriously and is even reported to have said that Luther was simply "some drunken German who will amend his ways when he sobers up." Thousands of copies of a German translation of the Ninety-Five Theses were quickly printed and were received sympathetically in a Germany that had a long tradition of dissatisfaction with papal policies and power.

Of course, Luther was not the first theologian to criticize the powers of the papacy. As we saw in Chapter 12, John Wyclif at the end of the fourteenth century and John Hus at the beginning of the fifteenth century had attacked the excessive power of the papacy. Luther was certainly well aware of John Hus's fate at the Council of Constance, where he was burned at the stake on charges of heresy.

THE QUICKENING REBELLION The controversy reached an important turning point with the Leipzig Debate in July 1519. In Leipzig, Luther's opponent, the capable Catholic theologian Johann Eck, forced Luther to move beyond indulgences and deny the authority of popes and councils. During the debate, Eck also identified Luther's ideas with those of John Hus, the condemned heretic. Luther was now compelled to see the consequences of his new theology. At the beginning of 1520, he proclaimed: "Farewell, unhappy, hopeless, blasphemous Rome! The Wrath of God has come upon you, as you deserve. We have cared for Babylon, and she is not healed: let us then, leave her, that she may be the habitation of dragons, spectres, and witches."[5] At the same time, Luther was convinced that he was doing God's work and had to proceed regardless of the consequences.

In three pamphlets published in 1520, Luther moved toward a more definite break with the Catholic Church. The *Address to the Nobility of the German Nation* was a political tract written

LUTHER AND THE NINETY-FIVE THESES

TO MOST HISTORIANS, THE PUBLICATION of Luther's Ninety-Five Theses marks the beginning of the Reformation. To Luther, they were simply a response to what he considered Johann Tetzel's blatant abuses in selling indulgences. Although written in Latin, Luther's statements were soon translated into German and disseminated widely across Germany. They made an immense impression on Germans already dissatisfied with the ecclesiastical and financial policies of the papacy.

Martin Luther, *Selections from the Ninety-Five Theses*

5. The Pope has neither the will nor the power to remit any penalties, except those which he has imposed by his own authority, or by that of the canons [canon law].

20. Therefore the Pope, when he speaks of the plenary remission of all penalties, does not mean simply of all, but only of those imposed by himself.

21. Thus those preachers of indulgences are in error who say that, by the indulgences of the Pope, a man is loosed and saved from all punishment.

27. They preach man [It is mere human talk], who say that the soul flies out of purgatory as soon as the money thrown into the chest rattles.

28. It is certain, that, when the money rattles in the chest, avarice and gain may be increased, but the suffrage of the Church depends on the will of God alone.

50. Christians should be taught, that, if the Pope were acquainted with the exactions of the preachers of pardons, he would prefer that the Basilica of St. Peter should be burnt to ashes, than that it should be built up with the skin, flesh, and bones of his sheep.

81. This license in the preaching of pardons makes it no easy thing, even for learned men, to protect the reverence due to the Pope against the calumnies, or, at all events, the keen questionings, of the laity;

82. As, for instance: Why does not the Pope empty purgatory for the sake of most holy charity and of the supreme necessity of souls,—this being the most just of all reasons,—if he redeems an infinite number of souls for the sake of that most fatal thing, money, to be spent on building a basilica—this being a slight reason?

86. Again: Why does not the Pope, whose riches are at this day more ample than those of the wealthiest of the wealthy, build the one Basilica of St. Peter with his own money, rather than with that of poor believers?

90. To repress these scruples and arguments of the laity by force alone, and not to solve them by giving reasons, is to expose the Church and the Pope to the ridicule of their enemies, and to make Christian men unhappy.

94. Christians should be exhorted to strive to follow Christ their head through pains, deaths, and hells;

95. And thus trust to enter heaven through many tribulations, rather than in the security of peace.

Q *What were the major ideas of Luther's Ninety-Five Theses? Why did they have such a strong appeal in Germany?*

Source: P. Schaff, *History of the Christian Church*, vol. VI (New York: Charles Scribner's Sons, 1916), pp. 161–166.

in German in which Luther called on the German princes to overthrow the papacy in Germany and establish a reformed German church. The *Babylonian Captivity of the Church*, written in Latin for theologians, attacked the sacramental system as the means by which the pope and church had held the real meaning of the Gospel captive for a thousand years. Luther called for the reform of monasticism and for the clergy to marry. Though virginity is good, he argued, marriage is better, and freedom of choice is best. *On the Freedom of a Christian Man* was a short treatise on the doctrine of salvation. It is faith alone, not good works, that justifies, frees, and brings salvation through Jesus. Being saved and freed by his faith in Jesus, however, does not free the Christian from doing good works. Rather, he performs good works out of gratitude to God. "Good works do not make a good man, but a good man does good works."[6]

Unable to accept Luther's forcefully worded dissent from traditional Catholic teachings, the church excommunicated him in January 1521. He was also summoned to appear before the Reichstag (RYKHSS-tahk), the imperial diet of the Holy Roman Empire, in Worms (WURMZ *or* VORMPS), convened by the recently elected Emperor Charles V (1519–1556). Expected to recant the heretical doctrines he had espoused, Luther refused and made the famous reply that became the battle cry of the Reformation:

> Since then Your Majesty and your lordships desire a simple reply, I will answer without horns and without teeth. Unless I am convicted by Scripture and plain reason—I do not accept the authority of popes and councils, for they have contradicted each other—my conscience is captive to the Word of God. I cannot and I will not recant anything, for to go against conscience is neither right nor safe. Here I stand, I cannot do otherwise. God help me. Amen.[7]

Emperor Charles was outraged at Luther's audacity and gave his opinion that "a single friar who goes counter to all Christianity for a thousand years must be wrong." By the Edict of Worms, Martin Luther was made an outlaw within the empire. His works were to be burned, and Luther himself was to be captured and delivered to the emperor. Instead, Luther's prince, the Elector of Saxony, sent him into hiding at the Wartburg (VART-bayrk) Castle, where he remained for nearly a year (see "Film & History" on p. 372).

The Rise of Lutheranism

At the beginning of 1522, Luther returned to Wittenberg in Electoral Saxony and began to organize a reformed church. While at the Wartburg Castle, Luther's foremost achievement was his translation of the New Testament into German. Within twelve years, his German New Testament had sold almost 200,000 copies. Lutheranism had wide appeal and spread rapidly, but not primarily through the written word since only 4 to 5 percent of people in Germany were literate. And most of these were in urban areas.

Instead, the primary means of disseminating Luther's ideas was the sermon. The preaching of evangelical sermons, based on a return to the original message of the Bible, found favor throughout Germany. In city after city, the arrival of preachers presenting Luther's teachings was soon followed by a public debate in which the new preachers proved victorious. State authorities then instituted a reform of the church.

Also useful to the spread of the Reformation were pamphlets illustrated with vivid woodcuts portraying the pope as a hideous Antichrist and titled with catchy phrases such as "I Wonder Why There Is No Money in the Land" (which, of course, was an attack on papal greed). Luther also insisted on the use of music as a means to teach the Gospel, and his own composition, "A Mighty Fortress Is Our God," became the battle hymn of the Reformation:

> With our power nothing is done.
>   We are soon lost.
> But for us fights the mighty one
>   Whom God himself has chosen.
> You ask, who is this?
> He is called Jesus Christ
> The Lord God of hosts.
> And there is no other God.
> He must hold the field forever.[8]

THE SPREAD OF LUTHER'S IDEAS Lutheranism spread to both princely and ecclesiastical states in northern and central Germany as well as to two-thirds of the free imperial cities,

Woodcut: Luther Versus the Pope. In the 1520s, after Luther's return to Wittenberg, his teachings began to spread rapidly, ending ultimately in a reform movement supported by state authorities. Pamphlets containing picturesque woodcuts were important in the spread of Luther's ideas. In the woodcut shown here, the crucified Jesus attends Luther's service on the left, while on the right the pope is at a table selling indulgences.

especially those of southern Germany, where prosperous burghers, for both religious and secular reasons, became committed to Luther's cause. Nuremberg, where an active city council led by the dynamic city secretary Lazarus Spengler (SCHPEN-ler) brought about a conversion as early as 1525, was the first imperial city to convert to Lutheranism. Luther had visited the city in 1518 and made a number of friends and supporters there, including some prominent men. Albrecht Dürer, the artist (see Chapter 12) said, "In my opinion, it is exactly here that Luther has helped to clarify the situation by making it a point to trust God more than oneself, worldly works, and the laws of human beings."[9] At its outset, the Reformation in Germany was largely an urban phenomenon. Three-fourths of the early converts to the reform movement were from the clergy, many of them from the upper classes, which made it easier for them to work with the ruling elites in the cities.

A series of crises in the mid-1520s made it apparent, however, that spreading the word of God was not as easy as Luther had originally envisioned—the usual plight of most reformers. Luther experienced dissent within his own ranks in Wittenberg from people such as Andreas Carlstadt (KARL-shtaht), who wished to initiate a more radical reform by abolishing all relics, images, and the Mass. Luther had no sooner dealt with them than he began to face opposition from the Christian humanists. Many had initially supported Luther, believing that he shared their goal of reforming the abuses within the church. But when it became apparent that Luther's movement threatened the unity of Christendom, the older generation of Christian humanists, including Erasmus, broke with the reformer. A younger generation of Christian humanists, however, played a significant role in Lutheranism. When Philip Melanchthon (muh-LANK-tun) (1497–1560) arrived in Wittenberg in 1518 at the age of twenty-one to teach Greek and Hebrew, he was immediately attracted to Luther's ideas and became a staunch supporter.

THE PEASANTS' WAR Luther's greatest challenge in the mid-1520s, however, came from the Peasants' War. Peasant dissatisfaction in Germany stemmed from several sources. Many peasants had not been touched by the gradual economic improvement of the early sixteenth century. In some areas, especially southwestern Germany, influential local lords continued to abuse their peasants, and new demands for taxes and other services caused them to wish for a return to "the good old days." Social discontent soon became entangled with religious revolt as peasants looked to Martin Luther, believing that he would support them. It was not Luther, however, but one of his ex-followers, the radical Thomas Müntzer (MOON-tsur), himself a pastor, who inflamed the peasants against their rulers with his fiery language: "Strike while the iron is hot!" Revolt first erupted in southwestern Germany in June 1524 and spread northward and eastward.

Luther reacted quickly and vehemently against the peasants. In his pamphlet *Against the Robbing and Murdering Hordes of Peasants*, he called on the German princes to "smite, slay and stab" the stupid and stubborn peasantry (see the box on p. 374). Luther, who knew how much his reformation of the

CHRONOLOGY	Luther's Reform Movement
Ninety-Five Theses	1517
Leipzig Debate	1519
Diet and Edict of Worms	1521
Peasants' War	1524–1525

church depended on the full support of the German princes and magistrates, supported the rulers, although he also blamed them for helping to set off the rebellion by their earlier harsh treatment of the peasants. To Luther, the state and its rulers were ordained by God and given the authority to maintain the peace and order necessary for the spread of the Gospel. It was the duty of princes to put down all revolts. By May 1525, the German princes had ruthlessly suppressed the peasant hordes. By this time, Luther found himself ever more dependent on state authorities for the growth and maintenance of his reformed church.

Organizing the Church

Justification by faith alone was the starting point for most of Protestantism's major doctrines. Since Luther downplayed the role of good works in salvation, the sacraments also had to be redefined. No longer regarded as merit-earning works, they were now viewed as divinely established signs signifying the promise of salvation. Based on his interpretation of scriptural authority, Luther kept only two of the Catholic Church's seven sacraments—baptism and the Lord's Supper. Baptism signified rebirth through grace. Regarding the Lord's Supper, Luther denied the Catholic doctrine of **transubstantiation**, which taught that the substance of the bread and wine consumed in the rite is miraculously transformed into the body and blood of Jesus. Yet he continued to insist on the real presence of Jesus's body and blood in the bread and wine given as a testament to God's forgiveness of sin.

Luther's emphasis on the importance of Scripture led him to reject the Catholic belief that the authority of Scripture must be supplemented by the traditions and decrees of the church. The word of God as revealed in the Bible was sufficient authority in religious affairs. A hierarchical priesthood was thus unnecessary since all Christians who followed the word of God were their own priests, constituting a "priesthood of all believers." Even though Luther thus considered the true church to be an invisible entity, the difficulties of actually establishing a reformed church led him to believe that a tangible, organized church was needed. Since the Catholic ecclesiastical hierarchy had been scrapped, Luther came to rely increasingly on the princes or state authorities to organize and guide the new Lutheran reformed churches. He had little choice. Secular authorities in Germany, as elsewhere, were soon playing an important role in church affairs. By 1530, in the German states that had converted to Lutheranism, both princes and city councils appointed officials who visited churches in their territories and regulated matters of worship. The Lutheran churches in Germany (and later in Scandinavia) quickly became territorial

LUTHER AND THE "ROBBING AND MURDERING HORDES OF PEASANTS"

THE PEASANTS' WAR OF 1524–1525 encompassed a series of uprisings by German peasants who were suffering from economic changes they did not comprehend. Led by radical religious leaders, the revolts quickly became entangled with the religious revolt set in motion by Luther's defiance of the church. But it was soon clear that Luther himself did not believe in any way in social revolution. This excerpt is taken from Luther's pamphlet written in May 1525 at the height of the peasants' power but not published until after their defeat.

Martin Luther, *Against the Robbing and Murdering Hordes of Peasants*

The peasants have taken on themselves the burden of three terrible sins against God and man, by which they have abundantly merited death in body and soul. In the first place they have sworn to be true and faithful, submissive and obedient, to their rulers, as Christ commands, when he says, "Render unto Caesar the things that are Caesar's," and in Romans XIII, "Let everyone be subject unto the higher powers." Because they are breaking this obedience, and are setting themselves against the higher powers, willfully and with violence, they have forfeited body and soul, as faithless, perjured, lying, disobedient knaves and scoundrels are wont to do. . . .

In the second place, they are starting a rebellion, and violently robbing and plundering monasteries and castles which are not theirs, by which they have a second time deserved death in body and soul, if only as highwaymen and murderers. . . . For rebellion is not simple murder, but is like a great fire, which attacks and lays waste a whole land. . . . Therefore, let everyone who can, smite, slay and stab, secretly or openly, remembering that nothing can be more poisonous, hurtful or devilish than a rebel. . . .

In the third place, they cloak this terrible and horrible sin with the Gospel, call themselves "Christian brothers," receive oaths and homage, and compel people to hold with them to these abominations. Thus, they become the greatest of all blasphemers of God and slanderers of his holy Name, serving the devil, under the outward appearance of the Gospel, thus earning death in body and soul ten times over. . . . It does not help the peasants, when they pretend that, according to Genesis I and II, all things were created free and common, and that all of us alike have been baptized. . . . For baptism does not make men free in body and property, but in soul; and the Gospel does not make goods common. . . . Since the peasants, then, have brought both God and man down upon them and are already so many times guilty of death in body and soul . . . I must instruct the worldly governors how they are to act in the matter with a clear conscience.

First, I will not oppose a ruler who, even though he does not tolerate the Gospel, will smite and punish these peasants without offering to submit the case to judgment. For he is within his rights, since the peasants are not contending any longer for the Gospel, but have become faithless, perjured, disobedient, rebellious murderers, robbers and blasphemers, whom even heathen rulers have the right and power to punish; nay, it is their duty to punish them, for it is just for this purpose that they bear the sword, and are "the ministers of God upon him that doeth evil."

 What does this passage tell you about the political interests and sympathies of key religious reformers like Luther? Were the reformers really interested in bringing about massive social changes to accompany their religious innovations?

Source: E. G. Rupp and B. Drewery, *Martin Luther: Documents of Modern History* (London: Palgrave Macmillan, 1970).

or state churches in which the state supervised and disciplined church members.

As part of the development of these state-dominated churches, Luther also instituted new religious services to replace the Mass. These featured a worship service consisting of a vernacular liturgy that focused on Bible reading, preaching the word of God, and song. Following his own denunciation of clerical celibacy, Luther married a former nun, Katherina von Bora (kat-uh-REE-nuh fun BOH-rah), in 1525. His union provided a model of married and family life for the new Protestant minister.

Germany and the Reformation: Religion and Politics

From its very beginning, the fate of Luther's movement was closely tied to political affairs. In 1519, Charles I, king of Spain and grandson of Emperor Maximilian (see Chart 13.1), was elected Holy Roman Emperor as Charles V. Charles ruled over an immense empire, consisting of Spain and its overseas possessions, the traditional Austrian Habsburg lands, Bohemia, Hungary, the Low Countries, and the kingdom of Naples in southern Italy (see Map 13.1). The extent of his possessions was reflected in the languages he used. He said once that he spoke Spanish to God, Italian to women, French to men, and German to his horse. Politically, Charles wanted to maintain his dynasty's control over his enormous empire; religiously, he hoped to preserve the unity of the Catholic faith throughout his empire. Despite Charles's strengths, his empire was overextended, and he spent a lifetime in futile pursuit of his goals. Four major problems—the French, the papacy, the Turks, and Germany's internal situation—cost him both his dream and his health. At the same time, the emperor's problems gave Luther's

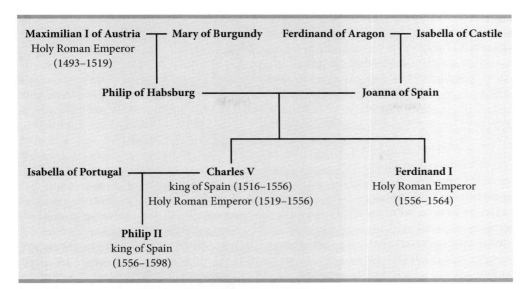

Chart 13.1 The Habsburgs as Holy Roman Emperors and Kings of Spain

Maximilian I of Austria ⌐ **Mary of Burgundy**   **Ferdinand of Aragon** ⌐ **Isabella of Castile**
Holy Roman Emperor
(1493–1519)

Philip of Habsburg ——————— **Joanna of Spain**

Isabella of Portugal ———— **Charles V**   **Ferdinand I**
king of Spain (1516–1556)   Holy Roman Emperor
Holy Roman Emperor (1519–1556)   (1556–1564)

Philip II
king of Spain
(1556–1598)

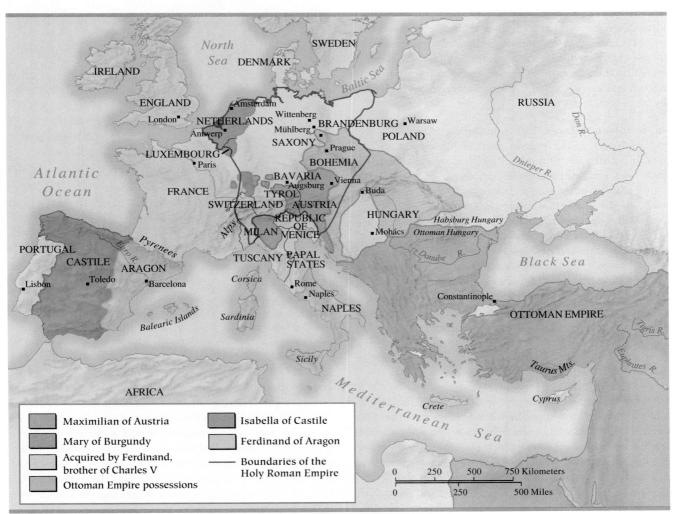

MAP 13.1 The Empire of Charles V. Charles V spent much of his reign fighting wars in Italy, against France and the Ottoman Empire, and within the borders of the Holy Roman Empire. He failed in his main goal to secure Europe for Catholicism: the Peace of Augsburg in 1555 recognized the equality of Catholicism and Lutheranism and let each German prince choose his realm's religion.

Q *Why would France feel threatened by the empire of Charles V?*

movement time to grow and organize before facing the concerted onslaught of the Catholic forces.

THE FRENCH AND THE PAPACY Charles V's chief political concern was his rivalry with the Valois king of France, Francis I (1515–1547). Encircled by the possessions of the Habsburg empire, Francis became embroiled in a series of conflicts with Charles over disputed territories in southern France, the Netherlands, the Rhineland, northern Spain, and Italy. These conflicts, known as the Habsburg-Valois Wars, were fought intermittently for twenty-four years (1521–1544), preventing Charles from concentrating on the Lutheran problem in Germany.

Meanwhile, Charles faced two other enemies. The Habsburg emperor expected papal cooperation in dealing with the Lutheran heresy. Papal policy, however, was guided by political considerations, not religious ones, a clear indication that, like the Catholic king of France, a pope could act against his religious interests because of the political situation. Fearful of Charles's power in Italy, Pope Clement VII (1523–1534) joined the side of Francis I in the second Habsburg-Valois War (1527–1529), with catastrophic results. In April 1527, the Spanish-imperial army of Charles V went berserk while attacking Rome and gave the capital of Catholicism a fearful and bloody sacking. Sobered by the experience, Clement came to terms with the emperor, and by 1530, Charles V stood supreme over much of Italy.

THE OTTOMAN EMPIRE In the meantime, Charles V also faced problems in the eastern part of his empire. In the fifteenth century, the Ottoman Turks had overrun Constantinople and established control over much of the Balkans in southeastern Europe (see Chapter 12). Now, in the first decades of the sixteenth century, the Ottomans posed a new threat to Europe. Ottoman armies had taken control of much of the North African coast and captured the Christian island of Rhodes. Under their new leader, Suleiman (SOO-lay-mahn) the Magnificent (1520–1566), Ottoman forces had defeated and killed King Louis of Hungary, Charles's brother-in-law, at the Battle of Mohács (MOH-hach) in 1526. Subsequently, the Ottomans overran most of Hungary, moved into Austria, and advanced as far as Vienna, where they were finally repulsed in 1529. The emperor and much of Christian Europe breathed a sigh of relief but still remained fearful of another Ottoman attack.

POLITICS IN GERMANY By the end of 1529, Charles was ready to deal with Germany. The second Habsburg-Valois War had ended, the Turks had been defeated temporarily, and the pope had been subdued. The internal political situation in the Holy Roman Empire was not in his favor, however. Germany was a land of several hundred territorial states: princely states, ecclesiastical principalities, and free imperial cities. Though all owed loyalty to the emperor, Germany's medieval development had enabled these states to become quite independent of imperial authority. They had no desire to have a strong emperor.

Charles's attempt to settle the Lutheran problem at the Diet of Augsburg in 1530 proved completely inadequate,

Charles V. Charles V sought to maintain religious unity throughout his vast empire by keeping all his subjects within the bounds of the Catholic Church. Due to his conflict with Francis I of France and his difficulties with the Turks, the papacy, and the German princes, Charles was never able to check the spread of Lutheranism. This portrait of Charles V is by the Venetian painter Titian.

Alte Pinakothek, Munich, Germany/Bridgeman Images

and the emperor wound up demanding that the Lutherans return to the Catholic Church by April 15, 1531. In February 1531, fearful of Charles's intentions, eight princes and eleven imperial cities—all Lutheran—formed a defensive alliance known as the Schmalkaldic League. These Protestant German states vowed to assist each other "whenever any one of us is attacked on account of the Word of God and the doctrine of the Gospel." Religion was dividing the empire into two armed camps.

The renewed threat of the Turks against Vienna forced Charles once again to seek compromise instead of war with the Protestant authorities. From 1532 to 1535, Charles was forced to fight off an Ottoman, Arab, and Barbary attack on the Mediterranean coasts of Italy and Spain. Two additional

CHRONOLOGY	Politics and the German Reformation	
First Habsburg-Valois War		1521–1525
Second Habsburg-Valois War		1527–1529
Defeat of the Turks at Vienna		1529
Diet of Augsburg		1530
Third Habsburg-Valois War		1535–1538
Fourth Habsburg-Valois War		1542–1544
Schmalkaldic Wars		1546–1555
Peace of Augsburg		1555

Habsburg-Valois Wars (1535–1538 and 1542–1544) soon followed and kept Charles preoccupied with military campaigns in southern France and the Low Countries. Finally, Charles made peace with Francis in 1544 and the Turks in 1545. Fifteen years after the Diet of Augsburg, Charles was finally free to resolve his problem in Germany.

By the time of Luther's death in February 1546, all hopes of a peaceful compromise had faded. Charles brought a sizable imperial army of German, Dutch, Italian, and Spanish troops to do battle with the Protestants. In the first phase of the Schmalkaldic Wars (1546–1547), the emperor's forces decisively defeated the Lutherans at the Battle of Mühlberg (MOOL-bayrk). Charles V was at the zenith of his power, and the Protestant cause seemed doomed.

Appearances proved misleading, however. The Schmalkaldic League was soon reestablished, and the German Protestant princes allied themselves with the new French king, Henry II (1547–1559)—a Catholic—to revive the war in 1552. This time Charles was less fortunate and had to negotiate a truce. Exhausted by his efforts to maintain religious orthodoxy and the unity of his empire, Charles abandoned German affairs to his brother Ferdinand, abdicated all of his titles in 1556, and retired to his country estate in Spain to spend the remaining two years of his life in solitude.

An end to religious warfare in Germany came in 1555 with the Peace of Augsburg, which marked an important turning point in the history of the Reformation. The agreement formally acknowledged the division of Christianity, with Lutheranism granted equal legal standing with Catholicism. Moreover, the peace settlement accepted the right of each German ruler to determine the religion of his subjects (but not the right of the subjects to choose their religion). Charles's hope for a united empire had been completely dashed, and the ideal of medieval Christian unity was irretrievably lost. The rapid proliferation of new Protestant groups served to underscore that new reality.

The Swiss Cantons

The Spread of the Protestant Reformation

FOCUS QUESTIONS: What were the main tenets of Lutheranism, Zwinglianism, Anabaptism, and Calvinism, and how did they differ from each other and from Catholicism? What impact did political, economic, and social conditions have on the development of these four reform movements?

For both Catholics and Protestant reformers, Luther's heresy raised the question of what constituted the correct interpretation of the Bible. The inability to agree on this issue led not only to theological confrontations but also to bloody warfare as each Christian group was unwilling to admit that it could be wrong.

Lutheranism in Scandinavia

In 1397, the Union of Kalmar had brought about the unification of Denmark, Norway, and Sweden under the rule of one monarch, the king of Denmark. This union, however, failed to achieve any real social or political unification of the three states, particularly since the independent-minded landed nobles worked to frustrate any increase in monarchical centralization. By the beginning of the sixteenth century, the union was on the brink of disintegration. In 1520, Christian II (1513–1523) of Denmark, ruler of the three Scandinavian kingdoms, was overthrown by Swedish barons led by Gustavus Vasa. Three years later, Vasa became king of an independent Sweden (1523–1560) and took the lead in establishing a Lutheran Reformation in his country and by the 1530s had created a Swedish Lutheran National Church.

Meanwhile, the Danish nobility had also deposed Christian II as the king of Denmark. He was succeeded by his uncle, who became Frederick I (1523–1533). Frederick encouraged Lutheran preachers to spread their evangelical doctrines and to introduce a Lutheran liturgy into the Danish church service. In the 1530s, under Frederick's successor, Christian III (1534–1559), a Lutheran state church was installed with the king as the supreme authority in all ecclesiastical affairs. Christian was also instrumental in spreading Lutheranism to Norway. By the 1540s, Scandinavia had become a Lutheran stronghold. Like the German princes, the Scandinavian monarchs had been the dominant force in establishing state-run churches.

The Zwinglian Reformation

In the sixteenth century, the Swiss Confederation was a loose association of thirteen self-governing states called cantons. Theoretically part of the Holy Roman Empire, they had become virtually independent in 1499. The six forest cantons were democratic republics; the seven urban cantons, which included Zürich, Bern, and Basel, were for the most part governed by city councils controlled by narrow oligarchies of wealthy citizens.

Ulrich Zwingli (OOL-rikh TSFING-lee) (1484–1531) was a product of the Swiss forest cantons. The precocious son of a relatively prosperous peasant, the young Zwingli eventually obtained both bachelor of arts and master of arts degrees. During his university education at Vienna and Basel, Zwingli was strongly influenced by Christian humanism. Ordained a priest in 1506, he accepted a parish post in rural Switzerland until his appointment as a cathedral priest in the Great Minster of Zürich in 1518. Through his preaching there, Zwingli began the Reformation in Switzerland.

Zwingli's preaching of the Gospel caused such unrest that in 1523 the city council held a public disputation or debate in the town hall. The disputation became a standard method of spreading the Reformation to many cities. It gave an advantage to reformers, since they had the power of new ideas and Catholics were not used to defending their teachings. The victory went to Zwingli's party, and the council declared that "Mayor, Council and Great Council of Zürich, in order to do away with disturbance and discord, have upon due deliberation and consultation decided and resolved that Master Zwingli should continue as heretofore to proclaim the Gospel and the pure sacred Scripture."[10]

REFORMS IN ZÜRICH Over the next two years, a city council strongly influenced by Zwingli promulgated evangelical reforms in Zürich. Zwingli looked to the state to supervise the church. He declared that a church without the magistrate is "mutilated and incomplete." The city council abolished relics and images, removed all paintings and decorations from the churches, and replaced them with whitewashed walls. As Zwingli remarked, "The images are not to be endured; for all that God has forbidden, there can be no compromise."[11] A new liturgy consisting of Scripture reading, prayer, and sermons replaced the Mass, and music was eliminated from the service as a distraction from the pure word of God. Monasticism, pilgrimages, the veneration of saints, clerical celibacy, and the pope's authority were all abolished as remnants of papal Christianity. Zwingli's movement soon spread to other cities in Switzerland, including Bern in 1528 and Basel in 1529.

A FUTILE SEARCH FOR UNITY By 1528, Zwingli's reform movement faced a serious political problem as the forest cantons remained staunchly Catholic. Zürich feared that they would ally with the Habsburgs. To counteract this danger, Zwingli attempted to build a league of evangelical cities by seeking an agreement with Luther and the German reformers. An alliance between them seemed possible, since the Reformation had spread to the southern German cities, especially Strasbourg, where Martin Bucer (1491–1551) had instituted a moderate reform movement containing characteristics of both Luther's and Zwingli's movements. Both the German and the Swiss reformers realized the need for unity to defend against imperial and conservative opposition.

Gianni Dagli Orti/The Art Archive at Art Resource, NY

Zwingli. Ulrich Zwingli began the Reformation in Switzerland through his preaching in Zürich. Zwingli's theology was accepted in Zürich and soon spread to other Swiss cities. This portrait of Zwingli was done by an unknown artist in the early sixteenth century.

Protestant political leaders, especially Landgrave Philip of Hesse, fearful that Charles V would take advantage of the division between the reformers, attempted to promote an alliance of the Swiss and German reformed churches by persuading the leaders of both groups to attend a colloquy (conference) at Marburg to resolve their differences. Able to agree on virtually everything else, the gathering splintered over the interpretation of the Lord's Supper (see the box on p. 379). Zwingli believed that the scriptural words "This is my body" and "This is my blood" should be taken symbolically, not literally. To Zwingli, the Lord's Supper was only a meal of remembrance, and he refused to accept Luther's insistence on the real presence of the body and blood of Jesus "in, with, and under the bread and wine." The Marburg Colloquy of 1529 produced no agreement and no evangelical alliance. It was a foretaste of the issues that would divide one reform group from another and lead to the creation of different Protestant groups.

In October 1531, war erupted between the Swiss Protestant and Catholic cantons. Zürich's army was routed, and Zwingli was found wounded on the battlefield. His enemies killed him, cut up his body, burned the pieces, and scattered the ashes. This Swiss civil war of 1531 provided an early indication of what religious passions would lead to in the sixteenth century. Unable to find peaceful ways to agree on the meaning of the Gospel, the disciples of Christianity resorted to violence and decision by force. When he heard of Zwingli's death, Martin Luther, who

A Reformation Debate: Conflict at Marburg

DEBATES PLAYED A CRUCIAL ROLE in the Reformation period. They were a primary instrument in introducing the Reformation into innumerable cities as well as a means of resolving differences among like-minded Protestant groups. This selection contains an excerpt from the vivacious and often brutal debate between Luther and Zwingli over the sacrament of the Lord's Supper at Marburg in 1529. The two protagonists failed to reach agreement.

The Marburg Colloquy, 1529

THE HESSIAN CHANCELLOR FEIGE: My gracious prince and lord [Landgrave Philip of Hesse] has summoned you for the express and urgent purpose of settling the dispute over the sacrament of the Lord's Supper. . . . Let everyone on both sides present his arguments in a spirit of moderation, . . . Now then, Doctor Luther, you may proceed.

LUTHER: Noble prince, gracious lord! Undoubtedly the colloquy is well intentioned. . . . Although I have no intention of changing my mind, which is firmly made up, I will nevertheless present the grounds of my belief and show where the others are in error. . . . Your basic contentions are these: In the last analysis you wish to prove that a body cannot be in two places at once, and you produce arguments about the unlimited body which are based on natural reason. I do not question how Christ can be God and man and how the two natures can be joined. For God is more powerful than all our ideas, and we must submit to his word.

Prove that Christ's body is not there where the Scripture says, "This is my body!" Rational proofs I will not listen to. It is God who commands, "Take, eat, this is my body." I request, therefore, valid scriptural proof to the contrary.

ZWINGLI: I insist that the words of the Lord's Supper must be figurative. This is ever apparent, and even required by the article of faith: "taken up into heaven, seated at the right hand of the Father." Otherwise, it would be absurd to look for him in the Lord's Supper at the same time that Christ is telling us that he is in heaven. One and the same body cannot possibly be in different places. . . .

LUTHER: I call upon you as before: your basic contentions are shaky. Give way, and give glory to God!

ZWINGLI: And we call upon you to give glory to God and to quit begging the question. The issue at stake is this: Where is the proof of your position? . . . You're trying to outwit me. I stand by this passage in the sixth chapter of John, verse 63, and shall not be shaken from it. You'll have to sing another tune.

LUTHER: You're being obnoxious.

ZWINGLI: (*excitedly*) Don't you believe that Christ was attempting in John 6 to help those who did not understand?

LUTHER: You're trying to dominate things! You insist on passing judgment . . . It is your point that must be proved, not mine. But let us stop this sort of thing. It serves no purpose.

ZWINGLI: It certainly does! It is for you to prove that the passage in John 6 speaks of a physical repast.

LUTHER: You express yourself poorly and make about as much progress as a cane standing in a corner. You're going nowhere.

ZWINGLI: No, no, no! This is the passage that will break your neck!

LUTHER: Don't be so sure of yourself. Necks don't break this way. You're in Hesse, not Switzerland.

 How did the positions of Zwingli and Luther on the sacrament of the Lord's Supper differ? What was the purpose of this debate? Based on this example, why do you think Reformation debates led to further hostility rather than compromise and unity between religious and sectarian opponents? What implications did this have for the future of the Protestant Reformation?

Source: "The Marburg Colloquy," in *Great Debates of the Reformation*, ed. D. Ziegler (New York: Modern Library, 1969).

had not forgotten the confrontation at Marburg, is supposed to have remarked that Zwingli "got what he deserved."

The Radical Reformation: The Anabaptists

Although many reformers were ready to allow the state to play an important, if not dominant, role in church affairs, some people rejected this kind of magisterial reformation and favored a far more radical reform movement. Collectively called the Anabaptists, these radicals were actually members of a large variety of groups who shared some common characteristics.

Anabaptism was especially attractive to the peasants, weavers, miners, and artisans who had been adversely affected by the economic changes of the age.

THE IDEAS OF THE ANABAPTISTS Anabaptists everywhere held certain ideas in common. All felt that the true Christian church was a voluntary association of believers who had undergone spiritual rebirth and had then been baptized into the church. Anabaptists advocated adult rather than infant baptism. No one, they believed, should be forced to accept the truth of the Bible. They also tried to return literally to the practices and spirit of early Christianity. Adhering to the accounts of early Christian communities in the New Testament, they followed a strict sort of democracy in which all believers were considered equal. Each church chose its own minister, who might be any member of the community, since all Christians were considered priests (though women were often excluded). Those chosen as ministers had the duty to lead services, which were very simple and contained nothing not found in the early church. Like early Christians, Anabaptists, who called themselves "Christians" or "Saints," accepted that they would have to suffer for their faith. Anabaptists rejected theological speculation in favor of simple Christian living according to what they believed was the pure word of God. The Lord's Supper was interpreted as a remembrance, a meal of fellowship celebrated in the evening in private houses according to Jesus's example.

Unlike the Catholics and other Protestants, most Anabaptists believed in the complete separation of church and state. Not only was government to be excluded from the realm of religion, but it was not even supposed to exercise political jurisdiction over real Christians. Human law had no power over those whom God had saved. Anabaptists refused to hold political office or bear arms because many took the commandment "Thou shall not kill" literally, although some Anabaptist groups did become quite violent. Their political beliefs as much as their religious beliefs caused the Anabaptists to be regarded as dangerous radicals who threatened the very fabric of sixteenth-century society. Indeed, the chief thing Protestants and Catholics could agree on was the need to stamp out the Anabaptists.

VARIETIES OF ANABAPTISTS One early group of Anabaptists known as the Swiss Brethren arose in Zürich. Their ideas, especially adult baptism, frightened Zwingli, and they were expelled from the city in 1523. Because the first members of the Swiss Brethren who were baptized as adults had already been baptized as children (in the Catholic Church), their opponents labeled them Anabaptists or Rebaptists. Under Roman law, such people were subject to the death penalty.

As the teachings of the Swiss Brethren spread through southern Germany, the Austrian Habsburg lands, and Switzerland, Anabaptists suffered ruthless persecution, especially after the Peasants' War of 1524–1525, when the upper classes resorted to repression. Virtually eradicated in Germany, Anabaptist survivors emerged in Moravia and Poland, and in the Netherlands, Anabaptism took on a strange form.

In the 1530s, the city of Münster, in Westphalia in northwestern Germany near the Dutch border, was the site of an Anabaptist uprising that determined the fate of Dutch Anabaptism. Seat of a powerful Catholic prince-bishop, Münster had experienced severe economic disasters, including crop failure and plague. Although converted to Lutheranism in 1532, Münster experienced a more radical mass religious hysteria that led to legal recognition for the Anabaptists. Soon Münster became a haven for Anabaptists from the surrounding neighborhood, especially the more wild-eyed variety known as Melchiorites, who adhered to a vivid **millenarianism**. They believed that the end of the world was at hand and that they would usher in the kingdom of God with Münster as the New Jerusalem. By the end of February 1534, these millenarian Anabaptists had taken control of the city, driven out everyone they considered godless or unbelievers, burned all books except the Bible, and proclaimed communal ownership of all property. Eventually, the leadership of this New Jerusalem fell into the hands of one man, John of Leiden, who proclaimed himself king of the New Jerusalem. As king, he would lead the elect from Münster out to cover the entire world and purify it of evil by the sword in preparation for Jesus's Second Coming and the creation of a New Age. In this new kingdom, John of Leiden believed, all goods would be held in common and the saints would live without suffering.

But it was not to be. As the Catholic prince-bishop of Münster gathered a large force and laid siege to the city, the new king repeatedly had to postpone the ushering forth from Münster. Finally, after many inhabitants had starved, a joint army of Catholics and Lutherans recaptured the city in June 1535 and executed the radical Anabaptist leaders in gruesome fashion. The New Jerusalem had ceased to exist.

Purged of its fantasies and its more extreme elements, Dutch Anabaptism reverted to its pacifist tendencies, especially evident in the work of Menno Simons (1496–1561), the man most responsible for rejuvenating Dutch Anabaptism. A popular leader, Menno dedicated his life to the spread of a peaceful, evangelical Anabaptism that stressed separation from the world in order to truly emulate the life of Jesus. Simons imposed strict discipline on his followers and banned those who refused to conform to the rules. The Mennonites, as his followers were called, spread from the Netherlands into northwestern Germany and eventually into Poland and Lithuania as well as the New World. Both the Mennonites and the Amish, who are also descended from the Anabaptists, maintain communities in the United States and Canada today.

The Reformation in England

The English Reformation was initiated by King Henry VIII (1509–1547), who wanted to divorce his first wife, Catherine of Aragon, because she had failed to produce a male heir. Furthermore, Henry had fallen in love with Anne Boleyn (BUH-lin *or* buh-LIN), a lady-in-waiting to Queen Catherine. Anne's unwillingness to be only the king's mistress and the king's desire to have a legitimate male heir made their marriage imperative, but the king's first marriage stood in the way.

Henry relied on Cardinal Wolsey, the highest-ranking English church official and lord chancellor to the king, to obtain from Pope Clement VII an annulment of the king's marriage. Normally, the pope might have been willing to oblige, but the sack of Rome in 1527 had made the pope dependent on the Holy Roman Emperor Charles V, who happened to be the nephew of Queen Catherine. Discretion dictated delay in granting the English king's request. Impatient with the process, Henry dismissed Wolsey in 1529.

Two new advisers now became the king's agents in fulfilling his wishes. These were Thomas Cranmer (1489–1556), who became archbishop of Canterbury in 1532, and Thomas Cromwell (1485–1540), the king's principal secretary after the fall of Wolsey. They advised the king to obtain an annulment of his marriage in England's own ecclesiastical courts. The most important step toward this goal was an act of Parliament cutting off all appeals from English church courts to Rome, a piece of legislation that essentially abolished papal authority in England. Henry no longer needed the pope to obtain his annulment. He was now in a hurry because Anne Boleyn had become pregnant and he had secretly married her in January 1533 to legitimize the expected heir. In May, as archbishop of Canterbury and head of the highest ecclesiastical court in England, Thomas Cranmer ruled that the king's marriage to Catherine was "null and absolutely void" and then validated Henry's marriage to Anne. At the beginning of June, Anne was crowned queen. Three months later, a child was born. Much to the king's disappointment, the baby was a girl, whom they named Elizabeth.

In 1534, Parliament completed the break of the Church of England with Rome by passing the Act of Supremacy, which declared that the king was "taken, accepted, and reputed the only supreme head on earth of the Church of England." This meant that the English monarch now controlled the church in all matters of doctrine, clerical appointments, and discipline. In addition, Parliament passed the Treason Act, making it punishable by death to deny that the king was the supreme head of the church.

One who challenged the new order was Thomas More, the humanist and former lord chancellor, who saw clearly to the heart of the issue: loyalty to the pope in Rome was now treason in England. More refused to support the new laws and was duly tried for treason. At his trial, he asked, rhetorically, what the effect of the actions of the king and Parliament would be: "Therefore am I not bound . . . to conform my conscience to the Council of one realm [England] against the general Council of Christendom?"[12] Because his conscience could not accept the victory of the national state over the church, nor would he, as a Christian, bow his head to a secular ruler in matters of faith, More was beheaded in London on July 6, 1535.

Recent research that emphasizes the strength of Catholicism in England suggests that Thomas More was not alone in his view of the new order. In fact, one historian has argued that Catholicism was vibrant in England in both the fifteenth and sixteenth centuries; in his view, the English Reformation was alien to many English people.

THE NEW ORDER Thomas Cromwell worked out the details of the Tudor government's new role in church affairs based on the centralized power exercised by the king and Parliament. Cromwell also came to his extravagant king's financial rescue with a daring plan for the dissolution of the monasteries. About four hundred religious houses were closed in 1536, and the king confiscated their lands and possessions. Many were sold to nobles, gentry, and some merchants. The king added enormously to his treasury and also to his ranks of supporters, who now had a stake in the new Tudor order.

Although Henry VIII had broken with the papacy, little change occurred in matters of doctrine, theology, and ceremony. Some of his supporters, such as Archbishop Thomas Cranmer, wished to have a religious reformation as well as an administrative one, but Henry was unyielding. Nevertheless, some clergymen ignored Henry on the matter of priestly celibacy and secretly married.

The final decade of Henry's reign was preoccupied with foreign affairs, factional intrigue, and a continued effort to find the perfect wife. Henry soon tired of Anne Boleyn and had her beheaded in 1536 on a charge of adultery. His third wife, Jane Seymour, produced the long-awaited male heir but died twelve

Henry VIII and His Successors. This allegorical painting of the Tudor succession, entitled *The Family of Henry VIII*, was done by an English artist about forty years after the death of Henry VIII. King Henry sits on his throne under the Tudor Coat of arms. At the far left is the figure of a Roman soldier representing the god of war. Next is Philip II of Spain, the husband of Mary Tudor, who stands at his right. To the right of Henry stand Edward, Elizabeth, and two female figures who represent peace and plenty.

days later. His fourth marriage, to Anne of Cleves, a German princess, was arranged for political reasons. Henry relied on a painted portrait of Anne when he made the arrangements, but he was disappointed at her physical appearance when he saw her in person and soon divorced her. His fifth wife, Catherine Howard, was more attractive but less moral. When she committed adultery, Henry had her beheaded. His last wife was Catherine Parr, who married the king in 1543 and outlived him. Henry was succeeded by the underage and sickly Edward VI (1547–1553), the son of his third wife.

Since the new king was only nine years old at the time of his accession to the throne, real control of England passed to a council of regency. During Edward's reign, Archbishop Cranmer and others inclined toward Protestant doctrines were able to move the Church of England in a more Protestant direction. New acts of Parliament instituted the right of the clergy to marry, eliminated images, and authorized a revised Protestant liturgy that was elaborated in a new prayer book and liturgical guide known as the Book of Common Prayer. These rapid changes in doctrine and liturgy aroused much opposition and prepared the way for the reaction that occurred when Mary, Henry's first daughter by Catherine of Aragon, came to the throne.

REACTION UNDER MARY Mary (1553–1558) was a Catholic who fully intended to restore England to the Roman Catholic fold. But her restoration of Catholicism, achieved by joint action of the monarch and Parliament, aroused opposition. There was widespread antipathy to Mary's unfortunate marriage to Philip II, son of Charles V and the future king of Spain. Philip was strongly disliked in England, and Mary's foreign policy of alliance with Spain aroused further hostility, especially when her forces lost Calais, the last English possession in France after the Hundred Years' War. The burning of more than three hundred Protestant heretics aroused further ire against "bloody Mary." As a result of her policies, Mary managed to achieve the opposite of what she had intended: England was more Protestant by the end of her reign than it had been at the beginning. When she came to power, Protestantism had become identified with church destruction and religious anarchy. Now people identified it with English resistance to Spanish interference. Mary's death in 1558 ended the restoration of Catholicism in England.

John Calvin and Calvinism

Of the second generation of Protestant reformers, one stands out as the systematic theologian and organizer of the Protestant movement—John Calvin (1509–1564). Calvin received a remarkably diverse education in humanistic studies and law in his native France. He was also influenced by Luther's writings, which were being circulated and read by French intellectuals as early as 1523. In 1533, Calvin experienced a religious crisis that determined the rest of his life's work. He described it in these words:

> God, by a sudden conversion, subdued and brought my mind
> to a teachable frame, which was more hardened in such
> matters than might have been expected from one at my early

period of life. Having thus received some taste and knowledge of true godliness, I was immediately inflamed with so intense a desire to make progress therein, although I did not leave off other studies, I yet pursued them with less ardor.[13]

Calvin's conversion was solemn and straightforward. He was so convinced of the inner guidance of God that he became the most determined of all the Protestant reformers.

After his conversion and newfound conviction, Calvin was no longer safe in Paris, since King Francis I periodically persecuted Protestants. Eventually, Calvin made his way to Basel, where in 1536 he published the first edition of the *Institutes of the Christian Religion*, a masterful synthesis of Protestant thought that immediately secured his reputation as one of the new leaders of Protestantism.

CALVIN'S IDEAS On most important doctrines, Calvin stood very close to Luther. He adhered to the doctrine of justification by faith alone to explain how humans achieved salvation. Calvin also placed much emphasis on the absolute sovereignty of God or the "power, grace, and glory of God." Thus, "God asserts his possession of omnipotence, and claims our

John Calvin. After a conversion experience, John Calvin abandoned his life as a humanist and became a reformer. In 1536, Calvin began working to reform the city of Geneva, where he remained until his death in 1564. This is a seventeenth-century portrait of Calvin done by a member of the Swiss school.

acknowledgment of this attribute; not such as is imagined by sophists, vain, idle, and almost asleep, but vigilant, efficacious, operative and engaged in continual action."[14]

One of the ideas derived from his emphasis on the absolute sovereignty of God—**predestination**—gave a unique cast to Calvin's teachings, although Luther also believed in this principle. This "eternal decree," as Calvin called it, meant that God had predestined some people to be saved (the elect) and others to be damned (the reprobate). According to Calvin, "He has once for all determined, both whom he would admit to salvation, and whom he would condemn to destruction.[15] Calvin identified three tests that might indicate possible salvation: an open profession of faith, a "decent and godly life," and participation in the sacraments of baptism and communion. In no instance did Calvin ever suggest that worldly success or material wealth was a sign of election. Significantly for the future of Calvinism, although Calvin himself stressed that there could be no absolute certainty of salvation, some of his followers did not always make this distinction. The practical psychological effect of predestination was to give some later Calvinists an unshakable conviction that they were doing God's work on earth. It is no accident that Calvinism became the activist international form of Protestantism.

To Calvin, the church was a divine institution responsible for preaching the word of God and administering the sacraments. Calvin kept the same two sacraments as other Protestant reformers, baptism and the Lord's Supper. Baptism was a sign of the remission of sins. Calvin believed in the real presence of Jesus in the sacrament of the Lord's Supper, but only in a spiritual sense. Jesus's body is at the right hand of God and thus cannot be in the sacrament, but to the believer, Jesus is spiritually present in the Lord's Supper.

CALVIN'S GENEVA Before 1536, John Calvin had essentially been a scholar. But in that year, he took up a ministry in Geneva that lasted, except for a brief exile (1538–1541), until his death in 1564. Calvin achieved a major success in 1541 when the city council accepted his new church constitution, known as the Ecclesiastical Ordinances.

This document created a church government that used both clergy and laymen in the service of the church. The Consistory, a special body for enforcing moral discipline, was set up as a court to oversee the moral life and doctrinal purity of Genevans (see the box on p. 384). As its power increased, the Consistory went from "fraternal corrections" to the use of public penance and excommunication. More serious cases could be turned over to the city council for punishments greater than excommunication. During Calvin's last years, stricter laws against blasphemy were enacted and enforced with banishment and public whippings.

Calvin's success in Geneva enabled the city to become a vibrant center of Protestantism. John Knox, the Calvinist reformer of Scotland, called it "the most perfect school of Christ on earth." Following Calvin's lead, missionaries trained in Geneva were sent to all parts of Europe. Calvinism became established in France, the Netherlands, Scotland, and central and eastern Europe. By the mid-sixteenth century, Calvinism had replaced Lutheranism as the international form of Protestantism, and Calvin's Geneva stood as the fortress of the Reformation.

The Social Impact of the Protestant Reformation

 FOCUS QUESTION: What impact did the Protestant Reformation have on society in the sixteenth century?

Because Christianity was such an integral part of European life, it was inevitable that the Reformation would have an impact on the family, education, and popular religious practices.

The Family

For centuries, Catholicism had praised the family and sanctified its existence by making marriage a sacrament. But the Catholic Church's high regard for abstinence from sex as the surest way to holiness made the celibate state of the clergy preferable to marriage. Nevertheless, because not all men could remain chaste, marriage offered the best means to control sexual intercourse and give it a purpose, the procreation of children. To some extent, this attitude persisted among the Protestant reformers; Luther, for example, argued that sex in marriage allowed one to "make use of this sex in order to avoid sin," and Calvin advised that every man should "abstain from marriage only so long as he is fit to observe celibacy." If "his power to tame lust fails him," then he must marry.

But the Reformation did bring some change to the conception of the family. Both Catholic and Protestant clergy preached sermons advocating a more positive approach to family relationships. The Protestants were especially important in

CHRONOLOGY	New Reform Movements	
The Zwinglian Reformation		
Zwingli made cathedral priest at Zürich	1518	
Reform adopted in Zürich	1523	
Marburg Colloquy	1529	
The Anabaptists		
Anabaptists expelled from Zürich	1523	
New Jerusalem in Münster	1534–1535	
The Reformation in England		
Henry VIII	1509–1547	
Act of Supremacy	1534	
Edward VI	1547–1553	
Mary	1553–1558	
Calvin and Calvinism		
Institutes of the Christian Religion	1536	
Calvin begins ministry in Geneva	1536	
Ecclesiastical Ordinances	1541	

CALVIN'S RULES FOR THE CHURCH IN GENEVA

JOHN CALVIN HAD EMPHASIZED IN HIS reform movement that the church should have the ability to enforce proper behavior. Consequently, the Ecclesiastical Ordinances of 1541, the constitution of the church in Geneva, provided for an order of elders whose function was to cooperate with the pastors in maintaining discipline, "to watch over the conduct of every individual," as Calvin expressed it. These selections from Calvin's plan demonstrate the organization of the elders and some of the rules that were expected to be followed in Geneva.

Plan for the Elders and Consistory and Rules for the Church in Geneva

The office of the elders is to watch over the conduct of every individual, to admonish lovingly those whom they see doing wrong or leading an irregular life. When there is need, they should lay the matter before the body deputed to inflict paternal disciple [that is, the Consistory] of which they are members. As the Church is organized, it is best that the elders be chosen, two from the small council, four from the council of sixty, and six from the council of two hundred [the councils constituted the government of the city of Geneva]; they should be men of good life and honest, without reproach and beyond suspicion, above all, God-fearing without reproach and endowed with spiritual prudence. And they should be so chosen they be distributed in each quarter of the city, so that they can have an eye on everything. . . .

The elders, who have been described, shall assemble once a week with the ministers, namely Thursday morning, to see if there be any disorders in the Church and discuss together such remedies as shall be necessary. . . . If any one shall in contempt refuse to appear before them, it shall be their duty to inform the council, so that it may supply a remedy. . . .

Those who are found to have rosaries or idols to adore, let them be sent before the consistory, and in addition to the reproof they receive there, let them be sent before the council. Let the same be done with those who go on a pilgrimage. Those who observe feasts or [Catholic] fasts should only be admonished. Those who go to mass shall, besides being admonished, be sent before the council, and it shall consider the propriety of punishing the offenders by imprisonment or special fines, as it judges best.

He who blasphemes, swearing by the body or blood of our Lord, or in like manner, shall kiss the earth for the first offense, pay five sous for the second and ten for the third. He who contradicts the word of God shall be sent before the consistory for reproof, or before the council for punishment, as the case may require. If any one sings indecent songs, or dances or otherwise, he shall be kept in prison three days and then sent to the council.

 Why did Calvin and Geneva put so much emphasis on the role of the Consistory? What specific Catholic practices did Calvin and Geneva wish to stop?

Source: J. H. Robinson, *Readings in European History*, vol. 2 (Boston: Ginn & Company, 1906), pp. 133–134.

---

developing this new view of the family. Because Protestantism had eliminated any idea of special holiness for celibacy, abolishing both monasticism and a celibate clergy, the family could be placed at the center of human life, and a new stress on "mutual love between man and wife" could be extolled. But were doctrine and reality the same? For more radical religious groups, at times they were (see the box on p. 385). One Anabaptist wrote to his wife before his execution, "My faithful helper, my loyal friend. I praise God that he gave you to me, you who have sustained me in all my trial."[16] But more often reality reflected the traditional roles of husband as the ruler and wife as the obedient servant whose chief duty was to please her husband. Luther stated it clearly:

> The rule remains with the husband, and the wife is compelled to obey him by God's command. He rules the home and the state, wages war, defends his possessions, tills the soil, builds, plants, etc. The woman on the other hand is like a nail driven into the wall . . . so the wife should stay at home and look after the affairs of the household, as one who has been deprived of the ability of administering those affairs that are outside and that concern the state. She does not go beyond her most personal duties.[17]

Obedience to her husband was not a wife's only role; her other important duty was to bear children. To Calvin and Luther, this function of women was part of the divine plan. God punishes women for the sins of Eve by the burdens of procreation and feeding and nurturing their children, but, said Luther, "it is a gladsome punishment if you consider the hope of eternal life and the honor of motherhood which had been left to her."[18] Although the Protestant reformers sanctified this role of woman as mother and wife, viewing it as a holy vocation, Protestantism also left few alternatives for women. Because monasticism had been destroyed, life as a nun was no longer available; for most Protestant women, family life was their only destiny. At the same time, by emphasizing the father as "ruler" and hence the center of household religion, Protestantism even removed the woman from her traditional role as controller of religion in the home.

Protestant reformers called on men and women to read the Bible and participate in religious services together. In this way, the reformers did provide a stimulus for the education of girls so that they could read the Bible and other religious literature. The city council of Zwickau, for example, established a girls' school in 1525. But these schools were designed to encourage

A PROTESTANT WOMAN

IN THE INITIAL ZEAL OF THE PROTESTANT REFORMATION, women were frequently allowed to play unusual roles. Katherine Zell of Germany (ca. 1497–1562) first preached beside her husband in 1527. After the deaths of her two children, she devoted the rest of her life to helping her husband and their reform faith. This selection is taken from one of her letters to the city of Strasbourg to defend herself against Ludwig Rabus, a Lutheran minister who had criticized her activities.

A Letter to the Whole Citizenship of the City of Strasbourg from Katherine Zell

So that you, dear Strasbourg, may know why I have first introduced this long speech about how I was loved in my youth and marriage (a speech that should be unnecessary!) so read now also what disrespect and judgment I have received in my old age. Therefore I have put here the letter that Mr. Ludwig sent to me. See how he ascribes to me insult, dishonor and godlessness together with all errors and heresies before God and human beings. He hands me over to the devil, with whom (God be praised) I have nothing to do forever, but I belong to my Lord Jesus Christ, who with His own blood redeemed me from the devil. So besides showing Rabus's letter I also seek to give a full accounting of my faith to anyone who wants it. In this account you may see whether my good husband's faith and mine are alike or unlike or whether my confidence and faith in the Lord Jesus have changed or not. However, I will clearly show Rabus that he and others have not kept to the pure knowledge of Jesus Christ as the old architects of our church taught us, . . .

Well then, this is now enough. However, if Mr. Ludwig is not satisfied with his injudicious condemnation of me, a poor solitary women, then I want to take God as my helper and further recount my dear husband's and my faith, teaching and life, and let anyone who wants to do so judge who has fallen away or climbed out of the right way! Now, dear Strasbourg, read this letter that Mr. Ludwig Rabus sent to me and judge without any favor and ill humor toward him or me. If I am owed this and have behaved as he describes, then I will gladly bear my punishment. But I believe that no Jew would give me such a testimony and bring such a judgment on me. I am also assured in my heart that I stand before my Lord Christ and His heavenly Father in a fitting way through the power of His Spirit; I stand before Him through the great and high merit of Christ in whom I believe, who also will bring to light this wicked letter or witness by Mr. Ludwig (which lies about me) on the great day of His glorious appearance, when all the books of the conscience with stand open. Yes, here I stand also before many people who know me, who know my life story and have seen me from youth: as a young woman in my father's house, in my marriage, and now in my grieving widowhood—let them also judge this matter between Mr. Ludwig and me.

 What was Katherine Zell's argument against Ludwig Rabus? Of what Protestant sect do you think she was a member?

Source: Elsie McKee, *Church Mother: The Writings of a Protestant Reformer in Sixteenth-Century Germany* (Chicago: University of Chicago Press, 2006), pp. 230–231.

proper moral values rather than intellectual development and really did little to improve the position of women in society. Likewise, when women attempted to take more active roles in religious life, reformers—Lutheran and Calvinist alike—shrank back in horror. To them, the equality of the Gospel did not mean overthrowing the inequality of social classes or the sexes. Calvin also made clear what he thought of women rulers: "the government of women . . . is utterly at variance with the legitimate order of nature. . . . For a female rule badly organized is like a tyranny, and is to be tolerated until God sees fit to overthrow it."[19] Overall, the Protestant Reformation did not noticeably transform women's subordinate place in society.

Education in the Reformation

The Reformation had an important effect on the development of education in Europe. Renaissance humanism had significantly altered the content of education, and Protestant educators were very successful in implementing and using humanist methods in Protestant secondary schools and universities. Unlike the humanist schools, however, which had been mostly for an elite, the sons and a few daughters of the nobility and wealthier bourgeoisie, Protestant schools were aimed at a much wider audience. Protestantism created an increased need for at least a semiliterate body of believers who could read the Bible for themselves.

While adopting the classical emphasis of humanist schools, Protestant reformers broadened the base of the people being educated. Convinced of the need to provide the church with good Christians and good pastors as well as the state with good administrators and citizens, Martin Luther advocated that all children should have the opportunity of an education provided by the state. To that end, he urged the cities and villages of Saxony to establish schools paid for by the public. Luther's ideas were shared by his Wittenberg co-worker Philip Melanchthon, whose educational efforts earned him the title of *Praecepter Germaniae* (PREE-sep-tur gayr-MAHN-ee-ee), the Teacher of Germany. In his scheme for education in Saxony, Melanchthon divided students into three classes or divisions based on their age or capabilities.

Following Melanchthon's example, the Protestants in Germany were responsible for introducing the gymnasium, or secondary school, where the humanist emphasis on the liberal arts based on instruction in Greek and Latin was combined with religious instruction. Most famous was the school in Strasbourg

A Sixteenth-Century Classroom. Protestants in Germany developed secondary schools that combined instruction in the liberal arts with religious education. This scene from a painting by Ambrosius Holbein shows a schoolmaster instructing a pupil in the alphabet while his wife helps a little girl.

founded by Johannes Sturm in 1538, which served as a model for other Protestant schools. John Calvin's Genevan Academy, founded in 1559, was organized in two distinct parts. The "private school" or gymnasium was divided into seven classes for young people who were taught Latin and Greek grammar and literature as well as logic. In the "public school," students were taught philosophy, Hebrew, Greek, and theology. The Genevan Academy, which eventually became a university, came to concentrate on preparing ministers to spread the Calvinist view of the Gospel.

Religious Practices and Popular Culture

The Protestant reformers' attacks on the Catholic Church led to radical changes in religious practices. The Protestant Reformation abolished or severely curtailed such customary practices as indulgences, the veneration of relics and saints, pilgrimages, monasticism, and clerical celibacy. The elimination of saints put an end to the numerous celebrations of religious holy days and changed a community's sense of time. Thus, in Protestant communities, religious ceremonies and imagery, such as processions and statues, tended to be replaced with individual private prayer, family worship, and collective prayer and worship at the same time each week on Sunday.

In addition to abolishing saints' days and religious carnivals, some Protestant reformers even tried to eliminate customary forms of entertainment. The Puritans (as English Calvinists were called), for example, attempted to ban drinking in taverns, dramatic performances, and dancing. Dutch Calvinists denounced the tradition of giving small presents to children on the feast of Saint Nicholas, in early December. Many of these Protestant attacks on popular culture were unsuccessful, however. The importance of taverns in English social life made it impossible to eradicate them, and celebrating at Christmastime persisted in the Dutch Netherlands.

The Catholic Reformation

 FOCUS QUESTION: What measures did the Roman Catholic Church take to reform itself and to combat Protestantism in the sixteenth century?

By the mid-sixteenth century, Lutheranism had become established in parts of Germany and Scandinavia, and Calvinism in parts of Switzerland, France, the Netherlands, and eastern Europe (see Map 13.2). In England, the split from Rome had resulted in the creation of a national church. The situation in Europe did not look particularly favorable for the Roman Catholic Church. Yet constructive, positive forces were already at work within the Catholic Church.

HISTORIANS DEBATE ## Catholic Reformation or Counter-Reformation?

There is no doubt that the Catholic Church underwent a revitalization in the sixteenth century. But was this reformation a **Catholic Reformation** or a Counter-Reformation? Some historians prefer to call it a "Counter-Reformation" to focus on the aspects that were a direct reaction against the Protestant movement. Historians who prefer to use "Catholic Reformation" point out that elements of reform were already present in the Catholic Church at the end of the fifteenth century and the beginning of the sixteenth, and that by the mid-sixteenth century, they came to be directed by a revived and reformed papacy, giving the church new strength.

No doubt, both positions on the nature of the reformation of the Catholic Church contain elements of truth. The Catholic Reformation revived the best features of medieval Catholicism and then adjusted them to meet new conditions, as is most apparent in the revival of mysticism and monasticism. The emergence of a new mysticism, closely tied to the traditions of Catholic piety, was especially evident in the life of the Spanish mystic Saint Teresa of Avila (1515–1582). A nun of the Carmelite

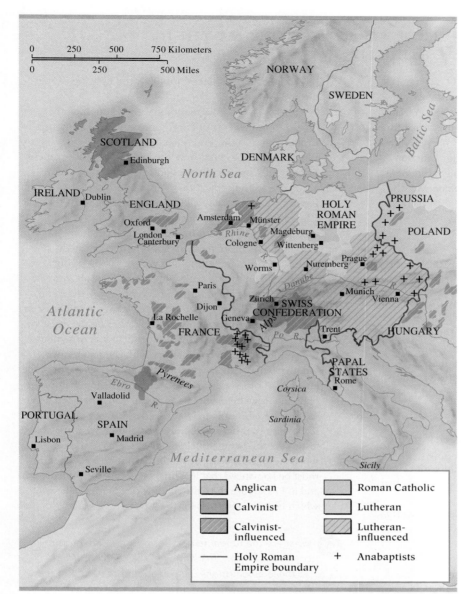

MAP 13.2 Catholics and Protestants in Europe by 1560. The Reformation continued to evolve beyond the basic split of the Lutherans from the Catholics. Several Protestant sects broke away from the teachings of Martin Luther, each with a separate creed and different ways of worship. In England, Henry VIII broke with the Catholic Church for political and dynastic reasons.

Q *Which areas of Europe were solidly Catholic, which were solidly Lutheran, and which were neither?*

order, Teresa experienced mystical visions that she claimed resulted in the ecstatic union of her soul with God. But Teresa also believed that mystical experience should lead to an active life of service on behalf of her Catholic faith. Consequently, she founded a new order of barefoot Carmelite nuns and worked to foster their mystical experiences.

The regeneration of religious orders also proved valuable to the reform of Catholicism. Old orders, such as the Benedictines and Dominicans, were reformed and renewed. The Capuchins emerged when a group of Franciscans decided to return to the simplicity and poverty of Saint Francis of Assisi, the medieval founder of the Franciscan order. In addition to caring for the sick and the poor, the Capuchins focused on preaching the Gospel directly to the people and emerged as an effective force against Protestantism. New religious orders and brotherhoods were also created. The Theatines, founded in 1524, placed their emphasis on reforming the secular clergy and encouraging those clerics to fulfill their duties among the laity. The Theatines also founded orphanages and hospitals to care for the victims of war and plague. The Ursulines, a new order of nuns founded in Italy in 1535, focused their attention on establishing schools for the education of girls.

The Society of Jesus

Of all the new religious orders, the most important was the Society of Jesus, known as the Jesuits, who became the chief instrument of the Catholic Reformation. The Society of Jesus was founded by a Spanish nobleman, Ignatius of Loyola (ig-NAY-shuss of loi-OH-luh) (1491–1556), whose injuries in battle cut short his military career. Loyola experienced a spiritual torment similar to Luther's but, unlike Luther, resolved his problems not by a new doctrine but by a decision to submit his will to the will of the church. Unable to be a real soldier, he vowed to be a soldier of God. Over a period of twelve years, Loyola prepared for his

LOYOLA AND OBEDIENCE TO "OUR HOLY MOTHER, THE HIERARCHICAL CHURCH"

IN HIS *SPIRITUAL EXERCISES*, Ignatius of Loyola developed a systematic program for "the conquest of self and the regulation of one's life" for service to the hierarchical Catholic Church. Ignatius's supreme goal was the commitment of the Christian to active service under Jesus's banner in the Church of Christ (the Catholic Church). In the final section of *The Spiritual Exercises*, Loyola explained the nature of that commitment in a series of "Rules for Thinking with the Church."

Ignatius of Loyola, "Rules for Thinking with the Church"

The following rules should be observed to foster the true attitude of mind we ought to have in the Church militant.

1. We must put aside all judgment of our own, and keep the mind ever ready and prompt to obey in all things the true Spouse of Jesus Christ, our holy Mother, the hierarchical Church.
2. We should praise sacramental confession, the yearly reception of the Most Blessed Sacrament [the Lord's Supper], and praise more highly monthly reception, and still more weekly Communion. . . .
3. We ought to praise the frequent hearing of Mass, the singing of hymns, psalmody, and long prayers whether in the church or outside. . . .
4. We must praise highly religious life, virginity, and continency; and matrimony ought not be praised as much as any of these.
5. We should praise vows of religion, obedience, poverty, chastity, and vows to perform other works of supererogation conducive to perfection. . . .
6. We should show our esteem for the relics of the saints by venerating them and praying to the saints. We should praise visits to the Station Churches,

pilgrimages, indulgences, jubilees, the lighting of candles in churches.
7. We must praise the regulations of the Church, with regard to fast and abstinence, for example, in Lent, on Ember Days, Vigils, Fridays, and Saturdays.
8. We ought to praise not only the building and adornment of churches, but also images and veneration of them according to the subject they represent.
9. Finally, we must praise all the commandments of the Church, and be on the alert to find reasons to defend them, and by no means in order to criticize them.
10. We should be more ready to approve and praise the orders, recommendations, and way of acting of our superiors than to find fault with them. Though some of the orders, etc., may not have been praiseworthy, yet to speak against them, either when preaching in public or in speaking before the people, would rather be the cause of murmuring and scandal than of profit. As a consequence, the people would become angry with their superiors, whether secular or spiritual. But while it does harm in the absence of our superiors to speak evil of them before the people, it may be profitable to discuss their bad conduct with those who can apply a remedy. . . .
13. If we wish to proceed securely in all things, we must hold fast to the following principle: What seems to me white, I will believe black if the hierarchical Church so defines. For I must be convinced that in Christ our Lord, the bridegroom, and in His spouse the Church, only one Spirit holds sway, which governs and rules for the salvation of souls.

 What are the fundamental assumptions that inform Loyola's rules for "thinking with the church"? What do these assumptions tell you about the nature of the Catholic reform movement?

Source: Ignatius of Loyola, "Rules for Thinking with the Church," in *The Spiritual Exercises of St. Ignatius of Loyola*, trans. L. J. Puhl (Baltimore: Loyola University Press, 1951).

lifework by prayer, pilgrimages, going to school, and working out a spiritual program in his brief but powerful book, *The Spiritual Exercises*. This was a training manual for spiritual development emphasizing exercises by which the human will could be strengthened and made to follow the will of God as manifested through his instrument, the Catholic Church (see the box above).

Loyola gathered together a small group of individuals who were eventually recognized as a religious order, the Society of Jesus, by a papal bull in 1540. The new order was grounded on the principles of absolute obedience to the papacy, a strict hierarchical order for the society, the use of education to achieve its goals, and a dedication to engage in "conflict for God." The Jesuits' organization came to resemble the structure of a

military command. A two-year novitiate weeded out all but the most dedicated adherents. Executive leadership was put in the hands of a general, who nominated all important positions in the order and was to be revered as the absolute head of the order. Loyola served as the first general of the order until his death in 1556. A special vow of absolute obedience to the pope made the Jesuits an important instrument for papal policy.

ACTIVITIES OF THE JESUITS The Jesuits pursued three major activities. They established highly disciplined schools, borrowing freely from humanist schools for their educational methods. To the Jesuits, the thorough education of young people was crucial to combating the advance of Protestantism.

A Revived Papacy

The involvement of the Renaissance papacy in dubious finances and Italian political and military affairs had given rise to numerous sources of corruption. The meager steps taken to control corruption left the papacy still in need of serious reform, and it took the jolt of the Protestant Reformation to bring it about.

The pontificate of Pope Paul III (1534–1549) proved to be a turning point in the reform of the papacy. Raised in the lap of Renaissance luxury, Paul III continued Renaissance papal practices by appointing his nephews as cardinals, involving himself in politics, and patronizing arts and letters on a lavish scale. Nevertheless, he perceived the need for change and expressed it decisively. He made advocates of reform, such as Gasparo Contarini (GAHS-puh-roh kahn-tuh-REE-nee) and Gian Pietro Caraffa (JAHN PYAY-troh kuh-RAH-fuh), cardinals. In 1535, Paul took the audacious step of appointing a reform commission to study the condition of the church. The commission's report in 1537 blamed the church's problems on the corrupt policies of popes and cardinals. Paul III also formally recognized the Jesuits and summoned the Council of Trent (see the next section).

A decisive turning point in the direction of the Catholic Reformation and the nature of papal reform came in the 1540s. In 1541, a colloquy had been held at Regensburg in a final attempt to settle the religious division peacefully. Here Catholic moderates, such as Cardinal Contarini, who favored concessions to Protestants in the hope of restoring Christian unity, reached a compromise with Protestant moderates on a number of doctrinal issues. When Contarini returned to Rome with these proposals, Cardinal Caraffa and other hardliners, who regarded all compromise with Protestant innovations as heresy, accused him of selling out to the heretics. It soon became apparent that the conservative reformers were in the ascendancy when Caraffa was able to persuade Paul III to establish the Roman Inquisition or Holy Office in 1542 to ferret out doctrinal errors. There was to be no compromise with Protestantism.

When Cardinal Caraffa was chosen pope as Paul IV (1555–1559), he so increased the power of the Inquisition that even liberal cardinals were silenced. This "first true pope of the Catholic Counter-Reformation," as he has been called, also created the Index of Forbidden Books, a list of books that Catholics were not allowed to read. It included all the works of Protestant theologians as well as authors considered "unwholesome," a category general enough to include the works of Erasmus. Rome, the capital of Catholic Christianity, was rapidly becoming Fortress Rome; any hope of restoring Christian unity by compromise was fast fading. The activities of the Council of Trent made compromise virtually impossible.

The Council of Trent

In 1542, Pope Paul III took the decisive step of calling for a general council of Christendom to resolve the religious differences created by the Protestant revolt. It was not until March 1545, however, that a group of cardinals, archbishops, bishops, abbots, and theologians met in the city of Trent on the border between Germany and Italy and initiated the Council of Trent. But a variety of problems, including an outbreak of plague,

Ignatius of Loyola. The Jesuits became the most important new religious order of the Catholic Reformation. Shown here in a sixteenth-century painting by an unknown artist is Ignatius of Loyola, founder of the Society of Jesus. Loyola is seen kneeling before Pope Paul III, who officially recognized the Jesuits in 1540.

In the course of the sixteenth century, the Jesuits took over the premier academic posts in Catholic universities, and by 1600, they were the most famous educators in Europe.

Another prominent Jesuit activity was the propagation of the Catholic faith among non-Christians. Francis Xavier (ZAY-vee-ur) (1506–1552), one of the original members of the Society of Jesus, carried the message of Catholic Christianity to the East. After converting tens of thousands in India, he traveled to Malacca and the Moluccas before reaching Japan in 1549. He spoke highly of the Japanese: "They are a people of excellent morals—good in general and not malicious.[20] Thousands of Japanese, especially in the southernmost islands, became Christians. In 1552, Xavier set out for China but died of a fever before he reached the mainland.

Although conversion efforts in Japan proved short-lived, Jesuit activity in China, especially that of the Italian Matteo Ricci (ma-TAY-oh REE-chee) (1552–1610), was more long-lasting. Recognizing the Chinese pride in their own culture, the Jesuits attempted to draw parallels between Christian and Confucian concepts and to show the similarities between Christian morality and Confucian ethics. For their part, the missionaries were impressed with many aspects of Chinese civilization, and reports of their experiences heightened European curiosity about this great society on the other side of the world.

The Jesuits were also determined to carry the Catholic banner and fight Protestantism. Jesuit missionaries succeeded in restoring Catholicism to parts of Germany and eastern Europe. Poland was largely won back for the Catholic Church through Jesuit efforts.

Pope Paul III	1534–1549
Papal recognition of Society of Jesus (Jesuits)	1540
Establishment of Roman Inquisition (Holy Office)	1542
Council of Trent	1545–1563
Pope Paul IV	1555–1559

war between France and Spain, and the changing of popes, prevented the council from holding regular annual meetings. Nevertheless, the council met intermittently in three major sessions between 1545 and 1563. Moderate Catholic reformers hoped that the council would make compromises in formulating doctrinal definitions that would encourage Protestants to return to the church. Conservatives, however, favored an uncompromising restatement of Catholic doctrines in strict opposition to Protestant positions. After a struggle, the latter group won.

The final doctrinal decrees of the Council of Trent reaffirmed traditional Catholic teachings in opposition to Protestant beliefs. The council affirmed Scripture and tradition as equal authorities in religious matters; only the church could interpret Scripture. Other decrees declared both faith and good works to be necessary for salvation and upheld the seven sacraments, the Catholic doctrine of transubstantiation, and clerical celibacy. The council also affirmed the belief in purgatory and in the efficacy of indulgences, although it prohibited the hawking of indulgences. Of the reform decrees that were passed, the most important established theological seminaries in every diocese for the training of priests.

After the Council of Trent, the Roman Catholic Church possessed a clear body of doctrine and a unified church under the acknowledged supremacy of the popes, who had triumphed over bishops and councils. The Roman Catholic Church had become one Christian denomination among many with an organizational framework and doctrinal pattern that would not be significantly altered for four hundred years. With renewed confidence, the Catholic Church entered a new phase of its history.

Politics and the Wars of Religion in the Sixteenth Century

 FOCUS QUESTION: What role did politics, economic and social conditions, and religion play in the European wars of the sixteenth century?

By the middle of the sixteenth century, Calvinism and Catholicism had become activist religions dedicated to spreading the word of God as they interpreted it. Although this struggle for the minds and hearts of Europeans is at the heart of the religious wars of the sixteenth century, economic, social, and political forces also played an important role in these conflicts. Of the sixteenth-century religious wars, none were more momentous or shattering than the French civil wars known as the French Wars of Religion.

The French Wars of Religion (1562–1598)

Religion was the engine that drove the French civil wars of the sixteenth century. Concerned by the growth of Calvinism, the French kings tried to stop its spread by persecuting Calvinists but had little success. **Huguenots** (HYOO-guh-nots), as the French Calvinists were called, came from all levels of society: artisans and shopkeepers hurt by rising prices and a rigid guild system, merchants and lawyers in provincial towns whose local privileges were tenuous, and members of the nobility. Possibly 40 to 50 percent of the French nobility became Huguenots, including the house of Bourbon (boor-BOHN), which stood next to the Valois (val-WAH) in the royal line of succession and ruled the southern French kingdom of Navarre (nuh-VAHR). The conversion of so many nobles made the Huguenots a potentially dangerous political threat to monarchical power. Though the Calvinists constituted only about 10 percent of the population, they were a strong-willed and well-organized minority.

The Catholic majority greatly outnumbered the Calvinist minority. The Valois monarchy was staunchly Catholic, and its control of the Catholic Church gave it little incentive to look on Protestantism favorably. When King Henry II was killed accidentally in a tournament in 1559, he was succeeded by a series of weak and neurotic sons, two of whom were dominated by their mother, Catherine de' Medici (1519–1589). As regent for her sons, the moderate Catholic Catherine looked to religious compromise as a way to defuse the political tensions but found to her consternation that both sides possessed their share of religious fanatics unwilling to make concessions. The extreme Catholic party—known as the ultra-Catholics—favored strict opposition to the Huguenots and was led by the Guise (GEEZ) family. Possessing the loyalty of Paris and large sections of northern and northwestern France through their client-patronage system, the Guises could recruit and pay for large armies and received support abroad from the papacy and Jesuits who favored the family's uncompromising Catholic position.

But religion was not the only factor contributing to the French civil wars. Resentful of the growing power of monarchical centralization, towns and provinces were only too willing to join a revolt against the monarchy. This was also true of the nobility, and because so many of them were Calvinists, they formed an important base of opposition to the crown. The French Wars of Religion, then, presented a major constitutional crisis for France and temporarily halted the development of the French centralized territorial state. The claim of the state's ruling dynasty to a person's loyalties was temporarily superseded by loyalty to one's religious belief. For some people, the unity of France was less important than religious truth. But there also emerged in France a group of public figures who placed politics before religion and believed that no religious truth was worth the ravages of civil war. These **politiques** (puh-lee-TEEKS) ultimately prevailed, but not until both sides were exhausted by bloodshed.

COURSE OF THE STRUGGLE The wars erupted in 1562 when the powerful duke of Guise massacred a peaceful congregation of Huguenots at Vassy. In the decade of the 1560s, the Huguenots held their own. Though too small a group to conquer France, their armies were so good at defensive campaigns that they could not be defeated either, despite the infamous Saint Bartholomew's Day massacre.

This massacre of Huguenots occurred in August 1572 at a time when the Catholic and Calvinist parties had apparently been reconciled through the marriage of the sister of the reigning Valois king, Charles IX (1560–1574), and Henry of Navarre, the Bourbon ruler of Navarre. Henry was the son of Jeanne d'Albret (ZHAHN dahl-BRAY), queen of Navarre, who had been responsible for introducing Calvinist ideas into her kingdom. Henry was also the acknowledged political leader of the Huguenots, and many Huguenots traveled to Paris for the wedding.

But the Guise family persuaded the king and his mother, Catherine de' Medici, that this gathering of Huguenots posed a threat to them. Charles and his advisers decided to eliminate the Huguenot leaders with one swift blow. According to one French military leader, Charles and his advisers believed that civil war would soon break out anyway and that "it was better to win a battle in Paris, where all the leaders were, than to risk it in the field and fall into a dangerous and uncertain war."[21]

The massacre began early in the day on August 24 when the king's guards sought out and killed some prominent Huguenot leaders. These murders soon unleashed a wave of violence that gripped the city of Paris. For three days, frenzied Catholic mobs roamed the streets of Paris, killing Huguenots in an often cruel

and bloodthirsty manner. According to one eyewitness account: "Then they took her [Françoise Lussault] and dragged her by the hair a long way through the streets, and spying the gold bracelets on her arms, without having the patience to unfasten them, cut off her wrists."[22] Three days of killing left three thousand Huguenots dead, although not Henry of Navarre, who saved his life by promising to turn Catholic. Thousands more were killed in provincial towns. The massacre boomeranged, however, because it discredited the Valois dynasty without ending the conflict.

The fighting continued. The Huguenots rebuilt their strength, and in 1576, the ultra-Catholics formed a "Holy League," vowing to exterminate heresy and seat a true Catholic champion—Henry, duke of Guise—on the French throne in place of the ruling king, Henry III (1574–1589), who had succeeded his brother Charles IX. The turning point in the conflict came in the War of the Three Henries in 1588–1589. Henry, duke of Guise, in the pay of Philip II of Spain, seized Paris and forced King Henry III to make him chief minister. To rid himself of Guise influence, Henry III assassinated the duke of Guise and then joined with Henry of Navarre (who meanwhile had returned to Calvinism), who was next in line to the throne, to crush the Catholic Holy League and retake the city of Paris. Although successful, Henry III was assassinated in 1589 by a monk who was repelled by the spectacle of a Catholic

The Saint Bartholomew's Day Massacre. Although the outbreak of religious war seemed unlikely in France, the collapse of the strong monarchy with the death of Henry II unleashed forces that led to a series of civil wars. Pictured here is the Saint Bartholomew's Day massacre of 1572. This contemporary painting by the Huguenot artist François Dubois vividly depicts a number of the incidents of that day when approximately three thousand Huguenots were murdered in Paris.

CHRONOLOGY	The French Wars of Religion (1562–1598)	
Duke of Guise massacres Huguenot congregation at Vassy	1562
Saint Bartholomew's Day massacre	1572
Henry III	1574–1589
Formation of the Holy League	1576
War of the Three Henries	1588–1589
Assassination of Henry III	1589
Coronation of Henry IV	1594
Edict of Nantes	1598

district and allowed them to retain a number of fortified towns for their protection. In addition, Huguenots were allowed to enjoy all political privileges, including the holding of public offices. Although the Edict of Nantes recognized the rights of the Protestant minority and ostensibly the principle of religious toleration, it did so only out of political necessity, not out of conviction.

Philip II and Militant Catholicism

The greatest advocate of activist Catholicism in the second half of the sixteenth century was King Philip II of Spain (1556–1598), the son and heir of Charles V. Philip's reign ushered in an age of Spanish greatness, both politically and culturally.

The first major goal of Philip II was to consolidate and secure the lands he had inherited from his father. These included Spain, the Netherlands, and possessions in Italy (see Map 13.3) and the New World. For Philip, this meant strict conformity to Catholicism, enforced by aggressive use of the Spanish Inquisition, and the establishment of strong, monarchical authority. The latter was not an easy task because Philip had inherited a governmental structure in which each of the various states and territories of his empire stood in an individual relationship to the king. Philip did manage, however, to expand royal power in Spain by making the monarchy less dependent on the traditional landed

king cooperating with a Protestant. Henry of Navarre now claimed the throne. Realizing, however, that Catholic France would never accept him, Henry took the logical way out and converted once again to Catholicism. With his coronation in 1594, the French Wars of Religion finally came to an end.

Nevertheless, the religious problem persisted until the Edict of Nantes (NAHNT) was issued in 1598. The edict acknowledged Catholicism as the official religion of France but guaranteed the Huguenots the right to worship in selected places in every

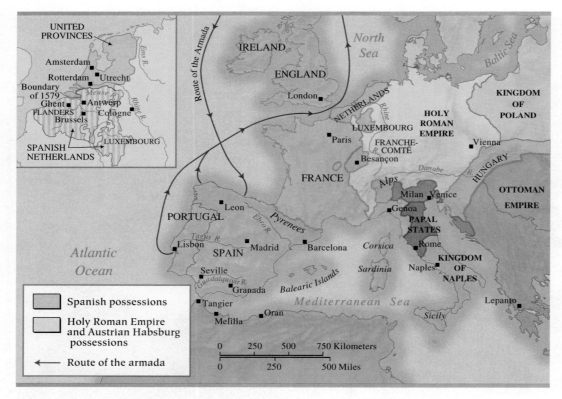

MAP 13.3 The Height of Spanish Power Under Philip II. Like his father, Charles V, Philip II, the "Most Catholic King," was a champion of the Catholic cause against Protestantism. He sought to maintain Habsburg control in the Netherlands by combating a Protestant revolt, a rebellion eventually supported by Queen Elizabeth of England. Spain's attempt to invade England in 1588 ended in disaster.

 Why would England feel threatened by Spanish territory in the Netherlands?

Scala/Art Resource, NY

Philip of Spain. This portrait by Titian depicts Philip II of Spain. The king's attempts to make Spain a great power led to large debts and crushing taxes, and his military actions in defense of Catholicism ended in failure and misfortune in both France and the Netherlands.

aristocracy. Philip tried to be the center of the whole government and supervised the work of all departments, even down to the smallest details. Unwilling to delegate authority, he failed to distinguish between important and trivial matters and fell weeks behind on state correspondence, where he was inclined to make marginal notes and even correct spelling. One Spanish official said, "If God used the Escorial [the royal palace where Philip worked] to deliver my death sentence, I would be immortal."

One of Philip's aims was to make Spain a dominant power in Europe. To a great extent, Spain's preeminence depended on a prosperous economy fueled by its importation of gold and silver from its New World possessions, its agriculture, its commerce, and its industry, especially in textiles, silk, and leather goods. The importation of silver also had detrimental effects,

however, as it helped set off a spiraling inflation that disrupted the Spanish economy, eventually hurting both textile production and agriculture. Moreover, the expenses of war, especially after 1580, proved devastating to the Spanish economy. American gold and silver never constituted more than 20 percent of the royal revenue, leading the government to impose a crushing burden of direct and indirect taxes. Even then the government was forced to borrow. Philip repudiated his debts seven times; still, two-thirds of state income went to pay interest on the debt by the end of his reign. The attempt to make Spain a great power led to its decline after Philip's reign.

Crucial to an understanding of Philip II is the importance of Catholicism to the Spanish people and their ruler. Driven by a heritage of crusading fervor, the Spanish had little difficulty seeing themselves as a nation of people divinely chosen to save Catholic Christianity from the Protestant heretics. Philip II, the "Most Catholic King," became the champion of Catholicism throughout Europe, a role that led to spectacular victories and equally spectacular defeats for the Spanish king. Spain's leadership of a holy league against Turkish encroachments in the Mediterranean, especially the Muslim attack on the island of Cyprus, resulted in a stunning victory over the Turkish fleet at the Battle of Lepanto (LEH-pahn-toh *or* LIH-pan-toh) in 1571. Philip's greatest misfortunes came from his attempt to crush the revolt in the Netherlands and his tortured relations with Queen Elizabeth of England.

Revolt of the Netherlands

As one of the richest parts of Philip's empire, the Spanish Netherlands was of great importance to the Most Catholic King. The Netherlands consisted of seventeen provinces (the modern Netherlands, Belgium, and Luxembourg). The seven northern provinces were largely Germanic in culture and Dutch speaking, while the French- and Flemish-speaking southern provinces were closely tied to France. Situated at the commercial crossroads of northwestern Europe, the Netherlands had become prosperous through commerce and a flourishing textile industry. Because of its location, the Netherlands was open to the religious influences of the age. Though some inhabitants had adopted Lutheranism or Anabaptism, by the time of Philip II, Calvinism was also making inroads. These provinces had no real political bond holding them together except their common ruler, and that ruler was Philip II, a foreigner who was out of touch with the local situation.

Philip II hoped to strengthen his control in the Netherlands, regardless of the traditional privileges of the separate provinces. This was strongly opposed by the nobles, towns, and provincial states, which stood to lose politically if their jealously guarded privileges and freedoms were weakened. Resentment against Philip increased when the residents of the Netherlands realized that the taxes they paid were being used for Spanish interests. Finally, religion became a major catalyst for rebellion when Philip attempted to crush Calvinism. Violence erupted in 1566 when Calvinists—especially nobles—began to destroy statues and stained-glass windows in Catholic churches. Philip responded by sending the duke of Alva with 10,000 veteran Spanish and Italian troops to crush the rebellion.

The repressive policies of the duke proved counterproductive. The levying of a permanent sales tax alienated many merchants and commoners, who now joined the nobles and Calvinists in the struggle against Spanish rule. A special tribunal, known as the Council of Troubles (nicknamed the Council of Blood by the Dutch), inaugurated a reign of terror in which even powerful aristocrats were executed. As a result, the revolt now became organized, especially in the northern provinces, where William of Nassau, the prince of Orange, also known as William the Silent, and Dutch pirates known as the "Sea Beggars" mounted growing resistance. In 1573, Philip removed the duke of Alva and shifted to a more conciliatory policy to bring an end to the costly revolt.

William of Orange wished to unify all seventeen provinces, a goal seemingly realized in 1576 with the Pacification of Ghent. This agreement stipulated that all the provinces would stand together under William's leadership, respect religious differences, and demand that the Spanish troops be withdrawn. But religious differences proved too strong for any lasting union. When the duke of Parma, the next Spanish leader, arrived in the Netherlands, he astutely played on the religious differences of the provinces and split their united front. The southern provinces formed a Catholic union—the Union of Arras—in 1579 and accepted Spanish control. To counter this, William of Orange organized the seven northern, Dutch-speaking states into a Protestant union—the Union of Utrecht—determined to oppose Spanish rule. The Netherlands was now divided along religious, geographic, and political lines into two hostile camps. The struggle dragged on until 1609, when a twelve-year truce

CHRONOLOGY	Philip II and Militant Catholicism
Philip II	1556–1598
Outbreak of revolt in the Netherlands	1566
Battle of Lepanto	1571
Spanish armada	1588
Twelve-year truce (Spain and Netherlands)	1609
Independence of the United Provinces	1648

ended the war, virtually recognizing the independence of the northern provinces. These "United Provinces" soon emerged as the Dutch Republic, although the Spanish did not formally recognize them as independent until 1648. The ten southern provinces remained a Spanish possession (see Map 13.3).

The England of Elizabeth

After the death of Queen Mary in 1558, her half-sister Elizabeth (1558–1603) ascended the throne of England. During Elizabeth's reign, England rose to prominence as the relatively small island kingdom became the leader of the Protestant nations of Europe, laid the foundations for a world empire, and experienced a cultural renaissance.

The daughter of King Henry VIII and Anne Boleyn, Elizabeth had had a difficult early life. During Mary's reign, she had even been imprisoned for a while and had learned early to hide

Stapleton Collection/Corbis

Procession of Queen Elizabeth I. Intelligent and learned, Elizabeth Tudor was familiar with Latin and Greek and spoke several European languages. Served by able administrators, Elizabeth ruled for nearly forty-five years and generally avoided open military action against any major power. This picture, painted near the end of her reign, shows the queen in a ceremonial procession with her courtiers.

QUEEN ELIZABETH I: "I HAVE THE HEART OF A KING"

QUEEN ELIZABETH I RULED ENGLAND from 1558 to 1603 with a consummate skill that contemporaries considered unusual in a woman. Though shrewd and paternalistic, Elizabeth, like other sixteenth-century monarchs, depended for her power on the favor of her people. When England faced the threat of an invasion by the Spanish armada of Philip II in 1588, Elizabeth sought to rally her troops with a speech at Tilbury, a town on the Thames River. This selection is taken from her speech.

Queen Elizabeth I, Speech to the Troops at Tilbury

My loving people, we have been persuaded by some, that are careful of our safety, to take heed how we commit ourselves to armed multitudes, for fear of treachery; but I assure you, I do not desire to live to distrust my faithful and loving people. Let tyrants fear; I have always so behaved myself that, under God, I have placed my chiefest strength and safeguard in the loyal hearts and good will of my subjects. And therefore I am come amongst you at this time, not as for my recreation or sport, but being resolved, in the midst and heat of the battle, to live or die amongst you all; to lay down, for my God, and

for my kingdom, and for my people, my honor and my blood, even in the dust. I know I have but the body of a weak and feeble woman; but I have the heart of a king, and of a king of England, too; and think foul scorn that Parma or Spain, or any prince of Europe, should dare to invade the borders of my realm: to which, rather than any dishonor should grow by me, I myself will take up arms; I myself will be your general, judge, and rewarder of every one of your virtues in the field. I know already, by your forwardness, that you have deserved rewards and crowns; and we do assure you, on the word of a prince, they shall be duly paid you. In the mean my lieutenant general shall be in my stead, than whom never prince commanded a more noble and worthy subject; not doubting by your obedience to my general, by your concord in the camp and by your valor in the field, we shall shortly have a famous victory over the enemies of my God, of my kingdom, and of my people.

 What qualities evident in Elizabeth's speech would have endeared her to her listeners? How was her popularity connected to the events of the late sixteenth century?

Source: Elizabeth I's Speech to the Troops at Tilbury in 1588.

---

her true feelings from both private and public sight. Intelligent, cautious, and self-confident, she moved quickly to solve the difficult religious problem she had inherited from Mary, who had become extremely unpopular when she tried to return England to the Catholic fold.

RELIGIOUS POLICY Elizabeth's religious policy was based on moderation and compromise. As a ruler, she wished to prevent England from being torn apart over matters of religion. Parliament cooperated with the queen in initiating the Elizabethan religious settlement in 1559. The Catholic legislation of Mary's reign was repealed, and the new Act of Supremacy designated Elizabeth as "the only supreme governor of this realm, as well in all spiritual or ecclesiastical things or causes, as temporal." She used this title rather than "supreme head of the church," which had been used by both Henry VIII and Edward VI, because she did not want to upset the Catholics, who considered the pope the supreme head, or radical Protestants, who thought that Christ alone was head of the church. The Act of Uniformity restored the church service of the Book of Common Prayer from the reign of Edward VI with some revisions to make it more acceptable to Catholics. The Thirty-Nine Articles, a new confession of faith, defined theological issues midway between Lutheranism and Calvinism. Elizabeth's religious settlement was basically Protestant, but it was a moderate Protestantism that avoided overly subtle distinctions and extremes.

The new religious settlement worked, at least to the extent that it smothered religious differences in England in the second half of the sixteenth century. Two groups, however, the Catholics and the Puritans, continued to oppose it. One of Elizabeth's greatest challenges came from her Catholic cousin, Mary, queen of Scots, who was next in line to the English throne. Mary was ousted from Scotland by rebellious Calvinist nobles in 1568 and fled for her life to England. There Elizabeth placed her under house arrest and for fourteen years tolerated her involvement in a number of ill-planned Catholic plots designed to kill Elizabeth and replace her on the throne with the Catholic Mary. Finally, in 1587, after Mary became embroiled in a far more serious plot, Elizabeth had her cousin beheaded to end the threats to her regime.

Potentially more dangerous to Anglicanism in the long run were the **Puritans** The word *Puritan* first appeared in 1564 when it was used to refer to Protestants within the Anglican Church who, inspired by Calvinist theology, wanted to remove any trace of Catholicism from the Church of England. Elizabeth managed to keep the Puritans in check during her reign.

Elizabeth proved as adept in government and foreign policy as in religious affairs (see the box above). She was well served administratively by the principal secretary of state. The talents of Sir William Cecil and Sir Francis Walsingham, who together held the office for thirty-two years, ensured much of Elizabeth's success in foreign and domestic affairs. Elizabeth also handled Parliament with much skill; it met only thirteen times during her entire reign.

FOREIGN POLICY Caution, moderation, and expediency also dictated Elizabeth's foreign policy. Fearful of other countries' motives, Elizabeth realized that war could be disastrous for her island kingdom and her own rule. Unofficially, however, she encouraged English seamen to raid Spanish ships and colonies. Francis Drake was especially adept at plundering Spanish fleets loaded with gold and silver from Spain's New World empire.

surely an act in accordance with the will of God. Accordingly, Philip ordered preparations for a fleet of warships that would rendezvous with the army of the duke of Parma in Flanders and escort his troops across the English Channel for the invasion.

THE SPANISH ARMADA The armada proved to be a disaster. The Spanish fleet that finally set sail had neither the ships nor the troops that Philip had planned to send. A conversation between a papal emissary and an officer of the Spanish fleet before the armada departed reveals the fundamental flaw:

> "And if you meet the English armada in the Channel, do you expect to win the battle?" "Of course," replied the Spaniard.
> "How can you be sure?" [asked the emissary].
> "It's very simple. It is well known that we fight in God's cause. So, when we meet the English, God will surely arrange matters so that we can grapple and board them, either by sending some strange freak of weather or, more likely, just by depriving the English of their wits. If we can come to close quarters, Spanish valor and Spanish steel (and the great masses of soldiers we shall have on board) will make our victory certain. But unless God helps us by a miracle the English, who have faster and handier ships than ours, and many more long-range guns, and who know their advantage just as well as we do, will never close with us at all, but stand aloof and knock us to pieces with their culverins [cannons], without our being able to do them any serious hurt. So," concluded the captain, and one fancies a grim smile, "we are sailing against England in the confident hope of a miracle."[23]

The hoped-for miracle never materialized. The Spanish fleet, battered by a number of encounters with the English, sailed back to Spain by a northward route around Scotland and Ireland, where it was further battered by storms. Although the English and Spanish would continue their war for another sixteen years, the defeat of the Spanish armada guaranteed for the time being that England would remain a Protestant country. Although Spain made up for its losses within a year and a half, the defeat was a psychological blow to the Spaniards.

While encouraging English piracy and providing clandestine aid to French Huguenots and Dutch Calvinists to weaken France and Spain, Elizabeth pretended complete aloofness and avoided alliances that would force her into war with any major power (see "Film & History" above). Gradually, however, Elizabeth was drawn into more active involvement in the Netherlands. This move accelerated the already mounting friction between Spain and England. After years of resisting the idea of invading England as impractical, Philip II of Spain was finally persuaded to do so by advisers who assured him that the people of England would rise against their queen when the Spaniards arrived. Moreover, Philip was easily convinced that the revolt in the Netherlands would never be crushed as long as England provided support for it. In any case, a successful invasion of England would mean the overthrow of heresy and the return of England to Catholicism,

CHAPTER SUMMARY

When the Augustinian monk Martin Luther burst onto the scene with a series of theses on indulgences, few people suspected that his observations would eventually split all of Europe along religious lines. But the yearning for reform of the church and meaningful religious experiences caused a seemingly simple dispute to escalate into a powerful movement.

Martin Luther established the twin pillars of the Protestant Reformation: the doctrine of justification by faith alone and the Bible as the sole authority in religious affairs. Although Luther felt that his revival of Christianity based on his interpretation

of the Bible should be acceptable to all, others soon appeared who also read the Bible but interpreted it in different ways. Protestantism fragmented into different sects—Zwinglianism, Calvinism, Anglicanism, Anabaptism—which, though united in their dislike of Catholicism, were themselves divided over the interpretation of the sacraments and religious practices. As reform ideas spread, religion and politics became ever more intertwined.

Although the peace of Augsburg in 1555 legally acknowledged Lutheranism in the Holy Roman Empire, it had lost much of its momentum and outside of Scandinavia had scant ability to attract new supporters. Its energy was largely replaced by the new Protestant form of Calvinism, which had a clarity of doctrine and a fervor that made it attractive to a whole new generation

of Europeans. But while Calvinism's activism enabled it to spread across Europe, Catholicism was also experiencing its own revival. New religious orders based on reform, a revived and reformed papacy, and the Council of Trent, which reaffirmed traditional Catholic doctrine, gave the Catholic Church a renewed vitality.

By the middle of the sixteenth century, it was apparent that the religious passions of the Reformation era had brought an end to the religious unity of medieval Europe. The religious division (Catholics versus Protestant) was instrumental in beginning a series of religious wars that were complicated by economic, social, and political forces that also played a role. The French Wars of Religion, the revolt of the Netherlands against

Philip II of Spain, and the conflict between Philip II and Elizabeth of England, which led to the failed attempt of the Spanish armada to invade England, were the major struggles in the sixteenth-century religious wars.

That people who were disciples of the Apostle of Peace would kill each other over their beliefs aroused skepticism about Christianity itself. As one German writer put it, "Lutheran, popish, and Calvinistic, we've got all these beliefs here, but there is some doubt about where Christianity has got."[24] It is surely no accident that the search for a stable, secular order of politics and for order in the universe through natural laws soon came to play important roles. Before we look at this search for order in the seventeenth century, however, we need first to look at the adventures that plunged Europe into its new role in the world.

CHAPTER TIMELINE

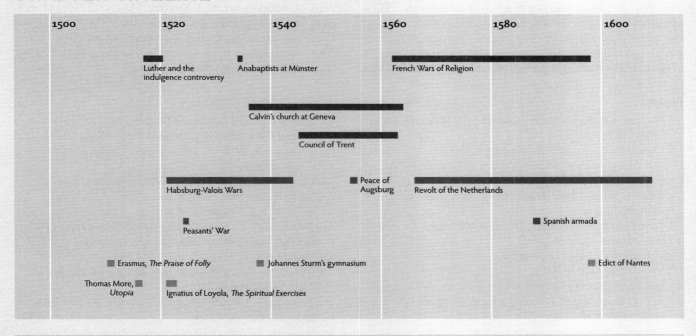

CHAPTER REVIEW

Upon Reflection

Q If attempts at reform of the Catholic Church were unsuccessful in the fifteenth century, why did they succeed during the sixteenth-century Reformation?

Q What role did politics play in the establishment of Lutheranism and Anglicanism?

Q Elizabeth of England and Philip II of Spain were two of Europe's most famous monarchs in the second half of the sixteenth century. Compare and contrast their methods of ruling and their foreign policy. Which was a more successful ruler? Why?

Key Terms

Christian (northern Renaissance) humanism (p. 366)
pluralism (p. 368)
confession (p. 369)
justification (p. 370)
transubstantiation (p. 373)
millenarianism (p. 380)

predestination (p. 383)
Catholic Reformation (p. 386)
Huguenots (p. 390)
politiques (p. 390)
Puritans (p. 395)

Suggestions for Further Reading

THE REFORMATION For a general history of the era of the Reformation, see **M. Greengrass, *Christendom Destroyed: Europe 1517–1648*** (New York, 2014). Basic surveys of the Reformation period include **J. D. Tracy, *Europe's Reformations, 1450–1650*,** 2nd ed. (Oxford, 2006), and **D. MacCulloch, *The Reformation*** (New York, 2003).

NORTHERN RENAISSANCE HUMANISM The development of humanism outside Italy is examined in **C. G. Nauert Jr., *Humanism and the Culture of Renaissance Europe*,** 2nd ed. (Cambridge, 2006).

LUTHER AND LUTHERANISM On Martin Luther's life, see **H. A. Oberman, *Luther: Between God and the Devil*** (New Haven, Conn., 2006), and the brief biography by **M. Marty, *Martin Luther*** (New York, 2004). On the role of Charles V, see **W. Maltby, *The Reign of Charles V*** (New York, 2002).

SPREAD OF THE PROTESTANT REFORMATION **W. P. Stephens's** *Zwingli* (Oxford, 1994) is an important study of the man's ideas. The most comprehensive account of the various groups and individuals who are called Anabaptists is **G. H. Williams, *The Radical Reformation*,** 2nd ed. (Kirksville, Mo.,

1992). On the English Reformation, see **N. L. Jones, *English Reformation: Religion and Cultural Adaptation*** (London, 2002). On Calvinism, see **W. G. Naphy, *Calvin and the Consolidation of the Genevan Reformation*** (Philadelphia, 2003).

SOCIAL IMPACT OF THE REFORMATION On the impact of the Reformation on the family, see **J. F. Harrington, *Reordering Marriage and Society in Reformation Germany*** (New York, 1995). On women, see **K. Stjerna, *Women and the Reformation*** (New York, 2008).

CATHOLIC REFORMATION A good introduction to the Catholic Reformation can be found in **M. A. Mullett, *The Catholic Reformation*** (London, 1999). Also valuable is **R. P. Hsia, *The World of Catholic Renewal, 1540–1770*,** 2nd ed. (Cambridge, 2006).

WARS OF RELIGION For a good introduction to the French Wars of Religion, see **R. J. Knecht, *The French Wars of Religion, 1559–1598*,** 3rd ed. (New York, 2010). On Philip II, see **G. Parker, *Imprudent King: A New Life of Philip II*** (New Haven, Conn. 2014). Elizabeth's reign can be examined in **D. Loades, *Elizabeth I*** (New York, 2006).

Notes

1. Quoted in R. Bainton, *Here I Stand: A Life of Martin Luther* (Nashville, 1978), p. 183.
2. Desiderius Erasmus, *The Paraclesis*, in *Christian Humanism and the Reformation: Selected Writings of Erasmus*, 3rd ed., J. Olin, ed. (New York, 1987), p. 101.
3. Thomas More, *Utopia*, trans. Paul Turner (Harmondsworth, U.K., 1965), p. 76.
4. Quoted in A. E. McGrath, *Reformation Thought: An Introduction* (Oxford, 1988), p. 72.
5. Quoted in G. Rupp, *Luther's Progress to the Diet of Worms* (New York, 1964), p. 82.
6. Martin Luther, *On the Freedom of a Christian Man*, quoted in E. G. Rupp and B. Drewery, eds., *Martin Luther* (New York, 1970), p. 50.
7. Quoted in R. Bainton, *Here I Stand: A Life of Martin Luther*, pp. 181–182.
8. Author's translation of Martin Luther's lyrics, second verse of *Ein feste Burg ist unser Gott.*
9. Quoted in A. Dürer, *The Writings of Albrecht Dürer*, ed. and trans. (New York, 1958), p. 157.
10. Quoted in D. L. Jensen, *Reformation Europe* (Lexington, Mass., 1981), p. 83.
11. Quoted in L. P. Wandel, *Voracious Idols and Violent Hands: Iconoclasm in Reformation Zürich, Strasbourg, and Basel* (New York, 1995), p. 81.

12. Quoted in A. G. Dickens and D. Carr, eds., *The Reformation in England to the Accession of Elizabeth I* (New York, 1968), p. 72.
13. Quoted in L. W. Spitz, *The Renaissance and Reformation Movements* (Chicago, 1971), p. 414.
14. John Calvin, *Institutes of the Christian Religion*, trans. J. Allen (Philadelphia, 1936), vol. 1, p. 220.
15. Ibid., vol. 1, p. 228; vol. 2, p. 181.
16. Quoted in R. Bainton, *Women of the Reformation in Germany and Italy* (Minneapolis, 1971), p. 154.
17. Quoted in B. S. Anderson and J. P. Zinsser, *A History of Their Own: Women in Europe from Prehistory to the Present* (New York, 1988), vol. 1, p. 259.
18. Quoted in J. A. Phillips, *Eve: The History of an Idea* (New York, 1984), p. 105.
19. Quoted in J. Zophy, *A Short History of Renaissance and Reformation Europe*, 3rd ed. (Upper Saddle River, N.J., 2003), p. 227.
20. Quoted in J. O'Malley, *The First Jesuits* (Cambridge, Mass., 1993), p. 76.
21. Quoted in R. J. Knecht, *The French Wars of Religion, 1559–1598*, 2nd ed. (New York, 1996), p. 47.
22. Quoted in M. P. Holt, *The French Wars of Religion, 1562–1629* (Cambridge, 1995), p. 86.
23. Quoted in G. Mattingly, *The Armada* (Boston, 1959), pp. 216–217.
24. Quoted in T. Schieder, *Handbuch der Europäischen Geschichte* (Stuttgart, 1979), vol. 3, p. 579.

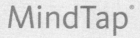 **MindTap®** is a fully online, highly personalized learning experience built upon Cengage Learning content. MindTap combines student learning tools—readings, multimedia, activities, and assessments—into a singular Learning Path that guides students through the course.

EUROPE AND THE WORLD: NEW ENCOUNTERS, 1500–1800

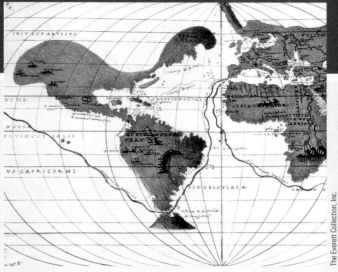

A 1536 Mercator projection map showing the route of Ferdinand Magellan's first circumnavigation of the world

The Everett Collection, Inc.

CHAPTER OUTLINE AND FOCUS QUESTIONS

On the Brink of a New World

Q Why did Europeans begin to embark on voyages of discovery and expansion at the end of the fifteenth century?

New Horizons: The Portuguese and Spanish Empires

Q How did Portugal and Spain acquire their overseas empires, and how did their empires differ?

New Rivals on the World Stage

Q How did the arrival of the Dutch, British, and French on the world scene in the seventeenth and eighteenth centuries affect Africa, Southeast Asia, India, China, and Japan? What were the main features of the African slave trade, and what effects did it have on Africa?

The Impact of European Expansion

Q How did European expansion affect both the conquered and the conquerors?

Toward a World Economy

Q What was mercantilism, and what was its relationship to colonial empires?

Critical Thinking

Q *What was the relationship between European overseas expansion and political, economic, and social developments in Europe?*

Connections to Today

Q *Considering both the benefits and the consequences, what are the similarities and differences between the overseas trade that developed in the seventeenth and eighteenth centuries and the global trade of the twenty-first century?*

WHILE MANY EUROPEANS were occupied with the problems of dynastic expansion and religious reform, others were taking voyages that propelled Europeans far beyond the medieval walls in which they had been enclosed for almost a thousand years. One of these adventurers was the Portuguese explorer Ferdinand Magellan. Convinced that he could find a sea passage to Asia through America, Magellan persuaded the king of Spain to finance an exploratory voyage. On August 10, 1519, Magellan set sail on the Atlantic with five ships and a Spanish crew of 277 men. After a stormy and difficult crossing of the Atlantic, Magellan's fleet moved down the coast of South America, searching for the elusive strait that would take him through. His Spanish ship captains thought he was crazy: "The fool is obsessed with his search for a strait," one remarked. "On the flame of his ambition he will crucify us all." At last, in October 1520, he found it, passing through a narrow waterway (later named the Strait of Magellan) and emerging into an unknown ocean that he called the Pacific Sea. Magellan reckoned that it would then be a short distance to the Spice Islands of the East, but he was badly mistaken. Week after week, he and his crew sailed on across the Pacific as their food supplies dwindled. According to one account, "When their last biscuit had gone, they scraped the maggots out of the casks, mashed them and served them as gruel. They made cakes out of sawdust soaked with the urine of rats—the rats themselves, as delicacies, had long since been hunted to extinction." At last they reached the islands that would later be called the Philippines (after King Philip II of Spain), where Magellan met his death at the hands of the natives. Although only one of his original fleet of five ships survived and returned to Spain, Magellan is still remembered as the first person to circumnavigate the world.

At the beginning of the sixteenth century, European adventurers like Magellan had begun launching small fleets into the vast reaches of the Atlantic Ocean. They were hardly aware that they were beginning a new era, not only for Europe, but for the peoples of Asia, Africa, and the Americas as well. Nevertheless, the voyages of these Europeans marked the beginning of a process that led to radical changes in the political, economic, and cultural life of the entire world.

Between 1500 and 1800, European power engulfed the world. In the Americas, Europeans established colonies that spread their laws, religions, and cultures. In the island regions of Southeast Asia, Europeans firmly established their rule. In other parts of Asia and in Africa, their activities ranged from trading goods to trafficking in humans, permanently altering the lives of the local peoples. In all regions touched by European expansion, the indigenous peoples faced exposure to new diseases, alteration of their religions and customs, and the imposition of new laws.

On the Brink of a New World

 FOCUS QUESTION: Why did Europeans begin to embark on voyages of discovery and expansion at the end of the fifteenth century?

Nowhere has the dynamic and even ruthless energy of Western civilization been more apparent than in its expansion into the rest of the world. By the late sixteenth century, the Atlantic seaboard had become the center of a commercial activity that raised Portugal and Spain and later the Dutch Republic, England, and France to prominence. The age of expansion was a crucial factor in the European transition from the agrarian economy of the Middle Ages to a commercial and industrial capitalistic system. Expansion also brought Europeans into new and lasting contacts with non-European peoples that inaugurated a new age of world history in the sixteenth century.

The Motives for Expansion

For almost a millennium, Catholic Europe had been confined to one geographic area. Its one major attempt to expand beyond those frontiers, the Crusades, had largely failed. Of course, Europe had never completely lost touch with the outside world: the goods of Asia and Africa made their way into medieval castles, the works of Muslim philosophers were read in medieval universities, and in the ninth and tenth centuries, the Vikings had even made their way to the eastern fringes of North America. But in all cases, contacts with non-European civilizations remained limited until the end of the fifteenth century, when Europeans embarked on a remarkable series of overseas journeys. What caused Europeans to undertake such dangerous voyages to the ends of the earth?

FANTASTIC LANDS Europeans had long felt the lure of lands outside Europe as a result of a large body of fantasy literature about "other worlds" that blossomed in the Middle Ages. In the fourteenth century, the author of *The Travels of John Mandeville* spoke of realms (which he had never seen) filled with precious stones and gold. Other lands were more frightening and considerably less appealing. In one country, "the folk be great giants of twenty-eight foot long, or thirty foot long. . . . And they eat more gladly man's flesh than any other flesh." Farther north was a land inhabited by "full cruel and evil women. And they have precious stones in their eyes. And they be of that kind that if they behold any man with wrath they slay him at once with the beholding."[1] Other writers, however, enticed Europeans with descriptions of mysterious Christian kingdoms: the magical kingdom of Prester John in Africa and a Christian community in southern India that was supposedly founded by Thomas, an apostle of Jesus.

ECONOMIC MOTIVES Although Muslim control of Central Asia cut Europe off from the countries farther east, the Mongol conquests in the thirteenth century had reopened the doors. The most famous medieval travelers to the East were the Polos of Venice. Niccolò and Maffeo, merchants from Venice, accompanied by Niccolò's son Marco, undertook the lengthy journey to the court of the great Mongol ruler Khubilai Khan (1259–1294) in 1271. An account of Marco's experiences, the *Travels*, was the most informative of all the descriptions of Asia by medieval European travelers (see the box on p. 401). Others followed the Polos, but in the fourteenth century, the conquests of the Ottoman Turks and then the breakup of the Mongol Empire reduced Western traffic to the East. With the closing of the overland routes, a number of people in Europe became interested in the possibility of reaching Asia by sea to gain access to the spices and other precious items of the region. Christopher Columbus had a copy of Marco Polo's *Travels* in his possession when he began to envision his epoch-making voyage across the Atlantic Ocean.

An economic motive thus loomed large in European expansion in the Renaissance. Merchants, adventurers, and government officials had high hopes of finding new areas of trade, especially more direct access to the spices of the East. These continued to come to Europe via Arab intermediaries but were

MARCO POLO'S *TRAVELS*

ONE OF THE MOST POPULAR TEXTS in late medieval Europe was *The Travels of Marco Polo*, in which the Venetian merchant Marco Polo recounted the story of his journeys throughout East and South Asia. His description of the city of Kinsay—modern Hangzhou (HAHNG-joh) in eastern China— heavily influenced Europeans' conception of Asia.

Marco Polo, "Description of the Great City of Kinsay"

When you have left the city of Changan and have traveled for three days through a splendid country, passing a number of towns and villages, you arrive at the most noble city of Kinsay, a name which is as much as to say in our tongue "The City of Heaven," as I told you before. . . .

First and foremost, then, the document stated the city of Kinsay to be so great that it hath a hundred miles of compass. And there are in it twelve thousand bridges of stone, for the most part so lofty that a great fleet could pass beneath them. . . .

The document aforesaid also stated that the number and wealth of the merchants, and the amount of goods that passed through their hands, was so enormous that no man could form a just estimate thereof. . . .

All the streets are paved with stone or brick, as indeed are all the highways throughout Manzi, so that you ride and travel in every direction without inconvenience. . . .

There is another thing I must tell you. It is the custom for every burgess of this city, and in fact for every description of person in it, to write over his door his own name, the name of his wife, and those of his children, his slaves, and all the inmates of his house, and also the number of animals that he keeps. And if any one dies in the house then the name of that person is erased, and if any child is born its name is added. So in this way the sovereign is able to know exactly the population of the city. . . .

In this part [of the city] are ten principal markets, though besides these there are a vast number of others in the different parts of the town. . . . In each of the squares is held a market three days in the week, frequented by 40,000 or 50,000 persons, who bring thither for sale every possible necessary of life, so that there is always an ample supply of every kind of meat and game, as of roebuck, red-deer, fallow-deer, hares, rabbits, partridges, pheasants, francolins, quails, fowls, capons, and of ducks and geese an infinite quantity; for so many are bred on the Lake that for a Venice groat of silver you can have a couple of ducks. . . .

Those markets make a daily display of every kind of vegetables and fruits; and among the latter there are in particular certain pears of enormous size, weighing as much as ten pounds apiece. . . .

To give you an example of the vast consumption in this city let us take the article of *pepper*; and that will enable you in some measure to estimate what must be the quantity of victual, such as meat, wine, groceries, which have to be provided for the general consumption. Now Messer Marco heard it stated by one of the Great Khan's officers of customs that the quantity of pepper introduced daily for consumption into the city of Kinsay amounted to 43 loads, each load being equal to 223 lbs.

The houses of the citizens are well built and elaborately finished; and the delight they take in decoration, in painting and in architecture, leads them to spend in this way sums of money that would astonish you.

 What does this description of the city of Kinsay tell us about Europe in the late thirteenth century? Why would Asia appeal to European merchants who read Marco Polo's account?

Source: H. Yule, ed., trans., *The Book of Ser Marco Polo*, vol. 1 (London: John Murray, 1903), pp. 185–193, 200–208.

---

outrageously expensive. In addition to the potential profits to be made from the spice trade, many European explorers and conquerors did not hesitate to express their desire for material gain in the form of gold and other precious metals. One Spanish conquistador (kahn-KEESS-tuh-dor) explained that the purpose of their mission to the New World was to "serve God and His Majesty, to give light to those who were in darkness, and to grow rich, as all men desire to do."[2]

RELIGIOUS ZEAL The conquistador's statement expressed another major reason for the overseas voyages—religious zeal. A crusading mentality was particularly strong in Portugal and Spain, where the Muslims had largely been driven out in the Middle Ages. Contemporaries of Prince Henry the Navigator of Portugal (see "The Development of a Portuguese Maritime Empire" later in this chapter) said that he was motivated by "his great desire to make increase in the faith of our Lord Jesus Christ and to bring him all the souls that should be saved." Although most scholars believe that the religious motive was secondary to economic considerations, it would be foolish to overlook the genuine desire of explorers and conquistadors, let alone missionaries, to convert the heathen to Christianity. Hernàn Cortés (hayr-NAHN kor-TAYSS *or* kor-TEZ), the conqueror of Mexico, asked his Spanish rulers if it was not their duty to ensure that the native Mexicans "are introduced into and instructed in the holy Catholic faith" and predicted that if "the devotion, trust and hope which they now have in their idols turned so as to repose with the divine power of the true God . . . they would work many miracles."[3] Spiritual and secular affairs were closely intertwined in the sixteenth century. No doubt, the desire for grandeur and glory as well as plain intellectual curiosity and a spirit of adventure also played some role in European expansion.

The Means for Expansion

If "God, glory, and gold" were the primary motives, what made the voyages possible? First of all, the expansion of Europe was connected to the growth of centralized monarchies during the Renaissance. Although historians still debate the degree of that centralization, the reality is that Renaissance expansion was a state enterprise. By the second half of the fifteenth century, European monarchies had increased both their authority and their resources and were in a position to turn their energies beyond their borders. For France, that meant the invasion of Italy, but for Portugal, a state not strong enough to pursue power in Europe, it meant going abroad. The Spanish monarchy was strong enough by the sixteenth century to pursue power both in Europe and beyond.

MAPS At the same time, Europeans had achieved a level of wealth and technology that enabled them to make a regular series of voyages beyond Europe. Although the highly schematic and symbolic medieval maps were of little help to sailors, the **portolani** (pohr-tuh-LAH-nee), or charts made by medieval navigators and mathematicians in the thirteenth and fourteenth centuries, were more useful. With details on coastal contours, distances between ports, and compass readings, these charts proved of great value for voyages in European waters. But because the portolani were drawn on a flat scale and took no account of the curvature of the earth, they were of little use for longer overseas voyages. Only when seafarers began to venture beyond the coast of Europe did they begin to accumulate information about the actual shape of the earth. By the end of the fifteenth century, cartography had developed to the point that Europeans possessed fairly accurate maps of the known world.

One of the most important world maps available to Europeans at the end of the fifteenth century was that of Ptolemy (TAHL-uh-mee), an astronomer of the second century C.E. Ptolemy's work, the *Geography*, had been known to Arab geographers as early as the eighth century, but it was not until the fifteenth century that a Latin translation was made of the work. Printed editions of Ptolemy's *Geography*, which contained his world map, became available from 1477 on. Ptolemy's map (see the accompanying illustration) showed the world as spherical with three major landmasses—Europe, Asia, and Africa—and only two oceans. In addition to showing the oceans as considerably smaller than the landmasses, Ptolemy had also drastically underestimated the circumference of the earth, which led Columbus and other adventurers to believe that it would be feasible to sail west from Europe to reach Asia.

SHIPS AND SAILING Europeans had also developed remarkably seaworthy ships as well as new navigational techniques. European shipbuilders had mastered the use of the axial rudder (an import from China) and had learned to combine the use of lateen sails with a square rig. With these innovations, they could construct ships mobile enough to sail against the wind and engage in naval warfare and also large enough to mount heavy cannons and carry a substantial amount of goods over long distances. Previously, sailors had used a quadrant and their knowledge of

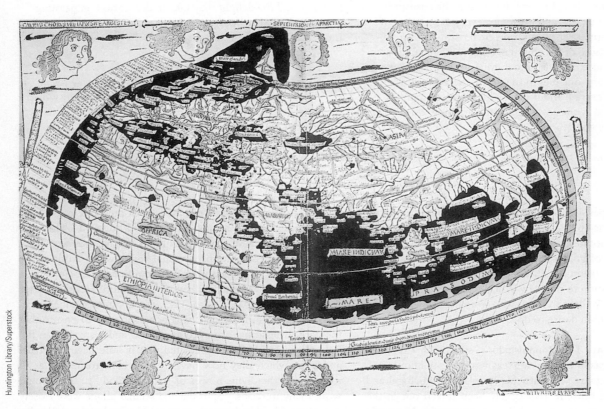

Ptolemy's World Map. Contained in the Latin translation of Ptolemy's *Geography* was this world map, which did not become available to Europeans until the late 1400s. Scholars quickly accepted it as the most accurate map of its time. The twelve "wind faces," meant to show wind currents around the earth, were a fifteenth-century addition to the ancient map.

the position of the Pole Star to ascertain their latitude. Below the equator, however, this technique was useless. Only with the assistance of new navigational aids such as the compass and the astrolabe were they able to explore the high seas with confidence.

A final spur to exploration was the growing knowledge of the wind patterns in the Atlantic Ocean. The first European fleets sailing southward along the coast of West Africa had found their efforts to return hindered by the strong winds that blew steadily from the north along the coast. By the late fifteenth century, however, sailors had learned to tack out into the ocean, where they were able to catch westerly winds in the vicinity of the Azores that brought them back to the coast of western Europe. Christopher Columbus used this technique in his voyages to the Americas, and others relied on their new knowledge of the winds to round the continent of Africa in search of the Spice Islands.

New Horizons: The Portuguese and Spanish Empires

 FOCUS QUESTION: How did Portugal and Spain acquire their overseas empires, and how did their empires differ?

Portugal took the lead in the European age of expansion when it began to explore the coast of Africa under the sponsorship of Prince Henry the Navigator (1394–1460). His motives were a blend of seeking a Christian kingdom as an ally against the Muslims, acquiring trade opportunities for Portugal, and spreading Christianity.

The Development of a Portuguese Maritime Empire

In 1419, Prince Henry founded a school for navigators on the southwestern coast of Portugal. Shortly thereafter, Portuguese fleets began probing southward along the western coast of Africa in search of gold, which had been carried northward from south of the Atlas Mountains in central Morocco for centuries. In 1441, Portuguese ships reached the Senegal River, just north of Cape Verde, and brought home a cargo of black Africans, most of whom were then sold as slaves to wealthy buyers elsewhere in Europe. Within a few years, an estimated one thousand slaves were shipped annually from the area back to Lisbon.

Through regular expeditions, the Portuguese gradually crept down the African coast, and in 1471, they discovered a new source of gold along the southern coast of the hump of West Africa (an area that would henceforth be known to Europeans as the Gold Coast). A few years later, they established contact with the state of Bakongo, near the mouth of the Zaire (Congo) River in Central Africa. To facilitate trade in gold, ivory, and slaves (some slaves were brought back to Lisbon, while others were bartered to local merchants for gold), the Portuguese leased land from local rulers and built stone forts along the coast.

THE PORTUGUESE IN INDIA Hearing reports of a route to India around the southern tip of Africa, Portuguese sea captains continued their probing. In 1488, Bartholomeu Dias (bar-toh-loh-MAY-oo DEE-ush) (ca. 1450–1500) took advantage of westerly

winds in the South Atlantic to round the Cape of Good Hope, but he feared a mutiny from his crew and returned (see Map 14.1). Ten years later, a fleet under the command of Vasco da Gama (VAHSH-koh dah GAHM-uh) (ca. 1460–1524) rounded the cape and stopped at several ports controlled by Muslim merchants along the coast of East Africa. Da Gama's fleet then crossed the Arabian Sea and reached the port of Calicut, on the southwestern coast of India, on May 18, 1498. On arriving in Calicut, da Gama announced to his surprised hosts that he had come in search of "Christians and spices." He found no Christians, but he did find the spices he sought. Although he lost two ships en route, da Gama's remaining vessels returned to Europe with their holds filled with ginger and cinnamon, a cargo that earned the investors a profit of several thousand percent.

Portuguese fleets returned annually to the area, seeking to destroy Arab shipping and establish a monopoly in the spice trade. In 1509, a Portuguese armada defeated a combined fleet of Turkish and Indian ships off the coast of India and began to impose a blockade on the entrance to the Red Sea to cut off the flow of spices to Muslim rulers in Egypt and the Ottoman Empire. The following year, seeing the need for a land base in

BRITISH LIBRARY/British Library, London, UK/Bridgeman Images

Portuguese in India. The Portuguese continued their exploration of India after gaining control of Goa in 1509 by moving northwards into the territory of Gujarat. This painting by a Mughal artist portrays the killing of Bahadur Shah, leader of the Gujarat sultanate, by a Portuguese convoy in 1537 after Bahadur Shah had formed an alliance with the Portuguese in an attempt to regain control of his sultanate after it was conquered by the Mughals.

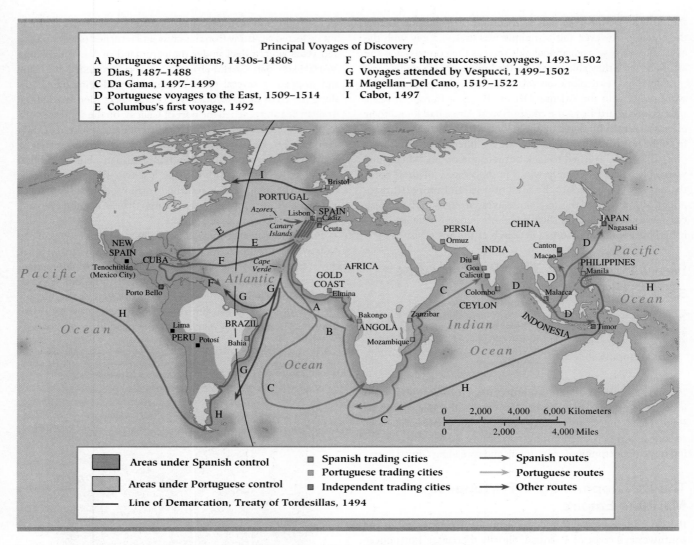

Principal Voyages of Discovery

A Portuguese expeditions, 1430s–1480s
B Dias, 1487–1488
C Da Gama, 1497–1499
D Portuguese voyages to the East, 1509–1514
E Columbus's first voyage, 1492

F Columbus's three successive voyages, 1493–1502
G Voyages attended by Vespucci, 1499–1502
H Magellan–Del Cano, 1519–1522
I Cabot, 1497

Areas under Spanish control
Areas under Portuguese control
—— Line of Demarcation, Treaty of Tordesillas, 1494

■ Spanish trading cities
■ Portuguese trading cities
■ Independent trading cities

→ Spanish routes
→ Portuguese routes
→ Other routes

MAP 14.1 **Discoveries and Possessions in the Fifteenth and Sixteenth Centuries.** Desire for wealth was the main motivation of the early explorers, though spreading Christianity was also an important factor. Portugal under Prince Henry the Navigator initiated the first voyages in the early fifteenth century; Spain's explorations began at the century's end.

Q *Which regions of the globe were primarily explored by Portugal, and which were the main focus of Spain's voyages?*

the area, Admiral Afonso de Albuquerque (ah-FAHN-soh day AL-buh-kur-kee) (ca. 1462–1515) set up port facilities at Goa (GOH-uh), on the western coast of India south of present-day Mumbai (Bombay). Goa henceforth became the headquarters for Portuguese operations throughout the entire region.

IN SEARCH OF SPICES In the early sixteenth century, the Portuguese expanded their search for spices (see "Images of Everyday Life" on p. 405). In 1511, Albuquerque sailed into the harbor of Malacca (muh-LAK-uh) on the Malay peninsula. Its Muslim rulers had transformed Malacca into a thriving port and a major stopping point in the spice trade. After a short but bloody battle, the Portuguese seized the city and massacred the local Arab population. This slaughter initiated a fierce and brutal struggle between the Portuguese and the Arabs. According

to one account, "To enhance the terror of his name he [Albuquerque] always separated Arabs from the other inhabitants of a captured city, and cut off the right hand of the men, and the noses and ears of the women."[4] By seizing Malacca, the Portuguese had not only weakened Arab control of the spice trade but obtained a major port en route to the Moluccas (muh-LUHK-uhz), then known as the Spice Islands.

From Malacca, the Portuguese launched expeditions farther east, to China and the Spice Islands. There they signed a treaty with a local ruler for the purchase and export of cloves to the European market. The new trading empire was now complete. Within a few years, the Portuguese had managed to seize control of the spice trade from Muslim traders and had garnered substantial profits for the Portuguese monarchy. Nevertheless, the Portuguese Empire remained limited, consisting only of trading posts on the coasts of

Spices and World Trade

PEPPER, CINNAMON, NUTMEG, AND other spices from the East had long been a part of European life. The illustration at the top right from a fifteenth-century French manuscript shows pepper being harvested in Malabar, in southwestern India. Europeans' interest in finding a direct route to the Spice Islands intensified after the fall of Constantinople to the Ottoman Turks in 1453 caused the price of pepper to increase thirtyfold. The Venetians had played a dominant role in the spice trade via Constantinople, as is evident in the Venetian fresco shown at the bottom right. It depicts a spice seller's shop with a wide variety of spices for sale. Vasco da Gama's success in locating a route to the East by sailing around Africa shifted much of the control over the spice trade into Portuguese hands. Following the establishment in 1518 of a fort in Ceylon, the center of cinnamon production, the Portuguese were able to dominate Europe's

cinnamon trade. The third illustration shows a portrait of da Gama from ca. 1600. The artist depicted the explorer holding a large stick of cinnamon in his right hand, an indication of the significance of the spice to his legacy and its role in his expeditions. Without the desire for spices, men such as da Gama and Christopher Columbus might not have ventured around Africa or across the Atlantic Ocean, thereby opening and forever altering European trade.

Gianni Dagli Orti/The Art Archive at Art Resource, NY

Bibliothèque Nationale, Paris/Archives Charmet/The Bridgeman Art Library

Scala/Art Resource, NY

India and China. The Portuguese lacked the power, the population, and the desire to colonize the Asian regions.

Why were the Portuguese so successful? Basically, their success was a matter of guns and seamanship. The first Portuguese fleet to arrive in Indian waters was relatively modest in size, consisting of three ships and twenty guns, a force sufficient for self-defense and intimidation but not for serious military operations. Later Portuguese fleets, which began to arrive with regularity early in the sixteenth century, were more

heavily armed and were able not only to intimidate but also to inflict severe defeats if necessary on local naval and land forces. The Portuguese by no means possessed a monopoly on the use of firearms and explosives, but their effective use of naval technology, their heavy guns that could be mounted in the hulls of their sturdy vessels, and their tactics gave them military superiority over lightly armed rivals that they were able to exploit until the arrival of other European forces several decades later.

Voyages to the New World

While the Portuguese were seeking access to the spice trade of the Indies by sailing eastward through the Indian Ocean, the Spanish were attempting to reach the same destination by sailing westward across the Atlantic. Although the Spanish came to overseas discovery and exploration after the initial efforts of Henry the Navigator, their greater resources enabled them to establish a far grander overseas empire than that of the Portuguese—and one that was quite different.

THE VOYAGES OF COLUMBUS An important figure in the history of Spanish exploration was an Italian known as Christopher Columbus (1451–1506). Knowledgeable Europeans were aware that the world was round but had little understanding of its circumference or the extent of the continent of Asia. Convinced that the circumference of the earth was less than contemporaries believed and that Asia was larger than people thought, Columbus felt that Asia could be reached by sailing west instead of around Africa. After being rejected by the Portuguese, he persuaded Queen Isabella of Spain to finance his exploratory expedition.

With a crew of ninety men and three ships, the *Santa María*, the *Niña*, and the *Pinta*, Columbus set sail on August 3, 1492.

Museo Navale, Genova-Pegli/SuperStock

Christopher Columbus. Columbus was an Italian explorer who worked for the queen of Spain. He has become a symbol for two entirely different perspectives. To some, he was a great and heroic explorer who discovered the New World; to others, especially in Latin America, he was responsible for beginning a process of invasion that led to the destruction of an entire way of life. Because Columbus was never painted during his lifetime, the numerous portraits of him are more fanciful than accurate. The portrait shown here was probably done by the Italian painter Ridolfo Ghirlandaio.

CHRONOLOGY	The Portuguese and Spanish Empires in the Sixteenth Century
Bartholomeu Dias sails around the tip of Africa	1488
The voyages of Columbus	1492–1502
Treaty of Tordesillas	1494
Vasco da Gama lands at Calicut in India	1498
Portuguese seize Malacca	1511
Landing of Portuguese ships in southern China	1514
Magellan's voyage around the world	1519–1522
Spanish conquest of Mexico	1519–1522
Pizarro's conquest of the Inca	1530–1535

On October 12, he reached the Bahamas and then went on to explore the coastline of Cuba and the northern shores of Hispaniola (present-day Haiti and the Dominican Republic). Columbus believed that he had reached Asia, and in his reports to Queen Isabella and King Ferdinand upon his return to Spain, he assured them not only that he would eventually find gold but also that they had a golden opportunity to convert the natives—whom Columbus persisted in calling "Indians"—to Christianity (see the box on p. 407). In three subsequent voyages (1493, 1498, 1502), Columbus sought in vain to find a route to the Asian mainland. In his four voyages, Columbus landed on all the major islands of the Caribbean and the mainland of Central America, still convinced that he had reached the Indies in Asia.

NEW VOYAGES Although Columbus clung to his belief until his death, other explorers soon realized that he had discovered a new frontier altogether. State-sponsored explorers joined the race to the New World. A Venetian seaman, John Cabot, explored the New England coastline of the Americas under a license from King Henry VII of England. The continent of South America was discovered accidentally by the Portuguese sea captain Pedro Cabral (kuh-BRAL) in 1500. Amerigo Vespucci (ahm-ay-REE-goh vess-POO-chee), a Florentine, accompanied several voyages and wrote a series of letters describing the geography of the New World. The publication of these letters led to the use of the name "America" (after Amerigo) for the new lands.

The first two decades of the sixteenth century witnessed numerous overseas voyages that explored the eastern coasts of both North and South America. Vasco Nuñez de Balboa (VAHS-koh NOON-yez day bal-BOH-uh) (1475–1519), a Spanish explorer, led an expedition across the Isthmus of Panama and reached the Pacific Ocean in 1513. Perhaps the most dramatic of all these expeditions was the journey of Ferdinand Magellan (1480–1521) in 1519. After passing through the strait named after him at the southern tip of South America, he sailed across the Pacific Ocean and reached the Philippines, where he was killed by the natives. Although only one of his fleet of five ships completed the return voyage to Spain, Magellan's name is still associated with the first known circumnavigation of the earth.

COLUMBUS LANDS IN THE NEW WORLD

ON RETURNING FROM AMERICA, which he believed was the coast of Asia, Christopher Columbus wrote about his experience. In this passage from a letter describing his first voyage, he tells of his arrival on the island of Hispaniola (Haiti). Historians believe that Columbus wrote this letter for public consumption.

Letter to Raphael Sanchez, Treasurer to the King and Queen of Spain

Thirty-three days after my departure from Cadiz I reached the Indian sea, where I discovered many islands, thickly peopled, of which I took possession without resistance in the name of our most illustrious Monarch, by public proclamation and with unfurled banners. To the first of these islands, I gave the name of the blessed Savior (San Salvador), relying upon whose protection I had reached this as well as the other islands; to each of these I also gave a name. . . .

The inhabitants of both sexes in this island, and in all the others which I have seen, or of which I have received information, go always naked as they were born, with the exception of some of the women, who use the covering of a leaf, or small bough, or an apron of cotton which they prepare for that purpose. None of them are possessed of any iron, neither have they weapons, being unacquainted with, and indeed incompetent to use them, not from any deformity of body (for they are well-formed), but because they are timid and full of fear. . . . As soon however as they see that they are safe, and have laid aside all fear, they are very simple and honest, and exceedingly liberal with all they have; none of them refusing any thing he may possess when he is asked for it. . . . They also give objects of great value for trifles, and content themselves with very little or nothing in return.

I however forbade that these trifles and articles of no value (such as pieces of dishes, plates, and glass, keys, and leather straps) should be given to them, although if they could obtain them, they imagined themselves to be possessed of the most beautiful trinkets in the world. . . . Thus, they bartered, like idiots, cotton and gold for fragments of bows, glasses, bottles, and jars. . . .

In all these islands there is no difference of physiognomy, of manners, or of language, but they all clearly understand each other, a circumstance very propitious for the realization of what I conceive to be the principal wish of our most serene King, namely, the conversion of these people to the holy faith of Christ, to which indeed, as far as I can judge, they are very favorable and well-disposed. . . .

Finally, to compress into a few words the entire summary of my voyage and speedy return, and of the advantages derivable there from, I promise, that with a little assistance afforded me by our most invincible sovereigns, I will procure them as much gold as they need, and as great a quantity of spices and cotton. . . . Let Christ rejoice on earth, as he rejoices in heaven in the prospect of the salvation of the souls of so many nations hitherto lost. Let us also rejoice as well on account of the exaltation of our faith as on account of the increase of our temporal prosperity, of which not only Spain but all Christendom will be partakers.

 What evidence in Columbus's comments suggests that his remarks were made mainly for public consumption and not just for the Spanish court? What elements in society might have responded to his statements, and why?

Source: R. H. Major, ed., trans., *Letters by Christopher Columbus* (London: Hakluyt Society, 1843), pp. 35–43.

The Europeans referred to the newly discovered territories as the New World, even though they held flourishing civilizations populated by millions of people. But the Americas were indeed new to the Europeans, who quickly saw opportunities for conquest and exploitation. The Spanish, in particular, were interested because the 1494 Treaty of Tordesillas (tor-day-SEE-yass) had divided up the newly discovered world into separate Portuguese and Spanish spheres of influence, and it turned out that most of South America (except for the eastern hump) fell within the Spanish sphere (see Map 14.1 on p. 404). Hereafter the route east around the Cape of Good Hope was to be reserved for the Portuguese while the route across the Atlantic was assigned to Spain.

The Spanish Empire in the New World

The Spanish conquerors known as **conquistadors** were hardy individuals motivated by a typical sixteenth-century blend of glory, greed, and religious crusading zeal. Although authorized by the Castilian crown, these groups were financed and outfitted privately, not by the government. Their superior weapons, organizational skills, and determination brought the conquistadors incredible success. They also benefited from rivalries among the native peoples and the decimation of the native peoples by European diseases (see "Disease in the New World" later in this chapter).

EARLY CIVILIZATIONS IN MESOAMERICA Before the Spaniards arrived in the New World, Mesoamerica (modern Mexico and Central America) had already hosted a number of flourishing civilizations. Beginning around 300 C.E., on the Yucatán peninsula a people known as the Maya (MY-uh) had built one of the most sophisticated civilizations in the Americas. The Maya built splendid temples and pyramids, were accomplished artists, and developed a sophisticated calendar, as accurate as any in existence in the world at that time. The Maya were an agrarian people who cleared the dense rain forests, developed farming,

The Maya

and built a patchwork of city-states. Mayan civilization came to include much of Central America and southern Mexico. For unknown reasons, Mayan civilization began to decline around 800 and had collapsed less than a hundred years later.

Sometime during the early twelfth century C.E., a people known as the Aztecs began a long migration that brought them to the Valley of Mexico. They established their capital at Tenochtitlán (tay-nawch-teet-LAHN) between 1325 and 1345 on an island in the middle of Lake Texcoco (now the location of Mexico City). For the next hundred years, the Aztecs built their city, constructing temples, other public buildings, houses, and causeways of stone across Lake Texcoco to the north, south, and west, linking the many islands to the mainland. At the beginning of the fifteenth century, they built an aqueduct to bring fresh water from a spring 4 miles away. Tenochtitlán benefited from commercial routes that brought goods from as far away as the Gulf of Mexico and the Inca Empire in northern South America. By 1500, flourishing trade and agricultural growth supported cities of over 80,000 inhabitants, with some estimates as high as 200,000 inhabitants, larger than most European cities of the time.

The Aztecs

The Aztecs were outstanding warriors, and while they were building their capital city, they also set out to bring the entire area around the city under their control. By the early fifteenth century, they had become the leading city-state in the lake region. For the remainder of the fifteenth century, the Aztecs consolidated their rule over much of what is modern Mexico, from the Atlantic to the Pacific Ocean and as far south as the Guatemalan border. The new kingdom was not a centralized state but a collection of semi-independent territories governed by local lords. The Aztec ruler confirmed these rulers in their authority in return for the payment of tribute. This loose political organization would later contribute to the downfall of the Aztec Empire.

SPANISH CONQUEST OF THE AZTEC EMPIRE In 1519, a Spanish expedition under the command of Hernán Cortés (1485–1547) landed at Veracruz, on the Gulf of Mexico. He marched to the city of Tenochtitlán (see the box on p. 409) at the head of a small contingent of troops (550 soldiers and 16 horses); as he went, he made alliances with city-states that had tired of the oppressive rule of the Aztecs. Especially important was Tlaxcala (tuh-lah-SKAH-lah), a state that the Aztecs had not been able to conquer. In November, Cortés arrived at Tenochtitlán, where he received a friendly welcome from the Aztec monarch Moctezuma (mahk-tuh-ZOO-muh) (often called Montezuma). At first, Moctezuma believed that his visitor was a representative of Quetzalcoatl (KWET-sul-koh-AHT-ul), the god who had departed from his homeland centuries before and had promised that he would return. Riddled with fears, Moctezuma offered gifts of gold to the foreigners and gave them a palace to use while they were in the city.

But the Spaniards quickly wore out their welcome. They took Moctezuma hostage and proceeded to pillage the city. In the fall of 1520, one year after Cortés had arrived, the local population revolted and drove the invaders from the city. Many of the Spaniards were killed, but the Aztecs soon experienced new disasters. As one Aztec related, "At about the time that the Spaniards had fled from Mexico, there came a great sickness, a pestilence, the smallpox." With no natural immunity to the diseases of the Europeans, many Aztecs fell sick and died (see "Disease in the New World" later in this chapter). Meanwhile, Cortés received fresh soldiers from his new allies; the state of Tlaxcala alone provided 50,000 warriors. After four months, the city capitulated.

The Spaniards then embarked on a new wave of destruction. The pyramids, temples, and palaces were leveled, and the stones were used to build Spanish government buildings and churches. The rivers and canals were filled in. The mighty Aztec Empire on mainland Mexico was no more. Between 1531 and 1550, the Spanish gained control of northern Mexico.

THE INCA In the late fourteenth century, the Inca were a small community in the area of Cuzco (KOOS-koh), a city located at an altitude of 10,000 feet in the mountains of southern Peru. In the

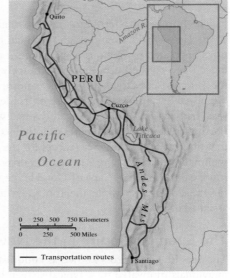

The Inca

THE SPANISH CONQUISTADOR: CORTÉS AND THE CONQUEST OF MEXICO

HERNÁN CORTÉS WAS A MINOR SPANISH nobleman who came to the New World in 1504 to seek his fortune. Contrary to his superior's orders, Cortés waged an independent campaign of conquest and overthrew the Aztec Empire in Mexico (1519–1522). Cortés wrote a series of five reports to Emperor Charles V to justify his action. The second report includes a description of Tenochtitlán, the capital of the Aztec Empire. The Spanish conquistador and his men were obviously impressed by this city, awesome in its architecture yet built by people who lacked European technology, such as wheeled vehicles and tools of hard metal.

Cortés's Description of Tenochtitlán

The great city Tenochtitlán is built in the midst of this salt lake, and it is two leagues from the heart of the city to any point on the mainland. Four causeways lead to it, all made by hand and some twelve feet wide. The city itself is as large as Seville or Cordoba. The principal streets are very broad and straight, the majority of them being of beaten earth, but a few and at least half of the smaller thoroughfares are waterways along which they pass in their canoes. Moreover, even the principal streets have openings at regular distances so that the water can freely pass from one to another, and these openings which are very broad are spanned by great bridges of huge beams, very stoutly put together, so firm indeed that over many of them ten horsemen can ride at once. . . .

The city has many open squares in which markets are continuously held and the general business of buying and selling proceeds. One square in particular is twice as big as that of Salamanca and completely surrounded by arcades where there are daily more than 60,000 folk buying and selling. Every kind of merchandise such as may be met with in every land is for sale there, whether of food and victuals, or ornaments of gold and silver, or lead, brass, copper, tin, precious stones, bones, shells, snails and feathers; limestone for building is likewise sold there, stone both rough and polished, bricks burnt and unburnt, wood of all kinds and in all stages of preparation. . . . There are houses as it were of apothecaries where they sell medicines made from these herbs, both for drinking and for use as ointments and salves. There are barbers' shops where you may have your hair washed and cut. There are other shops where you may obtain food and drink. . . .

Finally, to avoid being wordy in telling all the wonders of this city, I will simply say that the manner of living among the people is very similar to that in Spain, and considering that this is a barbarous nation shut off from a knowledge of the true God or communication with enlightened nations, one may well marvel at the orderliness and good government which is everywhere maintained.

The actual service of Montezuma and those things which call for admiration by their greatness and state would take so long to describe that I assure your Majesty I do not know where to begin with any hope of ending. For as I have already said, what could there be more astonishing than that a barbarous monarch such as he should have reproductions made in gold, silver, precious stones, and feathers of all things to be found in his land, and so perfectly reproduced that there is no goldsmith or silversmith in the world who could better them, nor can one understand what instrument could have been used for fashioning the jewels. . . .

 What did Cortés focus on in his description of this Aztec city? Why do you think he felt justified in overthrowing the Aztec Empire?

Source: J. H. Parry, *The European Reconnaissance: Selected Documents* (New York: Harper & Row, 1968).

1440s, however, under the leadership of their powerful ruler Pachakuti (pah-chah-KOO-tee), the Inca launched a campaign of conquest that eventually brought the entire region under their control. Pachakuti created a highly centralized state. Cuzco, the capital, was transformed from a city of mud and thatch into an imposing city of stone. Under Pachakuti and his immediate successors, Topa Inca and Huayna Inca (the word *Inca* means "ruler"), the boundaries of the Inca Empire were extended as far as Ecuador, central Chile, and the edge of the Amazon basin. The empire included perhaps 12 million people.

Pachakuti divided his realm into four quarters, each ruled by a governor. The quarters were in turn divided into provinces, each also ruled by a governor. The governors were usually chosen from relatives of the royal family. Each province was supposed to contain about 10,000 residents. At the top of the entire system was the emperor, who was believed to be descended from the sun god.

The Inca were great builders. One major project was a system of 24,800 miles of roads that extended from the border of modern-day Colombia to a point south of modern-day Santiago, Chile. Two major roadways extended in a north-south direction, one through the Andes Mountains and the other along the coast, with connecting routes between them. Rest houses, located a day's walk apart, and storage depots were placed along the roads. The Inca also built various types of bridges, including some of the finest examples of suspension bridges in premodern times, over the ravines and waterways.

SPANISH CONQUEST OF THE INCA EMPIRE The Inca Empire was still flourishing when the first Spanish expeditions arrived in the area. In December 1530, Francisco Pizarro (frahn-CHESS-koh puh-ZAHR-oh) (ca. 1475–1541) landed on the Pacific coast of South America with a band of about 180 men, but like Cortés, he had steel weapons, gunpowder, and horses, none of which were familiar to his hosts. Pizarro was also lucky because the Inca Empire had already succumbed to an epidemic of smallpox. Like the Aztecs, the Inca had no immunities to European diseases, and all too soon, smallpox was devastating entire villages. In another stroke of good fortune for Pizarro, even the Inca emperor was a victim. Upon the emperor's death, two sons claimed the throne, setting off a civil war. Pizarro took advantage of the situation by seizing Atahualpa (ah-tuh-WAHL-puh), whose forces had just defeated his brother's. Armed only with stones, arrows, and light spears, Incan soldiers were no match for the charging horses of the Spanish, let alone their guns and cannons. After executing Atahualpa, Pizarro and his soldiers, aided by their Incan allies, marched on Cuzco and captured the Incan capital. By 1535, Pizarro had established a capital at Lima for a new colony of the Spanish Empire.

ADMINISTRATION OF THE SPANISH EMPIRE Spanish policy toward the Indians of the New World was a combination of confusion, misguided paternalism, and cruel exploitation. Whereas the conquistadors made decisions based on expediency and their own interests, Queen Isabella declared the native peoples to be subjects of Castile and instituted the Spanish *encomienda* (en-koh-MYEN-dah), an economic and social system that permitted the conquering Spaniards to collect tribute from the Indians and use them as laborers. In return, the holders of an encomienda were supposed to protect the Indians, pay them wages, and supervise their spiritual needs. In practice, this meant that the settlers were free to implement the paternalistic system of the government as they pleased. Three thousand miles from Spain, Spanish settlers largely ignored their government and brutally used the Indians to pursue their own economic interests. Indians were put to work on plantations and in the lucrative gold and silver mines. In Peru, the Spanish made use of the mita, a system that allowed authorities to draft native labor to work in the silver mines.

Forced labor, starvation, and especially disease took a fearful toll of Indian lives. Voices were raised to protest the harsh treatment of the Indians, especially by Dominican friars. In a 1510 sermon, Antón Montecino startled churchgoers in Santo Domingo by saying:

> And you are heading for damnation . . . for you are destroying an innocent people. For they are God's people, these innocents, whom you destroyed. By what right do you make them die? Mining gold for you in your mines or working for you in your fields, by what right do you unleash enslaving wars upon them? They lived in peace in this land before you came, in peace in their own homes. They did nothing to harm you to cause you to slaughter them wholesale.[5]

In 1542, largely in response to the publications of Bartolomé de Las Casas (bahr-toh-loh-MAY day lahs KAH-sahs), a Dominican friar who championed the Indians (see the box on p. 411), the government abolished the encomienda system and provided more protection for the natives.

In the New World, Spanish nobles recreated the urban cities of Spain by constructing ordered towns built around a central plaza. The Spanish built their first town, Santo Domingo, in 1501 on the island of Hispaniola; by 1580, they had constructed 240 towns, with Mexico City and Lima being the largest. By 1600, over 250 thousand Spanish émigrés had arrived from Spain to fill their streets.

The Spanish developed an administrative system based on viceroys to administer their new territories. Spanish possessions were initially divided into two major administrative units: New Spain (Mexico, Central America, and the Caribbean islands), with its center in Mexico City, and Peru (western South America), governed by a **viceroy** in Lima. According to legislation of 1542, "the kingdoms of New Spain and Peru are to be ruled and governed by viceroys, who shall represent our royal person, hold the superior government, do and administer justice equally to all our subjects and vassals, and concern themselves with everything that will promote the calm, peace, ennoblement and pacification of those provinces."[6] Each viceroy served as the king's chief civil and military officer and was aided by advisory groups called *audiencias* (ow-dee-en-SEE-uss), which also functioned as supreme judicial bodies.

By papal agreement, the Catholic monarchs of Spain were given extensive rights over ecclesiastical affairs in the New World. They could appoint all bishops and clergy, build churches, collect fees, and supervise the various religious orders that sought to convert the heathen. Catholic missionaries converted and baptized hundreds of thousands of Indians in the early years of the conquest.

The mass conversion of the Indians brought the organizational and institutional structures of Catholicism to the New World. Dioceses, parishes, cathedrals, schools, and hospitals—all the trappings of civilized European society—soon appeared in the Spanish Empire. So, too, did the Spanish Inquisition, established first in Peru in 1570 and in Mexico the following year.

Disease in the New World

When Columbus reached the Caribbean island of Hispaniola in 1492, he brought more than gunpowder, horses, attack dogs, and soldiers to the shores of the New World. With no natural resistance to European diseases, the Indians of America were ravaged by smallpox, influenza, measles, and pneumonic plague, and later by typhus, yellow fever, and cholera.

Smallpox, a highly contagious disease, was spread through droplets in the air or direct contact with contaminated objects, such as clothing. In 1518, a smallpox epidemic erupted and quickly spread along trade routes from the Caribbean to Mesoamerica, killing a third of the Indian population. The disease ultimately reached Tenochtitlán and helped make

LAS CASAS AND THE SPANISH TREATMENT OF THE AMERICAN NATIVES

BARTOLOMÉ DE LAS CASAS (1474–1566) participated in the conquest of Cuba and received land and Indians in return for his efforts. But in 1514 he underwent a radical transformation and came to believe that the Indians had been cruelly mistreated by his fellow Spaniards. He became a Dominican friar and spent the remaining years of his life (he lived to the age of ninety-two) fighting for the Indians. This selection is taken from his most influential work, which is known to English readers as *The Tears of the Indians*. This work was largely responsible for the "black legend" of the Spanish as inherently "cruel and murderous fanatics." Most scholars feel that Las Casas may have exaggerated his account in order to shock his contemporaries into action.

Bartolomé de Las Casas, *The Tears of the Indians*

There is nothing more detestable or more cruel, than the tyranny which the Spaniards use toward the Indians for the getting of pearl. Surely the infernal torments cannot much exceed the anguish that they endure, by reason of that way of cruelty; for they put them under water some four or five ells [15 to 18 feet] deep, where they are forced without any liberty of respiration, to gather up the shells wherein the pearls are; sometimes they come up again with nets full of shells to take breath, but if they stay any while to rest themselves, immediately comes a hangman row'd in a little boat, who as soon as he has well beaten them, drags them again to their labor. Their food is nothing but filth, and the very same that contains the pearl, with a small portion of that bread which that country affords; in the first where of there is little nourishment; and as for the latter,

it is made with great difficulty, besides that they have not enough of that neither for sustenance; they lie upon the ground in fetters, lest they should run away; and many times they are drown'd in this labor, and are never seen again till they swim upon the top of the waves: oftentimes they also are devoured by certain sea monsters, that are frequent in those seas. Consider whether this hard usage of the poor creatures be consistent with the precepts which God commands concerning charity to our neighbor, by those that cast them so undeservedly into the dangers of a cruel death, causing them to perish without any remorse or pity, or allowing them the benefit of the sacraments, or the knowledge of religion; it being impossible for them to live any time under the water; and this death is so much the more painful, by reason that by the constricting of the breast, while the lungs strive to do their office, the vital parts are so afflicted that they die vomiting the blood out of their mouths. Their hair also, which is by nature black, is hereby changed and made of the same color with that of the sea wolves; their bodies are also so besprinkled with the froth of the sea, that they appear rather like monsters than men.

 In what ways did this account help create the image of the Spaniards as "cruel and murderous fanatics"? What motives may have prompted Las Casas to make this critique, and how might his opinions have affected the broader standing of Spain in the global politics of the age?

Source: Bartolomé de Las Casas, *The Tears of the Indians* (Williamstown, Mass.: The John Lilburne Company Publishers, 1970).

---

possible its conquest by Hernán Cortés. When the Spaniards reentered the city in 1521, they found an appalling scene, as reported by Bernal Díaz (ber-NAHL DEE-ass), who accompanied Cortés:

> We could not walk without treading on the bodies and heads of dead Indians. I have read about the destruction of Jerusalem, but I do not think the mortality was greater there than here in Mexico, where most of the warriors who had crowded in from all the provinces and subject towns had died. As I have said, the dry land and the stockades were piled with corpses. Indeed, the stench was so bad that no one could endure it. . . . Even Cortés was ill from the odors which assailed his nostrils.[7]

Smallpox ravaged the Aztecs. The Inca suffered a similar fate from smallpox and measles as well.

Throughout the sixteenth century, outbreaks of Old World diseases continued to spark epidemics that killed off large proportions of the local populations. By 1630, smallpox had reached New England. The ferocity of the epidemics left few survivors to tend the crops, leading to widespread starvation and higher mortality rates. Although scholarly estimates vary drastically, a reasonable guess is that 30 to 40 percent of the local populations died. On Hispaniola alone, out of an initial population of 100,000 Indians when Columbus arrived in 1492, only 300 survived by 1570. The population of central Mexico, estimated at roughly 11 million in 1519, had declined to 6.5 million by 1540 and 2.5 million by the end of the sixteenth century.

The high mortality rates among the native populations resulted in a shortage of workers for the Europeans, which led them to turn to Africa for the labor needed for the silver

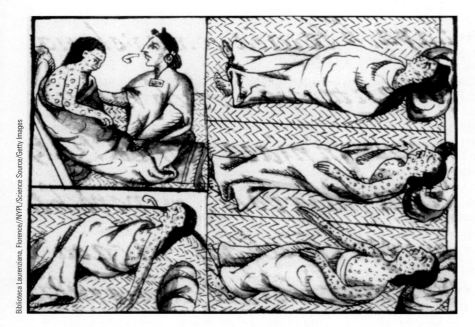

Aztec Victims of Smallpox. The indigenous populations of the New World had no immunities to the diseases of the Old World, such as smallpox. By 1520, smallpox had spread throughout the Caribbean and Mesoamerica. This sixteenth-century drawing by a Franciscan friar portrays Native Americans afflicted with smallpox. The pustules that often covered the body are clearly depicted. The figure at the lower right twists in agony, reflecting the immense pain experienced by those who contracted the disease.

mines and sugar plantations (see "Africa: The Slave Trade" later in this chapter). Despite the Europeans' technological advantages, the biological weapons that they brought with them from the Old World proved to have an even greater impact on the Americas.

New Rivals on the World Stage

 FOCUS QUESTIONS: How did the arrival of the Dutch, British, and French on the world scene in the seventeenth and eighteenth centuries affect Africa, Southeast Asia, India, China, and Japan? What were the main features of the African slave trade, and what effects did it have on Africa?

Portugal and Spain had been the first Atlantic nations to take advantage of the age of exploration, starting in the late fifteenth century, and both had become great colonial powers. In the seventeenth century, however, their European neighbors to the north—first the Dutch and then the French and English—moved to replace the Portuguese and Spanish and create their own colonial empires. The new rivals and their rivalry soon had an impact on much of the rest of the world—in Africa, Asia, and the Americas.

Africa: The Slave Trade

Although the primary objective of the Portuguese in sailing around Africa was to find a sea route to the Spice Islands, they soon discovered that profits could be made in Africa itself. So did other Europeans.

The Portuguese built forts on both the western and eastern coasts of Africa and tried, above all, to dominate the trade

in gold. During the mid-seventeenth century, however, the Dutch seized a number of Portuguese forts along the West African coast and at the same time took control of much of the Portuguese trade across the Indian Ocean.

The Dutch East India Company, a trading company established in 1602 under government sponsorship, also set up a settlement in southern Africa, at the Cape of Good Hope, to serve as a base to supply food and other provisions to Dutch ships en route to the Spice Islands. Eventually, however, it developed into a permanent colony. Dutch farmers, known as Boers, began to settle in areas outside the city of Cape Town. The area's moderate climate and freedom from tropical diseases made it attractive for Europeans to settle there.

The European exploration of the African coastline did not affect most Africans living in the interior of the continent, but for peoples living on or near the coast, the impact was great indeed. As the trade in slaves increased during the sixteenth through the eighteenth centuries, thousands and then millions of Africans were removed from their homes and forcibly shipped to plantations in the New World.

ORIGINS OF THE SLAVE TRADE Traffic in slaves was not new. As in other areas of the world, slavery had been practiced in Africa since ancient times. In the fifteenth century, it continued at a fairly steady level. The primary market for African slaves was the Middle East, where most were used as domestic servants. Slavery also existed in many European countries, where some slaves from Africa or war captives from the regions north of the Black Sea were used as household help or agricultural workers.

At first, the Portuguese simply replaced European slaves with African ones. During the second half of the fifteenth century, about a thousand slaves were taken to Portugal each year. Most ended up serving as domestic servants for affluent families in Europe. But the discovery of the Americas in the 1490s and the planting of sugarcane in South America and the islands of the Caribbean changed the situation drastically.

Cane sugar had first been introduced to Europeans from the Middle East during the Crusades. At the end of the fifteenth century, the Portuguese set up sugar plantations worked by African laborers on an island off the central coast of Africa. During the sixteenth century, sugarcane plantations were set up along the eastern coast of Brazil and on several islands in the Caribbean, reaching 195 in number by 1600. Because the growing of cane sugar demands both skill and large quantities of labor, the new plantations required more workers than could be provided by the small American Indian population in the New World, decimated by diseases imported from the Old World. Since the climate and soil of much of West Africa were not conducive to the cultivation of sugar, African slaves began to be shipped to Brazil and the Caribbean to work on the plantations. The first were sent from Portugal, but in 1518, a Spanish ship carried the first boatload of African slaves directly from Africa to the New World.

GROWTH OF THE SLAVE TRADE During the next two centuries, the trade in slaves grew dramatically and became part of the **triangular trade** connecting Europe, Africa, and the American continents that characterized the new Atlantic economy (see Map 14.2). European merchant ships (primarily those of England, France, Spain, Portugal, and the Dutch Republic) carried European manufactured goods, such as guns, gin, and cloth, to Africa, where they were traded for a cargo of slaves. The slaves were then shipped to the Americas and sold. European merchants then bought tobacco, molasses, sugar, rum, coffee, and raw cotton and shipped them back to Europe to be sold in European markets.

An estimated 275,000 enslaved Africans were exported to other countries during the sixteenth century, with 2,000 going annually to the Americas alone. The total climbed to over a million in the seventeenth century and jumped to 6 million in the eighteenth century, when the trade spread from West and Central Africa to East Africa. Even during the nineteenth century, when Great Britain and other European countries tried to end the slave trade, nearly 2 million were exported. Altogether as many as 10 million African slaves were transported to the Americas between the sixteenth and nineteenth centuries. About half were transported in British ships, with the rest divided among French, Dutch, Portuguese, Danish, and later, American ships.

One reason for the astonishing numbers of slaves, of course, was the high death rate. The journey of slaves from Africa to the Americas became known as the **Middle Passage**, the middle leg of the triangular trade route. African slaves were closely

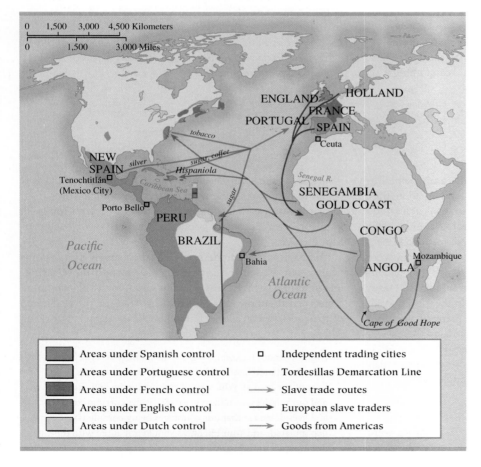

MAP 14.2 **Triangular Trade Route in the Atlantic Economy.** As the trade in slaves grew, it became part of the triangular trade route that characterized the Atlantic economy, involving the exchange of goods and slaves between the western coast of Europe, the slave depots on the African coast, and the ports of North and South America.

 What were the important source regions for slaves, and where were most of the slaves taken?

Areas under Spanish control	□ Independent trading cities
Areas under Portuguese control	— Tordesillas Demarcation Line
Areas under French control	→ Slave trade routes
Areas under English control	→ European slave traders
Areas under Dutch control	→ Goods from Americas

THE ATLANTIC SLAVE TRADE

ONE OF THE MOST ODIOUS PRACTICES of early modern Western society was the Atlantic slave trade, which reached its height in the eighteenth century. Blacks were transported in densely packed cargo ships from the western coast of Africa to the Americas to work as slaves in the plantation economy. Not until late in the eighteenth century did a rising chorus of voices raise serious objections to this trade in human beings. This excerpt presents a criticism of the slave trade from an anonymous French writer.

Diary of a Citizen

As soon as the ships have lowered their anchors off the coast of Guinea, the price at which the captains have decided to buy the captives is announced to the Negroes who buy prisoners from various princes and sell them to Europeans. Presents are sent to the sovereign who rules over that particular part of the coast, and permission to trade is given. Immediately the slaves are brought by inhuman brokers like so many victims dragged to a sacrifice. White men who covet that portion of the human race receive them in a little house they have erected on the shore, where they have entrenched themselves with two pieces of cannon and twenty guards. As soon as the bargain is concluded, the Negro is put in chains and led aboard the vessel, where he meets his fellow sufferers. . . .

The vessel sets sail for the Antilles, and the Negroes are chained in a hold of the ship. . . . Twice a day some disgusting food is distributed to them. Their consuming sorrow and the sad state to which they are reduced would make them commit suicide if they were not deprived of all the means for an attempt upon their lives. Without any kind of clothing it would be difficult to conceal from the watchful eyes of the sailors in charge any instrument apt to alleviate their despair. The fear of a revolt, such as sometimes happens on the voyage from Guinea, is the basis of a common concern and produces as many guards as there are men in the crew. The slightest noise or a secret conversation among two Negroes is punished with utmost severity. All in all, the voyage is made in a continuous state of alarm on the part of the white men, who fear a revolt, and in a cruel state of uncertainty on the part of the Negroes, who do not know the fate awaiting them.

When the vessel arrives at a port in the Antilles, they are taken to a warehouse where they are displayed, like any merchandise, to the eyes of buyers. The plantation owner pays according to the age, strength, and health of the Negro he is buying. He has him taken to his plantation, and there he is delivered to an overseer who then and there becomes his tormentor. In order to domesticate him, the Negro is granted a few days of rest in his new place, but soon he is given a hoe and a sickle and made to join a work gang. Then he ceases to wonder about his fate; he understands that only labor is demanded of him. But he does not know yet how excessive this labor will be. As a matter of fact, his work begins at dawn and does not end before nightfall; it is interrupted for only two hours at dinnertime. The food a full-grown Negro is given each week consists of two pounds of salt beef or cod and two pots of tapioca meal. . . .

 What does this account reveal about the nature of the slave trade and white attitudes toward blacks in the eighteenth century?

Source: R. Foster and E. Foster, eds., *European Society in the Eighteenth Century* (New York: Walker & Co., 1969).

---

packed into cargo ships, 300 to 450 per ship, and chained in holds without sanitary facilities or room to stand up; there they remained during the voyage to America, which took at least 100 days (see the box above). Mortality rates averaged 10 percent; longer journeys due to storms or adverse winds resulted in even higher death rates. The Africans who survived the journey were subject to high death rates from diseases to which they had little or no immunity and dysentery from poor sanitation. Death rates were lower for slaves born and raised in the New World: the new generation developed immunity to many of the more fatal diseases. Owners, however, rarely encouraged their slaves to have children. Many slave owners, especially in the West Indies, believed that buying a new slave was less expensive than raising a child from birth to working age at adolescence.

CONDUCT OF THE SLAVE TRADE Before the coming of Europeans in the fifteenth century, most slaves in Africa were prisoners of war. Many served as domestic servants or as wageless workers for the local ruler. When Europeans first began to take part in the slave trade, they bought slaves from local African merchants at slave markets in return for gold, guns, or other European goods such as textiles or copper or iron utensils.

At first, local slave traders obtained their supply from regions nearby, but as demand increased, they had to move farther inland to find their victims. In a few cases, local rulers became concerned about the impact of the slave trade on the well-being of their societies. In a letter to the king of Portugal in 1526, King Affonso of Congo (Bakongo) complained:

> And we cannot reckon how great the damage is, since the mentioned merchants are taking every day our natives, sons of the land and the sons of our noblemen and vassals and our relatives . . . and so great, Sir, is the corruption and licentiousness that our country is being completely depopulated, and Your Highness should not agree with this nor accept it as in your service.[8]

The Sale of Slaves. In the eighteenth century, the slave trade was a highly profitable commercial enterprise. This painting shows a Western slave merchant negotiating with a local African leader over slaves at Gorée, Senegal, in West Africa in the late eighteenth century.

But Europeans as well as other Africans generally ignored protests from Africans. As a general rule, local rulers viewed the slave trade as a source of income, and many sent raiders into defenseless villages in search of unsuspecting victims.

Historians once thought that Europeans controlled the terms of the slave trade and were able to obtain victims at bargain prices. It is now clear, however, that African middlemen—merchants, local elites, or rulers—were active in the process and were often able to dictate the price and number of slaves to European purchasers. Payment to the slave merchant was often made in goods, such as textiles, furniture, and guns.

EFFECTS OF THE SLAVE TRADE The effects of the slave trade varied from area to area. Of course, it had tragic effects on the lives of the slaves and their families. There was also an economic price as the importation of cheap manufactured goods from Europe undermined local cottage industries and forced countless families into poverty. The slave trade also led to the depopulation of some areas and deprived many African communities of their youngest and strongest men and women.

The political effects of the slave trade were also devastating. The need to maintain a constant supply of slaves led to increased warfare and violence as African chiefs and their followers, armed with guns acquired from the trade in slaves, increased their raids and wars on neighboring peoples. A few Europeans lamented what they were doing to traditional African societies. One Dutch slave trader remarked, "From us they have learned strife, quarrelling, drunkenness, trickery, theft, unbridled desire for what is not one's own, misdeeds unknown to them before, and the accursed lust for gold."[9] Nevertheless, the slave trade continued, with devastating effects for some African states.

Despite a rising chorus of humanitarian sentiments from European intellectuals, the use of black slaves remained largely acceptable to Western society. Europeans continued to view blacks as inferior beings fit primarily for slave labor. Not until the Society of Friends, known as the Quakers, began to criticize slavery in the 1770s and exclude from their church any member adhering to slave trafficking did European sentiment for the abolition of slavery begin to build. Even then, it was not until the radical stage of the French Revolution in the 1790s that the French abolished slavery. The British followed suit in 1807. Despite the elimination of the African source, slavery continued in the newly formed United States until the Civil War of the 1860s.

The West in Southeast Asia

Portugal's efforts to dominate the trade of Southeast Asia were never totally successful. The Portuguese lacked both the numbers and the wealth to overcome local resistance and colonize the Asian regions. Portugal's empire was simply too large and Portugal too small to maintain it. One Portuguese chronicler lamented, "My country, oh my country. Too heavy is the task that has been laid on your shoulders. Day after day I watch the ships leaving your shores filled always with your best and bravest men. And too many do not return. . . . Who then is left to till the fields, to harvest the grapes, to keep the enemy on our frontiers at bay?"[10] By the end of the sixteenth century, new European rivals had entered the fray.

One of them was Spain. The Spanish had established themselves in the region when Magellan landed in the Philippines. Although he was killed there, the Spanish were able to gain control over the Philippines, which eventually became a major Spanish base in the trade across the Pacific. Spanish ships carried silk and other luxury goods to Mexico in return for silver from the mines of Mexico.

The primary threat to the Portuguese Empire in Southeast Asia, however, came with the arrival of the Dutch and the English, who were better financed than the Portuguese. The shift in power began in the early seventeenth century when the Dutch seized a Portuguese fort in the Moluccas and then gradually pushed the Portuguese out of the spice trade. During the next fifty years, the Dutch occupied most of the Portuguese coastal forts along the trade routes throughout the Indian Ocean, including the island of Ceylon (today's Sri Lanka), and seized Malacca in 1641. The aggressive Dutch drove the English traders out of the spice market as well, eventually restricting the English to a single port on the southern coast of Sumatra.

The Dutch also began to consolidate their political and military control over the entire area. On the island of Java, where they had established a fort at Batavia (buh-TAY-vee-uh) (modern Jakarta) in 1619, the Dutch found that it was necessary to bring the inland regions under their control to protect their position. On Java and the neighboring island of Sumatra, the Dutch East

India Company established pepper plantations, which soon became the source of massive profits for Dutch merchants in Amsterdam. By the end of the eighteenth century, the Dutch had succeeded in bringing almost the entire Indonesian archipelago under their control.

The arrival of the Europeans had less impact on mainland Southeast Asia, where strong monarchies in Burma—now Myanmar (MYAN-mahr)—Thailand, and Vietnam resisted foreign encroachment. In the sixteenth century, the Portuguese established limited trade relations with several mainland states, including Thailand, Burma, Vietnam, and the remnants of the old Angkor kingdom in Cambodia. By the early seventeenth century, other nations had followed and had begun to compete actively for trade and missionary privileges. To obtain economic advantages, the Europeans soon became involved in local factional disputes. In general, however, these states were able to unite and drive the Europeans out.

Southeast Asia, ca. 1700

In Vietnam, the arrival of Western merchants and missionaries coincided with a period of internal conflict among ruling groups in the country. Expansion had led to a civil war that temporarily divided the country into two separate states, one in the south and one in the north. After their arrival in the mid-seventeenth century, the European powers began to take sides in local politics, with the Portuguese and the Dutch supporting rival factions. The Europeans also set up trading posts for their merchants, but by the end of the seventeenth century, when it became clear that economic opportunities were limited, most of them were abandoned. French missionaries attempted to remain, but their efforts were blocked by the authorities, who viewed converts to Catholicism as a threat to the prestige of the Vietnamese emperor (see "Global Perspectives" on p. 417).

Europe in Asia. As Europeans began to move into parts of Asia, they reproduced many of the physical surroundings of their homeland in the port cities they built there. This is evident in comparing these two scenes. Below is a seventeenth-century view of Batavia, which the Dutch built as their headquarters on the northern coast of Java in 1619. The scene at the left is from a sixteenth-century engraving of Amsterdam. This Dutch city had become the financial and commercial capital of Europe. It was also the chief port for the ships of the Dutch East India Company, which brought the spices of the East to Europe.

West Meets East: An Exchange of Royal Letters

ECONOMIC GAIN WAS NOT THE ONLY motivation of Western rulers who wished to establish a European presence in the East. In 1681, King Louis XIV of France wrote a letter to the king of Tonkin (the Trinh family head, then acting as viceroy to the Vietnamese emperor) asking permission for Christian missionaries to proselytize in Vietnam. The king of Tonkin politely declined the request.

A Letter to the King of Tonkin from Louis XIV

Most high, most excellent, most mighty and most magnanimous Prince, our very dear and good friend, may it please God to increase your greatness with a happy end!

We hear from our subjects who were in your Realm what protection you accorded them. We appreciate this all the more since we have for you all the esteem that one can have for a prince as illustrious through his military valor as he is commendable for the justice which he exercises in his Realm. We have even been informed that you have not been satisfied to extend this general protection to our subjects but, in particular, that you gave effective proofs of it to Messrs. Deydier and de Bourges. We would have wished that they might have been able to recognize all the favors they received from you by having presents worthy of you offered you; but since the war which we have had for several years, in which all of Europe had banded together against us, prevented our vessels from going to the Indies, at the present time, when we are at peace after having gained many victories and expanded our Realm through the conquest of several important places, we have immediately given orders to the Royal Company to establish itself in your kingdom as soon as possible, and have commanded Messrs. Deydier and de Bourges to remain with you in order to maintain a good relationship between our subjects and yours, also to warn us on occasions that might present themselves when we might be able to give you proofs of our esteem and of our wish to concur with your satisfaction as well as with your best interests.

By way of initial proof, we have given orders to have brought to you some presents which we believe might be agreeable to you. But the one thing in the world which we desire most, both for you and for your Realm, would be to obtain for your subjects who have already embraced the law of the only true God of heaven and earth, the freedom to profess it, since this law is the highest, the noblest, the most sacred and especially the most suitable to have kings reign absolutely over the people.

We are even quite convinced that, if you knew the truths and the maxims which it teaches, you would give first of all to your subjects the glorious example of embracing it. We wish you this incomparable blessing together with a long and happy reign, and we pray God that it may please Him to augment your greatness with the happiest of endings.

Written at Saint-Germain-en-Laye, the 10th day of January, 1681,

Your very dear and good friend,
Louis

Answer from the King of Tonkin to Louis XIV

The King of Tonkin sends to the King of France a letter to express to him his best sentiments, saying that he was happy to learn that fidelity is a durable good of man and that justice is the most important of things. Consequently practicing of fidelity and justice cannot but yield good results. Indeed, though France and our Kingdom differ as to mountains, rivers, and boundaries, if fidelity and justice reign among our villages, our conduct will express all of our good feelings and contain precious gifts. Your communication, which comes from a country which is a thousand leagues away, and which proceeds from the heart as a testimony of your sincerity, merits repeated consideration and infinite praise. Politeness toward strangers is nothing unusual in our country. There is not a stranger who is not well received by us. How then could we refuse a man from France, which is the most celebrated among the kingdoms of the world and which for love of us wishes to frequent us and bring us merchandise? These feelings of fidelity and justice are truly worthy to be applauded. As regards your wish that we should cooperate in propagating your religion, we do not dare to permit it, for there is an ancient custom, introduced by edicts, which formally forbids it. Now, edicts are promulgated only to be carried out faithfully; without fidelity nothing is stable. How could we disdain a well-established custom to satisfy a private friendship? . . .

We beg you to understand well that this is our communication concerning our mutual acquaintance. This then is my letter. We send you herewith a modest gift, which we offer you with a glad heart.

This letter was written at the beginning of winter and on a beautiful day.

 What are the underlying beliefs and approaches of these two rulers? How are they alike? How are they different? What is King Tonkin's justification for refusing Louis XIV's request? What is the significance of the way the two rulers date their letters?

Source: H. J. Benda and J. A. Larkin, eds. *The World of Southeast Asia: Selected Historical Readings* (New York: Harper & Row, 1967).

Why were the mainland states better able to resist the European challenge than the states in the Malay world? One factor, no doubt, was the cohesive nature of these states. The mainland states in Burma, Thailand, and Vietnam had begun to define themselves as distinct political entities. The Malay states had less cohesion. Moreover, the Malay states were victims of their own resources. The spice trade was enormously profitable. European merchants and rulers were determined to gain control of the sources of the spices, and that determination led them to take direct control of the Indonesian archipelago.

The French and British in India

When a Portuguese fleet arrived at the port of Calicut in the spring of 1498, the Indian subcontinent was divided into a number of Hindu and Muslim kingdoms. But it was on the verge of a new era of unity that would be brought about by a foreign dynasty called the Mughals (MOO-guls).

THE MUGHAL EMPIRE The founders of the Mughal Empire were not natives of India but came from the mountainous region north of the Ganges River valley. The founder of the dynasty, Babur (BAH-burr) (1483–1530), had an illustrious background. His father was descended from the great Asian conqueror Tamerlane; his mother, from the Mongol conqueror Genghis Khan. It was Akbar (AK-bar) (1556–1605), Babur's grandson, however, who brought Mughal rule to most of India, creating the greatest Indian empire since the Mauryan dynasty nearly two thousand years earlier. By the mid-seventeenth century, however, wars of succession and declining revenue led to the collapse of the Mughal Empire as Mughal nobles asserted their control over various territories. By the mid-eighteenth century the Mughals controlled little more territory than Delhi and its surrounding area. The vacuum of power created by the demise of the Mughals opened the door for European trading companies seeking to capitalize on the lucrative trade between India and Europe.

THE IMPACT OF THE WESTERN POWERS As we have seen, the first Europeans to arrive in India were the Portuguese. At first, Portugal dominated regional trade in the Indian Ocean, but at the end of the sixteenth century, the English and the Dutch arrived on the scene. Soon both powers were competing with Portugal, and with each other, for trading privileges in the region.

During the first half of the seventeenth century, the English presence in India steadily increased. By 1650, English trading posts had been established at Surat (a thriving port along the northwestern coast of India), Fort William (now the great city of Calcutta) near the Bay of Bengal, and Madras (now Chennai) on the southeastern coast. From Madras, English ships carried Indian-made cotton goods to the East Indies, where they were bartered for spices, which were shipped back to England.

English success in India attracted rivals, including the Dutch and the French. The Dutch abandoned their interests to concentrate on the spice trade in the middle of the seventeenth century, but the French were more persistent and established their own forts on the east coast. For a brief period, the French competed successfully with the British, even capturing the British fort at Madras.

But the British were saved by the military genius of Sir Robert Clive (CLYV), an aggressive British empire-builder who eventually became the chief representative of the East India Company in India. (The East India Company had been founded as a joint-stock company in 1600—see "The Growth of Commercial Capitalism" later in this chapter.) The British were aided as well by the refusal of the French government to provide financial support for French efforts in far-off India. Eventually, the French were restricted to the fort at Pondicherry and a handful of small territories on the southeastern coast.

In the meantime, Clive began to consolidate British control in Bengal, where the local ruler had attacked Fort William and imprisoned the local British population in the "Black Hole of Calcutta" (an underground prison for holding the prisoners, many of whom died in captivity). In 1757, a small British force numbering about three thousand defeated a Mughal-led army more than ten times its size in the Battle of Plassey (PLASS-ee). As part of the spoils of victory, the British East India Company received from the now-decrepit Mughal court the authority to impose and collect taxes from over 20 million people in the area surrounding Calcutta. During the Seven Years' War (1756–1763), the British forced the French to withdraw completely from India (see Chapter 18).

To officials of the East India Company, the expansion of their authority into the interior of the subcontinent probably seemed like a simple economic decision. It made sense to seek regular revenues that would pay for increasingly expensive military operations in India. In a letter to the company's directors

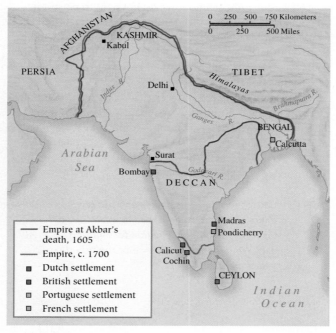

The Mughal Empire

Empire at Akbar's death, 1605
Empire, c. 1700
■ Dutch settlement
■ British settlement
□ Portuguese settlement
□ French settlement

in London, Clive described the potential of the East India Company's future in India:

> I can assert with some degree of confidence that this rich and flourishing kingdom may be totally subdued by so small a force as two thousand Europeans . . . [The Indians are] indolent, luxurious, ignorant and cowardly beyond all conception . . . [They] attempt everything by treachery rather than force . . . What is it, then, can enable us to secure our present acquisitions or improve upon them but such a force as leaves nothing to the power of treachery and ingratitude?"[11]

To historians, it marks a major step in the gradual transfer of all of the Indian subcontinent to the British East India Company and later, in 1858, to the British crown as a colony (see Chapter 24).

China

In 1514, a Portuguese fleet dropped anchor off the coast of China. It was the first direct contact between the Chinese Empire and Europe since the journeys of Marco Polo two hundred years earlier. At the time, the Chinese thought little of the event. China appeared to be at the height of its power as the most magnificent civilization on earth. Its empire stretched from the steppes of Central Asia to the China Sea, from the Gobi Desert to the tropical rain forests of Southeast Asia. From the lofty perspective of the imperial throne in Beijing, the Europeans could only be seen as an unusual form of barbarian. To the Chinese ruler, the rulers of all other countries were simply "younger brothers" of the Chinese emperor, who was regarded as the Son of Heaven.

THE MING AND QING DYNASTIES By the time the Portuguese fleet arrived off the coast of China, the Ming dynasty, which ruled from 1369 to 1644, had already begun a new era of greatness in Chinese history. Under a series of strong rulers, China extended its rule into Mongolia and Central Asia. The Ming even briefly reconquered Vietnam. Along the northern frontier, they strengthened the Great Wall and made peace with the nomadic tribesmen who had troubled China for centuries.

But the days of the Ming dynasty were numbered. In the 1630s, a major epidemic devastated the population in many areas. The suffering caused by the epidemic helped spark a peasant revolt led by Li Zicheng (lee zee-CHENG). In 1644, Li and his forces occupied the capital of Beijing. The last Ming emperor committed suicide by hanging himself from a tree in the palace gardens.

The overthrow of the Ming dynasty created an opportunity for the Manchus, a farming and hunting people who lived northeast of China in the area known today as Manchuria. The Manchus conquered Beijing, and Li Zicheng's army fell. The victorious Manchus then declared the creation of a new dynasty with the reign title of the Qing ("Pure").

The Qing (CHING) were blessed with a series of strong early rulers who pacified the country, corrected the most serious social and economic ills, and restored peace and prosperity. Two Qing monarchs, Kangxi (KAHNG-shee) and Qian-long (CHAN-loong), ruled China for well over a century, from the middle of the seventeenth century to the end of the eighteenth. They were responsible for much of the greatness of Manchu China.

WESTERN INROADS Although China was at the height of its power and glory in the mid-eighteenth century, the first signs of internal decay in the Manchu dynasty were beginning to appear. Qing military campaigns along the frontier were expensive and placed heavy demands on the treasury. At the same time, increasing pressure on the land because of population growth led to economic hardship for many peasants and even rebellion.

Unfortunately for China, the decline of the Qing dynasty occurred just as Europe was increasing pressure for more trade. The first conflict had come from the north, where Russian traders sought skins and furs. Formal diplomatic relations between China and Russia were established in 1689 and provided for regular trade between the two countries.

Dealing with the foreigners who arrived by sea was more difficult. By the end of the seventeenth century, the English had replaced the Portuguese as the dominant force in European trade. Operating through the East India Company, which served as both a trading unit and the administrator of English territories in Asia, the English established their first trading post at Canton in 1699.

Over the next several decades, trade with China, notably the export of tea and silk to England, increased rapidly. To limit contacts between Europeans and Chinese, the Qing government confined all European traders to a small island just outside the city walls of Canton and permitted them to reside there only from October through March.

For a while, the British accepted this system, which brought considerable profit to the East India Company. But by the end of the eighteenth century, some British traders had begun to demand access to other cities along the Chinese coast and insist that the country be opened to British manufactured goods. In 1793, a British mission under Lord Macartney visited Beijing to press for liberalization of trade restrictions.

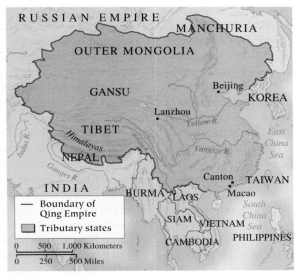

The Qing Empire

RUSSIAN EMPIRE
MANCHURIA
OUTER MONGOLIA
GANSU
Beijing
KOREA
Lanzhou
Yellow R.
TIBET
Himalayas
East China Sea
NEPAL
Yangtze R.
Indus R.
Ganges R.
INDIA
Canton TAIWAN
BURMA
Macao
South China Sea
LAOS
SIAM
VIETNAM
CAMBODIA
PHILIPPINES

— Boundary of Qing Empire
▢ Tributary states

0   500   1,000 Kilometers
0   250   500 Miles

AN IMPERIAL EDICT TO THE KING OF ENGLAND

IN 1793, THE BRITISH EMISSARY Lord Macartney visited the Qing Empire to request the opening of trading relations between his country and China. Emperor Qianlong's reply, addressed to King George III of England, illustrates how the imperial court in Beijing viewed the world. King George cannot have been pleased.

An Imperial Edict to the King of England

You, O King, are so inclined toward our civilization that you have sent a special envoy across the seas to bring to our Court your memorial of congratulations on the occasion of my birthday and to present your native products as an expression of your thoughtfulness. On perusing your memorial, so simply worded and sincerely conceived, I am impressed by your genuine respectfulness and friendliness and greatly pleased.

As to the request made in your memorial, O King, to send one of your nationals to stay at the Celestial Court to take care of your country's trade with China, this is not in harmony with the state system of our dynasty and will definitely not be permitted. Traditionally people of the European nations who wished to tender some service under the Celestial Court have been permitted to come to the capital. But after their arrival they are obliged to wear Chinese court costumes, are placed in a certain residence and are never allowed to return to their own countries. This is the established rule of the Celestial Dynasty with which presumably you, O King, are familiar. Now you, O King,

wish to send one of your nationals to live in the capital, but he is not like the Europeans, who come to Beijing as Chinese employees, live there and never return home again, nor can he be allowed to go and come and maintain any correspondence. This is indeed a useless undertaking. . . .

The Celestial Court has pacified and possessed the territory within the four seas. Its sole aim is to do its utmost to achieve good government and to manage political affairs, attaching no value to strange jewels and precious objects. The various articles presented by you, O King, this time are accepted by my special order to the office in charge of such functions in consideration of the offerings having come from a long distance with sincere good wishes. As a matter of fact, the virtue and prestige of the Celestial Dynasty having spread far and wide, the kings of the myriad nations come by land and sea with all sorts of precious things. Consequently there is nothing we lack, as your principal envoy and others have themselves observed. We have never set much store on strange objects, nor do we need any more of your country's manufactures.

 What reasons does Qianlong give for denying Britain's request to open diplomatic and trading relations with China? Do his comments indicate any ignorance about the West at the end of the eighteenth century? If he had known more, would his response have been different? Why or why not?

Source: S. Teng and J. K. Fairbank, *China's Response to the West: A Documentary Survey* (Cambridge, Mass.: Harvard University Press, 1982).

But Emperor Qianlong expressed no interest in British products (see the box above). An exasperated Macartney compared the Chinese Empire to "an old, crazy, first-rate man-of-war" that had once awed its neighbors "merely by her bulk and appearance" but was now destined under incompetent leadership to be "dashed to pieces on the shore." The Chinese would later pay for their rejection of the British request (see Chapter 24).

Japan

At the end of the fifteenth century, Japan was at a point of near anarchy, but in the course of the sixteenth century, a number of powerful individuals achieved the unification of Japan. One of them, Tokugawa Ieyasu (toh-koo-GAH-wah ee-yeh-YAH-soo) (1543–1616), took the title of shogun ("general") in 1603, an act that initiated the most powerful and longest lasting of all the Japanese shogunates. The Tokugawa rulers completed the restoration of central authority and remained in power until 1868.

OPENING TO THE WEST Portuguese traders had landed on the islands of Japan in 1543, and in a few years, Portuguese ships began stopping at Japanese ports on a regular basis to take part

in the regional trade between Japan, China, and Southeast Asia. The first Jesuit missionary, Francis Xavier, arrived in 1549 and had some success in converting the local population to Christianity.

Initially, the visitors were welcomed. Tobacco, clocks, eyeglasses, and other European goods fascinated the curious Japanese, and local nobles were interested in purchasing all types of European weapons and armaments. Japanese rulers found the new firearms especially helpful in defeating their enemies and unifying the islands. The effect on Japanese military architecture was especially striking, as local lords began to erect castles in stone on the European model.

The success of the Catholic missionaries, however, provoked a strong reaction against the presence of Westerners. When the missionaries interfered in local politics, Tokugawa Ieyasu, newly come to power, expelled all missionaries. Japanese Christians were now persecuted. When a group of Christian peasants on the island of Kyushu revolted in 1637, they were bloodily suppressed.

The European merchants were the next to go. The government closed the two major foreign trading posts on the island of Hirado and at Nagasaki (nah-gah-SAH-kee). Only a small Dutch community in Nagasaki was allowed to remain in Japan.

The Portuguese Arriving at Nagasaki. Portuguese traders landed accidentally in Japan in 1543. In a few years, they arrived regularly, taking part in a regional trade network involving Japan, China, and Southeast Asia. In these panels, done in black lacquer and gold leaf, we see a late-sixteenth-century Japanese interpretation of the first Portuguese landing at Nagasaki.

The Dutch, unlike the Spanish and Portuguese, had not allowed missionary activities to interfere with their trade interests. But the conditions for staying were strict. Dutch ships were allowed to dock at Nagasaki harbor just once a year and could remain for only two or three months.

The Americas

In the sixteenth century, Spain and Portugal had established large colonial empires in the Americas. Portugal continued to profit from its empire in Brazil. The Spanish also maintained an enormous South American empire, but Spain's importance as a commercial power declined rapidly in the seventeenth century because of a drop in the output of the silver mines and the poverty of the Spanish monarchy. By the beginning of the seventeenth century, both Portugal and Spain found themselves with new challenges to their American empires from the Dutch, English, and French, who increasingly sought to create their own colonial empires in the New World.

WEST INDIES Both the French and English colonial empires in the New World included large parts of the West Indies. The English held Barbados, Jamaica, and Bermuda, and the French possessed Saint-Domingue, Martinique, and Guadeloupe. On these tropical islands, both the English and the French developed plantation economies, worked by African slaves, which produced

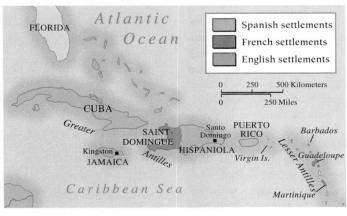

The West Indies

tobacco, cotton, coffee, and sugar, all products increasingly in demand in Europe.

The "sugar factories," as the sugar plantations in the Caribbean were called, played an especially prominent role. By the early eighteenth century, sugar was Britain's main export from its American colonies. By the last two decades of the century, the British colony of Jamaica, one of Britain's most important, was producing 50,000 tons of sugar annually with the slave labor of 200,000 blacks. The French colony of Saint-Domingue (later Haiti) had 500,000 slaves working on three thousand plantations. This colony produced 100,000 tons of sugar a year, but at the expense of a high death rate from the brutal treatment of the slaves. It is not surprising that Saint-Domingue was the site of the first successful slave uprising in 1793 (see Chapter 19).

BRITISH NORTH AMERICA Although Spain claimed all of North America as part of its American overseas empire, other nations largely ignored its claim. The British argued that "prescription without possession availeth nothing." The Dutch were among the first to establish settlements on the North American continent. Their activities began after 1609 when Henry Hudson, an English explorer hired by the Dutch, discovered the river that bears his name. Within a few years, the Dutch had established the mainland colony of New Netherland, which stretched from the mouth of the Hudson River as far north as

SACCHARARIÆ MOLÆ.

1. *Hic sacchari arundines demetuntur.*
2. *Hic frondes iis adimunt.*
3. *Hic molæ teruntur, succus polei excipitur.*
4. *Hic succus ahenis infusæ igne coquitur et purgatur.*
5. *Hic ex ahenis in ollas transportatur.*
6. *Hoce modo ad indurandum exponitur, arcu includitur ac transportatur.*

A Sugar Mill in the West Indies. Cane sugar was one of the most valuable products produced in the West Indies. By 1700, sugar was replacing honey as a sweetener for increasing numbers of Europeans. This seventeenth-century French illustration shows the operation of a sugar mill in the French West Indies.

Albany, New York. Present-day names such as Staten Island and Harlem remind us that it was the Dutch who initially settled the Hudson River valley. In the second half of the seventeenth century, competition from the English and French and years of warfare with those rivals led to the decline of the Dutch commercial empire. In 1664, the English seized the colony of New Netherland and renamed it New York; soon afterward, the Dutch West India Company went bankrupt.

In the meantime, the English had begun to establish their own colonies in North America. The first permanent English settlement in America was Jamestown, founded in 1607 in modern Virginia. It barely survived, making it evident that the colonizing of American lands was not necessarily conducive to quick profits. But the desire to practice one's own religion, combined with economic interests, could lead to successful colonization, as the Massachusetts Bay Company demonstrated. The Massachusetts colony had 4,000 settlers in its early years but by 1660 had swelled to 40,000. By the end of the seventeenth century, the English had established control over most of the eastern seaboard of the present United States.

British North America came to consist of thirteen colonies. They were thickly populated, containing about 1.5 million people by 1750, and were also prosperous. Supposedly run by the British Board of Trade, the Royal Council, and Parliament, these thirteen colonies had legislatures that tended to act independently. Merchants in such port cities as Boston, Philadelphia, New York, and Charleston resented and resisted regulation from the British government.

The British colonies in both North America and the West Indies were assigned roles in keeping with mercantilist theory (see "Mercantilism" later in this chapter). They provided raw materials, such as cotton, sugar and tobacco, for the mother country while buying the latter's manufactured goods. Navigation acts regulated what could be taken from and sold to the colonies. Theoretically, the system was supposed to provide a balance of trade favorable to the mother country.

FRENCH NORTH AMERICA The French also established a colonial empire in North America. Already in 1534, the French explorer Jacques Cartier (ZHAK kar-TYAY) had discovered the Saint Lawrence River and laid claim to Canada as a French possession. It was not until 1608, however, when Samuel de Champlain (shahm-PLAN *or* SHAM-playn) established a settlement at Quebec that the French began to take a more serious interest in Canada as a colony. In 1663, Canada was made the property of the French crown and administered by a French governor like a French province.

CHRONOLOGY	New Rivals on the World Stage
Portuguese traders land in Japan	1543
British East India Company formed	1600
Dutch East India Company formed	1602
English settlement at Jamestown	1607
Champlain establishes settlement at Quebec	1608
Dutch fort established at Batavia	1619
Dutch seize Malacca from the Portuguese	1641
English seize New Netherland	1664
English establish trading post at Canton	1699
Battle of Plassey	1757
French cede Canada to British	1763
British mission to China	1793

French North America was run autocratically as a vast trading area, where valuable furs, leather, fish, and timber were acquired. The inability of the French state to get its people to emigrate to its Canadian possessions, however, left the territory thinly populated. By the mid-eighteenth century, there were only about 15,000 French Canadians, most of whom were hunters, trappers, missionaries, or explorers. The French failed to provide adequate men or money, allowing their European wars to take precedence over the conquest of the North American continent. Already in 1713, by the Treaty of Utrecht, the French began to cede some of their American possessions to their British rival. As a result of the Seven Years' War, they would surrender the rest of their Canadian lands in 1763 (see Chapter 18).

British and French rivalry was also evident in the Spanish and Portuguese colonial empires in Latin America. The decline of Spain and Portugal had led these two states to depend even more on resources from their colonies, and they imposed strict mercantilist rules to keep others out. Spain, for example, tried to limit all trade with its colonies to Spanish ships. But the British and French were too powerful to be excluded. The British cajoled the Portuguese into allowing them into the lucrative Brazilian trade. The French, however, were the first to break into the Spanish Latin American market when the French Bourbons became kings of Spain at the beginning of the eighteenth century. Britain's first entry into Spanish American markets came in 1713, when the British were granted the privilege, known as the *asiento* (ah-SYEN-toh), of transporting 4,500 slaves a year to Spanish Latin America.

The Impact of European Expansion

 FOCUS QUESTION: How did European expansion affect both the conquered and the conquerors?

Between 1500 and 1800, the Atlantic nations of Europe moved into all parts of the world. The first had been Spain and Portugal, the two great colonial powers of the sixteenth century, followed by the Dutch, who built their colonial empire in the seventeenth century as Portugal and Spain declined. The Dutch were soon challenged by the British and French, who outstripped the others in the eighteenth century while becoming involved in a bitter rivalry. By the end of the eighteenth century, it appeared that Great Britain would become the great European imperial power. European expansion had a great impact on both the conquered and the conquerors.

The Conquered

Different regions experienced different effects from the European expansion. The native American civilizations, which had their own unique qualities and a degree of sophistication not much appreciated by Europeans, were virtually destroyed. In addition to devastating losses of population from European diseases, ancient social and political structures were ripped up and replaced by European institutions, religion, language, and culture. In Africa, the real demographic impact of the slave trade is uncertain due to a lack of records; however, estimates of the population in West Africa suggest that the slave trade negated any population growth, rather than causing a decline. Politically and socially, the slave trade encouraged the growth of territories in West Africa, such as Dahomey and Benin, where the leaders waged internal wars to secure more slaves to trade for guns and gunpowder. Without the slave trade, these territories became susceptible to European control in the nineteenth century. The Portuguese trading posts in the East had little direct impact on native Asian civilizations, although Dutch control of the Indonesian archipelago was more pervasive. China and Japan were still little affected by Westerners, although India was subject to ever-growing British encroachment.

In Central and South America, a new civilization arose that we have come to call Latin America. It was a multiracial society. Spanish and Portuguese settlers who arrived in the Western Hemisphere were few in number relative to the native Indians; many of the newcomers were males who not only used female natives for their sexual pleasure but married them as well. Already by 1501, Spanish rulers had authorized intermarriage between Europeans and native American Indians, whose offspring became known as mestizos (mess-TEE-zohz). Another group of people brought to Latin America were the Africans. Over a period of three centuries, possibly as many as 8 million slaves were brought to Spanish and Portuguese America to work the plantations. Africans also contributed to Latin America's multiracial character. Mulattoes (muh-LAH-toh)—the offspring of Africans and whites—joined mestizos and descendants of whites, Africans, and native Indians to produce a unique society in Latin America. Unlike Europe, and unlike British North America, which remained a largely white offshoot of Europe, Latin America developed a multiracial society with less rigid attitudes about race.

The European presence also affected the ecology of the conquered areas. Europeans brought horses, sheep, goats, pigs and cattle to the Americas, which revolutionized the life of the Indians. The Americas were well suited for the European animals. Since they had few predators and plenty of land to roam, the new animals rapidly increased in number. Explorer Hernando De Soto arrived in Florida in 1539 with thirteen pigs; they increased to 700 by 1542. Cattle farming supplanted the Indian agricultural practice of growing maize (Indian corn), eventually leading to the development of large estates for raising cattle. South America would later become a great exporter of beef. Europeans also brought new crops, such as wheat and cane sugar, to be cultivated on large plantations by native or imported slave labor. In their trips to other parts of the world, Europeans also carried New World plants with them. Thus, Europeans introduced sweet potatoes and maize to Africa in the sixteenth century.

CATHOLIC MISSIONARIES Although there were some Protestant missionaries in the world outside Europe, Catholic missionaries were far more active in spreading Christianity. From the beginning of their conquest of the New World, Spanish and Portuguese rulers were determined to Christianize the native peoples. This policy gave the Catholic Church an

THE MISSION

IN 1609, TWO JESUIT PRIESTS EMBARKED on a missionary calling with the Guaraní Indians in eastern Paraguay. Eventually, the Jesuits established more than thirty missions in the region. Well organized and zealous, the Jesuits transformed their missions into profitable businesses. This description of a Jesuit mission in Paraguay was written by Félix de Azara, a Spanish soldier and scientist.

Félix de Azara, Description and History of Paraguay and Rio de la Plata

Having spoken of the towns founded by the Jesuit fathers, and of the manner in which they were founded, I shall discuss the government which they established in them. . . . In each town resided two priests, a curate and a subcurate, who had certain assigned functions. The subcurate was charged with all the spiritual tasks, and the curate with every kind of temporal responsibility. . . .

The curate allowed no one to work for personal gain; he compelled everyone, without distinction of age or sex, to work for the community, and he himself saw to it that all were equally fed and dressed. For this purpose the curates placed in storehouses all the fruits of agriculture and the products of industry, selling in the Spanish towns their surplus of cotton, cloth, tobacco, vegetables, skins, and wood, transporting them in their own boats down the nearest rivers, and returning with implements and whatever else was required.

From the foregoing one may infer that the curate disposed of the surplus funds of the Indian towns, and that no Indian could aspire to own private property. This deprived them of any incentive to use reason or talent, since the most industrious, able, and worthy person had the same food, clothing, and pleasures as the most wicked, dull, and indolent.

It also follows that although this form of government was well designed to enrich the communities it also caused the Indian to work at a languid pace, since the wealth of his community was of no concern to him.

It must be said that although the Jesuit fathers were supreme in all respects, they employed their authority with a mildness and a restraint that command admiration. They supplied everyone with abundant food and clothing. They compelled the men to work only half a day, and did not drive them to produce more. Even their labor was given a festive air, for they went in procession to the fields, to the sound of music . . . and the music did not cease until they had returned in the same way they had set out. They gave them many holidays, dances, and tournaments, dressing the actors. . . . in the most costly European garments, but they permitted the women to act only as spectators.

They likewise forbade the women to sew; this occupation was restricted to the musicians, sacristans, and acolytes. But they made them spin cotton; and the cloth that the Indians wove, after satisfying their own needs, they sold together with the surplus cotton in the Spanish towns, as they did with the tobacco, vegetables, wood, and skins. The curate and . . . subcurate had their own plain dwellings, and they never left them except to take the air in the great enclosed yard of their college. They never walked through the streets of the town or entered the house of any Indian or let themselves be seen by any woman—or indeed, by any man, except for those indispensable few through whom they issued their orders.

 How were the missions organized to enable the missionaries to control most aspects of the Indians' lives? Why was this deemed necessary?

Source: B. Keen, ed., *Latin American Civilization*, vol. I (Boston: Houghton Mifflin, 1974), pp. 223–224.

---

important role to play in the New World, one that added considerably to church power. Catholic missionaries—especially the Dominicans, Franciscans, and Jesuits—fanned out to different parts of the Spanish Empire.

To facilitate their efforts, missionaries brought Indians together into villages, where they could be converted, taught trades, and encouraged to grow crops. These missions enabled the missionaries to control the lives of the Indians and helped ensure that they would remain docile members of the empire (see the box above and "Film & History"). Missions generally benefited the missionaries more than the Indians. In frontier districts such as California and Texas, missions also served as military barriers to foreign encroachment.

The Catholic Church constructed hospitals, orphanages, and schools. Monastic schools instructed Indian students in the rudiments of reading, writing, and arithmetic. The Catholic Church also provided outlets for women other than marriage.

Nunneries were places of prayer and quiet contemplation, but women in religious orders, many of them of aristocratic background, often lived well and worked outside their establishments by running schools and hospitals. Indeed, one of these nuns, Sor Juana Inés de la Cruz (SAWR HWAH-nuh ee-NAYSS day lah KROOZ) (1651–1695), was one of seventeenth-century Latin America's best-known literary figures. She wrote poetry and prose and promoted the education of women.

Christian missionaries also made the long voyage to China on European merchant ships. The Jesuits were among the most active and the most effective. Many of the early Jesuit missionaries to China were highly educated men who were familiar with European philosophical and scientific developments. They brought along clocks and various other instruments that impressed Chinese officials and made them more open to Western ideas.

The Jesuits used this openness to promote Christianity. To make it easier for the Chinese to accept Christianity, the Jesuits pointed to similarities between Christian morality and Confucian ethics. The Italian priest Matteo Ricci described the Jesuit approach:

> In order that the appearance of a new religion might not arouse suspicion among the Chinese people, the Jesuit Fathers did not speak openly about religious matters when they began to appear in public. . . . They did, however, try to teach this pagan people in a more direct way, namely, by virtue of their example and by the sanctity of their lives. In this way they attempted to win the good will of the people and little by little to dispose their minds to receive what they could not be persuaded to accept by word of mouth. . . . From the time of their entrance they wore the ordinary Chinese outer garment, which was somewhat similar to their own religious habits; a long robe reaching down to the heels and with very ample sleeves, which are much in favor with the Chinese.[12]

The efforts of the Christian missionaries reached their height in the early eighteenth century. Several hundred Chinese officials became Catholics, as did an estimated 300,000 ordinary Chinese. But ultimately squabbling among the religious orders themselves undermined the Christian effort. To make it easier for the Chinese to convert, the Jesuits had allowed the new Catholics to continue the practice of ancestor worship. Jealous Dominicans and Franciscans complained to the pope, who condemned the practice. Soon Chinese authorities began to suppress Christian activities throughout China.

The Jesuits also had some success in Japan, where they converted a number of local nobles. By the end of the sixteenth century, thousands of Japanese on the southernmost islands of Kyushu and Shikoku had become Christians. But the Jesuit practice of destroying local idols and shrines and turning some temples into Christian schools or churches caused a severe reaction. When a new group of Spanish Franciscans continued the same policies, the government ordered the execution of nine missionaries and a number of their Japanese converts. When missionaries continued to interfere in local politics, Tokugawa Ieyasu expelled all missionaries. Japanese Christians were now persecuted.

The Conquerors

For some Europeans, expansion abroad brought the possibility of obtaining land, riches, and social advancement. One Spaniard commented in 1572 that many "poor young men" had left Spain for Mexico, where they hoped to acquire landed estates and call themselves "gentlemen." Although some wives accompanied their husbands abroad, many ordinary European women found new opportunities for marriage in the New World because of the lack of white women. Indeed, as one commentator bluntly put it, even "a whore, if handsome, [can] make a wife for some rich planter."[13] In the violence-prone world of early Spanish America, a number of women also found themselves rich after their husbands were killed unexpectedly. In one area of Central America, women owned about 25 percent of the landed estates by 1700.

European expansion also had other economic effects on the conquerors. Wherever they went in the New World, Europeans looked for sources of gold and silver. One Aztec commented that the Spanish conquerors "longed and lusted for gold. Their bodies swelled with greed, and their hunger was ravenous; they hungered like pigs for that gold."[14] Rich silver deposits were found and exploited in Mexico and southern Peru (modern Bolivia). When the mines at Potosí in Peru opened in 1545, the value of precious metals imported into Europe quadrupled. Between 1503 and 1650, an estimated 16 million kilograms (more than 35 million pounds) of silver and 185,000 kilograms (407,000 pounds) of gold entered the port of Seville and set off a price revolution that affected the Spanish economy.

But gold and silver were only two of the products that became part of the exchange between the New World and the Old. Historians refer to the reciprocal importation and exportation of plants and animals between Europe and the Americas as the **Columbian Exchange** (see Map 14.3). While Europeans were bringing horses, cattle, and wheat to the New World, they were taking new agricultural products such as potatoes, chocolate, corn, tomatoes, and tobacco back to Europe. Potatoes became especially popular as a dietary staple in some areas of Europe. High in carbohydrates and rich in vitamins A and C, potatoes could be easily stored for winter use and enabled more people to survive on smaller plots of land. This improvement in nutrition was soon reflected in a rapid increase in population. Other products, such as cochineal, a red dye discovered in Mexico, gave European artists and artisans a "perfect red" for their paintings and cloth.

The European lifestyle was greatly affected by new products from abroad. In addition to new foods, new drinks also appeared in Europe. Chocolate, which had been brought to Spain from Aztec Mexico, became a common drink by 1700. The first coffee and tea houses opened in London in the 1650s and spread rapidly to other parts of Europe. In the eighteenth century, a craze for Chinese furniture and porcelain spread among the upper classes. Chinese ideas would also have an impact on intellectual attitudes (see Chapter 17).

European expansion, which was in part a product of European rivalries, also deepened that competition and increased the tensions among European states. Bitter conflicts arose over the cargoes coming from the New World and Asia. The

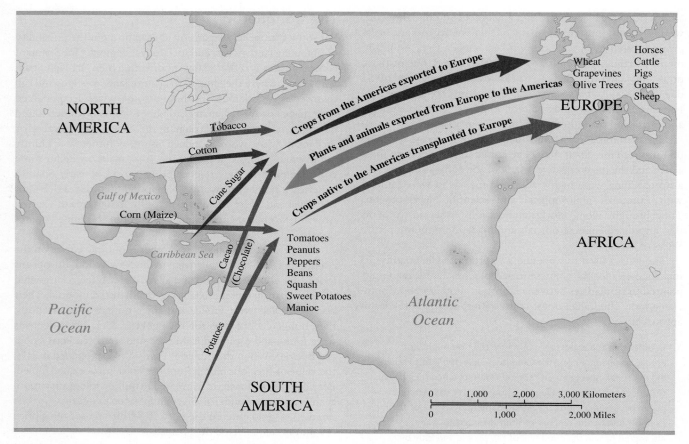

MAP 14.3 The Columbian Exchange. In addition to their diseases, which killed vast numbers of indigenous inhabitants of the Americas, Europeans transplanted many of their crops and domestic animals to the New World. Europeans also imported plants from the New World that improved food production and nutrition in Europe.

 Where were the main source regions for native plants imported into Europe?

Anglo-Dutch trade wars and the British-French rivalry over India and North America became part of a new pattern of worldwide warfare in the eighteenth century (see Chapter 18). Bitter rivalries also led to state-sponsored piracy as governments authorized private captains to attack enemy shipping and keep part of the proceeds for themselves.

In the course of their expansion, Europeans also came to have a new view of the world. When the travels began in the fifteenth century, Europeans were dependent on maps that were often fanciful and inaccurate. Their explorations helped them create new maps that gave a more realistic portrayal of the world, as well as new techniques called map projections that allowed them to represent the round surface of a sphere on a flat piece of paper. The most famous of these is the Mercator projection, the work of a Flemish cartographer, Gerardus Mercator (juh-RAHR-dus mur-KAY-tur) (1512–1594). A Mercator projection is what mapmakers call a conformal projection. It tries to show the true shape of landmasses, but only in a limited area. On the Mercator projection, the shapes of lands near the equator are quite accurate, but the farther away from the equator they lie, the more exaggerated their size becomes. For example,

the island of Greenland on a Mercator projection appears to be larger than the continent of South America. In fact, Greenland is about one-ninth the size of South America. Nevertheless, the Mercator projection was valuable to ship captains. Every straight line on a Mercator projection is a line of true direction, whether north, south, east, or west. For four centuries, ship captains were very grateful to Mercator.

The psychological impact of colonization on the colonizers is difficult to evaluate but hard to deny. Europeans were initially startled by the discovery of new peoples in the Americas. Some deemed them inhuman and thus fit to be exploited for labor. Others, however, found them to be refreshingly natural and as yet untouched by European corruption. But even the latter group still believed that the Indians should be converted—if not forcefully, at least peacefully—to Christianity. Overall, the relatively easy European success in dominating native peoples (be they Africans or Indians) reinforced Christian Europe's belief in the inherent superiority of European civilization and religion. The Scientific Revolution of the seventeenth century (see Chapter 16), the Enlightenment of the eighteenth (see Chapter 17), and the imperialism

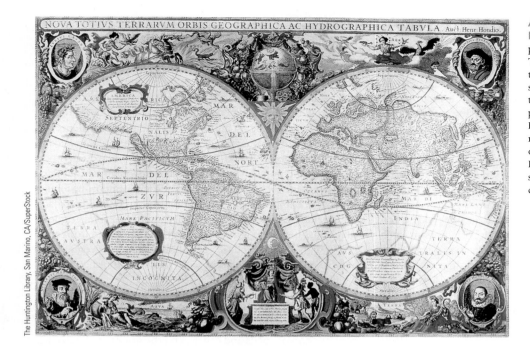

NOVA TOTIVS TERRARVM ORBIS GEOGRAPHICA AC HYDROGRAPHICA TABVLA Auct Henr Hondio.

A Seventeenth-Century World Map. This beautiful world map was prepared in 1630 by Henricus Hondius. The four portraits are of Caesar, the Roman statesman; Ptolemy, the second-century astronomer; Mercator, the Flemish cartographer whose map projection Hondius followed; and Hondius himself. By comparing this map with the map created by Ptolemy on p. 402, one can see how much Europeans had learned about the shape of the world by the seventeenth century.

The Huntington Library, San Marino, CA/SuperStock

of the nineteenth (see Chapter 24) would all bolster this Eurocentric perspective, which has pervaded Western civilization's relations with the rest of the world.

Toward a World Economy

Q **FOCUS QUESTION:** What was mercantilism, and what was its relationship to colonial empires?

During the High Middle Ages, Europeans had engaged in a commercial revolution that created new opportunities for townspeople in a basically agrarian economy. Although this commercial thrust was slowed by the devastating crises of the fourteenth century, Europe's discovery of the world outside in the fifteenth century led to an even greater burst of commercial activity and the inception of a world market.

Economic Conditions in the Sixteenth Century

Inflation became a major economic problem in the sixteenth and early seventeenth centuries. This so-called **price revolution** was a Europe-wide phenomenon, although it affected different areas at different times. Though the inflation rate was probably a relatively low 2 to 3 percent a year, it was noticeable in a Europe accustomed to stable prices. Foodstuffs were most subject to price increases, especially evident in the price of wheat. An upward surge in wheat prices was first noticed in the Mediterranean area—in Spain, southern France, and Italy—and reached its peak there in the 1590s.

Although precise data are lacking, economic historians believe that as a result of the price revolution, wages failed to keep up with price increases. Wage earners, especially

agricultural laborers and salaried workers in urban areas, saw their standard of living drop. At the same time, landed aristocrats, who could raise rents, managed to prosper. Commercial and industrial entrepreneurs also benefited from the price revolution because of rising prices, expanding markets, and relatively cheaper labor costs. Some historians regard this profit inflation as a valuable stimulus to investment and the growth of capitalism, helping to explain the economic expansion and prosperity of the sixteenth century. Governments were likewise affected by inflation. They borrowed heavily from bankers and imposed new tax burdens on their subjects, often stirring additional discontent.

The causes of the price revolution are a subject of much historical debate. Already in the 1560s, European intellectuals associated the rise in prices with the great influx of precious metals from the New World. Although this view was accepted for a long time, many economic historians now believe that the increase in population in the sixteenth century played an important role in creating inflationary pressures. A growing population increased the demand for land and food and drove up prices for both.

The Growth of Commercial Capitalism

The flourishing European trade of the sixteenth century revolved around three major areas: the Mediterranean in the south, the Low Countries and the Baltic region in the north, and central Europe, whose inland trade depended on the Rhine and Danube Rivers. As overseas trade expanded, however, the Atlantic seaboard began to play a more important role, linking the Mediterranean, Baltic, and central European trading areas together and making the whole of Europe into a more integrated market that was all the more vulnerable to price shifts. With their cheaper and faster ships, the Dutch came to monopolize both European and world trade, although they were increasingly challenged by the English and French in the seventeenth century.

The commercial expansion of the sixteenth and seventeenth centuries was made easier by new forms of commercial organization, especially the **joint-stock company**. Individuals bought shares in a company and received dividends on their investment while a board of directors ran the company and made the important business decisions. The return on investments could be spectacular. During its first ten years, investors received 30 percent on their money from the Dutch East India Company, which opened the Spice Islands and Southeast Asia to Dutch activity. The joint-stock company made it easier to raise large amounts of capital for world trading ventures.

Enormous profits were also being made in shipbuilding and in mining and metallurgy, where technological innovations, such as the use of pumps and new methods of extracting metals from ores, proved highly successful. The mining industry was closely tied to sixteenth-century family banking firms. In exchange for arranging large loans to Charles V, Jacob Fugger (YAH-gawp FOO-gurr) was given a monopoly over silver, copper, and mercury mines in the Habsburg possessions of central Europe that produced profits in excess of 50 percent per year. Though these close relationships between governments and entrepreneurs could lead to stunning successes, they could also be precarious. The House of Fugger went bankrupt at the end of the sixteenth century when the Habsburgs defaulted on their loans.

By the seventeenth century, the traditional family banking firms were no longer able to supply the numerous services needed for the expanding commercial capitalism. New institutions arose to take their place. The city of Amsterdam created the Bank of Amsterdam in 1609 as both a deposit and a transfer institution and the Amsterdam Bourse, or Exchange, where the trading of stocks replaced the exchange of goods. By the first half of the seventeenth century, the Amsterdam Exchange had emerged as the hub of the European business world, just as Amsterdam itself had replaced Antwerp as the greatest commercial and banking center of Europe.

Despite the growth of commercial capitalism, most of the European economy still depended on an agricultural system that had experienced few changes since the thirteenth century. At least 80 percent of Europeans still worked on the land. Almost all of the peasants of western Europe were free of serfdom, although many still owed a variety of feudal dues to the nobility. Despite the expanding markets and rising prices, European peasants saw little or no improvement in their lot as they faced increased rents and fees and higher taxes imposed by the state. In eastern Europe, the peasants' position even worsened as they were increasingly tied to the land in a new serfdom enforced by powerful landowners (see Chapter 15).

Mercantilism

In the seventeenth century, a set of economic tendencies that historians call **mercantilism** came to dominate economic practices. Fundamental to mercantilism was the belief that the total volume of trade was unchangeable. Therefore, states protected their economies by following certain practices: hoarding precious metals, implementing protectionist trade policies,

promoting colonial development, increasing shipbuilding, supporting trading companies, and encouraging the manufacturing of products to be used in trade.

According to the mercantilists, the prosperity of a nation depended on a plentiful supply of bullion (gold and silver). For this reason, it was desirable to achieve a favorable balance of trade in which goods exported were of greater value than those imported, promoting an influx of gold and silver payments that would increase the quantity of bullion. Furthermore, to encourage exports, governments should stimulate and protect export industries and trade by granting trade monopolies, encouraging investment in new industries through subsidies, importing foreign artisans, and improving transportation systems by building roads, bridges, and canals. By imposing high tariffs on foreign goods, they could be kept out of the country and prevented from competing with domestic industries. Colonies were also deemed valuable as sources of raw materials and markets for finished goods.

The mercantilists also focused on the role of the state, believing that state intervention in some aspects of the economy was desirable for the sake of the national good. Government regulations to ensure the superiority of export goods, the construction of roads and canals, and the granting of subsidies to create trade companies were all predicated on government involvement in economic affairs.

Overseas Trade and Colonies: Movement Toward Globalization

Mercantilist theory on the role of colonies was matched in practice by Europe's overseas expansion. With the development of colonies and trading posts in the Americas and the East, Europeans embarked on an adventure in international commerce in the seventeenth century. Although some historians speak of a nascent world economy, we should remember that local, regional, and intra-European trade still predominated. At the end of the seventeenth century, for example, English imports totaled 360,000 tons, but only 5,000 tons came from the East Indies. About one-tenth of English and Dutch exports were shipped across the Atlantic; slightly more went to the East. What made the transoceanic trade rewarding, however, was not the volume but the value of its goods. Dutch, English, and French merchants were bringing back products that were still consumed largely by the wealthy but were beginning to make their way into the lives of artisans and merchants. Pepper and spices from the Indies, West Indian and Brazilian sugar, and Asian coffee and tea were becoming more readily available to European consumers.

Trade within Europe remained strong throughout the eighteenth century as wheat, timber, and naval stores from the Baltic, wines from France, wool and fruit from Spain, and silk from Italy were exchanged along with a host of other products. But this trade increased only slightly while overseas trade boomed. From 1716 to 1789, total French exports quadrupled; intra-European trade, which constituted 75 percent of these exports in 1716, accounted for only 50 percent of the total in 1789. This increase in overseas trade has led some historians to proclaim the emergence of a truly global economy in the eighteenth century. Trade patterns now interlocked Europe, Africa, the East, and the Americas.

At the end of the fifteenth century, Europeans sailed out into the world in all directions. Beginning in the mid-fifteenth century with a handful of Portuguese ships that ventured southward along the West African coast, bringing back slaves and gold, the process of European expansion accelerated with the epochal voyages of Christopher Columbus to the Americas and Vasco da Gama to the Indian Ocean in the 1490s. The Portuguese Empire was based on trade; Portugal's population was too small for it to establish large colonies. But Spain had greater resources: Spanish conquistadors overthrew both the Aztec and Inca Empires, and Spain created two major administrative units in New Spain and Peru that subjected the native population to Spanish control. Catholic missionaries, under the control of the Spanish crown, brought Christianity, including cathedrals and schools.

Soon a number of other European peoples, including the Dutch, British, and French, had joined in the process of expansion, and by the end of the eighteenth century, they had created a global trade network dominated by Western ships and Western power. Although originally less prized than gold and spices, slaves became a major object of trade, and by the nineteenth century 10 million African slaves had been shipped to the Americas. Slavery was common in Africa, and the African

terminus of the trade was in the hands of the Africans, but the insatiable demand for slaves led to increased warfare on that unfortunate continent. It was not until the late 1700s that slavery came under harsh criticism in Europe.

In less than three hundred years, the European age of exploration had changed the shape of the world. In some areas, such as the Americas and the Spice Islands in Asia, it led to the destruction of indigenous civilizations and the establishment of European colonies. In others, such as Africa, India, and mainland Southeast Asia, it left native regimes intact but had a strong impact on local societies and regional trade patterns. Japan and China were least affected.

At the time, many European observers viewed the process in a favorable light. They believed that it not only expanded wealth through world trade and exchanged crops and discoveries between the Old World and the New but also introduced "heathen peoples" to the message of Jesus. No doubt, the conquest of the Americas and expansion into the rest of the world brought out the worst and some of the best of European civilization. The greedy plundering of resources and the brutal repression and enslavement were hardly balanced by attempts to create new institutions, convert the natives to Christianity, and foster the rights of the indigenous peoples. In any event, Europeans had begun to change the face of the world and increasingly saw their culture, with its religion, languages, and technology, as a coherent force to be exported to all corners of the world.

CHAPTER TIMELINE

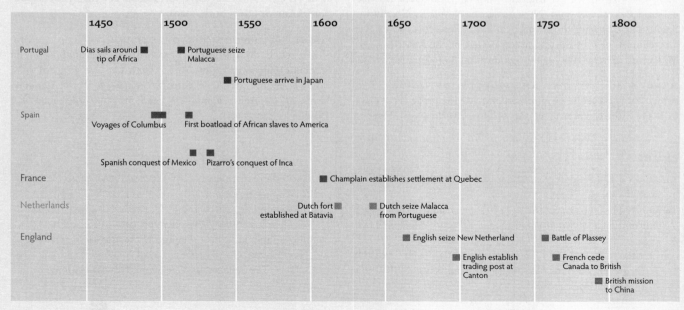

	1450	1500	1550	1600	1650	1700	1750	1800
Portugal	Dias sails around tip of Africa	Portuguese seize Malacca / Portuguese arrive in Japan						
Spain	Voyages of Columbus	First boatload of African slaves to America / Spanish conquest of Mexico / Pizarro's conquest of Inca						
France				Champlain establishes settlement at Quebec				
Netherlands			Dutch fort established at Batavia	Dutch seize Malacca from Portuguese				
England					English seize New Netherland / English establish trading post at Canton		Battle of Plassey / French cede Canada to British / British mission to China	

CHAPTER REVIEW

Upon Reflection

Q How did the experiences of the Spanish and Portuguese during the age of exploration differ from those of their French, Dutch, and English counterparts?

Q What role did religion play as a motivation in the age of exploration? Was it as important a motive as economics? Why or why not?

Q Why and how did Japan succeed in keeping Europeans largely away from its territory in the seventeenth century?

Key Terms

portolani (p. 402)
conquistadors (p. 407)
encomienda (p. 410)
viceroy (p. 410)
audiencias (p. 410)
triangular trade (p. 413)

Middle Passage (p. 413)
Columbian Exchange (p. 425)
price revolution (p. 427)
joint-stock company (p. 428)
mercantilism (p. 428)

Suggestions for Further Reading

GENERAL WORKS For general accounts of European discovery and expansion, see **D. Arnold**, *Age of Discovery*, 2nd ed. (London, 2002); **R. Fritze**, *New Worlds: The Great Voyages of Discovery, 1400–1600* (Westport, Conn., 2002); **G. J. Ames**, *The Globe Encompassed: The Age of European Discovery, 1500–1700* (Upper Saddle River, N.J., 2007); **P. Morgan** and **N. Canny, eds.**, *The Oxford Handbook of the Atlantic World, 1450–1850* (New York, 2011); and **A. Suranyi**, *The Atlantic Connection: A History of the Atlantic World, 1450–1900* (New York, 2015).

PORTUGUESE AND SPANISH EXPANSION On Portuguese expansion, see **R. Crowley**, *Conquerors: How Portugal Forged the First Global Empire* (New York, 2015). On Columbus, see **W. D. Phillips** and **C. R. Phillips**, *The Worlds of Christopher Columbus* (Cambridge, 1992). On the Spanish Empire in the New World, see **H. Kamen**, *Empire: How Spain Became a World Power, 1492–1763* (New York, 2003), and **R. Goodwin**, *Spain: The Centre of the World, 1519–1682* (New York, 2015). For a revisionist view of the Spanish conquest of the Americas, see **M. Restall**, *Seven Myths of the Spanish Conquest* (Oxford, 2003).

MERCANTILE EMPIRES AND WORLDWIDE TRADE The subject of mercantile empires and worldwide trade is covered in **J. H. Elliott**, *Empires of the Atlantic World* (New Haven,

Conn., 2006), and **M. J. Seymour**, *Transformation of the North Atlantic World, 1492–1763* (Westport, Conn., 2004). On the African slave trade, see **J. K. Thornton**, *Africa and Africans in the Making of the Atlantic World, 1400–1800* (Cambridge, 1998). On slavery in the New World see **D. B. Davis**, *Inhuman Bondage: The Rise and Fall of Slavery in the New World* (New York, 2008).

IMPACT OF EXPANSION The impact of expansion on European consciousness is explored in **A. Pagden**, *European Encounters with the New World: From Renaissance to Romanticism* (New Haven, Conn., 1993). On the impact of disease, see **N. D. Cook**, *Born to Die: Disease and the New World* (New York, 1998). The human and ecological effects of the interaction of New World and Old World cultures are examined thoughtfully in **A. W. Crosby**, *Ecological Imperialism: The Biological Expansion of Europe* (New York, 1986).

ECONOMIC DIMENSIONS OF EXPANSION On mercantilism, see **L. Magnusson**, *Mercantilism: The Shaping of an Economic Language* (New York, 1994). On the concept of a world economy, see **A. K. Smith**, *Creating a World Economy: Merchant Capital, Colonialism, and World Trade, 1400–1825* (Boulder, Colo., 1991).

Notes

1. Quoted in J. R. Hale, *Renaissance Exploration* (New York, 1968), p. 32.
2. Quoted in J. H. Parry, *The Age of Reconnaissance: Discovery, Exploration, and Settlement, 1450 to 1650* (New York, 1963), p. 33.
3. Quoted in R. B. Reed, "The Expansion of Europe," in R. D. Molen, ed., *The Meaning of the Renaissance and Reformation* (Boston, 1974), p. 308.
4. Quoted in I. Cameron, *Explorers and Exploration* (New York, 1991), p. 42.
5. Quoted in J. H. Parry and R. G. Keith, eds., *New Iberian World*, vol. 2 (New York, 1984), pp. 309–310.
6. Quoted in J. H. Elliott, *Empires of the Atlantic World* (New Haven, Conn., 2006), p. 125.
7. B. Diaz, *The Conquest of New Spain* (New York, 1963) pp. 405–406.

8. Quoted in A. Andrea and J. H. Overfield, *The Human Record: Sources of Global History*, 3rd ed. (Boston, 1998), p. 460.

9. Quoted in B. Davidson, *Africa in History: Themes and Outlines* (New York, 1991), p. 198.

10. Quoted in Cameron, *Explorers and Exploration*, p. 42.

11. Quoted in N. Ferguson, *Empire: The Rise and Demise of the British World Order and the Lessons for Global Power* (New York, 2002), p. 43.

12. Quoted in L. J. Gallagher, ed., trans., *China in the Sixteenth Century: The Journals of Matthew Ricci* (New York, 1953), p. 154.

13. Quoted in G. V. Scammell, *The First Imperial Age: European Overseas Expansion, c. 1400–1715* (London, 1989), p. 62.

14. M. Leon-Portilla, ed., *The Broken Spears: The Aztec Account of the Conquest of Mexico* (Boston, 1969), p. 51.

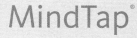

MindTap® is a fully online, highly personalized learning experience built upon Cengage Learning content. MindTap combines student learning tools—readings, multimedia, activities, and assessments—into a singular Learning Path that guides students through the course.

STATE BUILDING AND THE SEARCH FOR ORDER IN THE SEVENTEENTH CENTURY

Nicolas-René Jollain the Elder's portrait of Louis XIV captures the king's sense of royal grandeur

CHAPTER OUTLINE AND FOCUS QUESTIONS

Social Crises, War, and Rebellions

 What economic, social, and political crises did Europe experience in the first half of the seventeenth century?

The Practice of Absolutism: Western Europe

Q What was absolutism in theory, and how did its actual practice in France reflect or differ from the theory?

Absolutism in Central, Eastern, and Northern Europe

Q What developments enabled Brandenburg-Prussia, Austria, and Russia to emerge as major powers in the seventeenth century?

Limited Monarchy and Republics

Q What were the main issues in the struggle between king and Parliament in seventeenth-century England, and how were they resolved?

The Flourishing of European Culture

Q How did the artistic and literary achievements of this era reflect the political and economic developments of the period?

Critical Thinking

Q What theories of government were proposed by Jacques Bossuet, Thomas Hobbes, and John Locke, and how did their respective theories reflect concerns and problems of the seventeenth century?

Connections to Today

Q How does the exercise of state power in the seventeenth century compare with the exercise of state power in the twenty-first century? What, if anything, has changed?

BY THE END of the sixteenth century, Europe was beginning to experience a decline in religious passions and a growing secularization that affected both the political and the intellectual worlds (on the intellectual effects, see Chapter 16). Some historians like to speak of the seventeenth century as a turning point in the evolution of a modern state system in Europe. The ideal of a united Christian Europe gave way to the practical realities of a system of secular states in which matters of state took precedence over the salvation of subjects' souls. By the seventeenth century, the credibility of Christianity had been so weakened through religious wars that more and more Europeans came to think of politics in secular terms.

One response to the religious wars and other crises of the time was a yearning for order. As the internal social and political rebellions and revolts died down, it became apparent that the privileged classes of society—the aristocrats—remained in control, although the various states exhibited important differences in political forms. The most general trend saw an extension of monarchical power as a stabilizing force. This development, which historians have called absolute monarchy or absolutism, was most evident in France during the flamboyant reign of Louis XIV, regarded by some as the perfect embodiment of an absolute monarch. In his memoirs, the duc de Saint-Simon (dook duh san-see-MOHN), who had firsthand experience of French court life, said that Louis was "to the manner born, for he stood out like a king bee because of his height, grace, and beauty (even in the tone of his voice), and because of his princely bearing which was better than good looks." The king's natural grace gave him a special charm as well. He spoke well and learned quickly. He was naturally kind and "he loved glory; he desired peace and good government. He was born prudent, temperate, master of his emotions and his tongue . . . he was born good and just." His life was orderly, and his self-control was impeccable. But even absolute monarchs had imperfections, and Saint-Simon had the courage to point them out: "the king's intelligence was below the average. . . . Praise, or better, adulation pleased him so much that the most fulsome was welcome and the most servile even more delectable." Indeed, "he acquired a pride so colossal that, truly, had not God implanted in his heart the fear of the devil . . . he would have allowed himself to be worshipped."[1]

But absolutism was not the only response to the search for order in the seventeenth century. Other states, such as England, reacted differently to domestic crisis, and another very different system emerged in which monarchs were limited by the power of their representative assemblies. Absolute and limited monarchy were the two poles of seventeenth-century state building.

Social Crises, War, and Rebellions

 FOCUS QUESTION: What economic, social, and political crises did Europe experience in the first half of the seventeenth century?

The inflation-fueled prosperity of the sixteenth century showed signs of slackening by the beginning of the seventeenth. Economic contraction was evident in some parts of Europe in the 1620s. In the 1630s and 1640s, as imports of silver from the Americas declined, economic recession intensified, especially in the Mediterranean area. Once the industrial and financial center of Europe in the Renaissance, Italy was now becoming an economic backwater. Spain's economy was also seriously failing by the 1640s.

Population trends of the sixteenth and seventeenth centuries also reveal Europe's worsening conditions. The sixteenth century was a period of expanding population, possibly related to a warmer climate and increased food supplies. It has been estimated that the population of Europe increased from 60 million in 1500 to 85 million by 1600, the first major recovery of the European population since the devastation of the Black Death in the mid-fourteenth century. Records also indicate a leveling

off of the population by 1620, however, and even a decline by 1650, especially in central and southern Europe. Only the Dutch, English, and French grew in number in the first half of the seventeenth century. Europe's longtime adversaries—war, famine, and plague—continued to affect population levels. After the middle of the sixteenth century, another "little ice age," when average temperatures fell, affected harvests and caused famines. These problems created social tensions that came to a boil in the witchcraft craze.

The Witchcraft Craze

Hysteria over witchcraft affected the lives of many Europeans in the sixteenth and seventeenth centuries. Witchcraft trials were held in England, Scotland, Switzerland, Germany, some parts of France and the Low Countries, and even in New England in America.

Witchcraft was not a new phenomenon. Its practice had been part of traditional village culture for centuries, but it came to be viewed as both sinister and dangerous when the medieval church began to connect witches to the activities of the devil, thereby transforming witchcraft into a heresy that had to be wiped out. After the establishment of the Inquisition in the thirteenth century, some people were accused of a variety of witchcraft practices and, following the biblical injunction "Thou shalt not suffer a witch to live," were turned over to secular authorities for burning at the stake or, in England, hanging.

THE SPREAD OF WITCHCRAFT What distinguished witchcraft in the sixteenth and seventeenth centuries from these previous developments was the increased number of trials and executions of presumed witches. Perhaps more than 100,000 people throughout Europe were prosecuted on charges of witchcraft. Although larger cities were affected first, the trials spread to smaller towns and rural areas as the hysteria persisted well into the seventeenth century (see the box on p. 434).

The accused witches usually confessed to a number of practices, most often after intense torture. Many said that they had sworn allegiance to the devil and attended sabbats or nocturnal gatherings where they feasted, danced, and even copulated with the devil in sexual orgies. More common, however, were admissions of using evil incantations and special ointments and powders to wreak havoc on neighbors by killing their livestock, injuring their children, or raising storms to destroy their crops.

A number of contributing factors have been suggested to explain why the witchcraft frenzy became so widespread in the sixteenth and seventeenth centuries. Religious uncertainties clearly played some part. Many witchcraft trials occurred in areas where Protestantism had recently been victorious or in regions, such as southwestern Germany, where Protestant-Catholic controversies still raged. As religious passions became inflamed, accusations of being in league with the devil became common on both sides. After all, both Martin Luther and John Calvin had described their personal battles with Satan.

Recently, however, historians have emphasized the importance of social conditions, especially the problems of a society

A WITCHCRAFT TRIAL IN FRANCE

PERSECUTIONS FOR WITCHCRAFT REACHED their high point in the sixteenth and seventeenth centuries when tens of thousands of people were brought to trial. In this excerpt from the minutes of a trial in France in 1652, we can see why the accused witch stood little chance of exonerating herself.

The Trial of Suzanne Gaudry

28 May, 1652. . . . Interrogation of Suzanne Gaudry, prisoner at the court of Rieux. . . . [During interrogations on May 28 and May 29, the prisoner confessed to a number of activities involving the devil.]

Deliberation of the Court—June 3, 1652

The undersigned advocates of the Court have seen these interrogations and answers. They say that the aforementioned Suzanne Gaudry confesses that she is a witch, that she had given herself to the devil, that she had renounced God, Lent, and baptism, that she has been marked on the shoulder, that she has cohabited with the devil and that she has been to the dances. . . .

Third Interrogation—June 27

This prisoner being led into the chamber, she was examined to know if things were not as she had said and confessed at the beginning of her imprisonment.

—Answers no, and that what she has said was done so by force.

Pressed to say the truth, that otherwise she would be subjected to torture . . .

—Answers that she is not a witch. . . .

She was placed in the hands of the officer in charge of torture. . . .

The Torture

This prisoner, before being strapped down, was admonished to maintain herself in her first confessions. . . .

—Says that she denies everything she has said. . . . Feeling herself being strapped down, says that she is not a witch . . .

and being a little stretched [on the rack] screams ceaselessly that she is not a witch. . . .

Asked if she did not confess that she had been a witch for twenty-six years.

—Says that she said it, that she retracts it, crying that she is not a witch. . . .

The mark having been probed . . . it was adjudged by the aforesaid doctor and officer truly to be the mark of the devil.

Being more tightly stretched upon the torture-rack, urged to maintain her confessions.

—Said that it was true that she is a witch. Asked how long she has been in subjugation to the devil.

—Answers that it was twenty years ago that the devil appeared to her, being in her lodgings in the form of a man dressed in a little cow-hide and black breeches. . . .

Verdict

July 9, 1652. In the light of the interrogations, answers and investigations made into the charge against Suzanne Gaudry . . . seeing by her own confessions that she is said to have made a pact with the devil, received the mark from him . . . and that following this, she had renounced God, Lent, and baptism and had let herself be known carnally by him. . . . Also, seeing that she is said to have been a part of nocturnal carols and dances.

For expiation of which the advice of the undersigned is that the office of Rieux can legitimately condemn the aforesaid Suzanne Gaudry to death, tying her to a gallows, and strangling her to death, then burning her body and burying it here in the environs of the woods.

 Why were women, particularly older women, especially vulnerable to accusations of witchcraft? What "proofs" are offered here that Suzanne Gaudry had consorted with the devil? What does this account tell us about the spread of witchcraft accusations in the seventeenth century?

Source: A. C. Kors and E. Peters, eds., *Witchcraft in Europe, 1100–1700: A Documentary History* (Philadelphia: University of Pennsylvania Press, 1972).

in turmoil, in explaining the witchcraft hysteria. At a time when the old communal values that stressed working together for the good of the community were disintegrating before the onslaught of a new economic ethic that emphasized looking out for oneself, property owners became more fearful of the growing numbers of poor in their midst and transformed them psychologically into agents of the devil. Old women were particularly susceptible to suspicion. Many of them, no longer the recipients of the local charity available in traditional society, may even have tried to survive by selling herbs, potions, or secret remedies for healing. When problems arose—and

there were many in this crisis-laden period—these people were handy scapegoats. Of special concern was the fear that witches harmed mothers and their households or caused male impotence and thus disrupted the social order.

That women were most often the victims of the witch-hunt has led some scholars to argue that the witch hunt was really a woman hunt or "genderized mass murder," arguing that men hunted witches because they caused disorder and were sexual beings in a patriarchal society. Other scholars have rejected this approach and argue first, that men were also accused of witchcraft, and second, that women accused other women of witchcraft. These scholars believe that people in the sixteenth and seventeenth century believed in witchcraft as a constant threat in their society.

Despite scholarly differences about the nature of the witch hunts, there is no doubt that women were the primary victims. Current estimates are that there were 100,000 to 110,000 witch trials between 1450 and 1750 with about 50 percent of the trials leading to executions. Of those executed, 75 to 80 percent were women, many of them older women. A study of the Würzburg, Germany, witch trials reveals that of the 255 executed, 190 were women, 140 were women over forty, and 112 were over fifty.

That women should be the chief victims of witchcraft trials was hardly accidental. Nicholas Rémy, a witchcraft judge in France in the 1590s, found it "not unreasonable that this scum of humanity [witches] should be drawn chiefly from the feminine sex." To another judge, it came as no surprise that witches would confess to sexual experiences with Satan: "The Devil uses them so, because he knows that women love carnal pleasures, and he means to bind them to his allegiance by such agreeable provocations."[2] Of course, witch hunters were not the only ones who held women in such low esteem. Most theologians, lawyers, and philosophers in early modern Europe believed in the natural inferiority of women and thus would have found it plausible that women would be more susceptible to witchcraft.

DECLINE By the mid-seventeenth century, the witchcraft hysteria began to subside. The destruction caused by the religious wars had forced people to accept at least a grudging toleration, tempering religious passions. Moreover, as governments began to stabilize after the period of crisis, fewer magistrates were willing to accept the unsettling and divisive conditions generated by the trials of witches. Finally, by the turn of the eighteenth century, more and more educated people were questioning traditional attitudes toward religion and finding it contrary to reason to believe in the old view of a world haunted by evil spirits.

The Thirty Years' War

Although many Europeans responded to the upheavals of the second half of the sixteenth century with a desire for peace and order, the first fifty years of the seventeenth century continued to be plagued by crises. A devastating war that affected much of Europe and rebellions seemingly everywhere protracted the atmosphere of disorder and violence.

BACKGROUND TO THE WAR Religion, especially the struggle between Catholicism and Calvinism, played an important role in the outbreak of the Thirty Years' War (1618–1648), often called the "last of the religious wars." As the war progressed, however, it became increasingly clear that secular, dynastic-nationalist considerations were far more important. Although much of the fighting during the Thirty Years' War took place in the Germanic lands of the Holy Roman Empire, it became a Europe-wide struggle (see Map 15.1). In fact, some historians view it as part of a larger conflict for European leadership between the Bourbon dynasty of France and the Habsburg

dynasties of Spain and the Holy Roman Empire and date it from 1609 to 1659.

The Peace of Augsburg in 1555 had brought an end to religious warfare between German Catholics and Lutherans. Religion, however, continued to play a divisive role in German life as Lutherans and Catholics persisted in vying for control of various principalities. In addition, although the treaty had not recognized the rights of Calvinists, a number of German states had adopted Calvinism as their state church. At the beginning of the seventeenth century, the Calvinist ruler of the Palatinate (puh-LAT-uh-nuht *or* puh-LAT-uh-nayt), the Elector Palatine (PAL-uh-tyn) Frederick IV, assumed the leadership in forming a league of German Protestant states called the Protestant Union. To counteract it, Duke Maximilian of the south German state of Bavaria organized the Catholic League of German states. By 1609, then, Germany was dividing into two armed camps in anticipation of religious war.

A constitutional issue exacerbated the religious division. The desire of the Habsburg emperors to consolidate their authority in the Holy Roman Empire was resisted by the princes, who fought for their "German liberties," their constitutional rights and prerogatives as individual rulers. To pursue their policies, the Habsburg emperors looked to Spain (ruled by another branch of the family) for assistance while the princes turned to the enemies of Spain, especially France, for help against the emperors. The divisions in the Holy Roman Empire and Europe made it almost inevitable that if war did erupt, it would be widespread and difficult to stop.

THE BOHEMIAN PHASE Historians have traditionally divided the Thirty Years' War into four major phases. The Bohemian phase (1618–1625) began in one of the Habsburgs' own territories. In 1617, the Bohemian Estates (primarily the nobles) accepted the Habsburg Archduke Ferdinand as their king but soon found themselves unhappy with their choice. Though many of the nobles were Calvinists, Ferdinand was a devout Catholic who began a process of re-Catholicizing Bohemia and strengthening royal power. The Protestant nobles rebelled against Ferdinand in May 1618 and proclaimed their resistance by throwing two of the Habsburg governors and a secretary out of a window in the royal castle in Prague, the seat of Bohemian government. The Catholic side claimed that their seemingly miraculous escape from death in the 70-foot fall from the castle was due to the intercession of the Virgin Mary, while Protestants pointed out that they fell into a manure pile. The Bohemian rebels now seized control of Bohemia, deposed Ferdinand, and elected as his replacement the Protestant ruler of the Palatinate, Elector Frederick V, who was also the head of the Protestant Union.

Ferdinand, who in the meantime had been elected Holy Roman Emperor, refused to accept his deposition. Realizing that the election of Frederick V, if allowed to stand, could upset the balance of religious and political power in central Europe and give the Protestant forces greater control of the Holy Roman Empire, Ferdinand sought the aid of the imposing forces of Duke Maximilian of Bavaria and the Catholic League. With

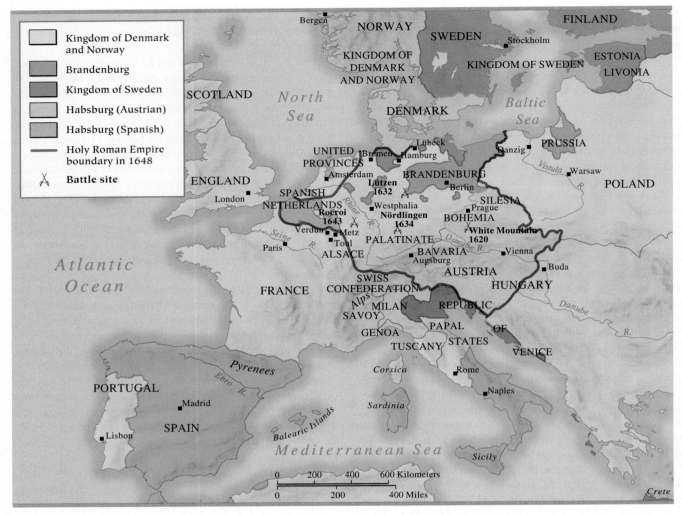

MAP 15.1 The Thirty Years' War. The conflict began in the German states as Europe's major powers backed either the northern Protestant Union or the southern Catholic League. As the war progressed, religion receded in importance, replaced by a dynastic struggle between the French Bourbons and the Spanish and Austrian Habsburgs.

Q *Compare this map with Map 13.2. Which countries engaged in the war were predominantly Protestant, which were predominantly Catholic, and which were mixed?*

their help, the imperial forces defeated Frederick and the Bohemian nobles at the Battle of White Mountain outside Prague on November 8, 1620. Spanish troops took advantage of Frederick's predicament by invading the Palatinate and conquering it by the end of 1622. The unfortunate Frederick fled into exile in the United Provinces. Reestablished as king of Bohemia, Emperor Ferdinand declared Bohemia a hereditary Habsburg possession, confiscated the land of the Protestant nobles, and established Catholicism as the sole religion. The Spanish renewed their attack on the Dutch, and the forces of Catholicism seemed on the road to victory. But the war was far from over.

THE DANISH PHASE The second phase of the war, the Danish phase (1625–1629), began when King Christian IV of Denmark (1588–1648), a Lutheran, intervened on behalf of the Protestant cause by leading an army into northern Germany. Christian had made an anti-Habsburg and anti-Catholic alliance with

the United Provinces and England. He also wanted, however, to gain possession of some Catholic territories in northern Germany to benefit his family.

In the meantime, Ferdinand had gained a new commander for the imperial forces in Albrecht von Wallenstein (AWL-brekht fun VAHL-en-shtyn). A brilliant and enigmatic commander, Wallenstein was a Bohemian nobleman who had taken advantage of Ferdinand's victory to become the country's wealthiest landowner. Wallenstein's forces defeated a Protestant army at Dessau and then continued to operate in northern Germany. The forces of Christian IV, despite substantial aid from their allies, were defeated in 1626 by an army of the Catholic League under Count Tilly and then suffered an even more devastating loss to Wallenstein's forces the following year. Wallenstein now occupied parts of northern Germany, including the Baltic ports of Hamburg, Lübeck, and Bremen. Christian IV's defeat meant the end of Danish supremacy in the Baltic.

The Thirty Years' War: Soldiers Plundering a Farm. This 1620 painting shows a group of soldiers running amok and plundering a farm. This scene was typical of many that occurred during the Thirty Years' War, especially in Germany, where the war caused enormous destruction.

After the success of the imperial armies, Emperor Ferdinand II was at the height of his power and took this opportunity to issue the Edict of Restitution in March 1629. His proclamation prohibited Calvinist worship and restored all property taken by Protestant princes or cities during the past seventy-five years to the Catholic Church. But this sudden growth in the power of the Habsburg emperor frightened many German princes, who feared for their independent status and reacted by forcing the emperor to dismiss Wallenstein.

THE SWEDISH PHASE The Swedish phase (1630–1635) marked the entry of Gustavus Adolphus (goo-STAY-vus uh-DAHL-fuss), king of Sweden (1611–1632), into the war. Gustavus Adolphus was responsible for reviving Sweden and transforming it into a great Baltic power. A military genius, he brought a disciplined and well-equipped Swedish army to northern Germany. He was also a devout Lutheran who felt compelled to aid his coreligionists in Germany.

Gustavus's army swept the imperial forces out of the north and moved into the heart of Germany. In desperation, the imperial side recalled Wallenstein, who was given command of the imperial army that met Gustavus's troops near Leipzig.

At the Battle of Lützen (LOOT-sun) in 1632, the Swedish forces prevailed but paid a high price for the victory when the Swedish king was killed in the battle. Although the Swedish forces remained in Germany, they proved much less effective. Despite the loss of Wallenstein, who was assassinated in 1634 on the orders of Emperor Ferdinand, the imperial army decisively defeated the Swedes at the Battle of Nördlingen at the end of 1634 and drove them out of southern Germany. This imperial victory guaranteed that southern Germany would remain Catholic. The emperor used this opportunity to make peace with the German princes by agreeing to annul the Edict of Restitution of 1629. But peace failed to come to war-weary Germany. The Swedes wished to continue, while the French, under the direction of Cardinal Richelieu (REESH-uh-lyoo), the chief minister of King Louis XIII, entered the war directly, beginning the fourth and final phase of the war, the Franco-Swedish phase (1635–1648).

THE FRANCO-SWEDISH PHASE By this time, religious issues were losing their significance. The Catholic French were now supporting the Protestant Swedes against the Catholic Habsburgs of Germany and Spain. The Battle of Rocroi (roh-KRWAH) in 1643 proved decisive as the French beat the Spanish and brought an end to Spanish military greatness. The French then moved on to victories over the imperialist-Bavarian armies in southern Germany. By this time, all parties were ready for peace, and after five years of protracted negotiations, the Peace of Westphalia in 1648 officially ended the war in Germany. The war between France and Spain, however, continued until the Peace of the Pyrenees in 1659. By that time, Spain had become a second-class power, and France had emerged as the dominant nation in Europe.

OUTCOMES OF THE WAR What were the results of what one historian has called a "basically meaningless conflict"? The Peace of Westphalia ensured that all German states, including the Calvinist ones, were free to determine their own religion. Territorially, France gained parts of western Germany, part of Alsace, and the three cities of Metz, Toul, and Verdun, giving the French control of the Franco-German border area. While Sweden and the German states of Brandenburg and Bavaria gained some territory in Germany, the Austrian Habsburgs did not really lose any but did see their authority as rulers of Germany further diminished. The more than three hundred states that made up the Holy Roman Empire were recognized as virtually independent, since each received the power to conduct its own foreign policy. The Habsburg emperor had been reduced to a figurehead in the Holy Roman Empire. The Peace of Westphalia also made it clear that religion and politics were now separate. The pope was completely ignored in all decisions at Westphalia, and political motives became the guiding forces in public affairs as religion moved closer to becoming primarily a matter of personal conviction and individual choice. Some historians also argue that the Peace of Westphalia marks the beginning of a modern international order in which sovereign states began to operate as equals within a secular framework.

The economic and social effects of the Thirty Years' War on Germany are still debated. Some areas of Germany were completely devastated, but others remained relatively untouched and even experienced economic growth. The most recent work pictures a damaged economy and a population decline of 15 to 20 percent in the Holy Roman Empire. Although historians may debate the degree of devastation, many people in Germany would have understood this description by a traveler journeying along the Main River in 1636:

> [We] came to a wretched little village called Neukirchen, which we found quite uninhabited yet with one house on fire. Here, since it was now late, we were obliged to stay all night, for the nearest town was four miles away; but we spent that night walking up and down with guns in our hands, and listening fearfully to the sound of shots in the woods around us. . . . Early next morning, His Excellency went to inspect the church and found it had been plundered and that the pictures and the altar had been desecrated. In the churchyard we saw a dead body, scraped out of the grave, while outside the churchyard we found another dead body.[3]

The Thirty Years' War was undoubtedly the most destructive conflict Europeans had yet experienced (see the box on p. 439).

HISTORIANS DEBATE ## Was There a Military Revolution?

By the seventeenth century, war played an increasingly important role in European affairs. Military power was considered essential to a ruler's reputation and power; thus, the pressure to build an effective military machine was intense. Some historians believe that the changes that occurred in the science of warfare between 1560 and 1660 warrant the title of military revolution.

Medieval warfare, with its mounted knights and supplementary archers, had been transformed in the Renaissance by the employment of infantry armed with pikes and halberds (long-handled weapons combining an axe with a spike) and arranged in massed rectangles known as squadrons or battalions. The use of firearms required adjustments to the size and shape of the massed infantry and made the cavalry less effective.

It was Gustavus Adolphus, the king of Sweden, who developed the first standing army of conscripts, notable for the flexibility of its tactics. The infantry brigades of Gustavus's army were composed of equal numbers of musketeers and pikemen, standing six men deep. They employed the salvo, in which all rows of the infantry fired at once instead of row by row. These salvos of fire, which cut up the massed ranks of the opposing infantry squadrons, were followed by a pike charge, giving the infantry a primarily offensive deployment. Gustavus also used his cavalry in a more mobile fashion. After shooting a pistol volley, they charged the enemy with their swords. Additional flexibility was obtained by using lighter artillery pieces that were more easily moved during battle. All of these changes required coordination, careful training, and better discipline, forcing rulers to move away from undisciplined mercenary forces. Naturally, the success of Gustavus Adolphus led to imitation.

AFTER GUSTAVUS ADOLPHUS entered the war, he was finally joined by German Protestant forces after the fall of the Protestant city of Magdeburg to the imperial forces. In this excerpt, a writer of this period gives a vivid description of what happened to Magdeburg and its inhabitants.

An Account of the Destruction of Magdeburg

Thus it came about that the city and all its inhabitants fell into the hands of the enemy, whose violence and cruelty were due in part to their common hatred of the adherents of the Augsburg Confession [Lutherans], and in part to their being embittered by the chain shot which had been fired at them and by the derision and insults that the Magdeburgers had heaped upon them from the ramparts.

Then was there naught but beating and burning, plundering, torture, and murder. Most especially was every one of the enemy bent on securing much booty. When a marauding party entered a house, if its master had anything to give he might thereby purchase respite and protection for himself and his family till the next man, who also wanted something should come along. It was only when everything had been brought forth and there was nothing left to give that the real trouble commenced. Then, what with blows and threats of shooting, stabbing, and hanging, the poor people were so terrified that if they had had anything left they would have brought it forth if it had been buried in the earth or hidden away in a thousand castles. In this frenzied rage, the great and splendid city that had stood like a fair princess in the land was now, in its hour of direct need and unutterable distress and woe, given over to the flames, and thousands of innocent men, women, and children, in the midst of a horrible din of heartrending shrieks and cries, were tortured and put to death in so cruel and shameful a manner that no words would suffice to describe, nor no tears to bewail it . . .

Thus, in a single day this noble and famous city, the pride of the whole country, went up in fire and smoke; and the remnant of its citizens, with their wives and children, were taken prisoner and driven away by the enemy with a noise of weeping and wailing that could be heard from afar, while the cinders and ashes from the town were carried by the wind to . . . distant places . . .

In addition to all this, quantities of sumptuous and irreplaceable house furnishings and movable property of all kinds, such as books, manuscripts, paintings, memorials of all sorts . . . which money could not buy, were either burned or carried away by the soldiers as booty. The most magnificent garments, hangings, silk stuffs, gold and silver lace, linen of all sorts, and other household goods were bought by the army soldiers for a mere song and peddled about by the cart load all throughout the archbishopric of Magdeburg. . . . Gold chains and rings, jewels, and every kind of gold and silver utensils were to be bought from the common soldiers for a tenth of their real value . . .

 What does this document reveal about the effect of war on ordinary Europeans? Compare this description with the descriptions of the treatment of civilians in other wars. Does this author exaggerate, or is this description similar to the others?

Source: J. H. Robinson, *Readings in European History*, vol. 2 (Boston: Ginn & Company, 1906), pp. 211–212.

Some historians have questioned the use of the phrase "military revolution" to describe the military changes from 1560 to 1660, arguing instead that military developments were gradual. In any case, for the rest of the seventeenth century, warfare continued to change. Standing armies, based partly on conscription, grew ever larger and more expensive. Standing armies necessitated better-disciplined and better-trained soldiers and led to the education of officers in military schools. Armies also introduced the use of linear rather than square formations to provide greater flexibility and mobility in tactics. There was also an increased use of firearms as the musket with attached bayonet increasingly replaced the pike in the ranks of the infantry. A naval arms race in the seventeenth century led to more and bigger warships or capital ships known as "ships of the line." By the end of the seventeenth century, most of these had two or three decks and were capable of carrying between fifty and one hundred heavy cannon.

Larger armies and navies could be maintained only by levying heavier taxes, making war a greater economic burden and an ever more important part of the early modern European state. The creation of large bureaucracies to supervise the military resources of the state led to growth in the power of state governments.

Rebellions

Before, during, and after the Thirty Years' War, a series of rebellions and civil wars stemming from the discontent of both nobles and commoners rocked the domestic stability of many European governments. To increase their power, monarchs attempted to extend their authority at the expense of traditional powerful elements who resisted the rulers' efforts. At the same time, to fight their battles, governments increased taxes and created such hardships that common people also rose in opposition.

Between 1590 and 1640, peasant and lower-class revolts erupted in central and southern France, Austria, and Hungary. In the decades of the 1640s and 1650s, even greater unrest occurred. Portugal and Catalonia rebelled against the Spanish government in 1640. The common people in Naples and Sicily revolted against both the government and the landed nobility in 1647. Russia, too, was rocked by urban uprisings in 1641,

1645, and 1648. Nobles rebelled in France from 1648 to 1652 in an effort to halt the growth of royal power. The northern states of Sweden, Denmark, and the United Provinces were not immune from upheavals involving clergy, nobles, and mercantile groups. The most famous and widest-ranging struggle, however, was the civil war and rebellion in England, commonly known as the English Revolution (discussed later in this chapter).

The Practice of Absolutism: Western Europe

 FOCUS QUESTION: What was absolutism in theory, and how did its actual practice in France reflect or differ from the theory?

Absolute monarchy or **absolutism** meant that the sovereign power or ultimate authority in the state rested in the hands of a king who claimed to rule by divine right. But what did sovereignty mean? The late-sixteenth-century political theorist Jean Bodin (ZHAHN boh-DAN) believed that sovereign power consisted of the authority to make laws, tax, administer justice, control the state's administrative system, and determine foreign policy. These powers made a ruler sovereign.

One of the chief theorists of **divine-right monarchy** in the seventeenth century was the French theologian and court preacher Bishop Jacques Bossuet (ZHAHK baw-SWAY) (1627–1704), who expressed his ideas in a book titled *Politics Drawn from the Very Words of Holy Scripture*. Bossuet argued first that government was divinely ordained so that humans could live in an organized society. God established kings and through them reigned over all the peoples of the world. Since kings received their power from God, their authority was absolute. They were responsible to no one (including parliaments) except God. For Bossuet, though, his last point was especially important. Because God would hold a king accountable for his actions, Bossuet believed that kings faced serious responsibilities as well as real limits on their power. There was also a large gulf between the theory of absolutism as expressed by Bossuet and the practice of absolutism. A monarch's absolute power was often limited greatly by practical realities.

Absolute Monarchy in France

France during the reign of Louis XIV (1643–1715) has traditionally been regarded as the best example of the practice of absolute monarchy in the seventeenth century. French culture, language, and manners influenced all levels of European society. French diplomacy and wars shaped the political affairs of western and central Europe. The court of Louis XIV seemed to be imitated everywhere in Europe. Of course, the stability of Louis's reign was magnified by the instability that had preceded it.

FOUNDATIONS OF FRENCH ABSOLUTISM: CARDINAL RICHELIEU In the half century before Louis XIV came to power, royal and ministerial governments struggled to avoid the breakdown of the French state. The line between order

and anarchy was often a narrow one. The situation was complicated by the fact that both Louis XIII (1610–1643) and Louis XIV were only boys when they succeeded to the throne in 1610 and 1643, respectively, leaving the government dependent on royal ministers. Two especially competent ministers played crucial roles in maintaining monarchical authority.

Cardinal Richelieu, Louis XIII's chief minister from 1624 to 1642, initiated policies that eventually strengthened the power of the monarchy. By eliminating the political and military rights of the Huguenots while preserving their religious privileges, Richelieu transformed the Huguenots into more reliable subjects. Richelieu acted more cautiously in "humbling the pride of the great men," the important French nobility. He understood the influential role played by the nobles in the French state. The dangerous ones were those who asserted their territorial independence when they were excluded from participating in the central government. Proceeding slowly but determinedly, Richelieu developed an efficient network of spies to uncover noble plots and then crushed the conspiracies and executed the conspirators, thereby eliminating a major threat to royal authority.

Cardinal Richelieu. A key figure in the emergence of a strong monarchy in France was Cardinal Richelieu, pictured here in a portrait by Philippe de Champaigne. Chief minister to Louis XIII, Richelieu strengthened royal authority by eliminating the private armies and fortified cities of the Huguenots and by crushing aristocratic conspiracies.

Hulton Archive/Stringer/Getty Images

To reform and strengthen the central administration, initially for financial reasons, Richelieu sent out royal officials called **intendants** (anh-tahnh-DAHNHZ *or* in-TEN-dunts) to the provinces to execute the orders of the central government. As the functions of the intendants grew, they came into conflict with provincial governors. Since the intendants were victorious in most of these disputes, they further strengthened the power of the crown. Richelieu proved less capable in financial matters, however. Not only was the basic system of state finances corrupt, but so many people benefited from the system's inefficiency and injustice that the government faced strong resistance when it tried to institute reforms. The *taille* (TY) (an annual direct tax usually levied on land or property) was increased—in 1643 it was two and a half times what it had been in 1610. Richelieu's foreign policy goal of confronting the growing power of the Habsburgs in the Thirty Years' War, however, led to ever-increasing expenditures, which soon outstripped the additional revenues. French debt continued its upward spiral under Richelieu.

CARDINAL MAZARIN Richelieu died in 1642, followed five months later by King Louis XIII, who was succeeded by his son Louis XIV, then but four years old. This necessitated a regency under Anne of Austria, the mother of Louis XIV. But she allowed Cardinal Mazarin (maz-uh-RANH), Richelieu's trained successor, to dominate the government. An Italian who had come to France as a papal legate and then become naturalized, Mazarin attempted to carry on Richelieu's policies until his death in 1661.

The most important event during Mazarin's rule was a revolt of the nobles known as the Fronde (FROHND). As a foreigner, Mazarin was greatly disliked by all elements of the French population. The nobles, who particularly resented the centralized administrative power being built up at the expense of the provincial nobility, temporarily allied with the members of the Parlement (par-luh-MAHNH) of Paris, who opposed the new taxes levied by the government to pay the costs of the Thirty Years' War (Mazarin continued Richelieu's anti-Habsburg policy), and with the people of Paris, who were also angry at the additional taxes. The Parlement of Paris was the most important court in France, with jurisdiction over half of the kingdom, and its members formed the nobles of the robe, the service nobility of lawyers and administrators. These nobles of the robe led the first Fronde (1648–1649), which broke out in Paris and was ended by compromise. The second Fronde, begun in 1650, was led by the nobles of the sword, who were descended from the medieval nobility. They were interested in overthrowing Mazarin for their own purposes: to secure their positions and increase their own power. The second Fronde was crushed by 1652, a task made easier when the nobles began fighting each other instead of Mazarin. With the end of the Fronde, the vast majority of the French concluded that the best hope for stability in France lay in the crown. When Mazarin died in 1661, the greatest of the seventeenth-century monarchs, Louis XIV, took over supreme power.

The Reign of Louis XIV (1643–1715)

The day after Cardinal Mazarin's death, Louis XIV, age twenty-three, expressed his determination to be a real king and the sole ruler of France:

Up to this moment I have been pleased to entrust the government of my affairs to the late Cardinal. It is now time that I govern them myself. You [secretaries and ministers of state] will assist me with your counsels when I ask for them. I request and order you to seal no orders except by my command. . . . I order you not to sign anything, not even a passport . . . without my command; to render account to me personally each day and to favor no one.[4]

His mother, who was well aware of Louis's proclivity for fun and games and getting into the beds of the maids in the royal palace, laughed aloud at these words. But Louis was quite serious.

Louis proved willing to pay the price of being a strong ruler. He established a conscientious routine from which he seldom deviated. Eager for glory (in the French sense of achieving what was expected of one in an important position), Louis created a grand and majestic spectacle at the court of Versailles (vayr-SY). Consequently, Louis and his court came to set the standard for monarchies and aristocracies all over Europe. Just a few decades after the king's death, the great French writer Voltaire dubbed the period from 1661 to 1715 the "Age of Louis XIV," and historians have tended to call it that ever since.

Although Louis may have believed in the theory of absolute monarchy and consciously fostered the myth of himself as the Sun King, the source of light for all of his people (see "Global Perspectives" on p. 442), historians are quick to point out that the realities fell far short of the aspirations. Despite the centralizing efforts of Cardinals Richelieu and Mazarin, seventeenth-century France still possessed a bewildering system of overlapping authorities. Provinces had their own regional courts, their own local Estates (parliaments), their own sets of laws. Members of the high nobility, with their huge estates and clients among the lesser nobility, still exercised much authority. Both towns and provinces possessed privileges and powers seemingly from time immemorial that they would not easily relinquish.

ADMINISTRATION OF THE GOVERNMENT One of the keys to Louis's power was that he was able to restructure the central policy-making machinery of government because it was part of his own court and household. The royal court located outside the city of Paris at Versailles was an elaborate structure that served different purposes: it was the personal household of the king, the location of central governmental machinery, and the place where powerful subjects came to find favors and offices for themselves and their clients as well as the main arena where rival aristocratic factions jostled for power. The greatest danger to Louis's personal rule came from the very high nobles and princes of the blood (the royal princes), who considered it their natural function to assert the policy-making role of royal ministers. Louis eliminated this threat by removing them from the royal council, the chief administrative body of the king and overseer of the central machinery of government, and enticing them to his court, where he could keep them preoccupied with court life and out of politics. Instead of using the high nobility and royal princes, Louis relied on other nobles for his ministers. His ministers were expected to be subservient; Louis said that he had no intention of "sharing my authority with them."

Sun Kings, West and East

AT THE END OF THE SEVENTEENTH CENTURY, two powerful rulers held sway in kingdoms that dominated the affairs of the regions around them. Both rulers saw themselves as favored by divine authority—Louis XIV of France as a divine-right monarch and Kangxi (GANG-zhee) of China as possessing the mandate of Heaven. Thus, both rulers saw themselves not as divine beings but as divinely ordained beings whose job was to govern organized societies. On the left, Louis, who ruled France from 1643 to 1715, is seen in a portrait by Hyacinthe Rigaud (ee-ah-SANT ree-GOH) that captures the king's sense of royal dignity and grandeur. One person at court said of the

king: "Louis XIV's vanity was without limit or restraint." On the right, Kangxi, who ruled China from 1661 to 1722, is seen in a portrait that shows him seated in majesty on his imperial throne. A dedicated ruler, Kangxi once wrote, "One act of negligence may cause sorrow all through the country, and one moment of negligence may result in trouble for hundreds and thousands of generations."

 Although these rulers practiced very different religions, why did they justify their powers in such a similar fashion?

Louis's domination of his ministers and secretaries gave him control of the central policy-making machinery of government and thus authority over the traditional areas of monarchical power: the formulation of foreign policy, the making of war and peace, the assertion of the secular power of the crown against any religious authority, and the ability to levy taxes to

fulfill these functions. Louis had considerably less success with the internal administration of the kingdom, however. The traditional groups and institutions of French society—the nobles, officials, town councils, guilds, and representative Estates in some provinces—were simply too powerful for the king to have direct control over the lives of his subjects. Consequently,

The Palace of Versailles. Louis XIV spent untold sums of money on the construction of a new palace at Versailles. As is evident from this exterior view, the palace was enormous—more than a quarter of a mile long. In addition to being the royal residence, it also housed the members of the king's government and served as home for thousands of French nobles. As the largest royal residence in Europe, Versailles impressed foreigners and became a source of envy for other rulers.

control of the provinces and the people was achieved largely by bribing the individuals responsible for executing the king's policies. Nevertheless, local officials could still obstruct the execution of policies they disliked, indicating clearly that a so-called absolute monarch was not always absolute. A recent study of Louis's relationship with the **parlements**, however, asserts that he was able to exercise both political and economic control over these provincial law courts, which were responsible for registering new laws sent to them by the king.

RELIGIOUS POLICY The maintenance of religious harmony had long been considered an area of monarchical power. The desire to keep it brought Louis into conflict with the French Huguenots. Louis XIV did not want to allow Protestants to practice their faith in largely Catholic France. Perhaps he was motivated by religion, but it is more likely that Louis, who believed in the motto "One king, one law, one faith," felt that the existence of this minority undermined his own political authority. In October 1685, Louis issued the Edict of Fontainebleau (fawnh-ten-BLOH). In addition to revoking the Edict of Nantes, the new edict provided for the destruction of Huguenot churches and the closing of Protestant schools. It is estimated that 200,000 Huguenots defied the prohibition against their leaving France and sought asylum in England, the United Provinces, and the German states. Although it was once believed that this exodus weakened the French economy, others

maintain that an influx of English and Irish political and religious refugees into France offset the loss. Support for the expulsion of the Protestants came from Catholic lay-people, who rejected Protestant legal rights, banned them from government meetings, and destroyed Protestant churches in an effort to regain Catholic control of heavily populated Protestant regions.

FINANCIAL ISSUES The cost of building Versailles and other palaces, maintaining his court, and pursuing his wars made finances a crucial issue for Louis XIV. He was most fortunate in having the services of Jean-Baptiste Colbert (ZHAHNH-bah-TEEST kohl-BAYR) (1619–1683) as controller general of finances. Colbert sought to increase the wealth and power of France through general adherence to mercantilism, which stressed government regulation of economic activities to benefit the state. To decrease the need for imports and increase exports, Colbert founded new luxury industries, such as the royal tapestry works at Beauvais; invited Venetian glass-makers and Flemish clothmakers to France; drew up instructions regulating the quality of goods produced; oversaw the training of workers; and granted special privileges, including tax exemptions, loans, and subsidies, to individuals who established new industries. To improve communications and the transportation of goods internally, he built roads and canals. To decrease imports directly, Colbert raised tariffs on foreign manufactured goods and created a merchant marine to carry French goods.

Although Colbert's policies are given much credit for fostering the development of manufacturing in France, some historians are dubious about the usefulness of many of his mercantilistic policies and question whether Colbert stuck to rigid mercantilistic convictions. Regulations were often evaded, and the imposition of high tariffs brought foreign retaliation. French trading companies entered the scene too late to be really competitive with the English and the Dutch. And above all, Colbert's economic policies, which were geared to making his king more powerful, were ultimately self-defeating. The more revenue Colbert collected to enable the king to make war, the faster Louis depleted the treasury. At the same time, the burden of taxes fell increasingly on the peasants, who still constituted the overwhelming majority of the French population. Nevertheless, some historians argue that although Louis bankrupted the treasury in order to pay for his wars, the economic practices implemented under Colbert, including investment in the shipping and textile industries and improvements in transportation facilities, allowed for greater economic growth in the eighteenth century.

DAILY LIFE AT THE COURT OF VERSAILLES The court of Louis XIV at Versailles set a standard that was soon followed by other European rulers. In 1660, Louis decided to convert a hunting lodge at Versailles, not far from the capital city of Paris, into a chateau. Not until 1688, after untold sums of money had been spent and tens of thousands of workers had labored incessantly, was construction completed on the enormous palace.

Versailles served many purposes. It was the residence of the king, a reception hall for state affairs, an office building for the members of the king's government, and the home of thousands of royal officials and aristocratic courtiers. Versailles also served a practical political purpose. It became home to the high nobility and princes of the blood. By keeping them involved in the myriad activities that made up daily life at the court of Versailles, Louis excluded them from real power while allowing them to share in the mystique of power as companions of the king. Versailles became a symbol for the French absolutist state and the power of the Sun King, Louis XIV. As a visible manifestation of France's superiority and wealth, this lavish court was intended to overawe subjects and impress foreign powers.

Interior of Versailles: The Hall of Mirrors. Pictured here is the exquisite Hall of Mirrors at Versailles. Located on the second floor, the hall overlooks the park below. Three hundred and fifty-seven mirrors were placed on the wall opposite the windows to create an illusion of even greater width. Careful planning went into every detail of the interior decoration. Even the doorknobs were specially designed to reflect the magnificence of Versailles. This photo shows the Hall of Mirrors after the restoration work that was completed in June 2007, a project that took three years, cost 12 million euros (more than $16 million), and included the restoration of the Bohemian crystal chandeliers.

THE KING'S DAY BEGINS

THE DUC DE SAINT-SIMON (1675–1755) WAS ONE of many noble courtiers who lived at Versailles and had firsthand experience of court life there. In his *Memoirs*, he left a controversial and critical account of Louis XIV and his court. In this selection, Saint-Simon describes the scene in Louis's bedroom at the beginning of the day.

Duc de Saint-Simon, *Memoirs*

At eight o'clock the chief valet of the room on duty, who alone had slept in the royal chamber, and who had dressed himself, awoke the King. The chief physician, the chief surgeon, and the nurse (as long as she lived) entered at the same time. The latter kissed the King; the others rubbed and often changed his shirt, because he was in the habit of sweating a great deal. At the quarter, the grand chamberlain was called (or, in his absence, the first gentleman of the chamber), and those who had, what was called the grandes entrées [grand entry]. The chamberlain (or chief gentleman) drew back the curtains which had been closed again, and presented the holy water from the vase, at the head of the bed. These gentlemen stayed but a moment, and that was the time to speak to the King, if any one had anything to ask of him; in which case the rest stood aside. When, contrary to custom, nobody had anything to say, they were there but for a few moments. He who had

opened the curtains and presented the holy water, presented also a prayer-book. Then all passed into the cabinet [a small room] of the council. A very short religious service being over, the King called, they reentered. The same officer gave him his dressing-gown; immediately after, other privileged courtiers entered, and then everybody, in time to find the King putting on his shoes and stockings, for he did almost everything himself and with address and grace. Every other day we saw him shave himself; and he had a little short wig in which he always appeared, even in bed, and on medicine days. . . .

As soon as he was dressed, he prayed to God, at the side of his bed, where all the clergy present knelt, the cardinals without cushions, all the laity remaining standing; and the captain of the guards came to the balustrade during the prayer, after which the king passed into his cabinet.

He found there, or was followed by all who had the entrée, a very numerous company, for it included everybody in any office. He gave orders to each for the day; thus within a half a quarter of an hour it was known what he meant to do; and then all this crowd left directly.

 What were the message and purpose of the royal waking and dressing ceremony for both the nobles and the king? Do you think this account might be biased? Why?

Source: B. St. John, trans., *The Memoirs of the Duke of Saint-Simon on the Reign of Louis XIV and the Regency*, vol. 3, 8th ed. (London: George Allen, 1913), pp. 221–222.

Life at Versailles became a court ceremony with Louis XIV at the center of it all. The king had little privacy; only when he visited his wife or mother or mistress or met with ministers was he free of the noble courtiers who swarmed about the palace. Most daily ceremonies were carefully staged, such as those attending Louis's rising from bed, dining, praying, attending Mass, and going to bed. A mob of nobles aspired to assist the king in carrying out these solemn activities. It was considered a great honor for a noble to be chosen to hand the king his shirt while dressing (see the box above). But why did nobles participate in so many ceremonies, some of which were so obviously demeaning? Active involvement in the activities at Versailles was the king's prerequisite for obtaining the offices, titles, and pensions that only he could grant. This policy reduced great nobles and ecclesiastics, the "people of quality," to a plane of equality, allowing Louis to exercise control over them and prevent them from interfering in the real lines of power. To maintain their social prestige, the "people of quality" were expected to adhere to rigid standards of court etiquette appropriate to their rank.

Indeed, court etiquette became a complex matter. Nobles and royal princes were arranged in an elaborate order of seniority and expected to follow certain rules of precedence. Who could sit down and on what kind of chair was a subject of much debate. When Philip of Orléans, the king's brother, and

his wife Charlotte sought to visit their daughter, the duchess of Lorraine, they encountered problems with Louis. Charlotte explained why in one of her letters:

> The difficulty is that the Duke of Lorraine claims that he is entitled to sit in an armchair in the presence of Philip and myself because the Emperor gives him an armchair. To this the King [Louis] replied that the Emperor's ceremonial is one thing and the King's another, and that, for example, the Emperor gives the cardinals armchairs, whereas here they may never sit at all in the King's presence.[5]

Louis refused to compromise; the duke of Lorraine was only entitled to a stool. The duke balked, and Philip and Charlotte canceled their visit.

Daily life at Versailles also included numerous forms of entertainment. Walks through the gardens, boating trips, performances of tragedies and comedies, ballets, and concerts all provided sources of pleasure. Three evenings a week, from seven to ten, Louis also held an *appartement* (uh-par-tuh-MAHNH) where he was "at home" to his court. The appartement was characterized by a formal informality. Relaxed rules of etiquette even allowed people to sit down in the presence of their superiors. The evening's entertainment began with a concert, followed by games of billiards or cards, and ended with a sumptuous buffet.

THE WARS OF LOUIS XIV Both the increase in royal power that Louis pursued and his desire for military glory led the king to wage war. Under the secretary of war, François-Michel Le Tellier (frahnh-SWAH-mee-SHEL luh tel-YAY), the marquis of Louvois (loo-VWAH), France developed a professional army numbering 100,000 men in peacetime and 400,000 in time of war. Louis made war an almost incessant activity of his reign. To achieve the prestige and military glory befitting the Sun King as well as to ensure the domination of his Bourbon dynasty over European affairs, Louis waged four wars between 1667 and 1713 (see Map 15.2).

In 1667, Louis began his first war by invading the Spanish Netherlands to his north and Franche-Comté to the east. But the Triple Alliance of the Dutch, English, and Swedes forced Louis to sue for peace in 1668 and accept a few towns in the Spanish Netherlands for his efforts. He never forgave the Dutch for arranging the Triple Alliance, and in 1672, after isolating the Dutch, France invaded the United Provinces with some initial success. But the French victories led Brandenburg, Spain, and the Holy Roman Empire to form a new coalition that forced Louis to end the Dutch War by making peace at Nimwegen (NIM-vay-gun) in 1678. While Dutch territory remained intact, France received Franche-Comté from Spain, which served merely to stimulate Louis's appetite for even more land.

This time, Louis moved eastward against the Holy Roman Empire, which he perceived from his previous war as feeble and unable to resist. The gradual annexation of the provinces of Alsace and Lorraine was followed by the occupation of the city of Strasbourg, a move that led to widespread protest and the formation of a new coalition. The creation of this League of Augsburg, consisting of Spain, the Holy Roman Empire, the United Provinces, Sweden, and England, led to Louis's third war, the War of the League of Augsburg (1689–1697). This bitterly contested eight-year struggle brought economic depression and famine to France. The Treaty of Ryswick (RYZ-wik) ending the war forced Louis to give up most of his conquests in the empire, although he was allowed to keep Strasbourg and part of Alsace. The gains were hardly worth the bloodshed and the misery he had caused the French people.

Louis's fourth war, the War of the Spanish Succession (1702–1713), was over bigger stakes, the succession to the Spanish throne. Charles II, the sickly and childless Habsburg ruler,

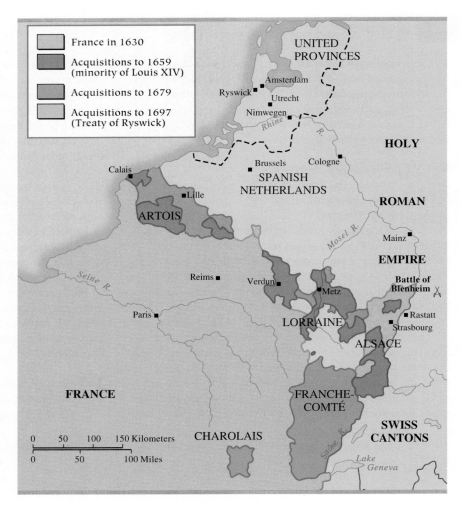

MAP 15.2 The Wars of Louis XIV. The Sun King instigated several wars in his efforts to expand the power of France and the Bourbon dynasty. A coalition of European states met each military thrust, however, so Louis's gains were minimal despite the amount of blood spilled and capital spent.

Q *At the expense of what countries did Louis XIV make most of his territorial acquisitions?*

left the throne of Spain in his will to a grandson of Louis XIV. When the latter became King Philip V of Spain after Charles's death, the suspicion that Spain and France would eventually be united in the same dynastic family caused the formation of a new coalition, determined to prevent a Bourbon hegemony that would mean the certain destruction of the European balance of power. This coalition of England, the United Provinces, Habsburg Austria, and German states opposed France and Spain in a war that dragged on in Europe and the colonial empires in North America for eleven years. In a number of battles, including the memorable defeat of the French forces at Blenheim (BLEN-im) in 1704 by allied troops led by the English commander, John Churchill, duke of Marlborough, the coalition wore down Louis's forces. An end to the war finally came with the Peace of Utrecht in 1713 and of Rastatt in 1714. Although these peace treaties confirmed Philip V as the Spanish ruler, initiating a Spanish Bourbon dynasty that would last into the twentieth century, they also affirmed that the thrones of Spain and France were to remain separated. The Spanish Netherlands, Milan, and Naples were given to Austria, and the emerging state of Brandenburg-Prussia gained additional territories. The real winner at Utrecht, however, was England, which received Gibraltar as well as the French possessions of Newfoundland, Hudson Bay Territory, and Nova Scotia in America. Though France, by its sheer size and position, remained a great power, England had emerged as a formidable naval force.

Only two years after the treaty, the Sun King was dead, leaving France in debt and surrounded by enemies. On his deathbed, the seventy-six-year-old monarch seemed remorseful when he told his successor:

> Soon you will be King of a great kingdom. I urge you not to forget your duty to God; remember that you owe everything to Him. Try to remain at peace with your neighbors. I loved war too much. Do not follow me in that or in overspending. Take advice in everything; try to find the best course and follow it. Lighten your people's burden as soon as possible, and do what I have had the misfortune not to do myself.[6]

Did Louis mean it? Did Louis ever realize how tarnished the glory he had sought had become? Ten years before the end of his reign one of his subjects wrote: "Even the people . . . who have so much loved you, and have placed such trust in you, begin to lose their love, their trust, and even their respect. . . . They believe you have no pity for their sorrows, that you are devoted only to your power and your glory."[7] In any event, the advice to his successor was probably not remembered; his great-grandson was only five years old.

The Decline of Spain

At the beginning of the seventeenth century, Spain possessed the most populous empire in the world, controlling almost all of South America and a number of settlements in Asia and Africa. To most Europeans, Spain still seemed the greatest power of the age, but the reality was quite different. The treasury was empty; Philip II went bankrupt in 1596 from excessive expenditures on war, and his successor, Philip III, did the same in 1607 by spending a fortune on his court. The armed forces were out-of-date, the government was inefficient, and the commercial class was weak in the midst of a suppressed peasantry, a luxury-loving class of nobles, and an oversupply of priests and monks. Spain continued to play the role of a great power, but appearances were deceiving.

During the reign of Philip III (1598–1621), many of Spain's weaknesses became apparent. Interested only in court luxury or miracle-working relics, Philip III allowed his first minister, the greedy duke of Lerma, to run the country. The aristocratic Lerma's primary interest was accumulating power and wealth for himself and his family. As important offices were filled with his relatives, crucial problems went unsolved.

THE REIGN OF PHILIP IV The reign of Philip IV (1621–1665) seemed to offer hope for a revival of Spain's energies, especially

CHRONOLOGY	Absolutism in Western Europe
France	
Louis XIII	1610–1643
Cardinal Richelieu as chief minister	1624–1642
Ministry of Cardinal Mazarin	1642–1661
First Fronde	1648–1649
Second Fronde	1650–1652
Louis XIV	1643–1715
First war (versus Triple Alliance)	1667–1668
Dutch War	1672–1678
Edict of Fontainebleau	1685
War of the League of Augsburg	1689–1697
War of the Spanish Succession	1702–1713
Spain	
Philip III	1598–1621
Philip IV	1621–1665

in the capable hands of his chief minister, Gaspar de Guzman (gahs-PAR day goos-MAHN), the count of Olivares (oh-lee-BAH-rayss). This clever, hardworking, and power-hungry statesman dominated the king's every move and worked to revive the interests of the monarchy. A flurry of domestic reform decrees, aimed at curtailing the power of the Catholic Church and the landed aristocracy, was soon followed by a political reform program whose purpose was to further centralize the government of all Spain and its possessions in monarchical hands. All of these efforts met with little real success, however, because both the number (estimated at one-fifth of the population) and the power of the Spanish aristocrats made them too strong to curtail in any significant fashion.

At the same time, most of the efforts of Olivares and Philip were undermined by their desire to pursue Spain's imperial glory and by a series of internal revolts. Spain's involvement in the Thirty Years' War led to a series of frightfully expensive military campaigns that incited internal revolts and years of civil war. Unfortunately for Spain, the campaigns also failed to produce victory. As Olivares wrote to King Philip IV, "God wants us to make peace; for He is depriving us visibly and absolutely of all the means of war."[8] At the Battle of Rocroi in 1643, much of the Spanish army was destroyed.

The defeats in Europe and the internal revolts of the 1640s ended any illusions about Spain's greatness. The actual extent of Spain's economic difficulties is still debated, but there is no question about its foreign losses. The Peace of Westphalia formally recognized Dutch independence in 1648, and the Peace of the Pyrenees with France in 1659 meant the surrender of Artois and the outlying defenses of the Spanish Netherlands as well as certain border regions that went to France.

Absolutism in Central, Eastern, and Northern Europe

 FOCUS QUESTION: What developments enabled Brandenburg-Prussia, Austria, and Russia to emerge as major powers in the seventeenth century?

During the seventeenth century, a development of great importance for the modern Western world took place in central and eastern Europe, as three new powers made their appearance: Prussia, Austria, and Russia.

The German States

The Peace of Westphalia, which officially ended the Thirty Years' War in 1648, left each of the states in the Holy Roman Empire virtually autonomous and sovereign. Properly speaking, there was no longer a German state but rather more than three hundred little Germanies. Of these, two emerged as great European powers in the seventeenth and eighteenth centuries.

THE RISE OF BRANDENBURG-PRUSSIA The evolution of Brandenburg into a powerful state was largely the work of the Hohenzollern (hoh-en-TSULL-urn) dynasty, which in 1415 had come to rule the insignificant principality in northeastern Germany. In 1609, the Hohenzollerns inherited some lands in the Rhine valley in western Germany; nine years later, they received the duchy of Prussia (East Prussia). By the seventeenth century, then, the dominions of the house of Hohenzollern, now called Brandenburg-Prussia, consisted of three disconnected masses in western, central, and eastern Germany; only the person of the Hohenzollern ruler connected them (see Map 15.3).

Frederick William the Great Elector (1640–1688), who came to power in the midst of the Thirty Years' War, laid the foundation for the Prussian state. Realizing that Brandenburg-Prussia was a small, open territory with no natural frontiers for defense, Frederick William built a competent and efficient standing army. By 1678, he possessed a force of 40,000 men that absorbed more than 50 percent of the state's revenues. To sustain the army and his own power, Frederick William established the General War Commissariat to levy taxes for the army and oversee its growth and training. The Commissariat soon evolved into an agency for civil government as well. Directly responsible to the elector, the new bureaucratic machine became his chief instrument for governing the state. Many of its officials were members of the Prussian landed aristocracy, the Junkers (YOONG-kers), who also served as officers in the all-important army.

The nobles' support for Frederick William's policies derived from the tacit agreement that he made with them. In order to eliminate the power that the members of the nobility could exercise in their provincial Estates-General, Frederick William made a deal with the nobles. In return for a free hand in running the government (in other words, for depriving the provincial Estates of their power), he gave the nobles almost unlimited power over their peasants, exempted the nobles from taxation, and awarded them the highest ranks in the army and the Commissariat with the understanding that they would not challenge his political control. As for the peasants, the nobles were allowed to appropriate their land and bind them to the soil as serfs. Serfdom was not new to Brandenburg-Prussia, but Frederick William reinforced it through his concessions to the nobles.

To build Brandenburg-Prussia's economy, Frederick William followed the fashionable mercantilist policies, constructing roads and canals and using high tariffs, subsidies, and monopolies for manufacturers to stimulate domestic industry. At the same time, however, he continued to favor the interests of the nobility at the expense of the commercial and industrial middle classes in the towns.

Frederick William laid the groundwork for the Prussian state. His son Frederick III (1688–1713) made one further significant

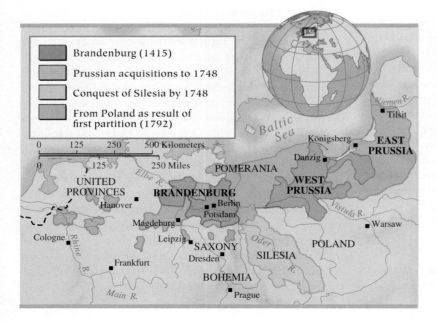

MAP 15.3 The Growth of Brandenburg-Prussia. Frederick William the Great Elector laid the foundation for a powerful state when he increased the size and efficiency of the army, raised taxes and created an efficient bureaucracy to collect them, and gained the support of the landed aristocracy. Later rulers added more territory.

 Why were the acquisitions of Pomerania and West Prussia important for Brandenburg-Prussia's continued rise to power?

contribution: in return for aiding the Holy Roman Emperor, he was officially granted the title of king-in-Prussia. Thus was Elector Frederick III transformed into King Frederick I, ruler of an important new player on the European stage.

THE EMERGENCE OF AUSTRIA The Austrian Habsburgs had long played a significant role in European politics as Holy Roman Emperors, but by the end of the Thirty Years' War, the Habsburg hopes of creating an empire in Germany had been dashed. In the seventeenth century, the house of Austria made an important transition; the German empire was lost, but a new empire was created in eastern and southeastern Europe.

The nucleus of the new Austrian Empire remained the traditional Austrian hereditary possessions: Lower and Upper Austria, Carinthia, Carniola, Styria, and Tyrol (see Map 15.4). To these had been added the kingdom of Bohemia and parts of northwestern Hungary in the sixteenth century.

In the seventeenth century, Leopold I (1658–1705) encouraged the eastward movement of the Austrian Empire, but he was sorely challenged by the revival of Ottoman power. Having moved into Transylvania, the Ottomans eventually pushed westward and laid siege to Vienna in 1683. A European army, led by the Austrians, counterattacked and decisively defeated the Ottomans in 1687. By the Treaty of Karlowitz (KARL-oh-vits) in 1699, Austria took control of Hungary, Transylvania, Croatia, and Slovenia, thus establishing an Austrian Empire in southeastern Europe. At the end of the War of the Spanish Succession,

Austria gained the Spanish Netherlands and received formal recognition of its occupation of the Spanish possessions in Italy, namely, Milan, Mantua, Sardinia, and Naples. By the beginning of the eighteenth century, the house of Austria had acquired an empire of considerable size.

The Austrian monarchy, however, never became a highly centralized, absolutist state, primarily because it included so many different national groups. The Austrian Empire remained a collection of territories held together by a personal union. The Habsburg emperor was archduke of Austria, king of Bohemia, and king of Hungary. Each of these territories had its own laws, Estates-General, and political life. The landed aristocrats throughout the empire were connected by a common bond of service to the house of Habsburg, as military officers or government bureaucrats, but no other common sentiment tied the regions together. Nevertheless, by the beginning of the eighteenth century, Austria was a populous empire in central Europe of great potential military strength.

Italy: From Spanish to Austrian Rule

By 1530, Emperor Charles V had managed to defeat the French armies in Italy and become the arbiter of Italy (see Chapter 13). Initially, he was content to establish close ties with many native Italian rulers and allowed them to rule, provided that they recognized his dominant role. But in 1540, he gave the duchy of Milan to his son Philip II and transferred all imperial rights over Italy to the Spanish monarchy.

MAP 15.4 The Growth of the Austrian Empire. The Habsburgs had hoped to establish a German empire, but the results of the Thirty Years' War crushed that dream. So Austria expanded to the east and the south, primarily at the expense of the Ottoman Empire, and also gained the Spanish Netherlands and former Spanish territories in Italy.

Q *In which areas did the Austrian Empire have access to the Mediterranean Sea, and why would that potentially be important?*

From the beginning of Philip II's reign in 1556 until 1713, the Spanish presence was felt everywhere in Italy. Only Florence, the Papal States, and Venice managed to maintain relatively independent policies. At the same time, the influence of the papacy became oppressive in Italy as the machinery of the Catholic Counter-Reformation—the Inquisition, the Index, and the Jesuits—was used to stifle all resistance to the Catholic orthodoxy created by the Council of Trent (see Chapter 13).

At the beginning of the eighteenth century, Italy suffered further from the struggles between France and Spain. But it was Austria, not France, that benefited the most from the War of the Spanish Succession. By gaining Milan, Mantua, Sardinia, and Naples, Austria supplanted Spain as the dominant power in Italy.

Russia: From Fledgling Principality to Major Power

A new Russian state had emerged in the fifteenth century under the leadership of the principality of Moscow and its grand dukes (see Chapter 12). In the sixteenth century, Ivan IV the Terrible (1533–1584), who was the first ruler to take the title of tsar ("Caesar"), expanded the territories of Russia eastward after finding westward expansion blocked by the powerful Swedish and Polish states. Ivan also extended the autocracy of the tsar by crushing the power of the Russian nobility, known as the **boyars** (boh-YARS). Ivan's dynasty came to an end in 1598 and was followed by a resurgence of aristocratic power in a period of anarchy known as the Time of Troubles. It did not end until the Zemsky Sobor (ZEM-skee suh-BOR), or national assembly, chose Michael Romanov (ROH-muh-nahf) (1613–1645) as the new tsar, beginning a dynasty that lasted until 1917.

In the seventeenth century, Muscovite society was highly stratified. At the top was the tsar, who claimed to be a divinely ordained autocratic ruler. Russian society was dominated by an upper class of landed aristocrats who, in the course of the seventeenth century, managed to bind their peasants to the land. An abundance of land and a shortage of peasants made serfdom desirable to the landowners. Townspeople were also controlled. Many merchants were not allowed to move from their cities without government permission or to sell their businesses to anyone outside their class. In the seventeenth century, merchant and peasant revolts as well as a schism in the Russian Orthodox Church created very unsettled conditions. In the midst of these political and religious upheavals, seventeenth-century Moscow was experiencing more frequent contacts with the West, and Western ideas were beginning to penetrate a few Russian circles. Nevertheless, Russia remained largely outside the framework of the West: the Renaissance, the Reformation, and the geographic discoveries of the sixteenth and seventeenth centuries made little impact on Russia. At the end of the seventeenth century, Peter the Great (1689–1725) noticeably accelerated the westernizing process.

THE REIGN OF PETER THE GREAT (1689–1725) Peter the Great was an unusual character. A strong man, towering 6 feet 9 inches tall, Peter was coarse in his tastes and rude in his behavior. He enjoyed a low kind of humor—belching contests, crude jokes, comical funerals—and vicious punishments including floggings, impalings, roastings, and beard burnings (see the box on p. 451). Peter gained a firsthand view of the West when he made a trip there in 1697–1698 and returned to Russia with a firm determination to westernize or Europeanize his realm. He admired European technology and gadgets and desired to transplant these to Russia. Only this kind of modernization could give him the army and navy he needed to make Russia a great power.

As could be expected, one of Peter's first priorities was the reorganization of the army and the creation of a navy. Employing both Russians and Europeans as officers, he conscripted peasants for twenty-five-year stints of service to build a standing army of 210,000 men. Peter has also been given credit for forming the first Russian navy.

Peter also reorganized the central government, partly along Western lines. In 1711, he created the Senate to supervise the administrative machinery of the state while he was away on military campaigns. In time, the Senate became something like a ruling council, but its ineffectiveness caused Peter to borrow the Western institution of "colleges," or boards of administrators entrusted with specific functions, such as foreign affairs, war, and justice. To impose the rule of the central government more effectively throughout the land, Peter divided Russia into eight provinces and later, in 1719, into fifty. Although he hoped to create a "police state," by which he meant a well-ordered community governed in accordance with law, few of his bureaucrats shared his concept of honest service and duty to the state. Peter hoped for a sense of civic duty, but his own forceful personality created an atmosphere of fear that prevented it. He wrote to one administrator, "According to these orders act, act, act. I won't write more, but you will pay with your head if you interpret orders again."[9]

To further his administrative aims, Peter demanded that all members of the landholding class serve in either military or civil offices. Moreover, in 1722, Peter instituted the Table of Ranks to create opportunities for nonnobles to serve the state and join the nobility. He had all civil offices ranked according to fourteen levels and created a parallel list of fourteen grades for all military offices. Every official was then required to begin at level one and work his way up the ranks. When a nonnoble reached the eighth rank, he acquired noble status. Peter's successors did not continue his attempt to create a new nobility based on merit, however.

To obtain the enormous amount of money needed for an army and navy that absorbed as much as four-fifths of the state revenue, Peter adopted Western mercantilistic policies to stimulate economic growth. He tried to increase exports and develop new industries while exploiting domestic resources like the iron mines in the Urals. But his military needs were endless, and he came to rely on the old expedient of simply raising taxes, imposing additional burdens on the hapless peasants, who were becoming ever more oppressed in Peter's Russia.

Peter also sought to establish state control over the Russian Orthodox Church. In 1721, he abolished the position of patriarch and created a body called the Holy Synod to make decisions for the church. At its head stood a **procurator**, a layman

PETER THE GREAT DEALS WITH A REBELLION

DURING HIS FIRST VISIT TO THE WEST IN 1697–1698, Peter received word that the Streltsy, an elite military unit stationed in Moscow, had revolted against his authority. Peter hurried home and crushed the revolt in a very savage fashion. This selection is taken from an Austrian account of how Peter dealt with the rebels.

Peter and the Streltsy

How sharp was the pain, how great the indignation, to which the tsar's Majesty was mightily moved, when he knew of the rebellion of the Streltsy, betraying openly a mind panting for vengeance! He was still tarrying at Vienna, quite full of the desire of setting out for Italy; but, fervid as was his curiosity of rambling abroad, it was, nevertheless, speedily extinguished on the announcement of the troubles that had broken out in the bowels of his realm. Going immediately to Lefort . . . he thus indignantly broke out: "Tell me, Francis, how I can reach Moscow by the shortest way, in a brief space, so that I may wreak vengeance on this great perfidy of my people, with punishments worthy of their abominable crime. Not one of them shall escape with impunity. Around my royal city, which, with their impious efforts, they planned to destroy, I will have gibbets and gallows set upon the walls and ramparts, and each and every one of them will I put to a direful death." Nor did he long delay the plan for his justly excited wrath; he took the quick post, as his ambassador suggested, and in four weeks'

time he had got over about 300 miles without accident, and arrived the 4th of September, 1698—a monarch for the well disposed, but an avenger for the wicked.

His first anxiety after his arrival was about the rebellion— in what it consisted, what the insurgents meant, who dared to instigate such a crime. And as nobody could answer accurately upon all points, and some pleaded their own ignorance, others the obstinacy of the Streltsy, he began to have suspicions of everybody's loyalty. . . . No day, holy or profane, were the inquisitors idle; every day was deemed fit and lawful for torturing. There was as many scourges as there were accused, and every inquisitor was a butcher. . . . The whole month of October was spent in lacerating the backs of culprits with the knout and with flames; no day were those that were left alive exempt from scourging or scorching; or else they were broken upon the wheel, or driven to the gibbet, or slain with the ax. . . .

To prove to all people how holy and inviolable are those walls of the city which the Streltsy rashly meditated scaling in a sudden assault, beams were run out from all the embrasures in the walls near the gates, in each of which two rebels were hanged. This day beheld about two hundred and fifty die that death. There are few cities fortified with as many palisades as Moscow has given gibbets to her guardian Streltsy.

 How did Peter deal with the revolt of the Streltsy? What does his approach to this problem tell us about the tsar?

Source: J. H. Robinson, *Readings in European History*, vol. 2 (Boston: Ginn & Co., 1906).

---

who represented the interests of the tsar and assured Peter of effective domination of the church.

Shortly after his return from the West in 1698, Peter had begun to introduce Western customs, practices, and manners into Russia. He ordered the preparation of the first Russian book of etiquette to teach Western manners. Among other things, it pointed out that it was not polite to spit on the floor or to scratch oneself at dinner. Because Europeans at that time did not wear beards or traditional long-skirted coats, Russian beards had to be shaved and coats shortened, a reform Peter personally enforced at court by shaving off his nobles' beards and cutting their coats at the knees with his own hands. Outside the court, barbers and tailors planted at town gates enforced the edicts by cutting the beards and cloaks of those who entered or left. Many Russians, as a result, according to one observer, regarded the tsar as a tyrant, "and there were many old Russians who, after having their beards shaved off, saved them preciously, in order to have them placed in their coffins, fearing that they would not be allowed to enter heaven without their beards."[10]

One group of Russians benefited greatly from Peter's cultural reforms—women. Having watched women mixing freely with men in Western courts, Peter shattered the seclusion of

upper-class Russian women and demanded that they remove the traditional veils that covered their faces. Peter also decreed that social gatherings be held three times a week in the large houses of Saint Petersburg where men and women could mix for conversation, card games, and dancing, which Peter had learned in the West. The tsar also now insisted that women could marry of their own free will.

RUSSIA AS A MILITARY POWER The object of Peter's domestic reforms was to make Russia into a great state and a military power. His primary goal was to "open a window to the West," meaning a port easily accessible to Europe. This could only be achieved on the Baltic, but at that time the Baltic coast was controlled by Sweden, the most important power in northern Europe. Desirous of these lands, Peter, with the support of Poland and Denmark, attacked Sweden in the summer of 1700 believing that the young king of Sweden, Charles XII, could easily be defeated. Charles, however, proved to be a brilliant general. He smashed the Danes, flattened the Poles, and with a well-disciplined force of only 8,000 men, routed the Russian army of 40,000 at the Battle of Narva (1700). The Great Northern War (1701–1721) soon ensued.

Peter the Great. Peter the Great wished to westernize Russia, especially in the realm of technical skills. His goal was the creation of a strong army and navy and the acquisition of new territory in order to make Russia a great power. Jean Marc Nattier, a French artist, painted this portrait of the tsar dressed in military armor in 1717.

But Peter fought back. He reorganized his army along western lines and at the Battle of Poltava (pul-TAH-vuh) in 1709 defeated Charles's army decisively. Although the war dragged on for another twelve years, the Peace of Nystadt (NEE-shtaht) in 1721 gave formal recognition to what Peter had already achieved: the acquisition of Estonia, Livonia, and Karelia (see Map 15.5). Sweden had become a second-rate power, and Russia was now the great European state Peter had wanted. And he was building it a fine capital. Early in the war, in the northern marshlands along the Baltic, Peter had begun to construct a new city, Saint Petersburg, his window on the West and a symbol that Russia was looking westward to Europe. Though its construction cost the lives of thousands of peasants, Peter completed the city during his lifetime. It remained the Russian capital until 1917.

Peter modernized and westernized Russia to the extent that it became a great military power and, by his death in 1725, an important member of the European state system. But his policies were also detrimental to Russia. Westernization was a bit of a sham because Western culture reached only the upper classes, and the real object of the reforms, the creation of a strong military, only added more burdens to the masses of the Russian people. The forceful way in which Peter the Great

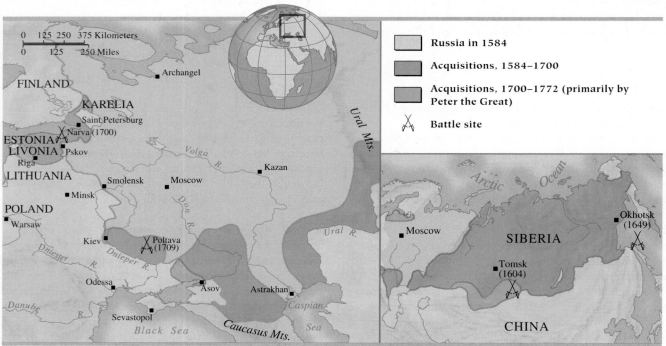

MAP 15.5 Russia: From Principality to Nation-State. Russia had expanded its territory since its emergence in the fifteenth century. Peter the Great modernized the country, instituting administrative and tax reforms and building up the military. He won territory on the Baltic from Sweden, enabling Russia to have a port at Saint Petersburg.

Q *Why would the westward expansion of Russia during Peter's reign affect the international balance of power in Europe?*

imposed westernization led his people to distrust Europe and Western civilization rather than embrace them.

The Great Northern States

As the economic thoroughfare for the products of eastern Europe and the West, the Baltic Sea bestowed special importance on the lands surrounding it. In the sixteenth century, Sweden had broken its ties with Denmark and emerged as an independent state (see Chapter 13). Despite their common Lutheran religion, Denmark's and Sweden's territorial ambitions in northern Europe kept them in almost constant rivalry during the seventeenth century.

DENMARK Under Christian IV (1588–1648), Denmark seemed a likely candidate for expansion, but it met with little success. The system of electing monarchs forced the kings to share their power with the Danish nobility, who exercised strict control over the peasants who worked their lands. Danish ambitions for ruling the Baltic were severely curtailed by the losses they sustained in the Thirty Years' War and later in the so-called Northern War (1655–1660) with Sweden.

Danish military losses led to a constitutional crisis in which a meeting of Denmark's Estates brought to pass a bloodless revolution in 1660. The power of the nobility was curtailed, a hereditary monarchy was reestablished, and a new absolutist constitution was proclaimed in 1665. Under Christian V (1670–1699), a centralized administration was instituted with the nobility as the chief officeholders.

SWEDEN Compared with Denmark, Sweden seemed a relatively poor country, and historians have had difficulty explaining why it played such a large role in European affairs in the seventeenth century. Sweden's economy was weak, and the monarchy was still locked in conflict with the powerful Swedish nobility. During the reign of Gustavus Adolphus (1611–1632), his wise and dedicated chief minister, Axel Oxenstierna (AHK-sul OOK-sen-shur-nah), persuaded the king to adopt a new policy in which the nobility formed a "First Estate" occupying the bureaucratic positions of an expanded central government. This created a stable monarchy and freed the king to raise a formidable army and participate in the Thirty Years' War, only to be killed in battle in 1632.

Sweden entered a period of severe political crisis after the death of Gustavus Adolphus. His daughter Christina (1633–1654) proved to be far more interested in philosophy and religion than ruling. Her tendency to favor the interests of the nobility caused the other estates of the Riksdag (reeks-TAGH), Sweden's parliament—the burghers, clergy, and peasants—to protest. In 1654, tired of ruling and wishing to become a Catholic, which was forbidden in Sweden, Christina abdicated in favor of her cousin, who became King Charles X (1654–1660). His accession to the throne defused a potentially explosive peasant revolt against the nobility.

Charles X reestablished domestic order, but it was his successor, Charles XI (1660–1697), who did the painstaking work of building the Swedish monarchy along the lines of an absolute monarchy. By retaking control of the crown lands and the revenues attached to them from the nobility, Charles managed to weaken the independent power of the nobles. He built up a

Sweden in the Seventeenth Century

bureaucracy, subdued both the Riksdag and the church, improved the army and navy, and left to his son, Charles XII (1697–1718), a well-organized Swedish state that dominated northern Europe. In 1693, he and his heirs were acclaimed as "absolute, sovereign kings, responsible for their actions to no man on earth."

Charles XII was primarily interested in military affairs. Though he was energetic and regarded as a brilliant general, his grandiose plans and strategies, which involved Sweden in conflicts with Poland, Denmark, and Russia, proved to be Sweden's undoing. By the time he died in 1718, Charles XII had lost much of Sweden's northern empire to Russia, and Sweden was no longer a first-class northern power.

The Ottoman Empire

After conquering Constantinople in 1453, the Ottoman Turks tried to complete their conquest of the Balkans, where they had been established since the fourteenth century (see Map 15.6).

Although they were successful in taking the Romanian territory of Wallachia in 1476, the resistance of the Hungarians kept them from advancing up the Danube valley. From 1480 to 1520, internal problems and the need to consolidate their eastern frontiers kept the Turks from any further attacks on Europe. The reign of Sultan Suleiman (SOO-lay-mahn) I the Magnificent (1520–1566), however, brought the Turks back to Europe's attention. Advancing up the Danube, the Turks seized Belgrade in 1521 and Hungary by 1526, although their attempts to conquer Vienna in 1529 were repulsed. At the same time, the Turks extended their power into the western Mediterranean, threatening to turn it into a Turkish lake until the Spanish destroyed a large Turkish fleet at Lepanto (in modern-day Greece) in 1571. Despite the defeat, the Turks continued to hold nominal control over the southern shores of the Mediterranean.

Although Europeans frequently spoke of new Christian Crusades against the "infidel" Turks, by the beginning of the

seventeenth century European rulers seeking alliances and trade concessions were treating the Ottoman Empire like another European power. The Ottoman Empire possessed a highly effective governmental system, especially when it was led by strong sultans or powerful grand viziers (prime ministers). The splendid capital, Constantinople, had a population far larger than that of any European city. Nevertheless, Ottoman politics periodically degenerated into bloody intrigues as factions fought each other for influence and the throne. In one particularly gruesome practice, a ruling sultan would murder his brothers to avoid challenges to his rule. Despite the periodic bouts of civil chaos, a well-trained bureaucracy of civil servants continued to administer state affairs efficiently.

A well-organized military system also added to the strength of the Ottoman Empire. Especially outstanding were the **Janissaries** (JAN-nih-say-reez), composed of Christian boys who had been taken from their parents, converted to the

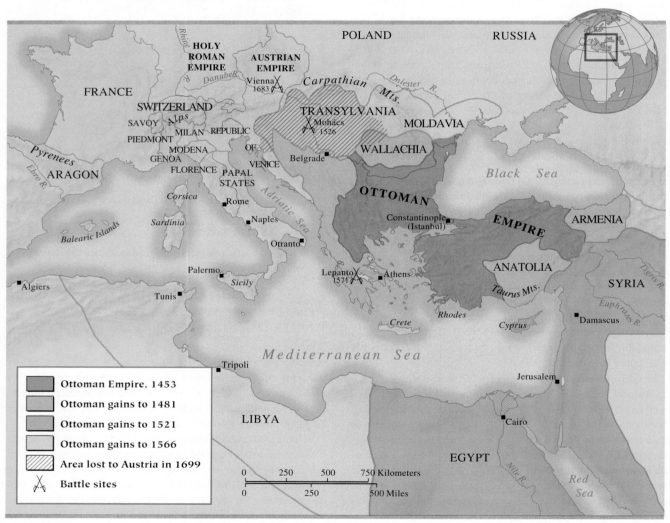

MAP 15.6 The Ottoman Empire. In the sixteenth and seventeenth centuries, the Ottoman Empire possessed an effective bureaucracy and military. During this period, it conquered much of the Balkans and made inroads into eastern Europe; by 1699, however, it had lost the farthest reaches of its European territory and would never again pose a serious threat to Europe.

Q *In what region did the Ottomans make the greatest territorial gains in the sixteenth century?*

Muslim faith, and subjected to rigid military discipline to form an elite core of 8,000 troops personally loyal to the sultan.

In the first half of the seventeenth century, the Ottoman Empire was a "sleeping giant." Occupied by domestic bloodletting and severely threatened by a challenge from Persia, the Ottomans were content with the status quo in eastern Europe. But under a new line of grand viziers in the second half of the seventeenth century, the Ottoman Empire again took the offensive. By 1683, the Ottomans had marched through the Hungarian plain and laid siege to Vienna. Repulsed by a mixed army of Austrians, Poles, Bavarians, and Saxons, the Turks retreated and were pushed out of Hungary by a new European coalition. Although they retained the core of their empire, the Ottoman Turks would never again be a threat to Europe.

The Limits of Absolutism

In recent decades, historical studies of local institutions have challenged the traditional picture of absolute monarchs. We now recognize that their power was far from absolute, and it is misleading to think that they actually controlled the lives of their subjects.

CHRONOLOGY	Absolutism in Central, Eastern, and Northern Europe
Brandenburg Prussia	
Hohenzollerns established in Brandenburg	1415
Hohenzollerns acquire East Prussia	1618
Frederick William the Great Elector	1640–1688
Elector Frederick III (King Frederick I)	1688–1713
Austrian Empire	
Leopold I	1658–1705
Turkish siege of Vienna	1683
Treaty of Karlowitz	1699
Russia	
Ivan IV the Terrible	1533–1584
Time of Troubles	1598–1613
Michael Romanov	1613–1645
Peter the Great	1689–1725
First trip to the West	1697–1698
Great Northern War	1701–1721
Construction of Saint Petersburg begins	1703
Battle of Poltava	1709
Denmark	
Christian IV	1588–1648
Christian V	1670–1699
Sweden	
Gustavus Adolphus	1611–1632
Christina	1633–1654
Charles X	1654–1660
Charles XI	1660–1697
Charles XII	1697–1718

In 1700, government for most people still meant the local institutions that affected their lives: local courts, local tax collectors, and local organizers of armed forces. Kings and ministers might determine policies and issue guidelines, but they still had to function through local agents and had no guarantee that their wishes would be carried out. A mass of urban and provincial privileges, liberties, and exemptions (including from taxation) and a whole host of corporate bodies and interest groups—provincial and national Estates, clerical officials, officeholders who had bought or inherited their positions, and provincial nobles—limited what monarchs could achieve. The most successful rulers were not those who tried to destroy the old system but rather those like Louis XIV, who knew how to use the old system to their advantage. Above all other considerations stood the landholding nobility. Everywhere in the seventeenth century, the landed aristocracy played an important role in the European monarchical system. As military officers, judges, officeholders, and landowners in control of vast, untaxed estates, their power remained immense. In some places, their strength put severe limits on how effectively even absolute monarchs could rule.

Limited Monarchy and Republics

 FOCUS QUESTION: What were the main issues in the struggle between king and Parliament in seventeenth-century England, and how were they resolved?

Almost everywhere in Europe in the seventeenth century, kings and their ministers were in control of central governments that sought to impose order by strengthening their powers. But not all European states followed the pattern of absolute monarchy. In eastern Europe, the Polish aristocracy controlled a virtually powerless king. In western Europe, two great states—the Dutch Republic and England—successfully resisted the power of hereditary monarchs.

The Weakness of the Polish Monarchy

Much of Polish history revolved around the bitter struggle between the crown and the landed nobility. The dynastic union of Jagiello (yahg-YEL-oh), grand prince of Lithuania, with the Polish queen Jadwiga (yahd-VEE-guh) resulted in a large Lithuanian-Polish state in 1386, although it was not until 1569 that a formal merger occurred between the two crowns. The union of Poland and Lithuania under the Jagiello dynasty had created the largest kingdom in Christendom at the beginning of the fifteenth century. As a result, Poland-Lithuania played a major role in eastern Europe in the fifteenth century and also ruled much of Ukraine by the end of the sixteenth century. Poland-Lithuania had a rather unique governmental system in that assemblies of nobles elected the king and carefully limited royal power. The power of the nobles also enabled them to keep the Polish peasantry in a state of serfdom.

In 1572, when the Jagiello dynasty came to an end, a new practice arose of choosing outsiders as kings, with the idea that they would bring in new alliances. When the throne was awarded to the Swede Sigismund III (1587–1631), the new king dreamed of creating a vast Polish empire that would include Russia and possibly Finland and Sweden. Poland not only failed to achieve this goal but by the end of the seventeenth century had become a weak, decentralized state.

It was the elective nature of the Polish monarchy that reduced it to impotence. The Sejm (SAYM), or Polish diet, was a two-chamber assembly in which landowners completely dominated the few townspeople and lawyers who were also members. To be elected to the kingship, prospective monarchs had to agree to share power with the Sejm (in effect with the nobles) in matters of taxation, foreign and military policy, and the appointment of state officials and judges. The power of the Sejm had disastrous results for central monarchical authority, for the real aim of most of its members was to ensure that central authority would not affect their local interests. The acceptance of the liberum veto in 1652, whereby the meetings of the Sejm could be stopped by a single dissenting member, reduced government to virtual chaos.

Poland in the Seventeenth Century

Poland, then, was basically a confederation of semi-independent estates of landed nobles. By the late seventeenth century, it had also become a battleground for foreign powers, who found the nation easy to invade but difficult to rule.

The Golden Age of the Dutch Republic

The seventeenth century has often been called the golden age of the Dutch Republic as the United Provinces held center stage as one of Europe's great powers. Like France and England, the United Provinces was an Atlantic power, underlining the importance of the shift of political and economic power from the Mediterranean basin to the countries on the Atlantic seaboard. As a result of the sixteenth-century revolt of the Netherlands, the seven northern provinces, which began to call themselves the United Provinces of the Netherlands in 1581, became the core of the modern Dutch state. The Peace of Westphalia officially recognized the new state in 1648.

With independence came internal dissension. There were two chief centers of political power in the new state. Each province had an official known as a stadholder (STAD-hohl-dur) who was responsible for leading the army and maintaining order. Beginning with William of Orange and his heirs, the house of Orange occupied the stadholderate in most of the seven provinces and favored the development of a centralized government with themselves as hereditary monarchs. The States General, an assembly of representatives from every province, opposed the Orangist ambitions and advocated a decentralized or republican form of government. For much of the seventeenth century, the republican forces were in control. But in 1672, burdened with war against both France and England, the United Provinces turned to William III (1672–1702) of the house of Orange to establish a monarchical regime. But his death in 1702 without a direct heir enabled the republican forces to gain control once more, although the struggle persisted throughout the eighteenth century.

Underlying Dutch prominence in the seventeenth century was economic prosperity, fueled by the role of the Dutch as carriers of European trade. But warfare proved disastrous to the Dutch Republic. Wars with France and England placed heavy burdens on Dutch finances and manpower. English shipping began to challenge what had been Dutch commercial supremacy, and by 1715, the Dutch were experiencing a serious economic decline.

LIFE IN SEVENTEENTH-CENTURY AMSTERDAM By the beginning of the seventeenth century, Amsterdam had replaced Antwerp as the financial and commercial capital of Europe. In 1570, Amsterdam had 30,000 inhabitants; by 1610, that number had doubled as refugees poured in, especially from the Spanish Netherlands. In 1613, this rapid growth caused the city government to approve an "urban expansion plan" that increased the city's territory from 500 to 1,800 acres through the construction of three large concentric canals. Builders prepared plots for the tall, narrow-fronted houses that were characteristic of the city by hammering wooden columns through the mud to the firm sand underneath. The canals in turn made it possible for merchants and artisans to use the upper stories of their houses as storerooms for their goods. Wares carried by small boats were hoisted to the top windows of these dwellings by block and tackle beams fastened to the gables of the roofs. Amsterdam's physical expansion was soon matched by its population as the city grew to 200,000 by 1660.

The exuberant expansion of Amsterdam in the seventeenth century owed much to the city's role as the commercial and financial center of Europe. But what had made this possible? For one thing, Amsterdam merchants possessed vast fleets of ships, many of which were used for the lucrative North Sea herring catch. Amsterdam-based ships were also important carriers for the products of other countries. The Dutch invention of the *fluyt* (FLYT), a shallow-draft ship of large capacity, enabled them to transport enormous quantities of cereals, timber, and iron.

Amsterdam merchants unloaded their cargoes at Dam Square, and the city soon became a crossroads for the exchange of many of Europe's chief products. Amsterdam was also, of course, the chief port for the Dutch West Indian and East Indian trading companies. Moreover, city industries turned imported raw materials into finished goods, making Amsterdam an important producer of woolen cloth, refined sugar and tobacco products, glass, beer, paper, books, jewelry, and leather goods. Some of the city's great wealth came from war profits: by 1700, Amsterdam was the principal supplier of military goods in Europe; its gun foundries had customers throughout the Continent.

Another factor in Amsterdam's prosperity was its importance as a financial center. Trading profits provided large quantities of capital for investment. The city's financial role was greatly facilitated by the foundation in 1609 of the Exchange Bank of Amsterdam, long the greatest public bank in northern Europe. The city also founded the Amsterdam Stock Exchange for speculating in commodities.

Dutch Domesticity

DURING THE GOLDEN AGE OF THE DUTCH REPUBLIC, Dutch painters delighted in painting scenes of domestic life, especially the lives of the wealthy burghers who prospered from trade, finance, and manufacturing. The Dutch painter Pieter de Hooch (PEE-ter duh HOHKH) specialized in painting pictures of Dutch interiors, as can be seen in three of his paintings. In *The Mother* (below left), de Hooch portrays a tranquil scene of a mother with her infant and small daughter. The spotless, polished floors reflect the sunlight streaming in through the open door. The rooms are clean and in good order. Household manuals, such as The *Experienced and Knowledgeable Hollands Householder,* provided detailed outlines of the cleaning tasks that should be performed each day of the week. In *The Linen Cupboard* (below right), a Dutch mother, assisted by her daughter, is shown storing her clean sheets in an elegant cupboard in another well-polished Dutch room. The Chinese porcelain on top of the cupboard and the antique statue indicate that this is the residence of a wealthy family. In *Two Women Teach a Child to Walk* (at the right), the artist again shows a well-furnished and spotless interior. A small girl is learning to walk, assisted by a servant holding straps attached to a band around the girl's head to keep her from falling.

Erich Lessing/Art Resource, NY

bpk, Berlin/Art Resource, NY

Rijksmuseum, Amsterdam//Alinari/Art Resource, NY

At the very top of Amsterdam's society stood a select number of very prosperous manufacturers, shipyard owners, and merchants whose wealth enabled them to control the city's government. In the first half of the seventeenth century, the Calvinist background of the wealthy Amsterdam burghers led them to adopt a simple lifestyle. They wore dark clothes and lived in substantial but simply furnished houses known for their steep, narrow stairways. The oft-quoted phrase that "cleanliness is next to godliness" was literally true for these self-confident Dutch burghers. Their houses were spotless and orderly (see "Images of Everyday Life" above); foreigners often commented that Dutch housewives always seemed to be scrubbing. But in the second half of the seventeenth century, the wealthy burghers began to reject their Calvinist heritage, a transformation that is especially evident in their more elaborate and colorful clothes.

England and the Emergence of Constitutional Monarchy

One of the most prominent examples of resistance to absolute monarchy came in seventeenth-century England, where king and Parliament struggled to determine the role each should play in governing the nation. But a deep and profound religious controversy complicated the struggle over this political issue. With the victory of Parliament came the foundation for constitutional monarchy by the end of the seventeenth century.

KING JAMES I AND PARLIAMENT Upon the death of Queen Elizabeth in 1603, the Tudor dynasty became extinct, and the Stuart line of rulers was inaugurated with the accession to the throne of Elizabeth's cousin, King James VI of Scotland (son of Mary, queen of Scots), who became James I (1603–1625) of England. Although used to royal power as king of Scotland, James understood little about the laws, institutions, and customs of the English. He espoused the divine right of kings, the belief that kings receive their power directly from God and are responsible to no one except God. This viewpoint alienated Parliament, which had grown accustomed under the Tudors to act on the premise that monarch and Parliament together ruled England as a "balanced polity." Parliament expressed its displeasure with James's claims by refusing his requests for additional monies needed by the king to meet the increased cost of government. Parliament's power of the purse proved to be its trump card in its relationship with the king.

James's religious policy also alienated some members of Parliament. The Puritans—Protestants in the Anglican Church inspired by Calvinist theology—wanted James to eliminate the episcopal system of church organization used in the Church of England (in which the bishop or *episcopos* played the major administrative role) in favor of a Presbyterian model (used in Scotland and patterned after Calvin's church organization in Geneva, where ministers and elders—also called presbyters—played an important governing role). James refused because he realized that the Anglican Church, with its bishops appointed by the crown, was a major support of monarchical authority. But the Puritans were not easily cowed and added to the rising chorus of opposition to the king. Many of England's **gentry**, mostly well-to-do landowners below the level of the nobility, had become Puritans, and these Puritan gentry not only formed an important and substantial part of the House of Commons, the lower house of Parliament, but also held important positions locally as justices of the peace and sheriffs. It was not wise to alienate them.

CHARLES I AND THE MOVE TOWARD REVOLUTION The conflict that had begun during the reign of James came to a head during the reign of his son, Charles I (1625–1649). In 1628, Parliament passed the Petition of Right, which the king was supposed to accept before being granted any tax revenues. This petition prohibited taxation without Parliament's consent, arbitrary imprisonment, the quartering of soldiers in private houses, and the declaration of martial law in peacetime. Although he initially accepted it, Charles later reneged on the agreement because of its limitations on royal power. In 1629, Charles decided that since he could not work with Parliament,

he would not summon it to meet. From 1629 to 1640, Charles pursued a course of personal rule, which forced him to find ways to collect taxes without the cooperation of Parliament. One expedient was a tax called ship money, a levy on seacoast towns to pay for coastal defense, which was now collected annually by the king's officials throughout England and used to finance other government operations besides defense. This use of ship money aroused opposition from middle-class merchants and landed gentry, who objected to the king's attempts to tax without Parliament's consent.

The king's religious policy also proved disastrous. His marriage to Henrietta Maria, the Catholic sister of King Louis XIII of France, aroused suspicions about the king's own religious inclinations. Even more important, however, the efforts of Charles and William Laud, the archbishop of Canterbury, to introduce more ritual into the Anglican Church struck the Puritans as a return to Catholic popery. Grievances mounted. Charles might have survived unscathed if he could have avoided calling Parliament, which alone could provide a focus for the many cries of discontent throughout the land. But when the king and Archbishop Laud attempted to impose the Anglican Book of Common Prayer on the Scottish Presbyterian Church, the Scots rose up in rebellion against the king. Financially strapped and unable to raise troops to defend against the Scots, the king was forced to call Parliament into session. Eleven years of frustration welled up to create a Parliament determined to deal the king his due.

In its first session, from November 1640 to September 1641, the so-called Long Parliament (because it lasted in one form or another from 1640 to 1660) took a series of steps that placed severe limitations on royal authority. These included the abolition of arbitrary courts; the abolition of taxes that the king had collected without Parliament's consent, such as ship money; and the passage of the revolutionary Triennial Act, which specified that Parliament must meet at least once every three years, with or without the king's consent. By the end of 1641, one group in Parliament was prepared to go no further, but a group of more radical parliamentarians pushed for more change, including the elimination of bishops in the Anglican Church. When the king tried to take advantage of the split by arresting some members of the more radical faction in Parliament, a large group in Parliament led by John Pym and his fellow Puritans decided that the king had gone too far. England slipped into civil war.

CIVIL WAR IN ENGLAND Parliament proved victorious in the first phase of the English Civil War (1642–1646). Most important to Parliament's success was the creation of the New Model Army, which was composed primarily of more extreme Puritans known as the Independents, who believed they were doing battle for the Lord. It is striking to read in the military reports of Oliver Cromwell (1599–1658), one of the group's leaders, such statements as "Sir, this is none other but the hand of God; and to Him alone belongs the glory." We might also attribute some of the credit to Cromwell himself, since his crusaders were well disciplined and trained in the latest military tactics. Supported by the New Model Army, Parliament ended the first phase of the civil war with the capture of King Charles I in 1646.

Civil War in England

A split now occurred in the parliamentary forces. A Presbyterian majority wanted to disband the army and restore Charles I with a Presbyterian state church. The army, composed mostly of the more radical Independents, who opposed an established Presbyterian church, marched on London in 1647 and began negotiations with the king. Charles took advantage of this division to flee and seek help from the Scots. Enraged by the king's treachery, Cromwell and the army engaged in a second civil war (1648) that ended with Cromwell's victory and the capture of the king. This time, Cromwell was determined to achieve a victory for the army's point of view. The Presbyterian members of Parliament were purged, leaving a Rump Parliament of fifty-three members of the House of Commons who then tried and condemned the king on a charge of treason and adjudged that "he, the said Charles Stuart, as a tyrant, traitor, murderer, and public enemy to the good people of this nation, shall be put to death by the severing of his head from his body." On January 30, 1649, Charles was beheaded, a most uncommon act in the seventeenth century. The revolution had triumphed, and the monarchy in England had been destroyed, at least for the moment.

CROMWELL AND NEW GOVERNMENTS After the death of the king, the Rump Parliament abolished the monarchy and the House of Lords and proclaimed England a republic or commonwealth (1649–1653). This was not an easy period for Cromwell. As commander in chief of the army, he had to crush a Catholic uprising in Ireland, which he accomplished with a brutality that earned him the eternal enmity of the Irish people, as well as an uprising in Scotland on behalf of the son of Charles I.

Cromwell also faced opposition at home, especially from more radically minded groups who took advantage of the upheaval in England to push their agendas. The Levellers, for example, advocated such advanced ideas as freedom of speech, religious toleration, and a democratic republic, arguing for the right to vote for all male householders over the age of twenty-one. The Levellers also called for annual Parliaments, women's equality with men, and government programs to care for the poor. As one Leveller said, "The poorest he that is in England has a life to live as the greatest he." To Cromwell, a country gentleman, only people of property had the right to participate in the affairs of state, and he warned in a fit of rage: "I tell you . . . you have no other way to deal with these men but to break them or they will break you; and make void all that work that, with so many years' industry, toil, and pains, you have done . . . I tell you again, you are necessitated to break them."[11] And break them he did; Cromwell smashed the radicals by force. More

Oliver Cromwell. Oliver Cromwell was a dedicated Puritan who helped form the New Model Army and defeat the forces supporting King Charles I. Unable to work with Parliament, he came to rely on military force to rule England. Cromwell is pictured here in 1649, on the eve of his military campaign in Ireland.

than a century would pass before their ideas of democracy and equality became fashionable.

At the same time that Cromwell was dealing with the Levellers, he also found it difficult to work with the Rump Parliament and finally dispersed it by force. As the members of Parliament departed (in April 1653), he shouted after them, "It's you that have forced me to do this. . . . I have sought the Lord night and day that He would slay me rather than put upon me the doing of this work."[12] With the certainty of one who is convinced he is right, Cromwell had destroyed both king and Parliament (see "Opposing Viewpoints" on p. 460).

The army provided a new government when it drew up the Instrument of Government, England's first and only written constitution. Executive power was vested in the Lord Protector (a position held by Cromwell) and legislative power in a reconstituted Parliament. But the new system failed to work. Cromwell found it difficult to work with Parliament, especially when its members debated his authority and advocated once again the creation of a Presbyterian state church. In 1655, Cromwell dissolved Parliament and divided the country into eleven regions, each ruled by a major general who served virtually as a military governor. To meet the cost of military government, Cromwell levied a 10 percent land tax on all former Royalists. Unable to establish a constitutional basis for a working

Oliver Cromwell: Three Perspectives

OLIVER CROMWELL WAS A STRONG LEADER with firm religious convictions. The first selection, taken from a letter written after the defeat of the king's forces at Naseby in 1645, reveals Cromwell's feelings about the reasons for his military victory. The next selection, also by Cromwell, is taken from his comments after his army's massacre of Catholic forces at Drogheda (DRAW ih-duh) in Catholic Ireland. The third selection is by Edmund Ludlow, a general on Cromwell's side who broke with Cromwell after the latter had become Lord Protector. The final selection by Edward Hyde, the first earl of Clarendon, a supporter of King Charles I and later Charles II, presents a royalist view of Cromwell.

Oliver Cromwell on the Victory at Naseby

Sir, this is none other but the hand of God; and to Him alone belongs the glory, wherein none are to share with Him. The general [Fairfax] served you with all faithfulness and honor: and the best commendations I can give him is, that I dare say he attributes all to God, and would rather perish than assume to himself. Which is an honest and a thriving way, and yet as much for bravery may be given to him, in this action, as to a man.

Cromwell on the Massacre at Drogheda

The next day, the other two towers were summoned, in one of which was about six or seven score; but they refused to yield themselves, and we knowing that hunger must compel them, set only good guards to secure them from running away until their stomachs were come down. From one of the said towers, notwithstanding their condition, they killed and wounded some of our men. When they submitted, their officers were knocked on the head, and every tenth man of the soldiers killed, and the rest shipped for the Barbados. The soldiers in the other tower were all spared, as to their lives only, and shipped likewise for the Barbados.

I am persuaded that this is a righteous judgment of God upon these barbarous wretches, who have imbrued their hands in so much innocent blood; and that it will tend to prevent the effusion of blood for the future, which are the satisfactory grounds to such actions, which otherwise cannot but work remorse and regret.

Edmund Ludlow, *Memoirs*

Then I drew near to the council-table, where Cromwell charged me with dispersing treasonable books in Ireland, and with endeavoring to render the officers of the army disaffected, by discoursing to them concerning new models of Government. I acknowledged that I had caused some papers to be dispersed in Ireland, but denied that they justly could be called treasonable. . . .

"You do well," said he, "to reflect on our fears. . . . I now require you to give assurance not to act against the Government." I desired to be excused in that particular, reminding him of the reasons I had formerly given him for my refusal, adding that I was in his power, and that he might use me as he thought fit. "Pray then," said he, "what is it that you would have? May not every man be as good as he will? What can you desire more than you have?" "It were easy," said I, "to tell what we would have." "What is that, I pray?" said he. "That which we fought for," said I, "that the nation might be governed by its own consent." "I am," said he, "as much for a government by consent as any man; but where shall we find that consent? Amongst the Prelatical, Presbyterian, Independent, Anabaptist, or Leveling Parties?" I answered, "Amongst those of all sorts who had acted with fidelity and affection to the public."

Lord Clarendon, *The History of the Rebellion and Civil Wars in England*

He was one of those men . . . whom his very enemies could not condemn without commending him at the same time: for he could never have done half that mischief without great parts of courage, industry, and judgment. He must have had a wonderful understanding in the natures and humors of men, and as great a dexterity in applying them; who, from a private and obscure birth (though of a good family), without interest or estate, alliance or friendship, could raise himself to such a height, and compound and knead such opposite and contradictory tempers, humors, and interests into a consistence, that contributed to his designs, and to their own destruction; whilst himself grew insensibly powerful enough to cut off those by whom he had climbed, in the instant that they projected to demolish their own building. What [a Roman writer] said of Cinna [a Roman politician] may very justly be said of him: he attempted those things which no good man dared have ventured on; and achieved those in which none but a valiant and great man could have succeeded. Without doubt, no man with more wickedness ever attempted any thing, or brought to pass what he desired more wickedly, more in the face and contempt of religion, and moral honesty; yet wickedness as great as his could never have accomplished those trophies, without the assistance of a great spirit, an admirable circumspection and sagacity, and a most magnanimous resolution.

 What motivated Cromwell's political and military actions? What was Edmund Ludlow's criticism of Cromwell, and how did Cromwell respond? In what ways did Edward Hyde see both good and bad features in Cromwell? How do you explain the differences in these three perspectives?

Sources: Oliver Cromwell on the Victory at Naseby and on the Massacre at Drogheda, in T. Carlyle, ed., *The Letters and Speeches of Oliver Cromwell*, vols. 1 and 3 (New York: G.P. Putnam's Sons, 1904); E. Ludlow, *Memoirs*, in C. H. Firth, *The Memoirs of Edmund Ludlow*, vol. 2 (Oxford: Oxford University Press, 1894); Lord Clarendon, *The History of the Rebellion and Civil Wars in England*, vol. 6 (Oxford: Oxford University Press, 1839).

government, Cromwell had resorted to military force to maintain the rule of the Independents, ironically using even more arbitrary policies than those of Charles I.

Oliver Cromwell died in 1658. After floundering for eighteen months, the military establishment decided that arbitrary rule by the army was no longer feasible and reestablished the monarchy in the person of Charles II, the eldest son of Charles I (see Chart 15.1). The restoration of the Stuart monarchy ended England's time of troubles, but it was not long before yet another constitutional crisis arose.

RESTORATION OF THE MONARCHY After eleven years of exile, Charles II (1660–1685) returned to England. As he entered London amid the acclaim of the people, he remarked cynically, "I never knew that I was so popular in England." The restoration of the monarchy and the House of Lords did not mean, however, that the work of the English Revolution was undone. Parliament kept much of the power it had won: its role in government was acknowledged, the necessity for its consent to taxation was accepted, and arbitrary courts were still abolished. Yet Charles continued to push his own ideas, some of which were clearly out of step with many of the English people. A serious religious problem disturbed the tranquility of Charles II's reign. After the restoration of the monarchy, a new Parliament (the Cavalier Parliament) met in 1661 and restored the Anglican Church as the official church of England. In addition, laws were passed to force everyone, particularly Catholics and Puritan Dissenters, to conform to the Anglican Church. Charles, however, was sympathetic to and perhaps even inclined toward Catholicism. Moreover, Charles's brother James, heir to the throne, did not hide the fact that he was a Catholic. Parliament's suspicions were therefore aroused in 1672 when Charles took the audacious step of issuing the Declaration of Indulgence, which suspended the laws that Parliament had passed against Catholics and Puritans. Parliament would have none of it and induced the king to suspend the declaration. Propelled by a strong anti-Catholic sentiment, Parliament then passed the Test Act of 1673, specifying that only Anglicans could hold military and civil offices.

A purported Catholic plot to assassinate King Charles and place his brother James on the throne, though soon exposed as imaginary, inflamed Parliament to attempt to pass a bill that would have barred James from the throne as a professed Catholic. Although these attempts failed, the debate over the bill created two political groupings: the Whigs, who wanted to exclude James and establish a Protestant king with toleration of Dissenters, and the Tories, who supported the king, despite their dislike of James as a Catholic, because they believed that Parliament should not tamper with the lawful succession to the throne. To foil these efforts, Charles dismissed Parliament in 1681, relying on French subsidies to rule alone. When he died in 1685, his Catholic brother came to the throne.

The accession of James II (1685–1688) virtually guaranteed a new constitutional crisis for England. An open and devout Catholic, his attempt to further Catholic interests made religion once more a primary cause of conflict between king and Parliament. Contrary to the Test Act, James named Catholics to high positions in the government, army, navy, and universities.

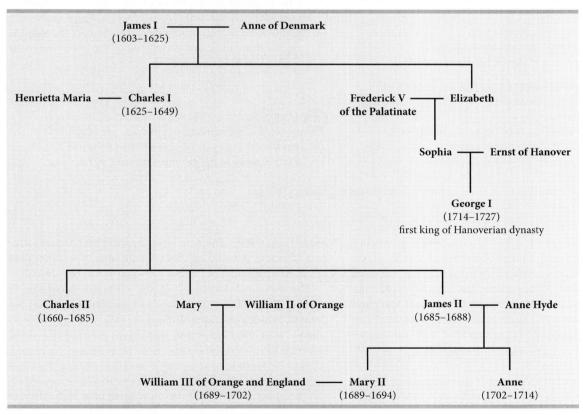

Chart 15.1 A Simplified Look at the Stuart Dynasty

THE BILL OF RIGHTS

IN 1688, THE ENGLISH EXPERIENCED yet another revolution, a bloodless one in which the Stuart king James II was replaced by Mary, James's daughter, and her husband, William of Orange. After William and Mary had assumed power, Parliament passed the Bill of Rights, which specified the rights of Parliament and laid the foundation for a constitutional monarchy.

The Bill of Rights

Whereas the said late King James II having abdicated the government, and the throne being thereby vacant, his Highness the prince of Orange (whom it has pleased Almighty God to make the glorious instrument of delivering this kingdom from popery and arbitrary power) did (by the device of the lords spiritual and temporal, and diverse principal persons of the Commons) cause letters to be written to the lords spiritual and temporal, being Protestants, and other letters to the several counties, cities, universities, boroughs, and Cinque Ports, for the choosing of such persons to represent them, as were of right to be sent to parliament, to meet and sit at Westminster upon the two and twentieth day of January, in this year 1689, in order to such an establishment as that their religion, laws, and liberties might not again be in danger of being subverted; upon which letters elections have been accordingly made.

And thereupon the said lords spiritual and temporal and Commons, pursuant to their respective letters and elections, being now assembled in a full and free representation of this nation, taking into their most serious consideration the best means for attaining the ends aforesaid, do in the first place (as their ancestors in like case have usually done), for the vindication and assertion of their ancient rights and liberties, declare:

1. That the pretended power of suspending laws, or the execution of laws, by regal authority, without consent of parliament is illegal.
2. That the pretended power of dispensing with the laws, or the execution of law by regal authority, as it has been assumed and exercised of late, is illegal.
3. That the commission for erecting the late court of commissioners for ecclesiastical causes, and all other commissions and courts of like nature, are illegal and pernicious.
4. That levying money for or to the use of the crown by pretense of prerogative, without grant of parliament, for longer time or in other manner than the same is or shall be granted, is illegal.
5. That it is the right of the subjects to petition the king, and all commitments and prosecutions for such petitioning are illegal.
6. That the raising or keeping a standing army within the kingdom in time of peace, unless it be with consent of parliament, is against law.
7. That the subjects which are Protestants may have arms for their defense suitable to their conditions, and as allowed by law.
8. That election of members of parliament ought to be free.
9. That the freedom of speech, and debates or proceedings in parliament, ought not to be impeached or questioned in any court or place out of parliament.
10. That excessive bail ought not to be required, nor excessive fines imposed, nor cruel and unusual punishments inflicted.
11. That jurors ought to be duly impaneled and returned, and jurors which pass upon men in trials for high treason ought to be freeholders.
12. That all grants and promises of fines and forfeitures of particular persons before conviction are illegal and void.
13. And that for redress of all grievances, and for the amending, strengthening, and preserving of the laws, parliament ought to be held frequently.

 How did the Bill of Rights lay the foundation for a constitutional monarchy? What key aspects of this document testify to the exceptional nature of English state politics in the seventeenth century?

Source: *The Statutes: Revised Edition*, vol. 2 (London: Eyre and Spottiswoode, 1871), pp. 10–12.

In 1687, he issued a new Declaration of Indulgence, which suspended all laws barring Catholics and Dissenters from office. Parliamentary outcries against James's policies stopped short of rebellion because members knew that he was an old man and that his successors were his Protestant daughters Mary and Anne, born to his first wife. But on June 10, 1688, a son was born to James II's second wife, also a Catholic. Suddenly, the specter of a Catholic hereditary monarchy loomed large.

A GLORIOUS REVOLUTION A group of seven prominent English noblemen invited William of Orange, husband of James's daughter Mary, to invade England. William and Mary raised an army and invaded England while James, his wife, and their infant son fled to France. With almost no bloodshed, England had embarked on a "Glorious Revolution," not over the issue of whether there would be a monarchy but rather over who would be monarch.

The events of late 1688 set the Glorious Revolution in motion. The far more important part was the Revolution Settlement, which confirmed William and Mary as monarchs. In January 1689, the Convention Parliament asserted that James had tried to subvert the constitution "by breaking the original contract between king and people" and declared the throne of England vacant. It then offered the throne to William and Mary, who accepted it along with the provisions of a declaration of rights, later enacted into law as the Bill of Rights in 1689 (see the box above). The Bill of Rights affirmed Parliament's right to make laws and levy taxes and made it impossible for kings to oppose or do without Parliament by stipulating that standing armies could be raised only with the consent of Parliament. Both elections of members and debates in Parliament had to be free, meaning that the king could not interfere. The rights of citizens to petition the sovereign, keep arms, have a jury trial, and not be subject to excessive bail were also confirmed. The Bill of Rights helped fashion a system of government based on the rule of law and a freely elected Parliament, thus laying the foundation for a constitutional monarchy.

The Bill of Rights did not settle the religious questions that had played such a large role in England's troubles in the seventeenth century. The Toleration Act of 1689 granted Puritan Dissenters the right of free public worship (Catholics were still excluded), although they did not yet have full civil and political equality since the Test Act was not repealed. Although the Toleration Act did not mean complete religious freedom and equality, it marked a departure in English history: few people would ever again be persecuted for religious reasons.

Many historians have viewed the Glorious Revolution as the end of the seventeenth-century struggle between king and Parliament. By deposing one king and establishing another, Parliament had demolished the divine-right theory of kingship (William was, after all, king by grace of Parliament, not God) and confirmed its right to participate in the government. Parliament did not have complete control of the government, but it now had an unquestioned role in affairs of state. Over the next century, it would gradually prove to be the real authority in the English system of constitutional monarchy.

RESPONSES TO REVOLUTION The English revolutions of the seventeenth century prompted very different responses from two English political thinkers—Thomas Hobbes and John Locke. Thomas Hobbes (1588–1679), who lived during the English Civil War, was alarmed by the revolutionary upheavals in his contemporary England. Hobbes's name has since been associated with the state's claim to absolute authority over its subjects, a topic that he elaborated in his major treatise on political thought known as the *Leviathan* (luh-VY-uh-thun), published in 1651.

Hobbes claimed that in the state of nature, before society was organized, human life was "solitary, poor, nasty, brutish, and short." Humans were guided not by reason and moral ideals but by animalistic instincts and a ruthless struggle for self-preservation. To save themselves from destroying each other (the "war of every man against every man"), people contracted to form a commonwealth, which Hobbes called "that great Leviathan (or rather, to speak more reverently, that mortal god) to which we owe our peace and defense." This commonwealth placed its collective power into the hands of a sovereign authority, preferably a single ruler, who served as executor, legislator, and judge. This absolute ruler possessed unlimited power. In Hobbes's view, subjects may not rebel; if they do, they must be suppressed.

John Locke (1632–1704) viewed the exercise of political power quite differently from Hobbes and argued against the absolute rule of one man. Locke's experience of English politics during the Glorious Revolution was incorporated into a political work called *Two Treatises of Government*. Like Hobbes, Locke began with the state of nature before human existence became organized socially.

But unlike Hobbes, Locke believed that humans lived then in a state of equality and freedom rather than a state of war. In this state of nature, humans had certain inalienable natural rights—to life, liberty, and property. Like Hobbes, Locke did not believe all was well in the state of nature. Since there was no impartial judge in the state of nature, people found it difficult to protect these rights. So they mutually agreed to establish a government to ensure the protection of their rights. This agreement established mutual obligations: government would protect the rights of the people while the people would act reasonably toward government. But if a government broke this agreement—for example, if a monarch failed to live up to his obligation to protect the people's rights or claimed absolute authority and made laws without the consent of the community—the people might form a new government. For Locke, however, the community of people was primarily the landholding aristocracy who were represented in Parliament, not the landless masses. Locke was hardly an advocate of political democracy, but his ideas proved important to both the Americans and the French in the eighteenth century and were used to support demands for constitutional government, the rule of law, and the protection of rights.

CHRONOLOGY	Limited Monarchy and Republics
Poland	
Merger of Poland and Lithuania	1569
Sigismund III	1587–1631
Beginning of liberum veto	1652
United Provinces	
Official recognition of United Provinces	1648
House of Orange	
William III	1672–1702
England	
James I	1603–1625
Charles I	1625–1649
Petition of Right	1628
First Civil War	1642–1646
Second Civil War	1648
Execution of Charles I	1649
Commonwealth	1649–1653
Death of Cromwell	1658
Restoration of monarchy	1660
Charles II	1660–1685
Cavalier Parliament	1661
Declaration of Indulgence	1672
Test Act	1673
James II	1685–1688
Declaration of Indulgence	1687
Glorious Revolution	1688
Bill of Rights	1689

The Flourishing of European Culture

FOCUS QUESTION: How did the artistic and literary achievements of this era reflect the political and economic developments of the period?

In the midst of religious wars and the growth of absolutism, European culture continued to flourish. The era was blessed with a number of prominent artists and writers.

The Changing Faces of Art

After the Renaissance, European art passed through a number of stylistic stages. The artistic Renaissance came to an end when a new movement called Mannerism emerged in Italy in the 1520s and 1530s.

MANNERISM The Reformation's revival of religious values brought much political turmoil. Especially in Italy, the worldly enthusiasm of the Renaissance gave way to anxiety, uncertainty, suffering, and a yearning for spiritual experience. **Mannerism** reflected this environment in its deliberate attempt to break down the High Renaissance principles of balance, harmony, and moderation (the term *Mannerism* derives from critics who considered their contemporary artists to be second-rate imitators, painting "in the manner of" Michelangelo's late style). Italian Mannerist painters deliberately distorted the rules of proportion by portraying elongated figures that conveyed a sense of suffering and a strong emotional atmosphere filled with anxiety and confusion.

Mannerism spread from Italy to other parts of Europe and perhaps reached its apogee in the work of El Greco (1541–1614). Doménikos Theotocópoulos (called "the Greek"—El Greco) was from Crete, but after studying in Venice and Rome, he moved in the 1570s to Spain, where he became a church painter in Toledo. El Greco's elongated and contorted figures, portrayed in unusual shades of yellow and green against an eerie background of turbulent grays, reflect the artist's desire to create a world of intense emotion.

THE BAROQUE PERIOD A new movement—the **Baroque** (buh-ROHK)—eventually replaced Mannerism. The Baroque began in Italy in the last quarter of the sixteenth century and spread to the rest of Europe, where it was most wholeheartedly embraced by the Catholic reform movement, and especially at the Catholic courts of the Habsburgs in Madrid, Prague, Vienna, and Brussels. Although it was resisted in France, England, and the Netherlands, eventually the Baroque style spread to all of Europe and to Latin America.

Baroque artists sought to bring together the classical ideals of Renaissance art with the spiritual feelings of the sixteenth-century religious revival. The Baroque painting style was known for its use of dramatic effects to arouse the emotions. In large part, though, Baroque art and architecture reflected the search for power that was so important to the seventeenth-century ethos. Baroque churches and palaces were magnificent and richly detailed. Kings and princes wanted other kings and princes as well as their subjects to be in awe of their power.

El Greco, *Laocoön.* Mannerism reached its height in the work of El Greco. Born in Crete, trained in Venice and Rome, and settling finally in Spain, El Greco worked as a church painter in Toledo. Pictured here is his version of the *Laocoön*, a Hellenistic sculpture discovered in Rome in 1506. The elongated, contorted bodies project a world of suffering while the somber background scene of the city of Toledo and the threatening sky add a sense of terror and doom.

National Gallery of Art, Washington, DC//SuperStock

Baroque painting was known for its use of dramatic effects to heighten emotional intensity. This style was especially evident in the works of the Flemish master Peter Paul Rubens (1577–1640), a prolific artist and an important figure in the spread of the Baroque from Italy to other parts of Europe. In his artistic masterpieces, bodies in violent motion, heavily fleshed nudes, a dramatic use of light and shadow, and rich, sensuous pigments converge to express intense emotions. The restless forms and constant movement blend together into a dynamic unity.

Perhaps the greatest figure of the Baroque was the Italian architect and sculptor Gian Lorenzo Bernini (ZHAHN loh-RENT-zoh bur-NEE-nee) (1598–1680), who completed Saint Peter's Basilica at the Vatican and designed the vast colonnade enclosing the piazza in front of it. Action, exuberance, profusion, and dramatic effects mark the work of Bernini in the interior of Saint Peter's, where his *Throne of Saint Peter* hovers in midair, held by the hands of the four great doctors of the Catholic Church. Above the chair, rays of golden light drive a mass of clouds and angels toward the spectator. In his most striking sculptural work, the *Ecstasy of Saint Theresa*, Bernini depicts a moment of mystical experience in the life of the sixteenth-century Spanish saint. The elegant draperies and the expression on her face create a sensuously real portrayal of physical ecstasy.

Less well known than the male artists who dominated the art world of seventeenth-century Italy but prominent in her own right was Artemisia Gentileschi (ar-tuh-MEE-zhuh jen-tuh-LESS-kee) (1593–1653). Born in Rome, she studied painting under her father's direction. In 1616, she moved to Florence and began a successful career as a painter. At the age of twenty-three, she became the first woman to be elected to the Florentine Academy of Design. Although she was known internationally in her day as a portrait painter, her fame now rests on a series of pictures of heroines from the Old Testament. Most famous is *Judith Beheading Holofernes*, a dramatic rendering of the biblical scene in which Judith slays the Assyrian general Holofernes to save her besieged town from the Assyrian army.

FRENCH CLASSICISM In the second half of the seventeenth century, France replaced Italy as the cultural leader of Europe. Rejecting the Baroque style as overly showy and impassioned, the French remained committed to the classical values of the High Renaissance. French late classicism, with its emphasis

Peter Paul Rubens, *The Landing of Marie de'Mediciat Marseilles.* Peter Paul Rubens played a key role in spreading the Baroque style from Italy to other parts of Europe. In *The Landing of Marie de' Medici at Marseilles*, Rubens made dramatic use of light and color, bodies in motion, and luxurious nudes to heighten the emotional intensity of the scene. This was one of a cycle of twenty-one paintings dedicated to the queen mother of France.

Gian Lorenzo Bernini, *Ecstasy of Saint Theresa.* One of the great artists of the Baroque period was the Italian sculptor and architect Gian Lorenzo Bernini. The *Ecstasy of Saint Theresa*, created for the Cornaro Chapel in the Church of Santa Maria della Vittoria in Rome, was one of Bernini's most famous sculptures. Bernini sought to convey visually Theresa's mystical experience when, according to her description, an angel pierced her heart repeatedly with a golden arrow.

on clarity, simplicity, balance, and harmony of design, was a rather austere version of the High Renaissance style. Its triumph reflected the shift in seventeenth-century French society from chaos to order. Though it rejected the emotionalism and high drama of the Baroque, French classicism continued the Baroque's conception of grandeur in the portrayal of noble subjects, especially those from classical antiquity.

DUTCH REALISM A brilliant flowering of Dutch painting paralleled the supremacy of Dutch commerce in the seventeenth century. Wealthy patricians and burghers of Dutch urban society commissioned works of art for their guild halls, town halls, and private dwellings. The subject matter of many Dutch paintings reflected the interests of this burgher society: portraits of themselves, group portraits of their military companies and guilds, landscapes, seascapes, genre scenes, still lives, and the interiors of their residences. Neither classical nor Baroque, Dutch painters were primarily interested in the realistic portrayal of secular everyday life.

This interest in painting scenes of everyday life is evident in the work of Judith Leyster (LESS-tur) (ca. 1609–1660), who established her own independent painting career, a remarkable occurrence in seventeenth-century Europe. Leyster became the first female member of the painting Guild of Saint Luke

Judith Leyster, *Self-Portrait*. Although Judith Leyster was a well-known artist to her Dutch contemporaries, her fame diminished soon after her death. In the late nineteenth century, a Dutch art historian rediscovered her work. In Leyster's *Self-Portrait*, painted in 1635, she is seen pausing in her work painting one of the scenes of daily life that made her such a popular artist in her own day.

in Haarlem, which enabled her to set up her own workshop and take on three male pupils. Musicians playing their instruments, women sewing, children laughing while playing games, and actors performing all form the subject matter of Leyster's paintings of everyday Dutch life.

The finest product of the golden age of Dutch painting was Rembrandt van Rijn (REM-brant vahn RYN) (1606–1669). During his early career, Rembrandt painted opulent portraits and grandiose scenes that were often quite colorful. He was prolific and successful, but he turned away from materialistic success to follow his own artistic path; in the process, he lost public support and died bankrupt.

Although Rembrandt shared the Dutch predilection for realistic portraits, he became more introspective as he grew older. He refused to follow his contemporaries, whose pictures were largely secular; half of his own paintings depicted scenes from biblical tales. Since the Protestant tradition of hostility to religious pictures had discouraged artistic expression, Rembrandt stands out as the one great Protestant painter of the seventeenth century.

A Wondrous Age of Theater

In England and Spain, writing reached new heights between 1580 and 1640. All of these impressive new works were written in the vernacular. Except for academic fields, such as theology, philosophy, jurisprudence, and the sciences, Latin was no longer

Artemisia Gentileschi, *Judith Beheading Holofernes*. Artemisia Gentileschi painted a series of pictures portraying scenes from the lives of courageous Old Testament women. In this painting, a determined Judith, armed with her victim's sword, struggles to saw off the head of Holofernes. Gentileschi realistically and dramatically shows the gruesome nature of Judith's act.

Rembrandt van Rijn, *The Night Watch*. The Dutch enjoyed a golden age of painting during the seventeenth century. The burghers and patricians of Dutch urban society commissioned works of art, and these quite naturally reflected the burghers' interests. In his painting *The Night Watch*, Rembrandt portrays the two leaders and sixteen members of a civic militia preparing for a parade in the city of Amsterdam.

a universal literary language. The greatest age of English literature is often called the Elizabethan era because much of the English cultural flowering of the late sixteenth and early seventeenth centuries occurred during the reign of Queen Elizabeth I. Elizabethan literature exhibits the exuberance and pride associated with England's international exploits at the time. Of all the forms of Elizabethan literature, none expressed the energy and intellectual versatility of the era better than drama. And of all the dramatists, none is more famous than William Shakespeare (1564–1616).

WILLIAM SHAKESPEARE Shakespeare was the son of a prosperous glovemaker from Stratford-upon-Avon. When he appeared in London in 1592, Elizabethans were already addicted to the stage. In Greater London, as many as six theaters were open six afternoons a week. London theaters ranged from the Globe, which was a circular unroofed structure holding three thousand spectators, to the Blackfriars, which was roofed and held only five hundred. In the former, an admission charge of a penny or two enabled even the lower classes to attend; the

higher prices in the latter ensured an audience of the well-to-do. Elizabethan audiences varied greatly, putting pressure on playwrights to write works that pleased nobles, lawyers, merchants, and even vagabonds.

William Shakespeare was a "complete man of the theater." Although best known for writing plays, he was also an actor and shareholder in the chief company of the time, the Lord Chamberlain's Company, which played in theaters as diverse as the Globe and the Blackfriars. Shakespeare has long been recognized as a universal genius. A master of the English language, he was instrumental in codifying a language that was still in transition. His technical proficiency, however, was matched by an incredible insight into human psychology. In tragedies as well as comedies, Shakespeare exhibited a remarkable understanding of the human condition (see the box on p. 468).

SPAIN'S GOLDEN CENTURY The theater was also one of the most creative forms of expression during Spain's golden century. As in England, actors' companies ran the first professional

WILLIAM SHAKESPEARE: IN PRAISE OF ENGLAND

WILLIAM SHAKESPEARE IS ONE OF THE MOST famous playwrights of the Western world. He was a universal genius, outclassing all others in his psychological insights, depth of characterization, imaginative skills, and versatility. His historical plays reflected the patriotic enthusiasm of the English in the Elizabethan era, as this excerpt from *Richard II* illustrates.

William Shakespeare, *Richard II*

This royal throne of kings, this sceptered isle,
This earth of majesty, this seat of Mars,
This other Eden, demi-Paradise,
This fortress built by Nature for herself
Against infection and the hand of war,
This happy breed of men, this little world,
This precious stone set in the silver sea,
Which serves it in the office of a wall
Or as a moat defensive to a house
Against the envy of less happier lands—
This blessed plot, this earth, this realm, this England,
This nurse, this teeming womb of royal kings,
Feared by their breed and famous by their birth,
Renowned for their deeds as far from home,

For Christian service and true chivalry,
As is the sepulcher in stubborn Jewry [the Holy Sepulcher
in Jerusalem]
Of the world's ransom, blessed Mary's Son—
This land of such dear souls, this dear dear land,
Dear for her reputation through the world,
Is now leased out, I die pronouncing it,
Like a tenement or pelting farm.
England, bound in with the triumphant sea,
Whose rocky shore beats back the envious siege
Of watery Neptune, is now bound in with shame,
With inky blots and rotten parchment bonds.
That England, what was wont to conquer others,
Hath made a shameful conquest of itself.
Ah, would the scandal vanish with my life,
How happy then were my ensuing death!

 Why is William Shakespeare aptly described as not merely a playwright, but a "complete man of the theater"? Which countries might Shakespeare have meant by the phrase "the envy of less happier lands"?

Source: G. B. Harrison, ed. *Shakespeare, The Complete Works* (New York: Harcourt Brace & World, 1952).

---

theaters, which were established in Seville and Madrid in the 1570s. Soon a public playhouse could be found in every large town, including Mexico City in the New World. Touring companies brought the latest Spanish plays to all parts of the Spanish Empire.

Beginning in the 1580s, Lope de Vega (LOH-pay day VAY-guh) (1562–1635) set the agenda for playwrights. Like Shakespeare, he was from a middle-class background. He was an incredibly prolific writer; almost one-third of his fifteen hundred plays survive, which have been characterized as witty, charming, action packed, and realistic. Lope de Vega made no apologies for the fact that he wrote his plays to please his audiences. In a treatise on drama written in 1609, he stated that the foremost duty of the playwright was to satisfy public demand. Shakespeare undoubtedly believed the same thing, since his livelihood depended on public approval, but Lope de Vega was considerably more cynical about it: he remarked that if anyone thought he had written his plays for fame, "undeceive him and tell him that I wrote them for money."

FRENCH DRAMA As the great age of theater in England and Spain was drawing to a close around 1630, a new dramatic era began to dawn in France that lasted into the 1680s. Unlike Shakespeare in England and Lope de Vega in Spain,

French playwrights wrote more for an elite audience and were forced to depend on royal patronage. Louis XIV used theater as he did art and architecture—to attract attention to his monarchy.

French dramatists cultivated a style that emphasized the clever, polished, and correct over the emotional and imaginative. Many of the French works of the period derived both their themes and their plots from classical Greek and Roman sources, especially evident in the works of Jean-Baptiste Racine (ZHAHNH-bah-TEEST ra-SEEN) (1639–1699). In *Phèdre*, which has been called his best play, Racine followed closely the plot of *Hippolytus* by the Greek tragedian Euripides. Like the ancient tragedians, Racine, who perfected the French neoclassical tragic style, focused on conflicts, such as between love and honor or inclination and duty, that characterized and revealed the tragic dimensions of life.

Jean-Baptiste Molière (ZHAHNH-bah-TEEST mohl-YAYR) (1622–1673) enjoyed the favor of the French court and benefited from the patronage of King Louis XIV. Molière wrote, produced, and acted in a series of comedies that often satirized the religious and social world of his time. In *Tartuffe*, he ridiculed religious hypocrisy. His satires, however, sometimes got him into trouble. The Paris clergy did not find *Tartuffe* funny and had it banned for five years. Only the protection of the king saved Molière from more severe harassment.

To many historians, the seventeenth century has assumed extraordinary proportions. The divisive effects of the Reformation had been assimilated and the concept of a united Christendom, held as an ideal since the Middle Ages, had been irrevocably destroyed by the religious wars, making possible the emergence of a system of nation-states in which power politics took on an increasing significance. The growth of political thought focusing on the secular origins of state power reflected the changes that were going on in seventeenth-century society.

Within those states, there slowly emerged some of the machinery that made possible a growing centralization of power. In those states called absolutist, strong monarchs with the assistance of their aristocracies took the lead in providing the leadership for greater centralization. In this so-called age of absolutism, Louis  XIV, the Sun King of France, was the model for other rulers. His palace of Versailles, where the nobles were entertained and controlled by ceremony and etiquette, symbolized his authority. Louis revoked his grandfather's Edict of Nantes, and he fought four costly wars, mainly to acquire lands on France's eastern borders. Strong monarchy also prevailed in central and eastern Europe, where three new powers made their appearance: Prussia, Austria, and Russia. Peter the Great attempted to westernize Russia, especially militarily, and built Saint Petersburg, a new capital city, as his window on the west.

But not all European states followed the pattern of absolute monarchy. Especially important were developments in England, where a series of struggles between king and Parliament took place in the seventeenth century. The conflict between the Stuart kings, who were advocates of divine-right monarchy, and Parliament led to civil war and the creation of a republic and then a military dictatorship under Oliver Cromwell. After his death, the Stuart  monarchy was restored, but a new conflict led to the overthrow of James II and the establishment of a new order. The landed aristocracy gained power at the expense of the monarchs, thus laying the foundations for a constitutional government in which Parliament provided the focus for the institutions of centralized power. In all the major European states, a growing concern for power and dynamic expansion led to larger armies and greater conflict. War remained an endemic feature of Western civilization.

But the search for order and harmony continued, evident in art and literature. At the same time, religious preoccupations and values were losing ground to secular considerations. The seventeenth century was a period of  transition toward the more secular spirit that has characterized modern Western civilization to the present. No stronger foundation for this spirit could be found than in the new view of the universe that was ushered in by the Scientific Revolution of the seventeenth century, and it is to that story that we turn in the next chapter.

CHAPTER TIMELINE

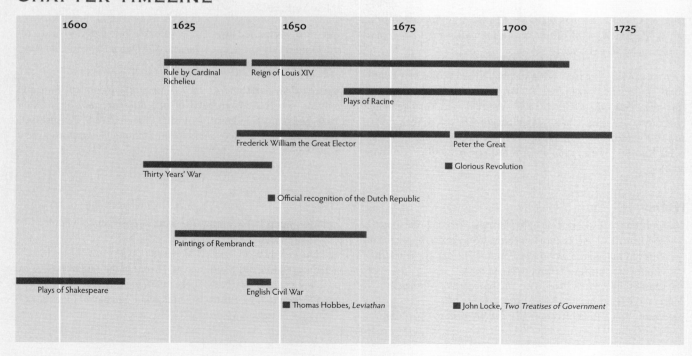

1600	1625	1650	1675	1700	1725

Rule by Cardinal Richelieu

Reign of Louis XIV

Plays of Racine

Frederick William the Great Elector

Peter the Great

■ Glorious Revolution

Thirty Years' War

■ Official recognition of the Dutch Republic

Paintings of Rembrandt

Plays of Shakespeare

English Civil War

■ Thomas Hobbes, *Leviathan*

■ John Locke, *Two Treatises of Government*

CHAPTER REVIEW

Upon Reflection

Q What does the witchcraft craze tell us about European society in the sixteenth and seventeenth centuries?

Q What did Louis XIV hope to accomplish in his domestic and foreign policies? To what extent did he succeed?

Q What role did the nobility play in Poland and England?

Key Terms

absolutism (p. 440)
divine-right monarchy (p. 440)
intendants (p. 441)
parlements (p. 443)
boyars (p. 450)

procurator (p. 450)
Janissaries (p. 454)
gentry (p. 458)
Mannerism (p. 464)
Baroque (p. 464)

Suggestions for Further Reading

GENERAL WORKS   For general works on the seventeenth century, see T. Munck, *Seventeenth-Century Europe, 1598–1700*, 2nd ed. (London, 2005); Q. Deakin, *Expansion, War, and Rebellion, 1598–1661* (Cambridge, 2000); and J. Bergin, *Seventeenth-Century Europe, 1598–1715* (Oxford, 2001).

WITCHCRAFT CRAZE   The story of the witchcraft frenzy can be examined in R. Briggs, *Witches and Neighbors: The Social and Cultural Context of European Witchcraft*, 2nd ed. (Oxford, 2002), L. Roper, *Witch Craze: Terror and Fantasy in Baroque Germany* (New Haven, Conn., 2006).

THIRTY YEARS' WAR   The fundamental study of the Thirty Years' War is P. H. Wilson, *The Thirty Years War: Europe's Tragedy* (Cambridge, Mass., 2009). For a brief study, see R. Bonney, *The Thirty Years' War, 1618–1648* (Oxford, 2002).

THE MILITARY REVOLUTION   On the military revolution, see J. M. Black, *A Military Revolution? Military Change and European Society* (London, 1996).

FRANCE AND SPAIN   For a succinct account of seventeenth-century French history, see R. Briggs, *Early Modern France, 1560–1715*, 2nd ed. (Oxford, 1998). A solid and very readable biography of Louis XIV is A. Levi, *Louis XIV* (New York, 2004). A good general work on seventeenth-century Spanish history is H. Kamen, *Spain, 1469–1714: A Society of Conflict* (London, 2014).

CENTRAL AND EASTERN EUROPE   On the German states, see P. H. Wilson, *The Holy Roman Empire, 1495–1806*, 2nd ed. (New York, 2011). On the creation of Austria, see P. S. Fichtner, *The Habsburg Monarchy, 1490–1848* (New York, 2003). On Austria and Prussia, see P. H. Wilson, *Absolutism in Central Europe* (New York, 2000).

RUSSIA   On *Peter the Great*, see P. Bushkovitz, *Peter the Great* (Oxford, 2001).

ENGLISH REVOLUTIONS   Good general works on the period of the English Revolutions include M. A. Kishlansky, *A Monarchy Transformed* (London, 1997), and D. Purkiss, *The English Civil War* (New York, 2006). On Oliver Cromwell, see P. Gaunt, M. Weems, and B. Wallis, *Oliver Cromwell* (New York, 2004), and P. Little, *Oliver Cromwell: New Perspectives* (New York, 2008).

UNITED PROVINCES   For a valuable but lengthy study on the United Provinces, see J. Israel, *The Dutch Republic: Its Rise, Greatness, and Fall* (New York, 1998).

EUROPEAN CULTURE   For a general survey of Baroque culture, see F. C. Marchetti et al., *Baroque, 1600–1770* (New York, 2005). For a biography of Shakespeare, see S. Greenblatt, *Will in the World: How Shakespeare Became Shakespeare* (New York, 2005).

Notes

1. Quoted in Louis, duc de Saint-Simon, *Versailles, the Court and Louis XIV*, ed. L. Norton (New York, 1958), pp. 247–248.
2. Quoted in J. Klaits, *Servants of Satan: The Age of the Witch Hunts* (Bloomington, Ind., 1985), p. 68.
3. Quoted in P. H. Wilson, *The Thirty Years War: Europe's Tragedy* (Cambridge, Mass., 2009), p. 783.
4. Quoted in J. B. Wolf, *Louis XIV* (New York, 1968), p. 134.

5. Quoted in J. B. Collins, *The State in Early Modern France* (Cambridge, 1995), p. 130.
6. Quoted in Wolf, *Louis XIV*, p. 618.
7. Quoted in D. H. Pennington, *Europe in the Seventeenth Century*, 2nd ed. (New York, 1989), p. 494.
8. Quoted in J. H. Elliot, *Imperial Spain, 1469–1716* (New York, 1963), p. 306.

9. Quoted in B. H. Sumner, *Peter the Great and the Emergence of Russia* (New York, 1962), p. 122.
10. Quoted in the account of Peter by an eighteenth-century French writer in J. H. Robinson, *Readings in European History*, vol. 2 (Boston, 1906), p. 311.
11. Quoted in S. Schama, *A History of Britain*, vol. 2: *The Wars of the British, 1603–1776* (New York, 2001), pp. 182, 185.
12. T. Carlyle, *Oliver Cromwell's Letters and Speeches: with Elucidations*, vol. II, (London: Chapman & Hall, 1893), p. 250.

MindTap® **MindTap®** is a fully online, highly personalized learning experience built upon Cengage Learning content. MindTap combines student learning tools—readings, multimedia, activities, and assessments—into a singular Learning Path that guides students through the course.

TOWARD A NEW HEAVEN AND A NEW EARTH: THE SCIENTIFIC REVOLUTION AND THE EMERGENCE OF MODERN SCIENCE

A nineteenth-century painting of Galileo before the Holy Office in the Vatican in 1633

Erich Lessing/Art Resource, NY

CHAPTER OUTLINE AND FOCUS QUESTIONS

Background to the Scientific Revolution

Q What developments during the Middle Ages and the Renaissance contributed to the Scientific Revolution of the seventeenth century?

Toward a New Heaven: A Revolution in Astronomy

Q What did Copernicus, Kepler, Galileo, and Newton contribute to a new vision of the universe, and how did it differ from the Ptolemaic conception of the universe?

Advances in Medicine and Chemistry

Q What did Paracelsus, Vesalius, and Harvey contribute to a scientific view of medicine?

Women in the Origins of Modern Science

Q What role did women play in the Scientific Revolution?

Toward a New Earth: Descartes, Rationalism, and a New View of Humankind

Q Why is Descartes considered the "founder of modern rationalism"?

The Scientific Method and the Spread of Scientific Knowledge

Q How were the ideas of the Scientific Revolution spread, and what impact did they have on society and religion?

Critical Thinking

Q *In what ways were the intellectual, political, social, and religious developments of the seventeenth century related?*

Connections to Today

Q *What scientific discoveries of the twentieth and twenty-first centuries have had as great an impact on society as those of the Scientific Revolution?*

IN ADDITION TO the political, economic, social, and international crises of the seventeenth century, we need to add an intellectual one. The Scientific Revolution questioned and ultimately challenged conceptions and beliefs about the nature of the external world and reality that had crystallized into a rather strict orthodoxy by the Later Middle Ages. Derived from the works of ancient Greeks and Romans and grounded in Christian thought, the medieval worldview had become formidable. But the breakdown of Christian unity during the Reformation and the subsequent religious wars had created an environment in which Europeans became more comfortable with challenging both the ecclesiastical and the political realms. Should it surprise us that a challenge to intellectual authority soon followed?

The Scientific Revolution taught Europeans to view the universe and their place in it in a new way. The shift from an earth-centered to a sun-centered cosmos had an emotional as well as an intellectual effect on the people who understood it. Thus, the Scientific Revolution, popularized in the eighteenth-century Enlightenment, stands as the major force in the transition to the largely secular, rational, and materialistic perspective that has defined the modern Western mentality since its full acceptance in the nineteenth and twentieth centuries.

The transition to a new worldview, however, was far from easy. In the seventeenth century, the Italian scientist Galileo Galilei (gal-li-LAY-oh GAL-li-lay), an outspoken advocate of the new worldview, found that his ideas were strongly opposed by the authorities of the Catholic Church. Galileo's position was clear: "I hold the sun to be situated motionless in the center of the revolution of the celestial bodies, while the earth rotates on its axis and revolves about the sun." Moreover, "nothing physical that sense-experience sets before our eyes . . . ought to be called in question (much less condemned) upon the testimony of Biblical passages."[1] But the church had a different view, and in 1633, Galileo, now sixty-eight and in ill health, was called before the dreaded Inquisition in Rome. He was kept waiting for two months before he was tried and found guilty of heresy and disobedience. Completely shattered by the experience, he denounced his errors: "I curse and detest the said errors and heresies contrary to the Holy Church." Legend holds that when he left the trial room, Galileo muttered to himself: "And yet it does move!" Galileo had been silenced, but his writings remained, and they spread throughout Europe. The Inquisition had failed to stop the new ideas of the Scientific Revolution.

In one sense, the Scientific Revolution was not a revolution. It was not characterized by the explosive change and rapid overthrow of traditional authority that we normally associate with the word *revolution*. The Scientific Revolution did overturn centuries of authority, but only in a gradual and piecemeal fashion. Nevertheless, its results were truly revolutionary. The Scientific Revolution was a key factor in setting Western civilization along its modern secular and materialistic path.

Background to the Scientific Revolution

 FOCUS QUESTION: What developments during the Middle Ages and the Renaissance contributed to the Scientific Revolution of the seventeenth century?

To say that the **Scientific Revolution** brought about a dissolution of the medieval worldview is not to say that the Middle Ages was a period of scientific ignorance. Many educated Europeans took an intense interest in the world around them since it was, after all, "God's handiwork" and therefore an appropriate subject for study. Late medieval scholastic philosophers had advanced mathematical and physical thinking in many ways, but the subjection of these thinkers to a strict theological framework and their unquestioning reliance on a few ancient authorities, especially Aristotle and Galen, limited where they could go.

Many "natural philosophers," as medieval scientists were called, preferred refined logical analysis to systematic observations of the natural world. A number of changes and advances in the fifteenth and sixteenth centuries may have played a major role in helping "natural philosophers" abandon their old views and develop new ones.

Ancient Authors and Renaissance Artists

Whereas medieval scholars had made use of Aristotle, Galen, and Ptolemy in Latin translations to develop many of their positions in the fields of physics, medicine, and astronomy, the Renaissance humanists had mastered Greek and made available new works of Galen, Ptolemy, and Archimedes as well as Plato and the pre-Socratics. These writings made it apparent that other thinkers in antiquity had contradicted the unquestioned authorities of the Middle Ages, Aristotle and Galen. The desire to discover which school of thought was correct stimulated new scientific work that sometimes led to a complete rejection of the classical authorities.

Renaissance artists have also been credited with making an impact on scientific study. Their desire to imitate nature led them to a close observation of nature. Their accurate renderings of rocks, plants, animals, and human anatomy established new standards for the study of natural phenomena. At the same time, the "scientific" study of the problems of perspective and correct anatomical proportions led to new insights. "No painter," one Renaissance artist declared, "can paint well without a thorough knowledge of geometry."[2] Renaissance artists were frequently called on to be practicing mathematicians as well. Leonardo da Vinci devised "war machines," and Albrecht Dürer made designs for the fortifications of cities.

Technological Innovations and Mathematics

Technical problems such as accurately calculating the tonnage of ships also stimulated scientific activity because they required careful observation and precise measurements. The discovery of the New World and increased trading furthered the need for improved navigational and mathematical knowledge. The relationship between technology and the Scientific Revolution was not a simple one, however, for many technological experts did not believe in abstract or academic learning. Moreover, the early institutions that supported the academic study of technology, such as Spain's Casa de Contractación, or House of Trade, regarded their technological discoveries as state secrets and kept them hidden from the public. Indeed, many of the technical innovations of the Middle Ages and the Renaissance were accomplished outside the universities by people who emphasized practical rather than theoretical knowledge. In any case, the invention of new instruments and machines, such as the telescope and the microscope, often made new scientific discoveries possible. The printing press had an indirect but crucial role in spreading innovative ideas quickly and easily.

Mathematics, so fundamental to the scientific achievements of the sixteenth and seventeenth centuries, was promoted in the Renaissance by the rediscovery of the works of ancient mathematicians and the influence of Plato, who had emphasized the importance of mathematics in explaining the universe. Applauded as the key to navigation, military science, and geography, mathematics was also regarded as the key to understanding the nature of things. According to Leonardo da Vinci, since God eternally geometrizes, nature is inherently mathematical: "Proportion is not only found in numbers and measurements but also in sounds, weights, times, positions, and in whatsoever power there may be."[3] Moreover, mathematical reasoning was seen as promoting a degree of certainty that was otherwise impossible. In the words of Leonardo da Vinci: "There is no certainty where one can neither apply any of the mathematical sciences nor any of those which are based upon the mathematical sciences."[4] Copernicus, Kepler, Galileo, and Newton were all great mathematicians who believed that the secrets of nature were written in the language of mathematics.

Renaissance Magic

Another factor in the origins of the Scientific Revolution may have been magic. Renaissance magic was the preserve of an intellectual elite from all of Europe. By the end of the sixteenth century, Hermetic magic had become fused with alchemical thought into a single intellectual framework. This tradition believed that the world was a living embodiment of divinity. Humans, who it was believed also had that spark of divinity within, could use magic, especially mathematical magic, to understand and dominate the world of nature or employ the powers of nature for beneficial purposes. Hermetic magicians, who experimented with natural objects, were considered to be practitioners of idolatry because of their practice of distorting nature. However, it was their engagement with experimentation that perhaps contributed to the later practice of "experimental philosophy" or empirical science based upon observation. Was it Hermeticism, then, that inaugurated the shift in consciousness that made the Scientific Revolution possible, since the desire to control and dominate the natural world was a crucial motivating force in the Scientific Revolution? One scholar has argued:

> It is a movement of the will which really originates an intellectual movement. A new center of interest arises, surrounded by emotional excitement; the mind turns where the will has directed it and new attitudes, new discoveries follow. Behind the emergence of modern science there was a new direction of the will toward the world, its marvels, and mysterious workings, a new longing and determination to understand those workings and to operate with them.[5]

"This time," the author continues, "the return to the occult [Hermetic tradition] stimulates the genuine science."[6] Scholars debate the issue, but histories of the Scientific Revolution frequently overlook the fact that the great names we associate with the revolution in cosmology—Copernicus, Kepler, Galileo, and Newton—all had a serious interest in Hermetic ideas and the fields of astrology and alchemy. The mention of these names also reminds us of one final consideration in the origins of the Scientific Revolution: it largely resulted from the work of a handful of great intellectuals.

Toward a New Heaven: A Revolution in Astronomy

FOCUS QUESTION: What did Copernicus, Kepler, Galileo, and Newton contribute to a new vision of the universe, and how did it differ from the Ptolemaic conception of the universe?

The greatest achievements in the Scientific Revolution of the sixteenth and seventeenth centuries came in the fields most dominated by the ideas of the Greeks—astronomy, mechanics, and medicine. The cosmological views of the Later Middle Ages had been built on a synthesis of the ideas of Aristotle, Ptolemy (the greatest astronomer of antiquity, who lived in the second century C.E.), and Christian theology. In the resulting Ptolemaic (tahl-uh-MAY-ik) or **geocentric conception**, the

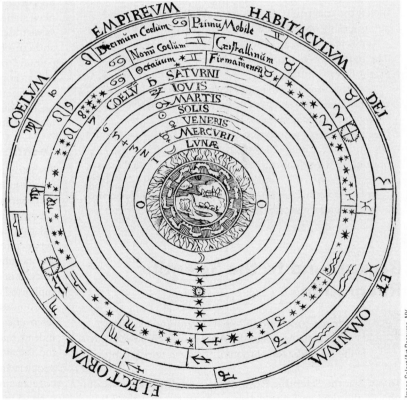

Image Select/Art Resource, NY

Medieval Conception of the Universe. As this sixteenth-century illustration shows, the medieval cosmological view placed the earth at the center of the universe, surrounded by a series of concentric spheres. The earth was imperfect and constantly changing, whereas the heavenly bodies that surrounded it were perfect and incorruptible. Beyond the tenth and final sphere was heaven, where God and all the saved souls were located. (The circles read from the center outward as follows: 1. Moon, 2. Mercury, 3. Venus, 4. Sun, 5. Mars, 6. Jupiter, 7. Saturn, 8. Firmament (of the Stars), 9. Crystalline Sphere, 10. Prime Mover; and around the outside, Empyrean Heaven—Home of God and All the Elect, that is, saved souls.)

universe was seen as a series of concentric spheres with a fixed or motionless earth at its center. Composed of the material substances of earth, air, fire, and water, the earth was imperfect and constantly changing. The spheres that surrounded the earth were made of a crystalline, transparent substance and moved in circular orbits around the earth. Circular movement, according to Aristotle, was the most "perfect" kind of motion and hence appropriate for the "perfect" heavenly bodies thought to consist of a nonmaterial, incorruptible "quintessence." These heavenly bodies, pure orbs of light, were embedded in the moving, concentric spheres, which in 1500 were believed to number ten. Working outward from the earth, eight spheres contained the moon, Mercury, Venus, the sun, Mars, Jupiter, Saturn, and the fixed stars. The ninth sphere imparted to the eighth sphere of the fixed stars its motion, and the tenth sphere was frequently described as the prime mover that moved itself and imparted motion to the other spheres. Beyond the tenth sphere was the Empyrean Heaven—the location of God and all the saved souls. This Christianized Ptolemaic universe, then, was finite. It had a fixed outer boundary in harmony with Christian thought and expectations. God and the saved souls were at one end of the universe, and humans were at the center. They had been given power over the earth, but their real purpose was to achieve salvation.

This conception of the universe, however, did not satisfy professional astronomers, who wished to ascertain the precise paths of the heavenly bodies across the sky. Finding that their observations did not always correspond to the accepted scheme, astronomers tried to "save appearances" by developing an elaborate system of devices. They proposed, for example, that the planetary bodies traveled on epicycles, concentric spheres within spheres, that would enable the paths of the planets to correspond more precisely to observations while adhering to Aristotle's ideas of circular planetary movement.

Copernicus

Nicolaus Copernicus (nee-koh-LAU-uss kuh-PURR-nuh-kuss) (1473–1543) had studied both mathematics and astronomy first at Krakow in his native Poland and later at the Italian universities of Bologna and Padua. Before he left Italy in 1506, he had become aware of ancient views that contradicted the Ptolemaic, earth-centered conception of the universe. Between 1506 and 1530, he completed the manuscript of his famous book, *On the Revolutions of the Heavenly Spheres*, but his own timidity and fear of ridicule from fellow astronomers kept him from publishing it until May 1543, shortly before his death.

Copernicus was not an accomplished observational astronomer and relied on his predecessors for his data. But he was a mathematician who felt that Ptolemy's geocentric system was too complicated and failed to accord with the observed motions of the heavenly bodies (see the box on p. 476). Copernicus hoped that his **heliocentric** or sun-centered **conception** would offer a simpler and more accurate explanation.

Copernicus argued that the universe consisted of eight spheres with the sun motionless at the center and the sphere of the fixed stars at rest in the eighth sphere. The planets revolved around the sun in the order of Mercury, Venus, the earth, Mars, Jupiter, and Saturn. The moon, however, revolved

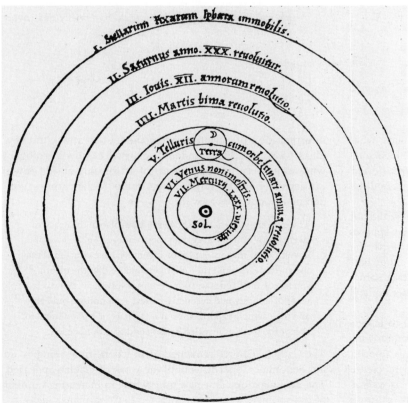

The Copernican System. The Copernican system was presented in *On the Revolutions of the Heavenly Spheres*, published shortly before Copernicus's death. As shown in this illustration from the first edition of the book, Copernicus maintained that the sun was the center of the universe and that the planets, including the earth, revolved around it. Moreover, the earth rotated daily on its axis. (The circles read from the inside out as follows: 1. Sun; 2. Mercury, orbit of 80 days; 3. Venus; 4. Earth, with the moon, orbit of one year; 5. Mars, orbit of 2 years; 6. Jupiter, orbit of 12 years; 7. Saturn, orbit of 30 years; 8. Immobile Sphere of the Fixed Stars.)

ON THE REVOLUTIONS OF THE HEAVENLY SPHERES

NICOLAUS COPERNICUS BEGAN A REVOLUTION in astronomy when he argued that the sun and not the earth was at the center of the universe. Expecting controversy and scorn, Copernicus hesitated to publish the work in which he put forth his heliocentric theory. He finally relented, however, and managed to see a copy of it just before he died.

Nicolaus Copernicus, *On the Revolutions of the Heavenly Spheres*

For a long time, then, I reflected on this confusion in the astronomical traditions concerning the derivation of the motions of the universe's spheres. I began to be annoyed that the movements of the world machine, created for our sake by the best and most systematic Artisan of all [God], were not understood with greater certainty by the philosophers, who otherwise examined so precisely the most insignificant trifles of this world. For this reason I undertook the task of rereading the works of all the philosophers which I could obtain to learn whether anyone had ever proposed other motions of the universe's spheres than those expounded by the teachers of astronomy in the schools. And in fact first I found in Cicero that Hicetas supposed the earth to move. Later I also discovered in Plutarch that certain others were of this opinion. I have decided to set his words down here, so that they may be available to everybody:

> Some think that the earth remains at rest. But Philolaus the Pythagorean believes that, like the sun and moon, it revolves around the fire in an oblique circle. Heraclides of Pontus and Ecphantus the Pythagorean make the earth move, not in a progressive motion, but like a wheel in a rotation from the west to east about its own center.

Therefore, having obtained the opportunity from these sources, I too began to consider the mobility of the earth. And even though the idea seemed absurd, nevertheless I knew that others before me had been granted the freedom to imagine any circles whatever for the purpose of explaining the heavenly phenomena. Hence I thought that I too would be readily permitted to ascertain whether explanations sounder than those of my predecessors could be found for the revolution of the celestial spheres on the assumption of some motion of the earth.

Having thus assumed the motions which I ascribe to the earth later on in the volume, by long and intense study I finally found that if the motions of the other planets are correlated with the orbiting of the earth, and are computed for the revolution of each planet, not only do their phenomena follow therefrom but also the order and size of all the planets and spheres, and heaven itself is so linked together that in no portion of it can anything be shifted without disrupting the remaining parts and the universe as a whole . . .

Hence I feel no shame in asserting that this whole region engirdled by the moon, and the center of the earth, traverse this grand circle amid the rest of the planets in an annual revolution around the sun. Near the sun is the center of the universe. Moreover, since the sun remains stationary, whatever appears as a motion of the sun is really due rather to the motion of the earth.

 What major new ideas did Copernicus discuss in this excerpt? What was the source of these ideas? Why might one say that European astronomers had finally destroyed the Middle Ages?

Source: Copernicus, in E. Rosen, trans., *The Complete Works* (London: Palgrave Macmillan, 1978).

---

around the earth. Moreover, according to Copernicus, what appeared to be the movement of the sun and the fixed stars around the earth was really explained by the daily rotation of the earth on its axis and the journey of the earth around the sun each year.

Copernicus, however, was basically conservative. He did not reject Aristotle's principle of the existence of heavenly spheres moving in circular orbits. As a result, when he put forth the calculations to prove his new theory, he retained about half of Ptolemy's epicycles and wound up with a system somewhat simpler than that of the Alexandrian astronomer but still extremely complicated.

Nevertheless, the shift from an earth-centered to a sun-centered system was significant and raised serious questions about Aristotle's astronomy and physics despite Copernicus's own adherence to Aristotle. It also seemed to create uncertainty about the human role in the universe as well as God's location. Protestant reformers, adhering to a literal interpretation of Scripture, were the first to attack the new ideas. Martin Luther thundered against "the new astrologer" who wants to turn the whole art of astronomy upside down. Luther's cohort at Wittenberg, Philip Melanchthon, condemned Copernicus as well:

> The eyes are witness that the heavens revolve in the space of twenty-four hours. But certain men, either from the love of novelty, or to make a display of ingenuity, have concluded that the earth moves, and they maintain that neither the eighth sphere [of the fixed stars] nor the sun revolves. . . . Now it is a want of honesty and decency to assert such notions publicly, and the example is pernicious. It is the part of a good mind to accept the truth as revealed by God and to acquiesce in it.[7]

The Catholic Church remained silent for the time being; it did not denounce Copernicus until the work of Galileo appeared. The denunciation came at a time when an increasing number of astronomers were being attracted to Copernicus's ideas.

Brahe

Copernicus did not have a great impact immediately, but doubts about the Ptolemaic system were growing. Johannes Kepler took the next step in destroying the geocentric conception and supporting the Copernican system. It has been argued, however, that Kepler's work would not have occurred without the material provided by Tycho Brahe (TY-koh BRAH).

A Danish nobleman, Tycho Brahe (1546–1601) was granted possession of an island near Copenhagen by King Frederick II. On it, Brahe built the elaborate Uraniborg Castle, which he outfitted with a library, observatories, and instruments he had designed for more precise astronomical observations. For twenty years, Brahe patiently concentrated on compiling a detailed record of his observations of the positions and movements of the stars and planets, a series of observations described as the most accurate up to that time. This body of data led him to reject the Aristotelian-Ptolemaic system, but at the same time he was unable to accept Copernicus's suggestion that the earth actually moved. Brahe's last years were spent in Prague as imperial mathematician to Emperor Rudolf II, who took a keen interest in astronomy, astrology, and the Hermetic tradition. While he was in Prague, Brahe took on an assistant by the name of Johannes Kepler.

The Art Archive/Art Resource, NY

Tycho Brahe. His work at the Uraniborg observatory provided astronomers with the best data on the position of the celestial bodies. He published his results in *Of More Recent Phenomena of the Ethereal World* in 1588. He is depicted here in a sixteenth-century Dutch oil painting with a silver nose; his own nose was cut off during a duel.

Kepler

Johannes Kepler (yoh-HAHN-us KEP-lur) (1571–1630) had been destined by his parents for a career as a Lutheran minister. While studying theology at the university at Tübingen (TOO-bing-un), however, he fell under the influence of Michael Mästlin (MEST-lin), Germany's best-known astronomer, and spent much time pursuing his real interests—mathematics and astronomy. He abandoned theology and became a teacher of mathematics and astronomy at Graz in Austria.

Kepler's work illustrates well the narrow line that often separated magic and science in the early Scientific Revolution. An avid astrologer, Kepler had a keen interest in Hermetic mathematical magic. In a book written in 1596, he elaborated on his theory that the universe was constructed on the basis of geometric figures, such as the pyramid and the cube. Believing that the harmony of the human soul (a divine attribute) was mirrored in the numerical relationships existing between the planets, he focused much of his attention on discovering the "music of the spheres." Kepler was also a brilliant mathematician and astronomer and, after Brahe's death, succeeded him as imperial mathematician to Rudolf II. There he gained possession of Brahe's detailed astronomical data and, using them, arrived at his three laws of planetary motion. These laws may have confirmed Kepler's interest in the "music of the spheres," but more important, they confirmed Copernicus's heliocentric theory while modifying it in some ways. Above all, they drove another nail into the coffin of the Aristotelian-Ptolemaic system.

Kepler published his first two laws of planetary motion in 1609. Although at Tübingen he had accepted Copernicus's heliocentric ideas, in his first law he rejected Copernicus by showing that the orbits of the planets around the sun were not circular but elliptical, with the sun at one focus of the ellipse rather than at the center. In his second law, he demonstrated that the speed of a planet is greater when it is closer to the sun and decreases as its distance from the sun increases. This proposition destroyed a fundamental Aristotelian tenet that Copernicus had shared—that the motion of the planets was steady and unchanging. Published ten years later, Kepler's third law established that the square of a planet's period of revolution is proportional to the cube of its average distance from the sun. In other words, planets with larger orbits revolve at a slower average velocity than those with smaller orbits.

Kepler's three laws effectively eliminated the idea of uniform circular motion as well as the idea of crystalline spheres revolving in circular orbits. The basic structure of the traditional Ptolemaic system had been disproved, and people had been freed to think in new ways about the actual paths of planets revolving around the sun in elliptical orbits. By the end of Kepler's life, the Ptolemaic system was rapidly losing ground to the new ideas (see the box on p. 478). Important questions remained unanswered, however: What were the planets made of? And how could motion in the universe be explained? It was an Italian scientist who achieved the next important breakthrough to a new cosmology by answering the first question and making important strides toward answering the second.

KEPLER AND THE EMERGING SCIENTIFIC COMMUNITY

THE EXCHANGE OF LETTERS BETWEEN INTELLECTUALS was an important avenue for scientific communication. After receiving a copy of Johannes Kepler's first major work, the Italian Galileo Galilei wrote to Kepler, inaugurating a correspondence between them. This selection contains samples of their letters to each other.

Galileo to Kepler, Padua, August 4, 1597

Your book . . . reached me not days ago but only a few hours ago, and as this Paulus just informed me of his return to Germany, I should think myself indeed ungrateful if I should not express to you my thanks by this letter. I thank you . . . for having deemed me worthy of such a proof of your friendship. . . . So far I have read only the introduction, but have learned from it . . . your intentions and congratulate myself on the good fortune of having found such a man as a companion in the exploration of truth. For it is deplorable that there are so few who seek the truth. . . . But this is not the place to mourn about the misery of our century but to rejoice with you about such beautiful ideas proving the truth. . . . I would certainly dare to approach the public with my ways of thinking if there were more people of your mind. As this is not the case, I shall refrain from doing so. . . . I shall always be at your service. Farewell, and do not neglect to give me further good news of yourself.

> Yours in sincere friendship,
> Galilaeus Galilaeus
> Mathematician at the Academy of Padua

Kepler to Galileo, Graz, October 13, 1597

I received your letter of August 4 on September 1. It was a double pleasure to me. First because I became friends with you, the Italian, and second because of the agreement in which we find ourselves concerning Copernican cosmography. . . .

I would, however, have wished that you who have such a keen insight into everything would choose another way to reach your practical aims. By the strength of your personal example you advise us . . . to go out of the way of general ignorance and warn us against exposing ourselves to the furious attacks of the scholarly crowd. . . . But after the beginning of a tremendous enterprise has been made in our time, and furthered by so many learned mathematicians, and after the statement that the earth moves can no longer be regarded as something new, would it not be better to pull the rolling wagon to its destination with united effort? . . . For it is not only you Italians who do not believe that they move unless they feel it, but we in Germany, too, in no way make ourselves popular with this idea. Yet there are ways in which we protect ourselves against these difficulties. . . . Be of good cheer, Galileo, and appear in public. If I am not mistaken there are only a few among the distinguished mathematicians of Europe who would dissociate themselves from us. So great is the power of truth. If Italy seems less suitable for your publication and if you have to expect difficulties there, perhaps Germany will offer us more freedom. . . . Please let me know, at least privately if you do not want to do so publicly, what you have discovered in favor of Copernicus.

 What does the correspondence between Galileo and Kepler reveal about an emerging spirit of scientific inquiry? What other notable achievements must European society have reached even to make this exchange of letters possible? What aspects of European material culture made the work of these scientists easier?

Source: C. Baumgardt, *Johannes Kepler, Life and Letters* (New York: Philosophical Library, 1951).

Galileo

Galileo Galilei (1564–1642) taught mathematics, first at Pisa and later at Padua, one of the most prestigious universities in Europe. Galileo was the first European to make systematic observations of the heavens by means of a telescope, thereby inaugurating a new age in astronomy. He had heard of a Flemish lens grinder who had created a "spyglass" that magnified objects seen at a distance and soon constructed his own after reading about it. Instead of peering at terrestrial objects, Galileo turned his telescope to the skies and made a remarkable series of discoveries: mountains and craters on the moon, four moons revolving around Jupiter, the phases of Venus, and sunspots. Galileo's observations demolished yet another aspect of the traditional cosmology in that the universe seemed to be composed of material substance similar to that of the earth rather than ethereal or perfect and unchanging substance.

Galileo's revelations, published in *The Starry Messenger* in 1610 (see the box above), stunned his contemporaries and probably did more to make Europeans aware of the new picture of the universe than the mathematical theories of Copernicus and Kepler did. The English ambassador in Venice wrote to the chief minister of King James I in 1610:

> I send herewith unto His Majesty the strangest piece of news . . . that he has ever yet received from any part of the world; which is the annexed book of the Mathematical Professor at Padua [Galileo], who by the help of an optical instrument . . . has discovered four new planets rolling about the sphere of Jupiter. . . . So upon the whole subject he has first overthrown all former astronomy. . . . By the next ship your Lordship shall receive from me one of the above instruments [a telescope], as it is bettered by this man.[8]

THE STARRY MESSENGER

THE ITALIAN GALILEO GALILEI WAS THE FIRST
European to use a telescope to make systematic observations of the heavens. His observations, as reported in *The Starry Messenger* in 1610, stunned European intellectuals by revealing that the celestial bodies were not perfect and immutable but composed of material substance similar to that of the earth. In this selection, Galileo describes how he devised a telescope and what he saw with it.

Galileo Galilei, *The Starry Messenger*

About ten months ago a report reached my ears that a Dutchman had constructed a telescope, by the aid of which visible objects, although at a great distance from the eye of the observer, were distinctly seen as if near; and some proofs of its most wonderful performances were reported, which some gave credence to, but others contradicted. A few days after, I received confirmation of the report in a letter written from Paris by a noble Frenchman, Jacques Badovere, which finally determined me to give myself up to inquire into the principle of the telescope, and then to consider the means by which I might compass the invention of a similar instrument, which a little while after I succeeded in doing, through deep study of the theory of Refraction; and I prepared a tube, at first of lead, in the ends of which I fitted two glass lenses, both plane on one side, but on the other side one spherically convex, and the other concave. Then bringing my eye to the concave lens I saw objects satisfactorily large and near, for they appeared one-third of the distance off and nine times larger than when they are seen with the natural eye alone. I shortly afterwards constructed another telescope with more nicety, which magnified objects more than sixty times. At length, by sparing neither labour nor expense, I succeeded in constructing for myself an instrument so superior that objects seen through it appear magnified nearly a thousand times, and more than thirty times nearer than if viewed by the natural powers of sight alone.

It would be altogether a waste of time to enumerate the number and importance of the benefits which this instrument may be expected to confer, when used by land or sea. But without paying attention to its use for terrestrial objects, I betook myself to observations of the heavenly bodies; and first of all, I viewed the Moon as near as if it was scarcely two semi-diameters of the Earth distant. After the Moon, I frequently observed other heavenly bodies, both fixed stars and planets, with incredible delight; and, when I saw their very great number, I began to consider about a method by which I might be able to measure their distances apart. . . .

Now let me review the observations made by me during the two months just past, again inviting the attention of all who are eager for true philosophy to the beginnings which led to the sight of the most important phenomena.

Let me speak first of the surface of the Moon, which is turned towards us. For the sake of being understood more easily, I distinguish two parts in it, which I call respectively the brighter and the darker. The brighter part seems to surround and to pervade the whole hemisphere; but the darker part discolors, like a sort of cloud, discolors the Moon's surface and makes it appear covered with spots. . . . These spots have never been observed by any one before me; and from my observations of them, often repeated, I have been led to the opinion which I have expressed, namely that I feel sure that the surface of the Moon is not perfectly smooth, free from inequalities, and exactly spherical, as a large school of philosophers considers with regard to the Moon and the other heavenly bodies, but that, on the contrary, it is full of inequalities, uneven, full of hollows and protuberances, just like the surface of the Earth itself, which is varied everywhere by lofty mountains and deep valleys.

 What was the significance of Galileo's invention? What impressions did he receive of the moon? Why were his visual discoveries so stunning, and how did he go about publicizing them?

Source: E. S. Carlo, *The Sidereal Messenger of Galileo Galilei: And a Part of the Preface to Kepler's Dioptrics Containing the Original Account of Galileo's Astronomical Discoveries* (London: Rivingtons, 1880), pp. 10–11, 14–15.

During a trip to Rome, scholars received Galileo as a conquering hero. Grand Duke Cosimo II of Florence offered him a new position as his court mathematician, which Galileo readily accepted. But even in the midst of his newfound acclaim, Galileo found himself increasingly suspect by the authorities of the Catholic Church.

GALILEO AND THE INQUISITION In *The Starry Messenger*, Galileo had revealed himself as a firm proponent of Copernicus's heliocentric system. The Roman Inquisition (or Holy Office) of the Catholic Church condemned Copernicanism and ordered Galileo to reject the Copernican thesis. As one cardinal commented, "The intention of the Holy Spirit is to teach us not how the heavens go, but how to go to heaven." The report of the Inquisition ran:

> That the doctrine that the sun was the center of the world and immovable was false and absurd, formally heretical and contrary to Scripture, whereas the doctrine that the earth was not the center of the world but moved, and has further a daily motion, was philosophically false and absurd and theologically at least erroneous.[9]

Galileo was told, however, that he could continue to discuss Copernicanism as long as he maintained that it was not a fact but a mathematical supposition. It is apparent from the Inquisition's response that the church attacked the Copernican system

SuperStock

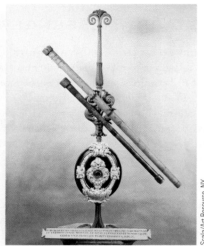

Scala/Art Resource, NY

The Telescope. The invention of the telescope enabled Europeans to inaugurate a new age in astronomy. Shown here is Johannes Hevelius (huh-VAY-lee-uss), an eminent German-Polish astrologer (1611–1697), making an observation with his telescope. Hevelius's observations were highly regarded. He located his telescope on the roof of his own house, and by the 1660s, his celestial observatory was considered one of the best in Europe. The photograph above shows Galileo's original telescope, built in 1609.

because it threatened not only Scripture but also an entire conception of the universe (see "Opposing Viewpoints" on p. 481). The heavens were no longer a spiritual world but a world of matter. Humans were no longer at the center, and God was no longer in a specific place. The new system raised such uncertainties that it seemed prudent simply to condemn it.

Galileo, however, never really accepted his condemnation. In 1632, he published his most famous work, *Dialogue on the Two Chief World Systems: Ptolemaic and Copernican.* Unlike most scholarly treatises, it was written in Italian rather than Latin, making it more widely available to the public, which no doubt alarmed the church authorities. The work took the form of a dialogue among Simplicio, a congenial but somewhat stupid supporter of Aristotle and Ptolemy; Sagredo, an open-minded layman; and Salviati, a proponent of Copernicus's ideas. There is no question who wins the argument, and the *Dialogue* was quickly perceived as a defense of the Copernican system. Galileo was dragged once more before the Inquisition in 1633, found guilty of teaching the condemned Copernican system, and forced to recant his errors. Placed under house arrest on his estate near Florence, he spent the remaining eight years of his life studying mechanics, a field in which he made significant contributions.

GALILEO AND THE PROBLEM OF MOTION One of the problems that fell under the heading of mechanics was the principle of motion. The Aristotelian conception, which dominated the late medieval world, held that an object remained at rest unless a force was applied against it. If a force was constantly exerted, then the object moved at a constant rate, but if it was removed, then the object stopped. This conception encountered some difficulties, especially with a projectile thrown out of a cannon. Late medieval theorists had solved this problem by arguing that the rush of air behind the projectile kept it in motion. The Aristotelian principle of motion also raised problems in the new Copernican system. In the Ptolemaic system, the concentric spheres surrounding the earth were weightless, but in the Copernican system, if a constant force had to be applied to objects to cause movement, then what power or force kept the heavy earth and other planets in motion?

Galileo made two contributions to the problem of motion. First, he demonstrated by experiments that if a uniform force was applied to an object, it would move at an accelerated speed rather than a constant speed. Moreover, Galileo discovered the principle of inertia when he argued that a body in motion continues in motion forever unless deflected by an external force. Thus, a state of uniform motion is just as natural as a state of rest. Before Galileo, natural philosophers had tried to explain motion; now their task was to explain changes in motion.

The condemnation of Galileo by the Inquisition, coming at a time of economic decline, seriously undermined further scientific work in Italy, which had been at the forefront of scientific innovation. Leadership in science now passed to the northern countries, especially England, France, and the Dutch Netherlands. By the 1630s and 1640s, no reasonable

A New Heaven? Faith Versus Reason

IN 1614, GALILEO WROTE A LETTER TO THE Grand Duchess Christina of Tuscany in which he explained why his theory that the earth rotated around the sun was not necessarily contrary to Scripture. To Galileo, it made little sense for the church to determine the nature of physical reality on the basis of biblical texts that were subject to different interpretations. One year later, Cardinal Robert Bellarmine, a Jesuit and now a member of the church's Inquisition, wrote a letter to one of Galileo's followers that laid out the Catholic Church's approach to the issue of Galileo's theory.

Galileo, Letter to the Grand Duchess Christina, 1614

Some years ago, as Your Serene Highness well knows, I discovered in the heavens many things that had not been seen before our own age. The novelty of these things, as well as some consequences which followed from them in contradiction to the physical notions commonly held among academic philosophers, stirred up against me no small number of professors—as if I had placed these things in the sky with my own hands in order to upset nature and overturn the sciences. . . .

Contrary to the sense of the Bible and the intention of the holy Fathers, if I am not mistaken, they would extend such authorities until even in purely physical matters—where faith is not involved—they would have us altogether abandon reason and the evidence of our senses in favor of some biblical passage, though under the surface meaning of its words this passage may contain a different sense. . . .

The reason produced for condemning the opinion that the earth moves and the sun stands still is that in many places in the Bible one may read that the sun moves and the earth stands still. Since the Bible cannot err, it follows as a necessary consequence that anyone takes an erroneous and heretical position who maintains that the sun is inherently motionless and the earth movable.

With regard to this argument, I think in the first place that it is very pious to say and prudent to affirm that the holy Bible can never speak untruth—whenever its true meaning is understood. But I believe nobody will deny that it is often very abstruse, and may say things which are quite different from what its bare words signify. Hence, in expounding the Bible if one were always to confine oneself to the unadorned grammatical meaning, one might fall into error. Not only contradictions and propositions far from true might thus be made to appear in the Bible, but even grave heresies and follies. Thus, it would be necessary to assign to God feet, hands, and eyes, as well as corporeal and human affections, such as anger, repentance, hatred, and sometimes even the forgetting of things past and ignorance of those to come. These propositions uttered by the Holy Ghost were set down in that manner by the sacred scribes in order to accommodate them to the capacities of the common people, who are rude and unlearned. For the sake of those who deserve to be separated from the herd, it is necessary that wise expositors should produce the true senses of such passages, together with the special reasons for which they were set down in these words. . . .

This being granted, I think that in discussions of physical problems we ought to begin not from the authority of scriptural passages, but from sense-experiences and necessary demonstrations; for the holy Bible and the phenomena of nature proceed alike from the divine Word. . . . For that reason it appears that nothing physical which sense-experience sets before our eyes, or which necessary demonstrations prove to us, ought to be called in question (much less condemned) upon the testimony of biblical passages which may have some different meaning beneath their words.

Robert Bellarmine, Letter to Paolo Foscarini, 1615

First. I say that it seems to me that Your Reverence and Galileo did prudently to content yourself with speaking hypothetically, and not absolutely, as I have always believed that Copernicus spoke. For to say that, assuming the earth moves and the sun stands still, all the appearances are saved better than with eccentrics and epicycles, is to speak well; there is no danger in this, and it is sufficient for mathematicians. But to want to affirm that the sun really is fixed in the center of the heavens and only revolves around itself (i.e., turns upon its axis) without traveling from east to west, and that the earth is situated in the third sphere and revolves with great speed around the sun, is a very dangerous thing, not only by irritating all the philosophers and scholastic theologians, but also by injuring our holy faith and rendering the Holy Scriptures false. For Your Reverence has demonstrated many ways of explaining Holy Scripture, but you have not applied them in particular, and without a doubt you would have found it most difficult if you had attempted to explain all the passages which you yourself have cited.

Second. I say that, as you know, the Council [of Trent] prohibits expounding the Scriptures contrary to the common agreement of the holy Fathers. And if Your Reverence would read not only the Fathers but also the commentaries of modern writers on Genesis, Psalms, Ecclesiastes and Josue, you would find that all agree in explaining literally (*ad litteram*) that the sun is in the heavens and moves swiftly around the earth, and that the earth is far from the heavens and stands immobile in the center of the universe. Now consider whether in all prudence the Church could encourage giving to Scripture a sense contrary to the holy Fathers and all the Latin and Greek commentators. Nor may it be answered that this is not a matter of faith, for if it is not a matter of faith from the point of view of the subject matter, it is on the part of the ones who have spoken. . . .

(continued)

(Continued)

Third. I say that if there were a true demonstration that the sun was in the center of the universe and the earth in the third sphere, and that the sun did not travel around the earth but the earth circled the sun, then it would be necessary to proceed with great caution in explaining the passages of Scripture which seemed contrary, and we would rather have to say that we did not understand them than to say that something was false which has been demonstrated. But I do not believe that there is any such demonstration; none has been shown to me. It is not the same thing to show that the appearances are saved by assuming that the sun really is in the center and the earth in the heavens. I believe that the first demonstration might

exist, but I have grave doubts about the second, and in a case of doubt, one may not depart from the Scriptures as explained by the holy Fathers.

 What does Galileo think is the difference between knowledge about the natural world and knowledge about the spiritual world? What does Galileo suggest that his opponents should do before dismissing his ideas? In what ways does Cardinal Bellarmine attempt to refute Galileo's ideas? Why did Galileo's ideas represent a threat to the Catholic Church?

Source: Galileo, *Letter to the Grand Duchess Christina*, 1614, in S. Drake, trans., *Discoveries and Opinions of Galileo* (New York: Doubleday, 1957); Robert Bellarmine, *Letter to Paolo Foscarini*, 1615, in J. J. Langford, *Galileo, Science, and the Church* (New York: Desclee, 1966).

---

astronomer could overlook that Galileo's discoveries, combined with Kepler's mathematical laws, had made nonsense of the Aristotelian-Ptolemaic world system and clearly established the reasonableness of the Copernican model. Nevertheless, the problem of explaining motion in the universe and tying together the ideas of Copernicus, Galileo, and Kepler had not yet been solved. This would be the work of an Englishman who has long been considered the greatest genius of the Scientific Revolution.

Newton

Born in the English village of Woolsthorpe in 1642, Isaac Newton was an unremarkable young man until he attended Cambridge University. His first great burst of creative energy came in 1666, when fear of the plague closed Cambridge and forced him to return to Woolsthorpe for eighteen months. There Newton discovered his creative talents: "In those days I was in the prime of my life for invention and minded mathematics and philosophy more than at any time since."[10] During this period, he invented the calculus, a mathematical means of calculating rates of change; began his investigations into the composition of light; and inaugurated his work on the law of universal gravitation. Two years after his return to Cambridge, in 1669, he accepted a chair in mathematics at the university. During a second intense period of creativity from 1684 to 1686, he wrote his famous *Principia* (prin-SIP-ee-uh) (see the box on p. 483). After a nervous breakdown in 1693, he sought and received an administrative post as warden of the royal mint and was advanced to master of the mint by 1699, a post he held until his death in 1727. Made president of the Royal Society (see "The Scientific Societies" later in this chapter) in 1703 and knighted in 1705 for his great achievements, Sir Isaac Newton is to this day the only English scientist to be buried in Westminster Abbey.

NEWTON AND THE OCCULT Although Newton occupies a very special place in the history of modern science, we need

to remember that he, too, remained extremely interested in aspects of the occult world. He left behind hundreds of manuscript pages of his studies of alchemy, and in fact, his alchemical experiments were a major feature of his life until he moved to London in 1696 to become warden of the royal mint. The British economist John Maynard Keynes said of Newton after examining his manuscripts in 1936:

> Newton was not the first of the age of reason. He was the last of the magicians. . . . He looked on the whole universe and all that is in it as a riddle, as a secret which could be read by applying pure thought to certain evidence, certain mystic clues which God had laid about the world to allow a sort of philosopher's treasure hunt to the esoteric brotherhood. He believed that these clues were to be found partly in the evidence of the heavens and in the constitution of elements . . . but also partly in certain papers and traditions handed down by the brethren in an unknown chain back to the original cryptic revelation in Babylonia.[11]

Although Newton may have considered himself a representative of the Hermetic tradition, he chose, it has been recently argued, for both political and psychological reasons to repress that part of his being, and it is as the "symbol of Western science" that he came to be viewed.

UNIVERSAL LAW OF GRAVITATION Newton's major work, the "hinge point of modern scientific thought," was his *Mathematical Principles of Natural Philosophy*, known simply as the *Principia*, the first word of its Latin title. In this work, the last highly influential book in Europe to be written in Latin, Newton spelled out the mathematical proofs demonstrating his universal law of gravitation. Newton's work was the culmination of the theories of Copernicus, Kepler, and Galileo. Though each had undermined some part of the Aristotelian-Ptolemaic cosmology, until Newton no one had pieced together a coherent synthesis for a new cosmology.

In the first book of the *Principia*, Newton defined the basic concepts of mechanics by elaborating the three laws of motion:

NEWTON'S RULES OF REASONING

IN 1687, ISAAC NEWTON PUBLISHED HIS MASTERPIECE, the *Mathematical Principles of Natural Philosophy*, or *Principia*. In this work, Newton demonstrated the mathematical proofs for his universal law of gravitation and completed the new cosmology begun by Copernicus, Kepler, and Galileo. He also described the rules of reasoning by which he arrived at his universal law.

Isaac Newton, *Rules of Reasoning in Philosophy*

Rule 1

We are to admit no more causes of natural things than such as are both true and sufficient to explain their appearances.

To this purpose the philosophers say that Nature does nothing in vain, and more is in vain when less will serve; for Nature is pleased with simplicity, and affects not the pomp of superfluous causes.

Rule 2

Therefore to the same natural effects we must, as far as possible, assign the same causes.

As to respiration in a man and in a beast; the descent of stones in Europe and in America; the light of our culinary fire and of the sun; the reflection of light in the earth and in the planets.

Rule 3

The qualities of bodies, which admit neither intensification nor remission of degrees, and which are found to belong to all bodies within the reach of our experiments, are to be esteemed the universal qualities of all bodies whatsoever.

For since qualities of bodies are only known to us by experiments, we are to hold for universal all such as universally agree with experiments; and such as are not liable to diminution can never be quite taken away.

Rule 4

In experimental philosophy we are to look upon propositions inferred by general induction from phenomena as accurately or very nearly true, notwithstanding any contrary hypotheses that may be imagined, till such time as other phenomena occur, by which they may either be made more accurate, or liable to exceptions.

This rule we must follow, that the argument of induction may not be evaded by hypotheses.

 What are Newton's rules of reasoning? How important were they to the development of the Scientific Revolution? How would following these rules change a person's view of the world, of European religious traditions, and of ancient "science"?

Source: Newton, *The Mathematical Principles of Natural Philosophy* (London, 1803), pp. 160–162.

every object continues in a state of rest or uniform motion in a straight line unless deflected by a force, the rate of change of motion of an object is proportional to the force acting on it, and to every action there is always an equal and opposite reaction. In book 3, Newton applied his theories of mechanics to the problems of astronomy by demonstrating that these three laws of motion govern the planetary bodies as well as terrestrial objects. Integral to his whole argument was the universal law of gravitation, which explained why the planetary bodies did not go off in straight lines but continued in elliptical orbits about the sun. In mathematical terms, Newton explained that every object in the universe was attracted to every other object with a force (gravity) that is directly proportional to the product of their masses and inversely proportional to the square of the distances between them.

The implications of Newton's universal law of gravitation were enormous, even though another century would

Isaac Newton. With a single law, that of universal gravitation, Isaac Newton was able to explain all motion in the universe. His great synthesis of the work of his predecessors created a new picture of the cosmos, one in which the universe was viewed as a great machine operating according to natural laws. Enoch Seeman painted this portrait of Newton one year before his death.

CHRONOLOGY	Important Works of the Scientific Revolution	
Copernicus, *On the Revolutions of the Heavenly Spheres*	1543
Vesalius, *On the Fabric of the Human Body*	1543
Galileo, *The Starry Messenger*	1610
Harvey, *On the Motion of the Heart and Blood*	1628
Galileo, *Dialogue on the Two Chief World Systems*	1632
Cavendish, *Grounds of Natural Philosophy*	1668
Newton, *Principia*	1687

pass before they were widely recognized. Newton had demonstrated that one universal law, mathematically proved, could explain all motion in the universe, from the movements of the planets in the celestial world to an apple falling from a tree in the terrestrial world. The secrets of the natural world could be known by human investigations. At the same time, the Newtonian synthesis created a new cosmology in which the world was seen largely in mechanistic terms. The universe was one huge, regulated, and uniform machine that operated according to natural laws in absolute time, space, and motion. Although Newton believed that God was "everywhere present" and acted as the force that moved all bodies on the basis of the laws he had discovered, later generations dropped his spiritual assumptions. Newton's **world-machine**, conceived as operating absolutely in time, space, and motion, dominated the Western worldview until the twentieth century, when the Einsteinian revolution, based on the concept of relativity, superseded the Newtonian mechanistic concept.

Newton's ideas were soon accepted in England, possibly out of national pride and conviction and, as has been argued recently, for political reasons (see "Science and Society" later in this chapter). Natural philosophers on the continent resisted Newton's ideas, and it took much of the eighteenth century before they were generally accepted everywhere in Europe. They were also reinforced by developments in other fields, especially medicine.

Advances in Medicine and Chemistry

 FOCUS QUESTION: What did Paracelsus, Vesalius, and Harvey contribute to a scientific view of medicine?

Although the Scientific Revolution of the sixteenth and seventeenth centuries is associated primarily with the dramatic changes in astronomy and mechanics that precipitated a new perception of the universe, a third field that had been dominated by Greek thought in the Later Middle Ages, that of

medicine, also experienced a transformation. Late medieval medicine was dominated not by the teachings of Aristotle but by those of the Greek physician Galen (GAY-len), who had lived in the second century C.E.

Galen's influence on the medieval medical world was pervasive in anatomy, physiology, and disease. Galen had relied on animal, rather than human, dissection to arrive at a picture of human anatomy that was quite inaccurate in many instances. Even when Europeans began to practice human dissection in the Later Middle Ages, instruction in anatomy still relied on Galen. While a professor read a text of Galen, an assistant dissected a cadaver for illustrative purposes. Physiology, or the functioning of the body, was also dominated by Galenic hypotheses, including the belief that there were two separate blood systems. One controlled muscular activities and contained bright red blood moving upward and downward through the arteries; the other governed the digestive functions and contained dark red blood that ebbed and flowed in the veins.

Treatment of disease was highly influenced by Galen's doctrine of four bodily humors: blood, considered warm and moist; yellow bile, warm and dry; phlegm, cold and moist; and black bile, cold and dry. Since disease was supposedly the result of an imbalance of humors that could be discerned from the quantity and color of urine, the examination of a patient's urine became the chief diagnostic tool. Although purging and bleeding to remedy the imbalance were often harmful to patients, treatment with traditional herbal medicines sometimes proved beneficial.

Paracelsus

Three figures are associated with the changes in medicine in the sixteenth and seventeenth centuries: Paracelsus (par-uh-SELL-suss), Andreas Vesalius (ahn-DRAY-uss vuh-SAY-lee-uss), and William Harvey. Philippus Aureolus von Hohenheim (1493–1541), who renamed himself Paracelsus ("greater than Celsus," an ancient physician), traveled widely and may have been awarded a medical degree from the University of Ferrara in Italy. He achieved a moment of glory when he was appointed city physician and professor of medicine at Basel in 1527. But this, like so many other appointments, proved short-lived due to his vanity and quick temper. He could never disguise his contempt for universities and physicians who did not agree with his new ideas:

> I am *monarcha medicorum*, monarch of physicians, and I can prove to you what you cannot prove. . . . It was not the constellations that made me a physician: God made me. . . . I need not don a coat of mail or a buckler against you, for you are not learned or experienced enough to refute even one word of mine. . . . Let me tell you this: every little hair on my neck knows more than you and all your scribes, and my shoebuckles are more learned than your Galen and Avicenna, and my beard has more experience than all your high colleges.[12]

Paracelsus was not easy to get along with, and he was forced to wander from one town to another until his death in 1541.

Paracelsus rejected the work of both Aristotle and Galen and attacked the universities as centers of their moribund philosophy. He and his followers hoped to replace the traditional system with a new chemical philosophy that was based on a new understanding of nature derived from fresh observation and experiment. This chemical philosophy was in turn closely connected to a view of the universe based on the macrocosm-microcosm analogy. According to this view, a human being was a small replica (microcosm) of the larger world (macrocosm). All parts of the universe were represented within each person. As Paracelsus said, "For the sun and the moon and all planets, as well as the stars and the whole chaos, are in man. . . . For what is outside is also inside; and what is not outside man is not inside. The outer and the inner are one thing."[13] In accordance with the macrocosmic-microcosmic principle, Paracelsus believed that the chemical reactions of the universe as a whole were reproduced in human beings on a smaller scale. Disease, then, was not caused by an imbalance of the four humors, as Galen had argued, but was due to chemical imbalances that were localized in specific organs and could be treated by chemical remedies.

Although others had used chemical remedies, Paracelsus and his followers differed from them in giving careful attention to the proper dosage of their chemically prepared metals and minerals. Paracelsus had turned against the Galenic principle that "contraries cure" in favor of the ancient Germanic folk principle that "like cures like." The poison that caused a disease would be its cure if used in proper form and quantity. Despite the apparent effectiveness of this use of toxic substances as treatment (Paracelsus did have a strong reputation for actually curing his patients), his opponents viewed it as the practice of a "homicide physician." Later generations came to regard Paracelsus more favorably, and historians who have stressed Paracelsus's concept of disease and recognition of "new drugs" for medicine have viewed him as a father of modern medicine. Others have argued that his macrocosmic-microcosmic philosophy and use of "like cures like" drugs make him the forerunner of both homeopathy and the holistic medicine of the postmodern era.

Vesalius

The new anatomy of the sixteenth century was the work of Andreas Vesalius (1514–1564). His study of medicine at Paris involved him in the works of Galen. Especially important to him was a recently discovered text of Galen, *On Anatomical Procedures*, that led Vesalius to emphasize practical research as the principal avenue for understanding human anatomy. After receiving a doctorate in medicine at the University of Padua in 1536, he accepted a position there as professor of surgery. In 1543, he published his masterpiece, *On the Fabric of the Human Body*.

This book was based on his personal dissection of a body to illustrate what he was discussing. Vesalius's anatomical treatise presented a careful examination of the individual organs and general structure of the human body. The book would not have been feasible without both the artistic advances of the Renaissance and technical developments in the art of printing.

Andreas Vesalius. In this seventeenth-century French portrait of Andreas Vesalius, Vesalius is portrayed with one of his cadavers. His work established new understanding of the human body while the developments in artistic representation during the Renaissance allowed for more accurate representations of his findings, as seen here.

Together, they made possible the creation of illustrations superior to any done before.

Vesalius's hands-on approach to teaching anatomy enabled him to rectify some of Galen's most glaring errors. He did not hesitate, for example, to correct Galen's assertion that the great blood vessels originated from the liver since his own observations made it apparent that they came from the heart. Nevertheless, Vesalius still clung to a number of Galen's erroneous assertions, including the Greek physician's ideas on the ebb and flow of two kinds of blood in the veins and arteries. It was not until William Harvey's work on the circulation of the blood nearly a century later that this Galenic misperception was corrected.

William Harvey

William Harvey (1578–1657) attended Cambridge University and later Padua, where he received a doctorate in medicine in 1602. His reputation rests on his book *On the Motion of the Heart and Blood*, published in 1628. Although questions had been raised in the sixteenth century about Galen's physiological principles, no major break from his system had occurred. Harvey's work, which was based on meticulous observations and experiments, led him to demolish the ancient Greek's erroneous contentions. Harvey demonstrated that the heart and not the liver was the beginning point of the circulation of blood in the body, that the same blood flows in both veins and arteries, and most important, that the blood makes a complete circuit as it passes through the body. His efforts did not come without an ethical cost, however. Harvey chose as his experimental subjects people who had been convicted of murder or treason and operated on them while they were alive in order to assess certain organ function, such as the process of digestion. Although Harvey's work dealt a severe blow to Galen's theories, his ideas did not begin to achieve general recognition until the 1660s, when capillaries, which explained how the blood passed from the arteries to the veins, were discovered. Harvey's theory of the circulation of the blood laid the foundation for modern physiology.

Chemistry

Although Paracelsus had proposed a new chemical philosophy in the sixteenth century, it was not until the seventeenth and eighteenth centuries that a science of chemistry arose. Robert Boyle (1627–1691) was one of the first scientists to conduct controlled experiments. His pioneering work on the properties of gases led to Boyle's law, which states that the volume of a gas varies with the pressure exerted on it. Boyle also rejected the medieval belief that all matter consisted of the same components in favor of the view that matter is composed of atoms, which he called "little particles of all shapes and sizes" and which would later be known as the chemical elements.

In the eighteenth century, Antoine Lavoisier (AHN-twahn lah-vwah-ZYAY) (1743–1794) invented a system of naming the chemical elements, much of which is still used today. In helping to show that water is a compound of oxygen and hydrogen, he demonstrated the fundamental rules of chemical combination. Many regard him as the founder of modern chemistry. Lavoisier's wife, Marie-Anne, was her husband's scientific collaborator. She learned English in order to translate the work of British chemists for her husband and made engravings to illustrate his scientific experiments. Marie-Anne Lavoisier is a reminder that women too played a role in the Scientific Revolution.

Women in the Origins of Modern Science

 FOCUS QUESTION: What role did women play in the Scientific Revolution?

During the Middle Ages, except for members of religious orders, women who sought a life of learning were severely hampered by the traditional attitude that a woman's proper role was as a daughter, wife, and mother. But in the late fourteenth and early fifteenth centuries, new opportunities for elite women emerged as enthusiasm for the new secular learning called humanism led Europe's privileged and learned men to encourage women to read and study classical and Christian texts. The ideal of a

humanist education for some of the daughters of Europe's elite persisted into the seventeenth century, but only for some privileged women.

Margaret Cavendish

Much as they were drawn to humanism, women were also attracted to the Scientific Revolution. Unlike females educated formally in humanist schools, women interested in science had to obtain a largely informal education. European nobles had the leisure and resources that gave them easy access to the world of learning. This door was also open to noblewomen who could participate in the informal scientific networks of their fathers and brothers. One of the most prominent female scientists of the seventeenth century, Margaret Cavendish (KAV-un-dish) (1623–1673), came from an aristocratic background. Cavendish was not a popularizer of science for women but a participant in the crucial scientific debates of her time. Despite her achievements, however, she was excluded from membership in the Royal Society (see "The Scientific Societies" later in this chapter), although she was once allowed to attend a meeting. She wrote a number of works on scientific matters, including *Observations upon Experimental Philosophy* and *Grounds of Natural Philosophy*, published in 1668. In these works, she did not hesitate to attack what she considered the defects of the rationalist and empiricist approaches to scientific knowledge and was especially critical of the growing belief that through science,

AS400 DB/Bettman/Corbis

Margaret Cavendish. Shown in this portrait is Margaret Cavendish, the duchess of Newcastle. She was a prolific writer, responsible for plays, biographies, poetry, and prose romances, as well as works in philosophy and science. Unlike most female authors of the time, who wrote anonymously, she used her own name on her works.

MARGARET CAVENDISH: THE EDUCATION OF WOMEN

MARGARET CAVENDISH'S HUSBAND, WHO WAS THIRTY YEARS HER SENIOR, encouraged her to pursue her literary interests. In addition to scientific works, she wrote plays, an autobiography, and a biography of her husband titled *The Life of the Thrice Noble, High and Puissant Prince William Cavendish, Duke, Marquess and Earl of Newcastle*. The autobiography and biography led one male literary critic to call her "a mad, conceited and ridiculous woman." In an essay titled "The Philosophical and Physical Opinions," she discussed the constraints placed upon women, including education.

Margaret Cavendish, "The Philosophical and Physical Opinions"

But to answer those objections that are made against me, as first how should I come by so much experience as I have expressed in my several books to have? I answer: I have had by relation the long and much experience of my lord, who hath lived to see and be in many changes of fortune and to converse with many men of sundry nations, ages, qualities, tempers, capacities, abilities, wits, humours, fashions and customs.

And as many others, especially wives, go from church to church, from ball to ball . . . gossiping from house to house, so when my lord admits me to his company I listen with attention to his edifying discourse and I govern myself by his doctrine: I dance a measure with the muses, feast with sciences, or sit and discourse with the arts.

The second is that, since I am no scholar, I cannot know the names and terms of art and the divers and several opinions of several authors. I answer: that I must have been a natural fool if I had not known and learnt them, for they are customarily taught all children from the nurse's breast, being ordinarily discoursed of in every family that is of quality, and the family from whence I sprung are neither natural idiots or ignorant fools, but the contrary, for they were rational, learned, understanding and witty. . . .

But as I have said my head was so full of my own natural fantasies, as it had not room for strangers to board therein, and certainly natural reason is a better tutor than education. For though education doth help natural reason to a more sudden maturity, yet natural reason was the first educator: for natural reason did first compose commonwealths, invented arts and science, and if natural reason hath composed, invented and discovered, I know no reason but natural reason may find out what natural reason hath composed, invented and discovered with the help of education. . . .

 What arguments does Cavendish make to defend her right and ability to be an author?

Source: K. Aughterson, *Renaissance Woman: A Sourcebook* (London: Routledge, 1995); pp. 286–288.

---

humans would be masters of nature: "We have no power at all over natural causes and effects . . . for man is but a small part. . . . His powers are but particular actions of Nature, and he cannot have a supreme and absolute power."[14]

As an aristocrat (she was the duchess of Newcastle), Cavendish was a good example of the women in France and England who worked in science (see the box above). In Germany, women interested in science came from a different background. There the tradition of female participation in craft production enabled some women to become involved in observational science, especially entomology and astronomy. Between 1650 and 1710, one of every seven German astronomers was a woman.

Maria Merian

A good example of female involvement in the Scientific Revolution stemming from the craft tradition was Maria Sibylla Merian (MAY-ree-un) (1647–1717), who had established a reputation as an important entomologist by the beginning of the eighteenth century. Merian's training came from working in her father's workshop, where she learned the art of illustration, a training of great importance since her exact observation of insects and plants was demonstrated through the superb illustrations she made. In 1699, she undertook an expedition into the wilds of the Dutch colony of Surinam in South America to collect and draw samples of plants and insect life. This led to her major scientific work, the *Metamorphosis of the Insects of Surinam*, in which she used sixty illustrations to show the reproductive and developmental cycles of Surinam's insect life.

Maria Winkelmann

The craft organization of astronomy also gave women opportunities to become involved in science. Those who did worked in family observatories; hence, daughters and wives received training as apprentices to fathers or husbands. The most famous of the female astronomers in Germany was Maria Winkelmann (VINK-ul-mahn) (1670–1720). She was educated by her father and uncle and received advanced training in astronomy from a nearby self-taught astronomer. When she married Gottfried Kirch, Germany's foremost astronomer, she became his assistant at the astronomical observatory operated in Berlin by the Academy of Science. She made some original contributions, including a hitherto undiscovered comet, as her husband related:

Early in the morning (about 2:00 A.M.) the sky was clear and starry. Some nights before, I had observed a variable star, and my wife (as I slept) wanted to find and see it for herself. In so doing, she found a comet in the sky. At which time she woke me, and I found that it was indeed a comet. . . . I was surprised that I had not seen it the night before.[15]

Moreover, Winkelmann corresponded with the famous scientist Gottfried Leibniz (who invented the calculus independently of Newton), who praised her effusively as "a most learned woman who could pass as a rarity." When her husband died in 1710, she applied for a position as assistant astronomer for which she was highly qualified. As a woman—with no university degree—she was denied the post by the Berlin Academy, which feared that it would establish a precedent by hiring a woman ("mouths would gape"). Winkelmann continued to do much of the work at the Berlin Academy once her son Christoph was appointed astronomer.

Winkelmann's difficulties with the Berlin Academy reflect the obstacles women faced in being accepted in scientific work, which was considered a male preserve. Although no formal statutes excluded women from membership in the new scientific societies, no woman was invited to join either the Royal Society of England or the French Academy of Sciences until the twentieth century. All of these women scientists were exceptional, since a life devoted to any kind of scholarship was still viewed as being at odds with the domestic duties women were expected to perform.

Debates on the Nature of Women

The nature and value of women had been the subject of an ongoing, centuries-long debate known as the **querelles des femmes** (keh-REL day FAHM)—arguments about women. Male opinions in the debate were largely a carryover from medieval times and were not favorable. Women were portrayed as inherently base, prone to vice, easily swayed, and "sexually insatiable." Hence, men needed to control them. Learned women were viewed as having overcome female liabilities to become like men. One man in praise of a woman scholar remarked that her writings were so good that you "would hardly believe they were done by a woman at all."

In the early modern era, women joined this debate by arguing against these male images of women. They argued that women also had rational minds and could grow from education. Further, since most women were pious, chaste, and temperate, there was no need for male authority over them. These female defenders of women emphasized education as the key to women's ability to move into the world. How, then, did the changes brought by the Scientific Revolution affect this debate over the nature of women? In an era of intellectual revolution in which traditional authorities were being overthrown, we might expect significant change in men's views of women. But by and large, instead of becoming an instrument for liberation, science was used to find new support for the old, stereotypical views about a woman's place in the scheme of things.

An important project in the new anatomy of the sixteenth and seventeenth centuries was the attempt to illustrate the human body and skeleton. For Vesalius, the portrayal of physical differences between males and females was limited to external bodily form (the outlines of the body) and the sexual organs. Vesalius saw no difference in skeletons and portrayed them as the same for men and women. It was not until the eighteenth century, in fact, that a new anatomy finally prevailed. Drawings of female skeletons between 1730 and 1790 varied, but females tended to have a larger pelvic area, and, in some instances, female skulls were portrayed as smaller than those of males. Eighteenth-century studies on the anatomy and physiology of sexual differences provided "scientific evidence" to reaffirm the traditional inferiority of women. The larger pelvic area "proved" that women were meant to be childbearers, and the larger skull "demonstrated" the superiority of the male mind. Male-dominated science had been used to "prove" male social dominance.

At the same time, during the seventeenth and eighteenth centuries, women even lost the traditional spheres of influence they had possessed, especially in the science-related art of midwifery. Women serving as midwives had traditionally been responsible for birthing. Similar to barber-surgeons or apothecaries (see Chapter 17), midwives had acquired their skills through apprenticeship. But the impact of the Scientific Revolution caused traditional crafts to be upgraded and then even professionalized as males took over. When medical men entered this arena, they also began to use devices and techniques derived from the study of anatomy. These were increasingly used to justify the male takeover of the traditional role of midwives. By the end of the eighteenth century, midwives were simply accessories to the art they had once controlled, except among the poor. Since little money was to be made in serving the lower classes, midwives were allowed to continue to practice their traditional art among them.

Overall, the Scientific Revolution reaffirmed traditional ideas about women. Male scientists used the new science to spread the view that women were inferior by nature, subordinate to men, and suited by nature to play a domestic role as nurturing mothers. The widespread distribution of books ensured the continuation of these ideas. Jean de La Bruyère (ZHAHNH duh lah broo-YARE), the seventeenth-century French moralist, was typical when he remarked that an educated woman was like a gun that was a collector's item, "which one shows to the curious, but which has no use at all, any more than a carousel horse."[16]

Toward a New Earth: Descartes, Rationalism, and a New View of Humankind

 FOCUS QUESTION: Why is Descartes considered the founder of modern rationalism?

The fundamentally new conception of the universe contained in the cosmological revolution of the sixteenth and seventeenth centuries inevitably had an impact on the Western

Descartes. Renè Descartes was one of the primary figures in the Scientific Revolution. Claiming to use reason as his sole guide to truth, Descartes posited a sharp distinction between mind and matter. He is shown here in a portrait done around 1649 by Frans Hals, one of the painters of the Dutch golden age who was famous for his portraits, especially that of Descartes.

view of humankind. Nowhere is this more evident than in the work of Renè Descartes (ruh-NAY day-KART) (1596–1650), an extremely important figure in Western history. Descartes began by reflecting the doubt and uncertainty that seemed pervasive in the confusion of the seventeenth century and ended with a philosophy that dominated Western thought until the twentieth century.

Descartes was born into a family of the French lower nobility. After a Jesuit education, he studied law at Poitiers but traveled to Paris to study by himself. In 1618, at the beginning of the Thirty Years' War, Descartes volunteered for service in the army of Maurice of Nassau, but he seems to have been interested less in military action than in traveling and finding leisure time to think. On the night of November 10, 1619, Descartes underwent what one historian has called an experience comparable to the "ecstatic illumination of the mystic." Having perceived in one night the outlines of a new rational-mathematical system, with a sense of divine approval he made a new commitment to mind, mathematics, and a mechanical universe. For the rest of his life, Descartes worked out the details of his vision.

The starting point for Descartes's new system was doubt, as he explained at the beginning of his most famous work, the *Discourse on Method*, written in 1637:

> From my childhood, I have been familiar with letters; and as I was given to believe that by their help a clear and certain knowledge of all that is useful in life might be acquired, I was ardently desirous of instruction. But as soon as I had finished the entire course of study, at the close of which it is customary to be admitted into the order of the learned, I completely changed my opinion. For I found myself involved in so many doubts and errors, that I was convinced I had advanced no farther in all my attempts at learning, than the discovery of my own ignorance.[17]

Descartes decided to set aside all that he had learned and begin again. One fact seemed beyond doubt—his own existence:

> But immediately upon this I observed that [while] I thus wished to think that all was false, it was absolutely necessary that I who thus thought, should be [something]; and as I observed that this truth, *I think, [therefore] I am*, was so certain and of such evidence, that no ground of doubt, however extravagant, could be alleged by the Sceptics capable of shaking it, I concluded that I might without scruple accept it as the first principle of the Philosophy of which I was in search.[18]

With this emphasis on the mind, Descartes asserted that he would accept only those things that his reason said were true.

From his first postulate, Descartes deduced an additional principle, the separation of mind and matter. Descartes argued that since "the mind cannot be doubted but the body and material world can, the two must be radically different." From this came an absolute duality between mind and body that has been called **Cartesian dualism**. Using mind or human reason, the path to certain knowledge, and its best instrument, mathematics, humans can understand the material world because it is pure mechanism, a machine that is governed by its own physical laws because it was created by God, the great geometrician.

Descartes's conclusions about the nature of the universe and human beings had important implications. His separation of mind and matter allowed scientists to view matter as dead or inert, as something that was totally separate from themselves and could be investigated independently by reason. The split between mind and body led Westerners to equate their identity with mind and reason rather than with the whole organism. Descartes has rightly been called the father of modern **rationalism** (see the box on p. 490). His books were placed on the papal Index of Forbidden Books and condemned by many Protestant theologians. The radical Cartesian split between mind and matter, and between mind and body, had devastating implications not only for traditional religious views of the universe but also for how Westerners viewed themselves.

THE FATHER OF MODERN RATIONALISM

RENÉ DESCARTES HAS LONG BEEN VIEWED as the founder of modern rationalism and modern philosophy because he believed that human beings could understand the world—itself a mechanical system—by the same rational principles inherent in mathematical thinking. In his *Discourse on Method,* he elaborated on his approach to discovering truth.

Renè Descartes, *Discourse on Method*

In place of the numerous precepts which have gone to constitute logic, I came to believe that the four following rules would be found sufficient, always provided I took the firm and unswerving resolve never in a single instance to fail in observing them.

The first was to accept nothing as true which I did not evidently know to be such, that is to say, scrupulously to avoid precipitance and prejudice, and in the judgments I passed to include nothing additional to what had presented itself to my mind so clearly and so distinctly that I could have no occasion for doubting it.

The second, to divide each of the difficulties I examined into as many parts as may be required for its adequate solution.

The third, to arrange my thoughts in order, beginning with things the simplest and easiest to know, so that I may then ascend little by little, as it were step by step, to the knowledge of the more complex, and in doing so, to assign an order of

thought even to those objects which are not of themselves in any such order of precedence.

And the last, in all cases to make enumerations so complete, and reviews so general, that I should be assured of omitting nothing.

Those long chains of reasonings, each step simple and easy, which geometers are wont to employ in arriving even at the most difficult of their demonstrations, have led me to surmise that all the things we human beings are competent to know are interconnected in the same manner, and that none are so remote as to be beyond our reach or so hidden that we cannot discover them—that is, provided we abstain from accepting as true what is not thus related, i.e., keep always to the order required for their deduction one from another. And I had no great difficulty in determining what the objects are with which I should begin, for that I already knew, namely, that it was with the simplest and easiest. Bearing in mind, too, that of all those who in time past have sought for truth in the sciences, the mathematicians alone have been able to find any demonstrations, that is to say, any reasons which are certain and evident, I had no doubt that it must have been by a procedure of this kind that they had obtained them.

 Describe Descartes's principles of inquiry and compare them with Newton's rules of reasoning. What are the main similarities between these systems of thinking?

Source: N. K. Smith, trans., *Descartes' Philosophical Writings* (London: Palgrave Macmillan, 1958).

The Scientific Method and the Spread of Scientific Knowledge

 FOCUS QUESTION: How were the ideas of the Scientific Revolution spread, and what impact did they have on society and religion?

During the seventeenth century, scientific learning and investigation began to increase dramatically. Major universities in Europe established new chairs of science, especially in medicine. Royal and princely patronage of individual scientists became an international phenomenon.

The Scientific Method

Of great importance to the work of science was establishing the proper means to examine and understand the physical realm. This development of a **scientific method** was crucial to the evolution of science in the modern world.

FRANCIS BACON Curiously enough, it was an Englishman with few scientific credentials who attempted to put forth a

new method of acquiring knowledge that made an impact on English scientists in the seventeenth century and other European scientists in the eighteenth century. Francis Bacon (1561–1626), a lawyer and lord chancellor, rejected Copernicus and Kepler and misunderstood Galileo. And yet in his unfinished work, *The Great Instauration,* he called for his contemporaries "to commence a total reconstruction of sciences, arts, and all human knowledge, raised upon the proper foundations." Bacon did not doubt humans' ability to know the natural world, but he believed that they had proceeded incorrectly: "The entire fabric of human reason which we employ in the inquisition of nature is badly put together and built up, and like some magnificent structure without foundation."

Bacon's new foundation—a correct scientific method—was to be built on inductive principles. Rather than beginning with assumed first principles from which logical conclusions could be deduced, he urged scientists to proceed from the particular to the general. From carefully organized experiments and thorough, systematic observations, correct generalizations could be developed.

Bacon was clear about what he believed his method could accomplish. His concern was for practical results rather than for pure science. He stated that "the true and lawful goal of the sciences is none other than this: that human life be endowed with new discoveries and power." He wanted science to contribute to the "mechanical arts" by creating devices that would benefit industry, agriculture, and trade. Bacon was prophetic when he said that he was "laboring to lay the foundation, not of any sect or doctrine, but of human utility and power." And how would this "human power" be used? To "conquer nature in action."[19] The control and domination of nature became a central proposition of modern science and the technology that accompanied it. Only in the twentieth century did some scientists begin to ask whether this assumption might not be at the heart of the earth's ecological crisis.

DESCARTES Descartes proposed a different approach to scientific methodology by emphasizing deduction and mathematical logic. As Descartes explained in the *Discourse on Method*, each step in an argument should be as sharp and well founded as a mathematical proof:

> Those long chains of reasonings, each step simple and easy, which geometers are wont to employ in arriving even at the most difficult of their demonstrations, have led me to surmise that all the things we human beings are competent to know are interconnected in the same manner, and that none are so remote as to be beyond our reach or so hidden that we cannot discover them—that is, provided we abstain from accepting as true what is not thus related, i.e., keep always to the order required for their deduction one from another.[20]

Descartes believed, then, that one could start with self-evident truths, comparable to geometric axioms, and deduce more complex conclusions. His emphasis on deduction and mathematical order complemented Bacon's stress on experiment and induction. It was Sir Isaac Newton who synthesized them into a single scientific methodology by uniting Bacon's **empiricism** with Descartes's rationalism. This scientific method began with systematic observations and experiments, which were used to arrive at general concepts. New deductions derived from these general concepts could then be tested and verified by precise experiments.

The scientific method, of course, was valuable in answering the question of *how* something works, and its success in doing this gave others much confidence in the method. It did not attempt to deal with the question of *why* something happens or the purpose and meaning behind the world of nature. This allowed religion to retain its central importance in the seventeenth century (see "Science and Religion" later in this chapter).

The Spread of Scientific Knowledge

Also important to the work of science was the emergence of new learned societies and journals that enabled the new scientists to communicate their ideas to each other and to disseminate them to a wider, literate public.

THE SCIENTIFIC SOCIETIES The first of these scientific societies appeared in Italy, but those of England and France were ultimately of greater significance. The English Royal Society evolved out of informal gatherings of scientists at London and Oxford in the 1640s, although it did not receive a formal charter from King Charles II until 1662. The French Royal Academy of Sciences also arose out of informal scientific meetings in Paris during the 1650s. In 1666, Louis XIV formally recognized the group. The French Academy received abundant state support and remained under government control; the state appointed its members and paid their salaries. In contrast, the Royal Society of England received little government encouragement, and its fellows simply co-opted new members.

Louis XIV and Colbert Visit the Academy of Sciences. In the seventeenth century, individual scientists received royal and princely patronage, and a number of learned societies were established. In France, Louis XIV, urged on by his controller general, Jean-Baptiste Colbert, gave formal recognition to the French Academy in 1666. In this painting by Henri Testelin, Louis XIV is shown seated, surrounded by Colbert and members of the French Royal Academy of Sciences.

RMN-Grand Palais/Art Resource, NY

The Science of Collecting

THE ART OF COLLECTING WAS AN IMPORTANT part of scientific culture. Early scientists maintained their relevance to the scientific community by their collections of drawings and specimens. Wealthy patrons were able to amass thousands of species of plants and insects as well as gems and scientific instruments for academic study. The prestige of one's collection could lead to scientific posts. Sir Hans Sloane (1660–1753), portrayed with his drawings of plants (see photo, right), was an English physician who had spent fifteen months in Jamaica as a personal physician to the West Indies fleet in 1687. He collected around 800 species to bring back to England. His large collection fostered his position as president of the Royal College of Physicians and the Royal Society and also served as the foundation for the British Museum. Various collections were kept in drawers, seen in this photo of specimens of beetles in the Jans Sloane collection (see below, left). These private collections consisted of objects collected around the globe, as did the public collections found in botanical gardens. In France, the Royal Botanical Garden, founded in 1640, served as the leading center of botany in Europe; its gardens were divided into quarters representing Europe, Asia, Africa, and the Americas, as seen in a French drawing (see below, right).

National Portrait Gallery, London, UK/Bridgeman Images

National History Museum, London, UK/Bridgeman Images

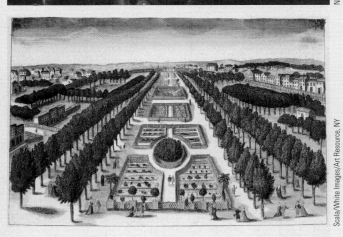

Scala/White Images/Art Resource, NY

Early on, both the English and the French scientific societies formally emphasized the practical value of scientific research. The Royal Society created a committee to investigate technological improvements for industry; the French Academy collected tools and machines (see "Images of Everyday Life" above). This concern with the practical benefits of science proved short-lived, however, as both societies came to focus their primary interest on theoretical work in mechanics and astronomy. The construction of observatories at Paris in 1667 and at Greenwich, England, in 1675 greatly facilitated research in astronomy by both groups. Although both the English and the French societies made useful contributions to scientific knowledge in the second half of the seventeenth century, their true significance was that they demonstrated the benefits of science proceeding as a cooperative venture.

Scientific journals furthered this concept of cooperation. The French *Journal des Savants* (zhoor-NAHL day sah-VAHNH), published weekly beginning in 1665, printed results of experiments as well as general scientific knowledge. Its format appealed to both scientists and the educated public interested in the new science. In contrast, the *Philosophical Transactions* of the Royal Society, also initiated in 1665, published papers of its members and learned correspondence and was aimed at practicing scientists. It became a prototype for the scholarly journals of later learned and academic societies and a crucial instrument for circulating news of scientific and academic activities.

SCIENCE AND SOCIETY The importance of science in the history of modern Western civilization is usually taken for granted. No doubt the Industrial Revolution of the nineteenth century provided tangible proof of the effectiveness of science and ensured its victory over Western minds. But how did science become such an integral part of Western culture in the seventeenth and eighteenth centuries? Recent research has stressed that one cannot simply assert that people perceived that science was a rationally superior system. Several factors, however, might explain the relatively rapid acceptance of the new science.

It has been argued that the literate mercantile and propertied elites of Europe were attracted to the new science because it offered new ways to exploit resources for profit. Some of the early scientists made it easier for these groups to accept the new ideas by showing how they could be applied directly to specific industrial and technological needs. Galileo, for example, consciously sought an alliance between science and the material interests of the educated elite when he assured his listeners that the science of mechanics would be quite useful "when it becomes necessary to build bridges or other structures over water." At the same time, Galileo stressed that science was fit for the "minds of the wise" and not for "the shallow minds of the common people." This made science part of the high culture of Europe's wealthy elites at a time when that culture was being increasingly separated from the popular culture of the lower classes (see Chapter 17).

It has also been argued that political interests used the new scientific conception of the natural world to bolster social stability. One scholar has argued that "no single event in the history of early modern Europe more profoundly shaped the integration of the new science into Western culture than did the English Revolution (1640–1660)."[21] Fed by their millenarian expectations that the end of the world would come and usher in a thousand-year reign of the saints, Puritan reformers felt it was important to reform and renew their society. They seized on the new science as a socially useful instrument to accomplish this goal. The Puritan Revolution's role in the acceptance of science, however, stemmed even more from the reaction to the radicalism spawned by the revolutionary ferment. The upheavals of the Puritan Revolution gave rise to groups, such as the Levellers, Diggers, and Ranters, who advocated not only radical political ideas but also a new radical science based on

Paracelsus and the natural magic associated with the Hermetic tradition. The propertied and educated elites responded vigorously to these challenges to the established order by supporting the new mechanistic science and appealing to the material benefits of science. Hence, the founders of the Royal Society were men who wanted to pursue an experimental science that would remain detached from radical reforms of church and state. Although willing to make changes, they now viewed those changes in terms of an increase in food production and commerce.

At the same time, princes and kings who were providing patronage for scientists were doing so not only for prestige but also for practical reasons, especially the military applications of the mathematical sciences. The use of gunpowder, for example, gave new importance to ballistics and metallurgy. Rulers, especially absolute ones, were also concerned about matters of belief in their realms and recognized the need to control and manage the scientific body of knowledge, as we have seen in the French Academy. In appointing its members and paying their salaries, Louis XIV was also ensuring that the members and their work would be under his control.

Science and Religion

In Galileo's struggle with the inquisitorial Holy Office of the Catholic Church, we see the beginning of the conflict between science and religion that has marked the history of modern Western civilization. Since time immemorial, theology had seemed to be the queen of the sciences. It was natural that the churches would continue to believe that religion was the final measure of all things. The emerging scientists, however, tried to draw lines between the knowledge of religion and the knowledge of "natural philosophy" or nature. Galileo had clearly felt that it was unnecessary to pit science against religion when he wrote:

> In discussions of physical problems we ought to begin not from the authority of scriptural passages, but from sense-experiences and necessary demonstrations; for the holy Bible and the phenomena of nature proceed alike from the divine word, the former as the dictate of the Holy Ghost and the latter as the observant executrix of God's commands. It is necessary for the Bible, in order to be accommodated to the understanding of every man, to speak many things which appear to differ from the absolute truth so far as the bare meaning of the words is concerned. But Nature, on the other hand, is inexorable and immutable; she never transgresses the laws imposed upon her, or cares a whit whether her abstruse reasons and methods of operation are understandable to men.[22]

To Galileo, it made little sense for the church to determine the nature of physical reality on the basis of biblical texts that were subject to radically divergent interpretations. The church, however, decided otherwise in Galileo's case and lent its great authority to one scientific theory, the Aristotelian-Ptolemaic cosmology, no doubt because it fit so well with its own philosophical views of reality. But the church's decision had tremendous consequences, just as the rejection of Darwin's ideas did in the nineteenth century. For educated individuals, it established a dichotomy between scientific investigations and religious beliefs. As the scientific beliefs triumphed, it became almost inevitable that religious beliefs would suffer, leading to a growing secularization in European intellectual life—precisely what the church had hoped to combat by opposing Copernicanism. Many seventeenth-century intellectuals were both religious and scientific and believed that the implications of this split would be tragic. Some believed that the split was largely unnecessary, while others felt the need to combine God, humans, and a mechanistic universe into a new philosophical synthesis. Two individuals—Spinoza and Pascal—illustrate the wide diversity in the response of European intellectuals to the implications of the cosmological revolution of the seventeenth century.

SPINOZA Benedict de Spinoza (spi-NOH-zuh) (1632–1677) was a philosopher who grew up in the relatively tolerant atmosphere of Amsterdam. He was excommunicated from the Amsterdam synagogue at the age of twenty-four for rejecting the tenets of Judaism. Ostracized by the local Jewish community and major Christian churches alike, Spinoza lived a quiet, independent life, earning a living by grinding optical lenses and refusing to accept an academic position in philosophy at the University of Heidelberg for fear of compromising his freedom of thought. Spinoza read a great deal of the new scientific literature and was influenced by Descartes.

Spinoza was unwilling to accept the implications of Descartes's ideas, especially the separation of mind and matter and the apparent separation of an infinite God from the finite world of matter. God was not simply the creator of the universe; he was the universe. All that is is in God, and nothing can be apart from God. This philosophy of pantheism (or monism) was set out in Spinoza's book *Ethics Demonstrated in the Geometrical Manner*, which was not published until after his death.

To Spinoza, human beings are not "situated in nature as a kingdom within a kingdom" but are as much a part of God or nature or the universal order as other natural objects. The failure to understand God had led to many misconceptions—for one, that nature exists only for one's use:

> As they find in themselves and outside themselves many means which assist them not a little in their search for what is useful, for instance, eyes for seeing, teeth for chewing, herbs and animals for yielding food, the sun for giving light, the sea for breeding fish, they come to look on the whole of nature as a means for obtaining such conveniences.[23]

Furthermore, unable to find any other cause for the existence of these things, they attributed them to a creator-God who must be worshiped to gain their ends: "Hence also it follows, that everyone thought out for himself, according to his abilities, a different way of worshiping God, so that God might love him more than his fellows, and direct the whole course of nature for the satisfaction of his blind cupidity and insatiable avarice." Then, when nature appeared unfriendly in the form of storms, earthquakes, and diseases, "they declared that such things happen, because the gods are angry at some

wrong done them by men, or at some fault committed in their worship," rather than realizing "that good and evil fortunes fall to the lot of pious and impious alike."[24] Likewise, human beings made moral condemnations of others because they failed to understand that human emotions, "passions of hatred, anger, envy and so, considered in themselves, follow from the same necessity and efficacy of nature" and "nothing comes to pass in nature in contravention to her universal laws." To explain human emotions, like everything else, we need to analyze them as we would the movements of planets: "I shall, therefore, treat of the nature and strength of my emotions according to the same method as I employed heretofore in my investigations concerning God and the mind. I shall consider human actions and desires in exactly the same manner as though I were concerned with lines, planes, and solids."[25] Everything has a rational explanation, and humans are capable of finding it. In using reason, people can find true happiness. Their real freedom comes when they understand the order and necessity of nature and achieve detachment from passing interests.

PASCAL Blaise Pascal (BLEZ pass-KAHL) (1623–1662) was a French scientist who sought to keep science and religion united.

Blaise Pascal (1623–62) (oil on canvas), Champaigne, Philippe de (1602–74)/Private Collection/Bridgeman Images

Blaise Pascal. Blaise Pascal was a brilliant scientist and mathematician who hoped to keep science and Christianity united. In his *Pensées*, he made a passionate argument on behalf of the Christian religion. He is pictured here in a portrait by Philippe de Champaigne, a well-known French portrait painter of the Baroque period.

CHRONOLOGY	Consequences of the Revolution: Important Works	
Bacon, *The Great Instauration*		1620
Descartes, *Discourse on Method*		1637
Pascal, *Pensées*		1669
Spinoza, *Ethics Demonstrated in the Geometrical Manner*		1677

An accomplished scientist and a brilliant mathematician, he excelled at both the practical, by inventing a calculating machine, and the abstract, by devising a theory of chance or probability and doing work on conic sections. After a profound mystical vision on the night of November 23, 1654, which assured him that God cared for the human soul, he devoted the rest of his life to religious matters. He planned to write an "apology for the Christian religion" but died before he could do so. He did leave a set of notes for the larger work, however, which in published form became known as the *Pensées* (pahn-SAY) (*Thoughts*).

In the *Pensées* (see the box below), Pascal tried to convert rationalists to Christianity by appealing to both their reason and their emotions. Humans were, he argued, frail creatures, often deceived by their senses, misled by reason, and battered by their emotions. And yet they were beings whose very nature involved thinking: "Man is but a reed, the weakest in nature; but he is a thinking reed."[26]

Pascal was determined to show that the Christian religion was not contrary to reason: "If we violate the principles of reason, our religion will be absurd, and it will be laughed at." Christianity, he felt, was the only religion that recognized people's true state of being as both vulnerable and great. To a Christian, a human being was both fallen and at the same time God's special creation. But it was not necessary to emphasize one at the expense of the other—to view humans as only rational or only hopeless. Pascal even had an answer for skeptics in his famous wager. God is a reasonable bet; it is worthwhile to assume that God exists. If he does, then we win all; if he does not, we lose nothing.

Despite his own background as a scientist and mathematician, Pascal refused to rely on the scientist's world of order and rationality to attract people to God: "If we submit

PASCAL: "WHAT IS A MAN IN THE INFINITE?"

PERHAPS NO INTELLECTUAL IN THE SEVENTEENTH CENTURY gave greater expression to the uncertainties generated by the cosmological revolution than Blaise Pascal, himself a scientist. Pascal's work, the *Pensées*, consisted of notes for a large unfinished work justifying the Christian religion. In this selection, Pascal presents his musings on the human place in an infinite world.

Blaise Pascal, *Pensées*

Let man then contemplate the whole of nature in her full and grand majesty, and turn his vision from the low objects which surround him. Let him gaze on that brilliant light, set like an eternal lamp to illumine the universe; let the earth appear to him a point in comparison with the vast circle described by the sun; and let him wonder at the fact that this vast circle is itself but a very fine point in comparison with that described by the stars in their revolution round the firmament. But if our view be arrested there, let our imagination pass beyond; it will sooner exhaust the power of conception than nature that of supplying material for conception. The whole visible world is only an imperceptible atom in the ample bosom of nature. No idea approaches it. We may enlarge our conceptions beyond all imaginable space; we only produce atoms in comparison with the reality of things. It is an infinite sphere, the centre of which is everywhere, the circumference nowhere.

In short it is the greatest sensible mark of the almighty power of God, that imagination loses itself in that thought.

Returning to himself, let man consider what he is in comparison with all existence; let him regard himself as lost in this remote corner of nature; and from the little cell in which he finds himself lodged, I mean the universe, let him estimate at their true value the earth, kingdoms, cities, and himself. What is a man in the Infinite? . . .

For in fact what is man in nature? A Nothing in comparison with the Infinite, an All in comparison with the Nothing, a mean between nothing and everything. Since he is infinitely removed from comprehending the extremes, the end of things and their beginning are hopelessly hidden from him in an impenetrable secret, he is equally incapable of seeing the nothing from which he was made, and the Infinite in which he is swallowed up. What will he do then, but perceive the appearance of the middle of things, in an eternal despair of knowing either their beginning or their end. All things proceed from the Nothing, and are borne towards the Infinite. Who will follow these marvellous processes? The Author of these wonders understands them. None other can do so.

 Why did Pascal question whether human beings could achieve scientific certainty? What is the significance of Pascal's thoughts for modern science?

Source: The Project Gutenberg EBook of Pascal's *Pensées*. Accessed from http://www.gutenberg.org/files/18269/18269-h/18269-h.htm.

everything to reason, there will be no mystery and no supernatural element in our religion." In the new cosmology of the seventeenth century, "finite man," Pascal believed, was lost in the new infinite world, a realization that frightened him: "The eternal silence of those infinite spaces strikes me with terror." The world of nature, then, could never reveal God: "Because they have failed to contemplate these infinites, men have rashly plunged into the examination of nature, as though they bore some proportion to her. . . . Their assumption is as infinite as their object." A Christian could only rely on a God who through Jesus cared for human beings. In the final analysis, after providing reasonable arguments for Christianity, Pascal came to rest on faith. Reason, he believed, could take people only so far: "The heart has its reasons of which

the reason knows nothing." As a Christian, faith was the final step: "The heart feels God, not the reason. This is what constitutes faith: God experienced by the heart, not by the reason."[27]

In retrospect, it is obvious that Pascal failed to achieve his goal of uniting Christianity and science. The gap between science and traditional religion grew ever wider as Europe continued along its path of secularization. Of course, traditional religions were not eliminated, nor is there any evidence that churches had yet lost their followers. That would happen later. Nevertheless, more and more of the intellectual, social, and political elites began to act on the basis of secular rather than religious assumptions.

CHAPTER SUMMARY

The Scientific Revolution represents a major turning point in modern Western civilization. In the Scientific Revolution, the Western world overthrew the medieval, Aristotelian-Ptolemaic worldview and geocentric universe and arrived at a new conception of the universe: the sun at the center, the planets as material bodies revolving around the sun in elliptical orbits, and an infinite rather than finite world. This new conception of the heavens was the work of a number of brilliant individuals: Nicolaus Copernicus, who theorized a heliocentric, or sun-centered, universe; Johannes Kepler, who discovered that planetary orbits were elliptical; Galileo Galilei, who, by using a telescope and observing the moon and sunspots, discovered that the universe seemed to be composed of material substance; and Isaac Newton, who tied together all of these ideas with his universal law of gravitation. The contributions of each individual built on the work of the others, thus establishing one of the basic principles of the new science—cooperation in the pursuit of new knowledge.

With the changes in the conception of "heaven" came changes in the conception of "earth." The work of Bacon and Descartes left Europeans with the separation of mind and matter and the belief that by using only reason they could in fact understand and dominate the world of nature. The development of a scientific methodology

furthered the work of the scientists, and the creation of scientific societies and learned journals spread its results. The Scientific Revolution was more than merely intellectual theories. It also appealed to nonscientific elites because of its practical implications for economic progress and for maintaining the social order, including the waging of war.

Although traditional churches stubbornly resisted the new ideas and a few intellectuals pointed to some inherent flaws, nothing was able to halt the supplanting of the traditional ways of thinking by new ways of thinking that created a more fundamental break with the past than that represented by the breakup of Christian unity in the Reformation.

The Scientific Revolution forced Europeans to change their conception of themselves. At first, some were appalled and even frightened by its implications. Formerly, humans on earth had viewed themselves as being at the center of the universe. Now the earth was only a tiny planet revolving around a sun that was itself only a speck in a boundless universe. Most people remained optimistic despite the apparent blow to human dignity. After all, had Newton not demonstrated that the universe was a great machine governed by natural laws? Newton had found one— the universal law of gravitation. Could others not find other laws? Were there not natural laws governing every aspect of human endeavor that could be found by the new scientific method? Thus, as we shall see in the next chapter, the Scientific Revolution leads us logically to the Enlightenment in the eighteenth century.

CHAPTER TIMELINE

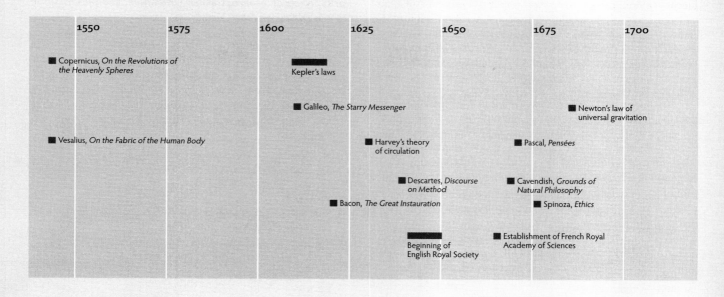

| | 1550 | 1575 | 1600 | 1625 | 1650 | 1675 | 1700 |

■ Copernicus, *On the Revolutions of the Heavenly Spheres*

Kepler's laws

■ Galileo, *The Starry Messenger*

■ Vesalius, *On the Fabric of the Human Body*

■ Harvey's theory of circulation

■ Newton's law of universal gravitation

■ Pascal, *Pensées*

■ Descartes, *Discourse on Method*

■ Cavendish, *Grounds of Natural Philosophy*

■ Bacon, *The Great Instauration*

■ Spinoza, *Ethics*

Beginning of English Royal Society

■ Establishment of French Royal Academy of Sciences

CHAPTER REVIEW

Upon Reflection

Q How do you explain the emergence of the Scientific Revolution?

Q What do we mean by the "Newtonian world-machine," and what is its significance?

Q Compare the methods used by Bacon and Descartes. Would Pascal agree with their methods and interests? Why or why not?

Key Terms

Scientific Revolution (p. 473)
geocentric conception (p. 474)
heliocentric conception (p. 475)
world-machine (p. 484)
querelles des femmes (p. 488)

Cartesian dualism (p. 489)
rationalism (p. 489)
scientific method (p. 490)
empiricism (p. 491)

Suggestions for Further Reading

GENERAL WORKS   General surveys of the entire Scientific Revolution include **J. Henry, *The Scientific Revolution and the Origins of Modern Science***, 2nd ed. (London, 2002), and **D. Wootton, *The Invention of Science: A New History of the Scientific Revolution*** (New York, 2015). See also **P. Dear, *Revolutionizing the Sciences: European Knowledge and Its Ambitions, 1500–1700*** (Princeton, N.J., 2001). On the Scientific Revolution in global perspective, see **T. Hoff, *Intellectual Curiosity and the Scientific Revolution: A Global Perspective*** (Cambridge, U.K., 2011), and **W. E. Burns, *The Scientific Revolution in Global Perspective*** (New York, 2015). On the relationship of magic to the beginnings of the Scientific Revolution, see the pioneering work by **F. Yates, *The Rosicrucian Enlightenment*** (London, 1975). On the relationship between Renaissance artists and the Scientific Revolution, see **P. H. Smith, *Body of the Artisan: Art and Experience in the Scientific Revolution*** (Chicago, 2006).

A REVOLUTION IN ASTRONOMY   On the important figures of the revolution in astronomy, see **H. Margolis, *It Started with Copernicus: How Turning the World Inside Out Led to the Scientific Revolution*** (New York, 2002); **D. Wootton, *Galileo: Watcher of the Stars*,** (New Haven, Conn., 2013); **M. Casper, *Johannes Kepler*,** trans. **C. D. Hellman** (London, 1959), the standard biography; **R. S. Westfall, *The Life of Isaac Newton*** (New York, 1993); and **P. Fara, *Newton: The Making of Genius*** (New York, 2004).

ADVANCES IN MEDICINE   For a general survey of medicine and the Scientific Revolution, see **M. Lindemann, *Medicine and Society in Early Modern Europe*** (Cambridge, 2010). The worldview of Paracelsus can be examined in **P. Ball, *The Devil's Doctor: Paracelsus and the World of Renaissance Magic and Science*** (New York, 2006). The standard biography of Vesalius is **C. D. O'Malley, *Andreas Vesalius of Brussels, 1514–1564***

(Berkeley, Calif., 1964). The work of Harvey is discussed in **G. Whitteridge, *William Harvey and the Circulation of the Blood*** (London, 1971).

IMPACT OF SCIENCE The importance of Francis Bacon in the early development of science is underscored in **P. Zagorin, *Francis Bacon*** (Princeton, N.J., 1998). A good introduction to the work of Descartes can be found in **G. Radis-Lewis, *Descartes: A Biography*** (Ithaca, N.Y., 1998).

WOMEN AND SCIENCE On the subject of women and early modern science, see the comprehensive and highly informative work by **L. Schiebinger, *The Mind Has No Sex? Women in the Origins of Modern Science*** (Cambridge, Mass., 1989) and **K. Park, *Secrets of Women: Gender, Generation, and the Origins of Human Dissection*** (New York, 2010).

SCIENCE AND SOCIETY The social and political context for the triumph of science in the seventeenth and eighteenth centuries is examined in **M. C. Jacobs, *The Cultural Meaning of the Scientific Revolution*** (New York, 1988). On the relationship of science and industry, see **S. Gaukroger, *The Emergence of a Scientific Culture: Science and the Shaping of Modernity, 1210–1685*** (Oxford, 2006).

Notes

1. Galileo, *Discoveries and Opinions*, tr. and ed. S. Drake (Garden City, N.Y., 1957), pp. 177, 180.
2. Quoted in A. G. R. Smith, *Science and Society in the Sixteenth and Seventeenth Centuries* (London, 1972), p. 59.
3. E. MacCurdy, *The Notebooks of Leonardo da Vinci* (London, 1948), vol. 1, p. 634.
4. Ibid., p. 636.
5. F. Yates, *Giordano Bruno and the Hermetic Tradition* (New York, 1964), p. 448.
6. Ibid., p. 450.
7. Quoted in Smith, *Science and Society*, p. 97.
8. L. P. Smith, *Life and Letters of* Sir Henry Wotton (Oxford, 1907), vol. 1, pp. 486–487.
9. Quoted in J. H. Randall, *The Making of the Modern Mind* (Boston, 1926), p. 234.
10. Quoted in Smith, *Science and Society*, p. 124.
11. Quoted in B. J. Dobbs, *The Foundations of Newton's Alchemy* (Cambridge, 1975), pp. 13–14.
12. Jolande Jacobi, ed., *Paracelsus: Selected Writings* (New York, 1965), pp. 5–6.
13. Ibid., p. 21.
14. Quoted in L. Schiebinger, *The Mind Has No Sex? Women in the Origins of Modern Science* (Cambridge, Mass., 1989), pp. 52–53.
15. Ibid., p. 85.
16. Quoted in P. Stock, *Better than Rubies: A History of Women's Education* (New York, 1978), p. 16.
17. *The Method, Meditations, and Selections from the Principles of Descartes*, Sixth Edition, John Veitch, trans. (William Blackwood and Sons: Edinburgh and London, 1879), pp. 5–6.
18. Ibid., p. 33.
19. Francis Bacon, *The Great Instauration*, trans. Jerry Weinberger (Arlington Heights, Ill., 1989), pp. 2, 8, 16, 21.
20. Descartes, *Discourse on Method*, in *Philosophical Writings*, p. 75.
21. M. C. Jacob, *The Cultural Meaning of the Scientific Revolution* (New York, 1988), p. 73.
22. Stillman Drake, ed., trans., *Discoveries and Opinions of Galileo* (New York, 1957), p. 182.
23. Benedict de Spinoza, *Ethics*, trans. R. H. M. Elwes (New York, 1955), pp. 75–76.
24. Ibid., p. 76.
25. Spinoza, *Letters*, quoted in Randall, *The Making of the Modern Mind*, p. 247.
26. Blaise Pascal, *Pensées*, trans. J. M. Cohen (Harmondsworth, U.K., 1961), p. 100.
27. Ibid., pp. 31, 52–53, 164, 165.

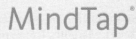 **MindTap®** is a fully online, highly personalized learning experience built upon Cengage Learning content. MindTap combines student learning tools—readings, multimedia, activities, and assessments—into a singular Learning Path that guides students through the course.

THE EIGHTEENTH CENTURY: AN AGE OF ENLIGHTENMENT

Portrait of Madame Geoffrin

© RMN-Grand Palais/Art Resource, NY

CHAPTER OUTLINE AND FOCUS QUESTIONS

The Enlightenment

Q What intellectual developments led to the emergence of the Enlightenment? Who were the leading figures of the Enlightenment, and what were their main contributions? In what type of social environment did the philosophes thrive, and what role did women play in that environment?

Culture and Society in the Enlightenment

Q What innovations in art, music, and literature occurred in the eighteenth century? How did popular culture differ from high culture in the eighteenth century?

Religion and the Churches

Q How did popular religion differ from institutional religion in the eighteenth century?

Critical Thinking

Q *What was the relationship between the Scientific Revolution and the Enlightenment?*

Connections to Today

Q *What intellectual movements today parallel the philosophes of the Enlightenment in challenging accepted ideas about government, religion, women, and the economy?*

THE EARTH-SHATTERING WORK of the "natural philosophers" in the Scientific Revolution had affected only a relatively small number of Europe's educated elite. In the eighteenth century, this changed dramatically as a group of intellectuals known as the philosophes popularized the ideas of the Scientific Revolution and used them to undertake a dramatic reexamination of all aspects of life. In Paris, the cultural capital of Europe, women took the lead in bringing together groups of men and women to discuss the new ideas of the philosophes. At her fashionable home on the rue Saint-Honoré, Marie-Thérèse de Geoffrin (ma-REE-tay-RAYZ duh zhoh-FRANH), the wife of a wealthy merchant, held sway over gatherings that became the talk of France and even Europe. Distinguished foreigners, including a future king of Sweden and a future king of Poland, competed to receive invitations. When Madame Geoffrin made a visit to Vienna, she was so well received that she exclaimed, "I am better known here than a couple of yards from my own house." Madame Geoffrin was an amiable but firm hostess who allowed wide-ranging discussions as long as they remained in good taste. When she found that artists and philosophers did not mix particularly well (the artists were high-strung and the philosophers talked too much), she set up separate meetings. Artists were invited only on Mondays, philosophers, on Wednesdays. These gatherings were among the many avenues for the spread of the ideas of the philosophes. And those ideas had such a widespread impact on their society that historians ever since have called the eighteenth century the Age of Enlightenment.

For most of the philosophes, "enlightenment" included the rejection of traditional Christianity. The religious wars and intolerance of the sixteenth and seventeenth centuries had so alienated intellectuals that they were open and even eager to embrace the new ideas of the Scientific Revolution. Whereas the great scientists of the seventeenth century believed that their work exalted God, the intellectuals of the eighteenth century read those scientific conclusions a different way and increasingly turned their backs on Christian orthodoxy. Consequently, European intellectual life in the eighteenth century was marked by the emergence of the secularization that has characterized the modern Western mentality ever since. Ironically, at the same time that reason and materialism were beginning to replace faith and worship, a great outburst of religious sensibility manifested itself in music and art. Clearly, the growing secularization of the eighteenth century had not yet captured the hearts and minds of all European intellectuals and artists.

The Enlightenment

 FOCUS QUESTIONS: What intellectual developments led to the emergence of the Enlightenment? Who were the leading figures of the Enlightenment, and what were their main contributions? In what type of social environment did the philosophes thrive, and what role did women play in that environment?

In 1784, the German philosopher Immanuel Kant (i-MAHN-yoo-el KAHNT) (1724–1804) defined the **Enlightenment** as "man's leaving his self-caused immaturity." Whereas earlier periods had been handicapped by the inability to "use one's intelligence without the guidance of another," Kant proclaimed as the motto of the Enlightenment: "Dare to know! Have the courage to use your own intelligence!" The eighteenth-century Enlightenment was a movement of intellectuals who dared to know. They were greatly impressed with the accomplishments of the Scientific Revolution, and when they used the word *reason*—one of their favorite words—they were advocating the application of the scientific method to the understanding of all life. All institutions and all systems of thought were subject to the rational, scientific way of thinking if only people would free themselves from the shackles of old, worthless traditions, especially religious ones. If Isaac Newton could discover the natural laws regulating the world of nature, they too, by using reason, could find the laws that governed human society. This belief in turn led them to hope that they could make progress toward a better society than the one they had inherited. *Reason, natural law, hope, progress*—these were the buzz words in the heady atmosphere of the eighteenth century.

The Paths to Enlightenment

The intellectuals of the eighteenth century were especially influenced by the revolutionary thinkers of the seventeenth

century. What were the major intellectual changes that culminated in the intellectual movement of the Enlightenment?

THE POPULARIZATION OF SCIENCE Although the intellectuals of the eighteenth century were much influenced by the scientific ideas of the seventeenth, they did not always acquire this knowledge directly from the original sources. Newton's *Principia* was not an easy book to read or comprehend. Scientific ideas were spread to ever-widening circles of educated Europeans not so much by scientists themselves as by popularizers. Especially important as the direct link between the Scientific Revolution of the seventeenth century and the philosophes of the eighteenth was Bernard de Fontenelle (bayr-NAHR duh fawnt-NELL) (1657–1757), secretary of the French Royal Academy of Science from 1691 to 1741.

Although Fontenelle performed no scientific experiments and made no scientific discoveries, he possessed a deep knowledge of all the scientific work of earlier centuries and his own time. Moreover, he was able to communicate that body of scientific knowledge in a clear and even witty fashion that appealed to his upper-class audiences in a meaningful way. One of his most successful books, *Plurality of Worlds*, was actually presented in the form of an intimate conversation between a lady aristocrat and her lover who are engaged in conversation under the stars. What are they discussing? "Tell me," she exclaims, "about these stars of yours." Her lover proceeds to tell her of the tremendous advances in cosmology after the foolish errors of their forebears:

> There came on the scene a certain German, one Copernicus, who made short work of all those various circles, all those solid skies, which the ancients had pictured to themselves. The former he abolished; the latter, he broke in pieces. Fired with the noble zeal of a true astronomer, he took the earth and spun it very far away from the center of the universe, where it had been installed, and in that center he put the sun, which had a far better title to the honor.[1]

In the course of two evenings under the stars, the lady learned the basic fundamentals of the new mechanistic universe. So too did scores of the educated elite of Europe.

Thanks to Fontenelle, science was no longer the monopoly of experts but part of literature. He was especially fond of downplaying the religious backgrounds of the seventeenth-century scientists. Himself a skeptic, Fontenelle contributed to the growing **skepticism** toward religion at the end of the seventeenth century by portraying the churches as enemies of scientific progress.

A NEW SKEPTICISM The great scientists of the seventeenth century, including Kepler, Galileo, and Newton, had pursued their work in a spirit of exalting God, not undermining Christianity. But as scientific knowledge spread, more and more educated men and women began to question religious truths and values. Skepticism about religion and a growing secularization of thought were especially evident in the work of Pierre Bayle (PYAYR BELL) (1647–1706), who remained a Protestant while becoming a leading critic of traditional religious attitudes.

The Popularization of Science in the Age of Enlightenment. During the Enlightenment, the ideas of the Scientific Revolution were spread and popularized in a variety of ways. Scientific societies funded by royal and princely patrons were especially valuable in providing outlets for the spread of new scientific ideas. This illustration shows the German prince Frederick Christian visiting his Academy of Sciences in 1739. Note the many instruments of the new science around the rooms—human skeletons, globes, microscopes, telescopes, and orreries (mechanical models of the solar system).

Archivio di Stato, Bologna//Alinari/Art Resource, NY

Bayle attacked superstition, religious intolerance, and dogmatism. In his view, compelling people to believe a particular set of religious ideas (as Louis XIV was doing at the time in Bayle's France) was wrong. It simply created hypocrites and in itself was contrary to what religion should be about. Individual conscience should determine one's actions. Bayle argued for complete religious toleration, maintaining that the existence of many religions would benefit rather than harm the state.

THE IMPACT OF TRAVEL LITERATURE Skepticism about both Christianity and European culture itself was nourished by travel reports. As we saw in Chapter 14, Europeans had embarked on voyages of discovery to other parts of the world in the late fifteenth and sixteenth centuries. In the course of the seventeenth century, traders, missionaries, medical practitioners, and explorers began to publish an increasing number of travel books that gave accounts of many different cultures. Then, too, the new geographic adventures of the eighteenth century, especially the discovery of the Pacific island of Tahiti and of New Zealand and Australia by James Cook, aroused much enthusiasm. Cook's *Travels*, an account of his journey, became a best-seller. Educated Europeans responded to these accounts of lands abroad in different ways. For some intellectuals, exotic peoples, such as the natives of Tahiti, presented an image of a "natural man" who was far happier than many Europeans. One intellectual wrote:

> The life of savages is so simple, and our societies are such complicated machines! The Tahitian is close to the origin of the world, while the European is closer to its old age. . . . [The Tahitians] understand nothing about our manners or our laws, and they are bound to see in them nothing but shackles disguised in a hundred different ways. Those shackles could only provoke the indignation and scorn of creatures in whom the most profound feeling is a love of liberty.[2]

The idea of the "noble savage" would play an important role in the political work of some philosophes.

The travel literature of the seventeenth and eighteenth centuries also led to the realization that there were highly developed civilizations with different customs in other parts of the world. China was especially singled out. One German university professor praised Confucian morality as superior to the intolerance of Christianity. Some European intellectuals began to evaluate their own civilization relative to others. Practices that had seemed to be grounded in reason now appeared to be merely matters of custom. Certainties about European practices gave way to **cultural relativism**.

Cultural relativism was accompanied by religious skepticism. As these travel accounts made clear, the Christian perception of God was merely one of many. Some people were devastated by this revelation: "Some complete their demoralization by extensive travel, and lose whatever shreds of religion remained to them. Every day they see a new religion, new customs, new rites."[3]

As Europeans were exposed to growing numbers of people around the world who were different from themselves, some intellectuals also began to classify people into racial groups. One group espoused polygenesis, or the belief in separate human species; others argued for monogenesis, or the belief in one human species characterized by racial variations. Both groups were especially unsympathetic to Africans and placed them in the lowest rank of humankind. In his *Encyclopedia*, the intellectual Denis Diderot (see "Diderot and the *Encyclopedia*" later in this chapter) maintained that all Africans were black and characterized the Negro as a "new species of mankind."

THE LEGACY OF LOCKE AND NEWTON The intellectual inspiration for the Enlightenment came primarily from two Englishmen, Isaac Newton and John Locke, acknowledged by the philosophes as great minds. Newton was frequently singled out for praise as the "greatest and rarest genius that ever rose for the ornament and instruction of the species." One English poet declared: "Nature and Nature's Laws lay hid in Night; God said, 'Let Newton be,' and all was Light." Enchanted by the grand design of the Newtonian world-machine, the intellectuals of the Enlightenment were convinced that by following Newton's rules of reasoning, they could discover the natural laws that governed politics, economics, justice, religion, and the arts.

John Locke's theory of knowledge especially influenced the philosophes. Locke studied medicine at Oxford University before joining the household of Lord Ashley as a general counselor before fleeing for the Netherlands in 1683 where he wrote his *Essay Concerning Human Understanding* in 1690. Locke denied Descartes's belief in innate ideas, instead he argued that every person was born with a *tabula rasa* (TAB-yuh-luh RAH-suh), a blank mind:

> Let us then suppose the mind to be, as we say, white paper, void of all characters, without any ideas. How comes it to be furnished? Whence comes it by that vast store which the busy and boundless fancy of man has painted on it with an almost endless variety? Whence has it all the materials of reason and knowledge? To this I answer, in one word, from experience. . . . Our observation, employed either about external sensible objects or about the internal operations of our minds perceived and reflected on by ourselves, is that which supplies our understanding with all the materials of thinking.[4]

Our knowledge, then, is derived from our environment, not from heredity; from reason, not from faith. Locke's philosophy implied that people were molded by their environment, by the experiences that they received through their senses from their surrounding world. By changing the environment and subjecting people to proper influences, they could be changed and a new society created. And how should the environment be changed? Newton had already paved the way by showing how reason enabled enlightened people to discover the natural laws to which all institutions should conform. No wonder the philosophes were enamored of Newton and Locke. Taken together, their ideas seemed to offer the hope of a "brave new world" built on reason.

The Philosophes and Their Ideas

The intellectuals of the Enlightenment were known by the French term *philosophe* (fee-loh-ZAWF), although not all of them were French and few were actually philosophers. The **philosophes** were literary people, professors, journalists, statesmen, economists, political scientists, and above all, social reformers. They came from both the nobility and the middle class, and a few even stemmed from lower origins. Although it was a truly international and **cosmopolitan** movement, the Enlightenment also enhanced the dominant role being played by French culture. Paris was its recognized capital, and most of the leaders of the Enlightenment were French (see Map 17.1). The French philosophes in turn affected intellectuals elsewhere and created a movement that engulfed the entire Western world, including the British and Spanish colonies in America.

Although the philosophes faced different political circumstances depending on the country in which they lived, they shared common bonds as part of a truly international movement. They were called philosophers, but what did philosophy mean to them? The role of philosophy was to change the world, not just discuss it. As one writer said, the philosophe is one who "applies himself to the study of society with the purpose of making his kind better and happier." To the philosophes, rationalism did not mean the creation of a grandiose system of thought to explain all things. Reason was scientific method, an appeal to facts and experience. A spirit of rational criticism was to be applied to everything, including religion and politics.

The philosophes' call for freedom of expression is a reminder that their work was done in an atmosphere of censorship. The philosophes were not free to write whatever they chose. State censors decided what could be published, and protests from any number of government bodies could result in the seizure of books and the imprisonment of their authors, publishers, and sellers. The philosophes found ways to get around state censorship. Some published under pseudonyms or anonymously or abroad, especially in Holland. The use of double meanings, such as talking about the Persians when they meant the French, became standard procedure for many. Books were also published and circulated secretly or in manuscript form to avoid the censors.

Although the philosophes constituted a kind of "family circle" bound together by common intellectual bonds, they often disagreed. Spanning almost a century, the Enlightenment evolved over time, with each succeeding generation becoming more radical as it built on the contributions of the previous one. A few people, however, dominated the landscape completely, and we might best begin our survey of the ideas of the philosophes by looking at three French giants—Montesquieu, Voltaire, and Diderot.

MONTESQUIEU AND POLITICAL THOUGHT Charles de Secondat, the baron de Montesquieu (MOHN-tess-kyoo) (1689–1755), came from the French nobility. He received a classical education and then studied law. In his first work, the *Persian Letters*, published in 1721, he used the format of two Persians supposedly traveling in western Europe and sending their impressions back home to enable him to criticize French institutions, especially the Catholic Church and the French monarchy. Much of the program of the French Enlightenment is contained in this work: the attack on traditional religion, the advocacy of religious toleration, the denunciation of slavery, and the use of reason to liberate human beings from their prejudices.

Montesquieu's most famous work, *The Spirit of the Laws*, was published in 1748. This treatise was a comparative study of governments in which Montesquieu attempted to apply the scientific method to the social and political arena to ascertain the "natural laws" governing the social relationships of human beings. Montesquieu distinguished three basic kinds of governments: republics, suitable for small states and based on citizen involvement; monarchy, appropriate for middle-sized states and grounded in the ruling class's adherence to law; and despotism, apt for large empires and dependent on fear to inspire obedience. Montesquieu used England as an example of the

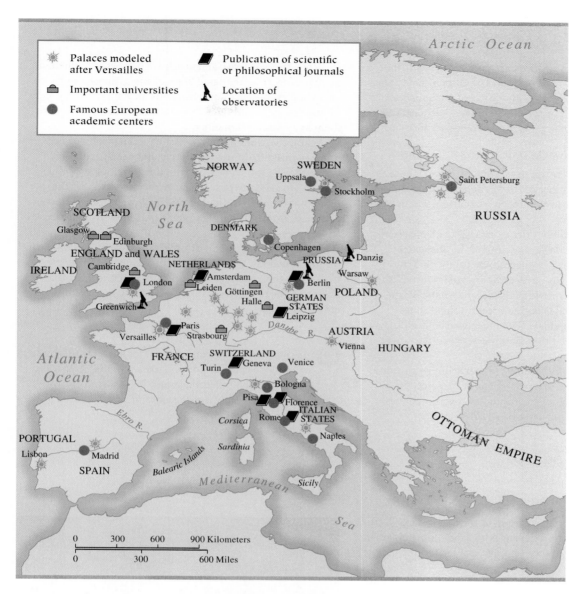

MAP 17.1 The Enlightenment in Europe. "Have the courage to use your own intelligence!" Kant's words epitomize the role of the individual in using reason to understand all aspects of life— the natural world and the sphere of human nature, behavior, and institutions.

Q *Which countries or regions were at the center of the Enlightenment, and what could account for peripheral regions being less involved?*

Legend:
- Palaces modeled after Versailles
- Important universities
- Famous European academic centers
- Publication of scientific or philosophical journals
- Location of observatories

second category, and it was his praise and analysis of England's constitution that led to his most far-reaching and lasting contribution to political thought—the importance of checks and balances created by means of a **separation of powers** (see the box on p. 504). He believed that England's system, with its separate executive, legislative, and judicial powers that served to limit and control each other, provided the greatest freedom and security for a state. In large part, Montesquieu misread the English situation and insisted on a separation of powers because he wanted the nobility of France (of which he was a member) to play an active role in running the French government. The translation of his work into English two years after publication ensured that it would be read by American philosophes, such

as Benjamin Franklin, James Madison, John Adams, Alexander Hamilton, and Thomas Jefferson, who incorporated its principles into the U.S. Constitution (see Chapter 19).

VOLTAIRE AND THE ENLIGHTENMENT The greatest figure of the Enlightenment was François-Marie Arouet (frahn-SWAH-ma-REE ahr-WEH), known simply as Voltaire (vohl-TAYR) (1694–1778). Son of a prosperous middle-class family from Paris, Voltaire received a classical education in Jesuit schools. Although he studied law, he wished to be a writer and achieved his first success as a playwright. By his mid-twenties, Voltaire had been hailed as the successor to Racine (see Chapter 15) for his tragedy *Œdipe* and his epic *Henriade* on his favorite king,

THE SEPARATION OF POWERS

THE ENLIGHTENMENT AFFECTED THE NEW WORLD of America as much as it did the old world of Europe. American philosophes were well aware of the ideas of European Enlightenment thinkers. This selection from Montesquieu's *Spirit of the Laws* enunciates the "separation of powers" doctrine.

Montesquieu, "Of the Constitution of England"

In every government there are three sorts of power: the legislative; the executive in respect to things dependent on the law of nations; and the executive in regard to matters that depend on the civil law.

By virtue of the first, the prince or magistrate enacts temporary or perpetual laws, and amends or abrogates those that have been already enacted. By the second, he makes peace or war, sends or receives embassies, establishes the public security, and provides against invasions. By the third, he punishes criminals, or determines the disputes that arise between individuals. The latter we shall call the judiciary power, and the other simply the executive power of the state.

The political liberty of the subject is a tranquility of mind arising from the opinion each person has of his safety. In order to have this liberty, it is requisite the government be so constituted as one man need not be afraid of another.

When the legislative and executive powers are united in the same person, or in the same body of magistrates, there can be no liberty; because apprehensions may arise, lest the same monarch or senate should enact tyrannical laws, to execute them in a tyrannical manner.

Again, there is no liberty, if the judiciary power be not separated from the legislative and executive. Were it joined with the legislative, the life and liberty of the subject would be exposed to arbitrary control; for the judge would be then the legislator. Were it joined to the executive power, the judge might behave with violence and oppression.

There would be an end of everything, were the same man or the same body, whether of the nobles or of the people, to exercise those three powers, that of enacting laws, that of executing the public resolutions, and of trying the causes of individuals.

 As seen in this excerpt, what is Montesquieu's doctrine of the separation of powers? What are the underlying moral and political justifications for this system of government? How was this doctrine incorporated into the U.S. Constitution?

Source: N. L. Torrey, *Les Philosophes* (New York: G. P. Putnam's Sons, 1961).

Henry IV. His wit made him a darling of the Parisian intellectuals but also involved him in a quarrel with a dissolute nobleman that forced him to flee France and live in England for almost two years.

Well received in English literary and social circles, the young playwright was much impressed by England. His *Philosophic Letters on the English*, written in 1733, expressed a deep admiration of English life, especially its freedom of the press, its political freedom, and its religious toleration. In judging the English religious situation, he made the famous remark that if there were two religions, they would cut each other's throats; but since there are thirty religions, "they live together peacefully and happily." Although he clearly exaggerated the freedoms England possessed, in a roundabout way Voltaire had managed to criticize many of the ills oppressing France, especially royal absolutism and the lack of religious toleration and freedom of thought. The criticism of absolute monarchy by Voltaire and other philosophes reflected the broader dissatisfaction of middle-class individuals with their society. In the course of

Voltaire. François-Marie Arouet, better known as Voltaire, achieved his first success as a playwright. A philosophe, Voltaire was well known for his criticism of traditional religion and his support of religious toleration. Maurice-Quentin de La Tour painted this portrait of Voltaire holding one of his books in 1736.

RMN-Grand Palais/Art Resource, NY

THE ATTACK ON RELIGIOUS INTOLERANCE

VOLTAIRE'S LUCID PROSE, BITING SATIRE, AND clever wit caused his works to be widely read and all the more influential. These two selections present different sides of Voltaire's attack on religious intolerance. The first is from a straightforward treatise, *The Ignorant Philosopher*, and the second is from his only real literary masterpiece, the novel *Candide*, in which he used humor to make the same fundamental point about religious intolerance.

Voltaire, *The Ignorant Philosopher*

The contagion of fanaticism then still subsists. . . . The author of the *Treatise upon Toleration* has not mentioned the shocking executions wherein so many unhappy victims perished in the valleys of Piedmont. He has passed over in silence the massacre of six hundred inhabitants of Valtelina, men, women, and children, who were murdered by the Catholics in the month of September, 1620. I will not say it was with the consent and assistance of the archbishop of Milan, Charles Borome, who was made a saint. Some passionate writers have averred this fact, which I am very far from believing; but I say, there is scarce any city or borough in Europe, where blood has not been spilt for religious quarrels; I say, that the human species has been perceptibly diminished, because women and girls were massacred as well as men; I say, that Europe would have had a third larger population, if there had been no theological disputes. In fine, I say, that so far from forgetting these abominable times, we should frequently take a view of them, to inspire an eternal horror for them; and that it is for our age to make reparation by toleration, for this long collection of crimes, which has taken place through the want of toleration, during sixteen barbarous centuries. Let it not then be said, that there are no traces left of that shocking fanaticism, of the want of toleration; they are still everywhere to be met with, even in those countries that are esteemed the most humane. The Lutheran and Calvinist preachers, were they masters, would, perhaps, be as little inclined to pity, as obdurate, as insolent as they upbraid their antagonists with being.

Voltaire, *Candide*

At last he [Candide] approached a man who had just been addressing a big audience for a whole hour on the subject of charity. The orator peered at him and said:

"What is your business here? Do you support the Good Old Cause?"

"There is not effect without a cause," replied Candide modestly. "All things are necessarily connected and arranged for the best. It was my fate to be driven from Lady Cunégonde's presence and made to run the gantlet, and now I have to beg my bread until I can earn it. Things should not have happened otherwise."

"Do you believe that the Pope is Antichrist, my friend?" said the minister.

"I have never heard anyone say so," replied Candide; "but whether he is or he isn't, I want some food."

"You don't deserve to eat," said the other. "Be off with you, you villain, you wretch! Don't come near me again or you'll suffer for it."

The minister's wife looked out of the window at that moment, and seeing a man who was not sure that the Pope was Antichrist, emptied over his head a chamber pot, which shows to what lengths ladies are driven by religious zeal.

 Compare the two approaches that Voltaire uses to address the problem of religious intolerance. Do you think one is more effective? Why?

Sources: Voltaire, *The Ignorant Philosopher* and *Candide*, in J. Butt, trans., *Candide or Optimism* (London: Penguin Classics, 1947).

the eighteenth century, this would help lead to revolutionary upheavals in France and other countries (see Chapter 19).

Voltaire returned to France to discover his *Philosophic Letters* banned by the state, sending Voltaire into exile to Cirey, near France's eastern border, where he lived in semi-seclusion on the estate of his mistress, the marquise du Châtelet (mahr-KEEZ duh shat-LAY) (1706–1749). Herself an early philosophe, the marquise was one of the first intellectuals to adopt the ideas of Isaac Newton, and in 1759 her own translation of Newton's famous *Principia* was published. While Voltaire lived with her at her château at Cirey, the two collaborated on a book about the natural philosophy of Newton.

Voltaire eventually settled on a magnificent estate at Ferney. Located in France near the Swiss border, Ferney gave Voltaire the freedom to write what he wished. By this time, through his writings, inheritance, and clever investments, Voltaire had become wealthy and now had the leisure to write an almost endless stream of pamphlets, novels, plays, letters, and histories.

Although he touched on all of the themes of importance to the philosophes, Voltaire was especially well known for his criticism of traditional religion and his strong attachment to the ideal of religious toleration (see the box above). He lent his prestige and skills as a polemicist to fighting cases of intolerance in France. The most famous incident was the Calas affair. Jean Calas (ZHAHNH ka-LAH) was a Protestant from Toulouse who was accused of murdering his own son to stop him from becoming a Catholic. Tortured to confess his guilt, Calas died shortly thereafter. An angry and indignant Voltaire published devastating broadsides that aroused public opinion and forced a retrial in which Calas was exonerated when it was proved that his son had actually committed suicide. The family was paid an indemnity, and Voltaire's appeals for toleration appeared all the more reasonable. In 1763, he penned

DIDEROT QUESTIONS CHRISTIAN SEXUAL STANDARDS

DENIS DIDEROT WAS ONE OF THE BOLDEST thinkers of the Enlightenment. In his *Supplement to the Voyage of Bougainville,* he constructed a dialogue between Orou, a Tahitian who symbolizes the wisdom of a philosophe, and a chaplain who defends Christian sexual mores. The dialogue gave Diderot the opportunity to criticize the practice of sexual chastity and monogamy.

Denis Diderot, *Supplement to the Voyage of Bougainville*

[Orou, speaking to the Chaplain:] "You are young and healthy and you have just had a good supper. He who sleeps alone sleeps badly; at night a man needs a woman at his side. Here is my wife and here are my daughters. Choose whichever one pleases you most, but if you would like to do me a favor, you will give your preference to my youngest girl, who has not yet had any children. . . ."

The chaplain replied that his religion, his holy orders, his moral standards and his sense of decency all prevented him from accepting Orou's invitation.

Orou answered: "I don't know what this thing is that you call religion, but I can only have a low opinion of it because it forbids you to partake of an innocent pleasure to which Nature, the sovereign mistress of us all, invites everybody. It seems to prevent you from bringing one of your fellow creatures into the world, from doing a favor asked of by a father, a mother and their children, from repaying the kindness of a host, and from enriching a nation by giving it an additional citizen. . . . Look at the distress you have caused to appear on the faces of these four women—they are afraid you have noticed some defect in them that arouses your distaste. . . ."

The Chaplain: "You don't understand—it's not that. They are all four of them equally beautiful. But there is my religion! My holy orders! . . . [God] spoke to our ancestors and gave them laws . . . he ordained that certain actions are good and others he forbade them to do as being evil."

Orou: "I see. And one of these evil actions which he has forbidden is that of a man who goes to bed with a woman or girl. But in that case, why did he make two sexes?"

The Chaplain: "In order that they might come together—but only when certain conditions are satisfied and only after certain initial ceremonies one man belongs to one woman and only to her; one woman belongs to one man and only to him."

Orou: "For their whole lives?"

The Chaplain: "For their whole lives. . . ."

Orou: "I find these strange precepts contrary to nature, and contrary to reason. . . . Furthermore, your laws seem to me to be contrary to the general order of things. For in truth is there anything so senseless as a precept that forbids us to heed the changing impulses that are inherent in our being, or commands that require a degree of constancy which is not possible, that violate the liberty of both male and female by chaining them perpetually to one another? . . . I don't know what your great workman [God] is, but I am very happy that he never spoke to our forefathers, and I hope that he never speaks to our children, for if he does, he may tell them the same foolishness, and they may be foolish enough to believe it."

 What attack does Diderot make on Christian sexual standards? What does this passage say about enlightened conceptions of nature and the place of physical pleasure in healthy human life?

Source: J. Barzun and R. Bowen, trans., *Diderot: Rameau's Nephew and Other Works* (Indianapolis: Hackett Publishing Company, 1956).

---

his *Treatise on Toleration*, in which he argued that religious toleration had created no problems for England and Holland and reminded governments that "all men are brothers under God." As he grew older, Voltaire became ever more strident in his denunciations. "Crush the infamous thing," he thundered repeatedly—the infamous thing being religious fanaticism, intolerance, and superstition.

Throughout his life, Voltaire championed not only religious tolerance but also **deism**, a religious outlook shared by most other philosophes. Deism was built on the Newtonian world-machine, which suggested the existence of a mechanic (God) who had created the universe. Voltaire said, "In the opinion that there is a God, there are difficulties, but in the contrary opinion there are absurdities." To Voltaire and most other philosophes, God had no direct involvement in the world he had created and allowed it to run according to its own natural laws. God did not extend grace or answer prayers or perform miracles, as Christians liked to believe. Jesus might be a "good fellow,"

as Voltaire called him, but he was not divine, as Christianity claimed.

DIDEROT AND THE *ENCYCLOPEDIA* Denis Diderot (duh-NEE DEE-droh) (1713–1784), the son of a skilled craftsman from eastern France, became a freelance writer so that he could study many subjects and read in many languages. One of his favorite topics was Christianity, which he condemned as fanatical and unreasonable. As he grew older, his literary attacks on Christianity grew more vicious. Of all religions, he maintained, Christianity was the worst, "the most absurd and the most atrocious in its dogma" (see the box above). Near the end of his life, he argued for an essentially materialistic conception of life: "This world is only a mass of molecules."

Diderot's most famous contribution to the Enlightenment was the twenty-eight-volume *Encyclopedia, or Classified Dictionary of the Sciences, Arts, and Trades,* that he edited and called the "great work of his life." Its purpose, according to Diderot, was to "change the general way of thinking." It did precisely that in becoming a major weapon of the philosophes' crusade against the old French society. The contributors included many philosophes who expressed their major concerns. They attacked religious superstition and advocated toleration as well as a program for social, legal, and political improvements that would lead to a society that was more cosmopolitan, more tolerant, more humane, and more reasonable. In later editions, the price of the *Encyclopedia* was drastically reduced, dramatically increasing its sales and making it available to doctors, clergy, teachers, lawyers, and even military officers. The ideas of the Enlightenment were spread even further as a result.

THE NEW "SCIENCE OF MAN" The Enlightenment belief that Newton's scientific methods could be used to discover the natural laws underlying all areas of human life led to the emergence in the eighteenth century of what the philosophes called the "science of man," or what we would call the social sciences. In a number of areas, philosophes arrived at natural laws that they believed governed human actions. If these "natural laws" seem less than universal to us, it reminds us how much the philosophes were people of their times reacting to the conditions they faced. Nevertheless, their efforts did at least lay the foundations for the modern social sciences.

That a science of man was possible was a strong belief of the Scottish philosopher David Hume (1711–1776). An important figure in the history of philosophy, Hume has also been called "a pioneering social scientist." In his *Treatise on Human Nature*, which he subtitled "An Attempt to Introduce the Experimental Method of Reasoning into Moral Subjects," Hume argued that observation and reflection, grounded in "systematized common sense," made conceivable a "science of man." Careful examination of the experiences that constituted human life would lead to the knowledge of human nature that would make this science possible.

The Physiocrats and Adam Smith have been viewed as founders of the modern discipline of economics. The leader of the Physiocrats was François Quesnay (frahn-SWAH keh-NAY) (1694–1774), a highly successful French court physician. Quesnay and the Physiocrats claimed they would discover the natural economic laws that governed human society. Their first principle was that land constituted the only source of wealth and that wealth itself could be increased only by agriculture because all other economic activities were unproductive and sterile. Even the state's revenues should come from a single tax on land rather than the hodgepodge of inequitable taxes and privileges currently in place. In stressing the economic primacy of agricultural production, the Physiocrats were rejecting the mercantilist emphasis on the significance of money—that is, gold and silver—as the primary determinants of wealth (see Chapter 14).

Their second major "natural law" of economics also represented a repudiation of mercantilism, specifically, its emphasis on a controlled economy for the benefit of the state. Instead, the Physiocrats stressed that the existence of the natural economic forces of supply and demand made it imperative that individuals should be left free to pursue their own economic self-interest. In doing so, all of society would ultimately benefit.

Consequently, they argued that the state should in no way interrupt the free play of natural economic forces by government regulation of the economy but rather should just leave it alone, a doctrine that subsequently became known by its French name, *laissez-faire* (less-ay-FAYR) (noninterference; literally, "let people do as they choose").

The best statement of laissez-faire was made in 1776 by a Scottish philosopher, Adam Smith (1723–1790), in his *Inquiry into the Nature and Causes of the Wealth of Nations*, known simply as *The Wealth of Nations*. In the process of enunciating three basic principles of economics, Smith presented a strong attack on mercantilism. First, he condemned the mercantilist use of tariffs to protect home industries. If one country can supply another country with a product cheaper than the latter can make it, it is better to purchase the product than to produce it. To Smith, free trade was a fundamental economic principle. Smith's second principle was his labor theory of value. Like the Physiocrats, he claimed that gold and silver were not the source of a nation's true wealth, but unlike the Physiocrats, he did not believe that land was either. Rather labor—the labor of individual farmers, artisans, and merchants—constituted the true wealth of a nation. Finally, like the Physiocrats, Smith believed that the state should not interfere in economic matters; indeed, he assigned to government only three basic functions: to protect society from invasion (army), defend individuals from injustice and oppression (police), and keep up certain public works, such as roads and canals, that private individuals could not afford. Thus, in Smith's view, the state should stay out of the lives of individuals. In emphasizing the economic liberty of the individual, the Physiocrats and Adam Smith laid the foundation for what became known in the nineteenth century as **economic liberalism**.

THE LATER ENLIGHTENMENT By the late 1760s, a new generation of philosophes who had grown up with the worldview of the Enlightenment began to move beyond their predecessors' beliefs. Baron Paul d'Holbach (dawl-BAHK) (1723–1789), a wealthy German aristocrat who settled in Paris, preached a doctrine of strict atheism and materialism. In his *System of Nature*, written in 1770, he argued that everything in the universe consisted of matter in motion. Human beings were simply machines; God was a product of the human mind and was unnecessary for leading a moral life. People needed only reason to live in this world: "Let us persuade men to be just, beneficent, moderate, sociable; not because the gods demand it, but because they must please men. Let us advise them to abstain from vice and crimes; not because they will be punished in the other world, but because they will suffer for it in this."[5] Holbach shocked almost all of his fellow philosophes with his uncompromising atheism. Most intellectuals remained more comfortable with deism and feared the effect of atheism on society.

Marie-Jean de Condorcet (ma-REE-ZHAHNH duh kohn-dor-SAY) (1743–1794), another French philosophe, made an exaggerated claim for progress. Condorcet was a victim of the turmoil of the French Revolution and wrote his chief work, *The Progress of the Human Mind*, while in hiding during the Reign of Terror (see Chapter 19). His survey of human history convinced him that humans had progressed through nine stages of history. Now, with the spread of science and reason, humans were about to enter the tenth stage, one of perfection, in which they will see that "there is no limit to the perfecting of the powers of man; that human perfectibility is in reality indefinite, that the progress of this perfectibility . . . has no other limit than the duration of the globe upon which nature has placed us." Shortly after composing this work, the prophet of humankind's perfection died in a French revolutionary prison.

ROUSSEAU AND THE SOCIAL CONTRACT No one was more critical of the work of his predecessors than Jean-Jacques Rousseau (ZHAHNH-ZHAHK roo-SOH) (1712–1778). Born in Geneva, he was orphaned at a young age and spent his youth wandering about France and Italy holding various jobs. Largely self-educated, he returned to school for a while to study music and the classics (he could afford to do so after becoming the paid lover of an older woman). Eventually, he made his way to Paris, where he was introduced into the circles of the philosophes. He never really liked the social life of the cities, however, and frequently withdrew into long periods of solitude.

Jean-Jacques Rousseau. By the late 1760s, a new generation of philosophes arose who began to move beyond and even to question the beliefs of their predecessors. Of the philosophes of the late Enlightenment, Rousseau was perhaps the most critical of his predecessors. Shown here is a portrait of Rousseau by Maurice-Quentin de La Tour.

Musée d'Art et d'Histoire, Geneva/Erich Lessing/Art Resource, NY

Rousseau's political beliefs were presented in two major works. In his *Discourse on the Origins of the Inequality of Mankind*, Rousseau began with humans in their primitive condition (or state of nature—see Chapter 15), where they were happy. There were no laws, no judges; all people were equal. But what had gone wrong?

> The first man who, having enclosed a piece of ground, thought of saying, This is mine, and found people simple enough to believe him, was the true founder of civil society. How many crimes, wars, murders; how much misery and horror the human race would have been spared if someone had pulled up the stakes and filled in the ditch, and cried to his fellow men: "Beware of listening to this impostor. You are lost if you forget that the fruits of the earth belong to everyone and that the earth itself belongs to no one!"[6]

To preserve their private property, people adopted laws and governors. In so doing, they rushed headlong not to liberty but into chains. "What then is to be done? Must societies be totally abolished? . . . Must we return again to the forest to live among bears?" No, civilized humans could "no longer subsist on plants or acorns or live without laws and magistrates." Government was an evil, but a necessary one.

In his celebrated treatise *The Social Contract*, published in 1762, Rousseau tried to harmonize individual liberty with governmental authority (see the box on p. 509). The social contract was basically an agreement on the part of an entire society to be governed by its general will. If any individual wished to follow his own self-interest, he should be compelled to abide by the general will. "This means nothing less than that he will be forced to be free," said Rousseau, because the general will represented a community's highest aspirations, whatever was best for the entire community. Thus, liberty was achieved through being forced to follow what was best for all people because, he believed, what was best for all was best for each individual. True freedom is adherence to laws that one has imposed on oneself. To Rousseau, because everybody was responsible for framing the general will, the creation of laws could never be delegated to a parliamentary institution:

> Thus, the people's deputies are not and could not be its representatives; they are merely its agents; and they cannot decide anything finally. Any law which the people has not ratified in person is void; it is not law at all. The English people believes itself to be free; it is gravely mistaken; it is free only during the election of Members of Parliament; as soon as the Members are elected, the people is enslaved; it is nothing.[7]

This is an extreme and idealistic statement, but it is the ultimate statement of participatory democracy.

Another influential treatise by Rousseau also appeared in 1762. Titled *Émile*, it is one of the Enlightenment's most important works on education. Written in the form of a novel, the work is really a general treatise "on the education of the natural man." Rousseau's fundamental concern was that education should foster rather than restrict children's natural instincts. Life's experiences had shown Rousseau the importance of the promptings of the heart, and what he sought was a balance

A SOCIAL CONTRACT

ALTHOUGH JEAN-JACQUES ROUSSEAU WAS ONE of the French philosophes, he has also been called "the father of Romanticism." His political ideas have proved extremely controversial. Though some people have hailed him as the prophet of democracy, others have labeled him an apologist for totalitarianism. This selection is taken from one of his most famous books, *The Social Contract*.

Jean-Jacques Rousseau, *The Social Contract*

Book 1, Chapter 6: "The Social Pact"

"How to find a form of association which will defend the person and goods of each member with the collective force of all, and under which each individual, while uniting himself with the others, obeys no one but himself, and remains as free as before." This is the fundamental problem to which the social contract holds the solution. . . .

Book 1, Chapter 7: "The Sovereign"

Despite their common interest, subjects will not be bound by their commitment unless means are found to guarantee their fidelity.

For every individual as a man may have a private will contrary to, or different from, the general will that he has as a citizen. His private interest may speak with a very different voice from that of the public interest; his absolute and naturally independent existence may make him regard what he owes to the common cause as a gratuitous contribution, the loss of which would be less painful for others than the payment is onerous for him; and fancying that the artificial person which constitutes the state is a mere rational entity, he might seek to enjoy the rights of a citizen without doing the duties of a subject. The growth of this kind of injustice would bring about the ruin of the body politic.

Hence, in order that the social pact shall not be an empty formula, it is tacitly implied in that commitment—which alone can give force to all others—that whoever refused to obey the general will shall be constrained to do so by the whole body, which means nothing other than that he shall be forced to be free; for this is the condition which, by giving each citizen to the nation, secures him against all personal dependence, it is the condition which shapes both the design and the working of the political machine, and which alone bestows justice on civil contracts—without it, such contracts would be absurd, tyrannical and liable to the grossest abuse.

 What was Rousseau's concept of the social contract? What implications did it have for political thought, especially in regard to the development of democratic ideals?

Source: Jean-Jacques Rousseau, *The Social Contract*, trans. M. Cranston (London: Penguin Classics, 1968).

---

between heart and mind, between sentiment and reason. This emphasis on heart and sentiment made him a precursor of the intellectual movement called **Romanticism** that dominated Europe at the beginning of the nineteenth century.

But Rousseau did not necessarily practice what he preached. His own five children born to his illiterate serving girl were sent to foundling homes, where many children died young. Rousseau also viewed women as "naturally" different from men: "To fulfill [a woman's] functions, an appropriate physical constitution is necessary to her. . . . She needs a soft sedentary life to suckle her babies. How much care and tenderness does she need to hold her family together." In *Émile*, Sophie, who was Émile's intended wife, was educated for her role as wife and mother by learning obedience and the nurturing skills that would enable her to provide loving care for her husband and children. Not everyone in the eighteenth century agreed with Rousseau, however, making ideas of gender an important issue in the Enlightenment.

THE "WOMAN'S QUESTION" IN THE ENLIGHTENMENT For centuries, men had dominated the debate about the nature and value of women. In general, many male intellectuals had argued that the base nature of women made them inferior to men and made male domination of women necessary (see Chapter 16). In the seventeenth and eighteenth centuries, many male thinkers reinforced this view by arguing that it was based on "natural" biological differences between men and women. Like Rousseau, they argued that the female constitution destined women to be mothers. Male writers, in particular, were critical of the attempts of some women in the Enlightenment to write on intellectual issues, arguing that women were by nature intellectually inferior to men. Nevertheless, some Enlightenment thinkers offered more positive views of women. Diderot, for example, maintained that men and women were not all that different, and Voltaire asserted that "women are capable of all that men are" in intellectual affairs.

It was women thinkers, however, who added new perspectives to the "woman's question" by making specific suggestions for improving the condition of women. Mary Astell (AST-ul) (1666–1731), daughter of a wealthy English coal merchant, argued in 1697 in *A Serious Proposal to the Ladies* that women needed to become better educated. Men, she believed, would resent her proposal, "but they must excuse me, if I be as partial to my own sex as they are to theirs, and think women as capable of learning as men are, and that it becomes them as well."[8] In a later work titled *Some Reflections upon Marriage*, Astell argued for the equality of the sexes in marriage: "If absolute sovereignty be not necessary in a state, how comes it to be so in a family?

CHRONOLOGY	Works of the Philosophes	
Montesquieu, *Persian Letters*		1721
Voltaire, *Philosophic Letters on the English*		1733
Hume, *Treatise on Human Nature*		1739–1740
Montesquieu, *The Spirit of the Laws*		1748
Voltaire, *The Age of Louis XIV*		1751
Diderot, *Encyclopedia*		1751–1765
Rousseau, *The Social Contract; Émile*		1762
Voltaire, *Treatise on Toleration*		1763
Beccaria, *On Crimes and Punishments*		1764
Holbach, *System of Nature*		1770
Smith, *The Wealth of Nations*		1776
Gibbon, *The Decline and Fall of the Roman Empire*		1776–1788
Wollstonecraft, *Vindication of the Rights of Woman*		1792
Condorcet, *The Progress of the Human Mind*		1794

For if arbitrary power is evil in itself, and an improper method of governing rational and free agents, it ought not be practiced anywhere. . . . If all men are born free, how is it that all women are born slaves?"[9]

The strongest statement for the rights of women in the eighteenth century was advanced by the English writer Mary Wollstonecraft (WULL-Stun-kraft) (1759–1797), viewed by many as the founder of modern European **feminism**. In *Vindication of the Rights of Woman*, written in 1792, Wollstonecraft pointed out two contradictions in the views of women held by such Enlightenment thinkers as Rousseau. To argue that women must obey men, she said, was contrary to the beliefs of the same individuals that a system based on the arbitrary power of monarchs over their subjects or slave owners over their slaves was wrong. The subjection of women to men was equally wrong. In addition, she argued, the Enlightenment was based on the ideal that reason is innate in all human beings. If women have reason, then they are entitled to the same rights that men have. Women, Wollstonecraft declared, should have equal rights with men in education and in economic and political life as well (see "Opposing Viewpoints" on p. 511).

The Social Environment of the Philosophes

The social background of the philosophes varied considerably, from the aristocratic Montesquieu to the lower-middle-class Diderot and Rousseau. The Enlightenment was not the preserve of any one class, although obviously its greatest appeal was to the aristocracy and upper middle classes of the major cities. The common people, especially the peasants, were little affected by the Enlightenment.

Of great importance to the Enlightenment was the spread of its ideas to the literate elite of European society. Although the publication and sale of books and treatises were crucial to this process, the salon was also a factor. **Salons** came into being in the seventeenth century but rose to new heights in the eighteenth. These were the elegant drawing rooms in the urban houses of the wealthy where invited philosophes and guests gathered to engage in witty, sparkling conversations that often centered on the ideas of the philosophes. In France's rigid hierarchical society, the salons were important in bringing together writers and artists with aristocrats, government officials, and wealthy bourgeoisie.

As hostesses of the salons, women found themselves in a position to affect the decisions of kings, sway political opinion, and influence literary and artistic taste. Salons provided havens for people and views unwelcome in the royal court. When French authorities suppressed the *Encyclopedia*, Marie-Thérèse de Geoffrin (1699–1777), a wealthy bourgeois widow whose father had been a valet, welcomed the encyclopedists to her salon and offered financial assistance to complete the work in secret. Madame Geoffrin was not without rivals, however. The marquise du Deffand (mahr-KEEZ duh duh-FAHNH) (1697–1780) had abandoned her husband in the provinces and established herself in Paris, where her ornate drawing room attracted many of the Enlightenment's great figures, including Montesquieu, Hume, and Voltaire.

Although women ran the salons, the reputation of a salon depended on the stature of the males a hostess was able to attract (see "Images of Everyday Life" on p. 512). Despite this male domination, both French and foreign observers complained that females exerted undue influence in French political affairs. Though exaggerated, this perception led to the decline of salons during the French Revolution.

The salons served an important role in promoting conversation and sociability between upper-class men and women as well as spreading the ideas of the Enlightenment. But other means of spreading Enlightenment ideas were also available. Coffeehouses, cafés, reading clubs, and public lending libraries established by the state were gathering places for the exchange of ideas. Learned societies were formed in cities throughout Europe and America. At such gatherings as the Select Society of Edinburgh, Scotland, and the American Philosophical Society in Philadelphia, lawyers, doctors, and local officials gathered to discuss enlightened ideas. Secret societies also developed. The most famous was the Freemasons, established in London in 1717, France and Italy in 1726, and Prussia in 1744. It was no secret that the Freemasons were sympathetic to the ideas of the philosophes.

Culture and Society in the Enlightenment

 FOCUS QUESTIONS: What innovations in art, music, and literature occurred in the eighteenth century? How did popular culture differ from high culture in the eighteenth century?

The intellectual adventure fostered by the philosophes was accompanied by both traditional practices and important changes in eighteenth-century culture and society.

Women in the Age of the Enlightenment: Rousseau and Wollstonecraft

THE "WOMAN'S QUESTION"—THE DEBATE ABOUT the nature and value of women—continued to be discussed in the eighteenth century. In *Émile*, Jean-Jacques Rousseau reflected the view of many male thinkers when he argued that there were natural biological differences between men and women that made women mothers rather than intellectuals. Some women thinkers, however, presented new perspectives. Mary Wollstonecraft, for example, responded to an unhappy childhood in a large family by seeking to lead an independent life. Few occupations were available for middle-class women in her day, but she survived by working as a teacher, chaperone, and governess to aristocratic children. All the while, she wrote and developed her ideas on the rights of women. The selection that follows is taken from her *Vindication of the Rights of Woman*, the work that won her a reputation as the foremost British feminist thinker of the eighteenth century.

Rousseau, *Émile* (1762)

It follows that woman is made specially to please men. If man ought to please her in turn, it is due to a less direct necessity. His merit is in his power; he pleases by the sole fact of his strength. . . .

The strictness of the relative duties of the two sexes is not and cannot be the same. When woman complains on this score about unjust man-made inequality, she is wrong. This inequality is not a human institution—or, at least, it is the work not of prejudice but of reason. It is up to the sex that nature has charged with the bearing of children to be responsible for them to the other sex. Doubtless it is not permitted to anyone to violate his faith, and every unfaithful husband who deprives his wife of the only reward of the austere duties of sex is an unjust and barbarous man. But the unfaithful woman does more; she dissolves the family and breaks all the bonds of nature. . . .

The good constitution of children initially depends on that of their mothers. The first education of men depends on the care of women. . . . Thus, the whole education of women ought to relate to men. To please men, to be useful to them, to make herself loved and honored by them, to raise them when young, to care for them when grown, to counsel them, to console them, to make their lives agreeable and sweet—these are the duties of women at all times, and they ought to be taught from childhood. . . .

The quest for abstract and speculative truths, principles, and axioms in the sciences, for everything that tends to generalize ideas, is not within the competence of women. All their studies ought to be related to practice. . . . Nor do women have sufficient precision and attention to succeed at the exact sciences. And as for the physical sciences, they are for the sex which is more active, gets around more, and sees more

objects, the sex which has more strength and uses it more to judge the relations of sensible beings and the laws of nature. Woman, who is weak and who sees nothing outside the house, estimates and judges the forces she can put to work to make up for her weakness.

Mary Wollstonecraft, *Vindication of the Rights of Woman* (1792)

It is a melancholy truth—yet such is the blessed effect of civilization—the most respectable women are the most oppressed; and, unless they have understandings far superior to the common run of understandings, taking in both sexes, they must, from being treated like contemptible beings, become contemptible. How many women thus waste life away the prey of discontent, who might have practiced as physicians, regulated a farm, managed a shop, and stood erect, supported by their own industry, instead of hanging their heads surcharged with the dew of sensibility, that consumes the beauty to which it at first gave luster. . . .

Proud of their weakness, however, [women] must always be protected, guarded from care, and all the rough toils that dignify the mind. If this be the fiat of fate, if they will make themselves insignificant and contemptible, sweetly to waste "life away," let them not expect to be valued when their beauty fades, for it is the fate of the fairest flowers to be admired and pulled to pieces by the careless hand that plucked them. In how many ways do I wish, from the purest benevolence, to impress this truth on my sex; yet I fear that they will not listen to a truth that dear-bought experience has brought home to many an agitated bosom, nor willingly resign the privileges of rank and sex for the privileges of humanity, to which those have no claim who do not discharge its duties. . . .

Would men but generously snap our chains, and be content with the rational fellowship instead of slavish obedience, they would find us more observant daughters, more affectionate sisters, more faithful wives, and more reasonable mothers—in a word, better citizens. We should then love them with true affection, because we should learn to respect ourselves; and the peace of mind of a worthy man would not be interrupted by the idle vanity of his wife.

 What did Rousseau believe was the role of women, and how did he think they should be educated? What arguments did Mary Wollstonecraft make on behalf of the rights of women? What picture did she paint of the women of her day? Why did Wollstonecraft suggest that both women and men were at fault for the "slavish" situation of women?

Sources: Jean-Jacques Rousseau, *Émile; Or on Education*, in A. Bloom, trans. (New York: Basic Books, 1979); Mary Wollstonecraft, *Vindication of the Rights of Woman* (1792).

Women and the Enlightenment Salon

AS HOSTESSES OF SALONS, WOMEN PLAYED a pivotal role in the spread of Enlightenment ideas by providing a place where philosophes could meet and discuss the topics of the day. Salons also offered women access to intellectual stimulus that was generally otherwise denied to them. Throughout Europe, women were barred from any other higher educational opportunities. A hostess of a salon not only provided food and a drawing room where the guests could mingle, but also set the agenda for the evening and dictated the guest list. Two of the most prominent Parisian hostesses were Madame Geoffrin and Madame Necker (neh-KAIR). In the painting on the left, Madame Geoffrin is seen (third on the right) in her salon surrounded by philosophes in her home on the rue Saint-Honore. Her salon was highly popular, with nobles, writers, artists, and financiers in regular attendance. Suzanne Necker, seen in the portrait at the lower right, was the wife of financier Jacques Necker and spent her days preparing for the evening discussions by reading and writing in her journal. Although the Parisian salons were the most famous, by the late eighteenth century, hostesses in Vienna and Berlin were also holding prominent salons. The painting at the lower left depicts Henriette Herz, whose father was the first Jewish physician to practice in Berlin. Herz was one of many notable wealthy women from Jewish families who sponsored salons in Berlin and Vienna.

© RMN-Grand Palais/Art Resource, NY

Antoine Watteau, *Return from Cythera*. Antoine Watteau was one of the most gifted painters in eighteenth-century France. His portrayal of aristocratic life reveals a world of elegance, wealth, and pleasure. In this painting, which is considered his masterpiece, Watteau depicts a group of aristocratic lovers about to depart from the island of Cythera, where they have paid homage to Venus, the goddess of love. Luxuriously dressed, they move from the woodlands to a golden barge that is waiting to take them from the island.

Innovations in Art, Music, and Literature

Although the Baroque and neoclassical styles that had dominated the seventeenth century continued into the eighteenth century, by the 1730s a new style known as **Rococo** (ruh-KOH-koh) had begun to influence decoration and architecture all over Europe. Following the death of Louis XIV in 1715, the great nobles of France returned to their townhouses in Paris to host soirées of intellectuals and aristocrats. Within these new spaces, a more delicate art form emerged. Unlike the Baroque, which stressed majesty, power, and movement, Rococo emphasized grace and gentle action. Rococo, derived from the French word *rocaille*, or pebble, rejected strict geometrical patterns and had a fondness for curves; it liked to follow the wandering lines of natural objects, such as seashells and flowers. It made much use of interlaced designs colored in gold with delicate contours and graceful curves. Highly secular, its lightness and charm spoke of the pursuit of pleasure, happiness, and love.

Some of Rococo's appeal is evident already in the work of Antoine Watteau (AHN-twahn wah-TOH) (1684–1721). Watteau created a specific type of Rococo; his paintings portrayed a lyrical view of aristocratic life—refined, sensual, civilized, with gentlemen and ladies in elegant dress—reflecting a world of upper-class pleasure and joy. Underneath that exterior, however, was an element of sadness as the artist revealed the fragility and transitory nature of pleasure, love, and life. Watteau relied upon the use of color rather than representational form to highlight his subjects. Watteau died at the age of thirty-six from tuberculosis. Later artists, such as Jean-Honoré Fragonard

(1732–1806), continued Watteau's use of color and subject matter of aristocratic life.

Another aspect of Rococo was that its decorative work could easily be used with Baroque architecture. The palace of Versailles had made an enormous impact on Europe. "Keeping up with the Bourbons" became important as the Austrian emperor, the Swedish king, German princes and prince-bishops, Italian princes, and even a Russian tsar built grandiose palaces. While emulating Versailles's size, they were modeled less after the French classical style of Versailles than after the seventeenth-century Italian Baroque, as modified by a series of brilliant German and Austrian sculptor-architects. This Baroque-Rococo architectural style of the eighteenth century was used in both palaces and churches, and often the same architects designed both. This is evident in the work of one of the greatest architects of the eighteenth century, Balthasar Neumann (BAHL-tuh-zahr NOI-mahn) (1687–1753).

Neumann's two masterpieces are the pilgrimage church of the Vierzehnheiligen (feer-tsayn-HY-li-gen) (Fourteen Saints) in southern Germany and the Bishop's Palace, known as the Residenz, the residential palace of the Schönborn (SHURN-bawn) prince-bishop of Würzburg (VOORTS-boork). Secular and spiritual become easily interchangeable in both buildings as the visitor is greeted by lavish and fanciful ornament; light, bright colors; and elaborate, rich detail. The church is designed without any straight lines, only ovals and circles, contrasting the traditional rectilinear nave, creating a fluidity of motion reflected in the curvilinear gilding on the ceiling.

Jean-Honoré Fragonard, *The Swing*. Fragonard captured the frivolity and decadence of France's aristocracy. In this painting, Fragonard portrays a young lady being pushed on a swing as her suitor sits below her. The lush environs and curvilinear landscape epitomize Rococo's love of nature, while the delicate light and color of the lady's dress highlight the playful moment of her kicking off her shoe.

Vierzehnheiligen, Interior View. Pictured here is the interior of the Vierzehnheiligen, the pilgrimage church designed by Balthasar Neumann. Elaborate detail, blazing light, rich colors, and opulent decoration blend together to create a work of stunning beauty. The pilgrim in search of holiness is struck by an incredible richness of detail. Persuaded by joy rather than fear, the believer is lifted toward heaven on a cloud of rapture.

Despite the popularity of the Rococo style, **neoclassicism** continued to maintain a strong appeal and in the late eighteenth century emerged in France as an established movement. Neoclassical artists wanted to recapture the dignity and simplicity of the classical style of ancient Greece and Rome. Some were especially influenced by the recent excavations of the ancient Roman cities of Herculaneum and Pompeii. Classical elements are evident in the work of Jacques-Louis David (ZHAHK-LWEE dah-VEED) (1748–1825). In the *Oath of the Horatii*, he re-created a scene from Roman history in which the three Horatius brothers swore an oath before their father, proclaiming their willingness to sacrifice their lives for their country. David's neoclassical style, with its moral seriousness and its emphasis on honor and patriotism, made him extremely popular during the French Revolution.

THE DEVELOPMENT OF MUSIC The seventeenth and eighteenth centuries were the formative years of classical music and saw the rise of the opera and oratorio, the sonata, the concerto, and the symphony. The Italians were the first to develop these genres but were soon followed by the Germans, Austrians, and English. As in previous centuries, most musicians depended on a patron—a prince, a well-endowed ecclesiastic, or an aristocrat. The many individual princes, archbishops, and bishops, each with his own court, provided the patronage that made Italy and Germany the musical leaders of Europe.

Many of the techniques of the Baroque musical style, which dominated Europe between 1600 and 1750, were perfected by two composers—Bach and Handel—who stand out as musical geniuses. Johann Sebastian Bach (yoh-HAHN suh-BASS-chun BAHK) (1685–1750) came from a family of musicians. Bach held the post of organist and music director at a number of small German courts before becoming director of church music at the Church of Saint Thomas in Leipzig in 1723. There Bach composed his Mass in B Minor, his *Saint Matthew's Passion*, and the cantatas and motets that have established his reputation as one of the greatest composers of all time. For Bach, music was above all a means to worship God; in his own words, his task in life was to make "well-ordered music in the honor of God."

The other great musical giant of the early eighteenth century, George Frederick Handel (HAN-dul) (1685–1759), was, like Bach, born in Saxony in Germany and in the same year. In contrast to Bach's quiet provincial life, however, Handel experienced a stormy international career and was profoundly secular in temperament. After studying in Italy, where he began his career by writing operas in the Italian manner, in 1712 he moved to England, where he spent most of his adult life attempting to run an opera company. Although patronized by the English royal court, Handel wrote music for large public audiences and was not averse to writing huge, unusual-sounding pieces. The band for his *Fireworks Music*, for example, was supposed to be accompanied by 101 cannons. Although he wrote more than forty operas and much other secular music, the worldly Handel

Jacques-Louis David, *Oath of the Horatii*. The Frenchman Jacques-Louis David was one of the most famous neoclassical artists of the late eighteenth century. To immerse himself in the world of classical antiquity, he painted the *Oath of the Horatii* in Rome. Thanks to its emphasis on patriotic duty, the work became an instant hit in both Paris and Rome.

is, ironically, probably best known for his religious music. His *Messiah* has been called "one of those rare works that appeal immediately to everyone, and yet is indisputably a masterpiece of the highest order."[10]

Although Bach and Handel composed many instrumental suites and concerti, orchestral music did not come to the fore until the second half of the eighteenth century, when new instruments such as the piano appeared. A new musical period, the classical era (1750–1830), also emerged, represented by two great innovators—Haydn and Mozart. Their renown caused the musical center of Europe to shift from Italy and Germany to the Austrian Empire.

Franz Joseph Haydn (FRAHNTS YO-zef HY-dun) (1732–1809) spent most of his adult life as musical director for the wealthy Hungarian princes, the Esterhazy brothers. Haydn was incredibly prolific, composing 104 symphonies in addition to string quartets, concerti, songs, oratorios, and Masses. His visits to England in 1790 and 1794 introduced him to another world, where musicians wrote for public concerts rather than princely patrons. This "liberty," as he called it, induced him to write his two great oratorios, *The Creation* and *The Seasons*, both of which were dedicated to the common people.

The concerto, symphony, and opera all reached their zenith in the works of Wolfgang Amadeus Mozart (VULF-gahng ah-muh-DAY-uss MOH-tsart) (1756–1791), a child prodigy who gave his first harpsichord concert at six and wrote his first opera

at twelve. He, too, sought a patron, but his discontent with the overly demanding archbishop of Salzburg forced him to move to Vienna, where his failure to find a permanent patron made his life miserable. Nevertheless, he wrote music prolifically and passionately until he died a debt-ridden pauper at thirty-five (see "Film & History" below). Mozart carried the tradition of

🎬 FILM & HISTORY

Watch *Amadeus*, which was based on the relationship of two eighteenth-century composers, Antonio Salieri and Wolfgang Amadeus Mozart. *Amadeus* is a brilliant film about the musical genius of Mozart. While the movie is accurate in presenting Mozart as a child prodigy and a great composer who died at the young age of thirty-five, the story of the rivalry between Salieri and Mozart is mostly fictional. Nevertheless, *Amadeus* provides viewers with a stunning portrayal of one of the world's greatest composers.

Q *How were musicians paid during the eighteenth century? How did this influence their work?*

Italian comic opera to new heights with *The Marriage of Figaro*, based on a Parisian play of the 1780s in which a valet outwits and outsings his noble employers, and *Don Giovanni*, a "black comedy" about the havoc Don Giovanni wrought on earth before he descended into hell. *The Marriage of Figaro, The Magic Flute,* and *Don Giovanni* are three of the world's greatest operas. Mozart composed with an ease of melody and a blend of grace, precision, and emotion that arguably no one has ever excelled. Haydn remarked to Mozart's father that "your son is the greatest composer known to me either in person or by reputation."

THE DEVELOPMENT OF THE NOVEL The eighteenth century was also decisive in the development of the novel. The novel was not a completely new literary genre but grew out of the medieval romances and the picaresque stories of the sixteenth century. The English are credited with establishing the modern novel as the chief vehicle for fiction writing. With no established rules, the novel was open to much experimentation. It also proved especially attractive to women readers and women writers.

Samuel Richardson (1689–1761) was a printer by trade and did not turn to writing until his fifties. His first novel, *Pamela: or, Virtue Rewarded*, focused on a servant girl's resistance to numerous seduction attempts by her master. Finally, by reading the girl's letters describing her feelings about his efforts, the master realizes that she has a good mind as well as an attractive body and marries her. Virtue is rewarded. *Pamela* won Richardson a large audience as he appealed to the growing cult of sensibility in the eighteenth century—the taste for the sentimental and emotional. Samuel Johnson, another great English writer of the century and an even greater wit, remarked, "If you were to read Richardson for the story . . . you would hang yourself. But you must read him for the sentiment."

Reacting against the moral seriousness of Richardson, Henry Fielding (1707–1754) wrote novels about people without scruples who survived by their wits. His best work was *The History of Tom Jones, a Foundling*, a lengthy novel about the numerous adventures of a young scoundrel. Fielding presented scenes of English life from the hovels of London to the country houses of the aristocracy. In a number of hilarious episodes, he described characters akin to real types in English society. Although he emphasized action rather than inner feeling, Fielding did his own moralizing by attacking the hypocrisy of his age.

THE WRITING OF HISTORY The philosophes were responsible for creating a revolution in the writing of history. Their secular orientation caused them to eliminate the role of God in history and freed them to concentrate on events themselves and search for causal relationships in the natural world. Earlier, the humanist historians of the Renaissance had also placed their histories in purely secular settings, but not with the same intensity and complete removal of God.

The philosophe-historians also broadened the scope of history from the humanists' preoccupation with politics. Politics still predominated in the work of Enlightenment historians, but they also paid attention to economic, social, intellectual, and cultural developments. As Voltaire explained in his masterpiece, *The Age of Louis XIV:* "It is not merely the life of Louis XIV that we propose to write; we have a wider aim in view. We shall endeavor to depict for posterity, not the actions of a single man, but the spirit of men in the most enlightened age the world has ever seen."[11] In seeking to describe the "totality of past human experience," Voltaire initiated the modern ideal of social history.

The weaknesses of these philosophe-historians stemmed from their preoccupations as philosophes. Following the ideals of the classics that dominated their minds, the philosophes sought to instruct as well as entertain. Their goal was to help civilize their age, and history could play a role by revealing its lessons according to their vision. Their emphasis on science and reason and their dislike of Christianity made them less than sympathetic to the period we call the Middle Ages. This is particularly noticeable in the other great masterpiece of eighteenth-century historiography, the six-volume *Decline and Fall of the Roman Empire* by Edward Gibbon (1737–1794). Although Gibbon thought that the decline of Rome had many causes, he portrayed the growth of Christianity as a major reason for Rome's eventual collapse. Like some of the philosophes, Gibbon believed in the idea of progress and, in reflecting on the decline and fall of Rome, expressed his optimism about the future of European civilization and the ability of Europeans to avoid the fate of the Romans.

The High Culture of the Eighteenth Century

Historians and cultural anthropologists have grown accustomed to distinguishing between a civilization's high culture and its popular culture. Whereas **high culture** usually refers to the literary and artistic world of the educated and wealthy ruling classes, **popular culture** refers to the written and unwritten lore of the masses, most of which is passed down orally. By the eighteenth century, European high culture consisted of a learned world of theologians, scientists, philosophers, intellectuals, poets, and dramatists, for whom Latin remained a truly international language. Their work was supported by a wealthy and literate lay group, the most important of whom were the landed aristocracy and the wealthier upper classes in the cities.

Especially noticeable in the eighteenth century was an expansion of both the reading public and publishing. One study revealed that French publishers were issuing about sixteen hundred titles yearly in the 1780s, up from three hundred titles in 1750. Though many of these titles were still aimed at small groups of the educated elite, many were also directed to the new reading public of the middle classes, which included women and even urban artisans. The growth of publishing houses made it possible for authors to make money from their works and be less dependent on wealthy patrons.

An important aspect of the growth of publishing and reading in the eighteenth century was the development of magazines for the general public. Great Britain, an important center for the new magazines, saw 25 periodicals published in 1700, 103 in 1760, and 158 in 1780. Although short-lived, the best known was Joseph Addison and Richard Steele's *Spectator*, begun in 1711.

A London Coffeehouse. Coffeehouses first appeared in Venice and Constantinople but quickly spread throughout Europe by the beginning of the eighteenth century. In addition to drinking coffee, patrons of coffeehouses could read magazines and newspapers, exchange ideas, play chess, smoke, and engage in business transactions. In this scene from a London coffeehouse of 1705, well-attired gentlemen make bids on commodities.

Its goal was "to bring Philosophy out of the closets and libraries, schools and colleges, to dwell in clubs and assemblies, at tea-tables and coffeehouses." In keeping with one of the chief intellectual goals of the philosophes, the *Spectator* wished to instruct and entertain at the same time. With its praise of family, marriage, and courtesy, the *Spectator* also had a strong appeal to women. Some of the new magazines were aimed specifically at women, such as *The Female Spectator* in England, which was also edited by a woman, Eliza Haywood, and featured articles by female writers.

Along with magazines came daily newspapers. The first was printed in London in 1702, but by 1780, thirty-seven other English towns had their own newspapers. Filled with news and special features, they were relatively cheap and were provided free in coffeehouses. In 1737, a German visitor to London described the atmosphere of public readership in a coffeehouse:

> The fine Gentleman . . . rises late, puts on a Frock . . . and leaving his Sword at Home . . . goes . . . to some Coffee-house, or Chocolate-house, frequented by the Person he would see; for 'tis a Sort of Rule with the English, to go once a Day at least, to Houses of this Sort, where they talk of Business and News, read the Papers, and often look at one another without opening their Lips; and 'tis very well they are so mute; for if they were as talkative as the People of many other Nations, the Coffee-houses would be intolerable, and there would be no hearing what one Man said, where there are so many.[12]

Books, too, received wider circulation through the development of public libraries in the cities as well as private circulating libraries, which offered books for rent.

EDUCATION AND UNIVERSITIES By the eighteenth century, Europe was home to a large number of privately endowed secondary schools, such as the grammar and public schools in England, the gymnasiums in German-speaking lands, and the *collèges* in France and Spain. These schools tended to be elitist, designed to meet the needs of the children of the upper classes of society. Basically, European secondary schools perpetuated the class hierarchy of Europe rather than creating avenues for social mobility. In fact, most of the philosophes reinforced the belief that education should function to keep people in their own social class. Baron d'Holbach said, "Education should teach . . . the rich to use their riches well, the poor to live by honest industry."

The curriculum of these secondary schools still largely concentrated on the Greek and Latin classics with little attention paid to mathematics, the sciences, and modern languages. Complaints from philosophe-reformers, as well as from merchants and other middle-class people who wanted their sons to have a more practical education, led to the development of new schools designed to provide a broader education. In Germany, the first *Realschule* (ray-AHL-shoo-luh) was opened in Berlin in 1747 and offered modern languages, geography,

THE PUNISHMENT OF CRIME

TORTURE AND CAPITAL PUNISHMENT REMAINED common features of European judicial systems well into the eighteenth century. Public spectacles were especially gruesome, as this excerpt from the *Nocturnal Spectator* of Restif de la Bretonne, a French novelist, demonstrates.

Restif de la Bretonne, "The Broken Man"

I went home by way of rue Saint-Antoine and the Place de Grève. Three murderers had been broken on the wheel there, the day before. I had not expected to see any such spectacle, one that I had never dared to witness. But as I crossed the square I caught sight of a poor wretch, pale, half dead, wracked by the pains of the interrogation inflicted on him twenty hours earlier; he was stumbling down from the Hotel de Ville supported by the executioner and the confessor. These two men, so completely different, inspired an inexpressible emotion in me! I watched the latter embrace a miserable man consumed by fever, filthy as the dungeons he came from, swarming with vermin! And I said to myself, "O Religion, here is your greatest glory!" . . .

I saw a horrible sight, even though the torture had been mitigated. . . . The wretch had revealed his accomplices. He was garroted before he was put to the wheel. A winch set under the scaffold tightened a noose around the victim's neck and he was strangled; for a long while the confessor and the hangman felt his heart to see whether the artery still pulsed, and the hideous blows were dealt only after it beat no longer. . . . I left, with my hair standing on end in horror.

 What does this selection reveal about the punishment of crime in the eighteenth century? What impact did such descriptions have on the philosophes' attitudes toward the administration of justice as it was carried out by their respective monarchical states?

Source: L. Asher and E. Fertig, trans., *Les Nuits de Paris; or, The Nocturnal Spectator: A Selection* (New York: Knopf, 1964).

---

and bookkeeping to prepare boys for careers in business. New schools of this kind were also created for upper-class girls, although they focused primarily on religion and domestic skills.

The most common complaint about universities, especially from the philosophes, was the old-fashioned curriculum that emphasized the classics and Aristotelian philosophy and provided no training in the sciences or modern languages. Before the end of the century, this criticism led to reforms that introduced new ideas in the areas of physics, astronomy, and even mathematics into the universities. It is significant, however, that very few of the important scientific discoveries of the eighteenth century occurred in the universities.

Crime and Punishment

By the eighteenth century, most European states had developed a hierarchy of courts to deal with crimes. Except in England, judicial torture remained an important means of obtaining evidence before a trial. Courts used the rack, thumbscrews, and other instruments to obtain confessions in criminal cases. Punishments for crimes were often cruel and even spectacular. Public executions were a basic part of traditional punishment and were regarded as necessary to deter potential offenders in an age when police forces were too weak to ensure the capture of criminals. Although nobles were executed by simple beheading, lower-class criminals condemned to death were tortured, broken on the wheel, or drawn and quartered (see the box above). The death penalty was still commonly used for property crimes as well as for violent offenses. By 1800, more than two hundred crimes were subject to the death penalty in England. In addition to executions, European states resorted to forced labor in mines, forts, and navies. England also sent criminals as indentured servants to colonies in the New World and, after the American Revolution, to Australia.

Appalled by the unjust laws and brutal punishments of their times, some philosophes sought to create a new approach to justice. The most notable effort was made by an Italian philosophe, Cesare Beccaria (CHAY-zuh-ray buh-KAH-ree-uh) (1738–1794). In his essay *On Crimes and Punishments*, written in 1764, Beccaria argued that punishments should serve only as deterrents, not as exercises in brutality: "Such punishments . . . ought to be chosen as will make the strongest and most lasting impressions on the minds of others, with the least torment to the body of the criminal."[13] Beccaria was also opposed to the use of capital punishment. It was spectacular, but it failed to stop others from committing crimes. Imprisonment—the deprivation of freedom—made a far more lasting impression. Moreover, capital punishment was harmful to society because it set an example of barbarism: "Is it not absurd that the laws, which detest and punish homicide, should, in order to prevent murder, publicly commit murder themselves?"

By the end of the eighteenth century, a growing sentiment against executions and torture led to a decline in both corporal and capital punishment. A new type of prison, in which criminals were placed in cells and subjected to discipline and regular work to rehabilitate them, began to replace the public spectacle of barbarous punishments.

The World of Medicine

In the eighteenth century, a hierarchy of practitioners practiced medicine. At the top stood the physicians, who were university graduates and enjoyed a high social status. Despite the scientific advances of the seventeenth and eighteenth centuries, however, university medical education was still largely conducted in Latin and was based primarily on Galen's work. New methods emphasizing clinical experience did begin to be introduced at the University of Leiden, which replaced Padua as the foremost medical school of Europe in the first half of the seventeenth century, only to be surpassed in the second half of that century by Vienna. A graduate with a doctorate in medicine from a university needed to receive a license before he could be a practicing member of the physicians' elite corporate body. In England, the Royal College of Physicians licensed only one hundred physicians in the early eighteenth century. Only officially licensed physicians could hold regular medical consultations with patients and receive payments, already regarded in the eighteenth century as outrageously high.

Below the physicians were the surgeons, who were still known as barber-surgeons well into the eighteenth century from their original dual occupation. Their primary functions were to bleed patients and perform surgery; the latter was often done crudely, without painkillers and in filthy conditions, because there was no understanding of anesthesia or infection. Bleeding was widely believed to be beneficial in reducing fevers and combating a variety of illnesses.

The surgeons underwent significant changes in the course of the eighteenth century. In the 1740s, they began to separate themselves from the barbers and organize their own guilds. At the same time, they started to undergo additional training by dissecting corpses and studying anatomy more systematically. As they became more effective, the distinction between physicians and surgeons began to break down, and surgeons were examining patients in a fashion similar to physicians by the end of the century. Moreover, surgeons also began to be licensed. In England, the Royal College of Surgeons required clinical experience before granting the license.

Other medical practitioners, such as apothecaries, midwives, and faith healers, primarily served the common people in the eighteenth century. Although their main function was to provide herbs and potions as recommended by physicians, apothecaries or pharmacists also acted independently in diagnosing illnesses and selling remedies. In the course of the eighteenth century, male doctors increasingly supplanted midwives in delivering babies. At the same time, the tradition of faith healing, so prominent in medieval medicine, continued to be practiced, especially in the rural areas of Europe.

Hospitals in the eighteenth century seemed more a problem than an aid in dealing with disease and illness. That conditions were bad is evident in this description by the philosophe Denis Diderot, who characterized the Hôtel-Dieu in Paris, France's "biggest, roomiest, and richest" hospital, in these words:

> Imagine a long series of communicating wards filled with sufferers of every kind of disease who are sometimes packed three, four, five or even six into a bed, the living alongside the dead and dying, the air polluted by this mass of unhealthy bodies, passing pestilential germs of their afflictions from one to the other, and the spectacle of suffering and agony on every hand. That is the Hôtel-Dieu. The result is that many of these poor wretches come out with diseases they did not have when they went in, and often pass them on to the people they go back to live with.[14]

Despite appeals, efforts at hospital reform in the eighteenth century remained ineffectual.

Popular Culture

Popular culture refers to the written and unwritten literature and the social activities and pursuits that are fundamental to the lives of most people. The distinguishing characteristic of popular culture is its collective and public nature. Group activity was especially evident in the festival, a broad name used to cover a variety of celebrations: community festivals in Catholic Europe that celebrated the feast day of the local patron saint; annual festivals, such as Christmas and Easter, that went back to medieval Christianity; and Carnival, the most spectacular form of festival, which was celebrated in Spain, Italy, France, Germany, and Austria. All of these festivals were special occasions when people ate, drank, and celebrated to excess (see "Global Perspectives" on p. 520). In traditional societies, festival was a time for relaxation and enjoyment because much of the rest of the year was a time of unrelieved work. As the poet Thomas Gray said of Carnival in Turin in 1739: "This Carnival lasts only from Christmas to Lent; one half of the remaining part of the year is passed in remembering the last, the other in expecting the future Carnival."[15]

CARNIVAL Carnival was celebrated in the weeks leading up to the beginning of Lent, the forty-day period of fasting and purification preceding Easter. Carnival was, understandably, a time of great indulgence, just the reverse of Lent, when people were expected to abstain from meat, sex, and most recreations. Hearty consumption of food, especially meat and other delicacies, and heavy drinking were the norm during Carnival; so was intense sexual activity. Songs with double meanings that would be considered offensive at other times could be sung publicly at this time of year. A float of Florentine "keymakers," for example, sang this ditty to the ladies: "Our tools are fine, new and useful; We always carry them with us; They are good for anything; If you want to touch them, you can."[16] Finally, Carnival was a time of aggression, a time to release pent-up feelings. Most often this took the form of verbal aggression, since people were allowed to openly insult other people and even criticize their social superiors and authorities. Certain acts of physical violence were also permitted. People pelted each other with apples, eggs, flour, and pigs' bladders filled with water.

TAVERNS AND ALCOHOL The same sense of community evident in festival was also present in the chief gathering places of the common people, the local taverns or cabarets. Taverns functioned as regular gathering places for neighborhood men to talk, play games, conduct small business matters, and drink. In some countries, the favorite drinks of poor people, such as gin in England and vodka in Russia, proved devastating as poor people regularly drank themselves into oblivion. Gin was cheap; the classic sign in English taverns, "Drunk for a penny, dead drunk for two pence," was literally true. In England, the consumption of gin rose from 2 million to 5 million gallons between 1714 and 1733 and declined only when complaints

Popular Culture in the West and East

BY THE SEVENTEENTH CENTURY, a popular culture distinct from the elite culture of the nobility was beginning to emerge in the urban worlds of both the West and the East. At the top is a scene from the celebration of Carnival on the Piazza Sante Croce in Florence, Italy. Carnival was a period of festivities before Lent, celebrated primarily in Roman Catholic countries. It became an occasion for indulgence in food, drink, games, and practical jokes as a prelude to the austerity of the forty-day Lenten season from Ash Wednesday to Easter. All of these activities are evident here. On the right below is a festival scene from the pleasure district of Kyoto known as the Gion. Spectators on a balcony are enjoying a colorful parade of floats and costumed performers. The festival originated as a celebration of the passing of a deadly epidemic in medieval Japan.

 Do festivals such as these still exist in our day? What purpose do they serve?

finally led to laws restricting sales in the 1750s. Of course, the rich drank too. Samuel Johnson once remarked that all the decent people in Lichfield got drunk every night and "were not the worse thought of." But unlike the poor, the rich drank port and brandy, usually in large quantities.

This difference in drinking habits between rich and poor reminds us of the ever-widening separation between the elite and the poor in the eighteenth century. In 1500, popular culture was for everyone; a second culture for the elite, it was the only culture for the rest of society. But between 1500 and 1800, the nobility, clergy, and bourgeoisie had abandoned popular culture to the lower classes. This was, of course, a gradual process, and in abandoning the popular festivals, the upper classes were also abandoning the popular worldview as well. The new scientific outlook had brought a new mental world for the upper classes, and they now viewed such things as witchcraft, faith healing, fortune telling, and prophecy as the beliefs of those who were, as one writer said, "of the weakest judgment and reason, as women, children, and ignorant and superstitious persons."

LITERACY AND PRIMARY EDUCATION Popular culture had always included a vast array of traditional songs and stories that were passed down from generation to generation. But popular culture was not entirely based on an oral tradition; a popular literature existed as well. So-called chapbooks, printed on cheap paper, were short brochures sold by itinerant peddlers to the lower classes. They contained both spiritual and secular material: lives of saints and inspirational stories competed with crude satires and adventure stories.

It is apparent from the chapbooks that popular culture did not have to remain primarily oral. Its ability to change was dependent on the growth of literacy. Studies in France indicate that literacy rates for men increased from 29 percent in the late seventeenth century to 47 percent in the late eighteenth century; for women, the increase was from 14 to 27 percent during the same period. Of course, certain groups were more likely to be literate than others. Upper-class elites and the upper middle classes in the cities were mostly all literate. Nevertheless, the figures also indicate dramatic increases for lower-middle-class artisans in urban areas. Recent research in the city of Marseilles, for example, indicates that literacy of male artisans and workers increased from 28 percent in 1710 to 85 percent in 1789, though the rate for women remained at 15 percent. Peasants, who constituted as much as 75 percent of the French population, remained largely illiterate.

The spread of literacy was closely connected to primary education. In Catholic Europe, primary education was largely a matter of local community effort, leading to little real growth. Only in the Habsburg Austrian Empire was a system of state-supported primary schools—*Volkschulen* (FULK-shoo-lun)—established, although only one in four school-age children actually attended.

The emphasis of the Protestant reformers on reading the Bible had led Protestant states to take a greater interest in primary education. Some places, especially the Swiss cantons, Scotland, and the German states of Saxony and Prussia, witnessed the emergence of universal primary schools that provided a modicum of education for the masses. But effective systems of primary education were hindered by the attitudes of the ruling classes, who feared the consequences of teaching the lower classes anything beyond the virtues of hard work and deference to their superiors. Hannah More, an English writer who set up a network of Sunday schools, made clear the philosophy of her charity school for poor children: "My plan of instruction is extremely simple and limited. They learn on weekdays such coarse work as may fit them for servants. I allow of no writing for the poor. My object is to train up the lower classes in habits of industry and piety."

Religion and the Churches

 FOCUS QUESTION: How did popular religion differ from institutional religion in the eighteenth century?

The music of Bach and the pilgrimage and monastic churches of southern Germany and Austria make us aware of a curious fact. Though much of the great art and music of the time was religious, the thought of the time was antireligious as life became increasingly secularized and men of reason attacked the established churches. And yet most Europeans were still Christians. Even many of those most critical of the churches accepted that society could not function without religious faith.

The Institutional Church

In the eighteenth century, the established Catholic and Protestant churches were basically conservative institutions that upheld society's hierarchical structure, privileged classes, and traditions. Although churches experienced change because of new state policies, they did not sustain any dramatic internal changes. In both Catholic and Protestant countries, the parish church run by a priest or pastor remained the center of religious practice. In addition to providing religious services, the parish church kept records of births, deaths, and marriages; provided charity for the poor; supervised whatever primary education there was; and cared for orphans.

CHURCH-STATE RELATIONS Early on, the Protestant Reformation had solved the problem of the relationship between church and state by establishing the principle of state control over the churches. In the eighteenth century, Protestant state churches flourished throughout Europe: Lutheranism in Scandinavia and the north German states; Anglicanism in England; and Calvinism (or Reformed churches) in Scotland, the United Provinces, and some of the Swiss cantons and German states (see Map 17.2). There were also Protestant minorities in other European countries.

In 1700, the Catholic Church still exercised much power in Catholic European states: Spain, Portugal, France, Italy, the Habsburg Empire, Poland, and most of southern Germany. The church also continued to possess enormous wealth. In Spain, three thousand monastic institutions housing 100,000 men and women controlled enormous landed estates.

The Catholic Church remained hierarchically structured. In most Catholic countries, the highest clerics, such as bishops, archbishops, abbots, and abbesses, were members of the upper class, especially the landed nobility, and received enormous revenues from their landed estates and tithes from the faithful. A wide gulf existed between the upper and lower clergy. While the French bishop of Strasbourg, for example, received 100,000 livres a year, parish priests were paid only 500.

In the eighteenth century, the governments of many Catholic states began to seek greater authority over the churches in their countries. This "nationalization" of the Catholic Church meant controlling the papacy and in turn the chief papal agent, the Society of Jesus. The Jesuits had proved extremely successful, perhaps too successful for their own good. They had created special enclaves, virtually states within states, in the French, Spanish, and Portuguese colonies in the New World. As advisers to Catholic rulers, the Jesuits exercised considerable political influence. But the high profile they achieved through their successes attracted a wide range of enemies, and a series of actions soon undermined Jesuit power. The Portuguese monarch destroyed the powerful Jesuit state in Paraguay and then in 1759 expelled the Jesuits from Portugal and confiscated their property. In 1764, they were expelled from France and three years later from Spain and the Spanish colonies. In 1773, when Spain and France demanded that the entire society be dissolved, Pope Clement XIV reluctantly complied. The dissolution of the Jesuit order, an important pillar of Catholic strength, was yet another victory for Catholic governments determined to win control over their churches.

The end of the Jesuits was paralleled by a decline in papal power. Already by the mid-eighteenth century, the papacy played only a minor role in diplomacy and international affairs. The nationalization of the churches by the states meant the loss of the papacy's power to appoint high clerical officials.

TOLERATION AND RELIGIOUS MINORITIES One of the chief battle cries of the philosophes was a call for religious toleration. Out of political necessity, a certain level of tolerance of different creeds had occurred in the seventeenth century, but many rulers still found it difficult to accept. Louis XIV had turned back the clock in France at the end of the seventeenth century, insisting on religious uniformity and suppressing the rights of the Huguenots (see Chapter 15). Many rulers continued to believe that there was only one path to salvation; it was the true duty of a ruler not to allow subjects to be condemned to hell by being heretics. Hence, persecution of heretics continued; the last burning of a heretic took place in 1781.

Nevertheless, some progress was made toward religious toleration. No ruler was more interested in the philosophes' call for religious toleration than Joseph II of Austria. His Toleration Patent of 1781, while recognizing Catholicism's public practice, granted Lutherans, Calvinists, and Greek Orthodox the right to worship privately. In all other ways, all subjects were now equal: "Non-Catholics are in future admitted under dispensation to buy houses and real property, to practice as master craftsmen, to take up academic appointments and posts in public service, and are not to be required to take the oath in any form contrary to their religious tenets."[17]

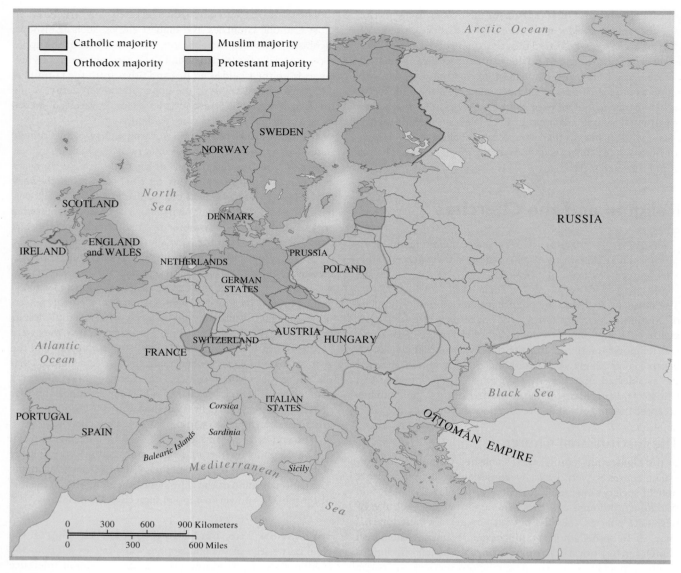

MAP 17.2 **Religious Populations of Eighteenth-Century Europe.** Christianity was still a dominant force in eighteenth-century Europe—even many of the philosophes remained Christians while attacking the authority and power of the established Catholic and Protestant churches. By the end of the century, however, most monarchs had increased royal power at the expense of religious institutions.

 To what extent were religious majorities geographically concentrated in certain areas, and what accounted for this?

In the Dutch Republic, however, toleration of various religious orders underwent significant changes during the eighteenth century, building upon centuries of varying degrees of religious tolerance towards dissenting groups. Toleration, however, did not equal freedom of religious expression, but rather freedom of conscience as prescribed in article 13 of the Union of Utrecht of 1579. To what degree this freedom was tolerated depended upon the political state, and by 1651, this privilege was granted to the Dutch Reformed Church, or Calvinist Church. All other religions could worship inconspicuously, and non-Reformed citizens were treated as second-class citizens. By the mid-eighteenth century, however, the writings of Enlightenment thinkers fueled heated public debates in the Dutch Republic. By 1796, a Declaration of Human Rights declared the separation of church and state, thus establishing the equality of all Protestant and Roman Catholic citizens in the United Provinces, while Jews were granted civil rights.

TOLERATION AND THE JEWS The Jews remained the despised religious minority of Europe. The largest number of Jews (known as the Ashkenazic Jews) lived in eastern Europe. Except in relatively tolerant Poland, Jews were restricted in their movements, forbidden to own land or hold many jobs, forced to pay burdensome special taxes, and also subject to periodic outbursts of popular wrath. The resulting **pogroms**, in which Jewish communities were looted and massacred, made Jewish existence precarious and dependent on the favor of their territorial rulers.

Another major group was the Sephardic Jews, who had been expelled from Spain in the fifteenth century. Although many had migrated to Turkish lands, some had settled in cities, such as Amsterdam, Venice, London, and Frankfurt, where they were relatively free to participate in the banking and commercial activities that Jews had practiced since the Middle Ages. The highly successful ones came to provide valuable services to rulers, especially in central Europe, where they were known as the court Jews. But even these Jews were insecure because their religion set them apart from the Christian majority and served as a catalyst to social resentment.

Some Enlightenment thinkers in the eighteenth century favored a new acceptance of Jews. They argued that Jews and Muslims were human and deserved the full rights of citizenship despite their religion. Many philosophes denounced persecution of the Jews but made no attempt to hide their hostility and ridiculed Jewish customs. Diderot, for example, said that the Jews had "all the defects peculiar to an ignorant and superstitious nation." Many Europeans favored the assimilation of the Jews into the mainstream of society, but only by the conversion of Jews to Christianity as the basic solution to the "Jewish problem." This, of course, was not acceptable to most Jews.

The Austrian emperor Joseph II attempted to adopt a new policy toward the Jews, although it too was limited. It freed Jews from nuisance taxes and allowed them more freedom of movement and job opportunities, but they were still restricted from owning land and worshiping in public. At the same time, Joseph II encouraged Jews to learn German and work toward greater assimilation into Austrian society.

Popular Religion in the Eighteenth Century

Despite the rise of skepticism and the intellectuals' belief in deism and natural religion, religious devotion remained strong in the eighteenth century.

CATHOLIC PIETY It is difficult to assess precisely the religiosity of Europe's Catholics. The Catholic parish church remained an important center of life for the entire community. How many people went to church regularly cannot be known exactly, but it has been established that 90 to 95 percent of Catholic populations did go to Mass on Easter Sunday, one of the church's most special celebrations. Catholic religiosity proved highly selective, however. Despite the Reformation, much popular devotion was still directed to an externalized form of worship focusing on prayers to saints, pilgrimages, and devotion to relics and images. This bothered many clergymen, who felt that their parishioners were "more superstitious than devout," as one Catholic priest put it. Many common people continued to fear witches and relied on the intervention of the saints and the Virgin Mary to save them from personal disasters caused by the devil.

PROTESTANT REVIVALISM: PIETISM After the initial century of religious fervor that created Protestantism in the sixteenth century, Protestant churches in the seventeenth century had settled down into well-established patterns controlled by state authorities and served by a well-educated clergy. Protestant churches became bureaucratized and bereft of religious enthusiasm. In Germany and England, where rationalism and deism had become influential and moved some theologians to a more "rational" Christianity, the desire of ordinary Protestant churchgoers for greater depths of religious experience led to new and dynamic religious movements.

Pietism (PY-uh-tiz-um) in Germany was a response to this desire for a deeper personal devotion to God. Begun in the seventeenth century by a group of German clerics who wanted their religion to be more personal, Pietism was spread by the teachings of Count Nikolaus von Zinzendorf (NEE-koh-LOWSS fun TSIN-sin-dorf) (1700–1760). To Zinzendorf and his Moravian Brethren, as his sect was called, true religious experience consisted of the mystical dimensions—the personal experience of God—in one's life. He was utterly opposed to what he perceived as the rationalistic approach of orthodox Lutheran clergy, who were being educated in new "rational" ideas. As Zinzendorf commented, "He who wishes to comprehend God with his mind becomes an atheist."

After the civil wars of the seventeenth century, England too had arrived at a respectable, uniform, and complacent state church. A pillar of the establishment, the Anglican Church seemed to offer little spiritual excitement, especially to the

John Wesley. In leading a deep spiritual revival in Britain, John Wesley founded a religious movement that came to be known as Methodism. He loved to preach to the masses, and this 1766 portrait by Nathaniel Hone shows him as he might have appeared before a crowd of people.

THE CONVERSION EXPERIENCE IN WESLEY'S METHODISM

AFTER HIS OWN CONVERSION EXPERIENCE, John Wesley traveled extensively to bring the "glad tidings" of Jesus to other people. It has been estimated that he preached more than 40,000 sermons, some of them to audiences numbering 20,000 listeners. Wesley gave his message wherever people gathered—in the streets, hospitals, private houses, and even pubs. In this selection from his journal, Wesley describes how emotional and even violent conversion experiences could be.

The Journal of the Reverend John Wesley

Sunday, May 20 [1759], being with Mr. B——ll at Everton, I was much fatigued, and did not rise: but Mr. B. did, and observed several fainting and crying out, while Mr. Berridge was preaching: afterwards at Church, I heard many cry out, especially children, whose agonies were amazing: one of the eldest, a girl of ten or twelve years old, was full in my view, in violent contortions of body, and weeping aloud, I think incessantly, during the whole service. . . . The Church was equally crowded in the afternoon, the windows being filled within and without, and even the outside of the pulpit to the very top; so that Mr. B. seemed almost stifled by their breath; yet feeble and sickly as he is, he was continually strengthened, and his voice, for the most part, distinguishable; in the midst of all the outcries. I believe there were present three times more men than women, a great part of whom came from far; thirty of them having set out at two in the morning, from a place thirteen miles off. The text was, *Having a form of godliness, but denying the power thereof.* When the power of religion began to be spoken of, the presence of God really filled the place: and while poor sinners felt the sentence of death in their souls, what sounds of distress did I hear! The greatest number of them who cried or fell, were men: but some women, and several children, felt the power of the same almighty Spirit, and seemed just sinking into hell. This occasioned a mixture of several sounds; some shrieking, some roaring aloud. The most general was a loud breathing, like that of people half strangled and gasping for life: and indeed almost all the cries were like those of human creatures, dying in bitter anguish. Great numbers wept without any noise: others fell down as death: some sinking in silence; some with extreme noise and violent agitation. I stood on the pew-seat, as did a young man in the opposite pew, an able-bodied, fresh, healthy countryman: but in a moment, while he seemed to think of nothing less, down he dropped with a violence inconceivable. The adjoining pews seemed to shake with his fall: I heard afterwards the stamping of his feet; ready to break the boards, as he lay in strong convulsions, at the bottom of the pew. Among several that were struck down in the next pew, was a girl, who was as violently seized as he. . . . Among the children who felt the arrows of the Almighty, I saw a sturdy boy, about eight years old, who roared above his fellows, and seemed in his agony to struggle with the strength of a grown man. His face was as red as scarlet: and almost all on whom God laid his hand, turned either very red or almost black. . . .

The violent struggling of many in the above-mentioned churches, has broken several pews and benches. Yet it is common for people to remain unaffected there, and afterwards to drop down on their way home. Some have been found lying as dead on the road: others, in Mr. B.'s garden; not being able to walk from the Church to his house, though it is not two hundred yards.

 What was a conversion experience? How does the emotionalism of this passage relate to enlightened thinkers' fascination with the passions and the workings of human reason?

Source: *The Journal of the Reverend John Wesley AM*, vol. 2. (Darlington, U.K.: J. M. Dent & Sons Ltd., 1920).

masses of people. The dissenting Protestant groups—Puritans, Quakers, Baptists—were relatively subdued, while the growth of deism seemed to challenge Christianity itself. The desire for deep spiritual experience seemed unmet until the advent of John Wesley.

WESLEY AND METHODISM An ordained Anglican minister, John Wesley (1703–1791) suffered a deep spiritual crisis and underwent a mystical experience: "I felt I did trust in Christ alone for salvation; and an assurance was given me, that He had taken away my sins, even mine, and saved me from the law of sin and death." To Wesley, "the gift of God's grace" assured him of salvation and led him to become a missionary to the English people, bringing the "glad tidings" of salvation to all people, despite opposition from the Anglican Church, which criticized this emotional mysticism or religious enthusiasm as superstitious nonsense. To Wesley, all could be saved by experiencing God and opening the doors to his grace.

In taking the Gospel to the people, Wesley preached to the masses in open fields, appealing especially to the lower classes neglected by the socially elitist Anglican Church. He tried, he said, "to lower religion to the level of the lowest people's capacities." Wesley's charismatic preaching often provoked highly charged and even violent conversion experiences (see the box above). Afterward, converts were organized into so-called Methodist societies or chapels in which they could aid each other in doing the good works that Wesley considered a component of salvation. Although Wesley sought to keep Methodism within the Anglican Church, after his death it became a separate and independent sect. Methodism was an important revival of Christianity and proved that the need for spiritual experience had not been expunged by the eighteenth-century search for reason.

The eighteenth century was a time of change but also of tradition. The popularization of the ideas of the Scientific Revolution, the impact of travel literature, a new skepticism, and the ideas of Locke and Newton led to what historians call the Age of Enlightenment. Its leading figures were the intellectuals known as philosophes who hoped that they could create a new society by using reason to discover the natural laws that governed it. Like the Christian humanists of the fifteenth and sixteenth centuries, they believed that education could create better human beings and a better human society. Such philosophes as Montesquieu, Voltaire, Diderot, Hume, Quesnay, Smith, Beccaria, Condorcet, and Rousseau attacked traditional religion as the enemy, advocated religious toleration and freedom of thought, criticized their oppressive societies, and created a new "science of man" in economics, politics, and education. In doing so, the philosophes laid the foundation for a modern worldview based on rationalism and secularism.

Although many of the philosophes continued to hold traditional views about women, female intellectuals like Mary Astell and Mary Wollstonecraft began to argue for the equality of the sexes and the right of women to be educated. The Enlightenment appealed largely to the urban middle classes and some members of the nobility, and its ideas were discussed in salons, coffeehouses, reading clubs, lending libraries, and societies like the Freemasons.

Innovation in the arts also characterized the eighteenth century. The cultural fertility of the age is evident in Rococo painting and architecture; the achievements of Bach, Handel, Haydn, and Mozart in music; the birth of the novel in literature; and new directions in education and historical writing.

Although the philosophes attacked the established Christian churches, many Europeans continued to practice their traditional faith. Moreover, a new wave of piety swept both Catholic and Protestant churches, especially noticeable in Protestant Europe with the advent of Pietism in Germany and John Wesley and Methodism in England.

Thus, despite the secular thought and secular ideas that began to pervade the mental world of the ruling elites, most people in eighteenth-century Europe still lived by seemingly eternal verities and practices—God, religious worship, and farming. The most brilliant architecture and music of the age were religious. And yet the forces of secularization were too strong to stop. In the midst of intellectual change, economic, political, and social transformations of great purport were taking shape and would lead, as we shall see in the next two chapters, to both political and social upheavals and even revolution before the century's end.

CHAPTER TIMELINE

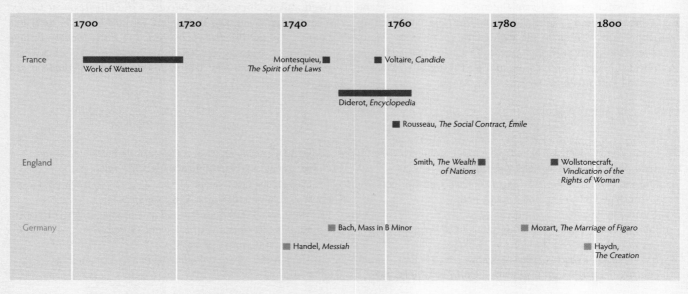

CHAPTER REVIEW

Upon Reflection

Q What contributions did Montesquieu, Voltaire, Diderot, and Rousseau make to the Enlightenment? What did they have in common? How did they differ?

Q What is popular culture, and how was it expressed in the eighteenth century?

Q What kinds of experiences do you associate with popular religion in the eighteenth century? How do you explain the continuing growth of popular religious devotion?

Key Terms

Enlightenment (p. 500)
skepticism (p. 500)
cultural relativism (p. 501)
philosophes (p. 502)
cosmopolitan (p. 502)
separation of powers (p. 503)
deism (p. 506)
laissez-faire (p. 507)
economic liberalism (p. 507)

Romanticism (p. 509)
feminism (p. 510)
salons (p. 510)
Rococo (p. 513)
neoclassicism (p. 514)
high culture (p. 516)
popular culture (p. 516)
pogroms (p. 523)
Pietism (p. 523)

Suggestions for Further Reading

EIGHTEENTH-CENTURY EUROPE Surveys of eighteenth-century Europe include **M. S. Anderson,** *Europe in the Eighteenth Century,* 4th ed. (London, 2000); **I. Woloch,** *Eighteenth-Century Europe, 1648–1789* (New York, 1986); and **T. C. W. Blanning, ed.,** *The Eighteenth Century: Europe, 1689–1815* (Oxford, 2000).

THE ENLIGHTENMENT Good introductions to the Enlightenment can be found in **D. Outram,** *The Enlightenment,* 2nd ed. (Cambridge, 2005), and **A. Pagden,** *The Enlightenment and Why It Still Matters* (New York, 2013). On the social history of the Enlightenment, see **T. Munck,** *The Enlightenment: A Comparative Social History, 1721–1794* (London, 2000). Studies of the major Enlightenment intellectuals include **R. Pearson,** *Voltaire Almighty: A Life in Pursuit of Freedom* (New York, 2005); **J. Fowler,** *New Essays on Diderot* (New York, 2011); and **L. Damrosch,** *Jean-Jacques Rousseau: Restless Genius* (Boston, 2007). On women in the eighteenth century, see **M. E. Wiesner-Hanks,** *Women and Gender in Early Modern Europe* (Cambridge, 2000), and **S. Knott and B. Taylor, eds.,** *Women, Gender and Enlightenment* (Basingstoke, 2005).

CULTURE AND SOCIETY On Rococo art, see **E. G. Bahr** and **I. F. Walther,** *Rococo* (New York, 2007). On the coffeehouse, see **E. Markman,** *The Coffee House: A Cultural History* (London, 2004).

POPULAR CULTURE Important studies on popular culture include **P. Burke,** *Popular Culture in Early Modern Europe,* 3rd ed. (New York, 2009), and **J. Mullan, ed.,** *Eighteenth-Century Popular Culture* (Oxford, 2000).

EIGHTEENTH-CENTURY RELIGIOUS HISTORY A good introduction to the religious history of the eighteenth century can be found in **G. R. Cragg,** *The Church and the Age of Reason, 1648–1789* (London, 1990). On religious toleration, see **O. P. Grell and R. Porter, eds.,** *Toleration in Enlightenment Europe* (Cambridge, 2000), and **B. Kaplan,** *Divided by Faith: Religious Conflict and the Practice of Toleration in Early Modern Europe* (Cambridge, Mass., 2007). On John Wesley, see **H. Rack,** *Reasonable Enthusiast: John Wesley and the Rise of Methodism,* 3rd ed. (New York, 2002).

Notes

1. Quoted in P. Hazard, *The European Mind, 1680–1715* (New York: Meridian Books, 1963), pp. 304–305.
2. Quoted in D. Outram, *The Enlightenment* (Cambridge: Cambridge University Press, 1995), p. 67.
3. Quoted in Hazard, *The European Mind,* p. 12.
4. John Locke, *An Essay Concerning Human Understanding* (New York, 1964), pp. 89–90.
5. Baron Paul d'Holbach, *Common Sense,* as quoted in F. E. Manuel, ed., *The Enlightenment* (Englewood Cliffs, N.J., 1965), p. 62.
6. Jean-Jacques Rousseau, *A Discourse on Inequality,* trans. M. Cranston (Harmondsworth, U.K., 1984), p. 109.
7. Jean-Jacques Rousseau, *The Social Contract,* trans. M. Cranston (Harmondsworth, U.K., 1968), p. 141.
8. Mary Astell, *A Serious Proposal to the Ladies,* in M. Ferguson, ed., *First Feminists: British Women Writers, 1578–1799* (Bloomington, Ind., 1985), p. 190.
9. Mary Astell, *Some Reflections upon Marriage,* in ibid., p. 193.

10. K. Clark, *Civilization* (New York: Harper & Row, 1969), p. 231.

11. Voltaire, *The Age of Louis XIV*, trans. M. P. Pollack (New York: Dutton, 1961), p. 1.

12. Quoted in B. Kümen, *The European World, 1500–1800* (London: Routledge, 2009), p. 230.

13. Cesare Beccaria, *An Essay on Crimes and Punishments*, trans. E. D. Ingraham (Philadelphia, 1819), pp. 59–60.

14. Quoted in R. Sand, *The Advance to Social Medicine* (London, 1952), pp. 86–87.

15. Quoted in P. Burke, *Popular Culture in Early Modern Europe* (New York, 1978), p. 179.

16. Quoted in ibid., p. 186.

17. Quoted in C. A. Macartney, *The Habsburg and Hohenzollern Dynasties in the Seventeenth and Eighteenth Centuries* (New York, 1970), p. 157.

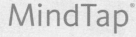 **MindTap®** is a fully online, highly personalized learning experience built upon Cengage Learning content. MindTap combines student learning tools—readings, multimedia, activities, and assessments—into a singular Learning Path that guides students through the course.

THE EIGHTEENTH CENTURY: EUROPEAN STATES, INTERNATIONAL WARS, AND SOCIAL CHANGE

A 1793 portrait of Catherine the Great of Russia by Johann Lampi

Hermitage, St. Petersburg, Russia/The Bridgeman Art Library

CHAPTER OUTLINE AND FOCUS QUESTIONS

The European States

Q What were the main developments in France, Great Britain, the Dutch Republic, the Mediterranean states, and the Scandinavian monarchies in the eighteenth century? What do historians mean by the term *enlightened absolutism*, and to what degree did eighteenth-century Prussia, Austria, and Russia exhibit its characteristics?

Wars and Diplomacy

Q How did the concepts of "balance of power" and "reason of state" influence international relations in the eighteenth century? What were the causes and results of the Seven Years' War?

Economic Expansion and Social Change

Q What changes occurred in agriculture, finance, industry, and trade during the eighteenth century?

The Social Order of the Eighteenth Century

Q Who were the main groups making up the European social order in the eighteenth century, and how did the conditions in which they lived differ both between groups and between different parts of Europe?

Critical Thinking

Q *What was the relationship among intellectual, political, economic, and social changes in the eighteenth century?*

Connections to Today

Q *How do the benefits and consequences of the agricultural revolution of the eighteenth century compare with the changes in agricultural production occurring in the twenty-first century?*

HISTORIANS OFTEN DEFINE the eighteenth century as the years from 1715 to 1789. Politically, this makes sense since 1715 marks the end of the age of Louis XIV and 1789 was the year in which the French Revolution erupted. This period has often been portrayed as the final phase of Europe's old order, before the violent upheaval and reordering of society associated with the French Revolution. Europe's old order—still largely agrarian, dominated by kings and landed aristocrats, and grounded in privileges for nobles, clergy, towns, and provinces—seemed to continue a basic pattern that had prevailed in Europe since medieval times. But new ideas and new practices were also beginning to emerge. Just as a new intellectual order based on rationalism and secularism was evolving from the Scientific Revolution and the Enlightenment, demographic, economic, and social patterns were beginning to change in ways that reflected a modern new order.

The ideas of the Enlightenment seemed to proclaim a new political age as well. Catherine the Great, who ruled Russia from 1762 to 1796, wrote to Voltaire, "Since 1746 I have been under the greatest obligations to you. Before that period I read nothing but romances, but by chance your works fell into my hands, and ever since then I have never ceased to read them, and have no desire for books less well written than yours, or less instructive." The empress of Russia also invited Diderot to Russia and, when he arrived, urged him to speak frankly "as man to man." Diderot did, offering her advice for a far-ranging program of political and financial reform. But Catherine's apparent eagerness to make enlightened reforms was tempered by skepticism. She said of Diderot, "If I had believed him everything would have been turned upside down in my kingdom; legislation, administration, finance—all would have been turned topsy-turvy to make room for impractical theories." For Catherine, enlightened reform remained more a dream than a reality, and in the end, the waging of wars to gain more power was more important.

In the eighteenth century, the process of centralization that had characterized the growth of states since the Middle Ages continued as most European states enlarged their bureaucratic machinery and consolidated their governments in order to collect the revenues and build the armies they needed to compete militarily with the other European states. International competition continued to be the favorite pastime of eighteenth-century rulers. Within the European state system, the nations that would dominate Europe until World War I—Britain, France, Austria, Prussia, and Russia—emerged as the five great powers of Europe. Their rivalries led to major wars, which some have called the first world wars because they were fought outside as well as inside Europe. In the midst of this state building and war making, dramatic demographic, economic, and social changes heralded the emergence of a radical transformation in the way Europeans would raise food and produce goods.

The European States

 FOCUS QUESTIONS: What were the main developments in France, Great Britain, the Dutch Republic, the Mediterranean states, and the Scandinavian monarchies in the eighteenth century? What do historians mean by the term *enlightened absolutism*, and to what degree did eighteenth-century Prussia, Austria, and Russia exhibit its characteristics?

Monarchs ruled most European states in the eighteenth century. Although the justifications of the previous century for strong monarchy continued to hold sway, divine-right assumptions were gradually superseded by influential utilitarian arguments as Europe became increasingly secularized. The Prussian king Frederick II expressed this new thinking well when explaining the services a monarch must provide for his people:

> These services consisted in the maintenance of the laws; a strict execution of justice; an employment of his whole powers to prevent any corruption of manners; and defending the state against its enemies. It is the duty of this magistrate

to pay attention to agriculture; it should be his care that provisions for the nation should be in abundance, and that commerce and industry should be encouraged. He is a perpetual sentinel, who must watch the acts and the conduct of the enemies of the state. . . . If he be the first general, the first minister of the realm, it is not that he should remain the shadow of authority, but that he should fulfill the duties of such titles. He is only the first servant of the state.[1]

The praises of the philosophes reinforced this utilitarian argument.

Enlightened Absolutism?

There is no doubt that Enlightenment thought had some impact on the political development of European states in the eighteenth century. Closely related to the Enlightenment idea of **natural laws** was the belief in **natural rights**, which were thought to be inalterable privileges that ought not to be withheld from any person. These natural rights included equality before the law, freedom of religious worship, freedom of speech and press, and the right to assemble, hold property, and seek happiness. The American Declaration of Independence summarized the Enlightenment concept of natural rights in its opening paragraph: "We hold these truths to be self-evident, that all men are created equal; that they are endowed by their creator with certain unalienable rights; that among these are life, liberty and the pursuit of happiness."

But how were these natural rights to be established and preserved? In the opinion of most philosophes, most people needed the direction provided by an enlightened ruler. What made rulers enlightened? They must allow religious toleration, freedom of speech and press, and the right to hold private property. They must foster the arts, sciences, and education. Above all, their rule must not be arbitrary; they must obey the laws and enforce them fairly for all subjects. Only strong monarchs seemed capable of overcoming vested interests and effecting the reforms society needed. Reforms then should come from above—from the rulers rather than from the people. Distrustful of the masses, the philosophes believed that absolute rulers, swayed by enlightened principles, were the best hope of reforming their societies.

The extent to which rulers actually did so is frequently discussed in the political analyses of Europe in the eighteenth century. Many historians once asserted that a new type of monarchy emerged in the late eighteenth century, which they called enlightened despotism or **enlightened absolutism**. Monarchs such as Frederick II of Prussia, Catherine the Great of Russia, and Joseph II of Austria supposedly followed the advice of the philosophes and ruled by enlightened principles, establishing a path to modern nationhood. Recent scholarship, however, has questioned the usefulness of the concept of enlightened absolutism. We can best determine the extent to which it can be applied by surveying the development of the European states in the eighteenth century and then making a judgment about the enlightened absolutism of the century's later years.

The Atlantic Seaboard States

As a result of the overseas voyages of the sixteenth century, the European economic axis began to shift from the Mediterranean to the Atlantic seaboard. In the seventeenth century, the

English and Dutch expanded as Spain and Portugal declined. By the eighteenth century, Dutch power had waned, and it was left to the English and French to build the commercial empires that created a true global economy.

FRANCE: THE PROBLEMS OF THE FRENCH MONARCHS In the eighteenth century, France experienced an economic revival as the Enlightenment gained strength. The French monarchy, however, was not overly influenced by the philosophes and resisted reforms even as the French aristocracy grew stronger.

Louis XIV had left France with enlarged territories, an enormous debt, an unhappy populace, and a five-year-old great-grandson as his successor. The governing of France fell into the hands first of the regent, the duke of Orléans, whose good intentions were thwarted by his drunken and immoral behavior, and later of Cardinal Fleury (floo-REE), the king's minister. France pulled back from foreign adventures while commerce and trade expanded and the government promoted the growth of industry, especially in coal and textiles. The budget was even balanced for a while. When Fleury died in 1743, Louis XV (1715–1774) decided to rule alone. But Louis was both lazy and weak, and ministers and mistresses soon began to influence the king, control the affairs of state, and undermine the prestige of the monarchy. One mistress—probably the most famous of eighteenth-century Europe—was Madame de Pompadour (ma-DAM duh POM-puh-door). An intelligent and beautiful woman, she charmed Louis XV and gained both wealth and power, often making important government decisions and giving advice on appointments and foreign policy. The loss of an empire in the Seven Years' War, accompanied by burdensome taxes, an ever-mounting public debt, more hungry people, and a court life at Versailles that remained frivolous and carefree, forced even Louis to recognize the growing disgust with his monarchy. Perhaps all might not have been in vain if a competent king had succeeded Louis. But the new king, Louis's twenty-year-old grandson who became Louis XVI (1774–1792), knew little about the operations

of the French government and lacked the energy to deal decisively with state affairs (see the box on p. 531). His wife, Marie Antoinette (ma-REE ahn-twahn-NET), was a spoiled Austrian princess who devoted much of her time to court intrigues (see "Film & History" above). As France's financial crises worsened, neither Louis nor his queen seemed able to fathom the depths of despair and discontent that soon led to violent revolution (see Chapter 19).

GREAT BRITAIN: KING AND PARLIAMENT The success of the Glorious Revolution in England had prevented absolutism without clearly inaugurating constitutional monarchy. The

National Portrait Gallery, London/The Bridgeman Art Library

The British House of Commons. A sharing of power between king and Parliament characterized the British political system in the eighteenth century. Parliament was divided into the House of Lords and the House of Commons. This painting shows the House of Commons in session in 1793 during a debate over the possibility of war with France. William Pitt the Younger is addressing the House.

THE FRENCH KING'S BEDTIME

LOUIS XIV HAD USED COURT ETIQUETTE to magnify the dignity of kingship. During the reign of Louis XVI, however, court etiquette degenerated to ludicrous depths. This excerpt from the *Memoirs of the Comtesse de Boigne* describes the king's *coucher* (KOO-shay), the formal ceremony in which the king retired for the night.

Comtesse de Boigne, *Memoirs*

The king [Louis XVI] went to his *coucher.* The so-called *coucher* took place every evening at half past nine. The gentlemen of the court assembled in the bedroom of Louis XVI (but Louis XVI did not sleep there). I believe that all those who had been presented at court were permitted to attend.

The king came in from an adjoining room, followed by his domestic staff. His hair was in curlers, and he was not wearing his decorations. Without paying attention to anybody, he stepped behind the handrail surrounding the bed, and the chaplain on duty was given the prayer book and a tall taperstand with two candles by one of the valets. He then joined the king behind the handrail, handed him the book, and held the taperstand during the king's prayer, which was short. The king then went to the part of the room where the courtiers were, and the chaplain gave the taperstand back to the first valet who, in turn, took it over to a person indicated by the king. This person held it as long as the *coucher* lasted. This distinction was very much sought after. . . .

The king had his coat, vest and finally shirt removed. He was naked to the waist, scratching and rubbing himself as if alone, though he was in the presence of the whole court and often a number of distinguished foreigners.

The first valet handed the nightshirt to the most qualified person. . . . If it was a person with whom the king was on familiar terms, he often played little tricks before donning it, missed it, passed it, and ran away, accompanying this charming nonsense with hearty laughter, making those who were sincerely attached to him suffer. Having donned the nightshirt, he put on his robe and three valets unfastened the belt and the knee buckles of his trousers, which fell down to his feet. Thus attired, hardly able to walk so absurdly encumbered, he began to make the round of the circle.

The duration of this reception was by no means fixed; sometimes it lasted only a few minutes, sometimes almost an hour; it depended on who was there. . . . When the king had enough, he dragged himself backward to an easy chair which had been pushed to the middle of the room and fell heavily into it, raising both legs. Two pages on their knees seized his shoes, took them off, and dropped them on the floor with a thump, which was part of the etiquette. When he heard it, the doorman opened the door and said, "This way, gentlemen." Everybody left, and the ceremony was over. However, the person who held the taperstand was permitted to stay if he had anything special to say to the king. This explains the high price attached to this strange favor.

 What does this account reveal about the condition of the French monarchy and the high French aristocracy during the reign of Louis XVI?

Source: From *Memoirs of the Comtesse de Boigne.* Ed. M. Charles Nicoullaud. New York: Heinemann, 1907.

---

eighteenth-century British political system was characterized by a sharing of power between king and Parliament, with Parliament gradually gaining the upper hand. (The United Kingdom of Great Britain came into existence in 1707 when the governments of England and Scotland were united; the term *British* came to refer to both English and Scots.) The king chose ministers responsible to himself who set policy and guided Parliament; Parliament had the power to make laws, levy taxes, pass the budget, and indirectly influence the king's ministers. The eighteenth-century British Parliament was dominated by a landed aristocracy that historians usually divide into two groups: the peers, who sat for life in the House of Lords, and the landed gentry, who sat in the House of Commons and served as justices of the peace in the counties. The two groups had much in common: both were landowners with similar economic interests, and they frequently intermarried.

The deputies to the House of Commons were chosen from the boroughs and counties, but not by popular voting. Who was eligible to vote in the boroughs varied wildly, enabling wealthy landed aristocrats to gain support by **patronage** and bribery; the result was a number of "pocket boroughs" controlled by a single person (hence "in his pocket"). The duke of Newcastle, for example, controlled the representatives from seven boroughs. It has been estimated that out of 405 borough deputies, 293 were chosen by fewer than 500 voters. This aristocratic control also extended to the county delegates, two from each of England's forty counties. Although all holders of property worth at least 40 shillings a year could vote, members of the leading landed gentry families were elected over and over again.

In 1714, a new dynasty—the Hanoverians—was established. When the last Stuart ruler, Queen Anne, died without an heir, the crown was offered to the Protestant rulers of the German state of Hanover. Because the first Hanoverian king, George I (1714–1727), did not speak English and neither he nor George II (1727–1760) had much familiarity with the British system, their chief ministers were allowed to handle Parliament. Many historians believe that this exercise of ministerial power was an important step in the development of the modern cabinet system in British government.

CHRONOLOGY	The Atlantic Seaboard States
France	
Louis XV	1715–1774
Louis XVI	1774–1792
Great Britain	
George 1	1714–1727
George II	1727–1760
Robert Walpole	1721–1742
William Pitt the Elder	1757–1761
George III	1760–1820
William Pitt the Younger	1783–1801

Robert Walpole served as prime minister from 1721 to 1742 and pursued a peaceful foreign policy to avoid new land taxes. But new forces were emerging in eighteenth-century England as growing trade and industry led an ever-increasing middle class to favor expansion of trade and world empire. The exponents of empire found a spokesman in William Pitt the Elder, who became prime minister in 1757 and furthered imperial ambitions by acquiring Canada and India in the Seven Years' War.

Despite his successes, Pitt the Elder was dismissed in 1761 by the new king, George III (1760–1820), and replaced by the king's favorite, Lord Bute. Discontent over the electoral system, however, and the loss of the American colonies (see Chapter 19) led to public criticism of the king. In 1780, the House of Commons affirmed that "the influence of the crown has increased, is increasing, and ought to be diminished." King George III managed to avoid drastic change by appointing William Pitt the Younger (1759–1806), son of William Pitt the Elder, as prime minister in 1783. Supported by the merchants, industrial classes, and the king, Pitt managed to stay in power. George III, however, remained an uncertain supporter because of periodic bouts of insanity (he once mistook a tree in Windsor Park for the king of Prussia). Nevertheless, thanks to Pitt's successes, serious reform of the corrupt parliamentary system was avoided for another generation.

THE DECLINE OF THE DUTCH REPUBLIC After its century in the sun, the Dutch Republic or United Netherlands suffered a decline in economic prosperity. Both local and national political affairs were dominated by the oligarchies that governed the Dutch Republic's towns. In the eighteenth century, the struggle continued between these oligarchs (or regents, as they were called, from their governing positions) and the house of Orange, who as stadholders headed the executive branch of government. The regents sought to reduce the power of the Orangists but soon became divided when Dutch burghers who called themselves the Patriots (artisans, merchants, and shopkeepers) began to agitate for democratic reforms that would open up the municipal councils to greater participation than that of the oligarchs. The success of the Patriots, however, led to foreign interference when the Prussian king sent troops to protect his sister, the wife of the Orangist stadholder. The

Patriots were crushed, and both Orangists and regents reestablished the old system. The intervention by Prussia serves to remind us of the growing power of the central European states.

Absolutism in Central and Eastern Europe

Of the five major European states, three were located in central and eastern Europe and came to play an increasingly important role in European international politics (see Map 18.1).

PRUSSIA: THE ARMY AND THE BUREAUCRACY Two able Prussian kings in the eighteenth century, Frederick William I and Frederick II, further developed the two major institutions—the army and the bureaucracy—that were the backbone of Prussia. Frederick William I (1713–1740) promoted the evolution of Prussia's highly efficient civil bureaucracy by establishing the General Directory. It served as the chief administrative agent of the central government, supervising military, police, economic, and financial affairs. Frederick William strove to maintain a highly efficient bureaucracy of civil service workers. It had its own code, in which the supreme values were obedience, honor, and service to the king as the highest duty. As Frederick William asserted, "One must serve the king with life and limb, with goods and chattels, with honor and conscience, and surrender everything except salvation. The latter is reserved for God. But everything else must be mine."[2] For his part, Frederick William personally kept a close watch over his officials to ensure that they performed their duties. As the Saxon minister at Berlin related:

> Every day His Majesty gives new proofs of his justice. Walking recently at Potsdam at six in the morning, he saw a post-coach arrive with several passengers who knocked for a long time at the post-house which was still closed. The King, seeing that no one opened the door, joined them in knocking and even knocked in some window-panes. The master of the post then opened the door and scolded the travelers, for no one recognized the King. But His Majesty let himself be known by giving the official some good blows of his cane and drove him from his house and his job after apologizing to the travelers for his laziness. Examples of this sort, of which I could relate several others, make everybody alert and exact.[3]

Close personal supervision of the bureaucracy became a hallmark of the eighteenth-century Prussian rulers.

Under Frederick William I, the rigid class stratification that had emerged in seventeenth-century Brandenburg-Prussia persisted. The nobility or landed aristocracy known as Junkers, who owned large estates with many serfs, still played a dominating role in the Prussian state. The Junkers held a complete monopoly over the officer corps of the Prussian army, which Frederick William passionately continued to expand. By the end of his reign, the army had grown from 45,000 to 83,000 men. Though tenth in geographic area and thirteenth in population among the European states, Prussia had the fourth largest army, after France, Russia, and Austria.

By using nobles as officers, Frederick William ensured a close bond between the nobility and the army and, in turn, the loyalty of the nobility to the absolute monarch. As officers, the Junker nobility became imbued with a sense of service to

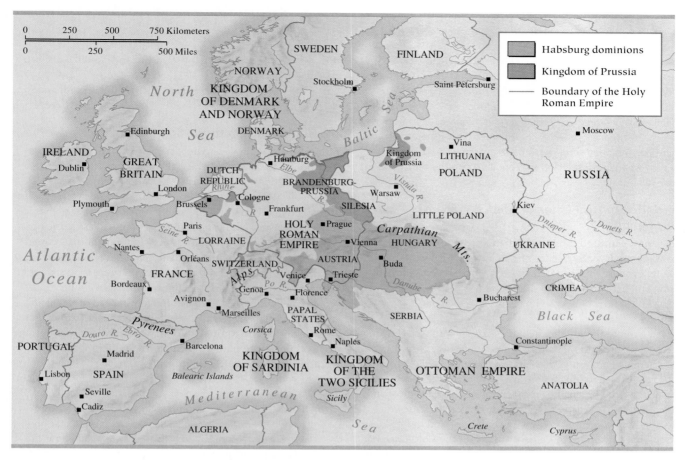

MAP 18.1 Europe in 1763. By the middle of the eighteenth century, five major powers dominated Europe—Prussia, Austria, Russia, Britain, and France. Each sought to enhance its power both domestically, through a bureaucracy that collected taxes and ran the military, and internationally, by capturing territory or preventing other powers from doing so.

Q *Given the distribution of Prussian and Habsburg holdings, in what areas of Europe were they most likely to compete for land and power?*

the king or state. All the virtues of the Prussian nobility were, in effect, military virtues: duty, obedience, sacrifice. At the same time, because of its size and reputation as one of the best armies in Europe, the Prussian army was the most important institution in the state. "Prussian militarism" became synonymous with the extreme exaltation of military virtues. Indeed, one Prussian minister around 1800 remarked that "Prussia was not a country with an army, but an army with a country which served as headquarters and food magazine."[4]

The remaining classes in Prussia were considerably less important than the nobility. The peasants were born on their lords' estates and spent most of their lives there or in the army. They had few real rights and even needed their Junker's permission to marry. For the middle class, the only opportunity for any social prestige was in the Prussian civil service, where the ideal of loyal service to the state became a hallmark of the middle-class official. Frederick William allowed and even encouraged men of non-noble birth to serve in important administrative posts. When he died in 1740, only three of his eighteen privy councillors were nobles.

Frederick II, known as the Great (1740–1786), was one of the best-educated and most cultured monarchs of the eighteenth century. He was well versed in Enlightenment thought and even invited Voltaire to live at his court for several years. His father had despised Frederick's intellectual interests and forced him to prepare for a career in ruling (see the box on p. 534). A believer in the king as the "first servant of the state," Frederick the Great became a conscientious ruler who made few innovations in the administration of the state. His diligence in overseeing its operation, however, made the Prussian bureaucracy famous for both its efficiency and its honesty.

For a time, Frederick seemed quite willing to follow the philosophes' recommendations for reform. He established a single code of laws for his territories that eliminated the use of torture except in treason and murder cases. He also granted limited freedom of speech and press as well as religious toleration—no difficult task since he had no strong religious convictions. He did exclude the Jews, levying special taxes on the Jewish subjects and barring them from civil service. Frederick attempted to improve the lives of the peasants by increasing agricultural

FREDERICK THE GREAT AND HIS FATHER

**AS A YOUNG MAN, THE FUTURE FREDERICK THE
GREAT** was quite different from his strict and austere father,
Frederick William I. Possessing a high regard for French
culture, poetry, and flute playing, Frederick resisted his father's
wishes that he immerse himself in governmental and military
affairs. Eventually, Frederick capitulated to his father's will and
accepted the need to master affairs of state. These letters,
written when Frederick was sixteen, illustrate the difficulties in
their relationship.

Frederick to His Father, Frederick William I (September 11, 1728)

I have not ventured for a long time to present myself before
my dear papa, partly because I was advised against it, but
chiefly because I anticipated an even worse reception than
usual and feared to vex my dear papa still further by the
favor I have now to ask; so I have preferred to put it in
writing.

I beg my dear papa that he will be kindly disposed toward
me. I do assure him that after long examination of my
conscience I do not find the slightest thing with which to
reproach myself; but if, against my wish and will, I have vexed
my dear papa, I hereby beg most humbly for forgiveness, and
hope that my dear papa will give over the fearful hate which
has appeared so plainly in his whole behavior and to which
I cannot accustom myself. I have always thought hitherto that
I had a kind father, but now I see the contrary. However, I will
take courage and hope that my dear papa will think this all
over and take me again into his favor. Meantime I assure him
that I will never, my life long, willingly fail him, and in spite of

his disfavor I am still, with most dutiful and childlike respect,
my dear papa's

> Most obedient and faithful servant and son,
> Frederick

Frederick William to His Son Frederick

A bad, obstinate boy, who does not love his father; for when
one does one's best, and especially when one loves one's
father, one does what he wishes not only when he is standing by but when he is not there to see. Moreover you know
very well that I cannot stand an effeminate fellow who has
no manly tastes, who cannot ride or shoot (to his shame be
it said!), is untidy about his person, and wears his hair curled
like a fool instead of cutting it; and that I have condemned
all these things a thousand times, and yet there is no sign of
improvement. For the rest, haughty, offish as a country lout,
conversing with none but a favored few instead of being affa-
ble and popular, grimacing like a fool, and never following my
wishes out of love for me but only when forced into it, caring
for nothing but to have his own way, and thinking nothing else
is of any importance. This is my answer.

> Frederick William

 Based on these documents, why was the relationship
between Frederick II and his father such a difficult one?
What does this troubled relationship tell you about the
effects of ruling on the great monarchs of Europe and
their families? What new duties and concerns of rulers
(like Frederick William) may have reshaped relations
between kings and sons?

Source: J. H. Robinson, *Readings in European History*, vol. 2 (Boston: Ginn & Co., 1906).

---

productivity—he imported clover and potatoes from Western
Europe and the iron plow, while draining swamps in the lower
Oder Valley. Although Frederick was well aware of the philosophes' condemnation of serfdom, he was too dependent on
the Prussian nobility to interfere with it or with the hierarchical structure of Prussian society. In fact, Frederick was a social
conservative who made Prussian society even more aristocratic
than it had been before. Frederick reversed his father's policy
of allowing commoners to rise to power in the civil service and
reserved the higher positions in the bureaucracy for members
of the nobility. Over time the upper ranks of the bureaucracy
came close to constituting a hereditary caste.

Like his predecessors, Frederick the Great took a great interest
in military affairs and enlarged the Prussian army (to 200,000 men).
Unlike his predecessors, he had no objection to using it. Freder-
ick did not hesitate to take advantage of a succession crisis in the
Habsburg monarchy to seize the Austrian province of Silesia (sy-
LEE-zhuh) for Prussia. This act aroused Austria's bitter hostility and
embroiled Frederick in two major wars, the War of the Austrian
Succession and the Seven Years' War (see "Wars and Diplomacy"

later in this chapter). Although the latter war left his country
exhausted, Frederick succeeded in keeping Silesia. After the wars,
the first partition of Poland with Austria and Russia in 1772 gave
him the Polish territory between Prussia and Brandenburg, bringing greater unity to the scattered lands of Prussia. By the end of his
reign, Prussia was recognized as a great European power.

THE AUSTRIAN EMPIRE OF THE HABSBURGS The Austrian Empire had become one of the great European states by
the beginning of the eighteenth century. The city of Vienna,
center of the Habsburg monarchy, was filled with magnificent
palaces and churches built in the Baroque style and became
the music capital of Europe. And yet Austria, a sprawling
empire composed of many different nationalities, languages,
religions, and cultures, found it difficult to provide common
laws and a centralized administration for its people.

Empress Maria Theresa (1740–1780), however, stunned by the
loss of Austrian Silesia to Prussia in the War of the Austrian
Succession, resolved to reform her empire in preparation for
the seemingly inevitable next conflict with rival Prussia. Maria

Frederick II. Frederick II was one of the most cultured and best-educated European monarchs. He is seen here in a portrait done five years before his death by the Swiss artist Anton Graff. The painting is regarded as Graff's masterpiece, and contemporaries considered it the best and most accurate portrait of the ruler.

bpk, Berlin/Charlottenburg Castle, Preussische Schlösser und Gärten, Berlin/Jörg P. Anders/Art Resource, NY

Franz Stephan I (1708–65) with his wife Marie-Therese (1717–80) and their children (oil on canvas), Mytens or Meytens, Martin II (1695–1770) (school of) / Château de Versailles, France/Bridgeman Images

Maria Theresa and Her Family. Maria Theresa governed the vast possessions of the Austrian Empire from 1740 to 1780. Of her ten surviving children, Joseph II (shown here in red standing beside his mother) succeeded her; Leopold became grand-duke of Tuscany and the ruler of Austria after Joseph's death; Ferdinand was made duke of Modena; and Marie Antoinette became the wife of King Louis XVI of France.

Theresa curtailed the role of the diets or provincial assemblies in taxation and local administration. Now clergy and nobles were forced to pay property and income taxes to royal officials rather than the diets. The Austrian and Bohemian lands were divided into ten provinces and subdivided into districts, all administered by royal officials rather than representatives of the diets, making part of the Austrian Empire more centralized and more bureaucratic. But these administrative reforms were done for practical reasons—to strengthen the power of the Habsburg state—and were accompanied by the expansion and modernization of the armed forces. Maria Theresa remained staunchly Catholic and conservative and was not open to the philosophes' calls for wider reforms. But her successor was.

Joseph II (1780–1790) was determined to make changes; at the same time, he carried on his mother's chief goal of enhancing Habsburg power within the monarchy and Europe. Joseph's reform program was far-reaching. He abolished serfdom and tried to give the peasants hereditary rights to their holdings. He also instituted a new penal code that abrogated the death penalty and established the principle of equality of all before the law. Joseph introduced drastic religious reforms as well, including complete religious toleration and restrictions on the Catholic Church. His government also supported public education, supplying textbooks and teachers for primary schools. Altogether, Joseph issued 6,000 decrees and 11,000 laws in his effort to transform Austria.

Joseph's reform program proved overwhelming for Austria, however. He alienated the nobility by freeing the serfs and alienated the church by his attacks on the monastic establishment. Even the peasants were unhappy, unable to comprehend the drastic changes inherent in Joseph's policies. His attempt to rationalize the administration of the empire by imposing German as the official bureaucratic language alienated the non-German nationalities. As Joseph complained, there were not enough people for the kind of bureaucracy he needed. His deep sense of failure is revealed in the epitaph he wrote for his gravestone: "Here lies Joseph II, who was unfortunate in everything that he undertook." His successors undid many of his reform efforts.

RUSSIA UNDER CATHERINE THE GREAT The six successors to Peter the Great of Russia all fell under the thumb of the palace guard. The last of these six was Peter III, whose German wife, Catherine, learned Russian and won the favor of the guard. When Peter was murdered by a faction of nobles, Catherine II the Great (1762–1796) emerged as autocrat of all Russia.

Catherine was an intelligent woman who was familiar with the works of the philosophes. She claimed that she wished to reform Russia along the lines of Enlightenment ideas, but she was always shrewd enough to realize that her success depended on the support of the palace guard and the gentry class from which it stemmed. She could not afford to alienate the Russian nobility (see the box "Opposing Viewpoints" on p. 536).

Initially, Catherine seemed eager to pursue reform. She called for the election of an assembly

Enlightened Absolutism: Enlightened or Absolute?

ALTHOUGH HISTORIANS HAVE USED THE TERM *enlightened absolutism* to describe a new type of monarchy in the eighteenth century, scholars have recently questioned the usefulness of the concept. The three selections below offer an opportunity to evaluate one so-called enlightened monarch, Catherine the Great of Russia. The first selection is from a letter written by the baron de Breteuil, the French ambassador to Russia, giving his impressions of Catherine. In 1767, Catherine convened a legislative commission to prepare a new code of laws for Russia. In her *Instruction*, parts of which form the second selection, she gave the delegates a detailed guide to the principles they should follow. Although the guidelines were culled from the liberal ideas of the philosophes, the commission itself accomplished nothing. The third selection, from a Decree on Serfs (also issued in 1767), reveals Catherine's authoritarian nature.

Letter of the Baron de Breteuil

[Catherine] seems to combine every kind of ambition in her person. Everything that may add luster to her reign will have some attraction for her. Science and the arts will be encouraged to flourish in the empire; projects useful for the domestic economy will be undertaken. She will endeavor to reform the administration of justice and to invigorate the laws; but her policies will be based on Machiavellianism; and I should not be surprised if in this field she rivals the king of Prussia. She will adopt the prejudices of her entourage regarding the superiority of her power and will endeavor to win respect not by the sincerity and probity of her actions but also by an ostentatious display of her strength. Haughty as she is, she will stubbornly pursue her undertakings and will rarely retrace a false step. Cunning and falsity appear to be vices in her character; woe to him who puts too much trust in her.

Catherine II, Proposals for a New Law Code

13. What is the true End of Monarchy? Not to deprive People of their natural Liberty; but to correct their Actions, in order to attain the supreme good. . . .

33. The Laws ought to be so framed, as to secure the Safety of every Citizen as much as possible.

34. The Equality of the Citizens consists in this; that they should all be subject to the same Laws. . . .

123. The Usage of Torture is contrary to all the Dictates of Nature and Reason; even Mankind itself cries out against it, and demands loudly the total Abolition of it. . . .

180. That Law, therefore, is highly beneficial to the Community where it is established, which ordains that every Man be judged by his Peers and Equals. For when the Fate of a Citizen is in Question, all Prejudices arising from the Difference of Rank or Fortune should be stifled; because they ought to have no Influence between the Judges and the Parties accused. . . .

194. No Man ought to be looked upon as guilty, before he has received his judicial Sentence; nor can the Laws deprive him of their Protection, before it is proved that he has forfeited all Right to it. What Right therefore can Power give to any to inflict Punishment upon a Citizen at a Time, when it is yet dubious, whether he is Innocent or guilty?

Catherine II, Decree on Serfs

The Governing Senate . . . has deemed it necessary to make known that the landlords' serfs and peasants . . . owe their landlords proper submission and absolute obedience in all matters, according to the laws that have been enacted from time immemorial by the autocratic forefathers of Her Imperial Majesty and which have not been repealed, and which provide that all persons who dare to incite serfs and peasants to disobey their landlords shall be arrested and taken to the nearest government office, there to be punished forthwith as disturbers of the public tranquillity, according to the laws and without leniency. And should it so happen that even after the publication of the present decree of Her Imperial Majesty any serfs and peasants should cease to give the proper obedience to their landlords . . . and should make bold to submit unlawful petitions complaining of their landlords, and especially to petition Her Imperial Majesty personally, then both those who make the complaints and those who write up the petitions shall be punished by the knout and forthwith deported to Nerchinsk to penal servitude for life and shall be counted as part of the quota of recruits which their landlords must furnish to the army.

 What impressions of Catherine do you get from the letter by the French ambassador to Russia? To what extent were the ideas expressed in the proposals for a new law code taken from the writings of the philosophes? What does the decree on serfs reveal about Catherine's view of power? Based on these documents, was Catherine an enlightened monarch? Why or why not?

Sources: Letter of the Baron de Breteuil and Catherine II, Decree on Serfs, in G. Vernadsky, *A Source Book for Russian History*, vol. 2 (New Haven, Conn.: Yale University Press, 1972); Catherine II, Proposals for a New Law Code, in W. F. Reddaway, *Documents of Catherine the Great* (Cambridge: Cambridge University Press, 1931).

in 1767 to debate the details of a new law code. In her *Instruction*, written as a guide to the deliberations, Catherine questioned the institutions of serfdom, torture, and capital punishment and even advocated the principle of the equality of all people in the eyes of the law. But a year and a half of negotiation produced little real change.

In fact, Catherine's subsequent policies had the effect of strengthening the landholding class at the expense of all others, especially the Russian serfs. To reorganize local government, Catherine divided Russia into fifty provinces, each of which was in turn subdivided into districts ruled by officials chosen by the nobles. In this way, the local nobility became responsible for the day-to-day governing of Russia. Moreover, the gentry were now formed into corporate groups with special legal privileges, including the right to trial by peers and exemption from personal taxation and corporal punishment. The Charter of the Nobility formalized these rights in 1785.

Catherine's policy of favoring the landed nobility led to even worse conditions for the Russian peasantry. The government's attempt to impose restrictions on free peasants in the border districts of the Russian Empire soon led to a full-scale revolt that spread to the Volga valley. It was intensified by the support of the Cossacks, independent tribes of fierce warriors who had at times fought for the Russians against the Turks but now resisted the government's attempt to absorb them into the empire.

An illiterate Cossack, Emelyan Pugachev (yim-yil-YAHN poo-guh-CHAWF), succeeded in welding the disparate elements of discontent into a mass revolt. Beginning in 1773, Pugachev's rebellion spread across southern Russia from the Urals to the Volga River. Initially successful, Pugachev won the support of many peasants when he issued a manifesto in July 1774 freeing all peasants from oppressive taxes and military service. Encouraged by Pugachev to seize their landlords' estates, the peasants responded by killing more than fifteen hundred estate owners and their families. The rebellion soon faltered, however, as government forces rallied and became more effective. Betrayed by his own subordinates, Pugachev was captured, tortured, and executed. The rebellion collapsed completely, and Catherine responded with even greater repression of the peasantry. All rural reform was halted, and serfdom was expanded into newer parts of the empire.

Catherine proved a worthy successor to Peter the Great by expanding Russia's territory westward into Poland and southward to the Black Sea. Russia spread southward by defeating the Ottoman Turks. In the Treaty of Kuchuk-Kainarji (koo-CHOOK-ky-NAR-jee) in 1774, the Russians gained some land and the privilege of protecting Greek Orthodox Christians in the Ottoman Empire. Russian expansion westward occurred at the expense of neighboring Poland. In the three partitions of Poland, Russia gained about 50 percent of Polish territory.

THE DESTRUCTION OF POLAND Poland was an excellent example of why a strong monarchy was needed in early modern Europe. The Polish king was elected by the Polish nobles and forced to accept drastic restrictions on his power, including limited revenues, a small bureaucracy, and a standing army of no more than 20,000 soldiers. For Polish nobles, these limitations eliminated an absolute king; for Poland's powerful neighbors, they were an invitation to meddle in its affairs.

The total destruction of the Polish state in the eighteenth century resulted from the rivalries of its three great neighbors, Austria, Russia, and Prussia. To avoid war, the leaders of these powers decided to compensate themselves by dividing Poland. To maintain the balance of power in central and eastern Europe, the three great powers cynically agreed to the acquisition of roughly equal territories at Poland's expense.

In 1772, Poland lost about 30 percent of its land and 50 percent of its population (see Map 18.2). Austria gained the agriculturally rich district of Galicia, Russia took the largest slice of land in eastern Poland, and Prussia acquired West Prussia, the smallest but most valuable territory because it united two of the chief sections of Prussia.

The remaining Polish state was supposedly independent; in truth, it was dominated by the Russians, who even kept troops on Polish territory. After the Poles attempted to establish a stronger state under a hereditary monarchy in 1791, the Russians gained the support of Austria and Prussia and intervened militarily in May 1792. In the following year, Russia and Prussia undertook a second partition of Polish territory. Finally, after a heroic but hopeless rebellion in 1794–1795 under General Thaddeus Kosciuszko (tah-DAY-oosh kaw-SHOOS-koh), the remaining Polish state was obliterated by Austria, Prussia, and Russia

Pugachev's Rebellion

Moscow
Don R.
Volga R.
RUSSIA
Aral Sea
Black Sea
Caspian Sea
0   600 Kilometers
0   600 Miles
▭ Area of rebellion
→ Pugachev's route

CHRONOLOGY	Central and Eastern Europe
Prussia	
Frederick William I	1713–1740
Frederick II the Great	1740–1786
Austrian Empire	
Maria Theresa	1740–1780
Joseph II	1780–1790
Russia	
Catherine II the Great	1762–1796
Pugachev's rebellion	1773–1775
Charter of the Nobility	1785
Poland	
First partition	1772
Second partition	1793
Third partition	1795

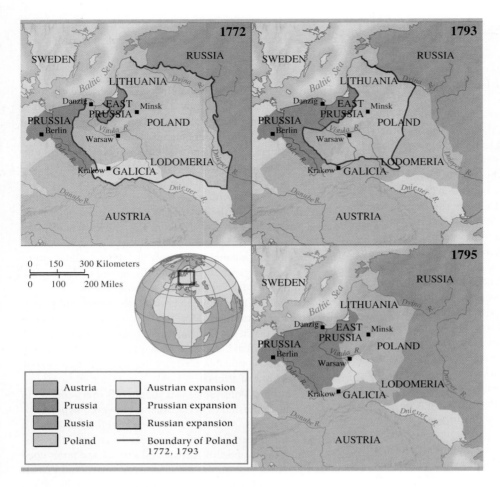

MAP 18.2 The Partitioning of Poland. Crowded by three great powers, Poland lay primarily on a plain with few easily defensible borders. This fact, combined with a weak and ineffectual monarchy, set the stage for Poland's destruction. By 1795, Austria, Prussia (Germany in 1870), and Russia had long borders with each other, a situation that would contribute to the outbreak of World War I in 1914.

Q *Which country gained the most territory at the expense of Poland?*

in the third partition of Poland (1795). Many historians have pointed to Poland's demise as a cogent example of why building a strong, absolutist state was essential to survival in the seventeenth and eighteenth centuries.

The Mediterranean World

At the beginning of the eighteenth century, Spain experienced a change of dynasties from the Habsburgs to the Bourbons. Bourbon rule temporarily rejuvenated Spain and at least provided an opportunity to centralize the institutions of the state. Under Philip V (1700–1746), the laws, administrative institutions, and language of Castile were established in the other Spanish kingdoms, making the king of Castile truly the king of Spain. Moreover, French-style ministries replaced the old conciliar system of government, and officials similar to French *intendants* were introduced into the various Spanish provinces. Since the Treaty of Utrecht in 1713 had taken the Italian territories and the Netherlands away from Spain, the latter now had fewer administrative problems and less drain on its already overtaxed economic resources. In the second half of the eighteenth century, especially during the reign of Charles III (1759–1788), the Catholic Church was also brought under royal control when the king banished the Jesuits and circumscribed the activities of the Inquisition. The king undertook ambitious economic reforms, establishing new roads, canals, textile mills, and banks. He also

attempted to reduce the authority of the landed aristocrats by curbing the privileges of the great sheep ranchers. The landed aristocracy continued to exercise substantial power throughout the eighteenth century, however.

PORTUGAL Portugal had experienced decline since the glorious days of empire in the sixteenth century. Nevertheless, during the long ministry of the marquis de Pombal (mar-KEE duh pum-BAHL) (1750–1777), who served as chief minister to a series of Portuguese kings, Portugal experienced a revival. The marquis secured his reputation after the devastating Lisbon earthquake of 1755 that destroyed eighty-five percent of the city's buildings, killing almost fifty thousand people. During his tenure, the nobility and Catholic Church were curtailed and the Portuguese Empire temporarily revived. After Pombal was removed from office, the nobility and church regained much of their power.

THE ITALIAN STATES After the Treaty of Utrecht, Austria had replaced Spain as the dominant force in Italy in the eighteenth century. The duchy of Milan, Sardinia, and the kingdom of Naples were all surrendered to the Habsburg emperors, and Sicily was given to the northern Italian state of Savoy, which was slowly emerging as a state with an appetite for territorial expansion. In 1734, the Bourbons of Spain reestablished control over Naples and Sicily. Though some Italian states, such as

CHRONOLOGY	The Mediterranean World and Scandinavia
Spain	
Philip V, the first Bourbon king	1700–1746
Charles III	1759–1788
Portugal	
Marquis de Pombal	1750–1777
Sweden	
Charles XII	1697–1718
Gustavus III	1771–1792
Denmark	
Christian VII	1766–1808

Venice and Genoa, remained independent, they grew increasingly impotent in international affairs.

The Scandinavian States

In the seventeenth century, Sweden had become the dominant power in northern Europe, but after the Battle of Poltava in 1709, Swedish power declined rapidly. Following the death of the powerful Charles XII in 1718, the Swedish nobility, using the Swedish diet as its instrument, gained control of public life and reduced the monarchy to puppet status. But the division of the nobility into pro-French and pro-Russian factions eventually enabled King Gustavus III (1771–1792) to reassert the power of the monarchy. Gustavus proved to be one of the most enlightened monarchs of his age. By decree, he established freedom of religion, speech, and press and instituted a new code of justice that eliminated the use of torture. Moreover, his economic reforms smacked of laissez-faire: he reduced tariffs, abolished tolls, and encouraged trade and agriculture. In 1792, however, a group of nobles, incensed at these reforms and their loss of power, assassinated the king, but they proved unable to fully restore the rule of the aristocracy.

Denmark also saw an attempt at enlightened reforms by King Christian VII (1766–1808) and his chief minister, John Frederick Struensee (SHTROO-un-zay). Aristocratic opposition stymied their efforts, however, and led to Struensee's death in 1772.

Enlightened Absolutism Revisited

Of the three major rulers traditionally associated most closely with enlightened absolutism—Joseph II, Frederick II, and Catherine the Great—only Joseph II sought truly radical changes based on Enlightenment ideas. Both Frederick and Catherine liked to be cast as disciples of the Enlightenment, expressed interest in enlightened reforms, and even attempted some, but neither ruler's policies seemed seriously affected by Enlightenment thought. Necessities of state and maintenance of the existing system took precedence over reform. Indeed, many historians feel that Joseph, Frederick, and Catherine were all guided primarily by a concern for the power and well-being of their states and that their policies were not all that different from those of their predecessors. In the final analysis, heightened state power was used to amass armies and wage wars to gain more power. Nevertheless, in their desire to build stronger state systems, these rulers did pursue such enlightened practices as legal reform, religious toleration, and the extension of education because these served to create more satisfied subjects and strengthened the state in significant ways.

It would be foolish, however, to overlook the fact that not only military but also political and social realities limited the ability of enlightened rulers to make reforms. Everywhere in Europe, the hereditary aristocracy still held the most power in society. Enlightened reforms were often limited to changes in the administrative and judicial systems that did not seriously undermine the powerful interests of the European nobility. Although aristocrats might join the populace in opposing monarchical extension of centralizing power, as the chief beneficiaries of a system based on traditional rights and privileges for their class, they were certainly not willing to support a political ideology that trumpeted the principle of equal rights for all.

Wars and Diplomacy

 FOCUS QUESTIONS: How did the concepts of "balance of power" and "reason of state" influence international relations in the eighteenth century? What were the causes and results of the Seven Years' War?

The philosophes condemned war as a foolish waste of life and resources in stupid quarrels of no value to humankind. Rulers, however, paid little attention to these comments and continued their costly struggles. By the eighteenth century, the European system of self-governing, individual states was grounded largely in the principle of self-interest. Because international relations were based on considerations of power, the eighteenth-century concept of a **balance of power** was predicated on how to counterbalance the power of one state by another to prevent any one state from dominating the others. This balance of power, however, did not imply a desire for peace. Large armies created to defend a state's security were often used for offensive purposes as well. As Frederick the Great of Prussia remarked, "The fundamental rule of governments is the principle of extending their territories." Nevertheless, the regular use of diplomacy served at times to lead to compromise.

The diplomacy of the eighteenth century still focused primarily on dynastic interests, or the desire of ruling families to provide for their dependents and extend their dynastic holdings. But the eighteenth century also saw the emergence of the concept of **reason of state**, on the basis of which a ruler such as Frederick II and a minister such as William Pitt the Elder looked beyond dynastic interests to the long-term future of their states.

International rivalry and the continuing centralization of the European states were closely related. The need for money to support the new standing armies, navies, and weapons of war that had originated in the seventeenth century created its own imperative for more efficient and effective control of power in the hands of bureaucrats who could collect taxes and organize states for the task of winning wars. At the same time, the development of large standing armies ensured that political disputes would periodically be resolved by armed conflict rather than diplomacy. Between 1715 and 1740, Europe seemed to prefer peace. But in 1740, a major conflict erupted over the succession to the Austrian throne.

The War of the Austrian Succession (1740–1748)

Unable to produce a male heir to the Austrian throne, the Habsburg emperor Charles VI (1711–1740) so feared the consequences of the succession of his daughter Maria Theresa that he spent much of his reign negotiating the Pragmatic Sanction, by which various European powers agreed to recognize his daughter as his legal heir.

After Charles's death, however, the Pragmatic Sanction was conveniently pushed aside, especially by Frederick II, who had recently succeeded to the throne of Prussia. The new Prussian ruler took advantage of the new empress to invade Austrian Silesia. The vulnerability of Maria Theresa encouraged France to enter the war against its traditional enemy Austria; in turn, Maria Theresa made an alliance with Great Britain, which feared

French hegemony over Continental affairs. All too quickly, the Austrian succession had set off a worldwide conflagration. The war was fought not only in Europe, where Prussia seized Silesia and France occupied the Austrian Netherlands, but in the East, where France took Madras (now Chennai) in India from the British, and in North America, where the British captured the French fortress of Louisbourg at the entrance to the Saint Lawrence River. By 1748, all parties were exhausted and agreed to stop. The peace treaty of Aix-la-Chapelle (ex-lah-shah-PELL) promised the return of all occupied territories except Silesia to their original owners. Prussia's refusal to return Silesia guaranteed another war, at least between the two hostile central European powers of Prussia and Austria.

The Seven Years' War (1756–1763)

Maria Theresa refused to accept the loss of Silesia and prepared for its return by rebuilding her army while working diplomatically through her able foreign minister, Count Wenzel von Kaunitz (VENT-sul fun KOW-nits), to separate Prussia from its chief ally, France. In 1756, Austria achieved what was soon labeled a diplomatic revolution. Bourbon-Habsburg rivalry had been a fact of European diplomacy since the late sixteenth century. But two new rivalries made this old one seem superfluous: Britain and France

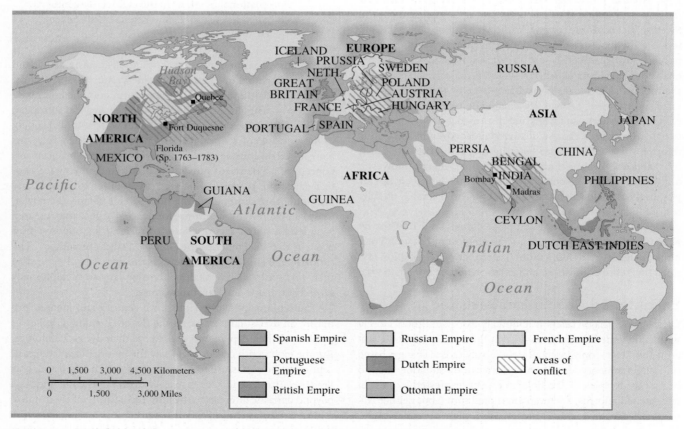

MAP 18.3 Battlefields of the Seven Years' War. A major struggle among the five great powers, the Seven Years' War was truly a worldwide conflict. In central Europe, Prussia survived against the combined forces of France, Austria, and Russia, while Britain emerged victorious against France in the struggle for empire, gaining control of French North America and India.

Q *Why were naval strength and ability important in the conflict between Britain and France?*

over colonial empires, and Austria and Prussia over Silesia. France now abandoned Prussia and allied with Austria. Russia, which saw Prussia as a major hindrance to Russian goals in central Europe, joined the new alliance. In turn, Great Britain allied with Prussia. This diplomatic revolution of 1756 now led to another war, with three major areas of conflict: Europe, India, and North America (see Map 18.3). Indeed, the Seven Years' War could be seen, as some historians have argued, as the first world war.

CONFLICT IN EUROPE Europe witnessed the clash of the two major alliances: the British and Prussians against the Austrians, Russians, and French. With his superb army and military prowess, Frederick the Great was able for some time to defeat the Austrian, French, and Russian armies. At the Battle of Rossbach (RAWSS-bahkh) in Saxony in 1757, he won a spectacular victory over combined French-Austrian forces that far outnumbered his own troops. Under attack from three different directions, however, Frederick's forces were gradually worn down and faced utter defeat when they were saved by the death of Tsarina Elizabeth of Russia (1741–1762), which brought her nephew Peter III to power. A great admirer of Frederick the Great, Peter withdrew the Russian troops from

British Library, London//Erich Lessing/Art Resource, NY

Robert Clive in India. Robert Clive was the leader of the army of the British East India Company. He had been commanded to fight the ruler of Bengal in order to gain trading privileges. After the Battle of Plassey in 1757, Clive and the East India Company took control of Bengal. In this painting by Edward Penny, Clive is shown receiving a grant of money for his injured soldiers from the local nabob or governor of Bengal.

the conflict and from the Prussian lands that they had occupied. His withdrawal guaranteed a stalemate and led to a desire for peace. The Peace of Hubertusburg (hoo-BERR-toos-bayrk) ended the European conflict in 1763. All occupied territories were returned, and Austria officially recognized Prussia's permanent control of Silesia.

WAR IN INDIA The Anglo-French struggle in the rest of the world had more decisive results. Known as the Great War for Empire, it was fought in India and North America. The French had returned Madras (muh-DRAS *or* muh-DRAHS) to Britain after the War of the Austrian Succession, but jockeying for power continued as the French and British supported opposing native Indian princes. The British under Robert Clive (1725–1774) ultimately won out, not because they had better forces but because they were more persistent (see the box on p. 542). By the Treaty of Paris in 1763, the French withdrew and left India to the British.

THE FRENCH AND INDIAN WAR By far the greatest conflicts of the Seven Years' War took place in North America, where it was known as the French and Indian War. There were two primary areas of contention. One consisted of the waterways of the Gulf of Saint Lawrence, guarded by the fortress of Louisbourg and by forts near the Great Lakes and Lake Champlain that protected French Quebec and French traders. The other was the unsettled Ohio River valley. As the French moved south from the Great Lakes and north from their garrisons along the Mississippi, they began to establish forts from the Appalachians to the Mississippi River. To British settlers in the thirteen colonies to the east, this French activity threatened to cut off a vast area from British expansion. The French found allies among the Indians, who considered the French traders less threatening than the British settlers.

Despite initial French successes, British fortunes were revived by the efforts of William Pitt the Elder, who was convinced that the destruction of the French colonial empire was a necessary prerequisite for the creation of Britain's own colonial empire. Accordingly, Pitt decided to make a minimal effort in Europe while concentrating resources, especially the British navy, on the colonial war. Although the French troops were greater in number, the ability of the French to use them in the New World was contingent on naval support. The defeat of French fleets in major naval battles in 1759 gave the British an advantage since the French could no longer easily reinforce their garrisons. A series of British victories soon followed. Already in 1758, the British had captured Forts Louisbourg and Duquesne. Then, on the night of September 13, 1759, British forces led by General James Wolfe scaled the heights outside Quebec and defeated the French under General Louis-Joseph Montcalm on the Plains of Abraham. Both generals died in the battle. The British

BRITISH VICTORY IN INDIA

THE SUCCESS OF THE BRITISH AGAINST THE French in India was due to Robert Clive. In this excerpt from one of his letters, he describes his famous victory at Plassey, north of Calcutta, on June 23, 1757. This battle demonstrated the inability of native Indian soldiers to compete with Europeans and signified the beginning of British control in Bengal (ben-GAHL). Clive claimed to have a thousand Europeans, two thousand sepoys (SEE-poiz) (local soldiers), and eight cannons available for this battle.

Robert Clive's Account of His Victory at Plassey

At daybreak we discovered the [governor's army] moving toward us, consisting, as we since found, of about fifteen thousand horse and thirty-five thousand foot, with upwards of forty pieces of cannon. They approached apace, and by six began to attack with a number of heavy cannon, supported by the whole army, and continued to play on us very briskly for several hours, during which our situation was of the utmost service to us, being lodged in a large grove with good mud banks. To succeed in an attempt on their cannon was next to impossible, as they were planted in a manner round us and at considerable distances from each other. We therefore remained quiet in our post, in expectation of a successful attack upon their camp at night. About noon the enemy drew off their artillery and retired to their camp. . . .

On finding them make no great effort to dislodge us, we proceeded to take possession of one or two more eminences

lying very near an angle of their camp, from whence, and an adjacent eminence in their possession, they kept a smart fire of musketry upon us. They made several attempts to bring out their cannon, but our advanced fieldpieces played so warmly and so well upon them that they were always driven back. Their horse exposing themselves a good deal on this occasion, many of them were killed, and among the rest four or five officers of the first distinction; by which the whole army being visibly dispirited and thrown into some confusion, we were encouraged to storm both the eminence and the angle of their camp, which were carried at the same instant, with little or no loss; though the latter was defended (exclusively of blacks) by forty French and two pieces of cannon; and the former by a large body of blacks, both horse and foot. On this a general rout ensued, and we pursued the enemy six miles, passing upwards of forty pieces of cannon they had abandoned, with an infinite number of carts and carriages filled with baggage of all kinds. . . . It is computed there are killed of the enemy about five hundred. Our loss amounted to only twenty-two killed and fifty wounded, and those chiefly blacks.

 In what ways, if any, would Clive's account likely have been different if the Battle of Plassey had occurred in Europe? According to the letter, what role did native Indians seemingly play in the battle? Why does Clive give them such little mention?

Source: J. H. Robinson, *Readings in European History*, vol. 2 (Boston: Ginn & Co., 1906).

---

went on to seize Montreal, the Great Lakes area, and the Ohio valley. The French were forced to make peace. By the Treaty of Paris, they ceded Canada and the lands east of the Mississippi to Britain. Their ally Spain transferred Spanish Florida to British control; in return, the French gave their Louisiana territory to the Spanish. By 1763, Great Britain had become the world's greatest colonial power.

European Armies and Warfare

The professional standing army, initiated in the seventeenth century, became a standard feature of eighteenth-century Europe. Especially noticeable was the increase in the size of armies, which paralleled the development of absolutist states. Between 1740 and 1780, the French army grew from 190,000 to 300,000 men; the Prussian, from 83,000 to 200,000; the Austrian, from 108,000 to 282,000; and the Russian, from 130,000 to 290,000.

COMPOSITION OF ARMIES The composition of these armies reflected the hierarchical structure of European society and the great chasm that separated the upper and lower classes. Officers came primarily from the landed aristocracy, which had for centuries regarded military activity as one of its major

CHRONOLOGY	The Mid-Century Wars
War of the Austrian Succession	1740–1748
Peace of Aix-la-Chapelle	1748
Seven Years' War	1756–1763
Diplomatic revolution	1756
Battle of Rossbach	1757
British capture of Forts Duquesne and Louisbourg	1758
Battle of Quebec	1759
Peace of Hubertusburg	1763
Treaty of Paris	1763

functions. Middle-class individuals could enter the middle ranks of the officer corps but were largely kept out of the higher ranks.

Rank-and-file soldiers came mostly from the lower classes of society. Some states, such as Prussia and Russia, conscripted able-bodied peasants. But many states realized that this was counterproductive since they could not afford to waste their farmers. For that reason, eighteenth-century armies were partly composed of foreign troops, many from Switzerland or the petty German states. Of the great powers, Britain alone had no regular standing army and relied on mercenaries, evident in its use of German troops in America. Most troops in European armies, especially the French and Austrian, were natives who enlisted voluntarily for six-year terms. Some were not exactly volunteers; often vagabonds and the unemployed were pressed into service. Most, however, came from the lower classes—peasants and also artisans from the cities—who saw the military as an opportunity to escape from hard times or personal problems.

The maritime powers, such as Britain and the Dutch Republic, regarded navies as more important than armies. In the second half of the eighteenth century, the British possessed 174 warships manned by 80,000 sailors. Conditions on these ships were often poor. Diseases such as scurvy and yellow fever were rampant, and crews were frequently press-ganged into duty.

THE NATURE OF WARFARE The dramatic increase in the size of armies and navies did not necessarily result in more destructive warfare in eighteenth-century Europe. For one thing, war was no longer driven by ideology as the religious conflicts of the sixteenth and seventeenth centuries had been. By their very nature, ideological wars are often violent and destructive. Moreover, since the larger armies depended on increased tax revenues, rulers regarded the wanton destruction of civilian taxpayers as foolish. Finally, the costliness of eighteenth-century armies as well as the technology and customary tactics of the age created a system of warfare based on limited objectives.

Since generals were extremely reluctant to risk the destruction of their armies in pitched battles, they came to rely on clever and elaborate maneuvers, rather than direct confrontation. A system of formalities accepted by all sides allowed defeated opponents to withdraw without being captured or destroyed. This mentality also encouraged the construction of vast fortresses to secure major roads and the enormous quantities of supplies needed by eighteenth-century armies. With its own set patterns of tactics, siege warfare often became, as one French critic said disgustedly, "the art of surrendering strongholds honorably after certain conventional formalities." Nevertheless, despite the maneuvering and the sieges, European warfare in the eighteenth century also involved many battles and considerable risk.

Economic Expansion and Social Change

 FOCUS QUESTION: What changes occurred in agriculture, finance, industry, and trade during the eighteenth century?

The depressed economic conditions of the seventeenth century began to improve in the early eighteenth century. Rapid population growth, expansion in banking and trade, an agricultural revolution (at least in Britain), the stirrings of industrialization, and an increase in worldwide trade and consumption characterized the economic patterns of the eighteenth century.

Growth of the European Population

Europe's population began to grow around 1750 and experienced a slow but steady rise, with some regional variations. It has been estimated that the total European population rose from around 120 million in 1700 to 140 million by 1750, and then grew to 190 million by 1790; thus, the growth rate in the second half of the century was double that of the first half. Individual states also experienced rapid growth between 1700 and 1790: Russia's population went from 14 million to 28 million (much of it due to territorial expansion); France's, from 20 to 26 or 27 million; Spain's, from 6 to 10 million; Brandenburg-Prussia's, from 1.5 to 5.5 million (over half of this came from territorial acquisition); and Britain's, from 5 or 6 to 9 million. These increases occurred during the same time that several million Europeans were going abroad as colonists.

Perhaps the most important cause of population growth was a decline in the death rate, thanks, no doubt, to more plentiful food and better transportation of food supplies, which led to improved diets and some relief from devastating famines. The introduction of new crops from the Americas, such as corn and potatoes, played an important role in creating a more bountiful and nutritious food supply (see "Was There an Agricultural Revolution?" later in this chapter). Some historians have estimated that at the beginning of the eighteenth century, farmers were producing about 20 to 30 percent more food than they needed to sustain themselves; by 1750, the surplus reached 50 percent.

But a more plentiful food supply was not the only factor contributing to population growth. Also of great significance was the end of the bubonic plague: the last great outbreak in western Europe occurred in 1720 in southern France. In England, a decline in the number of women who remained unmarried during their childbearing years may also have played an important role in population growth. It has been estimated that this number fell from 15 to 7 percent between 1700 and 1800.

Nevertheless, death was still a ubiquitous feature of everyday life. Diseases such as typhus, smallpox, influenza, and dysentery were rampant, especially since hygienic conditions remained poor—little bathing, dirty clothes, and no systematic elimination of human wastes. Despite the improved transportation, famine and hunger could still be devastating.

Family, Marriage, and Birthrate Patterns

The family, rather than the individual, was still at the heart of Europe's social organization. For the most part, people still thought of the family in traditional terms, as a patriarchal institution with the husband dominating his wife and children. The upper classes in particular were still concerned for the family as a "house," an association whose collective interests were more important than those of its individual members. In all social classes, parents, especially the fathers, still generally selected marriage partners for their children, based on the interests of the family (see the box on p. 544). One French noble responded to his son's inquiry about his upcoming marriage: "Mind your own business."

CHILD CARE At the beginning of the eighteenth century, traditional attitudes also prevailed in the care of children. Generally, lower-class women breast-fed their own children because

MARITAL ARRANGEMENTS

IN THE EIGHTEENTH CENTURY, UPPER-CLASS PARENTS continued to choose marriage partners for their children. This practice and the turmoil it could cause are evident in this selection from *The Rivals*, a play written in 1775 by Richard Sheridan. Sheridan was an Irish playwright who quit writing plays in order to pursue a political career. In this scene from *The Rivals*, a father, Sir Anthony Absolute, informs his son, Captain Jack Absolute, of the arrangements he has made for Jack's marriage. Jack, in love with another woman, is dumbfounded by his father's plans.

Richard Sheridan, *The Rivals*

ABSOLUTE: Now, Jack, I am sensible that the income of your commission, and what I have hitherto allowed you, is but a small pittance for a lad of your spirit.

CAPTAIN JACK: Sir, you are very good.

ABSOLUTE: And it is my wish, while yet I live, to have my boy make some figure in the world. I have resolved, therefore, to fix you at once in a noble independence.

CAPTAIN JACK: Sir, your kindness overpowers me—such generosity makes the gratitude of reason more lively than the sensations even of filial affection.

ABSOLUTE: I am so glad you are so sensible of my attention—and you shall be master of a large estate in a few weeks.

CAPTAIN JACK: Let my future life, sir, speak my gratitude; I cannot express the sense I have of your munificence.—Yet, sir, I presume you would not wish me to quit the army?

ABSOLUTE: Oh, that shall be as your wife chooses.

CAPTAIN JACK: My wife, sir!

ABSOLUTE: Ay, ay, settle that between you—settle that between you.

CAPTAIN JACK: A wife, sir, did you say?

ABSOLUTE: Ay, a wife—why, did I not mention her before?

CAPTAIN JACK: Not a word of her, sir.

ABSOLUTE: Odd, so! I musn't forget her though.—Yes, Jack, the independence I was talking of is by marriage—the fortune is saddled with a wife—but I suppose that makes no difference.

CAPTAIN JACK: Sir! Sir! You amaze me!

ABSOLUTE: Why, what the devil's the matter with you, fool? Just now you were all gratitude and duty.

CAPTAIN JACK: I was, sir—you talked of independence and a fortune, but not a word of a wife!

ABSOLUTE: Why—what difference does that make? Odds life, sir! If you had an estate, you must take it with the live stock on it, as it stands!

CAPTAIN JACK: If my happiness is to be the price, I must beg leave to decline the purchase. Pray, sir, who is the lady?

ABSOLUTE: What's that to you, sir? Come, give me your promise to love, and to marry her directly.

CAPTAIN JACK: Sure, sir, this is not very reasonable. . . . You must excuse me, sir, if I tell you, once for all, that in this point I cannot obey you. . . .

ABSOLUTE: Sir, I won't hear a word—not one word! . . .

CAPTAIN JACK: What, sir, promise to link myself to some mass of ugliness!

ABSOLUTE: Zounds! Sirrah! The lady shall be as ugly as I choose: she shall have a hump on each shoulder; she shall be as crooked as the crescent; her one eye shall roll like the bull's in Cox's Museum; she shall have a skin like a mummy, and the beard of a Jew—she shall be all this, sirrah! Yet I will make you ogle her all day, and sit up all night to write sonnets on her beauty.

 What does Sheridan suggest about marriage among the upper classes in the eighteenth century? What social, political, and economic considerations were significant in eighteenth-century marriages? Could he be overstating the issue? Why or why not?

Source: Richard Sheridan, *The Rivals* (London, 1775).

---

that provided the best nourishment. Moreover, since there were strong taboos in various parts of Europe against sexual intercourse while breastfeeding, mothers might also avoid another immediate pregnancy; if the infant died, they could then have another child. Lower-class women, however, also served as wet nurses for children of the aristocratic and upper middle classes. Mothers from these higher social strata considered breastfeeding undignified and hired wet nurses instead. Even the wives of artisans in the cities, for economic reasons, sent their babies to wet nurses in the countryside if they could, making the practice widespread in the eighteenth century.

In the second half of the eighteenth century, traditional attitudes began to alter, especially in western Europe. The impact of Enlightenment thought, such as Rousseau's *Émile*, and the increasing survival of more infants led to new attitudes toward

children. Childhood came to be viewed more and more as a distinct phase in human development. One result was a shift to dressing children in comfortable clothes appropriate to their age rather than in clothes modeled after adult styles. Shops for children's clothes appeared for the first time. The practice of **primogeniture**, in which the eldest son received all or the largest share of the parents' estate and thus was treated as the favorite, also came under attack. All children, it was argued, deserved their parents' attention. Appeals for women to breast-feed their children rather than use wet nurses soon followed. In England, games and toys specifically for children now appeared. The jigsaw puzzle was invented in the 1760s, and books, such as *Little Pretty Pocket-Book* (1744), aimed to please as well as teach children. These changes, however, were largely limited to the upper classes of western European society and did not extend to the peasants. For most Europeans, children were still a source of considerable anxiety. They represented a health risk to the mothers who bore them and more mouths to feed if they survived. In times of economic crisis, children proved such a burden to some families that they resorted to **infanticide** or abandoned their children at foundling homes.

Despite being punishable by death, infanticide remained a solution to the problem of too many children. So many children were being "accidentally" suffocated while in their parents' bed that in Austria in 1784 a law was enacted that forbade parents to place children under five years old in bed with them. More common than infanticide was simply leaving unwanted children at foundling homes or hospitals, which became a favorite charity of the rich in eighteenth-century Europe. The largest of its kind, located in Saint Petersburg, Russia, was founded by members of the nobility. By the end of the century, it was taking in 5,000 new babies a year and caring for 25,000 children at one time.

But severe problems arose as the system became overburdened. One historian has estimated that in the 1770s, one-third of all babies born in Paris were taken to foundling institutions by parents or desperate unmarried mothers, creating serious overcrowding. Foundling institutions often proved fatal for infants. Mortality rates ranged from 50 percent to as high as 90 percent (in a sense making foundling homes a legalized form of infanticide). Children who survived were usually sent to

miserable jobs. The suffering of poor children was one of the blackest pages of eighteenth-century European history.

MARRIAGE AND BIRTHRATES In most of Europe, newly married couples established their own households independent of their parents. This nuclear family, which had its beginning in the Middle Ages, had become a common pattern, especially in northwestern Europe. In order to save enough to establish their own households, both men and women (outside the aristocracy) married quite late; the average age for men in northwestern Europe was between twenty-seven and twenty-eight; for women, between twenty-five and twenty-seven.

Late marriages imposed limits on the birthrate; in fact, they might be viewed as a natural form of birth control. But was this limitation offset by the babies born illegitimately? From the low illegitimacy rate of 1 percent in some places in France and 5 percent in some English parishes, it would appear that it was not, at least in the first half of the eighteenth century. After 1750, however, illegitimacy appears to have increased. Studies in Germany, for example, show that rates of illegitimacy increased from 2 percent in 1700 to 5 percent in 1760 and to 10 percent in 1800, followed by an even more dramatic increase in the early nineteenth century.

For married couples, the first child usually appeared within one year of marriage, and additional children came at intervals of two or three years, producing an average of five births per

Children of the Upper Classes. This painting of John Bacon and his family illustrates an important feature of upper-class family life in Great Britain in the first half of the eighteenth century. The children appear as miniature adults, dressed in clothes modeled after the styles of their parents' clothes.

family. It would appear, then, that the birthrate had the potential of causing a significant increase in population. This possibility was restricted, however, because 40 to 60 percent of European women of childbearing age (between fifteen and forty-four) were not married at any given time. Moreover, by the end of the eighteenth century, especially among the upper classes in France and Britain, birth control techniques were being used to limit the number of children. Figures for the French aristocracy indicate that the average number of children declined from six in the period between 1650 and 1700 to three between 1700 and 1750 and to two between 1750 and 1780. These figures are even more significant when one considers that aristocrats married at younger ages than the rest of the population. Coitus interruptus remained the most commonly used form of birth control.

Among the working classes, whether peasants or urban workers, the contributions of women and children to the "family economy" were often crucial. In urban areas, both male and female children either helped in the handicraft manufacturing done in the home or were sent out to work as household servants. In rural areas, children worked on the land or helped in the activities of cottage industry. Married women grew vegetables in small plots, tended livestock, and sold eggs, vegetables, and milk. Wives of propertyless agricultural workers labored in the fields or as textile workers, spinning or knitting. In the cities, wives of artisans helped their husbands at their crafts or worked as seamstresses. The wives of unskilled workers labored as laundresses and cleaners for the rich or as peddlers of food or used clothing to the lower classes. But the family economy was often precarious. Bad harvests in the countryside or a downturn in employment in the cities often reduced people to utter poverty and a life of begging.

 Was There an Agricultural Revolution?

Did improvements in agricultural practices and methods in the eighteenth century lead to an **agricultural revolution**? The topic is much debated. Some historians have noted the beginning of agrarian changes already in the seventeenth century, especially in the Low Countries. Others, however, have questioned the use of the term, arguing that significant changes occurred only in England and that even there the upward trend in agricultural production was not maintained after 1750.

Traditional interpretations of the agricultural revolution are characterized by four interrelated factors: more farmland, increased crop yields per acre, healthier and more abundant livestock, and an improved climate. Climatologists believe that the "little ice age" of the seventeenth century declined in the eighteenth, especially evident in moderate summers that provided more ideal growing conditions.

Historians dispute the increase of the amount of land under cultivation and the rate at which more land entered cultivation. The amount of land under cultivation was increased by abandoning the old open-field system, in which part of the land was allowed to lie fallow to renew it and plow it for weeds. The formerly empty fields were now planted with new crops, such as alfalfa, turnips, and clover, which stored nitrogen in their roots and thereby restored the soil's fertility. Turnips could be hoed to remove weeds while the turnips were growing, allowing formerly fallow fields to be in continual use. Historians argue, however, that turnips were not common until the mid-eighteenth century and were not in constant rotation

Jethro Tull and the Seed Drill. A major innovation in the new agricultural practices of the eighteenth century was the development of seed drills that enabled farmers to plant seeds in rows and prevent them from being picked up by birds. The seed drill pictured here was invented by Jethro Tull (left), one of the many landed aristocrats who participated in the scientific experimentation of the age.

THE IMPACT OF AGRICULTURAL CHANGES

THE NEW AGRICULTURAL PRACTICES IN ENGLAND, which led to larger farms and increased productivity, also had social repercussions. As common lands were enclosed by large landowners, many small farmers became landless laborers, working for the larger farmers or in the emerging factories. This selection is from a work published in 1795 by David Davies (1742–1819), an English clergyman who analyzed the changes he saw in the countryside.

David Davies, *The Case of Labourers in Husbandry Stated and Considered*

The depriving of all landed property has beggared multitudes. It is plainly agreeable to sound policy, that as many individuals as possible in a state should possess an interest in the soil; because this attaches them strongly to the country and its constitution, and makes them zealous and resolute in defending them. But the gentry of this kingdom seem to have lost sight of this wise and salutary policy. Instead of giving to labouring people a valuable stake in the soil, the opposite measure has so long prevailed, that but few cottages, comparatively, have now any land about them. Formerly many of the lower sort of people [had land on which] they raised for themselves a considerable part of their subsistence. . . . But since these small parcels of ground have been swallowed up in the contiguous farms and enclosures, and the cottages themselves have been pulled down, the families which used to occupy them are crowded together in decayed farmhouses, with hardly ground enough about them for a cabbage garden; and being thus reduced to be mere hirelings, they are of course very liable to come to want. . . .

Thus an amazing number of people have been reduced from a comfortable state of partial independence to the precarious condition of hirelings, who, when out of work, must immediately come to their parish [for welfare]. And the great plenty of working hands always to be had when wanted, having kept down the price of labour below its proper level, the consequence is universally felt in the increased number of dependent poor.

 In Davies's eyes, how were the changes in agricultural practices affecting England's small farmers? What did he think would be the consequences of these changes?

Source: David Davies, *The Case of Labourers in Husbandry Stated and Considered* (London, 1795), pp. 55–56.

until the nineteenth century. Historians also argue that one of the reasons why output increased during this time was due to land reclamation, especially in eastern England. However, the increase of the new crops served another purpose; they provided winter fodder for livestock, enabling landlords to maintain an ever-larger number of animals.

The more numerous livestock increased the amount of meat in the European diet and enhanced food production by making available more animal manure, which was used to fertilize fields and produce larger yields per acre. Landed aristocrats with an interest in the scientific experimentation of the age also adopted innovations that increased yields. In England, Jethro Tull (1674–1741) discovered that using a hoe to keep the soil loose allowed air and moisture to reach plants and enabled them to grow better. He also used a drill to plant seeds in rows instead of scattering them by hand, a method that had lost much seed to the birds. However, some historians argue that the seed drill was not used by farmers on a large scale until the nineteenth century.

The eighteenth century witnessed greater yields of vegetables, including two important American crops, the potato and maize (Indian corn). Although they were not grown in quantity until after 1700, both had been brought to Europe from America in the sixteenth century. The potato became a staple in Germany, the Low Countries, and especially Ireland, where repression by English landlords forced large numbers of poor peasants to survive on small plots of marginal land. The potato took relatively little effort to produce in large quantities. High in carbohydrates and calories, rich in vitamins A and C, it could be easily stored for winter use.

Another argument of the agriculture revolution is whether or not the new crops and agricultural inventions increased food production while lowering the agricultural workforce, consequently altering the size and scale of farms and displacing agricultural workers. The new agricultural techniques were considered best suited to large-scale farms. Large landowners or yeomen farmers enclosed the old open fields, combining many small holdings into larger units. The end of the open-field system led to the demise of the cooperative farming of the village community. As crop yields increased, food prices began to decline, leaving landlords with the prospect of lowered profits. Their response was to enact legislation. Historians are still debating the causes of this legislation and whether or not it forced more innovative farming practices, leading to higher food yields. In England, Parliament was dominated by the landed aristocracy and enacted legislation to allow agricultural lands to be legally enclosed. As a result of these **enclosure acts**, England gradually became a land of large estates, and many small farmers were forced to become wage laborers or tenant farmers working farms of 100 to 500 acres. The enclosure acts allowed landlords to easily evict their tenants while converting the crop fields to meadows to raise sheep and generate income from their wool. The enclosure movement and new agricultural practices largely destroyed the traditional patterns of English village life (see the box above).

Historians continue to debate the timing and degree of an agricultural revolution in England, in part because some historians rely upon economics and pricing of food as a barometer for productivity. The lack of data makes this assessment problematic. However it is difficult to deny the rapid increase in agricultural production by the second half of the eighteenth century. English agriculture, with its noticeable increase in productivity, made possible the feeding of an expanding population while freeing the workforce from agriculture, enabling them to enter a new world of industrialization and urbanization. In other parts of Europe, however, noble privileges and heavy taxes on the peasants prevented the adoption of new agricultural practices. Nobles maintained rights of usage to all lands and often pastured animals on fallow fields; although the animals' manure could fertilize the soil, overgrazing could destroy the fields. In addition, lords often levied taxes on certain crops, such as wheat and rye, which prevented the introduction of fodder crops.

New Methods of Finance

A decline in the supply of gold and silver in the seventeenth century had created a chronic shortage of money that undermined the efforts of governments to meet their needs. The establishment of new public and private banks and the acceptance of paper notes made possible an expansion of credit in the eighteenth century.

Perhaps the best example of this process can be observed in England, where the Bank of England was founded in 1694. Unlike other banks accustomed to receiving deposits and exchanging foreign currencies, the Bank of England also made loans. In return for lending money to the government, the bank was allowed to issue paper "banknotes" backed by its credit. These soon became negotiable and provided a paper substitute for gold and silver coins. In addition, the issuance of government bonds paying regular interest, backed by the Bank of England and the London financial community, created the notion of a public or "national debt" distinct from the monarch's personal debts. This process meant that capital for financing larger armies and other government undertakings could be raised in ever-greater quantities.

These new financial institutions and methods were not risk-free, however. In both Britain and France in the early eighteenth century, speculators provided opportunities for people to invest in colonial trading companies. The French company under John Law was also tied to his attempt to create a national bank and paper currency for France. When people went overboard and drove the price of the stock to incredibly high levels, the bubble burst. Law's company and bank went bankrupt, leading to a loss of confidence in paper money that prevented the formation of a French national bank. Consequently, French public finance developed slowly in the eighteenth century (see Chapter 19).

This was not the case in Britain, however. Despite crises, public confidence in the new financial institutions enabled the British government to borrow large sums of money at relatively low rates of interest, giving it a distinct advantage in the struggle with France. According to a contemporary observer,

Britain's public credit was "the permanent miracle of her policy, which has inspired both astonishment and fear in the States of Europe."[5] Despite Britain's growing importance in finance, however, the Dutch Republic remained the leader in Europe's financial life, and Amsterdam continued to be the center of international finance until London replaced it in the nineteenth century. One observer noted in 1769:

> If ten or twelve businessmen of Amsterdam of the first rank meet for a banking operation, they can in a moment send circulating throughout Europe over two hundred million florins in paper money, which is preferred to cash. There is no Sovereign who could do as much. . . . This credit is a power which the ten or twelve businessmen will be able to exert over all the States of Europe, in complete independence of any authority.[6]

As Dutch trade, industry, and power declined, Dutch capitalists were inclined to lend money abroad because they had fewer opportunities at home.

European Industry

The most important product of European industry in the eighteenth century was textiles. Woolen cloth made up 75 percent of Britain's exports in the early part of the century. France, too, was a leader in the production of woolen cloth, and other major states emulated both France and Britain by encouraging the development of their own textile industries.

COTTAGE INDUSTRY Most textiles were still produced by traditional methods. In cities that were textile centers, master artisans used timeworn methods to turn out finished goods in their guild workshops. But by the eighteenth century, textile production was beginning to shift to the countryside in parts of Europe. In the countryside, textiles were produced by the "putting-out" or "domestic" system. A merchant-capitalist

Cottage Industry. One important source of textile production in the eighteenth century was the cottage industry, truly a family enterprise. Shown here is a family at work producing flax. It was customary in the cottage industry for women to spin and wind the yarn.

British Library, London, UK/Bridgeman Images

entrepreneur bought the raw materials, mostly wool and flax, and "put them out" to rural workers, who spun the raw material into yarn and then wove it into cloth on simple looms. Capitalist entrepreneurs sold the finished product, made a profit, and used it to manufacture more. This system became known as the **cottage industry** because spinners and weavers did their work in their own cottages. The cottage industry was truly a family enterprise: women and children could spin while men wove on the looms, enabling rural people to earn incomes to supplement their pitiful wages as agricultural laborers.

NEW METHODS AND NEW MACHINES The cottage system employed traditional methods of manufacturing and spread to many areas of rural Europe in the eighteenth century. But significant changes in industrial production also began to occur in the second half of the century, pushed along by the introduction of cotton, originally imported from India. The importation of raw cotton from slave plantations in the Americas encouraged the production of cotton cloth in Europe, where a profitable market developed because of the growing demand for lightweight cotton clothes that were less expensive than linens and woolens. But the traditional methods of the cottage industry proved incapable of keeping up with the growing demand, leading English cloth entrepreneurs to develop new methods and new machines. The flying shuttle sped up the process of weaving on a loom, thereby increasing the need for large quantities of yarn. In response, Richard Arkwright (1732–1792) invented a "water frame," powered by horse or water, which turned out yarn much faster than cottage spinning wheels. This abundance of yarn, in turn, led to the development of mechanized looms, invented in the 1780s but not widely adopted until the early nineteenth century. By that time, Britain was in the throes of the Industrial Revolution (see Chapter 20), but already at the end of the eighteenth century, rural workers, perceiving that the new machines threatened their traditional livelihood, had begun to call for the machines' destruction (see the box on p. 550).

THE NEW CONSUMERS As agricultural innovations in the eighteenth century reduced the need for agricultural workers, other occupations were expanding. Small merchants, craftspeople, and shopkeepers were growing in number, aided by the developments in industry. This led to the beginnings of a consumer revolution that was primarily centered in England in the eighteenth century. Consumers increasingly purchased a host of newly available goods including china, silverware, cut glass, mahogany furniture, teapots, and ready-made clothing. Porcelain had been imported from China for centuries; however, by the eighteenth century factories on the Continent and in England had bypassed Chinese production. Large showrooms opened in London. The most famous was that of Josiah Wedgwood, whose shop was illuminated by a large skylight and filled with opulent furnishings to show off his wares. By the late eighteenth century, Wedgwood's company exported nearly eighty percent of its wares. The consumer products of the eighteenth century quickly became international commodities.

Mercantile Empires and Worldwide Trade

As we saw in Chapter 14, the growth of commercial capitalism led to integrated markets, joint-stock trading companies, and banking and stock exchange facilities. Mercantilist theory had posited that a nation should acquire as much gold and silver as possible; that it should maintain a favorable balance of trade, or more exports than imports; and that the state should provide subsidies to manufacturers, grant monopolies to traders, build roads and canals, and impose high tariffs to limit imports. Colonies were also seen as valuable sources of raw materials and markets for finished goods. Mercantilist theory on the role of colonies was matched in practice by Europe's overseas expansion. With the development of colonies and trading posts in the Americas, Asia, and Africa, Europeans embarked on an adventure in international commerce. This increase in overseas trade has led some historians to speak of the emergence of a truly global economy in the eighteenth century.

Although trade within Europe still dominated total trade figures, overseas trade boomed in the eighteenth century. As we saw in Chapter 14, of all the goods traded in the eighteenth century, perhaps the most profitable were African slaves. The African slave trade and the plantation economy in the Americas that depended on it were an integral part of the new Atlantic economy, which enabled the nations of western Europe to experience greater prosperity than the states in central and eastern Europe.

During the eighteenth century, trade between European states and their colonies increased dramatically. In 1715, 19 percent of Britain's trade was with its American colonies; by 1785, that figure had risen to 34 percent. The growing trade of Europe with the Americas, Africa, and Asia was also visible in the expansion of merchant fleets. The British, for example, had 3,300 merchant ships carrying 260,000 tons in 1700; by

Bristol. After the discovery of the New World, Bristol became an important British shipping port. By the seventeenth century, it was the second-largest port in the kingdom. Portrayed here in a painting dated 1760 is Bristol's quay, where woods were unloaded and loaded.

THE BEGINNINGS OF MECHANIZED INDUSTRY: THE ATTACK ON NEW MACHINES

ALREADY BY THE END OF THE EIGHTEENTH CENTURY, mechanization was bringing changes to the traditional cottage industry of textile manufacturing. Rural workers who depended on the extra wages earned in their own homes often reacted by attacking the machinery that threatened their livelihoods. This selection is a petition that English woolen workers published in their local newspapers asking that machines no longer be used to prepare wool for spinning.

The Leeds Woolen Workers' Petition (1786)

To the Merchants, Clothiers and all such as wish well to the Staple Manufactory of this Nation.

The Humble ADDRESS and PETITION of Thousands, who labor in the Cloth Manufactory.

The Scribbling-Machines have thrown thousands of your petitioners out of employ, whereby they are brought into great distress, and are not able to procure a maintenance for their families, and deprived them of the opportunity of bringing up their children to labor: We have therefore to request, that prejudice and self-interest may be laid aside, and that you may pay that attention to the following facts, which the nature of the case requires.

The number of Scribbling-Machines extending about seventeen miles southwest of LEEDS, exceed all belief, being no less than *one hundred and seventy!* and as each machine will do as much work in twelve hours, as ten men can in that time do by hand (speaking within bounds) and they working night and day, one machine will do as much work in one day as would otherwise employ twenty men.

As we do not mean to assert any thing but what we can prove to be true, we allow four men to be employed at each machine twelve hours, working night and day, will take eight men in twenty-four hours; so that, upon a moderate computation twelve men are thrown out of employ for every single machine used in scribbling; and as it may be supposed the number of machines in all the other quarters together, nearly equal those in the South-West, full four thousand men are left to shift for a living how they can, and must of course fall to the Parish, if not time relieved. Allowing one boy to be bound apprentice from each family out of work, eight thousand hands are deprived of the opportunity of getting a livelihood.

We therefore hope, that the feelings of humanity will lead those who have it in their power to prevent the use of those machines, to give every discouragement they can to what has a tendency so prejudicial to their fellow-creatures. . . .

We wish to propose a few queries to those who would plead for the further continuance of these machines:

How are those men, thus thrown out of employ to provide for their families; and what are they to put their children apprentice to, that the rising generation may have something to keep them at work, in order that they may not be like vagabonds strolling about in idleness? Some say, Begin and learn some other business.—Suppose we do, who will maintain our families, whilst we undertake the arduous task; and when we have learned it, how do we know we shall be any better for all our pains; for by the time we have served our second apprenticeship, another machine may arise, which may take away that business also. . . .

But what are our children to do; are they to be brought up in idleness? Indeed as things are, it is no wonder to hear of so many executions; for our parts, though we may be thought illiterate men, our conceptions are, that bringing children up to industry, and keeping them employed, is the way to keep them from falling into those crimes, which an idle habit naturally leads to.

 What arguments did the Leeds woolen workers use against the new machines? What does the petition reveal about the concept of "progress" at the end of the eighteenth century?

Source: Leeds Woolen Workers' Petition (Leeds, 1786).

1775, those numbers had increased to 9,400 ships carrying 695,000 tons.

Flourishing trade also had a significant impact on the European economy, especially visible in the growth of towns and cities. The rise of the Atlantic trade led to great prosperity for such port cities as Bordeaux, Nantes, and Marseilles in France; Bristol and Liverpool in Britain; and Lisbon and Oporto in Portugal. Trade also led to the growth of related industries, such as textile manufacturing, sugar refining, and tobacco processing, and to an increase in dock workers, building tradesmen, servants, and numerous service people. Visitors' accounts of their visits to prosperous port cities detail the elegant buildings and affluent lifestyle they encountered.

The Social Order of the Eighteenth Century

 FOCUS QUESTION: Who were the main groups making up the European social order in the eighteenth century, and how did the conditions in which they lived differ both between groups and between different parts of Europe?

The pattern of Europe's social organization, first established in the Middle Ages, continued well into the eighteenth century. Social status was still largely determined not by wealth and economic standing but by the division into the traditional "orders" or "estates" determined by heredity. This divinely sanctioned division of society into traditional orders was supported by Christian teaching, which emphasized the need to fulfill the responsibilities of one's estate. Although Enlightenment intellectuals attacked these traditional distinctions, they did not die easily. In the Prussian law code of 1794, marriage between noble males and middle-class females was forbidden without a government dispensation. Even without government regulation, however, different social groups remained easily distinguished everywhere in Europe by the distinctive, traditional clothes they wore.

Nevertheless, some forces of change were at work in this traditional society. The ideas of the Enlightenment made headway as reformers argued that the concept of an unchanging social order based on privilege was hostile to the progress of society. Not until the revolutionary upheavals at the end of the eighteenth century, however, did the old order finally begin to crumble.

The Peasants

Because society was still mostly rural in the eighteenth century, the peasantry constituted the largest social group, making up as much as 85 percent of Europe's population. There were rather large differences, however, between peasants from area to area. The most important distinction, at least legally, was between the free peasant and the serf. Peasants in Britain, northern Italy, the Low Countries, Spain, most of France, and some areas of western Germany were legally free, though not exempt from burdens. Some free peasants in Andalusia in Spain, southern Italy, Sicily, and Portugal lived in poverty more desperate than that of many serfs in Russia and eastern Germany. In France, 40 percent of free peasants owned little or no land by 1789.

Small peasant proprietors or tenant farmers in western Europe were also not free from compulsory services. Most owed **tithes**, often one-third of their crops. Although tithes were intended for parish priests, in France only 10 percent of the priests received them. Instead the tithes wound up in the hands of towns and aristocratic landowners. Moreover, peasants could still owe a variety of dues and fees. Local aristocrats claimed hunting rights on peasant land and had monopolies over the flour mills, community ovens, and wine and oil presses needed by the peasants. Hunting rights, dues, fees, and tithes were all deeply resented.

Eastern Europe continued to be dominated by large landed estates owned by powerful lords and worked by serfs. Serfdom had come late to the east, having largely been imposed in the sixteenth and seventeenth centuries. Peasants in eastern Germany were bound to the lord's estate, had to perform labor services on the lord's land, and could not marry or move without permission and payment of a tax. By the eighteenth century, landlords also possessed legal jurisdiction, giving them control over the administration of justice. Only in the Habsburg empire had a ruler attempted to improve the lot of the peasants through a series of reforms. With the exception of the clergy and a small merchant class, eighteenth-century

Russia, unlike the rest of Europe, was still largely a society of landlords and serfs. Russian peasants were not attached to the land but to the landlord and thus existed in a condition approaching slavery.

THE VILLAGE The local village remained the center of social life for the peasants. The village, especially in western Europe, maintained public order; provided poor relief, a village church, and sometimes a schoolmaster; collected taxes for the central government; maintained roads and bridges; and established common procedures for sowing, plowing, and harvesting crops. But villages were often dominated by the wealthiest peasants and proved highly resistant to innovations, such as new agricultural practices.

THE PEASANT DIET The diet of the peasants in the eighteenth century had not changed much since the Middle Ages. Dark bread, made of roughly ground wheat and rye flour, remained the basic staple. It was quite nourishing and high in vitamins, minerals, and even proteins, since the bran and germ were not removed. Peasants drank water, wine, and beer and ate soups and gruel made of grains and vegetables. The new foods of the eighteenth century, potatoes and American corn, added important elements to the peasant diet. Of course, when harvests were bad, hunger and famine became the peasants' lot in life, making them even more susceptible to the ravages of disease.

The Nobility

The nobles, who constituted only 2 to 3 percent of the European population, played a dominating role in society. Being born a noble automatically guaranteed a place at the top of the social order, with all the attendant special privileges and rights. The legal privileges of the nobility included judgment by their peers, immunity from severe punishment, and exemption from many forms of taxation. Especially in central and eastern Europe, the rights of landlords over their serfs were overwhelming. In Poland until 1768, the nobility even possessed the right of life or death over their serfs.

In many countries, nobles were highly conscious of their unique lifestyle, which set them apart from the rest of society. This did not mean, however, that they were unwilling to bend the conventions of that lifestyle if there were profits to be made. For example, by convention, nobles were expected to live off the yields of their estates. But although nobles almost everywhere talked about trade being beneath their dignity, many were not averse to mercantile endeavors. Many were also all too eager to profit from the exploitation of raw materials found on their estates; as a result, many nobles were involved in industries such as mining, metallurgy, and glassmaking. Their diet also set them off from the rest of society. Aristocrats consumed enormous quantities of meat and fish accompanied by cheeses, nuts, and a variety of sweets.

Nobles also played important roles in military and government affairs. Since medieval times, landed aristocrats had served as military officers. Although monarchs found it impossible to exclude commoners from the ranks of officers, tradition maintained that nobles made the most natural and hence the best officers. Moreover, the eighteenth-century nobility played a significant role in the administrative machinery of state. In some countries, such as Prussia, the entire bureaucracy reflected aristocratic values. Moreover, in most of Europe, landholding nobles controlled much of the local government in their districts.

The nobility or landowning class was not a homogeneous social group, however. Landlords in England leased their land to tenant farmers, while those in eastern Europe used the labor services of serfs. Nobles in Russia and Prussia served the state, but those in Spain and Italy had few official functions. Differences in wealth, education, and political power also led to differences within countries as well. The gap between rich and poor nobles could be enormous. As the century progressed, poor nobles sometimes sank into the ranks of the unprivileged masses of the population. It has been estimated that the number of European nobles declined by one-third between 1750 and 1815.

Although the nobles clung to their privileged status and struggled to keep others out, almost everywhere a person with money found it possible to enter the ranks of the nobility. Rights of nobility were frequently attached to certain lands, so purchasing the lands made one a noble; the acquisition of government offices also often conferred noble status.

THE ARISTOCRATIC WAY OF LIFE: THE COUNTRY HOUSE One aristocrat who survived the French Revolution commented that "no one who did not live before the Revolution" could know the real sweetness of living. Of course, he spoke not for the peasants whose labor maintained the system but for the landed aristocrats. For them, the eighteenth century was a final century of "sweetness" before the Industrial Revolution and bourgeois society diminished their privileged way of life.

In so many ways, the court of Louis XIV had provided a model for other European monarchs, who built palaces and encouraged the development of a court society as a center of culture. As at Versailles, these courts were peopled by members of the aristocracy whose income from rents or officeholding enabled them to participate in this lifestyle. This court society, whether in France, Spain, or Germany, manifested common characteristics: participation in intrigues for the king's or prince's favor, serene walks in formal gardens, and duels to maintain one's honor.

The majority of aristocratic landowners, however, remained on their country estates and did not participate in court society; their large houses continued to give witness to their domination of the surrounding countryside. This was especially true in England, where the court of the Hanoverian kings (Georges I–III, from 1714 to 1820) made little impact on the behavior of upper-class society. English landed aristocrats invested much time, energy, and money in their rural estates, giving the English country house an important role in English social life. One American observer remarked, "Scarcely any persons who hold a leading place in the circles of their society live in London. They have houses in London, in which they stay while Parliament sits, and occasionally visit at other seasons; but their homes are in the country."[7]

Although there was much variety in country houses, many in the eighteenth century were built in the Georgian style (named after the Hanoverian kings). This style was greatly influenced by the classical serenity and sedateness of the sixteenth-century Venetian architect Andrea Palladio (ahn-DRAY-ah puh-LAH-dee-oh), who had specialized in the design of country villas. The Georgian country house combined elegance with domesticity, and its interior was often described as offering visual delight and utility along with the comfort of a home.

The country house also fulfilled a new desire for greater privacy that was reflected in the growing separation between the lower and upper floors. The lower floors were devoted to public activities—dining, entertaining, and leisure (see "Images of Everyday Life" on p. 553). A central entrance hall provided the setting for the ceremonial arrival and departure of guests on formal occasions. From the hall, guests could proceed to a series of downstairs common rooms. The largest was the drawing room (larger houses had two), which contained musical instruments and was used for dances or card games, a favorite pastime. Other common rooms included a formal dining room, informal breakfast room, library, study, gallery, billiard room, and conservatory. The entrance hall also featured a large staircase that led to the upstairs rooms, which consisted of bedrooms for husbands and wives, sons, and daughters. These rooms were used not only for sleeping but also for private activities, such as playing for the children and sewing, writing, and reading for wives. "Going upstairs" literally meant leaving the company of others in the downstairs common rooms to be alone in the privacy of one's bedroom. This eighteenth-century desire for privacy also meant keeping servants at a distance. They were now housed in their own wing of rooms and alerted to their employers' desire for assistance by a new invention—long cords connected to bells in the servants' quarters.

Although the arrangement of the eighteenth-century Georgian house originally reflected male interests, the influence of women was increasingly evident by the second half of the century. Already in the seventeenth century, it had become customary for the sexes to separate after dinner; while the men preoccupied themselves with brandy and cigars in the dining room, women would exit to a "withdrawing room" for their own conversation. In the course of the eighteenth century, the drawing room became a larger, more feminine room with comfortable pieces of furniture grouped casually in front of fireplaces to create a cozy atmosphere.

Aristocratic landowners, especially in Britain, also sought to expand the open space around their country houses to separate themselves from the lower classes in the villages and to remove farmland from their view. Often these open spaces were then enclosed by walls to create parks (as they were called in England) to provide even more privacy. Sometimes entire villages

The Aristocratic Way of Life

Collection of the Earl of Pembroke, Wilton House, Wilts./Bridgeman Images

Scala/Art Resource, NY

Art Resource, NY

Erich Lessing/Art Resource, NY

THE EIGHTEENTH-CENTURY COUNTRY HOUSE IN Britain fulfilled the desire of aristocrats for both elegance and greater privacy. The painting above at the left, by Richard Wilson, shows a typical English country house of the eighteenth century surrounded by a simple, serene landscape. Thomas Gainsborough's *Conversation in the Park*, above right, captures the relaxed life of two aristocrats in the park of their country estate. The illustration at the lower left shows the formal dining room of a great British country house. In the course of the eighteenth century, upper-class country houses

came to be furnished with upholstered furniture and elaborate carpets as aristocrats sought greater comfort. Cabinets with glass windows also became fashionable as a way to display fine china and other objects. Especially desirable were objects from the East, as vast amounts of Chinese and Japanese ceramics were imported into Europe in the eighteenth century. The illustration at the lower right shows Chinese cups without handles, which became extremely fashionable. As seen in the painting, it was even acceptable to pour tea into the saucer in order to cool it.

were destroyed to create a park, causing one English poet to lament the social cost:

The man of wealth and pride
Takes up the space that many poor supplied;
Space for his lake, his park's extended bounds,
Space for his horses, equipage and hounds.[8]

Along with a sense of privacy, parks gave landed aristocrats the ability to reshape their property to meet their leisure needs.

THE ARISTOCRATIC WAY OF LIFE: THE GRAND TOUR One characteristic of the high culture of the Enlightenment was its cosmopolitanism, reinforced by education in the Latin classics and the use of French as an international language. Travel was another manifestation of the Enlightenment's sophistication and interest in new vistas. An important aspect of eighteenth-century travel was the grand tour, in which the sons of aristocrats completed their education by making a tour of Europe's major cities. The English aristocracy in particular regarded the grand tour as crucial to their education. The great-aunt of Thomas Coke wrote to him upon his completion of school: "Sir, I understand you have left Eton and probably intend to go to one of those Schools of Vice, the Universities. If, however, you choose to travel I will give you 500 pounds [about $12,500] per annum."[9] Coke was no fool and went on the grand tour, along with many others. In one peak year alone, 40,000 Englishmen were traveling in Europe.

Travel was not easy in the eighteenth century. Crossing the English Channel could be difficult in rough seas and might take anywhere from three to twelve hours. The trip from France to Italy could be made by sea, where the traveler faced the danger of pirates, or overland by sedan chair over the Alps, where narrow passes made travel an adventure in terror. Inns, especially in Germany, were populated by thieves and the ubiquitous bedbugs. The English in particular were known for spending vast sums of money during their travels; as one observer recounted, "The French usually travel to save money, so that they sometimes leave the places where they sojourn worse off than they found them. The English, on the other hand, come over with plenty of cash, plenty of gear, and servants to wait on them. They throw their money about like lords."[10]

Since the trip was intended to be educational, young Englishmen in particular were usually accompanied by a tutor who ensured that his charges spent time looking at museum collections of natural history and antiquities. But tutors were not able to stop young men from also pursuing wine, women, and song. After crossing the Channel, English visitors went to Paris for a cram course on how to act sophisticated. They then went on to Italy, where their favorite destinations were Florence, Venice, and Rome. In Florence, the studious and ambitious studied art in the Uffizi Gallery. The less ambitious followed a less vigorous routine; according to the poet Thomas Gray, they "get up at twelve o'clock, breakfast till three, dine till five, sleep till six, drink cooling liquors till eight, go to the bridge till ten, sup till two, and so sleep till twelve again." In Venice, where sophisticated prostitutes had flourished since Renaissance times, women were the chief attraction for young English males. As Samuel Johnson remarked, "If a young man is wild, and must run after women and bad company, it is better this should be done abroad." Rome was another "great object of our pilgrimage," where travelers visited the "modern" sights, such as Saint Peter's and, above all, the ancient ruins. To a generation raised on a classical education, souvenirs of ruins and Piranesi's etchings of classical ruins were required purchases. After the accidental rediscovery of the ancient Roman towns of Herculaneum and Pompeii, they became a popular eighteenth-century tourist attraction.

The Inhabitants of Towns and Cities

Townspeople were still a distinct minority of the total population, except in the Dutch Republic, Britain, and parts of Italy. At the end of the eighteenth century, about one-sixth of the French population lived in towns of 2,000 people or more. The biggest city in Europe was London, with 1 million inhabitants, while Paris numbered between 550,000 and 600,000. Altogether, Europe had at least twenty cities in twelve countries with populations over 100,000, including Naples, Lisbon, Moscow, Saint Petersburg, Vienna, Amsterdam, Berlin, Rome, and Madrid. Although urban dwellers were vastly outnumbered by rural inhabitants, towns played an important role in Western culture. The contrasts between a large city, with its education, culture, and material consumption, and the surrounding, often poverty-stricken countryside were striking, evident in this British traveler's account of Russia's Saint Petersburg in 1741:

> The country about Petersburg has full as wild and desert a look as any in the Indies; you need not go above 200 paces out of the town to find yourself in a wild wood of firs, and such a low, marshy, boggy country that you would think God when he created the rest of the world for the use of mankind had created this for an inaccessible retreat for all sorts of wild beasts.[11]

Peasants often resented the prosperity of towns and their exploitation of the countryside to serve urban interests. Palermo in Sicily used one-third of the island's food production while paying only one-tenth of the taxes. Towns lived off the countryside not by buying peasant produce but by acquiring it through tithes, rents, and dues.

Many cities in western and even central Europe had a long tradition of patrician oligarchies that continued to control their communities by dominating town and city councils. Despite their domination, patricians constituted only a small minority of the urban population. Just below the patricians stood an upper crust of the middle classes: non-noble officeholders, financiers and bankers, merchants, wealthy rentiers who lived off their investments, and important professionals, including lawyers. Another large urban group was the petty bourgeoisie or lower middle class, made up of master artisans, shopkeepers, and small traders. Below them were the laborers or working classes. Much urban industry was still carried on in small guild workshops by masters, journeymen, and apprentices. Apprentices who acquired the proper skills became journeymen before entering the ranks of the masters, but increasingly in the eighteenth century, guilds became closed oligarchies as membership was restricted to the relatives of masters. Many skilled artisans were then often forced to become low-paid workers.

A Market Square in Naples. Below the wealthy patrician elites who dominated the towns and cities were a number of social groups with a wide range of incomes and occupations. This remarkable diversity is evident in this eighteenth-century painting by Angelo Costa, which shows a fair being held in the chief market square of the Italian city of Naples.

Urban communities also had a large group of unskilled workers who served as servants, maids, and cooks at pitifully low wages.

Despite an end to the ravages of plague, eighteenth-century cities still experienced high death rates, especially among children, because of unsanitary living conditions, polluted water, and a lack of sewerage facilities. One observer compared the stench of Hamburg to an open sewer that could be smelled for miles around. Overcrowding also exacerbated urban problems as cities continued to grow from an influx of rural immigrants. But cities proved no paradise for them as unskilled workers found few employment opportunities. The result was a serious problem of poverty in the eighteenth century.

THE PROBLEM OF POVERTY Poverty was a highly visible problem in the eighteenth century, both in cities and in the countryside (see the box on p. 556). In Venice, licensed beggars made up 3 to 5 percent of the population, and unlicensed beggars may have constituted as much as 13 to 15 percent. Beggars in Bologna were estimated at 25 percent of the population; in Mainz, figures indicate that 30 percent of the people were beggars or prostitutes. Prostitution was often an alternative to begging. In France and Britain by the end of the century, an estimated 10 percent of the people depended on charity or begging for their food.

Earlier in Europe, the poor had been viewed as blessed children of God; assisting them was a Christian duty. A change of attitude that had begun in the latter part of the sixteenth century became even more apparent in the eighteenth century. Charity to poor beggars, it was argued, simply encouraged their idleness and led them to vice and crime. A French official stated, "Beggary is the apprenticeship of crime; it begins by creating a love of idleness which will always be the greatest political and moral evil. In this state the beggar does not long resist the temptation to steal."[12] Although private charitable institutions such as the religious Order of Saint Vincent de Paul and the Sisters of Charity had been founded to help the poor, they were soon overwhelmed by the increased numbers of indigent in the eighteenth century.

Although some "enlightened" officials argued that the state should become involved in the problem, mixed feelings prevented concerted action. Since the sixteenth century, vagrancy and begging had been considered crimes. In the eighteenth century, French authorities attempted to round up vagrants and beggars and incarcerate them for eighteen months to act as a deterrent. This effort accomplished little, however, since the basic problem was socioeconomic. These people had no work. In the 1770s, the French tried to use public works projects, such as road building, to give people jobs, but not enough funds were available to accomplish much. The problem of poverty remained another serious blemish on the quality of eighteenth-century life.

POVERTY IN FRANCE

UNLIKE THE BRITISH, WHO HAD A SYSTEM OF public-supported poor relief, the French responded to poverty with ad hoc policies when conditions became acute. This selection is taken from an *intendant's* report to the controller general at Paris describing his suggestions for a program to relieve the grain shortages expected for the winter months.

M. de la Bourdonnaye, *Intendant* of Bordeaux, to the Controller General, September 30, 1708

Having searched for the means of helping the people of Agen in this cruel situation and having conferred with His Eminence, the Bishop, it seems to us that three things are absolutely necessary if the people are not to starve during the winter.

Most of the inhabitants do not have seed to plant their fields. However, we decided that we would be going too far if we furnished it, because those who have seed would also apply [for more]. Moreover, we are persuaded that all the inhabitants will make strenuous efforts to find some seed, since they have every reason to expect prices to remain high next year. . . .

But this project will come to nothing if the collectors of the *taille* [taxes] continue to be as strict in the exercise of their functions as they have been of late and continue to employ troops [to force collection]. Those inhabitants who have seed grain would sell it to be freed from an oppressive garrison, while those who must buy seed, since they have none left from their harvest and have scraped together a little money for this purchase, would prefer to give up that money [for taxes] when put under police constraint. To avoid this, I feel it is absolutely necessary that you order the receivers-general to reduce their operations during this winter, at least with respect to the poor. . . .

We are planning to import wheat for this region from Languedoc and Quercy, and we are confident that there will be enough. . . . As a protective measure, it would seem wise to establish two small storehouses. Ten thousand ecus [30,000 livres] would be sufficient for each. . . .

A third point demanding our attention is the support of beggars among the poor, as well as of those who have no other resources than their wages. Since there will be very little work, these people will soon be reduced to starvation. We should establish public workshops to provide work as was done in 1693 and 1694. . . . In this manner, we should rid ourselves of those who do not want to work and assure the others a moderate subsistence. For these workshops, we would need about 40,000 livres, or altogether 100,000 livres. The receiver-general of the *taille* of Agen could advance this sum. The 60,000 livres for the storehouses he would get back very soon. I shall await your orders on all of the above.

Marginal Comments by the Controller General

Operations for the collection of the *taille* are to be suspended. The two storehouses are to be established; great care must be taken to put them to good use. The interest on the advances will be paid by the king. His Majesty has agreed to the establishment of the public workshops for the able-bodied poor and is willing to spend up to 40,000 livres on them this winter.

 What does this document reveal about the nature of poverty in France in the eighteenth century? How would the growing ranks of the poor in Europe further destabilize society?

Source: R. Forster and E. Forster, *European Society in the Eighteenth Century* (London: Walker & Co., 1969).

CHAPTER SUMMARY

Everywhere in Europe at the beginning of the eighteenth century, the old order remained strong. Nobles, clerics, towns, and provinces all had privileges, some medieval in origin, others the result of the attempt of monarchies in the sixteenth and seventeenth centuries to gain financial support from their subjects. Everywhere in the eighteenth century, monarchs sought to enlarge their bureaucracies to raise taxes to support the new large standing armies that had originated in the seventeenth century. During the eighteenth century, royal authority was often justified by the service the monarch could give to the state and its

people rather than by divine right, creating a form of monarchy that some have labeled "enlightened absolutism." Three rulers, Frederick II of Prussia, Joseph II of Austria, and Catherine the Great of Russia, are traditionally associated with the concept of enlightened absolutism, although only Joseph II truly sought radical change based on Enlightenment ideas. Joseph abolished serfdom, reformed the laws, and granted religious toleration, but his reforms did not outlast his reign. Frederick and Catherine expressed interest in enlightened reforms, but maintenance of the existing political system took precedence over reform. Indeed, many historians believe that Frederick, Catherine, and Joseph were all guided by a policy of using state power to amass armies and wage wars to gain more power.

The existence of these armies made wars more likely. The emergence of five great powers, two of them (France and Britain) in conflict in the East and North America, initiated a new scale of confrontation. The mid-century War of the Austrian Succession and the Seven Years' War were fought not only in Europe but also in North America and India. Frederick the Great was the instigator, desiring Austrian Silesia, but Great Britain was the true victor, driving France from Canada and India. Britain emerged with a worldwide empire and became the world's greatest naval and colonial power. Standing armies became the norm, and everywhere in Europe, increased demands for taxes to support these conflicts led to attacks on the privileged orders and a desire for change not met by the ruling monarchs.

At the same time, the population grew, mainly as a result of a declining death rate and improvements in agriculture; paper money began to compensate for gold and silver; institutions such as the Bank of England mobilized the wealth of the nation through credit; and the beginnings of an industrial revolution emerged in the textile industry. This growth in population, along with dramatic changes in finance, trade, and industry and an increase in poverty, created tensions that undermined the traditional foundations of European society. The inability of the old order to deal meaningfully with these changes led to a revolutionary outburst at the end of the eighteenth century that marked the beginning of the end for that old order.

CHAPTER TIMELINE

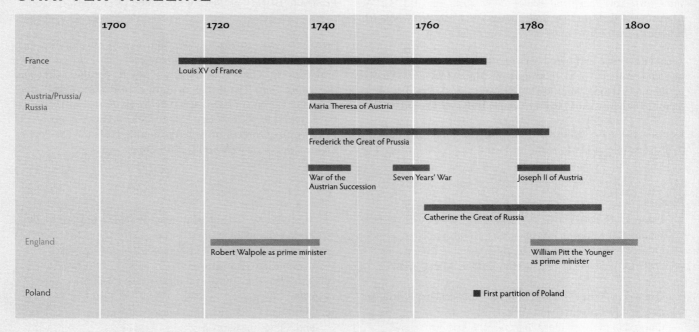

CHAPTER REVIEW

Upon Reflection

Q If you were a philosophe serving Joseph II of Austria or Catherine the Great of Russia, what advice would you give the monarch on the best way to rule his or her country?

Q What were the characteristics of war and diplomacy in the eighteenth century, and how would you compare the nature of war and diplomacy in the eighteenth century with that of the seventeenth century?

Q How and why did the nobility play a dominating role in the European society of the eighteenth century?

Key Terms

natural laws (p. 529)
natural rights (p. 529)
enlightened absolutism (p. 529)
patronage (p. 531)
balance of power (p. 539)
reason of state (p. 539)

primogeniture (p. 544)
infanticide (p. 545)
agricultural revolution (p. 546)
enclosure acts (p. 547)
cottage industry (p. 549)
tithes (p. 551)

Suggestions for Further Reading

GENERAL WORKS For a good introduction to the political history of the eighteenth century, see the relevant chapters in the general works by **Woloch, Anderson,** and **Blanning** listed in Chapter 17. See also **G. Treasure,** *The Making of Modern Europe, 1648–1780* (London, 2003), and **O. Hufton,** *Europe: Privilege and Protest, 1730–1789,* 2nd ed. (London, 2001). On enlightened absolutism, see **D. Beales,** *Enlightenment and Reform in Eighteenth-Century Europe* (New York, 2005). Good biographies of some of Europe's monarchs include **G. MacDonough,** *Frederick the Great* (New York, 2001); **V. Rounding,** *Catherine the Great: Love, Sex, and Power* (New York, 2007); **T. C. W. Blanning,** *Joseph II* (New York, 1994); and **J. Black,** *George III: America's Last King* (New Haven, Conn., 2006).

EIGHTEENTH-CENTURY WARFARE The warfare of this period is examined in **M. S. Anderson,** *War and Society in Europe of the Old Regime, 1615–1789* (New York, 1998). See also **A. J. Szabo,** *The Seven Years' War in Europe, 1756–1763* (Oxford, 2007).

ECONOMIC AND SOCIAL CHANGE A good introduction to European population can be found in **M. W. Flinn,** *The European Demographic System, 1500–1820* (Brighton, 1981). One of the best works on family and marriage patterns is **L. Stone,** *The Family, Sex, and Marriage in England, 1500–1800* (New York, 1977). On England's agricultural revolution debate, see **M. Overton,** *Agricultural Revolution in England* (Cambridge, 1996), and **R. C. Allen,** *Enclosure and the Yeoman: The Agricultural Development of the South Midlands, 1450–1850* (Oxford, 1992). On the consumer revolution, see **M. Berg,** *Luxury and Pleasure in Eighteenth-Century Britain* (Oxford, 2007), and **J. Mokyr,** *The Enlightened Economy: An Economic History of Britain 1700–1800* (New Haven, Conn., 2010).

THE SOCIAL ORDER On the European nobility, see **J. Dewald,** *The European Nobility, 1400–1800,* 2nd ed. (Cambridge, 2004). On the Grand Tour, see **R. Sweet,** *Cities and the Grand Tour: The British in Italy, c. 1620–1820* (Cambridge, 2013). On European cities, see **J. de Vries,** *European Urbanization, 1500–1800* (Cambridge, Mass., 1984). There is no better work on the problem of poverty than **O. Hufton,** *The Poor of Eighteenth-Century France* (Oxford, 1974).

Notes

1. Frederick II, *Forms of Government,* in E. Weber, *The Western Tradition* (Lexington, Mass., 1972), pp. 538, 544.
2. Quoted in R. A. Dorwart, *The Administrative Reforms of Frederick William I of Prussia* (Cambridge, Mass., 1953), p. 36.
3. Quoted in Sidney B. Fay, *The Rise of Brandenburg-Prussia to 1786,* rev. K. Epstein (New York, 1964), p. 92.
4. Quoted in H. Rosenberg, *Bureaucracy, Aristocracy, and Autocracy: The Prussian Experience, 1660–1815* (Cambridge, Mass., 1958), p. 40.
5. Quoted in F. Braudel, *Civilization and Capitalism,* vol. 3 (London, 1984), p. 378.
6. Quoted in ibid., p. 245.
7. Quoted in W. Rybczynski, *Home: A Short History of an Idea* (New York, 1986), p. 105.
8. Quoted in J. Dewald, *The European Nobility, 1400–1800* (Cambridge, 1996), pp. 91–92.
9. Quoted in P. Gay, *Age of Enlightenment* (New York, 1966), p. 87.
10. Quoted in P. Hazard, *The European Mind, 1680–1715* (Cleveland, Ohio, 1963), pp. 6–7.
11. I. Vinogradoff, "Russian Missions to London, 1711–1789: Further Extracts from the Cottrell Papers," *Oxford Slavonic Papers,* New Series (1982), 15: 76.
12. Quoted in J. Kaplow, *The Names of Kings: The Parisian Laboring Poor in the Eighteenth Century* (New York, 1972), p. 134.

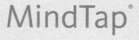 **MindTap®** is a fully online, highly personalized learning experience built upon Cengage Learning content. MindTap combines student learning tools—readings, multimedia, activities, and assessments—into a singular Learning Path that guides students through the course.

A REVOLUTION IN POLITICS: THE ERA OF THE FRENCH REVOLUTION AND NAPOLEON

The storming of the Bastille

CHAPTER OUTLINE AND FOCUS QUESTIONS

The Beginning of the Revolutionary Era: The American Revolution

Q What were the causes and results of the American Revolution, and what impact did it have on Europe?

Background to the French Revolution

Q What were the long-range and immediate causes of the French Revolution?

The French Revolution

Q What were the main events of the French Revolution between 1789 and 1799? What role did each of the following play in the French Revolution: lawyers, peasants, women, the clergy, the Jacobins, the sans-culottes, the French revolutionary army, and the Committee of Public Safety?

The Age of Napoleon

Q Which aspects of the French Revolution did Napoleon preserve, and which did he destroy?

Critical Thinking

Q *In what ways were the French Revolution, the American Revolution, and the seventeenth-century English revolutions alike? In what ways were they different?*

Connections to Today

Q *What similarities and differences do you see between the French Revolution and contemporary revolutions?*

ON THE MORNING OF JULY 14, 1789, a Parisian mob of eight thousand people in search of weapons streamed toward the Bastille (bass-STEEL), a royal armory filled with arms and ammunition. The Bastille was also a state prison, and although it now held only seven prisoners, in the eyes of these angry Parisians, it was a glaring symbol of the government's despotic policies. The armory was defended by the marquis de Launay (mar-KEE duh loh-NAY) and a small garrison of 114 men. The attack began in earnest in the early afternoon, and after three hours of fighting, de Launay and the garrison surrendered. Angered by the loss of ninety-eight of their members, the victorious mob beat de Launay to death, cut off his head, and carried it aloft in triumph through the streets of Paris. When King Louis XVI was told the news of the fall of the Bastille by the duc de La Rochefoucauld-Liancourt (dook duh lah-RUSH-foo-koh-lee-ahnh-KOOR), he exclaimed, "Why, this is a revolt." "No, Sire," replied the duc, "it is a revolution."

Historians have long assumed that the modern history of Europe began with two major transformations—the French Revolution (discussed in this chapter) and the Industrial Revolution (see Chapter 20). Accordingly, the French Revolution has been portrayed as the major turning point in European political and social history, when the institutions of the "old regime" were destroyed and a new order was created based on individual rights, representative institutions, and a concept of loyalty to the nation rather than the monarch. This perspective does have certain limitations, however.

France was only one of a number of areas in the Western world where the assumptions of the old order were challenged. Although some historians have called the upheavals of the eighteenth and early nineteenth

CCI/The Art Archive at Art Resource, NY

centuries a "democratic revolution," it is probably more appropriate to speak of a liberal movement to extend political rights and power to the bourgeoisie in possession of capital—citizens besides the aristocracy who were literate and had become wealthy through capitalist enterprises in trade, industry, and finance. The years preceding and accompanying the French Revolution included attempts at reform and revolt in the North American colonies, Britain, the Dutch Republic, some Swiss cities, and the Austrian Netherlands. The success of the American and French Revolutions makes them the center of attention for this chapter.

Not all of the decadent privileges that characterized the old European regime were destroyed in 1789, however. The revolutionary upheaval of the era, especially in France, did create new liberal and national political ideals, summarized in the French revolutionary slogan, "Liberty, Equality, Fraternity," that transformed France and were then spread to other European countries through the conquests of Napoleon. After Napoleon's defeat, however, the forces of reaction did their best to restore the old order and resist pressures for reform.

The Beginning of the Revolutionary Era: The American Revolution

 FOCUS QUESTION: What were the causes and results of the American Revolution, and what impact did it have on Europe?

At the end of the Seven Years' War in 1763, Great Britain had become the world's greatest colonial power. In North America, Britain controlled Canada and the lands east of the Mississippi (see Map 19.1). After the war, British policy makers sought to obtain new revenues from the thirteen American colonies to pay for expenses the British army had incurred in defending the colonists. An attempt to levy new taxes by a stamp act in 1765, however, led to riots and the law's quick repeal.

The Americans and the British had different conceptions of empire. The British envisioned a single empire with Parliament as the supreme authority throughout. Only Parliament could make laws for all the people in the empire, including the American colonists. The Americans, in contrast, had their own representative assemblies. They believed that neither the king nor Parliament had any right to interfere in their internal affairs and that no tax could be levied without the consent of an assembly whose members actually represented the people.

Crisis followed crisis in the 1770s until 1776, when the colonists decided to declare their independence from the British Empire. On July 4, 1776, the Second Continental Congress approved a declaration of independence written by Thomas Jefferson (1743–1826) (see the box on p. 562). A stirring political document, the declaration affirmed the Enlightenment's

natural rights of "life, liberty, and the pursuit of happiness" and declared the colonies to be "free and independent states absolved from all allegiance to the British crown." The war for American independence had formally begun.

The War for Independence

The war against Great Britain was a great gamble. Britain was a strong European military power with enormous financial resources. The Second Continental Congress had authorized the formation of a Continental Army under George Washington (1732–1799) as commander in chief. Washington, who had had political experience in Virginia and military experience in the French and Indian War, was a good choice for the job. As a southerner, he brought balance to an effort that until that point had been led by New Englanders. Nevertheless, compared with the British forces, the Continental Army consisted of undisciplined amateurs whose terms of service were usually very brief.

Complicating the war effort were the internal divisions within the colonies. Fought for independence, the Revolutionary War was also a civil war, pitting family members and neighbors against one another. The Loyalists, between 15 and 30 percent of the population, questioned whether British policies justified the rebellion. The Loyalists were strongest in New York and Pennsylvania and tended to be wealthy, older, and politically moderate.

Since probably half the colonial population was apathetic at the beginning of the struggle, the patriots, like the Loyalists, constituted a minority of the population. The patriots, however, managed to win over many of the uncommitted, either by persuasion or by force. There were patriots among the rich as well as Loyalists; George Washington owned an estate with 15,000 acres and 150 slaves. But the rich patriots joined an extensive coalition that included farmers and artisans. The wide social spectrum in this coalition had an impact on representative governments in the states after the war. The right to vote was often broadened; Pennsylvania, for example, dropped all property qualifications for voting.

Of great importance to the colonies' cause was the assistance provided by foreign countries that were eager to gain revenge for earlier defeats at the hands of the British. The French supplied arms and money to the rebels from the beginning of the war, and French officers and soldiers also served in Washington's Continental Army. When the British army of General Cornwallis was forced to surrender to a combined American and French army and French fleet under Washington at Yorktown in 1781, the British government decided to call it quits. The Treaty of Paris, signed in 1783, recognized the independence of the American colonies and granted the Americans control of the western territory from the Appalachians to the Mississippi River.

Forming a New Nation

The thirteen American colonies had gained their independence as the United States of America, but a fear of concentrated power and concern for their own interests caused them to have little enthusiasm for establishing a united nation with a strong

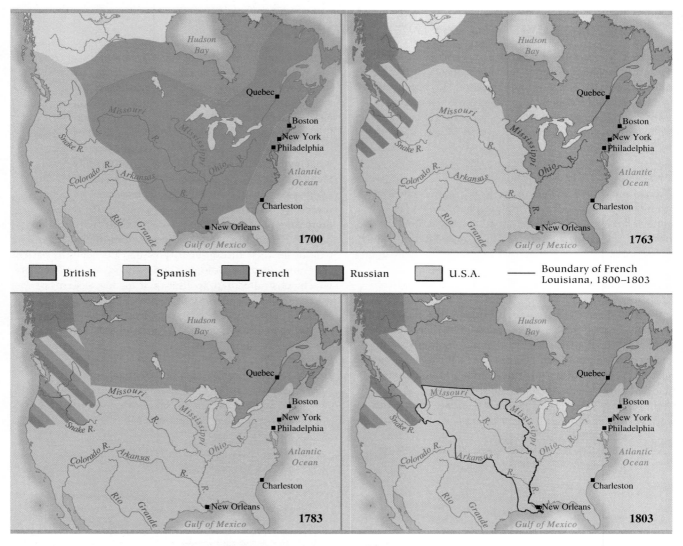

MAP 19.1 North America, 1700–1803. At the end of the Seven Years' War, Britain had gained much territory in eastern North America, but its efforts to obtain new revenues from the American colonies to help pay for the war sparked the American Revolution. The 1803 Louisiana Purchase nearly doubled the size of the United States and spurred westward expansion to the Pacific Ocean.

Q *In what periods was the Mississippi River a national boundary, and why was control of the river important for the United States?*

central government. The Articles of Confederation, ratified in 1781, did little to provide for a strong central government. A movement for a different form of national government soon arose. In the summer of 1787, fifty-five delegates attended a convention in Philadelphia to revise the Articles of Confederation. The convention's delegates—wealthy, politically experienced, well educated—rejected revision and decided to devise a new constitution.

The proposed constitution created a central government distinct from and superior to the governments of the individual states. The national government was given the power to levy taxes, raise a national army, regulate domestic and foreign trade, and create a national currency. The central or federal government was divided into three branches, each with some power

to check the functioning of the others. A president would serve as the chief executive with the power to execute laws, veto the legislature's acts, supervise foreign affairs, and direct military forces. Legislative power was vested in the second branch of government, a bicameral legislature composed of the Senate, elected by the state legislatures, and the House of Representatives, elected directly by the people. The Supreme Court and other courts "as deemed necessary" by Congress served as the third branch of government. They would enforce the Constitution as the "supreme law of the land."

The United States Constitution was approved by the states—by a slim margin—in 1788. Important to its success was a promise to add a bill of rights as the new government's first piece of business. Accordingly, in March 1789, the new Congress

THE ARGUMENT FOR INDEPENDENCE

ON JULY 2, 1776, THE SECOND CONTINENTAL CONGRESS adopted a resolution declaring the independence of the American colonies. Two days later, the delegates approved the Declaration of Independence, which gave the reasons for their action. Its principal author was Thomas Jefferson, who basically restated John Locke's theory of revolution (see Chapter 15).

The Declaration of Independence

When in the course of human events it becomes necessary for one people to dissolve the political bands which have connected them with another, and to assume among the Powers of the earth, the separate and equal station to which the Laws of Nature and of Nature's God entitle them, a decent respect to the opinions of mankind requires that they should declare the causes which impel them to the separation.

We hold these truths to be self-evident, that all men are created equal, that they are endowed by their Creator with certain unalienable Rights, that among these are Life, Liberty and the pursuit of Happiness. That to secure these rights, Governments are instituted among Men, deriving their just powers from the consent of the governed, That whenever any Form of Government becomes destructive of these ends, it is the Right of the People to alter or to abolish it and to institute new Government, laying its foundation on such principles and organizing its powers in such form, as to them shall seem most likely to effect their Safety and Happiness. Prudence, indeed, will dictate that Governments long established should not be changed for light and transient causes; and accordingly all experience has shown, that mankind are more disposed to suffer, while evils are sufferable, than to right themselves by abolishing the forms to which they are accustomed. But when a long train of abuses and usurpations, pursuing invariably the same Object evinces a design to reduce them under absolute Despotism, it is their right, it is their duty, to throw off such Government, and to provide new Guards for their future security.—Such has been the patient sufferance of these Colonies; and such is now the necessity which constrains them to alter their former Systems of government. The history of the present King of Great Britain is a history of repeated injuries and usurpations, all having in direct object the establishment of an absolute Tyranny over these States.

 What influence did John Locke's theory of revolution have on the American Declaration of Independence? How would a member of the British Parliament have responded to this declaration?

Source: S. N. Thorpe, *The Federal and State Constitutions* (Washington, DC, 1909), pp. 3–4.

The Declaration of Independence. The Declaration of Independence, approved on July 4, 1776, by the Second Continental Congress, opened the door to the war for American independence. John Trumbull's famous painting, *The Signing of the Declaration*, shows the members of the committee responsible for the Declaration of Independence (from left to right, John Adams, Roger Sherman, Robert Livingston, Thomas Jefferson, and Benjamin Franklin) standing before John Hancock, president of the Second Continental Congress.

proposed twelve amendments to the Constitution; the ten that were ratified by the states have been known ever since as the Bill of Rights. These guaranteed freedom of religion, speech, press, petition, and assembly, as well as the right to bear arms, protection against unreasonable searches and arrests, trial by jury, due process of law, and protection of property rights. Many of these rights were derived from the natural rights philosophy of the eighteenth-century philosophes, which was popular among the American colonists. Is it any wonder that many European intellectuals saw the American Revolution as the embodiment of the Enlightenment's political dreams?

Impact of the American Revolution on Europe

The year 1789 witnessed two far-reaching events, the beginning of a new United States of America and the eruption of the French Revolution. Was there a connection between the two great revolutions of the late eighteenth century?

There is no doubt that the American Revolution had an important impact on Europeans. Books, newspapers, and magazines provided the newly developing reading public with numerous accounts of American events. To many in Europe, it seemed to portend an era of significant changes, including new arrangements in international politics. The Venetian ambassador to Paris astutely observed in 1783 that "if only the union of the [American] provinces is preserved, it is reasonable to expect that, with the favorable effects of time, and of European arts and sciences, it will become the most formidable power in the world."[1] But the American Revolution also meant far more than that. To many Europeans, it proved that the liberal political ideas of the Enlightenment were not the vapid utterances of intellectuals. The rights of man, ideas of liberty and equality, popular sovereignty, the separation of powers, and freedom of religion, thought, and press were not utopian ideals. The Americans had created a new social contract, embodied it in a written constitution, and made the concepts of liberty and representative government a reality. The premises of the Enlightenment seemed confirmed; a new age and a better world could be achieved. As a Swiss philosophe expressed it, "I am tempted to believe that North America is the country where reason and humanity will develop more rapidly than anywhere else."[2]

Europeans obtained much of their information about America from returning soldiers, especially the hundreds of French officers who had served in the American war. One of them, the aristocratic marquis de Lafayette (mar-KEE duh lah-fay-ET), had volunteered for service in America in order to "strike a blow against England," France's old enemy. Closely associated with George Washington, Lafayette returned to France with ideas of individual liberties and notions of republicanism and popular sovereignty. He became a member of the Society of Thirty, a club composed of people from the Paris salons. These "lovers of liberty" would be influential in the early stages of the French Revolution. The Declaration of the Rights of Man and the Citizen (see "Destruction of the Old Regime" later in this chapter) showed unmistakable signs of the influence of the American Declaration of Independence as well as the American

state constitutions. Yet for all of its obvious impact, the American Revolution proved in the long run to be far less important to Europe than the French Revolution. The French Revolution was more complex, more violent, and far more radical in its attempt to construct both a new political order and a new social order. The French Revolution provided a model of revolution for Europe and much of the rest of the world; to many analysts, it remains the political movement that truly inaugurated the modern political world.

Background to the French Revolution

 FOCUS QUESTION: What were the long-range and immediate causes of the French Revolution?

Although we associate events like the French Revolution with sudden changes, the causes of such events involve long-range problems as well as immediate precipitating forces. **Revolutions**, as has been repeatedly shown, are not necessarily the result of economic collapse and masses of impoverished people hungering for change. In fact, in the fifty years before 1789, France had experienced a period of economic growth due to an expansion of foreign trade and an increase in industrial production, although many people, especially the peasants, failed to share in the prosperity. Thus, the causes of the French Revolution must be found in a multifaceted examination of French society and its problems in the late eighteenth century.

Social Structure of the Old Regime

The long-range or indirect causes of the French Revolution must first be sought in the condition of French society. Before the Revolution, French society was grounded in the inequality of rights or the idea of privilege. During the eighteenth century, the population had increased by forty-four percent from 18 million to 26 million. It was a young country, with 36 percent under the age of twenty, and 40 percent between twenty and forty; and it was divided, as it had been since the Middle Ages, into legal categories known as the three orders or estates.

THE FIRST ESTATE The First Estate consisted of the clergy and numbered about 130,000 people. The church owned approximately 10 percent of the land. Clergy were exempt from the *taille* (TY), France's chief tax, although the church had agreed to pay a "voluntary" contribution every five years to the state. The church was very wealthy; income from church property and other investments produced almost 300 million *livres* annually—half the income of the royal crown. Clergy were also radically divided, since the higher clergy, stemming from aristocratic families, shared the interests of the nobility and lived in palaces and townhouses, while the parish priests were often poor commoners.

THE SECOND ESTATE The Second Estate was the nobility, composed of no more than 350,000 people who nevertheless owned about 25 to 30 percent of the land. Under Louis XV

The Three Estates. This French political cartoon from 1789 reveals a critical view of France's privileged orders. Shown in the cartoon is a naked common man held in chains and being ridden by an aristocrat, a clergyman, and a judge. The message is clear: most ordinary French people (the Third Estate) are suffering horribly as a result of the privileges of the First and Second Estates.

and Louis XVI, the nobility had continued to play an important and even crucial role in French society, holding many of the leading positions in the government, the military, the law courts, and the higher church offices. Nobles also controlled much heavy industry in France, either through investment or by ownership of mining and metallurgical enterprises. The French nobility was also divided. The nobility of the robe derived their status from officeholding, a pathway that had often enabled commoners to attain noble rank. These nobles now dominated the royal law courts and important administrative offices. The nobility of the sword claimed to be descendants of the original medieval nobility. As a group, the nobles sought to expand their privileges at the expense of the monarchy—to defend liberty by resisting the arbitrary actions of monarchy, as some nobles asserted—and to maintain their monopoly over positions in the military, church, and government. In 1781, in reaction to the ambitions of aristocrats newly arrived from the bourgeoisie, the Ségur (say-GOO-uh) Law attempted to limit the sale of military officerships to fourth-generation nobles, thus excluding newly enrolled members of the nobility.

Although there were many poor nobles, on the whole the fortunes of the wealthy aristocrats outstripped those of most others in French society. Generally, the nobles tended to marry within their own ranks, making the nobility a fairly closed group. Although their privileges varied from region to region, the very possession of privileges remained a hallmark of the nobility. Common to all were tax exemptions, especially from the *taille*.

THE THIRD ESTATE The Third Estate, the commoners of society, constituted the overwhelming majority of the French population. They were divided by vast differences in occupation, level of education, and wealth. The peasants, who alone constituted 75 to 80 percent of the total population, were by far the largest segment of the Third Estate. They owned about 35 to 40 percent of the land, although their landholdings varied from area to area and more than half had no or little land on which to survive. The landless peasants were day laborers who increasingly migrated to Paris in search of work; they were the first to suffer in hard times. Serfdom no longer existed on any large scale in France, but French peasants still had obligations to their local landlords that they deeply resented. These relics of feudalism included the payment of fees for the use of village facilities, such as the flour mill, community oven, and winepress, as well as tithes to the clergy. The nobility also maintained the right to hunt on peasants' land.

Another part of the Third Estate consisted of skilled artisans, shopkeepers, and other wage earners in the cities. Although the eighteenth century had been a period of rapid urban growth, 90 percent of French towns had fewer than 10,000 inhabitants; only nine cities had more than 50,000. In the eighteenth century, consumer prices, especially the price of bread, rose faster than wages, causing these urban groups to experience a decline in purchasing power. The economic discontent of this segment of the Third Estate—and often simply their struggle for survival—led them to play an important role in the Revolution, especially in the city of Paris. Insubordination, one observer noted, "has been visible among the people for some years now and above all among craftsmen." The towns and cities were also home to large groups of unskilled and often unemployed workers. One magistrate complained that "misery . . . has thrown into the towns people who overburden them with their uselessness, and who find nothing to do, because there is not enough for the people who live there."[3]

About 8 percent, or 2.3 million people, constituted the bourgeoisie or middle class, who owned about 20 to 25 percent of the land. This group included the merchants, industrialists, and bankers who controlled the resources of trade, manufacturing, and finance and benefited from the economic prosperity after 1730. The bourgeoisie also included professional people—lawyers, holders of public offices, doctors, and writers. Many members of the bourgeoisie sought security and status through the purchase of land. They had their own set of grievances because they were often excluded from the social and political privileges monopolized by the nobles. These resentments of the middle class were for a long time assumed to be a major cause of the French Revolution. But although these tensions existed, the situation was not a simple case of a unified bourgeoisie against a unified noble class. As is evident, neither group was monolithic. Nobles were separated by vast differences in wealth and importance. A similar gulf separated wealthy financiers from local lawyers in French provincial towns.

At the upper levels of society, remarkable similarities existed between the wealthier bourgeoisie and the nobility. It was still possible for wealthy middle-class individuals to join the ranks of the nobility by obtaining public offices and entering the nobility of the robe. In fact, between 1774 and 1789, the not insignificant number of 2,500 wealthy bourgeoisie entered the ranks of the nobility. Over the century as a whole, 6,500 new noble families were created. In addition, as we saw in Chapter 18, the aristocrats were also engaging in capitalist activities on their landed estates, such as mining, metallurgy, and glassmaking, and were even investing in foreign trade. Viewed in terms of economic function, many members of the bourgeoisie and nobility formed a single class. Finally, the new and critical ideas of the Enlightenment proved attractive to both aristocrats and bourgeoisie. Members of both groups shared a common world of liberal political thought. The old view that the French Revolution was the result of the conflict between two rigid orders, the bourgeoisie and the nobility, has been enlarged and revised. Both aristocratic and bourgeois elites, long accustomed to a new socioeconomic reality based on wealth and economic achievement, were increasingly frustrated by a monarchical system resting on privileges and on an old and rigid social order based on the concept of estates. The opposition of these elites to the **old order** ultimately led them to take drastic action against the monarchical regime, although they soon split over the question of how far to proceed in eliminating traditional privileges. In a real sense, the Revolution had its origins in political grievances.

Other Problems Facing the French Monarchy

Although the long-range causes of the French Revolution can thus be found in part in the growing frustration at the monarchy's inability to deal with new social realities and problems, other factors were also present. The failure of the French monarchy was exacerbated by specific problems in the 1780s. Although the country had enjoyed fifty years of growth overall, periodic economic crises still occurred. Bad harvests in 1787 and 1788 and the beginnings of a manufacturing depression resulted in food shortages, rising prices for food and other necessities, and unemployment in the cities. The number of poor, estimated by some at almost one-third of the population, reached crisis proportions on the eve of the Revolution. An English traveler noted the misery of the poor in the countryside: "All the country girls and women are without shoes or stockings; and the plowmen at their work have neither sabots nor stockings to their feet. This is a poverty that strikes at the root of national prosperity."[4]

IDEAS OF THE PHILOSOPHES Existing privileges as well as social and political institutions were also coming under increasing criticism. Although the philosophes did not advocate revolution, their ideas circulated widely among the literate bourgeois and noble elites of France. The actual influence of the ideas of the philosophes is difficult to prove, but once the Revolution began, the revolutionary leaders frequently quoted Enlightenment writers, especially Rousseau.

FAILURE TO MAKE REFORMS The French parlements often frustrated efforts at reform. These thirteen law courts, which were responsible for registering royal decrees, could block royal edicts by not registering them. Although Louis XIV had forced them into submission, the parlements had gained new strength in the eighteenth century as they and their noble judges assumed the role of defenders of "liberty" against the arbitrary power of the monarchy. As noble defenders, however, they often pushed their own interests as well, especially by blocking new taxes. This last point reminds us that one of the fundamental problems facing the monarchy was financial.

FINANCIAL CRISIS The immediate cause of the French Revolution was the near collapse of government finances. France experienced a depression from 1778 to 1787 as a result of a loss of overseas markets and overproduction. Prices of grain and wine fell by forty and fifty percent. Peasants faced increasing uncertainty as rent prices remained high due to a rapidly growing population. Poor harvests in 1788 and 1789 sent prices of wheat and rye soaring—leaving many desperate. At a time when France was experiencing economic crises, the government was drastically short of money. Yet French governmental expenditures continued to grow due to costly wars and royal extravagance. The government responded by borrowing. Poor taxation policy contributed to the high debt, with most of the monarchy's funds coming from the peasantry. Unlike Britain, where the Bank of England financed the borrowing of money at low interest rates, France had no central bank, and instead relied on private loans. By 1788, the interest on the debt alone constituted half of government spending. Total debt had reached 4 billion livres (roughly $40 billion). Financial lenders, fearful they would never be repaid, were refusing to lend additional amounts.

The king's finance ministry wrestled with the problem but met with resistance. The parlements refused to assist in fiscal reform, fearing that it would involve higher taxes. In 1786, Charles de Calonne (SHAHRL duh ka-LUNN), the controller general of finance, finding himself unable to borrow any more, proposed a complete revamping of the fiscal and administrative system of the state. To gain support, Calonne convened an "assembly of notables" early in 1787. This gathering of nobles, prelates, and magistrates refused to cooperate, and the government's attempt to go it alone brought further disaster. On the verge of a complete financial collapse, the government was finally forced to call a meeting of the Estates-General, the French parliamentary body that had not met since 1614. By calling the Estates-General, the government was virtually admitting that the consent of the nation was required to raise taxes.

The French Revolution

FOCUS QUESTIONS: What were the main events of the French Revolution between 1789 and 1799? What role did each of the following play in the French Revolution: lawyers, peasants, women, the clergy, the Jacobins, the sans-culottes, the French revolutionary army, and the Committee of Public Safety?

In summoning the Estates-General, the government was merely looking for a way to solve the immediate financial crisis. The monarchy had no wish for a major reform of the government, nor did the delegates who arrived at Versailles come with plans for the revolutionary changes that ultimately emerged. Yet over the next years, through the interplay of the deputies meeting in various legislative assemblies, the common people in the streets of Paris and other cities, and the peasants in the countryside, much of the old regime would be destroyed, and Europe would have a new model for political and social change.

From Estates-General to a National Assembly

The Estates-General consisted of representatives from the three orders of French society. In the elections for the Estates-General, the government had ruled that the Third Estate should get double representation (it did, after all, constitute 97 percent of the population). Consequently, while both the First Estate (the clergy) and the Second (the nobility) had about 300 delegates each, the commoners had almost 600 representatives. Two-thirds of the latter were people with legal training, and three-fourths were from towns with more than two thousand inhabitants, giving the Third Estate a particularly strong legal and urban representation. Of the 282 representatives of the nobility, about 90 were liberal minded, urban oriented, and interested in the enlightened ideas of the century; half of them were under forty years of age. The activists of the Third Estate and the reform-minded individuals among the First and Second Estates had common ties in their youth, urban background, and hostility to privilege. The *cahiers de doléances* (ka-YAY duh doh-lay-AHNSS), or statements of local grievances, which were drafted throughout France during the elections to the Estates-General, advocated a regular constitutional government that would abolish the fiscal privileges of the church and nobility as the major way to regenerate the country.

The Estates-General opened at Versailles on May 5, 1789. It was divided from the start over the question of whether voting should be by order or by head (each delegate having one vote). The Parlement of Paris, consisting of nobles of the robe, had advocated voting by order according to the form used in 1614. Each order would vote separately; each would have veto power over the other two, thus guaranteeing aristocratic control over reforms. But opposition to the Parlement's proposal arose from a group of reformers calling themselves patriots or "lovers of liberty." Although they claimed to represent the nation, they consisted primarily of bourgeoisie and nobles. One group of patriots known as the Society of Thirty drew most of its members from the salons of Paris. The American Revolution had directly influenced some of this largely noble group, but all had been affected by the ideas of the Enlightenment and favored reforms made in the light of reason and utility.

THE NATIONAL ASSEMBLY The failure of the government to assume the leadership at the opening of the Estates-General created an opportunity for the Third Estate to push its demands for voting by head. Since it had double representation, with the assistance of liberal nobles and clerics, it could turn the three estates into a single-chamber legislature that would reform France in its own way. One representative, the Abbé Sieyès (ab-BAY syay-YESS), issued a pamphlet in which he asked, "What is the Third Estate? Everything. What has it been thus far in the political order? Nothing. What does it demand? To become something." Sieyès's sentiment, however, was not representative of the general feeling in 1789. Most delegates still wanted to make changes within a framework of respect for the authority of the king; revival or reform did not mean the overthrow of traditional institutions. When the First Estate declared in favor of voting by order, the Third Estate felt compelled to respond in a significant fashion. On June 17, 1789, the Third Estate voted to constitute itself a "National Assembly" and decided to draw up a constitution. Three days later, on June 20, the deputies of the Third Estate arrived at their meeting place only to find the doors locked; thereupon they moved to a nearby indoor tennis court and swore (in what has come to be known as the Tennis Court Oath) that they would continue to meet until they had produced a French constitution. These actions of June 17 and June 20 constituted the first step in the French Revolution, since the Third Estate had no legal right to act as the National Assembly. This revolution, largely the work of the lawyers of the Third Estate, was soon in jeopardy, however, as the king sided with the First Estate and threatened to dissolve the Estates-General. Louis XVI now prepared to use force. The revolution of the lawyers appeared doomed.

INTERVENTION OF THE COMMON PEOPLE The common people, however, in a series of urban and rural uprisings in July and August 1789, saved the Third Estate from the king's attempt to stop the Revolution. From now on, the common people would be mobilized by both revolutionary and counter-revolutionary politicians and used to support their interests. The common people had their own interests as well and would use the name of the Third Estate to wage a war on the rich, claiming that the aristocrats were plotting to destroy the Estates-General and retain their privileges. This war was not what the deputies of the Third Estate had planned.

The most famous of the urban risings was the fall of the Bastille (see the box on p. 568). The king's attempt to take defensive measures by increasing the number of troops at the arsenals in Paris and along the roads to Versailles served not to intimidate but rather to inflame public opinion. Increased mob activity in Paris led Parisian leaders to form the so-called Permanent Committee to keep order. Needing arms, they organized a popular force to capture the Invalides, a royal armory,

The Tennis Court Oath. Finding themselves locked out of their regular meeting place on June 20, 1789, the deputies of the Third Estate met instead in the nearby tennis courts of the Jeu de Paume and committed themselves to continue to meet until they established a new constitution for France. In this painting, the neoclassical artist Jacques-Louis David presents a dramatic rendering of the Tennis Court Oath.

and on July 14 attacked the Bastille, another royal armory. The Bastille had also been a state prison but now held only seven prisoners (five forgers and two insane persons). There were few weapons there except those in the hands of the small group of defenders. The Bastille was an imposing fortress with eight towers connected by 9-foot-thick walls. It was easily defended, but its commander, the marquis de Launay, was more inclined to negotiate. Although fighting erupted, de Launay refused to open fire with his cannon, and the garrison soon surrendered. In the minds of the Parisians who fought there, the fall of the Bastille was a great victory, and it quickly became a popular symbol of triumph over despotism.

Paris was abandoned to the insurgents, and Louis XVI was soon informed that the royal troops were unreliable. Louis's acceptance of that reality signaled the collapse of royal authority; the king could no longer enforce his will. Louis then confirmed the appointment of the marquis de Lafayette as commander of a newly created citizens' militia known as the National Guard.

At the same time, independently of what was going on in Paris, popular revolutions broke out in numerous cities. In Nantes, permanent committees and national guards were created to maintain order after crowds had seized the chief citadels. This collapse of royal authority in the cities was paralleled by peasant revolutions in the countryside.

PEASANT REBELLIONS AND THE GREAT FEAR A growing resentment of the entire seigneurial system, with its fees and obligations, greatly exacerbated by the economic and fiscal activities of the great estate holders—whether noble or bourgeois—in the difficult decade of the 1780s, created the conditions for a popular uprising. The fall of the Bastille and the king's apparent capitulation to the demands of the Third Estate now encouraged peasants to take matters into their own hands. From July 19 to August 3, peasant rebellions occurred in five major areas of France. Patterns varied. In some places,

peasants simply forced their lay and ecclesiastical lords to renounce dues and tithes; elsewhere they burned charters listing their obligations. The peasants were not acting in blind fury; they knew what they were doing. Many also believed that the king supported their actions. As a contemporary chronicler wrote, "For several weeks, news went from village to village. They announced that the Estates-General was going to abolish tithes, quitrents and dues, that the King agreed but that the peasants had to support the public authorities by going themselves to demand the destruction of titles."[5]

The agrarian revolts served as a backdrop to the Great Fear, a vast panic that spread like wildfire through France between July 20 and August 6. Fear of invasion by foreign troops, aided by a supposed aristocratic plot, encouraged the formation of more citizens' militias and permanent committees. The greatest impact of the agrarian revolts and the Great Fear was on the National Assembly meeting in Versailles. We will now examine its attempt to reform France.

Destruction of the Old Regime

One of the first acts of the National Assembly (also called the Constituent Assembly because from 1789 to 1791 it was writing a new constitution) was to destroy the relics of feudalism or aristocratic privileges. To some deputies, this measure was necessary to calm the peasants and restore order in the countryside, although many urban bourgeois were willing to abolish feudalism as a matter of principle. On the night of August 4, 1789, the National Assembly in an astonishing session voted to abolish seigneurial rights as well as the fiscal privileges of nobles, clergy, towns, and provinces.

THE DECLARATION OF THE RIGHTS OF MAN AND THE CITIZEN On August 26, the assembly provided the ideological foundation for its actions and an educational device for the

THE FALL OF THE BASTILLE

ON JULY 14, 1789, PARISIAN CROWDS IN SEARCH OF weapons attacked and captured the royal armory known as the Bastille. It had also been a state prison, and its fall marked the triumph of "liberty" over despotism. This intervention of the Parisian populace saved the Third Estate from Louis XVI's attempted counterrevolution.

A Parisian Newspaper Account of the Fall of the Bastille

First, the people tried to enter this fortress by the rue St.-Antoine, this fortress, which no one has even penetrated against the wishes of this frightful despotism and where the monster still resided. The treacherous governor had put out a flag of peace. So a confident advance was made; a detachment of French Guards, with perhaps five to six thousand armed bourgeois, penetrated the Bastille's outer courtyards, but as soon as some six hundred persons had passed over the first drawbridge, the bridge was raised and artillery fire mowed down several French Guards and some soldiers; the cannon fired on the town, and the people took fright; a large number of individuals were killed or wounded; but then they rallied and took shelter from the fire. . . . Meanwhile, they tried to locate some cannon; they attacked from the water's edge through the gardens of the arsenal, and from there made an orderly siege; they advanced from various directions, beneath a ceaseless round of fire. It was a terrible scene. . . . The fighting grew steadily more intense; the citizens had become hardened to the fire; from all directions they clambered onto the roofs or broke into the rooms; as soon as an enemy appeared among the turrets on the tower, he was fixed in the sights of a hundred guns and mown down in an instant; meanwhile cannon fire was hurriedly directed against the second drawbridge, which it pierced, breaking the chains;

in vain did the cannon on the tower reply, for most people were sheltered from it; the fury was at its height; people bravely faced death and every danger; women, in their eagerness, helped us to the utmost; even the children, after the discharge of fire from the fortress, ran here and there picking up the bullets and shot; [and so the Bastille fell and the governor, de Launay, was captured]. . . . Serene and blessed liberty, for the first time, has at last been introduced into this abode of horrors, this frightful refuge of monstrous despotism and its crimes.

Meanwhile, they get ready to march; they leave amidst an enormous crowd; the applause, the outbursts of joy, the insults, the oaths hurled at the treacherous prisoners of war; everything is confused; cries of vengeance and of pleasure issue from every heart; the conquerors, glorious and covered in honor, carry their arms and the spoils of the conquered, the flags of victory, the militia mingling with the soldiers of the fatherland, the victory laurels offered them from every side, all this created a frightening and splendid spectacle. On arriving at the square, the people, anxious to avenge themselves, allowed neither de Launay nor the other officers to reach the place of trial; they seized them from the hands of their conquerors, and trampled them underfoot one after the other. De Launay was struck by a thousand blows, his head was cut off and hoisted on the end of a pike with blood streaming down all sides. . . . This glorious day must amaze our enemies, and finally usher in for us the triumph of justice and liberty. In the evening, there were celebrations.

 Why did the fall of the Bastille come to mark the triumph of French "liberty" over despotism? Do you think this Parisian newspaper account might be biased? Why or why not?

Source: J. Gilchrist and W. J. Murray, eds., *The Press in the French Revolution: A Selection of Documents Taken from the Press of the Revolution for the Years 1789–1794* (London: Ginn & Company, 1971).

nation by adopting the Declaration of the Rights of Man and the Citizen (see "Opposing Viewpoints" on p. 570). This charter of basic liberties reflected the ideas of the major philosophes of the French Enlightenment and also owed much to the American Declaration of Independence and American state constitutions. The declaration began with a ringing affirmation of "the natural and imprescriptible rights of man" to "liberty, property, security, and resistance to oppression." It went on to affirm the destruction of aristocratic privileges by proclaiming an end to exemptions from taxation, freedom and equal rights for all men, and access to public office based on talent. The monarchy was restricted, and all citizens were to have the right to take part in the legislative process. Freedom of speech and press were coupled with the outlawing of arbitrary arrests.

The declaration also raised another important issue. Did the proclamation's ideal of equal rights for "all men" include women? Many deputies insisted that it did, at least in terms of civil liberties, provided that, as one said, "women do not aspire to exercise political rights and functions." Olympe de Gouges (oh-LAMP duh GOOZH), a playwright and pamphleteer, refused to accept this exclusion of women from political rights. Echoing the words of the official declaration, she penned a Declaration of the Rights of Woman and the Female Citizen in which she insisted that women should have the same rights as men (see "Opposing Viewpoints" on p. 570). The National Assembly ignored her demands.

THE WOMEN'S MARCH TO VERSAILLES In the meantime, Louis XVI had remained inactive at Versailles. He did refuse,

Revolution and Revolt in France and China

FRANCE AND CHINA EXPERIENCED REVOLUTIONARY upheaval at the end of the eighteenth century and well into the nineteenth. In both countries, common people often played an important role. At the top is a scene from the storming of the Bastille in Paris in 1789. This early action by the people of Paris ultimately led to the overthrow of the French monarchy. At the bottom is a scene from one of the struggles during the Taiping Rebellion, a major peasant revolt in the mid-nineteenth century in China. An imperial Chinese army is shown recapturing the city of Nanjing from Taiping rebels in 1864.

Q *What role did common people play in revolutionary upheavals in France and China in the eighteenth and nineteenth centuries?*

however, to promulgate the decrees on the abolition of feudalism and the declaration of rights, but an unexpected turn of events soon forced the king to change his mind. On October 5, after marching to the Hôtel de Ville, the city hall, to demand bread, crowds of Parisian women numbering in the thousands set off for Versailles, 12 miles away, to confront the king and the National Assembly. One eyewitness was amazed at the sight of "detachments of women coming up from every direction, armed with broomsticks, lances, pitchforks, swords, pistols and muskets." After meeting with a delegation of these women, who tearfully described how their children were starving for lack of bread, Louis XVI promised them grain supplies for Paris, thinking that this would end the protest. But the women's action had forced the Paris National Guard under Lafayette to follow their lead and march to Versailles. The crowd now insisted that the royal family return to Paris. On October 6, the king complied. As a goodwill gesture, he brought along wagonloads of flour from the palace stores. All were escorted by women armed with pikes (some of which held the severed heads of the king's guards), singing, "We are bringing back the baker, the baker's wife, and the baker's boy" (the king, queen, and their son). The king now accepted the National Assembly's decrees; it was neither the first nor the last occasion when Parisian crowds would affect national politics. The king was virtually a prisoner in Paris, and the National Assembly, now meeting in Paris, would also feel the influence of Parisian insurrectionary politics.

THE CATHOLIC CHURCH The Catholic Church was viewed as an important pillar of the old order, and it soon also felt the impact of reform. Because of the need for money, most of the lands of the church were confiscated, and *assignats* (ah-see-NYAH), a form of paper money, were issued based on the collateral of the newly nationalized church property. The church was also secularized. In July 1790, the new Civil Constitution of the Clergy was put into effect. Both bishops and priests of the Catholic Church were to be elected by the people and paid by the state. All clergy were also required to swear an oath of allegiance to the Civil Constitution. Since the pope forbade it, only 54 percent of the French parish clergy took the oath, and the majority of bishops refused. This was a critical development because the Catholic Church, still an important institution in the life of the French people, now became an enemy of the Revolution. The Civil Constitution has often been viewed as a serious tactical blunder on the part of the National Assembly, for by arousing the opposition of the church, it gave the counter-revolution a popular base from which to operate.

A NEW CONSTITUTION By 1791, the National Assembly had completed a new constitution that established a limited constitutional monarchy. There was still a monarch (now called "king of the French"), but he enjoyed few powers not subject to review by the new Legislative Assembly. The assembly, in which sovereign power was vested, was to sit for two years and consist of 745 representatives chosen by an indirect system of election that preserved power in the hands of the more affluent members of society. A distinction was drawn between active

The Natural Rights of the French People: Two Views

ONE OF THE IMPORTANT DOCUMENTS OF THE French Revolution, the Declaration of the Rights of Man and the Citizen, was adopted in August 1789 by the National Assembly. The declaration affirmed that "men are born and remain free and equal in rights," that government must protect these natural rights, and that political power is derived from the people. Olympe de Gouges (the pen name used by Marie Gouze) was a butcher's daughter who wrote plays and pamphlets. She argued that the Declaration of the Rights of Man and the Citizen did not apply to women and composed her own Declaration of the Rights of Woman and the Female Citizen in 1791.

Declaration of the Rights of Man and the Citizen

The representatives of the French people, organized as a national assembly, considering that ignorance, neglect, and scorn of the rights of man are the sole causes of public misfortunes and of corruption of governments, have resolved to display in a solemn declaration the natural, inalienable, and sacred rights of man, so that this declaration, constantly in the presence of all members of society, will continually remind them of their rights and their duties. . . . Consequently, the National Assembly recognizes and declares, in the presence and under the auspices of the Supreme Being, the following rights of man and citizen:

1. Men are born and remain free and equal in rights; social distinctions can be established only for the common benefit.
2. The aim of every political association is the conservation of the natural and imprescriptible rights of man; these rights are liberty, property, security, and resistance to oppression.
3. The source of all sovereignty is located in essence in the nation; no body, no individual can exercise authority which does not emanate from it expressly.
4. Liberty consists in being able to do anything that does not harm another person. . . .
6. The law is the expression of the general will; all citizens have the right to concur personally or through their representatives in its formation; it must be the same for all, whether it protects or punishes. All citizens being equal in its eyes are equally admissible to all honors, positions, and public employments, according to their capabilities and without other distinctions than those of their virtues and talents.
7. No man can be accused, arrested, or detained except in cases determined by the law, and according to the forms which it has prescribed. . . .
10. No one may be disturbed because of his opinions, even religious, provided that their public demonstration does not disturb the public order established by law.
11. The free communication of thoughts and opinions is one of the most precious rights of man: every citizen can therefore freely speak, write, and print. . . .
12. The guaranteeing of the rights of man and citizen necessitates a public force; this force is therefore instituted for the advantage of all, and not for the private use of those to whom it is entrusted. . . .
16. Any society in which guarantees of rights are not assured nor the separation of powers determined has no constitution.
17. Property being an inviolable and sacred right, no one may be deprived of it unless public necessity, legally determined, clearly requires such action, and then only on condition of a just and prior indemnity.

The Women's March on Versailles. On October 5, 1789, thousands of Parisian women marched to Versailles to confront King Louis XVI and to demand bread for their starving children. This contemporary print shows a group of dedicated marchers returning from Versailles with the King and his guard's heads on pikes.

Hulton Archive/Getty Images

Declaration of the Rights of Woman and the Female Citizen

Mothers, daughters, sisters, female representatives of the nation ask to be constituted as a national assembly. Considering that ignorance, neglect, or contempt for the rights of woman are the sole causes of public misfortunes and governmental corruption, they have resolved to set forth in a solemn declaration the natural, inalienable, and sacred rights of woman . . .

In consequence, the sex that is superior in beauty as in courage, needed maternal sufferings, recognizes and declares, in the presence and under the auspices of the Supreme Being, the following rights of woman and of the citizeness.

1. Woman is born free and remains equal to man in rights. Social distinctions may be based only on common utility.
2. The purpose of all political association is the preservation of the natural and imprescriptible rights of woman and man. These rights are liberty, property, security, and especially resistance to oppression.
3. The principle of all sovereignty rests essentially in the nation, which is but the reuniting of woman and man; no body and no individual may exercise authority which does not emanate expressly from the nation.
4. Liberty and justice consist in restoring all that belongs to another; hence, the exercise of the natural rights of woman has no other limits than those that the perpetual tyranny of man opposed to them; these limits must be reformed according to the laws of nature and reason. . . .
6. The law should be the expression of the general will; all citizenesses and citizens should take part, in person or by their representatives, in its formation. It must be the same for everyone. All citizenesses and citizens, being equal in its eyes, should be equally admissible to all public dignities, offices, and employments, according to their ability, with no other distinction than that of their virtues and talents.
7. No woman is exempted; she is indicted, arrested, and detained in the cases determined by law. Women like men obey this rigorous law. . . .
10. No one should be disturbed for his fundamental opinions; woman has the right to mount the scaffold; so she should have the right equally to mount the tribune, provided that these manifestations do not trouble public order as established by law.
11. The free communication of thought and opinions is one of the most precious rights of woman, since this liberty assures the recognition of children by their fathers. . . .
12. The safeguard of the rights of woman and citizeness requires public powers. These powers are instituted for the advantage of all, and not for the private benefit of those to whom they are entrusted. . . .
16. Any society in which the guaranteee of rights is not assured or the separation of powers not settled has no constitution. The constitution is null and void if the majority of individuals composing the nation has not cooperated in its drafting.
17. Property belongs to both sexes whether united or separate; it is for each of them an inviolable and sacred right, . . .

Q *What "natural rights" does the first document proclaim? To what extent was this document influenced by the writings of the philosophes? What rights for women does the second document enunciate? Given the nature and scope of the arguments in favor of natural rights and women's rights in these two documents, what key effects on European society would you attribute to the French Revolution?*

Sources: P. H. Beik, *The French Revolution* (New York: Walker & Co., 1970); Lynn Hunt, trans., *The French Revolution and Human Rights: A Brief Documentary History* (Boston: Beford/St. Martins, 1996), pp. 124–126.

and passive citizens. Although all had the same civil rights, only active citizens (men over the age of twenty-five paying taxes equivalent in value to three days' unskilled labor) could vote. The active citizens probably numbered 4.3 million in 1790. These citizens did not elect the members of the Legislative Assembly directly but voted for electors (men paying taxes equal in value to ten days' labor). This relatively small group of 50,000 electors chose the deputies. To qualify as a deputy, one had to pay at least a "silver mark" in taxes, an amount equivalent to fifty-four days' labor.

The National Assembly also undertook an administrative restructuring of France. In 1789, it abolished all the old local and provincial divisions and divided France into eighty-three departments, roughly equal in size and population. Departments were in turn divided into districts and communes, all supervised by elected councils and officials who oversaw financial, administrative, judicial, and ecclesiastical institutions within their territories. Although both bourgeois and aristocrats were eligible for offices based on property qualifications, few nobles were elected, leaving local and departmental governments in the hands of the bourgeoisie, especially lawyers of various types.

OPPOSITION FROM WITHIN By 1791, France had moved into a vast reordering of the old regime that had been achieved by a revolutionary consensus that was largely the work of the wealthier members of the bourgeoisie. By mid–1791, however, this consensus faced growing opposition from clerics angered by the Civil Constitution of the Clergy, lower classes hurt by the rise in the cost of living resulting from the inflation of the assignats, peasants who remained opposed to dues that had still not been abandoned, and political clubs offering more radical solutions to the nation's problems. Recent scholarship has placed a greater emphasis on the proliferation of political

RESPONSE TO THE KING'S FLIGHT TO VARENNES

FOLLOWING TWO YEARS OF ARDUOUS DELIBERATIONS, the National Assembly was completing a new constitution before handing over the reigns of power to the king and the Legislative Assembly. The king, however, demonstrated his unwillingness to rule as a constitutional monarch and deserted his people. The response by the people of Paris is described by well-known journalist Louis-Maris Prudhomme in his newspaper.

Response to the King's Flight to Varennes

Louis-Marie Prudhomme, *Révolutions de Paris* (1791)

It was not until ten o'clock in the morning that the municipal government announced, by firing a cannon thrice, the unexpected event of the day. But for three hours the news had already been passing from mouth to mouth and was circulating in all quarters of the city. During these three hours many outrages might have been committed. The king had gone. This news produced a moment of anxiety, and everybody ran in a crowd to the palace of the Tuileries to see if it were true; but every one turned almost immediately to the hall where the National Assembly met, declaring that their king was in there and that Louis XVI might go where he please.

Then the people became curious to visit the apartments vacated by the royal family; they traversed them all, and we questioned the sentinels we found there, "Where, and how, could he have escaped? How could this fat royal person, who complained of the meanness of his lodging, manage to make himself invisible to the sentries, –he whose girth could stop up any passage?" The soldiers of the guard had nothing to say to this. . . .

Far from being "famished for a glimpse of the king," the people proved, by the way in which they took the escape of Louis XVI, that they were sick of the throne and tired of paying for it. If they had known, moreover, that Louis XVI, in his message, which was just then being read in the National Assembly, complained "that he had not been able to find in the palace of the Tuileries the most simple conveniences of life," the people might have been roused to some excess; but they knew their own strength and did not permit themselves any of those little exhibitions of vengeance which are natural to irritated weakness.

They contented themselves with making sport, in their own way, of royalty and of the man who was invested with it. The portrait of the king was taken down from its place of honor and hung on the door. A fruit woman took possession of Antoinette's bed and used it to display her cherries, saying, "It's the nation's turn now to be comfortable." A young girl refused to let them put the queen's bonnet on her head and trampled it with indignation and contempt.

 What kinds of responses did the people of Paris have to the king's flight?

Source: J. H. Robinson, *Readings in European History* (New York: Ginn & Company, 1906), pp. 428–430.

clubs as a primary source of political instability during the revolution. The political clubs grew out of informal gatherings in the coffee houses and public spaces that had accompanied the elections to the Estates General. The most famous were the Jacobins (JAK-uh-binz), who first emerged as a gathering of more radical deputies at the beginning of the Revolution, especially during the events of the night of August 4, 1789. After October 1789, they occupied the former Jacobin convent in Paris. Jacobin clubs also formed in the provinces, where they served primarily as discussion groups. Eventually, they joined together in an extensive correspondence network and by spring 1790 were seeking affiliation with the Parisian club. One year later, there were nine hundred Jacobin clubs in France associated with the Parisian center. Members were usually the elite of their local societies, but they also included artisans and tradespeople.

In addition, by mid-1791, the government was still facing severe financial difficulties due to massive tax evasion. Despite all of their problems, however, the bourgeois politicians in charge remained relatively unified on the basis of their trust in the king. But Louis XVI disastrously undercut them. Quite upset with the whole turn of revolutionary events, he sought to flee France in June 1791 and almost succeeded. Louis XVI, however, stopped for several unplanned rests to have his meals prepared and missed his military escort. Once recognized in Varennes, he could have escaped, but while waiting for a larger military escort, the National Guardsmen and members of the National Assembly arrived instead and brought him back to Paris. The flight to Varennes shattered the illusion of a loyal king (see box above). Though radicals called for the king to be deposed, the members of the National Assembly, fearful of the popular forces in Paris calling for a republic, chose to ignore the king's flight and pretended that he had been kidnapped. In this unsettled situation, with a discredited and seemingly disloyal monarch, the new Legislative Assembly held its first session in October 1791.

Because the National Assembly had passed a "self-denying ordinance" that prohibited the reelection of its members, the composition of the Legislative Assembly turned out to be quite different from that of the National Assembly. The clerics and nobles were largely gone. Most of the representatives were men of property; many were lawyers. Although lacking national reputations, most had gained experience in the new revolutionary politics and prominence in their local areas through the National Guard, the Jacobin clubs, and the many elective offices spawned by the administrative reordering of France. The king made what seemed to be a genuine effort to work with the new Legislative Assembly, but France's relations with the rest of Europe soon led to Louis's downfall.

OPPOSITION FROM ABROAD By this time, most ultra royalists had emigrated, including the Count d'Artois, the king's younger brother, and the Count de Provence (later Louis XVIII). In October 1791, the Legislative Assembly ordered the émigré nobles to return to France or face the loss of their property and be legally classified as traitors. Louis XVI vetoed this law, raising doubts about his willingness to support the new constitution. Meanwhile, some European monarchs had become concerned about the French example and feared that revolution would spread to their countries. On August 27, 1791, Emperor Leopold II of Austria and King Frederick William II of Prussia had issued the Declaration of Pillnitz, which invited other European monarchs to take "the most effectual means . . . to put the king of France in a state to strengthen, in the most perfect liberty, the bases of a monarchical government equally becoming to the rights of sovereigns and to the well-being of the French Nation."[6] European monarchs were too suspicious of each other to undertake such a plan; however, an increasing number of monarchs openly supported the French émigrés, especially in the Rhineland where most émigrés had fled. In January 1791, the Legislative Assembly sent an ultimatum to Austria, demanding that the Holy Roman emperor, Leopold II, expel all French émigrés. The emperor refused, and the Legislative Assembly declared war on Austria on April 20, 1792. Why take such a step in view of its obvious dangers? Many people in France wanted war. Reactionaries hoped that a preoccupation with war would cool off the Revolution; French defeat, which seemed likely in view of the army's disintegration, might even lead to the restoration of the old regime. Leftists hoped that war would consolidate the Revolution at home and spread it to all of Europe.

The French fared badly in the initial fighting. A French army invaded the Austrian Netherlands (Belgium) but was routed, and Paris now feared invasion. In fact, if the Austrians and Prussians had cooperated, they might have seized Paris in May or June. Alarmed by the turn of events, the Legislative Assembly called for 20,000 National Guardsmen from the provinces to come and defend Paris. One group came from Marseilles singing a rousing war song, soon known as the "Marseillaise," that three years later became the French national anthem:

> Let's go, children of the fatherland
> The day of glory has arrived.
> Against us, is tyranny
> The bloody flag is raised.
> The bloody flag is raised.
> Do you hear in the countryside
> The roar of their fierce soldiers?
> They come right into our arms
> To slaughter your sons
> And your companions.
> To arm, citizens!
> Form up your battalions!
> Let us march, let us march!
> That their impure blood will water our fields.[7]

As fears of invasion grew, a frantic search for scapegoats began; as one observer noted, "Everywhere you hear the cry that the king is betraying us, the generals are betraying us, that nobody is to be trusted; . . . that Paris will be taken in six weeks by the Austrians. . . . We are on a volcano ready to spout flames."[8] Defeats in war coupled with economic shortages in the spring reinvigorated popular groups that had been dormant since the previous summer and led to renewed political demonstrations, especially against the king. Radical Parisian political groups, declaring themselves an insurrectionary commune, organized a mob attack on the royal palace and Legislative Assembly in August 1792, took the king captive, and forced the Legislative Assembly to suspend the monarchy and call for a national convention, chosen on the basis of universal male suffrage, to decide on the future form of government. The French Revolution was about to enter a more radical stage as power passed from the assembly to the new Paris Commune, composed of many who proudly called themselves the **sans-culottes** (sahn-koo-LUT *or* sanz-koo-LAHTSS), ordinary patriots without fine clothes. Although it has become customary to equate the more radical sans-culottes with working people or the poor, many were merchants and better-off artisans who were often the elite of their neighborhoods and trades.

The Radical Revolution

Before the National Convention met, the Paris Commune dominated the political scene. Led by the newly appointed minister of justice, Georges Danton (ZHORZH dahn-TAWNH) (1759–1794), the sans-culottes sought revenge on those who had aided the king and resisted the popular will. The advance of a Prussian army on Paris intensified the fears of treachery. Thousands of presumed traitors were arrested and then massacred as ordinary Parisian tradespeople and artisans solved the problem of overcrowded prisons by mass executions of their inmates. In September 1792, the newly elected National Convention began its sessions. Although it was called to draft a new constitution, it also acted as the sovereign ruling body of France.

Socially, the composition of the National Convention was similar to that of its predecessors. Dominated by lawyers, professionals, and property owners, it also included for the first time a handful of artisans. Two-thirds of the deputies were under age forty-five, and almost all had had political experience as a result of the Revolution. Almost all were also intensely distrustful of the king and his activities. It was therefore no surprise that the convention's first major step on September 21 was to abolish the monarchy and establish a republic. But that was about as far as members of the convention could agree, and the National Convention soon split into factions over the fate of the king. The two most important were the **Girondins** (juh-RAHN-dinz) (so-called because their leaders came from the department of Gironde, located in southwestern France) and the **Mountain** (so-called because its members' seats were on the side of the convention hall where the floor slanted upward). Both were members of the Jacobin club.

DOMESTIC CRISES Representing primarily the provinces, the Girondins came to fear the radical mobs in Paris and were

Execution of the King. At the beginning of 1793, the National Convention decreed the death of the king, and on January 21 of that year, Louis XVI was executed. As seen in this engraving, a new revolutionary device, the guillotine, was used to execute the king.

disposed to keep the king alive as a hedge against future eventualities. The Mountain represented the interests of the city of Paris and owed much of its strength to the radical and popular elements in the city, although the members of the Mountain themselves were middle class. The Mountain won out at the beginning of 1793 when the National Convention found the king guilty of treason by a vote of 387 to 334 and sentenced him to death. On January 21, 1793, the king was executed, and the destruction of the old regime was complete. Now there could be no turning back. But the execution of the king produced further challenges by creating new enemies for the Revolution both at home and abroad while strengthening those who were already its enemies.

Factional disputes between the Girondins and the Mountain were only one aspect of France's domestic crisis in 1792 and 1793. In Paris, the local government was controlled by the Commune, which drew a number of its leaders from the city's artisans and shopkeepers. The Commune favored radical change and put constant pressure on the National Convention, pushing it to ever more radical positions. As one man warned his fellow deputies, "Never forget that you were sent here by the sans-culottes."[9] At the end of May and the beginning of June 1793, the Commune organized a demonstration, invaded the National Convention, and forced the arrest and execution of the leading Girondins, thereby leaving the Mountain in control of the convention.

The National Convention itself still did not rule all of France. The authority of the convention was repudiated in western France, particularly in the department of the Vendée (vahnh-DAY), by peasants who revolted against the new military draft (see "A Nation in Arms" later in this chapter). The Vendean rebellion soon escalated into a full-blown counterrevolutionary appeal: "Long live the king and our good priests. We want our king, our priests and the old regime." Some of France's major provincial cities, including Lyons (LYOHNH) and Marseilles (mar-SAY), also began to break away from the central authority. Arguing as Marseilles did that "it is time for the anarchy of a few men of blood to stop,"[10] these cities favored a decentralized republic to free themselves from the ascendancy of Paris. In no way did they favor breaking up the "indivisible republic."

FOREIGN CRISIS Domestic turmoil was paralleled by a foreign crisis. Early in 1793, after Louis XVI had been executed, much of Europe—an informal coalition of Austria, Prussia, Spain, Portugal, Britain, and the Dutch Republic—was pitted against France. Carried away by initial successes and their own rhetoric, the French welcomed the struggle. Danton exclaimed to the convention, "They threaten you with kings! You have thrown down your gauntlet to them, and this gauntlet is a king's head, the signal of their coming death."[11] Grossly overextended, the French armies began to experience reverses, and by late spring some members of the anti-French coalition were poised for an invasion of France. If they succeeded, both the Revolution and the revolutionaries would be destroyed and the old regime reestablished. The Revolution had reached a decisive moment.

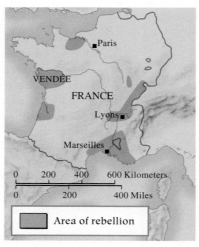

Rebellion in France

Citizens in the New French Army. To save the Republic from its foreign enemies, the National Convention created a revolutionary army of unprecedented size. The illustration above, from a book of paintings on the French Revolution by the Lesueur brothers, shows three citizens learning to drill, while a young volunteer is being armed and outfitted by his family. The illustration at the left, also by the Lesueur brothers, shows two volunteers joyfully going off to fight.

A NATION IN ARMS To meet the crisis and save the Republic from its foreign enemies, the Committee of Public Safety decreed a universal mobilization of the nation on August 23, 1793:

> Young men will fight, young men are called to conquer. Married men will forge arms, transport military baggage and guns and will prepare food supplies. Women, who at long last are to take their rightful place in the revolution and follow their true destiny, will forget their futile tasks: their delicate hands will work at making clothes for soldiers; they will make tents and they will extend their tender care to shelters where the defenders of the Patrie [nation] will receive the help that their wounds require. Children will make lint of old cloth. It is for them that we are fighting: children, those beings destined to gather all the fruits of the revolution, will raise their pure hands toward the skies. And old men, performing their missions again, as of yore, will be guided to the public squares of the cities where they will kindle the courage of young warriors and preach the doctrines of hate for kings and the unity of the Republic.[12]

In less than a year, the French revolutionary government had raised an army of 650,000; by September 1794, it numbered 1,169,000. The Republic's army—a **nation in arms**—was the largest Europe had ever seen. It now pushed the allies back across the Rhine and even conquered the Austrian Netherlands (see Map 19.2). By May 1795, the anti-French coalition of 1793 was breaking up.

Historians have focused on the importance of the French revolutionary army in the creation of modern nationalism. Previously, wars had been fought between governments or ruling dynasties by relatively small armies of professional soldiers.

To meet these crises, the National Convention adopted a program of curbing anarchy and counterrevolution at home while attempting to win the war by a vigorous mobilization of the people. To administer the government, the convention gave broad powers to an executive committee known as the Committee of Public Safety, which was dominated initially by Danton. For the next twelve months, virtually the same twelve members were reelected and gave the country the leadership it needed to weather the domestic and foreign crises of 1793. One of the most important members was Maximilien Robespierre (mak-see-meel-YENH ROHBZ-pyayr) (1758–1794), a small-town lawyer who had moved to Paris as a member of the Estates-General. Politics was his life, and he was dedicated to using power to benefit the people, whom he loved in the abstract though not on a one-to-one basis.

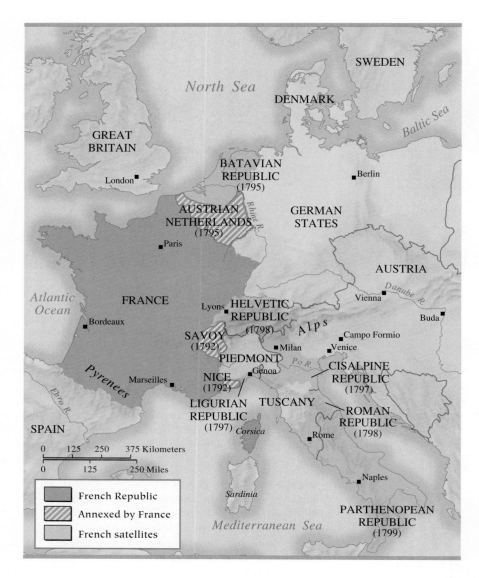

MAP 19.2 French Expansion During the Revolutionary Wars, 1792–1799. The conservative rulers of Europe, appalled at the republican character of the French Revolution, took up arms to restore the Bourbon monarchy. The French responded with a people's army, the largest ever seen, which pushed the invaders out of France, annexed the Austrian Netherlands and some Italian territory, and created a number of French satellite states.

Q *Why would Austria desire cooperation from the German states if it wanted to wage war on France?*

The new French army, however, was the creation of a "people's" government; its wars were now "people's" wars. The entire nation was to be involved in the war. But when dynastic wars became people's wars, warfare increased in ferocity and lack of restraint. Although innocent civilians had suffered in the earlier struggles, now the carnage became appalling at times. The wars of the French revolutionary era opened the door to the total war of the modern world.

THE COMMITTEE OF PUBLIC SAFETY AND THE REIGN OF TERROR To meet the domestic crisis, the National Convention and the Committee of Public Safety instituted the "Reign of Terror." Revolutionary courts were organized to protect the Republic from its internal enemies, "who either by their conduct, their contacts, their words or their writings, showed themselves to be supporters of tyranny or enemies of liberty" or "who have not constantly manifested their attachment to the revolution."[13] Victims of the Terror ranged from royalists, such as Queen Marie Antoinette, to former revolutionary Girondins, including Olympe de Gouges, the chief advocate

for political rights for women, and even included thousands of peasants. Many victims were persons who had opposed the radical activities of the sans-culottes. Robespierre forced through the Convention a law that denied suspects sent before the Revolutionary Tribunal all rights to defend themselves. This law increased the pace of executions. In the course of nine months, 16,000 people were officially killed under the blade of the guillotine, a revolutionary device for the quick and efficient separation of heads from bodies. But the true number of the Terror's victims was probably totaled closer to 250,000 (see the box on p. 577). The bulk of the Terror's executions took place during the Vendée revolt and in cities such as Lyons and Marseilles, places that had been in open rebellion against the authority of the National Convention.

Military force in the form of revolutionary armies was used to bring recalcitrant cities and districts back under the control of the National Convention. Marseilles fell to a revolutionary army in August. Starving Lyons surrendered early in October after two months of bombardment and resistance. Since Lyons was France's second city after Paris and had defied the National

JUSTICE IN THE REIGN OF TERROR

THE REIGN OF TERROR CREATED A REPRESSIVE environment in which revolutionary courts often acted quickly to condemn traitors to the revolutionary cause. In this account, an English visitor describes the court, the procession to the scene of execution, and the final execution procedure.

J. G. Milligen, *The Revolutionary Tribunal* (Paris, October 1793)

In the center of the hall, under a statue of Justice, holding scales in one hand, and a sword in the other, sat Dumas, the President, with the other judges. . . . To the right were benches on which the accused were placed in several rows, and *gendarmes* with carbines and fixed bayonets by their sides. To the left was the jury.

Never can I forget the mournful appearance of these funereal processions to the place of execution. The march was opened by a detachment of mounted *gendarmes*—the carts followed; they were the same carts as those that are used in Paris for carrying wood; four boards were placed across them for seats, and on each board sat two, and sometimes three victims; their hands were tied behind their backs, and the constant jolting of the cart made them nod their heads up and down, to the great amusement of the spectators. On the front of the cart stood Samson, the executioner, or one of his sons or assistants; *gendarmes* on foot marched by the side; then followed a hackney, in which was the reporting clerk, whose duty it was to witness the execution, and then return to the public accuser's office to report the execution of what they called the law.

The process of execution was also a sad and heartrending spectacle. In the middle of the Place de la Revolution was erected a guillotine, in front of a colossal statue of Liberty, represented seated on a rock, a cap on her head, a spear in her hand, the other reposing on a shield. On one side of the scaffold were drawn out a sufficient number of carts, with large baskets painted red, to receive the heads and bodies of the victims. Those bearing the condemned moved on slowly to the foot of the guillotine; the culprits were led out in turn, and if necessary, supported by two of the executioner's assistants, but their assistance was rarely required. Most of these unfortunates ascended the scaffold with a determined step—many of them looked up firmly on the menacing instrument of death, beholding for the last time the rays of the glorious sun, beaming on the polished axe; and I have seen some young men actually dance a few steps before they went up to be strapped to the perpendicular plane, which was then tilted to a horizontal plane in a moment, and ran on the grooves until the neck was secured and closed in by a moving board, when the head passed through what was called, in derision, "the republican toilet seat"; the weighty knife was then dropped with a heavy fall; and, with incredible dexterity and rapidity, two executioners tossed the body into the basket, while another threw the head after it.

 How were the condemned taken to the executioner? How did this serve to inflame the crowds? How were people executed? Why?

Source: J. M. Thompson, *English Witness of the French Revolution* (Oxford: Blackwell, 1938).

Convention during a time when the Republic was in peril, the Committee of Public Safety decided to make an example of it. By April 1794, some 1,880 citizens of Lyons had been executed. When guillotining proved too slow, cannon fire and grapeshot were used to blow condemned men into open graves. A German observed:

> Whole ranges of houses, always the most handsome, [were] burnt. The churches, convents, and all the dwellings of the former patricians were in ruins. When I came to the guillotine, the blood of those who had been executed a few hours beforehand was still running in the street. . . . I said to a group of sans-culottes that it would be decent to clear away all this human blood. Why should it be cleared? one of them said to me. It's the blood of aristocrats and rebels. The dogs should lick it up.[14]

In the Vendée, revolutionary armies were also brutal in defeating the rebel armies. After destroying one army on December 12, the commander of the revolutionary army ordered that no quarter be given: "The road to Laval is strewn with corpses. Women, priests, monks, children, all have been put to death. I have spared nobody." The Terror was at its most destructive in the Vendée. Forty-two percent of the death sentences during the Terror were passed in territories affected by the Vendée rebellion. Perhaps the most notorious act of violence occurred in Nantes, where victims were executed by sinking them in barges in the Loire River.

To a great extent, the Terror demonstrated little class prejudice. Estimates are that the nobles constituted 8 percent of its victims; the middle classes, 25; the clergy, 6; and the peasant and laboring classes, 60. To the Committee of Public Safety, this bloodletting was only a temporary expedient. Once the war and domestic emergency were over, "the republic of virtue" would ensue, and the Declaration of the Rights of Man and the Citizen would be fully established. Although theoretically a republic, the French government during the Terror was led by a group of twelve men who ordered the execution of people as national enemies. But how did they justify this? Louis Saint-Just (sanh-ZHOOST), one of the younger members of the Committee of Public Safety, explained their rationalization in a speech to the convention: "Since the French people has manifested its will, everything opposed to it is outside the sovereign.

ROBESPIERRE AND REVOLUTIONARY GOVERNMENT

IN ITS TIME OF TROUBLES, THE NATIONAL CONVENTION, under the direction of the Committee of Public Safety, instituted the Reign of Terror to preserve the Revolution from its internal enemies. In this selection, Maximilien Robespierre, one of the committee's leading members, tries to justify the violence to which these believers in republican liberty resorted.

Robespierre, Speech on Revolutionary Government

The theory of revolutionary government is as new as the Revolution that created it. . . . It behooves us to explain it to all in order that we may rally good citizens, at least, in support of the principles governing the public interest.

It is the function of government to guide the moral and physical energies of the nation toward the purposes for which it was established.

The object of constitutional government is to preserve the Republic; the object of the revolutionary government is to establish it.

Revolution is the war waged by liberty against its enemies; a constitution is that which crowns the edifice of freedom once victory has been won and the nation is at peace.

Source: G. Rude, ed., *Robespierre* (Upper Saddle River, N.J.: Prentice Hall, 1967).

The revolutionary government has to summon extraordinary activity to its aid precisely because it is at war. It is subjected to less binding and less uniform regulations, because the circumstances in which it finds itself are tempestuous and shifting above all because it is compelled to deploy, swiftly and incessantly, new resources to meet new and pressing dangers.

The principal concern of constitutional government is civil liberty; that of revolutionary government, public liberty. Under a constitutional government little more is required than to protect the individual against abuses by the state, whereas revolutionary government is obliged to defend the state itself against the factions that assail it from every quarter.

To good citizens revolutionary government owes the full protection of the state; to the enemies of the people it owes only death.

 How did Robespierre justify the violent activities of the French revolutionaries? In your opinion, do his explanations justify his actions? How does this document glorify the state and advance preservation of the state as the highest goal of modern politicians and policy makers?

Whatever is outside the sovereign is an enemy."[15] Clearly, Saint-Just was referring to Rousseau's concept of the general will, but it is equally apparent that these twelve men, in the name of the Republic, had taken upon themselves the right to ascertain the sovereign will of the French people (see the box above) and to kill their enemies as "outside the sovereign."

THE "REPUBLIC OF VIRTUE" Along with the Terror, the Committee of Public Safety took other steps both to control France and to create a new republican order and new republican citizens. By spring 1793, the committee was sending "representatives on mission" as agents of the central government to all departments to explain the war emergency measures and to implement the laws dealing with the wartime emergency.

The committee also attempted to provide some economic controls, especially since members of the more radical working class were advocating them. It established a system of requisitioning food supplies for the cities enforced by the forays of revolutionary armies into the countryside. The Law of the General Maximum established price controls on goods declared of first necessity, ranging from food and drink to fuel and clothing. The controls failed to work very well because the government lacked the machinery to enforce them.

THE ROLE OF WOMEN Women continued to play an active role in this radical phase of the French Revolution. As spectators at sessions of revolutionary clubs and the National Convention, women made the members and deputies aware of their demands. When on Sunday, February 25, 1793, a group of women appealed formally to the National Convention for lower bread prices, the convention reacted by adjourning until Tuesday. The women responded bitterly by accosting the deputies: "We are adjourned until Tuesday; but as for us, we adjourn ourselves until Monday. When our children ask us for milk we don't adjourn them until the day after tomorrow."[16] In 1793, two women—an actress and a chocolate manufacturer—founded the Society for Revolutionary Republican Women. Composed largely of working-class women, this Parisian group viewed itself as a "family of sisters" and vowed "to rush to the defense of the Fatherland."

Despite the importance of women to the revolutionary cause, male revolutionaries reacted disdainfully to female participation in political activity. In the radical phase of the Revolution, the Paris Commune outlawed women's clubs and forbade women to be present at its meetings. One of its members explained why:

> It is horrible, it is contrary to all laws of nature for a woman
> to want to make herself a man. The Council must recall
> that some time ago these denatured women, these viragos,
> wandered through the markets with the red cap to sully that
> badge of liberty and wanted to force all women to take off the
> modest headdress that is appropriate for them [the bonnet]. . . .
> Is it the place of women to propose motions? Is it the place of
> women to place themselves at the head of our armies?[17]

Most men—radical or conservative—agreed that a woman's place was in the home and not in military or political affairs. As one man asked, "Since when is it considered normal for a

Women Patriots. Women played a variety of roles in the events of the French Revolution. This picture shows a middle-class women's patriotic club discussing the decrees of the National Convention, an indication that some women had become highly politicized by the upheavals of the Revolution. The women are also giving coins to create a fund for impoverished families.

woman to abandon the pious care of her home, the cradle of her children, to listen to speeches in the public forum?"[18]

DE-CHRISTIANIZATION AND THE NEW CALENDAR In its attempt to create a new order, the National Convention also pursued a policy of **de-Christianization**. The word *saint* was removed from street names, churches were pillaged and closed by revolutionary armies, and priests were encouraged to marry. In Paris, the cathedral of Notre Dame was designated the Temple of Reason (see the box on p. 580). In November 1793, a public ceremony dedicated to the worship of reason was held in the former cathedral; patriotic maidens adorned in white dresses paraded before a temple of reason where the high altar once stood. At the end of the ceremony, a female figure personifying Liberty rose out of the temple. As Robespierre came to realize, de-Christianization backfired because France was still overwhelmingly Catholic. In fact, de-Christianization created more enemies than friends.

Yet another manifestation of de-Christianization was the adoption of a new republican calendar on October 5, 1793. Years would no longer be numbered from the birth of Jesus but from September 22, 1792, the day the French Republic was proclaimed. Thus, at the time the calendar was adopted, the French were already living in year II. The calendar contained twelve months; each month consisted of three ten-day weeks called *décades* (day-KAD) with the tenth day of each week a rest day (*décadi*). This eliminated Sundays and Sunday worship services and put an end to the ordering of French lives by a Christian calendar that emphasized Sundays, saints' days, and church holidays and festivals. Religious celebrations were to be replaced by revolutionary festivals. Especially important were the five days (six in leap years) left over in the calendar at the end of the year. These days were to form a half-week of festivals to celebrate the revolutionary virtues—Virtue, Intelligence, Labor, Opinion, and Rewards. The sixth extra day in a leap year would be a special festival day when French citizens would "come from all parts of the Republic to celebrate liberty and equality, to cement by their embraces the national fraternity." Of course, ending church holidays also reduced the number of nonworking holidays from fifty-six to thirty-two, a goal long recommended by eighteenth-century economic theorists.

The calendar's anti-Christian purpose was also apparent in the renaming of the months of the year. The months received names that were supposed to evoke the seasons, the temperature, or the state of the vegetation: Véndemiaire (vahnh-duh-MYAYR) (harvest—the first month of thirty days beginning September 22), Brumaire (broo-MAYR) (mist), Frimaire (free-MAYR) (frost), Nivose (nee-VOHZ) (snow), Pluviôse (ploo-VYOHZ) (rain), Ventose (vahnh-TOHZ) (wind), Germinal (jayr-mee-NAHL) (seeding), Floréal (floh-ray-AHL) (flowering), Prairial (pray-RYAL) (meadows), Messidor (MESS-i-dor) (wheat harvest), Thermidor (TAYR-mi-dor) (heat), and Fructidor (FROOK-ti-dor) (ripening).

The new calendar faced intense popular opposition, and the revolutionary government relied primarily on coercion to win its acceptance. Journalists, for example, were commanded to use republican dates in their newspaper articles. But many people refused to give up the old calendar, as one official reported:

> Sundays and Catholic holidays, even if there are ten in a row, have for some time been celebrated with as much pomp and splendor as before. The same cannot be said of *décadi*, which

DE-CHRISTIANIZATION

THE PHENOMENON OF DE-CHRISTIANIZATION PRODUCED some unusual spectacles during the radical stage of the French Revolution. This selection from the minutes of the National Convention describes how the cathedral of Notre Dame was put to new use as the Temple of Reason.

The Temple of Reason

A member puts in the form of a motion the demand of the citizens of Paris that the metropolitan cathedral [Notre Dame] be henceforth the Temple of Reason.

A member requests that the goddess of Reason place herself at the side of the president.

The attorney of the Commune conducts her to the desk. The president and the secretaries give her the fraternal kiss in the midst of applause. . . .

A member demands that the National Convention march in a body, in the midst of the People, to the Temple of Reason to sing the hymn of Liberty there.

This proposal is passed.

The Convention marches with the People to the Temple of Reason in the midst of general enthusiasm and joyful acclamations.

Source: P. H. Beik, *The French Revolution* (New York: Walker & Co., 1970).

Having entered the Temple of Reason, they sing the following hymn:

Descend, O Liberty, daughter of Nature:
The People have recaptured their immortal power;
Over the pompous remains of age-old imposture
Their hands raise thine altar.
Come, vanquisher of kings, Europe gazes upon you;
Come, vanquish the false gods.
Thou, holy Liberty, come dwell in this temple;
Be the goddess of the French. . . .
All kings make war on the sovereign People;
Let them henceforth fall at thy feet, O goddess;
Soon on the coffins of the world's tyrants
the world's peoples will swear peace.

Q What was the purpose of de-Christianization? Based on the ceremony described here, how effective do you think it was?

---

is observed by only a small handful of citizens. The first to disobey the law are the wives of public officials, who dress up on the holidays of the old calendar and abstain from work more religiously than anyone else.[19]

The government could hardly expect peasants to follow the new calendar when government officials were ignoring it. Napoleon later perceived that the revolutionary calendar was politically unpopular, and he simply abandoned it on January 1, 1806 (11 Nivôse XIV).

In addition to its anti-Christian function, the revolutionary calendar had also served to mark the Revolution as a new historical beginning, a radical break in time. Revolutionary upheavals often project millenarian expectations, the hope that a new age is dawning. The revolutionary dream of a new order presupposed the creation of a new human being freed from the old order and its symbols, a new citizen surrounded by a framework of new habits. Restructuring time itself offered the opportunity to forge new habits and create a lasting new order.

EQUALITY AND SLAVERY Early in the French Revolution, the desire for equality led to a discussion of what to do about slavery. A club called Friends of the Blacks advocated the abolition of slavery, which was achieved in France in September 1791. Nevertheless, French planters in the West

Revolt in Saint-Domingue (Haiti)

Indies, who profited greatly from the use of slaves on their sugar plantations, opposed the abolition of slavery in the French colonies. When the National Convention came into power, the issue was revisited, and on February 4, 1794, guided by ideals of equality, the government abolished slavery in the colonies.

In one French colony, slaves had already rebelled for their freedom. In 1791, black slaves in the French sugar colony of Saint-Domingue (san doh-MAYNG) (the western third of the island of Hispaniola), inspired by the ideals of the revolution occurring in France, revolted against French plantation owners. Slaves attacked, killing plantation owners and their families and burning their buildings. White planters retaliated with equal brutality. One wealthy French settler reported, "How can we stay in a country where slaves have raised their hands against their masters?"

Eventually, leadership of the revolt was taken over by Toussaint L'Ouverture (too-SANH loo-vayr-TOOR) (1746–1803), a son of African slaves, who seized control of all of Hispaniola by 1801. Although Napoleon had accepted the revolutionary ideal of equality, he did not deny the reports of white planters that the massacres of white planters by slaves demonstrated the savage nature of blacks. In 1802, he reinstated slavery in the French West Indian colonies and sent an army that captured L'Ouverture, who died in a French dungeon within a year. But the French soldiers, weakened by disease, soon succumbed to the slave forces. On January 1, 1804, the western part of Hispaniola, now called Haiti, announced its freedom and became the first independent state in Latin America. Despite Napoleon's efforts to the contrary, one of the French revolutionary ideals had triumphed abroad.

DECLINE OF THE COMMITTEE OF PUBLIC SAFETY Maintaining the revolutionary ideals in France proved not to be easy. By the Law of 14 Frimaire (passed on December 4, 1793), the Committee of Public Safety sought to centralize the administration of France more effectively and to exercise greater control in order to check the excesses of the Reign of Terror. The activities of both the representatives on mission and the revolutionary armies were scrutinized more carefully, and the campaign against Christianity was also dampened. Finally, in 1794, the Committee of Public Safety turned against its radical Parisian supporters, executed the leaders of the revolutionary Paris Commune, and turned it into a docile tool. This might have been a good idea for the sake of order, but in suppressing the people who had been its chief supporters, the National Convention alienated an important group. At the same time, the French had been successful against their foreign foes. The military successes meant that the Terror no longer served much purpose. But the Terror continued because Robespierre, now its dominant figure, had become obsessed with purifying the body politic of all the corrupt. Only then could the Republic of Virtue follow. Many deputies in the National Convention, however, feared that they were not safe while Robespierre was free to act. An anti-Robespierre coalition in the National Convention, eager now to destroy Robespierre before he destroyed them, gathered enough votes to condemn him. Robespierre was guillotined on July 28, 1794, beginning a reaction that brought an end to this radical stage of the French Revolution.

The National Convention and its Committee of Public Safety had accomplished a great deal. By creating a nation in arms, they preserved the French Revolution and prevented it from being destroyed by its foreign enemies, who, if they had succeeded, would have reestablished the old monarchical order. Domestically, the Revolution had also been saved from the forces of counterrevolution. The committee's tactics, however, provided an example for the use of violence in domestic politics that has continued to bedevil the Western world to this day.

Reaction and the Directory

After the execution of Robespierre, revolutionary fervor began to give way to the Thermidorean Reaction, named after the month of Thermidor. The Terror began to abate. The National Convention curtailed the power of the Committee of Public Safety, shut down the Jacobin club, and attempted to provide better protection for its deputies against the Parisian mobs. Churches were allowed to reopen for public worship, and a decree of February 21, 1795, gave freedom of worship to all cults. Economic regulation was dropped in favor of *laissez-faire* policies, another clear indication that moderate forces were regaining control of the Revolution. In addition, a new

Robespierre. Maximilien Robespierre, seen here in a portrait by an unknown artist, eventually became the dominant figure in the Committee of Public Safety. Fear of Robespierre, however, led many in the National Convention to condemn him, and on July 28, 1794, he was executed.

constitution, written in August 1795, reflected this more conservative republicanism or a desire for a stability that did not sacrifice the ideals of 1789.

To avoid the dangers of another single legislative assembly, the Constitution of 1795 established a national legislative assembly consisting of two chambers: a lower house, known as the Council of 500, whose function was to initiate legislation, and an upper house of 250 members, the Council of Elders, composed of married or widowed members over age forty, which would accept or reject the proposed laws. The 750 members of the two legislative bodies were chosen by electors who had to be owners or renters of property worth between one hundred and two hundred days' labor, a requirement that limited their number to 30,000, an even smaller base than the Constitution of 1791 had provided. The electors were chosen by the active citizens, now defined as all male taxpayers over the age of twenty-one. The executive authority or Directory consisted of five directors elected by the Council of Elders from a list presented by the Council of 500. To ensure some continuity from the old order to the new, the members of the National Convention ruled that two-thirds of the new members of the National Assembly must be chosen from their ranks. This decision set off disturbances in Paris and an insurrection at the beginning of October that was dispersed after fierce combat by an army contingent under the artillery general Napoleon Bonaparte. This would be the last time in the great French Revolution that the city of Paris would attempt to impose its wishes on the central government. Even more significant and ominous was this use of the army, which made it clear that the Directory from the beginning had to rely on the military for survival.

The period of the Directory was an era of materialistic reaction to the suffering and sacrifices that had been demanded in the Reign of Terror and the Republic of Virtue. Speculators made fortunes in property by taking advantage of the government's severe monetary problems. Elaborate fashions, which had gone out of style because of their identification with the nobility, were worn again. Gambling and roulette became popular once more. Groups of "gilded youth"—sons of the wealthy, with long hair and rumpled clothes—took to the streets to insult former supporters of the Revolution.

The government of the Directory had to contend with political enemies from both ends of the political spectrum. On the right, royalists who dreamed of restoring the monarchy continued their agitation; some still toyed with violent means. On the left, Jacobin hopes of power were revived by continuing economic problems, especially the total collapse in the value of the assignats. Some radicals even went beyond earlier goals, especially Gracchus Babeuf (GRAK-uss bah-BUFF), who sneered, "What is the French Revolution? An open war between patricians and plebeians, between rich and poor." Babeuf, who was appalled at the misery of the common people, wanted to abolish private property and eliminate private enterprise. His Conspiracy of Equals was crushed in 1796, and he was executed in 1797.

New elections in 1797 created even more uncertainty and instability. Battered by the left and right, unable to find a definitive solution to the country's economic problems, and still carrying on the wars left from the Committee of Public Safety, the Directory increasingly relied on the military to maintain its power. This led to a coup d'etat in 1799 in which the successful and popular general Napoleon Bonaparte was able to seize power.

The Age of Napoleon

 FOCUS QUESTION: Which aspects of the French Revolution did Napoleon preserve, and which did he destroy?

Napoleon (1769–1821) dominated both French and European history from 1799 to 1815. The coup that brought him to power occurred exactly ten years after the outbreak of the French Revolution. In a sense, Napoleon brought the Revolution to an end, but he was also its child; he even called himself the Son of the Revolution. The French Revolution had made possible his rise first in the military and then to supreme power in France. Even beyond this, Napoleon had once said, "I am the Revolution," and he never ceased to remind the French that they owed to him the preservation of all that was beneficial in the revolutionary program.

CHRONOLOGY	The French Revolution
Assembly of notables	1787
National Assembly (Constituent Assembly)	**1789–1791**
Meeting of Estates-General	May 5, 1789
Formation of National Assembly	June 17, 1789
Tennis Court Oath	June 20, 1789
Fall of the Bastille	July 14, 1789
Great Fear	Summer 1789
Declaration of the Rights of Man and the Citizen	August 26, 1789
Women's march to Versailles; king's return to Paris	October 5–6, 1789
Civil Constitution of the Clergy	July 12, 1790
Flight of the king	June 20–21, 1791
Legislative Assembly	**1791–1792**
France declares war on Austria	April 20, 1792
Attack on the royal palace	August 10, 1792
National Convention	**1792–1795**
Abolition of the monarchy	September 21, 1792
Execution of the king	January 21, 1793
Universal mobilization of the nation	August 23, 1793
Execution of Robespierre	July 28, 1794
Directory	**1795–1799**
Constitution of 1795 is adopted	August 22, 1795

The Rise of Napoleon

Napoleon was born in Corsica in 1769, only a few months after France had annexed the island. The son of an Italian lawyer whose family stemmed from the Florentine nobility, Napoleone Buonaparte (to use his birth name) grew up in the countryside of Corsica, a willful and demanding child who nevertheless developed discipline, thriftiness, and loyalty to his family. His father's connections in France enabled him to study first at a school in the French town of Autun, where he learned to speak French, and then to obtain a royal scholarship to study at a military school. At that time, he changed his first name to the more French-sounding Napoleon (he did not change his last name to Bonaparte until 1796).

Napoleon's military education led to his commission in 1785 as a lieutenant, although he was not well liked by his fellow officers because he was short, spoke with an Italian accent, and had little money. For the next seven years, Napoleon spent much of his time reading the works of the philosophes, especially Rousseau, and educating himself in military matters by studying the campaigns of great military leaders from the past, including Alexander the Great, Charlemagne, and Frederick the Great. The French Revolution and the European war that and in a series of stunning victories defeated the Austrians and dictated peace to them in 1797.

Throughout his Italian campaign, Napoleon won the confidence of his men by his energy, charm, and ability to comprehend complex issues quickly and make decisions rapidly. He was tough with his officers and drove them relentlessly. With rank-and-file soldiers, he took a different approach. He ate with them, provided good food and clothing, and charmed them with his words. "They knew I was their patron," Napoleon once remarked. Throughout the rest of his life, these qualities, combined with his keen intelligence, ease with words, and supreme confidence in himself, enabled Napoleon to influence people and win their firm support. Napoleon liked to see himself as a man of destiny and a great man who mastered luck. He once said:

> A consecutive series of great actions never is the result of chance and luck, it always is the product of planning and genius. Great men are rarely known to fail in their most perilous enterprises. . . . Is it because they are lucky that they become great? No, but being great, they have been able to master luck.[20]

Napoleon also saw himself as a military genius who had a "touch for leading, which could not be learned from books, nor by practice."

In 1797, Napoleon returned to France as a conquering hero and was given command of an army training to invade England. Believing that the French were unready for such an invasion, he proposed instead to strike indirectly at Britain by taking Egypt and threatening India, a major source of British wealth. But the British controlled the seas and by 1799 had cut off supplies from Napoleon's army in Egypt. Seeing no future in certain defeat, Napoleon did not hesitate to abandon his army and return to Paris, where he participated in the coup d'état that ultimately led to his virtual dictatorship of France. He was only thirty years old at the time.

NAPOLEON IN CONTROL With the coup of 1799, a new form of the Republic was proclaimed with a constitution that established a bicameral legislative assembly elected indirectly to reduce the role of elections. Executive power in the new government was vested in the hands of three consuls, although, as Article 42 of the constitution said, "the decision of the First Consul shall suffice." As first consul, Napoleon directly controlled the entire executive authority of government. He had overwhelming influence over the legislature, appointed members of the bureaucracy, controlled the army, and conducted foreign affairs. In 1802, Napoleon was made consul for life, and in 1804 he returned France to monarchy when he crowned himself Emperor Napoleon I. This step undoubtedly satisfied his enormous ego but also stabilized the regime and provided a permanence not possible in the consulate. The revolutionary era that had begun with an attempt to limit arbitrary government had ended with a government far more autocratic than the monarchy of the old regime. As his reign progressed and the demands of war increased, Napoleon's regime became ever more dictatorial.

Napoleon as a Young Officer. Napoleon rose quickly through the military ranks, being promoted to the rank of brigadier general at the age of twenty-five. This painting of Napoleon by the Romantic painter Baron Antoine-Jean Gros (GROH) presents an idealized, heroic image of the young leader.

followed broadened his sights and presented him with new opportunities.

NAPOLEON'S MILITARY CAREER Napoleon rose quickly through the ranks. In 1792, he became a captain and in the following year performed so well as an artillery commander in the capture of Toulon that he was promoted to the rank of brigadier general in 1794, when he was only twenty-five. In October 1795, he saved the National Convention from the Parisian mob, for which he was promoted to the rank of major general.

By this time, Napoleon had become a hero in some Parisian social circles, where he met Josephine de Beauharnais (zhoh-seff-FEEN duh boh-ar-NAY), widow of a guillotined general. Six years older than Napoleon, she lived a life of luxury, thanks to gifts from her influential male lovers. Napoleon fell deeply in love with her, married her in 1796, and remained committed to her for many years, despite her well-known affairs with other men.

Soon after his marriage, Napoleon was made commander of the French army in Italy (see the box on p. 584). There he turned a group of ill-disciplined soldiers into an effective fighting force

NAPOLEON AND PSYCHOLOGICAL WARFARE

IN 1796, AT THE AGE OF TWENTY-SEVEN, Napoleon Bonaparte was given command of the French army in Italy, where he won a series of stunning victories. His use of speed, deception, and surprise to overwhelm his opponents is well known. In this selection from a proclamation to his troops in Italy, Napoleon also appears to be a master of psychological warfare.

Napoleon Bonaparte, Proclamation to the French Troops in Italy (April 26, 1796)

Soldiers:

In a fortnight you have won six victories, taken twenty-one standards, fifty-five pieces of artillery, several strong positions, and conquered the richest part of Piedmont [in northern Italy]; you have captured 15,000 prisoners and killed or wounded more than 10,000 men. . . . You have won battles without cannon, crossed rivers without bridges, made forced marches without shoes, camped without brandy and often without bread. Soldiers of liberty, only republican troops could have endured what you have endured. Soldiers, you have our thanks! The grateful Patrie [nation] will owe its prosperity to you. . . .

The two armies which but recently attacked you with audacity are fleeing before you in terror; the wicked men who laughed at your misery and rejoiced at the thought of the triumphs of your enemies are confounded and trembling.

But, soldiers, as yet you have done nothing compared with what remains to be done. . . . Undoubtedly the greatest obstacles have been overcome; but you still have battles to fight, cities to capture, rivers to cross. Is there one among you whose courage is abating? No. . . . All of you are consumed with a desire to extend the glory of the French people; all of you long to humiliate those arrogant kings who dare to contemplate placing us in fetters; all of you desire to dictate a glorious peace, one which will indemnify the Patrie for the immense sacrifices it has made; all of you wish to be able to say with pride as you return to your villages, "I was with the victorious army of Italy!"

 What themes did Napoleon use to play on the emotions of his troops and inspire them to greater efforts? Do you think Napoleon believed these words? Why or why not?

Source: J. H. Stewart, *A Documentary Survey of the French Revolution* (London: Macmillan, 1951).

The Domestic Policies of Emperor Napoleon

Napoleon often claimed that he had preserved the gains of the Revolution for the French people. The ideal of republican liberty had, of course, been destroyed by Napoleon's thinly disguised autocracy. But were revolutionary ideals maintained in other ways? An examination of his domestic policies will enable us to judge the truth or falsehood of Napoleon's assertion.

NAPOLEON AND THE CATHOLIC CHURCH In 1801, Napoleon made peace with the oldest and most implacable enemy of the Revolution, the Catholic Church. Napoleon himself was devoid of any personal faith; he was an eighteenth-century rationalist who regarded religion at most as a convenience. In Egypt, he called himself a Muslim; in France, a Catholic. But Napoleon saw the necessity to come to terms with the Catholic Church in order to stabilize his regime. In 1800, he had declared to the clergy of Milan: "It is my firm intention that the Christian, Catholic, and Roman religion shall be preserved in its entirety. . . . No society can exist without morality; there is no good morality without religion. It is religion alone, therefore, that gives to the State a firm and durable support."[21] Soon after making this statement, Napoleon opened negotiations with Pope Pius VII to reestablish the Catholic Church in France.

Both sides gained from the Concordat that Napoleon arranged with the pope in 1801. Although the pope gained the right to depose French bishops, this gave him little real control over the French Catholic Church, since the state retained the right to nominate bishops. The Catholic Church was also permitted to hold processions again and reopen the seminaries. But Napoleon gained more than the pope. Just by signing the Concordat, the pope acknowledged the accomplishments of the Revolution. Moreover, the pope agreed not to raise the question of the church lands confiscated during the Revolution. Contrary to the pope's wishes, Catholicism was not reestablished as the state religion; Napoleon was only willing to recognize Catholicism as the religion of a majority of the French people. The clergy would be paid by the state, but to avoid the appearance of a state church, Protestant ministers were also put on the state payroll. As a result of the Concordat, the Catholic Church was no longer an enemy of the French government. At the same time, the agreement reassured those who had acquired church property during the Revolution that they could keep it, an assurance that obviously made them supporters of the Napoleonic regime.

A NEW CODE OF LAWS Before the Revolution, France did not have a single set of laws but rather some three hundred different legal systems. Efforts were made during the Revolution to codify laws for the entire nation, but it remained for Napoleon to bring the work to completion in seven codes, the most important of which was the Civil Code (also known as the Code Napoleon). This preserved most of the revolutionary

The Coronation of Napoleon. In 1804, Napoleon restored monarchy to France when he crowned himself emperor. In the coronation scene painted by Jacques-Louis David, Napoleon is shown crowning the empress Josephine while the pope looks on. Shown seated in the box in the background is Napoleon's mother, even though she was not at the ceremony.

gains by recognizing the principle of the equality of all citizens before the law, the right of individuals to choose their professions, religious toleration, and the abolition of serfdom and feudalism. Property rights continued to be carefully protected, while the interests of employers were safeguarded by outlawing trade unions and strikes. The Civil Code clearly reflected the revolutionary aspirations for a uniform legal system, legal equality, and protection of property and individuals. But the Civil Code strictly curtailed the rights of some people. During the radical phase of the French Revolution, new laws had made divorce an easy process for both husbands and wives, restricted the rights of fathers over their children (they could no longer have their children put in prison arbitrarily), and allowed all children (including daughters) to inherit property equally. Napoleon's Civil Code undid most of this legislation. The control of fathers over their families was restored. Divorce was still allowed but was made more difficult for women to obtain. A wife caught in adultery, for example, could be divorced by her husband and even imprisoned. A husband, however, could only be accused of adultery if he moved his mistress into his home. Women were now "less equal than men" in other ways as well. When they married, their property came under the control of

their husbands. In lawsuits, they were treated as minors, and their testimony was regarded as less reliable than that of men.

THE FRENCH BUREAUCRACY Napoleon also worked on rationalizing the bureaucratic structure of France by developing a powerful centralized administrative machine. During the Revolution, the National Assembly had divided France into eighty-three departments and replaced the provincial estates, nobles, and *intendants* with self-governing assemblies. Napoleon kept the departments but eliminated the locally elected assemblies and instituted new officials, the most important of which were the **prefects**. As the central government's agents, appointed by the first consul (Napoleon), the prefects were responsible for supervising all aspects of local government. Yet they were not local men, and their careers depended on the central government.

As part of Napoleon's overhaul of the administrative system, tax collection became systematic and efficient (which it had never been under the old regime). Professional collectors employed by the state who dealt directly with each individual taxpayer now collected taxes. No tax exemptions due to birth, status, or special arrangement were granted. In principle, these changes had been introduced in 1789, but not until Napoleon did they actually work. In 1802, the first consul proclaimed a balanced budget.

Administrative centralization required a bureaucracy of capable officials, and Napoleon worked hard to develop one. Early on, the regime showed its preference for experts and cared little whether that expertise had been acquired in royal or revolutionary bureaucracies. Not rank or birth but only demonstrated abilities now determined promotion in civil or military offices. This was, of course, what many bourgeois had wanted before the Revolution. Napoleon, however, also created a new aristocracy based on merit in the state service. Napoleon created 3,263 nobles between 1808 and 1814; nearly 60 percent were military officers, while the remainder came from the upper ranks of the civil service or were other state and local officials. Socially, only 22 percent of Napoleon's aristocracy came from the nobility of the old regime; almost 60 percent were of bourgeois origin.

NAPOLEON'S GROWING DESPOTISM In his domestic policies, then, Napoleon both destroyed and preserved aspects of the Revolution. Although equality was preserved in the law code and the opening of careers to talent, the creation of a new aristocracy, the strong protection accorded to property rights, and the use of conscription for the military make it clear that much equality had been lost. Liberty had been replaced by an initially benevolent despotism that grew increasingly arbitrary. Napoleon shut down sixty of France's seventy-three newspapers and insisted that all manuscripts be subjected to government scrutiny before they were published. Government police even opened the mail.

One prominent writer, Germaine de Staël (zhayr-MEN duh STAHL) (1766–1817), refused to accept Napoleon's growing despotism. Educated in Enlightenment ideas, she set up a salon in Paris that was a prominent intellectual center by 1800. She wrote novels and political works that denounced Napoleon's rule as tyrannical. Napoleon banned her books in France and exiled her to the German states, where she continued to write, although not without considerable anguish at being absent from France. "The universe is in France," she once wrote; "outside it there is nothing." After the overthrow of Napoleon, Germaine de Staël returned to her beloved Paris, where she died two years later.

Napoleon's Empire and the European Response

When Napoleon became consul in 1799, France was at war with a second European coalition of Russia, Great Britain, and Austria. Napoleon realized the need for a pause. He remarked to a Prussian diplomat "that the French Revolution is not finished so long as the scourge of war lasts. . . . I want peace, as much to settle the present French government as to save the world from chaos."[22] The peace he sought was achieved at Amiens (AH-mee-en) in March 1802 and left France with new frontiers and a number of client territories from the North Sea to the Adriatic. But the peace did not last because the British and French both

regarded it as temporary and had little intention of adhering to its terms.

In 1803, war was renewed with Britain, which was soon joined by Austria and Russia in the Third Coalition. At the Battle of Ulm in southern Germany in 1805, Napoleon surrounded an Austrian army, which quickly surrendered. Proceeding eastward from Ulm, Napoleon faced a large Russian army under Tsar Alexander I and some Austrian troops at Austerlitz (AWSS-tur-litz). The combined allied forces outnumbered Napoleon's forces, but the tsar chose poor terrain for the battle, and Napoleon devastated the allied forces. Austria sued for peace, and Tsar Alexander took his remaining forces back to Russia.

At first, Prussia had refused to join the Third Coalition, but after Napoleon began to reorganize the German states, Prussia reversed course. Acting quickly, Napoleon crushed the Prussian forces in two battles at Jena (YAY-nuh) and Auerstadt (AU-urr-shtaht) in October 1806 and then moved on to defeat the Russians, who had decided to reenter the fray, at Eylau (Y-lau) and Friedland (FREET-lahnt) in June 1807. The Treaties of Tilsit, signed by Napoleon and the rulers of Prussia and Austria at the beginning of July, ended the fighting and gave the French emperor the opportunity to create a new European order.

NAPOLEON'S GRAND EMPIRE The Grand Empire was composed of three major parts: the French empire, a series of dependent states, and allied states (see Map 19.3). The French empire, the inner core of the Grand Empire, consisted of an enlarged France extending to the Rhine in the east and including the western half of Italy north of Rome. Dependent states included Spain, the Netherlands, the kingdom of Italy, the Swiss Republic, the Grand Duchy of Warsaw, and the Confederation of the Rhine (a union of all German states except Austria and Prussia). Allied states were those defeated by Napoleon and forced to join his struggle against Britain; they included Prussia, Austria, and Russia. Although the internal structure of the Grand Empire varied outside its inner core, Napoleon considered himself the leader of the whole: "Europe cannot be at rest except under a single head who will have kings for his officers, who will distribute his kingdom to his lieutenants."

Within his empire, Napoleon demanded obedience, in part because he needed a common front against the British and in part because his growing egotism required obedience to his will. But as a child of the Enlightenment and the Revolution, Napoleon also sought acceptance everywhere of certain revolutionary principles, including legal equality, religious toleration, and economic freedom. As he explained to his brother Jerome, shortly after making him king of the new German state of Westphalia:

> What the peoples of Germany desire most impatiently is that talented commoners should have the same right to your esteem and to public employments as the nobles, that any trace of serfdom and of an intermediate hierarchy between the sovereign and the lowest class of the people should be completely abolished. The benefits of the Code Napoleon, the publicity of judicial procedure, the creation of juries must

MAP 19.3 Napoleon's Grand Empire in 1810. Napoleon's Grand Army won a series of victories against Austria, Prussia, and Russia that gave the French emperor full or partial control over much of Europe by 1807.

 On the continent, what is the overall relationship between distance from France and degree of French control, and how can you account for this?

be so many distinguishing marks of your monarchy. . . . What nation would wish to return under the arbitrary Prussian government once it had tasted the benefits of a wise and liberal administration? The peoples of Germany, the peoples of France, of Italy, of Spain all desire equality and liberal ideas. I have guided the affairs of Europe for many years now, and I have had occasion to convince myself that the buzzing of the privileged classes is contrary to the general opinion. Be a constitutional king.[23]

In the inner core and dependent states of his Grand Empire, Napoleon tried to destroy the old order. Nobility and clergy everywhere in these states lost their special privileges. He decreed equality of opportunity with offices open to talent, equality before the law, and religious toleration. This spread of French revolutionary principles was an important factor in the development of liberal traditions in these countries. These reforms have led some historians to view Napoleon as the last of the enlightened absolutists.

THE PROBLEM OF GREAT BRITAIN Like Hitler 130 years later, Napoleon hoped that his Grand Empire would last for centuries; like Hitler's empire, it collapsed almost as rapidly as it had been formed. Two major reasons help explain this: the survival of Great Britain and the force of nationalism. Britain's survival was due primarily to its sea power. As long as Britain ruled the waves, it was almost invulnerable to military attack. Although Napoleon contemplated an invasion of England and even collected ships for it, he could not overcome the British navy's decisive defeat of a combined French-Spanish fleet at Trafalgar (truh-FAL-ger) in 1805. Napoleon then turned

Francisco Goya, *The Third of May 1808*. After Napoleon imposed his brother Joseph on Spain as its king, the Spanish people revolted against his authority, and a series of riots broke out in Madrid. This painting by Francisco Goya shows the French response—a deliberate execution of Spanish citizens to frighten people into submission. Goya portrays the French troops as a firing squad, killing people (including a monk) reacting in terror. The peasant in the middle throws out his arms in a gesture reminiscent of crucifixion. Goya painted many scenes depicting the horrors of war in Napoleonic Spain.

to his **Continental System** to defeat Britain. Put into effect between 1806 and 1807, it attempted to prevent British goods from reaching the European continent in order to weaken Britain economically and destroy its capacity to wage war. But the Continental System failed. Allied states resented the ever-tightening French economic hegemony; some began to cheat and others to resist, thereby opening the door to British collaboration. New markets in the eastern Mediterranean and in Latin America also provided compensation for the British. Indeed, by 1810, British overseas exports were approaching record highs.

NATIONALISM A second important factor in the defeat of Napoleon was **nationalism**. This political creed had arisen during the French Revolution in the French people's emphasis on brotherhood (*fraternité*) and solidarity against other peoples. Nationalism involved the unique cultural identity of a people based on a common language, religion, and national symbols. The spirit of French nationalism had made possible the mass armies of the revolutionary and Napoleonic eras. But in spreading the principles of the French Revolution beyond France, Napoleon inadvertently brought about a spread of nationalism as well. The French aroused nationalism in two ways: by making themselves hated oppressors, and thus arousing the patriotism of others in opposition to French nationalism, and by showing the people of Europe what nationalism

was and what a nation in arms could do. The lesson was not lost on other peoples and rulers. A Spanish uprising against Napoleon's rule, aided by British support, kept a French force of 200,000 pinned down for years.

Nationalist movements also arose in the German states, where a number of intellectuals advocated a cultural nationalism based on the unity of the German people. The philosopher Johann Gottlieb Fichte (yoh-HAHN got-LEEP FIKH-tuh) (1762–1814), who had at first welcomed the French Revolution for freeing the human spirit, soon became a proponent of a German national spirit radically different from that of France. Although philosophical voices like Fichte's did little to overthrow the French, they did awaken a dream of German nationalism that would bear fruit later in the nineteenth century.

In Prussia, feeling against Napoleon led to a serious reform of the old order that had been so easily crushed by the French emperor. As one Prussian officer put it, the Prussians must learn from the French example and "place their entire national energies in opposition to the enemy." Under the direction of Baron Heinrich von Stein (HYN-rikh fun SHYTN) and later Prince Karl von Hardenberg (KARL fun HAR-den-berk), Prussia embarked on a series of political and military reforms, including the abolition of serfdom, election of city councils, and creation of a larger standing army. Prussia's reforms, instituted as a response to Napoleon, enabled it to again play an important role in European affairs.

The Fall of Napoleon

Napoleon once said, "If I had experienced pleasure, I might have rested; but the peril was always in front of me, and the day's victory was always forgotten in the preoccupation with the necessity of winning a new victory on the morrow."[24] Never at rest, Napoleon decided in 1812 to invade Russia. It was the beginning of his downfall, but Russia's defection from the Continental System had left him with little choice. Although aware of the risks in invading such a large country, Napoleon also knew that if the Russians were allowed to challenge the Continental System unopposed, others would soon follow suit. In June 1812, Napoleon's Grand Army of more than 600,000 men entered Russia. Napoleon's hopes for victory depended on quickly meeting and defeating the Russian armies, but the Russian forces refused to give battle and retreated hundreds of miles while torching their own villages and countryside to prevent Napoleon's army from finding food and forage. Heat and disease also took their toll of the army, and the vast space of Russian territory led many troops to desert. When the Russians did stop to fight at Borodino (bor-uh-DEE-noh), Napoleon's forces won an indecisive and costly victory. Forty-five thousand Russian troops were killed; the French lost 30,000 men, but they had no replacements nearby. When the remaining troops of the Grand Army arrived in Moscow, they found the city ablaze. Lacking food and supplies, Napoleon abandoned Moscow late in October and made the "Great Retreat" across Russia in terrible winter conditions. Only 40,000 troops managed to straggle back to Poland in January 1813. This military disaster then led to a war of liberation all over Europe, culminating in Napoleon's defeat in April 1814.

The defeated emperor of the French was allowed to play ruler on the island of Elba, off the coast of Tuscany, while the Bourbon monarchy was restored to France in the person of Louis XVIII, brother of the executed king. But the new king had little support, and Napoleon, bored on Elba, slipped back into France. When troops were sent to capture him, Napoleon opened his coat and addressed them: "Soldiers of the fifth regiment, I am your Emperor. . . . If there is a man among you would kill his Emperor, here I am!" No one fired a shot.

CHRONOLOGY	The Napoleonic Era, 1799–1815
Napoleon as first consul	1799–1804
Concordat with Catholic Church	1801
Emperor Napoleon I	1804–1815
Battle of Ulm (defeat of Austria)	1805
Battle of Austerlitz (defeat of Russia)	1805
Battle of Trafalgar (naval defeat of Napoleon's forces)	1805
Battles of Jena and Auerstadt (defeat of Prussia)	1806
Continental System established	1806
Battles of Eylau and Friedland (defeat of Russia)	1807
Invasion of Russia	1812
War of liberation	1813–1814
Exile to Elba	1814
Battle of Waterloo; exile to Saint Helena	1815
Death of Napoleon	1821

Shouting "Vive l'Empéreur! Vive l'Empéreur," the troops went over to his side, and Napoleon entered Paris in triumph on March 20, 1815.

The powers that had defeated him pledged once more to fight this person they called the "Enemy and Disturber of the Tranquillity of the World." Having decided to strike first at his enemies, Napoleon raised yet another army and moved to attack the nearest allied forces stationed in Belgium. At Waterloo on June 18, Napoleon met a combined British and Prussian army under the duke of Wellington and suffered a bloody defeat. This time, the victorious allies exiled him to Saint Helena, a small, forsaken island in the South Atlantic. Only Napoleon's memory would continue to haunt French political life.

CHAPTER SUMMARY

The late eighteenth century was a time of dramatic political transformation. Revolutionary upheavals, beginning in North America and continuing in France, produced movements for political liberty and equality. The documents created by these revolutions, the Declaration of Independence and the Declaration of the Rights of Man and the Citizen, embodied the fundamental ideas of the Enlightenment and set forth a liberal political agenda based on a belief in popular sovereignty—the people as the source of

political power—and the principles of liberty and equality. Liberty meant, in theory, freedom from arbitrary power as well as the freedom to think, write, and worship as one chose. Equality meant equality in rights and equality of opportunity based on talent rather than birth. In practice, equality remained limited; men who owned property had great opportunities for voting and officeholding, and there was certainly no equality between men and women.

The leaders of France's liberal revolution during the National and Legislative Assemblies between 1789 and 1791 were men of property, both bourgeois and noble, but they were assisted by commoners, both sans-culottes and peasants. In this first phase

of the Revolution, the old order was demolished as a new constitution established a limited constitutional monarchy. Yet, despite the hopes of the men of property, the liberal revolution was not the end of the Revolution. The decision of the revolutionaries to go to war with European monarchs who opposed the Revolution "revolutionized the revolution," opening the door to a more radical, democratic, and violent stage between 1792 and 1795 under the National Convention led by the Committee of Public Safety. During this phase, revolutionary courts persecuted those not sufficiently supportive of the revolutionary cause, creating the infamous Reign of Terror. The excesses of the Reign of Terror, however, led to a reaction and a government headed by a five-member Directory, which governed from 1795 to 1799. But it satisfied neither the radicals nor the royalists. In 1799, Napoleon Bonaparte overthrew this government and established first the Consulate and

then a new monarchy with himself as emperor. Napoleon, while diminishing freedom by establishing order and centralizing the government, shrewdly preserved equality of rights and the opening of careers to talent and integrated the bourgeoisie and old nobility into a new elite of property owners.

The French Revolution defined the modern revolutionary concept. No one had foreseen or consciously planned the upheaval that began in 1789, but after 1789, "revolutionaries" knew that mass uprisings could succeed in overthrowing unwanted governments. The French Revolution became the classic political and social model for revolution. At the same time, the liberal and national political ideals created by the Revolution and spread through Europe by Napoleon's conquests dominated the political landscape of the nineteenth and early twentieth centuries.

CHAPTER TIMELINE

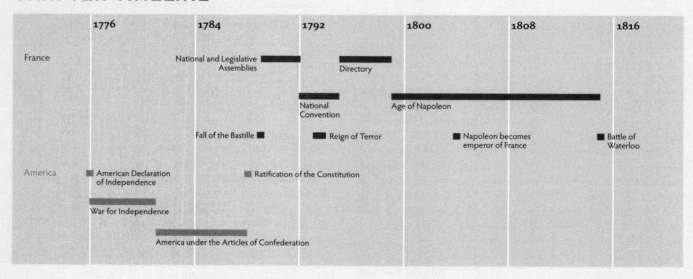

CHAPTER REVIEW

Upon Reflection

Q How was France changed by the revolutionary events of 1789 to 1792, and who benefited the most from these changes?

Q Why did the French Revolution enter a radical phase, and what did that radical phase accomplish?

Q In what ways did Napoleon's policies reject the accomplishments of the French Revolution? In what ways did his policies strengthen the Revolution's accomplishments?

Key Terms

revolution (p. 563)
old order (p. 565)
sans-culottes (p. 573)
Girondins (p. 573)
Mountain (p. 573)

nation in arms (p. 575)
de-Christianization (p. 579)
prefects (p. 585)
Continental System (p. 588)
nationalism (p. 588)

Suggestions for Further Reading

GENERAL WORKS A well-written introduction to the French Revolution can be found in **W. Doyle, *The Oxford History of the French Revolution***, 2nd ed. (Oxford, 2003). On the entire revolutionary and Napoleonic eras, see **O. Connelly, *The French Revolution and Napoleonic Era***, 3rd ed. (Fort Worth, Tex., 2000). A brief work is **J. D. Popkin et al., *A Short History of the French Revolution***, 4th ed. (Upper Saddle River, N.J., 2005). On the French Revolution in global perspective, see **S. Desan, L. Hunt, and W.M. Nelson, eds., *The French Revolution in Global Perspective*** (Ithaca, N.Y., 2013).

EARLY YEARS OF THE REVOLUTION The origins and early years of the French Revolution are examined in **W. Doyle, *Origins of the French Revolution***, 3rd ed. (Oxford, 1999), and **T. Tackett, *Becoming a Revolutionary*** (Princeton, N.J., 1996), on the deputies to the National Assembly. For an interesting insight into Louis XVI and French society, see **T. Tackett, *When the King Took Flight*** (Cambridge, Mass., 2003).

RADICAL REVOLUTION On the radical stage of the French Revolution, see **T. Tackett, *The Coming of the Terror in the French Revolution*** (Cambridge, Mass., 2015), and **D. Andress, *The Terror: The Merciless War for Freedom in Revolutionary France*** (New York, 2005). For a biography of Robespierre, one of the leading figures of this period, see **P. McPhee, *Robespierre: A Revolutionary Life*** (New Haven, Conn., 2013).

The importance of the revolutionary wars in the radical stage of the Revolution is underscored in **T. C. W. Blanning, *The French Revolutionary Wars, 1787–1802*** (New York, 1996). On the republican calendar, see **M. Shaw, *Time and the French Revolution*** (Rochester, N.Y., 2011).

WOMEN On the role of women in revolutionary France, see **O. J. Hufton, *Women and the Limits of Citizenship in the French Revolution*** (Toronto, 1992), and **J. Landes, *Women and the Public Sphere in the Age of the French Revolution*** (Ithaca, N.Y., 1988).

NAPOLEON The best biography of Napoleon is **S. Englund, *Napoleon: A Political Life*** (New York, 2004). See also **D. Bell, *Napoleon: A Concise Biography*** (Oxford, 2015), and **A. I. Grab, *Napoleon and the Transformation of Europe*** (New York, 2003), on Napoleon's Grand Empire. On Napoleon's wars, see **O. Connelly, *Blundering to Glory: Napoleon's Military Campaigns***, 3rd ed. (Lanham, Md., 2006), and **D. A. Bell, *The First Total War: Napoleon's Europe and the Birth of Warfare as We Know It*** (Boston, 2007).

AMERICAN REVOLUTION A history of the revolutionary era in America can be found in **S. Conway, *The War of American Independence, 1775–1783*** (New York, 1995), and **C. Bonwick, *The American Revolution*** (Charlottesville, Va., 1991).

Notes

1. Quoted in R. R. Palmer, *The Age of the Democratic Revolutions* (Princeton, N.J., 1959), vol. 1, p. 239.
2. Quoted in ibid., p. 242.
3. Quoted in O. J. Hufton, "Toward an Understanding of the Poor of Eighteenth-Century France," in J. F. Bosher, ed., *French Government and Society, 1500–1850* (London, 1973), p. 152.
4. Arthur Young, *Travels in France During the Years 1787, 1788, and 1789* (Cambridge, 1929), p. 23.
5. Quoted in D. M. G. Sutherland, *France, 1789–1815: Revolution and Counter-Revolution* (New York, 1986), p. 74.
6. Quoted in W. Doyle, *The Oxford History of the French Revolution* (Oxford, 1989), p. 156.
7. Author's translation of *La Marseillaise*.
8. Quoted in W. Doyle, *The Oxford History of the French Revolution*, p. 184.
9. Quoted in J. Hardman, ed., *French Revolution Documents* (Oxford, 1973), vol. 2, p. 23.
10. Quoted in W. Scott, *Terror and Repression in Revolutionary Marseilles* (London, 1973), p. 84.
11. Quoted in H. M. Stephens, *The Principal Speeches of the Statesmen and Orators of the French Revolution* (Oxford, 1892), vol. 2, p. 189.
12. Quoted in L. Gershoy, *The Era of the French Revolution* (Princeton, N.J., 1957), p. 157.
13. Quoted in J. M. Thompson, ed., *French Revolution Documents* (Oxford, 1933), pp. 258–259.
14. Quoted in Doyle, *Oxford History of the French Revolution*, p. 254.
15. Quoted in R. R. Palmer, *Twelve Who Ruled* (New York, 1965), p. 75.
16. Quoted in D. G. Levy, H. B. Applewhite, and M. D. Johnson, eds., *Women in Revolutionary Paris, 1789–1795* (Urbana, Ill., 1979), p. 132.
17. Ibid., pp. 219–220.
18. Quoted in E. G. Sledziewski, "The French Revolution as the Turning Point," in G. Fraisse and M. Perrot, eds., *A History of Women in the West* (Cambridge, 1993), vol. 4, p. 39.
19. Quoted in F. Furet and M. Ozouf, *A Critical Dictionary of the French Revolution*, trans. A. Goldhammer (Cambridge, Mass., 1989), p. 545.
20. Quoted in J. C. Herold, ed., *The Mind of Napoleon* (New York, 1955), p. 43.
21. Quoted in F. Markham, *Napoleon* (New York, 1963), pp. 92–93.
22. Quoted in Doyle, *Oxford History of the French Revolution*, p. 381.
23. Quoted in Herold, ed., *The Mind of Napoleon*, pp. 74–75.
24. Quoted in S. Englund, *Napoleon: A Political Life* (New York, 2004), p. 285.

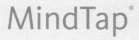 **MindTap®** is a fully online, highly personalized learning experience built upon Cengage Learning content. MindTap combines student learning tools—readings, multimedia, activities, and assessments—into a singular Learning Path that guides students through the course.

THE INDUSTRIAL REVOLUTION AND ITS IMPACT ON EUROPEAN SOCIETY

Power looms in an English textile factory

CHAPTER OUTLINE AND FOCUS QUESTIONS

The Industrial Revolution in Great Britain

Q Why was Great Britain the first state to have an Industrial Revolution? Why did it happen in Britain when it did? What were the basic features of the new industrial system created by the Industrial Revolution?

The Spread of Industrialization

Q How did the Industrial Revolution spread from Great Britain to the continent and the United States, and how did industrialization in those areas differ from British industrialization?

The Social Impact of the Industrial Revolution

Q What effects did the Industrial Revolution have on urban life, social classes, family life, and standards of living? What were working conditions like in the early decades of the Industrial Revolution, and what efforts were made to improve them?

Critical Thinking

Q *What role did government and trade unions play in the industrial development of the Western world? Who helped the workers the most?*

Connections to Today

Q *How do the locations of the centers of industrialization today compare with those during the Industrial Revolution, and how do you account for any differences?*

THE FRENCH REVOLUTION dramatically and quickly altered the political structure of France, and the Napoleonic conquests spread many of the revolutionary principles in an equally rapid and stunning fashion to other parts of Europe. During the late eighteenth and early nineteenth centuries, another revolution—an industrial one—was transforming the economic and social structure of Europe, although more slowly and somewhat less dramatically.

The Industrial Revolution caused a quantum leap in industrial production. New sources of energy and power, especially coal and steam, replaced wind and water to run machines that significantly decreased the use of human and animal labor and at the same time increased productivity. This in turn called for new ways of organizing human labor to maximize the benefits and profits from the new machines; factories replaced workshops and home workrooms. Many early factories were dreadful places with difficult working conditions. Reformers, appalled at these conditions, were especially critical of the treatment of married women. One reported, "We have repeatedly seen married females, in the last stage of pregnancy, slaving from morning to night beside these never-tiring machines, and when . . . they were obliged to sit down to take a moment's ease, and being seen by the manager, were fined for the offense." But there were also examples of well-run factories. William Cobbett described one in Manchester in 1830: "In this room, which is lighted in the most convenient and beautiful manner, there were five hundred pairs of looms at work, and five hundred persons attending those looms; and, owing to the goodness of the masters, the whole looking healthy and well-dressed."

During the Industrial Revolution, Europe experienced a shift from a traditional, labor-intensive economy based on farming and handicrafts to a more capital-intensive economy based on manufacturing by machines, specialized labor, and industrial factories. Although the Industrial Revolution took decades to spread, it was truly revolutionary in the way it fundamentally changed Europeans, their society, and their relationship to the rest of the world. The development of large factories encouraged mass movements of people from the countryside to urban areas, where impersonal coexistence replaced the traditional intimacy of rural life. Higher levels of productivity led to a search for new sources of raw materials, new consumption patterns, and a revolution in transportation that allowed raw materials and finished products to be moved quickly around the world. The creation of a wealthy industrial middle class and a huge industrial working class (or proletariat) substantially transformed traditional social relationships.

The Industrial Revolution in Great Britain

 FOCUS QUESTIONS: Why was Great Britain the first state to have an Industrial Revolution? Why did it happen in Britain when it did? What were the basic features of the new industrial system created by the Industrial Revolution?

Although the Industrial Revolution evolved over a long period of time, historians generally agree that it began in Britain sometime after 1750. By 1850, the Industrial Revolution had made Great Britain the wealthiest country in the world; it had also spread to the European continent and the New World. In another fifty years, both Germany and the United States would surpass Britain in industrial production.

Origins

A number of factors or conditions coalesced in Britain to produce the first Industrial Revolution. One of these was the **agricultural revolution** of the eighteenth century. The changes in the methods of farming and stock breeding that characterized this agricultural transformation led to a significant increase in food production. British agriculture could now feed more people at lower prices with less labor. Unlike people in the rest of Europe, even ordinary British families did not have to use most of their income to buy food, giving them the potential to purchase manufactured goods. At the same time, rapid population growth in the second half of the eighteenth century provided a pool of surplus labor for the new factories of the emerging British industry. Rural workers in cottage industries also provided a potential labor force for industrial enterprises.

SUPPLY OF CAPITAL Britain had a ready supply of **capital** for investment in the new industrial machines and the factories that

were needed to house them. In addition to profits from trade and cottage industry, Britain possessed an effective central bank and well-developed, flexible credit facilities. Nowhere in Europe were people so accustomed to using paper instruments to facilitate capital transactions. Many early factory owners were merchants and entrepreneurs who had profited from the eighteenth-century cottage industry. Of 110 cotton-spinning mills in operation in the area known as the Midlands between 1769 and 1800, fully 62 were established by hosiers, drapers, mercers, and others involved in some fashion in the cottage textile industry.

EARLY INDUSTRIAL ENTREPRENEURS But capital is only part of the story. Britain had a fair number of individuals who were interested in making profits if the opportunity presented itself (see the box on p. 594). The British were a people, as one historian has said, "fascinated by wealth and commerce, collectively and individually." No doubt the English revolutions of the seventeenth century had helped create an environment in Britain, unlike that of the absolutist states on the continent, where political power rested in the hands of a group of progressive people who favored innovation in economic matters.

Nevertheless, these early industrial entrepreneurs faced considerable financial hazards. Fortunes were made quickly and lost just as quickly. Early firms had a fluid structure. An individual or family proprietorship was the usual mode of operation, but entrepreneurs also brought in friends to help—and just as easily jettisoned them. John Marshall, who made money in flax spinning, threw his partners out: "As they could neither of them be of any further use, I released them from the firm and took the whole upon myself."[1]

MINERAL RESOURCES Britain had ample supplies of important mineral resources, such as coal and iron ore, needed in the manufacturing process. Britain was also small, so the resources had to be transported only relatively short distances. In addition to nature's provision of abundant rivers, from the mid-seventeenth century onward, both private and public investment poured into the construction of new roads, bridges, and, beginning in the 1750s and 1760s, canals. By 1780, roads, rivers, and canals linked the major industrial centers of the North, the Midlands, London, and the Atlantic. Unlike the continental countries, Britain had no internal customs barriers to hinder domestic trade.

ROLE OF GOVERNMENT Britain's government also played a significant role in the process of industrialization. Parliament contributed to the favorable business climate by providing a stable government and passing laws that protected private property. Moreover, Britain was remarkable for the freedom it provided for private enterprise. It placed fewer restrictions on private entrepreneurs than any other European state.

MARKETS Finally, a supply of markets gave British industrialists a ready outlet for their manufactured goods. British exports quadrupled between 1660 and 1760. In the course of its eighteenth-century wars and conquests, Great Britain had developed a vast colonial empire at the expense of its leading continental rivals, the Dutch Republic and France. Britain also possessed a well-developed merchant marine that was

THE TRAITS OF THE BRITISH INDUSTRIAL ENTREPRENEUR

RICHARD ARKWRIGHT (1732–1792), INVENTOR OF A spinning frame and founder of cotton factories, was a good example of the successful entrepreneur in the early Industrial Revolution in Britain. In this selection, Edward Baines, writing in 1835, discusses the traits that explain the success of Arkwright and presumably other British entrepreneurs.

Edward Baines, *The History of the Cotton Manufacture in Great Britain*

Richard Arkwright rose by the force of his natural talents from a very humble condition in society. He was born at Preston on the 23rd of December, 1732, of poor parents: being the youngest of thirteen children, his parents could only afford to give him an education of the humblest kind, and he was scarcely able to write. He was brought up to the trade of a barber at Kirkham and Preston, and established himself in that business at Bolton in the year 1760. Having become possessed of a chemical process for dyeing human hair, which in that day (when wigs were universal) was of considerable value, he traveled about collecting hair, and again disposing of it when dyed. In 1761, he married a wife from Leigh, and the connections he thus formed in that town are supposed to have afterwards brought him acquainted with Highs's experiments in making spinning machines. He himself manifested a strong bent for experiments in mathematics, which he is stated to have followed with so much devotedness as to have neglected his business and injured his circumstances. His natural disposition was ardent, enterprising, and stubbornly persevering: his mind was as coarse as it was bold and active, and his manners were rough and unpleasing. . . .

The most marked traits in the character of Arkwright were his wonderful ardor, energy, and perseverance. He commonly labored in his multifarious concerns from five o'clock in the morning till nine at night; and when considerably more than fifty years of age,—feeling that the defects of his education placed him under great difficulty and inconvenience in conducting his correspondence, and in the general management of his business,—he encroached upon his sleep, in order to gain an hour each day to learn English grammar, and another hour to improve his writing and orthography [spelling]! He was impatient of whatever interfered with his favorite pursuits; and the fact is too strikingly characteristic not to be mentioned, that he separated from his wife not many years after their marriage, because she, convinced that he would starve his family [because of the impractical nature of his schemes], broke some of his experimental models of machinery. Arkwright was a severe economist of time; and, that he might not waste a moment, he generally traveled with four horses, and at a very rapid speed. His concerns in Derbyshire, Lancashire, and Scotland were so extensive and numerous, as to [show] at once his astonishing power of transacting business and his all grasping spirit. In many of these he had partners, but he generally managed in such a way, that, whoever lost, he himself was a gainer.

 As seen in the life of Richard Arkwright, what traits did Edward Baines think were crucial to being a successful entrepreneur? To what extent are these still considered the necessary traits for a successful entrepreneur?

Source: E. Baines, *The History of the Cotton Manufacture in Great Britain* (London: Fisher, Fisher, and Jackson, 1835), pp. 195–196.

---

able to transport goods anywhere in the world. A crucial factor in Britain's successful industrialization was the ability to produce cheaply the articles most in demand abroad. And the best markets abroad were not in Europe, where countries protected their own incipient industries, but in the Americas, Africa, and the East, where people wanted sturdy, inexpensive clothes rather than costly, highly finished luxury items. Britain's machine-produced textiles fulfilled that demand. Nor should we overlook the British domestic market. Britain had the highest standard of living in Europe and a rapidly growing population. As Daniel Defoe noted already in 1728:

> For the rest, we see their Houses and Lodgings tolerably furnished, at least stuff'd well with useful and necessary household Goods: Even those we call poor People, Journeymen, working and Pains-taking People do thus; they lye warm, live in Plenty, work hard, and know no Want. These are the People that carry off the Gross of your Consumption; 'tis for these your Markets are kept open late on Saturday nights; because they usually receive their Week's Wages late. . . . In a Word, these are the Life of our whole Commerce, and all by their

Multitude: Their Numbers are not Hundreds or Thousands, or Hundreds of Thousands, but Millions; . . . by their Wages they are able to live plentifully, and it is by their expensive, generous, free way of living, that the Home Consumption is rais'd to such a Bulk, as well of our own, as of foreign Production.[2]

This demand from both domestic and foreign markets and the inability of the old system to fulfill it led entrepreneurs to seek and adopt the new methods of manufacturing that a series of inventions provided. In so doing, these individuals initiated the Industrial Revolution.

Technological Changes and New Forms of Industrial Organization

In the 1770s and 1780s, the cotton textile industry took the first major step toward the Industrial Revolution with the creation of the modern factory.

THE COTTON INDUSTRY Already in the eighteenth century, Great Britain had surged ahead in the production of cheap cotton goods using the traditional methods of the cottage

THE STEAM ENGINE AND COTTON

PRIOR TO THE INVENTION OF THE STEAM ENGINE, cotton was loomed by hand. In 1823, Richard Guest, an English economist, wrote of the advantages of steam weaving. It was not, however, advantageous for the handloom weavers; thousands lost their jobs as a result of the new invention.

Richard Guest, *A Compendius History of the Cotton-Manufacture*

The same powerful agent which so materially forwarded and advanced the progress of the Cotton Manufacture in the concluding party of the last century, has lately been further used as a substitute for manual labour, and the Steam Engine is now applied to the working of the loom as well as to the preparatory processes. . . .

It is a curious circumstance, that, when the Cotton Manufacture was in its infancy, all the operations, from the dress of the raw material to its being finally being turned out in the state of cloth, were completed under the roof of the weaver's cottage. The course of improved manufacture which followed, was to spin the yarn in factories and to weave it in cottages. . . . The Weaver's cottage with its rude apparatus of peg warping, hand card, hand wheels, and imperfect looms, was the Steam Loom factory in miniature. Those vast brick edifices in the vicinity of all the great manufacturing towns in the south of Lancashire, towering to the height of seventy or eighty feet, which strike the attention and excite the curiosity of the traveller, now perform the labors which formerly employed whole villages. In the Steam Loom factories, the cotton is carded, roved, spun, and woven into cloth, and the same quantum of labor is now performed in one of these structures which formerly occupied the industry of an entire district.

A very good Hand Weaver, a man twenty-five or thirty years of age, will weave two pieces of shirting per week, each twenty-four years long . . . A Steam Loom Weaver, fifteen years of age, will in the same time weave seven similar pieces. A Steam Loom factory containing two hundred Looms, with the assistance of one hundred persons under twenty years of age, and of twenty-five men, will weave seven hundred pieces per week. To manufacture one hundred similar pieces per week by the hand, it would be necessary to employ at least one hundred and twenty-five Looms, because many of the Weavers are females, and have cooking, washing, cleaning and various other duties to perform; others of them are children and, consequently, unable to weave as much as the men.

 In what ways did the new steam loom transform the cotton industry? Who was excluded from this new form of industry?

Source: R. Guest, *A Compendius History of the Cotton-Manufacture* (Manchester, 1823), pp. 44–48.

---

industry. The development of the flying shuttle had sped the process of weaving on a loom, enabling weavers to double their output. This caused shortages of yarn, however, until James Hargreaves's spinning jenny, perfected by 1768, enabled spinners to produce yarn in greater quantities. Richard Arkwright's water frame spinning machine, powered by water or horse, and Samuel Crompton's so-called mule, which combined aspects of the water frame and the spinning jenny, increased yarn production even more. Edmund Cartwright's power loom, invented in 1787, allowed the weaving of cloth to catch up with the spinning of yarn. Even then, early power looms were grossly inefficient, enabling home-based handloom weavers to continue to prosper, at least until the mid-1820s. After that, the new machines gradually replaced these workers. In 1813, there were 2,400 power looms in operation in Great Britain; they numbered 14,150 in 1820, 100,000 in 1833, and 250,000 by 1850. In the 1820s, there were still 250,000 handloom weavers in Britain; by 1860, only 3,000 were left.

The water frame, Crompton's mule, and power looms presented new opportunities to entrepreneurs. It was much more efficient to bring workers to the machines and organize their labor collectively in factories located next to rivers and streams, the sources of power for many of these early machines, than to leave the workers dispersed in their cottages. The concentration of labor in the new factories also brought the laborers and their families to live in the new towns that rapidly grew up around the factories.

The early devices used to speed up the processes of spinning and weaving were the products of weavers and spinners—in effect, of artisan tinkerers. But the subsequent expansion of the cotton industry and the ongoing demand for even more cotton goods created additional pressure for new and more complicated technology. The invention that pushed the cotton industry to even greater heights of productivity was the steam engine.

THE STEAM ENGINE The steam engine revolutionized the production of cotton goods and allowed the factory system to spread to other areas of production, thereby securing whole new industries. The steam engine thus ensured the triumph of the Industrial Revolution.

In the 1760s, a Scottish engineer, James Watt (1736–1819), created an engine powered by steam that could pump water from mines three times as quickly as previous engines. In 1782, Watt expanded the possibilities of the steam engine when he developed a rotary engine that could turn a shaft and thus drive machinery. Steam power could now be applied to spinning and weaving cotton, and before long, cotton mills using steam engines were multiplying across Britain. The introduction of the steam loom in the early 1820s revolutionized textile production (see the document above). Because steam engines

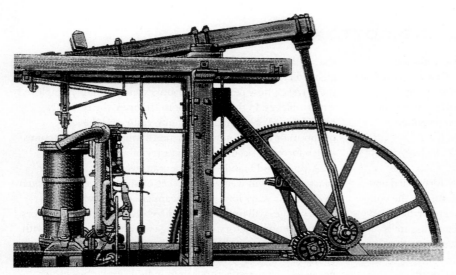

A Boulton and Watt Steam Engine. Encouraged by his business partner, Matthew Boulton, James Watt developed the first genuine steam engine. Pictured here is a typical Boulton and Watt engine. Steam pressure in the cylinder on the left drives the beam upward and sets the flywheel in motion.

Oxford Science Archive, Oxford//HIP/Art Resource, NY

were fired by coal, they did not need to be located near rivers; entrepreneurs now had greater flexibility in their choice of location.

The new boost given to cotton textile production by technological changes became readily apparent. In 1760, Britain had imported 2.5 million pounds of raw cotton, which was farmed out to cottage industries. In 1787, the British imported 22 million pounds of cotton; most of it was spun on machines, some powered by water in large mills. By 1840, fully 366 million pounds of cotton—now Britain's most important product in value—were imported. By this time, most cotton industry employees worked in factories. The cheapest labor in India could not compete in quality or quantity with Britain. British cotton goods sold everywhere in the world. And in Britain itself, cheap cotton cloth made it possible for millions of poor people to wear undergarments, long a luxury of the rich, who could afford expensive linen cloth. Cotton clothing was tough, comfortable, cheap, and easily washable.

The steam engine proved indispensable. Unlike horses, the steam engine was a tireless source of power and depended for fuel on a substance—coal—that seemed unlimited in quantity. The popular saying that "steam is an Englishman" had real significance by 1850. The success of the steam engine led to a need for more coal and an expansion in coal production; between 1815 and 1850, the output of coal quadrupled. In turn, new processes using coal furthered the development of the iron industry.

THE IRON INDUSTRY The British iron industry was radically transformed during the Industrial Revolution. Britain had large deposits of iron ore, but at the beginning of the eighteenth century, the basic process of producing iron had changed little since the Middle Ages and still depended heavily on charcoal. In the early eighteenth century, new methods of smelting iron ore to produce cast iron were devised, based on the use of

coke or "courke" that was made by slowly burning coal. Coke could heat iron ore at a faster rate than charcoal, thus yielding higher amounts. Still, a better quality of iron was not possible until the 1780s, when Henry Cort developed a process called puddling in which coke was used to burn away impurities in **pig iron** (the product of smelting iron ore with coke) to produce an iron of high quality called **wrought iron**. Wrought iron, with its lower carbon content, was malleable and able to withstand strain. A boom then ensued in the British iron industry. In 1740, Britain produced 17,000 tons of iron; in the 1780s, almost 70,000 tons; by the 1840s, more than 2 million tons; and by 1852, almost 3 million tons, more than the rest of the world combined.

The development of the iron industry was in many ways a response to the demand for the new machines. The high-quality wrought iron produced by the Cort process made it the most widely used metal until the production of cheaper steel in the 1860s. The growing supply of less costly metal encouraged the use of machinery in other industries, most noticeably in new means of transportation.

A REVOLUTION IN TRANSPORTATION The eighteenth century had witnessed an expansion of transportation facilities in Britain as entrepreneurs realized the need for more efficient means of moving resources and goods. Turnpike trusts constructed new roads, and between 1760 and 1830, a network of canals was built. But a new form of transportation that dazzled people with its promise soon overtook both roads and canals. To many economic historians, railroads were the "most important single factor in promoting European economic progress in the 1830s and 1840s." Again, Britain was the leader in the revolution.

The railways got their start in mining operations in Germany as early as 1500 and in British coal mines after 1600, where small handcarts filled with coal were pushed along parallel wooden rails. The rails reduced friction, enabling horses to haul more substantial loads. By 1700, some entrepreneurs began to replace wooden rails with cast-iron rails, and by the early nineteenth century, railways—still dependent on horsepower—were common in British mining and industrial districts. The development of the steam engine led to a radical transformation of the railways.

In 1804, Richard Trevithick (TREV-uh-thik) pioneered the first steam-powered locomotive on an industrial rail line in southern Wales. It pulled 10 tons of ore and seventy people at 5 miles per hour. Better locomotives soon followed. The engines built by George Stephenson and his son proved superior, and it was in their workshops in Newcastle-upon-Tyne that the locomotives for the first modern railways in Britain were built. George Stephenson's *Rocket* was used on the first public railway line, which opened in 1830, extending 32 miles from Liverpool to Manchester. *Rocket* sped along at 16 miles per hour. Within twenty years,

Railroad Line from Liverpool to Manchester. The railroad line from Liverpool to Manchester, opened in 1830, relied on steam locomotives. As is evident in this illustration, carrying passengers was the railroad's main business. First-class passengers rode in covered cars; second- and third-class passengers, in open cars.

locomotives had reached 50 miles per hour, an incredible speed to contemporary passengers accustomed to rides in horse-drawn stage-coaches. The new experience of railway transportation changed perceptions of time, space and nature. In 1837, Victor Hugo tried to capture this new experience by writing, "The flowers by the side of the road are no longer flowers but flecks, or rather streaks, of red or white; . . . the grain fields are great shocks of yellow hair; . . . the towns, the steeples, and the trees perform a crazy mingling dance on the horizon; from time to time, a shadow, a shape, a spectre appears and disappears with lightning speed: it's a railway guard."[3] During the same period, new companies were formed to build additional railroads as the infant industry proved successful financially as well as technically. Railroads created an entirely new industry, creating new jobs in upholstery, carriage-making, and glass production, while the engineering required to build bridges strong enough to support heavy trains prompted new engineering innovations. In 1840, Britain had almost 2,000 miles of railroads; by 1850, 6,000 miles of railroad track crisscrossed much of the country (see Map 20.1).

The railroad contributed significantly to the maturing of the Industrial Revolution. The railroad's demands for coal and iron furthered the growth of those industries. British supremacy in civil and mechanical engineering, so evident after 1840, was in large part based on the skills acquired in railway building. The huge capital demands necessary for railway construction encouraged a whole new group of middle-class investors to invest their money in joint-stock companies (see "Industrialization on the Continent" in Chapter 22). Railway construction created

MAP 20.1 The Industrial Revolution in Britain by 1850. The Industrial Revolution began in the mid-1700s. Increased food production, rapid population growth, higher incomes, plentiful capital, solid banking and financial institutions, an abundance of mineral resources, and easy transport all furthered the process, making Britain the world's wealthiest country by 1850.

Q *How well did the railroad system connect important British industrial areas?*

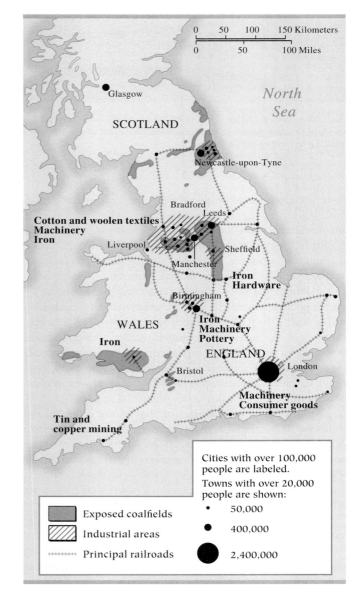

A British Textile Factory. The development of the factory changed the relationship between workers and employers as workers were encouraged to adjust to a new system of discipline that forced them to work regular hours under close supervision. This 1835 illustration shows women and men working in a British textile factory.

ARPL/HIP/The Image Works

new job opportunities, especially for farm laborers and peasants, who had long been accustomed to finding work outside their local villages. Perhaps most important, a cheaper and faster means of transportation had a rippling effect on the growth of an industrial economy. By reducing the price of goods, larger markets were created; increased sales necessitated more factories and more machinery, thereby reinforcing the self-sustaining nature of the Industrial Revolution, which marked a fundamental break with the traditional European economy. The great productivity of the Industrial Revolution enabled entrepreneurs to reinvest their profits in new capital equipment, further expanding the productive capacity of the economy. Continuous, even rapid, self-sustaining economic growth came to be seen as a fundamental characteristic of the new industrial economy.

The railroad was the perfect symbol of this aspect of the Industrial Revolution. The ability to transport goods and people at dramatic speeds also provided visible confirmation of a new sense of power. When railway engineers penetrated mountains with tunnels and spanned chasms with breathtaking bridges, contemporaries experienced a sense of power over nature not felt before in Western civilization.

THE INDUSTRIAL FACTORY Initially the product of the cotton industry, the factory became the chief means of organizing labor for the new machines. As the workplace shifted from the artisan's shop and the peasant's cottage to the factory, the latter

was not viewed as just a larger work unit. Employers hired workers who no longer owned the means of production but were simply paid wages to run the machines.

From its beginning, the factory system demanded a new type of discipline from its employees. Factory owners could not afford to let their expensive machinery stand idle. Workers were forced to work regular hours and in shifts to keep the machines producing at a steady pace for maximum output. This represented a massive adjustment for early factory laborers.

Preindustrial workers were not accustomed to a timed format. Agricultural laborers had always kept irregular hours; hectic work at harvest time might be followed by weeks of inactivity. Even in the burgeoning cottage industry of the eighteenth century, weavers and spinners who worked at home might fulfill their weekly quotas by working around the clock for two or three days and then proceeding at a leisurely pace until the next week's demands forced another work spurt.

Factory owners therefore faced a formidable task. They had to create a system of time-work discipline that would accustom employees to working regular, unvarying hours during which they performed a set number of tasks over and over again as efficiently as possible. One early industrialist said that his aim was "to make such machines of the men as cannot err." Such work, of course, tended to be repetitive and boring, and factory owners resorted to tough methods to accomplish their goals. Factory regulations were minute and detailed

DISCIPLINE IN THE NEW FACTORIES

WORKERS IN THE NEW FACTORIES OF THE Industrial Revolution had been accustomed to a lifestyle free of overseers. Unlike the cottages, where workers spun thread and wove cloth in their own rhythm and time, the factories demanded a new, rigorous discipline geared to the requirements of the machines. This selection is taken from a set of rules for a factory in Berlin in 1844. They were typical of company rules everywhere the factory system had been established.

Factory Rules, Foundry and Engineering Works of the Royal Overseas Trading Company, Berlin

In every large works, and in the co-ordination of any large number of workmen, good order and harmony must be looked upon as the fundamentals of success, and therefore the following rules shall be strictly observed.

1. The normal working day begins at all seasons at 6 A.M. precisely and ends, after the usual break of half an hour for breakfast, an hour for dinner and half an hour for tea, at 7 P.M. and it shall be strictly observed. . . . Workers arriving 2 minutes late shall lose half an hour's wages; whoever is more than 2 minutes late may not start work until after the next break; or at least shall lose his wages until then. Any disputes about the correct time shall be settled by the clock mounted above the gatekeeper's lodge. . . .

3. No workman, whether employed by time or piece, may leave before the end of the working day, without having first received permission from the overseer and having given his name to the gatekeeper. Omission of these two actions shall lead to a fine of ten silver groschen [pennies] payable to the sick fund.

4. Repeated irregular arrival at work shall lead to dismissal. This shall also apply to those who are found idling by an official or overseer, and refused to obey their order to resume work. . . .

6. No worker may leave his place of work otherwise than for reasons connected with his work.

7. All conversation with fellow-workers is prohibited; if any worker requires information about his work, he must turn to the overseer, or to the particular fellow-worker designated for the purpose.

8. Smoking in the workshops or in the yard is prohibited during working hours; anyone caught smoking shall be fined five silver groschen for the sick fund for every such offense. . . .

10. Natural functions must be performed at the appropriate places, and whoever is found soiling walls, fences, squares, etc., and similarly, whoever is found washing his face and hands in the workshop and not in the places assigned for the purpose, shall be fined five silver groschen for the sick fund. . . .

12. It goes without saying that all overseers and officials of the firm shall be obeyed without question, and shall be treated with due deference. Disobedience will be punished by dismissal.

13. Immediate dismissal shall also be the fate of anyone found drunk in any of the workshops. . . .

14. Every workman is obliged to report to his superiors any acts of dishonesty or embezzlement on the part of his fellow workmen. If he omits to do so, and it is shown after subsequent discovery of a misdemeanor that he knew about it at the time, he shall be liable to be taken to court as an accessory after the fact and the wage due to him shall be retained as punishment.

 What impact did factories have on the lives of workers? To what extent have such "rules" determined much of modern industrial life?

Source: S. Pollard and C. Holmes, eds., *Documents of European Economic History*, vol. I (London: Palgrave Macmillan, 1972).

(see the box above). Adult workers were fined for a wide variety of minor infractions, such as being a few minutes late for work, and dismissed for more serious misdoings, especially drunkenness. Drunkenness was viewed as particularly offensive because it set a bad example for younger workers and also courted disaster amid dangerous machinery. Employers found that dismissals and fines worked well for adult employees; in a time when great population growth had led to large numbers of unskilled workers, dismissal could be disastrous. Children were less likely to understand the implications of dismissal, so they were sometimes disciplined more directly—by beating.

The efforts of factory owners in the early Industrial Revolution to impose a new set of values were frequently reinforced by the new evangelical churches. Methodism, in particular, emphasized that people "reborn in Jesus" must forgo immoderation and follow a disciplined path. Laziness and wasteful habits were sinful. The acceptance of hardship in this life paved the way for the joys of the next. Evangelical values paralleled the efforts of the new factory owners to instill laborers with their own middle-class values of hard work, discipline, and thrift. In one crucial sense, the early industrialists proved successful. As the nineteenth century progressed, the second and third generations of workers came to view a regular working week as a natural way of life. It was, of course, an attitude that made possible Britain's incredible economic growth in that century.

Britain's Great Exhibition of 1851

In 1851, the British organized the world's first industrial fair. It was housed at Kensington in London in the Crystal Palace, an enormous structure made entirely of glass and iron, a tribute

The Great Exhibition of 1851. The Great Exhibition of 1851 was a symbol of the success of Great Britain, which had become the world's first industrial nation and its richest. More than 100,000 exhibits were housed in the Crystal Palace, a giant structure of cast iron and glass. The first illustration shows the front of the palace and some of its numerous visitors. The second shows the opening day ceremonies. Queen Victoria is seen at the center with her family, surrounded by visitors from all over the world. Note the large tree inside the building, providing a visible symbol of how the Industrial Revolution had supposedly achieved human domination over nature.

to British engineering skills. Covering 19 acres, the Crystal Palace contained 100,000 exhibits that displayed the wide variety of products created by the Industrial Revolution. Six million people visited the fair in six months. Though most of them were Britons who had traveled to London by train, foreign visitors were also prominent. The Great Exhibition displayed Britain's wealth to the world; it was a gigantic demonstration of British success. Even trees were brought inside the Crystal Palace as a visible symbol of how the Industrial Revolution had achieved human domination over nature. Prince Albert, Queen Victoria's husband, expressed the sentiments of the age when he described the exhibition as a sign that "man is approaching a more complete fulfillment of that great and sacred mission which he has to perform in this world . . . to conquer nature to his use." Not content with that, he also linked British success to divine will: "In promoting [the progress of the human race], we are accomplishing the will of the great and blessed God."[4]

In addition to demonstrating Britain's enormous industrial growth, the Crystal Palace exhibition also represented British imperial power. Goods from India were a highlight of the exhibition, and the East India Company drew attention to its role in India with exhibits of cotton, tea, and flax. But it was the display of Indian silks, jewels, shawls, and an elephant canopy that captured the attention of the British press and visitors. Despite the public interest in the ornate and intricate works from India, many British commentators, such as the scientist William Whewell, were less complimentary. They characterized the Indian handmade goods as typical of a system in which "tens of thousands" worked for a few despots. Moreover, these goods were examples of the "wasteful and ridiculous excess" of the labor-intensive production practices in the East, which could not compare to enlightened British labor practices.[5]

By the year of the Great Exhibition, Great Britain had become the world's first industrial nation and its wealthiest. Britain was the "workshop, banker, and trader of the world." It produced one-half of the world's coal and manufactured goods; its cotton industry alone in 1851 was equal in size to the industries of all other European countries combined. The quantity of goods produced was growing at three times the rate in 1780. Britain's certainty about its mission in the world in the nineteenth century was grounded in its incredible material success.

The Spread of Industrialization

 FOCUS QUESTION: How did the Industrial Revolution spread from Great Britain to the continent and the United States, and how did industrialization in those areas differ from British industrialization?

Beginning first in Great Britain, industrialization spread to the continental countries of Europe and the United States at different times and speeds during the nineteenth century. First to be industrialized on the continent were Belgium, France, and the German states; the first in North America was the new United States. Not until after 1850 did the Industrial Revolution spread to the rest of Europe and other parts of the world.

Industrialization on the Continent

In 1815, the Low Countries, France, and the German states were still largely agrarian. During the eighteenth century, some of the continental countries had experienced developments similar to those of Britain. They, too, had achieved population growth, made agricultural improvements, expanded their cottage industries, and witnessed growth in foreign trade. But whereas Britain's economy began to move in new industrial

directions in the 1770s and 1780s, continental countries lagged behind because they did not share some of the advantages that had made Britain's Industrial Revolution possible. Lack of good roads and problems with river transit made transportation difficult. Toll stations on important rivers and customs barriers along state boundaries increased the costs and prices of goods. Guild restrictions were also more prevalent, creating impediments that pioneer industrialists in Britain did not have to face. Finally, continental entrepreneurs were generally less enterprising than their British counterparts and tended to adhere to traditional business attitudes, such as a dislike of competition, a high regard for family security coupled with an unwillingness to take risks in investment, and an excessive worship of thriftiness. Thus, industrialization on the continent faced numerous hurdles, and as it proceeded in earnest after 1815, it did so along lines that were somewhat different from Britain's.

BORROWING TECHNIQUES AND PRACTICES Lack of technical knowledge was initially a major obstacle to industrialization. But the continental countries possessed an advantage here; they could simply borrow British techniques and practices. Of course, the British tried to prevent that. Until 1825, British artisans were prohibited from leaving the country; until 1842, the export of important machinery and machine parts, especially for textile production, was forbidden. But the British efforts to control the situation by legislation were never very effective. Already by 1825, there were at least two thousand skilled British mechanics on the continent, and British equipment was also being sold abroad, legally or illegally.

Gradually, the continent achieved technological independence as local people learned all the skills their British teachers had to offer. By the 1840s, new generations of skilled mechanics from Belgium and France were spreading their knowledge east and south, playing the same role that the British had earlier. Even more important, continental countries, especially France and the German states, began to establish a wide range of technical schools to train engineers and mechanics.

ROLE OF GOVERNMENT That government played an important role in this regard brings us to another difference between British and continental industrialization. Governments in most of the continental countries were accustomed to playing a significant role in economic affairs. Furthering the development of industrialization was a logical extension of that attitude. Hence, governments provided for the costs of technical education, awarded grants to inventors and foreign entrepreneurs, exempted foreign industrial equipment from import duties, and in some places even financed factories. Of equal if not greater importance in the long run, governments actively bore much of the cost of building roads and canals, deepening and widening river channels, and constructing railroads. By 1850, a network of iron rails had spread across Europe, although only Germany and Belgium had completed major parts of their systems by that time (see Map 20.2).

Governments on the continent also used **tariffs** to encourage industrialization. After 1815, cheap British goods flooded continental markets. The French responded with high tariffs

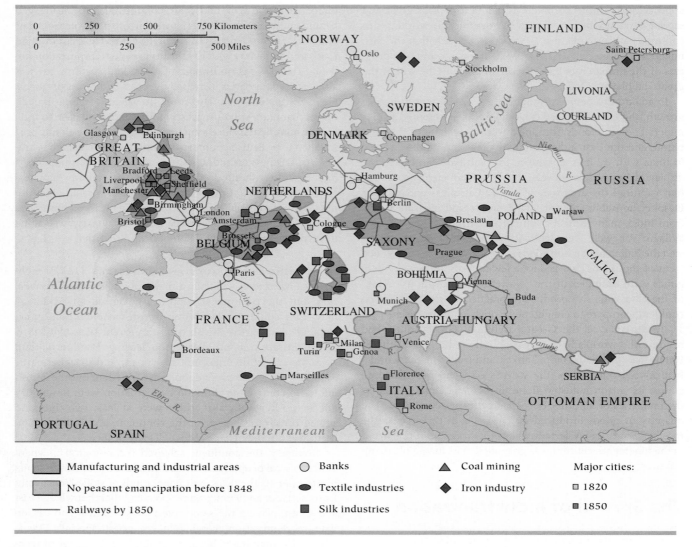

MAP 20.2 The Industrialization of Europe by 1850. Great Britain was Europe's first industrialized country; by the middle of the nineteenth century, however, several regions on the continent, especially in Belgium, France, and the German states, had made significant advances in industrialization.

Q *What reasons could explain why coal mining and iron industries are densely clustered in manufacturing and industrial areas?*

to protect their fledgling industries. The most systematic argument for the use of tariffs, however, was made by a German writer, Friedrich List (FREED-rikh LIST) (1789–1846), who emigrated to America and returned to Germany as a U.S. consul. In his *National System of Political Economy*, written in 1844, List advocated a rapid and large-scale program of industrialization as the surest path to develop a nation's strength. To ensure the growth of industry, he felt that a nation must use protective tariffs. If countries followed the British policy of free trade, then cheaper British goods would inundate national markets and destroy infant industries before they had a chance to grow. Germany, he insisted, could not compete with Britain without protective tariffs.

CENTERS OF CONTINENTAL INDUSTRIALIZATION As noted earlier, the Industrial Revolution on the continent occurred in three major centers between 1815 and 1850—Belgium, France, and the German states. As in Britain, cotton played an important role, although it was not as significant as heavy industry. France was the continental leader in the manufacture of cotton goods but still lagged far behind Great Britain. In 1849, France used 64,000 tons of raw cotton, Belgium, 11,000, and Germany, 20,000, whereas Britain used 286,000 tons. Continental cotton factories were older, used less efficient machines, and had less productive labor. In general, continental technology in the cotton industry was a generation behind Great Britain. But that is not the whole story. With its cheap coal and scarce water,

Belgium gravitated toward the use of the steam engine as the major source of power and invested in the new machines. By the mid-1840s, Belgium had the most modern cotton-manufacturing system on the continent.

The development of cotton manufacturing on the continent and in Britain differed in two significant ways. Unlike Britain, where cotton manufacturing was mostly centered in Lancashire (in northwestern England) and the Glasgow area of Scotland, cotton mills in France, Germany, and, to a lesser degree, Belgium were dispersed throughout many regions. Noticeable, too, was the mixture of old and new. The old techniques of the cottage system, such as the use of hand looms, held on much longer. In the French district of Normandy, for example, in 1849, eighty-three mills were still driven by hand or animal power. France's innovations in textiles were based less on high volume production and more on refined luxury goods for a specialized market. The success in Lyons, with the loom of Joseph-Marie Jacquard, enabled the production of patterned fine silk fabrics to be sold worldwide.

As traditional methods persisted alongside the new methods in cotton manufacturing, the new steam engine came to be used primarily in mining and metallurgy on the continent rather than in textile manufacturing. At first, almost all of the steam engines on the continent came from Britain; not until the 1820s was a domestic machine industry developed.

In Britain, the Industrial Revolution had been built on the cotton industry; on the continent, the iron and coal of heavy industry led the way. As in textiles, however, heavy industry on the continent before 1850 was a mixture of old and new. The adoption of new techniques, such as coke-smelted iron and puddling furnaces, coincided with the expansion of old-type charcoal blast furnaces. Before 1850, Germany lagged significantly behind both Belgium and France in heavy industry, and most German iron manufacturing was still based on old techniques. Not until the 1840s was coke-blast iron produced in the Rhineland. At that time, no one had yet realized the treasure of coal buried in the Ruhr valley. A German official wrote in 1852 that it was not to be expected that Germany would ever be able to reach the level of production of coal and iron currently attained in England. He said, "This is implicit in our far more limited resource endowment." Little did he realize that although the industrial development of continental Europe was about a generation behind Britain at midcentury, after 1850 an incredibly rapid growth in continental industry would demonstrate that Britain was not, after all, destined to remain the world's greatest industrial nation.

The Industrial Revolution in the United States

In 1800, the United States was an agrarian society. There were no cities with populations of more than 100,000, and six out of every seven American workers were farmers. By 1860, however, the population had grown from 5 million to 30 million people, larger than Great Britain's. Almost half of them lived west of the Appalachian Mountains. The number of states had more than doubled, from sixteen to thirty-four, and nine American cities had more than 100,000 in population. Only 50 percent of American workers were farmers. Between 1800 and the eve of the Civil War, the United States had experienced its own Industrial Revolution and the urbanization that accompanied it.

The initial application of machinery to production was accomplished, as in continental Europe, by borrowing from Great Britain. A British immigrant, Samuel Slater, established the first textile factory using water-powered spinning machines in Rhode Island in 1790. By 1813, factories were being established with power looms copied from British models. Soon thereafter, however, Americans began to equal or surpass British technical inventions. The Harpers Ferry arsenal, for example, built muskets with interchangeable parts. Because all the individual parts of the muskets were identical (for example, all triggers were the same), the final product could be put together quickly and easily; this enabled Americans to avoid the more costly system in which skilled workers fitted together individual parts made separately. The so-called American system reduced costs and revolutionized production by saving labor, important to a society that had few skilled artisans.

THE NEED FOR TRANSPORTATION Unlike Britain, the United States was a large country. The lack of a good system of internal transportation seemed to limit American economic development by making the transport of goods prohibitively expensive. This deficiency was gradually remedied by the introduction of the steamboat and the railroad as well as the construction of roads and canals. Thousands of miles of roads and canals were built linking east and west. The steamboat facilitated transportation on the Great Lakes, Atlantic coastal waters, and rivers. It was especially important to the Mississippi valley; by 1860, one thousand steamboats plied that river. Most important of all in the development of the American transportation system was the railroad. Beginning with 100 miles in 1830, by 1860 more than 27,000 miles of railroad track covered the United States. This transportation revolution turned the United States into a single massive market for the manufactured goods of the Northeast, the early center of American industrialization.

THE LABOR FORCE Labor for the growing number of factories came primarily from rural areas. The United States did not possess a large number of craftspeople, but it did have a rapidly expanding farm population, which soon outstripped the available farmland in the Northeast. While some of this excess population, especially men, went west, others, mostly women, found work in the new textile and shoe factories of New England. Indeed, women made up more than 80 percent of the labor force in the large textile factories. In Massachusetts mill towns, company boarding houses provided rooms for large numbers of young women who worked for several years before marriage. Outside Massachusetts, factory owners sought entire families, including children, to work in their mills; one mill owner ran this advertisement in a newspaper in Utica, New York: "Wanted: A few sober and industrious families of at least five children each, over the age of eight years, are wanted at the Cotton Factory in Whitestown. Widows

The Steamboat. The steamboat was an important means of transportation for American products and markets. Steamboats like the one shown in this illustration regularly plied the Mississippi River, moving the farm products of the Midwest and the Southern plantations to markets in New Orleans. After the American Civil War, railroads began to replace steamboats on many routes.

with large families would do well to attend this notice." When a decline in rural births threatened to dry up this labor pool in the 1830s and 1840s, European immigrants, especially poor and unskilled Irish, English, Scots, and Welsh, appeared in large numbers to replace American women and children in the factories.

Women, children, and immigrants had one thing in common as employees: they were largely unskilled laborers. Unskilled labor pushed American industrialization into a capital-intensive pattern. Factory owners invested heavily in machines that could produce in quantity at the hands of untrained workers. In Britain, the pace of mechanization was never as rapid because Britain's supply of skilled artisans made it more profitable to pursue a labor-intensive economy.

By 1860, the United States was well on its way to being an industrial nation. In the Northeast, the most industrialized section of the country, per capita income was 40 percent higher than the national average. Diets, it has been argued, were better and more varied; machine-made clothing was more abundant. Industrialization did not necessarily lessen economic disparities, however. Despite a growing belief in a myth of social mobility based on equality of economic opportunity, the reality was that the richest 10 percent of the population in the cities held 70 to 80 percent of the wealth, compared to 50 percent in 1800. Nevertheless, American historians generally argue that while the rich got richer, the poor, thanks to an increase in their purchasing power, did not get poorer.

Limiting the Spread of Industrialization in the Nonindustrialized World

Before 1870, the industrialization that had developed in western and central Europe and the United States did not extend in any significant way to the rest of the world. Even in eastern Europe, industrialization lagged far behind. Russia, for example, remained largely rural and agricultural, and its autocratic rulers kept the peasants in serfdom. There was not much of a middle class, and the tsarist regime, fearful of change, preferred to import industrial goods in return for the export of raw materials, such as grain and timber. Russia would not have its Industrial Revolution until the end of the nineteenth century.

THE EXAMPLE OF INDIA In other parts of the world where they had established control, newly industrialized European states pursued a deliberate policy of preventing the growth of mechanized industry. A good example is India. In the eighteenth century, India had been one of the world's greatest exporters of cotton cloth produced by hand labor; it produced 85 million pounds of yarn per year, versus 3 million for England. In the first half of the nineteenth century, much of India fell under the control of the British East India Company (see Chapter 24). The British intentionally limited the industrialization of India by cutting off credit, increasing land and rent prices, and raising transportation costs on goods that

British Ships in Calcutta. By the second half of the nineteenth century, the British had increased their trade and development in India. Shown here in this 1865 photograph are British clipper ships at the port of Calcutta, India.

were not approved by British authorities. With British control came inexpensive British factory-produced textiles, and soon thousands of Indian spinners and hand-loom weavers were unemployed. One British colonial officer observed that in Berar, a western Indian district renowned for its cotton, "Cotton is grown almost entirely for export. The manufacture of home cloth has been undermined by the importation of English Piece Goods, and many of the weaver class have become ordinary laborers."[6] British policy encouraged Indians to export their raw materials while buying British-made goods. In 1815, India imported less than one percent of cotton goods from Britain; by the early twentieth century, India was importing 40–50 percent of all cotton cloth produced in Lancashire. The example of India was repeated elsewhere as the rapidly industrializing nations of Europe worked to deliberately thwart the spread of the Industrial Revolution to their colonial dominions.

The Social Impact of the Industrial Revolution

FOCUS QUESTIONS: What effects did the Industrial Revolution have on urban life, social classes, family life, and standards of living? What were working conditions like in the early decades of the Industrial Revolution, and what efforts were made to improve them?

Eventually, the Industrial Revolution radically altered the social life of Europe and the world. Although much of Europe remained bound by its traditional ways, already in the first half of the nineteenth century, the social impact of the Industrial Revolution was being felt, and future avenues of growth were becoming apparent. Vast changes in the number of people and where they lived were already dramatically evident.

Population Growth

Population increases had already begun in the eighteenth century, but they accelerated dramatically in the nineteenth. They were also easier to discern because record keeping became more accurate. In the nineteenth century, governments began to take periodic censuses and systematically collect precise data on births, deaths, and marriages. Britain, for example, took its first census in 1801 and began the systematic registration of births, deaths, and marriages in 1836. In 1750, the total European population stood at an estimated 140 million; by 1800, it had increased to 187 million and by 1850 to 266 million, almost twice its 1750 level.

This population explosion cannot be explained by a higher birthrate, for birthrates were declining after 1790. Between 1790 and 1850, Germany's birthrate dropped from 40 per 1,000 to 36.1; Great Britain's, from 35.4 to 32.6; and France's, from 32.5 to 26.7. The key to the expansion of population was the decline in death rates evident throughout Europe. Historians now attribute this decline to two major causes. There was a drop in the number of deaths from famines, epidemics, and war. Major epidemic diseases, such as plague and smallpox, declined noticeably, although small-scale epidemics broke out now and then. The ordinary death rate also declined as a general increase in the food supply, already evident in the agricultural revolution of Britain in the late eighteenth century, spread to more areas. More food enabled a greater number of people to be better-fed and therefore more resistant to disease. Famine largely disappeared from western Europe, although there were dramatic exceptions in isolated areas, Ireland being the most significant.

Although industrialization itself did not cause population growth, industrialized areas did experience a change in the composition of the population. By 1850, the proportion of the population actively involved in manufacturing, mining, or building had risen to 48 percent in Britain, 37 percent in Belgium, and 27 percent in France. But the actual pockets of industrialization in 1850 were small and decentralized; one author characterized them as "islands in an agricultural sea."

THE GREAT IRISH POTATO FAMINE

THE GREAT IRISH FAMINE CAUSED BY THE potato blight was one of the nineteenth century's worst natural catastrophes, resulting in the decimation of the Irish population. Nicholas Cummins, a magistrate from County Cork, visited Skibbereen, one of the areas most affected by the famine, and sent a letter to the duke of Wellington reporting what he had seen. A copy of the letter was published in the London newspaper *The Times* on Christmas Eve in 1846 and became one of the most famous descriptions of the Irish crisis.

Nicholas Cummins, "The Famine in Skibbereen"

My Lord Duke,

Without apology or preface, I presume so far to trespass on your Grace as to state to you, and by the use of your illustrious name, to present to the British public the following statement of what I have myself seen within the last three days. Having for many years been intimately connected with the western portion of the County of Cork, and possessing some small property there, I thought it right personally to investigate the truth of several lamentable accounts which had reached me, of the appalling state of misery to which that part of the country was reduced. I accordingly went to . . . Skibbereen, and . . . I shall state simply what I there saw. . . . Being aware that I should have to witness scenes of frightful hunger, I provided myself with as much bread as five men could carry, and on reaching the spot I was surprised to find the wretched hamlet apparently deserted. I entered some of the hovels to ascertain the cause, and the scenes which presented themselves were such as no tongue or pen can convey the slightest idea of. In the first, six famished and ghastly skeletons, to all appearances dead, were huddled in a corner on some filthy straw, their sole covering what seemed a ragged horsecloth, their wretched legs hanging about, naked above the knees. I approached with horror, and found by a low moaning they were alive—they were in fever, four children, a woman and what had once been a man. It is impossible to go through the detail. Suffice it to say, that in a few minutes I was surrounded by at least 200 such phantoms, such frightful spectres as no words can describe, either from famine or from fever. . . .

In another case, decency would forbid what follows, but it must be told. My clothes were nearly torn off in my endeavor to escape from the throng of pestilence around, when my neckcloth was seized from behind by a grip which compelled me to turn, I found myself grasped by a woman with an infant just born in her arms and the remains of a filthy sack across her loins—the sole covering of herself and baby. The same morning the police opened a house on the adjoining lands, which was observed shut for many days, and two frozen corpses were found, lying upon the mud floor, half devoured by rats.

 What was the impact of the Great Irish Famine on the Irish people and on the broader Atlantic world? Why do you think the British government failed to provide relief for the Irish during the famine?

Source: C. Woodham Smith, *The Great Hunger* (New York: Harper Collins, 1962).

This minimal industrialization in light of the growing population meant severe congestion in the countryside, where ever-larger numbers of people divided the same amount of land into ever-smaller plots, and also gave rise to an ever-increasing mass of landless peasants. Overpopulation, especially noticeable in parts of France, northern Spain, southern Germany, Sweden, and Ireland, magnified the already existing problem of rural poverty. In Ireland, it produced the century's greatest catastrophe.

THE GREAT HUNGER Ireland was one of the most oppressed areas in western Europe. The predominantly Catholic peasant population rented land from mostly absentee British Protestant landlords whose primary concern was collecting their rents. Irish peasants lived in mud hovels in desperate poverty. The cultivation of the potato, a nutritious and relatively easy food to grow that produced three times as much food per acre as grain, gave Irish peasants a basic staple that enabled them to survive and even expand in numbers. As only an acre or two of potatoes was sufficient to feed a family, Irish men and women married earlier than elsewhere and started having children earlier as well. This led to significant growth in the population. Between 1781 and 1845, the Irish population doubled from 4 million to 8 million. Probably half of this population depended on the potato for survival. In the summer of 1845, the potato crop in Ireland was struck by blight due to a fungus that turned the potatoes black. Between 1845 and 1851, the Great Famine decimated the Irish population (see the box above). More than a million died of starvation and disease, and almost 2 million emigrated to the United States and Britain. Of all the European nations, only Ireland had a declining population in the nineteenth century. But other countries, too, faced problems of dire poverty and declining standards of living as their populations exploded.

EMIGRATION The flight of so many Irish to America reminds us that the traditional safety valve for overpopulation has always been emigration. Between 1821 and 1850, the number of emigrants from Europe averaged about 110,000 a year. Most of these emigrants came from places like Ireland and southern Germany, where peasant life had been reduced to marginal existence. Times of agrarian crisis resulted in great waves of emigration. Bad harvests in Europe in 1846–1847 (such as the catastrophe in Ireland) produced massive numbers of emigrants. In addition to the estimated 1.6 million from Ireland, for example, 935,000 people left Germany between 1847 and 1854.

More often than emigrating, however, the rural masses sought a solution to their poverty by moving to towns and cities within their own countries to find work. It should not astonish us, then, that the first half of the nineteenth century was a period of rapid urbanization.

The Growth of Cities

Although the Western world would not become a predominantly urban society until the twentieth century, cities and towns had already grown dramatically in the first half of the nineteenth century, a phenomenon related to industrialization. Cities had traditionally been centers for princely courts, government and military offices, churches, and commerce. By 1850, especially in Great Britain and Belgium, cities were rapidly becoming places for manufacturing and industry. With the steam engine, entrepreneurs could locate their manufacturing plants in urban centers where they had ready access to transportation facilities and unemployed people from the country looking for work.

In 1800, Great Britain had one major city, London, with a population of one million, and six cities between 50,000 and 100,000. Fifty years later, London's population had swelled to 2,363,000, and there were nine cities over 100,000 and eighteen cities with populations between 50,000 and 100,000. All together, these twenty-eight cities accounted for 5.7 million residents, or one-fifth of the total British population. When the populations of cities under 50,000 are added to this total, we realize that more than 50 percent of the British population lived in towns and cities by 1850. Britain was forced to become a food importer rather than an exporter as the number of people involved in agriculture declined to 20 percent of the population.

Urban populations also grew on the continent, but less dramatically. Paris had 547,000 inhabitants in 1800, but only two other French cities had populations of 100,000: Lyons and Marseilles. In 1851, Paris had grown to a million, but Lyons and Marseilles were still under 200,000. German and Austrian lands had only three cities with more than 100,000 inhabitants (Vienna had 247,000) in 1800; fifty years later, there were only five, but Vienna had grown to 440,000. As these figures show, urbanization did not proceed as rapidly here as in Britain; of course, neither had industrialization. Even in Belgium, the most heavily industrialized country on the continent, almost 50 percent of the male workforce was still engaged in agriculture at midcentury.

URBAN LIVING CONDITIONS IN THE EARLY INDUSTRIAL REVOLUTION The dramatic growth of cities in the first half of the nineteenth century produced miserable living conditions for many of the inhabitants. Of course, this had been true for centuries for many people in European cities, but the rapid urbanization associated with the Industrial Revolution intensified the problems and made these wretched conditions all the more apparent. Wealthy, middle-class inhabitants, as usual, insulated themselves as best they could, often living in suburbs or the outer ring of the city, where they could have individual houses and gardens. In the inner ring of the city stood the small row houses, some with gardens, of the artisans and the lower middle class. Finally, located in the center of most industrial towns were the row houses of the industrial workers (see "Images of Everyday Life" on p. 608). This report on working-class housing in the British city of Birmingham in 1843 gives an idea of the conditions they faced:

> The courts [of working-class row houses] are extremely numerous . . . a very large portion of the poorer classes of the inhabitants reside in them. . . . The courts vary in the number of the houses which they contain, from four to twenty, and most of these houses are three stories high, and built, as it is termed, back to back. There is a wash-house, an ash-pit, and a privy at the end, or on one side of the court, and not unfrequently one or more pigsties and heaps of manure. Generally speaking, the privies in the old courts are in a most filthy condition. Many which we have inspected were in a state which renders it impossible for us to conceive how they could be used; they were without doors and overflowing with filth.[7]

A New Industrial Town. Cities and towns grew dramatically in Britain in the first half of the nineteenth century, largely as a result of industrialization. Pictured here is Saltaire, a model textile factory and town founded near Bradford by Titus Salt in 1851. To facilitate the transportation of goods, the town was built on the Leeds and Liverpool canals.

HIP/Art Resource, NY

Living Conditions of London's Poor

ALTHOUGH SOME ENVIRONMENTAL HAZARDS existed before industrialization, others intensified in early industrial Britain, with a dramatic impact on living conditions. Burning coal filled the air with ash and soot, metal smelting gave off pungent fumes, and industrial plants belched clouds of smoke from the fires stoked in the steam engines. Water pollution was another problem, as slaughterhouses dumped their refuse into the streams and human waste found its way there as well due to a lack of proper sewerage. Consequently, working-class tenants in London found themselves living in crowded rooms surrounded by filth and putrid smells. Many of the houses for the poor were built back to back, leaving little room for sanitation. Despite efforts to improve conditions, the plight of London's workers remained dire. In 1869, an English writer, Blanchard Jerrold, commissioned the French illustrator Gustave Doré (goo-STAHV DOOR-ay) to create illustrations for a guide to London called *London: A Pilgrimage*. The book was published in 1872 with Doré's illustrations accompanying Jerrold's textual descriptions of the living conditions of London's poor. Doré's most haunting images are of tenement housing and its inhabitants in areas such as Whitechapel. In the first illustration, left, Doré shows a London slum district overshadowed by rail viaducts. The image directly below depicts an open air market on Dudley Street, where men, women, and children are attempting to sell their wares. In the third image, bottom left, children in ragged clothes play in the street.

Rooms were not large and were frequently overcrowded, as this government report of 1838 revealed: "I entered several of the tenements. In one of them, on the ground floor, I found six persons occupying a very small room, two in bed, ill with fever. In the room above this were two more persons in one bed ill with fever."[8] Another report said, "There were 63 families where there were at least five persons to one bed; and there were some in which even six were packed in one bed, lying at the top and bottom—children and adults."[9]

Sanitary conditions in these towns were appalling. Due to the lack of municipal direction, city streets were often used as sewers and open drains: "In the center of this street is a gutter, into which potato parings, the refuse of animal and vegetable matters of all kinds, the dirty water from the washing of clothes and of the houses, are all poured, and there they stagnate and putrefy."[10] Unable to deal with human excrement, cities in the new industrial era smelled horrible and were extraordinarily unhealthy. The burning of coal blackened towns and cities with soot, as Charles Dickens described in one of his novels: "A long suburb of red brick houses—some with patches of garden ground, where coal-dust and factory smoke darkened the shrinking leaves, and coarse rank flowers; and where the struggling vegetation sickened and sank under the hot breath of kiln and furnace."[11] Towns and cities were fundamentally death traps. As deaths outnumbered births in most large cities in the first half of the nineteenth century, only a constant influx of people from the countryside kept them alive and growing.

Adding to the deterioration of urban life was the adulteration of food. Consumers were defrauded in a variety of ways: alum was added to make bread look white and hence more expensive; beer and milk were watered down; and red lead, despite its poisonous qualities, was substituted for pepper. The government refused to intervene; a parliamentary committee stated that "more benefit is likely to result from the effects of a free competition . . . than can be expected to result from any regulations." It was not until 1875 that an effective food and drug act was passed in Britain.

Our knowledge of the pathetic conditions in the early industrial cities is largely derived from an abundance of social investigations. Such investigations began in France in the 1820s. During the next decade, Britain began its own investigations with the Poor Law Commission. The investigators were often struck by the physically and morally debilitating effects of urban industrial life on the poor. They observed, for example, that young working-class men were considerably shorter and scrawnier than the sons of middle-class families and much more subject to disease. They were especially alarmed by what they considered the moral consequences of such living conditions: prostitution, crime, and sexual immorality, all of which they saw as effects of living in such squalor.

URBAN REFORMERS To many of the well-to-do, this situation presented a clear danger to society. Were not these masses of workers, sunk in crime, disease, and immorality, a potential threat to their own well-being? Might not the masses be organized and used by unscrupulous demagogues to overthrow the established order? One of the most eloquent British reformers of the 1830s and 1840s, James Kay-Shuttleworth, described them as "volcanic elements, by whose explosive violence the structure of society may be destroyed." Another observer spoke more contemptuously in 1850:

> They live precisely like brutes, to gratify . . . the appetites of their uncultivated bodies, and then die, to go they have never thought, cared, or wondered whither. . . . Brought up in the darkness of barbarism, they have no idea that it is possible for them to attain any higher condition; they are not even sentient enough to desire to change their situation. . . . They eat, drink, breed, work and die; and . . . the richer and more intelligent classes are obliged to guard them with police.[12]

Some observers were less arrogant, however, and wondered if the workers should be held responsible for their fate.

One of the best of a new breed of urban reformers was Edwin Chadwick (1800–1890). With a background in law, Chadwick became obsessed with eliminating the poverty and squalor of the metropolitan areas. He became a civil servant and was soon appointed to a number of government investigatory commissions. As secretary of the Poor Law Commission, he initiated a passionate search for detailed facts about the living conditions of the working classes. After three years of investigation, Chadwick summarized the results in his *Report on the Condition of the Labouring Population of Great Britain*, published in 1842. In it, he concluded that "the various forms of epidemic, endemic, and other disease" were directly caused by the "atmospheric impurities produced by decomposing animal and vegetable substances, by damp and filth, and close overcrowded dwellings [prevailing] amongst the population in every part of the kingdom." Such conditions, he argued, could be eliminated. As to the means: "The primary and most important measures, and at the same time the most practicable, and within the recognized province of public administration, are drainage, the removal of all refuse of habitations, streets, and roads, and the improvement of the supplies of water."[13] In other words, Chadwick was advocating a system of modern sanitary reforms consisting of efficient sewers and a supply of piped water. Six years after his report and largely due to his efforts, Britain's first Public Health Act created the National Board of Health, empowered to form local boards that would establish modern sanitary systems.

Many middle-class citizens were quite willing to support the public health reforms of men like Chadwick because of their fear of **cholera**. Outbreaks of this deadly disease had ravaged Europe in the early 1830s and late 1840s and were especially rampant in the overcrowded cities. A single wave of cholera in 1832 killed 32,000 people in Paris and another 7,000 in London. As city authorities and wealthier residents became convinced that filthy conditions and poor sewage helped spread the disease, they began to support the call for new public health measures.

New Social Classes: The Industrial Middle Class

The rise of industrial capitalism produced a new middle-class group. The bourgeoisie or middle class was not new; it had existed since the emergence of cities in the Middle Ages. Originally, the bourgeois was the burgher or town dweller, active as a merchant, official, artisan, lawyer, or scholar, who enjoyed a

Attitudes of the Industrial Middle Class in Britain and Japan

IN THE NINETEENTH CENTURY, A NEW INDUSTRIAL
middle class in Great Britain took the lead in creating the
Industrial Revolution. Japan did not begin to industrialize until
after 1870. There, too, an industrial middle class emerged,
although there were important differences in the attitudes of
business leaders in Britain and Japan. Some of these differences
can be seen in these documents. The first is an excerpt from the
book *Self-Help*, first published in 1859 by Samuel Smiles, who
espoused the belief that people succeed through "individual
industry, energy, and uprightness." The other two selections are
by Shibusawa Eiichi (shih-boo-ZAH-wah EH-ee-chee), a Japanese
industrialist who supervised textile factories. Although he began
his business career in 1873, he did not write his autobiography,
the source of his first excerpt, until 1927.

Samuel Smiles, *Self-Help*

"Heaven helps those who help themselves" is a well-worn
maxim, embodying in a small compass the results of vast
human experience. The spirit of self-help is the root of all
genuine growth in the individual; and, exhibited in the lives
of many, it constitutes the true source of national vigor and
strength. Help from without is often enfeebling in its effects,
but help from within invariably invigorates. Whatever is done
for men or classes, to a certain extent takes away the stimulus
and necessity of doing for themselves; and where men are
subjected to overguidance and overgovernment, the inevitable
tendency is to render them comparatively helpless. . . .

National progress is the sum of individual industry, energy,
and uprightness, as national decay is of individual idleness, selfishness, and vice. What we are accustomed to decry as great
social evils, will, for the most part, be found to be only the outgrowth of our own perverted life; and though we may endeavor
to cut them down and extirpate them by means of law, they will
only spring up again with fresh luxuriance in some other form,
unless the individual conditions of human life and character are
radically improved. If this view be correct, then it follows that
the highest patriotism and philanthropy consist, not so much in
altering laws and modifying institutions as in helping and stimulating men to elevate and improve themselves by their own free
and independent action as individuals. . . .

Many popular books have been written for the purpose
of communicating to the public the grand secret of making

money. But there is no secret whatever about it, as the prov-
erbs of every nation abundantly testify. . . . "A penny saved is
a penny gained." —"Diligence is the mother of good-luck."—
"No pains, no gains." —"No sweat, no sweet." —"Sloth, the
Key of poverty." —"Work, and thou shalt have." —"He who
will not work, neither shall he eat." —"The world his, who has
patience and industry."

Shibusawa Eiichi, *Autobiography*

I . . . felt that it was necessary to raise the social standing of
those who engaged in commerce and industry. By way of
setting an example, I began studying and practicing the teachings of the *Analects* of Confucius. It contains teachings first
enunciated more than twenty-four hundred years ago. Yet it
supplies the ultimate in practical ethics for all of us to follow
in our daily living. It has many golden rules for businessmen.
For example, there is a saying: "Wealth and respect are what
men desire, but unless a right way is followed, they cannot be
obtained; poverty and lowly position are what men despise,
but unless a right way is found, one cannot leave that status
once reaching it." It shows very clearly how a businessman
must act in this world.

Shibusawa Eiichi on Progress

One must beware of the tendency of some to argue that it is
through individualism or egoism that the State and society can
progress most rapidly. They claim that under individualism,
each individual competes with the others, and progress results
from this competition. But this is to see merely the advantages
and ignore the disadvantages, and I cannot support such a
theory. Society exists, and a State has been founded. Although
people desire to rise to positions of wealth and honor, the
social order and the tranquillity of the State will be disrupted
if this is done egoistically. Men should not do battle in competition with their fellow men. Therefore, I believe that in
order to get along together in society and serve the State, we
must by all means abandon this idea of independence and self-
reliance and reject egoism completely.

 *What are the major similarities and differences between
the attitudes toward business of Samuel Smiles and
Shibusawa Eiichi? How do you explain the differences,
and what are their implications?*

Sources: Samuel Smiles, *Self-Help*, 1859; Shibusawa Eiichi, *The Autobiography of Shibusawa Eiichi: From Peasant to Entrepreneur* (Tokyo: University of Tokyo Press, 1994).

special set of rights from the charter of the town. As wealthy
townspeople bought land, the original meaning of the word
bourgeois became lost, and the term came to include people
involved in commerce, industry, and banking as well as professionals, such as lawyers, teachers, physicians, and government
officials at various levels. At the lower end of the economic
scale were master craftspeople and shopkeepers.

THE NEW INDUSTRIAL ENTREPRENEURS Lest we make
the industrial middle class too much of an abstraction, we need
to look at who the new industrial entrepreneurs actually were.
These were the people who constructed the factories, purchased the machines, and figured out where the markets were
(see "Global Perspectives" above). Their qualities included
resourcefulness, single-mindedness, resolution, initiative, vision,

ambition, and often, of course, greed. As Jedediah Strutt, the cotton manufacturer, said, the "getting of money . . . is the main business of the life of men."

But this was not an easy task. The early industrial entrepreneurs had to superintend an enormous array of functions that are handled today by teams of managers; they raised capital, determined markets, set company objectives, organized the factory and its labor, and trained supervisors who could act for them. The opportunities for making money were great, but the risks were also tremendous. The cotton trade, for example, which was so important to the early Industrial Revolution, was intensely competitive. Only through constant expansion could one feel secure, so early entrepreneurs reinvested most of their initial profits. Fear of bankruptcy was constant, especially among small firms. Furthermore, most early industrial enterprises were small. Even by the 1840s, only 10 percent of British industrial firms employed more than five thousand workers; 43 percent had fewer than one hundred. As entrepreneurs went bankrupt, new people could enter the race for profits, especially since the initial outlay required was not gigantic. In 1816, only one mill in five in the important industrial city of Manchester was in the hands of its original owner.

The new industrial entrepreneurs were from incredibly diverse social origins. Many of the most successful came from a mercantile background. Three London merchants, for example, founded a successful ironworks in Wales that owned eight steam engines and employed five thousand men. In Britain, land and domestic industry were often interdependent. Joshua Fielden, for example, acquired sufficient capital to establish a factory by running a family sheep farm while working looms in the farmhouse. Intelligent, clever, and ambitious apprentices who had learned their trades well could also strike it rich. William Radcliffe's family engaged in agriculture and spinning and weaving at home; he learned quickly how to succeed:

> Availing myself of the improvements that came out while I was in my teens . . . with my little savings and a practical knowledge of every process from the cotton bag to the piece of cloth . . . I was ready to commence business for myself and by the year 1789 I was well established and employed many hands both in spinning and weaving as a master manufacturer.[14]

By 1801, Radcliffe was operating a factory employing a thousand workers.

Members of dissenting religious minorities were often prominent among the early industrial leaders of Britain. The Darbys and Lloyds, who were iron manufacturers; the Barclays and Lloyds, who were bankers; and the Trumans and Perkins, who were brewers, were all Quakers. These were expensive trades and depended on the financial support that coreligionists in religious minorities provided for each other. Most historians believe that a major reason members of these religious minorities were so prominent in business was that they lacked other opportunities. Legally excluded from many public offices, they directed their ambitions into the new industrial capitalism.

It is interesting to note that in Britain in particular, aristocrats also became entrepreneurs. The Lambtons in Northumberland, the Curwens in Cumberland, the Norfolks in Yorkshire, and the Dudleys in Staffordshire all invested in mining enterprises. This close relationship between land and industry helped Britain assume the leadership role in the early Industrial Revolution.

SIGNIFICANCE OF THE INDUSTRIAL ENTREPRENEURS By 1850, in Britain at least, the kind of traditional entrepreneurship that had created the Industrial Revolution was declining and was being replaced by a new business aristocracy. This new generation of entrepreneurs stemmed from the professional and industrial middle classes, especially as sons inherited the successful businesses established by their fathers. It must not be forgotten, however, that even after 1850, a large number of small businesses existed in Britain, and some were still being founded by people from humble backgrounds. Indeed, the age of large-scale corporate capitalism did not begin until the 1890s (see Chapter 23).

Increasingly, the new industrial entrepreneurs—the bankers and owners of factories and mines—came to amass much wealth and play an important role alongside the traditional landed elites of their societies. The Industrial Revolution began at a time when the preindustrial agrarian world was still largely dominated by landed elites. As the new bourgeois bought great estates and acquired social respectability, they also sought political power, and in the course of the nineteenth century, their wealthiest members would merge with those old elites.

New Social Classes: Workers in the Industrial Age

At the same time that the members of the industrial middle class were seeking to reduce the barriers between themselves and the landed elite, they were also trying to separate themselves from the laboring classes below. The working class was actually a mixture of groups in the first half of the nineteenth century. Factory workers would eventually form an industrial proletariat, but in the first half of the century, they did not constitute a majority of the working class in any major city, even in Britain. According to the 1851 census, there were 1.8 million agricultural laborers and 1 million domestic servants in Britain but only 811,000 workers in the cotton and woolen industries. And one-third of these were still working in small workshops or at home.

In the cities, artisans or craftspeople remained the largest group of urban workers during the first half of the nineteenth century. They worked in numerous small industries, such as shoemaking, glovemaking, bookbinding, printing, and bricklaying. Some craftspeople, especially those employed in such luxury trades as coach building and clock making, formed a kind of aristocracy of labor and earned higher wages than others. Artisans were not factory workers; they were traditionally organized in guilds, where they passed on their skills to apprentices. But guilds were increasingly losing their power, especially in industrialized countries. Fearful of losing out to the new factories that could produce goods more cheaply, artisans tended to support movements against industrialization. Industrialists welcomed the decline of skilled craftspeople, as one perceptive old tailor realized in telling his life story:

It is upwards of 30 years since I first went to work at the tailoring trade in London. . . . I continued working for the honorable trade and belonging to the Society [for tailors] for about 15 years. My weekly earnings then averaged £1 16s. a week while I was at work, and for several years I was seldom out of work. . . . No one could have been happier than I was. . . . But then, with my sight defective . . . I could get no employment at the honorable trade, and that was the ruin of me entirely; for working there, of course, I got "scratched" from the trade society, and so lost all hope of being provided for by them in my helplessness. The workshop . . . was about seven feet square, and so low, that as you [sat] on the floor you could touch the ceiling with the tip of your finger. In this place seven of us worked. [The master] paid little more than half the regular wages, and employed such men as myself— only those who couldn't get anything better to do. . . . I don't think my wages there averaged above 12s. a week. . . . I am convinced I lost my eyesight by working in that cheap shop. . . . It is by the ruin of such men as me that these masters are enabled to undersell the better shops. . . . That's the way, sir, the cheap clothes is produced, by making blind beggars of the workmen, like myself, and throwing us on [the benevolence of] the parish [church] in our old age.[15]

Servants also formed another large group of urban workers, especially in major cities like London and Paris. Many were women from the countryside who became utterly dependent on their upper- and middle-class employers.

WORKING CONDITIONS FOR THE INDUSTRIAL WORKING CLASS Workers in the new industrial factories also faced wretched working conditions. We have already observed the psychological traumas workers experienced from their employers' efforts to break old preindustrial work patterns and create a well-disciplined labor force. But what were the physical conditions of the factories?

Unquestionably, in the early decades of the Industrial Revolution, "places of work," as early factories were called, were dreadful. Work hours ranged from twelve to sixteen hours a day, six days a week, with a half hour for lunch and for dinner. There was no security of employment and no minimum wage. The worst conditions were in the cotton mills, where temperatures were especially debilitating. One report noted that "in the cotton-spinning work, these creatures are kept, fourteen hours in each day, locked up, summer and winter, in a heat of from eighty to eighty-four degrees." Mills were also dirty, dusty, and unhealthy:

Not only is there not a breath of sweet air in these truly infernal scenes, but . . . there is the abominable and pernicious stink of the gas to assist in the murderous effects of the heat. In addition to the noxious effluvia of the gas, mixed with the steam, there are the dust, and what is called cotton-flyings or fuz, which the unfortunate creatures have to inhale; and . . . the notorious fact is that well constituted men

are rendered old and past labor at forty years of age, and that children are rendered decrepit and deformed, and thousands upon thousands of them slaughtered by consumptions [lung diseases], before they arrive at the age of sixteen.[16]

Thus ran a report on working conditions in the cotton industry in 1824.

Conditions in the coal mines were also harsh. The introduction of steam power meant only that steam-powered engines mechanically lifted coal to the top. Inside the mines, men still bore the burden of digging the coal out while horses, mules, women, and children hauled coal carts on rails to the lift. Dangers abounded in coal mines; cave-ins, explosions, and gas fumes (called "bad air") were a way of life. The cramped conditions—tunnels often did not exceed 3 or 4 feet in height— and constant dampness in the mines resulted in deformed bodies and ruined lungs.

Both children and women were employed in large numbers in early factories and mines (see the boxes on pp. 614 and 615). Children had been an important part of the family economy in preindustrial times, working in the fields or carding and spinning wool at home with the growth of the cottage industry. In the Industrial Revolution, however, child labor was exploited more than ever and in a considerably more systematic fashion. The owners of cotton factories appreciated certain features of child labor. Children had an especially delicate touch as spinners of cotton. Their smaller size made it easier for them to crawl under machines to gather loose cotton. Moreover, children were more easily broken to factory work. Above all, children represented a cheap supply of labor. In 1821, just about half of the British population was under twenty years of age. Hence, children made up a particularly abundant supply of labor, and they were paid only about one-sixth to one-third of what a man was paid. In the cotton factories in 1838, children under eighteen made up 29 percent of the total workforce; children as young as seven worked twelve to fifteen hours per day, six days a week, in cotton mills.

Especially terrible in the early Industrial Revolution was the use of so-called pauper apprentices. These were orphans or children abandoned by their parents who had wound up in the care of local parishes. To save on their upkeep, parish officials found it convenient to apprentice them to factory owners looking for a cheap source of labor. These children worked long hours under strict discipline and received inadequate food and recreation; many became deformed from being kept too long in contorted positions. Although economic liberals and some industrialists were against all state intervention in economic matters, Parliament eventually remedied some of the worst ills of child abuse in factories and mines (see "Efforts at Change: Reformers and Government" later in this chapter). The legislation of the 1830s and 1840s, however, primarily affected child labor in textile factories and mines. It did not touch the use of children in small workshops or the non-factory trades that were not protected. As these trades were in competition with the new factories, conditions there were often even worse. Pottery works, for example, were not investigated until the 1860s, when it was found that 17 percent

Women and Children in the Mines. Women and children were often employed in the factories and mines of the early nineteenth century. This illustration shows a woman and boy in a coal mine struggling to draw and push a barrel filled with coal. In 1842, the Coal Mines Act forbade the use of boys younger than ten and women in the mines.

of the workers were under eleven years of age. One investigator reported what he found:

> The boys were kept in constant motion throughout the day, each carrying from thirty to fifty dozen of molds into the stoves, and remaining . . . long enough to take the dried earthenware away. The distance thus run by a boy in the course of a day . . . was estimated at seven miles. From the very nature of this exhausting occupation children were rendered pale, weak and unhealthy. In the depth of winter, with the thermometer in the open air sometimes below zero, boys, with little clothing but rags, might be seen running to and fro on errands or to their dinners with the perspiration on their foreheads, "after laboring for hours like little slaves." The inevitable result of such transitions of temperature were consumption, asthma and acute inflammation.[17]

Little wonder that child labor legislation enacted in 1864 included pottery works.

By 1830, women and children made up two-thirds of the cotton industry's labor. As the number of children employed declined after the Factory Act of 1833, however, their places were taken by women, who came to dominate the labor forces of the early factories. Women made up 50 percent of the labor force in textile (cotton and woolen) factories before 1870. They were mostly unskilled labor and were paid half or less of what men received. Excessive working hours for women were outlawed in 1844, but only in textile factories and mines; not until 1867 were they outlawed in craft workshops.

The employment of children and women in large part represents a continuation of a preindustrial kinship pattern. The cottage industry had always involved the efforts of the entire family, and it seemed perfectly natural to continue this pattern. Men migrating from the countryside to industrial towns and cities took their wives and children with them into the factory or into the mines. Of 136 employees in Robert Peel's factory at Bury in 1801, 95 were members of the same twenty-six families. The impetus for this family work often came from the family itself. The factory owner Jedediah Strutt was opposed to child labor under age ten but was forced by parents to take children as young as seven.

The employment of large numbers of women in factories did not significantly transform female working patterns, as was once assumed. Studies of urban households in France and Britain, for example, have revealed that throughout the nineteenth century, traditional types of female labor still predominated in the women's work world. In 1851, fully 40 percent of the female workforce in Britain consisted of domestic servants. In France, the largest group of female workers, 40 percent, worked in agriculture. In addition, only 20 percent of female workers in Britain labored in factories, and only 10 percent did so in France. Regional and local studies have also found that most of the workers were single women. Few married women worked outside the home.

The factory acts that limited the work hours of children and women also began to break up the traditional kinship pattern of work and led to a new pattern based on a separation of work and home. Men came to be regarded as responsible for the primary work obligations as women assumed daily control of the family and performed low-paying jobs such as laundry work that could be done in the home. Domestic industry made it possible for women to continue their contributions to family survival.

Historians have also reminded us that if the treatment of children in the mines and factories seems particularly cruel and harsh, contemporary treatment of children in general was often brutal. Beatings, for example, had long been regarded, even by dedicated churchmen and churchwomen, as the best way to discipline children.

The problem of poverty among the working classes was also addressed in Britain by government action in the form

CHILD LABOR: DISCIPLINE IN THE TEXTILE MILLS

CHILD LABOR WAS NOT NEW, BUT IN THE early Industrial Revolution, it was exploited more systematically. These selections are taken from the Report of Sadler's Committee, an investigatory committee established by the government in 1832 to inquire into the condition of child factory workers.

Keeping the Children Awake

It is a very frequent thing at Mr. Marshall's [at Shrewsbury] where the least children were employed (for there were plenty working at six years of age), for Mr. Horseman to start the mill earlier in the morning than he formerly did; and provided a child should be drowsy, the overlooker walks round the room with a stick in his hand, and he touches that child on the shoulder, and says, "Come here." In a corner of the room there is an iron cistern; it is filled with water; he takes this boy, and takes him up by the legs, and dips him over head in the cistern, and sends him to work for the remainder of the day. . . .

What means were taken to keep the children to their work?—Sometimes they would tap them over the head, or nip them over the nose, or give them a pinch of snuff, or throw water in their faces, or pull them off where they were, and job them about to keep them waking.

The Sadistic Overlooker

Samuel Downe, age 29, factory worker living near Leeds; at the age of about ten began work at Mr. Marshall's mills at Shrewsbury, where the customary hours when work was brisk were generally 5 A.M. to 8 P.M., sometimes from 5:30 A.M. to 8 or 9.

What means were taken to keep the children awake and vigilant, especially at the termination of such a day's labor as you have described?—There was generally a blow or a box, or a tap with a strap, or sometimes the hand.

Have you yourself been strapped?—Yes, most severely, till I could not bear to sit upon a chair without having pillows, and through that I left. I was strapped both on my own legs, and then I was put upon a man's back, and then strapped and buckled with two straps to an iron pillar, and flogged, and all by one overlooker; after that he took a piece of tow, and twisted it in the shape of a cord, and put it in my mouth, and tied it behind my head.

He gagged you?—Yes; and then he orders me to run round a part of the machinery where he was overlooker, and he stood at one end, and every time I came there he struck me with a stick, which I believe was an ash plant, and which he generally carried in his hand, and sometimes he hit me, and sometimes he did not; and one of the men in the room came and begged me off, and that he let me go, and not beat me any more, and consequently he did.

You have been beaten with extraordinary severity?—Yes, I was beaten so that I had not power to cry at all, or hardly speak at one time. What age were you at that time?—Between 10 and 11.

 What kind of working conditions did children face in the textile mills during the early Industrial Revolution? Why were they beaten?

Source: E. R. Pike, *Human Documents of the Industrial Revolution in Britain* (London: Unwin & Hyman, 1966.)

---

of the Poor Law Act of 1834, which established workhouses where jobless poor people were forced to live. The intent of this policy, based on the assumption that the poor were responsible for their own pitiful conditions, was "to make the workhouses as like prisons as possible . . . to establish therein a discipline so severe and repulsive as to make them a terror to the poor." Within a few years, despite sporadic opposition, more than 200,000 poor people were locked up in workhouses, where family members were separated, forced to live in dormitories, given work assignments, and fed dreadful food. Children were often recruited from parish workhouses as cheap labor in factories.

HISTORIANS DEBATE **DID INDUSTRIALIZATION BRING AN IMPROVED STANDARD OF LIVING?** One of the most contested debates on the Industrial Revolution concerns the standard of living. Most historians conclude that in the long run, the Industrial Revolution improved living standards dramatically in the form of higher per capita incomes and greater consumer choices. But did the first

generation of industrial workers experience a decline in their living standards and suffer unnecessarily? During the first half of the nineteenth century, industrialization altered the lives of Europeans, especially the British, as they left their farms, moved to cities, and found work in factories. Historians have debated whether industrialization improved the standard of living during this time. Some historians have argued that industrialization increased employment and lowered prices of consumer goods, thereby improving the way people lived. However, they also maintain that household income rose because families became more industrious, sending multiple members of the family into wage-paying jobs. Other historians argue that wage labor made life worse for most families during the first half of the nineteenth century. They maintain that employment in the early factories was highly volatile and uncertain as employers dismissed workers whenever demand declined. Wages were not uniform, and inadequate housing in cities forced families to live in cramped and unsanitary conditions. Families continued to spend most of their incomes on food and clothing.

CHILD LABOR: THE MINES

AFTER EXAMINING CONDITIONS IN BRITISH coal mines, a government official commented that "the hardest labor in the worst room in the worst-conducted factory is less hard, less cruel and less demoralizing than the labor in the best of coal-mines." Yet it was not until 1842 that legislation was passed eliminating the labor of boys under ten from the mines. This selection is taken from a government report on the mines in Lancashire.

The Black Holes of Worsley

Examination of Thomas Gibson and George Bryan, witnesses from the coal mines at Worsley:

Have you worked from a boy in a coal mine?—(Both) Yes.

What had you to do then?—Thrutching the basket and drawing. It is done by little boys; one draws the basket and the other pushes it behind. Is that hard labor?—Yes, very hard labor.

For how many hours a day did you work?—Nearly nine hours regularly; sometimes twelve; I have worked about thirteen. We used to go in at six in the morning, and took a bit of bread and cheese in our pocket, and stopped two or three minutes; and some days nothing at all to eat.

How was it that sometimes you had nothing to eat?—We were over-burdened. I had only a mother, and she had nothing to give me. I was sometimes half starved. . . .

Do they work in the same way now exactly?—Yes, they do; they have nothing more than a bit of bread and cheese in their pocket, and sometimes can't eat it all, owing to the dust and damp and badness of air; and sometimes it is as hot as an oven; sometimes I have seen it so hot as to melt a candle.

What are the usual wages of a boy of eight?—They used to get 3d or 4d a day. Now a man's wages is divided into eight eighths; and when a boy is eight years old he gets one of those eighths; at eleven, two eighths; at thirteen, three eighths; at fifteen, four eighths; at twenty, man's wages.

What are the wages of a man?—About 15s if he is in full employment, but often not more than 10s, and out of that he has to get his tools and candles. He consumes about four candles in nine hours' work, in some places six; 6d per pound, and twenty-four candles to the pound.

Were you ever beaten as a child?—Yes, many a score of times; both kicks and thumps.

Are many girls employed in the pits?—Yes, a vast of those. They do the same kind of work as the boys till they get about 14 years of age, when they get the wages of half a man, and never get more, and continue at the same work for many years.

Did they ever fight together?—Yes, many days together. Both boys and girls; sometimes they are very loving with one another.

 What kind of working conditions did children face in the mines during the early Industrial Revolution? Why did entrepreneurs permit such conditions and such treatment of children?

Source: E. R. Pike, *Human Documents of the Industrial Revolution in Britain* (London: Unwin & Hyman, 1966).

Most historians do agree, however, that the gap between rich and poor increased substantially in the first half of the nineteenth century. One estimate, based on income tax returns in Britain, demonstrates that the wealthiest 1 percent of the population increased its share of the national product from 25 percent in 1801 to 35 percent in 1848. The real gainers in the early Industrial Revolution were members of the middle class—and some skilled workers whose jobs were not eliminated by the new machines. But industrial workers themselves would have to wait until the second half of the nineteenth century to reap the benefits of industrialization.

Efforts at Change: The Workers

Before long, workers looked to the formation of labor organizations to gain decent wages and working conditions. The British government, reacting against the radicalism of the French revolutionary working classes, had passed the Combination Acts in 1799 and 1800 outlawing associations of workers. The legislation failed to prevent the formation of **trade unions**, however. Similar to the craft societies of earlier times, these new associations were formed by skilled workers in a number of new industries, including the cotton spinners, ironworkers,

coal miners, and shipwrights. These unions served two purposes. One was to preserve their own workers' position by limiting entry into their trade; the other was to gain benefits from the employers. These early trade unions had limited goals. They favored a working-class struggle against employers, but only to win improvements for the members of their own trades.

THE TRADE UNION MOVEMENT Some trade unions were even willing to strike to attain their goals. Bitter strikes were carried out by miners in Northumberland and Durham in 1810, hand-loom weavers in Glasgow in 1813, and cotton spinners in Manchester in 1818. Such blatant illegal activity caused Parliament to repeal the Combination Acts in 1824, accepting the argument of some members that the acts themselves had so alienated workers that they had formed unions. Unions were now tolerated, but other legislation enabled authorities to keep close watch over their activities.

In the 1820s and 1830s, the union movement began to focus on the creation of national unions. One of the leaders in this effort was a well-known cotton magnate and social reformer, Robert Owen (1771–1858). Owen came to believe in the creation of voluntary associations that would demonstrate to

A Trade Union Membership Card. Skilled workers in a number of new industries formed trade unions in an attempt to gain higher wages, better working conditions, and special benefits. The scenes at the bottom of this membership card for the Associated Shipwrights Society illustrate some of the medical and social benefits it provided for its members.

LUDDITES Trade unionism was not the only type of collective action by workers in the early decades of the Industrial Revolution. The Luddites were skilled craftspeople in the Midlands and northern England who in 1812 attacked the machines that they believed threatened their livelihoods. These attacks failed to stop the industrial mechanization of Britain and have been viewed as utterly naive. Some historians, however, have also seen them as an intense eruption of feeling against unrestrained industrial capitalism. The inability of 12,000 troops to find the culprits provides stunning evidence of the local support they received in their areas.

CHARTISM A much more meaningful expression of the attempts of British workers to improve their condition occurred in the movement known as Chartism—the "first important political movement of working men organized during the nineteenth century." Its aim was to achieve political democracy. Chartism took its name from the People's Charter, a document drawn up in 1838 by the London Working Men's Association. The charter demanded universal male suffrage, payment for members of Parliament, the elimination of property qualifications for members of Parliament, and annual sessions of Parliament. Women, too, joined in the movement. Chartist groups in many large towns often had female sections. Although some women were quite active in the movement, they were fighting to win political rights for their husbands, not for themselves, as the Chartist platform did not include the right to vote for women.

Two national petitions incorporating the Chartist demands gained millions of signatures and were presented to Parliament in 1839 and 1842. Chartism attempted to encourage change through peaceful, constitutional means, although there was an underlying threat of force, as is evident in the Chartist slogan, "Peacefully if we can, forcibly if we must." In 1842, Chartist activists organized a general strike on behalf of their goals, but it had little success.

Despite the pressures exerted by the Chartists, members of Parliament, who were not at all ready for political democracy, rejected both national petitions. As one member said, universal male suffrage would be "fatal to all the purposes for which government exists" and was "utterly incompatible with the very existence of civilization." After 1848, Chartism as a movement had largely played itself out. It had never really posed a serious threat to the British establishment, but it had not been a total failure either. Its true significance stemmed from its ability to arouse and organize millions of working-class men and women, to give them a sense of working-class consciousness that they had not really possessed before. This political education of working people was important to the ultimate acceptance of all the points of the People's Charter in the future and would alter the political landscape in the nineteenth and twentieth centuries (see Chapters 22 and 23).

Efforts at Change: Reformers and Government

Efforts to improve the worst conditions of the industrial factory system also came from outside the ranks of the working classes. From its beginning, the Industrial Revolution had drawn

others the benefits of cooperative rather than competitive living (see Chapter 21). Although Owen's program was not directed specifically to trade unionists, his ideas had great appeal to some of their leaders. Under Owen's direction, plans emerged for the Grand National Consolidated Trades Union, which was formed in February 1834. As a national federation of trade unions, its primary purpose was to coordinate a general strike for the eight-hour working day. Rhetoric, however, soon outpaced reality, and by the summer of that year, the lack of real working-class support led to the federation's total collapse, and the union movement reverted to trade unions for individual crafts. The largest and most successful of these unions was the Amalgamated Society of Engineers, formed in 1850. Its provision of generous unemployment benefits in return for a small weekly payment was precisely the kind of practical gains these trade unions sought. Larger goals would have to wait.

much criticism. Romantic poets like William Wordsworth (see Chapter 21) decried the destruction of the natural world:

> I grieve, when on the darker side
> Of this great change I look; and there behold
> Such outrage done to nature as compels
> The indignant power to justify herself.[18]

Reform-minded individuals, be they factory owners who felt twinges of conscience or social reformers in Parliament, campaigned against the evils of the industrial factory, especially condemning the abuse of children. One hoped for the day "that these little ones should once more see the rising and setting of the sun."

GOVERNMENT ACTION As it became apparent that the increase in wealth generated by the Industrial Revolution was accompanied by ever-increasing numbers of poor people, more and more efforts were made to document and deal with the problems. As reports from civic-minded citizens and parliamentary commissions intensified and demonstrated the extent of poverty, degradation, and suffering, the reform efforts began to succeed.

Their first success was a series of factory acts passed between 1802 and 1819 that limited labor for children between the ages of nine and sixteen to twelve hours a day; the employment of children under nine years old was forbidden. Moreover, the laws stipulated that children were to receive instruction in reading and arithmetic during working hours. But these acts applied only to cotton mills, not to factories or mines where some of the worst abuses were taking place. Just as important, no provision was made for enforcing the acts through a system of inspection.

In the reform-minded decades of the 1830s and 1840s, new legislation was passed. The Factory Act of 1833 strengthened earlier labor legislation. All textile factories were now included. Children between the ages of nine and thirteen could work only eight hours a day; those between thirteen and eighteen, twelve hours. Factory inspectors were appointed with the power to fine those who broke the law. Another piece of legislation in 1833 required that children between nine and thirteen have at least two hours of elementary education during the working day. In 1847, the Ten Hours Act reduced the workday for children between thirteen and eighteen to ten hours. Women were also now included in the ten-hour limit. In 1842, the Coal Mines Act eliminated the employment of boys under ten and women in mines. Eventually, men too would benefit from the move to restrict factory hours.

CHAPTER SUMMARY

The Industrial Revolution was one of the major forces of change in the nineteenth century, as it led Western civilization into the machine-dependent modern world. It began in Britain, which had an agricultural revolution that increased the quantity of foodstuffs, population growth that created a supply of labor, capital for investment, a good supply of coal and iron ore, and a transportation revolution that created a system of canals, roads, and bridges. As the world's leading colonial power, Britain also had access to overseas markets. The cotton industry led the way, as new machines such as the spinning jenny and power loom enabled the British to produce cheap cotton goods. Most important was the steam engine, which led to factories and a

system of steam-powered railroads that moved people and goods efficiently. The Great Exhibition of 1851 in London showed the world the achievements of Britain's Industrial Revolution. Industrialization also spread to the continent, and by 1860, the United States was also well along that road. In the non-Western world, industrial development was much slower, in large part because European colonial powers deliberately pursued a policy of preventing the growth of mechanized industry, thus keeping the colonies as purchasers of industrial products.

The Industrial Revolution also transformed the social world of Europe. The creation of an industrial proletariat produced a whole new force for change. The work environment, especially in the new factories and mines, was dreadful, characterized by long hours, unsafe conditions, monotonous labor, and the use of child labor. Eventually, laws were passed to improve working conditions, especially for women and children. Labor unions were also formed to improve wages and conditions but met with limited success. Workers sometimes protested by destroying the factories and machines, as did the Luddites. The Chartist movement petitioned Parliament, calling for the right to vote and other reforms, but the members of Parliament refused the demands. The development of a wealthy industrial middle class presented a challenge to the long-term hegemony of landed wealth. Though that wealth had been threatened by the fortunes of commerce, it had never been overturned. But the new bourgeoisie became more demanding, as we shall see in the next chapter.

The Industrial Revolution seemed to prove to Europeans the underlying assumption of the Scientific Revolution of the seventeenth century—that human beings were capable of dominating nature. By rationally manipulating the material environment for human benefit, people could attain new levels of material prosperity and produce machines not dreamed of in their wildest imaginings. Lost in the excitement of the Industrial Revolution were the voices that pointed to the dehumanization of the workforce and the alienation from one's work, one's associates, oneself, and the natural world.

CHAPTER TIMELINE

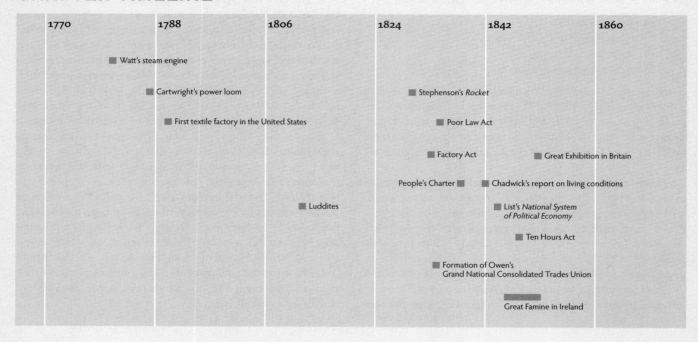

1770	1788	1806	1824	1842	1860

- Watt's steam engine
- Cartwright's power loom
- First textile factory in the United States
- Stephenson's *Rocket*
- Poor Law Act
- Factory Act
- Great Exhibition in Britain
- People's Charter
- Chadwick's report on living conditions
- Luddites
- List's *National System of Political Economy*
- Ten Hours Act
- Formation of Owen's Grand National Consolidated Trades Union
- Great Famine in Ireland

CHAPTER REVIEW

Upon Reflection

Q What made the factory system possible, and why was it such an important part of the early industrial system? What impact did it have on the lives of workers?

Q How are changes in population growth and the increase in urbanization related to the Industrial Revolution?

Q What efforts did workers make to ameliorate the harsh working conditions of the early Industrial Revolution?

Key Terms

agricultural revolution (p. 593)
capital (p. 593)
pig iron (p. 596)
wrought iron (p. 596)

tariffs (p. 601)
cholera (p. 609)
trade unions (p. 615)

Suggestions for Further Reading

GENERAL WORKS   For a brief introduction to the Industrial Revolution, see **J. Horn,** *The Industrial Revolution* (Westport, Conn., 2007). A more detailed account can be found in the classic work by **D. Landes,** *The Unbound Prometheus: Technological Change and Industrial Development in Western Europe from 1750 to the Present* (Cambridge, 1969). On the "makers" of the Industrial Revolution, see **G. Wightman,** *The Industrial Revolutionaries: The Making of the Modern World, 1776–1914* (New York, 2007).

BRITAIN IN THE INDUSTRIAL REVOLUTION   On the Industrial Revolution in Britain, see **P. Mathias,** *The First Industrial Nation: An Economic History of Britain, 1700–1914,*

3rd ed. (New York, 2001); **E. J. Evans,** *The Forging of the Modern State: Early Industrial Britain, 1783–1870,* 3rd ed. (London, 2001); **K. Morgan,** *The Birth of Industrial Britain: Social Change, 1750–1850* (New York, 2004); and **E. A. Wrigley,** *Energy and the English Industrial Revolution* (Cambridge, 2010). On the global dimensions of the British Industrial Revolution, see **R. Allen,** *The British Industrial Revolution in Global Perspective* (Cambridge, 2008). On the role of cotton in Britain's industrial history, see **S. Beckert,** *Empire of Cotton: A Global History* (New York, 2014). On the Crystal Palace, see **J. A. Auerbach,** *The Great Exhibition of 1851: A Nation on Display* (New Haven, Conn., 1999), and **L. Kriegel,** *Grand Designs: Labor, Empire, and the Museum in Victorian Culture* (Durham, N.C., 2007).

INDUSTRIALIZATION IN THE UNITED STATES   The early industrialization of the United States is examined in **B. Hindle** and **S. Lubar,** *Engines of Change: The American Industrial Revolution, 1790–1860* (Washington, DC, 1986).

SOCIAL IMPACT OF INDUSTRIALIZATION   For an examination of urban growth, see **J. G. Williamson,** *Coping with City Growth During the British Industrial Revolution* (Cambridge, 2002). On the Great Irish Famine, see **J. S. Donnelly,** *The Great Irish Potato Famine* (London, 2001). On city life, see **P. Pilbeam,** *The Middle Classes in Europe, 1789–1914* (Basingstoke, U.K., 1990). On female labor patterns, see **J. Rendall,** *Women in an Industrializing Society: England, 1750–1880* (Oxford, 2002), and **J. Burnette,** *Gender, Work, and Wages in Industrial Revolution Britain* (Cambridge, 2008).

Notes

1. Quoted in W. G. Rimmer, *Marshall's of Leeds, Flax-Spinners, 1788–1886* (Cambridge, 1960), p. 40.
2. D. Defoe, *A Plan of the English Commerce* (Oxford, 1928), pp. 76–77.
3. Quoted in W. Schivelbusch, *The Railway Journey* (Leamington Spa, U.K., 1977), p. 23.
4. Quoted in A. Tucker, *A History of English Civilization* (New York, 1972), p. 583.
5. Quoted in L. Kriegel, *Grand Designs: Labor, Empire, and the Museum in Victorian Culture* (Durham, N.C., 2007), p. 120.
6. Quoted in S. Beckert, *Empire of Cotton: A Global History* (New York, 2014), p. 296.
7. Quoted in *The Sessional Papers Printed by Order of The House of Lords, Or Presented by Royal Command in The Session 1842,* Vol. XXVII (London: W. Clowes and Sons, 1842), pp. 194–195.
8. Ibid., p. 314.
9. Ibid., p. 343.
10. Ibid., p. 315.
11. Charles Dickens, *The Old Curiosity Shop* (New York, 2000), p. 340.
12. Quoted in A. J. Donajgrodzi, ed., *Social Control in Nineteenth-Century Britain* (London, 1977), p. 141.
13. Quoted in *Report to Her Majesty's Principal Secretary of State for the Home Department, from the Poor Law Commissioners on An Inquiry into the Sanitary Condition of the Labouring Population of Great Britain* (London: W. Clowes and Sons, 1842), pp. 369–370.
14. Quoted in E. J. Evans, *Forging of the Modern State: Early Industrial Britain, 1783–1870* (Routledge, 2014), p. 113.
15. H. Mayhew, *London Labour and the London Poor* (London, 1851), vol.1, pp. 342–343.
16. Quoted in *Cobbett's Weekly Register,* Vol. LII from October to December 1824 (London: C. Clement, 1824), pp. 460–461.
17. Quoted in E. J. Evans, *Forging of the Modern State,* p. 158.
18. Quoted in A. J. George, ed., *The Complete Poetical Works of William Wordsworth,* Vol. 6 (Boston, 1919), p. 335.

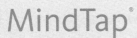 **MindTap**® is a fully online, highly personalized learning experience built upon Cengage Learning content. MindTap combines student learning tools—readings, multimedia, activities, and assessments—into a singular Learning Path that guides students through the course.

CHAPTER

21

REACTION, REVOLUTION, AND ROMANTICISM, 1815–1850

A gathering of statesmen at the Congress of Vienna

SuperStock/SuperStock

CHAPTER OUTLINE AND FOCUS QUESTIONS

The Conservative Order (1815–1830)

Q What were the goals of the Congress of Vienna and the Concert of Europe, and how successful were they in achieving those goals?

The Ideologies of Change

Q What were the main tenets of conservatism, liberalism, nationalism, and utopian socialism, and what role did each ideology play in Europe in the first half of the nineteenth century?

Revolution and Reform (1830–1850)

Q What forces for change were present in France, Great Britain, Belgium, Poland, and Italy between 1830 and 1848, and how did each nation respond? What were the causes of the revolutions of 1848, and why did the revolutions fail?

The Emergence of an Ordered Society

Q How did European states respond to the increase in crime in the late eighteenth and early nineteenth centuries?

Culture in an Age of Reaction and Revolution: The Mood of Romanticism

Q What were the characteristics of Romanticism, and how were they reflected in literature, art, and music?

Critical Thinking

Q In what ways were intellectual and artistic developments related to the political and social forces of the age?

Connections to Today

Q What are the dominant ideologies today, and how do they compare with those in the first half of the nineteenth century?

IN SEPTEMBER 1814, hundreds of foreigners began to converge on Vienna, the capital city of the Austrian Empire. Many were members of European royalty—kings, archdukes, princes, and their wives—accompanied by their diplomatic advisers and scores of servants. Their congenial host was the Austrian emperor, Francis I, who never tired of regaling Vienna's guests with concerts, glittering balls, sumptuous feasts, and countless hunting parties. One participant remembered, "Eating, fireworks, public illuminations. For eight or ten days, I haven't been able to work at all. What a life!" Of course, not every waking hour was spent in pleasure during this gathering of notables, known to history as the Congress of Vienna. These people were also representatives of all the states that had fought Napoleon, and their real business was to arrange a final peace settlement after almost a decade of war. On June 8, 1815, they finally completed their task.

The forces of upheaval unleashed during the French revolutionary and Napoleonic wars were temporarily quieted in 1815 as rulers sought to restore stability by reestablishing much of the old order to a Europe ravaged by war. Kings, landed aristocrats, and bureaucratic elites

620

regained their control over domestic governments, and internationally the forces of conservatism tried to maintain the new status quo; some states even used military force to intervene in the internal affairs of other countries in their desire to crush revolutions.

But the Western world had been changed, and it would not readily go back to the old system. New ideologies, especially liberalism and nationalism, both products of the revolutionary upheaval initiated in France, had become too powerful to be contained. Not content with the status quo, the forces of change gave rise first to the revolts and revolutions that periodically shook Europe in the 1820s and 1830s and then to the widespread revolutions of 1848. Some of the revolutions and revolutionaries were successful; most were not. Although the old order usually appeared to have prevailed, by 1850 it was apparent that its days were numbered. This perception was reinforced by the changes wrought by the Industrial Revolution. Together the forces unleashed by the dual revolutions—the French Revolution and the Industrial Revolution—made it impossible to return to prerevolutionary Europe. Nevertheless, although these events ushered in what historians like to call the modern European world, remnants of the old remained amid the new.

The Conservative Order (1815–1830)

 FOCUS QUESTION: What were the goals of the Congress of Vienna and the Concert of Europe, and how successful were they in achieving those goals?

The immediate response to the defeat of Napoleon was the desire to contain revolution and the revolutionary forces by restoring much of the old order.

The Peace Settlement

In March 1814, even before Napoleon had been defeated, his four major enemies—Great Britain, Austria, Prussia, and Russia—had agreed to remain united, not only to defeat France but also to ensure peace after the war. After Napoleon's defeat, this Quadruple Alliance restored the Bourbon monarchy to France in the person of Louis XVIII and agreed to meet at a congress in Vienna in September 1814 to arrange a final peace settlement.

The leader of the Congress of Vienna was the Austrian foreign minister, Prince Klemens von Metternich (KLAY-menss fun MET-ayr-nikh) (1773–1859). An experienced diplomat who was also conceited and self-assured, Metternich described himself in his memoirs in 1819: "There is a wide sweep about my mind. I am always above and beyond the preoccupation of most public men; I cover a ground much vaster than they can see. I cannot keep myself from saying about twenty times a day: 'How right I am, and how wrong they are.'"[1]

THE PRINCIPLE OF LEGITIMACY Metternich claimed that he was guided at Vienna by the **principle of legitimacy**. To reestablish peace and stability in Europe, he considered it necessary to restore the legitimate monarchs who would preserve traditional institutions. This had already been done in France and Spain with the restoration of the Bourbons, as well as in a number of the Italian states where rulers had been returned to their thrones. Elsewhere, however, the principle of legitimacy was largely ignored and completely overshadowed by more practical considerations of power. The congress's treatment of Poland, to which Russia, Austria, and Prussia all laid claim, illustrates this approach. Prussia and Austria were allowed to keep some Polish territory. A new, nominally independent Polish kingdom, about three-quarters of the size of the duchy of Warsaw, was established, with the Romanov dynasty of Russia as its hereditary monarchs. Although Poland was guaranteed its independence, the kingdom's foreign policy (and the kingdom itself) remained under Russian control. As compensation for the Polish lands it lost, Prussia received two-fifths of Saxony, the Napoleonic German kingdom of Westphalia, and the east bank of the Rhine. Austria was compensated for its loss of the Austrian Netherlands by being given control of two northern Italian provinces, Lombardy and Venetia (vuh-NEE-shuh) (see Map 21.1).

A NEW BALANCE OF POWER In making these territorial rearrangements, the diplomats at Vienna believed they were forming a new **balance of power** that would prevent any one country from dominating Europe. For example, to balance Russian gains, Prussia and Austria had been strengthened. According to Metternich, this arrangement had clearly avoided a great danger: "Prussia and Austria are completing their systems of defense; united, the two monarchies form an unconquerable barrier against the enterprises of any conquering prince who might perhaps once again occupy the throne of France or that of Russia."[2]

Considerations of the balance of power also dictated the allied treatment of France. France had not been significantly weakened; it remained a great power. The fear that France might again upset the European peace remained so strong that the conferees attempted to establish major defensive barriers against possible French expansion. To the north of France, they created a new enlarged kingdom of the Netherlands composed of the former Dutch Republic and the Austrian Netherlands (Belgium) under a new ruler, King William I of the house of Orange. To the southeast, Piedmont (officially part of the kingdom of Sardinia) was enlarged. On France's eastern frontier, Prussia was strengthened by giving it control of the territory along the east bank of the Rhine. The British at least expected Prussia to be the major bulwark against French expansion in central Europe, but the Congress of Vienna also created a new league of German states, the Germanic Confederation, to replace the Napoleonic Confederation of the Rhine.

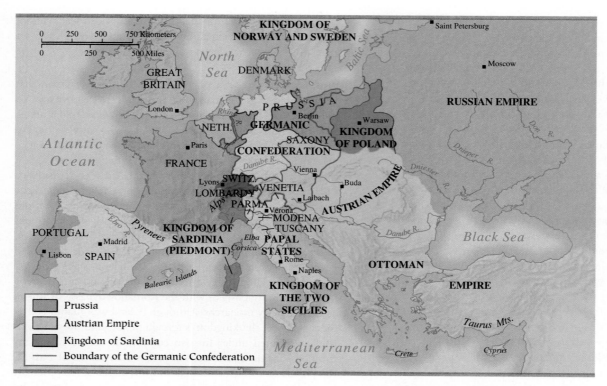

MAP 21.1 Europe After the Congress of Vienna, 1815. The Congress of Vienna imposed order on Europe based on the principles of monarchical government and a balance of power. Monarchs were restored in France, Spain, and other states recently under Napoleon's control, and much territory changed hands, often at the expense of the smaller, weaker states.

Q *How did Europe's major powers manipulate territory to decrease the probability that France could again threaten the continent's stability?*

Napoleon's escape from Elba and his return to France for one hundred days in the midst of the Congress of Vienna delayed the negotiations but did not significantly alter the overall agreement. It was decided, however, to punish the French people for their enthusiastic response to Napoleon's return. France's borders were pushed back to those of 1790, and the nation was forced to pay an indemnity and accept an army of occupation for five years. The order established by the Congress of Vienna managed to avoid a general European conflict for almost a century.

The Ideology of Conservatism

The peace arrangements of 1815 were the beginning of a conservative reaction determined to contain the liberal and nationalist forces unleashed by the French Revolution. Metternich and his kind were representatives of the ideology known as **conservatism** (see the box on p. 623). As a modern political philosophy, conservatism dates from 1790 when Edmund Burke (1729–1797) wrote his *Reflections on the Revolution in France* in reaction to the French Revolution, especially its radical republican and democratic ideas. Burke maintained that society was a contract, but "the state ought not to be considered as nothing better than a partnership agreement in a trade of pepper and

coffee, to be taken up for a temporary interest and to be dissolved by the fancy of the parties." The state was a partnership but one "not only between those who are living, but between those who are living, those who are dead and those who are to be born."[3] No one generation has the right to destroy this partnership; each generation has the duty to preserve and transmit it to the next. Burke advised against the violent overthrow of a government by revolution, but he did not reject all change. Sudden change was unacceptable but that did not mean that there should never be gradual or evolutionary improvements.

Burke's conservatism, however, was not the only kind. The Frenchman Joseph de Maistre (MESS-truh) (1753–1821) was the most influential spokesman for a counterrevolutionary and authoritarian conservatism. De Maistre espoused the restoration of hereditary monarchy, which he regarded as a divinely sanctioned institution. Only absolute monarchy could guarantee "order in society" and avoid the chaos generated by movements like the French Revolution.

Despite their differences, most conservatives held to a general body of beliefs. They favored obedience to political authority, believed that organized religion was crucial to social order, hated revolutionary upheavals, and were unwilling to accept either the liberal demands for civil liberties and representative governments or the nationalistic aspirations generated by the

THE VOICE OF CONSERVATISM: METTERNICH OF AUSTRIA

THERE WAS NO GREATER SYMBOL of conservatism in the first half of the nineteenth century than Prince Klemens von Metternich of Austria. Metternich played a crucial role at the Congress of Vienna and worked tirelessly for thirty years to repress the "revolutionary seed," as he called it, that had been spread to Europe by the "military despotism of Bonaparte."

Klemens von Metternich, *Memoirs*

We are convinced that society can no longer be saved without strong and vigorous resolutions on the part of the Governments still free in their opinions and actions.

We are also convinced that this may be, if the Governments face the truth, if they free themselves from all illusion, if they join their ranks and take their stand on a line of correct, unambiguous, and frankly announced principles.

By this course the monarchs will fulfill the duties imposed upon them by Him who, by entrusting them with power, has charged them to watch over the maintenance of justice, and the rights of all, to avoid the paths of error, and tread firmly in the way of truth. . . .

If the same elements of destruction which are now throwing society into convulsions have existed in all ages—for every age has seen immoral and ambitious men, hypocrites, men of heated imaginations, wrong motives, and wild projects—yet ours, by the single fact of the liberty of the press, possesses more than any preceding age the means of contact, seduction, and attraction whereby to act on these different classes of men.

We are certainly not alone in questioning if society can exist with the liberty of the press, a scourge unknown to the world before the latter half of the seventeenth century, and restrained until the end of the eighteenth, with scarcely any exceptions but England—a part of Europe separated from the continent by the sea, as well as by her language and by her peculiar manners.

The first principle to be followed by the monarchs, united as they are by the coincidence of their desires and opinions, should be that of maintaining the stability of political institutions against the disorganized excitement which has taken possession of men's minds; the immutability of principles against the madness of their interpretation; and respect for laws actually in force against a desire for their destruction. . . .

The first and greatest concern for the immense majority of every nation is the stability of the laws, and their uninterrupted action—never their change. Therefore, let the Governments govern, let them maintain the groundwork of their institutions, both ancient and modern; for if it is at all times dangerous to touch them, it certainly would not now, in the general confusion, be wise to do so. . . .

Let them maintain religious principles in all their purity, and not allow the faith to be attacked and morality interpreted according to the social contract or the visions of foolish sectarians.

Let them suppress Secret Societies, that gangrene of society. . . .

To every great State determined to survive the storm there still remain many chances of salvation, and a strong union between the States on the principles we have announced will overcome the storm itself.

 Based on Metternich's discussion, how would you define conservatism? What experiences conditioned Metternich's ideas? Based on this selection, what policies do you think Metternich would have wanted his government to pursue?

Source: Klemens von Metternich, *Memoirs*, trans. A. Naper (London: Richard Bentley & Sons, 1881).

French revolutionary era. The community took precedence over individual rights; society must be organized and ordered, and tradition remained the best guide for order. After 1815, the political philosophy of conservatism was supported by hereditary monarchs, government bureaucracies, landowning aristocracies, and revived churches, be they Protestant or Catholic. The conservative forces appeared dominant after 1815, both internationally and domestically.

Conservative Domination: The Concert of Europe

The European powers' fear of revolution and war led them to develop the Concert of Europe as a means to maintain the new status quo they had constructed. This accord grew out of the reaffirmation of the Quadruple Alliance in November 1815.

Great Britain, Russia, Prussia, and Austria renewed their commitment against any attempted restoration of Bonapartist power and agreed to meet periodically in conferences to discuss their common interests and examine measures that would be judged most helpful for "the maintenance of peace" in Europe.

In accordance with the agreement for periodic meetings, four congresses were held between 1818 and 1822. The first, held in 1818 at Aix-la-Chapelle (ex-lah-shah-PELL), was by far the most congenial. Metternich said that he had never known "a prettier little congress." The four great powers agreed to withdraw their army of occupation from France and to add France to the Concert of Europe. The Quadruple Alliance became a quintuple alliance.

The next congress proved far less pleasant. This session, at Troppau (TROP-ow), was called in the autumn of 1820 to deal with the outbreak of revolution in Spain and Italy. The revolt in Spain was directed against Ferdinand VII, the Bourbon king who had been restored to the throne in 1814. In southern Italy, the restoration of another Bourbon, Ferdinand I, as king of Naples and Sicily sparked a rebellion that soon spread to Piedmont in northern Italy.

THE PRINCIPLE OF INTERVENTION Metternich was especially disturbed by the revolts in Italy because he saw them as a threat to Austria's domination of the peninsula. At Troppau, he proposed a protocol that established the **principle of intervention**. It read:

> States which have undergone a change of Government due to revolution, the results of which threaten other states, *ipso facto* cease to be members of the European Alliance, and remain excluded from it until their situation gives guarantees for legal order and stability. If, owing to such situations, immediate danger threatens other states, the Powers bind themselves, by peaceful means, or if need be by arms, to bring back the guilty state into the bosom of the Great Alliance.[4]

The principle of intervention meant that the great powers of Europe had the right to send armies into countries where there were revolutions to restore legitimate monarchs to their thrones. Britain refused to agree to the principle, arguing that it had never been the intention of the Quadruple Alliance to interfere in the internal affairs of other states, except in France. Ignoring the British response, Austria, Prussia, and Russia met in a third congress at Laibach (LY-bahkh) in January 1821 and authorized the sending of Austrian troops to Naples. These forces crushed the revolt, restored Ferdinand I to the throne, and then moved north to suppress the rebels in Piedmont. At the fourth postwar conference, held at Verona in October 1822, the same three powers authorized France to invade Spain to crush the revolt against Ferdinand VII. In the spring of 1823, French forces restored the Bourbon monarch.

The success of this policy of intervention came at a price, however. The Concert of Europe had broken down when the British rejected Metternich's principle of intervention. And although the British had failed to thwart allied intervention in Spain and Italy, they were successful in keeping the continental powers from interfering with the revolutions in Latin America.

THE REVOLT OF LATIN AMERICA Although much of North America had been freed of European domination in the eighteenth century by the American Revolution, Latin America remained in the hands of the Spanish and Portuguese. By the

The Liberators of South America. José de San Martín of Argentina and Simón Bolívar are hailed as the leaders of the Latin American independence movement. In the painting on the left, San Martín is portrayed in the Andes mountains. His forces liberated Argentina, Chile, and Peru from Spanish authority. The painting on the right shows Bolívar leading his troops across the Andes in 1823 to fight in Peru. This depiction of impeccably uniformed troops moving in perfect formation through the snow of the Andes, by the Chilean artist Franco Gomez, is, of course, highly unrealistic.

end of the eighteenth century, the ideas of the Enlightenment and the new political ideals stemming from the successful revolution in North America were beginning to influence the Creole elites (descendants of Europeans who became permanent inhabitants of Latin America). The principles of the equality of all people in the eyes of the law, free trade, and a free press proved very attractive. Sons of Creoles, such as Simón Bolívar (see-MOHN buh-LEE-var) (1783–1830) of Venezuela and José de San Martín (hoh-SAY day san mar-TEEN) (1778–1850) of Argentina, who became the leaders of the independence movement, even attended European universities, where they imbibed the ideas of the Enlightenment. These Latin American elites, joined by a growing class of merchants, especially resented the domination of their trade by Spain and Portugal. At the beginning of the nineteenth century, Napoleon's European wars provided the Creoles with an opportunity for change. When Bonaparte toppled the monarchies of Spain and Portugal, the authority of the Spaniards and Portuguese in their colonial empires was weakened, and between 1807 and 1824, a series of revolts enabled most of Latin America to become independent.

Simón Bolívar has long been regarded as the George Washington of Latin America. Born into a wealthy Venezuelan family, he was introduced as a young man to the ideas of the Enlightenment. While in Rome to witness the coronation of Napoleon as king of Italy in 1805, he committed himself to free his people from Spanish control. When he returned to South America, Bolívar began to lead the bitter struggle for independence in Venezuela as well as other parts of northern South America. Although he was acclaimed as the "liberator" of Venezuela in 1813 by the people, it was not until 1821 that he definitively defeated Spanish forces there. He went on to liberate Colombia, Ecuador, and Peru. Already in 1819, he had become president of Venezuela, at the time part of a federation that included Colombia and Ecuador.

While Bolívar was busy liberating northern South America from the Spanish, José de San Martín was concentrating his efforts on the southern part of the continent. Son of a Spanish army officer in Argentina, San Martín went to Spain and pursued a military career in the Spanish army. In 1811, after serving twenty-two years, he learned of the liberation movement in his native Argentina, abandoned his military career in Spain, and returned to his homeland in March 1812. Argentina had already been freed from Spanish control, but San Martín believed that the Spaniards must be removed from all of South America if any nation was to remain free. In January 1817, he led his forces over the high Andes Mountains, an amazing feat in itself. Two-thirds of his pack mules and horses died during the difficult journey. Many of the soldiers suffered from lack of oxygen and severe cold while crossing mountain passes more than 2 miles above sea level. The arrival of San Martín's troops in Chile surprised the Spaniards, whose forces were routed at the Battle of Chacabuco (chahk-ah-BOO-koh) on February 12, 1817.

In 1821, San Martín moved on to Lima, Peru, the center of Spanish authority. Convinced that he was unable to complete the liberation of all of Peru, San Martín welcomed the arrival of Bolívar and his forces. As he wrote to Bolívar, "For me it would have been the height of happiness to end the war of independence under the orders of a general to whom [South] America owes its freedom. Destiny orders it otherwise, and one must resign oneself to it."[5] Highly disappointed, San Martín left South America for Europe, where he remained until his death outside Paris in 1850. Meanwhile, Bolívar took on the task of crushing the last significant Spanish army at Ayacucho (ah-ya-KOO-choh) on December 9, 1824. By then, Peru, Uruguay, Paraguay, Colombia, Venezuela, Argentina, Bolivia, and Chile had all become free states (see Map 21.2). In 1823, the Central American states became independent, and in 1838–1839, they divided into five republics (Guatemala, El Salvador, Honduras, Costa Rica, and Nicaragua). Earlier, in 1822, the prince regent of Brazil had declared Brazil's independence from Portugal.

The continental powers, however, flushed by their success in crushing the rebellions in Spain and Italy, favored the use of troops to restore Spanish control in Latin America. This time, British opposition to intervention prevailed. Eager to gain access to an entire continent for investment and trade, the British proposed joint action with the United States against European interference in Latin America. Distrustful of British motives, President James Monroe acted alone in 1823, guaranteeing the independence of the new Latin American nations and warning against any further European intervention in the New World in the famous Monroe Doctrine. Actually, British ships were more important to Latin American independence than American words. Britain's navy stood between Latin America and any European invasion force, and the continental powers were extremely reluctant to challenge British naval power.

Political independence did not mean economic independence, however, as old patterns were quickly reestablished, with Great Britain instead of Spain and Portugal now dominating the Latin American economy. British merchants moved in in large numbers, while British investors poured in funds, especially in the mining industry. Old trade patterns soon reemerged. Because Latin America served as a source of raw materials and foodstuffs for the industrializing nations of Europe and the United States, exports—especially of wheat, tobacco, wool, sugar, coffee, and hides—to the North Atlantic countries noticeably increased. At the same time, finished consumer goods, especially textiles, were imported in increasing quantities, causing a decline in industrial production in Latin America. The emphasis on exporting raw materials and importing finished products ensured the ongoing domination of the Latin American economy by foreigners.

THE GREEK REVOLT The principle of intervention proved to be a double-edged sword. Designed to prevent revolution, it could also be used to support revolution if the great powers found it in their interest to do so. In 1821, the Greeks revolted against their Ottoman Turkish masters. Although subject to Muslim control for four hundred years, the Greeks

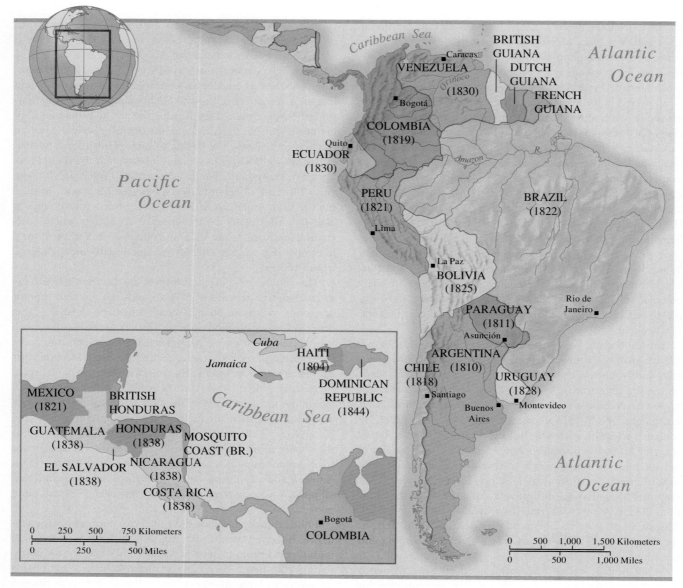

MAP 21.2 Latin America in the First Half of the Nineteenth Century. Latin American colonies took advantage of Spain's weakness during the Napoleonic wars to fight for independence, beginning with Argentina in 1810 and spreading throughout the region over the next decade with the help of leaders like Simón Bolívar and José de San Martín. The dates in parentheses show the years in which the countries received formal recognition.

 How many South American countries are sources of rivers that feed the Amazon, and roughly what percentage of the continent is contained within the Amazon's watershed?

had been allowed to maintain their language and their Greek Orthodox faith. A revival of Greek national sentiment at the beginning of the nineteenth century added to the growing desire for liberation "from the terrible yoke of Turkish oppression." The Greek revolt was soon transformed into a noble cause by an outpouring of European sentiment for the Greeks' struggle.

In 1827, a combined British and French fleet went to Greece and defeated a large Ottoman armada. A year later,

Russia declared war on the Ottoman Empire and invaded its European provinces of Moldavia and Wallachia. By the Treaty of Adrianople in 1829, which ended the Russian-Turkish war, the Russians received a protectorate over the two provinces. By the same treaty, the Ottoman Empire agreed to allow Russia, France, and Britain to decide the fate of Greece. In 1830, the three powers declared Greece an independent kingdom, and two years later, a new royal dynasty was established. The revolution had been successful only because the great powers

CHRONOLOGY	Conservative Domination: The Concert of Europe
Congress of Vienna	1814–1815
Congress of Aix-la-Chapelle	1818
Revolutions win independence for Latin America	1819–1824
Congress of Troppau	1820
Congress of Laibach	1821
Crushing of revolt in southern Italy	1821
Greek revolt against the Ottoman Empire	1821
Congress of Verona	1822
Crushing of revolt in Spain	1823
Monroe Doctrine	1823
Treaty of Adrianople	1829
Independence of Greece	1830

Peterloo Massacre This colored etching depicts the massacre on August 16, 1819, in St. Peter's Field in Manchester. The gathering was organized by the Manchester Patriotic Union Society, a group that had called for parliamentary reforms and the end of the Corn Laws. Over 60,000 people had gathered in the field. Soldiers forced their way toward the speakers by cutting their way through the crowds with their sabers, killing eleven and wounding many women and children.

The Balkans by 1830

themselves supported it. Until 1830, the Greek revolt was the only successful one in Europe; the conservative domination was still largely intact.

Conservative Domination: The European States

Between 1815 and 1830, the conservative domination of Europe evident in the Concert of Europe was also apparent in domestic affairs, as conservative governments throughout Europe worked to maintain the old order.

GREAT BRITAIN: RULE OF THE TORIES In 1815, the aristocratic landowning classes that dominated both houses of Parliament governed Great Britain. Suffrage for elections to the House of Commons, controlled by the landed gentry, was restricted and unequal, especially in light of the changing distribution of the British population due to the Industrial Revolution. Large new industrial cities such as Birmingham and Manchester had no representatives, while landowners used pocket and rotten boroughs (see Chapter 18) to control seats in the House of Commons. Although the monarchy was not yet powerless, in practice the power of the crown was largely in the hands of the ruling party in Parliament.

There were two political factions in Parliament, the Tories and the Whigs. Both were still dominated by members of the landed classes, although the Whigs were beginning to receive support from the new industrial middle class. Tory ministers largely dominated the government until 1830 and had little desire to change the existing political and electoral system.

Popular discontent grew after 1815 because of severe economic difficulties. The Tory government's response to falling agricultural prices was the Corn Law of 1815, which imposed extraordinarily high tariffs on foreign grain. Though the tariffs benefited the landowners, the price of bread rose substantially, making conditions for the working classes more difficult. Mass protest meetings took a nasty turn when a squadron of cavalry attacked a crowd of 60,000 demonstrators at Saint Peter's Fields in Manchester in 1819. The deaths of eleven people, called the Peterloo Massacre by government detractors, led Parliament to take even more repressive measures. The government restricted large public meetings and the dissemination of pamphlets among the poor, while extending police powers of search and arrest. At the same time, by making minor reforms in the 1820s, the Tories managed to avoid meeting the demands for electoral reforms—at least until 1830 (see "Reform in Great Britain" later in this chapter).

RESTORATION IN FRANCE In 1814, the Bourbon family was restored to the throne of France in the person of Louis XVIII (1814–1824). Louis understood the need to accept some of the changes brought to France by the revolutionary and Napoleonic eras. He accepted Napoleon's Civil Code with its recognition of the principle of equality before the law (see Chapter 19). The property rights of those who had purchased confiscated lands during the Revolution were preserved. A bicameral (two-house) legislature was established, consisting of the Chamber of Peers, chosen by the king, and the Chamber of Deputies, chosen by an electorate restricted to slightly fewer than 100,000 wealthy people.

Louis's grudging moderation, however, was opposed by liberals eager to extend the revolutionary reforms and by a group of **ultraroyalists** who criticized the king's willingness to compromise and retain so many features of the Napoleonic era. The ultras hoped to return to a monarchical system dominated by a privileged landed aristocracy and to restore the Catholic Church to its former position of influence.

The initiative passed to the ultraroyalists in 1824 when Louis XVIII died and was succeeded by his brother, the count of Artois (ar-TWAH), who became Charles X (1824–1830). In 1825, Charles granted an indemnity to aristocrats whose lands had been confiscated during the Revolution. Moreover, the king pursued a religious policy that encouraged the Catholic Church to reestablish control over the French educational system. Public outrage, fed by liberal newspapers, forced the king to compromise in 1827 and even to accept the principle of **ministerial responsibility**—that the ministers of the king were responsible to the legislature. But in 1829, he violated his commitment. A protest by the deputies led the king to dissolve the legislature in 1830 and call for new elections. France was on the brink of another revolution.

INTERVENTION IN THE ITALIAN STATES AND SPAIN The Congress of Vienna had established nine states in Italy, including Piedmont (part of the kingdom of Sardinia) in the north, ruled by the house of Savoy; the kingdom of the Two Sicilies (Naples and Sicily); the Papal States; a handful of small duchies ruled by relatives of the Austrian emperor; and the important northern provinces of Lombardy and Venetia, which were now part of the Austrian Empire. Much of Italy was under Austrian domination, and all the states had extremely reactionary governments eager to smother any liberal or nationalist sentiment. Nevertheless, secret societies motivated by nationalistic dreams and known as the Carbonari (kar-buh-NAH-ree) ("charcoal burners") continued to conspire and plan for revolution.

In Spain, another Bourbon dynasty had been restored in the person of Ferdinand VII in 1814. Ferdinand (1814–1833) had agreed to observe the liberal constitution of 1812, which allowed for the functioning of an elected parliamentary assembly known as the Cortes. But the king soon reneged on his promises, tore up the constitution, dissolved the Cortes, and persecuted its members, which led a combined group of army officers, upper-middle-class merchants, and liberal intellectuals to revolt. The king capitulated in March 1820 and promised once again to restore the constitution and the Cortes. But Metternich's policy of intervention came to Ferdinand's rescue.

Italy, 1815

In April 1823, a French army moved into Spain and forced the revolutionary government to flee Madrid. By August of that year, the king had been restored to his throne.

REPRESSION IN CENTRAL EUROPE After 1815, the forces of reaction were particularly successful in central Europe. The Habsburg empire and its chief agent, Prince Klemens von Metternich, played an important role. Metternich boasted, "You see in me the chief Minister of Police in Europe. I keep an eye on everything. My contacts are such that nothing escapes me."[6] Metternich's spies were everywhere, searching for evidence of liberal or nationalist plots. Although both liberalism and nationalism emerged in the German states and the Austrian Empire, they were initially weak as central Europe tended to remain under the domination of aristocratic landowning classes and autocratic, centralized monarchies.

The Vienna settlement in 1815 had recognized the existence of thirty-eight sovereign states in what had once been the Holy Roman Empire. Austria and Prussia were the two great powers; the other states varied considerably in size. Together these states formed the Germanic Confederation, but the confederation had little power. It had no real executive, and its only central organ was the federal diet, which needed the consent of all member states to take action, making it virtually powerless. Nevertheless, it also came to serve as Metternich's instrument to repress revolutionary movements within the German states.

Initially, Germans who favored liberal principles and German unity looked to Prussia for leadership. During the Napoleonic era, King Frederick William III (1797–1840), following the advice of his two chief ministers, Baron Heinrich von Stein and Prince Karl von Hardenberg, instituted political and institutional reforms in response to Prussia's defeat at the hands of Napoleon. The reforms included the abolition of serfdom, municipal self-government through town councils, the expansion of primary and secondary schools, and universal military conscription to form a national army. The reforms, however, did not include the creation of a legislative assembly or representative government as Stein and Hardenberg wished. After 1815, Frederick William grew more reactionary and was content to follow Metternich's lead. Though reforms had made Prussia strong, it remained largely an absolutist state with little interest in German unity.

Liberal and national movements in the German states were for the most part limited to university professors and students. The latter began to organize *Burschenschaften* (BOOR-shun-shahf-tuhn), student societies dedicated to fostering the goal of a free, united Germany (see the box on p. 629). Their ideas and their motto, "Honor, Liberty, Fatherland," were in part inspired by Friedrich Ludwig Jahn (FREED-rikh LOOD-vik YAHN), who had organized gymnastic societies during the Napoleonic wars to promote the regeneration of German youth and support the "War of German Liberation" against the French. Jahn encouraged Germans to pursue their Germanic heritage and urged his followers to disrupt the lectures of professors whose views were not nationalistic.

From 1817 to 1819, the *Burschenschaften* pursued a variety of activities that alarmed German governments. At an assembly held

UNIVERSITY STUDENTS AND GERMAN UNITY

IN THE EARLY NINETEENTH CENTURY, university students and professors were the chief supporters of German nationalism. Especially important were the *Burschenschaften,* student societies that espoused the cause of German unity. In this selection, the liberal Heinrich von Gagern explains the purpose of the *Burschenschaften* to his father.

Heinrich von Gagern, Letter to His Father

It is very hard to explain the spirit of the student movement to you, but I shall try. . . . It speaks to the better youth, the man of heart and spirit and love for all this good, and gives him nourishment and being. For the average student of the past, the university years were a time to enjoy life, and to make a sharp break with his own background in defiance of the philistine world, which seemed to him somehow to foreshadow the tomb. Their pleasures, their organizations, and their talk were determined by their *status* as students, and their university obligation was only to avoid failing the examination and scraping by adequately—bread-and-butter learning. . . . There are still many of those nowadays, indeed the majority overall. But at several universities, and especially here, another group—in my eyes a better one—has managed to get the upper hand in the sense that it sets the mood. . . .

Those who share in this spirit have then quite another tendency in their student life. Love of Fatherland is their guiding principle. Their purpose is to make a better future for the Fatherland . . . to spread national consciousness, or to use the much ridiculed and maligned Germanic expression, more folkishness, and to work for better constitutions. . . .

We want more sense of community among the several states of Germany, greater unity in their policies and in their

principles of government; no separate policy for each state, but the nearest possible relations with one another; above all, we want Germany to be considered *one* land and the German people one people. In the forms of our student comradeship we show how we want to approach this as nearly as possible in the real world. Regional fraternities are forbidden, and we live in a German comradeship, one people in spirit, as we want it for all Germany in reality. We give ourselves the freest of constitutions, just as we should like Germany to have the freest possible one, insofar as that is suitable for the German people. We want a constitution for the people that fits in with the spirit of the times and with the people's own level of enlightenment, rather than what each prince gives his people according to what he likes and what serves his private interest. Above all, we want the princes to understand and to follow the principle that they exist for the country and not the country for them. In fact, the prevailing view is that the constitution should not come from the individual states at all. The main principles of the German constitution should apply to all states in common, and should be expressed by the German federal assembly. This constitution should deal not only with the absolute necessities, like fiscal administration and justice, general administration and church and military affairs and so on; this constitution ought to be extended to the education of the young . . . and to many other such things.

 Would you call Heinrich von Gagern a nationalist? Why or why not? Based on this selection, why do you think the forces of nationalism and liberalism were allies during the first half of the nineteenth century?

Source: M. Walker, ed., *Metternich's Europe* (London: Walker & Co, 1968).

---

at the Wartburg Castle in 1817, marking the three hundredth anniversary of Luther's Ninety-Five Theses, the crowd burned books written by conservative authors. When a deranged student assassinated a reactionary playwright, Metternich had the diet of the Germanic Confederation draw up the Karlsbad (KARLSS-baht) Decrees of 1819. These closed the *Burschenschaften,* provided for censorship of the press, and placed the universities under close supervision and control. Thereafter, except for a minor flurry of activity from 1830 to 1832, Metternich and the cooperative German rulers maintained the conservative status quo.

The Austrian Empire was a multinational state, a collection of different peoples under the Habsburg emperor, who provided a common bond. The empire contained eleven peoples of different national origin, including Germans, Czechs, Magyars (Hungarians), Slovaks, Romanians, Slovenes, Poles, Serbians, and Italians. The Germans, though only a quarter of the population, were economically the most advanced and played a leading role in governing Austria. Essentially, the dynasty, the imperial civil service, the imperial army, and the Catholic

Church held the Austrian Empire together. But its national groups, especially the Hungarians, with their increasing desire for autonomy, acted as forces to break the empire apart.

Still Metternich managed to hold it all together. His antipathy to liberalism and nationalism was understandably grounded in the realization that these forces threatened to tear the empire apart. The growing liberal belief that each national group had the right to its own system of government could only mean disaster for the multinational Austrian Empire. While the forces of liberalism and nationalism grew, the Austrian Empire largely stagnated.

RUSSIA: AUTOCRACY OF THE TSARS At the beginning of the nineteenth century, Russia was overwhelmingly rural, agricultural, and autocratic. The Russian tsar was still regarded as a divine-right monarch. Alexander I (1801–1825) had been raised in the ideas of the Enlightenment and initially seemed willing to make reforms. With the aid of his liberal adviser Michael Speransky (spyuh-RAHN-skee), he relaxed censorship, freed political prisoners, and reformed the educational system. He refused, however, to grant a constitution or free the serfs in the face of opposition from the nobility. After the defeat of Napoleon, Alexander became a reactionary, and his government reverted to strict and arbitrary censorship. Soon opposition to Alexander arose from a group of secret societies.

One of these societies, known as the Northern Union, included both young aristocrats who had served in the Napoleonic wars and become aware of the world outside Russia and intellectuals alienated by the censorship and lack of academic freedom in Russian universities. The Northern Union favored the establishment of a constitutional monarchy and the abolition of serfdom. The sudden death of Alexander in 1825 offered them their opportunity.

Although Alexander's brother Constantine was the legal heir to the throne, he had renounced his claims in favor of his brother Nicholas. Constantine's abdication had not been made public, however, and during the ensuing confusion in December 1825, the military leaders of the Northern Union rebelled against the accession of Nicholas. This so-called Decembrist Revolt was soon crushed by troops loyal to Nicholas, and its leaders were executed.

The revolt transformed Nicholas I (1825–1855) from a conservative into a reactionary determined to avoid another rebellion. He strengthened both the bureaucracy and the secret police. The political police, known as the Third Section of the tsar's chancellery, were given sweeping powers over much of Russian life. They deported suspicious or dangerous persons, maintained close surveillance of foreigners in Russia, and reported regularly to the tsar on public opinion.

Matching Nicholas's fear of revolution at home was his fear of revolution abroad. There would be no revolution in Russia during the rest of his reign; if he could help it, there would be none in Europe either. Contemporaries called him the Policeman of Europe because of his willingness to use Russian troops to crush revolutions.

The Ideologies of Change

 FOCUS QUESTION: What were the main tenets of conservatism, liberalism, nationalism, and utopian socialism, and what role did each ideology play in Europe in the first half of the nineteenth century?

Although the conservative forces were in the ascendancy from 1815 to 1830, powerful movements for change were also at work. These depended on ideas embodied in a series of political philosophies or ideologies that came into their own in the first half of the nineteenth century.

Liberalism

One of these ideologies was **liberalism**, which owed much to the Enlightenment of the eighteenth century and to the American and French Revolutions at the end of that century. In addition, liberalism became even more significant as the Industrial

Revolution made rapid strides because the developing industrial middle class largely adopted the doctrine as its own. There were divergences of opinion among people classified as liberals, but all began with the belief that people should be as free from restraint as possible. This opinion is evident in both economic and political liberalism.

ECONOMIC LIBERALISM Also called classical economics, economic liberalism had as its primary tenet the concept of *laissez-faire*, the belief that the state should not interrupt the free play of natural economic forces, especially supply and demand. Government should not restrain the economic liberty of the individual and should restrict itself to only three primary functions: defense of the country, police protection of individuals, and the construction and maintenance of public works too expensive for individuals to undertake. If individuals were allowed economic liberty, ultimately they would bring about the maximum good for the maximum number and benefit the general welfare of society.

The case against government interference in economic matters was greatly enhanced by Thomas Malthus (MAWL-thuss) (1766–1834). In his major work, *Essay on the Principles of Population*, Malthus argued that population, when unchecked, increases at a geometric rate while the food supply correspondingly increases at a much slower arithmetic rate. The result will be severe overpopulation and ultimately starvation for the human race if this growth is not held in check. According to Malthus, nature imposes a major restraint with severe labor and exposure to the seasons, extreme poverty, bad nursing of children, excesses of all kinds, many common diseases, epidemics, wars, plague, and famine. Thus, misery and poverty were simply the inevitable result of the law of nature; no government or individual should interfere with its operation.

Malthus's ideas were further developed by David Ricardo (1772–1823). In *Principles of Political Economy*, written in 1817, Ricardo developed his famous "iron law of wages." Following Malthus, Ricardo argued that an increase in population means more workers; more workers in turn cause wages to fall below the subsistence level. The result is misery and starvation, which then reduce the population. Consequently, the number of workers declines, and wages rise above the subsistence level again, which in turn encourages workers to have larger families as the cycle is repeated. According to Ricardo, raising wages arbitrarily would be pointless since it would accomplish little but perpetuate this vicious circle.

POLITICAL LIBERALISM Politically, liberals came to hold a common set of beliefs. Chief among them was the protection of civil liberties or the basic rights of all people, which included equality before the law; freedom of assembly, speech, and press; and freedom from arbitrary arrest. All of these freedoms should be guaranteed by a written document, such as the American Bill of Rights or the French Declaration of the Rights of Man and the Citizen. In addition to religious toleration for all, most liberals advocated separation of church and state. The right of peaceful opposition to the government in and out of parliament and the making of laws by a

THE VOICE OF LIBERALISM: JOHN STUART MILL ON LIBERTY

JOHN STUART MILL WAS ONE OF BRITAIN'S most famous philosophers of liberalism. Mill's essay *On Liberty* is viewed as a classic statement of the liberal belief in the unfettered freedom of the individual. In this excerpt, Mill defends freedom of opinion from both government and the coercion of the majority.

John Stuart Mill, *On Liberty*

The object of this Essay is to assert one very simple principle, as entitled to govern absolutely the dealings of society with the individual in the way of compulsion and control, whether the means used be physical force in the form of legal penalties, or the moral coercion of public opinion. That principle is, that the sole end for which mankind are warranted, individually or collectively, interfering with the liberty of action of any of their number, is self-protection. That the only purpose for which power can be rightfully exercised over any member of a civilized community, against his will, is to prevent harm to others. His own good, either physical or moral, is not a sufficient warrant. . . . These are good reasons for remonstrating with him, or reasoning with him, or persuading him, or entreating him, but not for compelling him, or visiting him with any evil in case he do otherwise. To justify that, the conduct from which it is desired to deter him, must be calculated to produce evil to some one else. The only part of the conduct of any one, for which he is amenable to society, is that which concerns others. In the part which merely concerns himself, his independence is, of right, absolute. Over himself, over his own body and mind, the individual is sovereign. . . .

Society can and does execute its own mandates: and if it issues wrong mandates instead of right, or any mandates at all in things with which it ought not to meddle, it practices a social tyranny more formidable than many kinds of political oppression, since, though not usually upheld by such extreme penalties, it leaves fewer means of escape, penetrating more deeply into the details of life, and enslaving the soul itself. Protection, therefore, against the tyranny of the magistrate is not enough: there needs protection also against the tyranny of prevailing opinion and feeling, against the tendency of society to impose, by other means than civil penalties, its own ideas and practices as rules of conduct on those who dissent from them. . . .

But there is a sphere of action in which society, as distinguished from the individual has, if any, only an indirect interest; comprehending all that portion of a person's life and conduct which affects only himself, or if it also affects others, only with their free, voluntary and undeceived consent and participation. . . . This then is the appropriate region of human liberty. It comprises, first, the inward domain of consciousness; demanding liberty of conscience in the most comprehensive sense; liberty of thought and feeling; absolute freedom of opinion and sentiment on all subjects, practical or speculative, scientific, moral, or theological. . . .

Let us suppose, therefore, that the government is entirely at one with the people, and never thinks of exerting any power of coercion unless in agreement with what it conceives to be their voice. But I deny the right of the people to exercise such coercion, either by themselves or by their government. The power itself is illegitimate. The best government has no more title to it than the worst. It is as noxious, or more noxious, when exerted in accordance with public opinion, than when in opposition to it. If all mankind minus one were of one opinion, and only one person were of the contrary opinion, mankind would be no more justified in silencing that one person, than he, if he had the power, would be justified in silencing mankind. . . . The peculiar evil of silencing the expression of an opinion is, that it is robbing the human race; posterity as well as the existing generation; those who dissent from the opinion, still more than those who hold it. If the opinion is right, they are deprived of the opportunity of exchanging error for truth: if wrong, they lose, what is almost as great a benefit, the clearer perception and livelier impression of truth, produced by its collision with error.

 Based on the principles outlined here, how would you define liberalism? How do Mill's ideas fit into the concept of democracy? Which is more important in his thought: the individual or society?

Source: John Stuart Mill, *Utilitarianism, On Liberty, and Representative Government* (New York: Viking Press, 1914).

---

representative assembly (legislature) elected by qualified voters constituted two other liberal demands. Many liberals believed, then, in a constitutional monarchy or constitutional state with limits on the powers of government to prevent despotism and in written constitutions that would help guarantee these rights.

Many liberals also advocated ministerial responsibility, which would give the legislative branch a check on the power of the executive because the king's ministers would answer to the legislature rather than to the king. Liberals in the first half of the nineteenth century also believed in a limited suffrage. Although all people were entitled to equal civil rights, they should not have equal political rights. The right to vote and hold office should be open only to men who met certain property qualifications. As a political philosophy, liberalism was tied to middle-class men, especially industrial middle-class men who favored the extension of voting rights so that they could share power with the landowning classes. They had little desire to let the lower classes share that power. Liberals were not democrats.

One of the most prominent advocates of liberalism in the nineteenth century was the English philosopher John Stuart Mill (1806–1873). *On Liberty*, his most famous work, published in 1859, has long been regarded as a classic statement on the liberty of the individual (see the box above). Mill argued for an "absolute freedom of opinion and sentiment on all subjects" that needed to be protected from both government censorship and the tyranny of the majority.

Mill was also instrumental in expanding the meaning of liberalism by becoming an enthusiastic supporter of women's rights. When his attempt to include women in the voting reform bill of 1867 failed, Mill published an essay titled *On the Subjection of Women*, which he had written earlier with his wife, Harriet Taylor. He argued that the legal subordination of one sex to the other was wrong. Differences between women and men, he said, were due not to different natures but simply to social practices. With equal education, women could achieve as much as men. *On the Subjection of Women* would become an important work in the nineteenth-century movement for women's rights.

Nationalism

Nationalism was an even more powerful ideology for change in the nineteenth century. Nationalism arose out of an awareness of being part of a community that has common institutions, historical traditions, language, and customs. This community constitutes a "nation," and it, rather than a dynasty, city-state, or other political unit, becomes the focus of the individual's primary political loyalty. Nationalism, however, did not become a popular force for change until the French Revolution. From then on, nationalists came to believe that each nationality should have its own government. Thus, a divided people such as the Germans wanted national unity in a German nation-state with one central government. Subject peoples, such as the Hungarians, wanted national self-determination, or the right to establish their own autonomy rather than be subject to a German minority in a multinational empire.

Nationalism threatened to upset the existing political order, both internationally and nationally (see Map 21.3). A united Germany or united Italy would upset the balance of power established in 1815. By the same token, an independent Hungarian state would mean the breakup of the Austrian Empire. Because many European states were multinational, conservatives tried hard to repress the radical threat of nationalism.

At the same time, in the first half of the nineteenth century, nationalism and liberalism became strong allies. Most liberals believed that liberty could be realized only by peoples who ruled themselves. One British liberal argued that the boundaries of governments should coincide in the main with those of nationalities. Many nationalists believed that once each people obtained its own state, all nations could be linked together into a broader community of all humanity.

Early Socialism

In the first half of the nineteenth century, the pitiful conditions found in the slums, mines, and factories of the Industrial Revolution gave rise to another ideology for change known as **socialism**. The term eventually became associated with a Marxist analysis of human society (see Chapter 22), but early socialism was largely the product of political theorists or intellectuals who wanted to introduce equality into social conditions and believed that human cooperation was superior to the competition that characterized early industrial capitalism. To later Marxists, such ideas were impractical dreams, and they contemptuously labeled the theorists **utopian socialists**. The term has endured to this day.

The utopian socialists were against private property and the competitive spirit of early industrial capitalism. By eliminating these things and creating new systems of social organization, they thought that a better environment for humanity could be achieved. Early socialists proposed a variety of ways to accomplish that task.

FOURIER One group of early socialists sought to create voluntary associations that would demonstrate the advantages of cooperative living. Charles Fourier (SHAHRL foo-RYAY) (1772–1838) proposed the creation of small model communities called phalansteries. These were self-contained cooperatives, each consisting ideally of 1,620 people. Communally housed, the inhabitants of the **phalanstery** (fuh-LAN-stuh-ree) would live and work together for their mutual benefit. Work assignments would be rotated frequently to relieve workers of undesirable tasks. Fourier was unable to gain financial backing for his phalansteries, however, and his plan remained untested.

OWEN The British cotton manufacturer Robert Owen (1771–1858) also believed that humans would reveal their true natural goodness if they lived in a cooperative environment. At New Lanark in Scotland, he was successful in transforming a squalid factory town into a flourishing, healthy community. But when he attempted to create a self-contained cooperative community at New Harmony, Indiana, in the United States in the 1820s, bickering within the community eventually destroyed his dream. One of Owen's disciples, a wealthy woman named Frances Wright, bought slaves in order to set up a model community at Nashoba, Tennessee. The community failed, but Wright continued to work for women's rights.

BLANC The Frenchman Louis Blanc (LWEE BLAHNH) (1813–1882) offered yet another early socialist approach to a better society. In *The Organization of Work*, he maintained that social problems could be solved by government assistance. Denouncing competition as the main cause of the economic evils of his day, he called for the establishment of workshops that would manufacture goods for public sale. The state would finance these workshops, but the workers would own and operate them.

FEMALE SUPPORTERS With their plans for the reconstruction of society, utopian socialists attracted a number of female supporters who believed that only a reordering of society would help women. Zoé Gatti de Gamond (zoh-AY gah-TEE duh gah-MOHNH), a Belgian follower of Fourier, established her own phalanstery, which was supposed to provide men and women with the same educational and job opportunities.

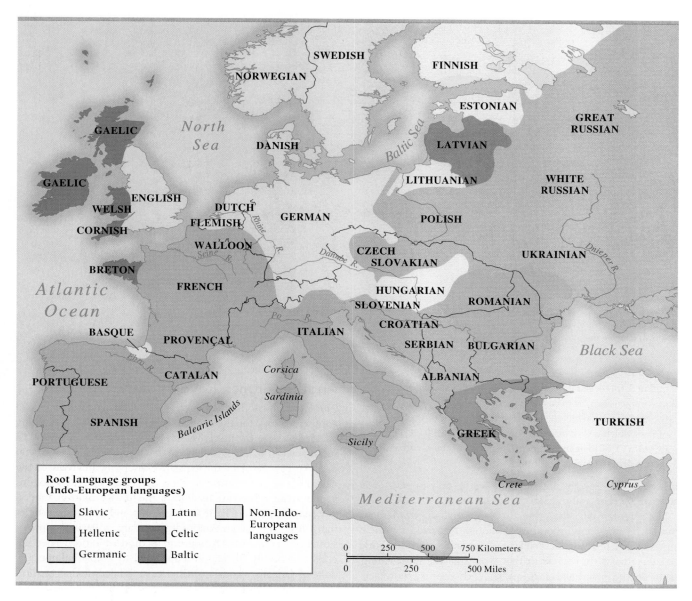

MAP 21.3 The Distribution of Languages in Nineteenth-Century Europe. Numerous languages were spoken in Europe. People who used the same language often had a shared history and culture, which laid the seeds for growing nationalism in the nineteenth century. Such nationalism eventually led to unification for Germany and Italy but spelled trouble for the polyglot Habsburg empire.

Q *Look at the distribution of Germanic, Latin, and Slavic languages. What patterns emerge, and how can you explain them?*

As part of collective living, men and women were to share responsibilities for child care and housecleaning. The ideas of the comte de Saint-Simón (san-see-MOHN), which combined Christian values, scientific thought, and socialist utopianism, proved especially attractive to a number of women who participated in the growing political activism of women that had been set in motion during the French Revolution. Saint-Simón's ideal cooperative society recognized the principle of equality between men and women, and a number of working-class women, including Suzanne Voilquin (soo-ZAHN vwahl-KANH), Claire Démar (DAY-mar), and Reine Guindorf (RY-nuh GWIN-dorf), published a newspaper dedicated to the emancipation of women.

TRISTAN One female utopian socialist, Flora Tristan (TRISS-tun) (1803–1844), even attempted to foster a "utopian synthesis of socialism and feminism." She traveled through France preaching the need for the liberation of women. Her *Worker's Union*, published in 1843, advocated the application of Fourier's ideas to reconstruct both family and work:

> Workers, be sure of it. If you have enough equity and justice to inscribe into your Charter the few points I have just

Children at New Lanark. Robert Owen created an early experiment in utopian socialism by establishing a model industrial community at New Lanark, Scotland. In this illustration, the children of factory workers are shown dancing the quadrille.

outlined, this declaration of the rights of women will soon pass into custom, from custom into law, and before twenty-five years pass you will then see inscribed in front of the book of laws which will govern French society: THE ABSOLUTE EQUALITY of man and woman. Then, my brothers, and only then, will human unity be constituted.[7]

She envisioned this absolute equality as the only hope to free the working class and transform civilization.

Flora Tristan, like the other utopian socialists, was largely ignored by her contemporaries. Although criticized for their impracticality, the utopian socialists at least laid the groundwork for later attacks on capitalism that would have a far-reaching result. In the first half of the nineteenth century, however, socialism remained a fringe movement largely overshadowed by liberalism and nationalism.

Revolution and Reform (1830–1850)

FOCUS QUESTIONS: What forces for change were present in France, Great Britain, Belgium, Poland, and Italy between 1830 and 1848, and how did each nation respond? What were the causes of the revolutions of 1848, and why did the revolutions fail?

Beginning in 1830, the forces of change began to break through the conservative domination of Europe, more successfully in some places than in others. Finally, in 1848, a wave of revolutionary fervor moved through Europe, causing liberals and nationalists everywhere to think that they were on the verge of creating a new order.

Another French Revolution

The new elections Charles X had called in 1830 produced another victory for the French liberals; at this point, the king decided to seize the initiative. On July 26, 1830, Charles issued a set of edicts (the July Ordinances) that imposed rigid censorship on the press, dissolved the legislative assembly, and reduced the electorate in preparation for new elections. Charles's actions produced an immediate rebellion—the July Revolution. Liberal newspapers defied Charles's censorship and published articles that fueled the revolt. Barricades went up in Paris as a provisional government led by a group of moderate, propertied liberals was hastily formed and appealed to Louis-Philippe, the duke of Orléans, a cousin of Charles X, to become the constitutional king of France. Charles X fled to Britain; a new monarchy had been born.

Louis-Philippe (1830–1848) was soon called the bourgeois monarch because political support for his rule came from the upper middle class. Louis-Philippe even dressed like a member of the middle class in business suits and hats. Constitutional changes that favored the interests of the upper bourgeoisie were instituted. Financial qualifications for voting were reduced yet remained sufficiently high that the number of voters increased only from 100,000 to barely 200,000, guaranteeing that only the wealthiest people would vote.

To the upper middle class, the bourgeois monarchy represented the stopping place for political progress. To the lesser bourgeoisie and the Parisian working class, who had helped overthrow Charles X in 1830, it was a severe disappointment because they had been completely excluded from political power. The rapid expansion of French industry in the 1830s and 1840s gave rise to an industrial working class concentrated in certain urban areas. Terrible working and living conditions and the periodic economic crises that created high levels of

The Revolution of 1830. In 1830, the forces of change began to undo the conservative domination of Europe. In France, the reactionary Charles X was overthrown and replaced by the constitutional monarch Louis-Philippe, a liberal and former revolutionary soldier. In this painting by Gustave Wappers, Louis-Philippe is seen riding to the Hôtel de Ville, the city hall, preceded by a man holding the French revolutionary tricolor flag, which had not been seen in France since 1815.

unemployment led to worker unrest and sporadic outbursts of violence.

Even in the legislature—the Chamber of Deputies—there were differences of opinion about the bourgeois monarchy and the direction it should take. Two groups rapidly emerged, both composed of upper-middle-class representatives. The Party of Movement, led by Adolphe Thiers (a-DAWLF TYAYR), favored ministerial responsibility, the pursuit of an active foreign policy, and limited expansion of the franchise. The Party of Resistance, led by François Guizot (frahnh-SWAH gee-ZOH), believed that France had finally reached the "perfect form" of government and needed no further institutional changes. After 1840, the Party of Resistance dominated the Chamber of Deputies. Guizot cooperated with Louis-Philippe in suppressing ministerial responsibility and pursuing a policy favoring the interests of the wealthier manufacturers and tradespeople.

Revolutionary Outbursts in Belgium, Poland, and Italy

Supporters of liberalism played a primary role in the July Revolution in France, but nationalism was the crucial force in three other revolutionary outbursts in 1830. In an effort to create a stronger, larger state on France's northern border, the Congress of Vienna had added the area once known as the Austrian Netherlands (Belgium) to the Dutch Republic. The merger of Catholic Belgium into the Protestant Dutch Republic never sat well with the Belgians, however, and in 1830, they rose up against the Dutch and succeeded in convincing the major European powers to accept their independence. Leopold of Saxe-Coburg, a minor German prince, was designated to be the new king, and a Belgian national congress established a constitutional monarchy for the new state.

The revolutionary scenarios in Italy and Poland were much less successful. Metternich sent Austrian troops to crush revolts in three Italian states. Poland, too, had a nationalist uprising in 1830 when revolutionaries tried to end Russian control of their country. But the Polish insurgents failed to get the hoped-for support from France and Britain, and by September 1831, the Russians had crushed the revolt and established an oppressive military dictatorship over Poland.

Reform in Great Britain

In 1830, new parliamentary elections brought the Whigs to power in Britain. At the same time, the successful July Revolution in France served to catalyze change in Britain. The Industrial Revolution had led to an expanding group of industrial leaders who objected to the corrupt British electoral system, which excluded them from political power. The Whigs, though also members of the landed classes, realized that concessions to reform were superior to revolution; the demands of the wealthy industrial middle class could no longer be ignored. In 1830, the Whigs introduced an election reform bill that was enacted in 1832 after an intense struggle (see "Opposing Viewpoints" on p. 636).

THE REFORM ACT OF 1832 The Reform Act gave explicit recognition to the changes wrought in British life by the Industrial Revolution. It disenfranchised fifty-six rotten boroughs and enfranchised forty-two new towns and cities and reapportioned others. This gave the new industrial urban communities some voice in government. A property qualification (of £10 annual rent) for voting was retained, however, so the number of voters increased only from 478,000 to 814,000, a figure that still meant that only one in every thirty people was represented in Parliament. Thus, the Reform Act of 1832 primarily

Response to Revolution: Two Perspectives

BASED ON THEIR POLITICAL BELIEFS, Europeans responded differently to the specter of revolution that haunted Europe in the first half of the nineteenth century. The first excerpt is taken from a speech given by Thomas Babington Macaulay (muh-KAHL-lee) (1800–1859), a historian and a Whig member of Parliament. Macaulay spoke in Parliament on behalf of the Reform Act of 1832, which extended the right to vote to the industrial middle classes of Britain. The Revolution of 1830 in France had influenced his belief that it was better to reform than to have a political revolution.

The second excerpt is taken from the *Reminiscences* of Carl Schurz (SHOORTS) (1829–1906). Like many liberals and nationalists in Germany, Schurz received the news of the February Revolution of 1848 in France with much excitement and great expectations for revolutionary change in the German states. After the failure of the German revolution, Schurz made his way to the United States and eventually became a U.S. senator.

Thomas Babington Macaulay, Speech of March 2, 1831

My hon. friend the member of the University of Oxford tells us that, if we pass this law, England will soon be a Republic. The reformed House of Commons will, according to him, before it has sat ten years, depose the King, and expel the Lords from their House. Sir, if my hon. friend could prove this, he would have succeeded in bringing an argument for democracy infinitely stronger than any that is to be found in the works of Paine. His proposition is, in fact, this—that our monarchical and aristocratic institutions have no hold on the public mind of England; that these institutions are regarded with aversion by a decided majority of the middle class. . . . Now, sir, if I were convinced that the great body of the middle class in England look with aversion on monarchy and aristocracy, I should be forced, much against my will, to come to this conclusion, that monarchical and aristocratic

institutions are unsuited to this country. Monarchy and aristocracy, valuable and useful as I think them, are still valuable and useful as means, and not as ends. The end of government is the happiness of the people; and I do not conceive that, in a country like this, the happiness of the people can be promoted by a form of government in which the middle classes place no confidence, and which exists only because the middle classes have no organ by which to make their sentiments known. But, sir, I am fully convinced that the middle classes sincerely wish to uphold the royal prerogatives, and the constitutional rights of the Peers. . . .

But let us know our interest and our duty better. Turn where we may—within, around—the voice of great events is proclaiming to us, "Reform, that you may preserve." Now, therefore, while everything at home and abroad forebodes ruin to those who persist in a hopeless struggle against the spirit of the age; now, while the crash of the proudest throne of the Continent is still resounding in our ears; . . . now, while the heart of England is still sound; now, while the old feelings and the old associations retain a power and a charm which may too soon pass away; now, in this your accepted time; now, in this your day of salvation, take counsel, not of prejudice, not of party spirit, not of the ignominious pride of a fatal consistency, but of history, of reason, of the ages which are past, of the signs of this most portentous time. Pronounce in a manner worthy of the expectation with which this great debate has been anticipated, and of the long remembrance which it will leave behind. Renew the youth of the State. Save property divided against itself. Save the multitude, endangered by their own ungovernable passions. Save the aristocracy, endangered by its own unpopular power. Save the greatest, and fairest, and most highly civilized community that ever existed, from calamities which may in a few days sweep away all the rich heritage of so many ages of wisdom and glory. The danger is terrible. The time is short. If this

---

benefited the upper middle class; the lower middle class, artisans, and industrial workers still had no vote. Moreover, the change did not significantly alter the composition of the House of Commons. One political leader noted that the Commons chosen in the first election after the Reform Act seemed "very much like every other Parliament." Nevertheless, a significant step had been taken. The industrial middle class had been joined to the landed interests in ruling Britain.

NEW REFORM LEGISLATION The 1830s and 1840s witnessed considerable reform legislation. The aristocratic landowning class was usually (but not always) the driving force for legislation that halted some of the worst abuses in the industrial system by instituting government regulation of working

conditions in the factories and mines. The industrialists and manufacturers now in Parliament opposed such legislation and were usually (but not always) the driving forces behind legislation that favored the principles of economic liberalism. The Poor Law of 1834 was based on the theory that giving aid to the poor and unemployed only encouraged laziness and increased the number of paupers. The Poor Law tried to remedy this by making paupers so wretched they would choose to work. Those unable to support themselves were crowded together in workhouses where living and working conditions were intentionally miserable so that people would be encouraged to find gainful employment.

Another piece of liberal legislation involved the repeal of the Corn Laws. This was primarily the work of the manufacturers

Bill should be rejected, I pray to God that none of those who concur in rejecting it may ever remember their votes with unavailing regret, amidst the wreck of laws, the confusion of ranks, the spoliation of property, and the dissolution of social order.

Carl Schurz, *Reminiscences*

One morning, toward the end of February, 1848, I sat quietly in my attic-chamber, working hard at my tragedy of "Ulrich von Hutten" [a sixteenth-century German knight] when suddenly a friend rushed breathlessly into the room, exclaiming: "What, you sitting here! Do you not know what has happened?"

"No; what?"

"The French have driven away Louis Philippe and proclaimed the republic."

I threw down my pen—and that was the end of "Ulrich von Hutten." I never touched the manuscript again. We tore down the stairs, into the street, to the market-square, the accustomed meeting-place for all the student societies after their midday dinner. Although it was still forenoon, the market was already crowded with young men talking excitedly. There was no shouting, no noise, only agitated conversation. What did we want there? This probably no one knew. But since the French had driven away Louis Philippe and proclaimed the republic, something of course must happen here, too. . . . We were dominated by a vague feeling as if a great outbreak of elemental forces had begun, as if an earthquake was impending of which we had felt the first shock, and we instinctively crowded together. . . .

The next morning there were the usual lectures to be attended. But how profitless! The voice of the professor sounded like a monotonous drone coming from far away. What he had to say did not seem to concern us. The pen that should have taken notes remained idle. At last we closed with a sigh the notebook and went away, impelled by a feeling that now we had something more important to do—to devote ourselves to the affairs of the fatherland. And this we did

by seeking as quickly as possible again the company of our friends, in order to discuss what had happened and what was to come. In these conversations, excited as they were, certain ideas and catchwords worked themselves to the surface, which expressed more or less the feelings of the people. Now had arrived in Germany the day for the establishment of "German Unity," and the founding of a great, powerful national German Empire. In the first line the convocation of a national parliament. Then the demands for civil rights and liberties, free speech, free press, the right of free assembly, equality before the law, a freely elected representation of the people with legislative power, responsibility of ministers, self-government of the communes, the right of the people to carry arms, the formation of a civic guard with elective officers, and so on—in short, that which was called a "constitutional form of government on a broad democratic basis." Republican ideas were at first only sparingly expressed. But the word democracy was soon on all tongues, and many, too, thought it a matter of course that if the princes should try to withhold from the people the rights and liberties demanded, force would take the place of mere petition. Of course the regeneration of the fatherland must, if possible, be accomplished by peaceable means. . . . Like many of my friends, I was dominated by the feeling that at last the great opportunity had arrived for giving to the German people the liberty which was their birthright and to the German fatherland its unity and greatness, and that it was now the first duty of every German to do and to sacrifice everything for this sacred object.

 What arguments did Macaulay use to support the Reform Act of 1832? Was he correct? Why or why not? Why was Carl Schurz so excited when he heard the news about the revolution in France? Do you think being a university student helps to explain his reaction? Why or why not? What differences do you see in the approaches of these two writers? What do these selections tell you about the development of politics in the German states and Britain in the nineteenth century?

Sources: Thomas Babington Macaulay, *Speeches, Parliamentary and Miscellaneous*, vol. 1 (New York: Hurst Co., 1853), pp. 20–21, 25–26; Carl Schurz, *Reminiscences*, vol. I (New York: The McClure Co., 1907), pp. 112–113.

Richard Cobden and John Bright, who formed the Anti-Corn Law League in 1838 to help workers by lowering bread prices. But abolishing the Corn Laws would also aid the industrial middle classes, who, as economic liberals, favored the principles of free trade. Repeal came in 1846 when Sir Robert Peel (1788–1850), the leader of the Tories, persuaded some of his associates to support free trade principles and abandon the Corn Laws.

While most of Europe experienced revolutions in 1848, the year ended without a major crisis in Britain. On the continent, middle-class liberals and nationalists were at the forefront of the revolutionary forces. In Britain, however, the middle class had been largely satisfied by the Reform Act of 1832 and the repeal of the Corn Laws in 1846.

The Revolutions of 1848

Despite the successes of revolutions in France, Belgium, and Greece, the conservative order remained in control of much of Europe. But liberalism and nationalism continued to grow. In 1848, these forces of change erupted once more. Yet again, revolution in France provided the spark for other countries, and soon most of central and southern Europe was ablaze with revolutionary fires (see Map 21.4). Tsar Nicholas I of Russia lamented to Queen Victoria in April 1848, "What remains standing in Europe? Great Britain and Russia."

YET ANOTHER FRENCH REVOLUTION A severe industrial and agricultural depression beginning in 1846 brought great

MAP 21.4 The Revolutions of 1848–1849. Beginning in Paris, revolutionary fervor fueled by liberalism and nationalism spread to the east and the south. After initial successes, the revolutionaries failed to maintain unity: propertied classes feared the working masses, and nationalists such as the Hungarians could not agree that all national groups deserved self-determination. The old order rallied its troops and prevailed.

 Which regions saw a great deal of revolutionary activity in 1848–1849, and which did not?

hardship to the French lower middle class, workers, and peasants. One-third of the workers in Paris were unemployed by the end of 1847. Scandals, graft, and corruption were rife, and the government's persistent refusal to extend the suffrage angered the disenfranchised members of the middle class.

As Louis-Philippe's government continued to refuse to make changes, opposition grew (see "Images of Everyday Life" on p. 639). Radical republicans and socialists, joined by the upper middle class under the leadership of Adolphe Thiers, agitated for the dismissal of Guizot. Since they were forbidden by law to stage political rallies, they used the political banquet to call for reforms. Almost seventy such banquets were held in France during the winter of 1847–1848; a grand culminating banquet was planned for Paris on February 22. When the government forbade it, people came anyway; students and workers threw

up barricades in Paris. Although Louis-Philippe now proposed reform, he was unable to form another ministry and abdicated on February 24 and fled to Britain. A provisional government was established by a group of moderate and radical republicans; the latter even included the socialist Louis Blanc. The provisional government ordered that a constituent assembly be convened to draw up a new constitution; the members of the assembly were to be elected by universal manhood suffrage.

The provisional government also established national workshops under the influence of Louis Blanc. As Blanc envisioned them, the workshops were to be cooperative factories run by the workers. In fact, the workshops primarily provided unskilled jobs, such as leaf raking and ditch digging, for unemployed workers. The cost of the program became increasingly burdensome to the government.

Political Cartoons: Attacks on the King

DURING THE EARLY YEARS OF HIS REIGN, Louis-Philippe relaxed censorship in an effort to appease the public. As political instability intensified during the 1830s and 1840s, he attempted to rein in the press. His efforts failed, however, in large part due to the lithograph, a new printing process that enabled artists to produce political cartoons quickly. For the first time in France, political caricatures began to be published regularly. Caricatures of Louis-Philippe often portrayed him with a pear-shaped head, both because there was a resemblance and because the French word for pear—*poire* (PWAHr)—had the slang meaning of simpleton or fool. The transformation of Louis-Philippe from king to pear is captured in the image on the left. In the image on the right, Louis-Philippe is shown with a pear-shaped head, running away from an angry crowd while carrying a bag of money.

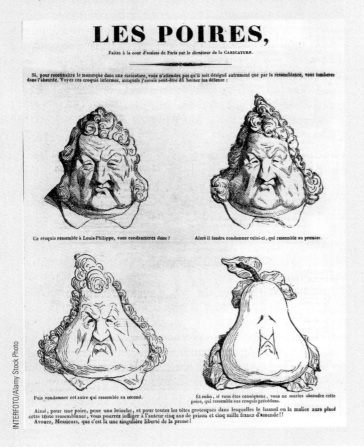

La poire tapée.

The result was a growing split between the moderate republicans, who had the support of most of France, and the radical republicans, whose main support came from the Parisian working class. In the elections for the National Assembly, five hundred seats went to moderate republicans and three hundred to avowed monarchists, while the radicals gained only one hundred. From March to June, the number of unemployed enrolled in the national workshops rose from 10,000 to almost 120,000, emptying the treasury and frightening the moderates, who responded by closing the workshops on June 23. The workers refused to accept this decision and poured into the streets. Four days of bitter and bloody fighting by government forces crushed the working-class revolt. Thousands were killed, and four thousand prisoners were deported to the French colony of Algeria in North Africa. The new constitution, ratified on November 4, 1848, established a republic (the Second Republic) with a unicameral (one-house) legislature of 750 elected by universal male suffrage for three years and a president, also elected by universal male suffrage, for four years. In the elections for the presidency held in December 1848, Charles Louis Napoleon Bonaparte, the nephew of Napoleon Bonaparte, resoundingly defeated four republicans who had been associated with the early months of the Second Republic. Within four years, President Napoleon would become Emperor Napoleon (see Chapter 22).

REVOLUTION IN THE GERMANIC STATES News of the revolution in Paris in February 1848 triggered upheavals in central Europe as well. Revolutionary cries for change caused many German rulers to promise constitutions, a free press, jury trials, and other liberal reforms. In Prussia, concessions were also made to appease the revolutionaries. King Frederick William IV (1840–1861) agreed to abolish censorship, establish a new constitution, and work for a united Germany. This last promise had its counterpart throughout all the German states as governments allowed elections by universal male suffrage for deputies to an all-German parliament to meet in Frankfurt, the seat of the Germanic Confederation. Its purpose was to fulfill a liberal and nationalist dream—the preparation of a constitution for a new united Germany.

Well-educated, articulate, middle-class delegates, many of them professors, lawyers, and bureaucrats, dominated this Frankfurt Assembly. When it came to nationalism, many were ahead of the times and certainly ahead of the governments of their respective states. From the beginning, the assembly aroused controversy by claiming to be the government for all of Germany. Then it became embroiled in a sticky debate over the composition of the new German state. Supporters of a *Grossdeutsch* (GROHS-doichM) ("Big German") solution wanted to include the German province of Austria, while proponents of a *Kleindeutsch* (KLYN-doich) ("Small German") solution favored excluding Austria and making the Prussian king the emperor of the new German state. The problem was solved when the Austrians withdrew, leaving the field to the supporters of the *Kleindeutsch* solution. Their victory was short-lived, however, as Frederick William IV gruffly refused the assembly's offer of the title of "emperor of the Germans" in March 1849 and ordered the Prussian delegates home.

The Frankfurt Assembly soon disbanded. Although some members spoke of using force, they had no real means of compelling the German rulers to accept the constitution they had drawn up. The attempt of the German liberals at Frankfurt to create a German state had failed.

UPHEAVAL IN THE AUSTRIAN EMPIRE The Austrian Empire also had its social, political, and nationalist grievances and needed only the news of the revolution in Paris to encourage it to erupt in flames in March 1848. The Hungarian liberals under Louis Kossuth (KAWSS-uth *or* KAW-shoot) agitated for "commonwealth" status; they were willing to keep the Habsburg monarch but wanted their own legislature. In March, demonstrations in Buda, Prague, and Vienna led to Metternich's dismissal, and the arch symbol of the conservative order fled abroad. In Vienna, revolutionary forces, carefully guided by the educated and propertied classes, took control of the capital and insisted that a constituent assembly be summoned to draw up a liberal constitution. Hungary was granted its wish for its own legislature, a separate national army, and control over its foreign policy and budget. Allegiance to the Habsburg dynasty was now Hungary's only tie to the Austrian Empire. In Bohemia, the Czechs began to demand their own government as well.

Although Emperor Ferdinand I (1835–1848) and Austrian officials had made concessions to appease the revolutionaries, they awaited an opportunity to reestablish their firm control. As in the German states, the conservatives were increasingly encouraged by the divisions between radical and moderate revolutionaries and played on the middle-class fear of a working-class social revolution. Their first success came in June 1848 when a military force under General Alfred Windischgrätz (VIN-dish-grets) ruthlessly suppressed the Czech rebels in Prague. In October, the death of the minister for war at the hands of a Viennese mob gave Windischgrätz the pretext for an attack on Vienna. By the end of the month, the radical rebels there had been crushed. In December, the feebleminded Ferdinand I agreed to abdicate in favor of his nephew, Francis Joseph I (1848–1916), who worked vigorously to restore the imperial government in Hungary. The Austrian armies, however, were unable to defeat Kossuth's forces, and it was only through the intervention of Nicholas I, who sent a Russian army of 140,000 men to aid the Austrians, that the Hungarian revolution was finally crushed in 1849. The revolutions in Austria had also failed. Autocratic government was restored; emperor and propertied classes remained in control, and the numerous nationalities were still subject to the Austrian government.

REVOLTS IN THE ITALIAN STATES The failure of revolutionary uprisings in Italy in 1830–1831 had encouraged the Italian movement for unification to take a new direction. This new generation of Italian nationalists came from the families who had participated in Italy's Napoleonic government. The leadership of Italy's **risorgimento** (ree-SOR-jee-men-toh) ("resurgence") passed into the hands of Giuseppe Mazzini (joo-ZEP-pay maht-SEE-nee) (1805–1872), a dedicated Italian nationalist who founded an organization known as Young Italy in 1831 (see the box on p. 641). This group set as its goal the creation of a united Italian republic. In *The Duties of Man*, Mazzini urged Italians to dedicate their lives to the Italian nation: "O my Brother! Love your Country. Our Country is our home." A number of Italian women also took up Mazzini's call. Especially notable was Cristina Belgioioso (bell-joh-YOH-soh), a wealthy aristocrat who worked to bring about Italian unification. Pursued by the Austrian authorities, she fled to Paris and started a newspaper espousing the Italian cause.

The dreams of Mazzini and Belgioioso seemed on the verge of fulfillment when a number of Italian states rose in revolt in 1848. Beginning in Sicily, rebellions spread northward as ruler after ruler granted a constitution to his people. Citizens in Lombardy and Venetia also rebelled against their Austrian overlords. The Venetians declared a republic in Venice. The king of the northern Italian state of Piedmont, Charles Albert (1831–1849), took up the call and assumed the leadership for a war of liberation from Austrian domination. His invasion of Lombardy proved unsuccessful, however, and by 1849, the Austrians had reestablished complete control over Lombardy and Venetia. Counterrevolutionary forces also prevailed throughout Italy. French forces helped Pope Pius IX regain control of Rome. Elsewhere Italian rulers managed to recover power on their own. Only Piedmont was able to keep its liberal constitution.

THE VOICE OF ITALIAN NATIONALISM: GIUSEPPE MAZZINI AND YOUNG ITALY

AFTER THE FAILURE OF THE UPRISINGS in Italy in 1830–1831, Giuseppe Mazzini emerged as the leader of the Italian *risorgimento*—the movement for Italian nationhood. In 1831, he founded an organization known as Young Italy whose goal was the creation of a united Italian republic. This selection is from the oath that the members of Young Italy were required to take.

Giuseppe Mazzini, *The Young Italy Oath*

Young Italy is a brotherhood of Italians who believe in a law of Progress and Duty, and are convinced that Italy is destined to become one nation,—convinced also that she possesses sufficient strength within herself to become one, and that the ill success of her former efforts is to be attributed not to the weakness, but to the misdirection of the revolutionary elements within her,—that the secret of force lies in constancy and unity of effort. They join this association in the firm intent of consecrating both thought and action to the great aim of reconstituting Italy as one independent sovereign nation of free men and equals. . . .

Each member will, upon his initiation into the association of Young Italy, pronounce the following form of oath, in the presence of the initiator: In the name of God and of Italy;

In the name of all the martyrs of the holy Italian cause who have fallen beneath foreign and domestic tyranny;

By the duties which bind me to the land wherein God has placed me, and to the brothers whom God has given me;

By the love—innate in all men—I bear to the country that gave my mother birth, and will be the home of my children. . . .

By the sufferings of the millions,—

I . . . believing in the mission intrusted by God to Italy, and the duty of every Italian to strive to attempt its fulfillment; convinced that where God has ordained that a nation shall be, He has given the requisite power to create it; that the people are the depositaries of that power, and that in its right direction for the people, and by the people, lies the secret of victory; convinced that virtue consists in action and sacrifice, and strength in union and constancy of purpose: I give my name to Young Italy, an association of men holding the same faith, and swear:

To dedicate myself wholly and forever to the endeavor with them to constitute Italy one free, independent, republican nation; to promote by every means in my power—whether by written or spoken word, or by action— the education of my Italian brothers toward the aim of Young Italy; toward association, the sole means of its accomplishment, and to virtue, which alone can render the conquest lasting; to abstain from enrolling myself in any other association from this time forth; to obey all the instructions, in conformity with the spirit of Young Italy, given me by those who represent with me the union of my Italian brothers; and to keep the secret of these instructions, even at the cost of my life; to assist my brothers of the association both by action and counsel—NOW AND FOREVER.

 Based on the principles outlined here, define nationalism. Why have some called nationalism a "secular religion"?

Source: *Joseph Mazzini: His Life, Writings, and Political Principles* (New York: Hurd & Houghton, 1872), pp. 62–69, 71–74.

THE FAILURES OF 1848 Throughout Europe in 1848, popular revolts had initiated revolutionary upheavals that had led to the formation of liberal constitutions and liberal governments. But how could so many immediate successes in 1848 be followed by so many disasters only months later? Two reasons stand out. The unity of the revolutionaries had made the revolutions possible, but divisions soon shattered their ranks. Except in France, moderate liberals from the propertied classes failed to extend suffrage to the working classes who had helped achieve the revolutions. But as radicals pushed for universal male suffrage, liberals everywhere pulled back. Concerned about their property and security, they rallied to the old ruling classes for the sake of order and out of fear of social revolution by the working classes. All too soon, established governments were back in power.

In 1848, nationalities everywhere had also revolted in pursuit of self-government. But here too, frightfully little was achieved as divisions among nationalities proved utterly disastrous. Though the Hungarians demanded autonomy from the Austrians, at the same time they refused the same to their minorities—the Slovenes, Croats, and Serbs. Instead of joining together against the old empire, minorities fought each other. No wonder that one Czech could remark in April 1848, "If the Austrian state had not already existed for so long, it would have been in the interests of Europe, indeed of humanity itself, to endeavor to create it as soon as possible."[8] The Austrians' efforts to recover the Hungarian provinces met with little success until they began to play off Hungary's rebellious minority nationalities against the Hungarians.

The Maturing of the United States

The U.S. Constitution, ratified in 1789, committed the United States to two of the major forces of the first half of the nineteenth century, liberalism and nationalism. Initially, divisions over the power of the federal government vis-à-vis the individual states challenged this constitutional commitment to national unity. Bitter conflict erupted between the Federalists and the Republicans. Led by Alexander Hamilton (1757–1804),

Great Britain	
Peterloo Massacre	1819
Reform Act	1832
Poor Law	1834
Repeal of Corn Laws	1846
France	
Louis XVIII	1814–1824
Charles X	1824–1830
July Revolution	1830
Louis-Philippe	1830–1848
Abdication of Louis-Philippe; formation of provisional government	1848 (February 22–24)
June Days: workers' revolt in Paris	1848 (June)
Establishment of Second Republic	1848 (November)
Election of Louis Napoleon as French president	1848 (December)
Low Countries	
Union of Netherlands and Belgium	1815
Belgian independence	1830
German States	
Frederick William III of Prussia	1797–1840
Germanic Confederation established	1815
Karlsbad Decrees	1819
Frederick William IV of Prussia	1840–1861
Revolution in Germany	1848
Frankfurt Assembly	1848–1849
Austrian Empire	
Emperor Ferdinand I	1835–1848
Revolt in Austrian Empire; Metternich dismissed	1848 (March)
Austrian forces under General Windischgrätz crush Czech rebels	1848 (June)
Viennese rebels crushed	1848 (October)
Francis Joseph I	1848–1916
Defeat of Hungarians with help of Russian troops	1849
Italian states	
Revolts in southern Italy and Sardinia crushed	1821
King Charles Albert of Piedmont	1831–1849
Revolutions in Italy	1848
Charles Albert attacks Austrians	1848
Austrians reestablish control in Lombardy and Venetia	1849
Russia	
Tsar Alexander I	1801–1825
Decembrist Revolt	1825
Tsar Nicholas I	1825–1855
Polish uprising	1830
Suppression of Polish revolt	1831

the Federalists favored a financial program that would establish a strong central government. The Republicans, guided by Thomas Jefferson (1743–1826) and James Madison (1751–1836), feared centralization and its consequences for popular liberties. European rivalries intensified these divisions because the Federalists were pro-British and the Republicans pro-French. The successful conclusion of the War of 1812 against Britain brought an end to the Federalists, who had opposed the war, while the surge of national feeling generated by the war served to heal the nation's divisions.

Another strong force for national unity came from the Supreme Court while John Marshall (1755–1835) was chief justice from 1801 to 1835. Marshall made the Supreme Court into an important national institution by asserting the right of the Court to overrule an act of Congress if the Court found it to be in violation of the Constitution. Under Marshall, the Supreme Court contributed further to establishing the supremacy of the national government by curbing the actions of state courts and legislatures.

The election of Andrew Jackson (1767–1845) as president in 1828 opened a new era in American politics, the era of mass democracy. The electorate was expanded by dropping traditional property qualifications; by the 1830s, suffrage had been extended to almost all adult white males. During the period from 1815 to 1850, the traditional liberal belief in the improvement of human beings was also given concrete expression. Americans developed detention schools for juvenile delinquents and new penal institutions, both motivated by the liberal belief that the right kind of environment would rehabilitate those in need of it.

The Emergence of an Ordered Society

 FOCUS QUESTION: How did European states respond to the increase in crime in the late eighteenth and early nineteenth centuries?

Everywhere in Europe, the revolutionary upheavals of the late eighteenth and early nineteenth centuries made the ruling elites nervous about social disorder and the potential dangers to their lives and property. At the same time, the influx of large numbers of people from the countryside into the rapidly growing cities had led to horrible living conditions, poverty, unemployment, and great social dissatisfaction. The first half of the nineteenth century witnessed a significant increase in crime, especially against property, in Britain, France, and Germany. The rise in property crimes provoked a severe reaction among middle-class urban residents, who feared that the urban poor posed a threat to their security and possessions. New police forces soon appeared to defend the propertied classes from criminals and social misfits.

New Police Forces

The first major contribution of the nineteenth century to the development of a disciplined or ordered society in Europe was a regular system of police. A number of European states established civilian police forces—groups of well-trained law enforcement officers who were to preserve property and lives, maintain domestic order, investigate crime, and arrest offenders. It was hoped that their very presence would prevent crime. That the new police existed to protect citizens eventually made them acceptable, and by the end of the nineteenth century, many Europeans viewed them approvingly.

FRENCH POLICE This new approach to policing made its first appearance in France in 1828 when Louis-Maurice Debelleyme (LWEE-moh-REESS duh-buh-LAYM), the prefect of Paris, proclaimed, "The essential object of our municipal police is the safety of the inhabitants of Paris. Safety by day and night, free traffic movement, clean streets, the supervision of and precaution against accidents, the maintenance of order in public places, the seeking out of offenses and their perpetrators."[9] In March 1829, the new police, known as *serjents*, appeared on Paris streets. They were dressed in blue uniforms to make them easily recognizable by all citizens. They were also lightly armed with a white cane during the day and a saber at night, underscoring the fact that they were a civilian, not a military, body. Initially, there were not many of the new police officers. Paris had eighty-five by August 1829 and only five hundred in 1850. Before the end of the century, their number had increased to four thousand.

BRITISH BOBBIES The British, fearful of the powers exercised by military or secret police in authoritarian continental states, had long resisted the creation of a professional police force. Instead, Britain depended on a system of unpaid constables recruited by local authorities. Often these local constables were incapable of keeping order, preventing crimes, or apprehending criminals. Such jobs could also be dangerous and involve incidents like the one reported by a man passing by a local pub in 1827:

> I saw Thomas Franklin [constable of the village of Leighton Buzzard] coming out backwards. John Brandon . . . was opposite and close to the constable. I saw the said John Brandon strike the said constable twice "bang full in the face"; the blows knocked the constable down on his back. John Brandon fell down with him. Sarah Adams . . . got on top of the constable and jostled his head against the ground. . . . The constable appeared very much hurt and his face was all over blood.[10]

The failure of the local constables led to a new approach. Between September 1829 and May 1830, three thousand uniformed police officers appeared on the streets of London. They came to be known as bobbies after Sir Robert Peel, who had introduced the legislation that created the force.

As is evident from the first instruction book for the new British police, their primary goal was to prevent crime: "Officers and police constables should endeavour to distinguish themselves by such vigilance and activity as may render it impossible for any one to commit a crime within that portion of the town under their charge."[11] The municipal authorities soon found, however, that the police were also useful for imposing order on working-class urban inhabitants. On Sundays, they were called on to clean up after Saturday night's drinking bouts. As demands for better pay and treatment led to improved working conditions, British police began to develop a sense of professionalism (see the box on p. 644).

SPREAD OF POLICE SYSTEMS Police systems were organized throughout the Western world during the nineteenth century. After the revolutions of 1848 in Germany, a state-financed police force called the *Schutzmannschaft* (SHOOTS-mun-shahft), modeled after the London police, was established for the city of Berlin. The *Schutzmannschaft* began as a civilian body, but already by 1851, the force had become organized more along military lines and was used for political purposes. Its military nature was reinforced by the force's weaponry, which included swords, pistols, and brass knuckles. One observer noted that "a German policeman on patrol is armed as if for war."[12]

OTHER APPROACHES TO THE CRIME PROBLEM Although the new police alleviated some of the fears about the increase in crime, contemporary reformers approached the problem in other ways. Some of them believed that the increase in crime was related to the dramatic increase in poverty. One commented in 1816 that poverty and misery were the parents

The London Police. One response to the revolutionary upheavals of the late eighteenth and early nineteenth centuries was the development of civilian police forces that would be responsible for protecting property, arresting criminals, and maintaining domestic order. This early photograph shows a group of London policemen, who came to be known as bobbies after Sir Robert Peel, the man responsible for introducing the legislation that initiated the London police force.

THE NEW BRITISH POLICE: "WE ARE NOT TREATED AS MEN"

THE NEW BRITISH POLICE FORCES, organized first in London in 1829, were well established throughout much of Britain by the 1840s. As professionalism rose in the ranks of the forces, so did demands for better pay and treatment. In this selection, police constables make clear their demands and complaints.

Complaints from Constables of D Division of the London Metropolitan Police

We are not treated as men but as slaves we englishmen do not like to be terrorized by a set of Irish Sergeants who are only lenient to their own countrymen . . . after we have done our night-Duty may we not have the privilege of going to Church or staying at home to Suit our own inclination when we are ordered by the Superintendent to go to church in our uniform on Wednesday we do not object to the going to church we like to go but we do not like to be ordered there and when we go on Sunday nights we are asked like so many schoolboys have we been to church should we say no let reason be what it may it does not matter we are forthwith ordered from Paddington to Marylebone lane the next night—about 2 hours before we go to Duty that is 2 miles from many of our homes being tired with our walk there and back we must either loiter about the streets or in some public house and there we do not want to go for we cannot spare our trifling wages to spend them there but there is no other choice left—for us to make our time out to go on Duty at proper time on Day we are ordered there for that offense another Man may faultlessly commit—the crime of sitting 4 minutes during the night—then we must be ordered there another to Shew his old clothes before they are given in even we must go to the expense of having them put in repair we have indeed for all these frightful crimes to walk 3 or 4 miles and then be wasting our time that makes our night 3 hours longer than they ought to be another thing we want to know who has the money that is deducted out of our wages for fines and many of us will be obliged to give up the duty unless we can have fair play as to the stationing of us on our beats why cannot we follow round that may all and each of us go over every beat and not for the Sergeants to put their favorites on the good beats. . . there are a great many of these things to try our temper.

 What were the complaints of the British constables? What was the main issue that the complaints raised? Why might it be said that the development of police forces is a defining characteristic of Western civilization in modern times?

Source: From C. Emsley, *Policing and Its Context, 1750–1870* (London: Palgrave Macmillan, 1983).

---

of crime. Strongly influenced by the middle-class belief that unemployment was the result of sheer laziness, European states passed poor laws that attempted to force paupers to either find work on their own or enter workhouses designed to make people so utterly uncomfortable that they would choose to reenter the labor market.

Meanwhile, another group of reformers was arguing that poor laws failed to address the real problem, which was that poverty was a result of the moral degeneracy of the lower classes, increasingly labeled the "dangerous classes" because of the perceived threat they posed to middle-class society. This belief led one group of secular reformers to form institutes to instruct the working classes in the applied sciences in order to make them more productive members of society. The London Mechanics' Institute, established in Britain, and the Society for the Diffusion of Useful Knowledge in the Field of Natural Sciences, Technical Science, and Political Economy, founded in Germany, are but two examples of this approach to the "dangerous classes."

Organized religion took a different approach. British evangelicals set up Sunday schools to improve the morals of working children, and in Germany, evangelical Protestants established nurseries for orphans and homeless children, women's societies to care for the sick and poor, and prison societies that prepared women to work in prisons. The Catholic Church attempted the same kind of work through a revival of its religious orders; dedicated priests and nuns used spiritual instruction and recreation to turn young male workers away from the moral vices of gambling and drinking and female workers from lives of prostitution.

Prison Reform

The increase in crime led to a rise in arrests. By the 1820s in most countries, the indiscriminate use of capital punishment, even for crimes against property, was increasingly being viewed as ineffective and was replaced by imprisonment. Although the British had shipped people convicted of serious offenses to their colonial territory of Australia, that practice began to slow down in the late 1830s when the colonists loudly objected. Incarceration, then, was the only alternative. Prisons served to isolate criminals from society, but a growing number of reformers questioned their purpose and effectiveness, especially when prisoners were subjected to harsh and even humiliating work as punishment. By the 1830s, European governments were seeking ways to reform their penal systems. Motivated by the desire not just to punish but to rehabilitate and transform criminals into new persons, the British and French sent missions to the United States in the early 1830s to examine how the two different systems then used in American prisons accomplished this goal. At the Auburn Prison in New York, for example, prisoners were separated at night but worked together in the same workshop during the day. At Walnut Street Prison in Philadelphia, prisoners were kept separated in individual cells.

After examining the American prisons, both the French and the British constructed prisons on the Walnut Street model with separate cells that isolated prisoners from one another. At Petite Roquette (puh-TEET rah-KET) in France and Pentonville in Britain, prisoners wore leather masks while they exercised and sat in separate stalls when in chapel. Solitary confinement, it was believed, forced prisoners to examine their consciences, led to greater remorse, and increased the possibility that they would change their evil ways. One supporter of the separate-cell system observed:

> A few months in the solitary cell renders a prisoner strangely impressible. The chaplain can then make the brawny navvy cry like a child; he can work on his feelings in almost any way he pleases; he can, so to speak, photograph his thoughts, wishes and opinions on his patient's mind, and fill his mouth with his own phrases and language.[13]

As prison populations increased, however, solitary confinement proved expensive and less feasible. The French even returned to their custom of sending prisoners to French Guiana to handle the overload.

Prison reform and police forces were geared toward one primary end, the creation of a more disciplined society. Disturbed by the upheavals associated with revolutions and the social discontent wrought by industrialization and urbanization, the ruling elites sought to impose some order on society.

Culture in an Age of Reaction and Revolution: The Mood of Romanticism

 FOCUS QUESTION: What were the characteristics of Romanticism, and how were they reflected in literature, art, and music?

At the end of the eighteenth century, a new intellectual movement known as Romanticism emerged to challenge the Enlightenment's preoccupation with reason in discovering truth. The Romantics tried to balance the use of reason by stressing the importance of intuition, feeling, emotion, and imagination as sources of knowing. One German Romantic exclaimed that it was his heart that counseled him to do it, and "my heart cannot err."

The Characteristics of Romanticism

Romantic writers emphasized emotion, sentiment, and inner feelings in their works. An important model for Romantics was the tragic figure in *The Sorrows of the Young Werther*, a novel by the great German writer Johann Wolfgang von Goethe (yoh-HAHN VULF-gahnk fun GUR-tuh) (1749–1832), who later rejected Romanticism in favor of Classicism. Werther was a Romantic figure who sought freedom in order to fulfill himself.

Misunderstood and rejected by society, he continued to believe in his own worth through his inner feelings, but his deep love for a girl who did not love him finally led him to commit suicide. After Goethe's *Sorrows of the Young Werther*, numerous novels and plays appeared whose plots revolved around young maidens tragically carried off at an early age (twenty-three was most common) by disease (usually tuberculosis, at that time a protracted disease that was usually fatal) to the sorrow and despair of their male lovers.

Another important characteristic of Romanticism was **individualism**, an interest in the unique traits of each person. The Romantics' desire to follow their inner drives led them to rebel against middle-class conventions. Long hair, beards, and outrageous clothes served to reinforce the individualism that young Romantics were trying to express.

Sentiment and individualism came together in the Romantics' stress on the heroic. The Romantic hero was a solitary genius who was ready to defy the world and sacrifice his life for a great cause. In the hands of the British writer Thomas Carlyle (1795–1881), however, the Romantic hero did not destroy himself in ineffective protests against society but transformed society instead. In his historical works, Carlyle stressed that historical events were largely determined by the deeds of such heroes.

Many Romantics possessed a passionate interest in the past. This historical focus was manifested in many ways. In Germany, the Grimm brothers collected and published local fairy tales, as did Hans Christian Andersen in Denmark. The revival of medieval Gothic architecture left the European countryside adorned with pseudo-medieval castles and cities bedecked with grandiose cathedrals, city halls, parliamentary buildings, and even railway stations. Literature, too, reflected this historical consciousness. The novels of Walter Scott (1771–1832) became European bestsellers in the first half of the nineteenth century. *Ivanhoe*, in which Scott tried to evoke the clash between Saxon and Norman knights in medieval England, became one of his most popular works.

To the history-mindedness of the Romantics could be added an attraction to the bizarre and unusual. In an exaggerated form, this preoccupation gave rise to so-called **Gothic literature**, chillingly evident in the short stories of horror by the American Edgar Allan Poe (1808–1849) and in *Frankenstein* by Mary Shelley (1797–1851). Shelley's novel was the story of a mad scientist who brings into being a humanlike monster who goes berserk. Some Romantics even sought the unusual in their own lives by pursuing extraordinary states of experience in dreams, nightmares, frenzies, and suicidal depression or by experimenting with cocaine, opium, and hashish to produce altered states of consciousness.

Romantic Poets

To the Romantics, poetry ranked above all other literary forms because they believed it was the direct expression of one's soul. The Romantic poets were viewed as seers who could reveal the invisible world to others. Their incredible sense of drama made some of them the most colorful figures of their era, living intense but short lives. Percy Bysshe Shelley (1792–1822),

Neo-Gothic Revival: British Houses of Parliament. The Romantic movement of the first half of the nineteenth century led, among other things, to a revival of medieval Gothic architecture that left European cities bedecked with neo-Gothic buildings. After the Houses of Parliament in London burned down in 1834, they were replaced with new buildings of neo-Gothic design, as seen in this photograph.

expelled from school for advocating atheism, set out to reform the world. His *Prometheus Unbound*, completed in 1820, is a portrait of the revolt of human beings against the laws and customs that oppress them. He drowned in a storm in the Mediterranean. Lord Byron (1788–1824) dramatized himself as the melancholy Romantic hero that he had described in his work *Childe Harold's Pilgrimage*. He participated in the movement for Greek independence and died in Greece fighting the Ottomans.

LOVE OF NATURE Romantic poetry gave full expression to one of the most important characteristics of Romanticism: love of nature, especially evident in the works of William Wordsworth (1770–1850). His experience of nature was almost mystical, as he claimed to receive "authentic tidings of invisible things":

> One impulse from a vernal wood
> May teach you more of man,
> Of Moral Evil and of good,
> Than all the sages can.[14]

To Wordsworth, nature contained a mysterious force that the poet could perceive and learn from. Nature served as a mirror into which humans could look to learn about themselves. Nature was, in fact, alive and sacred:

> To every natural form, rock, fruit or flower,
> Even the loose stones that cover the high-way,
> I gave a moral life, I saw them feel,
> Or link'd them to some feeling: the great mass
> Lay bedded in a quickening soul, and all
> That I beheld, respired with inward meaning.[15]

Other Romantics carried this worship of nature further into **pantheism** by identifying the great force in nature with God. The Romantics would have nothing to do with the deist God of the Enlightenment, the remote creator of the world-machine. As the German Romantic poet Friedrich Novalis (FREED-rikh noh-VAH-lis) said, "Anyone seeking God will find him anywhere."

CRITIQUE OF SCIENCE The worship of nature also led Wordsworth and other Romantic poets to critique the mechanistic materialism of eighteenth-century science, which, they believed, had reduced nature to a cold object of study. Against that view of the natural world, Wordsworth offered his own vivid and concrete experience. To him, the scientists' dry, mathematical approach left no room for the imagination or for the human soul. The poet who left to the world "one single moral precept, one single affecting sentiment," Wordsworth said, did more for the world than scientists who were soon forgotten. The monster created by Frankenstein in Mary Shelley's Gothic novel was a cautionary tale of the danger of science when it tries to conquer nature. Many Romantics were convinced that the emerging industrialization would cause people to become alienated from their inner selves and the natural world around them.

Romanticism in Art

Like the literary arts, the visual arts were also deeply affected by Romanticism. Although their works varied widely, Romantic artists shared at least two fundamental characteristics. All artistic expression to them was a reflection of the artist's inner feelings; a painting should mirror the artist's vision of the world and be the instrument of his own imagination. Moreover, Romantic artists deliberately rejected the principles of Classicism. Beauty was not a timeless thing; its expression depended on one's culture and one's age. The Romantics abandoned classical restraint for warmth, emotion, and movement. Through an examination of three painters, we can see how Romanticism influenced the visual arts.

FRIEDRICH The early life experiences of the German painter Caspar David Friedrich (kass-PAR dah-VEET FREED-rikh) (1774–1840) left him with a lifelong preoccupation with God and nature. Friedrich painted landscapes with an interest that transcended the mere presentation of natural details. His portrayal of mountains shrouded in mist, gnarled trees bathed in moonlight, and the stark ruins of monasteries surrounded by withered trees all conveyed a feeling of mystery and mysticism.

Caspar David Friedrich, *The Wanderer Above the Sea of Fog.* The German artist Caspar David Friedrich sought to express in painting his own mystical view of nature. "The divine is everywhere," he once wrote, "even in a grain of sand." In this painting, a solitary wanderer is shown from the back gazing at mountains covered in fog. Overwhelmed by the all-pervasive presence of nature, the figure expresses the human longing for infinity.

For Friedrich, nature was a manifestation of divine life, as is evident in *The Wanderer Above the Sea of Fog*. To Friedrich, the artistic process depended on one's inner vision. He advised artists, "Shut your physical eye and look first at your picture with your spiritual eye; then bring to the light of day what you have seen in the darkness."

TURNER Another artist who dwelt on nature and made landscape his major subject was the Englishman Joseph Malford William Turner (1775–1851). Turner was an incredibly prolific artist who produced more than 20,000 paintings, drawings, and watercolors. Many of his works addressed the encroachment of industrialization upon nature. Turner's concern with nature manifested itself in innumerable landscapes and seascapes, sunrises and sunsets. He did not idealize nature or reproduce it with realistic accuracy, however. He sought instead to convey its moods by using a skilled interplay of light and color to suggest natural effects. In allowing his objects to melt into their surroundings, he anticipated the Impressionist painters of the second half of the nineteenth century (see Chapter 24). John Constable, a contemporary English Romantic painter, described Turner's paintings as "airy visions, painted with tinted steam."

DELACROIX Eugène Delacroix (oo-ZHEN duh-lah-KRWAH) (1798–1863) was the most famous French Romantic artist. Largely self-taught, he was fascinated by the exotic and had a passion for color. Both characteristics are visible in *The Death of Sardanapalus*. Significant for its use of light and its patches of interrelated color and the sinuous nature of the bodily forms, this portrayal of the world of the last Assyrian king was criticized at the time for its garishness and overt eroticism. Delacroix rejoiced in combining theatricality and movement with a daring use of color. Many of his works reflect his own belief that "a painting should be a feast to the eye."

J. M. W. Turner, *Rain, Steam, and Speed—The Great Western Railway.* Although Turner began his artistic career by painting accurate representations of the natural world, he increasingly sought to create an atmosphere through the skillful use of light and color. In this painting, Turner eliminates specific details and uses general fields of color to convey the impression of a locomotive rushing toward the viewer.

Eugène Delacroix, *The Death of Sardanapalus.* Delacroix's *Death of Sardanapalus* was based on Lord Byron's verse account of the dramatic last moments of the decadent Assyrian king. Besieged by enemy troops and with little hope of survival, Sardanapalus orders that his harem women and prized horses go to their death with him. At the right, a guard stabs one of the women as the king looks on.

Erich Lessing/Art Resource, NY

Romanticism in Music

To many Romantics, music was the most Romantic of the arts because it enabled the composer to probe deeply into human emotions. One Romantic writer noted, "It has been rightly said that the object of music is the awakening of emotion. No other art can so sublimely arouse human sentiments in the innermost heart of man."[16] Although music historians have called the eighteenth century the age of Classicism and the nineteenth the era of Romanticism, there was much carryover of classical forms from one century to the next. One of the greatest composers of all time, Ludwig van Beethoven (BAY-toh-vunM), served as a bridge between Classicism and Romanticism.

BEETHOVEN Beethoven (1770–1827) is one of the few composers to singlehandedly transform the art of music. Set ablaze by the events in France, a revolutionary mood burned brightly across Europe, and Beethoven, like other creative personalities, yearned to communicate his cherished beliefs. He said, "I *must* write, for what weighs on my heart, I *must* express." For Beethoven, music had to reflect his deepest inner feelings.

Born in Bonn, Beethoven came from a family of musicians who worked for the electors of Cologne. He became an assistant organist at the court by the age of thirteen and soon made his way to Vienna, the musical capital of Europe, where he studied briefly under Haydn. Beginning in 1792, this city became his permanent residence.

During his first major period of composing (1792–1800), his work was largely within the classical framework of the eighteenth century, and the influences of Haydn and Mozart are apparent. But with the composition of the Third Symphony (1804), also called the *Eroica*, which was originally intended for Napoleon, Beethoven broke through to the elements of Romanticism in his use of uncontrolled rhythms to create dramatic

struggle and uplifted resolutions. E. T. A. Hoffman, a contemporary composer and writer, said, "Beethoven's music opens the flood gates of fear, of terror, of horror, of pain, and arouses that longing for the eternal which is the essence of Romanticism. He is thus a pure Romantic composer"[17] (see box on p. 649). Beethoven went on to write a vast quantity of works, but in the midst of this productivity and growing fame, he was more and more burdened by his growing deafness. One of the most moving pieces of music of all time, the chorale finale of his Ninth Symphony, was composed when Beethoven was totally deaf.

BERLIOZ Beethoven served as a bridge from the classical era to Romanticism; after him came a number of musical geniuses who composed in the Romantic style. The Frenchman Hector Berlioz (ek-TOR BAYR-lee-ohz) (1803–1869) was one of the most outstanding. His father, a doctor in Grenoble, intended that his son should also study medicine. The young Berlioz eventually rebelled, however, maintaining to his father's disgust that he would be "no doctor or apothecary but a great composer." Berlioz managed to fulfill his own expectations, achieving fame in Germany, Russia, and Britain, although the originality of his work kept him from receiving much recognition in his native France.

Berlioz was one of the founders of program music, which was an attempt to use the moods and sound effects of instrumental music to depict the actions and emotions inherent in a story, an event, or even a personal experience. This development of program music was evident in his most famous piece, the first complete program symphony, known as the *Symphonie Fantastique*. In this work, Berlioz used music to evoke the passionate emotions of a tortured love affair, including a fifth movement in which he musically creates an opium-induced nightmare of a witches' gathering.

BEETHOVEN'S INSTRUMENTAL MUSIC

ERNST THEODOR AMADEUS HOFFMANN (1776–1822) was a Prussian civil servant who served as a theatrical music director and producer as well as a music critic. His writings on Beethoven characterized the artist as the ultimate Romantic, whose instrumental music and complex compositions challenged the vocal music that had predominated in the eighteenth century. For Hoffmann, Beethoven's music exemplified the sublime experience the Romantics sought—one that would reveal the infinite found in nature.

Beethoven's Instrumental Music (1813)

When music is spoken of as an independent art, does not the term properly apply only to instrumental music, which scorns all aid, all admixture of other arts (poetry), and give pure expression to its own peculiar artistic nature? It is the most romantic of all arts, one might almost say the only one that is genuinely romantic, since its only subject-matter is infinity. . . . Music reveals to man an unknown realm, a world quite separate from the outer sensual world surrounding him, a world in which he leaves behind all precise feelings in order to embrace an inexpressible longing. . . .

It is certainly not merely an improvement in the means of expression (perfection of instruments, greater virtuosity of players), but also a deeper awareness of the peculiar nature of music, that has enabled great composers to raise instrumental music to its present level.

[Wolfgang Amadeus] Mozart and [Joseph] Hadyn, the creators of modern instrumental music, first showed us

the art in its full glory; but the one who regarded it with total devotion and penetrated to its innermost nature is Beethoven. The instrumental compositions of all three masters breathe the same romantic spirit for the very reason that they all intimately grasp the essential nature of the art; yet the character of their compositions is markedly different. Haydn's compositions are dominated by a feeling of childlike optimism. His symphonies lead us through endless, green forest-glades, through a motley throng of happy people. . . . Mozart leads us deep into the realm of spirits. . . .

In a similar way Beethoven's instrumental music unveils before us the realm of the mighty and the immeasurable. Here shining rays of light shoot through the darkness of night and we become aware of giant shadows swaying back and forth, moving ever closer around us and destroying *us* but not the pain of infinite yearning, in which every desire, leaping up in sounds of exultation, sinks back and disappears. Only in this pain, in which love, hope and joy are consumed without being destroyed, which threatens to burst our hearts with a full-chorused cry of all the passions, do we live on as ecstatic visionaries. . . .

Beethoven's music sets in motion the machinery of awe, of fear, of terror, of pain, and awakens that infinite yearning which is the essence of romanticism. He is therefore a purely romantic composer.

 What response does Beethoven's music elicit from the listener? Why does this make it Romantic?

Source: M. Clarke, trans., and D. Charlton, ed., *E. T. A. Hoffmann's Musical Writings. Kreisleriana: The Poet and the Composer, Musical Criticism* (New York: Cambridge University Press, 1989), pp. 96–103; reprinted in W. Breckman, *European Romanticism: A Brief History with Documents* (Boston: Bedford, 2008), pp. 127–128.

The Revival of Religion in the Age of Romanticism

After 1815, Christianity experienced a revival. In the eighteenth century, Catholicism had lost its attraction for many of the educated elite as even the European nobility flirted with the ideas of the Enlightenment. The restoration of the nobility brought a new appreciation for the Catholic faith as a force for order in society. This appreciation was greatly reinforced by the Romantic movement. The Romantics' attraction to the Middle Ages and their emphasis on emotion led them to their own widespread revival of Christianity.

CATHOLICISM Catholicism, in particular, benefited from this Romantic enthusiasm for religion. Especially among German Romantics, there were many conversions to the Catholic faith. One of the most popular expressions of this Romantic revival of Catholicism occurred in the work of the Frenchman François-René de Chateaubriand (frahnh-SWAH-ruh-NAY duh shah-TOH-bree-AHNH) (1768–1848). His book *Genius of Christianity*, published in 1802, was soon labeled the "Bible of Romanticism." His defense of Catholicism was based not on historical,

theological, or even rational grounds but largely on Romantic sentiment. As a faith, Catholicism echoed the harmony of all things. Its cathedrals brought one into the very presence of God; according to Chateaubriand, "You could not enter a Gothic church without feeling a kind of awe and a vague sentiment of the Divinity. . . . Every thing in a Gothic church reminds you of the labyrinths of a wood; every thing excites a feeling of religious awe, of mystery, and of the Divinity."[18]

PROTESTANTISM Protestantism also experienced a revival. That "awakening," as it was called, had already begun in the eighteenth century with the enthusiastic emotional experiences of Methodism in Britain and Pietism in Germany (see Chapter 17). Methodist missionaries from England and Scotland carried their messages of sin and redemption to liberal Protestant churches in France and Switzerland, winning converts to their strongly evangelical message. Germany, too, witnessed a Protestant awakening as enthusiastic evangelical preachers found that their messages of hellfire and their methods of emotional conversion evoked a ready response among people alienated by the highly educated establishment clergy of the state churches.

In 1815, a conservative order was reestablished throughout Europe at the Congress of Vienna, which made peace at the end of the Napoleonic wars and tried to restore Europe's "legitimate" rulers. The great powers, whose cooperation was embodied in the Concert of Europe, attempted to ensure the durability of the new conservative order by intervening to uphold conservative governments. Great Britain, however, seeking new markets, opposed intervention when the Latin American colonies of Spain and Portugal declared their independence. Within the European countries, conservative rulers worked to reestablish the old order.

But the revolutionary waves of the 1820s and 1830s made it clear that the ideologies of liberalism and nationalism, first unleashed by the French Revolution and now reinforced by the spread of the Industrial Revolution, were still alive and active. Liberalism favored freedom both in politics and in economics. Natural rights and representative government were essential, but most liberals favored limiting the right to vote to male property owners. Nationalism, with its belief in a community with common traditions, language, and customs, threatened the status quo in divided Germany and Italy and the multi-ethnic Austrian Empire. The forces of liberalism and nationalism, however, faced enormous difficulties, as failed revolutions in Poland, Russia, Italy, and Germany all testify. At the same time, reform legislation in Britain and successful revolutions in Greece, France, and Belgium demonstrated the continuing strength of these forces for change. In 1848, they erupted

once more as revolutions broke out all across Europe. A republic with universal manhood suffrage was established in France, but conflict emerged between socialist demands and the republican political agenda. The Frankfurt Assembly worked to create a unified Germany, but it also failed. In Austria, the liberal demands of Hungarians and other nationalities were eventually put down. In Italy, too, uprisings against Austrian rule failed when conservatives regained control. Although they failed, both liberalism and nationalism would succeed in the second half of the nineteenth century but in ways not foreseen by the idealistic liberals and nationalists. The disorder of the age also led European states to create civilian police forces.

Efforts at reform had a cultural side as well in the movement of Romanticism. Romantics reacted against what they viewed as the Enlightenment's excessive emphasis on reason. They favored intuition, feeling, and emotion, which became evident in the medieval fantasies of Walter Scott, the poetry of William Wordsworth and Percy Bysshe Shelley, the Gothic literature of Mary Shelley and Edgar Allan Poe, the paintings of Caspar David Friedrich and Eugène Delacroix, and the music of Ludwig van Beethoven and Hector Berlioz. Romanticism also brought a revival of religion evident in a renewed interest in Catholicism's medieval heritage and in a Protestant "awakening."

CHAPTER TIMELINE

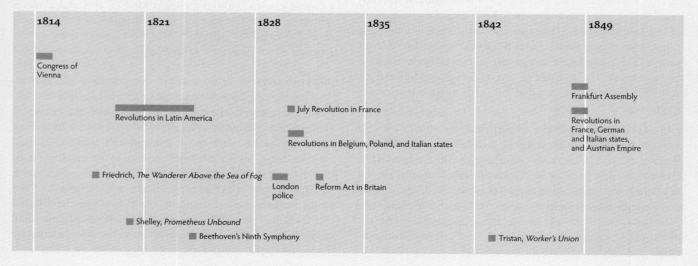

1814	1821	1828	1835	1842	1849

Congress of Vienna

Revolutions in Latin America

July Revolution in France

Revolutions in Belgium, Poland, and Italian states

Frankfurt Assembly

Revolutions in France, German and Italian states, and Austrian Empire

Friedrich, *The Wanderer Above the Sea of Fog*

London police

Reform Act in Britain

Shelley, *Prometheus Unbound*

Beethoven's Ninth Symphony

Tristan, *Worker's Union*

CHAPTER REVIEW

Upon Reflection

Q What were the chief ideas associated with the ideology of conservatism, and how were these ideas put into practice in the first half of the nineteenth century?

Q What were the chief ideas associated with the ideologies of liberalism and nationalism, and how were these ideas put into practice in the first half of the nineteenth century?

Q How was Great Britain able to avoid revolution in the 1830s and the 1840s?

Key Terms

principle of legitimacy (p. 621)
balance of power (p. 621)
ideology (p. 622)
conservatism (p. 622)
principle of intervention (p. 624)
ultraroyalists (p. 628)
ministerial responsibility (p. 628)
Burschenschaften (p. 628)

liberalism (p. 630)
socialism (p. 632)
utopian socialists (p. 632)
phalanstery (p. 632)
risorgimento (p. 640)
individualism (p. 645)
Gothic literature (p. 645)
pantheism (p. 646)

Suggestions for Further Reading

GENERAL WORKS For a good survey of the entire nineteenth century, see **R. Gildea, *Barricades and Borders: Europe, 1800–1914*,** 3rd ed. (Oxford, 2003), in the Short Oxford History of the Modern World series. Also valuable is **T. C. W. Blanning, ed., *Nineteenth Century: Europe 1789–1914*** (Oxford, 2000). For surveys of the period covered in this chapter, see **M. Lyons, *Postrevolutionary Europe 1815–1856*** (New York, 2006), and **C. Breunig** and **M. Levinger, *The Age of Revolution and Reaction, 1789–1850*,** 3rd ed. (New York, 2002). There are also some useful books on individual countries that cover more than the subject of this chapter. These include **R. Magraw, *France, 1815–1914: The Bourgeois Century*,** rev. ed. (Oxford, 2006); **D. Saunders, *Russia in the Age of Reaction and Reform, 1801–1881*** (London, 1992); **D. Blackbourn, *The Long Nineteenth Century: A History of Germany, 1789–1918*** (New York, 1998); **C. Clark, *Iron Kingdom: The Rise and Downfall of Prussia, 1608–1947*** (Cambridge, Mass., 2009); **A. Sked, *The Decline and Fall of the Habsburg Empire, 1815–1918*,** 2nd ed. (London, 2001); and **J. A. David, *Italy in the Nineteenth Century: 1796–1900*** (Oxford, 2001).

EUROPE, 1815–1830 On the peace settlement of 1814–1815, see **T. Chapman, *The Congress of Vienna*** (London, 1998).

A concise summary of the international events of the entire nineteenth century can be found in **R. Bullen** and **F. R. Bridge, *The Great Powers and the European States System, 1815–1914*,** rev. ed. (London, 2004). On Great Britain's reform legislation, see **E. J. Evans, *Great Reform Act of 1832*,** 2nd ed. (London, 1994). The Greek revolt is examined in detail in **D. Brewer, *Greek War of Independence*** (New York, 2001). On the rise of nationalism, see **B. Anderson, *Imagined Communities: Reflections on the Origin and Spread of Nationalism*** (London, 2006); **E. Gellner, *Nations and Nationalism*** (Ithaca, N.Y., 2009); and **T. Baycroft and M. Hewitson, eds., *What Is a Nation?: 1789–1914*** (Oxford, 2009).

REVOLUTIONS OF 1848 The best introduction to the revolutions of 1848 is **J. Sperber, *The European Revolutions, 1848–1851*,** 2nd ed. (New York, 2005). On Germany, see **M. Hewitson, *Nationalism in Germany 1848–1866: Revolutionary Nation*** (New York, 2010).

ROMANTICISM On the ideas of the Romantics, see **M. Cranston, *The Romantic Movement*** (Oxford, 1994). For an introduction to the arts, see **I. Ciseri, *Romanticism 1780–1860: The Birth of a New Sensibility*** (New York, 2003).

Notes

1. Quoted in C. Breunig, *The Age of Revolution and Reaction, 1789–1850* (New York, 1970), p. 119.
2. Quoted in M. S. Anderson, *The Ascendancy of Europe, 1815–1914*, 2nd ed. (London, 1985), p. 1.
3. Quoted in P. Viereck, *Conservatism* (Princeton, N.J., 1956), pp. 27, 114.
4. Quoted in R. Albrecht-Carrié, *The Concert of Europe* (New York, 1968), p. 48.
5. Quoted in M. C. Eakin, *The History of Latin America: Collision of Cultures* (New York, 2007), p. 188.
6. Quoted in G. de Berthier de Sauvigny, *Metternich and His Times* (London, 1962), p. 105.
7. Quoted in S. J. Moon, "Feminism and Socialism: The Utopian Synthesis of Flora Tristan," in Marilyn J. Boxer and Jean H. Quataert, eds., *Socialist Women* (New York, 1978), p. 38.

8. Quoted in S. Z. Pech, *The Czech Revolution of 1848* (Chapel Hill, N.C., 1969), p. 82.

9. Quoted in C. Emsley, *Policing and Its Context, 1750–1870* (New York, 1984), p. 58.

10. Quoted in C. Emsley, *Crime and Society in England, 1750–1900* (London, 1987), p. 173.

11. Quoted in C. Emsley, *Policing and Its Context*, p. 66.

12. Quoted in Ibid., p. 102.

13. Quoted in C. Emsley, *Crime and Society in England*, p. 226.

14. William Wordsworth, "The Tables Turned," *Poems of Wordsworth*, ed. M. Arnold (London, 1963), p. 138.

15. William Wordsworth, *The Prelude* (Harmondsworth, England, 1971), p. 109.

16. Quoted in H. G. Schenk, *The Mind of the European Romantics* (Garden City, N.Y., 1969), p. 205.

17. Quoted in S. Prawer, ed., *The Romantic Period in Germany* (London, 1970), p. 285.

18. Quoted in J. B. Halsted, ed., *Romanticism* (New York, 1969), p. 156.

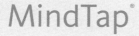

MindTap® is a fully online, highly personalized learning experience built upon Cengage Learning content. MindTap combines student learning tools—readings, multimedia, activities, and assessments—into a singular Learning Path that guides students through the course.

AN AGE OF NATIONALISM AND REALISM, 1850–1871

Proclamation of the German Empire in the Hall of Mirrors in the palace of Versailles

Schloss Friedrichsruhe, Germany/The Bridgeman Art Library

CHAPTER OUTLINE AND FOCUS QUESTIONS

The France of Napoleon III

Q What were the characteristics of Napoleon III's government, and how did his foreign policy contribute to the unification of Italy and Germany?

National Unification: Italy and Germany

Q What actions did Cavour and Bismarck take to bring about unification in Italy and Germany, respectively, and what role did war play in their efforts?

Nation Building and Reform: The National State in Midcentury

Q What efforts for reform occurred in the Austrian Empire, Russia, and Great Britain between 1850 and 1870, and how successful were they in alleviating each nation's problems?

Industrialization and the Marxist Response

Q What were the main ideas of Karl Marx?

Science and Culture in an Age of Realism

Q How did the belief that the world should be viewed realistically manifest itself in science, art, and literature in the second half of the nineteenth century?

Critical Thinking

Q *What was the relationship between nationalism and reform between 1850 and 1871?*

Connections to Today

Q *How do we define classes in society today, and in what ways are our definitions different from or similar to those that Marx and Engels used in* The Communist Manifesto *for the classes emerging in the wake of the Industrial Revolution?*

ACROSS THE EUROPEAN continent, the revolutions of 1848 had failed. The forces of liberalism and nationalism appeared to have been decisively defeated as authoritarian governments reestablished their control almost everywhere in Europe by 1850. And yet within twenty-five years, many of the goals sought by the liberals and nationalists during the first half of the nineteenth century seemed to have been achieved. National unity became a reality in Italy and Germany, and many European states were governed by constitutional monarchies, even though the constitutional-parliamentary features were frequently facades.

All the same, these goals were not achieved by liberal and nationalist leaders but by a new generation of conservative leaders who were proud of being practitioners of *Realpolitik* (ray-AHL-poh-lee-teek), the "politics of reality." One reaction to the failure of the revolutions of 1848 had been a new toughness of mind as people prided themselves on being realistic in their handling of power. The new conservative leaders used armies and power politics to achieve their foreign policy goals. And they did not hesitate to manipulate liberal means to achieve conservative ends at home. Nationalism had failed as a revolutionary movement in 1848–1849, but between 1850 and 1871, these new leaders found a variety of ways to pursue nation building. Winning wars was one means of nation building, but these rulers also sought to improve the economy and foster cultural policies that gave the citizens of their states a greater sense of national identity.

One of the most successful of these new conservative leaders was the Prussian Otto von Bismarck, who used both astute diplomacy and war to achieve the unification of Germany. On January 18, 1871, Bismarck and six hundred German princes, nobles, and generals filled the Hall of Mirrors in the palace of Versailles, outside Paris. The Prussian army had defeated the French, and the assembled notables were gathered for the proclamation of the Prussian king as the new emperor of a united German state. When the words "Long live His Imperial Majesty, the Emperor William!" rang out, the assembled guests took up the cry. One participant wrote that a thundering cheer went through the room while the flags waved over the head of the new emperor of Germany. European rulers who feared the power of the new German state were not so cheerful. The British prime minister declared that the balance of power had been "entirely destroyed."

The France of Napoleon III

 FOCUS QUESTION: What were the characteristics of Napoleon III's government, and how did his foreign policy contribute to the unification of Italy and Germany?

After 1850, a new generation of conservative leaders came to power in Europe. Foremost among them was Napoleon III (1852–1870) of France, who taught his contemporaries how authoritarian governments could use liberal and nationalistic forces to bolster their own power. It was a lesson others quickly learned.

Louis Napoleon: Toward the Second Empire

Even after his election as the president of the French Republic in 1848, many of his contemporaries dismissed "Napoleon the Small" as a nonentity whose success was due only to his name. But Louis Napoleon was a clever politician who was especially astute at understanding the popular forces of his day. After his election, he was clear about his desire to have personal power. He wrote, "I shall never submit to any attempt to influence me. . . . I follow only the promptings of my mind and heart. . . . Nothing, nothing shall trouble the clear vision of my judgment or the strength of my resolution."[1]

Louis Napoleon was a patient man. For three years, he persevered in winning the support of the French people, and when the National Assembly rejected his wish to revise the constitution

Emperor Napoleon III. On December 2, 1852, Louis Napoleon took the title of Napoleon III and then proceeded to create an authoritarian monarchy. As opposition to his policies intensified in the 1860s, Napoleon III began to liberalize his government. A disastrous military defeat at the hands of Prussia in 1870–1871, however, brought the collapse of his regime.

and be allowed to stand for reelection, Louis used troops to seize control of the government on December 1, 1851. After restoring universal male suffrage, Louis Napoleon asked the French people to restructure the government by electing him president for ten years (see "Opposing Viewpoints" on p. 655). By an overwhelming majority, 7.5 million yes votes to 640,000 no votes, they agreed. A year later, on November 21, 1852, Louis Napoleon returned to the people to ask for the restoration of the empire. This time, 97 percent responded affirmatively, and on December 2, 1852, Louis Napoleon assumed the title of Napoleon III (the first Napoleon had abdicated in favor of his son, Napoleon II, on April 6, 1814). The Second Empire had begun.

The Second Napoleonic Empire

The government of Napoleon III was clearly authoritarian in a Bonapartist sense. Louis Napoleon had asked, "Since France has carried on for fifty years only by virtue of the administrative, military, judicial, religious and financial organization of

The Practice of *Realpolitik:* Two Approaches

DURING THE MID-NINETEENTH CENTURY, a new generation of conservative leaders emerged who were proud of being practitioners of *Realpolitik*, the "politics of reality." Two of the most prominent were Louis Napoleon of France and Otto von Bismarck of Prussia. The first selection is taken from Louis Napoleon's proclamation to the French people in 1851, asking them to approve his actions after his coup d'état on December 1, 1851. The second and third selections are excerpts from Bismarck's famous "iron and blood" speech to a committee of the Prussian Reichstag and his 1888 speech to the German Reichstag on Germany's need for military preparation.

Louis Napoleon, Proclamation to the People, 1851

Frenchmen! The present situation cannot last much longer. Each passing day increases the danger to the country. The [National] Assembly, which ought to be the firmest supporter of order, has become a center of conspiracies. . . . It attacks the authority that I hold directly from the people; it encourages all evil passions; it jeopardizes the peace of France: I have dissolved it and I make the whole people judge between it and me. . . .

I therefore make a loyal appeal to the whole nation, and I say to you: If you wish to continue this state of uneasiness which degrades us and makes our future uncertain, choose another in my place, for I no longer wish an authority which is powerless to do good, makes me responsible for acts I cannot prevent, and chains me to the helm when I see the vessel speeding toward the abyss. . . .

Persuaded that the instability of authority and the preponderance of a single Assembly are permanent causes of trouble and discord, I submit to you the following fundamental bases of a constitution which the Assemblies will develop later.

1. A responsible chief elected for ten years.
2. Ministers dependent upon the executive power alone.
3. A Council of State composed of the most distinguished men to prepare the laws and discuss them before the legislative body.
4. A legislative body to discuss and vote the laws, elected by universal [male] suffrage.

This system, created by the First Consul [Napoleon I] at the beginning of the century, has already given France calm and prosperity; it will guarantee them to her again.

Such is my profound conviction. If you share it, declare that fact by your votes. If, on the contrary, you prefer a government without force, monarchical or republican, borrowed from I know not what past or from which chimerical future, reply in the negative. . . .

If I do not obtain a majority of your votes, I shall then convoke a new assembly, and I shall resign to it the mandate that I received from you. But if you believe that the cause of which my name is the symbol, that is, France regenerated by the revolution of 1789 and organized by the Emperor, is forever yours, proclaim it by sanctioning the powers that I ask from you. Then France and Europe will be saved from anarchy, obstacles will be removed, rivalries will disappear, for all will respect the decree of Providence in the decision of the people.

Bismarck, Speech to the Prussian Reichstag, 1862

It is true that we can hardly escape complications in Germany, although we do not seek them. Germany does not look to Prussia's liberalism, but to her power. The south German States—Bavaria, Württemberg, and Baden—would like to indulge in liberalism, and because of that no one will assign Prussia's role to them! Prussia must collect her forces and hold them in reserve for an opportune moment, which has already come and gone several times. Since the Treaty of Vienna, our frontiers have not been favorably designed for a healthy body politic. Not by speeches and majorities will the great questions of the day be decided—that was the mistake of 1848 and 1849—but by iron and blood.

Bismarck, Speech to the German Reichstag, 1888

When I say that it is our duty to endeavor to be ready at all times and for all emergencies, I imply that we must make greater exertions than other people for the same purpose, because of our geographical position. We are situated in the heart of Europe, and have at least three fronts open to an attack. France has only her eastern, and Russia only her western frontier where they may be attacked. We are also more exposed to the dangers of a coalition than any other nation, as is proved by the whole development of history, by our geographical position, and the lesser degree of cohesiveness, which until now has characterized the German nation in comparison with others. God has placed us where we are prevented, thanks to our neighbors, from growing lazy and dull. He has placed by our side the most warlike and restless of all nations, the French, and He has permitted warlike inclinations to grow strong in Russia, where formerly they existed to a lesser degree. Thus we are given the spur, so to speak, from both sides, and are compelled to exertions which we should perhaps not be making otherwise.

 Why did Louis Napoleon's argument to the French people have such a strong popular appeal? What are the similarities in the practice of Realpolitik by these two leaders? What are the noticeable differences in their approaches? Are the similarities more important than the differences? Why or why not? What can you learn about Realpolitik *from these three selections?*

Sources: F. M. Anderson, *The Constitutions and Other Select Documents Illustrative of the History of France 1789–1907* (Minneapolis: H. W. Wilson, 1904); L. L. Snyder, *Documents of German History* (Piscataway, N.J.: Rutgers University Press, 1958), p. 202; B. Tierney and J. Scott, eds., *Western Societies: A Documentary History*, vol. 2 (New York: Alfred A. Knopf, 1984), p. 366.

the Consulate and Empire, why should she not also adopt the political institutions of that period?"[2] As chief of state, Napoleon III controlled the armed forces, police, and civil service. Only he could introduce legislation and declare war. The Legislative Corps gave an appearance of representative government since its members were elected by universal male suffrage for six-year terms. But they could neither initiate legislation nor affect the budget.

EARLY DOMESTIC POLICIES The first five years of Napoleon III's reign were a spectacular success, as he reaped the benefits of worldwide economic prosperity as well as of some of his own economic policies. Napoleon believed in using the resources of government to stimulate the national economy and took many steps to encourage industrial growth. Government subsidies were used to foster the construction of railroads, harbors, roads, and canals. The major French railway lines were completed during Napoleon's reign, and industrial expansion was evident in the tripling of iron production. In his concern to reduce tensions and improve the social welfare of the nation, Napoleon provided hospitals and free medicine for the workers and advocated better housing for the working class.

In the midst of this economic expansion, Napoleon III undertook a vast reconstruction of the city of Paris. Under the direction of Baron Haussmann (HOWSS-mun), the medieval Paris of narrow streets and old city walls was destroyed and replaced by a modern Paris of broad boulevards, spacious buildings, circular plazas, public squares, an underground sewage system, a new public water supply, and gaslights (see Chapter 23). The new Paris served a military as well as an aesthetic purpose: broad streets made it more difficult for would-be insurrectionists to throw up barricades and easier for troops to move rapidly through the city to put down revolts.

LIBERALIZATION OF THE REGIME In the 1860s, as opposition to some of the emperor's policies began to mount, Napoleon III liberalized his regime. He reached out to the working class by legalizing trade unions and granting them the right to strike. He also began to liberalize the political process. The Legislative Corps had been closely controlled during the 1850s. In the 1860s, opposition candidates were allowed greater freedom to campaign, and the Legislative Corps was permitted more say in affairs of state, including debate over the budget. Initially, Napoleon's liberalization policies served to strengthen the government. In a plebiscite in May 1870 on whether to accept a new constitution that might have inaugurated a parliamentary regime, the French people gave Napoleon another resounding victory. This triumph was short-lived, however. Foreign policy failures led to growing criticism, and war with Prussia in 1870 turned out to be the death blow for Napoleon III's regime (see "The Franco-Prussian War" later in this chapter).

Foreign Policy: The Mexican Adventure

Napoleon III was considerably less accomplished at dealing with foreign policy, especially his imperialistic adventure in Mexico. Seeking to dominate Mexican markets for French goods, the emperor sent French troops to Mexico in 1861 to join British and Spanish forces in protecting their interests in the midst of the upheaval caused by a struggle between liberal and conservative Mexican factions. Although the British and Spanish withdrew their troops after order had been restored, French forces remained, and in 1864, Napoleon III installed Archduke Maximilian of Austria, his handpicked choice, as the new emperor of Mexico. When the French troops were needed in Europe, Maximilian became an emperor without an army. He surrendered to liberal Mexican forces in May 1867 and was executed in June. His execution was a blow to the prestige of the French emperor.

Foreign Policy: The Crimean War

Napoleon III's participation in the Crimean War (1854–1856) had been more rewarding. As heir to the Napoleonic empire, Napoleon III was motivated by the desire to free France from the restrictions of the peace settlements of 1814–1815 and to make France the chief arbiter of Europe. In the decline of the Ottoman Empire, he saw an opportunity to take steps toward these goals.

THE OTTOMAN EMPIRE The Crimean War was yet another attempt to answer the eastern question: Who would be the chief beneficiaries of the disintegration of the Ottoman Empire? In the seventeenth century, the Ottoman Empire had controlled southeastern Europe, but in 1699 it had lost Hungary, Transylvania, Croatia, and Slovenia to the expanding Austrian Empire. The Russian Empire to its north also encroached on the Ottoman Empire by seizing the Crimea in 1783 and Bessarabia in 1812 (see Map 22.1).

By the beginning of the nineteenth century, the Ottoman Empire had entered a fresh period of decline. A nationalist revolt had gained independence for Greece in 1830. Serbia claimed autonomy in 1827, which was recognized by the Ottoman Empire in 1830. In 1829, the Russians had obtained a protectorate over the Danubian provinces of Moldavia (mohl-DAY-vee-uh) and Wallachia (wah-LAY-kee-uh), gained control over the mouth of the Danube and eastern Black Sea coast, and secured passage of Russian ships through the Dardanelles Straights.

As Ottoman authority over the outlying territories in southeastern Europe waned, European governments began to take an active interest in the empire's apparent demise. Russia's proximity to the Ottoman Empire and the religious bonds between the Russians and the Greek Orthodox Christians in Ottoman-dominated southeastern Europe naturally gave it special opportunities to enlarge its sphere of influence. The Dardanelles Straights, a narrow sea-trading route connecting eastern and western Europe, was a valuable trading and military passage for Russia. Access to the Dardanelles enabled Russian warships to enter the heart of Europe. Other European powers not only feared Russian ambitions but also had objectives of their own in the area. Austria craved more land in the Balkans, a desire that inevitably meant conflict with Russia, and France and Britain were interested in commercial opportunities and naval bases in the eastern Mediterranean.

WAR IN THE CRIMEA War erupted between Russia and the Ottoman Empire in 1853 when the Russians demanded the right to protect Christian shrines in Palestine, a privilege that had already been extended to the French. When the Ottomans

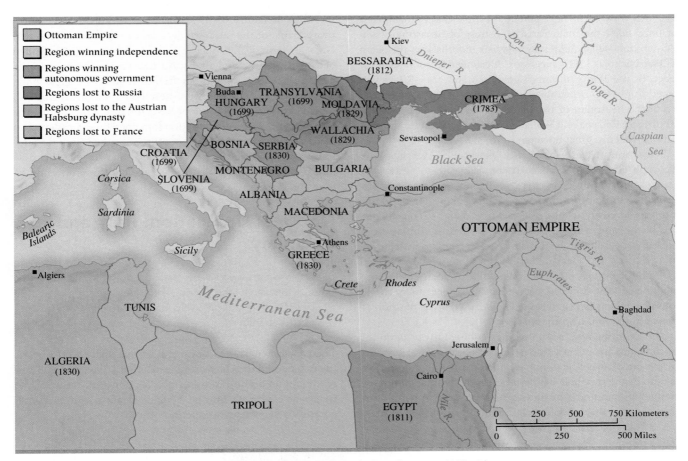

MAP 22.1 Decline of the Ottoman Empire. The decline in Ottoman fortunes began in 1699 with major losses to the Austrian Empire. The slide accelerated in the nineteenth century with nationalist revolts in the European provinces and defeat in the Crimean War. Being on the losing side in World War I would complete its destruction.

Q *What is the relationship between the distance from Constantinople and the date that a region was lost to the Ottoman Empire, and how can you explain it?*

refused, the Russians occupied Moldavia and Wallachia. Failure to resolve the dispute by negotiations led the Ottoman Empire to declare war on Russia on October 4, 1853. The following year, on March 28, Great Britain and France declared war on Russia.

Why did Britain and France take that step? Concern over the prospect of an upset in the balance of power was clearly one reason. The British in particular feared that an aggressive Russia would try to profit from the obvious weakness of the Ottoman government by seizing Ottoman territory or the long-coveted Dardanelles. Such a move would make Russia the major power in eastern Europe and would enable the Russians to challenge British naval control of the eastern Mediterranean. Napoleon III felt that the Russians had insulted France, first at the Congress of

The Crimean War

Vienna and now by their insistence on replacing the French as the protectors of Christians living in the Ottoman Empire. The French also feared the collapse of the Ottoman Empire and the growth of Russian influence there. Although the Russians assumed that they could count on support from the Austrians (since Russian troops had saved the Austrian government in 1849), the Austrian prime minister blithely observed that they would astonish the world "by our ingratitude," and Austria remained neutral. Since the Austrians had perceived that it was not in their best interest to intervene, Russia had to fight alone.

Poorly planned and poorly fought, the Crimean War is perhaps best remembered for the suicidal charge of the British Light Brigade at the Battle of Balaklava (bal-uh-KLAH-vauh). Britain and France decided to attack Russia's Crimean peninsula in the Black

Sea. After a two-year siege and at a terrible cost in manpower for both sides, the main Russian fortress of Sevastopol (suh-VAS-tuh-pohl) fell in September 1855, six months after the death of Tsar Nicholas I. His successor, Alexander II, soon sued for peace. By the Treaty of Paris, signed in March 1856, Russia was forced to give up Bessarabia at the mouth of the Danube and accept the neutrality of the Black Sea. In addition, the principalities of Moldavia and Wallachia were placed under the protection of all five great powers.

The Crimean War was the first "newspaper" war. The new telegraph allowed journalists to communicate to newspaper headquarters in European cities, while photographers and artists captured the horrors of war for the public. The Crimean War proved costly to both sides. More than 250,000 soldiers died in the war, with 60 percent of the deaths coming from disease (especially cholera) due to poor conditions, freezing temperatures, and a lack of food. Even more would have died on the British side if it had not been for the efforts of Florence Nightingale (1820–1910). Her insistence on strict sanitary conditions saved many lives and helped make nursing a profession of trained, middle-class women.

The Crimean War broke up longstanding European power relationships and effectively destroyed the Concert of Europe. Austria and Russia, the two chief powers maintaining the status quo in the first half of the nineteenth century, were now enemies because of Austria's unwillingness to support Russia in the war. Russia, defeated, humiliated, and weakened by the obvious failure of its serf-armies, withdrew from European affairs for the next two decades to set its house in order. Great Britain, disillusioned by its role in the war, also pulled back from continental affairs. Austria, paying the price for its neutrality, was now without friends among the great powers. Not until the 1870s were new combinations formed to replace those that had disappeared, and in the meantime, the European international situation remained fluid. Leaders who were willing to pursue the "politics of reality" found themselves in a situation rife with opportunity. It was this new international situation that made possible the unification of Italy and Germany.

National Unification: Italy and Germany

 FOCUS QUESTION: What actions did Cavour and Bismarck take to bring about unification in Italy and Germany, respectively, and what role did war play in their efforts?

The breakdown of the Concert of Europe opened the way for the Italians and the Germans to establish national states. Their successful unifications transformed the power structure of the European continent. Europe would be dealing with the consequences well into the twentieth century.

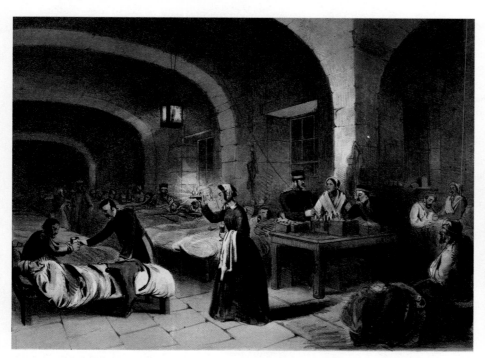

Florence Nightingale. Florence Nightingale is shown caring for wounded British soldiers in the military hospital at Scutari during the Crimean War. After a British journalist, W. H. Russell, issued a scathing denunciation of the quality of medical care afforded to wounded British soldiers, the British government allowed Nightingale to take a group of nurses to the Crimean front. Through her efforts in the Crimean War, Nightingale helped make nursing an admirable profession for middle-class women. At the right is a photograph of Nightingale.

Left: Eileen Tweedy/The Art Archive at Art Resource, NY

Right: Private Collection/The Bridgeman Art Library

The Unification of Italy

In 1850, Austria was still the dominant power on the Italian peninsula. After the failure of the revolution of 1848–1849, a growing number of advocates for Italian unification focused on the northern Italian state of Piedmont as their best hope to achieve their goal. The royal house of Savoy (suh-VOI) ruled the kingdom of Piedmont, which also included the island of Sardinia (see Map 22.2). Although soundly defeated by the Austrians in 1848–1849, Piedmont under King Charles Albert had made a valiant effort; it seemed reasonable that Piedmont would now assume the leading role in the cause of national unity. The little state seemed unlikely to supply the needed leadership, however, until the new king, Victor Emmanuel II (1849–1878), named Count Camillo di Cavour (kuh-MEEL-oh dee kuh-VOOR) (1810–1861) as his prime minister in 1852.

THE LEADERSHIP OF CAVOUR Cavour was a liberal-minded nobleman who had made a fortune in agriculture and went on to make even more money in banking, railroads, and shipping. Cavour was a moderate who favored constitutional government. He was a consummate politician with the ability to persuade others of the rightness of his convictions. After becoming prime minister in 1852, he pursued a policy of economic expansion, encouraging the building of roads, canals, and railroads and fostering business enterprise by expanding credit and stimulating investment in new industries. The growth in the Piedmontese economy and the subsequent increase in government revenues enabled Cavour to pour money into equipping a large army.

Cavour had no illusions about Piedmont's military strength and was well aware that he could not challenge Austria directly. He would need the French. In 1858, Cavour came to an agreement with Napoleon III. The emperor agreed to ally with Piedmont in driving the Austrians out of Italy. Once the Austrians were driven out, Italy would be reorganized. Piedmont would be extended into the kingdom of Upper Italy by adding Lombardy, Venetia, Parma, Modena, and part of the Papal States to its territory. In compensation for its efforts, France would receive the Piedmontese provinces of Nice (NEESS) and Savoy. A kingdom of Central Italy would be created for Napoleon III's cousin, Prince Napoleon, who would be married to the younger daughter of King Victor Emmanuel. This agreement between Napoleon and Cavour seemed to assure the French ruler of the opportunity to control Italy. Confident that the plan would work, Cavour provoked the Austrians into invading Piedmont in April 1859.

In the initial stages of fighting, it was the French who were largely responsible for defeating the Austrians in two major battles at Magenta (muh-JEN-tuh) and Solferino (sawl-fe-REE-noh). It was also the French who made peace with Austria on July 11, 1859, without informing their Italian ally. Why did Napoleon withdraw so hastily? For one thing, he realized that despite

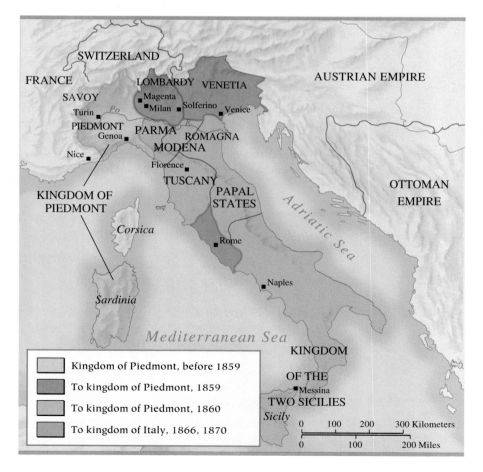

MAP 22.2 The Unification of Italy. Piedmont under the able guidance of Count Camillo di Cavour provided the nucleus for Italian unification. Alliances with France and Prussia, combined with the military actions of republican nationalists like Giuseppe Garibaldi, led to complete unification in 1870.

 Taking geographic factors and size of population into account, which of the countries shown on this map would likely have posed the greatest military threat to the new Italian state?

two losses, the Austrian army had not yet been defeated; the struggle might be longer and more costly than he had anticipated. Moreover, the Prussians were mobilizing in support of Austria, and Napoleon III had no desire to take on two enemies at once. As a result of Napoleon's peace with Austria, Piedmont received only Lombardy; Venetia remained under Austrian control. Cavour was furious at the French perfidy, but events in northern Italy now turned in his favor. Soon after the war with Austria had begun, some northern Italian states, namely, Parma, Modena, Tuscany, and part of the Papal States, had been taken over by nationalists. In plebiscites held in 1860, these states agreed to join Piedmont. Napoleon agreed to the annexations in return for Nice and Savoy.

THE EFFORTS OF GARIBALDI Meanwhile, in southern Italy, a new leader of Italian unification had come to the fore. Giuseppe Garibaldi (joo-ZEP-pay gar-uh-BAHL-dee) (1807–1882), a dedicated Italian patriot who had supported Mazzini

EDITIONS LAROUSSE/Archives Larousse, Paris, France/Bridgeman Images

Garibaldi. The Italian nationalists' dream of a united Italian state finally became a reality by 1870. An important figure in the cause of unification was Giuseppe Garibaldi, a determined Italian patriot. Garibaldi is shown here in an 1860 photograph taken by the French photographer Gustave Le Gray.

and the republican cause of Young Italy, raised an army of a thousand Red Shirts, as his volunteers were called because of their distinctive dress. On May 11, 1860, he landed in Sicily, where a revolt had broken out against the Bourbon king of the Two Sicilies.

Although his forces were greatly outnumbered, Garibaldi's daring tactics won the day (see the box on p. 661). By the end of July 1860, most of Sicily had been pacified under Garibaldi's control. In August, Garibaldi and his forces crossed over to the mainland and began a victorious march up the Italian peninsula. Naples and the Two Sicilies fell in early September. At this point, Cavour reentered the scene. Aware that Garibaldi planned to march on Rome, Cavour feared that such a move would bring war with France as the defender of papal interests. Moreover, Garibaldi and his men favored a democratic republicanism; Cavour did not and acted quickly to preempt Garibaldi. The Piedmontese army invaded the Papal States and, bypassing Rome, moved into the kingdom of Naples. Ever the patriot, Garibaldi chose to yield to Cavour's fait accompli rather than provoke a civil war and retired to his farm. Plebiscites in the Papal States and the Two Sicilies resulted in overwhelming support for union with Piedmont. On March 17, 1861, the new kingdom of Italy was proclaimed under a centralized government subordinated to the control of Piedmont and King Victor Emmanuel II (1861–1878) of the house of Savoy. Worn out by his efforts, Cavour died three months later.

Despite the proclamation of the new kingdom, the task of unification was not yet complete since Venetia in the north was still held by Austria and Rome was under papal control, supported by French troops. To attack either one meant war with a major European state, which the Italian army was not prepared to handle. It was the Prussian army that indirectly completed the task of Italian unification. In the Austro-Prussian War of 1866, the new Italian state became an ally of Prussia. Although the Italian army was defeated by the Austrians, Prussia's victory left the Italians with Venetia. In 1870, the Franco-Prussian War resulted in the withdrawal of French troops from Rome. The Italian army then annexed the city on September 20, 1870, and Rome became the new capital of the united Italian state.

CHRONOLOGY	The Unification of Italy
Victor Emmanuel II	1849–1878
Count Cavour becomes prime minister of Piedmont	1852
Agreement with Napoleon III	1858
Austrian War	1859
Plebiscites in the northern Italian states	1860
Garibaldi's invasion of the kingdom of the Two Sicilies	1860
Kingdom of Italy is proclaimed	1861
Italy's annexation of Venetia	1866
Italy's annexation of Rome	1870

GARIBALDI AND ROMANTIC NATIONALISM

GIUSEPPE GARIBALDI WAS ONE OF the most colorful figures involved in the unification of Italy. Accompanied by only one thousand of his famous Red Shirts, the Italian soldier of fortune left Genoa on the night of May 5, 1860, for an invasion of the kingdom of the Two Sicilies. The ragged band entered Palermo, the chief city on the island of Sicily, on May 31. This selection is taken from an account by a correspondent for the *Times* of London, the Hungarian-born Nandor Eber.

London Times, June 13, 1860

PALERMO, May 31—Anyone in search of violent emotions cannot do better than set off at once for Palermo. However blase he may be, or however milk-and-water his blood, I promise it will be stirred up. He will be carried away by the tide of popular feeling. . . .

In the afternoon Garibaldi made a tour of inspection round the town. I was there, but find it really impossible to give you a faint idea of the manner in which he was received everywhere. It was one of those triumphs which seem to be almost too much for a man. . . . The popular idol, Garibaldi, in his red flannel shirt, with a loose colored handkerchief around his neck, and his worn "wide-awake" [a soft-brimmed felt hat], was walking on foot among those cheering, laughing, crying, mad thousands; and all his few followers could do was to prevent him from being bodily carried off the ground. The people threw themselves forward to kiss his hands, or, at least, to touch the hem of his garment, as if it contained the panacea for all their past and perhaps coming suffering. Children were brought up, and mothers asked on their knees for his blessing; and all this while the object of this idolatry was calm and smiling as when in the deadliest fire, taking up the children and kissing them, trying to quiet the crowd,

stopping at every moment to hear a long complaint of houses burned and property sacked by the retreating soldiers, giving good advice, comforting, and promising that all damages should be paid for. . . .

One might write volumes of horrors on the vandalism already committed, for every one of the hundred ruins has its story of brutality and inhumanity. . . . In these small houses a dense population is crowded together even in ordinary times. A shell falling on one, and crushing and burying the inmates, was sufficient to make people abandon the neighboring one and take refuge a little further on, shutting themselves up in the cellars. When the Royalists retired they set fire to those of the houses which had escaped the shells, and numbers were thus burned alive in their hiding places. . . .

If you can stand the exhalation, try and go inside the ruins, for it is only there that you will see what the thing means and you will not have to search long before you stumble over the remains of a human body, a leg sticking out here, an arm there, a black face staring at you a little further on. You are startled by a rustle. You look round and see half a dozen gorged rats scampering off in all directions, or you see a dog trying to make his escape over the ruins. . . . I only wonder that the sight of these scenes does not convert every man in the town into a tiger and every woman into a fury. But these people have been so long ground down and demoralized that their nature seems to have lost the power of reaction.

 Why did Garibaldi become such a hero to the Italian people? How does Garibaldi's comportment as a political and military leader prefigure the conduct of later revolutionary military leaders and activists?

Source: *The Times*, June 13, 1860.

The Unification of Germany

After the failure of the Frankfurt Assembly to achieve German unification in 1848–1849, German nationalists focused on Austria and Prussia as the only two states powerful enough to dominate German affairs. Austria had long controlled the existing Germanic Confederation, but Prussian power had grown, strongly reinforced by economic expansion in the 1850s. Prussia had formed the **Zollverein** (TSOHL-fuh-ryn), a German customs union, in 1834. Before the Zollverein, there were 1800 customs tolls in Germany. By eliminating tolls on rivers and roads among member states, the Zollverein had stimulated trade and added to the prosperity of its members. By 1853, all the German states except Austria had joined the Prussian-dominated customs union. A number of middle-class liberals now began to see Prussia in a new light; some even looked openly to Prussia to bring about the unification of Germany.

In 1848, Prussia had framed a constitution that had at least the appearance of constitutional monarchy in that it had established a bicameral legislature with the lower house elected by universal male suffrage. The voting population, however, was divided into three classes determined by the amount of taxes they paid, a system that allowed the biggest taxpayers to gain the most seats. Unintentionally, by 1859, this system had allowed control of the lower house to fall largely into the hands of the rising middle classes, whose numbers were growing as a result of continuing industrialization. Their desire was to have a real parliamentary system, but the king's executive power remained too strong; royal ministers answered for their actions only to the king, not the parliament. Nevertheless, the parliament had been granted important legislative and taxation powers on which it could build.

In 1861, King Frederick William IV died and was succeeded by his brother. King William I (1861–1888) had definite ideas about the Prussian army because of his own military training. He and his advisers believed that the army was in dire need of change if Prussia was to remain a great power. The king planned to double the size of the army and institute three years of compulsory military service for all young men.

Middle-class liberals in the parliament, while willing to have reform, feared compulsory military service because they believed the government would use it to inculcate obedience to the monarchy and strengthen the influence of the conservative-military clique in Prussia. When the Prussian legislature rejected the new military budget submitted to parliament in March 1862, William I appointed a new prime minister, Count Otto von Bismarck (OT-toh fun BIZ-mark) (1815–1898). Bismarck, regarded even by the king as too conservative, came to determine the course of modern German history. Until 1890, he dominated both German and European politics.

BISMARCK Otto von Bismarck was born into the Junker class, the traditional, landowning aristocracy of Prussia, and remained loyal to it throughout his life. "I was born and raised as an aristocrat," he once said. As a university student, Bismarck indulged heartily in wine, women, and song, yet managed to read widely in German history. After earning a law degree, he embarked on a career in the Prussian civil service but soon tired of bureaucratic, administrative routine and retired to manage his country estates. Comparing the civil servant to a musician in an orchestra, he responded, "I want to play the tune the way it sounds good to me or not at all. . . . My pride bids me command rather than obey."[3] In 1847, desirous of more excitement and power than he could find in the country, he reentered public life. Four years later, he began to build a base of diplomatic experience as the Prussian delegate to the parliament of the Germanic Confederation. This, combined with his experience as Prussian ambassador to Russia and later to France, gave him opportunities to acquire a wide knowledge of European affairs and to learn how to assess the character of rulers.

Because Bismarck succeeded in guiding Prussia's unification of Germany, it is often assumed that he had determined on a course of action that led precisely to that goal. That is hardly the case. Bismarck was a consummate politician and opportunist. He was not a political gambler but a moderate who waged war only when all other diplomatic alternatives had been exhausted and when he was reasonably sure that all the military and diplomatic advantages were on his side. Bismarck has often been portrayed as the ultimate realist, the foremost nineteenth-century practitioner of **Realpolitik**. He was also quite open about his strong dislike of anyone who opposed him. He said one morning to his wife that he could not sleep the whole night: "I hated throughout the whole night."

In 1862, Bismarck resubmitted the army appropriations bill to parliament along with a passionate appeal to his liberal opponents: "Germany does not look to Prussia's liberalism, but to her power. . . . Not by speeches and majorities will the great questions of the day be decided—that was the mistake of 1848–1849—but by iron and blood"[4] (see "Opposing Viewpoints" on p. 655). His opponents were not impressed and rejected the bill once again. Bismarck went ahead, collected the taxes, and

Otto von Bismarck. Otto von Bismarck played a major role in leading Prussia to achieve the unification of the German states into a new German Empire, proclaimed on January 18, 1871. Bismarck then became chancellor of the new Germany. This photograph of Bismarck was taken in 1874, when he was at the height of his power and prestige.

reorganized the army anyway, blaming the liberals for causing the breakdown of constitutional government. From 1862 to 1866, Bismarck governed Prussia by largely ignoring parliament. Unwilling to revolt, parliament did nothing. In the meantime, opposition to his domestic policy determined Bismarck on an active foreign policy, which in 1864 led to his first war.

THE DANISH WAR (1864) In the three wars that he waged, Bismarck's victories were as much diplomatic and political as they were military. Before war was declared, Bismarck always saw to it that Prussia would be fighting only one power and that that opponent was isolated diplomatically.

The Danish War arose over the duchies of Schleswig (SHLESS-vik) and Holstein (HOHL-shtyn). In 1863, contrary to international treaty, the Danish government moved to incorporate the two duchies into Denmark. German nationalists were outraged since both duchies had large German populations and were regarded as German states. The diet of the Germanic Confederation urged its member states to send troops against Denmark, but Bismarck did not care to subject Prussian policy to the Austrian-dominated German parliament. Instead, he persuaded the Austrians to join Prussia in declaring war on Denmark on February 1, 1864. The

Danes were quickly defeated and surrendered Schleswig and Holstein to the victors (see Map 22.3). Austria and Prussia then agreed to divide the administration of the two duchies; Prussia took Schleswig while Austria administered Holstein. The plan was Bismarck's. By this time, Bismarck had come to the realization that for Prussia to expand its power by dominating the northern, largely Protestant part of the Germanic Confederation, Austria would have to be excluded from German affairs or, less likely, be willing to accept Prussian domination of Germany. The joint administration of the two duchies offered plenty of opportunities to create friction with Austria and provide a reason for war if it came to that. While he pursued negotiations with Austria, he also laid the foundations for the isolation of Austria.

THE AUSTRO-PRUSSIAN WAR (1866) Bismarck had no problem gaining Russia's agreement to remain neutral in the event

of an Austro-Prussian war because Prussia had been the only great power to support Russia's repression of a Polish revolt in 1863. Napoleon III was a thornier problem, but Bismarck was able to buy his neutrality with vague promises of territory in the Rhineland. Finally, Bismarck made an alliance with the new Italian state and promised it Venetia in the event of Austrian defeat.

With the Austrians isolated, Bismarck used the joint occupation of Schleswig-Holstein to goad the Austrians into a war on June 14, 1866. Many Europeans, including Napoleon III, expected a quick Austrian victory, but they overlooked the effectiveness of the Prussian military reforms of the 1860s. The Prussian breech-loading needle gun had a much faster rate of fire than the Austrian muzzleloader, and a superior network of railroads enabled the Prussians to mass troops quickly. At Königgrätz (kur-nig-GRETS) (Sadowa) on July 3, the Austrian army was defeated. Looking ahead, Bismarck refused to create

MAP 22.3 The Unification of Germany. Count Otto von Bismarck, the Prussian prime minister, skillfully combined domestic policies with wars with Denmark, Austria, and France to achieve the creation of the German Empire in 1871.

Q *In terms of increasing Prussia's military power and its ability to rule all of its lands, which was more important: the formation of the North German Confederation or the absorption of the South German Confederation?*

a hostile enemy by burdening Austria with a harsh peace as the Prussian king wanted. Austria lost no territory except Venetia to Italy but was excluded from German affairs. The German states north of the Main River were organized into the North German Confederation, controlled by Prussia. The southern German states, largely Catholic, remained independent but were coerced into signing military agreements with Prussia. In addition to Schleswig and Holstein, Prussia annexed Hanover and Hesse-Cassel because they had openly sided with Austria.

The Austrian war was a turning point in Prussian domestic affairs. After the war, Bismarck asked the Prussian parliament to pass a bill of indemnity, retroactively legalizing the taxes he had collected illegally since 1862. Even most of the liberals voted in favor of the bill because they had been won over by Bismarck's successful use of military power. With his victory over Austria and the creation of the North German Confederation, Bismarck had proved Napoleon III's dictum that nationalism and authoritarian government could be combined. In using nationalism to win support from liberals and prevent governmental reform, Bismarck showed that liberalism and nationalism, the two major forces of change in the early nineteenth century, could be separated.

He showed the same flexibility in the creation of a new constitution for the North German Confederation. Each German state kept its own local government, but the king of Prussia was head of the confederation, and the chancellor (Bismarck) was responsible directly to the king. Both the army and foreign policy remained in the hands of the king and his chancellor. Parliament consisted of two bodies: the Bundesrat (BOON-duhs-raht), or federal council, composed of delegates nominated by the states, and a lower house, the Reichstag (RYKHSS-tahk), elected by universal male suffrage. Like Napoleon, Bismarck believed that the peasants and artisans who made up most of the population were conservative at heart and could be used to overcome the advantages of the liberals.

THE FRANCO-PRUSSIAN WAR (1870–1871) Bismarck and William I had achieved a major goal by 1866. Prussia now dominated all of northern Germany, and Austria had been excluded from any significant role in German affairs. Nevertheless, unsettled business led to new international complications and further change. Bismarck realized that France would never be content with a strong German state to its east because of the potential threat to French security. At the same time, after a series of setbacks, Napoleon III needed a diplomatic triumph to offset his serious domestic problems. The French were not happy with the turn of events in Germany and looked for opportunities to humiliate the Prussians.

After a successful revolution had deposed Queen Isabella II, the throne of Spain was offered to Prince Leopold of Hohenzollern-Sigmaringen (hoh-en-TSULL-urn-zig-mah-RING-un), a distant relative of the Hohenzollern king of Prussia. Bismarck welcomed this possibility for the same reason that the French objected to it. If Leopold assumed the throne of Spain, France would be virtually encircled by members of the Hohenzollern dynasty. French objections caused King William I to force his relative to withdraw his candidacy. Bismarck was disappointed with the king's actions, but at this point, the French overreached.

Not content with their diplomatic victory, they pushed William I to make a formal apology to France and promise never to allow Leopold to be a candidate again. When Bismarck received a telegram from the king informing him of the French request, Bismarck edited it to make it appear even more insulting to the French, knowing that the French would be angry and declare war. The French reacted as Bismarck expected they would and declared war on Prussia on July 15, 1870. The French prime minister remarked that we go to war "with a light heart."

Unfortunately for the French, a "light heart" was not enough. They proved no match for the better-led and better-organized Prussian forces. The southern German states honored their military alliances with Prussia and joined the war effort against the French. The Prussian armies advanced into France, and at Sedan (suh-DAHN) on September 2, 1870, they captured an entire French army and Napoleon III himself. Napoleon III went into captivity in Germany and then exile in England, where he died in 1873. The Second French Empire collapsed, but the war was not yet over. After four months of bitter resistance, Paris finally capitulated on January 28, 1871, and an official peace treaty was signed in May. France had to pay an indemnity of 5 billion francs (about \$1 billion), support German occupying forces until the indemnity had been paid, and give up the provinces of Alsace (al-SASS) and Lorraine (luh-RAYN) to the new German state. The French defeat and the degrading treaty angered the French and left them burning for revenge.

Even before the war had ended, the southern German states had agreed to enter the North German Confederation. On January 18, 1871, in the Hall of Mirrors in Louis XIV's palace at Versailles, William I, with Bismarck standing at the foot of the throne, was proclaimed kaiser (KY-zur) or emperor of the Second German Empire (the first was the medieval Holy Roman Empire). The Prussian monarchy and the Prussian army had achieved German unity. In a real sense, Germany had been merged into Prussia, not Prussia into Germany. German liberals also rejoiced. They had dreamed of unity and freedom, but the achievement of unity now seemed much more important. One old liberal proclaimed:

> I cannot shake off the impression of this hour. I am no
> devotee of Mars; I feel more attached to the goddess of beauty

CHRONOLOGY	The Unification of Germany
King William I of Prussia	1861–1888
Bismarck becomes minister-president of Prussia	1862
Danish War	1864
Austro-Prussian War	1866
Battle of Königgrätz	1866 (July 3)
Franco-Prussian War	1870–1871
Battle of Sedan	1870 (September 2)
Fall of Paris	1871 (January 28)
German Empire proclaimed	1871 (January 18)

and the mother of graces than to the powerful god of war, but the trophies of war exercise a magic charm even upon the child of peace. One's view is involuntarily chained and one's spirit goes along with the boundless row of men who acclaim the god of the moment—success.[5]

The Prussian leadership of German unification meant the triumph of authoritarian, militaristic values over liberal, constitutional sentiments in the development of the new German state. With its industrial resources and military might, the new state had become the strongest power on the Continent. A new European balance of power was at hand.

Nation Building and Reform: The National State in Midcentury

 FOCUS QUESTION: What efforts for reform occurred in the Austrian Empire, Russia, and Great Britain between 1850 and 1870, and how successful were they in alleviating each nation's problems?

While European affairs were dominated by the unification of Italy and Germany, other states were also undergoing transformations (see Map 22.4). War, civil war, and changing political alignments served as catalysts for domestic reforms.

MAP 22.4 Europe in 1871. By 1871, most of the small states of Europe had been absorbed into larger ones, leaving the major powers uncomfortably rubbing shoulders with one another. Meanwhile, the power equation was shifting: the German Empire increased in power while Austria-Hungary and the Ottoman Empire declined.

Q *Of the great powers, which had the greatest overall exposure to the others in terms of shared borders and sea access?*

The Austrian Empire: Toward a Dual Monarchy

After the Habsburgs had crushed the revolutions of 1848–1849, they restored centralized, autocratic government to the empire. What seemed to be the only lasting result of the revolution of 1848 was the act of emancipation of September 7, 1848, that freed the serfs and eliminated all compulsory labor services. Nevertheless, the development of industrialization after 1850, especially in Vienna and the provinces of Bohemia and Galicia, served to bring economic and social change to the empire in the form of an urban proletariat, labor unrest, and a new industrial middle class.

In 1851, the revolutionary constitutions were abolished, and a system of centralized autocracy was imposed on the empire. Under the leadership of Alexander von Bach (1813–1893), local privileges were subordinated to a unified system of administration, law, and taxation implemented by German-speaking officials. Hungary was subjected to the rule of military officers, and the Catholic Church was declared the state church and given control of education. Economic troubles and war, however, soon brought change. After Austria's defeat in the Italian war in 1859, the Emperor Francis Joseph (1848–1916) attempted to establish an imperial parliament—the Reichsrat (RYKHSS-raht)—with a nominated upper house and an elected lower house of representatives. Although the system was supposed to provide representation for the nationalities of the empire, the complicated formula used for elections ensured the election of a German-speaking majority and thus served once again to alienate the ethnic minorities, particularly the Hungarians.

THE *AUSGLEICH* OF 1867 Only when military disaster struck again in the Austro-Prussian War did the Austrians deal with the fiercely nationalistic Hungarians. The result was the negotiated *Ausgleich* (OWSS-glykh), or Compromise, of 1867, which created the Dual Monarchy of Austria-Hungary. Each part of the empire now had a constitution, its own bicameral legislature, its own governmental machinery for domestic affairs, and its own capital (Vienna for Austria and Buda—soon to be united with Pest, across the river—for Hungary). Holding the two states together were a single monarch (Francis Joseph was emperor of Austria and king of Hungary) and a common army, foreign policy, and system of finances. In domestic affairs, the Hungarians had become an independent nation. The *Ausgleich* did not, however, satisfy the other nationalities that made up the multinational Austro-Hungarian Empire (see Map 22.5). The Dual Monarchy simply enabled the German-speaking Austrians and Hungarian Magyars to dominate the minorities, especially the Slavic peoples (Poles, Croats, Czechs, Serbs, Slovaks, Slovenes, and Little Russians), in their respective states. As the Hungarian nationalist Louis Kossuth remarked, "Dualism is the alliance of the conservative, reactionary and any apparently liberal elements in Hungary with those of the Austrian Germans who despise liberty, for the oppression of the other nationalities and races."[6] The nationalities problem persisted until the demise of the empire at the end of World War I.

Imperial Russia

Russia's defeat in the Crimean War at the hands of the British and French revealed the blatant deficiencies behind the facade of absolute power and made it clear even to staunch conservatives that Russia was falling hopelessly behind the western European powers. Tsar Alexander II (1855–1881), who came to power in the midst of the Crimean War, turned his energies to a serious overhaul of the Russian system.

Serfdom was the most burdensome problem in tsarist Russia. The continuing subjugation of millions of peasants to the land and their landlords was an obviously corrupt and failing system. Reduced to antiquated methods of production based on serf labor, Russian landowners were economically pressed and unable to compete with foreign agriculture. The serfs, who formed the backbone of the Russian infantry, were uneducated and consequently increasingly unable to deal with the more complex machines and weapons of war. Then, too, peasant dissatisfaction still led to local peasant revolts that disrupted the countryside. Alexander II seemed to recognize the inevitable: He told a group of Moscow nobles that serfdom could not remain unchanged and that it would be better to abolish serfdom from above than to wait "until it is abolished from below."

State Central Navy Museum, St. Petersburg, Russia//© culture-images/Lebrecht

Emancipation of the Serfs. On March 3, 1861, Tsar Alexander II issued an edict emancipating the Russian serfs. This watercolor by Alexei Kivshenko shows the tsar proclaiming the emancipation.

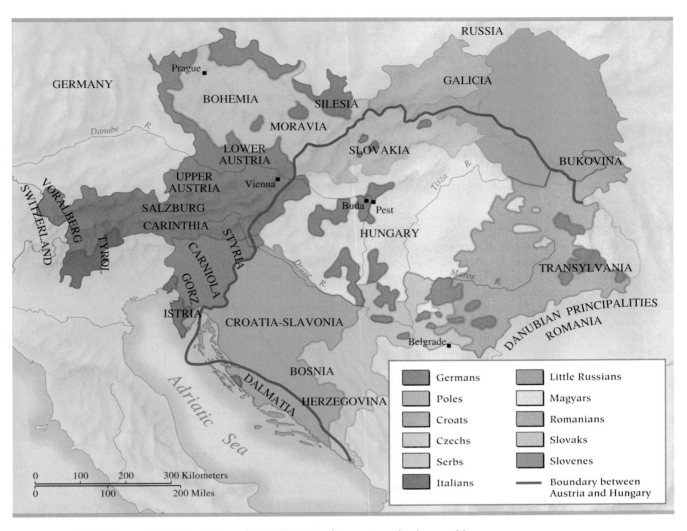

MAP 22.5 **Ethnic Groups in the Dual Monarchy, 1867.** Nationalism continued to be a problem in the Austrian Empire after the suppression of the 1848–1849 revolutions. Military defeats led Emperor Francis Joseph to create the Dual Monarchy, giving Hungary power over its domestic affairs. The demands of other ethnic minorities went largely unmet, however.

Q *Which ethnic group was most widely dispersed throughout the Dual Monarchy?*

ABOLITION OF SERFDOM On March 3, 1861, Alexander issued his emancipation edict (see the box on p. 668). Peasants could now own property, marry as they chose, and bring suits in the law courts. Nevertheless, the benefits of emancipation were limited. The government provided land for the peasants by purchasing it from the landowners, but the landowners often chose to keep the best lands. The Russian peasants soon found that they had inadequate amounts of good arable land to support themselves, a situation that worsened as the peasant population increased rapidly in the second half of the nineteenth century.

Nor were the peasants completely free. The state compensated the landowners for the land given to the peasants, but the peasants were expected to repay the state in long-term installments. To ensure that the payments were made, peasants were subjected to the authority of their *mir* (MEER), or village commune, which was collectively responsible for the land payments to the government. In a very real sense, then, the village commune, not the individual peasants, owned the land the peasants were purchasing. And since the village communes were responsible for the payments, they were reluctant to allow peasants to leave their land. Emancipation, then, led not to a free, landowning peasantry along the Western model but to an unhappy, land-starved peasantry that largely followed the old ways of farming.

OTHER REFORMS Alexander II also attempted other reforms. In 1864, he instituted a system of **zemstvos** (ZEMPST-vohz), or local assemblies, that provided a moderate degree of self-government. Representatives to the zemstvos were to be

EMANCIPATION: SERFS AND SLAVES

ALTHOUGH OVERALL THEIR HISTORIES have been quite different, Russia and the United States shared a common feature in the 1860s: They were the only states in the Western world that still had large enslaved populations (the Russian serfs were virtually slaves). The leaders of both countries issued emancipation proclamations within two years of each other. The first excerpt is taken from the Imperial Decree of March 3, 1861, which freed the Russian serfs. The second excerpt is from Abraham Lincoln's Emancipation Proclamation, issued on January 1, 1863.

Tsar Alexander II, Imperial Decree, March 3, 1861

By the grace of God, we, Alexander II, Emperor and Autocrat of all the Russias, King of Poland, Grand Duke of Finland, etc., to all our faithful subjects, make known:

Called by Divine Providence and by the sacred right of inheritance to the throne of our ancestors, we took a vow in our innermost heart to respond to the mission which is entrusted to us as to surround with our affection and our Imperial solicitude all our faithful subjects of every rank and of every condition, from the warrior, who nobly bears arms for the defense of the country to the humble artisan devoted to the works of industry; from the official in the career of the high offices of the State to the laborer whose plow furrows the soil. . . .

We thus came to the conviction that the work of a serious improvement of the condition of the peasants was a sacred inheritance bequeathed to us by our ancestors, a mission which, in the course of events, Divine providence called upon us to fulfill. . . .

In virtue of the new dispositions above mentioned, the peasants attached to the soil will be invested within a term fixed by the law with all the rights of free cultivators. . . .

At the same time, they are granted the right of purchasing their close, and, with the consent of the proprietors, they may acquire in full property the arable lands and other appurtenances which are allotted to them as a permanent holding. By the acquisition in full property of the quantity of land fixed, the peasants are free from their obligations toward the proprietors for land thus purchased, and they enter definitely into the condition of free peasants-landholders.

President Abraham Lincoln, Emancipation Proclamation, January 1, 1863

Now therefore, I, Abraham Lincoln, President of the United States, by virtue of the power in me vested as Commander-in-Chief of the Army and Navy of the United States in time of actual armed rebellion against the authority and government of the United States, and as a fit and necessary war measure for suppressing such rebellion, do, on this 1st day of January, A.D. 1863, and in accordance with my purpose to do so . . . order and designate as the States and parts of States wherein the people thereof, respectively, are this day in rebellion against the United States the following, to wit:

Arkansas, Texas, Louisiana, . . . Mississippi, Alabama, Florida, Georgia, South Carolina, North Carolina, and Virginia. . . .

And by virtue of the power for the purpose aforesaid, I do order and declare that all persons held as slaves within said designated States and parts of States are, and henceforward shall be free; and that the Executive Government of the United States, including the military and naval authorities thereof, will recognize and maintain the freedom of said persons.

 What changes did Tsar Alexander's emancipation of the serfs initiate in Russia? What effect did Lincoln's Emancipation Proclamation have on the southern "armed rebellion"? What reason did each leader give for his action? Were their actions equally effective?

Sources: *Annual Register* (London: Longman, 1861), p. 207; *U.S. Statutes at Large*, vol. 12 (Washington, DC: Government Printing Office, 1875), pp. 1268–1269.

---

elected from the noble landowners, townspeople, and peasants, but the property-based system of voting gave a distinct advantage to the nobles. Zemstvos were given a limited power to provide public services, such as education, famine relief, and road and bridge maintenance. They hired specialists to improve farming methods and healthcare, bringing medicine and education to the countryside. They could levy taxes to pay for these services, but their efforts were frequently disrupted by bureaucrats, who feared any hint of self-government. The hope of liberal nobles and other social reformers that the zemstvos would be expanded into a national parliament remained unfulfilled. The legal reforms of 1864, which created a regular system of local and provincial courts and a judicial code that accepted the principle of equality before the law, proved successful, however.

Even the autocratic tsar was unable to control the forces he unleashed by his reform program. Reformers wanted more and rapid change; conservatives opposed what they perceived as the tsar's attempts to undermine the basic institutions of Russian society. By 1870, Russia was witnessing an increasing number of reform movements. One of the most popular stemmed from the radical writings of Alexander Herzen (HAYRT-sun) (1812–1870), a Russian exile living in London who used his radical journal, *The Bell*, to extol his belief in "Land and Freedom," and to argue that a Russian peasant must be the chief instrument for social reform. Herzen believed that the peasant village commune could serve as an independent, self-governing body that would form the basis of a new Russia. Russian students and intellectuals who followed Herzen's ideas formed a movement called **populism** whose aim was to create a new society through the revolutionary acts of the peasants. The peasants' lack of interest in these revolutionary ideas, however, led some of the populists to resort to violent means to overthrow tsarist autocracy. One who advocated the use of violence to counteract the violent repression of the tsarist regime was Vera Zasulich (tsah-SOO-likh) (1849–1919). Daughter of a poor nobleman, she worked as a clerk before joining Land and Freedom, an underground populist organization advocating radical reform. In 1878, Zasulich shot and wounded the governor-general of Saint Petersburg. Put on trial, she was acquitted by a sympathetic jury.

Encouraged by Zasulich's successful use of violence against the tsarist regime, another group of radicals, known as the People's Will, succeeded in assassinating Alexander II in 1881. His son and successor, Alexander III (1881–1894), turned against reform and returned to the traditional methods of repression.

Great Britain: The Victorian Age

Like Russia, Britain was not troubled by revolutionary disturbances during 1848, although for quite different reasons. The Reform Act of 1832 had opened the door to political representation for the industrial middle class, and in the 1860s, Britain's liberal parliamentary system demonstrated once more its ability to make both social and political reforms that enabled the country to remain stable and prosperous.

One of the reasons for Britain's stability was its continuing economic growth. After 1850, middle-class prosperity was at last coupled with some improvements for the working classes. Real wages for laborers increased more than 25 percent

between 1850 and 1870. The British feeling of national pride was well reflected in Queen Victoria, whose reign from 1837 to 1901 was the longest in English history. Her sense of duty and moral respectability reflected the attitudes of her age, which has ever since been known as the Victorian Age (see "Film & History" below).

Politically, this was an era of uneasy stability as the aristocratic and upper-middle-class representatives who dominated Parliament blurred party lines by their internal strife and shifting positions. One political figure who stood out was Henry John Temple, Lord Palmerston (1784–1865), who was prime minister for most of the period from 1855 to 1865. Although a

☑ FILM & HISTORY

Watch *The Young Victoria* (2009), an imaginative yet still relatively realistic portrayal of the early struggles of the young woman who became Britain's longest-reigning monarch. Central to the film, however, is the romantic portrayal of the wooing of Victoria by her young German cousin, Prince Albert of Saxe-Coburg-Gotha (Rupert Friend), the nephew of the king of Belgium. The film accurately conveys the close bond and the deep and abiding love that developed between Victoria and Albert.

GK Films/The Kobal Collection

Q *How accurate is the film's portrayal of the young Victoria? As seen in the film, what character traits did the young queen possess that explain her ultimate success?*

Hulton Archive/Getty Images

Queen Victoria and Her Family. Queen Victoria, who ruled Britain from 1837 to 1901, married her German first cousin, Prince Albert of Saxe-Coburg-Gotha, in 1840 and subsequently gave birth to four sons and five daughters, who married into a number of European royal families. When she died at age eighty-one, she had thirty-seven great-grandchildren. Victoria is seated at the center of this 1881 photograph, surrounded by members of her family.

Whig, Palmerston had no strong party loyalty and found it easy to make political compromises. He was not a reformer, however, and opposed expanding the franchise.

DISRAELI AND THE REFORM ACT OF 1867 After Palmerston's death in 1865, the movement for the extension of the franchise only intensified. Although the Whigs (now called the Liberals), who had been responsible for the Reform Act of 1832, talked about passing additional reform legislation, it was actually the Tories (now called the Conservatives) who carried it through. The Tory leader in Parliament, Benjamin Disraeli (diz-RAY-lee) (1804–1881), was a charismatic speaker who was apparently motivated by the desire to win over the newly enfranchised groups to the Conservative Party. Political tensions over voting rights provoked massive demonstrations in 1866, and the Conservatives were forced to act. The Reform Act of 1867 was an important step toward the democratization of Britain. By lowering the monetary requirements for voting (taxes paid or income earned), it by and large enfranchised many male urban workers. The number of voters increased from about 1 million to slightly over 2 million (see Table 22.1). Although Disraeli believed that this would benefit the Conservatives, industrial workers helped produce a huge Liberal victory in 1868.

The extension of the right to vote had an important by-product, as it forced the Liberal and Conservative Parties to organize carefully in order to win over the electorate. Party discipline intensified, and the rivalry between the Liberals and Conservatives became a regular feature of parliamentary life. In large part this was due to the personal and political opposition of the two leaders of these parties, William Gladstone (GLAD-stun) (1809–1898) and Disraeli.

THE LIBERAL POLICIES OF GLADSTONE The first Liberal administration of William Gladstone, from 1868 to 1874, was responsible for a series of impressive reforms. Gladstone was a son of a merchant, whose father had made his fortune through trade with India. Gladstone based his policies on his deep moral and religious outrage at the living conditions of the poor. Legislation and government orders opened civil service positions to competitive exams rather than patronage, introduced the secret ballot for voting, and abolished the practice of purchasing military commissions. The Education Act of 1870 attempted to make elementary schools available for all children (see Chapter 24). These reforms were typically liberal. By eliminating abuses and enabling people with talent to compete fairly, they sought to strengthen the nation and its institutions.

The United States: Slavery and War

By the mid-nineteenth century, the issue of slavery increasingly threatened American national unity. Both North and South had grown dramatically in population during the first half of the nineteenth century. But their development was quite different. The cotton economy and social structure of the South were based on the exploitation of enslaved black Africans and their descendants. The importance of cotton is evident from production figures. In 1810, the South produced a raw cotton crop of 178,000 bales worth $10 million. By 1860, it was generating 4.5 million bales of cotton with a value of $249 million. Fully 93 percent of southern cotton in 1850 was produced by a slave population that had grown dramatically in fifty years. Although new slave imports had been barred in 1808, there were 4 million Afro-American slaves in the South by 1860—four times the number sixty years earlier. The cotton economy and plantation-based slavery were intimately related, and the attempt to maintain them in the course of the first half of the nineteenth century led the South to become increasingly defensive, monolithic, and isolated. At the same time, the rise of an abolitionist movement in the North challenged the southern order and created an "emotional chain reaction" that led to civil war.

By the 1850s, the slavery question had caused Andrew Jackson's Democratic Party to split along North-South lines. The Kansas-Nebraska Act of 1854, which allowed slavery in the Kansas and Nebraska territories to be determined by popular sovereignty, created a firestorm in the North and led to the creation of a new Republican Party. The Republicans were united by antislavery principles and were especially driven by the fear that the "slave power" of the South would attempt to spread the slave system throughout the country.

As polarization over the issue of slavery intensified, compromise became less feasible. When Abraham Lincoln, the man who had said in a speech in Illinois in 1858 that "this government cannot endure permanently half slave and half free," was elected president in November 1860, the die was cast. Lincoln carried only 2 of the 1,109 counties in the South; the Republicans were not even on the ballot in ten southern states. On December 20, 1860, a South Carolina convention voted to repeal the state's ratification of the U.S. Constitution. In February 1861, six more southern states did the same, and a rival nation—the Confederate States of America—was

TABLE 22.1	Expansion of the British Electorate	
	NUMBER OF VOTERS	PERCENTAGE OF TOTAL POPULATION
1831	516,000	2.1
(Reform Act of 1832)		
1833	812,000	3.4
1866	1,364,000	4.7
(Reform Act of 1867)		
1868	2,418,000	8.4
1883	3,152,000	9.0
(Reform Act of 1884)		
1885	5,669,000	16.3

Source: C. Cook and B. Keith, *British Historical Facts, 1830–1900* (Palgrave Macmillan: London: 1975), pp. 115, 232–233.

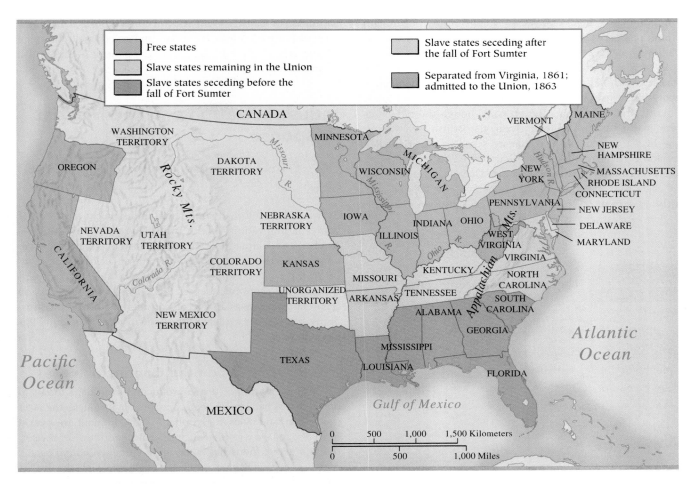

MAP 22.6 **The United States: The West and the Civil War.** By 1860, the North had developed an economy based on industry and commerce, whereas the South had remained a primarily agrarian economy based on black slave labor. The question of the continuance of slavery itself and the expansion of slavery into western territories led to the Civil War, in which the South sought to create an independent country.

Q *Why would its inhabitants want to create a separate state of West Virginia?*

formed (see Map 22.6). In April, fighting erupted between North and South at Fort Sumter near Charleston, South Carolina.

THE CIVIL WAR The American Civil War (1861–1865) was an extraordinarily bloody struggle, a foretaste of the total war to come in the twentieth century. More than 600,000 soldiers died, either in battle or from deadly infectious diseases spawned by filthy camp conditions. Over a period of four years, the Union states of the North mobilized their superior assets and gradually wore down the Confederate forces of the South. As the war dragged on, it had the effect of radicalizing public opinion in the North. What began as a war to save the Union became a war against slavery. On January 1, 1863, Lincoln's Emancipation Proclamation made most of the nation's slaves "forever free" (see the box on p. 668). The increasingly effective Union blockade of the South, combined with a shortage of fighting men, made the Confederate cause desperate by the end of 1864. The final push of Union troops under General Ulysses S. Grant forced General Robert E. Lee's Confederate Army to surrender on April 9, 1865. Although problems lay ahead, the Union victory confirmed that the United States would be "one nation, indivisible."

The Emergence of a Canadian Nation

North of the United States, the process of nation building was also making progress. By the Treaty of Paris in 1763, Canada—or New France, as it was called—passed into the hands of the British. By 1800, most Canadians favored more autonomy, although the colonists disagreed on the form this autonomy should take. Upper Canada (now Ontario) was predominantly English speaking, whereas Lower Canada (now Quebec) was dominated by French Canadians. A dramatic increase in immigration to Canada from Great Britain (almost one million immigrants between 1815 and 1850) also fueled the desire for self-government.

In 1837, a number of Canadian groups rose in rebellion against British authority. Rebels in Lower Canada demanded separation from Britain, creation of a republic, universal male suffrage, and freedom of the press. Although the rebellions were crushed by the following year, the British government now began to seek ways to satisfy some of the Canadian demands. The American Civil War proved to be a turning point. Fearful of American designs on Canada during the war and eager to reduce the costs of maintaining the colonies, the British government finally capitulated to Canadian demands. In 1867, Parliament established the Canadian nation—the

CHRONOLOGY	National States at Midcentury
France	
Louis Napoleon elected president	1848
Coup d'état by Louis Napoleon	1851
Creation of the Second Empire	1852
Emperor Napoleon III	1852–1870
"Authoritarian empire"	1852–1860
Crimean War	1854–1856
Treaty of Paris	1856
"Liberal empire"	1860–1870
Austrian Empire	
Establishment of imperial parliament	1859
Ausgleich, Dual Monarchy	1867
Russia	
Tsar Alexander II	1855–1881
Emancipation edict	1861 (March 3)
Creation of zemstvos and legal reforms	1864
Great Britain	
Queen Victoria	1837–1901
Ministry of Palmerston	1855–1865
Reform Act	1867
First Liberal ministry of William Gladstone	1868–1874
United States	
Kansas-Nebraska Act	1854
Election of Lincoln and secession of South Carolina	1860
Outbreak of Civil War	1861
Surrender of Lee	1865 (April 9)
Canada	
Formation of the Dominion of Canada	1867

Dominion of Canada—with its own constitution. Canada now possessed a parliamentary system and ruled itself, although foreign affairs still remained under the control of the British government.

Industrialization and the Marxist Response

 FOCUS QUESTION: What were the main ideas of Karl Marx?

Between 1850 and 1871, continental industrialization came of age. The innovations of the British Industrial Revolution—mechanized factory production, the use of coal, the steam engine, and the transportation revolution—all became regular features of economic expansion. Although marred periodically by economic depression (1857–1858) or recession (1866–1867), this was an age of considerable economic prosperity, particularly evident in the growth of domestic and foreign markets.

Industrialization on the Continent

The transformation of textile production from hand looms to power looms had largely been completed in Britain by the 1850s (for cotton) and 1860s (for wool). On the Continent, the period from 1850 to 1870 witnessed increased mechanization of the cotton and textile industries, although continental countries still remained behind Britain. By 1870, hand looms had virtually disappeared in Britain, whereas in France there were still 200,000 of them, along with 80,000 power looms. Nevertheless, this period of industrial expansion on the Continent was fueled not so much by textiles as by the growth of railroads. Between 1850 and 1870, European railroad track mileage increased from 14,500 to almost 70,000. The railroads, in turn, stimulated growth in both the iron and coal industries.

Between 1850 and 1870, continental iron industries made the transition from charcoal iron smelting to coke-blast smelting. Despite the dramatic increases in the production of pig iron, the continental countries had not yet come close to surpassing British iron production. In 1870, the British iron industry produced half the world's pig iron—four times as much as Germany and five times as much as France. In the middle decades of the nineteenth century, the textile, mining, and metallurgical industries on the Continent also rapidly converted to the use of the steam engine.

An important factor in the expansion of markets was the elimination of barriers to international trade. Essential international waterways were opened up by the elimination of restrictive tolls. The Danube River in 1857 and the Rhine in 1861, for example, were declared freeways for all ships. The negotiation of trade treaties in the 1860s reduced or eliminated protective tariffs throughout much of western Europe.

Governments also played a role by first allowing and then encouraging the formation of **joint-stock investment**

Opening of the Suez Canal.
Between 1850 and 1871, continental Europeans built railways, bridges, and canals as part of the ever-spreading process of industrialization. A French diplomat, Ferdinand de Lesseps (fer-DEE-nahn duh le-SEPS), was the guiding force behind the construction of the Suez Canal, which provided a link between the Mediterranean and Red Seas. Work on the canal began in 1859 and was completed ten years later. As seen here, an elaborate ceremony marked the opening of the canal. A French vessel led the first convoy of ships through the canal. The banks are lined with curious local inhabitants.

banks. These banks were crucial to continental industrial development because they mobilized enormous capital resources for investment. In the 1850s and 1860s, they were very important in the promotion of railway construction, although railroads were not always a safe investment. During a trip to Spain to examine possibilities for railroad construction, the locomotive manufacturer George Stephenson reported, "I have been a month in the country, but have not seen during the whole of that time enough people of the right sort to fill a single train."[7] His misgivings proved to be well founded. In 1864, the Spanish banking system, which depended largely on investments in railway shares, collapsed.

Before 1870, capitalist factory owners remained largely free to hire labor on their own terms based on market forces. Although workers formed trade unions in an effort to fight for improved working conditions and reasonable wages, the unions tended to represent only a small part of the industrial working class and proved largely ineffective. Real change for the industrial proletariat would come only with the development of socialist parties and socialist trade unions. These emerged after 1870, but the theory that made them possible had already been developed by midcentury in the work of Karl Marx.

Marx and Marxism

The beginnings of Marxism can be traced to the 1848 publication of *The Communist Manifesto*, a short treatise written by two Germans, Karl Marx (1818–1883) and Friedrich Engels (FREE-drikh ENG-ulz) (1820–1895). Marx was born into a relatively prosperous middle-class family in Trier in western

Karl Marx. Karl Marx was a radical journalist who joined with Friedrich Engels to write *The Communist Manifesto*, which proclaimed the ideas of a revolutionary socialism. After the failure of the 1848 revolution in Germany, Marx fled to Britain, where he continued to write and became involved in the work of the first International Working Men's Association.

Germany. He descended from a long line of rabbis, although his father, a lawyer, had become a Protestant to keep his job. Marx enrolled at the University of Bonn in 1835, but his carefree student ways soon led his father to send him to the more serious-minded University of Berlin, where he encountered the ideas of the German philosopher Georg Wilhelm Friedrich Hegel (GAY-awrk VIL-helm FREE-drikh HAY-guhl) (1770–1831). After receiving a Ph.D. in philosophy, Marx planned to teach at a university. Unable to obtain a position because of his professed atheism, Marx decided on a career in journalism and eventually became the editor of a liberal bourgeois newspaper in Cologne in 1842. After the newspaper was suppressed because of his radical views, Marx moved to Paris. There he met Friedrich Engels, who became his lifelong friend and financial patron.

Engels, the son of a wealthy German cotton manufacturer, had worked in Britain at one of his father's factories in Manchester. There he had acquired a firsthand knowledge of what he came to call the "wage slavery" of the British working classes, which he detailed in *The Conditions of the Working Class in England*, a damning indictment of industrial life written in 1844. Engels would contribute his knowledge of actual working conditions as well as monetary assistance to the financially strapped Marx.

In 1847, Marx and Engels joined a tiny group of primarily German socialist revolutionaries known as the Communist League. By this time, both Marx and Engels were enthusiastic advocates of the radical working-class movement and agreed to draft a statement of their ideas for the league. The resulting *Communist Manifesto*, published in German in January 1848, appeared on the eve of the revolutions of 1848. One would think from the opening lines of the preface that the pamphlet alone had caused this revolutionary upheaval: "A spectre is haunting Europe—the spectre of Communism. All the Powers of Old Europe have entered into a holy alliance to exorcise this spectre: Pope and Czar, Metternich and Guizot, French Radicals and German police spies."[8] In fact, *The Communist Manifesto* was known to only a few of Marx's friends. Although its closing words—"The proletarians have nothing to lose but their chains. They have a world to win. WORKING MEN OF ALL COUNTRIES, UNITE!"—were clearly intended to rouse the working classes to action, they passed unnoticed in 1848. The work, however, became one of the most influential political treatises in modern European history.

According to Engels, Marx's ideas were partly a synthesis of French and German thought. The French provided Marx with ample documentation for his assertion that a revolution could totally restructure society. They also provided him with several examples of socialism. From the German idealistic philosophers such as Hegel, Marx took the idea of dialectic: everything evolves, and all change in history is the result of conflicts between antagonistic elements. Marx was particularly impressed by Hegel, but he disagreed with Hegel's belief that history is determined by ideas manifesting themselves in historical forces. Instead, said Marx, the course of history is determined by material forces.

IDEAS OF *THE COMMUNIST MANIFESTO* Marx and Engels began the *Manifesto* with the statement that "the history of all hitherto existing society is the history of class struggles." Throughout history, oppressed and oppressor have "stood in constant opposition to one another." In an earlier struggle, the feudal classes of the Middle Ages were forced to accede to the emerging middle class or bourgeoisie. As the bourgeoisie took control in turn, its ideas became the dominant views of the era, and government became its instrument. Marx and Engels declared, "The executive of the modern State is but a committee for managing the common affairs of the whole bourgeoisie."[9] In other words, the government of the state reflected and defended the interests of the industrial middle class and its allies.

Although bourgeois society had emerged victorious out of the ruins of feudalism, Marx and Engels insisted that it had not triumphed completely. Now once again the members of the bourgeoisie were antagonists in an emerging class struggle, but this time they faced the **proletariat**, or the industrial working class. The struggle would be fierce, but eventually, so Marx and Engels predicted, the workers would overthrow their bourgeois masters. After this victory, the proletariat would form a dictatorship to reorganize the means of production. Then a classless society would emerge, and the state—itself an instrument of the bourgeoisie—would wither away since it no longer represented the interests of a particular class. Class struggles would then be over (see the box on p. 675). Marx believed that the emergence of a classless society would lead to progress in science, technology, and industry and to greater wealth for all.

After the failure of the revolutions of 1848, Marx went to London, where he spent the rest of his life. He continued his writing on political economy, especially his famous work *Das Kapital* (*Capital*), only one volume of which he completed. After his death, his friend Engels edited the remaining volumes.

ORGANIZING THE WORKING CLASS One of the reasons *Das Kapital* was not finished was Marx's preoccupation with organizing the working-class movement. In *The Communist Manifesto*, Marx had defined the communists as "the most advanced and resolute section of the working-class parties of every country." Their advantage was their ability to understand "the line of march, the conditions, and the ultimate general results of the proletarian movement." Marx saw his role in this light and participated enthusiastically in the activities of the International Working Men's Association. Formed in 1864 by British and French trade unionists, this "First International" served as an umbrella organization for working-class interests. Marx was the dominant personality on the organization's General Council and devoted much time to its activities. Internal dissension within the ranks soon damaged the organization, and it failed in 1872. Although it would be revived in 1889, the fate of socialism by that time was in the hands of national socialist parties.

THE CLASSLESS SOCIETY

IN *THE COMMUNIST MANIFESTO*, KARL MARX and Friedrich Engels projected the creation of a classless society as the end product of the struggle between the bourgeoisie and the proletariat. In this selection, they discuss the steps by which that classless society would be reached.

Karl Marx and Friedrich Engels, *The Communist Manifesto*

We have seen . . . that the first step in the revolution by the working class is to raise the proletariat to the position of ruling class. . . . The proletariat will use its political supremacy to wrest, by degrees, all capital from the bourgeoisie, to centralize all instruments of production in the hands of the State, i.e., of the proletariat organized as the ruling class; and to increase the total of productive forces as rapidly as possible.

Of course, in the beginning, this cannot be effected except by means of despotic inroads on the rights of property, and on the conditions of bourgeois production; by means of measures, therefore, which appear economically insufficient and untenable, but which, in the course of the movement, outstrip themselves, necessitate further inroads upon the old social order, and are unavoidable as a means of entirely revolutionizing the mode of production.

These measures will of course be different in different countries.

Nevertheless, in the most advanced countries, the following will be pretty generally applicable:

1. Abolition of property in land and application of all rents of land to public purposes.
2. A heavy progressive or graduated income tax.
3. Abolition of all right of inheritance. . . .
5. Centralization of credit in the hands of the State, by means of a national bank with State capital and an exclusive monopoly.
6. Centralization of the means of communication and transport in the hands of the State.
7. Extension of factories and instruments of production owned by the State. . . .
8. Equal liability of all to labor. Establishment of industrial armies, especially for agriculture.
9. Combination of agriculture with manufacturing industries; gradual abolition of the distinction between town and country, by a more equable distribution of the population over the country.
10. Free education for all children in public schools. Abolition of children's factory labor in its present form. . . .

When, in the course of development, class distinctions have disappeared, and all production has been concentrated in the whole nation, the public power will lose its political character. Political power, properly so called, is merely the organized power of one class for oppressing another. If the proletariat during its contest with the bourgeoisie is compelled, by the force of circumstances, to organize itself as a class, if, by means of a revolution, it makes itself the ruling class, and, as such, sweeps away by force the old conditions of production, then it will, along with these conditions, have swept away the conditions for the existence of class antagonisms and of classes generally, and will thereby have abolished its own supremacy as a class.

In place of the old bourgeois society, with its classes and class antagonisms, we shall have an association, in which the free development of each is the condition for the free development of all.

 How did Marx and Engels define the proletariat? The bourgeoisie? Why did Marxists come to believe that this distinction was paramount for understanding history? What steps did Marx and Engels believe would lead to a classless society? Marx criticized early socialists as utopian and regarded his own socialism as scientific, but do you think that his socialism was also utopian? Why or why not?

Source: Karl Marx and Frederick Engels, *The Communist Manifesto*, trans. Samuel Moore, 1888.

Science and Culture in an Age of Realism

 FOCUS QUESTION: How did the belief that the world should be viewed realistically manifest itself in science, art, and literature in the second half of the nineteenth century?

Between 1850 and 1870, two major intellectual developments are evident: the growth of scientific knowledge, with its rapidly increasing impact on the Western worldview, and the shift from Romanticism and its focus on the inner world of reality to Realism and its turning toward the outer, material world.

A New Age of Science

By the mid-nineteenth century, science was having an ever-greater impact on European life. The Scientific Revolution of the sixteenth and seventeenth centuries had fundamentally transformed the Western worldview and led to a modern, rational approach to the study of the natural world. Even in the eighteenth century, however, these intellectual developments had remained the preserve of an educated elite and resulted in few practical benefits. Moreover, the technical advances of the early Industrial Revolution had depended little on pure science and much more on the practical experiments of technologically oriented amateur inventors. Advances in industrial technology, however, fed an interest in basic scientific research, which in the 1830s and afterward resulted in a rash of basic scientific discoveries that were soon converted into technological improvements that affected everybody.

The development of the steam engine was important in encouraging scientists to work out its theoretical foundations, a preoccupation that led to thermodynamics, the science of the relationship between heat and mechanical energy. The laws of thermodynamics were at the core of nineteenth-century physics. In biology, the Frenchman Louis Pasteur (LWEE pas-TOOR) formulated the germ theory of disease, which had enormous practical applications in the development of modern scientific medical practices (see "A Revolution in Health Care" later in this chapter). In chemistry, in the 1860s, the Russian Dmitri Mendeleyev (di-MEE-tree men-duh-LAY-ef) (1834–1907) classified all the material elements then known on the basis of their atomic weights and provided the systematic foundation for the periodic law. The Englishman Michael Faraday (1791–1867) discovered the phenomenon of electromagnetic induction and put together a primitive generator that laid the foundation for the use of electricity, although economically efficient generators were not built until the 1870s.

The steadily increasing and often dramatic material gains generated by science and technology led to a growing faith in the benefits of science. The popularity of scientific and technological achievement produced a widespread acceptance of the scientific method, based on observation, experiment, and logical analysis, as the only path to objective truth and objective reality. This in turn undermined the faith of many people in religious revelation and truth. It is no accident that the nineteenth century was an age of increasing secularization, particularly evident in the growth of **materialism**, the belief that everything mental, spiritual, or ideal was simply a result of physical forces. Truth was to be found in the concrete material existence of human beings and not, as the Romantics imagined, in revelations gained by feeling or intuitive flashes. The importance of materialism was strikingly evident in the most important scientific event of the nineteenth century, the development of the theory of organic evolution according to natural selection. On the theories of Charles Darwin could be built a picture of humans as material beings that were simply part of the natural world.

Charles Darwin and the Theory of Organic Evolution

Charles Darwin (1809–1882), like many of the great scientists of the nineteenth century, was a scientific amateur. Born into an upper-middle-class family, he studied theology at Cambridge University while pursuing an intense side interest in geology and biology. In 1831, at the age of twenty-two, his hobby became his vocation when he accepted an appointment as a naturalist to study animals and plants on an official Royal Navy scientific expedition aboard the H.M.S. *Beagle*. Its purpose was to survey and study the landmasses of South America and the South

Pacific. Darwin's specific job was to study the structure of various forms of plant and animal life. He was able to observe animals on islands virtually untouched by external influence and compare them with animals on the mainland. As a result, Darwin came to discard the notion of a special creation and to believe that animals evolved over time and in response to their environment. When he returned to Britain, he eventually formulated an explanation for evolution in the principle of **natural selection**, a theory that he presented in 1859 in his celebrated book *On the Origin of Species by Means of Natural Selection*.

THE THEORY OF EVOLUTION The basic idea of Darwin's book was that all plants and animals had evolved over a long period of time from earlier and simpler forms of life, a principle known as **organic evolution**. Darwin was important in explaining how this natural process worked. He took the first step from Thomas Malthus's theory of population: in every species, "many more individuals of each species are born than can possibly survive." This results in a "struggle for existence." Darwin believed that "as more individuals are produced than can possibly survive, there must in every case be a struggle for existence, either one individual with another of the same species, or with the individuals of distinct species, or with the physical conditions of life." Those who succeeded in this struggle for existence had adapted better to their environment, a process made possible by the appearance of "variants." Chance variations that occurred in the process of inheritance enabled some organisms to be more adaptable to the environment than others, a process that Darwin called natural selection: "Owing to this struggle [for existence], variations, however slight, . . . if they be in any degree profitable to the individuals of a species, in their infinitely complex relations to other organic beings and to their physical conditions of life, will tend to the preservation of such individuals, and will generally be inherited by the offspring."[10] Those that were naturally selected for survival ("survival of the fit") survived. The unfit did not and became extinct. The fit who survived propagated and passed on the variations that enabled them to survive until, from Darwin's point of view, a new separate species emerged.

In *On the Origin of Species*, Darwin discussed plant and animal species only. He was not concerned with humans themselves and only later applied his theory of natural selection to humans. In *The Descent of Man*, published in 1871, he argued for the animal origins of human beings: "man is the co-descendant with other mammals of a common progenitor." Humans were not an exception to the rule governing other species (see the box on p. 677).

Darwin's ideas were highly controversial at first. Some people fretted that Darwin's theory made human beings ordinary products of nature rather than unique beings. Others were disturbed by the implications of life as a struggle for survival, of "nature red in tooth and claw." Was there a place in the Darwinian world for moral values? For those who believed in a rational order in the world, Darwin's theory seemed to eliminate purpose and design from the universe. Gradually, however, scientists and other intellectuals began to accept Darwin's theory. In the process, some people even tried to apply Darwin's ideas to society, yet another example of science's increasing prestige.

DARWIN AND THE DESCENT OF MAN

DARWIN PUBLISHED HIS THEORY of organic evolution in 1859, followed twelve years later by *The Descent of Man*, in which he argued that human beings, like other animals, evolved from lower forms of life. The theory provoked a firestorm of criticism, especially from the clergy. One critic described Darwin's theory as a "brutal philosophy—to wit, there is no God, and the ape is our Adam."

Charles Darwin, *The Descent of Man*

The main conclusion here arrived at, and now held by many naturalists, who are well competent to form a sound judgment, is that man is descended from some less highly organized form. The grounds upon which this conclusion rests will never be shaken, for the close similarity between man and the lower animals in embryonic development, as well as in innumerable points of structure and constitution, both of high and of the most trifling importance,—the rudiments which he retains, and the abnormal reversions to which he is occasionally liable,—are facts which cannot be disputed. They have long been known, but until recently they told us nothing with respect to the origin of man. Now when viewed by the light of our knowledge of the whole organic world, their meaning is unmistakable. The great principle of evolution stands up clear and firm, when these groups of facts are considered in connection with others, such as the mutual affinities of the members of the same group, their geographical distribution in past and present times, and their geological succession. It is incredible that all these facts should speak falsely. He who is not content to look, like a savage, at the phenomena of nature as disconnected, cannot any longer believe that man is the work of a separate act of creation. He will be forced to admit that the close resemblance of the embryo of man to that, for instance, of a dog—the construction of his skull, limbs and whole frame on the same plan with that of other mammals, independently of the uses to which the parts may be put—the occasional reappearance of various structures, for instance of several muscles, which man does not normally possess . . . —and a crowd of analogous facts—all point in the plainest manner to the conclusion that man is the co-descendant with other mammals of a common progenitor. . . .

Man may be excused for feeling some pride at having risen, though not through his own exertions, to the very summit of the organic scale; and the fact of his having thus risen, instead of having been aboriginally placed there, may give him hope for a still higher destiny in the distant future. But we are not here concerned with hopes or fears, only with the truth as far as our reason permits us to discover it; and I have given the evidence to the best of my ability. We must, however, acknowledge, as it seems to me, that man with all his noble qualities, with sympathy which feels for the most debased, with benevolence which extends not only to other men but to the humblest living creature, with his god-like intellect which has penetrated into the movements and constitution of the solar system—with all these exalted powers—Man still bears in his bodily frame the indelible stamp of his lowly origin.

 What was Darwin's basic argument in The Descent of Man? *Why did so many object to it? What forces in nineteenth-century European society do you think came together to stimulate Darwin's thinking and publications on this subject?*

Source: Charles Darwin, *The Descent of Man* (New York: Appleton, 1876), pp. 606–607, 619.

A Revolution in Health Care

The application of natural science to the field of medicine in the nineteenth century led to revolutionary breakthroughs in health care. The first steps toward a more scientific basis for medicine were taken in Paris hospitals during the first half of the nineteenth century. Clinical observation, consisting of an active physical examination of patients, was combined with the knowledge gained from detailed autopsies to create a new clinical medicine.

PASTEUR, KOCH, AND GERMS The major breakthrough toward a scientific medicine occurred with the discovery of microorganisms, or germs, as the agents causing disease. The germ theory of disease was largely the work of Louis Pasteur (1822–1895). Pasteur was not a doctor but a chemist who approached medical problems in a scientific fashion. In 1857, Pasteur became director of scientific studies at the École Normale in Paris. There he conducted experiments that proved microorganisms of various kinds were responsible for the process of fermentation, thereby launching the science of bacteriology.

Government and private industry soon perceived the inherent practical value of Pasteur's work. His examination of a disease threatening the wine industry led to the development in 1863 of a process—subsequently known as **pasteurization**—for heating a product to destroy the organisms causing spoilage. In 1877, Pasteur turned his attention to human diseases. His desire to do more than simply identify disease-producing organisms led him in 1885 to a preventive vaccination against rabies. In the 1890s, the principle of vaccination was extended to diphtheria, typhoid fever, cholera, and plague, creating a modern immunological science.

Robert Koch (ROH-berr KAWKH) (1843–1910), a German physician, took the study of bacteriology even further with his work on anthrax and tuberculosis. Koch developed new methods of culturing bacteria and staining microscope slides for examination. In 1882, his work led to the discovery of tuberculosis bacteria. Koch artificially reproduced these bacteria in animals, removed them, and re-infected healthy guinea pigs, successfully demonstrating that a specific bacterium was the causative agent of the disease. Koch and his students identified the specific organisms of at least twenty-one diseases, including gonorrhea, typhoid, pneumonia, meningitis, plague, and cholera.

The work of Pasteur, Koch, and the others who followed them in isolating the specific bacteriological causes of numerous diseases had a far-reaching impact. By providing a rational means of treating and preventing infectious diseases, they transformed the medical world. Both the practice of surgery and public health experienced a renaissance.

NEW SURGICAL PRACTICES Surgeons had already achieved a new professionalism by the end of the eighteenth century (see Chapter 17), but the discovery of germs and the introduction of anesthesia created a new environment for surgical operations. Surgeons had traditionally set broken bones, treated wounds, and amputated limbs, usually as a result of injuries in war. One major obstacle to more successful surgery was the inevitable postoperative infection, which was especially rampant in hospitals.

Joseph Lister (1827–1912), who developed the antiseptic principle, was one of the first people to deal with this problem. Following the work of Pasteur, Lister perceived that bacteria might enter a wound and cause infection. His use of carbolic acid, a newly discovered disinfectant, proved remarkably effective in eliminating infections during surgery. Lister's discoveries dramatically transformed surgery wards, as patients no longer succumbed regularly to what was called "hospital gangrene."

The second great barrier to large-scale surgery stemmed from the inability to lessen the pain of the patient. Alcohol and opiates had been used for centuries during surgical operations, but even their use did not allow unhurried operative maneuvers. After experiments with numerous agents, sulfuric ether was first used successfully in an operation at the Massachusetts General Hospital in 1846 (see the box on p. 679). Within a year, chloroform began to rival ether as an anesthetic agent.

NEW PUBLIC HEALTH MEASURES Although the great discoveries of bacteriology came after the emergence of the first public health movement, they significantly furthered its development. Based on the principle of preventive rather than curative medicine, the urban public health movement of the 1840s and 1850s was largely a response to the cholera epidemic (see Chapter 23). One medical man, in fact, called cholera "our best ally" in furthering public hygiene. The prebacteriological hygiene movement focused on providing clean water, adequate sewage disposal, and less crowded housing conditions. Bacterial discoveries led to greater emphasis on preventive measures, such as the pasteurization of milk, improved purification of water supplies, immunization against disease, and control of waterborne diseases. The public health movement also resulted in the government's hiring medical doctors not just to treat people but to deal with issues of public health as well.

NEW MEDICAL SCHOOLS The new scientific developments also had an important impact on the training of doctors for professional careers in health care. Although there were a few medical schools at the beginning of the nineteenth century, most medical instruction was still done by a system of apprenticeship. In the course of the nineteenth century, virtually every Western country founded new medical schools, but attempts

Thomas Eakins, *The Gross Clinic.* This painting, completed in 1875, shows Dr. Samuel Gross, one of the foremost surgeons in the United States, scalpel in hand, pausing midway in surgery on a young man's leg to discuss the operation with his students in the amphitheater of the Jefferson Medical College. Various tasks are performed by assistant doctors, including the anesthetist, who holds his cloth over the youth's face. Eakins's painting is a realistic portrayal of the new medical science at work.

Philadelphia Museum of Art, PA/ The Bridgeman Art Library

to impose uniform standards on them through certifying bodies met considerable resistance. Entrance requirements were virtually nonexistent, and degrees were granted after several months of lectures. Professional organizations founded around midcentury, such as the British Medical Association in 1832, the American Medical Association in 1847, and the German Doctors' Society in 1872, attempted to elevate professional standards but achieved little until the end of the century. The establishment of the Johns Hopkins University School of Medicine in 1893, with its four-year graded curriculum, clinical training for advanced students, and use of laboratories for teaching purposes, provided a new model for medical training that finally became standard practice in the twentieth century.

WOMEN AND MEDICAL SCHOOLS During most of the nineteenth century, medical schools in Europe and the United States were closed to female students. When Harriet Hunt applied to Harvard Medical School, the male students drew up resolutions that prevented her admission:

Resolved, that no woman of true delicacy would be willing in the presence of men to listen to the discussion of subjects

ANESTHESIA AND MODERN SURGERY

MODERN SCIENTIFIC MEDICINE BECAME established in the nineteenth century. Important to the emergence of modern surgery was the development of anesthetic agents that would block the patient's pain and enable surgeons to complete their surgery without the haste that had characterized earlier operations. This document is an eyewitness account of the first successful use of ether anesthesia, which took place at the Massachusetts General Hospital in 1846.

The First Public Demonstration of Ether Anesthesia, October 16, 1846

The day arrived; the time appointed was noted on the dial, when the patient was led into the operating-room, and Dr. Warren and a board of the most eminent surgeons in the State were gathered around the sufferer. "All is ready—the stillness oppressive." It had been announced "that a test of some preparation was to be made for which the astonishing claim had been made that it would render the person operated upon free from pain." These are the words of Dr. Warren that broke the stillness.

Those present were incredulous, and, as Dr. Morton had not arrived at the time appointed and fifteen minutes had passed, Dr. Warren said, with significant meaning, "I presume he is otherwise engaged." This was followed with a "derisive laugh," and Dr. Warren grasped his knife and was about to proceed with the operation. At that moment Dr. Morton entered a side door, when Dr. Warren turned to him and in a strong voice said, "Well, sir, your patient is ready." In a few minutes he was ready for the surgeon's knife, when Dr. Morton said, "Your patient is ready, sir."

Here the most sublime scene ever witnessed in the operating-room was presented, when the patient placed himself voluntarily upon the table, which was to become the altar of future fame. Not that he did so for the purpose of advancing the science of medicine, nor for the good of his fellow-men, for the act itself was purely a personal and selfish one. He was about to assist in solving a new and important problem of therapeutics, whose benefits were to be given to the whole civilized world, yet wholly unconscious of the sublimity of the occasion or the art he was taking.

That was a supreme moment for a most wonderful discovery, and, had the patient died upon the operation, science would have waited long to discover the hypnotic effects of some other remedy of equal potency and safety, and it may be properly questioned whether chloroform would have come into use as it has at the present time.

The heroic bravery of the man who voluntarily placed himself upon the table, a subject for the surgeon's knife, should be recorded and his name enrolled upon parchment, which should be hung upon the walls of the surgical amphitheater in which the operation was performed. His name was Gilbert Abbott.

The operation was for a congenital tumor on the left side of the neck, extending along the jaw to the maxillary gland and into the mouth, embracing a margin of the tongue. The operation was successful; and when the patient recovered he declared he had suffered no pain. Dr. Warren turned to those present and said, "Gentlemen, this is no humbug."

 In what ways does this account demonstrate the impact that modern science had made on Western society by the middle of the nineteenth century? What forces conjoined to encourage the practical application and refinement of new scientific discoveries?

Source: F. R. Packard, *The History of Medicine in the United States: A Collection of Facts and Figures* (Philadelphia: Lippincott, 1901).

---

that necessarily come under consideration of the students of medicine.

> Resolved, that we object to having the company of any female forced upon us, who is disposed to unsex herself, and to sacrifice her modesty by appearing with men in the lecture room.[11]

Elizabeth Blackwell (1821–1910) achieved the first major breakthrough for women in medicine. Although she had been admitted to the Geneva College of Medicine in New York by mistake, Blackwell's perseverance and intelligence won her the respect of her fellow male students. She received her M.D. in 1849 and eventually established a clinic in New York City.

European women experienced difficulties similar to Blackwell's. In Britain, Elizabeth Garret and Sophia Jex-Blake had to struggle for years before they were finally admitted to the practice of medicine. The unwillingness of medical schools to open their doors to women led to the formation of separate medical schools for women. The Female Medical College of Pennsylvania, established in 1850, was the first in the United States, and the London School of Medicine for Women was founded in 1874. But even after graduation from such institutions, women faced obstacles when they tried to practice as doctors. Many were denied licenses, and hospitals often closed their doors to them. In Britain, Parliament finally capitulated to pressure and passed a bill in 1876 giving women the right to take qualifying examinations. Soon women were entering medical schools in ever-larger numbers. By the 1890s, universities in Great Britain, Sweden, Denmark, Norway, Finland, Russia, and Belgium were admitting women to medical training and practice. Germany and Austria did not do so until after 1900. Even then, medical associations refused to accept women as equals in the medical profession. Women were not given full membership in the American Medical Association until 1915.

Science and the Study of Society

The importance of science in the nineteenth century perhaps made it inevitable that a scientific approach would be applied to the realm of human activity. The attempt to apply the methods of science systematically to the study of society was perhaps most evident in the work of the Frenchman Auguste Comte (ow-GOOST KOHNT) (1798–1857). His major work, *System of Positive Philosophy*, was published between 1837 and 1842 but had its real impact after 1850.

Comte created a system of "positive knowledge" based on a hierarchy of all the sciences and reinforced the Enlightenment's optimism in the potential of science. Mathematics was the foundation on which the physical sciences, earth sciences, and biological sciences were built. At the top was sociology, the science of human society, which for Comte incorporated economics, anthropology, history, and social psychology. Comte saw sociology's task as a difficult one. The discovery of the general laws of society would have to be based on the collection and analysis of data on humans and their social environment. Although his schemes were often complex and dense, Comte played an important role in the growing popularity of science and materialism in the mid-nineteenth century.

Realism in Literature

The belief that the world should be viewed realistically, frequently expressed after 1850, was closely related to the materialistic outlook. The term **Realism** was first employed in 1850 to describe a new style of painting and soon spread to literature.

The literary Realists of the mid-nineteenth century were distinguished by their deliberate rejection of Romanticism. The literary Realists wanted to deal with ordinary characters from real life rather than Romantic heroes in unusual settings. They also sought to avoid flowery and sentimental language by using careful observation and accurate description, an approach that led them to eschew poetry in favor of prose and the novel. Realists often combined their interest in everyday life with a searching examination of social questions. The

Realists were writing for a new bourgeois audience, including upper-middle-class women who were now free from work outside the home.

The leading novelist of the 1850s and 1860s, the Frenchman Gustave Flaubert (goo-STAHV floh-BAYR) (1821–1880), perfected the Realist novel. His *Madame Bovary* (1857) was a straightforward description of barren and sordid small-town life in France (see the box on p. 681). Emma Bovary, a woman of some vitality, is trapped in a marriage to a drab provincial doctor. Influenced by the images of romantic love she has read about in novels, she seeks the same thing for herself in adulterous affairs. Unfulfilled, she is ultimately driven to suicide, unrepentant to the end for her lifestyle. Flaubert's contempt for bourgeois society was evident in his portrayal of middle-class hypocrisy and smugness.

William Thackeray (1811–1863) wrote Britain's prototypical Realist novel, *Vanity Fair: A Novel Without a Hero*, in 1848. Thackeray deliberately flouted the Romantic conventions. A novel, Thackeray said, should convey the sentiment of reality as opposed to a tragedy or poem, "which may be heroical." Perhaps the greatest of the Victorian novelists was Charles Dickens (1812–1870), whose realistic novels focusing on the lower and middle classes in Britain's early industrial age became extraordinarily successful. His descriptions of the urban poor and the brutalization of human life were vividly realistic.

Realism in Art

In the first half of the nineteenth century, the classical school of painting had paralleled Romanticism in art, but both were superseded by the new mood of the mid-nineteenth century. In art, too, Realism became dominant after 1850, although Romanticism was by no means dead. Among the most important characteristics of Realism were a desire to depict the everyday life of ordinary people, be they peasants, workers, or prostitutes; an attempt at photographic realism; and an interest in the natural environment. The French became leaders in Realist painting.

COURBET Gustave Courbet (goo-STAHV koor-BAY) (1819–1877) was the most famous artist of the Realist school. In fact,

Gustave Courbet, *The Stonebreakers.* Realism, largely developed by French painters, aimed at a lifelike portrayal of the daily activities of ordinary people. Gustave Courbet was the most famous of the Realist artists. As is evident in *The Stonebreakers*, he sought to portray things as they really appear. He shows an old road builder and his young assistant in their tattered clothes, engrossed in their dreary work of breaking stones to construct a road. The use of browns and grays helps communicate the drudgery of their task.

FLAUBERT AND AN IMAGE OF BOURGEOIS MARRIAGE

IN *MADAME BOVARY*, GUSTAVE FLAUBERT PORTRAYS the tragic life of Emma Rouault, a farm girl whose hopes of escape from provincial life fail after she marries a doctor, Charles Bovary. After her initial attempts to find happiness in her domestic life, Emma seeks refuge in affairs and extravagant shopping. In this excerpt, Emma expresses her restlessness and growing boredom with her new husband. Flaubert's detailed descriptions of everyday life make *Madame Bovary* one of the seminal works of Realism.

Gustave Flaubert, *Madame Bovary*

If Charles only suspected, if his gaze had even once penetrated her thought, it seemed to her that a sudden abundance would have broken away from her heart, as the fruit falls from a tree when you shake it. But as their life together brought increased physical intimacy, she built up an inner emotional detachment that separated her from him.

Charles's conversation was as flat as a sidewalk, with everyone's ideas walking through it in ordinary dress, arousing neither emotion, nor laughter, nor dreams. He had never been curious, he said, the whole time he was living in Rouen to go see a touring company of Paris actors at the theater. He couldn't swim, or fence, or shoot, and once he couldn't even explain to Emma a term about horseback riding she had come across in a novel.

But a man should know everything, shouldn't he? Excel in many activities, initiate you into the excitements of passion, into life's refinements, into all its mysteries? Yet this man taught nothing, knew nothing, hoped for nothing. He thought she was happy, and she was angry at him for this placid stolidity, for this leaden serenity, for the very happiness she gave to him.

Sometimes she would draw. Charles was always happy watching her lean over her drawing board, squinting in order to see her work better, or rolling little bread pellets between her fingers. As for the piano, the faster her fingers flew over it, the more he marveled. She struck the keys with aplomb and ran from one end of the keyboard to the other without a stop. . . .

On the other hand, Emma did know how to run the house. She sent patients statements of their visits in well-written letters that didn't look like bills. When some neighbor came to dine on Sundays, she managed to offer some tasty dish, would arrange handsome pyramids of greengages on vine leaves, serve fruit preserves on a dish, and even spoke of buying finger bowls for dessert. All this reflected favorably on Bovary.

Charles ended up thinking all the more highly of himself for possessing such a wife. In the living room he pointed with pride to her two small pencil sketches that he had mounted in very large frames and hung against the wallpaper on long green cords. People returning from Mass would see him at his door wearing handsome needlepoint slippers.

He would come home late, at ten o'clock, sometimes at midnight. Then he would want something to eat and Emma would serve him because the maid was asleep. He would remove his coat in order to eat more comfortably. He would report on all the people he had met one after the other, the villages he had been to, the prescriptions he had written, and, content with himself, would eat the remainder of the stew, peel his cheese, bite into an apple, empty the decanter, then go to sleep, lying on his back and snoring. . . .

And yet, in line with the theories she admired, she wanted to give herself up to love. In the moonlight of the garden she would recite all the passionate poetry she knew by heart and would sing melancholy adagios to him with sighs, but she found herself as calm afterward as before and Charles didn't appear more amorous or moved because of it.

After she had several times struck the flint on her heart without eliciting a single spark, incapable as she was of understanding that which she did not feel or of believing things that didn't manifest themselves in conventional forms, she convinced herself without difficulty that Charles's passion no longer offered anything extravagant. His effusions had become routine; he embraced her at certain hours. It was one habit among others, like the established custom of eating dessert after the monotony of dinner.

 What does this passage reveal about bourgeois life in France during the mid-nineteenth century? What does this tell us about the roles of women during this time? How did Charles fail to live up to Emma's expectations of romantic love?

Source: Gustave Flaubert, *Madame Bovary*, trans. M. Marmur (New York: Penguin Press, 2011), pp. 39–43.

the word *Realism* was first coined in 1850 to describe one of his paintings. Courbet reveled in a realistic portrayal of everyday life. Courbet painted subjects that artists had previously deemed unworthy of painting—factory workers, peasants, and the wives of saloon keepers. "I have never seen either angels or goddesses, so I am not interested in painting them," he exclaimed. One of his famous works, *The Stonebreakers*, painted in 1849, shows two road workers, one old and one young, engaged in the deadening work of breaking stones to build a road. Courbet did not romanticize the laborers' work; instead he used browns and grays to convey the dreariness of the task. This representation of human misery was a scandal to those who objected to his "cult of ugliness." To Courbet, no subject was too ordinary, too harsh, or too ugly to interest him.

MILLET Jean-François Millet (ZHAHNH-frahnh-SWAH mil-YEH) (1814–1875) was preoccupied with scenes from rural life, especially peasants laboring in the fields, although his Realism still contained an element of Romantic sentimentality. Millet moved to the countryside near the village of Barbizon in the forest of Fontainbleau to paint his rural subjects in the fields. In *The Gleaners*, his most famous work, three peasant women gather grain in a field, a centuries-old practice that for Millet showed the symbiotic relationship between humans and nature. Millet made landscape and country life an important subject matter for French artists, but he, too, was criticized by his contemporaries for crude subject matter and unorthodox technique.

Music: The Twilight of Romanticism

The mid-nineteenth century witnessed the development of a new group of musicians known as the New German School. They emphasized emotional content rather than abstract form and championed new methods of using music to express literary or pictorial ideas.

LISZT The Hungarian-born composer Franz Liszt (FRAHNTS LIST) (1811–1886) best exemplifies the achievements of the New German School. A child prodigy, he established himself as an outstanding concert artist by the age of twelve. Liszt's performances and his dazzling personality made him the most highly esteemed virtuoso of his age. He has been called the greatest pianist of all time and has been credited with introducing the concept of the modern piano recital.

Jean-François Millet, *The Gleaners*. Jean-François Millet, another prominent French Realist painter, took a special interest in the daily activities of French peasants, although he tended to transform his peasants into heroic figures who dominated their environment. In *The Gleaners*, for example, the three peasant women engaged in the backbreaking work of gathering grain left after the harvest still appear as powerful figures, symbolizing the union of humans with the earth.

Liszt's compositions consist mainly of piano pieces, although he composed in other genres as well, including sacred music. He invented the term *symphonic poem* to refer to his orchestral works, which did not strictly obey traditional forms and were generally based on a literary or pictorial idea. Under the guidance of Liszt and the New German School, Romantic music reached its peak.

WAGNER Although Liszt was an influential mentor to a number of young composers, he was most closely associated with his eventual son-in-law Richard Wagner (RIKH-art VAHG-nur) (1813–1883). Building on the advances made by Liszt and the New German School, Wagner ultimately realized the German desire for a truly national opera. Wagner was not only a composer but also a propagandist and writer in support of his unique conception of dramatic music. Called both the culmination of the Romantic era and the beginning of the avant-garde, Wagner's music may be described as a monumental development in classical music.

Believing that opera is the best form of artistic expression, Wagner transformed opera into "music drama" through his *Gesamtkunstwerk* (guh-ZAHMT-koonst-vayrk) ("total art work"), a musical composition for the theater in which music, acting, dance, poetry, and scenic design are synthesized into a harmonious whole. He abandoned the traditional divisions of opera, which interrupted the dramatic line of the work, and instead used a device called a leitmotiv (LYT-moh-teef), a recurring musical theme in which the human voice combined with the line of the orchestra instead of rising above it. His operas incorporate literally hundreds of leitmotivs in order to convey the story. For his themes, Wagner looked to myth and epic tales from the past. His most ambitious work was *The Ring of the Nibelung*, a series of four music dramas dealing with the mythical gods of the ancient German epic.

CHAPTER SUMMARY

Between 1850 and 1871, the national state became the focus of people's loyalty, and the nations of Europe spent their energies in achieving unification or reform. France attempted to relive its memories of Napoleonic greatness through the election of Louis Napoleon, Napoleon's nephew, as president and later Emperor Napoleon III. Louis Napoleon was one of a new generation of conservative political leaders who were practitioners of *Realpolitik*.

Unification to achieve a national state preoccupied leaders in Italy and Germany. The dreams of Mazzini became a reality when the combined activities of Count Cavour and Giuseppe Garibaldi finally led to the unification of Italy in 1870. Under the guidance of Otto von Bismarck, Prussia engaged in wars with Denmark, Austria, and France before it finally achieved the goal of national unification in 1871.

Reform characterized developments in other Western states. Austria compromised with Hungarian nationalists and created the Dual Monarchy of Austria-Hungary. Russia's defeat in the Crimean War led to reforms under Alexander II, which included the freeing of the Russian serfs. In Great Britain, the pressures of industrialization led to a series of reforms that made the realm of Queen Victoria more democratic. The American Civil War ended with the union of the states preserved and slavery abolished. Canada achieved dominion status from Britain, which included the right to rule itself in domestic affairs.

Political nationalism had emerged during the French revolutionary era and had become a powerful force for change during the first half of the nineteenth century, but its triumph came only after 1850. Associated initially with middle-class liberals, it would have great appeal to the broad masses as well by the end of the century as people created their national "imagined communities." In 1871, however, the political transformations stimulated by the force of nationalism were by no means complete. Significantly large minorities, especially in the multiethnic empires controlled by the Austrians, Turks, and Russians, had not achieved the goal of their own national states. Moreover, the nationalism that had triumphed by 1871 was no longer the nationalism that had been closely identified with liberalism. Liberal nationalists had believed that unified nation-states would preserve individual rights and lead to a greater community of European peoples. Rather than unifying people, however, the new, loud, chauvinistic nationalism of the late nineteenth century divided them as the new national states became embroiled in bitter competition after 1871.

The period between 1850 and 1871 was also characterized by the emergence of Marxian socialism, new advances in science including the laws of thermodynamics, a germ theory of disease, and Darwin's theory of evolution. In the arts, Realism prevailed, evident in the writers and artists who were only too willing to portray realistically the grim world in which they lived.

CHAPTER TIMELINE

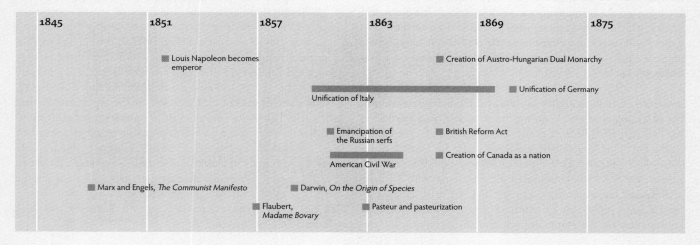

1845	1851	1857	1863	1869	1875

■ Louis Napoleon becomes emperor

■ Creation of Austro-Hungarian Dual Monarchy

Unification of Italy

■ Unification of Germany

■ Emancipation of the Russian serfs

■ British Reform Act

American Civil War

■ Creation of Canada as a nation

■ Marx and Engels, *The Communist Manifesto*

■ Darwin, *On the Origin of Species*

■ Flaubert, *Madame Bovary*

■ Pasteur and pasteurization

CHAPTER REVIEW

Upon Reflection

Q To what extent is it true to say that the forces of liberalism and nationalism triumphed in the Austrian Empire, Russia, and Great Britain between 1850 and 1871?

Q Despite Marx's claim for its scientific basis, can Marxism be viewed primarily as a product of its age? Why or why not?

Q How did Realism differ from Romanticism, and how did Realism reflect the economic and social realities of Europe during the middle decades of the nineteenth century?

Key Terms

Zollverein (p. 661)
Realpolitik (p. 662)
Ausgleich (p. 666)
mir (p. 667)
zemstvos (p. 667)
populism (p. 669)
joint-stock investment banks (p. 672)

proletariat (p. 674)
materialism (p. 676)
natural selection (p. 676)
organic evolution (p. 676)
pasteurization (p. 677)
Realism (p. 680)

Suggestions for Further Reading

GENERAL WORKS In addition to the general works on nineteenth-century Europe cited in Chapter 21, see two general surveys of the midcentury decades: **N. Rich,** *The Age of Nationalism and Reform, 1850–1890,* 2nd ed. (New York, 1980), and **J. A. S. Grenville,** *Europe Reshaped, 1848–1878,* 2nd ed. (London, 2000).

THE FRENCH SECOND EMPIRE For a good introduction to the French Second Empire, see **A. Plessis,** *The Rise and Fall of the Second Empire, 1852–1871,* trans. **J. Mandelbaum** (New York, 1985). The Crimean War and its impact are examined in **O. Figes,** *The Crimean War* (New York, 2010).

UNIFICATION OF ITALY AND GERMANY The unification of Italy can be examined in **B. Derek** and **E. F. Biagini,** *The*

Risorgimento and the Unification of Italy, 2nd ed. (London, 2002). The unification of Germany can be pursued in **W. Carr,** *The Origins of the Wars of German Unification* (New York, 1991). On Bismarck, see **E. Feuchtwanger,** *Bismarck* (London, 2002). On the Franco-Prussian War, see **G. Wawro,** *The Franco-Prussian War* (Cambridge, 2003).

THE NATIONAL STATE For a background discussion of the impact and character of nationalism, see **B. Anderson,** *Imagined Communities: Reflections on the Origins and Spread of Nationalism,* rev. ed. (New York, 2006). On the Austrian Empire, see **R. Okey,** *The Habsburg Monarchy* (New York, 2001), and **R. J. W. Evans,** *Austria, Hungary, and the Habsburgs: Central Europe 1683–1867* (Oxford, 2008). Imperial Russia is covered in **T. Chapman,** *Imperial Russia, 1801–1905* (London, 2001). On Victorian Britain, see **W. L. Arnstein,** *Queen Victoria* (New York, 2005). The definitive one-volume history of the American Civil War is **J. M. McPherson,** *Battle Cry of Freedom: The Civil War Era* (New York, 2003), in the Oxford History of the United States series, but see also the brief history by **G. W. Gallagher** and **J. Waugh,** *The American War: A History of the Civil War Era* (State College, Pa., 2015).

ECONOMIC DEVELOPMENTS AND THOUGHT See the general works on economic development listed in Chapters 20 and 21. On Marx, a standard work is **D. McLellan,** *Karl Marx: A Biography,* 4th ed. (New York, 2006). See also **F. Wheen,** *Karl Marx: A Life* (New York, 2001).

SCIENCE AND CULTURE For an introduction to the intellectual changes of the nineteenth century, see **H. McLeod,** *Secularisation in Western Europe, 1848–1914* (New York, 2000). A detailed biography of Darwin can be found in **J. Bowlby,** *Charles Darwin: A Biography* (London, 1990). On Realism, **J. Malpas,** *Realism* (Cambridge, 1997), is a good introduction.

Notes

1. Quoted in J. F. McMillan, *Napoleon III* (New York, 1991), p. 37.
2. Quoted in R. Gildea, *Barricades and Borders: Europe, 1800–1914,* 2nd ed. (Oxford, 1996), p. 170.
3. Quoted in O. Pflanze, *Bismarck and the Development of Germany: The Period of Unification, 1815–1871* (Princeton, N.J., 1963), p. 60.
4. L. L. Snyder, ed., *Documents of German History* (New Brunswick, N.J., 1958), p. 202.
5. Quoted in Pflanze, *Bismarck and the Development of Germany,* p. 327.
6. Quoted in G. Szabad, *Hungarian Political Trends Between the Revolution and the Compromise, 1849–1867* (Budapest, 1977), p. 163.
7. Quoted in R. Cameron, "Crédit Mobilier and the Economic Development of Europe," *Journal of Political Economy* 61 (1953): 470.
8. Karl Marx and Friedrich Engels, *The Communist Manifesto* (Harmondsworth, U.K., 1967), p. 79.
9. Ibid., pp. 79, 81, 82.
10. Charles Darwin, *On the Origin of Species* (New York, 1872), vol. 1, pp. 77, 79.
11. Quoted in A. Lyons and R. J. Petrucelli, *Medicine: An Illustrated History* (New York, 1978), p. 569.

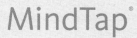 **MindTap**® is a fully online, highly personalized learning experience built upon Cengage Learning content. MindTap combines student learning tools—readings, multimedia, activities, and assessments—into a singular Learning Path that guides students through the course.

MASS SOCIETY IN AN "AGE OF PROGRESS," 1871–1894

The Museum of the City of New York/Art Resource, NY

Coney Island fun

CHAPTER OUTLINE AND FOCUS QUESTIONS

The Growth of Industrial Prosperity

Q What was the Second Industrial Revolution, and what effects did it have on European economic and social life? What roles did socialist parties and trade unions play in improving conditions for the working classes?

The Emergence of a Mass Society

Q What is a mass society, and what were its main characteristics? What role were women expected to play in society and family life in the latter half of the nineteenth century, and how closely did patterns of family life correspond to this ideal?

The National State

Q What general political trends were evident in the nations of western Europe in the last decades of the nineteenth century, and how did these trends differ from the policies pursued in Germany, Austria-Hungary, and Russia?

Critical Thinking

Q *What was the relationship among economic, social, and political developments between 1871 and 1894?*

Connections to Today

Q *In the late nineteenth century, new work opportunities for women emerged, but many middle- and upper-class women were still expected to remain in the home. What are the new opportunities and challenges for women today, and how do they compare with those in the nineteenth century?*

IN THE LATE 1800s, Europe entered a dynamic period of material prosperity. Bringing with it new industries, new sources of energy, and new goods, a second Industrial Revolution transformed the human environment, dazzled Europeans, and led them to believe that their material progress meant human progress. Scientific and technological achievements, many naively believed, would improve humanity's condition and solve all human problems. The doctrine of progress became an article of great faith.

The new urban and industrial world created by the rapid economic changes of the nineteenth century led to the emergence of a mass society by the late nineteenth century. Mass society meant improvements for the lower classes, who benefited from the extension of voting rights, a better standard of living, and education. It also brought mass leisure. New work patterns established the "weekend" as a distinct time of recreation and fun, and new forms of mass transportation—railroads and streetcars—enabled even ordinary workers to make excursions to amusement parks. Coney Island was only 8 miles from central New York City; Blackpool in England was a short train ride from nearby industrial towns. With their Ferris wheels and other daring rides that threw young men and women together, amusement parks offered a whole new world of entertainment. Thanks to the railroad, seaside resorts, once the preserve of the wealthy, became accessible to more people for weekend visits, much to the disgust of one upper-class regular, who complained about the new "day-trippers" who swarmed on the beach, wandering about aimlessly. Enterprising entrepreneurs in resorts like Blackpool welcomed the masses of new visitors, however, and built piers laden with food, drink, and entertainment to serve them.

The coming of mass society also created new roles for the governments of Europe's nation-states. In the early nineteenth century, "nations" functioned as communities of people bound together by common language, traditions, customs, and institutions. By the mid-nineteenth century, however, the "state"—the organized institutions of government—had come to dominate European lives. By 1871, the national states promoted economic growth and mass education, amassed national armies by conscription, and took more responsibility for public health and housing in their cities. By taking these steps, the governments of the national states hoped to foster national unity and national loyalty.

Within many of these national states, the growth of the middle class had led to the triumph of liberal practices: constitutional governments, parliaments, and principles of equality. The period after 1871 also witnessed the growth of political democracy as the right to vote was extended to all adult males; women, though, would still have to fight for the same political rights. With political democracy came a new mass politics and a new mass press. Both would become regular features of the twentieth century.

The Growth of Industrial Prosperity

 FOCUS QUESTIONS: What was the Second Industrial Revolution, and what effects did it have on European economic and social life? What roles did socialist parties and trade unions play in improving conditions for the working classes?

At the heart of Europeans' belief in progress after 1871 was the stunning material growth produced by what historians have called the Second Industrial Revolution. The First Industrial Revolution had given rise to textiles, railroads, iron, and coal. In the second revolution, steel, chemicals, electricity, and petroleum led the way to new industrial frontiers.

New Products

The first major change in industrial development after 1870 was the substitution of steel for iron. New methods of rolling and shaping steel made it useful in the construction of lighter, smaller, and faster machines and engines, as well as railways, ships, and armaments. In 1860, Great Britain, France, Germany, and Belgium together produced 125,000 tons of steel; by 1913, the total was 32 million tons. Whereas in the early 1870s Britain had produced twice as much steel as Germany, by 1910, German production was double that of Great Britain. The United States had surpassed them both in 1890.

CHEMICALS Great Britain also fell behind in the new chemical industry. A change in the method of making soda enabled France and Germany to take the lead in producing the alkaline used in the textile, soap, and paper industries. German

laboratories soon overtook the British in the development of new organic chemical compounds, such as artificial dyes and nitrates for fertilizer. By 1900, German firms had cornered 90 percent of the market for dye-stuffs and also led in the development of photographic plates and film.

ELECTRICITY Electricity was a major new form of energy that proved to be of great value since it could be easily converted into other forms of energy, such as heat, light, and motion, and moved relatively effortlessly through space over wires. In the 1870s, the first commercially practical generators of electrical current were developed. By 1881, Britain had its first public power station. By 1910, hydroelectric power stations and coal-fired steam-generating plants enabled entire districts to be tied in to a single power distribution system that provided a common source of power for homes, shops, and industrial enterprises.

Electricity spawned a whole series of inventions. The lightbulb, invented independently by the American Thomas Edison (1847–1931) and the Briton Joseph Swan (1828–1914), opened homes and cities to illumination by electric lights. A revolution in communications was fostered when Alexander Graham Bell (1847–1922) invented the telephone in 1876 and Guglielmo Marconi (gool-YEL-moh mahr-KOH-nee) (1874–1937) sent the first radio waves across the Atlantic in 1901. Although most electricity was initially used for lighting, it was eventually put to use in transportation. The first electric railway was installed in Berlin in 1879. By the 1880s, streetcars and subways had appeared in major European cities and had begun to replace horse-drawn buses. Electricity also transformed the factory. Conveyor belts, cranes, machines, and machine tools could all be powered by electricity and located anywhere. In the First Industrial Revolution, coal had been the major source of energy. Countries without adequate coal supplies lagged behind in industrialization. Thanks to electricity, they could now enter the industrial age.

THE INTERNAL COMBUSTION ENGINE The development of the internal combustion engine had a similar effect. The first internal combustion engine, fired by gas and air, was produced in 1878. It proved unsuitable for widespread use as a source of power in transportation until the development of liquid fuels—petroleum and its distilled derivatives. An oil-fired engine was made in 1897, and by 1902, the Hamburg-Amerika Line had switched from coal to oil on its new ocean liners. By the end of the nineteenth century, some naval fleets had been converted to oil burners as well.

The development of the internal combustion engine gave rise to the automobile and the airplane. The invention of a light engine by Gottlieb Daimler (GUHT-leeb DYM-lur) (1834–1900) in 1886 was the key to the development of the automobile. In 1900, world production stood at 9,000 cars; by 1906, Americans had overtaken the initial lead of the French. It was an American, Henry Ford (1863–1947), who revolutionized the car industry with the mass production of the Model T. By 1916, Ford's factories were producing 735,000 cars a year. Air transportation began with the Zeppelin (ZEP-puh-lin) airship in 1900. In 1903, at Kitty Hawk, North Carolina, Wilbur and Orville Wright made the first flight in a fixed-wing plane powered by a gasoline engine. It took

An Age of Progress. In the decades after 1871, the Second Industrial Revolution led many Europeans to believe that they were living in an age of progress when most human problems would be solved by scientific achievements. This illustration is taken from a special issue of the *Illustrated London News* celebrating the Diamond Jubilee of Queen Victoria in 1897. On the left are scenes from 1837, when Victoria came to the British throne; on the right are scenes from 1897. The vivid contrast underscored the magazine's conclusion: "The most striking . . . evidence of progress during the reign is the ever increasing speed which the discoveries of physical science have forced into everyday life. Steam and electricity have conquered time and space to a greater extent during the last sixty years than all the preceding six hundred years witnessed."

World War I to stimulate the aircraft industry, however, and the first regular passenger air service was not established until 1919.

New Markets

The growth of industrial production depended on the development of markets for the sale of manufactured goods. After 1870, the best foreign markets were already heavily saturated, forcing Europeans to take a renewed look at their domestic markets. As Europeans were the richest consumers in the world, those markets offered abundant possibilities. The dramatic population increases after 1870 (see "Population Growth" later in this chapter) were accompanied by a steady rise in national incomes. The leading industrialized nations, Britain and Germany, doubled or tripled their national incomes. Between 1850 and 1900, real wages increased by two-thirds in Britain and by one-third in Germany. As the prices of both food and manufactured goods declined due to lower transportation costs, Europeans could spend more on consumer products. Businesses soon perceived the value of using new techniques of mass marketing to sell the consumer goods made possible by the development of the steel and electrical industries. By bringing together a vast array of new products in one place, they created the department store (see the box on p. 689). The desire

to own sewing machines, clocks, bicycles, electric lights, and typewriters rapidly created a new consumer ethic that became a crucial part of the modern economy (see "Mass Consumption" later in this chapter).

TARIFFS AND CARTELS Meanwhile, increased competition for foreign markets and the growing importance of domestic demand led to a reaction against free trade. To many industrial and political leaders, protective **tariffs** guaranteed domestic markets for the products of their own industries. That is why, after a decade of experimentation with free trade in the 1860s, Europeans returned to tariff protection.

During this same period, **cartels** were being formed to decrease competition internally. In a cartel, independent enterprises worked together to control prices and fix production quotas, thereby restraining the kind of competition that led to reduced prices. In the United States, US Steel produced almost two-thirds of the industry's steel, while in Germany the Rhine-Westphalian Coal Syndicate controlled the majority of coal production. Cartels were especially strong in Germany, where banks moved to protect their investments by eliminating the "anarchy of competition." German businesses established cartels in potash, coal, steel, and chemicals.

THE DEPARTMENT STORE AND THE BEGINNINGS OF MASS CONSUMERISM

DOMESTIC MARKETS WERE ESPECIALLY IMPORTANT for the sale of the goods being turned out by Europe's increasing number of industrial plants. Techniques of mass marketing were developed to encourage people to purchase the new consumer goods. The Parisians pioneered the department store, and this selection is taken from a contemporary's account of the growth of these stores in the French capital city.

E. Lavasseur, *On Parisian Department Stores*

It was in the reign of Louis-Philippe that department stores for fashion goods and dresses, extending to material and other clothing, began to be distinguished. The type was already one of the notable developments of the Second Empire; it became one of the most important ones of the Third Republic. These stores have increased in number and several of them have become extremely large. Combining in their different departments all articles of clothing, toilet articles, furniture and many other ranges of goods, it is their special object so to combine all commodities as to attract and satisfy customers who will find conveniently together an assortment of a mass of articles corresponding to all their various needs. They attract customers by permanent display, by free entry into the shops, by periodic exhibitions, by special sales, by fixed prices, and by their ability to deliver the goods purchased to customers' homes, in Paris and to the provinces. Turning themselves into direct intermediaries between the producer and the consumer, even producing sometimes some of their articles in their own workshops, buying at lowest prices because of their large orders and because they are in a position to profit from bargains, working with large sums, and selling to most of their customers for cash only, they can transmit these benefits in lowered selling prices. . . . Taking 5–6 percent on 100 million brings them in more than 20 percent would bring to a firm doing a turnover of 50,000 francs.

The success of these department stores is only possible thanks to the volume of their business and this volume needs considerable capital and a very large turnover. Now capital, having become abundant, is freely combined nowadays in large enterprises, although French capital has the reputation of being more wary of the risks of industry than of State or railway securities. On the other hand, the large urban agglomerations, the ease with which goods can be transported by the railways, the diffusion of some comforts to strata below the middle classes, have all favored these developments.

As example we may cite some figures relating to these stores . . .

Le Louvre . . . did in 1893 a business of 120 million at a profit of 6.4 percent. *Le Bon Marché*, which was a small shop when Mr. Boucicaut entered it in 1852, already did a business of 20 million at the end of the Empire. During the republic its new buildings were erected; Mme. Boucicaut turned it by her will into a kind of cooperative society, with shares and an ingenious organization; turnover reached 150 million in 1893, leaving a profit of 5 percent. . . .

According to the tax records of 1891, these stores in Paris, numbering 12, employed 1,708 persons and were rated on their site values at 2,159,000 francs; the largest had then 542 employees. These same stores had, in 1901, 9,784 employees; one of them over 2,000 and another over 1,600; their site value has doubled (4,089,000 francs).

 Did the invention of department stores respond to or create the new "consumer ethic" in industrialized societies? What was the new turn-of-the-century ethic? According to Lavasseur, what were the positive effects of department stores for Parisian society?

Source: S. Pollard and C. Holmes, *Documents of European Economic History*, vol. 1 (London: Palgrave Macmillan, 1968).

LARGER FACTORIES The formation of cartels was paralleled by a move toward ever-larger manufacturing plants, especially in the iron and steel, machinery, heavy electrical equipment, and chemical industries. Although evident in Britain, France, and Belgium, the trend was most pronounced in Germany. Between 1882 and 1907, the number of people working in German factories with more than one thousand employees rose from 205,000 to 879,000. This growth in the size of industrial plants led to pressure for greater efficiency in factory production at the same time that competition led to demands for greater economy. The result was a desire to streamline or rationalize production as much as possible. One way to accomplish this was to cut labor costs by mechanizing transport within plants, such as using electric cranes to move materials. Even more important, the development of precision tools enabled manufacturers to produce interchangeable parts, which in turn led to the creation of the assembly line for production. First used in the United States for small arms and clocks, the assembly line had moved to Europe by 1850. In the second half of the nineteenth century, it was used primarily in manufacturing nonmilitary goods, such as sewing machines, typewriters, bicycles, and eventually automobiles. Principles of scientific management were also introduced by 1900 to maximize workers' efficiency.

New Patterns in an Industrial Economy

The Second Industrial Revolution played a role in the emergence of basic economic patterns that have characterized much of the modern European economy. Although the period after 1871 has been described as an age of material prosperity, recessions and crises were still very much a part of economic life. Although some historians question the appropriateness of characterizing the period from 1873 to 1895 as a great **depression**, Europeans did experience a series of economic crises during those years. Prices, especially those of agricultural products, fell dramatically. Slumps in the business cycle reduced profits, although recession occurred at different times in different countries. France and Britain, for example, sank into depression in the 1880s while Germany and the United States were recovering from their depression of the 1870s. From 1895 until World War I, however, Europe overall experienced an economic boom and achieved a level of prosperity that encouraged people later to look back to that era as *la belle époque* (lah BEL ay-PUK)—a golden age in European civilization.

GERMAN INDUSTRIAL LEADERSHIP After 1870, Germany replaced Great Britain as the industrial leader of Europe. Within two decades, Germany's superiority was evident in new areas of manufacturing, such as organic chemicals and electrical equipment, and increasingly apparent in its evergreater share of worldwide trade. Why had industrial leadership passed from Britain to Germany?

As a result of its early lead in industrialization, Britain had already established industrial plants and found it more difficult to shift to the new techniques of the Second Industrial Revolution. For example, the British chemist, William Henry Perkin, accidently discovered artificial dyes in 1856 while attempting to synthesize quinine, used for the treatment of malaria. However, it was Germany, not Britain, that capitalized on the discovery; by 1900, almost 90 percent of the world's dyes were made in Germany. As later entrants to the industrial age, the Germans could build the latest and most efficient plants. British entrepreneurs made the situation worse by their tendency to be suspicious of innovations and their reluctance to invest in new plants and industries. As one manufacturer remarked, "One wants to be thoroughly convinced of the superiority of a new method before condemning as useless a large plant that has hitherto done good service."[1] German managers, by contrast, were accustomed to change, and the formation of large cartels encouraged German banks to provide enormous sums for investment. Then, too, unlike the Germans, the British did not encourage formal scientific and technical education.

After 1870, the relationship of science and technology grew closer. Newer fields of industrial activity, such as organic chemistry and electrical engineering, required more scientific knowledge than the commonsense tinkering employed by amateur inventors. Companies began to invest capital in laboratory equipment for their own research or hired scientific consultants for advice. Nowhere was the relationship between science and technology more apparent than in Germany. In 1899, German technical schools were allowed to award doctorate degrees, and by 1900, they were turning out three to four thousand graduates a year. Many of these graduates made their way into industrial firms.

EUROPEAN ECONOMIC ZONES The struggle for economic (and political) supremacy between Great Britain and Germany should not cause us to overlook the other great polarization of

the age. By 1900, Europe was divided into two economic zones. Great Britain, Belgium, France, the Netherlands, Germany, the western part of the Austro-Hungarian Empire, and northern Italy constituted an advanced industrialized core that had a high standard of living, decent systems of transportation, and relatively healthy and educated populations (see Map 23.1). Another part of Europe, the backward and little industrialized area to the south and east, consisting of southern Italy, most of Austria-Hungary, Spain, Portugal, the Balkan kingdoms, and Russia, was still largely agricultural and relegated by the industrial countries to the function of providing food and raw materials. The presence of Romanian oil, Greek olive oil, and Serbian pigs and prunes in western Europe served as reminders of an economic division of Europe that continued well into the twentieth century.

The growth of an industrial economy also led to new patterns for European agriculture. An abundance of grain and lower transportation costs caused the prices of farm commodities to plummet. Some countries responded with tariff barriers against lower-priced foodstuffs. Where agricultural labor was scarce and hence expensive, as in Britain and Germany, landowners introduced machines for threshing and harvesting. Expensive agricultural labor forced Britain to import much of its food; in the early nineteenth century Britain imported 3 percent of its wheat, by 1895, 79 percent of Britain's wheat supply came from abroad. The slump in grain prices also led some countries to specialize in other food products. Denmark, for example, exported eggs, butter, and cheese; sugar beets predominated in Bohemia and northern France, fruit in Mediterranean countries, and wine in Spain and Italy. This age also witnessed the introduction of chemical fertilizers. Large estates could make these adjustments easily, but individual small farmers could not afford them and formed farm cooperatives that provided capital for making improvements and purchasing equipment and fertilizer.

Although the lower grain prices had a negative impact on farmers, the decline in prices benefited many working- and middle-class families in northern Europe. As less money was needed to purchase bread, the consumption of other foods increased during the second half of the nineteenth century. In Germany, meat consumption doubled between 1873 and 1914, and in France bread fell from 20 percent of the diet to 9 percent in 1900.

THE SPREAD OF INDUSTRIALIZATION After 1870, industrialization began to spread beyond western and central Europe and North America. Especially noticeable was its rapid development in Russia (see Chapter 24) and Japan. In Japan, the imperial government that came to power in 1867 (see Chapter 24) took the lead in promoting industry. The government financed industries, built railroads, brought foreign experts to train Japanese employees in new industrial techniques, and instituted a universal educational system based on applied science. By the end of the nineteenth century, Japan had developed key industries in tea, silk, armaments, and shipbuilding (see "Global Perspectives" on p. 692). Workers for these industries came from the large number of people who had abandoned their

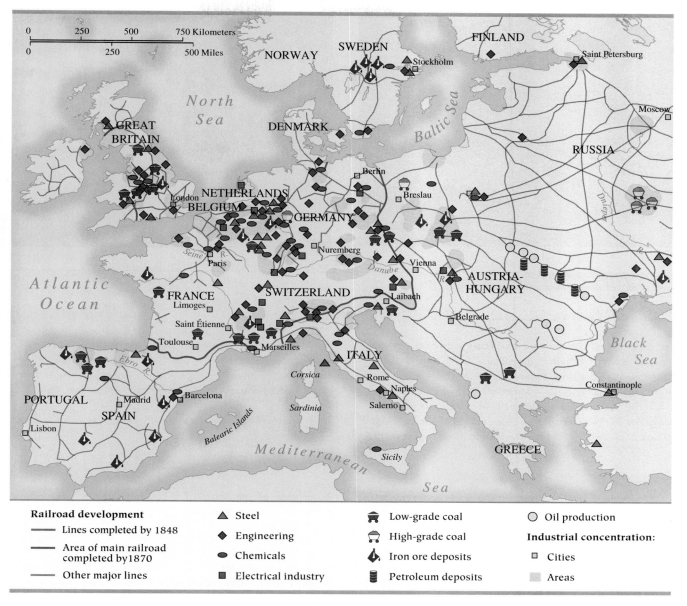

Railroad development

— Lines completed by 1848

— Area of main railroad completed by 1870

— Other major lines

▲ Steel

◆ Engineering

⬭ Chemicals

■ Electrical industry

🛒 Low-grade coal

🛒 High-grade coal

⬧ Iron ore deposits

⬢ Petroleum deposits

○ Oil production

Industrial concentration:

▫ Cities

▨ Areas

MAP 23.1 The Industrial Regions of Europe at the End of the Nineteenth Century. By the end of the nineteenth century, the Second Industrial Revolution—in steelmaking, electricity, petroleum, and chemicals—had spurred substantial economic growth and prosperity in western and central Europe; it also sparked economic and political competition between Great Britain and Germany.

 Look back at Map 20.2. What parts of Europe not industrialized in 1850 had become industrialized in the ensuing decades?

farms due to severe hardships in the countryside and fled to the cities, where they provided an abundant source of cheap labor.

As in Europe during the early decades of the Industrial Revolution, workers toiled for long hours in the coal mines and textile mills, often under horrendous conditions. Reportedly, coal miners employed on a small island in Nagasaki harbor worked naked in temperatures up to 130 degrees Fahrenheit. If they tried to escape, they were shot.

A WORLD ECONOMY The economic developments of the late nineteenth century, combined with the transportation

revolution that saw the growth of marine transport and railroads, also fostered a true world economy. By 1900, Europeans were importing beef and wool from Argentina and Australia, coffee from Brazil, nitrates from Chile, iron ore from Algeria, and sugar from Java. European capital was also invested abroad to develop railways, mines, electrical power plants, and banks. High rates of return, such as 11.3 percent on Latin American banking shares that were floated in London, provided plenty of incentive. Of course, foreign countries also provided markets for the surplus manufactured goods of Europe. With its capital, industries, and

The Granger Collection, New York.

Culver Pictures/The Art Archive/Picture Desk

East and West: Textile Factory Work

THE DEVELOPMENT OF THE FACTORY FORCED workers to adjust to a new system of discipline in which they worked regular hours under close supervision. Shown here is one of the earliest industrial factories in Japan, the Tomioka silk factory, built in the 1870s. Silk was one of the few Japanese products foreigners wanted to buy; thus, the success of silk factories created capital that could be invested in other industries.

Note that although women are doing the work in the factory, the managers are men. That was not unlike their counterparts in the textile factories in Europe and the United States, as seen in this 1890s photograph of garment workers in New York City.

 Are there any similarities or differences between the two factories?

military might, Europe dominated the world economy by the end of the nineteenth century.

Women and Work: New Job Opportunities

The Second Industrial Revolution had an enormous impact on the position of women in the labor market. During the course of the nineteenth century, considerable controversy erupted over a woman's "right to work." Working-class organizations tended to reinforce the underlying ideology of domesticity: women should remain at home to bear and nurture children and should not be allowed in the industrial workforce. Working-class men argued that keeping women out of industrial work would ensure the moral and physical well-being of families. In reality, keeping women out of the industrial workforce simply made it easier to exploit them when they needed income to supplement their husbands' wages or to support their families when their husbands were unemployed. The desperate need to work at times forced women to do marginal work at home or labor as pieceworkers in sweatshops. "Sweating" referred to the subcontracting of piecework usually, but not exclusively, in the tailoring trades; it was done at home since it required few skills or equipment. Pieceworkers were poorly paid and worked long hours. The poorest-paid jobs for the cheapest goods were called "slop work." In this

description of the room of a London slopper, we see how precarious her position was:

> I then directed my steps to the neighborhood of Drury-lane, to see a poor woman who lived in an attic on one of the closest courts in that quarter. On the table was a quarter of an ounce of tea. Observing my eye to rest upon it, she told me it was all she took. "Sugar," she said, "I broke myself of long ago; I couldn't afford it. A cup of tea, a piece of bread, and an onion is generally all I have for my dinner, and sometimes I haven't even an onion, and then I sops my bread."[2]

Often excluded from factories and in need of income, many women had no choice but to work for the pitiful wages of the sweated industries.

WHITE-COLLAR JOBS After 1870, however, new job opportunities for women became available. Although the growth of heavy industry in the mining, metallurgy, engineering, chemicals, and electrical sectors meant fewer jobs for women in manufacturing, the development of larger industrial plants and the expansion of government services created a large number of service or white-collar jobs. The increased demand for white-collar workers at relatively low wages, coupled with a shortage of male workers, led employers to hire women. Big businesses and retail shops needed clerks, typists, secretaries,

New Jobs for Women: The Telephone Exchange. The invention of the telephone in 1876 soon led to its widespread use. As is evident from this illustration of a telephone exchange in New York, most of the telephone operators were women. This was but one of a number of new job opportunities for women created by the Second Industrial Revolution.

file clerks, and salesclerks. The expansion of government services created opportunities for women to be secretaries and telephone operators and to take jobs in health and social services. Compulsory education necessitated more teachers, and the development of modern hospital services opened the way for an increase in nurses.

Many of the new white-collar jobs were unexciting. The work was routine and, except for teaching and nursing, required few skills beyond basic literacy. Although there was little hope for advancement, these jobs had distinct advantages for the daughters of the middle classes and especially the upward-aspiring working classes. For some middle-class women, the new jobs offered freedom from the domestic patterns expected of them. Nevertheless, because middle-class women did not receive an education comparable to that of men, the careers they could pursue were limited. Thus, they found it easier to fill the jobs at the lower end of middle-class occupations, such as teaching and civil service jobs, especially in the postal service.

Most of the new white-collar jobs, however, were filled by working-class women who saw them as an opportunity to escape from the "dirty" work of the lower-class world. Studies in France and Britain indicate that the increase in white-collar jobs did not lead to a rise in the size of the female labor force, but resulted only in a shift from industrial jobs to the white-collar sector of the economy.

PROSTITUTION Despite the new job opportunities, many lower-class women were forced to become prostitutes to survive. The rural, working-class girls who flocked into the cities in search of new opportunities were often naive and vulnerable. Employment was unstable, and wages were low. No longer protected by family or village community and church, some girls faced only one grim alternative—prostitution. In Paris, London, and many other large cities with transient populations, thousands of prostitutes plied their trade. One journalist estimated that there were 60,000 prostitutes in London in 1885 (see the box on p. 694). Most prostitutes were active for only a short time, usually from their late teens through their early twenties. Many eventually joined the regular workforce or married when they could.

In most European countries, prostitution was licensed and regulated by government and municipal authorities. Although the British government provided minimal regulation of prostitution, in the 1870s and 1880s it did attempt to enforce the Contagious Diseases Acts by giving authorities the right to examine prostitutes for venereal disease. Prostitutes found to be infected were confined for some time to special institutions called lock hospitals, where they were given moral instruction. But opposition to the Contagious Diseases Acts soon arose from middle-class female reformers. Their leader was Josephine Butler (1828–1906), who objected to laws that punished women but not men who suffered from venereal disease. Known as the "shrieking sisters" because they discussed sexual matters in public, Butler and her fellow reformers were successful in gaining the repeal of the acts in 1886.

Organizing the Working Classes

In the first half of the nineteenth century, many workers had formed trade unions that had functioned primarily as mutual aid societies (see Chapter 20). In return for a small weekly payment, the unions provided benefits to assist unemployed workers. In the late nineteenth century, the desire to improve their working and living conditions led many industrial workers to form political parties and labor unions, often based on the ideas of Karl Marx (see Chapter 22). One of the most important working-class or socialist parties was formed in Germany in 1875.

SOCIALIST PARTIES Under the direction of its two Marxist leaders, Wilhelm Liebknecht (VIL-helm LEEP-knekht)

PROSTITUTION IN VICTORIAN LONDON

AS CITIES GREW, MANY WOMEN LIVING without family support turned to prostitution to survive. The increase in prostitution led to the spread of venereal disease, prompting public health officials to call for laws against prostitutes. In England, the Contagious Diseases Acts of the 1860s allowed police to arrest women on suspicion of prostitution. Men who frequented prostitutes were rarely charged, however, and a public outcry against the laws led to their repeal and a more sympathetic view of prostitution by the end of the century. In the meantime, journalists such as Henry Mayhew began to interview prostitutes in an effort to understand their plight. This excerpt, which tells the story of a young London prostitute, was published in Mayhew's *London Labour and the London Poor* in 1862.

Henry Mayhew, *London Labour and the London Poor*

The narrative which follows—that of a prostitute, sleeping in the low-lodging houses, where boys and girls are huddled promiscuously together, discloses a system of depravity, atrocity, and enormity, which certainly cannot be paralleled in any nation, however, barbarous, nor in any age, however "dark.". . .

A good-looking girl of sixteen gave me the following awful statement:

"I am an orphan. When I was ten I was sent to service as maid of all-work, in a small tradesman's family. It was a hard place, and my mistress used me very cruelly, beating me often. When I had been in place three weeks, my mother died; my father having died . . . years before. I stood my mistress's ill-treatment for about six months. She beat me with sticks as well as her hands. I was black and blue, and at last I ran away. I got to Mrs. ___, a low lodging-house. I didn't know before that there was such a place. . . .

"During this time I used to see boys and girls from ten and twelve years old sleeping together, but understood nothing wrong. I had never heard of such places before I ran away. I can neither read nor write. My mother was a good woman, and I wish I'd had her to run away to. . . .

"At the month's end, when I was beat out, I met with a young man of fifteen—I myself was going on twelve years old—and he persuaded me to take up with him. I stayed with him three months in the same lodging house, living with him as his wife, though we were mere children, and being true to him. At the three months' end he was taken up for picking pockets, and got six months. I was sorry, for he was kind to me; . . . [I] was forced to go into the streets for a living. I continued walking the streets for three years, sometimes making a good deal of money, sometimes none, feasting one day and starving the next. . . .

"I lodged all this time at a lodging-house in Kent-street. They were all thieves and bad girls. I have known between three and four dozen boys and girls sleep in one room. The beds were filth and full of vermin. . . .

"At the house where I am [now] it is 3*d*. a night; but at Mrs. ___'s it is 1*d*. and 2*d*. a night, and just the same goings on. Many a girl—nearly all of them—goes out into the streets from this penny and two penny house, to get money for their favourite boys by prostitution. If the girl cannot get money she must steal something, or will be beaten by her 'chap' when she comes home."

 What role did poverty play in prostitution? Based on this account, what other options did a poor orphan girl have?

Source: H. Mayhew, *London Labour and the London Poor: Cyclopedia of the Conditions and Earnings of Those That Will Work, Those That Cannot Work, and Those That Will Not Work*, vol. 1 (London: Charles Griffin & Co., 1862), pp. 458–460.

(1826–1900) and August Bebel (ow-GOOST BAY-bul) (1840–1913), the German Social Democratic Party (SPD) espoused revolutionary Marxist rhetoric while organizing itself as a mass political party competing in elections for the Reichstag (the German parliament). Once in the Reichstag, SPD delegates worked to enact legislation to improve the condition of the working class. As August Bebel explained, "Pure negation would not be accepted by the voters. The masses demand that something should be done for today irrespective of what will happen on the morrow."[3] Despite government efforts to destroy it (see "Central and Eastern Europe: Persistence of the Old Order" later in this chapter), the SPD continued to grow. In 1890, it received 1.5 million votes and thirty-five seats in the Reichstag. When it received 4 million votes in the 1912 elections, it became the largest single party in Germany.

Socialist parties also emerged in other European states, although none proved as successful as the German Social Democrats. France had a variety of socialist parties, including a Marxist one. The leader of French socialism, Jean Jaurès (ZHAHNH zhaw-RESS) (1859–1914), was an independent socialist who looked to the French revolutionary tradition rather than Marxism to justify revolutionary socialism. In 1905, the French socialist parties succeeded in unifying themselves into a single, mostly Marxist-oriented socialist party. Social democratic parties on the German model were founded in Belgium, Austria, Hungary, Bulgaria, Poland, Romania, and the Netherlands before 1900. The Marxist Social Democratic Labor Party had been organized in Russia by 1898.

As the socialist parties grew, agitation for an international organization that would strengthen their position against international capitalism also grew. In 1889, leaders of the various socialist parties formed the Second International, which was organized as a loose association of national groups. Although the Second International took some coordinated actions—May

"Proletarians of the World, Unite." To improve their working and living conditions, many industrial workers, inspired by the ideas of Karl Marx, joined working-class or socialist parties. Pictured here is a socialist-sponsored poster that proclaims in German the closing words of *The Communist Manifesto*: "Proletarians of the World, Unite!"

Day (May 1), for example, was made an international labor day to be marked by strikes and mass labor demonstrations—differences often wreaked havoc at the organization's congresses. Two issues proved particularly divisive: revisionism and nationalism.

EVOLUTIONARY SOCIALISM Some Marxists believed in a pure **Marxism** that accepted the imminent collapse of capitalism and the need for socialist ownership of the means of production. The guiding light of the German Social Democrats, August Bebel, confided to another socialist that "every night I go to sleep with the thought that the last hour of bourgeois society strikes soon." Earlier, Bebel had said, "I am convinced that the fulfillment of our aims is so close, that there are few in this hall who will not live to see the day."[4] But a severe challenge to this orthodox Marxist position arose in the form of **evolutionary socialism**, also known as **revisionism**.

Most prominent among the evolutionary socialists was Eduard Bernstein (AY-doo-art BAYRN-shtyn) (1850–1932), a member of the German Social Democratic Party who had spent years in exile in Britain, where he had been influenced by moderate English socialism and the British parliamentary system. In 1899, Bernstein challenged Marxist orthodoxy with his book *Evolutionary Socialism* in which he argued that some of Marx's ideas had turned out to be quite wrong (see the box on p. 696). The capitalist system had not broken down, said Bernstein. Contrary to Marx's assertion, the middle class was actually expanding, not declining. At the same time, the proletariat was not sinking further down; instead, its position was improving as workers experienced a higher standard of living. In the face of this reality, Bernstein discarded Marx's emphasis on class struggle and revolution. The workers, he asserted, must continue to organize in mass political parties and even work together with the other advanced elements in a nation to bring about change. With the extension of the right to vote, workers were in a better position than ever to achieve their aims through democratic channels. Evolution by democratic means, not revolution, would achieve the desired goal of socialism. German and French socialist leaders, as well as the Second International, condemned evolutionary socialism as heresy and opportunism. But many socialist parties, including the German Social Democrats, while spouting revolutionary slogans, followed Bernstein's revisionist, gradualist approach.

THE PROBLEM OF NATIONALISM A second divisive issue for international socialism was nationalism. Marx and Engels had said that "the working men have no country" and that "national differences and antagonisms between peoples are daily more and more vanishing, owing to the development of the bourgeoisie."[5] They proved drastically wrong. Congresses of the Second International passed resolutions in 1907 and 1910 advocating joint action by workers of different countries to avert war but provided no real machinery to implement the resolutions. In truth, socialist parties varied from country to country and remained tied to national concerns and issues. Socialist leaders always worried that in the end, national loyalties might outweigh class loyalties among the masses. When World War I came in 1914, not only the working-class masses but even many of their socialist party leaders supported the war efforts of their national governments. Nationalism had proved a much more powerful force than socialism.

THE ROLE OF TRADE UNIONS Workers also formed trade unions to improve their working conditions. Attempts to organize the workers did not come until after unions had won the right to strike in the 1870s. Strikes proved necessary to achieve the workers' goals. A walkout by female workers in the match industry in 1888 and by dockworkers in London the following year led to the establishment of trade union organizations for both groups. By 1900, 2 million workers were enrolled in British unions, and by the outbreak of World War I, this number had risen to between 3 million and 4 million, although this was still less than one-fifth of the total workforce.

Trade unions failed to develop as quickly on the continent as they had in Britain. In France, the union movement was from the beginning closely tied to socialist ideology. As there were a number of French socialist parties, the socialist trade unions remained badly splintered. Not until 1895 did French unions

THE VOICE OF EVOLUTIONARY SOCIALISM: EDUARD BERNSTEIN

THE GERMAN MARXIST EDUARD BERNSTEIN was regarded as the foremost late-nineteenth-century theorist of Marxist revisionism. In his book *Evolutionary Socialism*, Bernstein argued that Marx had made some fundamental mistakes and that socialists needed to stress cooperation and evolution rather than class conflict and revolution.

Eduard Bernstein, *Evolutionary Socialism*

It has been maintained in a certain quarter that the practical deductions from my treatises would be the abandonment of the conquest of political power by the proletariat organized politically and economically. That is quite an arbitrary deduction, the accuracy of which I altogether deny.

I set myself against the notion that we have to expect shortly a collapse of the bourgeois economy, and that social democracy should be induced by the prospect of such an imminent, great, social catastrophe to adapt its tactics to that assumption. That I maintain most emphatically.

The adherents of this theory of a catastrophe base it especially on the conclusions of the *Communist Manifesto*. This is a mistake in every respect.

The theory which the *Communist Manifesto* sets forth of the evolution of modern society was correct as far as it characterized the general tendencies of that evolution. But it was mistaken in several special deductions, above all in the estimate of the time the evolution would take. . . . But it is evident that if social evolution takes a much greater period of time than was assumed, it must also take upon itself forms and lead to forms that were not foreseen and could not be foreseen then.

Social conditions have not developed to such an acute opposition of things and classes as is depicted in the *Manifesto*. It is not only useless, it is the greatest folly to attempt to conceal this from ourselves. The number of members of the possessing classes is today not smaller but larger. The enormous increase of social wealth is not accompanied by a decreasing number of large capitalists but by an increasing number of capitalists of all degrees. The middle classes change their character but they do not disappear from the social scale. . . .

In all advanced countries we see the privileges of the capitalist bourgeoisie yielding step by step to democratic organizations. Under the influence of this, and driven by the movement of the working classes which is daily becoming stronger, a social reaction has set in against the exploiting tendencies of capital, a counteraction which, although it still proceeds timidly and feebly, yet does exist, and is always drawing more departments of economic life under its influence. Factory legislation, the democratizing of local government, and the extension of its area of work, the freeing of trade unions and systems of cooperative trading from legal restrictions, the consideration of standard conditions of labor in the work undertaken by public authorities—all these characterize this phase of the evolution.

But the more the political organizations of modern nations are democratized the more the needs and opportunities of great political catastrophes are diminished. . . . But is the conquest of political power by the proletariat simply to be by a political catastrophe? Is it to be the appropriation and utilization of the power of the State by the proletariat exclusively against the whole non-proletarian world? . . .

No one has questioned the necessity for the working classes to gain the control of government. The point at issue is between the theory of a social cataclysm and the question whether, with the given social development in Germany and the present advanced state of its working classes in the towns and the country, a sudden catastrophe would be desirable in the interest of the social democracy. I have denied it and deny it again, because in my judgment a greater security for lasting success lies in a steady advance than in the possibilities offered by a catastrophic crash.

 Based on this selection, how would you define evolutionary socialism? What broader forces in nineteenth-century European society came together to promote this type of political thinking?

Source: Eduard Bernstein, *Evolutionary Socialism*, trans E. C. Harney (New York: B. W. Huebsch, 1911), pp. x–xii, xiv.

---

create a national organization called the General Confederation of Labor. Its decentralization and failure to include some of the more important individual unions, however, kept it weak and ineffective.

German trade unions, also closely attached to political parties, were first formed in the 1860s. Although there were liberal trade unions comprising skilled artisans and Catholic or Christian trade unions, the largest German trade unions were those of the socialists. By 1899, even the latter had accepted the practice of collective bargaining with employers. As strikes and collective bargaining achieved successes, German workers were increasingly inclined to forgo revolution for gradual improvements. By 1914, its 3 million members made the German trade union movement the second largest in Europe, after Great Britain's. Almost 85 percent of these 3 million belonged to socialist unions. Trade unions in the rest of Europe had varying degrees of success, but by 1914, they had made considerable progress in bettering the living and working conditions of the laboring classes.

THE ANARCHIST ALTERNATIVE Despite the revolutionary rhetoric, socialist parties and trade unions gradually became less radical in pursuing their goals. Indeed, this lack of revolutionary fervor drove some people from Marxist socialism into

anarchism, a movement that was especially prominent in less industrialized and less democratic countries.

Initially, anarchism was not a violent movement. Early anarchists believed that people were inherently good but had been corrupted by the state and society. True freedom could be achieved only by abolishing the state and all existing social institutions. In the second half of the nineteenth century, however, anarchists in Spain, Portugal, Italy, and Russia began to advocate using radical means to accomplish this goal. The Russian Michael Bakunin (buh-KOON-yun) (1814–1876), for example, believed that small groups of well-trained, fanatical revolutionaries could perpetrate so much violence that the state and all its institutions would disintegrate. To revolutionary anarchists, that would usher in the anarchist golden age. The Russian anarchist Lev Aleshker wrote shortly before his execution:

> Slavery, poverty, weakness, and ignorance—the external fetters of man—will be broken. Man will be at the center of nature. The earth and its products will serve everyone dutifully. Weapons will cease to be a measure of strength and gold a measure of wealth; the strong will be those who are bold and daring in the conquest of nature, and riches will be the things that are useful. Such a world is called "Anarchy." It will have no castles, no place for masters and slaves. Life will be open to all. Everyone will take what he needs—this is the anarchist ideal. And when it comes about, men will live wisely and well. The masses must take part in the construction of this paradise on earth.[6]

After Bakunin's death in 1876, anarchist revolutionaries used assassination as their primary instrument of terror. Their victims included a Russian tsar (1881), a president of the French Republic (1894), the king of Italy (1900), and a president of the United States (1901). Despite anarchist hopes, these states did not collapse.

The Emergence of a Mass Society

 FOCUS QUESTIONS: What is a mass society, and what were its main characteristics? What role were women expected to play in society and family life in the latter half of the nineteenth century, and how closely did patterns of family life correspond to this ideal?

The new patterns of industrial production, mass consumption, and working-class organization that we identify with the Second Industrial Revolution were only one aspect of the new **mass society** that emerged in Europe after 1870. A larger and vastly improved urban environment, new patterns of social structure, gender issues, mass education, and mass leisure were also important features of European society.

Population Growth

The European population increased dramatically between 1850 and 1910, rising from 270 million to more than 460 million by 1910 (see Table 23.1). Between 1850 and 1880, the main cause

TABLE 23.1	European Populations, 1851–1911 (in Thousands)		
	1851	**1881**	**1911**
England and Wales	17,928	25,974	36,070
Scotland	2,889	3,736	4,761
Ireland	6,552	5,175	4,390
France	35,783	37,406	39,192
Germany	33,413	45,234	64,926
Belgium	4,530	5,520	7,424
Netherlands	3,309	4,013	5,858
Denmark	1,415	1,969	2,757
Norway	1,490	1,819	2,392
Sweden	3,471	4,169	5,522
Spain	15,455	16,622	19,927
Portugal	3,844	4,551	5,958
Italy	24,351	28,460	34,671
Switzerland	2,393	2,846	3,753
Austria	17,535	22,144	28,572
Hungary	18,192	15,739	20,886
Russia	68,500	97,700	160,700
Romania	—	4,600	7,000
Bulgaria	—	2,800	4,338
Greece	—	1,679	2,632
Serbia	—	1,700	2,912

Source: B. R. Mitchell, *European Historical Statistics, 1750–1970* (New York: Macmillan, 1975).

of the population increase was a rising birthrate, at least in western Europe, but after 1880, a noticeable decline in death rates largely explains the increase in population. Although the causes of this decline have been debated, two major factors—medical discoveries and environmental conditions—stand out. Some historians have stressed the importance of developments in medical science. Smallpox vaccinations, for example, were compulsory in many European countries by the mid-1850s. More important were improvements in the urban environment in the second half of the nineteenth century that greatly reduced fatalities from such diseases as diarrhea, dysentery, typhoid fever, and cholera, which had been spread through contaminated water supplies and improper elimination of sewage. Improved nutrition also made a significant difference in the health of the population. The increase in agricultural productivity combined with improvements in transportation facilitated the shipment of food supplies from areas of surplus to regions with poor harvests. Better nutrition and food hygiene were especially instrumental in the decline in infant mortality by 1900. The pasteurization of milk reduced intestinal disorders that had been a major cause of infant deaths.

Emigration

Although growing agricultural and industrial prosperity supported an increase in the European population, it could not do so indefinitely, especially in areas that had little industrialization and severe rural overpopulation. Some of the excess labor from underdeveloped areas migrated to the industrial regions of Europe (see Map 23.2). By 1913, more than 400,000 Poles were working in the heavily industrialized Ruhr region of western Germany, and thousands of Italian laborers had migrated to France. The industrialized regions of Europe, however, were not able to absorb the entire surplus population of heavily agricultural regions like southern Italy, Spain, Hungary, and Romania, where the land could not support the growing numbers of people. The booming economies of North America after 1898 and cheap shipping fares after 1900 led to mass emigration from southern and eastern Europe to North America at the beginning of the twentieth century. In 1880, about 500,000 people left Europe each year on average; between 1906 and 1910, annual departures increased to 1.3 million, many of them from southern and eastern Europe. Altogether, between 1846 and 1932, probably 60 million Europeans left Europe, half of them bound for the United States and most of the rest for Canada or Latin America (see Table 23.2).

Other concerns besides economic motives also caused people to leave eastern Europe. Migrants from Austria and Hungary, for example, were not the dominant nationalities, the Germans and Magyars, but mostly their oppressed minorities, such as Poles, Slovaks, Serbs, Croats, Romanians, and Jews. Between 1880 and 1914, some 3.5 million Poles from Russia, Austria, and Germany went to the United States. Jews, who were severely persecuted, constituted 40 percent of the Russian emigrants to the United States between 1900 and 1913 and almost 12 percent of all emigrants to the United States during the first five years of the twentieth century.

Transformation of the Urban Environment

One of the most important consequences of industrialization and the population explosion of the nineteenth century was urbanization. In the course

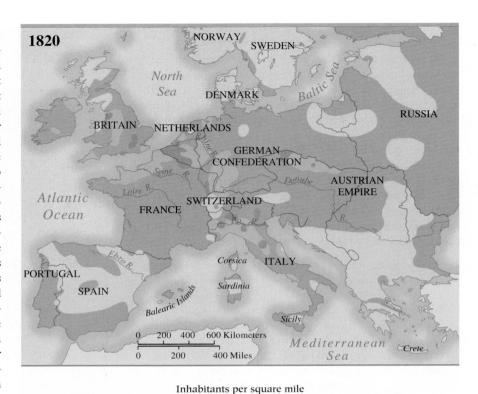

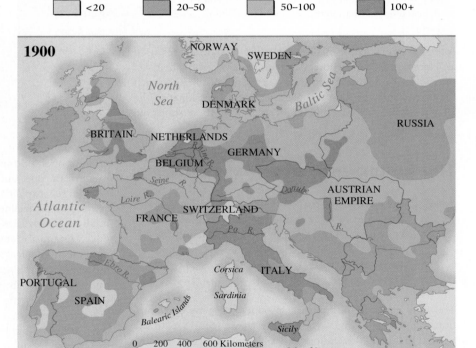

MAP 23.2 Population Growth in Europe, 1820–1900. Europe's population increased steadily throughout the nineteenth century. Advances in medical science, hygiene, nutrition, living conditions, and standards of living help account for the population increase, even though emigration to the United States, South America, and other regions reduced the total growth numbers.

Q *Which regions experienced the greatest population growth between 1820 and 1900, and how can you account for this?*

TABLE 23.2	European Emigration, 1876–1910 (Average Annual Emigration to Non-European Countries per 100,000 Population)						
	1876–1880	1881–1885	1886–1890	1891–1895	1896–1900	1901–1905	1906–1910
Europe	94	196	213	185	147	271	322
Ireland	650	1,422	1,322	988	759	743	662
Great Britain	102	174	162	119	88	127	172
Denmark	157	380	401	338	117	292	275
Norway	432	1,105	819	597	312	903	746
Sweden	301	705	759	587	249	496	347
Germany	108	379	207	163	47	50	44
Belgium	—	—	86	50	23	57	69
Netherlands	32	136	111	76	25	45	58
France	8	14	49	14	13	12	12
Spain	—	280	437	434	446	391	758
Portugal	258	356	423	609	417	464	694
Italy	396	542	754	842	974	1,706	1,938
Austria	48	90	114	182	182	355	469
Hungary	—	92	156	134	205	437	616
Russia	6	13	42	47	32	63	67

Source: R. Gildea, *Barricades and Borders: Europe, 1800–1914* (Oxford: Oxford University Press, 1987), p. 283.

PETER NEWARK'S PICTURES/Private Collection/Bridgeman Images

European Emigration. In the nineteenth century, nearly 34 million people emigrated from Europe to the United States. At mid-century, the average transatlantic voyage took one to three months; the introduction of larger ships and engines decreased the length of the journey by the end of the nineteenth century. However, most passengers could only afford to take the journey in the cramped conditions found in steerage. Shown here in an early twentieth-century photograph are steerage passengers enjoying fresh air as they enter the New York harbor.

of the nineteenth century, urban dwellers came to make up an ever-increasing percentage of the European population. In 1800, they constituted 40 percent of the population in Britain, 25 percent in France and Germany, and only 10 percent in eastern Europe. By 1914, urban inhabitants had increased to 80 percent of the population in Britain, 45 percent in France, 60 percent in Germany, and 30 percent in eastern Europe. The size of cities also expanded dramatically, especially in industrialized countries. In 1800, there were 21 European cities with populations over 100,000; by 1900, there were 147. Between 1800 and 1900, London's population grew from 960,000 to 6.5 million and Berlin's from 172,000 to 2.7 million.

Urban populations grew faster than the general population primarily because of the vast migration from rural areas to cities. People were driven from the countryside to the cities by sheer economic necessity—unemployment, land hunger, and physical want. Urban centers offered something positive as well, usually mass employment in factories and later in service trades and professions. But cities also grew faster in the second half of the nineteenth century because health and living conditions in them were improving.

IMPROVING LIVING CONDITIONS In the 1840s, a number of urban reformers, such as Edwin Chadwick in Britain (see Chapter 20) and Rudolf Virchow (ROO-dulf FEER-khoh) and Solomon Neumann (NOI-mahn) in Germany, had pointed to filthy living conditions as the primary cause of epidemic disease and urged sanitary reforms to correct the problem. Soon legislative acts created boards of health that brought governmental action to bear on public heath issues. Urban medical officers and building inspectors were authorized to inspect dwellings for public health hazards. New building regulations made it more difficult for private contractors to build shoddy housing. The Public Health Act of 1875 in Britain, for example, prohibited the construction of new buildings without running water and an internal drainage system. For the first time in Western history, the role of municipal governments had been expanded to include detailed regulations for the improvement of the living conditions of urban dwellers.

Essential to the public health of the modern European city was the ability to bring clean water into the city and to expel sewage from it. The accomplishment of those two tasks was a major engineering feat in the second half of the nineteenth century. With the construction of dams and reservoirs to store clean water and aqueducts and tunnels to carry it from the countryside to the city and into individual dwellings, people could bathe and drink water that was not contaminated with waterborne diseases such as cholera and typhoid. Regular private baths became accessible to more people as gas heaters in the 1860s and later electric heaters made hot baths possible. The shower had appeared by the 1880s.

The treatment of wastewater was improved by building mammoth underground pipes that carried raw sewage far from the city for disposal. In the late 1860s, a number of German cities began to construct sewer systems. Frankfurt began its program after a lengthy public campaign enlivened by the slogan "From the toilet to the river in half an hour." London devised a system of five enormous sewers that discharged their loads 12 miles from the city, where the waste was chemically treated. Unfortunately, in many places, new underground sewers simply discharged their raw sewage into what soon became highly polluted lakes and rivers. Nevertheless, the development of pure water and sewerage systems dramatically improved the public health of European cities.

Another effort to improve the urban environment involved the creation of public parks to help combat air pollution and provide a place where city dwellers could enjoy fresh air and sunshine. In many cities, reformers pushed for more green space. London devoted more than 190 acres to the creation of Victoria Park in 1842; by 1869, Paris had increased the size of its municipal parks from 47 to 4,500 acres.

HOUSING NEEDS Middle-class reformers who denounced the unsanitary living conditions of the working classes also focused on their housing needs. Overcrowded, disease-ridden slums were viewed as dangerous not only to physical health but also to the political and moral health of the entire nation. V. A. Huber (1800–1869), the foremost early German housing reformer, wrote in 1861, "Certainly it would not be too much to say that the home is the communal embodiment of family life. Thus, the purity of the dwelling is almost as important for the family as is the cleanliness of the body for the individual."[7] To Huber, good housing was a prerequisite for a stable family life and hence a stable society.

Early efforts to attack the housing problem emphasized the middle-class, liberal belief in the efficacy of private enterprise. Reformers such as Huber believed that the construction of model dwellings renting at a reasonable price would force other private landlords to elevate their housing standards. A fine example of this approach was the work of Octavia Hill (1838–1912), granddaughter of a celebrated social reformer (see the box on p. 701). With the financial assistance of a friend, she rehabilitated some old dwellings and constructed new ones to create housing for 3,500 tenants.

As the number and size of cities continued to mushroom, by the 1880s governments came to the conclusion—reluctantly—that private enterprise could not solve the housing crisis. In 1890, a British law empowered local town councils to collect new taxes and construct cheap housing for the working classes. London and Liverpool were the first communities to take advantage of their new powers. Similar activity had been set in motion in Germany by 1900. Everywhere, however, these lukewarm measures failed to do much to meet the real housing needs of the working classes. In housing, as in so many other areas of life in the late nineteenth century, the liberal principle that the government that governs least governs best had simply proved untrue. More and more, governments were stepping into areas of activity that they would never have touched earlier.

REDESIGNING THE CITIES Housing was but one area of urban reconstruction after 1870. As urban populations expanded in the nineteenth century, the older layout, confining the city to a compact area enclosed by defensive walls,

THE HOUSING VENTURE OF OCTAVIA HILL

OCTAVIA HILL WAS A PRACTICAL-MINDED British housing reformer who believed that workers and their families were entitled to happy homes. At the same time, she was convinced that the poor needed guidance and encouragement, not charity. In this selection, she describes her housing venture.

Octavia Hill, *Homes of the London Poor*

About four years ago I was put in possession of three houses in one of the worst courts of Marylebone. Six other houses were bought subsequently. All were crowded with inmates.

The first thing to be done was to put them in decent tenantable order. The set last purchased was a row of cottages facing a bit of desolate ground, occupied with wretched, dilapidated cow-sheds, manure heaps, old timber, and rubbish of every description. The houses were in a most deplorable condition—the plaster was dropping from the walls; on one staircase a pail was placed to catch the rain that fell through the roof. All the staircases were perfectly dark; the banisters were gone, having been burnt as firewood by tenants. The grates, with large holes in them, were falling forward into the rooms. The wash-house, full of lumber belonging to the landlord, was locked up; thus, the inhabitants had to wash clothes, as well as to cook, eat and sleep in their small rooms. The dustbin, standing in the front part of the houses, was accessible to the whole neighborhood, and boys often dragged from it quantities of unseemly objects and spread them over the court. The state of the drainage was in keeping with everything else. The pavement of the back-yard was all broken up, and great puddles stood in it, so that the damp crept up the outer walls. . . .

As soon as I entered into possession, each family had an opportunity of doing better: those who would not pay, or who led clearly immoral lives, were ejected. The rooms they vacated were cleansed; the tenants who showed signs of improvement moved into them, and thus, in turn, an opportunity was obtained for having each room distempered

[painted] and papered. The drains were put in order, a large slate cistern was fixed, the wash-house was cleared of its lumber, and thrown open on stated days to each tenant in turn. The roof, the plaster, the woodwork were repaired; the staircase walls were distempered; new grates were fixed; the layers of paper and rag (black with age) were torn from the windows, and glass put in; out of 192 panes only eight were found unbroken. The yard and footpath were paved.

The rooms, as a rule, were re-let at the same prices at which they had been let before; but tenants with large families were counseled to take two rooms, and for these much less was charged than if let singly: this plan I continue to pursue. In-coming tenants are not allowed to take a decidedly insufficient quantity of room, and no subletting is permitted. . . .

The pecuniary result has been very satisfactory. Five percent has been paid on all the capital invested. A fund for the repayment of capital is accumulating. A liberal allowance has been made for repairs. . . .

My tenants are mostly of a class far below that of mechanics. They are, indeed, of the very poor. And yet, although the gifts they have received have been next to nothing, none of the families who have passed under my care during the whole four years have continued in what is called "distress," except such as have been unwilling to exert themselves. Those who will not exert the necessary self-control cannot avail themselves of the means of livelihood held out to them. But, for those who are willing, some small assistance in the form of work has, from time to time, been provided—not much, but sufficient to keep them from want or despair.

 Did Octavia Hill's housing venture generate financial returns on her initial investment? What benefits did her tenants receive in turn? What feelings and beliefs about the lower classes are evident in Hill's account?

Source: From Octavia Hill, *Homes of the London Poor* (New York: Macmillan, 1875), pp. 15–16, 17–18, 23.

---

seemed restrictive and utterly useless. In the second half of the nineteenth century, many of the old defensive walls—worthless anyway from a military standpoint—were pulled down, and the areas were converted into parks and boulevards. In Vienna, for example, the great boulevards of the Ringstrasse replaced the old medieval walls. While the broad streets served a military purpose—the rapid deployment of troops to crush civil disturbances—they also offered magnificent views of the city hall, the university, and the parliament building, all powerful symbols of middle-class social values.

Like Vienna, many European urban centers were redesigned during the second half of the nineteenth century. The reconstruction of Paris after 1850 by Emperor Napoleon III was perhaps the most famous project and provided a model

for other cities. Paris was reshaped along wide boulevards, twice the width of previous streets and 12 percent longer to accommodate the new city structures. The old residential districts in the central city, many of them working-class slums, were demolished and replaced with town halls, government office buildings, retail stores including the new department stores, museums, cafés, and theaters, all of which provided for the shopping and recreational pleasures of the middle classes.

As cities expanded and entire groups of people were displaced from urban centers by reconstruction, city populations spilled over into the neighboring villages and countrysides, which were soon incorporated into the cities. The construction of streetcar and commuter train lines by the turn of

Paris Transformed. These two photographs, both of L'avenue de l'Opéra, show the degree of destruction that was needed to create the grand boulevards and monuments of late-nineteenth-century Paris. The first photograph was taken in 1865, and the second is from the 1880s. Evident in the latter photograph are the new uniform buildings, gas street lamps, and broad boulevards that linked the city's great cultural sites, such as the Opéra, shown in the background—the most expensive building constructed during the Second Empire.

THE UPPER CLASSES At the top of European society stood a wealthy elite, constituting only 5 percent of the population but controlling between 30 and 40 percent of its wealth. In the course of the nineteenth century, aristocrats coalesced with the most successful industrialists, bankers, and merchants to form this new elite. Big business had produced this group of wealthy **plutocrats**, while aristocrats, whose income from landed estates had declined, invested in railway shares, public utilities, government bonds, and businesses, sometimes on their own estates. Gradually, the greatest fortunes shifted into the hands of the upper middle class. In Great Britain, for example, landed aristocrats constituted 73 percent of the country's millionaires at midcentury, while commercial and financial magnates made up 14 percent. By the period 1900–1914, landowners had declined to 27 percent.

Increasingly, aristocrats and plutocrats fused as the wealthy upper middle class purchased landed estates to join the aristocrats in the pleasures of country living and the aristocrats bought lavish town houses for part-time urban life. Common bonds were also forged when the sons of wealthy middle-class families were admitted to the elite schools dominated by the children of the aristocracy. At Oxford, the landed upper class made up 40 percent of the student body in 1870 but only 15 percent in 1910, while undergraduates from business families went from 7 to 21 percent during the same period. This educated elite, whether aristocratic or middle class in background, assumed leadership roles in government bureaucracies and military hierarchies. Marriage also served to unite the two groups. Daughters of tycoons acquired titles, while aristocratic heirs gained new sources of cash. Wealthy American heiresses were especially in demand. When Consuelo Vanderbilt married the duke of Marlborough, the new duchess brought £2.5 million (approximately $67 million) to her husband.

the century enabled both working-class and middle-class populations to live in their own suburban neighborhoods far removed from their places of work. Cheap, modern transportation essentially separated home and work for many Europeans.

Social Structure of the Mass Society

Despite the improvements in living standards for many people in the last decades of the nineteenth century, wide disparities in wealth continued to exist. While the wealthiest members of the upper middle class were finding their way into the upper classes and the numbers of the middle classes were growing, most Europeans were still in the lower classes.

THE MIDDLE CLASSES The middle classes consisted of a variety of groups. Just below the upper middle class were such traditional groups as professionals in law, medicine, and the civil service as well as moderately well-to-do industrialists and merchants. The industrial expansion of the nineteenth century also added new groups to this segment of the middle class. These included business managers and new professionals, such as the engineers, architects, accountants, and chemists who formed professional associations as the symbols of their newfound importance. A lower middle class of small shopkeepers, traders, manufacturers, and prosperous peasants provided goods and services for the classes above them.

Standing between the lower middle class and the lower classes were new groups of white-collar workers who were the product of the Second Industrial Revolution. They included traveling sales representatives, bookkeepers, bank tellers, telephone operators, department store salesclerks, and secretaries. Although largely propertyless and often paid little more than skilled laborers, these white-collar workers were generally committed to middle-class ideals and optimistic about improving their status. In 1877, the French writer Emilé Zola (ay-MEEL ZOH-lah) (1840–1902) described the social mingling of the classes on a busy morning in a heavily working-class neighborhood:

> [By 8 o'clock] After the workmen came the workgirls— polishers, dressmakers, florists, huddled up in their thin dresses . . . chattering away and giggling, darting keen glances about them . . . Next the office workers passed along, blowing on their fingers and munching their penny rolls as they walked; lean young men in suits a size too small . . . or little old men with toddling gait and faces tired and pale from long hours at the desk, looking at their watches to regulate their speed within a second or two. And finally . . . the local well-to-do . . . taking their stroll in the sun.[8]

The moderately prosperous and successful middle classes shared a common lifestyle and values that dominated nineteenth-century society. The members of the middle class were especially active in preaching their worldview to their children and to the upper and lower classes of their society. This was particularly evident in Victorian Britain, often considered a model of middle-class society. It was the European middle classes who accepted and promulgated the importance of progress and science. They believed in hard work, which they viewed as the primary human good, open to everyone and guaranteed to have positive results. They were also regular churchgoers who believed in the good conduct associated with traditional Christian morality. The middle class was concerned with propriety, the right way of doing things, which gave rise to an incessant number of books aimed at the middle-class market with such titles as *The Habits of Good Society* and *Don't: A Manual of Mistakes and Improprieties More or Less Prevalent in Conduct and Speech*.

THE LOWER CLASSES Almost 80 percent of Europeans belonged to the lower classes. Many of them were landholding peasants, agricultural laborers, and sharecroppers, especially in eastern Europe. This was less true, however, in western and central Europe. About 10 percent of the British population worked in agriculture; in Germany, the figure was 25 percent. Many prosperous, landowning peasants shared the values of the middle class. Military conscription brought peasants into contact with the other groups of society, and state-run elementary schools forced the children of peasants to speak the national dialect and accept national loyalties.

The urban working class consisted of many different groups, including skilled artisans in such trades as cabinetmaking, printing, and jewelry making. Semiskilled laborers, who included such people as carpenters, bricklayers, and many factory workers, earned wages that were about two-thirds of those of highly skilled workers. At the bottom of the working-class hierarchy stood the largest group of workers, the unskilled laborers. They included day laborers, who worked irregularly for very low wages, and large numbers of domestic servants. One out of every seven employed persons in Great Britain in 1900 was a domestic servant. Most were women.

Urban workers did experience a real betterment in the material conditions of their lives after 1871. For one thing, urban improvements meant better living conditions. A rise in real wages, accompanied by a decline in many consumer costs, especially in the 1880s and 1890s, made it possible for workers to buy more than just food and housing. Workers' budgets now provided money for more clothes and even leisure at the same time that strikes and labor agitation were winning shorter (ten-hour) workdays and Saturday afternoons off.

"The Woman Question": The Role of Women

"The woman question" was the catchphrase used to refer to the debate over the role of women in society. In the nineteenth century, women remained legally inferior, economically dependent, and largely defined by family and household roles. Many women still aspired to the ideal of femininity popularized by writers and poets. Alfred, Lord Tennyson's poem *The Princess* expressed it well:

> *Man for the field and woman for the hearth:*
> *Man for the sword and for the needle she:*
> *Man with the head and woman with the heart:*
> *Man to command and woman to obey;*
> *All else confusion.*[9]

Historians have pointed out that this traditional characterization of the sexes, based on gender-defined social roles, was elevated to the status of universal male and female attributes in the nineteenth century, due largely to the impact of the Industrial Revolution on the family. As the chief family wage earners, men worked outside the home, while women were left with the care of the family, for which they were paid nothing. Of course, the ideal did not always match reality, especially for the lower classes, where the need for supplemental income drove women to do sweatwork.

MARRIAGE AND DOMESTICITY Throughout most of the nineteenth century, marriage was viewed as the only honorable career available for most women. Though the middle class glorified the ideal of domesticity (see the box on p. 704), for most women, marriage was a matter of economic necessity. The lack of meaningful work and the lower wages paid to women made it difficult for single women to earn a living. Retiring to convents as in the past was no longer an option; many spinsters who could not find sufficiently remunerative work therefore elected to enter domestic service as live-in servants. Most women chose instead to marry, which was reflected in an increase in marriage rates and a decline in illegitimacy rates in the course of the nineteenth century.

Advice to Women: Two Views

INDUSTRIALIZATION HAD A STRONG IMPACT on middle-class women as gender-based social roles became the norm. Men worked outside the home to support the family, while women provided for the needs of their children and husband at home. In the first selection, *Woman in Her Social and Domestic Character* (1842), Elizabeth Poole Sanford gives advice to middle-class women on their proper role and behavior.

Although a majority of women probably followed the nineteenth-century middle-class ideal of women as keepers of the household and nurturers of husband and children, an increasing number of women fought for the rights of women. The second selection is taken from the third act of Henrik Ibsen's 1879 play *A Doll's House*, in which the character Nora Helmer declares her independence from her husband's control.

Elizabeth Poole Sanford, *Woman in Her Social and Domestic Character*

The changes wrought by Time are many. It influences the opinions of men as familiarity does their feelings; it has a tendency to do away with superstition, and to reduce every thing to its real worth.

It is thus that the sentiment for woman has undergone a change. The romantic passion which once almost deified her is on the decline; and it is by intrinsic qualities that she must now inspire respect. She is no longer the queen of song and the star of chivalry. But if there is less of enthusiasm entertained for her, the sentiment is more rational, and, perhaps, equally sincere; for it is in relation to happiness that she is chiefly appreciated.

And in this respect it is, we must confess, that she is most useful and most important. Domestic life is the chief source of her influence; and the greatest debt society can owe to her is domestic comfort; for happiness is almost an element of virtue; and nothing conduces more to improve the character of men than domestic peace. A woman may make a man's home delightful, and may thus increase his motives for virtuous exertion. She may refine and tranquilize his mind,—may

turn away his anger or allay his grief. Her smile may be the happy influence to gladden his heart, and to disperse the cloud that gathers on his brow. And in proportion to her endeavors to make those around her happy, she will be esteemed and loved. She will secure by her excellence that interest and that regard which she might formerly claim as the privilege of her sex, and will really merit the deference which was then conceded to her as a matter of course. . . .

Perhaps one of the first secrets of her influence is adaptation to the tastes, and sympathy in the feelings, of those around her. This holds true in lesser as well as in graver points. It is in the former, indeed, that the absence of interest in a companion is frequently most disappointing. Where want of congeniality impairs domestic comfort, the fault is generally chargeable on the female side. It is for woman, not for man, to make the sacrifice, especially in indifferent matters. She must, in a certain degree, be plastic herself if she would mold others. . . .

Nothing is so likely to conciliate the affections of the other sex as a feeling that woman looks to them for support and guidance. In proportion as men are themselves superior, they are accessible to this appeal. On the contrary, they never feel interested in one who seems disposed rather to offer than to ask assistance. There is, indeed, something unfeminine in independence. It is contrary to nature, and therefore it offends. We do not like to see a woman affecting tremors, but still less do we like to see her acting the amazon. A really sensible woman feels her dependence. She does what she can; but she is conscious of inferiority, and therefore grateful for support. She knows that she is the weaker vessel, and that as such she should receive honor. In this view, her weakness is an attraction, not a blemish.

In every thing, therefore, that women attempt, they should show their consciousness of dependence. If they are learners, let them evince a teachable spirit; if they give an opinion, let them do it in an unassuming manner. There is something so unpleasant in female self-sufficiency that it not unfrequently deters instead of persuading, and prevents the adoption of advice which the judgment even approves.

BIRTHRATES AND BIRTH CONTROL Birthrates also dropped significantly at this time. A very important factor in the evolution of the modern family was the decline in the number of offspring born to the average woman. The change was not necessarily due to new technological products. Although the invention of vulcanized rubber in the 1840s made possible the production of condoms and diaphragms, they were not widely used as effective contraceptive devices until World War I. Some historians maintain that the change in attitude that led parents to deliberately limit the number of offspring was more important than the method used. Although some historians

attribute increased birth control to more widespread use of coitus interruptus, or male withdrawal before ejaculation, others have emphasized the ability of women to restrict family size through abortion and even infanticide or abandonment. That a change in attitude occurred was apparent in the emergence of a movement to increase awareness of birth control methods. Authorities prosecuted individuals who spread information about contraception for "depraving public morals" but were unable to stop them. In 1882 in Amsterdam, Dr. Aletta Jacob founded Europe's first birth control clinic. Initially, "family planning" was the suggestion of reformers who thought

Henrik Ibsen, *A Doll's House*

NORA (*Pause*): Does anything strike you as we sit here?

HELMER: What should strike me?

NORA: We've been married eight years; does it not strike you that this is the first time we two, you and I, man and wife, have talked together seriously?

HELMER: Seriously? What do you mean, *seriously?*

NORA: For eight whole years, and more—ever since the day we first met—we have never exchanged one serious word about serious things. . . .

HELMER: Why, my dearest Nora, what have you to do with serious things?

NORA: There we have it! You have never understood me. I've had great injustice done to me, Torvald; first by Father, then by you.

HELMER: What! Your father *and* me? We, who have loved you more than all the world!

NORA (*Shaking her head*): You have never loved me. You just found it amusing to think you were in love with me.

HELMER: Nora! What a thing to say!

NORA: Yes, it's true, Torvald. When I was living at home with Father, he told me his opinions and mine were the same. If I had different opinions, I said nothing about them, because he would not have liked it. He used to call me his doll-child and played with me as I played with my dolls. Then I came to live in your house.

HELMER: What a way to speak of our marriage!

NORA (*Undisturbed*): I mean that I passed from Father's hands into yours. You arranged everything to your taste and I got the same tastes as you; or pretended to—I don't know which—both, perhaps; sometimes one, sometimes the other. When I look back on it now, I seem to have been living here like a beggar, on handouts. I lived by performing tricks for you, Torvald. But that was how you wanted it. You and Father have done me a great wrong. It is your fault that my life has come to naught.

HELMER: Why, Nora, how unreasonable and ungrateful! Haven't you been happy here?

NORA: No, never. I thought I was, but I never was.

HELMER: Not—not happy! . . .

NORA: I must stand quite alone if I am ever to know myself and my surroundings; so I cannot stay with you.

HELMER: Nora! Nora!

NORA: I am going at once. I daresay [my friend] Christina will take me in for tonight.

HELMER: You are mad! I shall not allow it! I forbid it!

NORA: It's no use your forbidding me anything now. I shall take with me only what belongs to me; from you I will accept nothing, either now or later.

HELMER: This is madness!

NORA: Tomorrow I shall go home—I mean to what was my home. It will be easier for me to find a job there.

HELMER: On, in your blind inexperience—

NORA: I must try to gain experience, Torvald.

HELMER: Forsake your home, your husband, your children! And you don't consider what the world will say.

NORA: I can't pay attention to that. I only know that I must do it.

HELMER: This is monstrous! Can you forsake your holiest duties?

NORA: What do you consider my holiest duties?

HELMER: Need I tell you that? Your duties to your husband and children.

NORA: I have other duties equally sacred.

HELMER: Impossible! What do you mean?

NORA: My duties toward myself.

HELMER: Before all else you are a wife and a mother.

NORA: That I no longer believe. Before all else I believe I am a human being just as much as you are—or at least that I should try to become one. I know that most people agree with you, Torvald, and that they say so in books. But I can no longer be satisfied with what most people say and what is in books. I must think things out for myself and try to get clear about them.

 According to Elizabeth Sanford, what is the proper role of women? What forces in nineteenth-century European society merged to shape Sanford's understanding of "proper" gender roles? In Ibsen's play, what challenges does Nora Helmer make to Sanford's view of the proper role and behavior of wives? Why is her husband so shocked? Why did Ibsen title this play A Doll's House?

Sources: Elizabeth Poole Sanford, *Woman in Her Social and Domestic Character* (Boston: Otis, Broaders & Co., 1842), pp. 5–7, 15–16; Henrik Ibsen, *A Doll's House*, in W. D. Camp, *Roots of Western Civilization* (New York: Wiley, 1983).

---

that the problem of poverty could be solved by reducing the number of children among the lower classes. In fact, the practice spread quickly among the propertied classes, rather than among the impoverished, a good reminder that considerable differences still remained between middle-class and working-class families.

THE MIDDLE-CLASS FAMILY The family was the central institution of middle-class life (see "Images of Everyday Life" on p. 706). Men provided the family income, while women focused on household and child care. The use of domestic servants in many middle-class homes, made possible by an abundant supply of cheap labor, reduced the amount of time middle-class women had to spend on household work. At the same time, by limiting the number of children in the family, mothers could devote more time to child care and domestic leisure. The idea that leisure should be used for constructive purposes supported and encouraged the cult of middle-class domesticity.

The middle-class family fostered an ideal of togetherness. The Victorians created the family Christmas with its yule log, Christmas tree, songs, and exchange of gifts. In the United States, Fourth of July celebrations changed from drunken revels

The Middle-Class Family

NINETEENTH-CENTURY MIDDLE-CLASS MORALISTS considered the family the fundamental pillar of a healthy society. The family was a crucial institution in middle-class life, and togetherness constituted one of the important ideals of the middle-class family. The painting below by William P. Frith, titled *Many Happy Returns of the Day*, shows grandparents, parents, and children taking part in a family birthday celebration for a little girl. The servant at the left holds the presents for the little girl. New games and toys also appeared for middle-class children. The illustration on the bottom right shows a middle class family taking a vacation at the beach in France. New train lines and cheaper fares allowed for families to vacation together. The new freedom found playing at the beach would eventually alter the conservative fashions of the late nineteenth century. The final illustration shows the cover of *The Scout*, a magazine of the scouting movement founded by Robert Baden-Powell. The cover shows one of the new scouts wearing his uniform and watching a ship at sea, an activity that could later have military value in time of war.

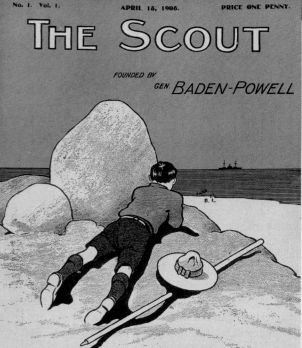

to family picnics by the 1850s. The education of middle-class females in domestic crafts, singing, and piano playing prepared them for their function of providing a proper environment for home recreation.

The new domestic ideal had an impact on child raising and children's play. Late-eighteenth-century thought, beginning with Rousseau, had encouraged a new view of children as unique beings, not small adults, which had carried over into the nineteenth century. They were entitled to a long childhood involved in activities with other children their own age. The early environment in which they were raised, it was thought, would determine how they turned out. And mothers were seen as the most important force in protecting children from the harmful influences of the adult world. New children's games and toys, including mass-produced dolls for girls, appeared in middle-class homes. The middle-class emphasis on the functional value of knowledge was also evident in these games. One advice manual maintained that young children should learn checkers because it called forth the resources of the mind in the "most gentle as well as the most successful manner."

Since middle-class sons were expected to follow careers like their father's, they were sent to schools where they were kept separate from the rest of society until the age of sixteen or seventeen. The schools used sport to "toughen boys up," and their leisure activities centered around both national military concerns and character building. This combination was especially evident in the establishment of the Boy Scouts in Britain in 1908. Boy Scouts provided organized recreation for boys between the ages of twelve and eighteen; adventure was combined with the discipline of earning merit badges and ranks in such a way as to instill ideals of patriotism, self-sacrifice, and masculinity.

The emphasis on manliness stemmed not only from military concerns but also from conceptions of masculinity formed during the late nineteenth century as the middle and upper classes looked for ways to control sexual licentiousness in the form of venereal disease or prostitution. Boy Scouts and *The Scout* magazine promoted an image of manliness with stories of youthful heroes who demonstrated their self-control by conquering the challenges of the wilderness. Thus, the Boy Scouts sought to reinforce Victorian and Edwardian codes of masculinity in an effort to counter the possible dangers that female domination of the home posed for male development. As one scout leader wrote, "The REAL Boy Scout is not a sissy. [He] adores his mother [but] is not hitched to [her] apron strings."

There was little organized recreational activity of this type for girls, although Robert Baden-Powell (BAD-un-POW-ul) (1857–1941), the founder of the Boy Scouts, did encourage his sister to establish a girls' division as an afterthought.

Its goal is evident from Agnes Baden-Powell's comment that "you do not want to make tomboys of refined girls, yet you want to attract, and thus raise, the slum girl from the gutter. The main object is to give them all the ability to be better mothers and Guides to the next generation."[10] Despite her comment, most organizations of this kind were for middle-class children, although some reformers tried to establish boys' clubs for working-class youths to reform them.

The new ideal of the middle-class woman as nurturing mother and wife who "determined the atmosphere of the household" through her character, not her work, frequently did not correspond to reality. In France, Germany, and even mid-Victorian Britain, relatively few families could actually afford to hire a host of servants. More often, middle-class families had one servant, usually a young working-class or country girl not used to middle-class lifestyles. Women, then, were often forced to work quite hard to maintain the expected appearance of the well-ordered household. A German housekeeping manual makes this evident:

> It often happens that even high-ranking ladies help at home with housework, and particularly with kitchen chores, scrubbing, etc., so that, above all, the hands have good cause to become very rough, hard, and calloused. When these ladies appear in society, they are extremely upset at having such rough-looking hands. In order to perform the hardest and most ordinary chores . . . and, at the same time, to keep a soft hand like those fine ladies who have no heavier work to do than embroidering and sewing, always keep a piece of fresh bacon, rub your hands with it just before bedtime, and you will fully achieve your goal. You will, as a result, have the inconvenience of having to sleep with gloves on, in order not to soil the bed.[11]

Thus, many middle-class wives were caught in a no-win situation. Often, for the sake of the advancement of her husband's career, she was expected to maintain in public the image of the "idle" wife, freed from demeaning physical labor and able to pass her days in ornamental pursuits. In truth, it was frequently the middle-class woman who paid the price for this facade in a life of unpaid work, carefully managing the family budget and participating in housework that could never be done by only one servant girl. As one historian has argued, the reality of many middle-class women's lives was that what appeared at first to be idleness was really "difficult and tiresome work."

THE WORKING-CLASS FAMILY Hard work was, of course, standard fare for women in working-class families. Daughters in working-class families were expected to work until they married; even after marriage, they often did piecework at home to help support the family. For the children of the working classes, childhood was over by the age of nine or ten, when they became apprentices or were employed in odd jobs.

Between 1890 and 1914, however, family patterns among the working class began to change. High-paying jobs in heavy industry and improvements in the standard of living made it possible for working-class families to depend on the income of husbands and the wages of grown children. By the early twentieth century, some working-class mothers could afford to stay at home, following the pattern of middle-class women. Women's work patterns varied by country, however; married French women were twice as likely to work outside the home as their British counterparts. In France, married women made up 20 percent of the nonagricultural labor force and contributed almost 15 percent of total family income. Nevertheless, working-class women were increasingly able to focus more on family life and to work only sporadically to supplement the family income.

The working classes also followed the middle classes in limiting the size of their families. Children began to be viewed as dependents rather than as potential wage earners as child labor laws and compulsory education moved children out of the workforce and into schools. Improvements in public health, as well as advances in medicine and a better diet, resulted in a decline in infant mortality rates for the lower classes, especially noticeable in the cities after 1890, and made it easier for working-class families to choose to have fewer children. At the same time, strikes and labor agitation led to laws that reduced work hours to ten per day by 1900 and eliminated work on Saturday afternoons, which enabled working-class parents to devote more attention to their children and develop deeper emotional ties with them. Even working-class fathers became involved in their children's lives. One observer in the French town of Belleville in the 1890s noted that "the workingman's love for his children borders on being an obsession."[12] Interest in educating children as a way to improve their future also grew.

Education in the Mass Society

Mass education was a product of the mass society of the late nineteenth century. Being "educated" in the early nineteenth century meant attending a secondary school or possibly even a university. Secondary schools emphasized a classical education based on the study of Greek and Latin. Secondary and university education was primarily for the elite, the sons of government officials, nobles, or wealthier middle-class families. After 1850, secondary education was expanded as more middle-class families sought employment in public service and the professions or entry into elite scientific and technical schools.

UNIVERSAL ELEMENTARY EDUCATION In the decades after 1870, the functions of the state were extended to include the development of mass education in state-run systems. Most Western governments began to offer at least primary education to both boys and girls between the ages of six and twelve. States also assumed responsibility for the quality of teachers by establishing teacher-training schools. By 1900, many European states, especially in northern and western Europe, were providing state-financed primary schools, salaried and trained teachers, and free, compulsory elementary education for the masses.

Why did European states make this commitment to mass education? Liberals believed that education was important to personal and social improvement and also sought, as in France, to supplant Catholic education with moral and civic training based on secular values. Even conservatives favored mass education as a means of improving the quality of military recruits and training people in social discipline. In 1875, a German military journal stated, "We in Germany consider education to be one of the principal ways of promoting the strength of the nation and above all military strength."[13]

Another incentive for mass education came from industrialization. In the early Industrial Revolution, unskilled labor was sufficient to meet factory needs, but the new firms of the Second Industrial Revolution demanded skilled labor. Both boys

and girls with an elementary education had new possibilities of jobs beyond their villages or small towns, including white-collar jobs in railways, subway stations, post offices, banking and shipping firms, teaching, and nursing. To industrialists, then, mass education furnished the trained workers they needed.

Nevertheless, the chief motive for mass education was political. For one thing, the expansion of voting rights necessitated a more educated electorate. Even more important, however, mass compulsory education instilled patriotism and nationalized the masses, providing an opportunity for even greater national integration. As people lost their ties to local regions and even to religion, nationalism supplied a new faith. The use of a single national language created greater national unity than loyalty to a ruler did.

A nation's motives for universal elementary education largely determined what was taught in its elementary schools. Indoctrination in national values took on great importance. At the core of the academic curriculum were reading, writing, arithmetic, national history (from a patriotic perspective), geography, literature, and some singing and drawing. The education of boys and girls differed, however. Where possible, the sexes were separated. Girls did less math and no science but concentrated on such domestic skills as sewing, washing, ironing, and cooking, all prerequisites for providing a good home for husband and children. Boys were taught some practical skills, such as carpentry, and even some military drill. Most of the elementary schools also inculcated the middle-class virtues of hard work, thrift, sobriety, cleanliness, and respect for the family. For most students, elementary education led to apprenticeship and a job.

FEMALE TEACHERS The development of compulsory elementary education created a demand for teachers, and most of them were female. In the United States, for example, women constituted two-thirds of all teachers by the 1880s. Many men viewed the teaching of children as an extension of women's "natural role" as nurturers of children. Moreover, females were paid lower salaries, in itself a considerable incentive for governments to encourage the establishment of teacher-training institutes for women. The first colleges for women were really teacher-training schools. In Britain, the women's colleges of Queen's and Bedford were established in the 1840s to provide teacher training for middle-class spinsters who needed to work. Barbara Bodichon (boh-di-SHOHNH) (1827–1891), a pioneer in the development of female education, established her own school where girls were trained for economic independence as well as domesticity. Not until the beginning of the twentieth century, however, were women permitted to enter the male-dominated universities. In France, 3 percent of university students in 1902 were women; by 1914, their number had increased to 10 percent of the total.

LITERACY AND NEWSPAPERS The most immediate result of mass education was an increase in literacy. In Germany, Great Britain, France, and the Scandinavian countries, adult illiteracy was virtually eliminated by 1900. Where there was less schooling, the story is very different. Adult illiteracy rates

A Women's College. Women were largely excluded from male-dominated universities before 1900. Consequently, women's desire for higher education led to the establishment of women's colleges, most of which were primarily teacher-training schools. This photograph shows female medical students dissecting cadavers in anatomy class at the Women's Medical College of Philadelphia, Pennsylvania.

were 79 percent in Serbia, 78 percent in Romania, 72 percent in Bulgaria, and 79 percent in Russia. All of these countries had made only a minimal investment in compulsory mass education.

With the dramatic increase in literacy after 1871 came the rise of mass-circulation newspapers, such as the *Evening News* (1881) and *Daily Mail* (1896) in London, which sold millions of copies a day. Known as the "yellow press" in the United States, these newspapers shared some common characteristics. They were written in an easily understood style and tended toward the sensational. Unlike eighteenth-century newspapers, which were full of serious editorials and lengthy political analyses, these tabloids provided lurid details of crimes, jingoistic diatribes, gossip, and sports news. There were other forms of cheap literature as well. Specialty magazines, such as the *Family Herald* for the entire family, and women's magazines began in the 1860s. Pulp fiction for adults included the extremely popular westerns with their innumerable variations on conflicts between cowboys and Indians. Literature for the masses was but one feature of the new mass culture; another was the emergence of new forms of leisure.

Mass Leisure

In the preindustrial centuries, play or leisure activities had been closely connected to work patterns based on the seasonal or daily cycles typical of the life of peasants and artisans. The process of industrialization in the nineteenth century had an enormous impact on those traditional patterns. The factory imposed new work patterns that were determined by the rhythms of machines and clocks and removed work time completely from the family environment of farms and workshops. Work and leisure became opposites as leisure came to be viewed as what people did for fun when not on the job. In fact, the new leisure hours created by the industrial system—evening hours after work, weekends, and later a week or two in the summer—largely determined the contours of the new **mass leisure**.

New technology and business practices also determined the forms of leisure pursuits. Gas street lamps and open boulevards enabled many urban dwellers to escape their cramped working and living conditions to promenade for pleasure. In 1901, an observer from Glasgow wrote, "Here come every night the young persons who have spent the day cooped in shops or warehouses, or offices, and who find sitting at home in dreary lodgings an intolerable torture. On Saturday they come in all the greater number. . . . The lighted street demands no admission money, and so they come in droves."[14] New technology also created novelties such as the Ferris wheel at amusement parks. The mechanized urban transportation systems of the 1880s meant that even the working classes were no longer dependent on neighborhood taverns but could make their way to athletic events, amusement parks, and dance halls. Likewise, railroads could take people to the beaches on weekends.

MUSIC AND DANCE HALLS Music and dance halls appeared in the second half of the nineteenth century. The first music hall in London was constructed in 1849 for a lower-class audience. As is evident from one Londoner's observation, music halls were primarily for males:

> [They were a] popular place of Saturday night resort with working men, as at them they can combine the drinking of the Saturday night glass and smoking of the Saturday night pipe, with the seeing and hearing of a variety of entertainments, ranging from magnificent ballets and marvelous scenic illusions to inferior tumbling, and from well-given operatic selections to the most idiotic of the so-called comic songs.[15]

By the 1880s, there were five hundred music halls in London. Promoters gradually made them more respectable and broadened their fare to entice both women and children to attend the programs. The new dance halls, which were all the rage by 1900, were more strictly oriented toward adults. The sight of young people engaged in sexually suggestive dancing often shocked contemporaries.

MASS TOURISM The upper and middle classes had created the first market for tourism, but as wages increased and workers were given paid vacations, tourism became another form of mass leisure. Thomas Cook (1808–1892) was a British pioneer of mass tourism. Secretary to a British temperance group, Cook had been responsible for organizing a railroad trip to temperance gatherings in 1841. This experience led him to offer trips on a regular basis after he found that he could make substantial profits by renting special trains, lowering prices, and increasing the number of passengers. In 1867, he offered tours to Paris and by the 1880s to Switzerland. In Paris, trains cut the travel time to the beaches; by the 1840s, the first "pleasure train" was run from Paris to the Norman coast. By 1850, the railway company sold discounted tickets for third and second classes, allowing working-class Parisians to sojourn to the coast for the weekend. By 1900, tourism and vacation time became a way of life for the middle and upper classes.

TEAM SPORTS Team sports had also developed into yet another form of mass leisure by the late nineteenth century. Sports were by no means a new activity. Unlike the old rural games, however, they were no longer chaotic and spontaneous activities but became strictly organized, with written rules and officials to enforce them. The rules were the products of organized athletic groups, such as the English Football Association (1863) and the American Bowling Congress (1895).

The new sports were not just for fun; like other forms of middle-class recreation, they were intended to provide training for people, especially adolescents. Not only could the participants develop individual skills, but they could also acquire a sense of teamwork useful for military service. These characteristics were already evident in the British public schools (which were really private boarding schools) in the 1850s and 1860s when such schools as Harrow, Uppingham, and Loretto placed organized sports at the center of the curriculum. At Loretto, for example, education was supposed to instill First—Character. Second—Physique. Third—Intelligence. Fourth—Manners. Fifth—Information.

The new team sports rapidly became professionalized. In Britain, soccer had its Football Association in 1863 and rugby its Rugby Football Union in 1871. In the United States, the first national association to recognize professional baseball players was formed in 1863. By 1900, the National League and American League had a monopoly over professional baseball. The development of urban transportation systems made possible the construction of stadiums where thousands could attend, making mass spectator sports a big business. In 1872, some 2,000 people watched the British Soccer Cup Final. By 1885, the crowd had increased to 10,000 and by 1901 to 100,000. Professional teams became objects of mass adulation by crowds of urbanites who compensated for their lost sense of identity in mass urban areas by developing these new loyalties. Spectator sports even reflected class differences. Upper-class soccer teams in Britain viewed working-class teams as vicious and prone to "money-grubbing, tricks, sensational displays, and utter rottenness."

Soccer Moments. Until 1863, football (soccer) in Britain was an aggressive sport with few set rules. One of the first things the new English Football Association did after it was established on October 26, 1863, was to set up fourteen rules of play. At the left, a magazine called *The Graphic* shows a scene from an international soccer match in 1872. The two players with the ball have the rose of England on their shirts. At the right, another sketch from *The Graphic* shows the first match of the Ladies' Football Club in 1895.

WOMEN'S SOCCER, 1881

BEFORE THE BRITISH LADIES FOOTBALL CLUB of the late nineteenth century, two teams claiming English nationality, although largely from Glasgow, Scotland, attempted to play soccer matches in Scotland and England in 1881. Their efforts were thwarted, however, by violent mobs of all-male crowds. Newspaper reports from the *Glasgow Herald* and *Nottinghamshire Guardian* chronicled the response to women playing soccer.

Ladies' International Match, Scotland V. England

A rather novel football match took place at Easter Road, Edinburgh on Saturday between teams of lady players representing England and Scotland—the former hailing from London and the latter, it is said, from Glasgow. A considerable amount of curiosity was evinced in the event, and upwards of a thousand persons witnessed it. The young ladies' ages appeared to range from eighteen to four-and-twenty, and they were very smartly dressed. The Scotch team wore blue jerseys, white knickerbockers, red stockings, a red belt, high heeled boots and blue and white cowl; while the English sisters were dressed in blue and white jerseys, blue stockings and belt, high-heeled boots, and red and white cowl. The game, judged from a player's point of view, was a failure, but some of the individual members of the teams showed that they had a fair idea of the game. During the first half the Scotch team, playing against the wind, scored a goal, and in the second half they added another two, making a total of three goals against their opponents' nothing.

Ladies "International" Football Match

What will probably be the first and last exhibition of a female football match in Glasgow took place on Monday evening on Shawfield Grounds. Upwards of 5,000 spectators were present, and the absence of the fair sex was especially noticeable. The teams were supposed to be representatives of England and Scotland, and as the Scotch team had won the recent match in Edinburgh, some excitement was thereby caused as to the result of the encounter. The meager training of the teams did not augur much for proficiency of play, and if the display of football tactics was of a sorry description, it was only what might have been expected, and not much worse than some of the early efforts of our noted football clubs. The costume was suitable, and at a distance the players could scarcely be distinguished from those in ordinary football matches. The game was continued without interruption till ends were changed, but the chaff of the spectators was anything but complimentary. Cries of "Go it, Fanny!" and "Well done, Nelly!" resounded from all parts of the field, but the players went on the even tenors of their way, regardless of interruptions. At last a few roughs broke into the enclosure, and as these were followed by hundreds soon after, the players were roughly jostled, and had prematurely to take refuge in the omnibus which had conveyed them to the ground. Their troubles were not, however, yet ended, for the crowd tore up the stakes and threw them at the departing vehicle, and but for the presence of the police some bodily injury to the females might have occurred. The team of four grey horses was driven rapidly from the ground amid the jeers of the crowd, and the players escaped with, let us hope, nothing worse than a serious fright.

 How did viewers respond to women playing soccer? How were the women described?

Source: *Glasgow Herald*, May 9, 1881; *Nottinghamshire Guardian*, May 20, 1881.

The sports cult of the late nineteenth century was mostly male oriented. Many men believed that females were not particularly suited for "vigorous physical activity," although it was permissible for middle-class women to indulge in less active sports such as croquet and lawn tennis. Women's attempt to play soccer during the 1880s was met with violent opposition (see the box above), although by 1895, the British Ladies Football Club played throughout England. Eventually, some athletics crept into women's colleges and girls' public schools in England.

Standardized forms of amusement drew mass audiences. Although some authorities argued that the new amusements were important for improving people, in truth, they served primarily to provide entertainment and distract people from the realities of their work lives. The new mass leisure also represented a significant change from earlier forms of popular culture. Festivals and fairs had been based on active and spontaneous community participation, whereas the new forms of mass leisure were businesses, standardized for largely passive mass audiences and organized to make profits.

Mass Consumption

Amusement parks, dance halls, organized tourist trips, and athletic events all offered new forms of leisure for masses of people, but they also quickly became part of the new mass consumption of the late nineteenth century. Earlier most people's purchases had been limited: some kitchen utensils, bedding, furniture, and a few select pieces of tailor-made clothing. Now middle- and upper-class Europeans were able to purchase and enjoy a wide variety of material goods. The new mass consumption was made possible by improvements in the standard of living, the factory system, population growth, expanded transportation systems, urbanization, and new modernized retailers, which sold standardized merchandise in large volumes.

When European cities were reconstructed in the late nineteenth century, space was allotted for department stores. Constructed of the new industrial materials—iron columns and plate-glass windows—department stores such as Paris's Le Bon Marché (luh BAHN mar-SHAY) offered consumers an endless variety of goods in large spaces (see the box on p. 689). In 1860, its merchandise included shawls, cloaks, bedding, and fabrics; by the 1880s, its stock had expanded to include women's, men's, and children's clothing, accessories, furniture, rugs, umbrellas, toothbrushes, stationery, perfume, toys, shoes, and cutlery. Sales at Le Bon Marché in 1877 registered 73 million francs. Omnibuses carried people throughout Paris, enabling them to travel beyond their neighborhoods to shop at the new stores. Advertising in mass newspapers introduced Europeans to the new products, while department store catalogs enabled people living outside the cities to also purchase the new goods.

Although most advertisements were directed toward women, men also took part in the new consumer culture of the late nineteenth century. Not only did men consume goods such as alcohol and tobacco, but they were also the chief purchasers of ready-made clothing in the late nineteenth century. In the United States in 1890, men bought 71 percent of all ready-made clothing. As work and leisure were separated, men needed to expand their wardrobes to include both clothes for work outside the home and clothes to be worn for entertaining at home or other leisure activities. Men also consumed such goods as shaving soaps, aftershave lotions, hair dyes, and sporting goods.

The National State

 FOCUS QUESTION: What general political trends were evident in the nations of western Europe in the last decades of the nineteenth century, and how did these trends differ from the policies pursued in Germany, Austria-Hungary, and Russia?

Within the major European states, considerable progress was made toward achieving such liberal practices as constitutions and parliaments, but it was largely in western European states that **mass politics** became a reality. Reforms encouraged the expansion of political democracy through voting rights for men and the creation of mass political parties. At the same time, however, these developments were strongly resisted in parts of Europe where the old political forces remained strong.

Western Europe: The Growth of Political Democracy

In general, parliamentary government was most firmly rooted in the western European states. Both Britain and France saw an expansion of the right to vote, but liberal reforms proved less successful in Spain and Italy.

REFORM IN BRITAIN By 1871, Great Britain had a functioning two-party parliamentary system, and the growth of political democracy became one of the preoccupations of British politics. Its cause was pushed along by the expansion of suffrage. Much

advanced by the Reform Act of 1867 (see Chapter 22), the right to vote was further extended during the second ministry of William Gladstone (1880–1885) with the passage of the Reform Act of 1884. It gave the vote to all men who paid regular rents or taxes; by largely enfranchising agricultural workers, a group previously excluded, the act added another 2 million male voters to the electorate (see Table 22.1 on p. 670). Women were still denied the right to vote. The following year, the Redistribution Act eliminated historic boroughs and counties and established constituencies with approximately equal populations and one representative each. The payment of salaries to members of the House of Commons beginning in 1911 further democratized that institution by at least opening the door to people other than the wealthy. The British system of gradual reform through parliamentary institutions had become the way of British political life.

Gradual reform failed to solve the problem of Ireland, however. The Irish had long been subject to British rule, and the Act of Union of 1801 had united the English and Irish Parliaments. Like other unfree ethnic groups in Europe, the Irish developed a sense of national self-consciousness. They detested the absentee British landlords and their burdensome rents.

In 1870, William Gladstone attempted to alleviate Irish discontent by enacting limited land reform, but as Irish tenants continued to be evicted in the 1870s, the Irish began to make new demands. In 1879, a group called the Irish Land League, which advocated independence, called on Parliament to at least institute land reform. Charles Parnell (1846–1891), a leader of the Irish representatives in Parliament, called for **home rule**, which meant self-government by having a separate Parliament but not complete independence. Soon Irish peasants were responding to British inaction with terrorist acts. When the British government reacted with more force, Irish Catholics began to demand independence.

The Liberal leader William Gladstone, continuing to hope for a peaceful solution to the "Irish Question," introduced a home rule bill in 1886 that would have created an Irish Parliament without granting independence. But even this compromise was voted down in Parliament, especially by Conservative members who believed that concessions would only result in more violence. Gladstone tried again when he was prime minister in 1893 but experienced yet another defeat. The Irish Question remained unresolved.

THE THIRD REPUBLIC IN FRANCE The defeat of France by the Prussian army in 1870 brought the downfall of Louis Napoleon's Second Empire. French republicans initially set up a provisional government, but the victorious Otto von Bismarck intervened and forced the French to choose a government by universal male suffrage. The French people rejected the republicans and overwhelmingly favored the monarchists, who won 400 of the 630 seats in the new National Assembly. In response, on March 26, 1871, radical republicans formed an independent republican government in Paris known as the Commune.

But the National Assembly refused to give up its power and decided to crush the revolutionary Commune. When vicious fighting broke out in April, many working-class men and women stepped forth to defend the Commune. At first, women's activities were the traditional ones: caring for the wounded soldiers and feeding the troops. Gradually, however, women expanded their activities to include taking care of weapons, working as scouts, and even setting up their own fighting brigades. Louise Michel (mee-SHEL) (1830–1905), a schoolteacher, emerged as one of the leaders of the Paris Commune. She proved tireless in forming committees for the defense of the Commune.

All of these efforts were in vain, however. In the last week of May, government troops massacred thousands of the Commune's defenders. Estimates are that 20,000 were shot; another 10,000 (including Louise Michel) were shipped to the French penal colony of New Caledonia in the South Pacific. The brutal repression of the Commune bequeathed a legacy of hatred that continued to plague French politics for decades. The split between the middle and working classes, begun in the revolutionary hostilities of 1848–1849, had widened immensely. The harsh punishment of women who participated in the revolutionary activity also served to discourage any future efforts by working-class women to improve their conditions.

Although a majority of the members of the monarchist-dominated National Assembly wished to restore a monarchy to France, inability to agree on who should be king caused the monarchists to miss their opportunity and led in 1875 to an improvised constitution that established a republican form of government as the least divisive compromise. This constitution established a bicameral legislature with an upper house, the Senate, elected indirectly and a lower house, the Chamber of Deputies, chosen by universal male suffrage; a president, selected by the legislature for a term of seven years, served as executive of the government. The Constitution of 1875, intended only as a stopgap measure, solidified the republic—the Third Republic—which lasted sixty-five years. New elections in 1876 and 1877 strengthened the hands of the republicans, who managed by 1879 to institute ministerial responsibility and establish the power of the Chamber of Deputies. The prime minister or premier and his ministers were now responsible not to the president but to the Chamber of Deputies.

Although the government's moderation gradually encouraged more and more middle-class and peasant support, the position of the Third Republic remained precarious because monarchists, Catholic clergy, and professional army officers still opposed it.

A major crisis in the 1880s, however, actually served to strengthen the republican government. General Georges Boulanger (ZHORZH boo-lahnh-ZHAY) (1837–1891) was a popular military officer who attracted the public attention of all those discontented with the Third Republic: monarchists, Bonapartists, aristocrats, and nationalists who favored a war of revenge against Germany. Boulanger appeared as the strong man on horseback, the savior of France. But in 1889, just when his strength had grown to the point when many expected a coup d'état, he lost his nerve and fled France, a completely discredited man. In the long run, the Boulanger crisis served to rally support for the resilient republic.

SPAIN In Spain, a new constitution, drafted in 1875 under King Alfonso XII (1874–1885), established a parliamentary government dominated by two political groups, the Conservatives and the Liberals, whose members stemmed from the same small social group of great landowners allied with a few wealthy industrialists. Because suffrage was limited to the propertied classes, Liberals and Conservatives alternated in power but followed basically the same conservative policies. Spain's defeat in the Spanish-American War in 1898 and the loss of Cuba and the Philippines to the United States increased the discontent with the status quo. When a group of young intellectuals known as the Generation of 1898 called for political and social reforms, both Liberals and Conservatives attempted to enlarge the electorate and win the masses' support for their policies. The attempted reforms did little to allay the unrest, however, and the growth of industrialization in some areas resulted in more workers being attracted to the radical solutions of socialism and anarchism. When violence erupted in Barcelona in July 1909, military forces brutally suppressed the rebels. The revolt and its repression made clear that reform would not be easily accomplished because the Catholic Church, the large landowners, and the army remained tied to a conservative social order.

ITALY By 1870, Italy had emerged as a geographically united state with pretensions to great power status. Its internal weaknesses, however, gave that claim a particularly hollow ring. One Italian leader said after unification, "We have made Italy; now we must make Italians." But many Italians continued to put loyalty to their families, towns, and regions above their loyalty to the new state.

Sectional differences—a poverty-stricken south and an industrializing north—also weakened any sense of community. Most of the Italian leaders were northerners who treated southern Italians with contempt. The Catholic Church, which had lost control of the Papal States as a result of unification, even refused to accept the existence of the new state. Chronic turmoil between workers and industrialists undermined the social fabric. And few Italians felt empowered in the new Italy: only 2.5 percent of the people could vote for the legislative body. In 1882, the number was increased, but only to 10 percent. The Italian government was unable to deal effectively with these problems because of the extensive corruption among government officials and the lack of stability created by ever-changing government coalitions.

Central and Eastern Europe: Persistence of the Old Order

Germany, Austria-Hungary, and Russia pursued political policies that were quite different from those of the western European nations. The central European states (Germany and Austria-Hungary) had the trappings of parliamentary government, including legislative bodies and elections by universal male suffrage, but authoritarian forces, especially powerful monarchies and conservative social groups, remained strong. In eastern Europe, especially Russia, the old system of autocracy was barely touched by the winds of change.

GERMANY Despite unification, important divisions remained in German society that could not simply be papered over by the force of nationalism. These divisions were already evident in the new German constitution that provided for a federal system with a bicameral legislature. The Bundesrat, or upper house, represented the twenty-five states that made up Germany. Individual states, such as Bavaria and Prussia, kept their own kings, their own post offices, and even their own armies in peacetime. The lower house of the German parliament, the Reichstag, was elected on the basis of universal male suffrage, but it did not have ministerial responsibility. Ministers of government, including the all-important chancellor, were responsible not to the parliament but to the emperor. The emperor also commanded the armed forces and controlled foreign policy and internal administration. Though the creation of a parliament elected by universal male suffrage presented opportunities for the growth of a real political democracy, it failed to develop in Germany before World War I. The army and Bismarck were two major reasons why it did not.

The German (largely Prussian) army viewed itself as the defender of monarchy and aristocracy and sought to escape any control by the Reichstag by operating under a general staff responsible only to the emperor. Prussian military tradition was strong, and military officers took steps to ensure the loyalty of their subordinates to the emperor, which was easy as long as Junker landowners were officers. As the growth of the army made it necessary to turn to the middle class for officers, extreme care was taken to choose only sons "of honorable bourgeois families."

The policies of Otto von Bismarck, who served as chancellor of the new German state until 1890, often served to prevent the growth of more democratic institutions. At first, Bismarck worked with the liberals to achieve greater centralization of Germany through common codes of criminal and commercial law. The liberals also joined Bismarck in his attack on the Catholic Church, the so-called *Kulturkampf* (kool-TOOR-kahmf), or "struggle for civilization." Like Bismarck, middle-class liberals distrusted Catholic loyalty to the new Germany. Bismarck's strong-arm tactics against the Catholic clergy and Catholic institutions proved counterproductive, however, and Bismarck welcomed an opportunity in 1878 to abandon the attack on Catholicism by making an abrupt shift in policy.

In 1878, Bismarck abandoned the liberals and began to persecute the socialists. When the Social Democratic Party elected twelve deputies to the Reichstag in 1877, Bismarck grew alarmed. He genuinely believed that the socialists' anti-nationalistic, anti-capitalistic, and antimonarchical stance represented a danger to the empire. In 1878, Bismarck got parliament to pass a stringent antisocialist law that outlawed the Social Democratic Party and limited socialist meetings and publications, although socialist candidates were still permitted to run for the Reichstag. In addition to these repressive measures, Bismarck also attempted to woo workers away from socialism by enacting social welfare legislation (see the box on p. 715). Between 1883 and 1889, the Reichstag passed laws that established sickness, accident, and disability benefits as well as old-age pensions financed by compulsory contributions from workers, employers, and the state. Bismarck's social security system was the most progressive the world had yet seen, although even his system left much to be desired, as the Social Democrats pointed out. A full pension, for example, was payable only at age seventy after forty-eight

Bismarck and William II. In 1890, Bismarck sought to undertake new repressive measures against the Social Democrats. Disagreeing with this policy, Emperor William II forced him to resign. This political cartoon shows William II reclining on a throne made of artillery and cannonballs and holding a doll labeled "socialism." Bismarck bids farewell as Germany, personified as a woman, looks on with grave concern.

BISMARCK AND THE WELFARE OF THE WORKERS

IN HIS ATTEMPT TO WIN WORKERS AWAY from socialism, Bismarck favored an extensive program of social welfare benefits, including old-age pensions and compensation for absence from work due to sickness, accident, or disability. This selection is taken from Bismarck's address to the Reichstag on March 10, 1884, in which he explained his motives for social welfare legislation.

Bismarck, Address to the Reichstag

The positive efforts began really only in the year . . . 1881 . . . with the imperial message . . . in which His Majesty William I said: "Already in February of this year, we have expressed our conviction that the healing of social ills is not to be sought exclusively by means of repression of Social Democratic excesses, but equally in the positive promotion of the welfare of the workers."

In consequence of this, first of all the insurance law against accidents was submitted. . . . And it reads . . . "But those who have, through age or disability, become incapable of working have a confirmed claim on all for a higher degree of state care than could have been their share heretofore. . . ."

The worker's real sore point is the insecurity of his existence. He is not always sure he will always have work. He is not sure he will always be healthy, and he foresees some day he will be old and incapable of work. But also if he falls into poverty as a result of long illness, he is completely helpless with his own powers, and society hitherto does not recognize

relief, even when he has worked ever so faithfully and diligently before. But ordinary poor relief leaves much to be desired, especially in the great cities where it is extraordinarily much worse than in the country. . . . We read in Berlin newspapers of suicide because of difficulty in making both ends meet, of people who died from direct hunger and have hanged themselves because they have nothing to eat, of people who announce in the paper they were tossed out homeless and have no income. . . . For the worker it is always a fact that falling into poverty and onto poor relief in a great city is synonymous with misery, and this insecurity makes him hostile and mistrustful of society. That is humanly not unnatural, and as long as the state does not meet him halfway, just as long will this trust in the state's honesty be taken from him by accusations against the government, which he will find where he wills; always running back again to the socialist quacks . . . and, without great reflection, letting himself be promised things, which will not be fulfilled. On this account, I believe that accident insurance, with which we show the way . . . will still work on the anxieties and ill-feeling of the working class.

 What arguments did Bismarck advance for social welfare legislation? How did Bismarck benefit politically from these moves toward state protection of workers' interests? To what broader forces in nineteenth-century European social and political life was Bismarck responding when he formulated these policies?

Source: F. B. M. Hollyday, ed., *Bismarck* (Upper Saddle River, N.J.: Prentice-Hall, 1970).

---

years of contributions. In the event of a male worker's death, no benefits were paid to his widow or children.

Both the repressive and the social welfare measures failed to stop the advance of socialism, however. The Social Democratic Party continued to grow. In his frustration, Bismarck planned still more repressive measures in 1890, but before he could carry them out, the new emperor, William II (1888–1918), eager to pursue his own policies, cashiered the aged chancellor.

AUSTRIA-HUNGARY After the creation of the Dual Monarchy of Austria-Hungary in 1867, the Austrian part received a constitution that established a parliamentary system with the principle of ministerial responsibility. But Emperor Francis Joseph (1848–1916) largely ignored ministerial responsibility and proceeded to personally appoint and dismiss his ministers and rule by decree when parliament was not in session.

The problem of the minorities continued to trouble the empire. The ethnic Germans, who made up only one-third of Austria's population, governed Austria but felt increasingly threatened by the Czechs, Poles, and other Slavic groups within the empire. The difficulties in dealing with this problem were especially evident from 1879 to 1893 when Count Edward von Taaffe (TAH-fuh) (1833–1895) served as prime minister. Taaffe

attempted to "muddle through" by relying on a coalition of German conservatives, Czechs, and Poles to maintain a majority in parliament. But his concessions to national minorities, such as allowing the Slavic languages as well as German to be used in education and administration, antagonized the German-speaking Austrian bureaucracy and aristocracy, two of the basic pillars of the empire. Opposition to Taaffe's policies brought his downfall in 1893 but did not solve the **nationalities problem**. While the dissatisfied non-German groups demanded concessions, the ruling Austrian Germans resisted change.

What held the Austro-Hungarian Empire together was a combination of forces. Francis Joseph, the emperor, was one unifying factor. Although strongly anti-Hungarian, the cautious emperor made an effort to take a position above national differences. Loyalty to the Catholic Church also helped keep such national groups as Czechs, Slovaks, and Poles loyal to the Catholic Habsburg dynasty. Finally, although dominated by German-speaking officials, the large imperial bureaucracy served as a unifying force for the empire.

Unlike Austria, Hungary had a working parliamentary system, but it was controlled by the great Magyar landowners who dominated both the Hungarian peasantry and the other ethnic groups in Hungary. The Hungarians attempted to solve their nationalities problem by systematic Magyarization. The Magyar language was imposed on all schools and was the only language that could be used by government and military officials.

RUSSIA In Russia, the government made no concession whatever to liberal and democratic reforms, eliminating altogether any possibility of a mass politics. The assassination of Alexander II in 1881 convinced his son and successor, Alexander III (1881–1894), that reform had been a mistake, and he quickly instituted what he said were "exceptional measures." The powers of the secret police were expanded. Advocates of constitutional monarchy and social reform, along with revolutionary groups, were persecuted. Entire districts of Russia were placed under martial law if the government suspected the inhabitants of treason. The powers of the zemstvos, created by the reforms of Alexander II, were sharply curtailed.

Alexander also pursued a radical Russification program of the numerous nationalities that made up the Russian Empire. Russians themselves constituted only 40 percent of the population, which did not stop the tsar from banning the use of all languages except Russian in schools. The policy of Russification served primarily to anger national groups and create new sources of opposition to tsarist policies.

When Alexander III died, his weak son and successor, Nicholas II (1894–1917), adopted his father's conviction that the absolute power of the tsars should be preserved: "I shall maintain the principle of autocracy just as firmly and unflinchingly as did my unforgettable father."[16] But conditions were changing, especially with the growth of industrialization, and the tsar's approach was not realistic in view of the new circumstances he faced.

CHRONOLOGY	National States of Europe, 1871–1894
Great Britain	
Second ministry of William Gladstone	1880–1885
Reform Act	1884
France	
Surrender of French provisional government to Germany	1871 (January 28)
Paris Commune	1871 (March–May)
Republican constitution (Third Republic)	1875
Boulanger is discredited	1889
Spain	
King Alfonso XII	1874–1885
New constitution	1875
Germany	
Bismarck as chancellor	1871–1890
Antisocialist law	1878
Social welfare legislation	1883–1889
Austria-Hungary	
Emperor Francis Joseph	1848–1916
Count Edward von Taaffe as prime minister	1879–1893
Russia	
Tsar Alexander III	1881–1894

CHAPTER SUMMARY

The Second Industrial Revolution helped create a new material prosperity that led Europeans to believe they had ushered in a new age of progress. In this second revolution, steel, chemicals, electricity, petroleum, and the internal combustion engine led the way to new industrial frontiers. Europe became divided into an industrialized north and a poorer south and east, while European manufactured goods and investment capital were exported abroad in exchange for raw materials, creating a true world economy. New jobs provided work opportunities for many women, although prostitution remained an avenue for survival for other women. Working-class socialist parties, such as Germany's Social Democratic Party, began working for change by forming trade unions and electing representatives to legislative bodies.

A major feature of this "new age of progress" was the emergence of a mass society. Better sanitation and improved diets led to a dramatic population increase, while emigration enabled Europe to avoid overcrowding. Class divisions continued to dictate styles of living, while industrialism reinforced traditional gender patterns: women stayed at home while men went out to work. Nevertheless, some women began to espouse birth control as an avenue for change. The lower classes benefited from the right to vote, a higher standard of living, and a modicum of education from new schools as most states assumed responsibility for mass compulsory education for children. New forms of mass transportation, combined with new work patterns, enabled large numbers of people to participate in new mass leisure activities, including weekend excursions to amusement parks and seaside resorts, dance halls, and sporting events.

New patterns of mass consumption arose, encouraging people to accumulate more material possessions.

By 1871, the national state had become the focus of people's lives. Especially in western Europe, liberal and democratic reforms brought new possibilities for greater participation in the political process, although women were still largely excluded from political rights. After 1871, the national state also began to expand its functions beyond all previous activities by adopting social insurance measures to protect workers against accidents, illness, and old age, and by enacting public health and housing measures, designed to curb the worst ills of urban living.

This extension of state functions took place in an atmosphere of increased national loyalty. After 1871, Western national states increasingly sought to solidify the social order and win the active loyalty and support of their citizens by deliberately cultivating national feelings. Yet this policy contained potentially great dangers. As we shall see in the next chapter, nations had discovered once again that imperialistic adventures and military successes could arouse nationalistic passions, but they also found that nationalistic feelings could lead to intense international rivalries that made war almost inevitable.

CHAPTER TIMELINE

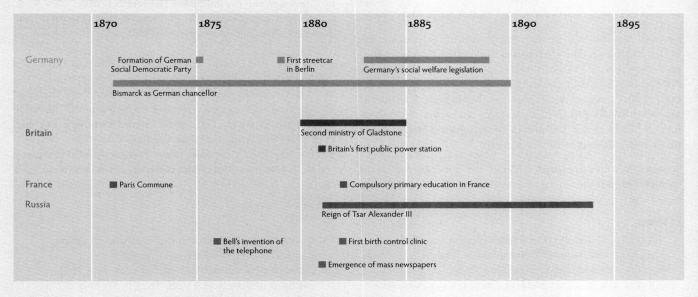

CHAPTER REVIEW

Upon Reflection

Q To what extent did the emergence and development of socialist parties and trade unions meet the needs of the working classes between 1871 and 1894?

Q How were the promises and problems of the new mass society reflected in education, leisure, and consumption?

Q Between 1871 and 1894, two major domestic political issues involved the achievement of liberal practices and the growth of political democracy. To what extent were these realized in Great Britain, France, Germany, Austria-Hungary, and Russia?

Key Terms

tariffs (p. 688)
cartels (p. 688)
depression (p. 690)
Marxism (p. 695)
evolutionary socialism (p. 695)
revisionism (p. 695)
anarchism (p. 697)
mass society (p. 697)

plutocrats (p. 702)
mass education (p. 708)
mass leisure (p. 709)
mass politics (p. 712)
home rule (p. 712)
Kulturkampf (p. 714)
nationalities problem (p. 715)

Suggestions for Further Reading

GENERAL WORKS   In addition to the general works on the nineteenth century and individual European countries cited in Chapters 21 and 22, a more specialized work on the subject matter of this chapter is available in **F. Gilbert** and **D. C. Large**, *The End of the European Era, 1890 to the Present*, 5th ed. (New York, 2002).

SECOND INDUSTRIAL REVOLUTION   The subject of the Second Industrial Revolution is well covered in **D. Landes**, *The Unbound Prometheus*, cited in Chapter 20. On the transformation of the marketplace during the late-nineteenth century, see **S. Topik** and **A. Wells**, *Global Markets Transformed, 1870–1945* (Cambridge, 2012). The impact of the new technology on European thought is imaginatively discussed in **S. Kern**, *The Culture of Time and Space, 1880–1918*, rev. ed. (Cambridge, Mass., 2003).

SOCIAL CLASSES   An interesting work on aristocratic life is **D. Cannadine**, *The Decline and Fall of the British Aristocracy* (New Haven, Conn., 1990). On the middle classes, see **P. Pilbeam**, *The Middle Classes in Europe, 1789–1914* (Basingstoke, U.K., 1990). On the working classes, see **R. Magraw**, *A History of the French Working Class* (Cambridge, Mass., 1992). On emigration, see **D. Hoerder**, *Cultures in Contact: World Migrations in the Second Millennium* (Durham, 2002).

WOMEN'S EXPERIENCES   There are good overviews of women's experiences in the nineteenth century in **B. G. Smith**, *Changing Lives: Women in European History Since 1700*, rev. ed. (Lexington, Mass., 2005). A good study is **M. J. Peterson**, *Family, Love and Work in the Lives of Victorian Gentlewomen* (Bloomington, Ind., 1989). For a new perspective on domestic life, see **J. Flanders**, *Inside the Victorian Home: A Portrait of Domestic Life in Victorian England* (New York, 2004).

MASS EDUCATION, LEISURE, AND CONSUMPTION   On various aspects of education, see **M. J. Maynes**, *Schooling in Western Europe: A Social History* (Albany, N.Y., 1985). A concise and well-presented survey of leisure patterns is **G. Cross**, *A Social History of Leisure Since 1600* (State College, Pa., 1990). On the rise of the department store, see **G. Crossick**, *Cathedrals of Consumption: The European Department Store* (New York, 1999). On mass sports, see **A. Harvey**, *Football: The First Hundred Years: The Untold Story* (Abingdon, 2005).

DOMESTIC POLITICS   The domestic politics of the period can be examined in the general works on individual countries listed in the bibliographies for Chapters 21 and 22. There are also specialized works on aspects of each country's history. On Britain, see **D. Read**, *The Age of Urban Democracy: England, 1868–1914* (New York, 1994). On the Paris Commune, see **D. A. Shafer**, *The Paris Commune* (New York, 2005). On Germany, see **W. J. Mommsen**, *Imperial Germany, 1867–1918* (New York, 1995).

Notes

1. Quoted in D. Landes, *The Unbound Prometheus: Technological Change and Industrial Development in Western Europe from 1750 to the Present* (Cambridge, 1969), p. 353.
2. Quoted in M. J. Boxer and J. H. Quataert, eds., *Connecting Spheres: Women in the Western World, 1500 to the Present* (New York, 1987), p. 151.
3. Quoted in W. L. Guttsman, *The German Social Democratic Party, 1875–1933* (London, 1981), p. 63.
4. Quoted in L. Derfler, *Socialism Since Marx: A Century of the European Left* (New York, 1973), p. 58.
5. Karl Marx and Friedrich Engels, *The Communist Manifesto* (Harmondsworth, U.K., 1967), p. 102.
6. Quoted in P. Avrich, *The Russian Anarchists* (Princeton, N.J., 1971), p. 67.
7. Quoted in N. Bullock and J. Read, *The Movement for Housing Reform in Germany and France, 1840–1914* (Cambridge, 1985), p. 42.
8. Quoted in T. C. W. Blanning, *The Nineteenth Century: Europe 1789–1914*, (Oxford, 2000), p. 120.
9. Quoted in J. Cuming Walters, *Tennyson: Poet, Philosopher, Idealist* (London: Kegan Paul, Trench, Trubner & Co., Ltd., 1893), p. 64.
10. Quoted in G. Cross, *A Social History of Leisure Since 1600* (State College, Pa., 1990), pp. 116, 119.
11. Quoted in Boxer and Quataert, *Connecting Spheres*, p. 161.
12. Quoted in L. R. Berlanstein, *The Working People of Paris, 1871–1914* (Baltimore, 1984), p. 141.
13. Quoted in R. Gildea, *Barricades and Borders: Europe, 1800–1914*, 2nd ed. (Oxford, 1996), pp. 240–241.
14. Quoted in A. Lees and L. H. Lees, *Cities and the Making of Modern Europe, 1750–1914* (Cambridge, 2007), p. 224.
15. Quoted in Cross, *Social History of Leisure*, p. 130.
16. Quoted in S. Galai, *The Liberation Movement in Russia, 1900–1905* (Cambridge, 1973), p. 26.

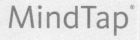 **MindTap®** is a fully online, highly personalized learning experience built upon Cengage Learning content. MindTap combines student learning tools—readings, multimedia, activities, and assessments—into a singular Learning Path that guides students through the course.

CHAPTER

24

AN AGE OF MODERNITY, ANXIETY, AND IMPERIALISM, 1894–1914

The Eiffel Tower at the World's Fair of 1900 in Paris

ND/Roger Viollet/Getty Images

CHAPTER OUTLINE AND FOCUS QUESTIONS

Toward the Modern Consciousness: Intellectual and Cultural Developments

Q What developments in science, intellectual affairs, and the arts in the late nineteenth and early twentieth centuries "opened the way to a modern consciousness," and how did this consciousness differ from earlier worldviews?

Politics: New Directions and New Uncertainties

Q What gains did women make in their movement for women's rights? How did a new right-wing politics affect the Jews in different parts of Europe? What political problems did Great Britain, Italy, France, Germany, Austria-Hungary, and Russia face between 1894 and 1914, and how did they solve them?

The New Imperialism

Q What were the causes of the new imperialism that took place after 1880, and what effects did European imperialism have on Africa and Asia?

International Rivalry and the Coming of War

Q What was the Bismarckian system of alliances, and how successful was it at keeping the peace? What issues lay behind the international crises that Europe faced in the late nineteenth and early twentieth centuries?

Critical Thinking

Q *What is the connection between the "new imperialism" of the late nineteenth century and the causes of World War I?*

Connections to Today

Q *What scientific discoveries of the past twenty years have challenged the modern consciousness that emerged in the late nineteenth and early twentieth centuries?*

IN 1889, THE EIFFEL TOWER stood above Paris as a beacon of progress, a symbol of what technology and industrialization could accomplish. Constructed from iron to mark the entrance to the World's Fair, it was the tallest structure in the world, extending 1,000 feet above the city. Over a period of five months, 3.5 million visitors paid to ascend the tower and overlook the grounds teeming with throngs of people. Almost 175,000 people a day came to visit the fair's 60,000 exhibits, which included an Algerian bazaar, Swiss chalet, Indian palace, and Japanese garden. Guidebooks for the fair posited that a visitor would need ten to twenty days to see all of the displays. One awestruck visitor declared, "There is only one cry; this is the most grandiose, the most dazzling, the most marvelous spectacle ever seen."[1] For most in attendance, the modern era was indeed an age of progress that was providing more opportunities, higher standards of living, better cities, more goods to consume, and greater democratization.

The optimism found at the World's Fair and throughout Europe's cities was not unchallenged, however. Some were still struggling to achieve progress. Many workers continued to endure pitiful housing conditions and low wages, while women fought for the right to vote. Beneath the apparent calm, political tensions were also building, fueled by imperialist adventures, international rivalries, and cultural uncertainties. After 1880, Europeans engaged in a great race for colonies around the world. This competition for lands abroad greatly intensified existing antagonisms among European states.

Ultimately, Europeans proved incapable of finding constructive ways to cope with their international rivalries. The development of two large alliance systems—the Triple Alliance and the Triple Entente—may have helped preserve peace for a time, but eventually the alliances made it easier for the European nations to be drawn into World War I.

The cultural life of Europe in the decades before 1914 reflected similar dynamic tensions. The advent of mass education produced better-informed citizens but also made it easier for governments to stir up the masses by nationalistic appeals through the new mass journalism. At the same time, despite the appearance of progress, European philosophers, writers, and artists were creating modern cultural expressions that questioned traditional ideas and values and initiated a crisis of confidence. Before 1914, many intellectuals had a sense of unease about the direction in which society was heading, accompanied by a feeling of imminent catastrophe. They proved remarkably prophetic.

Toward the Modern Consciousness: Intellectual and Cultural Developments

 FOCUS QUESTION: What developments in science, intellectual affairs, and the arts in the late nineteenth and early twentieth centuries "opened the way to a modern consciousness," and how did this consciousness differ from earlier worldviews?

Before 1914, most Europeans continued to believe in the values and ideals that had been generated by the Scientific Revolution and the Enlightenment. *Reason*, *science*, and *progress* were still important buzzwords in the European vocabulary. The ability of human beings to improve themselves and achieve a better society seemed to be well demonstrated by a rising standard of living, urban improvements, and mass education. Such products of modern technology as electric lights, phonographs, cinema, and automobiles reinforced the popular prestige of science and the belief in the ability of the human mind to comprehend the universe through the use of reason. Near the end of the nineteenth century, however, a dramatic transformation in the realm of ideas and culture challenged many of these assumptions. A new view of the physical universe, an appeal to

the irrational, alternative views of human nature, and radically innovative forms of literary and artistic expression shattered old beliefs and opened the way to a modern consciousness. These new ideas called forth a sense of confusion and anxiety that would become even more pronounced after World War I.

Developments in the Sciences: The Emergence of a New Physics

Science was one of the chief pillars supporting the optimistic and rationalistic view of the world that many Westerners shared in the nineteenth century. Supposedly based on hard facts and cold reason, science offered a certainty of belief in the orderliness of nature that was comforting to many people for whom traditional religious beliefs no longer had much meaning. Many naively believed that the application of already known scientific laws would give humanity a complete understanding of the physical world and an accurate picture of reality. The new physics dramatically altered that perspective.

Throughout much of the nineteenth century, Westerners adhered to the mechanical conception of the universe postulated by the classical physics of Isaac Newton. In this perspective, the universe was viewed as a giant machine in which time, space, and matter were objective realities that existed independently of the people observing them. Matter was thought to be composed of indivisible solid material bodies called atoms.

These views were first seriously questioned at the end of the nineteenth century. The French scientist Marie Curie (kyoo-REE) (1867–1934) and her husband Pierre (1859–1906) discovered that the element radium gave off rays of radiation that apparently came from within the atom itself. Atoms were not simply hard, material bodies but small worlds containing such subatomic particles as electrons and protons that behaved in seemingly random and inexplicable fashion. Inquiry into the disintegrative process within atoms became a central theme of the new physics.

Building on this work, in 1900, a Berlin physicist, Max Planck (PLAHNK) (1858–1947), rejected the belief that a heated body radiates energy in a steady stream but maintained instead that energy is radiated discontinuously, in irregular packets that he called "quanta." The quantum theory raised fundamental questions about the subatomic realm of the atom. By 1900, the old view of atoms as the basic building blocks of the material world was being seriously questioned, and Newtonian physics was in trouble.

THE WORK OF EINSTEIN Albert Einstein (YN-styn *or* YN-shtyn) (1879–1955), a German-born patent officer working in Switzerland, pushed these theories of thermodynamics into new terrain. In 1905, Einstein published a paper titled "The Electro-Dynamics of Moving Bodies" that contained his special theory of relativity. According to **relativity theory**, space and time are not absolute but relative to the observer, and both are interwoven into what Einstein called a four-dimensional space-time continuum. Neither space nor time had an existence independent of human experience. As Einstein later explained simply to a journalist, "It was formerly believed that if all

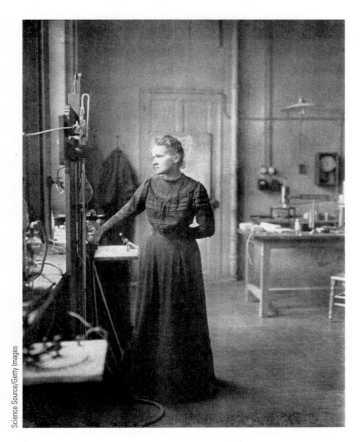

Marie Curie. Marie Curie was born in Warsaw, Poland, but studied at the University of Paris, where she received degrees in both physics and mathematics. She was the first woman to win two Nobel Prizes, one in 1903 in physics and another in 1911 in chemistry. She is shown here in her Paris laboratory in 1912. She died of leukemia, a result of her laboratory work with radioactivity.

material things disappeared out of the universe, time and space would be left. According to the relativity theory, however, time and space disappear together with the things."[2] Moreover, matter and energy reflected the relativity of time and space. Einstein concluded that matter was nothing but another form of energy. His epochal formula $E = mc^2$—each particle of matter is equivalent in energy to its mass times the square of the velocity of light—was the key theory explaining the vast energies contained within the atom. It led to the atomic age.

Many scientists were unable to comprehend Einstein's ideas, but during a total eclipse of the sun in May 1919, scientists were able to demonstrate that light was deflected in the gravitational field of the sun, just as Einstein had predicted. This confirmed Einstein's general theory of relativity and opened the scientific and intellectual world to his ideas. The 1920s would become the "heroic age" of physics.

Toward a New Understanding of the Irrational

Intellectually, the decades before 1914 witnessed a combination of contradictory developments. Thanks to the influence of science, confidence in human reason and progress still remained a dominant thread. At the same time, however, a small group of intellectuals attacked the idea of optimistic progress, dethroned reason, and glorified the irrational.

NIETZSCHE Friedrich Nietzsche (FREED-rikh NEE-chuh *or* NEE-chee) (1844–1900) was one of the intellectuals who glorified the irrational. According to Nietzsche, Western bourgeois society was decadent and incapable of any real cultural creativity, primarily because of its excessive emphasis on the rational faculty at the expense of emotions, passions, and instincts. Reason, Nietzsche claimed, actually played little role in human life because humans were at the mercy of irrational life forces.

Nietzsche believed that Christianity should shoulder much of the blame for Western civilization's enfeeblement. The "slave morality" of Christianity, he believed, had obliterated the human impulse for life and had crushed the human will:

> I call Christianity the one great curse, the one enormous and innermost perversion. . . . I call it the one immortal blemish of mankind. . . . Christianity has taken the side of everything weak, base, ill-constituted, it has made an ideal out of opposition to the preservative instincts of strong life. . . . Christianity is called the religion of pity.—Pity stands in antithesis to the basic emotions which enhance the energy of the feeling of life: it has a depressive effect. One loses force when one pities.[3]

How, then, could Western society be renewed? First, said Nietzsche, one must recognize that "God is dead." Europeans had killed God, he said, and it was no longer possible to believe in some kind of cosmic order. Eliminating God and hence Christian morality had liberated human beings and made it possible to create a higher kind of being Nietzsche called the superman: "I teach you the Superman. Man is something that is to be surpassed."[4] Superior intellectuals must free themselves from the ordinary thinking of the masses, create their own values, and lead the masses. Nietzsche rejected and condemned political democracy, social reform, and universal suffrage.

BERGSON Another popular revolutionary against reason in the 1890s was Henri Bergson (AHN-ree BERK-son) (1859–1941), a French philosopher whose lectures at the University of Paris made him one of the most important influences in French thought in the early twentieth century. Bergson accepted rational, scientific thought as a practical instrument for providing useful knowledge but maintained that it was incapable of arriving at truth or ultimate reality. To him, reality was the "life force" that suffused all things; it could not be divided into analyzable parts. Reality was a whole that could only be grasped intuitively and experienced directly. When we analyze it, we have merely a description, no longer the reality we have experienced.

SOREL Georges Sorel (ZHORZH soh-RELL) (1847–1922), a French political theorist, combined Bergson's and Nietzsche's ideas on the limits of rational thinking with his own passionate interest in **revolutionary socialism**. Sorel understood the political potential of the nonrational and advocated violent action as the only sure way to achieve the aims of socialism. To destroy capitalist society, he recommended the use of the **general strike**, envisioning it as a mythic image that had the power to inspire workers to take violent, heroic action against the capitalist order. Sorel also came to believe that the new socialist society would have to be governed by a small elite ruling body because the masses were incapable of ruling themselves.

Sigmund Freud and Psychoanalysis

Around the turn of the twentieth century, a Viennese doctor, Sigmund Freud (SIG-mund *or* ZIG-munt FROID) (1856–1939), put forth a series of theories that undermined optimism about the rational nature of the human mind. Freud's thought, like the new physics and the irrationalism of Nietzsche, added to the uncertainties of the age. His major ideas were published in 1900 in *The Interpretation of Dreams*, which contained the basic foundation of what came to be known as **psychoanalysis**.

Sigmund Freud. Freud was one of the intellectual giants of the nineteenth and twentieth centuries. Born in Moravia, Freud began to study medicine at the University of Vienna in 1873. After entering private practice, he began to study patients suffering from psychosomatic symptoms, which led him to believe that unconscious forces strongly determine human behavior. Freud is seen here in a photograph taken in 1921. He was addicted to tobacco and smoked up to twenty cigars a day, a habit that led to mouth cancer and a series of operations that were ultimately unsuccessful.

ROLE OF THE UNCONSCIOUS According to Freud, human behavior was strongly determined by the unconscious, by earlier experiences and inner forces of which people were largely oblivious. To explore the content of the unconscious, Freud relied not only on hypnosis but also on dreams, but the latter were cloaked in an elaborate code that had to be deciphered if the content was to be properly understood.

But why did some experiences whose influence persisted in controlling an individual's life remain unconscious? According to Freud, the answer was repression (see the box on p. 723), a process by which unsettling experiences were blotted from conscious awareness but still continued to influence behavior because they had become part of the unconscious. To explain how repression worked, Freud elaborated an intricate theory of the inner life of human beings.

According to Freud, a human being's inner life was a battleground of three contending forces: the id, ego, and superego. The id was the center of unconscious drives and was ruled by what Freud termed the pleasure principle. As creatures of desire, human beings directed their energy toward pleasure and away from pain. The id contained all kinds of lustful drives and desires and crude appetites and impulses. The ego was the seat of reason and hence the coordinator of the inner life. It was governed by the reality principle. Although humans were dominated by the pleasure principle, a true pursuit of pleasure was not feasible. The reality principle meant that people rejected pleasure so that they might live together in society. The superego was the locus of conscience and represented the inhibitions and moral values that society in general and parents in particular imposed on people. The superego served to force the ego to curb the unsatisfactory drives of the id.

The human being was thus a battleground among id, ego, and superego. Ego and superego exerted restraining influences on the unconscious id and repressed or kept out of consciousness what they wanted to. The most important repressions, according to Freud, were sexual, and he went on to develop a theory of infantile sexual drives embodied in the Oedipus complex (Electra complex for females), or the infant's craving for exclusive possession of the parent of the opposite sex. Repression began in childhood, and psychoanalysis was accomplished through a dialogue between psychotherapist and patient in which the therapist probed deeply into memory in order to retrace the chain of repression all the way back to its childhood origins. By making the conscious mind aware of the unconscious and its repressed contents, the patient's psychic conflict was resolved.

Although many of Freud's ideas have been shown to be wrong in many details, he is still regarded as an important figure because of the impact his theories have had.

The Impact of Darwin

In the second half of the nineteenth century, scientific theories were sometimes wrongly applied to achieve other ends. The application of Darwin's principle of organic evolution to the social order came to be known as **social Darwinism**.

SOCIAL DARWINISM The most popular exponent of social Darwinism was the British philosopher Herbert Spencer (1820–1903).

FREUD AND THE CONCEPT OF REPRESSION

FREUD'S PSYCHOANALYTICAL THEORIES RESULTED from his attempt to understand the world of the unconscious. This excerpt is taken from a lecture given in 1909 in which Freud described how he arrived at his theory of the role of repression. Although Freud valued science and reason, his theories of the unconscious produced a new image of the human being as governed less by reason than by irrational forces.

Sigmund Freud, *The Origin and Development of Psychoanalysis*

But I did not give [the technique of encouraging patients to reveal forgotten experiences] up without drawing definite conclusions from the data which I had gained. I had substantiated the fact that the forgotten memories were not lost.

They were in the possession of the patient, ready to emerge and form associations with his other mental content, but hindered from becoming conscious, and forced to remain in the unconscious by some sort of a force. The existence of this force could be assumed with certainty, for in attempting to drag up the unconscious memories into the consciousness of the patient, in opposition to this force, one got the sensation of his own personal effort striving to overcome it. One could get an idea of this force, which maintained the pathological situation, from the resistance of the patient.

It is on this idea of resistance that I based my theory of the psychic processes of hystericals. It had been found that in order to cure the patient it was necessary that this force should be overcome. Now with the mechanism of the cure as a starting point, quite a definite theory could be constructed. These same forces, which in the present situation as resistances opposed the emergence of the forgotten ideas into consciousness, must themselves have caused the forgetting, and repressed from consciousness the pathogenic experiences. I called this hypothetical process "repression" and considered that it was proved by the undeniable existence of resistance.

But now the question arose: what were those forces, and what were the conditions of this repression, in which we were now able to recognize the pathogenic mechanism of hysteria? A comparative study of the pathogenic situations, which the cathartic treatment has made possible, allows us to answer this question. In all those experiences, it had happened that a wish had been aroused, which was in sharp opposition to the other desires of the individual, and was not capable of being reconciled with the ethical, aesthetic and personal pretensions of the patient's personality. There had been a short conflict, and the end of this inner struggle was the repression of the idea that presented itself to consciousness as the bearer of this irreconcilable wish. This was, then, repressed from consciousness and forgotten. The incompatibility of the idea in question with the "ego" of the patient was the motive of the repression, the ethical and other pretensions of the individual were the repressing forces. The presence of the incompatible wish, or the duration of the conflict, had given rise to a high degree of mental pain; this pain was avoided by the repression. This latter process is evidently in such a case a device for the protection of the personality.

 According to Freud, how did he discover the existence of repression? What function does repression perform? What aspects of modern European society might have contributed to forcing individuals into repressive modes of thinking and acting?

Source: *The American Journal of Psychology*, vol. 21, no. 2 (1910), pp. 192–199.

Using Darwin's terminology, Spencer argued that societies were organisms that evolved through time from a struggle with their environment. Progress came from "the struggle for survival," as the "fit"—the strong—advanced while the weak declined. As Spencer expressed it in 1851 in his book *Social Statics*:

> Pervading all Nature we may see at work a stern discipline which is a little cruel that it may be very kind. . . . Meanwhile, the well-being of existing humanity and the unfolding of it into this ultimate perfection, are both secured by the same beneficial though severe discipline to which the animate creation at large is subject. It seems hard that an unskillfulness, which with all his efforts he cannot overcome, should entail hunger upon the artisan. It seems hard that a laborer, incapacitated by sickness from competing with his stronger fellows, should have to bear the resulting privations. It seems hard that widows and orphans should be left to struggle for life or death. Nevertheless, when regarded not separately but in connection with the interests of universal humanity, these harsh fatalities are seen to be full of beneficence—the same beneficence which brings to early graves the children of diseased parents, and singles out the intemperate and the debilitated as the victims of an epidemic.[5]

The state should not intervene in this natural process.

RACISM Rabid nationalists and racists also applied Darwin's ideas in an even more radical way. In their pursuit of national greatness, extreme nationalists argued that nations, too, were engaged in a "struggle for existence" in which only the fittest survived. The German general Friedrich von Bernhardi (FREED-rikh fun bayrn-HAR-dee) (1849–1930) argued in 1907:

> War is a biological necessity of the first importance, a regulative element in the life of mankind which cannot be

dispensed with, since without it an unhealthy development will follow, which excludes every advancement of the race, and therefore all real civilization. "War is the father of all things." The sages of antiquity long before Darwin recognized this.[6]

Numerous nationalist organizations preached the same doctrine as Bernhardi. The Nationalist Association of Italy, for example, founded in 1910, declared that "we must teach Italy the value of international struggle. But international struggle is war? Well, then, let there be war! And nationalism will arouse the will for a victorious war . . . the only way to national redemption."[7]

Racism, too, was dramatically revived and strengthened by new biological arguments. Perhaps nowhere was the combination of extreme nationalism and racism more evident and more dangerous than in Germany. The concept of the *Volk* (FULK) (nation, people, or race) had been an underlying idea in German history since the beginning of the nineteenth century. One of the chief propagandists for German **volkish thought** at the turn of the twentieth century was Houston Stewart Chamberlain (1855–1927), an Englishman who became a German citizen. His book *The Foundations of the Nineteenth Century*, published in 1899, made a special impact on Germany. Modern-day Germans, according to Chamberlain, were the only pure successors of the "Aryans," who were portrayed as the true and original creators of Western culture. The Aryan (AR-ee-un) race, under German leadership, must be prepared to fight for Western civilization and save it from the destructive assaults of such lower races as Jews, Negroes, and Orientals. Increasingly, Jews were singled out by German volkish nationalists as the racial enemy in biological terms and as parasites who wanted to destroy the Aryan race.

The Attack on Christianity

The growth of scientific thinking as well as the forces of modernization presented new challenges to the Christian churches. Industrialization and urbanization had an especially adverse effect on religious institutions. With the mass migration of people from the countryside to the city, the close-knit, traditional ties of the village in which the church had been a key force gave way to new urban patterns of social life from which the churches were often excluded. The established Christian churches had a weak hold on workers.

The political movements of the late nineteenth century were also hostile to the established Christian churches. Beginning during the eighteenth-century Enlightenment and continuing well into the nineteenth century, European governments, especially in predominantly Catholic countries, had imposed controls over church courts, religious orders, and appointments of the clergy. But after the failure of the revolutions of 1848, governments were eager to use the churches' aid in reestablishing order and relaxed these controls.

Eventually, however, the close union of state authorities with established churches produced a backlash in the form of **anticlericalism**, especially in the liberal nation-states of the late nineteenth century. As one example, in the 1880s, the French republican government substituted civic training for religious instruction in order to undermine the Catholic Church's control of education. In 1901, Catholic teaching orders were outlawed, and four years later, in 1905, church and state were completely separated.

Science became one of the chief threats to all the Christian churches and even to religion itself in the nineteenth century. Darwin's theory of evolution, accepted by ever-larger numbers of educated Europeans, seemed to contradict the doctrine of divine creation. By seeking to suppress Darwin's books and to forbid the teaching of the evolutionary hypothesis, the churches often caused even more educated people to reject established religions.

The scientific spirit also encouraged a number of biblical scholars to apply critical principles to the Bible, leading to the so-called higher criticism. One of its leading exponents was Ernst Renan (re-NAHNH) (1823–1892), a French Catholic scholar. In his *Life of Jesus*, Renan questioned the historical accuracy of the Bible and presented a radically different picture of Jesus. He saw Jesus not as the son of God but as a human being whose value lay in the example he provided by his life and teaching.

RESPONSE OF THE CHURCHES One response of the Christian churches to these attacks was the outright rejection of modern ideas and forces. Protestant fundamentalist sects were especially important in maintaining a literal interpretation of the Bible. The Catholic Church under Pope Pius IX (1846–1878) also took a rigid stand against modern ideas. In 1864, Pope Pius issued a papal encyclical called the *Syllabus of Errors* in which he stated that it is "an error to believe" that the pope ought to "agree with progress, liberalism, and modern civilization." He condemned nationalism, socialism, religious toleration, and freedom of speech and press.

Rejection of the new was not the churches' only response, however. A religious movement called Modernism included an attempt by the churches to reinterpret Christianity in the light of new developments. The modernists viewed the Bible as a book of useful moral ideas, encouraged Christians to become involved in social reforms, and insisted that the churches must provide a greater sense of community. The Catholic Church condemned Modernism in 1907 and had driven it underground by the beginning of World War I.

Yet another response of the Christian churches to modern ideas was compromise, an approach especially evident in the Catholic Church during the pontificate of Leo XIII (1878–1903). Pope Leo permitted the teaching of evolution as a hypothesis in Catholic schools and also responded to the challenges of modernization in the economic and social spheres. In his encyclical *De Rerum Novarum* (day RAYR-um noh-VAR-um), issued in 1891, he upheld the individual's right to private property but at the same time criticized "naked" capitalism for the poverty and degradation in which it had left the working classes. Much in socialism, he declared, was Christian in principle, but he condemned Marxist socialism for its materialistic and antireligious foundations. The pope recommended that Catholics form socialist parties and labor unions of their own to help the workers.

Other religious groups also made efforts to win support for Christianity among the working-class poor and to restore religious practice among the urban working classes. Sects of evangelical missionaries were especially successful; a prime example is the Salvation Army, founded in London in 1865 by William Booth (1829–1912), the army's first "general." The Salvation Army established food centers, shelters where the homeless could sleep, and "rescue homes" for women, but all these had a larger purpose, as Booth admitted: "It is primarily and mainly for the sake of saving the soul that I seek the salvation of the body."[8]

The Culture of Modernity: Literature

The revolution in physics and psychology was paralleled by a revolution in literature and the arts. Before 1914, writers and artists self-consciously rejected the traditional literary and artistic styles that had dominated European cultural life since the Renaissance. The changes that they produced have since been called **Modernism**.

NATURALISM Throughout much of the late nineteenth century, literature was dominated by Naturalism. Naturalists accepted the material world as real and felt that literature should be realistic. By addressing social problems, writers could contribute to an objective understanding of the world. Although Naturalism was a continuation of Realism, it lacked the underlying note of liberal optimism about people and society that had been prevalent in the 1850s. The Naturalists were pessimistic about Europe's future and often portrayed characters caught in the grip of forces beyond their control.

The novels of the French writer Émile Zola provide a good example of Naturalism. Against a backdrop of the urban slums and coalfields of northern France, Zola showed how alcoholism and different environments affected people's lives. He had read Darwin's *Origin of Species* and had been impressed by its emphasis on the struggle for survival and the importance of environment and heredity. These themes were central to his *Rougon-Macquart*, a twenty-volume series of novels on the "natural and social history of a family." Zola maintained that the artist must analyze and dissect life as a biologist would a living organism. He said that he had simply done on living bodies the work of analysis that "surgeons perform on corpses."

The second half of the nineteenth century was a golden age for Russian literature. The nineteenth-century realistic novel reached its high point in the works of Leo Tolstoy (TOHL-stoy) (1828–1910) and Fyodor Dostoevsky (FYUD-ur dos-tuh-YEF-skee) (1821–1881). Tolstoy's greatest work was *War and Peace*, a lengthy novel played out against the historical background of Napoleon's invasion of Russia in 1812. It is realistic in its vivid descriptions of military life and character portrayal. Each person is delineated clearly and analyzed psychologically. Upon a great landscape, Tolstoy imposed a fatalistic view of history that ultimately proved irrelevant in the face of life's enduring values of human love and trust.

Dostoevsky combined narrative skill and acute psychological and moral observation with profound insights into human nature. He maintained that the major problem of his age was a loss of spiritual belief. Western people were attempting to gain salvation through the construction of a materialistic paradise built only by human reason and human will. Dostoevsky feared that the failure to incorporate spirit would result in total tyranny. His own life experiences led him to believe that only through suffering and faith could the human soul be purified, views that are evident in his best-known works, *Crime and Punishment* and *The Brothers Karamazov* (see the box on p. 726).

SYMBOLISM At the turn of the century, a new group of writers, known as the Symbolists, reacted against Realism. Primarily interested in writing poetry, the Symbolists believed that an objective knowledge of the world was impossible. The external world was not real but only a collection of symbols that reflected the true reality of the individual human mind. Art, they believed, should function for its own sake instead of serving, criticizing, or seeking to understand society. In the works of such Symbolist poets as W. B. Yeats (YAYTS) and Rainer Maria Rilke (RY-nuhmah-REE-uh RILL-kuh), poetry ceased to be part of popular culture because only through a knowledge of the poet's personal language could one hope to understand what the poem was saying.

Modernism in the Arts

Since the Renaissance, artists had tried to represent reality as accurately as possible, carefully applying brushstrokes and employing perspective to produce realistic portrayals of their subjects. By the late nineteenth century, however, artists were seeking new forms of expression.

IMPRESSIONISM The preamble to modern painting can be found in **Impressionism**, a movement that originated in France in the 1870s when a group of artists rejected the studios and museums and went out into the countryside to paint nature directly. But the Impressionists did not just paint scenes from nature. Their subjects included streets and cabarets, rivers, and busy boulevards—wherever people congregated for work and leisure. In this sense, Impressionist subject matter reflected the pastimes of the new upper middle class. Instead of adhering to the conventional modes of painting and subject matter, the Impressionists sought originality and distinction from past artworks. Their paintings utilized bright colors, dynamic brushstrokes, and a smaller, more private scale than that of their predecessors. Camille Pissarro (kah-MEEL pee-SAH-roh) (1830–1903), one of Impressionism's founders, expressed what they sought:

> Precise drawing is dry and hampers the impression of the whole, it destroys all sensations. Do not define too closely the outlines of things; it is the brushstroke of the right value and color which should produce the drawing. . . . Work at the same time upon sky, water, branches, ground, keeping everything going on an equal basis and unceasingly rework until you have got it. . . . Don't proceed according to rules and principles, but paint what you observe and feel. Paint generously and unhesitatingly, for it is best not to lose the first impression.[9]

DOSTOEVSKY: AN ATTACK ON REASON

The Russian novelist and essayist Fyodor Dostoevsky (1821–1881), whose masterpieces include *Crime and Punishment* and *The Brothers Karamazov*, questioned the Enlightenment argument that reason and science could dictate human behavior. For Dostoevsky, the individual's happiness came from the expression of one's free will. In *Notes From Underground*, the narrator of the novel, called the Underground Man, addresses an imaginary audience in a long monologue in which he expresses his revulsion for the modern principles of progress.

Fyodor Dostoevsky, *Notes from Underground*

Oh, tell me, who first declared, who first proclaimed, that man only does nasty things because he does not know his own real interests; and that if he were enlightened, if his eyes were opened to his real normal interests, man would at once cease to do nasty things, would at once become good and noble because, being enlightened and understanding his real advantage, he would see his own advantage in the good and nothing else, and we all know that not a single man can knowingly act to his own disadvantage. Consequently, so to say, he would begin doing good through necessity. Oh, the babe! Oh, the pure, innocent child! Why, in the first place, when in all these thousands of years has there even been a time when man has acted only for his own advantage? What is to be done with the millions of facts that bear witness that men, knowingly, that is, fully understanding their real advantages, have left them in the background and have rushed headlong on another path, to risk, to chance, compelled to this course by nobody and by nothing, but, as it were, precisely because they did not want the beaten track, and stubbornly, willfully, went off on another difficult, absurd way seeking it almost in the darkness. . . .

You see, gentlemen, reason, gentlemen, is an excellent thing, there is no disputing that, but reason is only reason and can only satisfy man's rational faculty, while will is a manifestation of all life, that is, of all human life including reason as well as all impulses. And although our life, in this manifestation of it, is often worthless, yet it is life nevertheless and not simply extracting square roots. After all, here I, for instance, quite naturally want to live, and not simply my rational faculty, that is, not simply one-twentieth of all my faculties for life. What does reason know? Reason only knows what it has succeeded in learning . . .

Gentlemen, I am tormented by questions; answer them for me. Now you, for instance, want to cure men of their old habits and reform their will in accordance with science and common sense. But how do you know, not only that it is possible, but also that it is *desirable*, to reform man in that way? And what leads you to the conclusion that it is so *necessary* to reform man's desires? In short, how do you know that such a reformation will really be advantageous to man? And go to the heart of the matter, why are you *so sure* of your conviction that not to act against his real normal advantages guaranteed by the conclusions of reason and arithmetic is always advantageous for man and must be a law for all mankind?

 Why did Dostoevsky believe that people would choose not to adhere to reason?

Source: M. Perry, J. Peden, and T. H. Von Laue, eds., *Sources of the Western Tradition, Volume II: From the Renaissance to the Present* (Wadsworth Publishing: Boston, 2008), pp. 273–276.

Impressionists like Pissarro sought to put into their paintings their impressions of the changing effects of light on objects in nature.

Pissarro's ideas are visibly portrayed in the work of Claude Monet (CLOHD moh-NEH) (1840–1926). Monet was especially enchanted with water and painted many pictures in which he attempted to capture the interplay of light, water, and atmosphere, especially evident in *Impression, Sunrise*. It was Monet's *Impression, Sunrise* that gave the Impressionists their name. Following their first exhibition in 1874, a satirical magazine referred to "Impressionism" in mocking the loose brushwork of Monet's painting. By 1877, however, the artists had adopted the name for themselves.

The first Impressionist exhibition included paintings by three women, one of whom was Berthe Morisot (BAYRT mor-ee-ZOH) (1841–1895). Her work fetched the highest price at the first Impressionist auction. Morisot broke with the practice of women being only amateur artists and became a professional painter. Her dedication to the new style of painting won her the disfavor of the traditional French academic artists. Morisot believed that women had a special vision, which was, as she said, "more delicate than that of men." Her special touch is evident in the lighter colors and flowing brushstrokes of *Young Girl by the Window* (see "Global Perspectives" on p. 728). Near the end of her life, Morisot lamented the refusal of men to take her work seriously: "I don't think there has ever been a man who treated a woman as an equal, and that's all I would have asked, for I know I'm worth as much as they."[10]

POST-IMPRESSIONISM By the 1880s, a new movement known as **Post-Impressionism** had emerged in France and soon spread to other European countries. Post-Impressionism retained the Impressionist emphasis on light and color but revolutionized it even further by paying more attention to structure and form. Post-Impressionists sought to use both color and line to express inner feelings and produce a personal

Claude Monet, *Impression,* *Sunrise.* Impressionists rejected "rules and principles" and sought to paint what they observed and felt in order "not to lose the first impression." Monet entered this painting, *Impression, Sunrise,* in the first Impressionist show in 1874. He sought to capture his impression of the fleeting moments of sunrise through the simple interplay of light, water, and atmosphere.

statement of reality rather than an imitation of objects. Impressionist paintings had retained a sense of realism, but the Post-Impressionists shifted from objective reality to subjective reality and in so doing began to withdraw from the artist's traditional task of depicting the external world. Post-Impressionism was the real beginning of modern art.

Paul Cézanne (say-ZAHN) (1839–1906) was one of the most important Post-Impressionists. Initially, he was influenced by the Impressionists but soon rejected their work. In paintings, such as *Mont Sainte-Victoire,* Cézanne sought to express visually the underlying geometric structure and form of everything he painted. He accomplished this by pressing his wet brush directly

Paul Cézanne, *Mont Sainte-Victoire.* Post-Impressionists sought above all to express their inner feelings and capture on canvas their own vision of reality. In *Mont Sainte-Victoire,* depicting a mountain near his home that he painted more than sixty times, Cézanne challenged traditional landscape painting by eliminating a single perspective and replacing it with subtle color that created the form of the mountain.

Impressionist Painting: West and East

BERTHE MORISOT, the first female painter to join the Impressionists, developed her own unique style. Her gentle colors and strong use of pastels are especially evident in *Young Girl by the Window*, seen at the left. Many of her paintings focus on women and domestic scenes. The French Impressionist style also spread abroad. One of the most outstanding Japanese artists of the time was Kuroda Seiki (koor-OH-duh SAY-kee) (1866–1924), who returned from nine years in Paris to open a Western-style school of painting in Tokyo. Shown at the right is his *Under the Trees*, painted in 1898, an example of the fusion of contemporary French Impressionist painting with the Japanese tradition of courtesan prints.

 What differences and similarities do you notice in these two paintings?

Erich Lessing/Art Resource, NY

Christie's Images Ltd./SuperStock

onto the canvas, forming cubes of color on which he built the form of the mountain. His technique enabled him to break down forms to their basic components. Cézanne explained to one young painter that you must see in nature "the cylinder, the sphere, and the cone."

Another famous Post-Impressionist was a tortured and tragic figure, Vincent van Gogh (van GOH *or* vahn GOK) (1853–1890). For van Gogh, art was a spiritual experience. He was especially interested in color and believed that it could act as its own form of language. Van Gogh maintained that artists should paint what they feel, which is evident in his *Starry Night*. Despite his influence on later artists, Van Gogh considered himself an artistic failure—he sold only one of his paintings before committing suicide.

THE SEARCH FOR INDIVIDUAL EXPRESSION By the beginning of the twentieth century, the belief that the task of art was to represent "reality" had lost much of its meaning. By that time, psychology and the new physics had made it evident that many people were not sure what constituted reality anyway. Then, too, the development of photography gave artists another reason to reject visual realism. Invented in the 1830s, photography became popular and widespread after George Eastman produced the first Kodak camera for the mass market in 1888. What was the point of an artist doing what the camera did better? Unlike the camera, which could only mirror reality, artists could create reality. Individual consciousness became the source of meaning. Between 1905 and 1914, this search for individual expression produced a wide variety of

Vincent van Gogh, *The Starry Night*. The Dutch painter Vincent van Gogh was a major figure among the Post-Impressionists. His originality and power of expression made a strong impact on his artistic successors. In *The Starry Night*, painted in 1889, van Gogh's subjective vision was given full play as the dynamic swirling forms of the heavens above overwhelm the village below. The heavens seem alive with a mysterious spiritual force. Van Gogh painted this work in an asylum one year before he committed suicide.

schools of painting, all of which had their greatest impact after World War I.

In 1905, one of the most important figures in modern art was just beginning his career. Pablo Picasso (PAHB-loh pi-KAH-soh) (1881–1973) was from Spain but settled in Paris in 1904. Picasso was extremely flexible and painted in a remarkable variety of styles. He was instrumental in the development of a new style called **Cubism** that used geometric designs as visual stimuli to re-create reality in the viewer's mind. Picasso's 1907 work *Les Demoiselles d'Avignon* (lay dem-wah-ZEL dah-vee-NYONH), which portrays five women in a brothel, has been called the first Cubist painting. Picasso and other artists were inspired by collections of objects shipped from European colonies, such as African masks, textiles, tools, and weapons.

The modern artist's flight from "visual reality" reached a high point in 1910 with the beginning of **abstract painting**. Wassily Kandinsky (vus-YEEL-yee kan-DIN-skee) (1866–1944), a Russian

who worked in Germany, was one of the founders of abstract painting. As is evident in his *Square with White Border*, Kandinsky sought to avoid representation altogether. He believed that art should speak directly to the soul. To do so, it must avoid any reference to visual reality and concentrate on color.

Modernism in Music

In the first half of the nineteenth century, the Romantics' attraction to exotic and primitive cultures had sparked a fascination with folk music, which became increasingly important as musicians began to look for ways to express their national identities. In the second half of the century, new flames of nationalistic spirit were fanned in both literary and musical circles.

GRIEG One example of this new nationalistic spirit may be found in the Scandinavian composer Edvard Grieg (ED-vart GREEG) (1843–1907), who remained a dedicated supporter of

Pablo Picasso, *Les Demoiselles d'Avignon*. Pablo Picasso, a major pioneer of modern art, experimented with a remarkable variety of styles. *Les Demoiselles d'Avignon* (1907) was the first great example of Cubism, which one art historian has called the first style of the twentieth century to break radically with the past. Geometric shapes replace traditional forms, forcing the viewer to re-create reality in his or her own mind. Picasso said of this painting that he painted forms as he thought them, not as he saw them. The head at the upper right of the painting reflects Picasso's attraction to aspects of African art, as is evident from the Congo mask included at the left.

Norwegian nationalism throughout his life. Grieg's nationalism expressed itself in the lyric melodies found in the folk music of his homeland. Among his best-known works is the *Peer Gynt Suite* (1876), incidental music to a play by Henrik Ibsen. Grieg's music paved the way for the creation of a national music style in Norway.

DEBUSSY The Impressionist movement in music followed its artistic counterpart by some thirty years. Impressionist music stressed elusive moods and haunting sensations and is distinctive in its delicate beauty and elegance of sound. The composer most tangibly linked to the Impressionist movement was Claude Debussy (CLOHD duh-bus-SEE) (1862–1918), whose musical compositions were often inspired by the visual arts. One of Debussy's most famous works, *Prelude to the Afternoon of a Faun* (1894), was actually inspired by a poem, "Afternoon of a Faun," written by his friend, the Symbolist poet Stéphane Mallarmé (stay-FAHN mah-lahr-MAY) (1842–1898). But Debussy

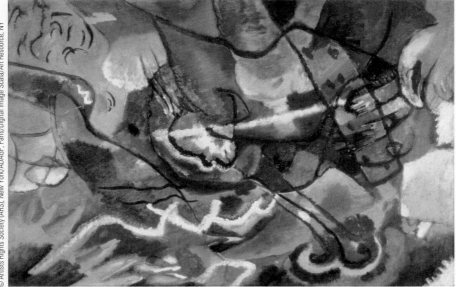

Wassily Kandinsky, *Square with White Border*. One of the originators of abstract painting was the Russian Wassily Kandinsky, who sought to eliminate representation altogether by focusing on color and avoiding any resemblance to visual reality. In *Square with White Border*, Kandinsky used color "to send light into the darkness of men's hearts." He believed that color, like music, could fulfill a spiritual goal of appealing directly to the human senses.

did not tell a story in music; rather, *Prelude to the Afternoon of a Faun* re-created in sound the overall feeling of the poem. Said Mallarmé upon hearing Debussy's piece, "I was not expecting anything like this. This music prolongs the emotion of my poem, and evokes the scene more vividly than color."[11]

Other composers adopted stylistic idioms that imitated presumably primitive forms in an attempt to express less refined and therefore more genuine feelings. A chief exponent of musical primitivism was Igor Stravinsky (EE-gor struh-VIN-skee) (1882–1971), one of the twentieth century's most important composers, both for his compositions and for his impact on other composers. He gained international fame as a ballet composer and together with the Ballet Russe, under the direction of Sergei Diaghilev (syir-GYAY DYAHG-yuh-lif) (1872–1929), revolutionized the world of music with a series of ballets. The three most significant ballets Stravinsky composed for Diaghilev's company were *The Firebird* (1910), *Petrushka* (1911), and *The Rite of Spring* (1913). All three were based on Russian folk tales. *The Rite of Spring* proved to be a revolutionary piece in the development of music. At its premiere on May 29, 1913, the pulsating rhythms, sharp dissonances, and unusual dancing overwhelmed the Paris audience and caused a riot at the theater. Like the intellectuals of his time, Stravinsky sought a new understanding of irrational forces in his music, which became an important force in inaugurating a modern musical movement.

Politics: New Directions and New Uncertainties

 FOCUS QUESTIONS: What gains did women make in their movement for women's rights? How did a new right-wing politics affect the Jews in different parts of Europe? What political problems did Great Britain, Italy, France, Germany, Austria-Hungary, and Russia face between 1894 and 1914, and how did they solve them?

The uncertainties in European intellectual and cultural life were paralleled by growing anxieties in European political life. The seemingly steady progress in the growth of liberal principles and **political democracy** after 1871 was soon slowed or even halted altogether after 1894. The new mass politics had opened the door to changes that many nineteenth-century liberals found unacceptable, and liberals themselves were forced to move in new directions. The appearance of a new right-wing politics based on racism added an ugly note to the already existing anxieties. With their newfound voting rights, workers elected socialists who demanded new reforms when they took their places in legislative bodies. Women, too, made new demands, insisting on the right to vote and using new tactics to gain it. In central and eastern Europe, tensions grew as authoritarian governments refused to meet the demands of reformers. And outside Europe, a new giant appeared in the Western world as the United States emerged as a great industrial power with immense potential.

The Movement for Women's Rights

In the 1830s, a number of women in the United States and Europe, who worked together in several reform movements, became frustrated by the apparent prejudices against females. They sought improvements for women by focusing on specific goals. Family and marriage laws were especially singled out because it was difficult for women to secure divorces and property laws gave husbands almost complete control over the property of their wives. These early efforts were not particularly successful, however. For example, women did not gain the right to their own property until 1870 in Britain, 1900 in Germany, and 1907 in France. Although the British legalized divorce in 1857, the French state permitted only a limited degree of divorce in 1884. In Catholic countries such as Spain and Italy, women had no success at all in achieving the right to divorce their husbands.

NEW PROFESSIONS Divorce and property rights were only a beginning for the women's movement, however. Some middle- and upper-middle-class women gained access to higher education, and others sought entry into occupations dominated by men. The first to fall was teaching. Because medical training was largely closed to women, they sought alternatives through the development of nursing. One nursing pioneer was Amalie Sieveking (uh-MAHL-yuh SEE-vuh-king) (1794–1859), who founded the Female Association for the Care of the Poor and Sick in Hamburg, Germany. As she explained, "To me, at least as important were the benefits which [work with the poor] seemed to promise for those of my sisters who would join me in such a work of charity. The higher interests of my sex were close to my heart."[12] Sieveking's work was followed by the more famous British nurse, Florence Nightingale (1820–1910), whose efforts during the Crimean War, along with those of Clara Barton (1821–1912) in the American Civil War, transformed nursing into a profession of trained, middle-class "women in white."

THE RIGHT TO VOTE By the 1840s and 1850s, the movement for women's rights had entered the political arena with the call for equal political rights. Many feminists believed that the right to vote was the key to all other reforms to improve the position of women. The British women's movement was the most vocal and active in Europe, but it divided over tactics. The liberal Millicent Fawcett (1847–1929) organized a moderate group who believed that women must demonstrate that they would use political power responsibly if they wanted Parliament to grant them the right to vote. Another group, however, favored a more radical approach. Emmeline Pankhurst (EM-uh-leen PANK-hurst) (1858–1928) and her daughters, Christabel and Sylvia, founded the Women's Social and Political Union in 1903, which enrolled mostly middle- and upper-class women. The members of Pankhurst's organization realized the value of the media and used unusual publicity stunts to call attention to their demands (see the box on p. 732 and "Images of Everyday Life" on p. 733). Derisively labeled "suffragettes" by male politicians, they pelted government officials with eggs, chained themselves to lampposts, smashed the windows of fashionable department stores, burned railroad cars, and went

THE STRUGGLE FOR THE RIGHT TO VOTE

EMMELINE PANKHURST, WITH THE HELP of her daughters, was the leader of the women's movement for the right to vote in Britain at the end of the nineteenth century and the beginning of the twentieth century. Believing that peaceful requests were achieving little from the members of Parliament, Pankhurst came to advocate more forceful methods, as is evident in this selection from *My Own Story*, her autobiography published in 1914. Although this confrontational approach was abandoned during World War I, the British government granted women the right to vote in 1918 at the end of the war.

Emmeline Pankhurst, *My Own Story*

I had called upon women to join me in striking at the Government through the only thing that governments are really very much concerned about—property—and the response was immediate. Within a few days the newspapers rang with the story of the attack made on letter boxes in London, Liverpool, Birmingham, Bristol, and half a dozen other cities. In some cases the boxes, when opened by postmen, mysteriously burst into flame; in others the letters were destroyed by corrosive chemicals; in still others the addresses were rendered illegible by black fluids. Altogether it was estimated that over 5,000 letters were completely destroyed and many thousands more were delayed in transit.

It was with a deep sense of their gravity that these letter-burning protests were undertaken, but we felt that something drastic must be done in order to destroy the apathy of the men of England who view with indifference the suffering of women oppressed by unjust laws. As we pointed out, letters, precious though they may be, are less precious than human bodies and souls. . . . And so, in order to call attention to greater crimes against human beings, our letter burnings continued.

In only a few cases were the offenders apprehended, and one of the few women arrested was a helpless cripple, a woman who could move about only in a wheeled chair. She received a sentence of eight months in the first division, and, resolutely hunger striking, was forcibly fed with unusual brutality, the prison doctor deliberately breaking one of her teeth in order to insert a gag. In spite of her disabilities and

her weakness the crippled girl persisted in her hunger strike and her resistance to prison rules, and within a short time had to be released. The excessive sentences of the other pillar box destroyers resolved themselves into very short terms because of the resistance of the prisoners, every one of whom adopted the hunger strike.

It was at this time, February, 1913, less than two years ago as I write these words, that militancy, as it is now generally understood by the public began—militancy in the sense of continued, destructive, guerrilla warfare against the Government through injury to private property. Some property had been destroyed before this time, but the attacks were sporadic, and were meant to be in the nature of a warning as to what might become a settled policy. Now we indeed lighted the torch, and we did it with the absolute conviction that no other course was open to us. We had tried every other measure, as I am sure that I have demonstrated to my readers, and our years of work and suffering and sacrifice had taught us that the Government would not yield to right and justice, what the majority of members of the House of Commons admitted was right and justice, but that the Government would, as other governments invariably do, yield to expediency. Now our task was to show the Government that it was expedient to yield to the women's just demands. In order to do that we had to make England and every department of English life insecure and unsafe. We had to make English law a failure and the courts farce comedy theatres; we had to discredit the Government and Parliament in the eyes of the world; we had to spoil English sports, hurt business, destroy valuable property, demoralize the world of society, shame the churches, upset the whole orderly conduct of life.

That is, we had to do as much of this guerrilla warfare as the people of England would tolerate. When they came to the point of saying to the Government: "Stop this, in the only way it can be stopped, by giving the women of England representation," then we should extinguish our torch.

 What methods did Emmeline Pankhurst advocate be used to achieve the right to vote for women? Why did she feel justified in using these methods? Do you think she was justified? Why or why not?

Source: Emmeline Pankhurst, *My Own Story* (New York: Hearst International Library, 1914).

on hunger strikes in jail. In 1913, Emily Davison accepted martyrdom for the cause when she threw herself in front of the king's horse at the Epsom Derby horse race (see "Film & History" on p. 734). **Suffragists** had one fundamental aim: the right of women to full citizenship in the nation-state.

Although few women elsewhere in Europe used the Pankhursts' confrontational methods, demands for women's rights were heard throughout Europe and the United States

before World War I. Nevertheless, only in Finland, Norway, and some American states did women actually receive the right to vote before 1914. It would take the dramatic upheaval of World War I before male-dominated governments capitulated on this basic issue (see Chapter 25).

EFFORTS FOR PEACE Women reformers took on other issues besides suffrage. In many countries, women supported

The Struggle for the Right to Vote

FOR MANY FEMINISTS, THE RIGHT TO VOTE came to represent the key to other reforms that would benefit women. In Britain, suffragists attracted attention to their cause by unusual publicity stunts. The photograph at the left shows the arrest of a suffragist who had chained herself to the railings of Buckingham Palace in London. Below is a photo of Emily Davison sacrificing her life for the cause by throwing herself under the king's horse at the Epsom Derby horse race. The third illustration shows police arresting Emmeline Pankhurst outside Buckingham Palace in 1914.

Central Press/Getty Images

STAPLETON COLLECTION/Private Collection/Bridgeman Images

Arthur Barrett/Getty Images

peace movements. Bertha von Suttner (ZOOT-nuh) (1843–1914) became the head of the Austrian Peace Society and protested against the growing arms race of the 1890s. Her novel *Lay Down Your Arms* became a best-seller and brought her the Nobel Peace Prize in 1905. Lower-class women also took up the cause of peace. In 1911, a group of female workers marched in Vienna and demanded, "We want an end to armaments, to the means of murder and we want these millions to be spent on the needs of the people."[13]

THE NEW WOMAN Bertha von Suttner was but one example of the "new women" who were becoming more prominent at the turn of the century. These women renounced traditional feminine roles. Although some of them supported political ideologies such as socialism that flew in the face of the ruling classes, others simply sought new freedom outside the household and new roles other than those of wives and mothers.

Maria Montessori (mahn-tuh-SOR-ee) (1870–1952) was a good example of the "new woman." Breaking with tradition, she attended medical school at the University of Rome. Although often isolated by the male students, she persisted and in 1896 became the first Italian woman to receive a medical degree. Three years later, she undertook a lecture tour in Italy on the subject of the "new woman," whom she characterized as a woman who followed a rational, scientific perspective. In keeping with this ideal, Montessori put her medical background to work in a school for mentally handicapped children. She devised new teaching materials that enabled these children to read and write and became convinced, as she later stated, that the same methods applied to normal students would develop their personality in a "marvelous and surprising way." Subsequently, she established a system of childhood education based on natural and spontaneous activities in which students learned at their own pace. By the 1930s, hundreds of Montessori schools had been established in Europe and the United States. As a professional woman and an unwed mother, Montessori also embodied some of the freedoms of the "new woman."

Jews in the European Nation-State

Near the end of the nineteenth century, a revival of racism combined with extreme nationalism to produce a new right-wing politics aimed primarily at the Jews. Of course, anti-Semitism was not new to European civilization. Since the Middle Ages, Jews had been portrayed as the murderers of Jesus and subjected to mob violence; their rights had been restricted, and they had been physically separated from Christians in quarters known as ghettos.

In the nineteenth century, as a result of the ideals of the Enlightenment and the French Revolution, Jews were increasingly granted legal equality in many European countries. The French revolutionary decrees of 1790 and 1791 emancipated the Jews and admitted them to full citizenship. After the revolutions of 1848, emancipation became a fact of life for Jews throughout western and central Europe. For many Jews, emancipation enabled them to leave the ghetto and become assimilated as hundreds of thousands of Jews entered what had been the closed worlds of parliaments and universities. In 1880, for example, Jews made up 10 percent of the population of the city of Vienna, Austria, but 39 percent of its medical students and 23 percent of its law students. A Jew could "leave his Jewishness behind," as the career of Benjamin Disraeli, who became prime minister of Great Britain, demonstrated. Many other Jews became successful bankers, lawyers, scientists, scholars, journalists, and stage performers.

ANTI-SEMITISM IN THE AUSTRIAN EMPIRE AND GERMANY These achievements represented only one side of the picture, however. In Austrian politics, for example, the Christian Socialists combined agitation for workers with a virulent **anti-Semitism**. They were most powerful in Vienna, where they were led by Karl Lueger (LOO-gur), mayor of Vienna from 1897 to 1910. Imperial Vienna at the turn of the century was a brilliant center of European culture, but it was also the home of an insidious German nationalism that blamed Jews for the corruption of German culture. It was in Vienna between 1907 and 1913 that Adolf Hitler later claimed to have found his worldview, one that was largely based on violent German nationalism and rabid anti-Semitism.

Germany, too, had its right-wing anti-Semitic parties, such as Adolf Stöcker's Christian Social Party. These parties used anti-Semitism to win the votes of traditional lower-middle-class groups who felt threatened by the new economic forces of the times. These German anti-Semitic parties were based on race. In medieval times, Jews could convert to Christianity and escape from their religion. To modern racial anti-Semites, Jews were racially stained; this could not be altered by conversion. One could not be both a German and a Jew. Hermann Ahlwardt (HER-mahn AHL-vart), an anti-Semitic member of the German Reichstag, made this clear in a speech to that body:

> The Jew is no German. . . . A Jew who was born in Germany does not thereby become a German; he is still a Jew. Therefore it is imperative that we realize that Jewish racial characteristics differ so greatly from ours that a common life of Jews and Germans under the same laws is quite impossible because the Germans will perish.[14]

After 1898, the political strength of the German anti-Semitic parties began to decline.

PERSECUTION OF JEWS IN EASTERN EUROPE The worst treatment of Jews in the last two decades of the nineteenth century and the first decade of the twentieth occurred in eastern Europe, where 72 percent of the entire world Jewish population lived. Russian Jews were admitted to secondary schools and universities only under a quota system and were forced to live in certain regions of the country. Persecutions and **pogroms** (organized massacres) were widespread. Between 1903 and 1906, pogroms took place in almost seven hundred Russian towns and villages, mostly in Ukraine. Hundreds of thousands of Jews decided to emigrate to escape the persecution. Between 1881 and 1899, an average of 23,000 Jews left Russia each year. Many of them went to the United States and Canada, although some (probably about 25,000) moved to Palestine, which soon became the focus for a Jewish nationalist movement called **Zionism**.

THE ZIONIST MOVEMENT The emancipation of the nineteenth century had presented vast opportunities for some Jews but dilemmas for others. Did emancipation mean full assimilation, and did assimilation mean the disruption of traditional Jewish life? Many Jews paid the price willingly, but others advocated a different answer, a return to Palestine. For many Jews, Palestine, the land of ancient Israel, had long been the land of their dreams.

During the nineteenth century, as nationalist ideas spread, the idea of national independence captured the imagination of some Jews. A key figure in the growth of political Zionism was Theodor Herzl (TAY-oh-dor HAYRT-sul) (1860–1904). In 1896, he published a book called *The Jewish State* (see the box on p. 736) in which he maintained that "the Jews who wish it will have their state." Financial support for the development of settlements in Palestine came from wealthy Jewish banking families who wanted a refuge in Palestine for persecuted Jews. Establishing settlements was difficult, though, because Palestine was then part of the Ottoman Empire and Ottoman authorities were opposed to Jewish immigration. In 1891, one Jewish essayist pointed to the problems this would create:

> We abroad are accustomed to believe that Erez Israel [the land of Israel] is almost totally desolate at present . . . but in reality it is not so. . . . Arabs, especially those in towns, see and understand our activities and aims in the country but keep quiet and pretend as if they did not know . . . and they try to exploit us, too, and profit from the new guests while laughing at us in their hearts. But if the time comes and our people

make such progress as to displace the people of the country . . . they will not lightly surrender the place.[15]

Despite the warnings, however, the First Zionist Congress, which met in Switzerland in 1897, proclaimed as its aim the creation of a "home in Palestine" secured by public law for the Jewish people. One thousand Jews migrated to Palestine in 1901, and the number rose to three thousand annually between 1904 and 1914; but on the eve of World War I, the Zionist dream remained just that.

The Transformation of Liberalism: Great Britain and Italy

In dealing with the problems created by the new mass politics, liberal governments often followed policies that undermined the basic tenets of liberalism. This was particularly true in Great Britain and Italy.

GREAT BRITAIN In Britain, the demands of the working-class movement caused Liberals to move away from their ideals. Liberals were forced to adopt significant social reforms due to the pressure of two new working-class organizations: trade unions and the Labour Party. Frustrated by the government's failure to enact social reform, trade unions began to advocate more radical change of the economic system, calling for "collective ownership" and control over production, distribution, and exchange. This "new unionism" also led to the union organization of many steel factory workers and to new confrontations in the streets of London as British workers struck for a minimum wage and other benefits.

At the same time, a movement for laborers emerged among a group of intellectuals known as the Fabian Socialists who stressed the need for the workers to use their right to vote to capture the House of Commons and pass legislation that would benefit the laboring class. Neither the Fabian Socialists nor the British trade unions were Marxist. They did not advocate class struggle and revolution but instead favored evolution toward a socialist state by democratic means. In 1900, representatives of the trade unions and Fabian Socialists coalesced to form the Labour Party. Although the new party won only one seat in 1900, it managed to elect twenty-nine members to the House of Commons in 1906.

The Liberals, who gained control of the House of Commons in that year and held the government from 1906 to 1914, perceived that they would have to enact a program of social welfare or lose the support of the workers. The policy of reform was especially advanced by David Lloyd George (1863–1945), a brilliant orator from Wales who had been deeply moved by the misery of Welsh coal miners and served as chancellor of the Exchequer from 1908 to 1915. The Liberals abandoned the classic principles of *laissez-faire* and voted for a series of social reforms. The National Insurance Act of 1911 provided benefits for workers in case of sickness and unemployment, to be paid for by compulsory contributions from workers, employers, and the state. Additional legislation provided a small pension for retirees over seventy and compensation for workers injured on the job. To pay for the new program, Lloyd George increased

Palestine

THE VOICE OF ZIONISM: THEODOR HERZL AND THE JEWISH STATE

THE AUSTRIAN JEWISH JOURNALIST Theodor Herzl wrote *The Jewish State* in the summer of 1895 in Paris while he was covering the Dreyfus case for his Vienna newspaper. During several weeks of feverish composition, he set out to analyze the fundamental causes of anti-Semitism and devise a solution to the "Jewish problem." In this selection, he discusses two of his major conclusions.

Theodor Herzl, *The Jewish State*

I do not intend to arouse sympathetic emotions on our behalf. That would be a foolish, futile, and undignified proceeding. I shall content myself with putting the following questions to the Jews: Is it true that, in countries where we live in perceptible numbers, the position of Jewish lawyers, doctors, technicians, teachers, and employees of all descriptions becomes daily more intolerable? True, that the Jewish middle classes are seriously threatened? True, that the passions of the mob are incited against our wealthy people? True, that our poor endure greater sufferings than any other proletariat?

I think that this external pressure makes itself felt everywhere. In our economically upper classes it causes discomfort, in our middle classes continual and grave anxieties, in our lower classes absolute despair.

Everything tends, in fact, to one and the same conclusion, which is clearly enunciated in that classic Berlin phrase: 'Juden raus!" (Out with the Jews!)

I shall now put the Jewish Question in the curtest possible form: Are we to "get out" now? And if so, to what place?

Or, may we yet remain? And if so, how long?

Let us first settle the point of staying where we are. Can we hope for better days, can we possess our souls in patience, can we wait in pious resignation till the princes and peoples of this earth are more mercifully disposed toward us? I say that we cannot hope for a change in the current of feeling. And why not? Were we as near to the hearts of princes as are their other subjects, even so they could not protect us. They would only feed popular hatred of Jews by showing us too much favor.

By "too much," I really mean less than is claimed as a right by every ordinary citizen, or by every race. The nations in whose midst Jews live are all, either covertly or openly, Anti-Semitic. . . .

The whole plan is in its essence perfectly simple, as it must necessarily be if it is to come within the comprehension of all.

Let the sovereignty be granted us over a portion of the globe large enough to satisfy the rightful requirements of a nation; the rest we shall manage for ourselves.

The creation of a new State is neither ridiculous nor impossible. We have in our day witnessed the process in connection with nations which were not in the bulk of the middle class, but poorer, less educated, and consequently weaker than ourselves. The Governments of all countries scourged by Anti-Semitism will be keenly interested in assisting us to obtain the sovereignty we want. . . .

Palestine is our ever-memorable historic home. The very name of Palestine would attract our people with a force of marvelous potency. Supposing his Majesty the Sultan were to give us Palestine, we could in return undertake to regulate the whole finances of Turkey. We should there form a portion of the rampart of Europe against Asia, an outpost of civilization as opposed to barbarism. We should as a neutral State remain in contact with all Europe, which would have to guarantee our existence. The sanctuaries of Christendom would be safeguarded by assigning to them an extra-territorial status such as is well known to the law of nations. We should form a guard of honor about these sanctuaries, answering for the fulfillment of this duty with our existence. This guard of honor would be the great symbol of the solution of the Jewish Question after eighteen centuries of Jewish suffering.

 What forces in European society came together to intensify anti-Semitism in the late nineteenth century? What was the relationship between nationalism and Zionism at this time? Was Herzl's Zionism simply a reaction to Western anti-Semitism, or did other developments also contribute to his movement?

Source: From Theodor Herzl, *The Jewish State*, 3rd ed., trans. S. d'Avigdor (New York: Federation of American Zionists, 1917), pp. 7–8, 11, 12.

---

the tax burden on the wealthy classes. Though both the benefits of the program and the tax increases were modest, they were the first hesitant steps toward the future British welfare state. Liberalism, which had been based on the principle that the government that governs least governs best, had been transformed.

In the effort to achieve social reform, Lloyd George was also forced to confront the power of the House of Lords. Composed of hereditary aristocrats, the House of Lords took a strong stance against Lloyd George's effort to pay for social reform measures by taxes, however modest, on the wealthy. In 1911, the Liberals pushed through a law that restricted the ability of the House of

Lords to impede legislation enacted by the House of Commons. After 1911, the House of Lords became largely a debating society.

The Liberals also tried to solve the Irish problem (see Chapter 23). Parliament finally granted home rule in 1914, but the explosive situation in Ireland itself created more problems. Irish Protestants in northern Ireland, especially in the province of Ulster, wanted no part of an Irish Catholic state. The outbreak of World War I enabled the British government to sidestep the potentially explosive issue and to suspend Irish home rule for the duration of the war. Failure to deal decisively with the issue simply led to more problems later.

David Lloyd George. David Lloyd George (on the left), the Chancellor of the Exchequer, walking with Winston Churchill to the House of Commons on Budget Day in April 1910. The 'People's Budget' put forth by Lloyd George in 1908 led to a constitutional crisis and passage of the Parliament Act in 1911.

ITALY Liberals had even greater problems in Italy. A certain amount of stability was achieved from 1903 to 1914 when the liberal leader Giovanni Giolitti (joh-VAHN-nee joh-LEE-tee) served intermittently as prime minister. Giolitti was a master of using *trasformismo*, or **transformism**, a system in which old political groups were transformed into new government coalitions by political and economic bribery. In the long run, however, Giolitti's devious methods made Italian politics even more corrupt and unmanageable. When urban workers turned to violence to protest their living and working conditions, Giolitti tried to appease them with social welfare legislation and universal male suffrage in 1912. To strengthen his popularity, he also aroused nationalistic passions by conquering Libya. Despite his efforts, however, worker unrest continued, and in 1914 government troops had to be used to quell rioting workers.

France: Travails of the Third Republic

In the 1890s, the fragile Third Republic remained divided over whether to embrace the republic or restore some form of limited monarchy. An unexpected crisis, which exposed the renewed anti-Semitism in Europe in the late nineteenth century, embroiled the country in a divisive struggle. Early in 1895,

Alfred Dreyfus (DRY-fuss), a wealthy Jew and a captain in the French general staff, was found guilty by a secret military court of selling army secrets and condemned to life imprisonment on Devil's Island. Evidence soon emerged that pointed to his innocence. Another officer, a Catholic aristocrat, was more obviously the traitor, but the army, a stronghold of aristocratic and Catholic officers, refused a new trial. Some right-wing journalists even used the case to push their own anti-Semitic views. After a wave of intense public outrage, however, the Republic's leaders insisted on a new trial. Although the new trial failed to set aside the guilty verdict, the government pardoned Dreyfus in 1899, and in 1906, he was finally exonerated.

The impact of the Dreyfus affair extended beyond France. It convinced Theodor Herzl, who covered the trial for a Viennese newspaper, that assimilation did not protect Jews from anti-Semitism. As a result, as we have seen, he came to advocate that Jews needed a country of their own, leading to the Zionist movement.

In France itself, the Dreyfus affair led to a change in government. Moderate republicans lost control to radical republicans who were determined to make greater progress toward a more democratic society by breaking the power of the Republic's enemies, especially the army and the Catholic Church. The army was purged of all high-ranking officers who had anti-republican reputations. Most of the Catholic religious orders that had controlled many French schools were forced to leave France. Moreover, church and state were officially separated in 1905, and during the next two years, the government seized church property and stopped paying clerical salaries.

These changes ended the political threat from the right to the Third Republic, which by now commanded the loyalty of most French people. Nevertheless, problems remained. As a nation of small businessmen and farmers, the French lagged far behind Great Britain, Germany, and the United States in industrial activity. Moreover, a surge of industrialization after 1896 left the nation with the realization that little had been done to appease the discontent of the French working classes and their abysmal working conditions. Since only a quarter of French wage earners worked in industry, the French parliament felt little pressure to enact labor legislation. This made the use of strikes more appealing to the working classes. The brutal government repression of labor walkouts in 1911 only further alienated the working classes.

Growing Tensions in Germany

The new imperial Germany begun by Bismarck in 1871 continued as an "authoritarian, conservative, military-bureaucratic power state" during the reign of Emperor William II (1888–1918). Unstable and aggressive, the emperor was inclined to tactless remarks, as when he told the soldiers of a Berlin regiment that they must be prepared to shoot their fathers and mothers if he ordered them to do so. A small group of about twenty powerful men joined William in setting government policy.

By 1914, Germany had become the strongest military and industrial power on the Continent. New social configurations had emerged, as more than 50 percent of German workers had jobs in industry while only 30 percent of the workforce was still in agriculture. Urban centers had mushroomed in number and size. The rapid changes in William's Germany helped produce a society torn between modernization and traditionalism.

The growth of industrialization led to even greater expansion for the Social Democratic Party. Despite the enactment of new welfare legislation to favor the working classes, William II was no more successful than Bismarck at slowing the growth of the Social Democrats. By 1912, it had become the largest single party in the Reichstag. At the same time, the party increasingly became less revolutionary and more revisionist in its outlook. Nevertheless, its growth frightened the middle and upper classes, who blamed labor for their own problems.

With the expansion of industry and cities came demands for more political participation and growing sentiment for reforms that would produce greater democratization. Conservative forces, especially the landowning nobility and representatives of heavy industry, two of the powerful ruling groups in Germany, tried to block it by supporting William II's activist foreign policy (see "New Directions and New Crises" later in this chapter). Expansionism, they believed, would divert people from further democratization.

The tensions in German society created by the conflict between modernization and traditionalism were also manifested in a new, radicalized, right-wing politics. A number of pressure groups arose to support nationalistic goals. Groups such as the Pan-German League stressed strong German nationalism and advocated imperialism as a tool to overcome social divisions and unite all classes. They were also anti-Semitic and denounced Jews as the destroyers of the national community.

Austria-Hungary: The Problem of the Nationalities

At the beginning of the 1890s, Austria-Hungary was still troubled by the problem of its numerous nationalities (see Chapter 23). The granting of universal male suffrage in 1907 served only to exacerbate the problem because nationalities that had played no role in the government now agitated in the parliament for autonomy. This led prime ministers after 1900 to ignore the parliament and rely increasingly on imperial emergency decrees to govern. Parliament itself became a bizarre forum in which, in the words of one incredulous observer, "about a score of men, all decently clad, were seated or standing, each at his little desk. Some made an infernal noise violently opening and shutting the lids of their desks. Others emitted a blaring sound from little toy trumpets; . . . still others beat snare drums."[16]

The threat the nationalities posed to the position of the dominant German minority in Austria also produced a backlash in the form of virulent German nationalism. As Austria industrialized in the 1870s and 1880s, two working-class parties came into existence, both strongly influenced by nationalism. The Social Democrats, although a Marxist party that argued for social and political gains such as universal suffrage and the eight-hour workday, supported the Austrian government, fearful that the autonomy of the different nationalities would hinder industrial development and prevent improvements for workers. Even more nationalistic, however, were the Christian Socialists, who, as we have seen, combined agitation for workers with a virulent anti-Semitism.

While subjugating their nationalities, the ruling Magyars in Hungary developed a movement for complete separation from Austria. In 1903, when they demanded that the Hungarian army be separated from the imperial army, Emperor Francis Joseph (as king of Hungary) responded quickly and forcefully. He threatened to impose universal male suffrage on Hungary, a move that would challenge Magyar domination of the minorities. Hungarian leaders fell into line, and the new Hungarian parliamentary leader, Count István Tisza (ISHT-vun TISS-ah), cooperated in maintaining the Dual Monarchy. Magyar rule in Hungary, he realized, was inextricably bound up with the Dual Monarchy; its death would only harm the rule of the Magyar landowning class.

Industrialization and Revolution in Imperial Russia

Starting in the 1890s, Russia experienced a massive surge of state-sponsored industrialism under the guiding hand of Sergei Witte (syir-GYAY VIT-uh) (1849–1915), the minister for finance from 1892 to 1903. Witte saw industrial growth as crucial to Russia's national strength. Believing that railroads were a powerful weapon in economic development, Witte pushed the government toward a program of massive railroad construction. By 1900, some 35,000 miles of railroads had been built, including large parts of the 5,000-mile trans-Siberian line between Moscow and Vladivostok, on the Pacific Ocean. Witte also encouraged a system of protective tariffs to help Russian industry and persuaded Tsar Nicholas II (1894–1917) that foreign capital was essential for rapid industrial development. Witte's program made possible the rapid growth of a modern steel and coal industry in Ukraine, making Russia by 1900 the fourth-largest producer of steel behind the United States, Germany, and Great Britain.

With industrialization came factories, an industrial working class, industrial suburbs around Saint Petersburg and Moscow, and the pitiful working and living conditions that accompanied the beginnings of industrialization everywhere. Socialist thought and socialist parties developed, although repression in Russia soon forced them to go underground and become revolutionary. The Marxist Social Democratic Party, for example, held its first congress in Minsk in 1898, but the arrest of its leaders caused the next one to be held in Brussels in 1903, attended by Russian émigrés. The Social Revolutionaries worked to overthrow the tsarist autocracy and establish peasant socialism. Having no other outlet for their opposition to the regime, they advocated political terrorism and attempted to assassinate government officials and members of the ruling dynasty. The growing opposition to the tsarist regime finally exploded into revolution in 1905.

THE REVOLUTION OF 1905 As had happened elsewhere in Europe in the nineteenth century, defeat in war led to political

Nicholas II. The last tsar of Russia hoped to preserve the traditional autocratic ways of his predecessors. In this photograph, Nicholas II and his wife, Alexandra, are shown in 1913 with their family at the Kremlin at the celebration of the three-hundredth anniversary of the founding of the Romanov dynasty.

upheaval at home. Russia's territorial expansion to the south and east, especially its designs on northern Korea, led to a confrontation with Japan. Japan made a surprise attack on the Russian eastern fleet at Port Arthur on February 8, 1904. In response, Russia sent its Baltic fleet halfway around the world to the East, only to be defeated by the new Japanese navy at Tsushima (TSOO-shee-mah) Strait off the coast of Japan. Much to the astonishment of many Europeans, who could not believe that an Asian state was militarily superior to a great European power, the Russians admitted defeat and sued for peace in 1905.

In the midst of the war, the growing discontent of increased numbers of Russians rapidly led to upheaval. A middle class of business and professional people longed for liberal institutions and a liberal political system. Nationalities were dissatisfied with their domination by an ethnic Russian population that constituted only 40 percent of the empire's total population. Peasants were still suffering from lack of land, and laborers felt oppressed by their working and living conditions in Russia's large cities. The breakdown of the transport system caused by the Russo-Japanese War led to food shortages in the major cities of Russia. As a result, on January 9, 1905, a massive procession of workers went to the Winter Palace in Saint Petersburg to present a petition of grievances to the tsar. Troops foolishly opened fire on the peaceful demonstration, killing hundreds and launching a revolution (see the box on p. 740).

This "Bloody Sunday" incited workers to call strikes and form unions; meanwhile the elected regional councils, or *zemstovs*, demanded parliamentary government, ethnic groups revolted, and peasants burned the houses of landowners. After a general strike in October 1905, the government capitulated. Nicholas II issued the October Manifesto, in which he granted civil liberties and agreed to create a legislative assembly known as the Duma (DOO-muh), elected directly by a broad franchise. This satisfied the middle-class moderates, who now supported the government's repression of a workers' uprising in Moscow at the end of 1905.

FAILURE OF THE REVOLUTION But real constitutional monarchy proved short-lived. Under Peter Stolypin (stuh-LIP-yin), who served as the tsar's chief adviser from late 1906 until his assassination in 1911, important agrarian reforms dissolved the village ownership of land and opened the door to private ownership by enterprising peasants. Nicholas II, however, was no friend of reform. Already by 1907, the tsar had curtailed the power of the Duma, and after Stolypin's murder, he fell back on the army and bureaucracy to rule Russia.

The Rise of the United States

Between 1860 and 1914, the United States made the shift from an agrarian to a mighty industrial nation. American heavy industry stood unchallenged in 1900. In that year, the Carnegie Steel

BLOODY SUNDAY

ON JANUARY 9, 1905, A MASSIVE PROCESSION of workers led by a Russian Orthodox priest loyal to the tsar, Father Gregory Gapon, carried pictures of the tsar and a petition to present to him at his imperial palace in Saint Petersburg. Although the tsar was not even there, government officials ordered troops to fire on the crowd. This account is by the leader of the procession, Father Gapon.

An Account of Bloody Sunday

We were not more than thirty yards from the soldiers, being separated from them only by the bridge over the Tarakanovskii Canal, which here marks the border of the city, when suddenly, without any warning and without a moment's delay, was heard the dry crack of many rifleshots. I was informed later on that a bugle was blown, but we could not hear it above the singing, and even if we had heard it we should not have known what it meant.

Vasiliev, with whom I was walking hand in hand, suddenly left hold of my arm and sank upon the snow. One of the workmen who carried the banners fell also. Immediately one of the two police officers to whom I had referred shouted out, "What are you doing? How dare you fire upon the portrait of the Tsar?" This, of course, had no effect, and both he and the other officer were shot down—as I learned afterwards, one was killed and the other dangerously wounded.

I turned rapidly to the crowd and shouted to them to lie down, and I also stretched myself out upon the ground. As we lay thus another volley was fired, and another, and yet another, till it seemed as though the shooting was continuous. The crowd first kneeled and then lay flat down, hiding their heads from the rain of bullets, while the rear rows of the procession began to run away. The smoke of the fire lay before us like a thin cloud, and I felt it stiflingly in my throat. An old man named Lavrentiev, who was carrying the Tsar's portrait, had been one of the first victims. Another old man caught the portrait as it fell from his hands and carried it till he too was killed by the next volley. With his last gasp the old man said, "I may die, but I will see the Tsar." One of the banner-carriers had his arm broken by a bullet. A little boy of ten years, who was carrying a church lantern, fell pierced by a bullet, but still held the lantern tightly and tried to rise again, when another shot struck him down. Both the smiths who had guarded me were killed, as well as all those who were carrying the icons and banners; and all these emblems now lay scattered on the snow. . . .

Horror crept into my heart. The thought flashed through my mind, "And this is the work of our Little Father, the Tsar." Perhaps this anger saved me, for now I knew in very truth that a new chapter was opened in the book of the history of our people. I stood up, and a little group of workmen gathered round me again. Looking backward, I saw that our line, though still stretching away into the distance, was broken and that many of the people were fleeing. It was in vain that I called to them, and in a moment I stood there, the center of a few scores of men, trembling with indignation amid the broken ruins of our movement.

 What may have led the troops to fire on the demonstrators? According to this selection, who was responsible for the shooting? Was the author justified in holding them responsible? Why or why not? What impact, if any, might the violence of 1905 have had on the events of 1917?

Source: George Gapon, *The Story of My Life* (New York: Dutton, 1906), pp. 182–185.

Company alone produced more steel than Great Britain's entire steel industry. Industrialization also led to urbanization. While established cities, such as New York, Philadelphia, and Boston, grew even larger, other moderate-size cities, such as Pittsburgh, grew by leaps and bounds because of industrialization. Whereas 20 percent of Americans lived in cities in 1860, over 40 percent did in 1900. Four-fifths of the population growth in cities came from migration. Eight to 10 million Americans moved from rural areas into the cities, and 14 million foreigners came from abroad. By 1910, the total population reached 91,972,000, which was greater than the populations of Germany and Great Britain.

The United States had become the world's richest nation and greatest industrial power. Yet serious questions remained about the quality of American life. In 1890, the richest 9 percent of Americans owned an incredible 71 percent of all the wealth. Labor unrest over unsafe working conditions, strict work discipline, and periodic cycles of devastating unemployment led workers to organize. By the turn of the century, one national organization, the American Federation of Labor, emerged as labor's dominant voice. Its lack of real power, however, was reflected in its membership figures. In 1900, it included only 8.4 percent of the American industrial labor force.

During the so-called Progressive Era after 1900, an age of reform swept across the United States. State governments enacted economic and social legislation, such as laws that governed hours, wages, and working conditions, especially for women and children. The realization that state laws were ineffective in dealing with nationwide problems, however, led to a Progressive movement at the national level. The Meat Inspection Act (1906) and Pure Food and Drug Act (1905)

CHRONOLOGY — Politics, 1894–1914

Reign of Emperor William II	1888–1918
Reign of Tsar Nicholas II	1894–1917
Dreyfus affair in France	1895–1899
Theodor Herzl, *The Jewish State*	1896
Austrian Christian Socialists under Karl Lueger	1897–1910
First congress of Social Democratic Party in Russia	1898
Beginning of the Progressive Era in the United States	1900
Formation of Labour Party in Britain	1900
Pankhursts establish Women's Social and Political Union	1903
Ministries of Giovanni Giolitti in Italy	1903–1914
Russo-Japanese War	1904–1905
Revolution in Russia	1905
National Insurance Act in Britain	1911
Universal male suffrage in Italy	1912
Social Democratic Party becomes largest party in Germany	1912

provided for a limited degree of federal regulation of corrupt industrial practices, while government led anti-trust suits that broke up large corporate trusts, such as Standard Oil Company, the company that controlled much of the petrochemical industry in the United States. The presidency of Woodrow Wilson (1913–1921) witnessed the enactment of a graduated federal income tax and the establishment of the Federal Reserve System, which permitted the federal government to play a role in important economic decisions formerly made by bankers. Like European nations, the United States was slowly adopting policies that extended the functions of the state.

The Growth of Canada

Canada faced problems of national unity at the end of the nineteenth century. In 1870, the Dominion of Canada had four provinces: Quebec, Ontario, Nova Scotia, and New Brunswick. With the addition of two more—Manitoba and British Columbia—the following year, Canada stretched from the Atlantic to the Pacific.

Real unity was difficult to achieve, however, because of the distrust between the English-speaking majority and the French-speaking Canadians, living primarily in Quebec. Wilfred Laurier (LOR-ee-ay) (1841–1919), who became the first French Canadian prime minister in 1896, was able to reconcile the two groups. During his administration, industrialization boomed, especially the production of textiles, furniture, and railway equipment.

Hundreds of thousands of immigrants, primarily from Europe, also flowed into Canada. Many settled on lands in the west, thus helping populate Canada's vast territories.

The New Imperialism

 FOCUS QUESTION: What were the causes of the new imperialism that took place after 1880, and what effects did European imperialism have on Africa and Asia?

In the 1880s, European states embarked on an intense scramble for overseas territory. This "**new imperialism**," as some have called it, led Europeans to carve up Asia and Africa. What explains the mad scramble for colonies after 1880?

Causes of the New Imperialism

The existence of competitive nation-states and growing nationalism after 1870 was undoubtedly a major determinant in the growth of the new imperialism. As European affairs grew tense, heightened competition spurred European states to acquire colonies abroad that provided ports and coaling stations for their navies. Great Britain, for example, often expanded into new regions not for economic reasons but to keep the French, Germans, or Russians from setting up bases that could harm British interests. Colonies were also a source of international prestige. Once the scramble for colonies began, failure to enter the race was perceived as a sign of weakness, totally unacceptable to an aspiring great power. As a British foreign minister wrote, "When I left the Foreign Office in 1880, nobody thought about Africa. When I returned to it in 1885, the nations of Europe were almost quarreling with each other as to the various portions of Africa which they should obtain."[17] Late-nineteenth-century imperialism was closely tied to nationalism.

Patriotic fervor was often used to arouse interest in imperialism. Schools used maps of colonial territories in teaching geography. Newspapers and magazines often featured soldiers' letters that made imperialism seem a heroic adventure on behalf of one's country. Volunteer groups, such as geographic societies and naval leagues, fostered enthusiasm for imperial adventures. Plays were even written to excite people about expansion abroad, while artists and photographers traveled with British colonial forces to provide images for British newspapers.

THE ROLE OF SOCIAL DARWINISM AND RACISM Imperialism was also tied to social Darwinism and racism. As noted earlier, social Darwinists believed that in the struggle between nations, the fit are victorious and survive. Superior races must dominate inferior races by military force to show how strong and virile they are. As British professor of mathematics Karl Pearson argued in 1900, "The path of progress is strewn with the wrecks of nations; traces are everywhere to be seen of the [slaughtered remains] of inferior races. . . . Yet these dead

The first step towards lightening

The White Man's Burden

is through teaching the virtues of cleanliness.

Pears' Soap

is a potent factor in brightening the dark corners of the earth as civilization advances, while amongst the cultured of all nations it holds the highest place—it is the ideal toilet soap.

Soap and the White Man's Burden. The concept of the "white man's burden" included the belief that the superiority of their civilization obligated Europeans to impose their practices on supposedly primitive nonwhites. This advertisement for Pears' Soap clearly communicates the Europeans' view of their responsibility toward other peoples.

people are, in very truth, the stepping stones on which mankind has arisen to the higher intellectual and deeper emotional life of today."[18] Others were equally blunt. One Englishman wrote, "To the development of the White Man, the Black Man and the Yellow must ever remain inferior, and as the former raised itself higher and yet higher, so did these latter seem to shrink out of humanity and appear nearer and nearer to the brutes."[19]

RELIGIOUS MOTIVES Some Europeans took a more religious or humanitarian approach to imperialism, arguing that Europeans had a moral responsibility to civilize ignorant peoples. This notion of the "white man's burden" (see "Opposing Viewpoints" on p. 743) helped at least the more idealistic individuals rationalize imperialism in their own minds. One British official declared that the British Empire was under God, "the greatest instrument for good that the

world has seen." Thousands of Catholic and Protestant missionaries went abroad to seek converts to their faith. Nevertheless, the belief that the superiority of their civilization obligated them to impose modern industries and new medicines on supposedly primitive nonwhites was yet another form of racism.

THE ECONOMIC MOTIVE Some historians have emphasized an economic motivation for imperialism. There was a great demand for natural resources and products not found in Western countries, such as rubber, oil, and tin. Instead of just trading for these products, European investors advocated direct control of the areas where the raw materials were found. The large surpluses of capital that bankers and industrialists were accumulating often encouraged them to seek higher rates of profit in underdeveloped areas. All of these factors combined to create an **economic imperialism**, whereby European finance dominated the economic activity of a large part of the world. This economic imperialism, however, was not necessarily the same thing as colonial expansion. Businesses invested where it was most profitable, not necessarily where their own countries had colonial empires. For example, less than 10 percent of French foreign investments before 1914 went to French colonies; most of the rest went to Latin American and European countries. Even the British had more trade with Belgium than with all of Africa in the 1890s. It should also be remembered that much of the colonial territory that was acquired was mere wasteland from the perspective of industrialized Europe and cost more to administer than it produced economically. Only the search for national prestige could justify such losses.

Followers of Karl Marx were especially eager to argue that imperialism was economically motivated because they associated imperialism with the ultimate demise of the capitalist system. Marx had hinted at this argument, but it was one of his followers, the Russian V. I. Lenin (see Chapter 25), who in *Imperialism, the Highest Stage of World Capitalism* developed the idea that capitalism leads to imperialism. According to Lenin, as the capitalist system concentrates more wealth in ever-fewer hands, the possibility for investment at home is exhausted, and capitalists are forced to invest abroad, establish colonies, and exploit small, weak nations. In his view, then, the only cure for imperialism was the destruction of capitalism.

The Scramble for Africa

Before 1880, Europeans controlled relatively little of the African continent. In 1875, Europeans ruled 11 percent of Africa; by 1902, 90 percent. Earlier, when their economic interests were more limited (in the case of Africa, primarily the slave trade), European states had generally been satisfied to deal with existing independent states rather than attempting to establish direct control over vast territories. For the most part, the Western presence in Africa had been limited to controlling the regional trade network and establishing a few footholds where the foreigners could carry on trade and missionary activity. During the last two decades of the nineteenth century, however, the quest

White Man's Burden Versus Black Man's Burden

ONE OF THE JUSTIFICATIONS FOR EUROPEAN imperialism was the notion that superior white peoples had a moral obligation to raise ignorant native peoples to a higher level of civilization. The British poet Rudyard Kipling (1865–1936) captured this notion in his poem "The White Man's Burden." The Western attempt to justify imperialism on the basis of moral responsibility, evident in Kipling's poem, was often hypocritical. Edward Morel, a British journalist who spent time in the Congo, pointed out the destructive effects of Western imperialism on Africans in his book *The Black Man's Burden*.

Rudyard Kipling, "The White Man's Burden"

Take up the White Man's burden—
Send forth the best ye breed—
Go bind your sons to exile
to serve your captives' needs;
To wait in heavy harness,
On fluttered folk and wild—
Your new-caught sullen peoples,
Half-devil and half-child.

Take up the White Man's burden—
In patience to abide,
To veil the threat of terror
And check the show of pride;
By open speech and simple,
An hundred times made plain
To seek another's profit,
And work another's gain.

Take up the White Man's burden—
The savage wars of peace—
Fill full the mouth of Famine
And bid the sickness cease;
And when your goal is nearest
The end for others sought,
Watch sloth and heathen Folly
Bring all your hopes to nought.

Take up the White Man's burden—
No tawdry rule of kings,
But toil of serf and sweeper—
The tale of common things.
The ports ye shall not enter,
The roads ye shall not tread,
Go mark them with your living,
And mark them with your dead.

Take up the White Man's burden—
And reap his old reward:
The blame of those ye better,
The hate of those ye guard—
The cry of hosts ye humour

(Ah, slowly!) toward the light—
"Why brought ye us from bondage,
Our loved Egyptian night?"

Take up the White Man's burden—
Ye dare not stoop to less—
Nor call too loud on Freedom
To cloak your weariness;
By all ye cry or whisper,
By all you leave or do,
The silent, sullen peoples
Shall weigh your gods and you.

Take up the White Man's burden—
Have done with childish days—
The lightly proferred laurel,
The easy, ungrudged praise.
Comes now, to search your manhood
Through all the thankless years,
Cold, edged with dear-bought wisdom,
The judgment of your peers!

Edward Morel, The *Black Man's Burden*

It is [the Africans] who carry the "Black man's burden." They have not withered away before the white man's occupation. Indeed . . . Africa has ultimately absorbed within itself every Caucasian and, for that matter, every Semitic invader, too. In hewing out for himself a fixed abode in Africa, the white man has massacred the African in heaps. The African has survived, and it is well for the white settlers that he has. . . .

What the partial occupation of his soil by the white man has failed to do; what the mapping out of European political "spheres of influence" has failed to do; what the Maxim [machine gun] and the rifle, the slave gang, labor in the bowels of the earth and the lash, have failed to do; what imported measles, smallpox and syphilis have failed to do; whatever the overseas slave trade failed to do; the power of modern capitalistic exploitation, assisted by modern engines of destruction, may yet succeed in accomplishing.

For from the evils of the latter, scientifically applied and enforced, there is no escape for the African. Its destructive effects are not spasmodic: they are permanent. . . . It kills not the body merely, but the soul. It breaks the spirit. It attacks the African at every turn, from every point of vantage. It wrecks his polity, uproots him from the land, invades his family life, destroys his natural pursuits and occupations, claims his whole time, enslaves him in his own home. . . .

In Africa, especially in tropical Africa, which a capitalistic imperialism threatens and has, in part, already devastated, man is incapable of reacting against unnatural conditions. In those regions man is engaged in a perpetual struggle against disease and an exhausting climate, which tells heavily upon

(continued)

(Continued)

childbearing. . . . The African of the tropics is capable of tremendous physical labors. But he cannot accommodate himself to the European system of monotonous, uninterrupted labor, with its long and regular hours, involving, moreover, as it frequently does, severance from natural surroundings and nostalgia, the condition of melancholy resulting from separation from home, a malady to which the African is specially prone. Climatic conditions forbid it. When the system is forced upon him, the tropical African droops and dies.

Nor is violent physical opposition to abuse and injustice henceforth possible for the African in any part of Africa. His chances of effective resistance have been steadily dwindling with the increasing perfectibility in the killing power of modern armament. . . .

Thus, the African is really helpless against the material gods of the white man, as embodied in the trinity of imperialism, capitalistic exploitation, and militarism. . . .

To reduce all the varied and picturesque and stimulating episodes in savage life to a dull routine of endless toil . . . to dislocate social ties and disrupt social institutions; . . . to graft upon primitive passions the annihilating evils of scientific slavery, and the bestial imaginings of civilized man, unrestrained by convention or law; in fine, to kill the soul in a people—this is a crime which transcends physical murder.

 What arguments did Kipling make to justify European expansion in Africa and Asia? How does the selection by Edward Morel challenge or undermine Kipling's beliefs?

Source: *Rudyard Kipling's Verse* (Garden City, N.Y.: Doubleday, 1919), pp. 371–372. Edward Morel, *The Black Man's Burden: The White Man in Africa from the Fifteenth Century to World War I* (London: National Labour Press, 1920).

for colonies became a scramble as all of the major European states engaged in a land grab (see Map 24.1). This new imperialism employed European military strength and industrial technology to control new territories, using locally trained military to carry out the oppression of local populations.

SOUTH AFRICA During the Napoleonic wars, the British had established themselves in South Africa by taking control of Cape Town, originally founded by the Dutch. After the wars, the British encouraged settlers to come to what they called the Cape Colony. British policies disgusted the Boers (BOORS *or* BORS) or Afrikaners (ah-fri-KAH-nurz), as the descendants of the Dutch colonists were called, and in 1835 led them to migrate north on the Great

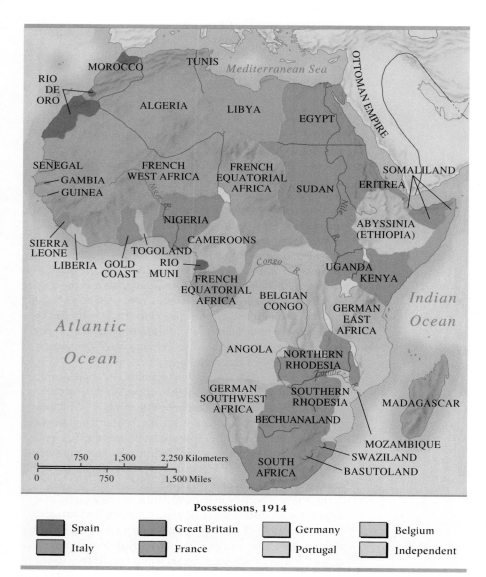

MAP 24.1 Africa in 1914. The major European powers' rush to acquire colonies was motivated by a combination of factors: the need for ports and fueling stations for navies, enhancement of international prestige, outlets for nationalist feelings, expression of social Darwinism, and a desire to "civilize" non-Europeans.

Possessions, 1914

Spain | Great Britain | Germany | Belgium
Italy | France | Portugal | Independent

 Of the two countries with the largest amount of territory in Africa, which one's colonies were more geographically concentrated, and what could be the benefits of this?

Trek to the region between the Orange and Vaal Rivers (later known as the Orange Free State) and north of the Vaal River (the Transvaal). Hostilities between the British and the Boers continued, however. In 1877, the British governor of the Cape Colony seized the Transvaal (trans-VAHL), but a Boer revolt led the British government to recognize Transvaal as the independent South African Republic. These struggles between the British and the Boers did not prevent either white group from massacring and subjugating the Zulu (ZOO-loo) and Xhosa (KHOH-suh) peoples of the region.

In the 1880s, Cecil Rhodes (1853–1902) largely determined British policy in South Africa. Rhodes founded both diamond and gold companies that monopolized production of these precious commodities and enabled him to gain control of a territory north of Transvaal that he named Rhodesia after himself. Rhodes was a great champion of British expansion. He said once that if there were a God, "I think he would like me to paint as much of Africa British red as possible." One of his goals was to create a series of British colonies "from the Cape to Cairo," all linked by a railroad. His imperialist ambitions led to his downfall in 1896, however, when the British government forced him to resign as prime minister of the Cape Colony after he conspired to overthrow the Boer government of the South African Republic without British approval. Although the British government had hoped to avoid war with the Boers, it could not stop extremists on both sides from precipitating a conflict.

THE BOER WAR The Boer War began in 1899 and dragged on until 1902 as the Boers proved to be an effective opponent. Due to the Boers' use of guerrilla tactics, the British sustained high casualties and immense expenses in securing victory. Almost 450,000 British and imperial forces were needed to defeat 87,000 Boers at a cost of 22,000 British deaths. The British implemented the concentration camp, rounding up thousands of Boer civilians and prisoners of war and placing them in enclosed camps. Mass newspapers in Britain reported on the high casualties, costs, and brutalities against Boer women and children, causing a public outcry and arousing antiwar sentiment at home. Britain had won, but the cost of the Boer War demonstrated that increased military and monetary investment would be needed to maintain the British Empire.

The Struggle for South Africa

British policy toward the defeated Boers was remarkably conciliatory. Transvaal and the Orange Free State had representative governments by 1907, and in 1910, the Union of South Africa was created. Like Canada, Australia, and New Zealand, it became a fully self-governing dominion within the British Empire.

PORTUGUESE AND FRENCH POSSESSIONS Before 1880, the French and the Portuguese had made the only other European settlements in Africa. The Portuguese had held on to their settlements in Angola on the west coast and Mozambique on the east coast. The French had started the conquest of Algeria in Muslim North Africa in 1830, although it was not until 1879 that French civilian rule was established there. The next year, 1880, the European scramble for possession of Africa began in earnest. By 1900, the French had added the huge area of French West Africa and Tunisia to their African empire. In 1912, they established a protectorate over much of Morocco; the rest was left to Spain.

OTHER BRITISH POSSESSIONS The British took an active interest in Egypt after the French opened the Suez Canal in 1869. Believing that the canal was their lifeline to India, the British sought to control the canal area. Egypt was a well-established state with an autonomous Muslim government, but that did not stop the British from landing an expeditionary force there in 1882. Although they claimed that their occupation was only temporary, they soon established a protectorate over Egypt. From Egypt, the British moved south into the Sudan and seized it after narrowly averting a war with France. Not to be outdone, Italy joined in the imperialist scramble. Their humiliating defeat by the Ethiopians in 1896 only led the Italians to try again in 1911, when they invaded and seized Ottoman Tripoli, which they renamed Libya.

BELGIUM AND CENTRAL AFRICA Central Africa was also added to the list of European colonies. Popular interest in the forbiddingly dense tropical jungles of Central Africa was first aroused in the 1860s and 1870s by explorers, such as the Scottish missionary David Livingstone and the British-American journalist Henry M. Stanley. But the real driving force for the colonization of Central Africa was King Leopold II (1865–1909) of Belgium, who rushed enthusiastically into the pursuit of empire in Africa. Profit, however, was far more important to Leopold than progress; his treatment of the Africans was so brutal that even other Europeans condemned his actions. In 1876, Leopold created the International Association for the Exploration and Civilization of Central Africa and engaged Henry Stanley to establish Belgian settlements in the Congo. Alarmed by Leopold's actions, the French also moved into the territory north of the Congo River.

GERMAN POSSESSIONS Between 1884 and 1900, most of the rest of Africa was carved up by the European powers. Germany entered the ranks of the imperialist powers at this time. Initially, Bismarck had downplayed the significance of colonies, but as domestic political pressures for a German empire intensified, Bismarck became a political convert to colonialism (see the box on p. 746). Bismarck explained that this colonial business was a sham, "but we need it for the elections." The Germans established colonies in South-West Africa, the Cameroons, Togoland, and Tanganyika.

DOES GERMANY NEED COLONIES?

AFTER ITS UNIFICATION IN 1871, Germany sought to join the other great European powers in establishing a colonial empire. Among the supporters of German colonial expansion was Friedrich Fabri, a colonial administrator in South-West Africa, who argued that colonization would encourage national growth and the spread of German culture. This excerpt is from Fabri's popular book *Does Germany Need Colonies?* published in Germany in 1879.

Friedrich Fabri, *Does Germany Need Colonies?*

Above all we need to regain ample, rewarding, and reliable sources of employment; we need new and reliable export markets; in short we need a well-designed and firmly implemented commercial and labor policy. Any far-reaching and perceptive attempt to execute such a policy will necessarily lead to the irrefutable conclusion that the German State needs colonial possessions. . . .

For us, the colonial question is not at all a question of political power. Whoever is guided by the desire for expanding German power has a poor understanding of it. It is rather a question of culture. Economic needs linked to broad national perspectives point to practical action. In looking for colonial possessions Germany is not prompted by the desire for expanding its power; it wants only to fulfill a national, we may even say a moral duty. . . .

In looking for commercial colonies the question is WHERE? German participation seems most important in the colonial exploitation of newly opened Central Africa. . . . The significance of Central Africa is much greater in every respect than has been assumed since antiquity. Should not Germany in its needs for colonies participate energetically in the competition for this massive territory? . . .

What matters above all is to raise our understanding about the significance and necessity of colonial possessions and thereby forcefully arouse the will of the nation in that direction. When we have overcome all opposition and turn to effective action, our first attempts with their inevitable troubles and difficulties will justify our effort. The German nation has long experience on the oceans, is skilled in industry and commerce, more capable than others in agricultural colonization, and furnished with an ample manpower like no other modern highly cultured nation. Should it not also enter successfully upon this new venture? The more we are convinced that the colonial question has become now a question of life and death for Germany, the fewer doubts we have. Well-planned and powerfully handled, it will have the most beneficial consequences for our economic situation, and for our entire national development. . . .

Even more important is the consideration that a people at the height of their political power can successfully maintain their historic position only as long as they recognize and prove themselves as the bearers of a cultural mission. . . .

It would be well if we Germans began to learn from the colonial destiny of our Anglo-Saxon cousins and emulate them in peaceful competition. When, centuries ago, the German empire stood at the head of the European states, it was the foremost commercial and maritime power. If the new Germany wants to restore and preserve its traditional powerful position in future, it will conceive of it as a cultural mission and no longer hesitate to practice its colonizing vocation.

 What were Fabri's justifications for colonization?

Source: From M. Perry, J. R. Peden, and T. H. von Laue, *Sources of the Western Tradition*, vol. 2 (New York: Houghton Mifflin, 2008), pp. 249–250.

IMPACT ON AFRICA By 1914, Britain, France, Germany, Belgium, Spain, and Portugal had carved up the entire African continent. Only Liberia, founded by emancipated American slaves, and Ethiopia remained free states. Despite the humanitarian rationalizations about the "white man's burden," Africa had been conquered by European states determined to create colonial empires. Any peoples who dared to resist (with the exception of the Ethiopians, who defeated the Italians) were simply devastated by the superior military force of the Europeans. In 1898, Sudanese tribesmen attempted to defend their independence and stop a British expedition armed with the recently developed machine gun. In the ensuing Battle of Omdurman (om-door-MAHN), the Sudanese were massacred. One observer noted, "It was not a battle but an execution. . . . The bodies were not in heaps—bodies hardly ever are; but they spread evenly over acres and acres. Some lay very composedly with their slippers placed under their heads for a last pillow; some knelt, cut short in the middle of a last prayer. Others were torn to pieces."[20] The

casualties at Omdurman tell the story of the one-sided conflicts between Europeans and Africans: twenty-eight British deaths to 11,000 Sudanese. Military superiority was frequently accompanied by brutal treatment of blacks. Nor did Europeans hesitate to deceive the Africans to gain their way. One South African king, Lo Bengula, informed Queen Victoria about how he had been cheated:

Some time ago a party of men came to my country, the principal one appearing to be a man called Rudd. They asked me for a place to dig for gold, and said they would give me certain things for the right to do so. I told them to bring what they could give and I would show them what I would give. A document was written and presented to me for signature. I asked what it contained, and was told that in it were my words and the words of those men. I put my hand to it. About three months afterwards I heard from other sources that I had given by that document the right to all the minerals of my country.[21]

CHRONOLOGY	The New Imperialism: Africa	
Great Trek of the Boers	1835	
Opening of the Suez Canal	1869	
Leopold of Belgium establishes settlements in the Congo	1876	
British seizure of Transvaal	1877	
French conquest of Algeria	1879	
British expeditionary force in Egypt	1882	
Ethiopians defeat the Italians	1896	
Battle of Omdurman in the Sudan	1898	
Boer War	1899–1902	
Union of South Africa	1910	
Italians seize Tripoli	1911	
French protectorate over Morocco	1912	

Imperialism in Asia

Although Asia had been open to Western influence since the sixteenth century, not much of its immense territory had fallen under direct European control. The Dutch were established in the East Indies, the Spanish were in the Philippines, and the French and Portuguese had trading posts on the Indian coast. China, Japan, Korea, and Southeast Asia had largely managed to exclude Westerners. The British and the Russians, however, had acquired the most Asian territory.

THE BRITISH IN ASIA It was not until the explorations of Australia by Captain James Cook between 1768 and 1771 that Britain took an active interest in the East. The availability of land for grazing sheep and the discovery of gold in Australia led to an influx of settlers who slaughtered many of the indigenous inhabitants. In 1850, the British government granted the various Australian colonies virtually complete self-government, and fifty years later, on January 1, 1901, all the colonies were unified into the Commonwealth of Australia. Nearby New Zealand, which the British had declared a colony in 1840, was granted dominion status in 1907.

A private trading company known as the British East India Company had been responsible for subjugating much of India. In 1858, however, after a revolt of the sepoys, or Indian troops of the East India Company's army, had been crushed, the British Parliament transferred the company's powers directly to the government in London. In 1876, the title Empress of India was bestowed on Queen Victoria; Indians were now her colonial subjects.

THE RUSSIANS IN ASIA Russian expansion in Asia was a logical outgrowth of Russia's traditional territorial aggrandizement. Russian explorers had penetrated the wilderness of Siberia in the seventeenth century and reached the Pacific coast in 1637. In the eighteenth century, Russians established a claim

on Alaska, which they sold to the United States in 1867. Gradually, Russian settlers moved into cold and forbidding Siberia. Altogether, 7 million Russians settled in Siberia between 1800 and 1914, by which time 90 percent of the Siberian population was Slavic, not Asiatic.

The Russians also moved south, attracted by warmer climates and the crumbling Ottoman Empire (see Map 24.2). By 1830, the Russians had established control over the entire northern coast of the Black Sea and then pressed on into Central Asia, securing the trans-Caspian area by 1881 and Turkestan in 1885. These advances brought the Russians to the borders of Persia and Afghanistan, where the British also had interests because of their desire to protect their holdings in India. In 1907, the Russians and British agreed to make Afghanistan a buffer state between Russian Turkestan and British India and to divide Persia into two spheres of influence. Halted by the British in their expansion to the south, the Russians moved east into Asia. The Russian occupation of Manchuria and an attempt to move into Korea brought war with the new imperialist power, Japan. After losing the Russo-Japanese War in 1905, the Russians agreed to a Japanese protectorate in Korea, and their Asian expansion was brought to a temporary halt.

CHINA The thrust of imperialism after 1880 led Westerners to move into new areas of Asia hitherto largely free of Western influence. By the nineteenth century, the ruling Manchu dynasty of the Chinese Empire was showing signs of decline. In 1842, the British had obtained (through war) the island of Hong Kong and trading rights in a number of Chinese cities. Other Western nations soon rushed in to gain similar trading privileges. Chinese attempts to resist this foreign encroachment led to military defeats and new demands. Only rivalry among the great powers themselves prevented the complete dismemberment of the Chinese Empire. Instead, Britain, France, Germany, Russia, the United States, and Japan established spheres of influence and long-term leases of Chinese territory. In 1899, urged along by the American secretary of state, John Hay, they agreed to an "open door" policy in which one country would not restrict the commerce of the other countries in its sphere of influence.

JAPAN AND KOREA Japan avoided Western intrusion until 1853–1854, when American naval forces under Commodore Matthew Perry forced the Japanese to grant the United States trading and diplomatic privileges. Japan, however, managed to avoid China's fate. Korea had also largely excluded Westerners. The fate of Korea was determined by the struggle first between China and Japan in 1894–1895 and later between Japan and Russia in 1904–1905. Japan's victories gave it clear superiority, and in 1910, Japan formally annexed Korea.

SOUTHEAST ASIA In Southeast Asia, Britain established control over Burma (modern Myanmar) and the Malay States, and France played an active role in subjugating Indochina. The city of Saigon (sy-GAHN) was occupied in 1858, and four years later, Cochin China was taken. In the 1880s, the French extended "protection" over Cambodia, Annam, Tonkin, and Laos and organized them into the Union of French Indochina.

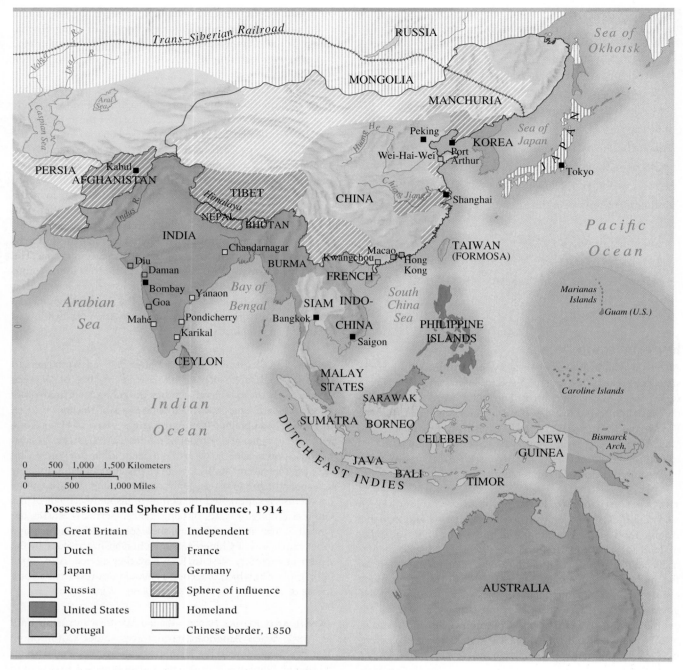

MAP 24.2 Asia in 1914. Asia became an important arena of international competition in the nineteenth and early twentieth centuries. Beset by economic stagnation and an inability to modernize, a weak China was unable to withstand the demands of the United States, the European powers, and a Westernizing Japan. Britain, France, Russia, Japan, and the United States had direct or indirect control of nearly all of Asia by 1914.

 Why would both Russia and Japan covet Manchuria?

Only Siam (Thailand) remained free as a buffer state because of British-French rivalry.

AMERICAN IMPERIALISM The Pacific islands were also the scene of great power competition and witnessed the entry of the United States onto the imperialist stage. The Samoan

Islands became the first important American colony; the Hawaiian Islands were the next to fall. Soon after Americans had made Pearl Harbor into a naval station in 1887, American settlers gained control of the sugar industry on the islands. When Hawaiian natives tried to reassert their authority, the U.S. Marines were brought in to "protect" American lives.

Britain obtains Hong Kong and trading rights from Chinese government	1842
Australian colonies receive self-government	1850
Mission of Commodore Perry to Japan	1853–1854
Rebellion of sepoys in India	1857–1858
French occupy Saigon	1858
Overthrow of the shogun in Japan	1867
Emperor Mutsuhito and the Meiji Restoration	1867–1912
Queen Victoria is made Empress of India	1876
Russians in Central Asia (trans-Caspian area)	1881
Formation of Indian National Congress	1883
Japanese defeat of China	1894–1895
Spanish-American War; United States annexes Philippines	1898
"Open door" policy in China	1899
Boxer Rebellion in China	1900–1901
Commonwealth of Australia	1901
Commonwealth of New Zealand	1907
Russian-British agreement over Afghanistan and Persia	1907
Japan annexes Korea	1910
Overthrow of Manchu dynasty in China	1912

Hawaii was annexed by the United States in 1898 during the era of American nationalistic fervor generated by the Spanish-American War. The American defeat of Spain encouraged Americans to extend their empire by acquiring Puerto Rico, Guam, and the Philippine Islands. Although the Filipinos hoped for independence, the Americans refused to grant it. As President William McKinley said, the United States had the duty "to educate the Filipinos and uplift and Christianize them," a remarkable statement in view of the fact that most of them had been Roman Catholics for centuries. It took three years and 60,000 troops to pacify the Philippines and establish American control.

Responses to Imperialism

When Europeans imposed their culture on peoples they considered inferior, how did the conquered peoples respond? Initial attempts to expel the foreigners only led to devastating defeats at the hands of Westerners, whose industrial technology gave them modern weapons of war with which to crush the indigenous peoples. Accustomed to rule by small elites, most people simply accepted their new governors, making Western rule relatively easy. The conquered peoples subsequently adjusted to foreign rule in different ways. Traditionalists sought to maintain their cultural traditions, but modernizers believed that adoption of Western ways would enable them to reform their societies and eventually challenge Western rule. Most people probably stood somewhere between these two extremes. Four examples illustrate different approaches to the question of how indigenous peoples responded to foreign rule.

AFRICA By the beginning of the twentieth century, a new class of African leaders had emerged. Educated in colonial schools and some even in the West, they were the first generation of Africans to know a great deal about the West and to write in the language of their colonial masters. Although this "new class" admired Western culture and even disliked the ways of their own countries, many came to resent the foreigners and their arrogant contempt for colonial peoples. Westerners had exalted democracy, equality, and political freedom, but these values were not applied in the colonies. There were few democratic institutions, and colonial peoples could hold only lowly jobs in the colonial bureaucracy. Equally important, the economic prosperity of the West never extended to the colonies. To many Africans, colonialism meant the loss of their farmlands or terrible jobs on plantations or in sweatshops and factories run by foreigners.

Although middle-class Africans did not suffer to the extent that poor peasants or workers on plantations did, they too had complaints. They usually qualified only for menial jobs in the government or business. The purported superiority of the Europeans over the natives was also expressed in a variety of ways. Segregated clubs, schools, and churches were set up as more European officials brought their wives and began to raise families. Europeans also had a habit of addressing natives by their first names or calling an adult male "boy."

Such conditions led many of the new urban educated class to have very complicated feelings about their colonial masters and the civilization they represented. Though willing to admit the superiority of many aspects of Western culture, these new intellectuals fiercely hated colonial rule and were determined to assert their own nationality and cultural destiny. Out of this mixture of hopes and resentments emerged the first stirrings of modern nationalism in Africa. During the first quarter of the twentieth century, in colonial societies across Africa, educated native peoples began to organize political parties and movements seeking the end of foreign rule.

CHINA The humiliation of China by the Western powers led to much antiforeign violence, but the Westerners used this lawlessness as an excuse to extort further concessions from the Chinese. A major outburst of violence against foreigners occurred in the Boxer Rebellion in 1900–1901. "Boxers" was the popular name given to Chinese who belonged to a secret organization called the Society of Harmonious Fists, whose aim was to push the foreigners out of China. The Boxers murdered foreign missionaries, Chinese who had converted to Christianity, railroad workers, foreign businessmen, and even the German envoy to Beijing. Response to the killings was immediate and overwhelming. An allied army consisting of eighteen thousand British, French, Russian, American, and Japanese troops attacked Beijing, restored order, and demanded more concessions from the Chinese government. The imperial government was so weakened that the forces of the revolutionary leader Sun Yat-sen (SOON yaht-SEN) (1866–1925), who adopted a program of "nationalism, democracy, and socialism," overthrew the Manchu dynasty in 1912. The new Republic of China remained weak and ineffective, and China's travails were far from over.

JAPAN In the late 1850s and early 1860s, it looked as if Japan would follow China's fate and be carved up into spheres of influence by aggressive Western powers. A remarkably rapid transformation, however, produced a very different result. Before 1868, the shogun (SHOH-gun), a powerful hereditary military governor assisted by a warrior nobility known as the samurai (SAM-uh-ry), exercised real power in Japan. The emperor's functions had become primarily religious. After the shogun's concessions to the Western nations, antiforeign sentiment led to a samurai revolt in 1867 and the restoration of the emperor as the head of the government. The new emperor was the astute, dynamic, young Mutsuhito (moo-tsoo-HEE-toh) (1867–1912), who called his reign the Meiji (MAY-jee) (Enlightened Government). The new leaders who controlled the emperor now inaugurated a remarkable transformation of Japan that has since been known as the Meiji Restoration.

Recognizing the obvious military and industrial superiority of the West, the new leaders decided to modernize Japan by absorbing and adopting Western methods. Thousands of young Japanese were sent abroad to receive Western educations, especially in the social and natural sciences. A German-style army and a British-style navy were established. The Japanese copied the industrial and financial methods of the United States and developed a modern commercial and industrial system. A highly centralized administrative system copied from the French replaced the old system. Initially, the Japanese adopted the French principles of social and legal equality, but by 1890, they had created a political system that was democratic in form but authoritarian in practice.

In imitating the West, Japan also developed a powerful military state. Universal military conscription was introduced in 1872, and a modern peacetime army of 240,000 was eventually established. The Japanese avidly pursued the Western imperialistic model. They defeated China in 1894–1895, annexed some Chinese territory, and established their own sphere of influence in China. After they had defeated the Russians in 1905, the Japanese made Korea a colony under harsh rule. The Japanese had proved that an Asian power could play the "white man's" imperialistic game and provided a potent example to peoples in other regions of Asia and Africa.

INDIA The British government had been in control of India since the mid-nineteenth century. After crushing a major revolt in 1858, the British ruled

The West and Japan. In their attempt to modernize, the Japanese absorbed and adopted Western methods. They were also influenced by Western culture, as Western fashions became the rage in elite circles. Baseball was even imported from the United States. This painting shows Western-style stone houses in Tokyo and streets filled with people dressed in a variety of styles.

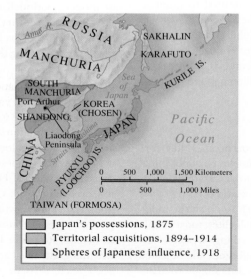

Japanese Expansion

Japan's possessions, 1875
Territorial acquisitions, 1894–1914
Spheres of Japanese influence, 1918

India directly. Under Parliament's supervision, a small group of British civil servants directed the affairs of India's almost 300 million people.

The British brought order to a society that had been divided by civil wars for some time and created a relatively honest and efficient government. They also brought Western technology—railroads, banks, mines, industry, medical knowledge, and hospitals. The British introduced Western-style secondary schools and colleges where the Indian upper and middle classes and professional classes were educated and taught English so that they could serve as trained subordinates in the government and army.

British legislation also affected the legal status of Indian women. In 1829, the British banned the practice of *sati* (suh-TEE), which called for a widow to immolate herself on her husband's funeral pyre. Some scholars question how extensive the practice was, however, and suggest that the abolition of sati became central to Britain's image of itself as culturally superior. Female infanticide was also discouraged. Although women's position in Indian society was not significantly altered, the recognition of women by the law did afford some protection against these practices.

The Indian people paid a high price for the peace and stability brought by British rule. Population had increased from 136 million in 1864 to 300 million by 1904. This population growth led to extreme poverty as a way of life for most Indians; almost two-thirds of the population was malnourished in 1901. British industrialization brought little improvement for the masses. British manufactured goods destroyed local industries, and Indian wealth was used to pay British officials and a large army. The new system of education implemented by the British served only the elite, upper-class Indians, and it was conducted only in the rulers' English language while 90 percent of the population remained illiterate. Even for the Indians who benefited the most from their Western educations, British rule was degrading. The best jobs and the best housing were reserved for Britons. Even well-educated Indians were never considered the equals of the British. As Lord Kitchener, one of Britain's foremost military commanders in India, said, "It is this consciousness of the inherent superiority of the European which has won for us India. However well educated and clever a native may be, and however brave he may prove himself, I believe that no rank we can bestow on him would cause him to be considered an equal of the British officer."[22] Such smug racial attitudes made it difficult for British rule, no matter how beneficent, ever to be ultimately accepted and led to the rise of an Indian nationalist movement. By 1883, when the Indian National Congress was formed, moderate, educated, upper-class Indians were beginning to seek self-government. By 1919, in response to British violence and British insensitivity, Indians were demanding complete independence.

Results of the New Imperialism

By 1900, almost all the societies of Africa and Asia were either under full colonial rule or, as in the case of China and the Ottoman Empire, at a point of virtual collapse. Only a handful of states, such as Japan in East Asia, Thailand in Southeast Asia, Afghanistan and Persia in the Middle East, and mountainous Ethiopia in East Africa, managed to escape internal disintegration or subjection to colonial rule. For the most part, the exceptions were the result of good fortune rather than design. Thailand escaped subjugation primarily because officials in Britain and France found it more convenient to transform the country into a buffer state than to fight over it. Ethiopia and Afghanistan survived due to their remote location and mountainous terrain. Only Japan managed to avoid the common fate through a concerted strategy of political and economic reform. With the coming of imperialism, a global economy was finally established, and the domination of Western civilization over those of Africa and Asia appeared to be complete. At the same time, the competition for lands abroad also heightened the existing rivalries among European states.

International Rivalry and the Coming of War

 FOCUS QUESTIONS: What was the Bismarckian system of alliances, and how successful was it at keeping the peace? What issues lay behind the international crises that Europe faced in the late nineteenth and early twentieth centuries?

Before 1914, Europeans had experienced almost fifty years of peace. There had been wars (including wars of conquest in the non-Western world), but none had involved the great powers. A series of crises had occurred that might easily have led to general war. One reason they did not is that until 1890, Bismarck of Germany exercised a restraining influence on the Europeans.

The Bismarckian System

Bismarck knew that the emergence of a unified Germany in 1871 had upset the balance of power established at Vienna in 1815. Fearing the French desire for revenge over their loss of Alsace-Lorraine in the Franco-Prussian War, Bismarck made an alliance first in 1873 and again in 1881 with the traditionally conservative powers Austria-Hungary and Russia. But the Three Emperors' League, as it was called, failed to work very well, primarily because of Russian-Austrian rivalry in the Balkans.

THE BALKANS: DECLINE OF OTTOMAN POWER The problem in the Balkans was a by-product of the disintegration of the Ottoman Empire. As subject peoples in the Balkans clamored for independence, corruption and inefficiency weakened the Ottoman government. Only the interference of the great European powers, who were fearful of each other's designs on its territories, kept the Ottoman Empire alive. Complicating the situation was the rivalry between Russia and Austria, which both had designs on the Balkans. For Russia, the Balkans provided the shortest overland route to Constantinople and the Mediterranean. Austria viewed the Balkans as fertile ground for Austrian expansion. Although Germany had no real interests in the Balkans, Bismarck was fearful of the consequences of a war between Russia and Austria over the region and served as a restraining influence on both powers. Events in the Balkans, however, precipitated a new crisis.

In 1876, the Balkan states of Serbia and Montenegro (mahn-tuh-NEE-groh) declared war on the Ottoman Empire. Both were defeated, but Russia, with Austrian approval, attacked and defeated the Ottomans. The Treaty of San Stefano in 1878 created a large Bulgarian state, extending from the Danube in the north to the Aegean Sea in the south. As Bulgaria was viewed as a Russian satellite, this Russian success caused the other great powers to call for a congress of European powers to discuss a revision of the treaty.

The Congress of Berlin, which met in the summer of 1878, was dominated by Bismarck. The congress effectively

The Balkans in 1878

New Directions and New Crises

Emperor William II embarked on an activist foreign policy dedicated to enhancing German power by finding, as he put it, Germany's rightful "place in the sun." One of his changes in Bismarck's foreign policy was to drop the Reinsurance Treaty with Russia, which he viewed as being at odds with Germany's alliance with Austria. The ending of the alliance achieved what Bismarck had feared: it brought France and Russia together. Long isolated by Bismarck's policies, republican France leaped at the chance to draw closer to tsarist Russia, and in 1894, the two powers concluded a military alliance.

During the next ten years, German policies abroad caused the British to draw closer to France. By 1907, a loose confederation of Great Britain, France, and Russia—known as the Triple Entente (ahn-TAHNT)—stood opposed to the Triple Alliance of Germany, Austria-Hungary, and Italy. Europe was divided into two opposing camps that became more and more inflexible and unwilling to compromise. When the members of the two alliances became involved in a new series of crises between 1908 and 1913 over control of the remnants of the Ottoman Empire in the Balkans, the stage was set for World War I.

CRISES IN THE BALKANS, 1908–1913 The Bosnian Crisis of 1908–1909 initiated a chain of events that eventually spun out of control. Since 1878, Bosnia and Herzegovina had been under the protection of Austria, but in 1908, Austria took the drastic step of annexing these two Slavic-speaking territories. Serbia became outraged at this action because it dashed the Serbs' hopes of creating a large Serbian kingdom that would include most of the southern Slavs. But this was why the Austrians had annexed Bosnia and Herzegovina. To the Austrians, a large Serbia would be a threat to the unity of the Austro-Hungarian Empire, with its large Slavic population. The Russians, as protectors of their fellow Slavs and desiring to increase their own authority in the Balkans, supported the Serbs and opposed the Austrian action. Backed by the Russians, the Serbs prepared for war against Austria. At this point, William II intervened and demanded that the Russians accept Austria's annexation of Bosnia and Herzegovina or face war with Germany. Weakened from their defeat in the Russo-Japanese War in 1904–1905, the Russians backed down. Humiliated, they vowed revenge.

European attention returned to the Balkans in 1912 when Serbia, Bulgaria, Montenegro, and Greece organized the Balkan League and defeated the Ottomans in the First Balkan War. When the victorious allies were unable to agree on how to divide the conquered Ottoman provinces of Macedonia and Albania, the Second Balkan War erupted in 1913. Greece, Serbia, Romania, and the Ottoman Empire attacked and defeated Bulgaria. As a result, Bulgaria obtained only a small part of Macedonia, and most of the rest was divided between Serbia and Greece (see Map 24.3). Yet Serbia's aspirations remained unfulfilled. The two Balkan wars left the inhabitants embittered and created more tensions among the great powers.

One of Serbia's major ambitions had been to acquire Albanian territory that would give it a port on the Adriatic. At the London Conference, arranged by Austria at the end of the two Balkan wars, the Austrians had blocked Serbia's wishes by

demolished the Treaty of San Stefano, much to Russia's humiliation. The new Bulgarian state was considerably reduced, and the rest of the territory was returned to Ottoman control. The three Balkan states of Serbia, Montenegro, and Romania, until then nominally under Ottoman control, were recognized as independent. The other Balkan territories of Bosnia and Herzegovina (HAYRT-suh-guh-VEE-nuh) were placed under Austrian protection; Austria could occupy but not annex them.

NEW ALLIANCES After the Congress of Berlin, the European powers sought new alliances to safeguard their security. Angered by the Germans' actions at the congress, the Russians terminated the Three Emperors' League in 1879. Bismarck then made an alliance with Austria in 1879 that was joined by Italy in 1882. The Triple Alliance of 1882 committed Germany, Austria, and Italy to support the existing political order while providing a defensive alliance against France or "two or more great powers not members of the alliance." At the same time, Bismarck sought to remain on friendly terms with the Russians and signed the Reinsurance Treaty with Russia in 1887, hoping to prevent a French-Russian alliance that would threaten Germany with the possibility of a two-front war. The Bismarckian system of alliances, geared to preserving peace and the status quo, had worked, but in 1890, Emperor William II dismissed Bismarck and began to chart a new direction for Germany's foreign policy.

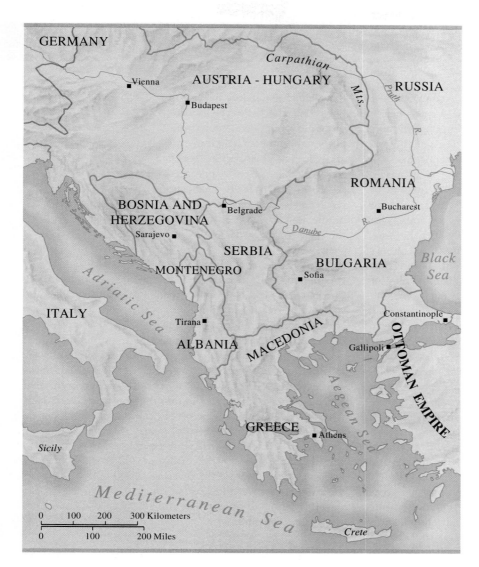

MAP 24.3 The Balkans in 1913. The First Balkan War (1912) liberated most of the region from Ottoman control; the Second Balkan War (1913) increased the size of Greece and Serbia at Bulgaria's expense. Russia supported the ambitions of its fellow Slavs in Serbia, who sought to create a large Slavic kingdom in the Balkans. Austria and its ally Germany opposed Serbia's ambitions.

Q *Look at the map on p. 752. What territories had the Ottomans lost by the end of 1913?*

creating an independent Albania. The Germans, as Austrian allies, had supported this move. In their frustration, Serbian nationalists increasingly portrayed the Austrians as monsters who were keeping the Serbs from becoming a great nation. As Serbia's chief supporters, the Russians were also upset by the turn of events in the region. A feeling had grown among Russian leaders that they could not back down again in the event of a confrontation with Austria or Germany in the Balkans.

Austria-Hungary had achieved another of its aims, but it was still convinced that Serbia was a mortal threat to its empire and must at some point be crushed. Meanwhile, the French and Russian governments renewed their alliance and promised each other that they would not back down at the next crisis. Britain drew closer to France. By the beginning of 1914, the two armed camps viewed each other with suspicion. An American in Europe observed that the whole of Europe was charged with electricity; it only needed a spark to "set the whole thing off." The German ambassador to France noted at the same time that "peace remains at the mercy of an accident." The European "age of progress" was about to come to an inglorious and bloody end.

CHRONOLOGY	European Diplomacy
Three Emperors' League	1873
Serbia and Montenegro attack the Ottoman Empire	1876
Treaty of San Stefano	1878
Congress of Berlin	1878
Defensive alliance: Germany and Austria	1879
Triple Alliance: Germany, Austria, and Italy	1882
Reinsurance Treaty: Germany and Russia	1887
Military alliance: Russia and France	1894
Triple Entente: France, Britain, and Russia	1907
First Balkan War	1912
Second Balkan War	1913

What many Europeans liked to call their "age of progress" in the decades before 1914 was also an era of anxiety. Driven by national rivalry, social Darwinism, religious and humanitarian concerns, and economic demands for raw materials and overseas investment, at the end of the nineteenth century Western nations began a renewed frenzy of imperialist expansion around the world. By 1914, European nations had carved up most of Africa into colonies and created spheres of influence in Asia. Both China and Japan were also affected by Western imperialism. The opening of China to Western trade concessions ultimately led to a revolution and the overthrow of the Manchu dynasty. Japan adopted Western military, educational, and governmental ways, even becoming an imperialist power in its own right. At the same time, Western treatment of non-Western peoples as racial inferiors caused educated, non-Western elites in the colonies to initiate movements for national independence. Before these movements could be successful, however, the power that Europeans had achieved through their mass armies and technological superiority had to be weakened. The Europeans soon inadvertently accomplished this task by demolishing their own civilization on the battlegrounds of Europe in World War I.

This war was a result of the growing tensions that arose as a result of national rivalry. In competing with and fearing each other, the European nations formed defensive alliances

that helped maintain a balance of power but also led to the creation of large armies, enormous military establishments, and immense arsenals. The alliances also generated tensions that were unleashed when Europeans were unable to resolve a series of crises, especially in the Balkans, and rushed into the catastrophic carnage of World War I.

The cultural revolutions before 1914 had also produced anxiety and a crisis of confidence in European civilization. Albert Einstein showed that time and space were relative to the observer, that matter was simply another form of energy, and that the old Newtonian view of the universe was no longer valid. Sigmund Freud argued that human behavior was governed not by reason but by the unconscious, adding to the uncertainties of the age. Some intellectuals used the ideas of Charles Darwin to argue that in the struggle of races and nations the fittest survive. Collectively, these new ideas helped create a modern consciousness that questioned most Europeans' optimistic faith in reason, the rational structure of nature, and the certainty of progress. As we shall see in the next two chapters, the devastating experiences of World War I would turn this culture of uncertainty into a way of life after 1918.

CHAPTER TIMELINE

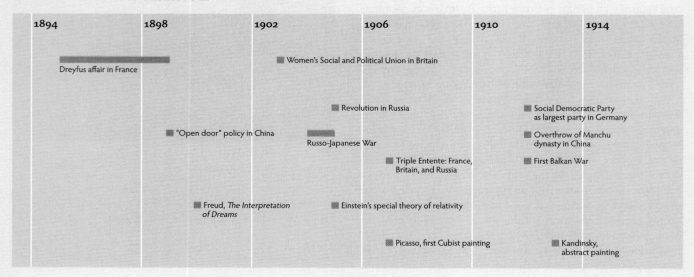

1894	1898	1902	1906	1910	1914

Dreyfus affair in France

Women's Social and Political Union in Britain

Revolution in Russia

Social Democratic Party as largest party in Germany

"Open door" policy in China

Russo-Japanese War

Overthrow of Manchu dynasty in China

Triple Entente: France, Britain, and Russia

First Balkan War

Freud, *The Interpretation of Dreams*

Einstein's special theory of relativity

Picasso, first Cubist painting

Kandinsky, abstract painting

CHAPTER REVIEW

Upon Reflection

Q How is Modernism evident in literature and the arts between 1894 and 1914? How do these literary and artistic products reflect the political and social developments of the age?

Q One historian has written that the history of colonial expansion was "one of long-range schemes that appear almost accidental when viewed singly." Does the practice of imperialism in Africa and Asia substantiate this statement? Why or why not?

Q What might European diplomats have done between 1894 and 1914 to avoid war?

Key Terms

relativity theory (p. 720)
revolutionary socialism (p. 721)
general strike (p. 722)
psychoanalysis (p. 722)
social Darwinism (p. 722)
volkish thought (p. 724)
anticlericalism (p. 724)
Modernism (p. 725)
Impressionism (p. 725)
Post-Impressionism (p. 726)

Cubism (p. 729)
abstract painting (p. 729)
political democracy (p. 731)
suffragists (p. 732)
anti-Semitism (p. 734)
pogroms (p. 735)
Zionism (p. 735)
transformism (p. 737)
new imperialism (p. 741)
economic imperialism (p. 742)

Suggestions for Further Reading

INTELLECTUAL AND CULTURAL DEVELOPMENTS   On Modernism, see **P. Gay, *Modernism: The Lure of Heresy*** (New York, 2007). On Freud, see **P. Gay, *Freud: A Life for Our Time*,** rev. ed. (New York, 2006). Nietzsche is examined in **L. Spinks, *Friedrich Nietzsche*** (London, 2003). Very valuable on modern art are **G. Crepaldi, *The Impressionists*** (New York, 2002), and **B. Denvir, *Post-Impressionism*** (New York, 1992).

POLITICS: NEW DIRECTIONS   The rise of feminism is examined in **J. Rendall, *The Origins of Modern Feminism: Women in Britain, France and the United States*** (London, 1985). On the "new woman," see **M. L. Roberts, *Disruptive Acts: The New Woman in Fin-de-Siècle France*** (Chicago, 2002). European racism is analyzed in **N. MacMaster, *Racism in Europe, 1870–2000*** (New York, 2001). Anti-Semitism in France is the subject of **L. Derfler, *The Dreyfus Affair*** (Westport, Conn., 2002). The beginnings of the Labour Party are examined in **R. J. H. Stewart, *Origins of the British Labour Party*** (New York, 2003). A good introduction to the political world of William II's Germany can

be found in **C. Clark, *Kaiser Wilhelm II*** (London, 2000). On Russia, see **A. Ascher, *Revolution of 1905: A Short History*** (Stanford, Calif., 2004).

THE NEW IMPERIALISM   For broad perspectives on imperialism, see **M. W. Doyle, *Empires*** (Ithaca, N.Y., 1986), and **P. Curtain, *The World and the West: The European Challenge and the Overseas Response in the Age of Empire*** (New York, 2000). Different aspects of imperialism are covered in **N. Ferguson, *Empire: The Rise and Demise of the British World Order*** (New York, 2002), a broad survey that emphasizes how the British Empire gave rise to many aspects of the modern world; and **T. Pakhenham, *The Scramble for Africa*** (New York, 1991). On gender and imperialism, see **P. Levine, *Gender and Empire*** (Oxford, 2004).

INTERNATIONAL RIVALRY   Two valuable works on the diplomatic history of the period are **N. Rich, *Great Power Diplomacy: 1814–1914*** (New York, 1991), and **C. J. Bartlett, *Peace, War and European Powers*,** rev. ed. (New York, 1996).

Notes

1. Quoted in C. Rearick, *Pleasures of the Belle Époque: Entertainment and Festivity in Turn-of-the-Century France* (New Haven, Conn., 1985), p. 120.
2. Quoted in A. E. E. McKenzie, *The Major Achievements of Science* (New York, 1960), vol. 1, p. 310.
3. Friedrich Nietzsche, *Twilight of the Idols and the Anti-Christ*, trans. R. J. Hollingdale (New York, 1972), pp. 117–118.
4. Friedrich Nietzsche, *Thus Spake Zarathustra*, in *The Philosophy of Nietzsche* (New York, 1954), p. 6.
5. Herbert Spencer, *Social Statics* (New York, 1896), pp. 146, 150.

6. Friedrich von Bernhardi, *Germany and the Next War*, trans. A. H. Powles (New York, 1914), pp. 18–19.

7. Quoted in E. R. Tannenbaum, *1900: The Generation Before the Great War* (Garden City, N.Y., 1976), p. 337.

8. William Booth, *In Darkest England and the Way Out* (London, 1890), p. 45.

9. Quoted in J. Rewald, *The History of Impressionism* (New York, 1961), pp. 456–458.

10. Quoted in A. Higonnet, *Berthe Morisot's Images of Women* (Cambridge, Mass., 1992), p. 19.

11. Quoted in C. Wright, *Listening to Music* (Saint Paul, Minn., 1992), p. 327.

12. Quoted in C. M. Prelinger, "Prelude to Consciousness: Amalie Sieveking and the Female Association for the Care of the Poor and the Sick," in J. C. Fout, ed., *German Women in the Nineteenth Century: A Social History* (New York, 1984), p. 119.

13. Quoted in B. G. Smith, *Changing Lives: Women in European History Since 1700* (Lexington, Mass., 1989), p. 379.

14. Quoted in P. Massing, *Rehearsal for Destruction: A Study of Political Anti-Semitism in Imperial Germany* (New York, 1949), p. 147.

15. Quoted in A. Eban, *Heritage: Civilization and the Jews* (New York, 1984), p. 249.

16. Quoted in J. Merriman, *A History of Modern Europe* (New York, 1996), p. 953.

17. Quoted in ibid., p. 965.

18. Karl Pearson, *National Life from the Standpoint of Science* (London, 1905), p. 184.

19. Quoted in J. Ellis, *The Social History of the Machine Gun* (New York, 1975), p. 80.

20. Quoted in ibid., p. 86.

21. Quoted in L. L. Snyder, ed., *The Imperialism Reader* (Princeton, N.J., 1962), p. 220.

22. Quoted in K. M. Panikkar, *Asia and Western Dominance* (London, 1959), p. 116.

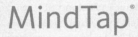 **MindTap®** is a fully online, highly personalized learning experience built upon Cengage Learning content. MindTap combines student learning tools—readings, multimedia, activities, and assessments—into a singular Learning Path that guides students through the course.

CHAPTER 25

THE BEGINNING OF THE TWENTIETH-CENTURY CRISIS: WAR AND REVOLUTION

British infantrymen prepare to advance during the Battle of the Somme

Universal History Archive/UIG/Getty Images

CHAPTER OUTLINE AND FOCUS QUESTIONS

The Road to World War I

Q What were the long-range and immediate causes of World War I?

The War

Q What did the belligerents expect at the beginning of World War I, and why did the course of the war turn out to be so different from their expectations? How did World War I affect the belligerents' governmental and political institutions, economic affairs, and social life?

War and Revolution

Q What were the causes of the Russian Revolution of 1917, and why did the Bolsheviks prevail in the civil war and gain control of Russia?

The Peace Settlement

Q What were the objectives of the chief participants at the Paris Peace Conference of 1919, and how closely did the final settlement reflect these objectives?

Critical Thinking

Q *What was the relationship between World War I and the Russian Revolution?*

Connections to Today

Q *What lessons from the outbreak of World War I are of value in considering international relations today?*

ON JULY 1, 1916, British and French infantry forces attacked German defensive lines along a 25-mile front near the Somme River in France. Each soldier carried almost 70 pounds of equipment, making it "impossible to move much quicker than a slow walk." German machine guns soon opened fire: "We were able to see our comrades move forward in an attempt to cross No-Man's Land, only to be mown down like meadow grass," recalled one British soldier. "I felt sick at the sight of this carnage and remember weeping."[1] In one day, more than 21,000 British soldiers died. After six months of fighting, the British had advanced 5 miles; one million British, French, and German soldiers had been killed or wounded.

Philip Gibbs, an English war correspondent, described what he saw in the German trenches that the British forces overran: "Victory! . . . Some of the German dead were young boys, too young to be killed for old men's crimes, and others might have been old or young. One could not tell because they had no faces, and were just masses of raw flesh in rags of uniforms. Legs and arms lay separate without any bodies thereabout."[2]

World War I (1914–1918) was the defining event of the twentieth century. It devastated the prewar economic, social, and political order of Europe, and its uncertain outcome served to prepare the way for an even more destructive war. Overwhelmed by the size of its battles, the number of its casualties, and the extent of its impact on all facets of European life, contemporaries referred to it simply as the Great War.

The Great War was all the more disturbing to Europeans because it came after a period that many believed to have been an age of progress. There had been international crises before 1914, but somehow

Europeans had managed to avoid serious and prolonged military confrontations. When smaller European states had gone to war, as in the Balkans in 1912 and 1913, the great European powers had shown the ability to keep the conflict localized. Material prosperity and a fervid belief in scientific and technological progress had convinced many people that Europe stood on the verge of creating the utopia that humans had dreamed of for centuries. The historian Arnold Toynbee expressed what the pre–World War I era had meant to his generation:

> [It was expected] that life throughout the World would become more rational, more humane, and more democratic and that, slowly, but surely, political democracy would produce greater social justice. We had also expected that the progress of science and technology would make mankind richer, and that this increasing wealth would gradually spread from a minority to a majority. We had expected that all this would happen peacefully. In fact we thought that mankind's course was set for an earthly paradise.[3]

After 1918, it was no longer possible to maintain naive illusions about the progress of Western civilization. As World War I was followed by the destructiveness of World War II and the mass murder machines of totalitarian regimes, it became all too apparent that instead of a utopia, European civilization had become a nightmare. The Great War resulted not only in great loss of life and property but also in the questioning of one of the basic intellectual precepts on which Western civilization had seemed to have been founded—the belief in progress. To many Europeans, especially intellectuals, a sense of hopelessness and despair soon replaced blind faith in progress. Recently, one historian in his history of Europe from 1914–1949 has used the title "To Hell and Back" to capture the history of this period. World War I and the revolutions it spawned can properly be seen as the first stage in the crisis of the twentieth century.

The Road to World War I

 FOCUS QUESTION: What were the long-range and immediate causes of World War I?

On June 28, 1914, the heir to the Austrian throne, Archduke Francis Ferdinand, was assassinated in the Bosnian city of Sarajevo (sar-uh-YAY-voh). Although this event precipitated the confrontation between Austria and Serbia that led to World War I, war was not inevitable. Previous assassinations of European leaders had not led to war, and European statesmen had managed to localize earlier conflicts. Although the decisions that European statesmen made during this crisis constitute the immediate cause and were crucial in leading to war, certain long-range underlying forces were also propelling Europeans

toward armed conflict. These long-range forces explain the origins of World War I.

Nationalism

In the first half of the nineteenth century, liberals had maintained that the organization of European states along national lines would lead to a peaceful Europe based on a sense of international fraternity. They had been very wrong. The system of nation-states that had emerged in Europe in the second half of the nineteenth century led not to cooperation but to competition. Rivalries over colonial, industrial, and commercial interests intensified during an era of frenzied imperialist expansion, and the division of Europe's great powers into two loose alliances (Germany, Austria, and Italy in one, and France, Great Britain, and Russia in the other) only added to the tensions (see Map 25.1). The series of crises that tested these alliances in the early years of the new century (see Chapter 24) had taught European states a dangerous lesson. Governments that had exercised restraint in order to avoid war wound up being publicly humiliated, whereas those that went to the brink of war to maintain their national interests had often been praised for having preserved national honor. In either case, by 1914, the major European states had come to believe that their allies were important and that their security depended on supporting those allies, even when they took foolish risks.

Diplomacy based on brinkmanship was especially frightening in view of the nature of the European state system. Each nation-state regarded itself as sovereign, subject to no higher interest or authority. Each state was motivated by its own self-interest and success. As Emperor William II of Germany remarked, "In questions of honor and vital interests, you don't consult others." Such attitudes made war an ever-present possibility, particularly since most statesmen considered war an acceptable way to preserve the power of their national states. And each state had its circles of political and military leaders who thought that war was inevitable and would provide an opportunity to achieve their goals. In Germany, there were those who advocated the creation of a German empire by acquiring parts of Russia and possibly even parts of Belgium and France. France wished to regain control of Alsace-Lorraine, which had been seized by the Germans in the Franco-Prussian War. Austria-Hungary sought to prevent Serbia from creating a large Serbian state at the expense of its own multinational empire. Britain wanted to preserve its world empire, and Russia felt compelled to maintain its great power status by serving as the protector of its fellow Slavic peoples in the Balkans.

Internal Dissent

The growth of nationalism in the nineteenth century had yet another serious consequence. Not all ethnic groups had achieved the goal of nationhood. Slavic minorities in the Balkans and the Austrian Empire, for example, still dreamed of creating their own national states. So did the Irish in the British Empire and the Poles in the Russian Empire.

National aspirations, however, were not the only source of internal strife at the beginning of the twentieth century.

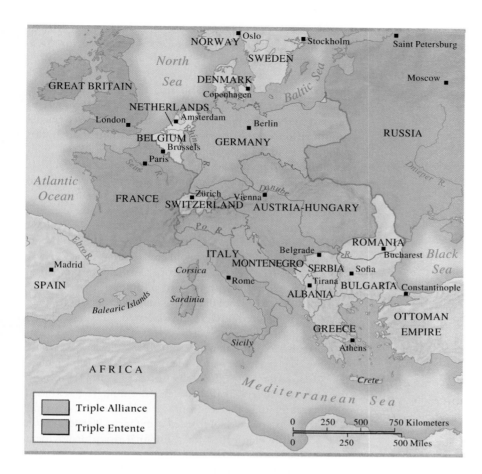

MAP 25.1 **Europe in 1914.** By 1914, two alliances dominated Europe: the Triple Entente of Britain, France, and Russia and the Triple Alliance of Germany, Austria-Hungary, and Italy. Russia sought to bolster its fellow Slavs in Serbia, whereas Austria-Hungary was intent on increasing its power in the Balkans and thwarting Serbia's ambitions. Thus, the Balkans became the flash point for World War I.

Q *Which nonaligned nations were positioned between the two alliances?*

Socialist labor movements had grown more powerful and were increasingly inclined to use strikes, even violent ones, to achieve their goals. Some conservative leaders, alarmed at the increase in labor strife and class division, even feared that European nations were on the verge of revolution. Did these statesmen opt for war in 1914 because they believed that "prosecuting an active foreign policy," as one leader expressed it, would smother "internal troubles"? Some historians have argued that the desire to suppress internal disorder may have encouraged some leaders to take the plunge into war in 1914.

Militarism

The growth of large mass armies after 1900 not only heightened the existing tensions in Europe but made it inevitable that if war did come, it would be highly destructive. **Conscription** had been established as a regular practice in most Western countries before 1914 (the United States and Britain were major exceptions). European military machines had doubled in size between 1890 and 1914. With its 1.3 million men, the Russian army was the largest, but the French and Germans were not far behind with 900,000 each. The British, Italian, and Austrian armies numbered between 250,000 and 500,000 soldiers. Most European land armies depended on peasants, since many young, urban working-class males were unable to pass the physical examinations required for military service.

Militarism, however, involved more than just large armies. As armies grew, so did the influence of military leaders, who drew up vast and complex plans for quickly mobilizing millions of men and enormous quantities of supplies in the event of war. Fearful that changes in these plans would create chaos in the armed forces, military leaders insisted that their plans could not be altered. In the crises during the summer of 1914, the generals' lack of flexibility forced European political leaders to make decisions for military instead of political reasons.

The Outbreak of War: The Summer of 1914

Militarism, nationalism, and the desire to stifle internal dissent may all have played a role in the origins of World War I, but the decisions made by European leaders in the summer of 1914 directly precipitated the conflict. It was another crisis in the Balkans that forced this predicament on European statesmen.

ANOTHER CRISIS IN THE BALKANS As we have seen, states in southeastern Europe had struggled to free themselves from Ottoman rule in the course of the nineteenth and early twentieth centuries. But the rivalry between Austria-Hungary and Russia for domination of these new states created serious tensions in the region. The crises between 1908 and 1913 had only intensified the antagonisms (see Chapter 24).

By 1914, Serbia, supported by Russia, was determined to create a large, independent Slavic state in the Balkans, but

Austria, which had its own Slavic minorities to contend with, was equally set on preventing that possibility. Many Europeans perceived the inherent dangers in this combination of Serbian ambition bolstered by Russian opposition to Austria and Austria's conviction that Serbia's success would mean the end of its empire. The British ambassador to Vienna wrote in 1913:

> Serbia will some day set Europe by the ears, and bring about a universal war on the Continent. . . . I cannot tell you how exasperated people are getting here at the continual worry which that little country causes to Austria under encouragement from Russia. . . . It will be lucky if Europe succeeds in avoiding war as a result of the present crisis. The next time a Serbian crisis arises . . . I feel sure that Austria-Hungary will refuse to admit of any Russian interference in the dispute and that she will proceed to settle her differences with her little neighbor by herself.[4]

It was against this backdrop of mutual distrust and hatred between Austria-Hungary and Russia, on the one hand, and Austria-Hungary and Serbia, on the other, that the events of the summer of 1914 were played out.

HISTORIANS DEBATE **THE ASSASSINATION OF FRANCIS FERDINAND: A "BLANK CHECK"?** A Bosnian activist who worked for the Black Hand, a Serbian terrorist organization dedicated to the creation of a pan-Slavic kingdom, carried out the assassination of the Austrian Archduke Francis Ferdinand and his wife, Sophia, on June 28, 1914. Although the Austrian government did not know whether the Serbian government had been directly involved in the archduke's assassination, it saw an opportunity to "render Serbia impotent once and for all by a display of force," as the Austrian foreign minister put it. Fearful of Russian intervention on Serbia's behalf, Austrian leaders sought the backing of their German allies. Emperor William II and his chancellor, Theobald von Bethmann-Hollweg (TAY-oh-bahlt fun BET-mun-HOHL-vek), responded with the infamous "blank check," their assurance that Austria-Hungary could rely on Germany's "full support," even if "matters went to the length of a war between Austria-Hungary and Russia." Much historical debate has focused on this "blank check" of July 5 extended to the Austrians. Did the Germans realize that an Austrian-Serbian war could lead to a wider war? If so, did they actually want one? Historians are still divided on the answers to these questions.

Led by Franz Conrad von Hotzendorf (FRAHNTS KON-raht fun HEHT-sen-dorf), chief of the Austro-Hungarian General Staff, who thought war with Serbia was both necessary and inevitable, Austrian leaders had already decided by July 14 to send Serbia an ultimatum that threatened war. But the Austrians decided to wait until the end of the official French state visit to Russia before issuing the ultimatum. On July 23, the day the French president left Russia, Austrian leaders issued their ultimatum to Serbia. Their demands were so extreme that Serbia had little choice but to reject some of them in order to preserve its sovereignty. Austria then declared war on Serbia on July 28.

Although Austria had hoped to keep the war limited to Serbia and Austria in order to ensure its success in the Balkans, these hopes soon vanished.

DECLARATIONS OF WAR Still smarting from its humiliation in the Bosnian crisis of 1908, Russia was determined to support Serbia. On July 28, Tsar Nicholas II ordered partial **mobilization** of the Russian army against Austria. At this point, the rigidity of the military war plans played havoc with diplomatic and political decisions. The Russian General Staff informed the tsar that their mobilization plans were based on a war against both Germany and Austria simultaneously. They could not execute partial mobilization without creating chaos in the army. Consequently, the Russian government ordered full mobilization of the Russian army on July 29, knowing that the Germans would consider this an act of war against them (see the box on p. 761). Germany responded to Russian mobilization with its own ultimatum that the Russians must halt their mobilization within twelve hours. When the Russians ignored it, Germany declared war on Russia on August 1.

German war plans then determined whether France would become involved in the war. Under General Alfred von Schlieffen (AHL-fret fun SHLEE-fun), chief of staff from 1891 to 1905, the German General Staff had devised a military plan based on the assumption of a two-front war with France and Russia, since the two powers had formed a military alliance in 1894. The Schlieffen Plan called for a minimal troop deployment against Russia while most of the German army would make a rapid invasion of western France by way of neutral Belgium. After the planned quick defeat of the French, the German army expected to redeploy to the east against Russia. Under the Schlieffen Plan, Germany could not mobilize its troops solely against Russia and therefore declared war on France on August 3 after issuing an ultimatum to Belgium on August 2 demanding the right of German troops to pass through Belgian territory.

On August 4, Great Britain declared war on Germany, officially over this violation of Belgian neutrality but in

CHRONOLOGY	The Road to World War I	
		1914
Assassination of Archduke Francis Ferdinand		June 28
The "blank check"		July 5
Austria's ultimatum to Serbia		July 23
Austria declares war on Serbia		July 28
Russia mobilizes		July 29
Germany's ultimatum to Russia		July 31
Germany declares war on Russia		August 1
Germany declares war on France		August 3
German troops invade Belgium		August 4
Great Britain declares war on Germany		August 4

"YOU HAVE TO BEAR THE RESPONSIBILITY FOR WAR OR PEACE"

AFTER AUSTRIA DECLARED WAR ON Serbia on July 28, 1914, Russian support of Serbia and German support of Austria threatened to escalate the conflict in the Balkans into a wider war. As we can see in these last-minute telegrams between the Russians and the Germans, neither side was able to accept the other's line of reasoning.

Communications between Berlin and Saint Petersburg on the Eve of World War I

Emperor William II to Tsar Nicholas II, July 28, 10:45 P.M.

I have heard with the greatest anxiety of the impression which is caused by the action of Austria-Hungary against Servia [Serbia]. The inscrupulous agitation which has been going on for years in Servia, has led to the revolting crime of which Archduke Franz Ferdinand has become a victim. The spirit which made the Servians murder their own King and his consort still dominates that country. Doubtless You will agree with me that both of us, You as well as I, and all other sovereigns, have a common interest to insist that all those who are responsible for this horrible murder shall suffer their deserved punishment. . . .

Your most sincere and devoted friend and cousin.

(*Signed*)
Wilhelm

Tsar Nicholas II to Emperor William II, July 29, 1:00 P.M.

I am glad that You are back in Germany. In this serious moment I ask You earnestly to help me. An ignominious war has been declared against a weak country and in Russia the indignation which I full share is tremendous. I fear that very soon I shall be unable to resist the pressure exercised upon me and that I shall be forced to take measures which will lead to war. To prevent a calamity as a European war would be, I urge You in the name of our old friendship to do all in Your power to restrain Your ally from going too far.

(*Signed*)
Nicolas

Emperor William II to Tsar Nicholas II, July 29, 6:30 P.M.

I have received Your telegram and I share Your desire for the conservation of peace. However: I cannot—as I told You in my first telegram—consider the action of Austria-Hungary as an "ignominious war." Austria-Hungary knows from experience that the promises of Servia as long as they are merely on paper are entirely unreliable. . . . I believe that a direct understanding is possible and desirable between Your Government and Vienna, an understanding which I—as I have already telegraphed You—my Government endeavors to aid with all possible effort. Naturally military measures by Russia, which might be construed as a menace by Austria-Hungary, would accelerate a calamity which both of us desire to avoid and would undermine my position as mediator which—upon Your appeal to my friendship and aid—I willingly accepted.

(*Signed*)
Wilhelm

Emperor William II to Tsar Nicholas II, July 30, 1:00 A.M.

My Ambassador has instructions to direct the attention of Your Government to the dangers and serious consequences of a mobilization. I have told You the same in my last telegram. Austria-Hungary has mobilized only against Servia, and only a part of her army. If Russia, as seems to be the case, according to Your advice and that of Your Government, mobilizes against Austria-Hungary, the part of the mediator with which You have entrusted me in such friendly manner and which I have accepted upon Your express desire, is threatened if not made impossible. The entire weight of decision now rests upon Your shoulders, You have to bear the responsibility for war or peace.

(*Signed*)
Wilhelm

German Chancellor to German Ambassador at Saint Petersburg, July 31, URGENT

In spite of negotiations still pending and although we have up to this hour made no preparations for mobilization, Russia has mobilized her entire army and navy, hence also against us. On account of these Russian measures, we have been forced, for the safety of the country, to proclaim the threatening state of war, which does not yet imply mobilization. Mobilization, however, is bound to follow if Russia does not stop every measure of war against us and against Austria-Hungary within 12 hours, and notifies us definitely to this effect. Please communicate this at once to M. Sasonof and wire hour of communication.

 How do the telegrams exchanged between William II and Nicholas II reveal why the Europeans foolishly went to war in 1914? What do they tell us about the nature of the relationship between these two monarchs?

Source: J. B. Scott, ed., *Diplomatic Documents Relating to the Outbreak of the European War* (New York: Oxford University Press, 1916).

---

fact over the British desire to maintain world power. As one British diplomat argued, if Germany and Austria were to win the war, "what would be the position of a friendless England?" By August 4, all the great powers of Europe were at war. Through all the maneuvering of the last few days before the war, one fact stands out—all the great powers seemed willing to risk war. They were not disappointed.

The War

FOCUS QUESTIONS: What did the belligerents expect at the beginning of World War I, and why did the course of the war turn out to be so different from their expectations? How did World War I affect the belligerents' governmental and political institutions, economic affairs, and social life?

Before 1914, many political leaders had become convinced that war involved so many political and economic risks that it was not worth fighting. Others had believed that "rational" diplomats could control any situation and prevent the outbreak of war. At the beginning of August 1914, both of these prewar illusions were shattered, but the new illusions that replaced them soon proved to be equally foolish.

1914–1915: Illusions and Stalemate

Many Europeans went to war in 1914 with remarkable enthusiasm (see the box on p. 763). Government propaganda had been successful in stirring up national antagonisms before the war. Now, in August 1914, the urgent pleas of governments for defense against aggressors found many receptive ears in every belligerent nation. Middle-class crowds, often composed of young students, were especially enthusiastic, but workers in the cities and peasants in the countryside were considerably less eager for war. Once the war began, however, most people seemed genuinely convinced that their nation's cause was just. Even domestic differences were temporarily shelved in the midst of war fever. Socialists had long derided "imperialist war" as a blow against the common interests that united the working classes of all countries. Nationalism, however, proved more powerful than working-class solidarity in the summer of 1914 as socialist parties everywhere dropped plans for strikes and workers expressed their readiness to fight for their country. The German Social Democrats, for example, decided that it was imperative to "safeguard the culture and independence of our own country."

A new set of illusions fed the enthusiasm for war. Almost everyone in August 1914 believed that the war would be over in a few weeks. People were reminded that the major battles of European wars since 1815 had in fact ended in a matter of weeks, conveniently overlooking the American Civil War (1861–1865), which was the true prototype for World War I. The illusion of a short war was also bolstered by another illusion, the belief that in an age of modern industry, war could not be conducted for more than a few months without destroying a nation's economy. Both the soldiers who exuberantly boarded the trains for the war front

The Excitement of War. World War I was greeted with incredible enthusiasm. Each of the major belligerents was convinced of the rightness of its cause. Everywhere in Europe, jubilant civilians sent their troops off to war with joyous fervor, as is evident in the photograph at the top showing French troops marching off to war. The photograph below shows a group of German soldiers marching off to battle with civilian support. The belief that the soldiers would be home by Christmas proved to be a pathetic illusion.

in August 1914 and the jubilant citizens who bombarded them with flowers as they departed believed that the warriors would be home by Christmas.

Then, too, war held a fatal attraction for many people. To some, war was an exhilarating release from humdrum bourgeois existence, from a "world grown old and cold and weary,"

THE EXCITEMENT OF WAR

THE INCREDIBLE OUTPOURING OF PATRIOTIC enthusiasm that greeted the declaration of war at the beginning of August 1914 demonstrated the power that nationalistic feeling had attained at the beginning of the twentieth century. Many Europeans seemingly believed that the war had given them a higher purpose, a renewed dedication to the greatness of their nations. These selections are taken from three sources: the autobiography of Stefan Zweig (SHTE-fahn TSVYK), an Austrian writer; the memoirs of Robert Graves, a British writer; and a letter by a German soldier, Walter Limmer, to his parents.

Stefan Zweig, *The World of Yesterday*

The next morning I was in Austria. In every station placards had been put up announcing general mobilization. The trains were filled with fresh recruits, banners were flying, music sounded, and in Vienna I found the entire city in a tumult. . . . There were parades in the street, flags, ribbons, and music burst forth everywhere, young recruits were marching triumphantly, their faces lighting up at the cheering. . . .

And to be truthful, I must acknowledge that there was a majestic, rapturous, and even seductive something in this first outbreak of the people from which one could escape only with difficulty. And in spite of all my hatred and aversion for war, I should not like to have missed the memory of those days. As never before, thousands and hundreds of thousands felt what they should have felt in peace time, that they belonged together. A city of two million, a country of nearly fifty million, in that hour felt that they were participating in world history, in a moment which would never recur, and that each one was called upon to cast his infinitesimal self into the glowing mass, there to be purified of all selfishness. All differences of class, rank, and language were flooded over at that moment by the rushing feeling of fraternity. . . .

What did the great mass know of war in 1914, after nearly half a century of peace? They did not know war, they had hardly given it a thought. It had become legendary, and distance had made it seem romantic and heroic. They still saw it in the perspective of their school readers and of paintings in museums; brilliant cavalry attacks in glittering uniforms, the fatal shot always straight through the heart, the entire campaign a resounding march of victory—"We'll be home at Christmas," the recruits shouted laughingly to their mothers in August of 1914. . . . A rapid excursion into the romantic, a wild, manly adventure—that is how the war of 1914 was painted in the imagination of the simple man, and the younger people were honestly afraid that they might miss this most wonderful and exciting experience of their lives; that is why they hurried and thronged to the colors, and that is why they shouted and sang in the trains that carried them to the slaughter; wildly and feverishly the red wave of blood coursed through the veins of the entire nation.

Robert Graves, *Goodbye to All That*

I had just finished with Charterhouse and gone up to Harlech, when England declared war on Germany. A day or two later I decided to enlist. In the first place, though the papers predicted only a very short war—over by Christmas at the outside—I hoped that it might last long enough to delay my going to Oxford in October, which I dreaded. Nor did I work out the possibilities of getting actively engaged in the fighting, expecting garrison service at home, while the regular forces were away. In the second place, I was outraged to read of the Germans' cynical violation of Belgian neutrality. Though I discounted perhaps twenty per cent of the atrocity details as wartime exaggeration, that was not, of course, sufficient.

Walter Limmer, "Letter to His Parents"

In any case I mean to go into this business. . . . That is the simple duty of every one of us. And this feeling is universal among the soldiers, especially since the night when England's declaration of war was announced in the barracks. We none of us got to sleep till three o'clock in the morning, we were so full of excitement, fury, and enthusiasm. It is a joy to go to the Front with such comrades. We are bound to be victorious! Nothing else is possible in the face of such determination to win.

 What do these excerpts reveal about the motivations of people to join and support World War I? Do the excerpts reveal anything about the power of nationalism in Europe in the early twentieth century?

Sources: Stefan Zweig, *The World of Yesterday*, trans. H. Ripperger (New York: Viking Press, 1943); Robert Graves, *Goodbye to All That* (London: Jonathan Cape, 1929); Walter Limmer, "Letter to His Parents," in J. E. Lewis, ed., *The Mammoth Book of Eyewitness: World War I* (New York: Carolland Graf Publishers, 2003), p. 24.

as one poet wrote. To some, war meant a glorious adventure, as a young German student wrote to his parents: "My dear ones, be proud that you live in such a time and in such a nation and that you . . . have the privilege of sending those you love into so glorious a battle."[5] And finally, some believed that the war would have a redemptive effect, that millions would abandon their petty preoccupations with material life, ridding the nation of selfishness and sparking a national rebirth based on self-sacrifice, heroism, and nobility. All of these illusions died painful deaths on the battlefields of World War I.

WAR IN THE WEST German hopes for a quick end to the war rested on a military gamble. The Schlieffen Plan had called for the German army to proceed through Belgium into northern France with a vast encircling movement that would sweep around Paris and surround most of the French army. But the

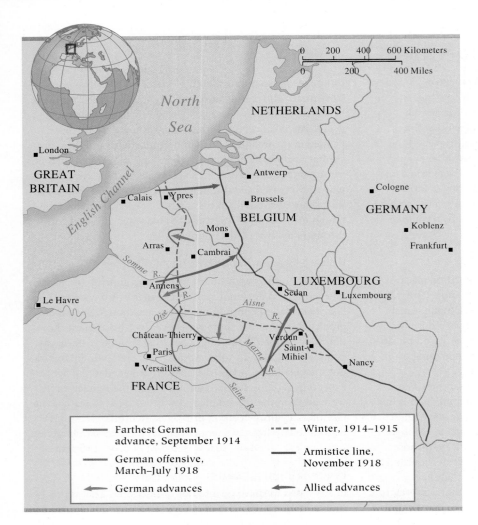

MAP 25.2 The Western Front, 1914–1918. The Western Front was the site of massive carnage: millions of soldiers died in offensives and counteroffensives as they moved battle lines only a few miles at a time in France and Belgium from 1914 to 1917. Soldiers in the trenches were often surrounded by the rotting bodies of dead comrades.

 What is the approximate distance between the armistice line near Sedan and the closest approach of the Germans to Paris?

Legend:
— Farthest German advance, September 1914
---- Winter, 1914–1915
— German offensive, March–July 1918
— Armistice line, November 1918
← German advances
← Allied advances

plan suffered a major defect from the beginning; it called for a strong right flank for the encircling of Paris, but German military leaders, concerned about a Russian invasion in the east, had moved forces from the right flank to strengthen the German army in the east.

On August 4, German troops crossed into Belgium. They encountered little resistance, but when they did, they responded with fierce measures, burning villages, killing civilians, and senselessly destroying a good part of the city of Louvain, including the university library.

By the first week of September, the Germans had reached the Marne River, only 20 miles from Paris. The Germans seemed on the verge of success but had underestimated the speed with which the British would be able to mobilize and put troops into battle in France. An unexpected counterattack by British and French forces under the French commander General Joseph Joffre (ZHUFF-ruh) stopped the Germans at the First Battle of the Marne (September 6–10) east of Paris (see Map 25.2). The German

The Schlieffen Plan

troops fell back, but the exhausted French army was unable to pursue its advantage. The war quickly turned into a stalemate as neither the Germans nor the French could dislodge the other from the trenches they had begun to dig for shelter. Two lines of trenches soon extended from the English Channel to the frontiers of Switzerland. The Western Front had become bogged down in **trench warfare**, which kept both sides in virtually the same positions for four years.

WAR IN THE EAST In contrast to the west, the war in the east was marked by much more mobility, although the cost in lives was equally enormous. At the beginning of the war, the Russian army moved into eastern Germany but was decisively defeated at the Battles of Tannenberg on August 30 and the Masurian Lakes on September 15 (see Map 25.3). These battles established the military reputations of the commanding general, Paul von Hindenburg (POWL fun HIN-den-boork), and his chief of staff, General Erich Ludendorff

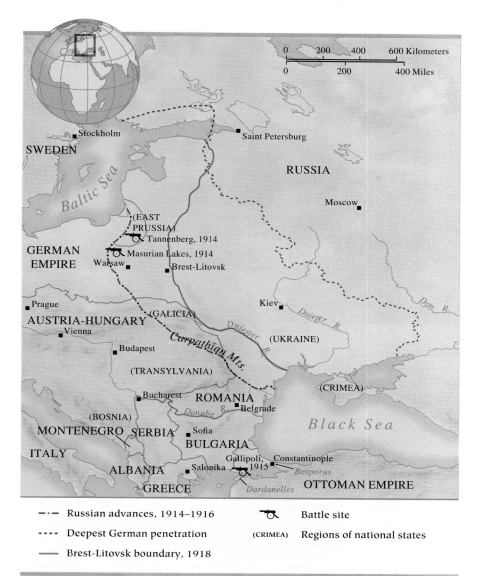

MAP 25.3 The Eastern Front, 1914–1918. Russia made early gains but then was pushed far back into its own territory by the German army. After the Bolsheviks seized power, they negotiated the Treaty of Brest-Litovsk, which extracted Russia from the war at the cost of substantial Russian territory (see Map 25.4).

 What is the approximate average distance between the farthest advances of Russia into Germany and the farthest advances of Germany into Russia?

- · — Russian advances, 1914–1916
- - - - Deepest German penetration
- —— Brest-Litovsk boundary, 1918

Battle site

(CRIMEA) Regions of national states

(AY-rikh LOO-dun-dorf). The Russians were no longer a threat to German territory.

The Austrians, Germany's allies, fared less well initially. They had been defeated by the Russians in Galicia and thrown out of Serbia as well. To make matters worse, the Italians broke their alliance with the Germans and Austrians and entered the war on the Allied side by attacking Austria in May 1915. By this time, the Germans had come to the aid of the Austrians. A German-Austrian army defeated and routed the Russian army in Galicia and pushed the Russians back 300 miles into their own territory. Russian casualties stood at 2.5 million killed, captured, or wounded; the Russians had almost been knocked out of the war. Buoyed by their success, the Germans and Austrians, joined by the Bulgarians in September 1915, attacked and eliminated Serbia from the war.

1916–1917: The Great Slaughter

The successes in the east enabled the Germans to move back to the offensive in the west. The early trenches dug in 1914 had by now become elaborate systems of defense. Both lines of trenches were protected by barbed wire entanglements 3 to 5 feet high and 30 yards wide, concrete machine-gun nests, and mortar batteries, supported further back by heavy artillery. Troops lived in holes in the ground, separated from each other by a "no-man's land."

The unexpected development of trench warfare baffled military leaders, who had been trained to fight wars of movement and maneuver. But public outcries for action put them under heavy pressure. The only plan generals could devise was to attempt a breakthrough by throwing masses of men against enemy lines that had first been battered by artillery barrages. Once the decisive breakthrough had been achieved, they thought, they could then return to the war of movement that they knew best. Periodically, the high command on either side would order an offensive that would begin with an artillery barrage to flatten the enemy's barbed wire and leave the enemy in a state of shock. After "softening up" the enemy in this fashion, a mass of soldiers would climb out of their trenches with fixed bayonets and try to work their way toward the enemy trenches. The attacks rarely worked; the

Impact of the Machine Gun. Trench warfare on the Western Front stymied military leaders, who had expected to fight a war based on movement and maneuver. Their efforts to effect a breakthrough by sending masses of men against enemy lines were the height of folly in view of the brutal efficiency of the machine gun. This photograph shows a group of German soldiers in their machine-gun nest.

machine gun put hordes of men advancing unprotected across open fields at a severe disadvantage. In 1916 and 1917, millions of young men were killed in the search for the elusive breakthrough. In the German offensive at Verdun (ver-DUN) in 1916, the British campaigns on the Somme (SUHM) in 1916 and at Ypres (EE-preh) in 1917, and the French attack in Champagne in 1917, the senselessness of trench warfare became all too obvious. In ten months at Verdun, 700,000 men lost their lives over a few square miles of terrain.

DAILY LIFE IN THE TRENCHES Warfare in the trenches of the Western Front produced unimaginable horrors (see the box on p. 767). Many participants commented on the cloud of confusion that covered the battlefields. When attacking soldiers entered "no-man's land," the noise, machine-gun fire, and exploding artillery shells often caused them to panic and lose

their bearings; they went forward only because they were carried on by the momentum of the soldiers beside them. Rarely were battles as orderly as they were portrayed on military maps and in civilian newspapers.

Battlefields were hellish landscapes of barbed wire, shell holes, mud, and injured and dying men (see "Film & History" on p. 768). The introduction of poison gas in 1915 produced new forms of injuries, as one British writer described:

> I wish those people who write so glibly about this being a holy war could see a case of mustard gas . . . could see the poor things burnt and blistered all over with great mustard-colored suppurating blisters with blind eyes all sticky . . . and stuck together, and always fighting for breath, with voices a mere whisper, saying that their throats are closing and they know they will choke.[6]

Victims of the Machine Gun. Masses of men weighed down with equipment and advancing slowly across open land made magnificent targets for opponents armed with machine guns. This photograph shows French soldiers moving across a rocky terrain, all open targets for their enemies manning the new weapons.

THE REALITY OF WAR: TRENCH WARFARE

THE ROMANTIC ILLUSIONS ABOUT THE excitement and adventure of war that filled the minds of so many young men who marched off to battle (see the box on p. 763) quickly disintegrated after a short time in the trenches on the Western Front. This description of trench warfare is taken from the most famous novel that emerged from World War I, *All Quiet on the Western Front* by Erich Maria Remarque (AY-rikh mah-REE-ah ruh-MAHRK), published in 1929. Remarque had fought in the trenches in France.

Erich Maria Remarque, *All Quiet on the Western Front*

We wake up in the middle of the night. The earth booms. Heavy fire is falling on us. We crouch into corners. We distinguish shells of every caliber.

Each man lays hold of his things and looks again every minute to reassure himself that they are still there. The dugout heaves, the night roars and flashes. We look at each other in the momentary flashes of light, and with pale faces and pressed lips shake our heads.

Every man is aware of the heavy shells tearing down the parapet, rooting up the embankment and demolishing the upper layers of concrete. . . . Already by morning a few of the recruits are green and vomiting. They are too inexperienced. . . .

The bombardment does not diminish. It is falling in the rear too. As far as one can see it spouts fountains of mud and iron. A wide belt is being raked.

The attack does not come, but the bombardment continues. Slowly we become mute. Hardly a man speaks. We cannot make ourselves understood.

Our trench is almost gone. At many places it is only eighteen inches high, it is broken by holes, and craters, and mountains of earth. A shell lands square in front of our post. At once it is dark. We are buried and must dig ourselves out. . . .

Towards morning, while it is still dark, there is some excitement. Through the entrance rushes in a swarm of fleeing rats that try to storm the walls. Torches light up the confusion. Everyone yells and curses and slaughters. The madness and despair of many hours unloads itself in this outburst. Faces are distorted, arms strike out, the beasts scream; we just stop in time to avoid attacking one another. . . .

Suddenly it howls and flashes terrifically, the dug-out cracks in all its joints under a direct hit, fortunately only a light one that the concrete blocks are able to withstand. It rings metallically, the walls reel, rifles, helmets, earth, mud, and dust fly everywhere. Sulphur fumes pour in. . . . The recruit starts to rave again and two others follow suit. One jumps up and rushes out, we have trouble with the other two. I start after the one who escapes and wonder whether to shoot him in the leg—then it shrieks again, I fling myself down and when I stand up the wall of the trench is plastered with smoking splinters, lumps of flesh, and bits of uniform. I scramble back.

The first recruit seems actually to have gone insane. He butts his head against the wall like a goat. We must try tonight to take him to the rear. Meanwhile we bind him, but so that in case of attack he can be released.

Suddenly the nearer explosions cease. The shelling continues but it has lifted and falls behind us, our trench is free. We seize the hand-grenades, pitch them out in front of the dug-out and jump after them. The bombardment has stopped and a heavy barrage now falls behind us. The attack has come.

No one would believe that in this howling waste there could still be men; but steel helmets now appear on all sides out of the trench, and fifty yards from us a machine-gun is already in position and barking.

The wire-entanglements are torn to pieces. Yet they offer some obstacle. We see the storm-troops coming. Our artillery opens fire. Machine-guns rattle, rifles crack. The charge works its way across. Haie and Kropp begin with the hand-grenades. They throw as fast as they can, others pass them, the handles with the strings already pulled. Haie throws seventy-five yards, Kropp sixty, it has been measured, the distance is important. The enemy as they run cannot do much before they are within forty yards.

We recognize the distorted faces, the smooth helmets: they are French. They have already suffered heavily when they reach the remnants of the barbed-wire entanglements. A whole line has gone down before our machine-guns; then we have a lot of stoppages and they come nearer.

I see one of them, his face upturned, fall into a wire cradle. His body collapses, his hands remain suspended as though he were praying. Then his body drops clean away and only his hands with the stumps of his arms, shot off, now hang in the wire.

 What does this excerpt from Erich Maria Remarque reveal about the realities of trench warfare? Would the surviving front-line victims of the war have been able to describe or explain their experiences there to those left behind on the home front? What effect would that have on postwar European society?

Source: Reproduced by permission of the Estate of the Late Paulette Goddard Remarque.

Soldiers in the trenches also lived with the persistent presence of death. Since combat went on for months, they had to carry on in the midst of countless bodies of dead men or the remains of men dismembered by artillery barrages. Many soldiers remembered the stench of decomposing bodies and the swarms of rats that grew fat in the trenches (see the box on p. 768).

Daily life in the trenches was predictable. Thirty minutes before sunrise, troops had to "stand to," ready to repel any attack.

THE REALITY OF WAR: THE VIEWS OF BRITISH POETS

PERHAPS NO ONE CAPTURED THE HORRORS of trench warfare and the use of poison gas better than British poets who served on the front lines of the war. Best known are Wilfred Owen and Siegfried Sassoon, both of whom served on the Western front and had firsthand knowledge of the conditions suffered by frontline soldiers. The first poem below is *Dulce et Decorum Est*, in which Owen uses striking descriptions to question why anyone would die fighting for one's country. The second poem is by Sassoon and relates how conditions in the trenches impacted the soldiers.

Wilfred Owen, *Dulce et Decorum Est*

Bent double, like old beggars under sacks,
Knock-kneed, coughing like hags, we cursed through sludge,
Till on the haunting flares we turned our backs,
And towards our distant rest began to trudge.
Men marched asleep. Many had lost their boots,
But limped on, blood-shod. All went lame, all blind;
Drunk with fatigue; deaf even to the hoots
Of gas-shells dropping softly behind.

Gas! GAS! Quick, boys!-An ecstasy of fumbling
Fitting the clumsy helmets [gas masks] just in time,
But someone still was yelling out and stumbling
And flound'ring like a man in fire or lime.
Dim though the misty panes and thick green light,
As under a green sea, I saw him drowning.

In all my dreams before my helpless sight
He plunges at me, guttering, choking, drowning.

If in some smothering dreams, you too could pace
Behind the wagon that we flung him,

And watch the white eyes writhing in his face,
His hanging face, like a devil's sick of sin,
If you could hear, at every jolt, the blood
Come gargling from the froth-corrupted lungs
Bitter as the cud
Of vile, incurable shores on innocent tongues,
My friend, you would not tell with such high zest
To children ardent [keen] for some desperate glory,
The old Lie: Dulce et decorum est
Pro patria mori. [the words taken from an ode by Horace: "it is sweet and right to die for your country]

Siegfried Sassoon, *Suicide in the Trenches*

I knew a simple soldier boy
Who grinned at life in empty joy,
Slept soundly through the lonesome dark,
And whistled early with the lark.

In winter trenches, cowed and glum,
With crumps and lice and lack of rum,
He put a bullet through his brain.
No one spoke of him again.

You smug-faced crowds with kindling eye
Who cheer when soldier lads march by,
Sneak home and pray you'll never know
The hell where youth and laughter go.

 What impressions of trench warfare do you learn from these two poems? Why would you characterize them as antiwar poems?

Source: Wilfred Owen, in *The Penguin Book of First World War Poetry*, 2nd ed. (New York: Penguin Books, 1981), pp. 182–183; Siegfried Sassoon, *The Complete War Poems*, p. 26.

 FILM & HISTORY

United Artists/The Kobal Collection at Art Resource, NY

Watch *Paths of Glory* (1957), a powerful antiwar film directed by Stanley Kubrick in 1957 and based on the novel with the same name by Humphrey Cobb. Set in France in 1916, the film deals with the time during World War I when the Western Front had become bogged down in brutal trench warfare. The novel was based loosely on a true story of five French soldiers who were executed for mutiny. The film realistically portrays the horrors of trench warfare in World War I and is also scathing in its portrayal of military leaders.

Q *How does the film capture the horrors of trench warfare? How is the film a realistic indictment of war and the military elites?*

If no attack was forthcoming that day, the day's routine consisted of breakfast followed by inspection, sentry duty, restoration of the trenches, care of personal items, or whiling away the time as best they could. Soldiers often recalled the boredom of life in the dreary, lice-ridden, muddy or dusty trenches (see "Images of Everyday Life" on p. 769).

At many places along the opposing lines of trenches, a "live and let live" system evolved based on the realization that neither side was going to drive out the other anyway. The "live and let live" system resulted in arrangements such as not shelling the latrines or attacking during breakfast. Some parties even worked out agreements to make noise before lesser raids so that the opposing soldiers could retreat to their bunkers.

On both sides, troops produced their own humorous magazines to help pass the time and fulfill the need to laugh in the midst of the daily madness. The British trench magazine, the *B.E.F. Times*, devoted one of its issues to defining military terms. A typical definition was "DUDS—These are of two kinds.

Life in the Trenches

THE SLAUGHTER OF MILLIONS OF men in the trenches of World War I created unimaginable horrors for the participants. For the sake of survival, many soldiers learned to harden themselves against the stench of decomposing bodies and the sight of bodies horribly dismembered by artillery barrages, as is evident in the photograph at the top left. Life in the trenches could also be boring, and soldiers whiled away the time as best they could when they were not fighting. Shown in the photograph at the top right is a group of German soldiers in their trench reading and writing letters during a lull in the fighting. The introduction of poison gas in 1915 led quickly to the use of protective gas masks. The bottom photograph shows Austrian soldiers in their trench demonstrating how to use the gas masks.

Hulton Archive/Getty Images

Three Lions/Getty Images

Hulton Archive/Getty Images

A shell on impact failing to explode is called a dud. They are unhappily not as plentiful as the other kind, which often draws a big salary and explodes for no reason. These are plentiful away from the fighting areas."[7]

Soldiers on the Western Front did not spend all of their time on the front line or in combat when they were on the front line. An infantryman spent one week out of every month in the front-line trenches, one week in the reserve lines, and the remaining two weeks somewhere behind the lines in rest camps where they might at least have a roof over their heads in wooden huts. But there was not much rest; drills in the morning and games in the afternoon were aimed at keeping soldiers fit. There was at least light entertainment in the evening: concerts, popular songs, and comedic sketches.

But what enabled soldiers to keep going amid the horrors in the trenches? For one thing, many soldiers believed that it was their duty, due to a combination of patriotism, sense of honor, and a deference to authority, to defend the homeland. Some even found self-fulfillment in doing their duty. One soldier wrote home, "I am much happier than I ever thought I should be in the Army. After all, I am in my destined place, and doing or about to do what I should be doing or about to do . . . and thank God I don't flinch from the sound of the guns."[8]

As the war dragged on, there developed a serious gap between the frontline soldiers and their families back home who did not know about the horrible conditions. This led the frontline soldiers to feel alone, who then turned to each other and developed a strong sense of comradeship. One soldier wrote that those years "will stand out in the memories of vast numbers of those who fought as the happiest period of their lives. . . . In spite of all the differences in rank, we were comrades, brothers, dwelling together in unity."[9]

At the same time, as the war never seemed to end, the sense of duty eventually gave rise to disillusionment. One soldier said, "Everybody is fed up with the war out here and doesn't care who wins so long as we can get it over."[10] In some cases, especially for the French and Germans, disillusionment led to mutinies that were mostly repressed.

The Widening of the War

As another response to the stalemate on the Western Front, both sides looked for new allies that might provide a winning advantage. The Ottoman Empire had already come into the war on Germany's side in the autumn of 1914. Russia, Great Britain, and France declared war on the Ottoman Empire in November. Although the forces of the British Empire attempted to open a Balkan front by landing forces at Gallipoli (gah-LIP-poh-lee), southwest of Constantinople, in April 1915, the entry of Bulgaria into the war on the side of the Central Powers (as Germany, Austria-Hungary, and the Ottoman Empire were called) and a disastrous campaign at Gallipoli caused them to withdraw. The Italians, as we have seen, entered the war on the Allied side after France and Britain promised to further their acquisition of Austrian territory. In the long run, however, Italian military incompetence forced the Allies to come to the assistance of Italy.

A GLOBAL CONFLICT Because the major European powers controlled colonial empires in other parts of the world, the war in Europe soon became a world war. In the Middle East, the British officer T. E. Lawrence (1888–1935), who came to be known as Lawrence of Arabia, incited Arab princes to revolt against their Ottoman overlords in 1916. In 1918, British forces from Egypt and Mesopotamia destroyed the rest of the Ottoman Empire in the Middle East. For their Middle East campaigns, the British mobilized forces from India, Australia, and New Zealand.

The Allies also took advantage of Germany's preoccupation in Europe and lack of naval strength to seize German colonies in Africa. But there too the war did not end quickly. The first British shots of World War I were actually fired in Africa when British African troops moved into the German colony of Togoland near the end of August 1914. But in East Africa, the German commander Colonel Paul von Lettow-Vorbeck (POWL fun LEH-toh-FOR-bek) managed to keep his African troops fighting one campaign after another for four years; he did not surrender until two weeks after the armistice ended the war in Europe.

In the battles in Africa, Allied governments drew mainly on African soldiers, but some states, especially France, also recruited African troops to fight in Europe. The French drafted more than 170,000 West African soldiers, many of whom fought in the trenches on the Western Front. African troops were also used as occupation forces in the German Rhineland at the end of the war. Many Africans were killed or injured in Europe, where they were often at a distinct disadvantage due to the unfamiliar terrain and climate (see "Global Perspectives" on p. 771).

Hundreds of thousands of Africans were also used for labor, especially for carrying supplies and building roads and bridges. In East Africa, both sides drafted African laborers as carriers for their armies. More than 100,000 of these laborers died from disease and starvation caused by neglect.

The immediate impact of World War I in Africa was the extension of colonial rule, since Germany's African colonies were simply transferred to the winning powers, especially the British and the French. But the war also had unintended consequences for the Europeans. African soldiers who had gone to war for the Allies, especially those who left Africa and fought in Europe, became politically aware and began to advocate political and social equality. As one African who had fought for the French said, "We were not fighting for the French, we were fighting for ourselves [to become] French citizens."[11] Moreover, educated African elites, who had aided their colonial overlords in enlisting local peoples to fight, did so in the belief that they would be rewarded with citizenship and new political possibilities after the war. When their hopes were frustrated, they soon became involved in anticolonial movements (see Chapter 26).

In East Asia and the Pacific, Japan joined the Allies on August 23, 1914, primarily to seize control of German territories in Asia. As one Japanese statesman declared, the war in Europe was "divine aid . . . for the development of the destiny of Japan."[12] The Japanese took possession of German territories in China, as well as the German-occupied islands in the Pacific.

GLOBAL PERSPECTIVES

Soldiers from Around the World

ALTHOUGH WORLD WAR I BEGAN IN EUROPE, it soon became a global conflict fought in different areas of the world and with soldiers from all parts of the globe. The French drafted more than 170,000 troops to fight in Europe. Shown in the photograph at the left are French Senegalese troops as they arrived in France in 1915. They would later fight in the Marne campaign on the western front. About 80,000 Africans were killed or injured in Europe. The photo at the right shows a group of American soldiers with a German machine captured during an offensive in 1918.

New Zealand and Australia quickly joined the Japanese in conquering the German-held parts of New Guinea.

ENTRY OF THE UNITED STATES The United States tried to remain neutral in the Great War but found it more difficult to do so as the war dragged on. Although there was considerable sentiment for the British side in the conflict, the immediate cause of American involvement grew out of the naval conflict between Germany and Great Britain. Only once did the German and British naval forces engage in direct combat—at the Battle of Jutland on May 31, 1916, when the Germans won an inconclusive victory.

Britain used its superior naval power to maximum effect, however, by imposing a naval blockade on Germany. Germany retaliated with a counterblockade enforced by the use of unrestricted submarine warfare. At the beginning of 1915, the German government declared the area around the British Isles a war zone and threatened to torpedo any ship caught in it. Strong American protests over the German sinking of passenger liners, especially the British ship *Lusitania* on May 7, 1915, when more than one hundred Americans lost their lives, forced the German government to modify its policy of unrestricted submarine warfare starting in September 1915 and to briefly suspend unrestricted submarine warfare a year later.

In January 1917, however, eager to break the deadlock in the war, the Germans decided on another military gamble by returning to unrestricted submarine warfare. German naval officers convinced Emperor William II that the use of unrestricted submarine warfare could starve the British into submission within five months. When the emperor expressed concern about the Americans, the chief of the German Naval Staff told him not to worry. The Americans, he said, were "disorganized and undisciplined," and the British would starve before the Americans could act. And even if the Americans did intervene, Admiral Henning von Holtzendorff (HOHLT-sen-dorf) assured the emperor, "I give your Majesty my word as an officer, that not one American will land on the Continent."

The return to unrestricted submarine warfare brought the United States into the war on April 6, 1917. Although American troops did not arrive in Europe in large numbers until the following year, the entry of the United States into the war in 1917 gave the Allied Powers a psychological boost when they needed it. The year 1917 was not a good one for them. Allied offensives on the Western Front were disastrously defeated. The Italian armies were smashed in October, and in November, the Bolshevik Revolution in Russia led to Russia's withdrawal from the war (see "The Russian Revolution" later in this chapter). The cause of the Central Powers looked favorable, although war weariness in the Ottoman Empire, Bulgaria, Austria-Hungary, and Germany was beginning to take its toll. The home front was rapidly becoming a cause for as much concern as the war front.

A New Kind of Warfare

By the end of 1915, airplanes appeared on the battlefront. The planes were first used to spot the enemy's position, but soon they began to attack ground targets, especially enemy communications. Fights for control of the air occurred and increased over time. At first, pilots fired at each other with hand-held pistols, but later machine guns were mounted on the noses of planes, which made the skies considerably more dangerous.

The Germans also used their giant airships—the zeppelins—to bomb London and eastern England. This caused little damage but frightened many people. Germany's enemies, however, soon found that zeppelins, which were filled with hydrogen gas, quickly became raging infernos when hit by antiaircraft guns.

TANKS Tanks also appeared on the battlefields of Europe in 1916. The first tank—a British model—used caterpillar tracks, which enabled it to move across rough terrain. Armed with mounted guns, tanks could attack enemy machine-gun positions as well as enemy infantry. But the first tanks were not very effective, and it was not until 1918, with the introduction of the British Mark V model, that tanks had more powerful engines and greater maneuverability. They could now be used in large numbers, and coordinated with infantry and artillery, they became effective instruments in pushing back the retreating German army.

The tank came too late to have a great effect on the outcome of World War I, but the lesson was not lost on those who realized the tank's potential for creating a whole new kind of warfare. In World War II (see Chapter 27), lightning attacks that depended on tank columns and massive air power enabled armies to cut quickly across battle lines and encircle entire enemy armies. It was a far cry from the trench warfare of World War I.

The Home Front: The Impact of Total War

The prolongation of World War I made it a **total war** that affected the lives of all citizens, however remote they might be from the battlefields. World War I transformed the governments, economies, and societies of the European belligerents in fundamental ways. The need to organize masses of men and matériel for years of combat (Germany alone had 5.5 million men in active units in 1916) led to increased centralization of government powers, economic regimentation, and manipulation of public opinion to keep the war effort going.

TOTAL WAR: POLITICAL CENTRALIZATION AND ECONOMIC REGIMENTATION As we have seen, the outbreak of World War I was greeted with a rush of patriotism; even socialists went enthusiastically into the fray. As the war dragged on, however, governments realized that more than patriotism would be needed. Since the war was expected to be short, little thought had been given to economic problems and long-term wartime needs. Governments had to respond quickly when the war machines failed to achieve their knockout blows and made ever-greater demands for men and matériel.

The extension of government power was a logical outgrowth of these needs. Most European countries had already devised some system of mass conscription or military draft. It was now carried to unprecedented heights as countries mobilized tens of millions of young men for that elusive breakthrough to victory. Even countries that traditionally relied on volunteers (Great Britain had the largest volunteer army in modern history—one

million men—in 1914 and 1915) were forced to resort to conscription, especially to ensure that skilled workers did not enlist but remained in factories that were crucial to the production of munitions. In 1916, despite widespread resistance to this extension of government power, compulsory military service was introduced in Great Britain.

Throughout Europe, wartime governments expanded their powers over their economies. Free market capitalistic systems were temporarily shelved as governments experimented with price, wage, and rent controls, the rationing of food supplies and materials, the regulation of imports and exports, and the **nationalization** of transportation systems and industries. Some governments even moved toward compulsory employment. In effect, to mobilize all of their resources for the war effort, European nations had moved toward planned economies directed by government agencies. Under total war mobilization, the distinction between soldiers at war and civilians at home narrowed. In the view of political leaders, all citizens constituted a national army dedicated to victory. As the American president Woodrow Wilson (1856–1924) expressed it, the men and women "who remain to till the soil and man the factories are no less a part of the army than the men beneath the battle flags."

Not all European nations made the shift to total war equally well. Germany had the most success in developing a planned economy. At the beginning of the war, the government asked Walter Rathenau (VAHL-tuh RAH-tuh-now), head of the German General Electric Company, to use his business methods to organize the War Raw Materials Board, which would allocate strategic raw materials to produce the goods that were most needed. Rathenau made it possible for the German war machine to be effectively supplied. The Germans were much less successful with the rationing of food, however. Even before the war, Germany had to import about 20 percent of its food supply. The British blockade of Germany and a decline in farm labor made food shortages inevitable. Daily food rations in Germany were cut from 1,350 calories in 1916 to 1,000 by 1917, barely adequate for survival. As a result of a poor potato harvest in the winter of 1916–1917, turnips became the basic staple for the poor. An estimated 750,000 German civilians died of hunger during World War I.

Eventually, the military assumed control of the German war government. The two popular military heroes of the war, General Paul von Hindenburg, chief of the General Staff, and Erich Ludendorff, deputy chief of staff, took charge of the government by 1916 and virtually became the military dictators of Germany. In 1916, Hindenburg and Ludendorff decreed a system of complete mobilization for total war. In the Auxiliary Service Law of December 2, 1916, they required all male noncombatants between the ages of seventeen and sixty to work only in jobs deemed crucial to the war effort.

Germany, of course, had an authoritarian political system before the war began. France and Britain did not, but even in those countries, the power of the central government dramatically increased. At first, Great Britain tried to fight the war by continuing its liberal tradition of limited government interference in the economy. The pressure of circumstances, however,

The Wartime Leaders of Germany. Over the course of the war, the power of central governments was greatly enlarged in order to meet the demands of total war. In Germany, the two military heroes of the war, Paul von Hindenburg (left) and Erich Ludendorff (right), became virtual military dictators by 1916. The two are shown here with Emperor William II (center), whose power declined as the war dragged on.

forced the British government to take a more active role in economic matters. The need to ensure adequate production of munitions led to the creation in July 1915 of the Ministry of Munitions under a dynamic leader, David Lloyd George. The Ministry of Munitions took numerous steps to ensure that private industry would produce war matériel at limited profits. It developed a vast bureaucracy of 65,000 clerks to oversee munitions plants. Beginning in 1915, it was given the power to take over plants manufacturing war goods that did not cooperate with the government. The British government also rationed food supplies and imposed rent controls.

The French were less successful than the British and Germans in establishing a strong war government during much of the war. For one thing, the French faced a difficult obstacle in organizing a total war economy. German occupation of northeastern France cost the nation 75 percent of its coal production and almost 80 percent of its steelmaking capacity. Then, too, the relationship between civil and military authorities in France was extraordinarily strained. For the first three years of the war, military and civil authorities struggled over who would oversee the conduct of the war. Not until the end of 1917 did the French war government find a strong leader in Georges Clemenceau (ZHORZH kluh-mahn-SOH) (1841–1929). Declaring that "war is

too important to be left to generals," Clemenceau established clear civilian control of a total war government.

The three other major belligerents—Russia, Austria-Hungary, and Italy—had much less success than Britain, Germany, and France in mobilizing for total war. The autocratic empires of Russia and Austria-Hungary had backward economies that proved incapable of turning out the quantity of war matériel needed to fight a modern war. The Russians, for example, conscripted millions of men but could arm only one-fourth of them. Unarmed Russian soldiers were sent into battle anyway and told to pick up rifles from their dead colleagues. With their numerous minorities, both the Russian and Austro-Hungarian Empires found it difficult to achieve the kind of internal cohesion needed to fight a prolonged total war. Italy, too, lacked both the public enthusiasm and the industrial resources needed to wage a successful total war.

PUBLIC ORDER AND PUBLIC OPINION As the Great War dragged on and both casualties and privations worsened, internal dissatisfaction replaced the patriotic enthusiasm that had marked the early stages of the war. By 1916, there were numerous signs that civilian morale was beginning to crack under the pressure of total war.

The first two years of the war witnessed only a few scattered strikes, but thereafter strike activity increased dramatically. In 1916, 50,000 German workers carried out a three-day work stoppage in Berlin to protest the arrest of a radical socialist leader. In France and Britain, the number of strikes also increased. Even worse was the violence that erupted in Ireland when members of the Irish Republican Brotherhood and Citizens Army occupied government buildings in Dublin on Easter Sunday (April 24) in 1916. British forces crushed the Easter Rebellion and then condemned its leaders to death.

Internal opposition to the war came from two major sources in 1916 and 1917, liberals and socialists. Liberals in both Germany and Britain sponsored peace resolutions calling for a negotiated peace without any territorial acquisitions. They were largely ignored. Socialists in Germany and Austria also called for negotiated settlements. By 1917, war morale had so deteriorated that more dramatic protests took place. Mutinies in the Italian and French armies were put down with difficulty. Czech leaders in the Austrian Empire openly called for an independent democratic Czech state. In April 1917, some 200,000 workers in Berlin went out on strike for a week to protest the reduction of bread rations. Only the threat of military force and prison brought them back to their jobs. Despite the strains, all of the belligerent countries except Russia survived the stresses of 1917 and fought on.

War governments also fought back against the growing opposition to the war. Authoritarian regimes, such as those of Germany, Russia, and Austria-Hungary, had always relied on force to subdue their populations. Under the pressures of the war, however, even parliamentary regimes resorted to an expansion of police powers to stifle internal dissent. At the very beginning of the war, the British Parliament passed the Defence of the Realm Act, which allowed the public authorities to arrest dissenters as traitors. The act was later extended to authorize

British Recruiting Poster. As the conflict persisted month after month, governments resorted to active propaganda campaigns to generate enthusiasm for the war. In this British recruiting poster, the government encourages men to "enlist now" to preserve their country. By 1916, the British were forced to adopt compulsory military service.

public officials to censor newspapers by deleting objectionable material and even to suspend newspaper publication. In France, government authorities had initially been lenient about public opposition to the war. But by 1917, they began to fear that open opposition to the war might weaken the French will to fight. When Georges Clemenceau became premier near the end of 1917, the lenient French policies came to an end, and basic civil liberties were suppressed for the duration of the war. The editor of an antiwar newspaper was even executed on a charge of treason.

Wartime governments made active use of propaganda to arouse enthusiasm for the war. At the beginning, public officials needed to do little to achieve this goal. The British and French, for example, exaggerated German atrocities in Belgium and found that their citizens were only too willing to believe these accounts. But as the war dragged on and morale sagged, governments were forced to devise new techniques to stimulate declining enthusiasm. In one British recruiting poster, for example, a small daughter asked her father, "Daddy, what did you do in the Great War?" while her younger brother played with toy soldiers and cannons.

THE SOCIAL IMPACT OF TOTAL WAR Total war made a significant impact on European society, most visibly by bringing an end to unemployment. The withdrawal of millions of men from the labor market to fight, combined with the heightened demand for wartime products, led to jobs for everyone able to work.

The cause of labor also benefited from the war. The enthusiastic patriotism of workers was soon rewarded with a greater acceptance of trade unions. To ensure that labor problems would not disrupt production, war governments in Britain, France, and Germany not only sought union cooperation but also for the first time allowed trade unions to participate in making important government decisions on labor matters. In return, unions cooperated on wage limits and production schedules. Labor gained two benefits from this cooperation: it opened the way to the collective bargaining practices that became more widespread after World War I and increased the prestige of trade unions, enabling them to attract more members.

World War I also created new roles for women. With so many men off fighting at the front, women were called on to take over jobs and responsibilities that had not been open to them before. These included certain clerical jobs that only small numbers of women had held earlier. In Britain, for example, the number of women who worked in banking rose from 9,500 to almost 64,000 in the course of the war, while the number of women in commerce rose from a half million to almost one million. Overall, 1,345,000 women in Britain obtained new jobs or replaced men during the war. Women were also now employed in jobs that had been considered "beyond the capacity of women." These included such occupations as chimney sweeps, truck drivers, farm laborers, and, above all, factory workers in heavy industry (see the box on p. 775). In France, 684,000 women worked in armaments plants for the first time; in Britain, the figure was 920,000. Thirty-eight percent of the workers in the Krupp (KROOP) armaments works in Germany in 1918 were women.

Male resistance, however, often made it difficult for women to enter these new jobs, especially in heavy industry. One Englishwoman who worked in a munitions factory recalled her experience: "I could quite see it was hard on the men to have women coming into all their pet jobs and in some cases doing them a good deal better. I sympathized with the way they were torn between not wanting the women to undercut them, and yet hating them to earn as much."[13] While male workers expressed concern that the employment of females at lower wages would depress their own wages, women began to demand equal pay. The French government passed a law in July 1915 that established a minimum wage for women homeworkers in textiles, an industry that had grown dramatically because of the need for military uniforms. In 1917, the government decreed that men and women should receive equal rates for piecework. Despite the noticeable increase in women's wages that resulted from government regulations, women's industrial wages still were not equal to men's wages at the end of the war.

WOMEN IN THE FACTORIES

DURING WORLD WAR I, WOMEN were called on to assume new job responsibilities, including factory work. In this selection, Naomi Loughnan, a young, upper-middle-class woman, describes the experiences in a munitions plant that considerably broadened her perspective on life.

Naomi Loughnan, "Munition Work"

We little thought when we first put on our overalls and caps and enlisted in the Munition Army how much more inspiring our life was to be than we had dared to hope. Though we munition workers sacrifice our ease we gain a life worth living. Our long days are filled with interest, and with the zest of doing work for our country in the grand cause of Freedom. As we handle the weapons of war we are learning great lessons of life. In the busy, noisy workshops we come face to face with every kind of class, and each one of these classes has something to learn from the others. . . .

Engineering mankind is possessed of the unshakable opinion that no woman can have the mechanical sense. If one of us asks humbly why such and such an alteration is not made to prevent this or that drawback to a machine, she is told, with a superior smile, that a man has worked her machine before her for years, and that therefore if there were any improvement possible it would have been made. As long as we do exactly what we are told and do not attempt to use our brains, we give entire satisfaction, and are treated as nice, good children. Any swerving from the easy path prepared for us by our males arouses the most scathing contempt in their manly bosoms. . . . Women have, however, proved that their entry into the munition world has increased the output.

Employers who forget things personal in their patriotic desire for large results are enthusiastic over the success of women in the shops. But their workmen have to be handled with the utmost tenderness and caution lest they should actually imagine it was being suggested that women could do their work equally well, given equal conditions of training—at least where muscle is not the driving force. . . .

The coming of the mixed classes of women into the factory is slowly but surely having an educative effect upon the men. "Language" is almost unconsciously becoming subdued. There are fiery exceptions who make our hair stand up on end under our close-fitting caps, but a sharp rebuke or a look of horror will often straighten out the most savage. . . . It is grievous to hear the girls also swearing and using disgusting language. Shoulder to shoulder with the children of the slums, the upper classes are having their eyes opened at last to the awful conditions among which their sisters have dwelt. Foul language, immorality, and many other evils are but the natural outcome of overcrowding and bitter poverty. . . . Sometimes disgust will overcome us, but we are learning with painful clarity that the fault is not theirs whose actions disgust us, but must be placed to the discredit of those other classes who have allowed the continued existence of conditions which generate the things from which we shrink appalled.

 What did Naomi Loughnan learn about men and lower-class women while working in the munitions factory? What did she learn about herself? What can one conclude about the effects of total war on European women?

Source: Naomi Loughnan, "Munition Work," in *Women War Workers*, ed. G. Stone (London: George Harrap and Company, 1917), pp. 25, 35–38.

Even worse, women had achieved little real security about their place in the workforce. Both men and women seemed to think that many of the new jobs for women were only temporary, an expectation quite evident in the British poem "War Girls," written in 1916:

> There's the girl who clips your ticket for the train,
> And the girl who speeds the lift from floor to floor,
> There's the girl who does a milk-round in the rain,
> And the girl who calls for orders at your door.
> Strong, sensible, and fit,
> They're out to show their grit,
> And tackle jobs with energy and knack.
> No longer caged and penned up,
> They're going to keep their end up
> Till the khaki soldier boys come marching back.[14]

At the end of the war, governments moved quickly to remove women from the jobs they had encouraged them to take earlier. By 1919, there were 650,000 unemployed women in Britain, and

wages for women who were still employed were also lowered. The work benefits for women from World War I seemed to be short-lived.

Nevertheless, in some countries, the role played by women in the wartime economies did have a positive impact on the women's movement for social and political emancipation. The most obvious gain was the right to vote, given to women in Germany and Austria immediately after the war (in Britain already in January 1918). The Nineteenth Amendment to the U.S. Constitution gave women in the United States the right to vote in 1920. Contemporary media, however, tended to focus on the more noticeable yet in some ways more superficial social emancipation of upper- and middle-class women. In ever-larger numbers, these young women took jobs, had their own apartments, and showed their new independence by smoking in public and wearing shorter dresses, cosmetics, and boyish hairstyles.

In one sense, World War I had been a great social leveler. Death in battle did not distinguish between classes. Although

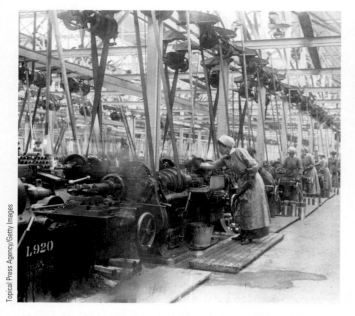

Women Munition Workers in a British Factory. World War I created new opportunities for women. They were now employed in jobs that had earlier been considered beyond their capacity. As seen in the picture at the left, British women, dressed in caps and smocks, are making munitions in an armaments factory. As the recruitment poster at the right shows, the British government encouraged women to work in the munitions factories to aid the war effort. Women working in these factories were often nicknamed "munitionettes."

all social classes suffered casualties in battle, two groups were especially hard-hit. Junior officers who led the charges across the "no-man's land" that separated the lines of trenches experienced death rates three times higher than regular casualty rates. Many of these junior officers were members of the aristocracy (see the box on p. 777). The unskilled workers and peasants who made up the masses of soldiers mowed down by machine guns also suffered heavy casualties. The fortunate ones were the skilled laborers who gained exemptions from military service because they were needed at home to train workers in the war industries.

The burst of patriotic enthusiasm that marked the beginning of the war deceived many into believing that the war was creating a new sense of community that meant the end of the class conflict that had marked European society in the decades before the war. David Lloyd George, who became the British prime minister in 1916, wrote in September 1914 that "all classes, high and low, are shedding themselves of selfishness. . . . It is bringing a new outlook to all classes. . . . We can see for the first time the fundamental things that matter in life, and that have been obscured from our vision by the . . . growth of prosperity."[15] Lloyd George's optimism proved to be quite misguided, however. The Great War did not eliminate the class conflict that had characterized pre-1914 Europe, and this became increasingly apparent as the war dragged on. The economic impact of the war was felt unevenly. One group of people who especially benefited were the owners of the large industries manufacturing the weapons

of war. Despite public outrage, governments rarely limited the enormous profits made by the industrial barons. In fact, in the name of efficiency, wartime governments tended to favor large industries when scarce raw materials were allocated. Small firms considered less essential to the war effort even had to shut down because of a lack of resources.

Inflation also caused inequities. The combination of full employment and high demand for scarce consumer goods caused prices to climb. Many skilled workers were able to earn wages that enabled them to keep up with inflation, but this was not true for unskilled workers or those in nonessential industries. Only in Great Britain did the wages of workers outstrip prices. Everywhere else in Europe, people experienced a loss of purchasing power.

Many middle-class people were hit especially hard by inflation. They included both those who lived on fixed incomes, such as retired people on pensions, and professional people, such as clerks, lesser civil servants, teachers, small shopkeepers, and members of the clergy, whose incomes remained stable at a time when prices were rising. By the end of the war, many of these people were actually doing less well economically than skilled workers. Their discontent would find expression after the war.

THE SELECTIONS BELOW ARE taken from *Letters from a Lost Generation*, a collection of letters between Vera Brittain, who gave up her university studies to become a nurse, and four young men—her fiance Roland Leighton, her younger brother, and their two close friends. All four were well-educated, upper-class individuals, and all four died in battle in World War I.

Letters from a Lost Generation
Roland to Vera: France, 20–21 April 1915

It is very nice sitting here now. At times I can quite forget danger and war and death, and think only of the beauty of life, and love—and you. Everything is such a grim contrast here. I went up yesterday morning to my fire trench, through the sunlit wood, and found the body of a dead British soldier hidden in the undergrowth a few yards from the path. He must have been shot there during the wood fighting in the early part of the war and lain forgotten all this time. . . . I am having a mound of earth thrown over him, to add one more to the other little graves in the wood.

You do not mind me telling you these gruesome things, do you? You asked me to tell you everything. It is of such things that my new life is made.

Wednesday, 21st

I had no opportunity to finish this yesterday.

We are going out of the trenches this afternoon at 4 o'clock. I shall be glad of the rest, as it has been a tiring four days here. I was up nearly all last night mending the barbed wire entanglements in front of our trenches, and this morning can hardly keep my eyes open. There is nothing glorious in trench warfare. It is all waiting and taking of petty advantages—and those who can wait longest win. And it is all for nothing—for an empty name, for an ideal perhaps—after all.

Vera to Roland: Oxford, England, 25 April 1915

I received your letter dated April 20th this morning. Yes, tell me all the gruesome things you see. . . . I want your new life to be mine to as great an extent as is possible, and this is the only way it can—Women are no longer the sheltered and protected darlings of man's playtime, fit only for the nursery and the drawing-room—at least, no woman that you are interested in could ever be just that. Somehow I feel it makes me stronger to realize what horrors there are. I shudder and grow cold when I hear about them, and then feel that next time I shall bear it, not more callously, yet in some way better. . . .

Is it really all for nothing—for an empty name—an ideal? Last time I saw you it was I who said that and you who denied it. Was I really right, and will the issue really not be worth one of the lives that have been sacrificed for it? Or did we need this gigantic catastrophe to wake up all that was dead within us? You can judge best of us two now. In the light of all that you have seen, tell me what you really think. Is it an ideal for which you personally are fighting, and is it one which justifies all the blood that has been and is to be shed? . . .

You speak of "anticipation"—it is very sweet to think that such a thing may be again, and that you in spite of everything have hope enough to look forward. Now you are in the midst of it all, do you still feel you will come through to the end? I always am thinking how you said "I am coming back," and that one day our dreams will come true.

 What do these letters tell you about the impact the war had on educated women? What does the tone of Roland's letter suggest about an officer's experiences during the war? How did they affect his view of the value and purpose of the war?

Source: M. S. Neiberg, ed., *The World War I Reader* (New York: New York University Press, 2007), pp. 227–229.

War and Revolution

 FOCUS QUESTION: What were the causes of the Russian Revolution of 1917, and why did the Bolsheviks prevail in the civil war and gain control of Russia?

By 1917, total war was creating serious domestic turmoil in all of the European belligerent states. Most countries were able to prop up their regimes and persuade their people to continue the war for another year, but others were coming close to collapse. In Austria, for example, a government minister warned that if the monarchs of the Central Powers could not make peace soon, "it will be made for them by their peoples." Russia, however, was the only belligerent that actually experienced the kind of complete collapse in 1917 that others were predicting might happen throughout Europe. Out of Russia's collapse came the Russian Revolution, whose impact would be widely felt in Europe for decades to come.

The Russian Revolution

After the Revolution of 1905 had failed to bring any substantial changes to Russia, Tsar Nicholas II relied on the army and bureaucracy to uphold his regime. But World War I magnified Russia's problems and severely challenged the tsarist government. The tsar, possessed of a strong sense of moral duty to his country, was the only European monarch to take personal charge of the armed forces, despite a lack of training for such an awesome responsibility. Russian industry was unable to produce the weapons needed for the army. Ill-led and ill-armed, Russian armies suffered incredible losses. Between 1914 and 1916, 2 million soldiers were killed, while another 4 to 6 million were wounded or captured.

The tsarist government was unprepared for the tasks that it faced in 1914. The surge of patriotic enthusiasm that greeted the outbreak of war was soon dissipated by a government that distrusted its own people. Although the middle classes and liberal aristocrats still hoped for a constitutional monarchy, they were sullen over the tsar's revocation of the political concessions made during the Revolution of 1905. Peasant discontent flourished as conditions worsened. The concentration of Russian industry in a few large cities made workers' frustrations all the more evident and dangerous. In the meantime, Nicholas was increasingly insulated from events by his wife, Alexandra. This German-born princess was a well-educated woman who had fallen under the influence of Rasputin (rass-PYOO-tin), a Siberian peasant whom the tsarina regarded as a holy man because he alone seemed able to stop the bleeding of her hemophiliac son, Alexis. Rasputin's influence made him a power behind the throne, and he did not hesitate to interfere in government affairs. As the leadership at the top experienced a series of military and economic disasters, the middle class, aristocrats, peasants, soldiers, and workers grew more and more disenchanted with the tsarist regime. Even conservative aristocrats who supported the monarchy felt the need to do something to reverse the deteriorating situation. For a start, they assassinated Rasputin in December 1916. By then it was too late to save the monarchy, and its fall came quickly in the first weeks of March 1917.

THE MARCH REVOLUTION At the beginning of March, a series of strikes broke out in the capital city of Petrograd (formerly Saint Petersburg). Here the actions of working-class women helped change the course of Russian history. Weeks earlier, the government had introduced bread rationing in the city after the price of bread skyrocketed. Many of the women who stood in line waiting for bread were also factory workers who put in twelve-hour days. The number of women working in Petrograd factories had doubled since 1914. The Russian government had become aware of the volatile situation in the capital from police reports, one of which stated:

> Mothers of families, exhausted by endless standing in line at stores, distraught over their half-starving and sick children, are today perhaps closer to revolution than [the liberal opposition leaders] and of course they are a great deal more dangerous because they are the combustible material for which only a single spark is needed to burst into flame.[16]

On March 8, a day celebrated since 1910 as International Women's Day, about 10,000 women marched through Petrograd shouting "Peace and bread" and "Down with autocracy." Soon other workers joined the women, and together they called for a general strike that succeeded in shutting down all the factories in the city on March 10. The tsarina wrote to Nicholas at the battlefront that "this is a hooligan movement. If the weather were very cold they would all probably stay at home." Believing his wife, Nicholas told his military commanders, "I command you tomorrow to stop the disorders in the capital, which are unacceptable in the difficult time of war with Germany and Austria."[17] The troops were ordered to disperse the crowds, shooting them if necessary. Initially, the troops obeyed, but soon significant numbers of the soldiers

Bettmann/Corbis

The Women's March in Petrograd. After the imposition of bread rationing in Petrograd, 10,000 women engaged in mass demonstrations and demanded "Peace and bread" for the families of soldiers. This photograph shows the women marching through the streets of Petrograd on March 8, 1917.

joined the demonstrators. The situation was now out of the tsar's control. The Duma, or legislature, which the tsar had tried to dissolve, met anyway and on March 12 declared that it was assuming governmental responsibility. It established a provisional government on March 15; the tsar abdicated the same day.

In just one week, the tsarist regime had fallen apart. Although no particular group had been responsible for the outburst, the moderate Constitutional Democrats assumed responsibility for establishing the provisional government. They represented primarily a middle-class and liberal aristocratic minority. Their program consisted of a liberal agenda that included working toward a parliamentary democracy and passing reforms that provided universal suffrage, civil equality, and an eight-hour workday.

The provisional government also faced another authority, the **soviets**, or councils of workers' and soldiers' deputies. The soviet of Petrograd had been formed in March 1917; around the same time, soviets sprang up spontaneously in army units and towns. The soviets represented the more radical interests of the lower classes and were largely composed of socialists of various kinds. Among them was the Marxist Social Democratic Party, which had formed in 1898 but divided in 1903 into two factions known as the Mensheviks (MENS-shuh-viks) and the **Bolsheviks** (BOHL-shuh-viks). The Mensheviks wanted the Social Democrats to be a mass electoral socialist party based on a Western model. Like the Social Democrats of Germany, they were willing to cooperate temporarily in a parliamentary democracy while working toward the ultimate achievement of a socialist state.

The Bolsheviks were a small faction of Russian Social Democrats who had come under the leadership of Vladimir Ulianov (VLAD-ih-meer ool-YA-nuf), known to the world as V. I. Lenin (LEH-nin) (1870–1924). Born in 1870, Lenin received a legal education and became a lawyer. In 1887, he turned into a dedicated enemy of tsarist Russia when his older brother was executed for planning to assassinate the tsar. Lenin's search for a revolutionary faith led him to Marxism, and in 1894 he moved to Saint Petersburg, where he helped organize an illegal group known as the Union for the Liberation of the Working Class. Arrested for this activity, Lenin was shipped to Siberia. After his release, he chose to go into exile in Switzerland and eventually assumed the leadership of the Bolshevik wing of the Russian Social Democratic Party.

Under Lenin's direction, the Bolsheviks became a party dedicated to a violent revolution that would destroy the capitalist system. He believed that a "vanguard" of activists must form a small party of well-disciplined professional revolutionaries to accomplish the task. Between 1900 and 1917, Lenin spent most of his time in Switzerland. The outbreak of war in 1914 gave him hope that all of Europe was ripe for revolution, and when the provisional government was formed in March 1917, he believed that an opportunity for the Bolsheviks to seize power in Russia had come. A few weeks later, with the connivance of the German High Command, who hoped to create disorder in Russia, Lenin, his wife, and a small group of his followers were shipped to Russia in a "sealed train" by way of Finland.

Lenin's arrival in Russia on April 3 opened a new stage in the Russian Revolution. In his "April Theses," issued on April 20, Lenin presented a blueprint for revolutionary action based on his own version of Marxist theory. According to Lenin, it was not necessary for Russia to experience a bourgeois revolution before it could move toward socialism, as orthodox Marxists had argued. Instead, Russia could move directly into socialism. In the April Theses, Lenin maintained that the soviets of soldiers, workers, and peasants were ready-made instruments of power. The Bolsheviks must work toward gaining control of these groups and then use them to overthrow the provisional government. At the same time, the Bolsheviks articulated the discontent and aspirations of the people, promising an end to the war, the redistribution of all land to the peasants, the transfer of factories and industries from capitalists to committees of workers, and the relegation of government power from the provisional government to the soviets. Three simple slogans summed up the Bolshevik program: "Peace, land, bread," "Worker control of production," and "All power to the soviets."

In late spring and early summer, while the Bolsheviks set about winning over the masses to their program and gaining a majority in the Petrograd and Moscow soviets, the provisional government struggled to gain control of Russia against almost overwhelming obstacles. Peasants began land reform by seizing property on their own in March. The military situation was also deteriorating. The Petrograd soviet had issued its Army Order No. 1 in March to all Russian military forces, encouraging them to remove their officers and replace them with committees composed of "the elected representatives of the lower ranks" of the army. Army Order No. 1 led to the collapse of all discipline and created military chaos. When the provisional government attempted to initiate a new military offensive in July, the army simply dissolved as masses of peasant soldiers turned their backs on their officers and returned home to join their families in seizing land.

THE BOLSHEVIK REVOLUTION In July 1917, Lenin and the Bolsheviks were falsely accused of inciting an attempt to overthrow the provisional government, and Lenin was forced to flee to Finland. But the days of the provisional government were numbered. In July 1917, Alexander Kerensky (kuh-REN-skee), a moderate socialist, had become prime minister in the provisional government. In September, when General Lavr Kornilov (LAH-vur kor-NYEE-luff) attempted to march on Petrograd and seize power, Kerensky released Bolsheviks from prison and turned to the Petrograd soviet for help. Although General Kornilov's forces never reached Petrograd, Kerensky's action had strengthened the hands of the Petrograd soviet and had shown Lenin how weak the provisional government really was.

By the end of October, the Bolsheviks had achieved a slight majority in the Petrograd and Moscow soviets. The number of party members had also grown from 50,000 to 240,000. Reports of unrest abroad had convinced Lenin that "we are on the threshold of a world proletarian revolution," and he tried to persuade his fellow Bolsheviks that the time was ripe for the overthrow of the provisional government. Although he faced

Lenin and Trotsky. V. I. Lenin and Leon Trotsky were important figures in the Bolsheviks' successful seizure of power in Russia. On the left, Lenin is seen addressing a rally in Moscow in 1917. On the right, Trotsky, who became commissar of war in the new regime, is shown haranguing the troops of the Red Guard in 1918.

formidable opposition within the Bolshevik ranks, he managed to gain support for his policy. With Leon Trotsky (TRAHT-skee) (1877–1940), a fervid revolutionary, as chairman of the Petrograd soviet, the Bolsheviks were in a position to seize power in the name of the soviets. During the night of November 6, pro-soviet and pro-Bolshevik forces took control of Petrograd under the immensely popular slogan "All power to the soviets." The provisional government quickly collapsed with little bloodshed. The following night, the all-Russian Congress of Soviets, representing local soviets from all over the country, affirmed the transfer of power. At the second session, on the night of November 8, Lenin announced the new Soviet government, the Council of People's Commissars, with himself as its head.

One immediate problem the Bolsheviks faced was the Constituent Assembly, which had been initiated by the provisional government and was scheduled to meet in January 1918. Elections to the assembly by universal suffrage had resulted in a defeat for the Bolsheviks, who had only 225 delegates whereas the Socialist Revolutionaries had garnered 420. But no matter. Lenin simply broke the Constituent Assembly by force. He said that to hand over power to the Constituent Assembly "would again be compromising with malignant bourgeoisie" (see the box on p. 781).

But the Bolsheviks (soon renamed the Communists) still had a long way to go. Lenin, ever the opportunist, realized the importance of winning mass support as quickly as possible by fulfilling Bolshevik promises. In his first law, issued on the new regime's first day in power, Lenin declared the land nationalized and turned it over to local rural land committees. In effect, this action merely ratified the peasants' seizure of the land and assured the Bolsheviks of peasant support, especially against

any attempt by the old landlords to regain their power. Lenin also met the demands of urban workers by turning over control of the factories to committees of workers. To Lenin, however, this was merely a temporary expedient.

The new government also introduced a number of social changes. Alexandra Kollontai (kul-lun-TY) (1872–1952), who had become a supporter of revolutionary socialism while in exile in Switzerland, took the lead in pushing a Bolshevik program for women's rights and social welfare reforms. As minister of social welfare, she tried to provide health care for women and children by establishing "palaces for the protection of maternity and children." Between 1918 and 1920, the new regime enacted a series of reforms that made marriage a civil act, legalized divorce, decreed the equality of men and women, and permitted abortions. Kollontai was also instrumental in establishing a women's bureau, known as Zhenotdel (zhen-ut-DELL), within the Communist Party. This bureau sent men and women to all parts of the Russian Empire to explain the new social order. Members of Zhenotdel were especially eager to help women with matters of divorce and women's rights. In the eastern provinces, several Zhenotdel members were brutally murdered by angry males who objected to any kind of liberation for their wives and daughters. Much to Kollontai's disappointment, many of these Communist social reforms were later undone as the Communists came to face more pressing matters, including the survival of the new regime.

Lenin had also promised peace, and that, he realized, was not an easy task because of the humiliating losses of Russian

SOLDIER AND PEASANT VOICES

IN 1917, RUSSIA EXPERIENCED a cataclysmic upheaval as two revolutions overthrew first the tsarist regime and then the provisional government that replaced it. Peasants, workers, and soldiers poured out their thoughts and feelings on these events, some of them denouncing the Bolsheviks for betraying their socialist revolution. These selections are taken from two letters, the first from a soldier and the second from a peasant. Both are addressed to Bolshevik leaders.

Letter from a Soldier in Leningrad to Lenin, January 6, 1918

Bastard! What the hell are you doing? How long are you going to keep on degrading the Russian people? After all, it's because of you they killed the former minister . . . and so many other innocent victims. Because of you, they might kill even other former ministers belonging to the [Socialist Revolutionary] party because you call them counterrevolutionaries and even monarchists. . . . And you, you Bolshevik gang leader hired either by Nicholas II or by Wilhelm II, are waging this pogrom propaganda against men who may have done time with you in exile.

Scoundrel! A curse on you from the politically conscious Russian proletariat, the conscious ones and not the kind who are following you—that is, the Red Guards, the tally clerks, who, when they are called to military service, all hide at the factories and now are killing . . . practically their own father, the way the soldiers did in 1905 when they killed their own, or the way the police and gendarmes did in [1917]. That's who they're more like. They're not pursuing the ideas of socialism because they don't understand them (if they did they wouldn't act this way) but because they get paid a good salary both at the factory and in the Red Guards. But not all the workers are like that—there are very politically aware ones and the soldiers—again not all of them—are like that but only former policemen, constables, gendarmes and the very very ignorant ones who under the old regime tramped with hay on one foot and straw on the other because they couldn't tell their right foot from their left and they are pursuing not the ideas of socialism that you advocate but to be able to lie on their cots in the barracks and do absolutely nothing not even be asked to sweep the floor, which is already piled with several inches of filth. And so the entire proletariat of Russia is following you, by count fewer than are against you, but they are only physically or rather technically stronger than the majority, and that is what you're abusing when you disbanded

the Constituent Assembly the way Nicholas II disbanded the Duma.

You point out that counterrevolutionaries gathered there. You lie, scoundrel, there wasn't a single counterrevolutionary and if there was then it was you, the Bolsheviks, which you proved by your actions when you encroached on the gains of the revolution: you are shutting down newspapers, even socialist ones, arresting socialists, committing violence and deceiving the people; you promised loads but did none of it.

Letter from a Peasant to the Bolshevik Leaders, January 10, 1918

TO YOU!

Rulers, plunderers, rapists, destroyers, usurpers, oppressors of Mother Russia, citizens Lenin, Trotsky, Uritsky, Zinoviev, Spiridonova, Antonov, Lunacharsky, Krylenko, and Co. [leaders of the Bolshevik party]:

Allow me to ask you how long you are going to go on degrading Russia's millions, its tormented and exhausted people. Instead of peace, you signed an armistice with the enemy, and this gave our opponent a painful advantage, and you declared war on Russia. You moved the troops you had tricked to the Russian-Russian front and started a fratricidal war. Your mercenary Red Guards are looting, murdering, and raping everywhere they go. A fire has consumed all our dear Mother Russia. Rail transport is idle, as are the plants and factories; the entire population has woken up to find itself in the most pathetic situation, without bread or kerosene or any of the other essentials, unclothed and unshod in unheated houses. In short: hungry and cold. . . . You have strangled the entire press, and freedom with it, you have wiped out the best freedom fighters, you have destroyed all Russia. Think it over, you butchers, you hirelings of the Kaiser [William II]. Isn't your turn about up, too? For all you are doing, we, politically aware Great Russians, are sending you butchers, you hirelings of the Kaiser, our curse. May you be damned, you accursed one, you bloodthirsty butchers, you hirelings of the Kaiser—don't think you're in the clear, because the Russian people will sober up and that will be the end of you. I'm writing in red ink to show that you are bloodthirsty. . . . I'm writing these curses, a Great Russian native of Orel Province, peasant of Mtsensk Uezd.

 What arguments do the writers of these letters use against Lenin and the Bolsheviks? Why do they feel so betrayed by the Bolsheviks?

Source: M. D. Steinberg, *Voices of Revolution*, 1917 (New Haven, Conn.: Yale University Press, 2001).

---

territory that it would entail. There was no real choice, however. On March 3, 1918, the new Communist government signed the Treaty of Brest-Litovsk (BREST-li-TUFFSK) with Germany and gave up eastern Poland, Ukraine, Finland, and the Baltic provinces. To his critics, Lenin argued that it made

no difference since the spread of socialist revolution throughout Europe would make the treaty largely irrelevant. In any case, he had promised peace to the Russian people, but real peace did not occur, for the country soon lapsed into civil war.

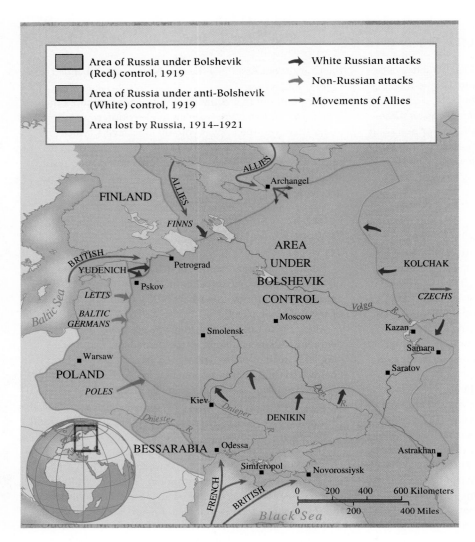

MAP 25.4 The Russian Revolution and Civil War. The Russian Civil War lasted from 1918 to 1921. A variety of disparate groups, including victorious powers from World War I, sought to either overthrow the Bolsheviks or seize Russian territory. Lack of cohesion among their enemies helped the Bolsheviks triumph, but at the cost of much hardship and bloodshed.

 How did the area under Bolshevik control make it easier for the Bolsheviks to defeat the White forces?

CIVIL WAR The new Bolshevik regime faced great opposition, not only from groups loyal to the tsar but also from bourgeois and aristocratic liberals and anti-Leninist socialists, including Mensheviks and Socialist Revolutionaries. In addition, thousands of Allied troops were eventually sent to different parts of Russia in the hope of bringing Russia back into the Great War.

Between 1918 and 1921, the Bolshevik (Red) Army was forced to fight on many fronts (see Map 25.4). The first serious threat to the Bolsheviks came from Siberia, where a White (anti-Bolshevik) force under Admiral Alexander Kolchak (kul-CHAHK) pushed westward and advanced almost to the Volga River before being stopped. Attacks also came from the Ukrainians in the southeast and from the Baltic regions. In mid-1919, White forces under General Anton Denikin (ahn-TOHN dyin-YEE-kin), probably the most effective of the White generals, swept through Ukraine and advanced almost to Moscow. At one point in late 1919, three separae White armies seemed to be closing in on the Bolsheviks but were eventually pushed back. By 1920, the major White forces had been defeated, and Ukraine was retaken. The next year, the Communist regime regained control over the independent nationalist governments in the Caucasus: Georgia, Russian Armenia, and Azerbaijan.

The royal family was yet another victim of the civil war. After the tsar had abdicated, he, his wife, and their five children had been taken into custody. They were moved in August 1917 to Tobolsk in Siberia and in April 1918 to Ekaterinburg (i-kat-tuh-RIN-burk), a mining town in the Urals. On the night of July 16, members of the local soviet murdered the tsar and his family and burned their bodies in a nearby mine shaft.

How had Lenin and the Bolsheviks triumphed over what seemed at one time to be overwhelming forces? For one thing, the Red Army became a well-disciplined and formidable fighting force, thanks largely to the organizational genius of Leon Trotsky. As commissar of war, Trotsky reinstated the draft and even recruited and gave commands to former tsarist army officers. Trotsky insisted on rigid discipline; soldiers who deserted or refused to obey orders were summarily executed. The Red Army also had the advantage of interior lines of defense and was able to move its troops rapidly from one battlefront to the other.

The disunity of the anti-Communist forces seriously weakened their efforts. Political differences created distrust among the Whites and prevented them from cooperating effectively with each other. Some Whites, such as Admiral Kolchak, insisted on restoring the tsarist regime, but others understood that only a more liberal and democratic program had any chance of success. Since the White forces were forced to operate on the fringes of the Russian Empire, it was difficult enough to achieve military cooperation. Political differences made it virtually impossible.

The Whites' inability to agree on a common goal contrasted sharply with the Communists' single-minded sense of purpose. Inspired by their vision of a new socialist order, the Communists had the advantage of possessing the determination that comes from revolutionary fervor and revolutionary convictions.

The Communists also succeeded in translating their revolutionary faith into practical instruments of power. A policy of **war communism**, for example, was used to ensure regular supplies for the Red Army. War communism included the nationalization of banks and most industries, the forcible requisition of grain from peasants, and the centralization of state administration under Bolshevik control. Another Bolshevik instrument was "revolutionary terror." Although the old tsarist secret police had been abolished, a new Red secret police—known as the Cheka (CHEK-uh)—replaced it. The Red Terror instituted by the Cheka aimed at nothing less than the destruction of all opponents of the new regime. "Class enemies"—the bourgeoisie—were especially singled out, at least according to a Cheka officer who said that the first questions you should put to the accused person are: to what class does he belong, what is his origin, what was his education, and what is his profession? According to the officer, "these should determine the fate of the accused." In practice, however, the Cheka promulgated terror against members of all classes, including the proletariat, if they opposed the new regime. Thousands were executed. The Red Terror added an element of fear to the Bolshevik regime.

Finally, the intervention of foreign armies enabled the Communists to appeal to the powerful force of Russian patriotism. Although the Allied Powers had initially intervened in Russia to encourage the Russians to remain in the war, the end of the war on November 11, 1918, had made that purpose inconsequential. Nevertheless, Allied troops remained, and Allied countries did not hide their anti-Bolshevik feelings. At one point, British, American, French, and (in Siberia) Japanese forces were stationed on Russian soil. These forces rarely engaged in pitched battles, however, nor did they pursue a common strategy, although they did give material assistance to the anti-Bolsheviks. This intervention by the Allies enabled the Communist government to appeal to patriotic Russians to fight the attempts of foreigners to control their country. Allied interference was never substantial enough to make a military difference in the civil war, but it did serve indirectly to help the Bolshevik cause.

By 1921, the Communists had succeeded in retaining control of Russia (though not without an enormous loss of life and destruction in the country; see Chapter 27). In the course of

CHRONOLOGY	The Russian Revolution
	1917
March of women in Petrograd	March 8
General strike in Petrograd	March 10
Establishment of provisional government	March 15
Tsar abdicates	March 15
Formation of Petrograd soviet	March
Lenin arrives in Russia	April 3
Lenin's "April Theses"	April 20
Bolsheviks gain majority in Petrograd soviet	October
Bolsheviks overthrow provisional government	November 6–7
	1918
Lenin disbands Constituent Assembly	January
Treaty of Brest-Litovsk	March 3
Civil war	1918–1921

the civil war, the Bolshevik regime had also transformed Russia into a bureaucratically centralized state dominated by a single party. It was also a state that was largely hostile to the Allied Powers that had sought to assist the Bolsheviks' enemies in the civil war. To most historians, the Russian Revolution is unthinkable without the total war of World War I, for only the collapse of Russia made it possible for a radical minority like the Bolsheviks to seize the reins of power. In turn, the Russian Revolution had an impact on the course of World War I.

The Last Year of the War

For Germany, the withdrawal of the Russians from the war in March 1918 offered renewed hope for a favorable outcome. The victory over Russia persuaded Ludendorff and most German leaders to make one final military gamble—a grand offensive in the west to break the military stalemate. The German attack was launched in March and lasted into July. The German forces succeeded in advancing 40 miles to the Marne River, within 35 miles of Paris. But an Allied counterattack, led by the French General Ferdinand Foch (FAYR-dee-nawnh FUSH) and supported by the arrival of 140,000 fresh American troops, defeated the Germans at the Second Battle of the Marne on July 18. Ludendorff's gamble had failed. Having used up his reserves, Ludendorff knew that defeat was now inevitable. With the arrival of one million more American troops on the continent, Allied forces began making a steady advance toward Germany.

To avoid certain defeat as a result of the entry of fresh American troops into the war, army leaders Paul von Hindenburg and Erich Ludendorff sought an armistice even though German armies were still fighting outside Germany. On September 29, 1918, General Ludendorff informed German leaders that the

1914	
Battle of Tannenberg	August 26–30
First Battle of the Marne	September 6–10
Battle of Masurian Lakes	September 15
Russia, Great Britain, and France declare war on Ottoman Empire	November
1915	
Battle of Gallipoli begins	April 25
Italy declares war on Austria-Hungary	May 23
Entry of Bulgaria into the war	September
1916	
Battle of Verdun	February 21–December 18
Battle of Jutland	May 31
Somme offensive	July 1–November 19
1917	
Germany returns to unrestricted submarine warfare	January
United States enters the war	April 6
Champagne offensive	April 16–29
1918	
Last German offensive	March 21–July 18
Second Battle of the Marne	July 18
Allied counteroffensive	July 18–November 10
Armistice between Allies and Germany	November 11
1919	
Paris Peace Conference begins	January 18
Peace of Versailles	June 28

war was lost. Unwilling to place the burden of defeat on the army, Ludendorff demanded that the government sue for peace at once. When German officials discovered that the Allies were unwilling to make peace with the autocratic imperial government, they instituted reforms to set up a liberal government. Implicit among the Allied demands, however, was the abdication of the emperor. William II refused to abdicate, but on November 3, naval units in Kiel mutinied, and within days, councils of workers and soldiers, German versions of the Russian soviets, were forming throughout northern Germany and taking over the supervision of civilian and military administrations. William II capitulated to public pressure and left the country on November 9, while the socialists under Friedrich Ebert (FREED-rikh AY-bert) announced the establishment of a republic. Two days later, on November 11, 1918, an armistice

agreed to by the new German government went into effect. The way in which the war ended, with German armies still fighting outside Germany, later led German nationalists, especially Adolf Hitler (see the next chapter), to argue that the German army had not been defeated but stabbed in the back by the "Jewish-Marxist" civilians who had established the republic. Moreover, at the end of World War II, the Allied armies would be sure to occupy defeated Germany rather than repeat the experience of World War I (see Chapter 27). The Great War was over, but the revolutionary forces set in motion by the war were not yet exhausted.

THE CASUALTIES OF THE WAR World War I devastated European civilization. Between 8 and 9 million soldiers died on the battlefields; another 22 million were wounded. Many of those who survived had suffered the loss of arms or legs or other forms of mutilation; many died later from war injuries. The birthrate in many European countries declined noticeably as a result of the death or maiming of so many young men. World War I also created a "lost generation" of war veterans who had become accustomed to violence and who would form the postwar bands of fighters who supported Mussolini and Hitler in their bids for power (see Chapter 26).

Nor did the killing affect only soldiers. Untold numbers of civilians died from war, civil war, or starvation. In 1915, using the excuse of a rebellion by the Armenian minority and their supposed collaboration with the Russians, the Turkish government began systematically to kill Armenian men and expel women and children. Within seven months, 600,000 Armenians had been killed, and 500,000 had been deported. Of the latter, 400,000 died while marching through the deserts and swamps of Syria and Iraq. By September 1915, as many as one million, and possibly more, Armenians were dead, the victims of **genocide**.

Revolutionary Upheavals in Germany and Austria-Hungary

Like Russia, Germany and Austria-Hungary experienced political revolution as a result of military defeat. In November 1918, when Germany began to disintegrate in a convulsion of mutinies and mass demonstrations (known as the November Revolution), only the Social Democrats were numerous and well organized enough to pick up the pieces. But the German socialists had divided into two groups during the war. A majority of the Social Democrats still favored parliamentary democracy as a gradual approach to social democracy and the elimination of the capitalist system. A minority of German socialists, however, disgusted with the Social Democrats' support of the war, had formed their own Independent Social Democratic Party in 1916. In 1918, the more radical members of the Independent Socialists favored an immediate social revolution carried out by the councils of soldiers, sailors, and workers. Led by Karl Liebknecht (LEEP-knekht) and Rosa Luxemburg (LOOK-sumboork), these radical, left-wing socialists formed the German Communist Party in December 1918. In effect, two parallel governments were established in Germany: the parliamentary republic proclaimed by the majority Social Democrats and the revolutionary socialist republic declared by the radicals.

Unlike Russia's Bolsheviks, Germany's radicals failed to achieve control of the government. By ending the war on November 11, the moderate socialists had removed a major source of dissatisfaction. When the radical socialists (now known as Communists) attempted to seize power in Berlin in January 1919, Friedrich Ebert and the moderate socialists called on the regular army and groups of antirevolutionary volunteers known as Free Corps to crush the rebels. The victorious forces brutally murdered Liebknecht and Luxemburg. The Free Corps and the regular army also crushed a similar attempt at Communist revolution in the city of Munich in southern Germany. The German republic had been saved, but only because the moderate socialists had relied on the traditional army—in effect, the same conservatives who had dominated the old imperial regime. Moreover, this "second revolution" of January 1919, bloodily crushed by the republican government, created a deep fear of communism among the German middle classes. All too soon, a politician named Adolf Hitler would cleverly manipulate this fear.

Austria-Hungary, too, experienced disintegration and revolution. When it attacked Serbia in 1914, the imperial regime had tried to crush the nationalistic forces that it believed were destroying the empire. By 1918, those same nationalistic forces had brought about the complete breakup of the Austro-Hungarian Empire. As war weariness took hold of the empire, ethnic minorities increasingly sought to achieve national independence, a desire encouraged by Allied war aims that included calls for the independence of the subject peoples. By the time the war ended, the Austro-Hungarian Empire had been replaced by the independent republics of Austria, Hungary, and Czechoslovakia and a new southern Slavic monarchical state that eventually came to be called Yugoslavia. Other regions clamored to join Italy, Romania, and a reconstituted Poland. Rivalries among the nations that succeeded Austria-Hungary would weaken eastern Europe for the next eighty years. Ethnic pride and national statehood proved far more important to these states than class differences. Only in Hungary was there an attempt at social revolution when Béla Kun (BAY-luh KOON) established a Communist state. It was crushed after a brief five-month existence.

The Peace Settlement

 FOCUS QUESTION: What were the objectives of the chief participants at the Paris Peace Conference of 1919, and how closely did the final settlement reflect these objectives?

In January 1919, the delegations of the victorious Allied nations gathered in Paris to conclude a final settlement of the Great War. By that time, the reasons for fighting World War I had been transformed from selfish national interests to idealistic principles. At the end of 1917, after they had taken over the Russian government, Lenin and the Bolsheviks had publicly revealed the contents of secret wartime treaties found in the archives of the Russian foreign ministry. The documents made it clear that European nations had gone to war primarily to achieve territorial gains. At the beginning of 1918, however, the American president, Woodrow Wilson, had attempted to shift the discussion of war aims from territorial gains to a higher ground.

Peace Aims

On January 8, 1918, President Wilson submitted to the U.S. Congress an outline known as the "Fourteen Points" that he believed justified the enormous military struggle as being fought for a moral cause. Later, Wilson spelled out additional steps for a truly just and lasting peace. Wilson's proposals included "open covenants of peace, openly arrived at" instead of secret diplomacy; the reduction of national armaments to a "point consistent with domestic safety"; and the **self-determination** of peoples so that "all well-defined national aspirations shall be accorded the utmost satisfaction." Wilson characterized World War I as a people's war waged against "absolutism and militarism," two scourges of liberty that could only be eliminated by creating democratic governments and a "general association of nations" that would guarantee the "political independence and territorial integrity to great and small states alike" (see the box on p. 786). As the spokesman for a new world order based on democracy and international cooperation, Wilson was enthusiastically cheered by many Europeans when he arrived in Europe for the peace conference. Wilson's rhetoric on self-determination was also heard by peoples in the colonial world and was influential in inspiring anticolonial nationalist movements in Africa, Asia, and the Middle East (see Chapter 26).

Wilson soon found, however, that other states at the Paris Peace Conference were guided by considerably more pragmatic motives. The secret treaties and agreements, for example, that had been made before the war could not be totally ignored, even if they did conflict with the principle of self-determination enunciated by Wilson. National interests also complicated the deliberations of the Paris Peace Conference. David Lloyd George, prime minister of Great Britain, had won a decisive electoral victory in December 1918 on a platform of making the Germans pay for this dreadful war.

France's approach to peace was primarily determined by considerations of national security. Georges Clemenceau, the feisty premier of France, believed that the French people had borne the brunt of German aggression and deserved revenge and security against future German aggression (see the box on p. 786). Clemenceau wanted a demilitarized Germany, vast German reparations to pay for the costs of the war, and a separate Rhineland as a buffer state between France and Germany—demands that Wilson viewed as vindictive and contrary to the principle of national self-determination.

Yet another consideration affected the negotiations at Paris: the fear that Bolshevik revolution would spread from Russia to other European countries. This concern led the Allies to enlarge and strengthen such eastern European states as Poland, Czechoslovakia, and Romania at the expense of both Germany and Bolshevik Russia.

Three Voices of Peacemaking

WHEN THE ALLIED POWERS MET in Paris in January 1919, it soon became apparent that the victors had different opinions on the kind of peace they expected. The first selection is a series of excerpts from the speeches of Woodrow Wilson in which the American president presented his idealistic goals for a peace based on justice and reconciliation.

The French leader Georges Clemenceau had a vision of peacemaking quite different from that of Woodrow Wilson. The French sought revenge and security. In the selection from his book *Grandeur and Misery of Victory*, Clemenceau revealed his fundamental dislike and distrust of Germany.

Yet a third voice of peacemaking was heard in Paris in 1919, although not at the peace conference. W. E. B. Du Bois (doo BOISS), an African American writer and activist, had organized the Pan-African Congress to meet in Paris during the sessions of the Paris Peace Conference. The goal of the Pan-African Congress was to present a series of resolutions that promoted the cause of Africans and people of African descent. As can be seen in the selection presented here, the resolutions did not call for immediate independence for African nations.

Woodrow Wilson, Speeches

May 26, 1917

We are fighting for the liberty, the self-government, and the undictated development of all peoples, and every feature of the settlement that concludes this war must be conceived and executed for that purpose. Wrongs must first be righted and then adequate safeguards must be created to prevent their being committed again. . . .

No people must be forced under sovereignty under which it does not wish to live. No territory must change hands except for the purpose of securing those who inhabit it a fair chance of life and liberty. No indemnities must be insisted on except those that constitute payment for manifest wrongs done. No readjustments of power must be made except such as will tend to secure the future peace of the world and the future welfare and happiness of its peoples.

And then the free peoples of the world must draw together in some common covenant, some genuine and practical cooperation that will in effect combine their force to secure peace and justice in the dealings of nations with one another.

April 6, 1918

We are ready, whenever the final reckoning is made, to be just to the German people, deal fairly with the German power, as with all others. There can be no difference between peoples in the final judgment, if it is indeed to be a righteous judgment. To propose anything but justice, even-handed and dispassionate justice, to Germany at any time, whatever the outcome of the war, would be to renounce and dishonor our own cause. For we ask nothing that we are not willing to accord.

Although twenty-seven nations were represented at the Paris Peace Conference, Wilson, Clemenceau, and Lloyd George made the most important decisions. Italy was considered one of the so-called Big Four powers but played a much less important role than the other three countries. Germany, of course, was not invited to attend, and Russia could not because of civil war, although the Allies were also unwilling to negotiate with the Communist regime that was then fighting for power in Russia.

In view of the many conflicting demands at the conference table, it was inevitable that the Big Three would quarrel. Wilson was determined to create a "league of nations" to prevent future wars. Clemenceau and Lloyd George were equally determined to punish Germany. In the end, only compromise made it possible to achieve a peace settlement. On January 25, 1919, the conference adopted the principle of the League of Nations. The details of its structure were left for later sessions, and Wilson willingly agreed to make compromises on territorial arrangements to guarantee the establishment of the League, believing that a functioning League could later rectify bad arrangements. Clemenceau also compromised to obtain some guarantees for French security. He renounced France's desire for a separate Rhineland and instead accepted a defensive alliance with Great Britain and the United States. Both states pledged to help France if it was attacked by Germany.

The Treaty of Versailles

The final peace settlement of Paris consisted of five separate treaties with the defeated nations—Germany, Austria, Hungary, Bulgaria, and the Ottoman Empire. The Treaty of Versailles with Germany, signed on June 28, 1919, was by far the most important. The victorious Allies wrote the treaty without German involvement. The Germans considered it a harsh peace, conveniently overlooking that the Treaty of Brest-Litovsk, which they had imposed on Bolshevik Russia, was even more severe. The Germans were particularly unhappy with Article 231, the so-called **War Guilt Clause**, which declared Germany (and Austria) responsible for starting the war and ordered Germany to pay **reparations** for all the damage that the Allied governments and their people suffered as a result of the war "imposed upon them by the aggression of

January 3, 1919

Our task at Paris is to organize the friendship of the world, to see to it that all the moral forces that make for right and justice and liberty are united and are given a vital organization to which the peoples of the world will readily and gladly respond. In other words, our task is no less colossal than this, to set up a new international psychology, to have a new atmosphere.

Georges Clemenceau, *Grandeur and Misery of Victory*

War and peace, with their strong contrasts, alternate against a common background. For the catastrophe of 1914 the Germans are responsible. Only a professional liar would deny this. . . .

What after all is this war, prepared, undertaken, and waged by the German people, who flung aside every scruple of conscience to let it loose, hoping for a peace of enslavement under the yoke of a militarism, destructive of all human dignity? It is simply the continuance, the recrudescence, of those never-ending acts of violence by which the first savage tribes carried out their depredations with all the resources of barbarism. . . .

I have sometimes penetrated into the sacred cave of the Germanic cult, which is, as every one knows, the *Bierhaus* [beer hall]. A great aisle of massive humanity where there accumulate, amid the fumes of tobacco and beer, the popular rumblings of a nationalism upheld by the sonorous brasses blaring to the heavens the supreme voice of Germany, *Deutschland uber alles! Germany above everything!* Men, women, and children, all petrified in reverence before the divine stoneware pot, brows furrowed with irrepressible power, eyes lost in a dream of infinity, mouths twisted by the intensity of willpower, drink in long draughts the celestial hope of vague expectations. These only remain to be

realized presently when the chief marked out by Destiny shall have given the word. There you have the ultimate framework of an old but childish race.

Pan-African Congress

Resolved

That the Allied and Associated Powers establish a code of law for the international protection of the natives of Africa. . . .

The Negroes of the world demand that hereafter the natives of Africa and the peoples of African descent be governed according to the following principles:

1. The Land: the land and its natural resources shall be held in trust for the natives and at all times they shall have effective ownership of as much land as they can profitably develop. . . .

3. Labor: slavery and corporal punishment shall be abolished and forced labor except in punishment for crime. . . .

5. The State: the natives of Africa must have the right to participate in the government as fast as their development permits, in conformity with the principle that the government exists for the natives, and not the natives for the government.

 How did the peacemaking aims of Wilson and Clemenceau differ? How did their different views affect the deliberations of the Paris Peace Conference and the nature of the final peace settlement? How and why did the views of the Pan-African Congress differ from those of Wilson and Clemenceau?

Sources: Woodrow Wilson, Speeches, May 26, 1917; April 6, 1918; January 3, 1919; Georges Clemenceau, *Grandeur and Misery of Victory* (New York: Harcourt, 1930), pp. 105, 107, 280; excerpts from Resolution from the Pan-African Congress, Paris, 1919.

Germany and her allies." Reparations were a logical consequence of the wartime promises that Allied leaders had made to their people that the Germans would pay for the war effort. The treaty did not establish the amount to be paid but left that to be determined later by a reparations commission (see Chapter 26).

The military and territorial provisions of the treaty also rankled the Germans. Germany had to reduce its army to 100,000 men, limit its weapons, cut back its navy, and eliminate its air force. Germany was virtually disarmed. German territorial losses included colonies in Africa to Belgium, islands in the Pacific in Japan, the cession of Alsace and Lorraine to France and large sections of Prussia to the new Polish state. German land west and as far as 30 miles east of the Rhine was established as a demilitarized zone and stripped of all armaments or fortifications to serve as a barrier to any future German military moves westward against France. Outraged by the "dictated peace," the new German government vowed to resist rather than accept the treaty, but it had no real alternative. Rejection meant a renewal of the war, and as the army pointed out, that was no longer practicable. After the war, radical politicians like

Adolf Hitler were able to gain popularity by raving against this "dictated peace."

The Other Peace Treaties

The separate peace treaties made with the other Central Powers extensively redrew the map of eastern Europe. Many of these changes merely ratified what the war had already accomplished. The empires that had controlled eastern Europe for centuries had been destroyed or weakened, and a number of new states appeared on the map of Europe (see Map 25.5).

Both the German and Russian Empires lost considerable territory in eastern Europe, and the Austro-Hungarian Empire disappeared altogether. New nation-states emerged from the lands of these three empires: Finland, Latvia, Estonia, Lithuania, Poland, Czechoslovakia, Austria, and Hungary. Territorial rearrangements were also made in the Balkans. Romania acquired additional lands from Russia, Hungary, and Bulgaria. Serbia formed the nucleus of the new state of Yugoslavia.

Although the Paris Peace Conference was supposedly guided by the principle of self-determination, the mixtures of

Fair play gegen Deutschland

Ist das englisch?

The Treaty of Versailles. Shown here are the three most important decision makers at the Paris Peace Conference, Georges Clemenceau, Woodrow Wilson, and David Lloyd George, shortly after the signing of the Treaty of Versailles. The Germans' reaction to what they considered a harsh and unfair peace treaty is captured on the cover of *Simplicissimus*, a German satirical magazine published in Munich. A black man representing France is seen beating a German tied to a tree trunk while an Englishman looks on with a grin on his face.

peoples in eastern Europe made it impossible to draw boundaries along neat ethnic lines. Compromises had to be made, sometimes to satisfy the national interest of the victors. France, for example, had lost Russia as its major ally on Germany's eastern border and wanted to strengthen and expand Poland, Czechoslovakia, Yugoslavia, and Romania as much as possible so that those states could serve as barriers against Germany and Communist Russia. As a result of compromises, virtually every eastern European state was left with a minorities problem that could lead to future conflicts. Germans in Poland; Hungarians, Poles, and Germans in Czechoslovakia; and Serbs, Croats, Slovenes, Macedonians, and Albanians in Yugoslavia all became sources of later conflict.

The centuries-old Ottoman Empire was dismembered by the peace settlement after the war. To gain Arab support against the Ottomans during the war, the Allies had promised to recognize the independence of Arab states in the Middle Eastern lands of the Ottoman Empire. But the imperialist habits of Europeans died hard. After the war, France took control of Lebanon and Syria, and Britain

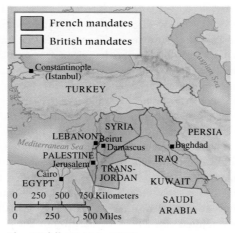

French mandates
British mandates

Constantinople
(Istanbul)
TURKEY
SYRIA
LEBANON
Beirut
Mediterranean Sea Damascus
PALESTINE
Jerusalem
Cairo TRANS-
EGYPT JORDAN
PERSIA
Baghdad
IRAQ
KUWAIT
SAUDI
ARABIA
Caspian Sea

0   250   500   750 Kilometers
0   250   500 Miles

The Middle East in 1919

received Iraq and Palestine. Officially, both acquisitions were called **mandates**. Since Woodrow Wilson had opposed the outright annexation of colonial territories by the Allies, the peace settlement had created a system of mandates whereby a nation officially administered a territory on behalf of the League of Nations. The system of mandates could not hide the fact that the principle of national self-determination at the Paris Peace Conference was largely for Europeans.

The peace settlement negotiated at Paris soon came under attack, not only by the defeated Central Powers but also by others who felt that the peacemakers had been shortsighted. Some people agreed, however, that the settlement was the best that could be achieved under the circumstances. They believed that self-determination had served reasonably well as a central organizing principle, and the establishment of the League of Nations gave some hope that future conflicts could be resolved peacefully. Yet within twenty years, Europe would again be engaged in deadly conflict. As some historians have suggested, perhaps a lack of enforcement, rather than the

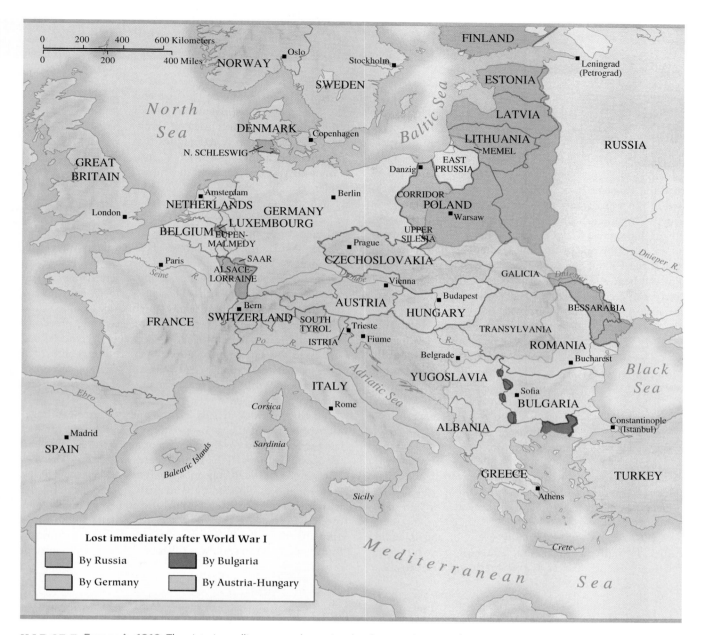

MAP 25.5 Europe in 1919. The victorious allies met to determine the shape and nature of postwar Europe. At the urging of the American president Woodrow Wilson, the peace conference created several new countries from the prewar territory of Austria-Hungary, Germany, and Russia in an effort to satisfy the nationalist aspirations of many former imperial subjects.

Q *What new countries emerged, and what countries gained territory when Austria-Hungary was dismembered?*

structure of the settlement, may account for the failure of the peace of 1919.

Successful enforcement of the peace necessitated the active involvement of its principal architects, especially in helping the new German state develop a peaceful and democratic republic. The failure of the U.S. Senate to ratify the Treaty of Versailles, however, meant that the United States never joined the League of Nations. The Senate also rejected Wilson's defensive alliance with Great Britain and France. Already by the end of 1919, the United States was pursuing

policies intended to limit its direct involvement in future European wars.

This retreat had dire consequences. American withdrawal from the defensive alliance with Britain and France led Britain to withdraw as well. By removing itself from European affairs, the United States forced France to stand alone facing its old enemy, leading the embittered nation to take strong actions against Germany that only intensified German resentment. By the end of 1919, it appeared that the peace established mere months earlier was already beginning to unravel.

The assassination of Archduke Francis Ferdinand of Austria-Hungary in the Bosnian capital of Sarajevo in the summer of 1914 led within six weeks to a major war among the major powers of Europe. The Germans drove the Russians back in the east, but a stalemate developed in the west, where trenches extending from the Swiss border to the English Channel were defended by barbed wire and machine guns. The Ottoman Empire joined Germany, and Italy became one of the Allies. After German submarine attacks, the United States entered the war in 1917, but even from the beginning of the war, battles also took place in the African colonies of the Great Powers as well as in the East, making this a truly global war.

Unprepared for war, Russia soon faltered and collapsed, leading to a revolution against the tsar. But the new provisional government in Russia also soon failed, enabling the revolutionary Bolsheviks of V. I. Lenin to seize power. Lenin established a dictatorship and made a costly peace with Germany. After Russia's withdrawal from the war, Germany launched a massive attack in the west but had been severely weakened by the war. In the fall of 1918, after American troops entered the conflict, the German government collapsed, leading to the armistice on November 11, 1918.

World War I was the defining event of the twentieth century. It shattered the liberal and rational assumptions of late-nineteenth and early-twentieth-century European society. The incredible destruction and the deaths of almost 10 million people undermined the whole idea of progress. New propaganda techniques had manipulated entire populations into sustaining their involvement in a meaningless slaughter.

World War I was a total war that required extensive mobilization of resources and populations. As a result, government centralization increased, as did the power of the state over the lives of its citizens. Civil liberties, such as freedom of the press, speech, assembly, and movement, were circumscribed in the name of national security. Governments' need to plan the production and distribution of goods and to ration consumer goods led to restrictions on economic freedom. Although the late nineteenth and early twentieth centuries had witnessed the extension of government authority into such areas as mass education, social welfare legislation, and mass conscription, World War I made the practice of strong central authority a way of life.

Finally, World War I ended the age of European hegemony over world affairs. In 1917, the Russian Revolution had laid the foundation for the creation of a new Eurasian power, the Soviet Union, and the United States had entered the war. The waning of the European age was not evident to all, however, for it was clouded by American isolationism and the withdrawal of the Soviets from world affairs while they nurtured the growth of their own socialist system. These developments, though temporary, created a political vacuum in Europe that all too soon was filled by the revival of German power.

CHAPTER TIMELINE

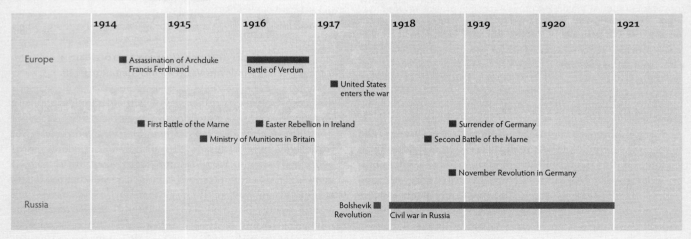

CHAPTER REVIEW

Upon Reflection

Q Which nation, if any, was most responsible for causing World War I? Why?

Q Why can 1917 be viewed as the year that witnessed the decisive turning point of the war?

Q How did Lenin and the Bolsheviks manage to seize and hold power despite their small numbers?

Key Terms

conscription (p. 759)
militarism (p. 759)
mobilization (p. 760)
trench warfare (p. 764)
total war (p. 772)
nationalization (p. 772)
soviets (p. 779)

Bolsheviks (p. 779)
war communism (p. 783)
genocide (p. 784)
self-determination (p. 785)
War Guilt Clause (p. 786)
reparations (p. 786)
mandates (p. 788)

Suggestions for Further Reading

GENERAL WORKS ON TWENTIETH-CENTURY EUROPE A number of general works on European history in the twentieth century provide a context for understanding both World War I and the Russian Revolution. See **N. Ferguson**, *The War of the World: Twentieth-Century Conflict and the Descent of the West* (New York, 2006); **R. Paxton**, *Europe in the Twentieth Century*, 5th ed. (New York, 2011); and **I. Kershaw**, *To Hell and Back: Europe 1914–1949* (New York, 2015).

CAUSES OF WORLD WAR I The historical literature on the causes of World War I is enormous. Good starting points are **J. Joll** and **G. Mattel**, *The Origins of the First World War*, 3rd ed. (London, 2006), and **A. Mombauer**, *The Origins of the First World War: Controversies and Consensus* (London, 2002).

WORLD WAR I The best brief account of World War I is **H. Strachan**, *The First World War* (New York, 2005). See also **S. Audoin-Rouzeau** and **A. Becker**, *14–18: Understanding the Great War* (New York, 2002). On the global nature of World War I, see **M. S. Neiberg**, *Fighting the Great War: A Global History* (Cambridge, Mass., 2005), and **W. K. Storey**, *The First World War: A Concise Global History* (New York, 2009).

WOMEN IN WORLD WAR I On the role of women in World War I, see **S. Grayzel**, *Women and the First World War* (London, 2002).

THE RUSSIAN REVOLUTION A good introduction to the Russian Revolution can be found in **R. A. Wade**, *The Russian Revolution, 1917*, 2nd ed. (Cambridge, 2005). For a study that puts the Russian Revolution into the context of World War I, see **P. Holquist**, *Making War, Forging Revolution* (Cambridge, Mass., 2002). On Lenin, see **R. Service**, *Lenin: A Biography* (Cambridge, Mass., 2000).

THE PEACE SETTLEMENT On the Paris Peace Conference, see **M. MacMillan**, *Paris 1919: Six Months That Changed the World* (New York, 2002), and **E. Goldstein**, *The First World War Peace Settlements* (London, 2002). On the impact of Woodrow Wilson's ideas on the colonial world, see **E. Manela**, *The Wilsonian Moment: Self-Determination and the International Origins of Anticolonial Nationalism* (Oxford, 2007).

Notes

1. M. Gilbert, *The First World War: A Complete History* (New York, 1994), p. 259.
2. Quoted in ibid., p. 264.
3. A. Toynbee, *Surviving the Future* (New York, 1971), pp. 106–107.
4. Quoted in J. Remak, "1914—The Third Balkan War: Origins Reconsidered," *Journal of Modern History* 43 (1971): 364–365.
5. Quoted in R. G. L. Waite, *Vanguard of Nazism* (New York, 1969), p. 22.
6. Quoted in J. M. Winter, *The Experience of World War I* (New York, 1989), p. 142.
7. Quoted in ibid., p. 137.
8. Quoted in J. Ellis, *Eye Deep in Hell: Trench Warfare in World War I* (Baltimore, 1989), p. 166.
9. Quoted in ibid., p. 202.
10. Quoted in ibid., p. 177.
11. Quoted in H. Strachan, *The First World War* (New York, 2004), pp. 94–95.
12. Quoted in ibid., p. 72.
13. Quoted in G. Braybon, *Women Workers in the First World War: The British Experience* (London, 1981), p. 79.
14. "War Girls" by Jessie Pope, *Simple Rhymes for Stirring Times* (London, C. Arthur Pearson, 1916), p. 42.
15. Quoted in R. Paxton, *Europe in the Twentieth Century*, 2nd ed. (New York, 1985), p. 110.
16. Quoted in W. M. Mandel, *Soviet Women* (Garden City, N.Y., 1975), p. 43.
17. Quoted in M. D. Steinberg, *Voices of Revolution, 1917* (New Haven, Conn., 2001), p. 55.

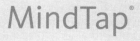

MindTap® is a fully online, highly personalized learning experience built upon Cengage Learning content. MindTap combines student learning tools—readings, multimedia, activities, and assessments—into a singular Learning Path that guides students through the course.

THE FUTILE SEARCH FOR STABILITY: EUROPE BETWEEN THE WARS, 1919–1939

A "Hooverville" on the streets of the United States

CHAPTER OUTLINE AND FOCUS QUESTIONS

An Uncertain Peace

Q What was the impact of World War I, and what problems did European countries face in the 1920s?

The Democratic States in the West

Q How did France, Great Britain, and the United States respond to the various crises, including the Great Depression, that they faced in the interwar years? How did World War I affect Europe's colonies in Asia and Africa?

The Authoritarian and Totalitarian States

Q Why did many European states experience a retreat from democracy in the interwar years? What are the characteristics of so-called totalitarian states, and to what degree were these characteristics present in Fascist Italy, Nazi Germany, and Stalinist Russia?

The Expansion of Mass Culture and Mass Leisure

Q What new dimensions in mass culture and mass leisure emerged during the interwar years, and what role did these activities play in Italy, Germany, and the Soviet Union?

Cultural and Intellectual Trends in the Interwar Years

Q What were the main cultural and intellectual trends in the interwar years?

Critical Thinking

Q Why have some historians called the 1920s both an age of anxiety and a period of hope?

Connections to Today

Q What lessons for dealing with the Western world's current economic crises can you learn from the responses of European states to the Great Depression?

ONLY TWENTY YEARS after the Treaty of Versailles, Europeans were again at war. Yet in the 1920s, many people assumed that the world was about to enter a new era of international peace, economic growth, and political democracy. In all of these areas, the optimistic hopes of the 1920s failed to be realized. After 1919, most people wanted peace but were unsure how to maintain it. The League of Nations, conceived as a new instrument to provide for collective security, failed to work well. New treaties that renounced the use of war looked good on paper but had no means of enforcement. Then, too, virtually everyone favored disarmament, but few could agree on how to achieve it.

Europe faced serious economic and social hardships after World War I. The European economy did not begin to recover from the war until 1922, and even then it was beset by financial problems left over from the war and, most devastating of all, the severe depression that began at the end of 1929. The Great Depression brought misery to millions of people. Begging for food on the streets became widespread, especially when soup kitchens were unable to keep up with the demand. Larger and larger numbers of people were homeless and moved from place to place looking for work and shelter. In the United

States, the homeless set up shantytowns they derisively named "Hoovervilles" after the U.S. president, Herbert Hoover. Some of the destitute saw but one solution; one unemployed person expressed that in view of what he was experiencing, that " I think I should prefer to do away with myself, to take gas, to jump into the river, or leap from some high place. . . . Would I really come to such a decision?" Social unrest spread rapidly, and some unemployed staged hunger marches to get attention. In democratic countries, more and more people began to listen to and vote for radical voices calling for extreme measures.

According to Woodrow Wilson, World War I had been fought to make the world safe for democracy, and for a while after 1919, political democracy seemed well on its way. But hope soon faded as authoritarian regimes spread into Italy and Germany and across eastern Europe.

An Uncertain Peace

 FOCUS QUESTION: What was the impact of World War I, and what problems did European countries face in the 1920s?

Four years of devastating war had left many Europeans with a profound sense of despair and disillusionment. The Great War indicated to many people that something was dreadfully wrong with Western values. In The *Decline of the West*, the German writer Oswald Spengler (1880–1936) reflected this disillusionment when he emphasized the decadence of Western civilization and posited its collapse (see the box on p. 794).

The Impact of World War I

The enormous suffering and the deaths of almost 10 million people shook traditional society to its foundations and undermined the whole idea of progress. New propaganda techniques had manipulated entire populations into maintaining their involvement in a senseless slaughter. How did Europeans deal with such losses? In France, for example, probably two-thirds of the population was in mourning over the deaths of these young people.

An immediate response was the erection of war memorials accompanied by ceremonies to honor the dead. Battlefields also became significant commemorative sites with memorial parks, large monuments, and massive cemeteries, including ossuaries or vaults where the bones of thousands of unidentified soldiers were interred. Virtually all belligerent countries adopted national ceremonies for the burial of an Unknown Soldier, a telling reminder of the brutality of World War I. Businesses, schools, universities, and other corporate bodies all set up their own war memorials.

It is impossible to calculate the social impact of the mourning for the lost soldiers. One French mother explained, "No matter how proud as Frenchwomen we poor mothers may be

of our sons, we nevertheless carry wounds in our hearts that nothing can heal. It is strongly contrary to nature for our children to depart before us." Another Frenchman wrote, "Why should the old people remain alive, when the children who might have initiated the most beautiful era in French history march off to the sacrifice?"[1]

World War I created a lost generation of war veterans who had become accustomed to violence. In the course of the war, extreme violence and brutality became a way of life and a social reality. As one Frenchman recounted: "Not only did war make us dead, impotent or blind. In the midst of beautiful actions, of sacrifice and self-abnegation, it also awoke in us, . . . ancient instincts of cruelty and barbarity. At times, I, who have never punched anyone, who loathes disorder and brutality, took pleasure in killing."[2] After the war, some veterans became pacifists, but for many veterans, the violence of the war seemed to justify the use of violence in the new political movements of the 1920s and 1930s (see "The Authoritarian and Totalitarian States" later in this chapter). These men were fiercely nationalistic and eager to restore the national interests they felt had been betrayed in the peace treaties.

The Search for Security

The peace treaties at the end of World War I had tried to fulfill the nineteenth-century dream of nationalism by redrawing boundaries and creating new states. Nevertheless, this peace settlement had left many nations unhappy. Conflicts over disputed border regions poisoned mutual relations in eastern Europe for years, and many Germans viewed the Peace of Versailles as a dictated peace and vowed to seek its revision.

The U.S. president Woodrow Wilson had recognized that the peace treaties contained unwise provisions that could serve as new causes for conflicts and had put many of his hopes for the future in the League of Nations. Although it had some success in guaranteeing protection for the rights of the many ethnic and religious minorities that remained in some of the newly formed states, the League was not particularly effective at maintaining the peace. The failure of the United States to join the League and the subsequent American determination to be less involved in European affairs undermined the League's effectiveness from the beginning. Moreover, the League's sole weapon for halting aggression was the imposition of economic sanctions such as trade embargoes that often failed to prevent League members from engaging in military action. Efforts to promote disarmament were also ineffective, despite provisions in both the League's covenant and the Treaty of Versailles.

The weakness of the League of Nations and the failure of the United States to honor its promise to form a defensive military alliance with France left the French feeling embittered and alone. Fear of German aggression led them to reject the possibility of disarmament. Before World War I, France's alliance with Russia had served to threaten Germany with the possibility of a two-front war. But Communist Russia was now a hostile power. To compensate, France built a network of alliances in eastern Europe with Poland and the members of the so-called Little Entente (Czechoslovakia, Romania, Yugoslavia).

THE DECLINE OF EUROPEAN CIVILIZATION

THE DUTCH HISTORIAN JOHAN HUIZINGA (yoh-HAHN HY-zin-guh) (1872–1945) was one of many European intellectuals who questioned the very survival of European civilization as a result of the crises that ensued in the aftermath of World War I. In his book *In the Shadow of Tomorrow*, written in 1936, Huizinga lamented the decline of civilization in his own age, which he attributed in large part to World War I.

Johan Huizinga, *In the Shadow of Tomorrow*

We are living in a demented world. And we know it. It would not come as a surprise to anyone if tomorrow the madness gave way to a frenzy which would leave our poor Europe in a state of distracted stupor, with engines still turning and flags streaming in the breeze, but with the spirit gone.

Everywhere there are doubts as to the solidity of our social structure, vague fears of the imminent future, a feeling that our civilization is on the way to ruin. They are not merely the shapeless anxieties which beset us in the small hours of the night when the flame of life burns low. They are considered expectations founded on observation and judgment of an overwhelming multitude of facts. How to avoid the recognition that almost all things which once seemed sacred and immutable have now become unsettled, truth and humanity, justice and reason? We see forms of government no longer capable of functioning, production systems on the verge of collapse, social forces gone wild with power. The roaring engine of this tremendous time seems to be heading for a breakdown. . . .

The first ten years of this century have known little if anything in the way of fears and apprehensions regarding the future of our civilization. Friction and threats, shocks and dangers, there were then as ever. But except for the revolutionary menace which Marxism had hung over the world, they did not appear as evils threatening mankind with ruin. . . .

Today, however, the sense of living in the midst of a violent crisis of civilization, threatening complete collapse, has spread far and wide. Oswald Spengler's *The Decline of the West* has been the alarm signal for untold numbers the world over. . . . It has jolted [people] out of their unreasoning faith in the providential nature of Progress and familiarized them with the idea of a decline of existing civilization and culture in our own time. Unperturbed optimism is at present only possible for those who . . . in their social or political creed of salvation think to have the key to the hidden treasure-room of earthly weal from which to scatter on humanity the blessings of the civilization to come. . . .

How naïve the glad and confident hope of a century ago, that the advance of science and the general extension of education assured the progressive perfection of society, seems to us today! Who can still seriously believe that the translation of scientific triumphs into still more marvelous technical achievements is enough to save civilization. . . . Modern society, with its intensive development and mechanization, indeed looks very different from the dream vision of Progress!

 What problems does Huizinga describe in this excerpt? Why does he think these problems negate the prewar vision of progress?

Source: From Johan Huizinga, *In the Shadow of Tomorrow* (W.W. Norton, 1936), p. 386.

Although these alliances looked good on paper as a way to contain Germany and maintain the new status quo, they overlooked the fundamental military weaknesses of those nations. Poland and the Little Entente states were not substitutes for Russia.

THE FRENCH POLICY OF COERCION (1919–1924) Unable to secure military support through the League of Nations, France sought security between 1919 and 1924 by relying primarily on a strict enforcement of the Treaty of Versailles. This tough policy toward Germany began with the issue of reparations, the payments that the Germans were supposed to make to compensate for the "damage done to the civilian population of the Allied and Associated Powers and to their property," as the treaty asserted. In April 1921, the Allied Reparations Commission settled on a sum of 132 billion marks ($33 billion) for

The Little Entente

German reparations, payable in annual installments of 2.5 billion (gold) marks. Confronted with Allied threats to occupy the Ruhr valley, Germany's chief industrial and mining center, the new German republic accepted the reparations settlement and made its first payment in 1921. The following year, however, facing financial problems, the German government announced that it was unable to pay any more. Outraged by what it considered Germany's violation of the peace settlement, the French government sent troops to occupy the Ruhr valley. If the Germans would not pay reparations, the French would collect reparations in kind by operating and using the Ruhr mines and factories.

Both Germany and France suffered from the French occupation of the Ruhr. The German government adopted a policy of passive resistance that was largely financed by printing more paper money, but this only

The Effects of Inflation. The inflationary pressures that had begun in Germany at the end of World War I intensified during the French occupation of the Ruhr. By the early 1920s, the value of the German mark had fallen precipitously. This photograph shows German children using bundles of worthless money as building blocks. The wads of money were cheaper than toys.

intensified the inflationary pressures that had already appeared in Germany by the end of the war. The German mark soon became worthless. In 1914, a dollar was worth 4.2 marks; by November 1, 1923, the rate had reached 130 billion marks to the dollar, and by the end of November, it had snowballed to an incredible 4.2 trillion marks to the dollar. Economic disaster fueled political upheavals as Communists staged uprisings in October 1923, and Adolf Hitler's band of Nazis attempted to seize power in Munich in November (see "Hitler and Nazi Germany" later in this chapter). But the French were hardly victorious. Their gains from the occupation were not enough to offset the costs. Meanwhile, pressure from the United States and Great Britain forced the French to agree to a new conference of experts to reassess the reparations problem. By the time the conference did its work in 1924, both France and Germany were willing to pursue a more conciliatory approach toward each other.

The Hopeful Years (1924–1929)

The formation of new governments in both Great Britain and France opened the door to conciliatory approaches to Germany and the reparations problem. At the same time, a new German government led by Gustav Stresemann (GOOS-tahf SHTRAY-zuh-mahn) (1878–1929) ended the policy of passive resistance and committed Germany to carry out most of the provisions of the Treaty of Versailles while seeking a new settlement of the reparations question. At the same time, the German government stabilized the currency and ended the extreme inflation by issuing a new temporary currency, the Rentenmark, equal to 3 trillion old marks.

In August 1924, an international commission produced a new plan for reparations. Named the Dawes Plan after the American banker who chaired the commission, it reduced reparations and stabilized Germany's payments on the basis of its ability to pay. The Dawes Plan also granted an initial $200 million loan for German recovery, which opened the door to heavy American investments in Europe that helped usher in a new era of European prosperity between 1924 and 1929.

THE SPIRIT OF LOCARNO With prosperity came new efforts at European diplomacy. The foreign ministers of Germany and France, Gustav Stresemann and Aristide Briand (ah-ruh-STEED bree-AHNH) (1862–1932), fostered a spirit of international cooperation by concluding the Treaty of Locarno (loh-KAHR-noh) in 1925. This guaranteed Germany's new western borders with France and Belgium. Although Germany's new eastern borders with Poland were conspicuously absent from the agreement, a clear indication that Germany did not accept those borders as permanent, many viewed the Locarno pact as the beginning of a new era of European peace. On the day after the pact was concluded, the headline in the *New York Times* ran "France and Germany Ban War Forever," and the *London Times* declared, "Peace at Last."[3]

Germany's entry into the League of Nations in March 1926 soon reinforced the new spirit of conciliation engendered at Locarno. Two years later, similar optimistic attitudes prevailed in the Kellogg-Briand pact, drafted by the American secretary of state Frank B. Kellogg and the French foreign minister Aristide Briand. Sixty-three nations eventually agreed to the pact, in which they pledged "to renounce war as an instrument of national policy." Nothing was said, however, about what would be done if anyone violated the treaty.

The spirit of Locarno was based on little real substance. Germany lacked the military power to alter its western borders even if it wanted to. And the issue of disarmament soon proved that even the spirit of Locarno could not induce nations to cut back on their weapons. The League of Nations Covenant had suggested the "reduction of national armaments to the lowest point consistent with national safety." Germany, of course, had been disarmed with the expectation that other states would do likewise. Numerous disarmament conferences, however, failed to achieve anything substantial as states proved unwilling to trust their security to anyone but their own military forces.

COEXISTENCE WITH SOVIET RUSSIA One other hopeful sign in the years between 1924 and 1929 was the new coexistence of the West with Soviet Russia. By the beginning of 1924,

Soviet hopes for Communist revolutions in Western states had largely dissipated. In turn, these states had realized by then that the Bolshevik regime could not be ousted. By 1924, Germany, Britain, France, and Italy, as well as several smaller European countries, had established full diplomatic relations with Soviet Russia. Nevertheless, Western powers remained highly suspicious of Soviet intentions.

The Great Depression

After World War I, most European states hoped to return to the liberal ideal of a market economy based on private enterprise and largely free of state intervention. But the war had vastly strengthened business cartels and labor unions, making some government regulation of these powerful organizations appear necessary. Then, too, the economic integration of Europe before 1914 that had been based on free trade was soon undermined by a wave of protectionism and trade barriers, and reparations and war debts further damaged the postwar international economy. Consequently, the prosperity that did occur between 1924 and 1929 was uncommonly fragile, and the dream of returning to a self-regulating market economy was mere illusion. Then, to dash the dream altogether, along came the Great Depression.

CAUSES Two factors played an important role in bringing on the Great Depression: a downturn in domestic economies and an international financial crisis caused by the collapse of the American stock market in 1929. Already in the mid-1920s, prices for agricultural goods were beginning to decline rapidly due to overproduction of basic commodities, such as wheat. During the war, farmers in Argentina, Australia, Canada, and the United States had expanded food production to meet the demands of the warring European nations. After the war, these farmers did not curtail production, expecting that Europe

would not recover from the devastation of its fields and the loss of farmers. By 1927, however, European production returned to prewar levels, causing a sharp decline in commodity prices. Prices fell by 30 percent between 1924 and 1929. Meanwhile, an increase in the use of oil and hydroelectricity led to a slump in the coal industry even before 1929.

Furthermore, much of Europe's prosperity between 1924 and 1929 had been built on American bank loans to Germany. Twenty-three billion new marks had been invested in German municipal bonds and German industries since 1924. Already in 1928 and 1929, American investors had begun to pull money out of Germany in order to invest in the booming New York stock market. The crash of the American stock market in October 1929 led panicky American investors to withdraw even more of their funds from Germany and other European markets. The withdrawal of funds seriously weakened the banks of Germany and other central European states. The Credit-Anstalt, Vienna's most prestigious bank, collapsed on May 31, 1931. By that time, trade was slowing down, industrialists were cutting back production, and unemployment was increasing as the ripple effects of international bank failures had a devastating impact on domestic economies.

UNEMPLOYMENT Economic depression was by no means a new phenomenon in European history. But the depth of the economic downturn after 1929 fully justifies the "Great Depression" label. During 1932, the worst year of the depression, one British worker in four was unemployed, and 6 million Germans—40 percent of the German labor force—were out of work. Between 1929 and 1932, industrial production plummeted almost 50 percent in the United States and nearly as much in Germany. The unemployed and homeless filled the streets of cities throughout the advanced industrial countries (see the box on p. 797).

The Great Depression: Bread Lines in Paris. The Great Depression devastated the European economy and had serious political repercussions. Because of its more balanced economy, France did not feel the effects of the depression as quickly as other European countries. By 1931, however, even France was experiencing lines of unemployed people at free-food centers.

Harlingue/Roger Viollet/Getty Images

THE GREAT DEPRESSION: UNEMPLOYED AND HOMELESS IN GERMANY

IN 1932, GERMANY HAD 6 MILLION unemployed workers, many of them wandering aimlessly through the country, begging for food and seeking shelter in city lodging houses for the homeless. The Great Depression was an important factor in the rise to power of Adolf Hitler and the Nazis. This selection presents a description of the unemployed homeless in 1932.

Heinrich Hauser, "With Germany's Unemployed"

An almost unbroken chain of homeless men extends the whole length of the great Hamburg-Berlin highway. . . . All the highways in Germany over which I have traveled this year presented the same aspect. . . .

Most of the hikers paid no attention to me. They walked separately or in small groups, with their eyes on the ground. And they had the queer, stumbling gait of barefooted people, for their shoes were slung over their shoulders. . . . There was something else that had never been seen before—whole families that had piled all their goods into baby carriages and wheelbarrows that they were pushing along as they plodded forward in dumb despair. . . .

I saw them—and this was the strongest impression that the year 1932 left with me—I saw them, gathered into groups of fifty or a hundred men, attacking fields of potatoes. I saw them digging up the potatoes and throwing them into sacks while the farmer who owned the field watched them in despair and the local policeman looked on gloomily from the distance. I saw them staggering toward the lights of the city as night fell, with their sacks on their backs. . . .

I saw that the individual can know what is happening only by personal experience. I know what it is to be a tramp. I know what cold and hunger are. . . . But there are two things that I have only recently experienced—begging and spending the night in a municipal lodging house.

I entered the huge Berlin municipal lodging house in a northern quarter of the city. . . .

Distribution of spoons, distribution of enameled-ware bowls with the words "Property of the City of Berlin" written on their sides. Then the meal itself. A big kettle is carried. Men with yellow smocks have brought it in and men with yellow smocks ladle out the food. These men, too, are homeless and they have been expressly picked by the establishment and given free food and lodging and a little pocket money in exchange for their work about the house. . . .

Now the men are standing in a long row, dressed in their plain nightshirts that reach to the ground . . . The men lean far over the kettle so that the warm steam from the food envelops them and they hold out their bowls as if begging. . . . A piece of bread is handed out with every bowl.

My next recollection is sitting at a table in another room on a crowded bench that is like a seat in a fourth-class railway carriage. Hundreds of hungry mouths make an enormous noise eating their food. The men sit bent over their food like animals who feel that someone is going to take it away from them. They hold their bowl with their left arm part way around it, so that nobody can take it away, and they also protect it with their other elbow and with their head and mouth, while they move the spoon as fast as they can between their mouth and the bowl.

 Why did Hauser compare the scene he describes from 1932 with conditions in the years 1917 and 1918? How did the growing misery of many ordinary Germans promote the rise of extremist political parties like the Nazis?

Source: *Living Age*, vol. 344, no. 4398 (March 1933), pp. 27–31, 34–38.

SOCIAL AND POLITICAL REPERCUSSIONS The economic crisis also had unexpected social repercussions. Women were often able to secure low-paying jobs as servants, house-cleaners, or laundresses while many men remained unemployed, either begging on the streets or staying at home to do household tasks. Many unemployed men, resenting this reversal of traditional gender roles, were open to the shrill cries of demagogues with simple solutions to the economic crisis. High unemployment rates among young males often led them to join gangs that gathered in parks or other public places, arousing fear among local residents.

Governments seemed powerless to deal with the crisis. The classical liberal remedy for depression, a deflationary policy of balanced budgets, which involved cutting costs by lowering wages and raising tariffs to exclude other countries' goods from home markets, only served to worsen the economic crisis and create even greater mass discontent. This in turn led to serious political repercussions. Increased government activity in the economy was one reaction, even in countries like the United States that had a strong *laissez-faire* tradition. Another effect was a renewed interest in Marxist doctrines, since Marx had predicted that capitalism would destroy itself through overproduction. Communism took on new popularity, especially among workers and intellectuals. Finally, the Great Depression increased the attractiveness of simplistic dictatorial solutions, especially from a new movement known as **fascism**. Everywhere in Europe, democracy seemed on the defensive in the 1930s.

The Democratic States in the West

 FOCUS QUESTIONS: How did France, Great Britain, and the United States respond to the various crises, including the Great Depression, that they faced in the interwar years? How did World War I affect Europe's colonies in Asia and Africa?

Woodrow Wilson proclaimed that World War I had been fought to make the world safe for democracy, and in 1919, there seemed to be some justification for that claim. Four major European states and a host of minor ones had functioning political democracies. In a number of nations, universal male suffrage had even been replaced by universal suffrage as male politicians rewarded women for their contributions to World War I by granting them the right to vote (except in Italy, France, and Spain, where women had to wait until the end of World War II). Women also began to enter political life as deputies to parliamentary bodies. In the new German republic, for example, almost 10 percent of the deputies elected to the Reichstag in 1919 were women, although the number dropped to 6 percent by 1926.

Great Britain

After World War I, Great Britain went through a period of painful readjustment and serious economic difficulties. During the war, Britain had lost many of the markets for its industrial products, especially to the United States and Japan. The postwar decline of such staple industries as coal, steel, and textiles led to a rise in unemployment, which reached the 2 million mark in 1921. The continuing wartime coalition government led by Liberal David Lloyd George proved unable to change this situation.

By 1923, British politics experienced a major transformation when the Labour Party surged ahead of the Liberals as the second most powerful party in Britain after the Conservatives. In fact, after the elections of November 1923, a Labour-Liberal agreement enabled Ramsay MacDonald (1866–1937) to become the first Labour prime minister of Britain. Dependent on Liberal support, MacDonald rejected any extreme social or economic experimentation. His government lasted only ten months, however, as the Conservative Party's charge that his administration was friendly toward communism proved to be a highly successful campaign tactic.

Under Stanley Baldwin (1867–1947) as prime minister, the Conservatives guided Britain during an era of recovery from 1925 to 1929. This recovery, however, was relatively superficial. British exports in the 1920s never compensated for the overseas investments lost during the war, and unemployment remained at a startling 10 percent level. Coal miners suffered especially as the antiquated and inefficient British coal mines were hard-hit by a world glut of coal. Attempts by mine owners to lower coal miners' wages led to a national strike (the General Strike of 1926) by miners and sympathetic trade unions. A compromise settled the strike, but many miners refused to accept the settlement and were eventually forced back to work at lower wages for longer hours.

In 1929, just as the Great Depression was beginning, a second Labour government came into power, but it failed to solve the nation's economic problems and fell in 1931. A National Government (a coalition of Liberals and Conservatives) claimed credit for bringing Britain out of the worst stages of the depression, primarily by using the traditional policies of balanced budgets and protective tariffs. By 1936, unemployment had dropped to 1.6 million after reaching a depression high of 3 million in 1932.

British politicians largely ignored the new ideas of a Cambridge economist, John Maynard Keynes (KAYNZ) (1883–1946), who published his *General Theory of Employment, Interest and Money* in 1936. He condemned the traditional view that in a free economy, depressions should be left to work themselves out. Instead, Keynes argued that unemployment stemmed not from overproduction but from a decline in demand and that demand could be increased by public works, financed, if necessary, by deficit spending to stimulate production.

France

After the defeat of Germany, France had become the strongest power on the European continent. Its greatest need was to rebuild the devastated areas of northern and eastern France. But no French government seemed capable of solving France's financial problems between 1921 and 1926. Like other European countries, though, France did experience a period of relative prosperity between 1926 and 1929.

France began to feel the full effects of the Great Depression in 1932, and that economic instability soon had political repercussions. During a nineteen-month period in 1932 and 1933, six different cabinets were formed as France faced political chaos. During the same time, French right-wing groups, espousing policies similar to those of the Fascists in Italy and the Nazis in Germany, marched through the streets in numerous demonstrations. Riots in February 1934, fomented by a number of right-wing leagues, frightened many into believing that the extremists intended to seize power. These fears began to drive the French leftist parties together despite their differences and led in 1936 to the formation of the Popular Front.

The first Popular Front government was formed in June 1936 and was a coalition of the two French leftist parties, the Socialists and the Radicals. These parties shared a belief in antimilitarism, anticlericalism, and the importance of education. But despite their name, the Radicals were a democratic party of small property owners, whereas the Socialists were nominally committed to Marxist socialism. The Socialist leader, Leon Blum (LAY-ohnn BLOOM) (1872–1950), served as prime minister. The Popular Front succeeded in initiating a program for workers that some have called the French New Deal. It established the right of collective bargaining, a forty-hour workweek, two-week paid vacations, and minimum wages. The Popular Front's policies failed to solve the problems of the depression, however. By 1938, the French were experiencing a serious decline of confidence in their political system that left them unprepared to deal with their aggressive Nazi enemy to the east.

The Scandinavian States

The Scandinavian states were particularly successful in coping with the Great Depression. Socialist parties had grown steadily in the late nineteenth and early twentieth centuries, and between the wars, they came to head the governments of Sweden, Denmark, Norway, and Finland. These Social Democratic governments encouraged the development of rural and industrial cooperative enterprises. Ninety percent of the Danish milk industry, for example, was organized on a cooperative basis by 1933. Privately owned and managed, Scandinavian cooperatives seemed to avoid the pitfalls of either Communist or purely capitalist economic systems.

Social Democratic governments also greatly expanded social services. Not only did Scandinavian governments increase old-age pensions and unemployment insurance, but they also provided such novel forms of assistance as subsidized housing, free prenatal care, maternity allowances, and annual paid vacations for workers. To achieve their social welfare states, the Scandinavian governments required high taxes and large bureaucracies, but these did not prevent both private and cooperative enterprises from prospering. Indeed, between 1900 and 1939, Sweden experienced a greater rise in real wages than any other European country.

The United States

After Germany, no Western nation was more affected by the Great Depression than the United States. By the end of 1932, industrial production was down almost 50 percent. By 1933, there were 15 million unemployed. Under these circumstances, the Democrat Franklin Delano Roosevelt (1882–1945) won the 1932 presidential election by a landslide.

Roosevelt and his advisers pursued a policy of active government intervention in the economy that came to be known as the New Deal. The first New Deal created a variety of agencies designed to bring relief, recovery, and reform. To support the nation's banks, the Federal Deposit Insurance Corporation was established; it insured the safety of bank deposits up to $5,000. The Federal Emergency Relief Administration provided funds to help states and local communities meet the needs of the destitute and the homeless. The Civilian Conservation Corps employed more than 2 million people on reforestation projects and federal road and conservation projects.

By 1935, it was becoming apparent that the initial efforts of Roosevelt's administration had produced only a slow recovery at best. As his policies came under increasing criticism by people who advocated more radical change, Roosevelt inaugurated new efforts that collectively became known as the Second New Deal. These included a stepped-up program of public works, such as the Works Progress Administration (WPA), established in 1935. This government organization employed between 2 and 3 million people who worked at building bridges, roads, post offices, and airports. The Roosevelt administration was also responsible for social legislation that launched the American welfare state. In 1935, the Social Security Act created a system of old-age pensions and unemployment insurance. The National Labor Relations Act of 1935 encouraged the rapid growth of

CHRONOLOGY	The Democratic States
Great Britain	
First Labour Party government	1924
Conservative Party government	1924–1929
General strike	1926
Second Labour Party government	1929–1931
Beginning of National Government coalition	1931
France	
Formation of the Popular Front	1936
United States	
Election of Franklin D. Roosevelt	1932
Beginning of the New Deal	1933
Second New Deal	1935

labor unions. The New Deal provided some social reform measures that perhaps averted the possibility of social revolution in the United States. It did not, however, solve the unemployment problems of the Great Depression. After partial recovery between 1933 and 1937, the economy experienced another downturn during the winter of 1937–1938. In May 1937, American unemployment still stood at 7 million; by the following year, it had increased to 11 million. Only World War II and the subsequent growth of armaments industries brought American workers back to full employment.

European States and the World: The Colonial Empires

World War I and the Great Depression also had an impact on Europe's colonial empires. Despite the war, the Allied nations had managed to hold on to their colonial empires. Great Britain and France had even added to their empires by dividing up many of Germany's colonial possessions and, as we have seen, taking control of large parts of the Middle East through a system of mandates. In the years after the war, however, a rising tide of unrest against European political domination began to emerge in Asia and Africa and led to movements for change.

THE MIDDLE EAST For the countries of the Middle East, the period between the two world wars was a time of transition. With the fall of the Ottoman and Persian empires, new modernizing regimes emerged in Turkey and Iran. A fiercely independent government was established in Saudi Arabia in 1932. Iraq, too, gained its independence from Britain in the same year. Elsewhere in the Middle East, however, European influence remained strong as the British and French maintained their mandates in Syria, Lebanon, Jordan, and Palestine.

Although Britain and France had made plans to divide up Ottoman territories in the Middle East, General Mustafa Kemal (MOOS-tah-fah kuh-MAHL) (1881–1938) led Turkish forces in creating a new republic of Turkey in 1923. Kemal wanted to modernize Turkey along Western lines. The trappings of a

Dinodia Photos/Alamy Stock Photo

Gandhi. Mahatma Gandhi, India's "Great Soul," became the spiritual leader of India's struggle for independence from British colonial rule. Unlike many other nationalist leaders, Gandhi rejected the materialistic culture of the West and urged his followers to return to the native traditions of the Indian village. To illustrate his point, as seen in this illustration, Gandhi dressed in the simple Indian *dhoti* rather than in the Western fashion favored by many of his colleagues. He is also using a manual spinning wheel to make cotton thread to protest imports of British textiles.

democratic system were put in place, although the new president did not tolerate opposition. In addition to introducing a state-run industrial system, Kemal also westernized Turkish culture. The Latin alphabet was now used in writing the Turkish language. Popular education was introduced, and old aristocratic titles were abolished. All Turkish citizens were forced to adopt family names, in the European style; Kemal himself adopted the name Atatürk (ah-tah-TIRK), meaning "Father Turk." Atatürk made Turkey a secular republic and broke the power of the Islamic religion. New laws gave women equal rights with men in all aspects of marriage and inheritance, and in 1934, women received the right to vote. Education and the professions were now open to citizens of both sexes. By and large, the Turkish republic was the product of Atatürk's determined efforts to use nationalism and Western ways to create a modern Turkish nation.

INDIA By the time of World War I, the Indian people had already begun to refer to Mohandas Gandhi (moh-HAHN-dus GAHN-dee) as India's "Great Soul," or Mahatma (mah-HAHT-muh). Gandhi (1869–1948) began a movement based on nonviolent resistance whose aim was to force the British to improve the lot of the poor and grant independence to India. Relations between the British and Indians deteriorated following the

1919 Amritsar Massacre, wherein British troops fired on crowds of protestors and pilgrims who had journeyed to Punjab for religious celebrations. The massacre took place in an enclosed space where British troops prevented the crowd from dispersing by blocking the exits. In response, Gandhi urged his followers to follow a peaceful policy of **civil disobedience** refusing to obey British regulations. Gandhi also began to manufacture his own clothes and dressed in a simple *dhoti* (DOH-tee) or loincloth made of coarse homespun cotton. He adopted the spinning wheel as a symbol of India's resistance to imports of British textiles.

Although the British resisted Gandhi's movement, in 1935 they granted India internal self-government to be implemented gradually. Legislative councils at the local level were enlarged and given responsibility for education, local affairs, and public health, and Indian participation in government slowly increased. Responsibility for law and order, land revenue, and famine relief remained under the control of the British, however. Complete independence would have to wait until after World War II.

AFRICA Black Africans who fought in World War I in the armies of the British and the French hoped for independence after the war. As one newspaper in the Gold Coast put it, if African volunteers who fought on European battlefields were "good enough to fight and die in the Empire's cause, they were good enough to have a share in the government of their countries." Many shared this feeling. The peace settlement after World War I turned out be a great disappointment. It stripped Germany of its African colonies and awarded them to the British and the French to administer as mandates for the League of Nations.

After World War I, Africans became more active politically. Africans who had fought in the war had learned new ideas in the West about freedom and nationalism. Even in Africa itself, missionary schools had often taught their African pupils about liberty and equality. As more Africans became aware of the enormous gulf between Western ideals and practices, they decided to seek reform. As yet independence remained only a dream.

Protest took different forms. In Nigeria and South Africa, workers organized trade unions that tried to gain benefits for workers. But there were also incidents of violent protest. In British Nigeria, a growing middle class supported increasing protest movements. In 1929, a group of women protested the high taxes that were levied on the goods they were selling in the markets. During the riot that ensued, women called for all white men to leave their country. The British crushed the riot, killing fifty women in the process. Although colonial powers responded to these protest movements with force, they also began to make some reforms in the hope of satisfying the indigenous peoples. The reforms, however, were too few and too late, and by the 1930s, an increasing number of African leaders were calling for independence, not reform.

The clearest calls came from a new generation of young African leaders who had been educated in Europe and the United States. Those who went to the United States were especially influenced by the pan-African ideas of W. E. B. Du Bois (doo BOISS) (1868–1963) and Marcus Garvey (1887–1940). Du Bois, an African American educated at Harvard, was the leader of a movement that tried to make all Africans aware of their own cultural heritage. Garvey, a Jamaican who lived in Harlem in New York, also stressed the need for the unity of all Africans. Leaders and movements also appeared in individual African nations. In his book *Facing Mount Kenya*, Jomo Kenyatta (JOH-moh ken-YAHT-uh) (1894–1978) of Kenya, who had been educated in Great Britain, argued that British rule was destroying the traditional culture of the peoples of black Africa.

The Authoritarian and Totalitarian States

 FOCUS QUESTIONS: Why did many European states experience a retreat from democracy in the interwar years? What are the characteristics of so-called totalitarian states, and to what degree were these characteristics present in Fascist Italy, Nazi Germany, and Stalinist Russia?

The apparent triumph of liberal democracy in 1919 proved extremely short-lived. By 1939, only two major states (Great Britain and France) and several minor ones (the Low Countries, the Scandinavian states, Switzerland, and Czechoslovakia) remained democratic. What had happened to Woodrow Wilson's claim that World War I had been fought to make the world safe for democracy? Actually, World War I turned out to have had the opposite effect.

HISTORIANS DEBATE **The Retreat from Democracy: Did Europe Have Totalitarian States?**

The postwar expansion of the electorate made mass politics a reality and seemed to enhance the spread of democracy in Europe. But the war itself had created conditions that led the new mass electorate to distrust democracy and move toward a more radicalized politics.

Many postwar societies were badly divided, especially along class lines. During the war, to maintain war production, governments had been forced to make concessions to trade unions and socialist parties, so the working class had been strengthened. At the same time, the position of many middle-class people had declined, as consumer industries had been curtailed during the war and war bonds, which had been purchased by the middle classes as their patriotic contribution to the war effort, sank in value and even became worthless in some countries.

Gender divisions also weakened social cohesion. After the war, as soldiers returned home, women were forced out of jobs they had taken during the war, jobs that many newly independent women wanted to retain. The loss of so many men during the war had also left many younger women with no marital prospects and widows with no choice but to find jobs in the labor force. At the same time, fears about a declining population because of the war led many male political leaders to encourage women to return to their traditional roles as wives and mothers. Many European countries outlawed abortions and curtailed the sale of birth control devices while providing increased welfare benefits to entice women to remain at home and bear children.

The Great Depression served to deepen social conflict. Larger and larger numbers of people felt victimized, first by the war, and now by socioeconomic conditions that seemed beyond their control. Postwar politics became more and more polarized as people reverted to the wartime practice of dividing into friends and enemies, downplaying compromise and emphasizing conflict. Moderate centrist parties that supported democracy soon found themselves with fewer and fewer allies as people became increasingly radicalized politically, supporting the extremes of left-wing communism or right-wing fascism. In the 1920s, Italy had become the first Fascist state while the Soviet Union moved toward a repressive Communist state. In the 1930s, a host of other European states adopted authoritarian structures of various kinds. Is it justified to call any of them **totalitarian states**?

The word *totalitarian* was first used by Benito Mussolini (buh-NEE-toh moos-suh-LEE-nee) in Italy to describe his new Fascist state: "Fascism is totalitarian," he declared. A number of historians eventually applied the term to both Nazi Germany and the Soviet Union (Fascist Italy, Nazi Germany, and the Soviet Union are discussed later in the chapter). Especially during the Cold War between the United States and the Soviet Union in the 1950s and 1960s, Western leaders were inclined to refer to both the Soviet Union and the Eastern European states that had been brought under Soviet control as "totalitarian."

What did the historians who used the term think were the characteristics of a totalitarian state? Totalitarian regimes, it was argued, extended the functions and power of the central state far beyond what they had been in the past. The totalitarian state expected the active loyalty and commitment of its citizens to the regime's goals and used modern mass **propaganda** techniques and high-speed modern communications to conquer the minds and hearts of its subjects. The total state aimed to control not only the economic, political, and social aspects of life but the intellectual and cultural aspects as well. The purpose of that control was the active involvement of the masses in the achievement of the regime's goal, whether it be war, a socialist state, or a thousand-year Reich (RYKH). Moreover, the totalitarian state was led by a single leader and a single party and ruthlessly rejected the liberal ideal of limited government power and constitutional guarantees of individual freedoms. Indeed, individual freedom was subordinated to the collective will of the masses, organized and determined for them by a leader. Furthermore, modern technology gave these states unprecedented ability to use police controls to enforce their wishes on their subjects.

By the 1970s and 1980s, however, revisionist historians were questioning the usefulness of the term *totalitarian* and regarded it as crude and imprecise. Certainly, some regimes, such as Fascist Italy, Nazi Germany, and the Soviet Union, sought total control, but these states exhibited significant differences and none of them was successful in establishing total control of its society.

Nevertheless, these three states did transcend traditional political labels and led to some rethinking of these labels. Fascism in Italy and Nazism in Germany grew out of extreme rightist preoccupations with nationalism and, in the case of Germany, with racism. Communism in the Soviet Union emerged out of Marxist socialism, a radical leftist program. Thus, extreme right-wing and left-wing regimes no longer appeared to be at opposite ends of the political spectrum but came to be viewed as similar to each other in at least some respects.

Fascist Italy

In the early 1920s, in the wake of economic turmoil, political disorder, and the general insecurity and fear stemming from World War I, Benito Mussolini burst onto the Italian scene with the first fascist movement in Europe.

IMPACT OF WORLD WAR I As a new European state after 1861, Italy faced a number of serious problems that were only magnified when it became a belligerent in World War I. An estimated 700,000 Italian soldiers died, and the treasury reckoned the cost of the war at 148 billion lire, twice the sum of all government expenditures between 1861 and 1913. Italy did gain some territory, namely, Trieste, and a new northern border that included the formerly Austrian South Tyrol area. Italy's demands for Fiume and Dalmatia on the Adriatic coast were rejected, however, which gave rise to the myth that Italy had been cheated of its just rewards by the other victors. The war created immense domestic confusion. Inflation undermined middle-class security. Demobilization of the troops created high unemployment and huge groups of dissatisfied veterans. The government proved unable to deal effectively with these problems.

Territory Gained by Italy

THE BIRTH OF FASCISM Benito Mussolini (1883–1945) was an unruly and rebellious child who ultimately received a diploma as an elementary school teacher. After an unsuccessful stint as a teacher, Mussolini became a socialist and gradually became well known in Italian socialist circles. In 1912, he obtained the important position of editor of *Avanti* (Forward), the official socialist daily newspaper. After editorially switching his position from ardent neutrality, the socialist position, to intervention in World War I, he was expelled from the Socialist Party.

In 1919, Mussolini laid the foundations for a new political movement that came to be called fascism after the name of his group, the *Fascio di Combattimento* (FASH-ee-oh dee com-bat-ee-MEN-toh) (League of Combat). It received little attention in the elections of 1919, but political stalemate in Italy's parliamentary system and strong nationalist sentiment saved Mussolini and the Fascists.

The new parliament elected in November quickly proved incapable of governing Italy. Three major parties, the Socialists, Liberals, and Popolari (or Christian Democrats, a new Catholic party formed in January 1919), were unable to form an effective coalition. The Socialists, who had now become the largest party, spoke theoretically of the need for revolution, which alarmed conservatives, who quickly associated them with Bolsheviks or Communists. Thousands of industrial and agricultural strikes in 1919 and 1920 created a climate of class warfare and continual violence. Mussolini shifted quickly from leftist to rightist politics and began to gain support from middle-class industrialists fearful of working-class agitation and large landowners who objected to the agricultural strikes. Mussolini also perceived that Italians were angry over Italy's failure to receive more fruits of victory in the form of territorial acquisitions after World War I. He realized then that anticommunism, antistrike activity, and nationalist rhetoric combined with the use of brute force might help him obtain what he had been unable to achieve in free elections.

In 1920 and 1921, he formed bands of armed Fascists called *squadristi* (skwah-DREES-tee) and turned them loose in attacks on Socialist offices and newspapers. Strikes by trade unionists and Socialist workers and peasant leagues were broken up by force. At the same time, Mussolini entered into a political alliance with the Liberals under Giovanni Giolitti, then the prime minister. No doubt, Giolitti and the Liberals believed that the Fascists could be used to crush socialism temporarily and then be dropped. In this game of mutual deceit, Mussolini soon proved to be the more skillful player. By allying with the government coalition, he gained respectability and a free hand for his violent squadristi. Mussolini's efforts were rewarded when the Fascists won thirty-five parliamentary seats, or 7 percent of the total, in the election of May 1921.

The use of violence was crucial to Mussolini's plans. By 1921, the black-shirted Fascist squads numbered 200,000 and had become a regular feature of Italian life. World War I veterans and students were especially attracted to the squadristi and relished the opportunity to use unrestrained violence. Administering large doses of castor oil to unwilling victims became one of their favorite tactics.

Mussolini and the Fascists believed that these terrorist tactics would eventually achieve political victory. They deliberately created conditions of disorder knowing that fascism would flourish in such an environment. The Fascists construed themselves as the party of order and drew the bulk of their support from the middle and upper classes; white-collar workers, professionals and civil servants, landowners, merchants and artisans, and students made up almost 60 percent of the membership of the

Fascist Party. The middle-class fear of socialism, Communist revolution, and disorder made the Fascists attractive.

As the Italian political situation deteriorated further, Mussolini and the Fascists were emboldened to plan a march on Rome in order to seize power. In a speech in Naples to Fascist Blackshirts on October 24, 1922, Mussolini exclaimed, "Either we are allowed to govern, or we will seize power by marching on Rome" to "take by the throat the miserable political class that governs us."[4] Bold words, but in truth the planned march on Rome was a calculated bluff to frighten the government into giving them power. The bluff worked, and the government capitulated even before the march occurred. On October 29, 1922, King Victor Emmanuel III (1900–1946) made Mussolini prime minister of Italy. Twenty-four hours later, the Fascist Blackshirts were allowed to march into Rome in order to create the myth that they had gained power by an armed insurrection after a civil war.

MUSSOLINI AND THE ITALIAN FASCIST STATE Since the Fascists constituted but a small minority in parliament, the new prime minister was forced to move slowly. In the summer of 1923, Mussolini began to prepare for a national election that would consolidate the power of his Fascist government and give him a more secure base from which to govern. The national elections that were held on April 6, 1924, resulted in an enormous victory for the Fascists. They won 65 percent of the votes and garnered 374 seats out of a total of 535 in parliament. Although the elections were conducted in an atmosphere of Fascist fraud, force, and intimidation, the size of the victory indicated the growing popularity of Mussolini and his Fascists.

By 1926, Mussolini had established his Fascist dictatorship. Press laws gave the government the right to suspend any publications that fostered disrespect for the Catholic Church, the monarchy, or the state. The prime minister was made "head of government" with the power to legislate by decree. A police law empowered the police to arrest and confine anybody for nonpolitical or political crimes without due process of law. The government was given the power to dissolve political and cultural associations. In 1926, all anti-Fascist parties were outlawed. A secret police, known as the OVRA, was also established. By the end of 1926, Mussolini ruled Italy as *Il Duce* (eel DOO-chay), the leader.

Mussolini conceived of the Fascist state as totalitarian: "Fascism is totalitarian, and the Fascist State, the synthesis and unity of all values, interprets, develops and gives strength to the whole life of the people"[5] (see the box on p. 804). Mussolini did try to create a police state, but police activities in Italy were never as repressive, efficient, or savage as those of Nazi Germany. Likewise, the Italian Fascists' attempt to exercise control over all forms of mass media, including newspapers, radio, and cinema, so that they could use propaganda as an instrument to integrate the masses into the state, failed to achieve its major goals. Most commonly, Fascist propaganda was disseminated through simple slogans, such as "Mussolini is always right," plastered on walls all over Italy.

Mussolini and the Fascists also attempted to mold Italians into a single-minded community by pursuing a Fascist educational policy and developing Fascist organizations. Because the secondary schools maintained considerable freedom from Fascist control, the regime relied more and more on the activities

Mussolini, the Iron Duce. One of Mussolini's favorite images of himself was that of the Iron Duce—the strong leader who is always right. Consequently, he was often seen in military-style uniforms and military poses. This photograph shows Mussolini in one of his numerous uniforms with his Blackshirt bodyguards giving the Fascist salute.

THE VOICE OF ITALIAN FASCISM

IN 1932, AN ARTICLE ON FASCISM appeared in the *Italian Encyclopedia*. Attributed to Mussolini, it was largely written by the philosopher Giovanni Gentile (joh-VAHN-nee jen-TEE-lay). Mussolini had always argued that fascism was based only on the need for action, not on doctrines, but after its success, he felt the need to summarize the basic political and social ideas of fascism. These excerpts are taken from that article.

Benito Mussolini, "The Political and Social Doctrine of Fascism"

Above all, Fascism . . . believes neither in the possibility nor the utility of perpetual peace. It thus repudiates the doctrine of Pacifism—born of a renunciation of struggle and an act of cowardice in the face of sacrifice. War alone brings up to its highest tension all human energy and puts the stamp of nobility upon the peoples who have the courage to meet it. All other trials are substitutes, which never really put men into the position where they have to make the great decision—the alternative of life or death. Thus, a doctrine which is founded upon this harmful postulate of peace is hostile to Fascism. . . . Thus, the Fascist accepts life and loves it, knowing nothing of and despising suicide: he rather conceives of life as duty and struggle and conquest. . . . Fascism is the complete opposite of Marxian socialism, the materialist conception of history; according to which the history of human civilization can be explained simply through the conflict of interests among the various social groups and by the change and development in the means and instruments of production. That the changes in the economic field have their importance no one can deny; but that these factors are sufficient to explain the history of humanity excluding all others is an absurd delusion. Fascism, now and always, believes in holiness and in heroism; that is to say, in actions influenced by no economic motive, direct or indirect. . . .

After Socialism, Fascism combats the whole complex system of democratic ideology, and repudiates it, whether in its theoretical premises or in its practical application. Fascism denies that the majority, by the simple fact that it is a majority, can direct human society; it denies that numbers alone can govern by means of a periodical consultation, and it affirms the immutable, beneficial, and fruitful inequality of mankind, which can never be permanently leveled through the mere operation of a mechanical process such as universal suffrage.

The foundation of Fascism is the conception of the State, its character, its duty and its aim. Fascism conceives of the State as an absolute, in comparison with which all individuals or groups are relative, only to be conceived of in their relation to the State. . . . The Fascist state organizes the nation, but leaves a sufficient margin of liberty to the individual; the latter is deprived of all useless and possibly harmful freedom, but retains what is essential; the deciding power in the question cannot be the individual, but the State alone. . . .

For Fascism, the growth of empire . . . is an essential manifestation of vitality, and its opposite a sign of decadence. Peoples which are rising . . . are always imperialist; any renunciation is a sign of decay and of death. Fascism is the doctrine best adapted to represent the tendencies and the aspirations of a people, like the people of Italy, who are rising again after many centuries of foreign servitude. But Empire demands discipline . . . and a deeply felt sense of duty and sacrifice.

 In Mussolini's view, what were the basic principles of Italian Fascism? Why might such principles have appealed to a broad public in the aftermath of World War I?

Source: Reprinted by permission of the publisher from *International Conciliation*, no. 306 (Washington, D.C.: Carnegie Endowment for International Peace, 1935), pp. 5–17.

of youth organizations, known as the Young Fascists, to indoctrinate the young people of the nation in Fascist ideals. By 1939, about 6.8 million children, teenagers, and young adults of both sexes, or 66 percent of the population between eight and eighteen, were enrolled in some kind of Fascist youth group. Activities for these groups included unpopular Saturday afternoon marching drills and calisthenics, seaside and mountain summer camps, and competitions. An underlying motif for all of these activities was the Fascist insistence on militarization. Beginning in the 1930s, all male groups were given some kind of premilitary exercises to develop discipline and provide training for war. Results were mixed. Italian teenagers, who liked neither military training nor routine discipline of any kind, simply refused to attend Fascist youth meetings on a regular basis.

The Fascist organizations hoped to create a new Italian—hardworking, physically fit, disciplined, intellectually sharp,

and martially inclined. In practice, the Fascists largely reinforced traditional social attitudes in Italy, as is evident in their policies regarding women. The Fascists portrayed the family as the pillar of the state and women as the basic foundation of the family. "Woman into the home" became the Fascist slogan. Women were to be homemakers and baby producers, "their natural and fundamental mission in life," according to Mussolini, who viewed population growth as an indicator of national strength. To Mussolini, female emancipation was "un-Fascist." Employment outside the home was an impediment distracting women from conception. "It forms an independence and consequent physical and moral habits contrary to child bearing."[6] A practical consideration also underlay the Fascist attitude toward women: eliminating women from the job market reduced male unemployment figures in the depression economy of the 1930s.

CHRONOLOGY	Fascist Italy	
Creation of *Fascio di Combattimento*		1919
Squadristi violence		1920–1921
Fascists win thirty-five seats in Parliament		1921
Mussolini is made prime minister		1922
Electoral victory for Fascists		1924
Establishment of Fascist dictatorship		1925–1926
Lateran Accords with Catholic Church		1929

In the 1930s, the Fascists translated their attitude toward women into law with a series of enactments aimed at encouraging larger families. Families with many offspring were offered supplementary pay, loans, prizes, and subsidies, and mothers of many children received gold medals. A national "Mother and Child" holiday was celebrated on December 24, with prizes awarded for fertility. Also in the 1930s, decrees were passed that set quotas on the employment of women, but they failed to accomplish their goal.

Despite the instruments of repression, the use of propaganda, and the creation of numerous Fascist organizations, Mussolini failed to attain the degree of control achieved in Hitler's Germany or Stalin's Soviet Union. Mussolini and the Fascist Party never really destroyed the old power structure. Some institutions, including the armed forces and the monarchy, were never absorbed into the Fascist state and managed to maintain their independence. Mussolini had boasted that he would help the workers and peasants, but instead he generally allied himself with the interests of the industrialists and large landowners at the expense of the lower classes.

Even more indicative of Mussolini's compromise with the traditional institutions of Italy was his attempt to gain the support of the Catholic Church. In the Lateran Accords of February 1929, Mussolini's regime recognized the sovereign independence of a small enclave of 109 acres within Rome, known as Vatican City, which had remained in the church's possession since the unification of Italy in 1870; in return, the papacy recognized the Italian state. The Lateran Accords also guaranteed the church a large grant of money and recognized Catholicism as the "sole religion of the state." In return, the Catholic Church urged Italians to support the Fascist regime.

In all areas of Italian life under Mussolini and the Fascists, there was a noticeable dichotomy between Fascist ideals and practice. The Italian Fascists promised much but delivered considerably less, and they were soon overshadowed by a much more powerful fascist movement to the north.

Hitler and Nazi Germany

In 1923, a small rightist party, known as the Nazis, led by an obscure Austrian rabble-rouser named Adolf Hitler (1889–1945), tried to seize power in southern Germany in conscious imitation of Mussolini's march on Rome in 1922. Although the attempt failed, Hitler and the Nazis achieved sudden national prominence. Within ten years, they had taken over complete power.

WEIMAR GERMANY After Germany's defeat in World War I, a German democratic state known as the Weimar (VY-mar) Republic had been established. Formed by a coalition of Social Democrats, the Catholic Center Party, and German Democrats, the fragmented republic had no outstanding political leader and proved to be unstable. In 1925, Paul von Hindenburg, the World War I military hero, was elected president. Hindenburg was a traditional military man, monarchist in sentiment, who at heart was not in favor of the republic. The young republic suffered politically from attempted uprisings and attacks from both the left and the right.

Another of the republic's problems was its inability to change Germany's basic governmental structure. The government never really controlled the army, which operated as a state within a state. Other institutions maintained their independence as well. Hostile judges, teachers, and bureaucrats remained in office and used their positions to undermine democracy from within. At the same time, important groups of landed aristocrats and leaders of powerful business cartels refused to accept the overthrow of the imperial regime and remained hostile to the republic.

The Weimar Republic also faced serious economic difficulties. The runaway inflation of 1922 and 1923 had serious social repercussions. Widows, orphans, the retired elderly, army officers, teachers, civil servants, and others who lived on fixed incomes all watched their monthly stipends become worthless and their lifetime savings disappear. Their economic losses increasingly pushed the middle class to the rightist parties that were hostile to the republic. To make matters worse, after a period of prosperity from 1924 to 1929, Germany faced the Great Depression. Unemployment increased to nearly 4.4 million by December 1930. The depression paved the way for social discontent, fear, and extremist parties. The political, economic, and social problems of the Weimar Republic provided an environment in which Hitler and the Nazis were able to rise to power.

THE EMERGENCE OF ADOLF HITLER Born in 1889, Adolf Hitler was the son of an Austrian customs official. He was a total failure in secondary school and eventually made his way to Vienna to become an artist. Though he was rejected by the Vienna Academy of Fine Arts, Hitler stayed on in Vienna to live the bohemian lifestyle of an artist. In his autobiography, *Mein Kampf* (myn KAHMPF) (My Struggle), Hitler characterized his years in Vienna from 1908 to 1913 as an important formative period in his life: "In this period there took shape within me a world picture and a philosophy which became the granite foundation of all my acts. In addition to what I then created, I have had to learn little, and I have had to alter nothing."[7]

In Vienna, then, Hitler established the basic ideas of an ideology from which he never deviated for the rest of his life. At the core of Hitler's ideas was racism, especially anti-Semitism (see the box on p. 806). His hatred of the Jews lasted to the very end of his life. Hitler also became an extreme German

ADOLF HITLER'S HATRED OF THE JEWS

A BELIEVER IN ARYAN RACIAL supremacy, Adolf Hitler viewed the Jews as the archenemies of the Aryans. He believed that the first task of a true Aryan state would be the elimination of the Jewish threat. This is why Hitler's political career both began and ended with a warning against the Jews. In this excerpt from his autobiography, *Mein Kampf*, Hitler describes how he came to be an anti-Semite when he lived in Vienna in his early twenties.

Adolf Hitler, *Mein Kampf*

My views with regard to anti-Semitism thus succumbed to the passage of time, and this was my greatest transformation of all. . . .

Once, as I was strolling through the Inner City [of Vienna], I suddenly encountered an apparition in a black caftan and black hair locks. Is this a Jew? was my first thought.

For, to be sure, they had not looked like that in Linz. I observed the man furtively and cautiously, but the longer I stared at this foreign face, scrutinizing feature for feature, the more my first question assumed a new form:

Is this a German?

As always in such cases, I now began to try to relieve my doubts by books. For a few pennies I bought the first anti-Semitic pamphlets of my life. . . .

Yet I could no longer very well doubt that the objects of my study were not Germans of a special religion, but a people in themselves; for since I had begun to concern myself with this question and to take cognizance of the Jews, Vienna appeared to me in a different light than before. Wherever I went, I began to see Jews, and the more I saw, the more sharply they became distinguished in my eyes from the rest of humanity. . . .

In a short time I was made more thoughtful than ever by my slowly rising insight into the type of activity carried on by the Jews in certain fields.

Was there any form of filth or profligacy, particularly in cultural life, without at least one Jew involved in it? . . .

Sometimes I stood there thunderstruck.

I didn't know what to be more amazed at: the agility of their tongues or their virtuosity at lying.

Gradually I began to hate them.

 What was Hitler's attitude toward the Jews? Why do you think such crazed views became acceptable (or at least tolerable) to large numbers of ordinary Germans in the aftermath of World War I?

Source: Adolf Hitler, *Mein Kampf*, trans. R. Manheim (Boston: Houghton Mifflin, 1971).

nationalist who learned from the mass politics of Vienna how political parties could effectively use propaganda and terror. Finally, in his Viennese years, Hitler also came to a firm belief in the need for struggle, which he saw as the "granite foundation of the world."

In 1913, Hitler moved to Munich, still without purpose and with no real future in sight. World War I saved him: "Overpowered by stormy enthusiasm, I fell down on my knees and thanked Heaven from an overflowing heart for granting me the good fortune of being permitted to live at this time."[8] As a dispatch runner on the Western Front, Hitler distinguished himself by his brave acts. At the end of the war, finding again that his life had no purpose or meaning, he returned to Munich and decided to enter politics and found, at last, his true profession.

THE RISE OF THE NAZIS Hitler joined the obscure German Workers' Party, one of a number of right-wing extreme nationalist parties in Munich. By the summer of 1921, Hitler had assumed total control of the party, which he renamed the National Socialist German Workers' Party, or Nazi for short (from the first two syllables of its German name). His idea was that the party's name would distinguish the Nazis from the socialist parties while gaining support from both working-class and nationalist circles. Hitler worked assiduously to develop the party into a mass political movement with flags, badges, uniforms, its own newspaper, and its own police force or

militia known as the SA, the *Sturmabteilung* (SHTOORM-ap-ty-loonk), or Storm Troops. The SA was used to defend the party in meeting halls and to break up the meetings of other parties. Hitler's oratorical skills were largely responsible for attracting an increasing number of followers. By 1923, the party had grown from its early hundreds into a membership of 55,000, plus another 15,000 in the SA.

When it appeared that the Weimar Republic was on the verge of collapse in the fall of 1923, the Nazis and other right-wing leaders in the south German state of Bavaria decided to march on Berlin to overthrow the Weimar government. When his fellow conspirators reneged, Hitler and the Nazis decided to act on their own by staging an armed uprising in Munich on November 8. The so-called Beer Hall Putsch was quickly crushed. Hitler was arrested, put on trial for treason, and sentenced to prison for five years, a lenient sentence indeed from sympathetic right-wing judges.

During his brief stay in prison, Hitler wrote *Mein Kampf*, an autobiographical account of his movement and its underlying ideology. Extreme German nationalism, virulent anti-Semitism, and vicious anticommunism are linked together by a social Darwinian theory of struggle that stresses the right of superior nations to **Lebensraum** (LAY-benz-rowm) (living space) through expansion and the right of superior individuals to secure authoritarian leadership over the masses. What is perhaps most remarkable about *Mein Kampf* is its elaboration of a

Hitler and the Blood Flag Ritual. In developing his mass political movement, Adolf Hitler used ritualistic ceremonies as a means of binding party members to his own person. Here Hitler is shown touching the "blood flag," which had supposedly been stained with the blood of Nazis killed during the Beer Hall Putsch, to an SS banner while the SS standard-bearer makes a "blood oath" of allegiance: "I vow to remain true to my Führer, Adolf Hitler. I bind myself to carry out all orders conscientiously and without reluctance." The SS originated as Hitler's personal bodyguard and later became a secret police force and instrument of terror in the Nazi state.

series of ideas that directed Hitler's actions once he took power. That others refused to take Hitler and his ideas seriously was one of his greatest advantages.

HITLER'S NEW TACTICS The Beer Hall Putsch proved to be a major turning point in Hitler's career. Rather than discouraging him, his trial and imprisonment reinforced his faith in himself and in his mission. He now clearly understood the need for a change in tactics. If the Nazis could not overthrow the Weimar Republic by force, they would have to use constitutional means to gain power. This implied the formation of a mass political movement that would actively compete for votes with the other political parties.

After his release from prison, Hitler set about organizing the Nazi Party for the lawful takeover of power. His position on leadership in the party was quite clear. There was to be no discussion of ideas in the party, and the party was to follow the *Führerprinzip* (FYOOR-ur-prin-TSEEP), the leadership principle, which entailed nothing less than a single-minded party under one leader. As Hitler expressed it, "A good National Socialist is one who would let himself be killed for his Führer at any time."[9]

In the late 1920s, Hitler reorganized the Nazi Party on a regional basis and expanded it to all parts of Germany. By 1929, the Nazis had a national party organization. The party also grew from 27,000 members in 1925 to 178,000 by the end of 1929. Especially noticeable was the youthfulness of the regional, district, and branch leaders of the Nazi organization. Many were under thirty and were fiercely committed to Hitler because he gave them the kind of active politics they sought. Rather than democratic debate, they wanted brawls in beer halls, enthusiastic speeches, and comradeship in the building of a new Germany. One new young Nazi member expressed his excitement about the party:

> For me this was the start of a completely new life. There was only one thing in the world for me and that was service in the movement. All my thoughts were centered on the movement. I could talk only politics. I was no longer aware of anything else. At the time I was a promising athlete; I was very keen on sport, and it was going to be my career. But I had to give this up too. My only interest was agitation and propaganda.[10]

Such youthful enthusiasm gave Nazism the aura of a "young man's movement" and a sense of dynamism that the other parties could not match.

By 1929, the Nazi Party had also made a significant shift in strategy. Between 1925 and 1927, Hitler and the Nazis had pursued an urban strategy geared toward winning workers from the socialists and Communists. But failure in the 1928 elections, when the Nazis gained only 2.6 percent of the vote and twelve seats in the Reichstag, convinced Hitler of the need for a change. By 1929, the party began to pursue middle-class and lower-middle-class votes in small towns and rural areas, especially in northern, central, and eastern Germany.

Germany's economic difficulties paved the way for the Nazis' rise to power. Unemployment rose dramatically, from 4.35 million in 1931 to 6 million by the winter of 1932. The economic and psychological impact of the Great Depression made the radical solutions offered by extremist parties appear more attractive. Already in the Reichstag elections of September 1930, the Nazis polled 18 percent of the vote and gained 107 seats, making the Nazi Party one of the largest in Germany.

By 1930, Chancellor Heinrich Brüning (HYN-rikh BROO-ning) (1885–1970) had been unable to form a working parliamentary majority in the Reichstag and relied on the use of emergency decrees by President Hindenburg to rule. In a real sense, then, parliamentary democracy was already dying in 1930, three years before Hitler destroyed it.

THE NAZI SEIZURE OF POWER Hitler's quest for power from late 1930 to early 1933 depended on political maneuvering around President Hindenburg. Nevertheless, the elections from 1930 through 1932 were indirectly responsible for the Nazis' rise to power since they showed the importance of the Nazi Party. The party itself grew dramatically during this period, from 289,000 members in September 1930 to 800,000 by 1932. The SA also rose to 500,000 members.

The Nazis proved very effective in developing modern electioneering techniques. In their election campaigns, party members pitched their themes to the needs and fears of different social groups. But even as they were making blatant appeals to class interests, the Nazis were denouncing conflicts of interest and maintaining that they stood above classes and parties. Hitler, in particular, claimed to stand above all differences and promised to create a new Germany free of class differences and party infighting. His appeal to national pride, national honor, and traditional militarism struck chords of emotion in his listeners.

Elections, however, proved to have their limits. In the elections of July 1932, the Nazis won 230 seats, making them the largest party in the Reichstag. But four months later, in November, they declined to 196 seats. It became apparent to many Nazis that they would not gain power simply by the ballot box. Hitler saw clearly, however, that after 1930 the Reichstag was not all that important, since the government ruled by decree with the support of President Hindenburg. Increasingly, the right-wing elites of Germany—the industrial magnates, landed aristocrats, military establishment, and higher bureaucrats—came to see Hitler as the man who had the mass support to establish a right-wing, authoritarian regime that would save Germany and their privileged positions from a Communist takeover. These people almost certainly thought that they could control Hitler and, like many others, may well have underestimated his abilities. Under pressure from these elites, President Hindenburg agreed to allow Hitler to become chancellor (on January 30, 1933) and form a new government.

Within two months, Hitler had laid the foundations for the Nazis' complete control over Germany. One of Hitler's important cohorts, Hermann Göring (GUR-ing) (1893–1946), had been made minister of the interior and hence head of the police of the Prussian state, the largest of the federal states in Germany. He used his power to purge the police of non-Nazis and to establish an auxiliary police force composed of SA members. This action legitimized Nazi terror. On the day after a fire broke out in the Reichstag building (February 27), supposedly set by the Communists, Hitler was also able to convince President Hindenburg to issue a decree that gave the government emergency powers. It suspended all basic rights of citizens for the full duration of the emergency, thus enabling the Nazis to arrest and imprison anyone without redress.

The crowning step of Hitler's "legal seizure" of power came after the Nazis had gained 288 Reichstag seats in the elections of March 5, 1933. Since they still did not possess an absolute majority, on March 23 the Nazis sought the passage of an Enabling Act, which would empower the government to dispense with constitutional forms for four years while it issued laws to deal with the country's problems. Since the act was to be an amendment to the Weimar constitution, the Nazis needed and obtained a two-thirds vote to pass it. Only the Social Democrats had the courage to oppose Hitler. The Enabling Act provided the legal basis for Hitler's subsequent acts. He no longer needed either the Reichstag or President Hindenburg. In effect, Hitler became a dictator appointed by the parliamentary body itself.

With their new source of power, the Nazis acted quickly to enforce Gleichschaltung (glykh-SHAHL-toonk), the coordination of all institutions under Nazi control. They purged the civil service of Jews and democratic elements, established concentration camps for opponents of the new regime, eliminated the autonomy of the federal states, dissolved the trade unions and replaced them with the gigantic Labor Front, and abolished all political parties except the Nazis. By the end of the summer of 1933, within seven months of being appointed chancellor, Hitler and the Nazis had established a powerful control over Germany.

Why had this seizure of power been so quick and easy? The Nazis were not only ruthless in their use of force but ready to take control. The depression and the Weimar Republic's failure to resolve it had weakened what little faith the Germans had in their democratic state. But negative factors alone cannot explain the Nazi success. To many Germans, the Nazis offered a national awakening. "Germany awake," one of the many Nazi slogans, had a powerful appeal to a people psychologically crushed by their defeat in World War I. The Nazis presented a strong image of a dynamic new Germany that was above parties and above classes.

By the end of 1933, there were only two sources of potential danger to Hitler's authority: the armed forces and the SA within his own party. The SA, under the leadership of Ernst Röhm (RURM), openly criticized Hitler and spoke of the need for a "second revolution" and the replacement of the regular army by the SA. Neither the army nor Hitler favored such a possibility. Hitler solved both problems simultaneously on June 30, 1934, by having Röhm and a number of other SA leaders killed in return for the army's support in allowing Hitler to succeed Hindenburg when the president died. When Hindenburg died on August 2, 1934, the office of president was abolished, and Hitler became sole ruler of Germany. Public officials and soldiers were all required to take a personal oath of loyalty to Hitler as the "Führer of the German Reich and people." The Third Reich had begun.

THE NAZI STATE (1933–1939) Having smashed the parliamentary state, Hitler now felt that the real task was at hand: to develop the "total state." Hitler's aims had not been simply power for power's sake or a tyranny based on personal ambition. He had larger ideological goals. The development of an Aryan racial state that would dominate Europe and possibly the world for generations to come required a massive

PROPAGANDA AND MASS MEETINGS IN NAZI GERMANY

PROPAGANDA AND MASS RALLIES were two of the chief instruments that Hitler used to prepare the German people for the tasks he set before them. In the first selection, taken from a speech to a crowd at Nuremberg, Hitler describes the kind of mystical bond he hoped to create through his mass rallies. In the second excerpt, a Hamburg schoolteacher gives her impression of a Hitler rally.

Adolf Hitler, Speech at the Nuremberg Party Rally, 1936

Do we not feel once again in this hour the miracle that brought us together? Once you heard the voice of a man, and it struck deep into your hearts; it awakened you, and you followed this voice. Year after year you went after it, though him who had spoken you never even saw. You heard only a voice, and you followed it. When we meet each other here, the wonder of our coming together fills us all. Not everyone of you sees me, and I do not see everyone of you. But I feel you, and you feel me. It is the belief in our people that has made us small men great, that has made us poor men rich, that has made brave and courageous men out of us wavering, spiritless, timid folk; this belief made us see our road when we were astray; it joined us together into one whole! . . . You come, that . . . you may, once in a while, gain the feeling that now we are together; we are with him and he with us, and we are now Germany!

A Teacher's Impression of a Hitler Rally, 1932

The April sun shone hot like in summer and turned everything into a picture of gay expectation. There was immaculate order and discipline, although the police left the whole square to the stewards and stood on the sidelines. Nobody spoke of "Hitler," always just "the Führer," "the Führer says," "the Führer wants," and what he said and wanted seemed right

and good. The hours passed, the sun shone, expectations rose. In the background, at the edge of the track there were columns of carriers like ammunition carriers. . . . Aeroplanes above us. Testing of the loudspeakers, buzzing of the cine-cameras. It was nearly 3 P.M. "The Führer is coming!" A ripple went through the crowds. Around the speaker's platform one could see hands raised in the Hitler salute. A speaker opened the meeting, abused the "system," nobody listened to him. A second speaker welcomed Hitler and made way for the man who had drawn 120,000 people of all classes and ages. There stood Hitler in a simple black coat and looked over the crowd, waiting—a forest of swastika pennants swished up, the jubilation of this moment was given vent in a roaring salute. Main theme: Out of parties shall grow a nation, the German nation. He censured the "system" ("I want to know what there is left to be ruined in this state!"). "On the way here Socialists confronted me with a poster, 'Turn back, Adolf Hitler.' Thirteen years ago I was a simple unknown soldier. I went my way. I never turned back. Nor shall I turn back now." Otherwise he made no personal attacks, nor any promises, vague or definite. His voice was hoarse after all his speaking during the previous days. When the speech was over, there was roaring enthusiasm and applause. Hitler saluted, gave his thanks, the Horst Wessel song sounded out across the course. Hitler was helped into his coat. Then he went.—How many look up to him with touching faith! as their helper, their savior, their deliverer from unbearable distress—to him who rescues the Prussian prince, the scholar, the clergyman, the farmer, the worker, the unemployed, who rescues them from the parties back into the nation.

 In Hitler's view, what would mass meetings accomplish for his movement? How do mass rallies further the development of nationalism?

Sources: Adolf Hitler, Speech at the Nuremberg Party Rally, 1936; A Teacher's Impression of a Hitler Rally, 1932, in L Solmitz, "Diary," trans. and quoted in J. Noakes and G. Pridham, *Documents on Nazism, 1919–45* (New York: Viking Press, 1974), p. 161.

---

movement in which the German people would be actively involved, not passively cowed by force. Hitler stated:

> We must develop organizations in which an individual's entire life can take place. Then every activity and every need of every individual will be regulated by the collectivity represented by the party. There is no longer any arbitrary will, there are no longer any free realms in which the individual belongs to himself. . . . The time of personal happiness is over.[11]

The Nazis pursued the creation of this unified state in a variety of ways. They employed mass demonstrations and spectacles to integrate the German nation into a collective fellowship and to mobilize it as an instrument for Hitler's policies. These mass demonstrations, especially the Nuremberg party rallies that were held every September and the Harvest Festivals

celebrated at the Bückeberg (BOOK-uh-bayrk) near Hamelin every fall, combined the symbolism of a religious service with the merriment of a popular amusement. They had great appeal and usually evoked mass enthusiasm and excitement (see the box above).

Some features of the state apparatus of Hitler's total state seem contradictory. One usually thinks of Nazi Germany as having an all-powerful government that maintained absolute control and order. In truth, Nazi Germany was the scene of almost constant personal and institutional conflict, which resulted in administrative chaos. Incessant struggle characterized relationships within the party, within the state, and between party and state. By fostering rivalry within the party and between party and state, Hitler became the ultimate decision maker.

The Nazi Mass Spectacle. Hitler and the Nazis made clever use of mass spectacles to rally the German people behind the Nazi regime. These mass demonstrations evoked intense enthusiasm, as is evident in this photograph of Hitler arriving at the Bückeberg near Hamelin for the Harvest Festival in 1937. Almost one million people were present for the celebration.

In the economic sphere, Hitler and the Nazis also established control, but industry was not nationalized, as the left wing of the Nazi Party wanted. Hitler felt that it was irrelevant who owned the means of production so long as the owners recognized their master. Although the regime pursued the use of public works projects and "pump-priming" grants to private construction firms to foster employment and end the depression, there is little doubt that rearmament did far more to solve the unemployment problem. Unemployment, which had stood at 6 million in 1932, dropped to 2.6 million in 1934 and less than 500,000 in 1937. The regime claimed full credit for solving Germany's economic woes, and the improved economy was an important factor in convincing many Germans to accept the new regime, despite its excesses.

The German Labor Front under Robert Ley regulated the world of labor. The Labor Front was a state-run union. To control all laborers, it used the workbook. Every salaried worker had to have one in order to hold a job. Only by submitting to the policies of the Nazi-controlled Labor Front could a worker obtain and retain a workbook. The Labor Front also sponsored activities to keep the workers happy (see "Mass Leisure" later in this chapter).

For those who needed coercion, the Nazi state had its instruments of terror and repression. Especially important was the SS, the *Schutzstaffeln* (SHOOTS-shtah-fuhn), or Protection Squads. Originally created as Hitler's personal bodyguard, the SS, under the direction of Heinrich Himmler (1900–1945), came to control all of the regular and secret police forces. Himmler and the SS functioned on the basis of two principles: terror and ideology. Terror included the instruments of repression and murder: the secret police, criminal police, concentration camps, and later the execution squads and death camps for the extermination of the Jews (see Chapter 27). For Himmler,

the SS was a crusading order whose primary goal was to further the Aryan master race. SS members, who constituted a carefully chosen elite, were thoroughly indoctrinated in racial ideology.

Other institutions, such as the Catholic and Protestant churches, primary and secondary schools, and universities, were also brought under the control of the Nazi state. Nazi professional organizations and leagues were formed for civil servants, teachers, women, farmers, doctors, and lawyers. Because the early indoctrination of the nation's youth would lay the foundation for a strong state, special attention was given to youth organizations: the *Hitler Jugend* (YOO-gunt) (Hitler Youth) and its female counterpart, the *Bund Deutscher Mädel* (BOONT DOIT-chuh MAY-dul) (German Girls Association). The oath required of Hitler Youth members demonstrates the dedication expected of youth in the Nazi state: "In the presence of this blood banner, which represents our Führer, I swear to devote all my energies and my strength to the savior of our country, Adolf Hitler. I am willing and ready to give up my life for him, so help me God."

Women played a crucial role in the Aryan racial state as bearers of the children who would bring about the triumph of the Aryan race. To the Nazis, the differences between men and women were quite natural. Men were warriors and political leaders; women were destined to be wives and mothers. Motherhood was exalted in an annual ceremony on August 12, Hitler's mother's birthday, when Hitler awarded the German Mother's Cross to a select group of German mothers. Those with four children received a bronze cross, those with six a silver cross, and those with eight or more a gold cross.

Nazi ideas determined employment opportunities for women. The Nazis hoped to drive women out of heavy industry or other jobs that might hinder them from bearing healthy

Hitler as Munich politician	1919–1923
Beer Hall Putsch	1923
Nazis win 107 seats in Reichstag	1930 (September)
Hitler is made chancellor	1933 (January 30)
Reichstag fire	1933 (February 27)
Enabling Act	1933 (March 23)
Purge of the SA	1934 (June 30)
Hindenburg dies; Hitler as sole ruler	1934 (August 2)
Nuremberg laws	1935
Kristallnacht	1938 (November 9–10)

children, as well as certain professions, including university teaching, medicine, and law, which were considered inappropriate for women, especially married women. The Nazis encouraged women to pursue professional occupations that had direct practical application, such as social work and nursing. In addition to restrictive legislation against females, the Nazi regime pursued its campaign against working women with such poster slogans as "Get hold of pots and pans and broom and you'll sooner find a groom!" Nazi policy toward female workers remained inconsistent, however. Especially after the rearmament boom and increased conscription of males for military service resulted in a labor shortage, the government encouraged women to work, even in areas previously dominated by males.

The Nazi total state was intended to be an Aryan racial state. From its beginning, the Nazi Party reflected Hitler's strong anti-Semitic beliefs. Once in power, the Nazis translated anti-Semitic ideas into anti-Semitic policies. Already on April 1, 1933, the new Nazi government initiated a two-day boycott of Jewish businesses. A series of laws soon followed that excluded "non-Aryans" (defined as anyone "descended from non-Aryans, especially Jewish parents or grandparents") from the legal profession, civil service, judgeships, the medical profession, teaching positions, cultural and entertainment enterprises, and the press.

In September 1935, the Nazis announced new racial laws at the annual party rally in Nuremberg. These "Nuremberg laws" excluded German Jews from German citizenship and forbade marriages and extramarital relations between Jews and German citizens. The Nuremberg laws essentially separated Jews from the Germans politically, socially, and legally and were the natural extension of Hitler's stress on the preservation of a pure Aryan race.

Another considerably more violent phase of anti-Jewish activity took place in 1938 and 1939; it was initiated on November 9–10, 1938, the infamous *Kristallnacht* (kri-STAHL-nahkht), or Night of Shattered Glass. The assassination of a third secretary in the German embassy in Paris by a young Polish Jew became the excuse for a Nazi-led destructive rampage against the Jews in which synagogues were burned, seven thousand Jewish businesses were destroyed, and at least one hundred Jews were killed. Moreover, 30,000 Jewish males were rounded up and sent to concentration camps. *Kristallnacht* also led to further drastic steps. Jews were barred from all public buildings and prohibited from owning, managing, or working in any retail store. Finally, under the direction of the SS, Jews were encouraged to "emigrate from Germany." After the outbreak of World War II, the policy of emigration was replaced by a more gruesome one.

Anti-Semitism in Nazi Germany. Soon after seizing power, Hitler and the Nazis began to translate their anti-Semitic ideas into anti-Semitic policies. This photograph shows one example of Nazi action against the Jews as Germans are seen passing by the broken windows of a Jewish shop in Berlin the morning after *Kristallnacht*, the Night of Shattered Glass, when thousands of Jewish businesses were destroyed.

The Soviet Union

The civil war in Russia had come to an end by the beginning of 1921. It had taken an enormous toll of life, but the Red Terror and the victories of the Red Army had guaranteed the survival of the Communist regime. During the civil war, Lenin had pursued a policy of "war communism." Under this policy of expedience, the government had nationalized transportation and communication facilities as well as banks, mines, factories, and businesses that employed more than ten workers. The government had also assumed the right to requisition food from the peasants, who often resisted fiercely, slaughtering their own animals and destroying their crops, though without much success. Hunger led to an untold number of deaths in the countryside. Added to this problem was drought, which caused a great famine between 1920 and 1922 that claimed as many as 5 million lives. Industrial collapse paralleled the agricultural disaster. By 1921, industrial output was at only 20 percent of its 1913 levels. Russia was exhausted. As Leon Trotsky observed, "The collapse of the productive forces surpassed anything of the kind that history had ever seen. The country, and the government with it, were at the very edge of the abyss."[12]

THE NEW ECONOMIC POLICY In March 1921, Lenin pulled Russia back from the abyss by establishing his **New Economic Policy** (NEP). The NEP was a modified version of the old capitalist system. Peasants were now allowed to sell their produce openly, and retail stores as well as small industries that employed fewer than twenty employees could operate under private ownership; heavy industry, banking, and mines remained in the hands of the government. In 1922, Lenin and the Communists formally created a new state called the Union of Soviet Socialist Republics, known by its initials as the USSR and commonly called the Soviet Union. Already in that year, a revived market and good harvest had brought the famine to an end; Soviet agriculture climbed to 75 percent of its prewar level. Industry, especially state-owned heavy industry, fared less well and continued to stagnate. Only coal production had reached prewar levels by 1926. Overall, the NEP had saved the Soviet Union from complete economic disaster even though Lenin and other leading Communists intended it to be only a temporary, tactical retreat from the goals of communism.

In the meantime, Lenin and the Communists were strengthening their one-party state. The number of bureaucrats increased dramatically and soon constituted a new elite with the best jobs, food, and dwellings. Even Lenin issued warnings about the widening power of the bureaucracy that he had helped create.

THE STRUGGLE FOR POWER Between 1922 and 1924, Lenin suffered a series of strokes that finally led to his death on January 21, 1924. Although Communist control theoretically rested on a principle of collective leadership, Lenin had in fact provided one-man rule. His death inaugurated a struggle for power among the members of the Politburo (POL-it-byoor-oh), the institution that had become the leading organ of the party.

In 1924, the Politburo of seven members was severely divided over the future direction of the nation. The Left, led by Leon Trotsky, wanted to end the NEP and launch the Soviet Union on the path of rapid industrialization, primarily at the expense of the peasantry. This same group wanted to continue the revolution, believing that the survival of the Russian Revolution ultimately depended on the spread of communism abroad. Another group in the Politburo, called the Right, rejected the cause of world revolution and wanted instead to concentrate on constructing a socialist state. Believing that too rapid industrialization would worsen the living standards of the Soviet peasantry, this group also favored a continuation of Lenin's NEP.

These ideological divisions were underscored by an intense personal rivalry between Leon Trotsky and Joseph Stalin. Trotsky had been a key figure in the success of the Bolshevik Revolution and the Red Army. In 1924, he held the post of commissar of war and was the leading spokesman for the Left in the Politburo. Joseph Stalin (1879–1953) had joined the Bolsheviks in 1903 and had come to Lenin's attention after staging a daring bank robbery to obtain funds for the Bolshevik cause. Stalin, who was neither a dynamic speaker nor a forceful writer, was content to hold the dull bureaucratic job of party general secretary while other Politburo members held party positions that enabled them to display their brilliant oratorical abilities. He was a good organizer (his fellow Bolsheviks called him "Comrade Card-Index"), and the other members of the Politburo soon found that the position of party secretary was really the most important in the party hierarchy. The general secretary appointed the regional, district, city, and town party secretaries. In 1922, for example, Stalin had made some 10,000 appointments, many of them trusted followers whose holding of key positions proved valuable in the struggle for power. Although Stalin at first refused to support either the Left or the Right in the Politburo, he finally came to favor the goal of "socialism in one country" rather than world revolution.

Stalin used his post as party general secretary to gain complete control of the Communist Party. Trotsky was expelled from the party in 1927. Eventually, he made his way to Mexico, where he was murdered in 1940, no doubt on Stalin's orders. By 1929, Stalin had succeeded in eliminating the Old Bolsheviks of the revolutionary era from the Politburo and establishing a powerful dictatorship.

THE STALINIST ERA (1929–1939) The Stalinist era marked the beginning of an economic, social, and political revolution that was more sweeping in its results than the revolutions of 1917. Stalin made a significant shift in economic policy in 1928 when he launched his first five-year plan. Its real goal was nothing less than the transformation of the Soviet Union from an agricultural country into an industrial state virtually overnight. Instead of consumer goods, the first five-year plan emphasized maximum production of capital goods and armaments and succeeded in quadrupling the production of heavy machinery and doubling oil production. Between 1928 and 1937, during the first two five-year plans, steel production increased from 4 to 18 million tons per year, and hard coal output went from 36 to 128 million tons.

The social and political costs of industrialization were enormous. Little provision was made for absorbing the expanded labor force into the cities. Though the industrial labor force

Stalin and the First Five-Year Plan. After establishing his dictatorship, Stalin sought to achieve the rapid industrialization of the Soviet Union as well as the collectivization of agriculture by his first five-year plan. This poster, published in 1932 with a photograph of Stalin, celebrates the achievements of that plan. It reads, "At the end of the Plan, the basis of collectivization must be completed."

increased by millions between 1932 and 1940, total investment in housing actually declined after 1929; as a result, millions of workers and their families lived in pitiful conditions. Real wages in industry also declined by 43 percent between 1928 and 1940, and strict laws limited workers' freedom of movement. To inspire and pacify the workers, government propaganda stressed the need for sacrifice to create the new socialist state. Soviet labor policy stressed high levels of achievement, typified by the Stakhanov cult. Alexei Stakhanov (uh-LEK-say stuh-KHAH-nuf) was a coal miner who mined 102 tons of coal in one shift, exceeding the norm by 1,300 percent. He was held up as an example to others, even though his feat had been contrived for publicity purposes.

Rapid industrialization was accompanied by an equally rapid collectivization of agriculture. Stalin believed that the capital needed for industrial growth could be gained by creating agricultural surpluses through eliminating private farms and pushing people onto collective farms (see the box on p. 814). The first step was to eliminate the kulaks (KOO-laks), or wealthy farmers, who were sent to the Siberian camps beginning in 1930. By eliminating private property, a Communist ideal would also be achieved.

By 1930, some 10 million peasant households had been collectivized; by 1934, the Soviet Union's 26 million family farms had been collectivized into 250,000 units. This was done at tremendous cost since Stalin did not hesitate to starve the peasants to force them to comply with the policy of collectivization, especially in Ukraine, where 2.9 million died. Stalin himself supposedly told Winston Churchill during World War II that 10 million peasants died during the artificially created famines of 1932 and 1933. The only concession Stalin made to the peasants was to allow each household to have one tiny, privately owned garden plot.

Stalin's program of rapid industrialization entailed additional costs as well. To achieve his goals, Stalin strengthened the party bureaucracy under his control. Those who resisted were sent to forced labor camps in Siberia. Stalin's desire for sole control of decision making also led to purges of the Old Bolsheviks. Between 1936 and 1938, the most prominent Old Bolsheviks were put on trial and condemned to death. During this same time, Stalin undertook a purge of army officers, diplomats, union officials, party members, intellectuals, and numerous ordinary citizens. One old woman was sent to Siberia for saying, "If people prayed, they would work better." Estimates are that 8 million Russians were arrested; millions died in Siberian forced labor camps. This gave Stalin the distinction of being one of the greatest mass murderers in human history. The Stalinist bloodbath made what some Western intellectuals had hailed as the "new civilization" much less attractive by the late 1930s.

Disturbed by a rapidly declining birthrate, Stalin also reversed much of the permissive social legislation of the early 1920s. Advocating complete equality of rights for women, the Communists had made divorce and abortion easy to obtain while also encouraging women to work outside the home and liberate themselves sexually. After Stalin came to power, the family was praised as a miniature collective in which parents were responsible for inculcating values of duty, discipline, and hard work. Abortion was outlawed, and divorced fathers who did not support their children faced heavy fines. A new divorce law of June 1936 imposed fines for repeated divorces, and homosexuality was declared a criminal activity. The regime now praised motherhood and urged women to have large families as a patriotic duty. But by this time, many Soviet women worked in factories and spent many additional hours waiting in line to purchase increasingly scarce consumer goods. Despite the change in policy, no dramatic increase in the birthrate occurred.

CHRONOLOGY	The Soviet Union
New Economic Policy begins	1921
Death of Lenin	1924
Trotsky is expelled from the Communist Party	1927
First five-year plan begins	1928
Stalin's dictatorship is established	1929
Height of Stalin's purges	1936–1938

The Authoritarian and Totalitarian States ■ 813

THE FORMATION OF COLLECTIVE FARMS

ACCOMPANYING THE RAPID INDUSTRIALIZATION of the Soviet Union was the collectivization of agriculture, a feat that involved nothing less than transforming Russia's 26 million family farms into 250,000 collective farms, or *kolkhozes* (kuhl-KAW-zez). This selection provides a firsthand account of how the process worked.

Max Belov, *The History of a Collective Farm*

General collectivization in our village was brought about in the following manner: Two representatives of the [Communist] Party arrived in the village. All the inhabitants were summoned by the ringing of the church bell to a meeting at which the policy of general collectivization was announced. . . . The upshot was that although the meeting lasted two days, from the viewpoint of the Party representatives nothing was accomplished.

After this setback the Party representatives divided the village into two sections and worked each one separately. Two more officials were sent to reinforce the first two. A meeting of our section of the village was held in a stable which had previously belonged to a kulak. The meeting dragged on until dark. Suddenly someone threw a brick at the lamp, and in the dark the peasants began to beat the Party representatives who jumped out the window and escaped from the village barely alive. . . . The militia was called in and stayed in the village until the peasants . . . calmed down. . . .

By the end of 1930 there were two kolkhozes in our village. Though at first these collectives embraced at most only 70 percent of the peasant households, in the months that followed they gradually absorbed more and more of them.

In these kolkhozes the great bulk of the land was held and worked communally, but each peasant household owned a house of some sort, a small plot of ground and perhaps some livestock. All the members of the kolkhoz were required to work on the kolkhoz a certain number of days each month; the rest of the time they were allowed to work on their own holdings. They derived their income partly from what they grew on their garden strips and partly from their work in the kolkhoz.

When the harvest was over, and after the farm had met its obligations to the state and to various special funds (for instance, seed, etc.) and had sold on the market whatever undesignated produce was left, the remaining produce and the farm's monetary income were divided among the kolkhoz members according to the number of "labor days" each one had contributed to the farm's work. . . . It was in 1930 that the kolkhoz members first received their portions out of the "communal kettle." After they had received their earnings, at the rate of 1 kilogram of grain and 55 kopecks per labor day, one of them remarked, "You will live, but you will be very, very thin. . . ."

By late 1932 more than 80 percent of the peasant households . . . had been collectivized. . . . That year the peasants harvested a good crop and had hopes that the calculations would work out to their advantage These hopes were in vain. The kolkhoz workers received only 200 grams of flour per labor day for the first half of the year; the remaining grain, . . . was taken by the government. The peasants were told that industrialization of the country . . . demanded grain and sacrifices from them.

 What was the purpose of collectivizing Soviet agriculture? According to Belov, why did the peasants of his village assault the Communist Party representatives? What was the result of their protest?

Source: From Fedor Belov, *The History of a Soviet Collective Farm* (Westport, Conn.: Praeger).

The Stalinist era did witness some positive changes in the everyday lives of Soviet citizens. To create leaders for the new Communist society, Stalin began a program to enable workers, peasants, and young Communists to receive higher education, especially in engineering. There was also tremendous growth in part-time schools, where large numbers of adults took courses to become literate so that they could advance to technical school or college. Increasing numbers of people saw education as the key to better jobs and upward mobility in Soviet society. One woman of peasant background recounted: "In Moscow I had a burning desire to study. Where or what wasn't important; I wanted to study." For what purpose? "We had a saying at work: 'Without that piece of paper [the diploma] you are an insect; with it, a human being.' My lack of higher education prevented me from getting decent wages."[13]

Authoritarianism in Eastern Europe

A number of other states in Europe had conservative authoritarian governments that adopted some of the trappings of states like Nazi Germany and the Soviet Union, especially their wide police powers. For these states, however, the greatest concern was not the creation of a mass movement aimed at establishing a new kind of society but rather the defense of the existing social order. Consequently, the **authoritarian state** tended to limit the participation of the masses and was content with passive obedience rather than active involvement in the goals of the regime. A number of states in eastern Europe adopted this kind of authoritarian government.

Nowhere had the map of Europe been more drastically altered by World War I than in eastern Europe. The new states

Eastern Europe After World War I

of Austria, Poland, Czechoslovakia, and Yugoslavia adopted parliamentary systems, and the preexisting kingdoms of Romania and Bulgaria gained new parliamentary constitutions in 1920. Greece became a republic in 1924. Hungary's government was parliamentary in form but was controlled by its landed aristocrats. At the beginning of the 1920s, political democracy seemed well established, but almost everywhere in eastern Europe, parliamentary governments soon gave way to authoritarian regimes.

Several problems helped create this situation. Eastern European states had little tradition of liberalism or parliamentary politics and no substantial middle class to support them. Then, too, these states were largely rural and agrarian. Large landowners who feared the growth of agrarian peasant parties with their schemes for land redistribution still controlled much of the land. Ethnic conflicts also threatened to tear these countries apart. Fearful of land reform, Communist agrarian upheaval, and ethnic conflict, powerful landowners, the churches, and even some members of the small middle class looked to authoritarian governments to maintain the old system.

Already in the 1920s, some eastern European states began to move away from political democracy toward authoritarian structures. A military coup d'état established an authoritarian regime in Bulgaria in 1923. Poland established an authoritarian regime in 1926 when Marshal Joseph Pilsudski (peel-SOOT-skee) (1867–1935) created a military dictatorship. In Yugoslavia, King Alexander I (1921–1934) abolished the constitution and imposed a royal dictatorship in 1929. During the 1930s, all of the remaining parliamentary regimes except Czechoslovakia succumbed to authoritarianism. Eastern European states were increasingly attracted to the authoritarian examples of Fascist Italy and Nazi Germany.

Although Admiral Miklós Horthy (MIK-lohsh HOR-tee) (1868–1957) had ruled Hungary as "regent" since 1919, the appointment of Julius Gömbös (GUM-buhsh) (1886–1936) as prime minister in 1932 brought Hungary even closer to Italy and Germany. Romania witnessed the development of a strong fascist movement led by Corneliu Codreanu (kor-NELL-yoo kaw-dree-AH-noo) (1899–1938). Known as the Legion of the Archangel Michael, it possessed its own paramilitary squad called the Iron Guard. As Codreanu's fascist movement grew and became Romania's third largest political party, King Carol II (1930–1940) responded in 1938 by ending parliamentary rule, crushing the leadership of the legion, and imposing

authoritarian rule. In Greece, General Ioannis Metaxas (yah-AH-nees muh-tahk-SAHSS) (1871–1941) imposed a dictatorship in 1936.

Only Czechoslovakia, with its substantial middle class, liberal tradition, and strong industrial base, maintained its political democracy. Thomas Masaryk (MAS-uh-rik) (1850–1937), an able and fair leader who served as president from 1918 to 1935, was able to maintain an uneasy but stable alliance of reformist socialists, agrarians, and Catholics.

Dictatorship in the Iberian Peninsula

Parliamentary regimes also failed to survive in both Spain and Portugal. Both countries were largely agrarian, illiterate, and dominated by powerful landlords and Catholic clergy.

Spain's parliamentary monarchy was unable to deal with the social tensions generated by the industrial boom and inflation that accompanied World War I. Supported by King Alfonso XIII (1886–1931), General Miguel Primo de Rivera (PREE-moh day ri-VAY-ruh) (1870–1930) led a successful military coup in September 1923 and created a personal dictatorship that lasted until 1930. But a faltering economy because of the Great Depression led to the collapse of Primo de Rivera's regime in January 1930 as well as to a widespread lack of support for the monarchy. Alfonso XIII left Spain in 1931, and a new Spanish republic was instituted, governed by a coalition of democrats and reformist socialists. Political turmoil ensued as control of the government passed from leftists to rightists until the Popular Front, an antifascist coalition composed of democrats, socialists, Communists, and other leftist groups, took over in 1936. But the Popular Front was unacceptable to senior army officers. Led by General Francisco Franco (1892–1975), Spanish military forces revolted against the government and inaugurated a brutal and bloody civil war that lasted three years.

THE SPANISH CIVIL WAR The war split the country between left and right (see the box on p. 816). On the left were the Republicans who supported the Popular Front. They were concentrated in urban areas such as Madrid and Barcelona and favored modernization, workers' rights, the expansion of manufacturing, a civilian army, and secularization. On the right were the Nationalists who supported Franco's military coup, the monarchy, the military, an agrarian economy, and the Catholic Church.

The Spanish conflict was complicated by foreign intervention. In 1936, Great Britain, France, Germany, Italy, and the Soviet Union signed a nonintervention agreement declaring that they would not provide economic or military support for either side. Germany and Italy quickly rejected the agreement, however, and sent troops, weapons, and military advisers to assist Franco. Hitler used the Spanish Civil War as an opportunity to test the new weapons of his revived air force. The devastating air attack on Guernica (GWAIR-nih-kuh *or* gair-NEE-kuh) on April 26, 1937, initiated a new level of brutally destructive warfare. Meanwhile, the British and French adhered to their position of nonintervention, so the Republicans turned to the

SPAIN DIVIDED: A VIEW FROM BARCELONA

IN 1936, ENGLISH NOVELIST GEORGE ORWELL traveled to Barcelona to write newspaper articles; instead he joined the Republican forces and fought for six months before returning to England in June 1937. Published in 1938, Orwell's *Homage to Catalonia* is a first-hand account of Barcelona during the civil war.

George Orwell, Barcelona (1936)

I had come to Spain with some notion of writing newspaper articles, but I had joined the militia almost immediately, because at that time and in that atmosphere it seemed the only conceivable thing to do. The Anarchists were still in virtual control of Catalonia and the revolution was still in full swing. . . . It was the first time that I had ever been in a town where the working class was in the saddle. Practically every building of any size had been seized by the workers and was draped with red flags or with the red and black flag of the Anarchists; every wall was scrawled with the hammer and sickle . . . almost every church had been gutted and its images burnt. . . . Every shop and café had an inscription saying that it had been collectivised. . . . Waiters and shop-walkers looked you in the face and treated you as an equal. Servile and even ceremonial forms of speech had temporarily disappeared. . . . There were no private motor-cars, they had all been commandeered, and the trams and taxis and much of the other transport were painted red and black. . . . Down the Ramblas, the wide central artery of the town where crowds of people streamed constantly to and fro, the loud-speakers were bellowing revolutionary songs all day and far into the night. And it was the aspect of the crowds that was the queerest thing of all. In outward appearance it was a town in which the wealthy classes had practically ceased to exist. Except for a small number of women and foreigners there were no 'well-dressed' people at all. Practically everyone wore rough working-class clothes, or blue overalls or some variant of militia uniform. . . . Also, I believed that things were as they appeared, that this was really a workers' State and that the entire bourgeoisie had either fled, been killed or voluntarily come over to the workers' side; I did not realise that great numbers of well-to-do bourgeois were simply lying low and disguising themselves as proletarians for the time being. Together with all this there was something of the evil atmosphere of war. The town had a gaunt untidy look, roads and buildings were in poor repair, the streets at night were dimly lit for fear of air-raids, the shops were mostly shabby and half-empty. Meat was scarce and milk practically unobtainable, there was a shortage of coal, sugar and petrol, and a really serious shortage of bread. . . . Yet so far as one could judge the people were contented and hopeful. There was no unemployment, and the price of living was still extremely low; you saw very few conspicuously destitute people, and no beggars except the gypsies. Above all, there was a belief in the revolution and the future, a feeling of having suddenly emerged into an era of equality and freedom. Human beings were trying to behave as human beings and not as cogs in the capitalist machine.

 Why did Orwell join the revolutionaries? What kind of society were the revolutionaries trying to build in Barcelona? Why? Ultimately, why did they not succeed?

Source: George Orwell, *Homage to Catalonia* (London: Secker and Warburg, 1938).

Soviet Union for aid. The Soviets sent tanks, planes, and pilots. The Republicans also gained assistance from international brigades of volunteers, including the Abraham Lincoln Brigade from the United States.

Gradually, Franco's forces wore down the Popular Front, and after they captured Madrid on March 28, 1939, the Spanish Civil War finally came to an end. The war had been a brutal one. Probably 400,000 people died in the war, only one-fourth of them on the battlefield. Civilians died from air raids, disease, and bloody reprisals by both sides against their enemies and their supporters. Another 200,000 people were executed in the years following Franco's victory.

THE FRANCO REGIME General Franco soon established a dictatorship that lasted until his death in 1975. It was not a fascist government, although it was unlikely to oppose the Fascists in Italy or the Nazis in Germany. The fascist movement in Spain, known as the Falange (fuh-**LANJ**) and led by José Antonio Primo de Rivera, son of the former

CHRONOLOGY	The Authoritarian States	
Eastern Europe		
Pilsudski creates military dictatorship in Poland	1926	
Alexander I creates royal dictatorship in Yugoslavia	1929	
Gömbös is made prime minister in Hungary	1932	
Dictatorship of General Metaxas in Greece	1936	
Carol II crushes Iron Guard and imposes authoritarian rule in Romania	1938	
Spain		
Dictatorship of Primo de Rivera	1923–1930	
Creation of Spanish Republic	1931	
Spanish Civil War	1936–1939	
Dictatorship of Franco	1939–1975	

The Destruction of Guernica. On April 26, 1937, the German Condor Legion dropped 100,000 tons of explosives in three hours on the small Basque town of Guernica, killing 1,654 people and wounding 889. The first illustration shows the ruins of Guernica after the German attack. The scene was also captured in Pablo Picasso's *Guernica* (1937), a large (11 by 25 feet) Cubist piece that portrays the horror and human destruction caused by mass bombings. The fragmented bodies include a woman holding her dead child, dismembered limbs, and terrified horses.

dictator, contributed little to Franco's success and played a minor role in the new regime. Franco's government, which outlawed political opposition, favored large landowners, business, and the Catholic clergy, and curtailed the media, was yet another example of a traditional, conservative, authoritarian regime.

PORTUGAL In 1910, the Portuguese had overthrown their monarchy and established a republic. Severe inflation after World War I, however, undermined support for the republic and helped intensify political instability. In 1926, a group of army officers seized power, and by the early 1930s, the military junta's finance minister, Antonio Salazar (SAL-uh-zahr) (1889–1970), had become the strongman of the regime. Salazar controlled the Portuguese government for the next forty years.

The Expansion of Mass Culture and Mass Leisure

 FOCUS QUESTION: What new dimensions in mass culture and mass leisure emerged during the interwar years, and what role did these activities play in Italy, Germany, and the Soviet Union?

The decade of the 1920s came to be known as the Roaring Twenties for the exuberance of its popular culture. Berlin, the capital of Germany, became the entertainment center of Europe with its theaters, cabarets, cinemas, and jazz clubs. The Roaring Twenties were especially known for dance crazes. People danced in clubs and dance halls, at home, and in the streets, doing the Charleston, the Bunny Hug, and various

Sasha/Getty Images

The Charleston. Dancing became the rage during the Roaring Twenties, and the Charleston was the most popular and enduring dance of the decade. This photograph shows a couple dancing the Charleston in a scene from the London musical *Just a Kiss* in 1926.

other dances. Josephine Baker (1906–1975), an American singer and dancer, became especially well known in Europe, appearing at European clubs featuring American "Negro" jazz music. One critic said, "She dances for hours without the slightest trace of tiredness." She became a wonderful symbol of the popular "flapper," the unconventional and lively young woman of the 1920s. Jazz, a musical form that had originated with African American musicians in the United States, became so popular that the 1920s were also known as the Jazz Age. Admired for its improvised qualities and forceful rhythms, jazz spread throughout the Western world as King Oliver, Bix Beiderbecke (BIKS BY-der-bek), Jelly Roll Morton, and others wrote and played some of the greatest jazz music of the time.

Radio and Movies

A series of technological inventions in the late nineteenth century had prepared the way for a revolution in mass communications. Especially important was Guglielmo Marconi's discovery of "wireless" radio waves. But it was not until June 16, 1920, that a radio broadcast (of a concert by soprano Nellie Melba from London) for a mass audience was attempted. The United States, Europe, and Japan then constructed permanent broadcasting

facilities during 1921 and 1922, and mass production of radios (receiving sets) also began. In 1926, when the British Broadcasting Corporation (BBC) was made into a public corporation, there were 2.2 million radios in Great Britain. By the end of the 1930s, there were 9 million.

The technical foundation for motion pictures had already been developed in the 1890s when short movies were produced as novelties for music halls. The first short films were produced by the French Lumiére brothers in 1895; their film *The Train Arrives at the Station* caused a mixed reaction of fear and delight from its viewers in Finland in 1896: "The first picture we saw last night showed the arrival of a railway train to the station of a large city. . . . From afar, the arrival of the train could be approached so naturally that we almost feared being run over. It stopped in time, however, and . . . It all happened so naturally that we were quite dumbfounded."[14] Shortly before World War I, full-length features, such as the Italian film *Quo Vadis* and the American film *Birth of a Nation*, were released, and it quickly became apparent that cinema was a new form of entertainment for the masses. By 1939, about 40 percent of adults in the more advanced industrial countries were attending the movies once a week. That figure increased to 60 percent by the end of World War II.

Mass forms of communication and entertainment were not new, but the increased size of audiences and the ability of radio and cinema, unlike the printed word, to provide an immediate shared experience added new dimensions to mass culture. Favorite film actors and actresses became stars who then became the focus of public adoration and scrutiny. Sensuous actresses such as Marlene Dietrich, whose appearance in the early sound film *The Blue Angel* catapulted her to fame, popularized new images of women's sexuality.

Of course, radio and movies could also be used for political purposes. Hitler had said that "without motor cars, sound films, and wireless, no victory of National Socialism." Radio seemed to offer great opportunities for reaching the masses, especially when it became apparent that the emotional harangues of a demagogue such as Hitler had just as much impact on people when heard on radio as in person. The Nazi regime encouraged radio listening by urging manufacturers to produce cheap radios that could be bought on the installment plan. The Nazis also erected loudspeaker pillars in the streets to encourage communal radio listening, especially to broadcasts of mass meetings.

Film, too, had propaganda potential, a possibility not lost on Joseph Goebbels (GUR-bulz) (1897–1945), the propaganda minister of Nazi Germany. Believing that film constituted one of the "most modern and scientific means of influencing the masses," Goebbels created a special film section in his Propaganda Ministry and encouraged the production of both documentaries and popular feature films that carried the Nazi message. *Triumph of the Will*, for example, was a documentary of the 1934 Nuremberg party rally that forcefully conveyed the power of National Socialism to viewers (see "Film & History" on p. 819). Both Fascist Italy and Nazi Germany also controlled and exploited the content of newsreels shown in movie theaters.

Watch *Triumph of the Will* (1934), one of the best-known films of Nazi Germany, a documentary directed by Leni Riefenstahl (LAY-nee REE-fuhn-shtahl), an actress who turned to directing in 1932. Adolf Hitler invited her to make a film about the 1934 Nuremberg party rally. In filming this party day of unity—as it was called—Hitler was trying to demonstrate, in the wake of the purge of the SA on June 30, that the Nazi Party was strongly united behind its leader.

World History Archive/Image Asset Management Ltd./Alamy

In what ways is the film a piece of propaganda aimed at conveying to viewers the power of National Socialism? Riefenstahl maintained that it was "a pure historical film." Why was she criticized for that view?

Mass Leisure

Mass leisure activities had developed at the turn of the century, but new work patterns after World War I dramatically expanded the amount of free time available to take advantage of them. By 1920, the eight-hour day had become the norm for many office and factory workers in northern and western Europe.

SPORTS Professional sporting events for mass audiences became an especially important aspect of mass leisure. Attendance at association football (soccer) games increased dramatically, and the inauguration of the World Cup contest in 1930 added to the nationalistic rivalries that began to surround such mass sporting events. Increased attendance also made the 1920s and 1930s a great era of stadium building. For the 1936 Olympics, the Germans built a stadium in Berlin that seated 140,000 people.

TOURISM Travel opportunities also added new dimensions to mass leisure activities. The military use of aircraft during World War I spurred improvements in planes that made civilian air travel a reality. The first regular international airmail service began in 1919, and regular passenger service soon followed. Although air travel remained the preserve of the wealthy or the adventurous, trains, buses, and private cars made excursions to beaches or resorts more popular and more affordable. Beaches, such as the one at Brighton in England, were increasingly mobbed by crowds of people from all social classes, a clear reflection of the growth of democratic politics. In France, the Popular Front government passed legislation that provided paid vacations for all salaried employees or wage earners. Workers were granted a fifteen-day paid vacation in the summer, corresponding to school vacation. Whereas in Italy and Germany (see the next section) mass leisure activities were used to support state initiatives, in France paid vacations became a citizen's right.

Europeans living in the colonies of the European states also increasingly found opportunities for tourism. They flocked to colonial spas where they could find reminders of European culture and medicinal treatment. Hydrotherapy (treatment with mineral water) was employed to treat malaria and yellow fever, ailments that often afflicted Europeans living in the colonies, especially in Africa.

ORGANIZED MASS LEISURE IN ITALY AND GERMANY Mass leisure provided the Fascist and Nazi regimes with new ways to control their populations. Mussolini's Italy created the *Dopolavoro* (duh-puh-LAH-vuh-roh) (Afterwork) as a vast national recreation agency. The Dopolavoro established clubhouses with libraries, radios, and athletic facilities in virtually every town and village. Some clubhouses included auditoriums for plays and films, as well as travel agencies that arranged tours, cruises, and resort vacations on the Adriatic at reduced rates. Dopolavoro groups introduced many Italians to various facets of mass culture and mass leisure with activities such as band concerts, movies, choral groups, roller skating, and ballroom dancing. Essentially, the Dopolavoro enabled the Italian government to provide recreational activities and supervise them as well. By doing so, the state imposed new rules and regulations on previously spontaneous activities, thus breaking down old group solidarities and enabling these groups to be guided by the goals of the state.

The Nazi regime instituted a similar program called *Kraft durch Freude* (KRAHFT doorkh FROI-duh) (Strength Through Joy). The purpose of Kraft durch Freude was to coordinate the free time of the working class by offering a variety of leisure time activities, including concerts, operas, films, guided tours, and sporting events. Especially popular were inexpensive vacations, much like modern package tours, such as cruises to Scandinavia or the Mediterranean or, more likely for workers, short trips to various sites in Germany. Some 130,000 workers took cruises in 1938; 7 million took short trips.

More and more, mass culture and mass leisure had the effect of increasing the homogeneity of national populations, a process that had begun in the nineteenth century with the development of the national state and mass politics. Local popular culture was increasingly replaced by national and even international culture as new forms of mass production and consumption brought similar styles of clothing and fashion to people throughout Europe.

Cultural and Intellectual Trends in the Interwar Years

 FOCUS QUESTION: What were the main cultural and intellectual trends in the interwar years?

The artistic and intellectual innovations of the pre–World War I period, which had shocked many Europeans, had been the preserve primarily of a small group of avant-garde artists and intellectuals. In the 1920s and 1930s, they became more widespread as artists and intellectuals continued to work out the implications of the ideas developed before 1914. But what made the prewar avant-garde culture acceptable in the 1920s and the 1930s? Perhaps the most important factor was the impact of World War I.

To many people, the experiences of the war seemed to confirm the prewar avant-garde belief that human beings were violent and irrational animals who were incapable of creating a sane and rational world. The Great Depression of the late 1920s and early 1930s, as well as the growth of fascist movements based on violence and the degradation of individual rights, only added to the uncertainties generated by the Great War. The crisis of confidence in Western civilization ran deep and was well captured in the words of the French poet Paul Valéry (POHL vah-lay-REE) in the early 1920s:

> The storm has died away, and still we are restless, uneasy, as if the storm were about to break. Almost all the affairs of men remain in a terrible uncertainty. We think of what has disappeared, and we are almost destroyed by what has been destroyed; we do not know what will be born, and we fear the future. . . . Doubt and disorder are in us and with us. There is no thinking man, however shrewd or learned he may be, who can hope to dominate this anxiety, to escape from this impression of darkness.[15]

Political and economic uncertainties were paralleled by social insecurities. The war had served to break down many traditional middle-class attitudes, especially toward sexuality. In the 1920s, women's physical appearance changed dramatically. Short skirts, short hair, the use of cosmetics that were once thought to be the preserve of prostitutes, and the new practice of sun tanning gave women a new image. This change in physical appearance, which stressed more exposure of a woman's body, was also accompanied by frank discussions of sexual matters. In England in 1918, Marie Stopes published *Married Love*, which emphasized sexual pleasure in marriage and soon became a best-seller. In 1926, the Dutch physician Theodore van de Velde (TAY-oh-dor vahn duh VELL-duh) published *Ideal Marriage: Its Physiology and Technique*. Translated into a number of languages, it became an international bestseller. Van de Velde described female and male anatomy, discussed birth control techniques, and glorified sexual pleasure in marriage. Family planning clinics, such as those of Margaret Sanger in the United States and Marie Stopes in Britain, began to spread new ideas on sexuality and birth control to the working classes.

Nightmares and New Visions: Art and Music

Uncertainty also pervaded the cultural and intellectual achievements of the interwar years. Postwar artistic trends were largely a working out of the implications of prewar developments. Abstract painting, for example, became ever more popular as many pioneering artists of the early twentieth century matured in the decades after the war. In addition, prewar fascination with the absurd and the unconscious contents of the mind seemed even more appropriate after the nightmare landscapes of World War I battlefronts. This gave rise to both the Dada movement and Surrealism, but it was German Expressionist artists who best directly captured the disturbingly destructive effects of World War I.

GERMAN EXPRESSIONISTS Although Expressionism as a movement began before World War I, the war itself had a devastating impact on a group of German Expressionist artists who focused on the suffering and shattered lives caused by the war. George Grosz (GROHS) (1893–1959), one of these artists, expressed his anger in this way: "Of course, there was a kind of mass enthusiasm at the start. . . . And then after a few years when everything bogged down, when we were defeated, when everything went to pieces, all that remained, at least of me and most of my friends, were disgust and horror."[16] Another German artist who gave visual expression to the horrors of World War I was Otto Dix (1891–1969), who had also served in the war and was well versed in its effects. In *The War*, he gave a graphic presentation of the devastating effects of the Great War.

THE DADA MOVEMENT Dadaism (DAH-duh-iz-um) attempted to enshrine the purposelessness of life. Tristan Tzara (TRISS-tun TSAHR-rah) (1896–1945), a Romanian-French poet and one of the founders of Dadaism, expressed the Dadaist contempt for the Western tradition in a lecture in 1922 when he stated that the acts of life have no beginning or end. "Everything happens in a completely idiotic way. . . . Like everything in life, Dada is useless." Revolted by the insanity of life, especially the mass destruction of WWI, the Dadaists tried to give absurdity an expression by creating "anti-art." The 1918 Berlin Dada Manifesto maintained that "Dada is the international expression of our times, the great rebellion of artistic movements."

In the hands of Hannah Höch (HEKH) (1889–1978), Dada became an instrument to comment on women's roles in the new mass culture. Höch was the only female member of the Berlin Dada Club, which featured the use of photomontage. Her work was part of the first Dada show in Berlin in 1920. In *Dada Dance*, she seemed to criticize the "new woman" by making fun of the way women were inclined to follow new fashion styles. In other works, however, she created positive images of the modern woman and expressed a keen interest in new freedoms for women.

SURREALISM Perhaps more important as an artistic movement was **Surrealism**, which sought a reality beyond the material, sensible world and found it in the world of the unconscious through the portrayal of fantasies, dreams, or nightmares. Employing logic to portray the illogical, the Surrealists created disturbing and evocative images. The Spaniard Salvador Dalí (dah-LEE *or* DAH-lee) (1904–1989) became the high priest of Surrealism and in his mature phase became a master of representational Surrealism. In *The Persistence of Memory*, Dalí portrayed recognizable objects divorced from their normal context. By placing these objects in unrecognizable relationships, he created a disturbing world in which the irrational had become tangible, forcing viewers to question the rational.

Hannah Höch, *Cut with the Kitchen Knife Dada Through the Last Weimar Beer Belly Cultural Epoch of Germany*. Hannah Höch, a prominent figure in the postwar Dada movement, used photomontage to create images that reflected on women's issues. In *Cut with the Kitchen Knife* (1919), she combined pictures of German political leaders with sports stars, Dada artists, and scenes from urban life. The arrangement and various sizes of letters and figures throughout create a sense of dislocation. One major theme emerged: the confrontation between the anti-Dada world of German political leaders and the Dada world of revolutionary ideals. Höch associated women with Dada and the new world.

and engineering were to be unified, and all unnecessary ornamentation was to be stripped away. Functionalism was based on the architects' belief that art had a social function and could help create a new civilization.

The United States was a leader in these pioneering architectural designs. Unprecedented urban growth and the absence of restrictive architectural traditions allowed for new building methods, especially in the relatively "new city" of Chicago. The Chicago School of the 1890s, led by Louis H. Sullivan (1856–1924), used reinforced concrete, steel frames, and electric elevators to build skyscrapers virtually free of external ornamentation. One of Sullivan's most successful pupils was Frank Lloyd Wright (1867–1959), who became known for innovative designs in domestic architecture. Wright's private houses, built chiefly for wealthy patrons, featured geometric structures with long lines, overhanging roofs, and severe planes of brick and stone. The interiors were open spaces that included cathedral ceilings and built-in furniture and lighting fixtures. Wright pioneered the modern American house.

Especially important in the spread of functionalism was the Bauhaus (BOW-howss) School of Art, Architecture, and Design, founded in 1919 in Weimar, Germany, by the Berlin architect Walter Gropius (VAHL-tuh GROH-pee-uss) (1883–1969).

FUNCTIONALISM IN MODERN ARCHITECTURE The move to **functionalism** in modern architecture also became more widespread in the 1920s and 1930s. First conceived near the end of the nineteenth century, functionalism meant that buildings, like the products of machines, should be "functional" or useful, fulfilling the purpose for which they were constructed. Art

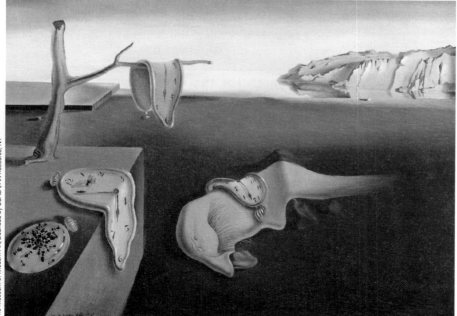

Salvador Dalí, *The Persistence of Memory*. Surrealism was another important artistic movement between the wars. Influenced by the theories of Freudian psychology, Surrealists sought to reveal the world of the unconscious, or the "greater reality" that they believed existed beyond the world of physical appearances. As is evident in this 1931 painting, Salvador Dalí sought to portray the world of dreams by putting time in a suspended state and placing recognizable objects in unrecognizable relationships.

Walter Gropius, The Bauhaus. Walter Gropius was one of Europe's pioneers in modern architecture. When the Bauhaus moved to Dessau in 1925, Gropius designed a building for its activities. His straightforward use of steel, reinforced concrete, and rows of windows reflects the move to functionalism in modern architecture.

The Bauhaus teaching staff consisted of architects, artists, and designers who worked together to blend the study of fine arts (painting and sculpture) with the applied arts (printing, weaving, and furniture making). Gropius urged his followers to foster a new union of arts and crafts to create the buildings and objects of the future. Gropius's own buildings were often unornamented steel boxes with walls of windows, reflecting his belief that the "sensibility of the artist must be combined with the knowledge of the technician to create new forms in architecture and design."

A POPULAR AUDIENCE Important to the development of artistic expression between the wars was the search for a new popular audience. To attract a wider audience, artists and musicians began to involve themselves in the new mass culture. The German Kurt Weill (VYL) (1900–1950), for example, had been a struggling composer of classical music before he turned to jazz rhythms and other popular musical idioms for the music for *The Threepenny Opera*. Some artists even regarded art as a means to transform society and located their studios in poor, working-class neighborhoods. Theater proved especially attractive as postwar artists sought to make an impact on popular audiences. The German director Erwin Piscator (AYR-vin PIS-kuh-tor) began his directing career by offering plays to workers on picket lines. Piscator hoped to reach workers by experimental drama with political messages. Like many other artists, however, he became frustrated by his failure to achieve a mass audience.

The postwar acceptance of modern art forms was by no means universal. Many traditionalists denounced what they considered degeneracy and decadence in the arts. Nowhere was this more evident than in Nazi Germany and the Soviet Union.

CULTURE OF NAZISM In the 1920s, Weimar Germany was one of the chief European centers for modern arts and sciences. In Nazi Germany, artists and writers were placed under the control of the state, and only works that supported the Nazi ideals were permitted, such as Ernest Jünger's *The Storm of Steel*, a memoir of a German officer during World War I that stressed military service and sacrifice. Hitler and the Nazis rejected modern art as "degenerate" or "Jewish" art, and began a systematic program of confiscation and destruction of thousands of paintings, drawings, prints, and sculpture by artists such as Cezanne, Picasso, and Van Gogh. In an address at the premiere of the Great German Art Exhibition in the newly opened House of German Art in July 1937, Hitler proclaimed, "The people regarded this art [modern art] as the outcome of an impudent and unashamed arrogance or of a simply shocking lack of skill; . . . these achievements—which might have been produced by untalented children of from eight to ten years old—could never be valued as an expression of our own times or of the German future."[17] Hitler and the Nazis believed that they had laid the foundation for a new and genuine German art, which would glorify the strong, the healthy, and the heroic—all supposedly attributes of the Aryan race. The new German art was actually the old nineteenth-century genre art with its emphasis on realistic scenes of everyday life and was intended to inculcate social values useful to the ruling regimes.

A NEW STYLE IN MUSIC At the beginning of the twentieth century, a revolution in music parallel to the revolution in art had begun with the work of Igor Stravinsky (see Chapter 24). But Stravinsky still wrote music in a definite key. The Viennese composer Arnold Schönberg (AR-nawlt SHURN-bayrk) (1874–1951) began to experiment with a radically new style by creating musical pieces in which tonality is completely abandoned, a system that he called atonal music. Since the use of traditional forms was virtually impossible in atonal music, Schönberg created a new system of composition—twelve-tone composition—which used a scale of twelve notes independent of any tonal key. Resistance to modern music was even greater than to modern painting, and atonal music did not begin to win favor until after World War II.

The Search for the Unconscious in Literature

The interest in the unconscious, heightened by the impact of World War I and evident in Surrealism, was also apparent in the new literary techniques that emerged in the 1920s. One of its most visible manifestations was the "stream-of-consciousness" technique in which the writer presented an interior monologue, or a report of the innermost thoughts of each character. One example of this genre was written by the Irish exile James Joyce (1882–1941). His *Ulysses*, published in 1922, told the story of one day in the life of ordinary people in Dublin by following the flow of their inner dialogue. Disconnected ramblings and veiled allusions pervade Joyce's work.

Another famous writer who used her own stream-of-consciousness technique was Virginia Woolf (1882–1942). Woolf belonged to a group of intellectuals and artists, known

THE NOVELS OF HERMANN HESSE made a strong impact on young people, first in Germany in the 1920s and then in the United States in the 1960s after they had been translated into English. Many of these young people shared Hesse's fascination with the unconscious and his dislike of modern industrial civilization. This excerpt from *Demian* spoke directly to many of them.

Hermann Hesse, Demian

The following spring I was to leave the preparatory school and enter a university. I was still undecided, however, as to where and what I was to study. I had grown a thin mustache, I was a full-grown man, and yet I was completely helpless and without a goal in life. Only one thing was certain: the voice within me, the dream image. I felt the duty to follow this voice blindly wherever it might lead me. But it was difficult and each day I rebelled against it anew. Perhaps I was mad, as I thought at moments; perhaps I was not like other men? But I was able to do the same things the others did;

with a little effort and industry I could read Plato, was able to solve problems in trigonometry or follow a chemical analysis. There was only one thing I could not do: wrest the dark secret goal from myself and keep it before me as others did who knew exactly what they wanted to be—professors, lawyers, doctors, artists, however long this would take them and whatever difficulties and advantages this decision would bear in its wake. This I could not do. Perhaps I would become something similar, but how was I to know? Perhaps I would have to continue my search for years on end and would not become anything, and would not reach a goal. Perhaps I would reach this goal but it would turn out to be an evil, dangerous, horrible one.

I wanted only to try to live in accord with the promptings which came from my true self. Why was that so very difficult?

 How does Hesse's interest in the unconscious appear in this excerpt? Why was a dislike of mechanized society particularly intense after World War I?

Source: Herman Hesse, *Demian* (New York: Bantam Books, 1966), p. 30.

---

as the Bloomsbury Circle, who sought to create new artistic and literary forms. In her novels *Mrs. Dalloway* and *Jacob's Room*, Woolf used the inner monologues of her main characters to reveal their world of existence. Woolf came to believe that for a woman to be a writer, she would need to have her own income to free herself from the expected roles of wife and mother.

The German writer Hermann Hesse (HESS-uh) (1877–1962) dealt with the unconscious in a different fashion. His novels reflected the influence of both Carl Jung's psychological theories and Eastern religions and focused among other things on the spiritual loneliness of modern human beings in a mechanized urban society. *Demian* was a psychoanalytic study of incest, and *Steppenwolf* mirrored the psychological confusion of modern existence. Hesse's novels made a large impact on German youth in the 1920s (see the box above). He won the Nobel Prize for Literature in 1946.

The Unconscious in Psychology: Carl Jung

The growing concern with the unconscious also led to greater popular interest in psychology. The full impact of Sigmund Freud's thought was not felt until after World War I. The 1920s witnessed a worldwide acceptance of his ideas. Freudian terms, such as *unconscious, repression, id, ego,* and *Oedipus complex,* entered the common vocabulary. Popularization of Freud's ideas led to the widespread misconception that an uninhibited sex life was necessary for a healthy mental life. Despite such misconceptions, psychoanalysis did develop into a major profession, especially in the United States. But Freud's ideas did not go unchallenged, even by his own pupils. One of the most prominent challenges came from Carl Jung (YOONG).

A disciple of Freud, Carl Jung (1856–1961) came to believe that Freud's theories were too narrow and reflected Freud's own personal biases. Jung's study of dreams—his own and those of others—led him to diverge sharply from Freud. Whereas for Freud the unconscious was the seat of repressed desires or appetites, for Jung it was an opening to deep spiritual needs and ever-greater vistas for humans.

Jung viewed the unconscious as twofold: a "personal unconscious" and, at a deeper level, a "collective unconscious." The collective unconscious was the repository of memories that all human beings share and consisted of archetypes, mental forms or images that appear in dreams. The archetypes are common to all people and have a special energy that creates myths, religions, and philosophies. To Jung, the archetypes proved that mind was only in part personal or individual because their origin was buried so far in the past that they seemed to have no human source. Their function was to bring the original mind of humans into a new, higher state of consciousness.

The "Heroic Age of Physics"

The prewar revolution in physics initiated by Max Planck and Albert Einstein continued in the interwar period. In fact, Ernest Rutherford (1871–1937), one of the physicists responsible for demonstrating that the atom could be split, dubbed the 1920s the "heroic age of physics." By the early 1940s, physicists had distinguished seven subatomic particles and achieved a sufficient understanding of the atom to lay the foundations for the development of a sophisticated new explosive device, the atomic bomb.

The new picture of the universe that was unfolding continued to undermine the old scientific certainties of classical physics. Classical physics had rested on the fundamental belief that all phenomena could be predicted if they could be completely understood; thus, the weather could be accurately predicted if we knew everything about the wind, sun, and water. In 1927, the German physicist Werner Heisenberg (VAYR-nur HY-zun-bayrk) (1901–1976) upset this belief when he posited the **uncertainty principle**. In essence, Heisenberg argued that no one could determine the path of an electron because the very act of observing the electron with light affected the electron's location. The uncertainty principle was more than an explanation for the path of an electron, however; it was a new worldview. Heisenberg shattered confidence in predictability and dared to propose that uncertainty was at the root of all physical laws.

CHAPTER SUMMARY

The devastation wrought by World War I destroyed the liberal optimism of the prewar era. Yet many in the 1920s still hoped that the progress of Western civilization, so seemingly evident before 1914, could somehow be restored. These hopes proved largely unfounded. France, feeling vulnerable to another invasion, sought to weaken Germany by occupying the Ruhr when Germany failed to pay reparations but gained little from the occupation. European recovery, largely the result of American loans and investments, ended when the Great Depression began at the end of the 1920s.

The democratic states—Great Britain, France, the Scandinavian countries, and the United States—spent much of the 1930s trying to recover from the Great Depression. New

governments that aimed at total control and required the active commitment of their citizens came to power in Italy, Germany, and the Soviet Union. Italian Fascism resulted from Italy's losses in World War I, economic problems, and incompetent politicians. Mussolini organized the Fascist movement in 1919 and by threatening to march on Rome was chosen as prime minister in 1922. Rival parties were outlawed, and Mussolini used repression and propaganda to create a Fascist state. Mussolini failed, however, to attain the degree of control achieved in Hitler's Germany. Heading the Nazi Party, Adolf Hitler became chancellor in 1933 and within

six months had seized dictatorial control. Hitler rearmed Germany, abolished all other political parties and the labor unions, and created a police state under the direction of the SS. Nazi Germany excluded Jews from citizenship and beginning in 1938 with *Kristallnacht* often persecuted and encouraged them to leave Germany.

After assuming leadership of the Soviet Union, Joseph Stalin followed his own path to establish total control. Five-year plans were instituted to turn the Soviet Union into an industrial society, while opponents were sent to Siberia, sentenced to labor camps, or liquidated. With the exception of Czechoslovakia, authoritarian governments appeared in eastern Europe as well as in Portugal and Spain. In the Spanish Civil War, the fascist states aided Francisco Franco, and the Soviet Union backed the Popular Front.

The new authoritarian governments not only restricted individual freedoms and the rule of law but, especially in Germany and the Soviet Union, sought even greater control over the lives of their subjects in order to manipulate and guide them to achieve the goals of their regimes. For many people, despite the loss of personal freedom, these mass movements offered some sense of security in a world that seemed fraught with uncertainty, an uncertainty that was also evident in popular culture, the arts, literature, and even physics. But the seeming security of these mass movements gave rise to even greater uncertainty as Europeans, after a brief twenty-year interlude of peace, again plunged into war.

CHAPTER TIMELINE

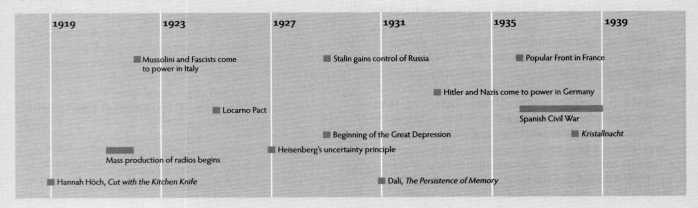

1919	1923	1927	1931	1935	1939
	Mussolini and Fascists come to power in Italy	Stalin gains control of Russia		Popular Front in France	
			Hitler and Nazis come to power in Germany		
	Locarno Pact			Spanish Civil War	
		Beginning of the Great Depression		Kristallnacht	
		Heisenberg's uncertainty principle			
Mass production of radios begins					
Hannah Höch, Cut with the Kitchen Knife		Dali, The Persistence of Memory			

CHAPTER REVIEW

Upon Reflection

Q What were the causes of the Great Depression, and how did European states respond to it?

Q What were Hitler's ideas, and how did he implement them once he and the Nazis had established the Nazi state in Germany?

Q How do the cultural and intellectual trends of the 1920s and 1930s reflect a crisis of confidence in Western civilization?

Key Terms

fascism (p. 797)
civil disobedience (p. 800)
totalitarian states (p. 801)
propaganda (p. 801)
squadristi (p. 802)
Lebensraum (p. 806)
Führerprinzip (p. 807)

New Economic Policy (p. 812)
authoritarian state (p. 814)
Dadaism (p. 820)
Surrealism (p. 820)
functionalism (p. 821)
uncertainty principle (p. 824)

Suggestions for Further Reading

GENERAL WORKS   For a general introduction to the interwar period, see **M. Kitchen, *Europe Between the Wars: A Political History*,** 2nd ed. (London, 2006). On the Great Depression, see **C. P. Kindleberger, *The World in Depression, 1929–39*,** rev. ed. (Berkeley, Calif., 1986).

THE DEMOCRATIC STATES   On Great Britain, see **R. Overy, *The Twilight Years: The Paradox of Britain Between the Wars*** (New York, 2009). France is covered in **A. P. Adamthwaite, *Grandeur and Misery: France's Bid for Power in Europe, 1914–1940*** (London, 1995). On Weimar Germany, see **E. D. Weitz, *Weimar Germany: Promise and Tragedy*** (Princeton, 2013).

FASCISM AND FASCIST ITALY   For general studies of fascist movements, see **R. O. Paxton, *The Anatomy of Fascism*** (New York, 2004). The best biography of Mussolini is **R. J. B. Bosworth, *Mussolini*** (London, 2002). On Fascist Italy, see **R. J. B. Bosworth, *Mussolini's Italy: Life Under the Fascist Dictatorship*** (New York, 2006).

NAZI GERMANY   A brief but sound survey of Nazi Germany is **J. J. Spielvogel** and **D. Redles, *Hitler and Nazi Germany: A History*,** 7th ed. (Upper Saddle River, N.J., 2014). A more detailed examination can be found in the three-volume history of Nazi Germany by **R. J. Evans: *The Coming***

of the Third Reich (New York, 2004), ***The Third Reich in Power: 1933–1939*** (New York, 2005), and ***The Third Reich at War*** (New York, 2009). The best biography of Hitler is **I. Kershaw, *Hitler, 1889–1936: Hubris*** (New York, 1999), and ***Hitler: Nemesis*** (New York, 2000).

THE STALINIST ERA   On Stalin, see **R. Service, *Stalin: A Biography*** (Cambridge, Mass., 2006). On everyday life in the Stalinist era, see **S. Fitzpatrick, *Everyday Stalinism*** (Oxford, 1999).

AUTHORITARIAN STATES   Starting points for the study of eastern Europe are **I. T. Berend, *Decades of Crisis: Central and Eastern Europe before World War II*** (Berkeley, Calif., 2001), and **J. R. Lampe, *Balkans into Southeastern Europe: A Century of War and Transition*** (London, 2006).

SOCIETY AND CULTURE   The use of cinema for propaganda purposes is well examined in **D. Welch, *Propaganda and the German Cinema*** (New York, 1985). Gender issues are discussed in **S. Petersen, *Family, Dependence, and the Origins of the Welfare State: Britain and France, 1914–1945*** (New York, 1994). On the cultural and intellectual environment of Weimar Germany, see **R. Metzger** and **C. Brandstetter, *Berlin: The Twenties*** (New York, 2007).

Notes

1. Quoted in S. Audoin-Rouzeau and A. Becker, *14–18: Understanding the Great War*, trans. Catherine Temerson (New York, 2002), pp. 212–213.
2. Quoted in ibid., p. 41.
3. Quoted in R. Paxton, *Europe in the Twentieth Century*, 2nd ed. (New York, 1985), p. 237.
4. Quoted in D. M. Smith, *Mussolini* (New York, 1982), p. 51.
5. Benito Mussolini, "The Doctrine of Fascism," in A. Lyttleton, ed., *Italian Fascisms from Pareto to Gentile* (London, 1973), p. 42.
6. Quoted in A. D. Grand, "Women Under Italian Fascism," *Historical Journal* 19 (1976): 958–959.
7. Adolf Hitler, *Mein Kampf*, trans. R. Manheim (Boston, 1943), p. 22.

8. Ibid., p. 161.

9. Quoted in J. Fest, *Hitler*, trans. R. Winston and C. Winston (New York, 1974), p. 241.

10. Quoted in J. Noakes and G. Pridham, eds., *Nazism, 1919–1945, A Documentary Reader*, vol. 1: *The Rise to Power 1919–1934* (Exeter, U.K., 1983), pp. 50–51.

11. Quoted in J. J. Spielvogel and D. Redles, *Hitler and Nazi Germany: A History*, 6th ed. (Upper Saddle River, N.J., 2010), p. 83.

12. I. Howe, ed., *The Basic Writings of Trotsky* (London, 1963), p. 162.

13. Quoted in S. Fitzpatrick, *Everyday Stalinism. Ordinary Life in Extraordinary Times: Soviet Russia in the 1930s* (New York, 1999), p. 87.

14. Quoted in H. Salmi, *Nineteenth-Century Europe: A Cultural History* (Cambridge, 2008), p. 105.

15. Paul Valéry, *Variety*, trans. M. Cowley (New York, 1927), pp. 27–28.

16. Quoted in M. Eberle, *World War I and the Weimar Artists: Dix, Grosz, Beckmann, Schlemmer* (New Haven, Conn., 1985), p. 54.

17. N. H. Baynes, ed., *The Speeches of Adolf Hitler, 1922–1939* (Oxford, 1942), vol. 1, p. 591.

MindTap®

MindTap® is a fully online, highly personalized learning experience built upon Cengage Learning content. MindTap combines student learning tools—readings, multimedia, activities, and assessments—into a singular Learning Path that guides students through the course.

THE DEEPENING OF THE EUROPEAN CRISIS: WORLD WAR II

Adolf Hitler salutes soldiers marching in Nuremberg during the party rally in 1938

Hugo Jaeger/Time Life Pictures/Getty Images

CHAPTER OUTLINE AND FOCUS QUESTIONS

Prelude to War (1933–1939)

Q What were Hitler's foreign policy goals, and what steps did he take to achieve them between 1933 and 1939? How did Japan's policies lead to war in Asia?

The Course of World War II

Q What were the major events of World War II in Europe and in Asia, and why were the Allies ultimately victorious?

The New Order

Q How was the Nazi empire organized? What was the Holocaust, and what was the relationship between Hitler's worldview, his foreign policy, and the Holocaust?

The Home Front

Q What were conditions like on the home front for Japan and the major Western nations involved in World War II?

Aftermath of the War

Q What were the costs of World War II? How did the Allies' visions of postwar Europe differ, and how did these differences contribute to the emergence of the Cold War?

Critical Thinking

Q What was the relationship between World War I and World War II, and how did the ways in which the wars were fought differ?

Connections to Today

Q In what ways are the results of World War II still having an impact today?

ON FEBRUARY 3, 1933, only four days after he had been appointed chancellor of Germany, Adolf Hitler met secretly with Germany's leading generals. He revealed to them his desire to remove the "cancer of democracy," create a new authoritarian leadership, and forge a new domestic unity. All Germans would need to realize that "only a struggle can save us and that everything else must be subordinated to this idea." Youth especially must be trained and their wills strengthened "to fight with all means." Since Germany's living space was too small for its people, Hitler said, Germany must rearm and prepare for "the conquest of new living space in the east and its ruthless Germanization."[1] Even before he had consolidated his power, Hitler had a clear vision of his goals, and their implementation meant another European war. World War II was clearly Hitler's war. Although other countries may have helped make the war possible by not resisting Hitler's Germany earlier, it was Nazi Germany's actions that made World War II inevitable.

World War II was more than just Hitler's war, however. This chapter will focus on the European theater of war, but both European and American armies were also involved in fighting around the world. World War II consisted of two conflicts: one provoked by the ambitions of Germany in Europe, the other by the ambitions of Japan in Asia. By 1941, with the involvement of the United States in both wars, the two had merged into one global conflict.

Although World War I has been described as a total war, World War II was even more so and was fought on a scale unknown in history. Almost everyone in the warring countries was involved in one way or another: as soldiers; as workers in wartime industries; as ordinary citizens subject to invading armies, military occupation, or bombing raids; as refugees; or as victims of mass extermination. The world had never witnessed such widespread willful death and destruction.

Prelude to War (1933–1939)

 FOCUS QUESTIONS: What were Hitler's foreign policy goals, and what steps did he take to achieve them between 1933 and 1939? How did Japan's policies lead to war in Asia?

Only twenty years after the "war to end all war," Europe plunged back into the nightmare of total war. The efforts at collective security in the 1920s—the League of Nations, the attempts at disarmament, the pacts and treaties—all proved meaningless in light of the growth of Nazi Germany and its deliberate scrapping of the postwar settlement in the 1930s. Still weary from the last war, France and Britain refused to accept the possibility of another war. The Soviet Union, treated as an outcast by the Western powers, had turned in on itself, and the United States had withdrawn into its traditional isolationism. The small successor states to Austria-Hungary were too weak to oppose Germany. Thus, the power vacuum in the heart of Europe encouraged a revived and militarized Germany to acquire the living space that Hitler claimed Germany needed for its rightful place in the world.

The Role of Hitler

World War II in Europe began in the mind of Adolf Hitler, who believed that only the Aryans were capable of building a great civilization. But to Hitler, the Germans, in his view the leading group of Aryans, were threatened from the east by a large mass of inferior peoples, the Slavs, who had learned to use German weapons and technology. Germany needed more land to support a larger population and be a great power. Hitler was a firm believer in the doctrine of *Lebensraum* (living space), espoused by Karl Haushofer (HOWSS-hoh-fuh), a professor of geography at the University of Munich. The doctrine of *Lebensraum* maintained that a nation's power depended on the amount and kind of land it occupied. Already in the 1920s, in the second volume of *Mein Kampf*, Hitler had indicated where a National Socialist regime would find this land: "And so we National Socialists . . . take up where we broke off six hundred years ago. We stop the endless German movement to the south and west, and turn

our gaze toward the land in the east. . . . If we speak of soil in Europe today, we can primarily have in mind only Russia and her vassal border states."[2]

In Hitler's view, the Russian Revolution had created the conditions for Germany's acquisition of land to its east. Imperial Russia had been strong only because of its German leadership. The seizure of power by the Bolsheviks (who, in Hitler's mind, were Jewish) had left Russia weak and vulnerable. Once it had been conquered, the land of Russia could be resettled by German peasants, and the Slavic population could be used as slave labor to build the Aryan racial state that would dominate Europe for the next thousand years. Hitler's conclusion was clear: Germany must prepare for its inevitable war with the Soviet Union. Hitler's ideas were by no means secret. He had spelled them out in *Mein Kampf*, a book readily available to anyone who wished to read it (see the box on p. 829).

Hitler and the Nazis were neither the first Europeans nor the first Germans to undertake European conquest and world power. A number of elite circles in Germany before World War I had argued that Germany needed to annex lands to its south, east, and west if it wished to compete with the large states and remain a great power. The defeat in World War I destroyed this dream of world power, but the traditional conservative elites in the German military and the Foreign Office supported Hitler's foreign policy until 1937, largely because it accorded with their own desires for German expansion. But, as they realized too late, Nazi policy went far beyond previous German goals. Hitler's desire to create an Aryan racial empire led to slave labor and even mass extermination on a scale that would have been incomprehensible to previous generations of Germans.

Although Hitler had defined his goals, he had no prearranged timetable for achieving them. During his rise to power, he had demonstrated the ability to be both ideologue and opportunist. After 1933, a combination of military and diplomatic situations, organizational chaos in the administration of Germany, and economic pressures, especially after 1936, caused Hitler periodically to take steps that seemed to contradict the foreign policy goals of *Mein Kampf*, but he always returned to his basic ideological plans for racial supremacy and empire. He was certain of one thing: only he had the ability to accomplish these goals, and his fears for his health pushed him to fulfill his mission as quickly as possible. His impatience would become a major cause of his own undoing.

The "Diplomatic Revolution" (1933–1936)

Between 1933 and 1936, Hitler and Nazi Germany achieved a "diplomatic revolution" in Europe. When Hitler became chancellor of Germany on January 30, 1933, Germany's position in Europe seemed weak. The Versailles treaty had created a demilitarized zone on Germany's western border that would allow the French to move into the heavily industrialized parts of Germany in the event of war. To Germany's east, the smaller states, such as Poland and Czechoslovakia, had defensive treaties with France. The Versailles treaty had also limited Germany's army to 100,000 troops with no air and limited naval forces.

HITLER'S FOREIGN POLICY GOALS

ADOLF HITLER WAS A FIRM believer in the geopolitical doctrine of *Lebensraum*, which advocated that nations must find sufficient living space to be strong. This idea was evident in *Mein Kampf*, but it was explained in even more detail in a treatise that Hitler wrote in 1928. It was not published in his lifetime.

Hitler's *Secret Book*, 1928

I have already dealt with Germany's various foreign policy possibilities in this book. Nevertheless I shall once more briefly present the possible foreign policy goals so that they may yield a basis for the critical examination of the relations of these individual foreign policy aims to those of other European states.

1. Germany can renounce setting a foreign policy goal altogether. This means that in reality she can decide for anything and need be committed to nothing at all. . . . [Hitler rejects this alternative.]
2. Germany desires to effect the sustenance of the German people by peaceful economic means, as up to now. Accordingly even in the future she will participate most decisively in world industry, export and trade. . . . From a folkish standpoint setting this foreign policy aim is calamitous, and it is madness from the point of view of power politics.
3. Germany establishes the restoration of the borders of the year 1914 as her foreign policy aim. This goal is insufficient from a national standpoint, unsatisfactory from a military point of view, impossible from a folkish standpoint with its eye on the future, and mad from the viewpoint of its consequences. . . .
4. Germany decides to go over to a clear, far-seeing territorial policy. Thereby she abandons all attempts at world-industry and world-trade and instead concentrates all her strength in order, through the allotment of sufficient living space for the next hundred years to our people, also to prescribe a path of life. Since this territory can be only in the East, the obligation to be a naval power also recedes into the background. Germany tries anew to champion her interests through the formation of a decisive power on land.

This aim is equally in keeping with the highest national as well as folkish requirements. It likewise presupposes great military power means for its execution, but does not necessarily bring Germany into conflict with all European great powers. As surely as France here will remain Germany's enemy, just as little does the nature of such a political aim contain a reason for England, and especially for Italy, to maintain the enmity of the World War.

 According to Hitler, what were Germany's possible foreign policy goals? Which one did Hitler prefer? Why? What were the consequences of his decisions in this realm?

Source: Adolf Hitler, *Hitler's Secret Book* (New York: Grove Press, 1961).

The Germans were not without advantages, however. Germany was the most populous European state after the Soviet Union and still possessed a great industrial capacity. Hitler was also well aware that Great Britain and France, dismayed by the costs and losses of World War I, wanted to avoid another war. Hitler knew that France posed a threat to an unarmed Germany, but he believed that if he could keep the French from acting against Germany in his first years, he could remove the restrictions imposed on Germany by Versailles and restore its strength.

Hitler's ability to rearm Germany and fulfill his expansionist policies depended initially on whether he could convince others that his intentions were peaceful. Posing as a man of peace in his public speeches, Hitler emphasized that Germany wished only to revise the unfair provisions of Versailles by peaceful means and achieve Germany's rightful place among the European states. During his first two years in office, Hitler pursued a prudent foreign policy without unnecessary risks. His dramatic action in October 1933, when he withdrew Germany from the Geneva Disarmament Conference and the League of Nations, was done primarily for domestic political reasons, to give the Germans the feeling that their country was no longer dominated by other European states.

GERMAN REARMAMENT By the beginning of 1935, Hitler had become convinced that Germany could break some of the provisions of the Treaty of Versailles without serious British and French opposition. Hitler had come to believe, based on their responses to his early actions, that both states wanted to maintain the international status quo, but without using force. Consequently, he decided to announce publicly what had been going on secretly for some time—Germany's military rearmament. On March 9, 1935, Hitler announced the creation of a new air force and, one week later, the introduction of a military draft that would expand Germany's army from 100,000 to 550,000 troops.

Hitler's unilateral repudiation of the disarmament clauses of the Versailles treaty brought a swift reaction as France, Great Britain, and Italy condemned Germany's action and warned against future aggressive steps. But nothing concrete was done. Even worse, Britain subsequently moved toward open acceptance of Germany's right to rearm when it agreed to the Anglo-German Naval Pact on June 18, 1935. This treaty allowed Germany to build a navy that would be 35 percent of the size of the British navy, with equality in submarines. The British were starting a policy of **appeasement**, based on the belief that if European states satisfied the reasonable demands of dissatisfied powers, the latter would be content, and stability and peace would be achieved in Europe. British appeasement was grounded in large part on Britain's desire to avoid another war, but British statesmen who believed that Nazi Germany offered a powerful bulwark against Soviet communism also fostered it.

OCCUPATION OF THE RHINELAND In March 7, 1936, buoyed by his conviction that the Western democracies had no intention of using force to maintain all aspects of the Treaty of Versailles, Hitler sent German troops into the demilitarized Rhineland. According to the Versailles treaty, the French had the right to use force against any violation of the demilitarized Rhineland. But France would not act without British support, and the British viewed the occupation of German territory by German troops as another reasonable action by a dissatisfied power. The London *Times* noted that the Germans were only "going into their own back garden." The French and British response only reinforced Hitler's growing conviction that they were weak nations unwilling to use force to defend the old order. At the same time, since the German generals had opposed his plan, Hitler became even more convinced of his own superior abilities. Many Germans expressed fresh enthusiasm for a leader who was restoring German honor.

NEW ALLIANCES Meanwhile, Hitler gained new allies. In October 1935, Benito Mussolini had committed Fascist Italy to imperial expansion by invading Ethiopia. Angered by French and British opposition to his invasion, Mussolini welcomed Hitler's support and began to draw closer to the German dictator he had once called a buffoon. The joint intervention of Germany and Italy on behalf of General Francisco Franco in the Spanish Civil War in 1936 also drew the two nations closer together. In October 1936, Mussolini and Hitler concluded an agreement that recognized their common political and economic interests, and one month later, Mussolini referred publicly to the new Rome-Berlin Axis. Also in November 1936, Germany and Japan (the rising military power in the East) concluded the Anti-Comintern Pact and agreed to maintain a common front against communism.

By the end of 1936, Hitler and Nazi Germany had achieved a "diplomatic revolution" in Europe. The Treaty of Versailles had been virtually scrapped, and Germany was once more a "world power," as Hitler proclaimed. Hitler had demonstrated a great deal of diplomatic skill in taking advantage of Europeans' burning desire for peace. He had used the tactic of peaceful revision as skillfully as he had used the tactic of legality in his pursuit of power in Germany. By the end of 1936, Nazi power had increased enough that Hitler could initiate an even more daring foreign policy. As Hitler perceived, if the Western states were so afraid of war that they resisted its use when they were strong and Germany was weak, then they would be even more reluctant to do so now that Germany was strong. Although many Europeans still wanted to believe that Hitler desired peace, his moves had actually made war more possible.

The Path to War in Europe (1937–1939)

On November 5, 1937, at a secret conference with his military leaders in Berlin, Adolf Hitler revealed his future aims. Germany's ultimate goal, he assured his audience, must be the conquest of living space in the east. Although this might mean war with France and Great Britain, Germany had no alternative if the basic needs of the German people were to be met. First, however, Germany must deal with Austria and Czechoslovakia and secure its eastern and southern flanks.

ONGOING REARMAMENT In the meantime, Hitler had continued Germany's rearmament at an ever-quickening pace. Expenditures on rearmament rose dramatically: in 1933, 1 billion Reichsmarks; in 1935, 5 billion; in 1937, 9.5 billion; and in 1939, 30 billion. Important to rearmament was the planning for a new type of warfare known as **blitzkrieg** (BLITZ-kreeg), or "lightning war." Hitler and some of his military commanders wanted to avoid the trench warfare of World War I and conceived a lightning warfare that depended on mechanized columns and massive air power to cut quickly across battle lines and encircle and annihilate entire armies. Blitzkrieg meant the quick defeat of an enemy and also determined much of Hitler's rearmament program: the construction of a large air force—the Luftwaffe (LOOFT-vahf-uh)—and immense numbers of tanks and armored trucks to carry infantry. The tanks, mechanized infantry, and mobile artillery formed the new strike forces called panzer divisions that, with air force support, would lead the blitzkrieg attack (each **panzer division** consisted of about three hundred tanks with accompanying forces and supplies). At the same time, the number of men in the German armed services rose from 550,000 in 1935 to 4.5 million in 1939. Naval rearmament also proceeded after the Anglo-German Naval Pact of 1935.

UNION WITH AUSTRIA By the end of 1937, Hitler was convinced that neither the French nor the British would provide much opposition to his plans. Neville Chamberlain (1869–1940), who had become prime minister of Britain in May 1937, was a strong advocate of appeasement and believed that the survival of the British Empire depended on an accommodation with Germany. Chamberlain had made it known to Hitler in November 1937 that he would not oppose changes in central Europe, provided that they were executed peacefully.

Hitler decided to move first on Austria. By threatening Austria with invasion, Hitler coerced the Austrian chancellor, Kurt von Schuschnigg (SHOOSH-nik) (1897–1977), into putting an Austrian Nazi in charge of the government. When German troops marched unopposed into Austria on March 12, 1938, they did so on the "legal basis" of the new Austrian

Hitler Arrives in Vienna. By threatening to invade Austria, Hitler forced the Austrian government to capitulate to his wishes. Austria was annexed to Germany. Shown here is the triumphal arrival of Hitler in Vienna on March 13, 1938. Sitting in the car beside Hitler is Arthur Seyss-Inquart, Hitler's new handpicked governor of Austria.

chancellor's request for German troops to assist in establishing law and order. One day later, on March 13, after his triumphal return to his native land, Hitler formally annexed Austria to Germany. Great Britain's ready acknowledgment of Hitler's action and France's inability to respond due to a political crisis only increased the German dictator's contempt for Western weakness.

The annexation of Austria improved Germany's strategic position in central Europe and put Germany in position for Hitler's next objective, the destruction of Czechoslovakia (see Map 27.1). On May 30, 1938, Hitler had already told his generals that it was his "unalterable decision to smash Czechoslovakia by military action in the near future."[3] This goal might have seemed unrealistic since democratic Czechoslovakia was quite prepared to defend itself and was well supported by pacts with France and Soviet Russia. Nevertheless, Hitler believed that France and Britain would not use force to defend Czechoslovakia.

CZECHOSLOVAKIA In the meantime, Hitler had stepped up his demands on the Czechs. Initially, the Germans had asked for autonomy for the Sudetenland (soo-DAY-tun-land), the mountainous northwestern border area of Czechoslovakia that was home to 3 million ethnic Germans. As Hitler knew, the Sudetenland also contained Czechoslovakia's most important frontier defenses and considerable industrial resources as well. But on September 15, 1938, Hitler demanded the cession of the Sudetenland to Germany and expressed his willingness to risk "world war" to achieve his objective. By that time, Hitler was convinced that France and Britain would not use force to defend Czechoslovakia. On paper, the Czech republic seemed well protected by a pact with France. Yet the French

made it clear that they would act only if the British supported them. The British refused to do so, and on September 29, at the hastily arranged Munich Conference, the British, French, Germans, and Italians (neither the Czechs nor the Russians were invited) reached an agreement that essentially met all of Hitler's demands. German troops were allowed to occupy the Sudetenland as the Czechs, abandoned by their Western allies, stood by helplessly. The Munich Conference was the high point of Western appeasement of Hitler. When Chamberlain returned to England from Munich, he boasted that the Munich agreement meant "peace for our time." Hitler had promised Chamberlain that he had made his last demand; all other European problems could be settled by negotiation. Like many German politicians, Chamberlain had believed Hitler's assurances (see the box "Opposing Viewpoints" on p. 833).

In fact, Munich confirmed Hitler's perception that the Western democracies were weak and would not fight. Increasingly, Hitler was convinced of his own infallibility, and he had by no means been satisfied at Munich. Already at the end of October 1938, Hitler told his generals to prepare for the final liquidation of the Czechoslovakian state. Using the internal disorder that he had deliberately fostered as a pretext, Hitler occupied the Czech lands (Bohemia and Moravia) while the Slovaks, with Hitler's encouragement, declared their independence from the Czechs and became a puppet state (Slovakia) of Nazi Germany. On the evening of March 15, 1939, Hitler triumphantly declared in Prague that he would be known as the greatest German of them all.

POLAND At last, the Western states reacted vigorously to Hitler's threat. After all, the Czechs were not Germans crying

MAP 27.1 **Changes in Central Europe, 1936–1939.** Hitler's main objectives in the late 1930s were the reoccupation of the Rhineland, the incorporation into a greater Germany of lands that contained German people (Austria and the Sudetenland), and the acquisition of *Lebensraum* (living space) in eastern Europe for the expansion of the German people.

Q *What aspects of Czechoslovakia's location would have made it difficult for France and Britain to come directly to its aid in 1938?*

Legend:

Germany

Italy

German advances:

Reoccupied Rhineland, March 1936

Annexed Albania, April 1939

Annexed Austria, March 1938

Annexed Sudetenland, October 1938

Poland and Hungary Annexed Czech territory, 1938 and 1939

Occupied Bohemia and Moravia, March 1939

( ) Former independent nations: Albania, Austria, and Czechoslovakia

Annexed Memel, March 1939

---

for reunion with Germany. Hitler's naked aggression made clear that his promises were utterly worthless. When Hitler began to demand the return to Germany of Danzig, which had been made a free city by the Treaty of Versailles to serve as a seaport for Poland, Britain recognized the danger and offered to protect Poland in the event of war. At the same time, both France and Britain, realizing that only the Soviet Union was powerful enough to help contain Nazi aggression, began political and military negotiations with Joseph Stalin and the Soviets. The West's distrust of Soviet communism, however, made an alliance unlikely.

Meanwhile, Hitler pressed on in the belief that the West would not really fight over Poland. He ordered his generals to prepare for the invasion of Poland on September 1, 1939.

The Munich Conference: Two Views

AT THE MUNICH CONFERENCE, the leaders of France and Great Britain capitulated to Hitler's demands on Czechoslovakia. Although the British prime minister, Neville Chamberlain, defended his actions at Munich as necessary for peace, another British statesman, Winston Churchill, characterized the settlement at Munich as "a disaster of the first magnitude."

Winston Churchill, Speech to the House of Commons, October 5, 1938

I will begin by saying what everybody would like to ignore or forget but which must nevertheless be stated, namely, that we have sustained a total and unmitigated defeat, and that France has suffered even more than we have. . . . The utmost my right honorable Friend the Prime Minister . . . has been able to gain for Czechoslovakia and in the matters which were in dispute has been that the German dictator, instead of snatching his victuals from the table, has been content to have them served to him course by course. . . . And I will say this, that I believe the Czechs, left to themselves and told they were going to get no help from the Western Powers, would have been able to make better terms than they have got. . . .

We are in the presence of a disaster of the first magnitude which has befallen Great Britain and France. Do not let us blind ourselves to that. . . .

And do not suppose that this is the end. This is only the beginning of the reckoning. This is only the first sip, the first foretaste of a bitter cup which will be proffered to us year by year unless by a supreme recovery of moral health and martial vigor, we arise again and take our stand for freedom as in the olden time.

Neville Chamberlain, Speech to the House of Commons, October 6, 1938

That is my answer to those who say that we should have told Germany weeks ago that, if her army crossed the border of Czechoslovakia, we should be at war with her. We had no treaty obligations and no legal obligations to Czechoslovakia. . . . When we were convinced, as we became convinced, that nothing any longer would keep the Sudetenland within the Czechoslovakian State, we urged the Czech Government as strongly as we could to agree to the cession of territory, and to agree promptly. . . . It was a hard decision for anyone who loved his country to take, but to accuse us of having by that advice betrayed the Czechoslovakian State is simply preposterous. What we did was to save her from annihilation and give her a chance of new life as a new State, which involves the loss of territory and fortifications, but may perhaps enable her to enjoy in the future and develop a national existence under a neutrality and security comparable to that which we see in Switzerland today. Therefore, I think the Government deserve the approval of this House for their conduct of affairs in this recent crisis which has saved Czechoslovakia from destruction and Europe from Armageddon.

 What were the opposing views of Churchill and Chamberlain on the Munich Conference? Why did they disagree so much? With whom do you agree? Why?

Sources: Winston Churchill, Speech to the House of Commons, October 5, 1938, in *Parliamentary Debates, House of Commons* (London: His Majesty's Stationery Office, 1938), vol. 339, pp. 361–369; Neville Chamberlain, Speech to the House of Commons, October 6, 1938, in *In Search of Peace* (New York: Putnam, 1939), pp. 213–215, 217.

To preclude an alliance between the West and the Soviet Union, which would create the danger of a two-front war, Hitler, ever the opportunist, negotiated his own nonaggression pact with Stalin and shocked the world with its announcement on August 23, 1939. A secret protocol to the treaty created German and Soviet spheres of influence in eastern Europe: Finland, the Baltic states of Estonia and Latvia, and eastern Poland would go to the Soviet Union, while Germany would acquire western Poland. The treaty with the Soviet Union gave Hitler the freedom to attack Poland. He told his generals: "Now Poland is in the position in which I wanted her. . . . I am only afraid that at the last moment some swine or other will yet submit to me a plan for mediation."[4] He need not have worried. On September 1, German forces invaded Poland; two days later, Britain and France declared war on Germany. Two weeks later, on September 17, Germany's newfound ally, the Soviet Union, sent its troops into eastern Poland. Europe was again at war.

The Path to War in Asia

The war in Asia arose from the ambitions of Japan, whose rise to the status of world power had been swift. Japan had defeated China in 1895 and Russia in 1905 and had taken over many of Germany's eastern and Pacific colonies in World War I. By 1933, the Japanese Empire included Korea, Formosa (Taiwan), Manchuria, and the Marshall, Caroline, and Mariana Islands in the Pacific.

By the early 1930s, Japan was experiencing severe internal tensions. Its population had exploded from 30 million in 1870 to 80 million by 1937. Much of Japan's ability to feed its population and to pay for industrial raw materials depended on the manufacture of heavy industrial goods (especially ships) and

Hitler Declares War. Adolf Hitler believed that it was necessary for Germany to gain living space through conquest in the east. This policy meant war. Hitler's nonaggression pact with the Soviet Union on August 23, 1939, paved the way for his invasion of Poland on September 1. On that day, Hitler spoke to the German Reichstag and announced the outbreak of war.

JAPANESE GOALS IN EAST ASIA In September 1931, Japanese soldiers had seized Manchuria, an area of northeastern China that had natural resources Japan needed. Eventually, after worldwide protests against the seizure, the League of Nations condemned Japan's action, which caused Japan to withdraw from the League. During the next several years, Japan consolidated its hold on Manchuria, which it renamed Manchukuo (man-CHOO-kwoh), and then began to expand its control in North China. By the mid-1930s, militant elements connected with the government and the armed forces were effectively in control of Japanese politics.

For the moment, the prime victim of Tokyo's militant strategy was China. When clashes between Chinese and Japanese troops broke out, the Chinese Nationalist leader, Chiang Kai-shek (CHANG ky-SHEK) (1887–1975), sought to appease Tokyo by granting Japan the authority to administer areas in North China. But as Japan moved steadily southward, popular protests in Chinese cities against Japanese aggression intensified. When Chinese and Japanese forces clashed at the Marco Polo Bridge, south of Beijing, in July 1937, China refused to apologize, and hostilities spread.

Japan had not planned to declare war on China, but neither side would compromise, and the 1937 incident eventually turned into a major conflict. The Japanese advanced up the Yangtze valley and seized the Chinese capital of Nanjing (nan-JING), raping and killing thousands of innocent civilians in the process. But Chiang Kai-shek refused to capitulate and moved his government upriver to Hankou (HAHN-kow). Japanese strategists had hoped to force Chiang to join a Japanese-dominated new order in East Asia, comprising Japan, Manchuria, and China. This aim was part of a larger plan to seize Soviet Siberia with its rich resources and create a new "Monroe Doctrine for Asia," in which Japan would guide its Asian neighbors on the path to development and prosperity.

During the late 1930s, Japan began to cooperate with Nazi Germany on the assumption that the two countries would ultimately launch a joint attack on the Soviet Union and divide up its resources between them. But when Germany surprised the world by signing a nonaggression pact with the Soviets in August 1939, Japanese strategists were compelled to reevaluate their long-term objectives. Japan was not strong enough to defeat the Soviet Union alone, so the Japanese began to shift their gaze southward to the vast resources of Southeast Asia—the oil of the Dutch East Indies, the rubber and tin of Malaya, and the rice of Burma and Indochina.

A move southward, of course, would risk war with the European colonial powers, especially Britain and France, as well as with the other rising power in the Pacific, the United States.

textiles. But in the 1930s, Western nations established tariff barriers to protect their own economies from the effects of the depression. Japan was devastated, both economically and politically.

Although political power had been concentrated in the hands of the emperor and his cabinet, Japan had also experienced a slow growth of political democracy with universal male suffrage in 1924 and the emergence of mass political parties. The economic crises of the 1930s stifled this democratic growth. Right-wing patriotic societies allied themselves with the army and navy to push a program of expansion at the expense of China and the Soviet Union, while the navy hoped to make Japan self-sufficient in raw materials by conquering British Malaya and the Dutch East Indies. In 1935, Japan began to construct a modern naval fleet, and after 1936, the armed forces exercised much influence over the government.

A Japanese Victory March in China. After consolidating its authority over Manchuria, Japan began to expand into northern China. Direct hostilities between Japanese and Chinese forces began in 1937. This photograph shows a Japanese victory march in Shanghai at the beginning of December 1937. By 1939, Japan had conquered most of eastern China.

CHRONOLOGY	Prelude to War, 1933–1939
Japan seizes Manchuria	September 1931
Hitler becomes chancellor	January 30, 1933
Hitler announces a German air force	March 9, 1935
Hitler announces military conscription	March 16, 1935
Anglo-German Naval Pact	June 18, 1935
Mussolini invades Ethiopia	October 1935
Hitler occupies demilitarized Rhineland	March 7, 1936
Mussolini and Hitler intervene in the Spanish Civil War	1936
Rome-Berlin Axis	October 1936
Anti-Comintern Pact (Japan and Germany)	November 1936
Japan invades China	1937
Germany annexes Austria	March 13, 1938
Munich Conference: Germany occupies Sudetenland	September 29, 1938
Germany occupies the rest of Czechoslovakia	March 1939
German-Soviet Nonaggression Pact	August 23, 1939
Germany invades Poland	September 1, 1939
Britain and France declare war on Germany	September 3, 1939
Soviet Union invades Poland	September 17, 1939

When the Japanese took military control of southern Vietnam in July 1941, the Americans responded by cutting off sales of vital scrap iron and oil to Japan. Japan's military leaders decided to preempt any further American response by attacking the American naval fleet in the Pacific.

The Course of World War II

FOCUS QUESTION: What were the major events of World War II in Europe and in Asia, and why were the Allies ultimately victorious?

Nine days before he attacked Poland, Hitler made clear to his generals what was expected of them: "When starting and waging a war it is not right that matters, but victory. Close your hearts to pity. Act brutally. Eighty million people must obtain what is their right. . . . The wholesale destruction of Poland is the military objective. Speed is the main thing. Pursuit until complete annihilation."[5] Hitler's remarks set the tone for what became the most destructive war in human history.

Victory and Stalemate

Unleashing an early form of blitzkrieg, or "lightning war," Hitler stunned Europe with the speed and efficiency of the German attack. Moving into Poland with about 1.5 million troops from two fronts, German forces used panzer divisions, or armored columns, supported by airplanes to break quickly through the Polish lines and encircle the outnumbered and poorly equipped Polish armies. The coordinated air and ground assaults included the use of Stuka dive bombers; as they descended from the skies, their sirens emitted a blood-curdling shriek, adding a frighteningly destructive element to the German attack. Regular infantry units, still on foot with their supplies drawn by horses, then marched in to hold the newly conquered territory. Soon afterward, Soviet military forces attacked eastern Poland. Within four weeks, Poland had surrendered. On September 28, 1939, Germany and the Soviet Union officially divided Poland between them.

HITLER'S ATTACK IN THE WEST Although Hitler's hopes of avoiding a war in the west were dashed when France and Britain declared war on September 3, he was confident that he could control the situation. Expecting another war of attrition and economic blockade, Britain and France refused to go on the offensive. Between 1930 and 1935, France had built a series of concrete and steel fortifications armed with heavy artillery—known as the Maginot (MA-zhi-noh) Line—along its border with Germany. Now France was quite happy to remain in its defensive shell.

After a winter of waiting (called the "phony war"), Hitler resumed the war on April 9, 1940, with another blitzkrieg, this time against Denmark and Norway. The invasion of Norway was dramatic; the Nazis landed troops at key positions along the coast and dropped paratroopers into airfields and major cities. The British landed a force of almost 50,000 troops but were eventually driven out. Norway surrendered on June 9, and Germany's northern flank was now secure.

One month later, on May 10, the Germans launched their attack on the Netherlands, Belgium, and France. The Netherlands fell in five days. Bombing devastated the Dutch city of Rotterdam, which quickly became a symbol of ruthless Nazi destruction of civilian life. The German forces pushed into Belgium as if to move into France as they had done in World War I, but this was only a trick. The Germans now unleashed their main assault through Luxembourg and the Ardennes, a move that was completely unexpected by the French and British forces. German panzer divisions broke through the weak French defensive positions there, outflanking the Maginot Line, raced across northern France, and reached the English Channel on May 21, splitting the Allied armies. The main Belgian army surrendered on May 28, and the other British and French forces were trapped at Dunkirk. At this point Hitler stopped the advance of the German armored units and ordered the Luftwaffe (the German air force) to destroy the Allied army on the beaches of Dunkirk. The Luftwaffe was ineffective in bombing the Allied forces, however, and by the time Hitler ordered his armored units to advance again, the British had rebuilt their defenses sufficiently to allow for a gigantic evacuation of 350,000 French and British troops by a fleet of small ships. The "miracle of Dunkirk" saved a well-trained army to fight another day.

On June 5, the Germans launched another offensive into southern France. Five days later, Benito Mussolini, believing that the war was over and eager to grab some of the spoils, declared war on France and invaded from the south. Dazed by the speed of the German offensive, the French were never able to mount an adequate resistance and surrendered on June 22. German armies occupied about three-fifths of France while the French hero of World War I, Marshal Henri Pétain (AHN-ree pay-TANH) (1856–1951), established an authoritarian regime—known as Vichy (VISH-ee) France—over the remainder. The Allies regarded the Pétain government as a Nazi puppet state, and a French government-in-exile took up residence in Britain. Germany was now in control of western and central Europe, but Britain still had not been defeated.

THE PROBLEM OF BRITAIN The German victories in Denmark and Norway had led to a change of government in Britain. Growing dissatisfaction with the apostle of appeasement, Neville Chamberlain, led a member of his own party to say to the prime minister, "You have sat too long for any good you have been doing. Depart, I say, and let us have done with you. In the name of God go!"[6] Chamberlain resigned, and on May 10, 1940, Winston Churchill (1874–1965), a longtime advocate of a hardline policy toward Nazi Germany, became prime minister. Churchill was confident that he could guide Britain to ultimate victory. He later wrote that he thought he knew a great deal about it all "and I was sure I should not fail." Churchill proved to be an inspiring leader who rallied the British people with stirring speeches. Hitler had hoped that the British could be persuaded to make peace so that he could fulfill his long-awaited opportunity to gain living space in the east. Led by the stubbornly determined Churchill, who believed there could be no compromise with Nazism, the British refused, and Hitler was forced to prepare for an invasion of Britain, a prospect that he faced with little confidence.

As Hitler realized, an amphibious invasion of Britain would be possible only if Germany gained control of the air. By August 1940, the Luftwaffe had launched a major offensive against British air and naval bases, harbors, communication centers, and war industries. The British fought back doggedly, supported by an effective radar system that gave them early warning of German attacks. Moreover, the Ultra intelligence operation, which had broken German military codes, gave the British air force information about the specific targets of German air attacks. Nevertheless, the British air force suffered critical losses by the end of August and was probably saved by Hitler's change of strategy. In September, in retaliation for a British attack on Berlin, Hitler ordered a shift from military targets to massive bombing of cities to break British morale. The British rebuilt their air strength quickly and were soon inflicting major losses on Luftwaffe bombers. By the end of September, Germany had lost the Battle of Britain, and the invasion of Britain had to be postponed.

At this point, Hitler pursued the possibility of a Mediterranean strategy, which would involve capturing Egypt and the Suez Canal and closing the Mediterranean to British ships, thereby shutting off Britain's supply of oil. Hitler's commitment to the Mediterranean was never wholehearted, however. His initial plan was to let the Italians, whose role was to secure the Balkan and Mediterranean flanks, defeat the British in North Africa, but this strategy failed when the British routed the Italian army. Although Hitler then sent German troops to the North African theater of war, his primary concern lay elsewhere: he had already decided to fulfill his lifetime obsession with the acquisition of living space in the east.

INVASION OF THE SOVIET UNION Already at the end of July 1940, Hitler had told his army leaders to begin preparations for the invasion of the Soviet Union. Although he had no desire for a two-front war, Hitler became convinced that Britain was remaining in the war only because it expected Soviet support. If the Soviet Union were smashed, Britain's last hope would be eliminated. Moreover, Hitler had convinced himself that the Soviet Union, with its Jewish-Bolshevik leadership and a pitiful army, could be defeated quickly and decisively. Although the invasion of the Soviet Union was scheduled for the spring of 1941, problems in the Balkans delayed the attack.

Hitler had already obtained the political cooperation of Hungary, Bulgaria, and Romania. Mussolini, however, who liked to think of the Balkans as being within the Italian sphere

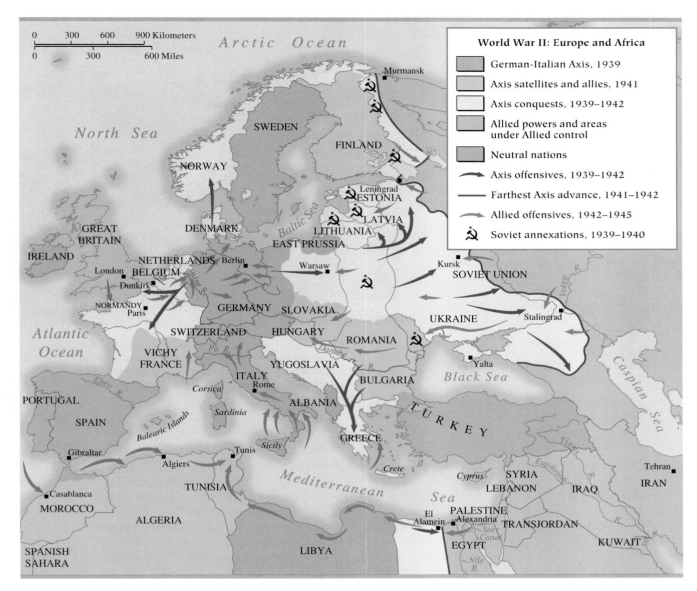

MAP 27.2 World War II in Europe and North Africa. With its fast and effective military, Germany quickly overwhelmed much of western Europe. Hitler had overestimated his country's capabilities, however, and underestimated those of his foes. By late 1942, his invasion of the Soviet Union was failing, and the United States had become a major factor in the war. The Allies successfully invaded Italy in 1943 and France in 1944.

 Which countries were neutral, and how did geography help make their neutrality an option?

of influence, became considerably upset over Germany's gains in southeastern Europe. To ensure the extension of Italian influence in that region, Mussolini launched an attack on Greece on October 28, 1940. But the Italians were militarily unprepared, and their invasion was quickly stopped. Hitler was furious because the disastrous invasion of Greece exposed his southern flank to British air bases in Greece. To secure his Balkan flank, Hitler first invaded Yugoslavia on April 6, 1941. After its surrender on April 17, he smashed Greece in six days. Now reassured, Hitler turned to the east and invaded the Soviet Union, believing that the Soviets could still be decisively defeated before winter set in.

On June 22, 1941, Nazi Germany launched its attack on the Soviet Union, by far the largest invasion the Germans had yet attempted. The German force consisted of 180 divisions, including 20 panzer divisions, 8,000 tanks, and 3,200 airplanes. German troops were stretched out along an 1,800-mile front (see Map 27.2). The Soviets had 160 infantry divisions but were able to mobilize another 300 divisions out of reserves within half a year. Hitler had badly miscalculated the Soviets' potential power.

The German troops advanced rapidly, capturing 2 million Soviet soldiers. By November, one German army group had swept through Ukraine while a second was besieging Leningrad; a third approached within 25 miles of Moscow, the

German Troops in the Soviet Union. At first, the German attack on the Soviet Union—known as Operation Barbarossa—was enormously successful, leading one German general to remark in his diary that the Russian campaign had been "won in the space of two weeks." These photos show German troops advancing by foot and by tank in the Soviet Union.

Soviet capital. But despite their successes, the Germans had failed to achieve their primary objective. They did not eliminate the Soviet army, nor did the Soviet state collapse in a few months, as Hitler thought it would.

An early winter and unexpected Soviet resistance brought the German advance to a halt. Armor and transport vehicles stalled in temperatures of 30 below zero. Hitler's commanders wished to withdraw and regroup for the following spring, but Hitler refused. Fearing the disintegration of his lines, he insisted that there would be no retreat. A Soviet counterattack in December 1941 by an army supposedly exhausted by Nazi victories came as an ominous ending to the year. Although the Germans managed to hold on and reestablish their lines, a war diary kept by a member of Panzer Group Three described their desperate situation: "Discipline is breaking down. More and more soldiers are heading west on foot without weapons. . . . The road is under constant air attack. Those killed by bombs are no longer being buried. All the hangers-on (cargo troops, Luftwaffe, supply trains) are pouring to the rear in full flight."[7] By December 1941, another of Hitler's decisions—the declaration of war on the United States—had probably made his defeat inevitable and turned another European conflict into a global war.

The War in Asia

On December 7, 1941, Japanese carrier-based aircraft attacked the U.S. naval base at Pearl Harbor in the Hawaiian Islands. The same day, other units launched additional assaults on the Philippines and began advancing toward the British colony of Malaya.

The next day, the United States declared war on Japan. Three days later, Hitler declared war on the United States, although he was by no means required to do so by his loose alliance with Japan. This action enabled President Franklin D. Roosevelt to overcome strong American isolationist sentiment and bring the United States into the European conflict.

Shortly after the American entry into the war, Japanese forces invaded the Dutch East Indies and occupied a number of islands in the Pacific Ocean (see Map 27.3). In some cases, as on the Bataan (buh-TAN or buh-TAHN) peninsula and the island of Corregidor (kuh-REG-ih-dor) in the Philippines, resistance was fierce, but by the spring of 1942, almost all of Southeast Asia and much of the western Pacific had fallen into Japanese hands. Tokyo declared the creation of the Great East Asia Co-Prosperity Sphere, encompassing the entire region under Japanese tutelage, and announced its intention to liberate the colonial areas of Southeast Asia from Western colonial rule. For the moment, however, Japan needed the resources of the region for its war machine and placed the countries under its rule on a wartime basis.

Japanese leaders had hoped that their lightning strike at American bases would destroy the U.S. Pacific Fleet and persuade the Roosevelt administration to accept Japanese domination of the Pacific. In the eyes of Japanese leaders, material indulgence had made the American people soft. But Tokyo had miscalculated. The attack on Pearl Harbor galvanized American opinion and won broad support for Roosevelt's war policy. The United States now joined with European nations and

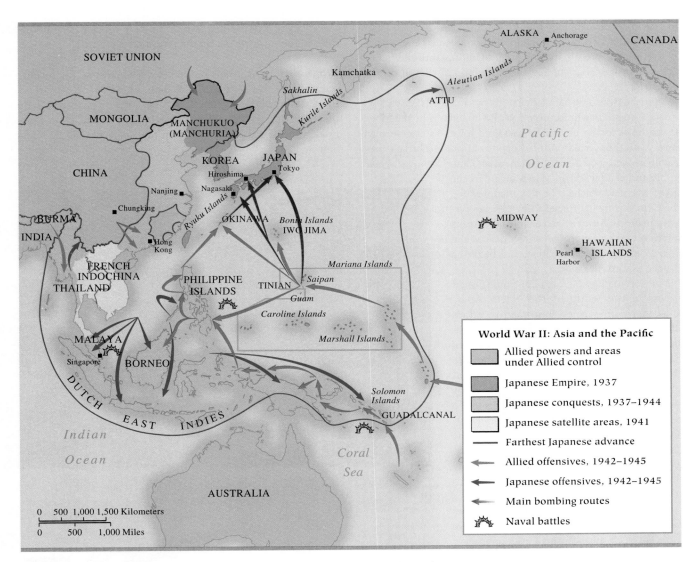

MAP 27.3 World War II in Asia and the Pacific. In 1937, Japan invaded northern China, beginning its effort to create a "Great East Asia Co-Prosperity Sphere." Further Japanese expansion caused the United States to end iron and oil sales to Japan. Deciding that war with the United States was inevitable, Japan engineered a surprise attack on Pearl Harbor.

Q *Why was control of the islands in the western Pacific of great importance both to the Japanese and to the Allies?*

Nationalist China in a combined effort to defeat Japan and bring its hegemony in the Pacific to an end.

The Turning Point of the War (1942–1943)

The entry of the United States into the war created a coalition (the Grand Alliance) that ultimately defeated the Axis powers (Germany, Italy, Japan). Nevertheless, the three major Allies—Britain, the United States, and the Soviet Union—had to overcome mutual suspicions before they could operate as an effective alliance. Two factors aided that process. First, Hitler's declaration of war on the United States made it easier for the Americans to accept the British and Soviet contention that the defeat of Germany should be the first priority of the United

States. For that reason, the United States increased the quantity of trucks, planes, and other arms that it sent to the British and Soviets. Also important to the alliance was the tacit agreement of the three chief Allies to stress military operations while ignoring political differences and larger strategic issues concerning any postwar settlement. At the beginning of 1943, the Allies agreed to fight until the Axis powers surrendered unconditionally. Although this principle of **unconditional surrender** might have discouraged dissident Germans and Japanese from overthrowing their governments in order to arrange a negotiated peace, it also had the effect of cementing the Grand Alliance by making it nearly impossible for Hitler to divide his foes.

Defeat was far from Hitler's mind at the beginning of 1942, however. As Japanese forces advanced into Southeast Asia and the Pacific after crippling the American naval fleet at Pearl Harbor, Hitler and his European allies continued the war in Europe against Britain and the Soviet Union. Until the fall of 1942, it appeared that the Germans might still prevail on the battlefield.

After the British defeat of Italian troops in North Africa, Hitler sent General Erwin Rommel (RAHM-ul), whom he described as "the most daring general of armored forces in the German army," with the German Afrika Korps to Libya in February 1941. Leading a combined force of Germans and Italians, Rommel attacked on March 30 and by the end of May had reached the Egyptian frontier, where he was finally forced to halt. Reinforcements in North Africa in 1942 enabled the Afrika Korps to break though the British defenses in Egypt, capture Tobruk in June, and begin an advance toward Alexandria.

The Germans were also continuing their success in the Battle of the North Atlantic as their submarines continued to attack Allied ships carrying supplies to Great Britain. Although the convoy system reduced ship losses, even convoys were still subject to attack. Hitler had increased the number of submarines from 56 in 1939 to almost 250 by the beginning of 1942. German attacks led to the loss of 4.5 million tons of shipping during the first six months of 1942, causing the British to worry about being forced into submission. Not until the middle of 1943 did the Allies begin to win the Battle of the North Atlantic.

In the spring of 1942, a renewed German offensive in the Soviet Union led to the capture of the entire Crimea, causing Hitler to boast in August 1942:

> As the next step, we are going to advance south of the Caucasus and then help the rebels in Iran and Iraq against the English. Another thrust will be directed along the Caspian Sea toward Afghanistan and India. Then the English will run out of oil. In two years we'll be on the borders of India. Twenty to thirty elite German divisions will do. Then the British Empire will collapse.[8]

But this would be Hitler's last optimistic outburst. By the fall of 1942, the war had turned against the Germans.

In North Africa, British forces had stopped Rommel's troops at El Alamein (ell ah-lah-MAYN) in the summer of 1942 and then forced them back across the desert. In November 1942, British and American forces invaded French North Africa and forced the German and Italian troops to surrender in May 1943. By that time, new detection devices had enabled

the Allies to destroy increasing numbers of German submarines in the shipping war in the Atlantic.

BATTLE OF STALINGRAD On the Eastern Front, the turning point of the war occurred at Stalingrad. After the capture of the Crimea, Hitler's generals wanted him to concentrate on the Caucasus and its oilfields, but Hitler decided that Stalingrad, a major industrial center on the Volga, should be taken first.

The Battle of Stalingrad. The Battle of Stalingrad was a major turning point on the Eastern Front. Shown in the first photograph is a German infantry platoon in the ruins of a tractor factory they had captured in the northern part of Stalingrad. This victory took place on October 15, 1942, at a time when Hitler still believed he was winning the battle for Stalingrad. That belief was soon dashed as a Soviet counteroffensive in November led to a total defeat for the Germans. The second photograph shows thousands of captured soldiers being marched across frozen Soviet soil to prison camps. The soldiers in white fur hats are Romanian. Fewer than 6,000 captured soldiers survived to go home; the remainder—almost 85,000 prisoners—died in captivity.

A GERMAN SOLDIER AT STALINGRAD

THE SOVIET VICTORY AT STALINGRAD was a major turning point in World War II. This excerpt comes from the diary of a German soldier who fought and died in the Battle of Stalingrad. His dreams of victory and a return home with medals were soon dashed by the realities of Soviet resistance.

Diary of a German Soldier

Today, after we'd had a bath, the company commander told us that if our future operations are as successful, we'll soon reach the Volga, take Stalingrad and then the war will inevitably soon be over. Perhaps we'll be home by Christmas.

July 29. The company commander says the Russian troops are completely broken, and cannot hold out any longer. To reach the Volga and take Stalingrad is not so difficult for us. The Führer knows where the Russians' weak point is. Victory is not far away. . . .

August 10. The Führer's orders were read out to us. He expects victory of us. We are all convinced that they can't stop us. . . .

September 4. We are being sent northward along the front toward Stalingrad. We marched all night and by dawn had reached Voroponovo Station. We can already see the smoking town. It's a happy thought that the end of the war is getting nearer. . . .

September 8. Two days of non-stop fighting. The Russians are defending themselves with insane stubbornness. Our regiment has lost many men. . . .

September 16. Our battalion, plus tanks, is attacking the [grain storage] elevator, from which smoke is pouring—the grain in it is burning, the Russians seem to have set light to it themselves. Barbarism. The battalion is suffering heavy losses. . . .

October 10. The Russians are so close to us that our planes cannot bomb them. We are preparing for a decisive attack.

Source: V. Chuikov, *The Battle for Stalingrad* (New York: HarperCollins, 1964).

The Führer has ordered the whole of Stalingrad to be taken as rapidly as possible. . . .

October 22. Our regiment has failed to break into the factory. We have lost many men; every time you move you have to jump over bodies. . . .

November 10. A letter from Elsa today. Everyone expects us home for Christmas. In Germany everyone believes we already hold Stalingrad. How wrong they are. If they could only see what Stalingrad has done to our army. . . .

November 21. The Russians have gone over to the offensive along the whole front. Fierce fighting is going on. So, there it is—the Volga, victory and soon home to our families! We shall obviously be seeing them next in the other world.

November 29. We are encircled. It was announced this morning that the Führer has said: "The army can trust me to do everything necessary to ensure supplies and rapidly break the encirclement."

December 3. We are on hunger rations and waiting for the rescue that the Führer promised. . . .

December 14. Everybody is racked with hunger. Frozen potatoes are the best meal, but to get them out of the ice-covered ground under fire from Russian bullets is not so easy. . . .

December 26. The horses have already been eaten. . . . The soldiers look like corpses or lunatics, looking for something to put in their mouths. They no longer take cover from Russian shells; they haven't the strength to walk, run away and hide. A curse on this war!

 What did this soldier believe about the Führer? Why? What was the source of his information? Why is the battle for Stalingrad considered a major turning point in World War II?

The German advance on Stalingrad encountered fierce resistance, but Hitler was determined to capture the city named after the Soviet dictator. Stalin had issued a war order called "Not a Step Back." Although the Germans destroyed much of the city, the Soviet troops used the bombed-out buildings and factories as well-fortified defensive positions. A deadly and brutal street-by-street conflict evolved during September, October, and November, in which both sides took severe losses. On November 8, Hitler announced that the German Sixth Army had taken Stalingrad, but in fact, on November 19 and 20, the Soviets attacked German positions north and south of Stalingrad, and by November 23 they had surrounded the German forces. Hitler commanded General Friedrich Paulus to stand firm with his Sixth Army and forbade attempts to break out of the encirclement. Winter privations and Soviet attacks,

however, forced the Germans to surrender on February 2, 1943 (see the box above). The entire German Sixth Army of 300,000 men was lost. By February 1943, German forces in the Soviet Union were back to their positions of June 1942. By the spring of 1943, even Hitler knew that the Germans would not defeat the Soviet Union.

BATTLE OF MIDWAY The tide of battle in Asia also turned dramatically in 1942. In the Battle of the Coral Sea on May 7–8, 1942, American naval forces stopped the Japanese advance and temporarily relieved Australia of the threat of invasion. On June 4, at the Battle of Midway Island, American planes destroyed all four of the attacking Japanese aircraft carriers and established American naval superiority in the Pacific. The victory came at a high cost; about two-fifths of the American planes were shot down in the encounter. By the fall of 1942, Allied forces were beginning to gather for offensive operations in three areas: from bases in north Burma and India into the rest of Burma; in the Solomon Islands and on New Guinea, with forces under the direction of American general Douglas MacArthur moving toward the Philippines; and across the Pacific where combined U.S. Army, Marine, and Navy forces would mount attacks against Japanese-held islands. After a series of bitter engagements in the waters off the Solomon Islands from August to November 1942, Japanese fortunes began to fade.

The Last Years of the War

By the beginning of 1943, the tide of battle had turned against Germany, Italy, and Japan, but it would take a long time to achieve the goal of unconditional surrender of the three Axis powers. After the Axis forces had surrendered in Tunisia on May 13, 1943, the Allies crossed the Mediterranean and carried the war to Italy, an area that Winston Churchill had called the "soft underbelly" of Europe. After taking Sicily, Allied troops began the invasion of mainland Italy in September. In the meantime, after the ouster and arrest of Benito Mussolini, a new Italian government offered to surrender to Allied forces. But Mussolini was liberated by the Germans in a daring raid and then set up as the head of a puppet German state in northern Italy while German troops moved in and occupied much of Italy. The new defensive lines established by the Germans in the hills south of Rome were so effective that the Allied advance up the Italian peninsula was a painstaking affair accompanied by heavy casualties. Rome did not fall to the Allies until June 4, 1944. By that time, the Italian war had assumed a secondary role anyway as the Allies opened their long-awaited "second front" in western Europe two days later.

ALLIED ADVANCES IN THE WEST Since the autumn of 1943, the Allies had been planning a cross-channel invasion of France from Britain. A series of Allied deceptions managed to trick the Germans into believing that the invasion would come on the flat plains of northern France. Instead, the Allies, under the direction of the American general Dwight D. Eisenhower (1890–1969), landed five assault divisions on the Normandy beaches on June 6 in history's greatest amphibious invasion. Three airborne divisions were also sent to secure the flanks of the areas where the troops went ashore. Putting 150,000 troops ashore in one day required the support of more than 7,000 naval ships. An initially indecisive German response enabled the Allied forces to establish a beachhead. Within three months, they had landed 2 million men and a half-million vehicles that pushed inland and broke through the German defensive lines.

After the breakout, Allied troops moved south and east and liberated Paris by the end of August. Supply problems as well as a last-minute, desperate (and unsuccessful) offensive by German troops in the Battle of the Bulge slowed the Allied advance. Nevertheless, by March 1945, Allied armies had crossed the Rhine River and advanced further into Germany. At the end of April, Allied forces in northern Germany moved toward the Elbe River, where they finally linked up with the Soviets.

SOVIET OFFENSIVE IN THE EAST The Soviets had come a long way since the Battle of Stalingrad in 1943. In the summer of 1943, Hitler's generals had urged him to build an "east wall" based on river barriers to halt the Soviets. Instead, Hitler gambled on using newly developed heavy tanks to take the offensive, but the Soviets soundly defeated the German forces at the Battle of Kursk (KOORSK) (July 5–12), the greatest tank battle of World War II. The Germans lost eighteen of their best panzer divisions. Soviet forces now began a relentless

Crossing the Rhine. After landing at Normandy, Allied forces liberated France and prepared to move into Germany. Makeshift bridges enabled the Allies to cross the Rhine in some areas and advance deeper into Germany. Units of the U.S. Seventh Army of General Patch are shown here crossing the Rhine at Worms on a pontoon bridge constructed by battalions of engineers alongside the ruins of the old bridge.

National Archives (111-C-273), Washington, DC

Germany and the Soviet Union divide Poland	September 1939
Blitzkrieg against Denmark and Norway	April 1940
Blitzkrieg against Belgium, Netherlands, and France	May 1940
Churchill becomes British prime minister	May 10, 1940
France surrenders	June 22, 1940
Battle of Britain	Summer 1940
Nazi seizure of Yugoslavia and Greece	April 1941
Germany invades the Soviet Union	June 22, 1941
Japanese attack on Pearl Harbor	December 7, 1941
Battle of the Coral Sea	May 7–8, 1942
Battle of Midway Island	June 4, 1942
Allied invasion of North Africa	November 1942
Soviets win Battle of Stalingrad	February 2, 1943
Axis forces surrender in North Africa	May 13, 1943
Battle of Kursk	July 5–12, 1943
Invasion of mainland Italy	September 1943
Allied invasion of France	June 6, 1944
Hitler commits suicide	April 30, 1945
Germany surrenders	May 7, 1945
Atomic bomb dropped on Hiroshima	August 6, 1945
Japan surrenders	August 14, 1945

advance westward. The Soviets had reoccupied Ukraine by the end of 1943 and lifted the siege of Leningrad and moved into the Baltic states by the beginning of 1944. Advancing along a northern front, Soviet troops occupied Warsaw in January 1945 and entered Berlin in April. Meanwhile, Soviet troops swept along a southern front through Hungary, Romania, and Bulgaria.

In January 1945, Adolf Hitler had moved into a bunker 55 feet under Berlin to direct the final stages of the war. Hitler continued to arrange his armies on worn-out battle maps as if it still made a difference. In his final political testament, Hitler, consistent to the end in his rabid anti-Semitism, blamed the Jews for the war: "Above all I charge the leaders of the nation and those under them to scrupulous observance of the laws of race and to merciless opposition to the universal poisoner of all peoples, international Jewry."[9] Hitler committed suicide on April 30, two days after Mussolini had been shot by partisan Italian forces. On May 7, German commanders surrendered. The war in Europe was over.

DEFEAT OF JAPAN The war in Asia continued. Beginning in 1943, American forces had gone on the offensive and advanced their way, slowly at times, across the Pacific. American forces took an increasing toll of enemy resources, especially at sea and in the air. Especially devastating to the Japanese were the losses they sustained at the Battle of Leyte Gulf in the Philippines, the largest naval battle of World War II. Combined American and Australian naval forces caused such heavy losses of Japanese ships that the Japanese navy was unable to sail to battle in any significant way.

When President Harry Truman (Roosevelt had died on April 12, 1945) and his advisers became convinced that American troops might suffer heavy casualties in the invasion of the Japanese homeland, they made the decision to drop the newly developed atomic bomb on Hiroshima (hee-roh-SHEE-muh) and Nagasaki (nah-gah-SAH-kee). The Japanese surrendered unconditionally on August 14. World War II was finally over.

The New Order

 FOCUS QUESTIONS: How was the Nazi empire organized? What was the Holocaust, and what was the relationship between Hitler's worldview, his foreign policy, and the Holocaust?

The initial victories of the Germans and the Japanese gave them the opportunity to create new orders in Europe and Asia. Although both countries presented positive images of these new orders for publicity purposes, in practice both followed policies of ruthless domination of their subject peoples.

The Nazi Empire

After the German victories in Europe, Nazi propagandists created glowing images of a new European order based on "equal chances" for all nations and an integrated economic community. This was not Hitler's conception of a European New Order. He saw the Europe he had conquered simply as subject to German domination. Only the Germans, he once said, "can really organize Europe."

The Nazi empire stretched across continental Europe from the English Channel in the west to the outskirts of Moscow in the east. In no way was this empire organized systematically or governed efficiently. Some states—Spain, Portugal, Switzerland, Sweden, and Turkey—remained neutral and outside the empire. Germany's allies—Italy, Romania, Bulgaria, Hungary, and Finland—kept their independence but found themselves increasingly restricted by the Germans as the war progressed. The remainder of Europe was largely organized in one of two ways. Some areas, such as western Poland, were directly annexed by Nazi Germany and made into German provinces. Most of occupied Europe was administered by German military or civilian officials, combined with varying degrees of indirect control from collaborationist regimes. Competing lines of authority by different offices in occupied Europe made German occupation inefficient.

HITLER'S PLANS FOR A NEW ORDER IN THE EAST

HITLER'S NIGHTLY MONOLOGUES TO his post-dinner guests, which were recorded by the Führer's private secretary, Martin Bormann, reveal much about the New Order he wished to create. On the evening of October 17, 1941, he expressed his views on what the Germans would do with their newly conquered territories in the east.

Hitler's *Secret Conversations*, October 17, 1941

In comparison with the beauties accumulated in Central Germany, the new territories in the East seem to us like a desert. . . . This Russian desert, we shall populate it. . . . We'll take away its character of an Asiatic steppe, we'll Europeanize it. With this object, we have undertaken the construction of roads that will lead to the southernmost point of the Crimea and to the Caucasus. These roads will be studded along their whole length with German towns, and around these towns our colonists will settle.

As for the two or three million men whom we need to accomplish this task, we'll find them quicker than we think. They'll come from Germany, Scandinavia, the Western countries and America. I shall no longer be here to see all that, but in twenty years the Ukraine will already be a home for twenty million inhabitants besides the natives. In three hundred years, the country will be one of the loveliest gardens in the world.

As for the natives, we'll have to screen them carefully. The Jew, that destroyer, we shall drive out. . . . We shan't settle in the Russian towns, and we'll let them fall to pieces without intervening. And, above all, no remorse on this subject! We're not going to play at children's nurses; we're absolutely without obligations as far as these people are concerned. To struggle against the hovels, chase away the fleas, provide German teachers, bring out newspapers—very little of that for us! We'll confine ourselves, perhaps, to setting up a radio transmitter, under our control. For the rest, let them know just enough to understand our highway signs, so that they won't get themselves run over by our vehicles. . . . There's only one duty: to Germanize this country by the immigration of Germans, and to look upon the natives as Redskins. If these people had defeated us, Heaven have mercy! But we don't hate them. That sentiment is unknown to us. We are guided only by reason. . . .

All those who have the feeling for Europe can join in our work.

In this business I shall go straight ahead, coldbloodedly. What they may think about me, at this juncture, is to me a matter of complete indifference. I don't see why a German who eats a piece of bread should torment himself with the idea that the soil that produces this bread has been won by the sword.

 What new order did Hitler envision in the east? What would its achievement have meant for the peoples of eastern Europe?

Source: H. Trevor-Roper, *Hitler's Secret Conversations 1941–1944* (New York: Farrar, Straus & Young, 1953).

Racial considerations played an important role in how conquered peoples were treated in the **Nazi New Order**. The Germans established civil administrations in Norway, Denmark, and the Netherlands because the Nazis considered their peoples Aryan, racially akin to the Germans and hence worthy of more lenient treatment. "Inferior" Latin peoples, such as the occupied French, were given military administrations. By 1943, however, as Nazi losses continued to multiply, all the occupied territories of northern and western Europe were ruthlessly exploited for material goods and workers for Germany's war needs.

PLANS FOR AN ARYAN RACIAL EMPIRE Because the conquered lands in the east contained the living space for German expansion and were populated in Nazi eyes by racially inferior Slavic peoples, Nazi administration there was considerably more brutal. Hitler's racial ideology and his plans for an Aryan racial empire were so important to him that he and the Nazis began to implement their racial program soon after the conquest of Poland. Heinrich Himmler, a strong believer in Nazi racial ideology and the leader of the SS, was put in charge of German resettlement plans in the east. Himmler's task was to evacuate the inferior Slavic peoples and replace them with Germans, a policy first applied to the new German provinces created from the lands of western Poland. One million Poles were uprooted and dumped in southern Poland. Hundreds of thousands of ethnic Germans (descendants of Germans who had migrated years earlier from Germany to various parts of southern and eastern Europe) were encouraged to colonize the designated areas in Poland. By 1942, 2 million ethnic Germans had settled in Poland.

The invasion of the Soviet Union inflated Nazi visions of German colonization in the east. Hitler spoke to his intimate circle of a colossal project of social engineering after the war, in which Poles, Ukrainians, and Soviets would become slave labor and German peasants would settle on the abandoned lands and Germanize them (see the box above). Nazis involved in this kind of planning were well aware of the human costs. Himmler told a gathering of SS officers that although the destruction of 30 million Slavs was a prerequisite for German plans in the east, "whether nations live in prosperity or starve to death interests me only insofar as we need them as slaves for our culture. Otherwise it is of no interest."[10]

ECONOMIC EXPLOITATION Economically, the Nazi New Order meant the ruthless exploitation of conquered Europe's resources. In eastern Europe, economic exploitation was direct and severe. The Germans seized raw materials, machines, and food, leaving only enough to maintain local peoples at a bare subsistence level. Although the Germans adopted legal formalities in their economic exploitation of western Europe, military supplies and important raw materials were taken outright. As Nazi policies created drastic shortages of food, clothing, and shelter, many Europeans suffered severely.

USE OF FOREIGN WORKERS Labor shortages in Germany led to a policy of forced mobilization of foreign labor for Germany. After the invasion of the Soviet Union, the 4 million Soviet prisoners of war captured by the Germans became a major source of heavy labor, but it was wasted by allowing 3 million of them to die from neglect. In 1942, a special office was created to recruit labor for German farms and industries. By the summer of 1944, 7 million foreign workers were laboring in Germany and constituted 20 percent of Germany's labor force. At the same time, another 7 million workers were supplying forced labor in their own countries on farms, in industries, and even in military camps. Forced labor often proved counterproductive, however, because it created economic chaos in occupied countries and disrupted industrial production that could have helped Germany. Even worse for the Germans, the brutal character of Germany's recruitment policies often caused more and more people to resist the Nazi occupation forces.

Resistance Movements

German policies toward conquered peoples quickly led to the emergence of resistance movements throughout Europe, especially in the east, where brutality toward the native peoples produced a strong reaction. In Ukraine and the Baltic states, for example, the Germans were initially hailed as liberators from Communist rule, but Hitler's policies of treating Slavic peoples as subhumans only drove those peoples to support and join guerrilla forces.

RESISTANCE MOVEMENTS IN NAZI-OCCUPIED EUROPE Resistance movements were formed throughout Europe. Active resisters committed acts of sabotage against German installations, assassinated German officials, disseminated anti-German newspapers, wrote anti-German sentiments on walls, and spied on German military positions for the Allies. Some anti-Nazi groups from occupied countries, such as the Free French movement under Charles de Gaulle (SHAHRL duh GOHL), created governments-in-exile in London. In some countries, resistance groups even grew strong enough to take on the Germans in pitched battles. In Yugoslavia, for example, Josip Broz (yaw-SEEP BRAWZ), known as Tito (TEE-toh) (1892–1980), led a band of guerrillas against German occupation forces. By 1944, his partisan army numbered 250,000, including 100,000 women.

After the invasion of the Soviet Union in 1941, Communists throughout Europe assumed leadership roles in underground resistance movements. This sometimes led to conflict with other local resistance groups who feared the postwar consequences of Communist power. Charles de Gaulle's Free French movement, for example, thwarted the attempt of French Communists to dominate the major French resistance groups.

Women, too, joined resistance movements in large numbers throughout Nazi-occupied Europe. Women served as message carriers, planted bombs in Nazi headquarters, assassinated Nazi officers, published and distributed anti-German underground newspapers, spied on German military movements and positions, and used shopping baskets to carry weapons, medicines, and money to help their causes. In Norway, women smuggled Jews into neutral Sweden. In Greece, wives dressed their husbands as women to save them when the Nazis tried to stop acts of sabotage by vicious reprisals in which they executed all the males of a village.

Resistance was, of course, a dangerous activity and could lead to family tragedies and death for the people who were captured. But even in smaller countries, resistance fighters emerged, even if not in great numbers. In the Netherlands, for example, about 25,000 joined the resistance by fall 1944; another 10,000 joined in the last year of the war. Only 25 percent survived the war.

RESISTANCE IN GERMANY Germany had its resistance movements, too, although the increased control of the SS over everyday life made resistance both dangerous and ineffectual. The White Rose movement involved an attempt by a small group of students and one professor at the University of Munich to distribute pamphlets denouncing the Nazi regime as lawless, criminal, and godless. Its members were caught, arrested, and promptly executed. Likewise, the Gestapo (guh-STAH-poh) (the secret police) crushed most Communist resistance groups.

Only one plot against Hitler and the Nazi regime came remotely close to success. It was the work primarily of a group of military officers and conservative politicians who were appalled at Hitler's warmongering and sickened by the wartime atrocities he had encouraged. One of their number, Colonel Count Claus von Stauffenberg (KLOWSS fun SHTOW-fen-berk) (1907–1944), believed that only the elimination of Hitler would bring the overthrow of the Nazi regime. On July 20, 1944, a bomb planted by Stauffenberg in Hitler's East Prussian headquarters exploded, but it failed to kill the dictator. The plot was then quickly uncovered and crushed. Five thousand people were executed, and Hitler remained in control of Germany.

The Holocaust

No aspect of the Nazi New Order was more terrifying than the deliberate attempt to exterminate the Jewish people of Europe. Racial struggle was a key element in Hitler's ideology and meant to him a clearly defined conflict of opposites: the Aryans, creators of human cultural development, against the Jews, parasites who were trying to destroy the Aryans. At a meeting of the Nazi Party in 1922, Hitler proclaimed, "There can be no compromise—there are only two possibilities: either victory of the Aryan or annihilation of the Aryan and the victory of the Jew."[11] Although Hitler later toned down his anti-Semitic message when his party sought mass electoral victories, anti-Semitism was a recurring theme in Nazism and resulted in a wave of legislative acts against the Jews between 1933 and 1939 (see Chapter 26).

EARLY NAZI POLICY By the beginning of 1939, Nazi policy focused on promoting the "emigration" of German Jews from Germany. At the same time, Hitler had given ominous warnings about the future of Europe's Jewish population. When he addressed the German Reichstag on January 30, 1939, he stated:

> I have often been a prophet in life and was generally laughed at. During my struggle for power, the Jews primarily received with laughter my prophecies that I would someday assume the leadership of the state and thereby of the entire Volk and then, among many other things, achieve a solution of the Jewish problem. . . . Today I will be a prophet again: if international finance Jewry within Europe and abroad should succeed once more in plunging the peoples into a world war, then the consequence will be not the Bolshevization of the world and therewith a victory of Jewry, but on the contrary, the destruction of the Jewish race in Europe.[12]

At the time, emigration was still the favored policy. Once the war began in September 1939, the so-called Jewish problem took on new dimensions. For a while, there was discussion of the Madagascar Plan, which aspired to the mass shipment of Jews to the island of Madagascar, off the eastern coast of Africa. When war contingencies made this plan impracticable, an even more drastic policy was conceived (see "Film & History" below).

▣ FILM & HISTORY

Watch *Europa, Europa* (1990), a harrowing story of one Jewish boy's escape from the horrors of Nazi persecution. It is based on the memoirs of Salomon "Solly" Perel, a German Jew of Polish background who survived by pretending to be an Aryan. Although there is no way of knowing if each detail of this movie is historically accurate (and a few are absurdly inaccurate, such as a bombing run by a plane that was not developed until after the war), overall the story has the ring of truth.

Les Films du Losange/CCC Filmkunst/ The Kobal Collection at Art Resource, NY

 What does this film reveal about the difficulties of being Jewish during World War II? How realistic is the film?

THE SS AND THE *EINSATZGRUPPEN* Heinrich Himmler and the SS organization closely shared Adolf Hitler's racial ideology. The SS was given responsibility for what the Nazis called their **Final Solution** to the Jewish problem—the annihilation of the Jewish people. Reinhard Heydrich (RYN-hart HY-drikh) (1904–1942), head of the SS's Security Service, was assigned administrative responsibility for the Final Solution. After the defeat of Poland, Heydrich ordered the special strike forces—*Einsatzgruppen* (YN-zahtz-groop-un)—that he had created to round up all Polish Jews and concentrate them in ghettos established in a number of Polish cities.

In June 1941, the *Einsatzgruppen* were given new responsibilities as mobile killing units. These SS death squads followed the regular army's advance into the Soviet Union. Their job was to round up Jews in their villages and execute and bury them in mass graves, often giant pits dug by the victims themselves before they were shot. The leader of one of these death squads described the mode of operation:

> The unit selected for this task would enter a village or city and order the prominent Jewish citizens to call together all Jews for the purpose of resettlement. They were requested to hand over their valuables to the leaders of the unit, and shortly before the execution to surrender their outer clothing. The men, women, and children were led to a place of execution which in most cases was located next to a more deeply excavated anti-tank ditch. Then they were shot, kneeling or standing, and the corpses thrown into the ditch.[13]

Such regular killing created morale problems among the SS executioners. During a visit to Minsk in the Soviet Union, SS leader Himmler tried to build morale by pointing out that "he would not like it if Germans did such a thing gladly. But their conscience was in no way impaired, for they were soldiers who had to carry out every order unconditionally. He alone had responsibility before God and Hitler for everything that was happening . . . and he was acting from a deep understanding of the necessity for this operation."[14]

THE DEATH CAMPS Although it has been estimated that the *Einsatzgruppen* killed as many as one million Jews, this approach to solving the Jewish problem was soon perceived as inadequate. Instead, the Nazis opted for the systematic annihilation of the European Jewish population in specially built death camps. The plan was simple. Jews from countries occupied by Germany (or sympathetic to Germany) would be rounded up, packed like cattle into freight trains, and shipped to Poland, where six extermination centers were built for this purpose (see Map 27.4). The largest and most infamous was Auschwitz-Birkenau (OWSH-vitz-BEER-kuh-now). Technical assistance for the construction of the camps was provided by experts from the T-4 program, which had been responsible for the extermination of 80,000 alleged racially unfit mental and physical defectives in Germany between 1938 and 1941.

The Holocaust: Activities of the *Einsatzgruppen.* The activities of the mobile killing units known as the *Einsatzgruppen* were the first stage in the mass killings of the Holocaust. This picture shows a soldier of Einsatzgruppe D about to shoot a Jew kneeling in front of a mass grave in Ukraine. Onlookers include members of the German army, the German Labor Service, and even Hitler Youth. When it became apparent that this method of killing was inefficient, it was replaced by the death camps.

Based on their experiences, medical technicians chose Zyklon B (the commercial name for hydrogen cyanide) as the most effective gas for quickly killing large numbers of people in gas chambers designed to look like shower rooms to facilitate the cooperation of the victims. After gassing, the corpses would be burned in specially built crematoria.

To inform party and state officials of the general procedures for the Final Solution, a conference was held at Wannsee (VAHN-zay), outside Berlin, on January 20, 1942. Reinhard Heydrich outlined the steps that would now be taken to "solve the Jewish question." He explained how in the course of executing the final solution Europe is to be "combed through from west to east" for Jews, who would then be brought into so-called transit ghettos, to be transported from there farther to the east. The conference then worked out all of the bureaucratic details so that party and state officials would cooperate fully in the final elimination of the Jews.

By the spring of 1942, the death camps were in operation. Although the elimination of the ghettos in Poland was the first priority, by the summer of 1942, Jews were also being shipped from France, Belgium, and the Netherlands. In 1943, there were shipments of Jews from the capital cities of Berlin, Vienna, and Prague and from Greece, southern France, Italy, and Denmark. Even as the Allies were making important advances in 1944, Jews were being shipped from Greece and Hungary. These shipments depended on the cooperation of Germany's Transport Ministry, and despite desperate military needs, the Final Solution had priority in using railroad cars for the transportation of Jews to the death camps. Even the military argument that Jews could be used to produce armaments was overridden by the demands of extermination.

A harrowing experience awaited the Jews when they arrived at one of the six death camps. Rudolf Hoss (HESS), commandant at Auschwitz-Birkenau, described it:

> We had two SS doctors on duty at Auschwitz to examine the incoming transports of prisoners. The prisoners would be marched by one of the doctors who would make spot decisions as they walked by. Those who were fit for work were sent into the camp. Others were sent immediately to the extermination plants. Children of tender years were invariably exterminated since by reason of their youth they were unable to work. . . . At Auschwitz we endeavored to fool the victims into thinking that they were to go through a delousing process. Of course, frequently they realized our true intentions and we sometimes had riots and difficulties due to that fact.[15]

About 30 percent of the arrivals at Auschwitz were sent to a labor camp; the remainder went to the gas chambers. A French doctor described the process:

> It is mid-day, when a long line of women, children, and old people enter the yard. . . . The senior official in charge . . . climbs on a bench to tell them that they are going to have a bath and that afterward they will get a drink of hot coffee. They all undress in the yard. . . . The doors are opened and an indescribable jostling begins. The first people to enter the gas chamber begin to draw back. They sense the death which awaits them. The SS men put an end to this pushing and shoving with blows from their rifle butts beating the heads of the horrified women who are desperately hugging their children. The massive oak double doors are shut. For two endless minutes one can hear banging on the walls and screams which are no longer human. And then—not a sound. Five minutes later the doors are opened. The corpses, squashed together and distorted, fall out like a waterfall. . . . The bodies which are still warm pass through the hands of the hairdresser who cuts their hair and the dentist who pulls out their gold teeth. . . . One more transport has just been processed through No. IV crematorium.[16]

MAP 27.4 The Holocaust. Hitler used the fiction of the Aryan race, to which Germans supposedly belonged, to help radicalize the German people and justify his hatred of Jews. Hitler's "Final Solution" to the "Jewish problem" was the mass execution of Europe's Jews in death camps.

Q *Which region lost the largest number of Jews in the camps, and what helps explain this?*

of at least another 9 to 10 million people. Because the Nazis also considered the Gypsies of Europe (like the Jews) a race containing alien blood, they were systematically rounded up for extermination. About 40 percent of Europe's one million Gypsies were killed in the death camps. The leading elements of the "subhuman" Slavic peoples—the clergy, intelligentsia, civil leaders, judges, and lawyers—were arrested and deliberately killed. Probably an additional 4 million Poles, Ukrainians, and Belorussians lost their lives as slave laborers for Nazi Germany, and at least 3 to 4 million Soviet prisoners of war were killed in captivity. The Nazis also singled out homosexuals for persecution, and thousands lost their lives in concentration camps.

The New Order in Asia

Once Japan's takeover was completed, Japanese war policy in the occupied areas in Asia became essentially defensive, as Japan hoped to use its new possessions to meet its needs for raw materials, such as tin, oil, and rubber, as well as to serve as an outlet for Japanese manufactured goods. To provide a structure for the arrangement, Japanese leaders set up the Great East Asia Co-Prosperity Sphere as a self-sufficient community designed to provide mutual benefits to the occupied areas and the home country.

The Japanese conquest of Southeast Asia had been accomplished under the slogan "Asia for the Asians." Japanese officials in occupied territories quickly promised that independent governments would be established under Japanese tutelage. Such governments were eventually established in Burma, the Dutch East Indies, Vietnam, and the Philippines.

In fact, however, real power rested with Japanese military authorities in each territory, and the local Japanese military command was directly subordinated to the army general staff in Tokyo. The economic resources of the colonies were exploited for the benefit of the Japanese war machine, while natives were recruited to serve in local military units or were conscripted to work on public works projects. In some cases, the people living in the occupied areas were subjected to severe hardships.

Like German soldiers in occupied Europe, Japanese military forces often had little respect for the lives of their

After they had been gassed, the bodies were burned in the crematoria. The victims' goods and even their bodies were used for economic gain. Female hair was cut off, collected, and turned into mattresses or cloth. Some inmates were also subjected to cruel and painful "medical" experiments. The Germans killed between 5 and 6 million Jews, more than 3 million of them in the death camps. Virtually 90 percent of the Jewish populations of Poland, the Baltic countries, and Germany were exterminated. Overall, the Holocaust was responsible for the death of nearly two out of every three European Jews (see the box on p. 849).

THE OTHER HOLOCAUST The Nazis were also responsible for the deliberate death by shooting, starvation, or overwork

HEINRICH HIMMLER: "WE HAD THE MORAL RIGHT"

ALTHOUGH NAZI LEADERS WERE reluctant to talk openly about their attempt to destroy the Jews of Europe, when they did, they had no qualms about justifying their actions. In 1943, Heinrich Himmler, the leader of the SS, who assumed responsibility for executing the Holocaust, gave a remarkable speech to the leaders of the SS in Poznan, Poland.

Heinrich Himmler, Speech to SS Leaders

I also want to talk to you, quite frankly, on a very grave matter. Among yourselves it should be mentioned quite frankly, and yet we will never speak of it publicly. I mean the clearing out of the Jews, extermination of the Jewish race. It's one of those things it is easy to talk about— "The Jewish race is being exterminated," says one party member, "that's quite clear, it's in our program—elimination of the Jews, and we're doing it, exterminating them." And then they come, 80 million worthy Germans, and each one had his decent Jew. Of course, the others are vermin, but this one is an A-1 Jew. Not one of those who talk this way has witnessed it, not one of them has been through it. Most of you must know what it means when 100 corpses are lying side by side, or 500 or 1,000. To have stuck it

Source: *Nazi Conspiracy and Aggression* (Washington, D.C., 1946), 4: 563–564.

out and at the same time . . . to have remained decent fellows, that is what has made us hard. This is a page of glory in our history which has never been written and is never to be written. . . . We have taken from them what wealth they had. I have issued a strict order . . . that this wealth should, as a matter of course, be handed over to [Germany] without reserve. We have taken none of it for ourselves. . . . We had the moral right, we had the duty to our people, to destroy this people which wanted to destroy us. But we have not the right to enrich ourselves with so much as a fur, a watch, a mark, or a cigarette or anything else. Because we have exterminated a bacterium we do not want, in the end, to be infected by the bacterium and die of it. I will not see so much as a small area of sepsis appear here or gain a hold. Wherever it may form, we will cauterize it. But altogether we can say that we have fulfilled this most difficult duty for the love of our people. And our spirit, our soul, our character has not suffered injury from it.

Q *How does Himmler justify the Holocaust? What is wrong with his argument, and how does it demonstrate the danger of ideological rigidity?*

The Holocaust: The Extermination Camp at Auschwitz. After their initial successes in the east, Hitler and the Nazis set in motion the machinery for the physical annihilation of Europe's Jews. Shown here is a group of Jews arriving at Auschwitz. It is estimated that 1.1 million people (90 percent of them Jews) were killed there.

Universal Images Group/Getty Images

subject peoples. In their conquest of Nanjing, China, in 1937, Japanese soldiers had spent several days killing, raping, and looting. Almost 800,000 Koreans were sent overseas, most of them as forced laborers, to Japan. Tens of thousands of Korean women were forced to serve as "comfort women" (prostitutes) for Japanese troops. In construction projects to help their war effort, the Japanese also made extensive use of labor forces composed of both prisoners of war and local peoples. In building the Burma-Thailand railway in 1943, for example, the Japanese used 61,000 Australian, British, and Dutch prisoners of war and almost 300,000 workers from Burma, Malaya, Thailand, and the Dutch East Indies. By the time the railway was completed, 12,000 Allied prisoners of war and 90,000 native workers had died from the inadequate diet and appalling working conditions in an unhealthy climate.

The Home Front

 FOCUS QUESTION: What were conditions like on the home front for Japan and the major Western nations involved in World War II?

World War II was even more of a total war than World War I. Fighting was much more widespread and covered most of the globe. Economic mobilization was more extensive; so too was the mobilization of women. The number of civilians killed was far higher; almost 20 million died as a result of bombing raids, mass extermination policies, and attacks by invading armies.

The Mobilization of Peoples

The home fronts of the major belligerents varied considerably, based on national circumstances.

GREAT BRITAIN The British mobilized their resources more thoroughly than their allies or even Germany. By the summer of 1944, fully 55 percent of the British people were in the armed forces or civilian "war work." The British were especially determined to make use of women. Most women under forty years of age were called on to do war work of some kind. By 1944, women held almost 50 percent of the civil service positions, and the number of women in agriculture doubled as "land girls" performed agricultural labor usually undertaken by men.

The government encouraged the "Dig for Victory" campaign to increase food production. Fields normally reserved for athletic events were turned over to citizens to plant gardens in "Grow Your Own Food" campaigns. Even with 1.4 million new gardens in 1943, Britain still faced a shortage of food as German submarines continued to sink hundreds of British merchant vessels. Food rationing, with its weekly allotments of bacon, sugar, fats, and eggs, intensified during the war as the British became accustomed to a diet dominated by bread and potatoes. Many people spent their hours after work in such wartime activities as "Dig for Victory," the Civil Defence, or the Home Guard. The Home Guard had been founded in 1940 to fight off

German invaders. Even elderly people were expected to help manufacture airplane parts in their homes.

During the war, the British placed much emphasis on a planned economy. In 1942, the government created a ministry for fuel and power to control the coal industry and a ministry for production to oversee supplies for the armed forces. Although controls and bureaucratic "red tape" became unpopular, especially with businesspeople, most British citizens seemed to accept that total war required unusual governmental interference in people's lives. The British did make substantial gains in manufacturing war materiel. Tank production quadrupled between 1940 and 1942, and the production of aircraft grew from 8,000 in 1939 to 26,000 in 1943 and 1944.

THE SOVIET UNION World War II had an enormous impact on the Soviet Union. Known to the Soviets as the Great Patriotic War, the German-Soviet war witnessed the greatest land battles in history as well as incredible ruthlessness. To Nazi Germany, it was a war of oppression and annihilation that called for merciless measures. Two out of every five persons killed in World War II were Soviet citizens.

The shift to a war footing necessitated only limited administrative changes in the Soviet Union. As the central authority, the dictator Joseph Stalin simply created a system of "super-centralization," by which he directed military and political affairs. All civil and military organizations were subjected to the control of the Communist Party and the Soviet police.

The initial defeats of the Soviet Union led to drastic emergency mobilization measures that affected the civilian population. Leningrad, for example, experienced nine hundred days of siege, during which its inhabitants became so desperate for food that they ate dogs, cats, and mice. As the German army made its rapid advance into Soviet territory, the factories in the western part of the Soviet Union were dismantled and shipped to the interior—to the Urals, western Siberia, and the Volga region. Machines were placed on the bare ground, and walls went up around them as workers began their work. The Kharkov Tank Factory produced its first twenty-five T-34 tanks only ten weeks after the plant had been rebuilt.

This widespread military, industrial, and economic mobilization created yet another industrial revolution for the Soviet Union. Stalin labeled it a "battle of machines," and the Soviets won, producing 78,000 tanks and 98,000 artillery pieces. Fifty-five percent of Soviet national income went for war materiel, compared to 15 percent in 1940. As a result of the emphasis on military goods, Soviet citizens experienced incredible shortages of both food and housing. Civilian food consumption fell by 40 percent during the war; in the Volga area, the Urals, and Siberia, workers lived in dugouts or dilapidated barracks.

Soviet women played a major role in the war effort. Women and girls worked in factories, mines, and railroads. Women constituted between 26 and 35 percent of the laborers in mines and 48 percent in the oil industry. Overall, the number of women working in industry increased almost 60 percent. Soviet women were also expected to dig antitank ditches and work as air-raid

Women in the Factories. Although only the Soviet Union used women in combat positions, the number of women working in industry increased dramatically in most belligerent countries. British women are shown here in a factory building Beaufort fighter planes for the British air force in 1940. At the right is a propaganda poster encouraging women to work in the factories.

wardens. In addition, the Soviet Union was the only country in World War II to use women as combatants. Soviet women served as snipers and also as aircrews in bomber squadrons. The female pilots who helped defeat the Germans at Stalingrad were known as the "Night Witches."

Soviet peasants were asked to bear enormous burdens. Not only did the peasants furnish 60 percent of the military forces, but at the same time, they were expected to feed the Red Army and the Soviet people under very trying conditions. The German occupation in the early months of the war resulted in the loss of 47 percent of the country's grain-producing regions. Although new land was opened in the Urals, Siberia, and Soviet Asia, a shortage of labor and equipment hindered the effort to expand agricultural production. Because farm tractors and trucks were requisitioned to carry guns for the military, women and children were literally harnessed to do the plowing, and everywhere peasants worked long hours on collective farms for no pay. In 1943, the Soviet harvest was only 60 percent of its 1940 figure, a shortfall that meant extreme hardship for many people.

Total mobilization produced victory for the Soviet Union. Stalin and the Communist Party had quickly realized after the start of the German invasion that the Soviet people would not fight for Communist ideology but would do battle to preserve "Mother Russia." Government propaganda played on patriotic feelings. In a speech on the anniversary of the Bolshevik Revolution in November 1941, Stalin rallied the Soviet people by speaking of the country's past heroes, including the famous tsars of imperial Russia.

THE UNITED STATES The home front in the United States was quite different from those of its two chief wartime allies, largely because the United States faced no threat of war in its own territory. Although the economy and labor force were slow to mobilize, eventually the United States became the arsenal of the Allied powers, producing the military equipment they needed. The mobilization of the United States also had a great impact on American social and economic developments.

The immediate impact of mobilization was a dramatic expansion of the American economy, which ultimately brought an end to the Great Depression. Old factories were converted from peacetime goods to war goods, and many new factories were built. Massive amounts of government money also financed new industries, such as chemicals and electronics. A new government Office of Scientific Research and Development provided funds for contracts with universities and scientists to create such new products as rocket engines. The Manhattan Project for the development of an atomic bomb, which employed 130,000 people and cost $2 billion, involved the cooperation of scientists, defense contractors, and the federal government.

American industry supplied not only the U.S. armed forces but also the other Allies with the huge quantities of tanks, trucks, jeeps, and airplanes needed to win the war. During the war years, gross national product (GNP) rose by 15 percent a year. During the high point of war production in the United States in November 1943, the nation was constructing six ships a day and $6 billion worth of other military equipment a month. The production of airplanes increased from 6,000 in 1939 to more than 96,000 in 1944.

Industrial mobilization led to an increased government role in the economy. The federal bureaucracy grew dramatically with the establishment of the War Production Board, which allocated resources and managed production; the War Labor Board, which settled labor disputes; and the Office of Price Administration, which controlled prices and rationed scarce goods, such as gasoline, rubber, and meat.

The mobilization of the American economy also caused social problems. The construction of new factories created boomtowns where thousands came to work but then faced a shortage of houses, health facilities, and schools. The dramatic transformation of small towns into large cities often brought a breakdown in traditional social mores, especially evident in the increase in teenage prostitution. Economic mobilization also led to a widespread movement of people, which in turn created new social tensions. Sixteen million men and women were enrolled in the military, and another 16 million, mostly wives and sweethearts of the servicemen or workers looking for jobs, also relocated. More than one million African Americans migrated from the rural South to the industrial cities of the North and West, looking for jobs in industry. The presence of African Americans in areas where they had not lived before led to racial tensions and sometimes even racial riots. In Detroit in June 1943, white mobs roamed the streets attacking African Americans. Many of the one million African Americans who enlisted in the military, only to be segregated in their own battle units, were angered by the way they were treated. Some became militant and prepared to fight for their civil rights.

Japanese Americans were treated even more shabbily. On the West Coast, 110,000 Japanese Americans, 65 percent of whom had been born in the United States, were removed to camps encircled by barbed wire and required to take loyalty oaths. Although public officials claimed that this policy was necessary for security reasons, no similar treatment of German Americans or Italian Americans ever took place. The racism inherent in this treatment of Japanese Americans was evident in the comment of the California governor, Culbert Olson: "You know, when I look out at a group of Americans of German or Italian descent, I can tell whether they're loyal or not. I can tell how they think and even perhaps what they are thinking. But it is impossible for me to do this with inscrutable orientals, and particularly the Japanese."[17]

GERMANY In August 1914, Germans had enthusiastically cheered their soldiers marching off to war. In September 1939, the streets were quiet. Many Germans were apathetic or, even worse for the Nazi regime, had a foreboding of disaster. Hitler was very aware of the importance of the home front. He believed that the collapse of the home front in World War I had caused Germany's defeat, and in his determination to avoid a repetition of that experience, he adopted economic policies that may indeed have cost Germany the war.

To maintain the morale of the home front during the first two years of the war, Hitler refused to convert production from consumer goods to armaments. Blitzkrieg enabled the Germans to win quick victories, after which they could plunder the food and raw materials of the conquered countries in order to avoid diverting resources away from the civilian economy. After the German defeats on the Soviet front and the American entry into the war, the economic situation changed. Early in 1942, Hitler finally ordered a massive increase in armaments production and the size of the army. Hitler's personal architect, Albert Speer (SHPAYR), was made minister for armaments and munitions in 1942. By eliminating waste and rationalizing procedures, Speer was able to triple the production of armaments between 1942 and 1943 despite the intense Allied air raids. Speer's urgent plea for a total mobilization of resources for the war effort went unheeded, however. Hitler, fearful of civilian morale problems that would undermine the home front, refused any dramatic cuts in the production of consumer goods. A total mobilization of the economy was not implemented until 1944, when schools, theaters, and cafés were closed and Speer was finally permitted to use all remaining resources for the production of a few basic military items. By that time, it was in vain. Total war mobilization was too little and too late in July 1944 to save Germany from defeat.

The war produced a reversal in Nazi attitudes toward women. Nazi resistance to female employment declined as the war progressed and more and more men were called up for military service. Nazi magazines now proclaimed, "We see the woman as the eternal mother of our people, but also as the working and fighting comrade of the man."[18] But the number of women working in industry, agriculture, commerce, and domestic service increased only slightly. The total number of employed women in September 1944 was 14.9 million, compared to 14.6 in May 1939. Many women, especially those of the middle class, resisted regular employment, particularly in factories. Even the introduction of labor conscription for women in January 1943 failed to achieve much as women found ingenious ways to avoid the regulations.

JAPAN Wartime Japan was a highly mobilized society. To ensure its control over all national resources, the government set up a planning board to control prices, wages, the utilization of labor, and the allocation of resources. Traditional habits of obedience and hierarchy, buttressed by the concept of imperial divinity, were emphasized to encourage citizens to sacrifice their resources, and sometimes their lives, for the national cause. Especially important was the code of *bushido* (BOO-shee-doh), or the way of the warrior, the old code of morality of the samurai, who had played a prominent military role in medieval and early modern Japan. The code of bushido was revived during the nationalistic fervor of the 1930s. Based on an ideal of loyalty and service, the code emphasized the obligation to honor and defend emperor, country, and family and to sacrifice one's life if one failed in this sacred mission.

THE BOMBING OF CIVILIANS

THE HOME FRONT BECAME a battlefront when civilian populations became the targets of mass bombing raids. Many people believed that mass bombing could effectively weaken the morale of the civilian population and shorten the war. Rarely did it achieve its goal. In these selections, British, German, and Japanese civilians relate their experiences during bombing raids.

London, 1940

Early last evening, the noise was terrible. My husband and Mr. P. were trying to play chess. I was playing draughts with Kenneth in the cupboard. . . . Presently I heard a stifled voice "Mummy! I don't know what's become of my glasses." "I should think they are tied up in my wool." My knitting had disappeared and wool seemed to be everywhere! We heard a whistle, a bang which shook the house, and an explosion. . . . Well, we straightened out, decided draughts and chess were no use under the circumstances, and waited for a lull so we could have a pot of tea.

Hamburg, 1943

As the many fires broke through the roofs of the burning buildings, a column of heated air rose more than two and a half miles high and one and a half miles in diameter. . . . This column was turbulent, and it was fed from its base by in-rushing cooler ground-surface air. One and one half miles from the fires this draught increased the wind velocity from eleven to thirty-three miles per hour. At the edge of the area the velocities must have been appreciably greater, as trees three feet in diameter were uprooted. In a short time the temperature reached ignition point for all combustibles, and the entire area was ablaze. In such fires complete burn-out occurred; that is, no trace of combustible material remained . . .

Hiroshima, August 6, 1945

I heard the airplane; I looked up at the sky, it was a sunny day, the sky was blue. . . . Then I saw something drop—and pow!—a big explosion knocked me down. Then I was unconscious—I don't know for how long. Then I was conscious but I couldn't see anything. . . . Then I see people moving away and I just follow them. It is not light like it was before, it is more like evening. I look around; houses are all flat! . . . I follow the people to the river. I couldn't hear anything, my ears are blocked up. I am thinking a bomb has dropped! . . . I didn't know my hands were burned, nor my face.

 What common elements do you find in these three different descriptions of bombing raids? What effect did aerial bombing have on the nature of modern warfare?

Source: J. Campbell, ed. *The Experience of World War II* (New York: Oxford University Press, 1989), p. 180.

The system culminated in the final years of the war when young Japanese were encouraged to volunteer en masse to serve as pilots in suicide missions—known as *kamikaze* (kah-mi-KAH-zee) ("divine wind")—against U.S. warships.

Women's rights, too, were to be sacrificed to the greater national cause. Already by 1937, Japanese women were being exhorted to fulfill their patriotic duty by bearing more children and by espousing the slogans of the Greater Japanese Women's Association. Nevertheless, Japan was extremely reluctant to mobilize women on behalf of the war effort. General Hideki Tojo (hee-DEK-ee TOH-joh), prime minister from 1941 to 1944, opposed female employment, arguing that "the weakening of the family system would be the weakening of the nation. . . . We are able to do our duties only because we have wives and mothers at home."[19] Female employment increased during the war, but only in areas where women traditionally had worked, such as the textile industry and farming. Instead of using women to meet labor shortages, the Japanese government brought in Korean and Chinese laborers.

Front-Line Civilians: The Bombing of Cities

Bombing was used in World War II in a variety of ways: against nonhuman military targets, against enemy troops, and against civilian populations. The use of bombs made World War II as devastating for civilians as for front-line soldiers (see the box above). A small number of bombing raids in the last year of World War I had given rise to the argument, first expressed by the Italian general Giulio Douhet (JOOL-yoh doo-AY) and then widely accepted, that the public outcry generated by the bombing of civilian populations would be an effective way to coerce governments into making peace. Consequently, European air forces began to develop long-range bombers in the 1930s.

LUFTWAFFE ATTACKS The first sustained use of civilian bombing contradicted Douhet's theory. Beginning in early September 1940, the German Luftwaffe subjected London and many other British cities and towns to nightly air raids, making the Blitz (as the British called the German air raids) a national experience. Londoners took the first heavy blows and set the standard for the rest of the British population by refusing to panic. One British woman expressed well what many others apparently felt:

> It was a beautiful summer night . . . and made more beautiful than ever by the red glow from the East, where the docks were burning. We stood and stared for a minute, and I tried to fix the scene in my mind, because one day this will be history, and I shall be one of those who actually saw it. I wasn't frightened any more.[20]

But London morale was helped by the fact that German raids were widely scattered over a very large city. Smaller communities were more directly affected by the devastation. On November 14, 1940, for example, the Luftwaffe destroyed hundreds of shops and 100 acres of the city center of Coventry. The destruction of smaller cities did produce morale problems as wild rumors of heavy casualties spread quickly in these communities. Nevertheless, morale was soon restored. In any case, war production in these areas seems to have been little affected by the raids.

THE BOMBING OF GERMANY The British failed to learn from their own experience, however, and soon proceeded to bomb German cities. Churchill and his advisers believed that destroying German communities would break civilian morale and bring victory. Major bombing raids began in 1942 under the direction of Arthur Harris, the wartime leader of the British air force's Bomber Command, which was rearmed with four-engine heavy bombers capable of taking the war into the center of occupied Europe. On May 31, 1942, Cologne became the first German city to be subjected to an attack by one thousand bombers.

With the entry of the Americans into the war, the bombing strategy changed. American planes flew daytime missions aimed at the precision bombing of transportation facilities and war industries, while the British Bomber Command continued nighttime saturation bombing of all German cities with populations over 100,000. Bombing raids added an element of terror to circumstances already made difficult by growing shortages of food, clothing, and fuel. Germans especially feared the incendiary bombs, which created firestorms that swept destructive paths through the cities. Four raids on Hamburg in August 1943 produced temperatures of 1,800 degrees Fahrenheit, obliterated half the city's buildings, and killed thousands of civilians. The ferocious bombing of Dresden from February 13 to 15, 1945, created a firestorm that may have killed as many as 35,000 inhabitants and refugees (see "Global Perspectives" on p. 855). Even some Allied leaders began to criticize what they saw as the unnecessary terror bombing of German cities. Urban dwellers became accustomed to living in air-raid shelters, usually cellars in businesses or houses. Occupants of shelters could be crushed to death, however, if the shelters were hit directly or die by suffocation from the effects of high-explosive bombs. Not until 1943 did Nazi leaders begin to evacuate women and children to rural areas. But evacuation created its own problems since people in country villages were often hostile to the urban newcomers.

Germany suffered enormously from the Allied bombing raids. Millions of buildings were destroyed, and possibly half a million civilians died in the raids. Nevertheless, it is highly unlikely that the Allied bombing sapped the morale of the German people. Instead, Germans, whether pro-Nazi or anti-Nazi, fought on stubbornly, often driven simply by a desire to live. Nor did the bombing destroy Germany's industrial capacity. The Allied Strategic Bombing survey revealed that the production of war matériel actually increased between 1942 and 1944. Even in 1944 and 1945, Allied raids cut German production of

armaments by only 7 percent. Nevertheless, the widespread destruction of transportation systems and fuel supplies made it extremely difficult for the new matériel to reach the German military. Because of strong German air defenses, air raids were also costly for the Allies. Nearly 40,000 Allied planes were destroyed, and 160,000 airmen lost their lives.

The destruction of German cities from the air did accomplish one major goal. There would be no stab-in-the-back myth after World War II as there had been after World War I. The loss of the war could not be blamed on the collapse of the home front. Many Germans understood that the home front had been a battlefront, and they had fought on their front just as the soldiers had on theirs.

THE BOMBING OF JAPAN: THE ATOMIC BOMB The bombing of civilians eventually reached a new level with the dropping of the first atomic bomb on Japan. Fearful of German attempts to create a superbomb through the use of uranium, the American government pursued a dual strategy. While sabotaging German efforts, the United States and Britain recruited scientists, including many who had fled from Germany, to develop an atomic bomb. Working under the direction of J. Robert Oppenheimer (1904–1967) at a secret laboratory in Los Alamos, New Mexico, Allied scientists built and tested the first atomic bomb by the summer of 1945. A new era in warfare was about to begin.

Japan was especially vulnerable to air raids because its air force had been virtually destroyed in the course of the war, and its crowded cities were built of flimsy materials. Attacks on Japanese cities by the new American B-29 Superfortresses, the biggest bombers of the war, had begun on November 24, 1944. By the summer of 1945, many of Japan's factories had been destroyed, along with one-fourth of its dwellings. After the Japanese government decreed the mobilization of all people between the ages of thirteen and sixty into a "people's volunteer corps," President Truman and his advisers feared that Japanese fanaticism might mean heavy American casualties. This concern led them to drop the atomic bomb on Hiroshima (August 6) and Nagasaki (August 9). The destruction was incredible. Of 76,000 buildings near the hypocenter of the explosion in Hiroshima, 70,000 were flattened; 140,000 of the city's 400,000 inhabitants died by the end of 1945. By the end of 1950, another 50,000 had perished from the effects of radiation.

Aftermath of the War

 FOCUS QUESTIONS: What were the costs of World War II? How did the Allies' visions of postwar Europe differ, and how did these differences contribute to the emergence of the Cold War?

World War II was the most destructive war in history. Much had been at stake. Nazi Germany followed a worldview based on racial extermination and the enslavement of millions in order to create an Aryan racial empire. The Japanese, fueled

The Impact of Total War in West and East

WORLD WAR II WAS A TOTAL WAR for civilians as political leaders came to see the bombing of civilians as a legitimate way to attempt to demoralize the population and end the war. The results of this policy are evident in these three scenes of life between 1941 and 1945. In the first photograph (top left), refugees walk past a bombed tenement building, where 800 people died and 800 more were injured during a German bombing raid on Clydebank near Glasgow in Scotland in March 1941. Only 7 of the city's 12,000 houses were left undamaged;

35,000 of the 47,000 inhabitants became homeless overnight. The raid on Clydebank was Scotland's only severe bombing experience. The city was attacked because of its proximity to nearby shipyards that were refitting ships to serve in the war. The second photograph (bottom left) shows the devastation in Dresden, Germany, as a result of British and American bombing raids on February 13 and 14, 1945. An area of 2.5 square miles in the city was destroyed, and as many as 35,000 people died. The most devastating destruction of civilians came near the end of the war when the United States dropped atomic bombs on the Japanese cities of Hiroshima and Nagasaki. The panoramic view of Hiroshima after the bombing in the third photograph shows the incredible devastation produced by the atomic bomb.

Keystone/Getty Images

Bettmann/Corbis

J. R. Eyerman//Time Life Pictures/Getty Images

by extreme nationalist ideals, also pursued dreams of empire in Asia that led to mass murder and untold devastation. Fighting the Axis powers in World War II required the mobilization of millions of ordinary men and women in the Allied countries who rose to the occasion and struggled to preserve a different way of life. As Winston Churchill once put it, "War is horrible, but slavery is worse."

The Costs of World War II

The costs of World War II were enormous. At least 21 million soldiers died. Civilian deaths were even greater and are now estimated at around 40 million, of whom more than 28 million were Russian and Chinese. The Soviet Union experienced the greatest losses: 10 million soldiers and 19 million civilians. In 1945, millions of people around the world faced starvation; in Europe, 100 million people depended on food relief of some kind.

Millions of people had also been uprooted by the war and became "displaced persons." Europe alone may have had 30 million displaced persons, many of whom found it hard to return home. After the war, millions of Germans were expelled from the Sudetenland in Czechoslovakia, and millions more were ejected from former eastern German territories that were turned over to Poland, all of which seemed reasonable to people who had suffered so much at the hands of the Germans. In Asia, millions of Japanese returned from the former Japanese empire to Japan, while thousands of Korean forced laborers returned to Korea.

Everywhere cities lay in ruins. In Europe, physical devastation was especially bad in eastern and southeastern Europe as well as in the cities of western and central Europe. In Asia, China had experienced extensive devastation from eight years of conflict. So too had the Philippines, while large parts of the major cities in Japan had been destroyed in air raids. At the same time, millions of tons of shipping now lay beneath the seas; factories, farms, transportation systems, bridges, and dams were in ruins. The total monetary cost of the war has been estimated at $4 trillion. The economies of most belligerents, with the exception of the United States, were left drained and on the brink of disaster.

The Impact of Technology

Before World War II, theoretical science and technology were largely separated. Pure science was the domain of university professors who were far removed from the practical technological concerns of technicians and engineers. But during World War II, governments recruited university scientists to develop new weapons and practical instruments of war. In 1940, British physicists played a crucial role in the development of an improved radar system that helped defeat the German air force in the Battle of Britain. German scientists created self-propelled rockets and jet airplanes to keep Hitler's hopes alive for a miraculous turnaround in the war. The computer, too, was a wartime creation. The British mathematician Alan Turing designed a primitive computer to assist British intelligence in breaking the secret codes of German ciphering machines

FILM & HISTORY

Watch *The Imitation Game* (2014), a drama based on the attempt of British intelligence to crack the Enigma, a Nazi ciphering machine used to send secret military messages. The film revolves around the heated attempt of Alan Turing and other mathematicians to successfully create a machine (the first primitive computer) to decipher the Nazi codes.

 How accurate is the film's depiction of Turing's achievements? How did Turing's personal life affect his achievement?

(see "Film & History" above). The most famous product of wartime scientific research was the atomic bomb, created by a team of American and European scientists under the guidance of the American physicist J. Robert Oppenheimer. Obviously, most wartime devices were created for destructive purposes, but merely to mention computers and jet airplanes demonstrates that they could easily be adapted for peacetime uses.

The Allied War Conferences

The total victory of the Allies in World War II was followed not by true peace but by a new conflict known as the **Cold War** that dominated European and world politics for more than forty years. The Cold War stemmed from military, political, and ideological differences, especially between the Soviet Union and the United States, that became apparent at the Allied war conferences held in the last years of the war. Although Allied leaders were mostly preoccupied with how to end the war, they also were strongly motivated by differing and often conflicting visions of postwar Europe.

THE CONFERENCE AT TEHRAN Stalin, Roosevelt, and Churchill, the leaders of the Big Three of the Grand Alliance, met at Tehran (teh-RAHN) (the capital of Iran) in November 1943 to decide the future course of the war. Their major tactical decision concerned the final assault on Germany, and after much debate, they decided on an American-British invasion of the continent through France, which they scheduled for the spring of 1944. The acceptance of this plan had important consequences. It meant that Soviet and British-American forces would meet in defeated Germany along a north-south dividing line and that, most likely, eastern Europe would be liberated by Soviet forces. The Allies also agreed to a partition of postwar Germany, but differences over questions like the frontiers of Poland were carefully set aside. Roosevelt was pleased with the accord with Stalin. Harry Hopkins, one of Roosevelt's advisers at the conference, remarked:

> We really believed in our hearts that this was the dawn of the new day. . . . We were absolutely certain that we had won the

The Victorious Allied Leaders at Yalta. Even before World War II ended, the leaders of the Big Three of the Grand Alliance, Churchill, Roosevelt, and Stalin (seated, left to right), met in wartime conferences to plan the final assault on Germany and negotiate the outlines of the postwar settlement. At the Yalta meeting (February 5–11, 1945), the three leaders concentrated on postwar issues. The American president, who died two months later, was already a worn-out man at Yalta.

first great victory of the peace—and by "we," I mean all of us, the whole civilized human race. The Russians had proved that they could be reasonable and far-seeing and there wasn't any doubt in the minds of the President or any of us that we could live with them and get along with them peacefully for as far into the future as any of us could imagine.[21]

THE YALTA CONFERENCE By the time of the conference at Yalta in Ukraine in February 1945, the defeat of Germany was a foregone conclusion. The Western powers, which had earlier believed that the Soviets were in a weak position, were now faced with the reality of 11 million Red Army soldiers taking possession of eastern and much of central Europe. Stalin was still operating under the notion of spheres of influence. He was deeply suspicious of the Western powers and desired a buffer to protect the Soviet Union from possible future Western aggression. At the same time, however, Stalin was eager to obtain economically important resources and strategic military positions. Roosevelt by this time was moving away from the notion of spheres of influence to the ideal of self-determination. He called for the end of the system of "unilateral action, exclusive alliances, and spheres of influence." The Grand Alliance approved the "Declaration on Liberated Europe." This was a pledge to assist liberated European nations in the creation of democratic institutions of "their own choice." Liberated countries were to hold free elections to determine their political systems.

At Yalta, Roosevelt sought Soviet military help against Japan. The atomic bomb was not yet assured, and American military planners feared the possible loss of many men in amphibious assaults on the Japanese home islands. Roosevelt therefore agreed to Stalin's price for military assistance against Japan: possession of Sakhalin and the Kurile Islands as well as two warm-water ports and railroad rights in Manchuria.

The creation of the United Nations was a major American concern at Yalta. Roosevelt hoped to ensure the participation of the Big Three powers in a postwar international organization before difficult issues divided them into hostile camps. After a number of compromises, both Churchill and Stalin accepted Roosevelt's plans for a United Nations organization and set the first meeting for San Francisco in April 1945.

The issues of Germany and eastern Europe were treated less decisively. The Big Three reaffirmed that Germany must surrender unconditionally and created four occupation zones. Churchill, over the objections of the Soviets and Americans, insisted that the French be given one occupation zone, carved out of the British and American zones. German reparations were set at $20 billion. A compromise was also worked out with regard to Poland. It was agreed that a provisional government would be established with members of both the Lublin (LOO-bleen) Poles, who were Polish Communists living in exile in the Soviet Union, and the London Poles, who were non-Communists exiled in Britain. Stalin also agreed to free elections in the future to determine a new government. But the issue of free elections in eastern Europe caused a serious rift between the Soviets and the Americans. The principle was that eastern European governments would be freely elected, but they were also supposed to be pro-Soviet. As Churchill expressed it, "The Poles will have their future in their own hands, with the single limitation that they must honestly follow in harmony with their allies, a policy friendly to Russia."[22] This attempt to reconcile two irreconcilable goals was doomed to failure, as soon became evident at the next conference of the Big Three powers.

INTENSIFYING DIFFERENCES Even before the conference at Potsdam (PAHTS-dam) took place in July 1945, Western relations with the Soviets were deteriorating rapidly. The Grand Alliance had been one of necessity in which disagreements had been subordinated to the pragmatic concerns of the war. The Allied powers' only common aim was the defeat of Nazism. Once this goal had been all but accomplished, the

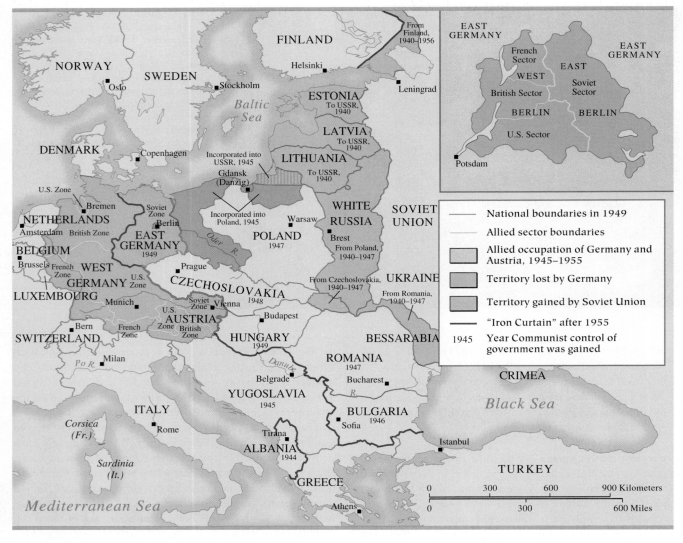

MAP 27.5 Territorial Changes After World War II. In the last months of World War II, the Red Army occupied much of eastern Europe. Stalin sought pro-Soviet satellite states in the region as a buffer against future invasions from western Europe, whereas Britain and the United States wanted democratically elected governments. Soviet military control of the territory settled the question.

Q Which country gained the greatest territory at the expense of Germany?

many differences that troubled East-West relations came to the surface. Each side committed acts that the other viewed as unbecoming of "allies."

From the perspective of the Soviets, the United States' termination of Lend-Lease aid before the war was over and its failure to respond to the Soviet request for a $6 billion loan for reconstruction exposed the Western desire to keep the Soviet state weak. On the American side, the Soviet Union's failure to fulfill its Yalta pledge on the "Declaration on Liberated Europe" as applied to eastern Europe set a dangerous precedent. This was evident in Romania as early as February 1945, when the Soviets engineered a coup and installed a new government under the Communist Petra Groza (PET-ruh GRO-zhuh), called the "Little Stalin." One month later, the Soviets sabotaged the Polish settlement by arresting the London Poles and their

sympathizers and installing the Soviet-backed Lublin Poles in power. To the Americans, the Soviets seemed to be asserting control of eastern European countries under puppet Communist regimes (see Map 27.5).

THE POTSDAM CONFERENCE The Potsdam Conference of July 1945 consequently began under a cloud of mistrust. Roosevelt had died on April 12 and had been succeeded by Harry Truman. During the conference, Truman received word that the atomic bomb had been successfully tested. Some historians have argued that this knowledge resulted in Truman's stiffened resolve against the Soviets. Whatever the reasons, there was a new coldness in the relations between the Soviets and the Americans. At Potsdam, Truman demanded free elections throughout eastern Europe. Stalin responded, "A freely

EMERGENCE OF THE COLD WAR: CHURCHILL AND STALIN

LESS THAN A YEAR AFTER the end of World War II, the major Allies that had fought together to destroy Hitler's Germany had divided into two hostile camps. These excerpts, taken from Winston Churchill's speech to an American audience on March 5, 1946, and Joseph Stalin's reply to Churchill only nine days later, reveal the divisions in the Western world that marked the beginning of the Cold War.

Churchill's Speech at Fulton, Missouri, March 5, 1946

From Stettin in the Baltic to Trieste in the Adriatic, an iron curtain has descended across the continent. Behind that line lie all the capitals of the ancient states of central and eastern Europe. Warsaw, Berlin, Prague, Vienna, Budapest, Belgrade, Bucharest, and Sofia, all these famous cities and the populations around them lie in the Soviet sphere and all are subject, in one form or another, not only to Soviet influence but to a very high and increasing measure of control from Moscow. . . .

The Russian-dominated Polish Government has been encouraged to make enormous and wrongful inroads upon Germany, and mass expulsions of millions of Germans on a scale grievous and undreamed of are now taking place. The Communist parties, which were very small in all these eastern states of Europe, have been raised to preeminence and power far beyond their numbers and are seeking everywhere to obtain totalitarian control. Police governments are prevailing in nearly every case, and so far, except in Czechoslovakia,

there is no true democracy. . . . Whatever conclusions may be drawn from these facts—and facts they are—this is certainly not the liberated Europe we fought to build up. Nor is it one which contains the essentials of permanent peace.

Stalin's Reply to Churchill, March 14, 1946

In substance, Mr. Churchill now stands in the position of a firebrand of war. And Mr. Churchill is not alone here. He has friends not only in England but also in the United States of America.

In this respect, one is reminded remarkably of Hitler and his friends. Hitler began to set war loose by announcing his racial theory, declaring that only people speaking the German language represent a fully valuable nation. Mr. Churchill begins to set war loose, also by a racial theory, maintaining that only nations speaking the English language are fully valuable nations, called upon to decide the destinies of the entire world.

The German racial theory brought Hitler and his friends to the conclusion that the Germans, as the only fully valuable nation, must rule over other nations. The English racial theory brings Mr. Churchill and his friends to the conclusion that nations speaking the English language, being the only fully valuable nations, should rule over the remaining nations of the world.

 What do the statements of Churchill and Stalin tell us about the origins and rhetoric of the Cold War? Why might it be said that both sides in this global conflict persistently misunderstood the other?

Source: *Congressional Record*, 79th Congress, 2nd Session, A (Washington, D.C.: U.S. Government Printing Office), pp. 1145–1147.

elected government in any of these East European countries would be anti-Soviet, and that we cannot allow."[23] After a bitterly fought and devastating war, Stalin sought absolute military security. To him, it could be gained only by the presence of Communist states in eastern Europe. Free elections might result in governments hostile to the Soviets. By the middle of 1945, only an invasion by Western forces could undo developments in eastern Europe, and after the world's most destructive conflict had ended, few people favored such a policy.

Emergence of the Cold War

The Soviets did not view their actions as dangerous expansionism but as legitimate security maneuvers. Was it not the West that had attacked the East? When Stalin sought help against the Nazis in the 1930s, had not the West turned a deaf ear? But there was little sympathy in the West for Soviet fears and even less trust in Stalin. When the American secretary of state, James Byrnes, proposed a twenty-five-year disarmament of Germany, the Soviet Union rejected it. In the West, many saw this as proof of Stalin's plans to expand in central Europe and create a Communist East German state. When Byrnes responded by

announcing that American troops would be needed in Europe for an indefinite time and made moves that foreshadowed the creation of an independent West Germany, the Soviets saw this as a direct threat to Soviet security in Europe.

As the war slowly receded into the past, the reality of conflicting ideologies had reappeared. Many in the West interpreted Soviet policy as part of a worldwide Communist conspiracy. The Soviets, for their part, viewed Western, especially American, policy as nothing less than global capitalist expansionism or, in Leninist terms, economic imperialism. Vyacheslav Molotov (vyich-chiss-SLAHF MAHL-uh-tawf) (1890–1986), the Russian foreign minister, referred to the Americans as "insatiable imperialists and warmongering groups of adventurers."[24] In March 1946, in a speech to an American audience, former British prime minister Winston Churchill declared that "an iron curtain" had "descended across the continent," dividing Germany and Europe into two hostile camps. Stalin branded Churchill's speech a "call to war with the Soviet Union" (see the box above). Only months after the world's most devastating conflict had ended, the world seemed once again bitterly divided. Would the twentieth-century crisis of Western civilization never end?

Between 1933 and 1939, Europeans watched as Adolf Hitler rebuilt Germany into a great military power. For Hitler, military power was an absolute prerequisite for the creation of a German racial empire that would dominate Europe and the

world for generations to come. During that same period, the nation of Japan fell under the influence of military leaders who conspired with right-wing forces to push a program of expansion at the expense of China and the Soviet Union as well as territories in Southeast Asia. The ambitions of Germany in Europe and those of Japan in Asia led to a global conflict that became the most devastating war in human history.

The Axis nations, Germany, Italy, and Japan, proved victorious during the first two years of the war, which began after the German invasion of Poland on September 1, 1939. By 1942, the war had begun to turn in favor of the Allies, an alliance of Great Britain, the Soviet Union, and the United States. The Japanese advance was ended at the naval battles of the Coral Sea and

Midway in 1942. In February 1943, the Soviets won the Battle of Stalingrad and began to push westward. By mid-1943, Germany and Italy had been driven out of North Africa; in June 1944, Rome fell to the Allies, and an Allied invasion force landed in Normandy in France. After the Soviets linked up with British and American forces in April 1945, Hitler committed suicide, and the war in Europe came to an end. After atomic bombs

were dropped on Hiroshima and Nagasaki in August 1945, the war in Asia also ended.

During its domination of Europe, the Nazi empire brought death and destruction to many, especially Jews, minorities, and others that the Nazis considered racially inferior peoples. The Japanese New Order in Asia, while claiming to promote a policy of "Asia for the Asians," also brought economic exploitation, severe hardships, and often death for the subject peoples under Japanese control. All sides bombed civilian populations, making World War II as devastating for civilians as for front-line soldiers.

If Hitler had been successful, the Nazi New Order, built on authoritarianism, racial extermination, and the brutal oppression of peoples, would have meant a triumph of barbarism and the end of freedom and equality, which, however imperfectly realized, had become important ideals in Western civilization.

The Nazis lost, but only after tremendous sacrifices and costs. Much of European civilization lay in ruins, and the old Europe had disappeared forever. Europeans, who had been accustomed to dominating the world at the beginning of the twentieth century, now watched helplessly at mid-century as the two new superpowers created by the two world wars took control of their destinies. Even before the last battles had been fought, the United States and the Soviet Union had arrived at different visions of the postwar European world. No sooner had the war ended than their differences gave rise to a new and potentially even more devastating conflict known as the Cold War.

CHAPTER TIMELINE

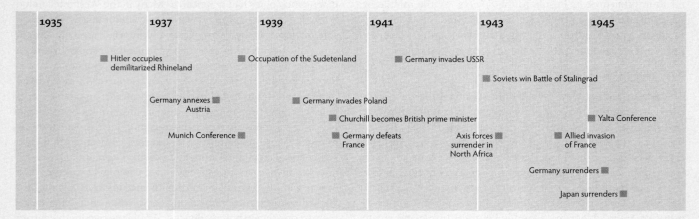

1935	1937	1939	1941	1943	1945
	Hitler occupies demilitarized Rhineland	Occupation of the Sudetenland	Germany invades USSR		
				Soviets win Battle of Stalingrad	
	Germany annexes Austria	Germany invades Poland			
		Churchill becomes British prime minister			Yalta Conference
	Munich Conference	Germany defeats France	Axis forces surrender in North Africa	Allied invasion of France	
				Germany surrenders	
				Japan surrenders	

CHAPTER REVIEW

Upon Reflection

Q How do you account for the early successes of the Germans from 1939 through 1941?

Q How did the Nazis attempt to establish a New Order in Europe after their military victories, and what were the results of their efforts?

Q How did the attempt to arrive at a peace settlement after World War II lead to the beginnings of a new conflict known as the Cold War?

Key Terms

appeasement (p. 830)
blitzkrieg (p. 830)
panzer division (p. 830)
unconditional surrender (p. 839)

Nazi New Order (p. 844)
Final Solution (p. 846)
Einsatzgruppen (p. 846)
Cold War (p. 856)

Suggestions for Further Reading

PRELUDE TO WAR On the causes of World War II, see **R. J. Overy,** *The Origins of the Second World War*, 3rd ed. (London, 2008). On the origins of the war in the Pacific, see **A. Iriye,** *The Origins of the Second World War in Asia and the Pacific* (London, 1987).

GENERAL WORKS General works on World War II include the comprehensive work by **G. Weinberg,** *A World at Arms: A Global History of World War II*, 2nd ed. (Cambridge, 2005), and **A. Roberts,** *The Storm of War: A New History of the Second World War* (New York, 2011). For a good military history of World War II, see **W. Murray** and **A. Millett,** *A War to Be Won: Fighting the Second World War* (Cambridge, Mass., 2000). On the Nazi-Soviet war, see **E. Mawdsley,** *Thunder in the East: The Nazi-Soviet War, 1941–1945* (London, 2015). On the impact of the war on civilians, see **J. Bourke,** *The Second World War: A People's History* (Oxford, 2003).

THE NEW ORDER A standard work on the German New Order in Russia is **A. Dallin,** *German Rule in Russia, 1941–1945*, rev. ed. (London, 1985). On Poland, see **P. T. Rutherford,** *Prelude to the Final Solution: The Nazi Program for Deporting Ethnic Poles, 1939–1941* (Lawrence, Kans., 2007). On foreign labor, see **U. Herbert,** *Hitler's Foreign Workers: Enforced Foreign Labor in Germany under the Third Reich*, trans. **W. Templer** (Cambridge, 1997).

THE HOLOCAUST The best studies of the Holocaust include **R. Hilberg,** *The Destruction of the European Jews*, rev. ed., 3 vols. (New York, 1985), and **S. Friedlander,** *The Years of Extermination: Nazi Germany and the Jews, 1939–1945* (New York, 2007). For a brief study, see **D. Dwork** and **R. J. van Pelt,** *Holocaust: A History* (New York, 2002). Other Nazi atrocities are examined in **R. C. Lukas,** *Forgotten Holocaust: The Poles Under German Occupation, 1939–44*, 2nd ed. (Lexington, Ky., 2001).

THE HOME FRONT On the home front in Germany, see **M. Kitchen,** *Nazi Germany at War* (New York, 1995), and **J. Stephenson,** *The Nazi Organisation of Women*, rev. ed. (London, 2013). On the home front in Britain, see **S. Rose,** *Which People's War? National Identity and Citizenship in Britain, 1939–1945* (Oxford, 2003). The Soviet Union during the war is examined in **M. Harrison** and **J. Barber,** *The Soviet Home Front 1941–1945* (London, 1991).

THE BOMBING CAMPAIGNS On the Allied bombing campaign against Germany, see **R. Hansen,** *Fire and Fury: The Allied Bombing of Germany, 1942–1945* (London, 2008). On the use of the atomic bomb in Japan, see **M. Gordin,** *Five Days in August: How World War II Became a Nuclear War* (Princeton, N.J., 2006).

Notes

1. Quoted in J. Noakes and G. Pridham, eds., *Nazism, 1919–1945: A Documentary Reader*, vol. 3: *Foreign Policy, War, and Racial Extermination* (Exeter, U.K., 1995), p. 629.
2. Adolf Hitler, *Mein Kampf*, trans. R. Manheim (Boston, 1971), p. 654.
3. *Documents on German Foreign Policy* (London, 1956), ser. D, vol. 2, p. 358.
4. Ibid., vol. 7, p. 204.
5. Quoted in N. Rich, *Hitler's War Aims* (New York, 1973), vol. 1, p. 129.
6. Quoted in W. Murray and A. Millett, *A War to Be Won: Fighting the Second World War* (Cambridge, Mass., 2000), p. 66.
7. Quoted in ibid., p. 137.
8. A. Speer, *Spandau*, trans. R. Winston and C. Winston (New York, 1976), p. 50.
9. *Nazi Conspiracy and Aggression* (Washington, D.C., 1946), vol. 6, p. 262.
10. International Military Tribunal, *Trial of the Major War Criminals* (Nuremberg, 1947–1949), vol. 22, p. 480.

11. Adolf Hitler, *My New Order*, ed. R. D. Roussy de Sales (New York, 1941), pp. 21–22.
12. Quoted in L. Dawidowicz, *The War Against the Jews* (New York, 1975), p. 106.
13. *Nazi Conspiracy and Aggression*, vol. 5, pp. 341–342.
14. Quoted in R. Hilberg, *The Destruction of the European Jews*, rev. ed. (New York, 1985), vol. 1, pp. 332–333.
15. *Nazi Conspiracy and Aggression*, vol. 6, p. 789.
16. Quoted in J. Noakes and G. Pridham, eds., *Nazism, 1919–1945: A Documentary Reader*, vol. 3: *Foreign Policy, War, and Racial Extermination*, p. 1182.
17. Quoted in J. Campbell, *The Experience of World War II* (New York, 1989), p. 170.
18. Quoted in C. Koonz, "Mothers in the Fatherland: Women in Nazi Germany," in R. Bridenthal and C. Koonz, eds., *Becoming Visible: Women in European History* (Boston, 1977), p. 466.
19. Quoted in Campbell, *The Experience of World War II*, p. 143.
20. Quoted in ibid., p. 177.
21. Quoted in R. E. Sherwood, *Roosevelt and Hopkins: An Intimate History* (New York, 1948), p. 870.
22. Quoted in N. Graebner, *Cold War Diplomacy, 1945–1960* (Princeton, N.J., 1962), p. 117.
23. Quoted in ibid., p. 117.
24. Quoted in W. Loth, *The Division of the World, 1941–1955* (New York, 1988), p. 81.

COLD WAR AND A NEW WESTERN WORLD, 1945–1965

Survivors in the ruins of Berlin, Germany, at the end of World War II

CHAPTER OUTLINE AND FOCUS QUESTIONS

Development of the Cold War

Q Why were the United States and the Soviet Union suspicious of each other after World War II, and what events between 1945 and 1949 heightened the tensions between the two nations? How and why did the Cold War become a global affair after 1949?

Europe and the World: Decolonization

Q Why and how did the European colonies in Africa, the Middle East, and Asia gain independence between 1945 and 1965?

Recovery and Renewal in Europe

Q What were the main developments in the Soviet Union, Eastern Europe, and Western Europe between 1945 and 1965?

The United States and Canada: A New Era

Q What were the main political developments in North America between 1945 and 1965?

Postwar Society and Culture in the Western World

Q What major changes occurred in Western society and culture between 1945 and 1965?

Critical Thinking

Q What were the similarities and differences in the political, social, and economic history of Eastern Europe and Western Europe between 1945 and 1965?

Connections to Today

Q In what ways are the developments in the Cold War between 1945 and 1965 still evident in international affairs today?

THE END OF WORLD WAR II in Europe had been met with great joy. One visitor to Moscow reported, "I looked out of the window [at 2 A.M.], almost everywhere there were lights in the window—people were staying awake. Everyone embraced everyone else, someone sobbed aloud." But after the victory parades and celebrations, Europeans awoke to a devastating realization: their civilization was in ruins. Some wondered if Europe would ever regain its former prosperity and importance. Winston Churchill wrote, "What is Europe now? A rubble heap, a charnel house, a breeding ground of pestilence and hate." There was ample reason for his pessimism. Almost 40 million people (soldiers and civilians) had been killed during the preceding six years. Massive air raids and artillery bombardments had reduced many of the great cities of Europe to heaps of rubble. The Polish capital of Warsaw had been almost completely obliterated. An American general described Berlin: "Wherever we looked we saw desolation. It was like a city of the dead."

Suffering and shock were visible in every face. Dead bodies still remained in canals and lakes and were being dug out from under bomb debris. Millions of Europeans faced starvation, as grain harvests were only half of what they had been in 1939. Millions were also homeless. In the parts of the Soviet Union that had been occupied by the Germans, almost 25 million people were without homes. The destruction of bridges, roads, and railroads had left transportation systems paralyzed. Untold millions of people had been uprooted by the war; now they became "displaced persons" trying to find food and then their way home. Eleven million prisoners of war had to be returned to their native countries while 15 million Germans and Eastern Europeans were driven out of countries where they were no longer wanted. Yet despite the chaos, Europe was soon on the road to a remarkable recovery. Already by 1950, Europe's industrial and agricultural output was 30 percent above prewar levels.

World War II had cost Europe more than physical destruction, however. European supremacy in world affairs had also been destroyed. After 1945, the colonial empires of the European nations disintegrated, and Europe's place in the world changed radically. As the Cold War conflict between the world's two superpowers—the United States and the Soviet Union—intensified, the European nations were divided into two armed camps dependent on one or the other of these two major powers. The United States and the Soviet Union, whose rivalry raised the specter of nuclear war, seemed to hold the survival of Europe and the world in their hands.

Development of the Cold War

 FOCUS QUESTIONS: Why were the United States and the Soviet Union suspicious of each other after World War II, and what events between 1945 and 1949 heightened the tensions between the two nations? How and why did the Cold War become a global affair after 1949?

Even before World War II had ended, the two major Allied powers—the United States and the Soviet Union—had begun to disagree on the nature of the postwar European world. Unity had been maintained during the war because of the urgent need to defeat the Axis powers, but once they were defeated, the differences between the Americans and Soviets again surged to the front.

HISTORIANS DEBATE Confrontation of the Superpowers: Who Started the Cold War?

There has been considerable historical debate about who was responsible for starting the Cold War. In the 1950s, most scholars in the West assumed that the bulk of the blame must fall on the shoulders of Joseph Stalin, whose determination to impose Soviet rule on Eastern Europe snuffed out hopes for freedom and self-determination there and aroused justifiable fears of Communist expansion in the West. During the next

decade, however, revisionist historians—influenced in part by their dislike of aggressive U.S. policies in Southeast Asia—began to argue that the fault lay primarily in the United States, where President Harry Truman and his anti-Communist advisers sought to encircle the Soviet Union with a group of pliant U.S. client states. More recently, many historians have adopted a more nuanced view, noting that both the United States and the Soviet Union took steps at the end of World War II that were unwise or might have been avoided.

Both nations, however, were working within a framework conditioned by the past. Ultimately, the rivalry between the two superpowers stemmed from their different historical perspectives and their irreconcilable political ambitions. Intense competition for political and military supremacy had long been a regular feature of Western civilization. The United States and the Soviet Union were the heirs of that European tradition of power politics, and it should not surprise us that two such different systems would seek to extend their way of life to the rest of the world. Because of its need to feel secure on its western border, the Soviet Union was not prepared to give up the advantages it had gained in Eastern Europe from Germany's defeat. But neither were American leaders willing to give up the power and prestige the United States had gained throughout the world. Suspicious of each other's motives, the United States and the Soviet Union soon raised their mutual fears to a level of intense competition (see "Opposing Viewpoints" on p. 865). In recent years, some historians have emphasized Soviet responsibility, especially in view of new evidence from previously closed Soviet archives that indicates that Stalin had even been willing to go to war to spread communism to all of Europe. Regardless of who was responsible, however, a number of events between 1945 and 1949 embroiled the Soviet Union and the United States in continual conflict.

DISAGREEMENT OVER EASTERN EUROPE Eastern Europe was the first area of disagreement. The United States and Great Britain had championed self-determination and democratic freedom for the liberated nations of Eastern Europe. Stalin, however, fearful that the Eastern European nations would return to traditional anti-Soviet attitudes if they were permitted free elections, opposed the West's plans. Having liberated Eastern Europe from the Nazis, the Red Army proceeded to install pro-Soviet governing regimes in Poland, Romania, Bulgaria, and Hungary. These pro-Soviet governments satisfied Stalin's desire for a buffer zone against the West, but the local populations and their sympathizers in the West saw the regimes as an expansion of Stalin's empire. Only another war could change this situation, and few people wanted another armed conflict.

THE TRUMAN DOCTRINE A civil war in Greece provided another arena for confrontation between the superpowers. In 1946, the Communist People's Liberation Army and the anti-Communist forces supported by the British were fighting each other for control of Greece. Great Britain had initially assumed primary responsibility for promoting postwar reconstruction in the eastern Mediterranean, but in 1947 ongoing postwar economic problems caused the British to withdraw from the active role they had been playing in both Greece and Turkey. The U.S.

Who Started the Cold War? American and Soviet Perspectives

ALTHOUGH THE UNITED STATES and the Soviet Union had cooperated during World War II to defeat the Germans and Japanese, differences began to appear as soon as victory became certain. The year 1946 was an especially important turning point in the relationship between the two new superpowers. George Kennan, an American diplomat regarded as an expert on Soviet affairs, was asked to write an analysis of one of Stalin's speeches. His U.S. Foreign Service dispatch, which came to be known as the Long Telegram, was sent to U.S. embassies, U.S. State Department officials, and military leaders. The Long Telegram gave a strong view of Soviet intentions. A response to Kennan's position was written by Nikolai Novikov (nyik-uh-LY NAH-vuh-kahf), a former Soviet ambassador to the United States. His response was read by Vyacheslav Molotov, the Soviet foreign minister, but historians are not sure if Stalin or other officials also read it and were influenced by it.

George Kennan, The Long Telegram, February 1946

At the bottom of [the Soviet] neurotic view of world affairs is a traditional and instinctive Russian sense of insecurity. Originally, this was the insecurity of a peaceful agricultural people trying to live on a vast exposed plain in the neighborhood of fierce nomadic peoples. To this was added, as Russia came into contact with the economically advanced West, the fear of more competent, more powerful, more highly organized societies. . . . For this reason they have always feared foreign penetration, feared direct contact between the Western world and their own. . . . And they have learned to seek security only in patient but deadly struggle for total destruction of rival power, never in compacts and compromises with it. . . .

In summary, we have here a political force committed fanatically to the belief that with the United State there can be no permanent modus vivendi, that it is desirable and necessary the internal harmony of our society be disrupted, our traditional way of life be destroyed, the international authority of our state be broken, if Soviet power is to be secure. . . . In addition it has an elaborate and far-flung apparatus for exertion of its influence in other countries, an apparatus of amazing flexibility and versatility, managed by people whose experience and skill in underground methods are presumably without parallel in history. Finally, it is seemingly inaccessible to considerations of reality in its basic reactions. . . . This is admittedly not a pleasant picture. . . . But I would like to record my conviction that the problem is within our power to

solve—and that without recourse to any general conflict. . . . I think we may approach calmly and with good heart the problem of how to deal with Russia . . . [but] we must have the courage and self-confidence to cling to our own methods and conceptions of human society. After all, the greatest danger that can befall us in coping with this problem of Soviet communism is that we shall allow ourselves to become like those with whom we are coping.

Nikolai Novikov, Telegram, September 27, 1946

One of the stages in the achievement of dominance over the world by the United States is its understanding with England concerning the partial division of the world on the basis of mutual concessions. The basic lines of the secret agreement between the United States and England regarding the division of the world consist, as shown by facts, in their agreement on the inclusion of Japan and China in the sphere of influence of the United States in the Far East. . . . The American policy in China is striving for the complete economic and political submission of China to the control of American monopolistic capital. . . .

Obvious indications of the U.S. effort to establish world dominance are also to be found in the increase in military potential in peacetime and in the establishment of a large number of naval and air bases both in the United States and beyond its borders. . . .

Careful note should be taken of the fact that the preparation by the United States for a future war is being conducted with the prospect of war against the Soviet Union, which in the eyes of American imperialists is the main obstacle in the path of the United States to world domination. This is indicated by facts such as the tactical training of the American army for war with the Soviet Union as the future opponent, the placing of American strategic bases in regions from which it is possible to launch strikes on Soviet territory, intensified training and strengthening of Arctic regions as close approaches to the USSR, and attempts to prepare Germany and Japan to use those countries in a war against the USSR.

 In Kennan's view, what was the Soviet policy after World War II? What did he believe determined that policy, and how did he think the United States should respond? In Novikov's view, what was the goal of U.S. foreign policy, and how did he believe the Americans planned to achieve it? Why was it so difficult to find a common ground between the two positions?

Source: K. M. Jensen, ed., *Origins of the Cold War: The Novikov, Kennan, and Roberts 'Long' Telegrams of 1946* (Washington, D.C.: Endowment of the United States Institute of Peace, 1993), pp. 20–21, 28–31, 8, 16.

president Harry Truman, alarmed by British weakness and the possibility of Soviet expansion into the eastern Mediterranean, responded with the **Truman Doctrine**. The Truman Doctrine said, in essence, that the United States would provide financial aid to countries that claimed they were threatened by Communist expansion. If the Soviets were not stopped in Greece, the United States would have to face the spread of communism throughout the free world. As Dean Acheson, the American secretary of state, explained, "Like apples in a barrel infected by disease, the corruption of Greece would infect Iran and all the East . . . likewise Africa . . . Italy . . . France. . . . Not since Rome and Carthage had there been such a polarization of power on this earth."[1] In March 1947, at Truman's request the U.S. Congress agreed to provide $400 million in economic and military aid for Greece and Turkey.

THE MARSHALL PLAN The proclamation of the Truman Doctrine was followed in June 1947 by the European Recovery Program, better known as the **Marshall Plan**. Intended to rebuild prosperity and stability, this program included $13 billion for the economic recovery of war-torn Europe. Underlying it was the belief that Communist aggression fed off economic turmoil. General George C. Marshall had noted in a commencement speech at Harvard, "Our policy is not directed against any country or doctrine but against hunger, poverty, desperation and chaos."[2] Nevertheless, the Marshall Plan, which did not include the Soviet Union, helped speed up the division of Europe into two competing blocs. According to the Soviet view, the Marshall Plan aimed at the "construction of a bloc of states bound by obligations to the USA, and to guarantee the American loans in return for the relinquishing by the European states of their economic and later also their political independence."[3] Some scholars believe that the Marshall Plan encouraged Stalin to push for even greater control of Eastern Europe to safeguard Soviet interests.

THE AMERICAN POLICY OF CONTAINMENT By 1947, the split in Europe between East and West had become a fact of life (see "Film & History" above). At the end of World War II, the United States had favored a quick end to its commitments in Europe. But American fears of Soviet aims caused the United States to play an increasingly important role in European affairs. In an article in *Foreign Affairs* in July 1947, George Kennan, a well-known American diplomat with much knowledge of Soviet affairs, advocated a policy of **containment** against further aggressive Soviet moves. Kennan favored the application of counter-force at a "series of constantly shifting geographical and political points, corresponding to the shifts and maneuvers of Soviet policy." After the Soviet blockade of Berlin in 1948, containment of the Soviet Union became formal American policy.

⏵ FILM & HISTORY

Watch *The Third Man* (1949), a classic thriller set in postwar Vienna about an American who travels to Vienna after the war in search of his friend, only to discover his friend has gone underground in the Russian sector of Vienna. Following the war, Vienna was divided into four zones, each with its suspicious officials from the four powers—United States, Britain, France, and the Soviet Union. The film captures the bleakness of postwar Europe and was filmed in Vienna, where piles of rubble and bomb craters still remained alongside architectural masterpieces.

Q *How does the film portray post-war Europe? How are the Russians portrayed in the film? Why?*

CONTENTION OVER GERMANY The fate of Germany also became a source of heated contention between East and West. Besides **denazification** and the partitioning of Germany (and Berlin) into four occupied zones, the Allied powers had agreed on little else with regard to the conquered nation. The Soviets, hardest hit by the war, took reparations from Germany in the form of booty. The technology-starved Soviets dismantled and removed to the Soviet Union 380 factories from the western zones of Berlin before transferring their control to the Western powers. By the summer of 1946, two hundred chemical, paper, and textile factories in the Soviets' East German zone had likewise been shipped to the Soviet Union. At the same time, the German Communist Party was reestablished under the control of Walter Ulbricht (VAHL-tuh OOL-brikkt) (1893–1973) and was soon in charge of the political reconstruction of the Soviet zone in eastern Germany.

At the same time, the British, French, and Americans gradually began to merge their zones economically and by February 1948 were making plans for the unification of these three western sections of Germany and the formal creation of a West German federal government. The Soviets responded with a blockade of West Berlin that allowed neither trucks nor trains to enter the three western zones of Berlin. The Soviets hoped to secure economic control of all Berlin and force the Western powers to halt the creation of a separate West German state.

The Western powers faced a dilemma. Direct military confrontation seemed dangerous, and no one wished to risk World War III. Therefore, an attempt to

The Berlin Air Lift

The Berlin Air Lift. During the Berlin Air Lift, the United States and its Western allies flew 13,000 tons of supplies daily to Berlin and thus were able to break the Soviet land blockade of the city. In this photograph, residents of West Berlin watch an American plane land at Berlin's Templehof Airport with supplies for the city.

break through the blockade with tanks and trucks was ruled out. But how could the 2.5 million people in the three western zones of Berlin be kept alive when the whole city was inside the Soviet zone? The solution was the Berlin Air Lift.

It was an enormous task. Western Allied air forces worked around the clock for almost a year to supply the city of Berlin with foodstuffs as well as the coal, oil, and gasoline needed to heat the city's dwellings and run its power stations, sewer plants, and factories. At the peak 13,000 tons of supplies were being flown to Berlin daily. Altogether the Western powers shipped 2.3 million tons of food on 277,500 flights. Seventy-three Allied airmen lost their lives due to accidents. The Soviets, also not wanting war, did not interfere and finally lifted the blockade in May 1949. The blockade of Berlin had severely increased tensions between the United States and the Soviet Union and brought about the separation of Germany into two states. At the end of May, a constitution was drafted for a Federal Republic of Germany (West Germany). Konrad Adenauer (AD-uh-now-ur) (1876–1967) was elected as the new German chancellor in September 1949. A month later, the separate German Democratic Republic was established in East Germany. Berlin remained a divided city and the source of much contention between East and West.

NEW MILITARY ALLIANCES The Soviet Union also detonated its first atomic bomb in 1949, and all too soon, both superpowers were involved in an escalating arms race that resulted in the construction of ever more destructive nuclear weapons. Soon the search for security took the form of **mutual deterrence**, the belief that an arsenal of nuclear weapons prevented war by assuring that if one nation launched its nuclear weapons in a preemptive first strike, the other nation would

still be able to respond and devastate the attacker. Therefore, the assumption was that neither side would risk using the massive arsenals that had been assembled. The search for security in the uncertain atmosphere of the Cold War also led to the formation of military alliances. The North Atlantic Treaty Organization (**NATO**) was formed in April 1949 when Belgium, Britain, Denmark, France, Iceland, Italy, Luxembourg, the Netherlands, Norway, and Portugal signed a treaty with the United States and Canada. A few years later West Germany, Greece, and Turkey joined NATO. All the powers agreed to provide mutual assistance if any one of them was attacked.

The Eastern European states soon followed suit. In 1949, they formed the Council for Mutual Economic Assistance (COMECON) for economic cooperation. Then in 1955, Albania, Bulgaria, Czechoslovakia, East Germany, Hungary, Poland, Romania, and the Soviet Union organized a formal military alliance in the **Warsaw Pact**. As had happened so many times before, Europe was divided into hostile alliance systems (see Map 28.1).

Globalization of the Cold War

The Cold War soon spread from Europe to the rest of the world. In 1949, the victory of the Chinese Communists in the Chinese civil war brought a new Communist regime and intensified American fears about the spread of communism. Shortly thereafter, the Korean War turned the Cold War into a world-wide struggle, eventually leading to a system of military alliances around the globe.

THE KOREAN WAR The removal of Korea from Japanese control had been one of the stated objectives of the Allies in World War II, and on the eve of the Japanese surrender in

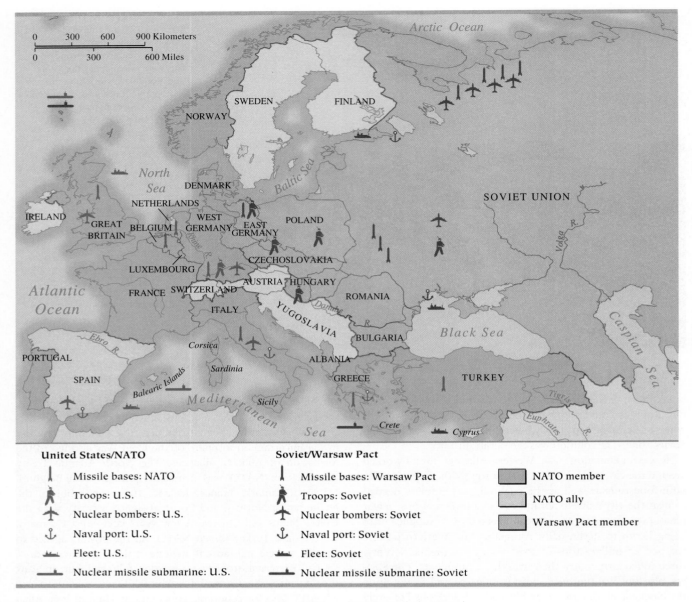

MAP 28.1 The New European Alliance Systems in the 1950s and 1960s. With the United States as its leader, NATO was formed in 1949 to counter the perceived military threat of the Soviet Union and its Eastern European satellites, which formally created the Warsaw Pact in 1955. Soviet and American troops, each backed by nuclear weapons, directly faced each other, heightening Cold War tensions.

 Which NATO countries shared a border with one or more Warsaw Pact countries?

August 1945, the Soviet Union and the United States agreed to divide the country into two separate occupation zones at the 38th parallel. They originally planned to hold national elections after the restoration of peace to reunify Korea under an independent government. But as U.S.-Soviet relations deteriorated, two separate governments emerged in Korea, a Communist one in the north (Democratic People's Republic of Korea or North Korea) and an anti-Communist one (Republic of Korea or South Korea) in the south.

Tensions between the two governments ran high along the dividing line, and on June 25, 1950, with the apparent approval of Stalin, North Korean troops invaded South Korea. The Americans, seeing this as yet another example of Communist aggression and expansion, gained the support of the United Nations and intervened by sending American troops to turn back the invasion. By September, United Nations forces (mostly Americans and South Koreans) under the command of General Douglas MacArthur marched northward across the 38th parallel with the aim of unifying Korea under a single non-Communist government. But Mao Zedong (mow zee-DAHNG) (1893–1976), the leader of Communist China, sent Chinese forces into the fray and forced MacArthur's troops back to South Korea.

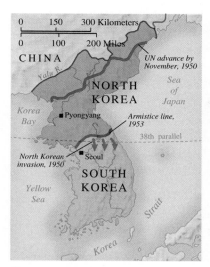

The Korean War

To many Americans, the Chinese intervention in Korea was clear evidence that China intended to promote communism throughout Asia. In fact, China's decision to enter the war was probably motivated in large part by the fear that hostile U.S. forces might be stationed on the Chinese frontier. When two more years of fighting failed to produce a conclusive victory, an armistice was finally signed in 1953. The boundary line between North and South Korea remained roughly at the 38th parallel. To many Americans, the policy of containing communism had succeeded in Asia, just as it had earlier in Europe, though at the cost of losing more than 33,000 men in the war. The Chinese invasion also hardened Western attitudes against the new Chinese government and led to China's isolation from the major capitalist powers for two decades. As a result, China was forced to rely almost entirely on the Soviet Union, with which it had signed a pact of friendship and cooperation in early 1950.

THE FIRST VIETNAM WAR A struggle began in French Indochina after World War II when the Indochinese Communist Party led by Ho Chi Minh (HOH CHEE MIN) (1890–1969) formed a multiparty nationalist alliance called the Vietminh (vee-et-MIN) Front and seized power in northern and central Vietnam. When the negotiations between Ho's government and the returning French collapsed, war broke out in December 1946.

For three years, the Vietminh gradually increased in size and effectiveness. What had begun as an anticolonial struggle by Ho Chi Minh's Vietminh Front against the French soon became the next Cold War struggle as both the United States and the new Communist government in China began to intervene in the conflict in the early 1950s. China began to provide military assistance to the Vietminh to protect its own borders from hostile forces. The Americans supported the French but pressured the French government to prepare for an eventual transition to a non-Communist government in Vietnam.

At the Geneva Conference in 1954, with the French public tired of fighting the "dirty war" in Indochina, the French agreed to a peace settlement with Ho Chi Minh's Vietminh. Vietnam was temporarily divided into a northern Communist half (known as the Democratic Republic of Vietnam) and a non-Communist southern half based in Saigon (sy-GAHN) (known eventually as the Republic of Vietnam). Elections were to be held in two years to create a unified government.

ESCALATION OF THE COLD WAR The Korean and Vietnamese experiences seemed to confirm American fears of Communist expansion and reinforced American determination to contain Soviet power. In the mid-1950s, the administration of President Dwight D. Eisenhower (1890–1969) adopted a policy of massive retaliation, which advocated the full use of American nuclear bombs to counteract even a Soviet ground attack in Europe, although there was no evidence that Stalin ever planned such an attack. Meanwhile, American military alliances were extended around the world. Eisenhower claimed the freedom "we cherish and defend in Europe and in the Americas" was no different from the "freedom that is imperiled in Asia." The Central Treaty Organization (CENTO) of Great Britain, Iran, Iraq, Pakistan, Turkey, and the United States was intended to prevent the Soviet Union from expanding at the expense of its southern neighbors. In addition, Australia, Britain, France, New Zealand, Pakistan, the Philippines, Thailand, and the United States formed the Southeast Asia Treaty Organization (SEATO). By the mid-1950s, the United States found itself allied militarily with forty-two states around the world.

Despite the escalation of the Cold War, hopes for a new era of peaceful coexistence also appeared. The death of Stalin in 1953 caused some people in the West to think that the new Soviet leadership might adopt more flexible policies. But this optimism proved premature. A summit conference at Geneva in 1955 between President Eisenhower and Nikolai Bulganin (nyik-uh-LY bool-GAN-yin) (1895–1975), then the leader of the Soviet government, produced no real benefits. A year later, all talk of **rapprochement** (ra-prohsh-MAHN) between East and West temporarily ceased when the Soviet Union used its armed forces to crush Hungary's attempt to assert its independence from Soviet control.

ANOTHER BERLIN CRISIS A crisis over Berlin also added to the tension in the late 1950s. In August 1957, the Soviet Union had launched its first intercontinental ballistic missile (ICBM) and, shortly thereafter, *Sputnik I*, the first space satellite. Fueled by partisan political debate, fears of a "missile gap" between the United States and the Soviet Union seized the American public. Nikita Khrushchev (nuh-KEE-tuh KHROOSH-chawf) (1894–1971), the new leader of the Soviet Union, attempted to take advantage of the American frenzy over missiles to solve the problem of West Berlin. Khrushchev had said that Berlin was like "the testicles of the West: every time I want to make the West scream, I squeeze on Berlin."[4] West Berlin had remained a "Western island" of prosperity in the midst of the relatively poverty-stricken East Germany. Many East Germans also managed to escape East Germany by fleeing through West Berlin.

In November 1958, Khrushchev announced that unless the West removed its forces from West Berlin within six months, he would turn over control of the access routes to Berlin to the East Germans. Unwilling to accept an ultimatum that would have abandoned West Berlin to the Communists, Eisenhower and the West stood firm, and Khrushchev eventually backed down.

The crisis was revived when John F. Kennedy (1917–1963) became the American president. During a summit meeting in Vienna in June 1961, Khrushchev threatened Kennedy with another six-month ultimatum over West Berlin. Kennedy left Vienna convinced of the need to deal firmly with the Soviet Union, and Khrushchev was forced once again to back off. Frustrated, Khrushchev conspired with Walter Ulbricht, the East German leader, to build a wall around West Berlin to cut off the flow of refugees to the West. On August 13, 1961, East German workers under military supervision began the construction of the Berlin Wall. Within a few months, more than 100 miles of wall, topped by numerous watchtowers, surrounded West Berlin. Since access from West Germany into West Berlin was still permitted, the Americans acquiesced and accepted the wall's existence. The Berlin Wall became a powerful symbol of a divided Europe. And Khrushchev, determined to achieve some foreign policy success, soon embarked on an even more dangerous venture in Cuba.

THE CUBAN MISSILE CRISIS The Cold War confrontation between the United States and the Soviet Union reached frightening levels during the Cuban Missile Crisis. In 1959, a left-wing revolutionary named Fidel Castro (fee-DELL KASS-troh) (b. 1927) had overthrown the Cuban dictator Fulgencio Batista (FULL-jen-see-oh bah-TEES-tuh) (1901–1973) and established a Soviet-supported totalitarian regime. In 1961, an American-supported attempt to invade Cuba via the Bay of Pigs and overthrow Castro's regime ended in utter failure. The next year, in 1962, the Soviet Union decided to station nuclear missiles in Cuba. The United States was not prepared to allow nuclear weapons within such close striking distance of the American mainland, even though it had placed nuclear weapons in Turkey within easy range of the Soviet Union. Khrushchev was quick to point out that "your rockets are in Turkey. You are worried by Cuba . . . because it is 90 miles from the American coast. But Turkey is next to us."[5] When U.S. intelligence discovered that a Soviet fleet carrying missiles was heading to Cuba, President Kennedy decided to blockade Cuba and prevent the fleet from reaching its destination. This approach to the problem had the benefit of delaying confrontation and giving the two sides time to find a peaceful solution (see the box on p. 871). Khrushchev agreed to turn back the fleet if Kennedy pledged not to invade Cuba. In a conciliatory letter to Kennedy, Khrushchev wrote:

> We and you ought not to pull on the ends of the rope in which you have tied the knot of war, because the more the two of us pull, the tighter that knot will be tied. And a moment may come when that knot will be tied too tight that even he who tied it will not have the strength to untie it. . . . Let us not only relax the forces pulling on the ends of the rope, let us take measures to untie that knot. We are ready for this.[6]

The Cuban Missile Crisis brought the world frighteningly close to nuclear war. Indeed, in 1992, a high-ranking Soviet officer revealed that short-range rockets armed with nuclear devices would have been used against American troops if the United States had invaded Cuba, an option that President Kennedy fortunately had rejected. The intense feeling that

CHRONOLOGY	The Cold War to 1962
Truman Doctrine	1947
European Recovery Program (Marshall Plan)	1947
Berlin blockade	1948–1949
Communists win civil war in China	1949
Soviet Union explodes first atomic bomb	1949
Formation of NATO	1949
Formation of COMECON	1949
Korean War	1950–1953
End of First Vietnam War	1954
Formation of Warsaw Pact	1955
Berlin Crisis	1958
Vienna summit	1961
Cuban Missile Crisis	1962

the world might have been annihilated in a few days had a profound influence on both sides. A hotline communication system between Moscow and Washington was installed in 1963 to expedite rapid communication between the two superpowers in a time of crisis. In the same year, the two powers agreed to ban nuclear tests in the atmosphere, a step that served to lessen the tensions between the two nations.

Europe and the World: Decolonization

 FOCUS QUESTION: Why and how did the European colonies in Africa, the Middle East, and Asia gain independence between 1945 and 1965?

As we saw in Chapter 26, movements for independence had begun in earnest in Africa and Asia in the years between the wars. After World War II, these movements grew even louder. The ongoing subjugation of peoples by colonial powers seemed at odds with the goals the Allies had pursued in overthrowing the repressive regimes of Germany, Italy, and Japan. Then, too, indigenous peoples everywhere took up the call for national self-determination and expressed their determination to fight for independence.

The ending of the European colonial empires did not come easy, however. In 1941, Winston Churchill had said that he had not become prime minister in order to "preside over the liquidation of the British Empire." Britain and France in particular seemed reluctant to let go of their colonies, but for a variety of reasons both eventually gave in to the obvious: the days of empire were over.

During the war, the Japanese had already humiliated the Western states by overrunning their colonial empires. In addition, colonial soldiers who had fought on behalf of the Allies were well aware that Allied war aims included the principle of self-determination for the peoples of the world. Equally

THE CUBAN MISSILE CRISIS FROM KHRUSHCHEV'S PERSPECTIVE

THE CUBAN MISSILE CRISIS WAS one of the sobering experiences of the Cold War. It led the two superpowers to seek new ways to lessen the tensions between them. This version of the events is taken from the memoirs of Nikita Khrushchev.

Nikita Khrushchev, *Khrushchev Remembers*

I will explain what the Caribbean crisis of October 1962, was all about. . . . At the time that Fidel Castro led his revolution to victory and entered Havana with his troops, we had no idea what political course his regime would follow. . . . All the while the Americans had been watching Castro closely. At first they thought that the capitalist underpinnings of the Cuban economy would remain intact. So by the time Castro announced that he was going to put Cuba on the road toward Socialism, the Americans had already missed their chance to do anything about it by simply exerting their influence. . . . That left only one alternative—invasion! . . .

After Castro's crushing victory over the counter-revolutionaries we intensified our military aid to Cuba. . . . We were sure that the Americans would never reconcile themselves to the existence of Castro's Cuba. They feared, as much as we hoped, that a Socialist Cuba might become a magnet that would attract other Latin American countries to Socialism. . . . It was clear to me that we might very well lose Cuba if we didn't take some decisive steps in her defense. . . . We had to establish a tangible and effective deterrent to American interference in the Caribbean. But what exactly? The logical answer was missiles. We knew that American missiles were aimed against us in Turkey and Italy, to say nothing of West Germany. . . . My thinking went like this: if we installed the missiles secretly and then if the United

States discovered the missiles were there after they were . . . ready to strike, the Americans would think twice before trying to liquidate our installations by military means. . . . I want to make one thing absolutely clear: when we put our ballistic missiles in Cuba we had no desire to start a war. On the contrary, our principal aim was only to deter America from starting a war. . . .

President Kennedy issued an ultimatum, demanding that we remove our missiles and bombers from Cuba. . . . We sent the Americans a note saying that we agreed to remove our missiles and bombers on the condition that the President give us his assurance that there would be no invasion of Cuba by the forces of the United States or anybody else. Finally Kennedy gave in and agreed to make a statement giving us such an assurance. . . . The two most powerful nations of the world had been squared off against each other . . . but both sides showed that if the desire to avoid war is strong enough, even the most pressing dispute can be solved by compromise. And a compromise over Cuba was indeed found. . . . It was a great victory for us, though, that we had been able to extract from Kennedy a promise that neither America nor any of her allies would invade Cuba. . . . The Caribbean crisis was a triumph of Soviet foreign policy and a personal triumph in my own career as a statesman and as a member of the collective leadership. We achieved . . . a spectacular success without having to fire a single shot!

 According to his memoirs, why did Khrushchev decide to install missiles in Cuba? Why did he later agree to remove them? What did each side "lose" and what did each side "win" in the Cuban Missile Crisis?

Source: S. Talbot, ed., *Khrushchev Remembers* (New York: Little, Brown and Company, 1990).

---

important to the process of **decolonization** after World War II, the exhaustive struggles of the war had destroyed the power of the European states. The greatest colonial empire builder, Great Britain, no longer had the energy or the wealth to maintain its colonial empire. Given the combination of circumstances, a rush of decolonization swept the world. Between 1947 and 1962, virtually every colony achieved independence and attained statehood. Although some colonial powers willingly relinquished their control, others had to be driven out by national wars of liberation. Decolonization was a difficult and even bitter process, but it created a new world as the non-Western states ended the long era of Western domination.

Africa: The Struggle for Independence

After World War II, Europeans reluctantly realized that colonial rule in Africa would have to come to an end, but little had been done to prepare Africans for self-rule. Political organizations

that had been formed by Africans before the war to gain their rights became formal political parties with independence as their goal. In the Gold Coast, a large middle class and growing economy enabled Kwame Nkrumah (KWAH-may en-KROO-muh) (1909–1972) to form the Convention People's Party, the first African political party in black Africa. In the late 1940s, Jomo Kenyatta (JOH-moh ken-YAHT-uh) (1894–1978) founded the Kenya African National Union, which focused on economic issues but also sought self-rule for Kenya.

For the most part, these political activities were nonviolent and were led by Western-educated African intellectuals. Their constituents were primarily merchants, urban professionals, and members of labor unions. But the demand for independence was not restricted to the cities. In Kenya, for example, the widely publicized Mau Mau movement among the Kikuyu (ki-KOO-yuh) peoples used terrorism to demand *uhuru* (oo-HOO-roo) (Swahili for "freedom") from the British. Mau Mau terrorism alarmed the European population and convinced the British in 1959 to promise eventual independence.

A similar process was occurring in Egypt, which had been a British protectorate since the 1880s. In 1918, a formal political party called the Wafd (WAHFT) was organized to promote Egyptian independence. Although Egypt gained its formal independence in 1922, it still remained under British control. Egyptian intellectuals, however, were opposed as much to the Egyptian monarchy as to the British, and in 1952, an army coup overthrew King Farouk (fuh-ROOK) and set up an independent republic.

In North Africa, the French, who were simply not strong enough to maintain control of their far-flung colonial empire, granted full independence to Morocco and Tunisia in 1956 (see Map 28.2). Since Algeria was home to 2 million French settlers, however, France attempted to retain its dominion there. But a group of Algerian nationalists organized the National Liberation Front (FLN) and in 1954 initiated a guerrilla war to liberate

Marc Riboud/Magnum Photos

Algerian Independence. Although the French wanted to retain control of their Algerian colony, a bloody war of liberation finally led to Algeria's freedom. This photograph shows Algerians celebrating the announcement of independence on July 3, 1962.

their homeland (see the box on p. 874). By mid-1956, France had sent 400,000 troops to Algeria to protect French settlers and capture FLN terrorist cells. As the war dragged on, the French people became so divided that their leader, Charles de Gaulle, accepted the inevitable and granted Algerian independence in 1962. The liberation of Algeria led to a massive movement of peoples as 2 million French settlers repatriated to France, and thousands of harkis (har-KEES), Muslim Algerians who had fought alongside the French, also fled in fear of retaliation. Their fears were not unwarranted; the new Algerian authorities executed almost 60,000 harkis who remained behind.

In areas such as South Africa, where European settlers dominated the political system, the transition to independence was more complicated. In South Africa, political activity by local blacks began with the formation of the African National Congress (ANC) in 1912. At first, it was a group of intellectuals whose goal was to gain economic and political reforms, including full equality for educated Africans, within the framework of the existing system. The ANC's efforts, however, met with little success. At the same time, by the 1950s, South African whites were strengthening the laws separating whites and blacks, creating a system of racial segregation in South Africa known as **apartheid** (uh-PAHRT-hyt). When blacks demonstrated against the apartheid laws, the white government brutally repressed the demonstrators. After the arrest of Nelson Mandela (1918–2013), the ANC leader, in 1962, members of the ANC called for armed resistance to the white government.

When both the British and the French decided to let go of their colonial empires, most black African nations achieved their independence in the late 1950s and 1960s. The Gold Coast, now renamed Ghana and under the guidance of Kwame Nkrumah, was first in 1957. Nigeria, the Belgian Congo (renamed Zaire), Kenya, Tanganyika (later, when joined with Zanzibar, renamed Tanzania), and others soon followed. Seventeen new African nations emerged in 1960. Another eleven followed between 1961 and 1965. By the late 1960s, only parts of southern Africa and the Portuguese possessions of Mozambique and Angola remained under European rule. After a series of brutal guerrilla wars, the Portuguese finally gave up their colonies in the 1970s.

The newly independent African countries faced immediate and severe challenges. Many of the countries were based upon artificial boundaries created by the European colonists. In Nigeria, the Royal Niger Company had decided on the boundaries in 1895, which did not account for the various religious and ethnic groups within the region. After independence in 1960, Nigeria was embroiled in a bloody civil war by 1967, only to emerge under the control of a military government by 1970. Religious and ethnic conflict became a reoccurring issue in the wake of decolonization, as many nations formed under the artificial boundaries of their colonial powers were unable to resolve their internal differences.

Conflict in the Middle East

Although Turkey, Iran, Saudi Arabia, and Iraq had become independent states between the two world wars, the end of World War II led to the emergence of other independent states

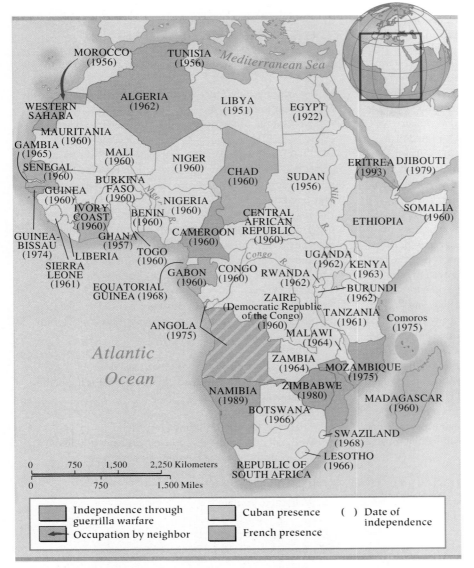

MAP 28.2 Decolonization in Africa. By the late 1950s, Britain and France had decided to allow independence for most of their African colonies, although France fought hard before relinquishing Algeria. Most of the new states had difficulty promoting economic growth and dealing with internal ethnic animosities.

Q *What is a significant characteristic shared by a majority of the countries that gained independence from 1975 onward?*

government, balancing power between Christians and Muslims. In Syria, the German occupation of France during World War II allowed for the declaration of Syrian independence in 1941, with full independence in 1946. The country adopted a republican government before a military coup in 1963 placed the military Ba'ath Party in power.

THE QUESTION OF PALESTINE The one issue on which all Muslim states in the area could agree was the question of Palestine. As tensions between Jews and Arabs intensified in that mandate during the 1930s, the British reduced Jewish immigration into the area and firmly rejected Jewish proposals for an independent state in Palestine. The Zionists, who wanted Palestine as a home for Jews, were not to be denied, however. Many people had been shocked at the end of World War II when they learned about the Holocaust, and sympathy for the Jewish cause grew dramatically. As a result, the Zionists turned for support to the United States, and in March 1948, the Truman administration approved the concept of an independent Jewish state in Palestine, even though Jews comprised only about one-third of the local population. When a United Nations resolution divided Palestine into a Jewish state and an Arab state, the Jews in Palestine acted. On May 14, 1948, they proclaimed the state of Israel.

Its Arab neighbors saw the new state as a betrayal of the Palestinian people, 90 percent of whom were Muslim. Outraged at the lack of Western support for Muslim interests in the area, several Arab countries invaded the new Jewish state. The invasion failed, but both sides remained bitter. The Arab states refused to recognize the existence of Israel.

in the Middle East. Jordan, Syria, and Lebanon, all European mandates before the war, became independent (see Map 28.3). Sympathy for the idea of Arab unity led to the formation of the Arab League in 1945, but different points of view among its members prevented it from achieving anything of substance.

BRITISH AND FRENCH TERRITORIES The British and French had maintained their mandates over Jordan, Syria and Lebanon until the end of World War II. The British recognized the constitutional independence of Jordan in 1922, but it was not until 1946 that full independence was granted. Jordan became a constitutional monarchy. Lebanon gained independence from the French in 1942 and established a multi-religious

NASSER AND PAN-ARABISM In Egypt, a new leader arose who would play an important role in the Arab world and the Arab-Israeli conflict. Colonel Gamal Abdel Nasser (guh-MAHL ahb-DOOL NAH-sur) (1918–1970) seized control of the Egyptian government in 1954 and two years later nationalized the Suez Canal Company, which had been under British and French administration. Seeing a threat to their route to the Indian Ocean, the British and French launched a joint attack on Egypt to protect their investment. They were joined by Israel, whose leaders had grown exasperated at sporadic Arab

FRANTZ FANON AND THE WRETCHED OF THE EARTH

BORN ON THE ISLAND OF MARTINIQUE, Frantz Fanon (FRAHNTS FAN-uhn) (1925–1961) studied psychiatry in France. His work as head of a psychiatric hospital in Algeria led him to favor violence as a necessary instrument to overthrow Western imperialism, which to Fanon was itself rooted in violence. *The Wretched of the Earth*, published in 1961, provided an argument for national liberation movements in the Third World. In the last part of the book, Fanon discussed the mental disorders that arose from Algeria's war of national liberation.

The Wretched of the Earth: Colonial War and Mental Disorders, Series B

We have here brought together certain cases or groups of cases in which the event giving rise to the illness is in the first place the atmosphere of total war which reigns in Algeria.

Case No. 1: The murder by two young Algerians, thirteen and fourteen years old respectively, of their European playmate.

We had been asked to give expert medical advice in a legal matter. Two young Algerians thirteen and fourteen years old, pupils in a secondary school, were accused of having killed one of their European schoolmates. They admitted having done it. The crime was reconstructed, and photos were added to the record. Here one of the children could be seen holding the victim while the other struck at him with a knife. The little defendants did not go back on their declarations. We had long conversations with them. We here reproduce the most characteristic of their remarks:

The boy fourteen years old:

This young defendant was in marked contrast to his school fellow. He was already almost a man, and an adult in his muscular control, his appearance, and the content of his replies. He did not deny having killed either. Why had he killed? He did not reply to the question but asked me had I ever seen a European in prison. Had there ever been a European arrested and sent to prison after the murder of an Algerian? I replied that in fact I had never seen any Europeans in prison.

"And yet there are Algerians killed every day, aren't there?"

"Yes."

"So why are only Algerians found in the prisons? Can you explain that to me?"

"No. But tell me why you killed this boy who was your friend."

"I'll tell you why. You've heard tell of the Rivet business?" [Rivet was a village near Algiers where in 1956 the French militia dragged forty men from their own beds and afterward murdered them.]

"Yes."

"Two of my family were killed then. At home, they said that the French had sworn to kill us all, one after the other. And did they arrest a single Frenchman for all those Algerians who were killed?"

"I don't know."

"Well, nobody at all was arrested. I wanted to take to the mountains, but I was too young. So [my friend] and I said we'd kill a European."

"Why?"

"In your opinion, what should we have done?"

"I don't know. But you are a child and what is happening concerns grown-up people."

"But they kill children too."

"That is no reason for killing your friend."

"Well, kill him I did. Now you can do what you like."

"Had your friend done anything to harm you?"

"Not a thing."

"Well?"

"Well, there you are."

 What does this selection tell you about some of the fundamental characteristics of European colonial regimes? What broader forces, perhaps liberated or focused by World War II, could have contributed to the uprisings and to the crimes the colonized committed against the colonizers in the postwar period?

commando raids on Israeli territory and now decided to strike back. But the Eisenhower administration in the United States, concerned that the attack smacked of a revival of colonialism, joined with the Soviet Union, its Cold War enemy, and supported Nasser. Together, they brought about the withdrawal of foreign forces from Egypt and of Israeli troops from the Sinai peninsula.

Nasser emerged from the conflict as a powerful leader and now began to promote Pan-Arabism, or Arab unity. In March 1958, Egypt formally united with Syria in the United Arab Republic (UAR), with Nasser as president of the new state. Egypt and Syria hoped that the union would eventually include all Arab states, but many other Arab leaders were suspicious of Pan-Arabism. Oil-rich Arab states such as Iraq and Saudi Arabia feared that they would be asked to share their vast oil revenues with the poorer states of the Middle East. In 1961, Nasser's plans and the UAR came to an end when military leaders seized control of Syria and withdrew it from its union with Egypt.

THE ARAB-ISRAELI DISPUTE The breakup of the UAR did not end the dream of Pan-Arabism. At a meeting of Arab leaders held in Jerusalem in 1964, Egypt took the lead

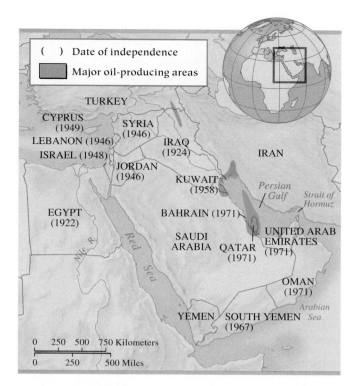

MAP 28.3 **Decolonization in the Middle East.** Under the control of the Ottoman Empire prior to World War I, much of the Middle East was ruled directly or indirectly by the British and French after the war. Britain, the main colonial power, granted independence to most of its holdings in the first years after World War II, although it did maintain control of small states in the Persian Gulf and Arabian Sea region until 1971.

 Which countries are major oil producers?

in forming the Palestine Liberation Organization (PLO) to represent the interests of the Palestinians. The PLO believed that only the Palestinian peoples (and not Jewish immigrants from abroad) had the right to form a state in Palestine. A guerrilla movement called al-Fatah (al-FAH-tuh), led by the PLO political leader Yasir Arafat (yah-SEER ah-ruh-FAHT) (1929–2004), began to launch terrorist attacks on Israeli territory.

During the 1960s, the dispute between Israel and other states in the Middle East intensified. Essentially alone except for the sympathy of the United States and a few Western European countries, Israel adopted a policy of immediate retaliation against any hostile act by the PLO and its Arab neighbors. By the spring of 1967, Nasser in Egypt had stepped up his military activities and imposed a blockade against Israeli shipping through the Gulf of Aqaba (AH-kuh-buh). Learning that an attack was imminent, on June 5, 1967, Israel launched preemptive air strikes against Egypt and several of its Arab neighbors. Israeli warplanes bombed seventeen Egyptian airfields and wiped out most of the Egyptian air force. Israeli armies then broke the blockade at the head of the Gulf of Aqaba and occupied the Sinai peninsula. Other Israeli forces seized Jordanian territory on the West Bank of the Jordan River, occupied all of Jerusalem (formerly divided between Israel and Jordan), and

attacked Syrian military positions in the Golan Heights area along the Israeli-Syrian border. In this brief Six-Day War, as it is called, Israel devastated Nasser's forces and tripled the size of its territory. The new Israel aroused even more bitter hatred among the Arabs. Furthermore, another million Palestinians now lived inside Israel's new borders, most of them on the West Bank.

Asia: Nationalism and Communism

In Asia, the United States initiated the process of decolonization in 1946 when it granted independence to the Philippines (see Map 28.4). Britain soon followed suit with India. But ethnic and religious differences made the process both difficult and violent.

At the end of World War II, the British negotiated with both the Indian National Congress, which was mostly Hindu, and the Muslim League. British India's Muslims and Hindus were bitterly divided and unwilling to accept a single Indian state. Britain soon realized that British India would have to be divided into two countries, one Hindu (India) and one Muslim (Pakistan). Pakistan would actually consist of two regions separated by more than 1,000 miles.

Among Congress leaders, only Mahatma Gandhi objected to the division of India. A Muslim woman, critical of his opposition to partition, asked him, "If two brothers were living together in the same house and wanted to separate and live in two different houses, would you object?" "Ah," Gandhi replied, "if only we could separate as two brothers. But we will not. It will be an orgy of blood. We shall tear ourselves asunder in the womb of the mother who bears us."[7]

On August 15, 1947, India and Pakistan became independent. But Gandhi had been right. The flight of millions of Hindus and Muslims across the new borders led to violence, and more than a million people were killed—including Gandhi, who was assassinated on January 30, 1948, by a Hindu militant. India's new beginning had not been easy.

Other areas of Asia also achieved independence. In 1948, Britain granted independence to Ceylon (modern Sri Lanka) and Burma (modern Myanmar). When the Dutch failed to reestablish control over the Dutch East Indies, Indonesia emerged as an independent nation in 1949. The French effort to remain in Indochina led to a bloody struggle with the Vietminh, led by Ho Chi Minh, the Communist and nationalist leader of the Vietnamese. After their defeat in 1954, the French granted independence to Laos and Cambodia, and Vietnam was temporarily divided in anticipation of elections in 1956 that would decide its fate. But the elections were never held, and the division of Vietnam under Communist and pro-Western regimes eventually led to the Second Vietnam War (see Chapter 29).

CHINA UNDER COMMUNISM At the end of World War II, two Chinese governments existed side by side. The Americans supported the Nationalist government of Chiang Kai-shek, based in southern and central China. The Communists, under the leadership of Mao Zedong, had built a strong base in North China. Their People's Liberation Army included nearly one million troops.

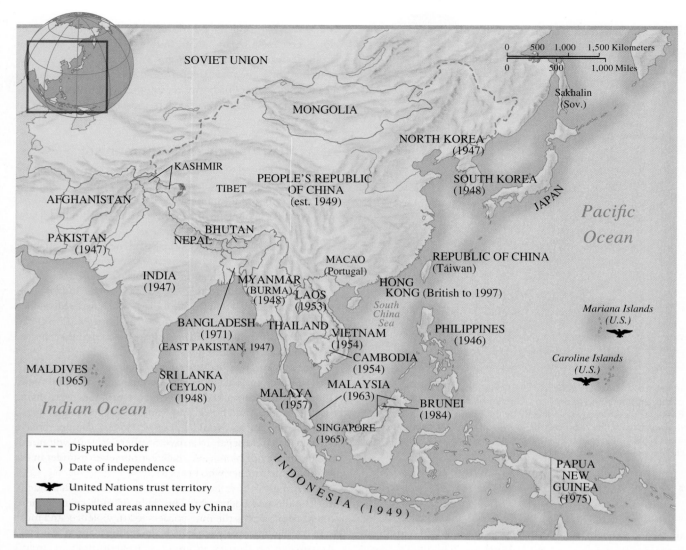

MAP 28.4 Decolonization in Asia. Britain and the United States granted independence to their possessions in Asia soon after World War II. France fought hard to hold Indochina but left after major military defeats. Cold War tensions in Asia led to both the Korean War and the Vietnam War.

Q *What two neighboring countries' presence helps explain why Korea has had difficulty maintaining complete independence throughout much of its history?*

When efforts to form a coalition government in 1946 failed, full-scale war between the Nationalists and the Communists broke out. In the countryside, millions of peasants were attracted to the Communists by promises of land, and many joined Mao's army. By 1948, the People's Liberation Army had surrounded Beijing. The following spring, the Communists crossed the Yangtze and occupied Shanghai. During the next few months, Chiang's government and 2 million of his followers fled to the island of Taiwan, off the coast of mainland China. On October 1, 1949, Mao mounted the rostrum of the Gate of Heavenly Peace in Beijing and made a victory statement to the thousands gathered in the square before him. The Chinese people have stood up, he said, and no one will be able to humiliate us again.

The newly victorious Communist Party, under the leadership of its chairman, Mao, had a long-term goal of building a socialist society. In 1955, the Chinese government collectivized all private farmland and nationalized most industry and commerce. When the collective farms failed to increase food production, Mao began a more radical program, known as the Great Leap Forward, in 1958. Existing collective farms, normally the size of the traditional village, were combined into vast "people's communes," each containing more than 30,000 people. Mao hoped this program would mobilize the people for a massive effort to speed up economic growth and reach the final stage of communism—the classless society—before the end of the twentieth century. But the Great Leap Forward was a disaster. Bad weather and peasant hatred of the new system combined to drive food production downward. Despite his failures, Mao was not yet ready to abandon his dream of a totally classless society, and in 1966 he launched China on a new forced march toward communism (see Chapter 29).

Decolonization and Cold War Rivalries

The process of decolonization also became embroiled in Cold War politics. As independent nations emerged in Asia and Africa, they often found themselves caught in the rivalry between the United States and the Soviet Union. In Vietnam, for example, the division of the country in 1954 left the northern half under the Communist leader Ho Chi Minh supported by the Soviet Union. Meanwhile, South Vietnam was kept afloat by American financial and military aid. The Second Vietnam War resulted from the American perception that it needed to keep communism from expanding, while Ho Chi Minh saw the struggle between North and South as an attempt to overthrow Western colonial masters (the Americans had simply replaced the French) and achieve self-determination for the Vietnamese people.

Many new nations tried to stay neutral in the Cold War. Under the leadership of Jawaharlal Nehru (juh-WAH-hur-lahl NAY-roo) (1889–1964), for example, India took a neutral stance in the Cold War and sought to provide leadership to all newly independent nations in Asia and Africa. India's neutrality put it at odds with the United States, which during the 1950s was trying to mobilize all nations against what it viewed as the menace of international communism.

Often, however, new nations found it difficult to remain nonaligned. In Indonesia, for example, which achieved its independence from the Dutch in 1949, President Sukarno (soo-KAHR-noh) (1901–1970), who was highly suspicious of the West, nationalized foreign-owned enterprises and sought economic aid from China and the Soviet Union while relying for domestic support on the Indonesian Communist Party. The army and conservative Muslims resented Sukarno's increasing reliance on the Communists, overthrew him in 1965, and established a military government under General Suharto (soo-HAHR-toh) (1921–2008), who quickly restored good relations with the West.

Recovery and Renewal in Europe

 FOCUS QUESTION: What were the main developments in the Soviet Union, Eastern Europe, and Western Europe between 1945 and 1965?

Just a few years after the defeat of Germany and Italy in World War II, economic revival brought renewed growth to European society, although major differences remained between Western and Eastern Europe.

The Soviet Union: From Stalin to Khrushchev

World War II had devastated the Soviet Union—a quarter of its buildings and roads were destroyed and nearly 27 million had died. To create a new industrial base, Stalin returned to the method that he had used in the 1930s—the acquisition of development capital from Soviet labor. Working hard for little pay, poor housing, and precious few consumer goods, Soviet laborers were expected to produce goods for export with little in return for themselves. The incoming capital from abroad could then be used to purchase machinery and Western technology. The loss of millions of men in the war meant that much of this tremendous workload fell upon Soviet women. They performed almost 40 percent of heavy manual labor.

Economic recovery in the Soviet Union was nothing less than spectacular. By 1947, industrial production had attained prewar levels; three years later, it had surpassed them by 40 percent. New power plants, canals, and giant factories were built, and new industries and oil fields were established in Siberia and Soviet Central Asia.

STALIN'S POLICIES Although Stalin's economic policy was successful in promoting growth in heavy industry, primarily for the benefit of the military, consumer goods were scarce. The development of thermonuclear weapons in 1953, MIG fighters from 1950 to 1953, and the first space satellite (*Sputnik*) in 1957 may have elevated the Soviet state's reputation as a world power abroad, but domestically, the Soviet people were shortchanged. Heavy industry grew at a rate three times that of personal consumption. High labor turnover and a failure to reinvest in new technologies led to a decline in the industrial economy by the 1970s. In addition to worker discontent, the housing shortage was acute. A British military attaché in Moscow reported that "all houses, practically without exception, show lights from every window after dark. This seems to indicate that every room is both a living room by day and a bedroom by night. There is no place in overcrowded Moscow for the luxury of eating and sleeping in separate rooms."[8]

When World War II ended in 1945, Stalin had been in power for more than fifteen years. During that time, he had removed all opposition to his rule. Although he was the undisputed master of the Soviet Union, Stalin's morbid suspicions fueled the constantly increasing repression that was a characteristic of his regime. In 1946, the government decreed that all literary and scientific works must conform to the political needs of the state. Along with this anti-intellectual campaign came political terror. A new series of purges seemed imminent in 1953 when a number of Jewish doctors were implicated in a spurious plot to kill high-level Party officials. Only Stalin's death on March 5, 1953, prevented more bloodletting.

KHRUSHCHEV'S RULE A new collective leadership succeeded Stalin until Nikita Khrushchev emerged as the chief Soviet policy maker. Khrushchev had been responsible for ending the system of forced-labor camps, a regular feature of Soviet life under Stalin. At the Twentieth Congress of the Communist Party in 1956, Khrushchev condemned Stalin for his "administrative violence, mass repression, and terror" (see the box on p. 878).

Once in power, Khrushchev took steps to undo some of the worst features of Stalin's repressive regime. A certain degree of intellectual freedom was now permitted; Khrushchev said that "readers should be given the chance to make

KHRUSHCHEV DENOUNCES STALIN

THREE YEARS AFTER THE DEATH of Stalin, the new Soviet premier, Nikita Khrushchev, addressed the Twentieth Congress of the Communist Party and denounced the former Soviet dictator for his crimes. This denunciation was the beginning of a policy of de-Stalinization.

Nikita Khrushchev, Address to the Twentieth Party Congress, February 1956

Comrades . . . quite a lot has been said about the cult of the individual and about its harmful consequences. . . . The cult of the person of Stalin . . . became at a certain specific stage the source of a whole series of exceedingly serious and grave perversions of Party principles, of Party democracy, of revolutionary legality.

Stalin absolutely did not tolerate collegiality in leadership and in work and . . . practiced brutal violence, not only toward everything which opposed him, but also toward that which seemed to his capricious and despotic character, contrary to his concepts.

Stalin abandoned the method of ideological struggle for that of administrative violence, mass repressions and terror. . . . Arbitrary behavior by one person encouraged and permitted arbitrariness in others. Mass arrests and deportations of many thousands of people, execution without trial and without normal investigation created conditions of insecurity, fear and even desperation.

Stalin showed in a whole series of cases his intolerance, his brutality and his abuse of power. . . . He often chose the path of repression and annihilation, not only against actual enemies, but also against individuals who had not committed any crimes against the Party and the Soviet government. . . .

Many Party, Soviet and economic activists who were branded in 1937–8 as "enemies" were actually never enemies, spies, wreckers and so on, but were always honest communists; they were only so stigmatized, and often, no longer able to bear barbaric tortures, they charged themselves (at the order of the investigative judges-falsifiers) with all kinds of grave and unlikely crimes.

This was the result of the abuse of power by Stalin, who began to use mass terror against the Party cadres. . . . Stalin put the Party and the NKVD [the secret police] up to the use of mass terror when the exploiting classes had been liquidated in our country and when there were no serious reasons for the use of extraordinary mass terror. The terror was directed . . . against the honest workers of the Party and the Soviet state. . . .

Stalin was a very distrustful man, sickly suspicious. . . . Everywhere and in everything he saw "enemies," "two-facers" and "spies." Possessing unlimited power, he indulged in great willfulness and choked a person morally and physically. A situation was created where one could not express one's own will. When Stalin said that one or another would be arrested, it was necessary to accept on faith that he was an "enemy of the people." What proofs were offered? The confession of the arrested. . . . How is it possible that a person confesses to crimes that he had not committed? Only in one way—because of application of physical methods of pressuring him, tortures, bringing him to a state of unconsciousness, deprivation of his judgment, taking away of his human dignity.

 According to Khrushchev, what were Stalin's crimes? What purposes, political and historical, do you think Khrushchev intended his denunciation of Stalin to serve?

Source: Reprinted from the Congressional Record, 84th Congress, 2nd Session, vol. 102, part 7 (Washington, D.C.: U.S. Government Printing Office), pp. 9389–9402.

their own judgments" regarding the acceptability of controversial literature and that "police measures shouldn't be used."[9] In 1962, he allowed Alexander Solzhenitsyn (sohl-zhuh-NEET-sin) (1918–2008) to publish his novel *A Day in the Life of Ivan Denisovich*, a grim portrayal of the horrors of the forced-labor camps. Most important, Khrushchev extended the process of **de-Stalinization** by reducing the powers of the secret police and closing some of the Siberian prison camps. Khrushchev's revelations about Stalin at the Twentieth Congress caused turmoil in Communist ranks everywhere, however, and encouraged a spirit of rebellion in Soviet satellite countries in Eastern Europe. Soviet troops reacted by crushing an uprising in Hungary in 1956, and Khrushchev and the Soviet leaders, fearful of further undermining the basic foundations of the regime, downplayed their de-Stalinization campaign.

Economically, Khrushchev tried to place more emphasis on light industry and consumer goods. Attempts to increase agricultural output by growing corn and cultivating vast lands east of the Ural Mountains proved less successful and damaged Khrushchev's reputation within the Party. These failures, combined with increased military spending, hurt the Soviet economy. The industrial growth rate, which had soared in the early 1950s, now declined dramatically from 13 percent in 1953 to 7.5 percent in 1964.

Khrushchev's personality also did not endear him to the higher Soviet officials, who frowned at his tendency to crack jokes and play the clown. Nor were the higher members of the Party bureaucracy pleased when Khrushchev tried to curb their privileges. Foreign policy failures caused additional damage to Khrushchev's reputation among his colleagues. His rash plan to place missiles in Cuba was the final straw. While he was on vacation in 1964, a special meeting of the Soviet Politburo voted him out of office (because of "deteriorating health") and forced him into retirement. Although a group of leaders succeeded him, real power came into the hands of Leonid Brezhnev (lee-oh-NYEET BREZH-neff) (1906–1982), the "trusted" supporter of Khrushchev who had engineered his downfall.

Eastern Europe: Behind the Iron Curtain

At the end of World War II, Soviet military forces remained in all the lands they had liberated from the Nazis in Eastern Europe and the Balkans except Greece, Albania, and Yugoslavia. All of the occupied states came to be part of the Soviet sphere of influence and, after 1945, experienced similar political developments. Between 1945 and 1947, one-party Communist governments became firmly entrenched in East Germany, Bulgaria, Romania, Poland, and Hungary. In Czechoslovakia, which had some tradition of democratic institutions, the Communists did not achieve their goals until 1948 when all other parties were dissolved and Klement Gottwald (GUT-vald) (1896–1953), the leader of the Communists, became the new president of Czechoslovakia.

ALBANIA AND YUGOSLAVIA Albania and Yugoslavia were exceptions to this progression of Soviet dominance in Eastern Europe. Both had had strong Communist resistance movements during the war, and in both countries, the Communist Party simply took over power when the war ended. In Albania, local Communists established a rigidly Stalinist regime that grew increasingly independent of the Soviet Union.

In Yugoslavia, Tito (Josip Broz), leader of the Communist resistance movement, seemed to be a loyal Stalinist. After the war, however, he moved toward the establishment of an independent Communist state in Yugoslavia. Stalin hoped to take control of Yugoslavia, just as he had done in other Eastern European countries, but Tito refused to capitulate to Stalin's demands and gained the support of the people by portraying the struggle as one of Yugoslav national freedom. In 1958, the Yugoslav party congress asserted that Yugoslav Communists did not see themselves as deviating from communism, only Stalinism. They considered their way closer to the Marxist-Leninist ideal. This included a more decentralized economic and political system in which workers could manage themselves and local communes could exercise some political power.

Between 1948 and Stalin's death in 1953, the Eastern European satellite states followed a policy of **Stalinization**. They instituted Soviet-type five-year plans with emphasis on heavy industry rather than consumer goods and the collectivization of agriculture. They eliminated all non-Communist parties and established the institutions of repression—secret police and military forces. But communism—a foreign import—had not developed deep roots among the peoples of Eastern Europe. Moreover, Soviet economic exploitation of Eastern Europe resulted in harsh living conditions for most people.

1956: UPHEAVAL IN EASTERN EUROPE After Stalin's death, many Eastern European states began to pursue a new, more nationalistically oriented course as the new Soviet leaders, including Khrushchev, interfered less in the internal affairs of their satellites. But in the late 1950s, the Soviet Union also made it clear, particularly in Poland and Hungary, that it would not allow its Eastern European satellites to become independent of Soviet control.

In 1956, after the circulation of Khrushchev's denunciation of Stalin, protests—especially by workers—erupted in Poland. In response, the Polish Communist Party adopted a series of reforms in October 1956 and elected Wladyslaw Gomulka (vlah-DIS-lahf goh-MOOL-kuh) (1905–1982) as first secretary. Gomulka declared that Poland had the right to follow its own socialist path. Fearful of Soviet armed response, however, the Poles compromised. Poland pledged to remain loyal to the Warsaw Pact, and the Soviets agreed to allow Poland to follow its own path to socialism.

The developments in Poland in 1956 inspired national Communists in Hungary to seek the same kinds of reforms and independence. Intense debates eventually resulted in the ouster of the ruling Stalinist and the selection of Imry Nagy (IM-ray NAHJ-uh) (1896–1958) as the new Hungarian leader. Internal dissent, however, was not directed simply against the Soviets but against communism in general, which was viewed as a creation of the Soviets, not the Hungarians. The Stalinist secret police had also bred much terror and hatred. This dissatisfaction, combined with economic difficulties, created a situation ripe for revolt. To quell the rising rebellion, Nagy declared Hungary a free nation on November 1, 1956. He promised free elections, and the mood of the country made it clear that this could mean the end of Communist rule in Hungary. But Khrushchev was in no position at home to allow a member of the Communist flock to fly the coop. Just three days after Nagy's declaration, the Red Army invaded the capital city of Budapest (see the box on p. 880). The Soviets reestablished control over the country, and János Kádár (YAH-nush KAH-dahr) (1912–1989), a reform-minded cabinet minister, replaced Nagy and worked with the Soviets to quash the revolt. By collaborating with the Soviet invaders, Kádár saved many of Nagy's economic reforms. The developments in Poland and Hungary in 1956 discouraged any similar upheavals elsewhere in Eastern Europe.

Erich Lessing/Art Resource, NY

Hungarian Revolt. Young fighters are shown walking with their weapons away from the Kilian barracks in the background. The Corvin Passage behind them was a strategic transportation route that the insurgents defended by resisting Soviet tanks during the Hungarian Revolution.

SOVIET REPRESSION IN EASTERN EUROPE: HUNGARY, 1956

DEVELOPMENTS IN POLAND IN 1956 inspired the Communist leaders of Hungary to begin to remove their country from Soviet control. But there were limits to Khrushchev's tolerance, and he sent Soviet troops to crush Hungary's movement for independence. The first selection is a statement by the Soviet government justifying the use of Soviet troops; the second is a brief and tragic final statement from Imry Nagy, the Hungarian leader.

Statement of the Soviet Government, October 30, 1956

The Soviet Government regards it as indispensable to make a statement in connection with the events in Hungary.

The course of the events has shown that the working people of Hungary, who have achieved great progress on the basis of their people's democratic order, correctly raise the question of the necessity of eliminating serious shortcomings in the field of economic building, the further raising of the material well-being of the population, and the struggle against bureaucratic excesses in the state apparatus.

However, this just and progressive movement of the working people was soon joined by forces of black reaction and counterrevolution, which are trying to take advantage of the discontent of part of the working people to undermine the foundations of the people's democratic order in Hungary and to restore the old landlord and capitalist order.

The Soviet Government and all the Soviet people deeply regret that the development of events in Hungary has led to bloodshed. On the request of the Hungarian People's Government the Soviet Government consented to the

entry into Budapest of the Soviet Army units to assist the Hungarian People's Army and the Hungarian authorities to establish order in the town.

The Last Message of Imry Nagy, November 4, 1956

This fight is the fight for freedom by the Hungarian people against the Russian intervention, and it is possible that I shall only be able to stay at my post for one or two hours. The whole world will see how the Russian armed forces, contrary to all treaties and conventions, are crushing the resistance of the Hungarian people. They will also see how they are kidnapping the Prime Minister of a country which is a Member of the United Nations, taking him from the capital, and therefore it cannot be doubted at all that this is the most brutal form of intervention. I should like in these last moments to ask the leaders of the revolution, if they can, to leave the country. I ask that all that I have said in my broadcast, and what we have agreed on with the revolutionary leaders during meetings in Parliament, should be put in a memorandum, and the leaders should turn to all the peoples of the world for help and explain that today it is Hungary and tomorrow, or the day after tomorrow, it will be the turn of other countries because the imperialism of Moscow does not know borders, and is only trying to play for time.

 Based on this selection, what was the Soviet Union's policy toward its Eastern European satellite states in the 1950s? Compare this policy with Soviet policy in Eastern Europe in the late 1980s (see Chapter 29). What impact did the change in policy have on Eastern Europe?

Source: Department of State Bulletin, Nov. 12, 1956, pp. 746–747.

CHRONOLOGY	The Soviet Union and Satellite States in Eastern Europe
Death of Stalin	1953
Khrushchev's denunciation of Stalin	1956
Attempt at reforms in Poland	1956
Hungarian revolt is crushed	1956
Berlin Wall is built	1961
Brezhnev replaces Khrushchev	1964

Western Europe: The Revival of Democracy and the Economy

All the countries of Western Europe faced similar kinds of problems at the end of World War II. They needed to rebuild their economies, re-create their democratic institutions, and contend with the growth of Communist parties.

The important role that Communists had played in the resistance movements against the Nazis gained them a new respectability and strength once the war was over. Communist parties did well in elections in Italy and France in 1946 and 1947, but Communist success was short-lived. After the hardening of the divisions in the Cold War, their advocacy of Soviet policies hurt the Communist parties at home, and support began to dwindle. Only in France and Italy, where social inequities remained their focus, did Communist parties retain significant support—about 25 percent of the vote.

As part of their electoral strategy, Communist parties had often joined forces with other left-wing parties, such as the Social Democrats. Socialist parties had also fared well immediately after the war as the desire to overthrow the old order led to the abandonment of conservative politics. But support for the socialists soon waned. In France, for example, socialists won 23 percent of the vote in 1945 but 18 percent in 1946 and only 12.6 percent in 1962. The Cold War also hurt the cause of socialism. Socialist parties had originally been formed in the late nineteenth century as Marxist parties, and their identification with Communist parties in postwar coalitions cost them dearly. In the late 1950s, many socialist parties on the continent perceived the need to eliminate their old doctrinal emphasis on class struggle and began to call for social justice and liberty. Although they advocated economic and social planning, they no longer demanded the elimination of the capitalist system.

By 1950, moderate political parties had made a remarkable comeback in Western Europe. Especially important was the rise of Christian Democratic parties. The new Christian Democrats were not connected to the prewar church-based parties that had been advocates of church interests and had crusaded against both liberal and socialist causes. The new Christian Democrats were sincerely interested in democracy and in significant economic reforms. They were especially strong in Italy and Germany.

Western European countries recovered relatively rapidly from the devastation of World War II. The Marshall Plan played a significant role in this process. Between 1947 and 1950, European countries received $9.4 billion to be used for new equipment and raw materials. By 1950, industrial output in Europe was 30 percent above prewar levels. Between 1947 and 1950, steel production alone expanded by 70 percent. And this economic recovery continued well into the 1950s and 1960s. Those years were a time of dramatic economic growth and prosperity in Western Europe, which experienced virtually full employment.

Charles de Gaulle. Charles de Gaulle returned to politics in 1958 in response to the crisis in Algeria. As president, he sought to revive the greatness of the French nation. He is shown here arriving in Algeria in 1958.

FRANCE: THE DOMINATION OF DE GAULLE The history of France for nearly a quarter century after the war was dominated by one man—Charles de Gaulle (1890–1970)—who possessed an unshakable faith that he had a historic mission to reestablish the greatness of the French nation. During the war, de Gaulle had assumed leadership of some resistance groups and played an important role in ensuring the establishment of a French provisional government after the war. The declaration of the Fourth Republic, with a return to a parliamentary system based on parties that de Gaulle considered weak, led him to withdraw from politics. Eventually, he formed the French Popular Movement, a decidedly rightist organization. It blamed the parties for France's political mess and called for a stronger presidency, a goal that de Gaulle finally achieved in 1958.

The fragile political stability of the Fourth Republic had been badly shaken by the Algerian crisis. The French army had suffered defeat in Indochina in 1954 and was determined to resist Algerian demands for independence. But a strong antiwar movement among French intellectuals and church leaders led to bitter divisions that opened the door to the possibility of civil war in France. The panic-stricken leaders of the Fourth Republic offered to let de Gaulle take over the government and revise the constitution.

In 1958, de Gaulle immediately drafted a new constitution for the Fifth Republic that greatly enhanced the power of the president, who would now have the right to choose the prime minister, dissolve parliament, and supervise both defense and foreign policy. As the new president, de Gaulle believed that the path to France as a great power was the participation in the nuclear arms race. France exploded its first nuclear bomb in 1960. Despite his successes, de Gaulle did not really achieve his ambitious goals of world power. Although his successors maintained that France was the "third nuclear power" after the United States and the Soviet Union, in truth France was too small for such global ambitions.

Although the cost of the nuclear program increased the defense budget, de Gaulle did not neglect the French economy. Economic decision making was centralized. Between 1958 and 1968, the French gross national product increased by 5.5 percent annually, faster than the U.S. economy was growing. By the end of de Gaulle's era, France was a major industrial producer and exporter, particularly in such areas as automobiles and armaments. Nevertheless, problems remained. The **nationalization** (government ownership) of traditional industries, such as coal, steel, and railroads, led to large government deficits. The cost of living increased faster than in the rest of Europe. Consumer prices were 45 percent higher in 1968 than they had been ten years earlier.

Increased dissatisfaction with the inability of de Gaulle's government to deal with these problems soon led to more violent action. In May 1968, a series of student protests (see Chapter 29), followed by a general strike by the labor unions, shook the government. Although de Gaulle managed to restore order, the events of May 1968 seriously undermined the French people's respect for their aloof and imperious president. Tired and discouraged, de Gaulle resigned from office in April 1969 and died within a year.

WEST GERMANY: A RECONCEIVED NATION Already by the end of 1945, the Western powers occupying Germany (the United States, Britain, and France) had allowed the reemergence of political parties in their zones. Three major parties came forth: the Social Democrats (SPD), the Christian Democrats (CDU), and the Free Democrats (FDP). Over the next three years, the occupation forces gradually allowed the political parties to play greater roles in their zones.

As a result of the pressures of the Cold War, the unification of the three Western zones into the Federal Republic of Germany became a reality in 1949. Konrad Adenauer, the leader of the CDU who served as chancellor from 1949 to 1963, became the "founding hero" of the Federal Republic. Adenauer sought respect for West Germany by cooperating with the United States and the other Western European nations. He was especially desirous of reconciliation with France, Germany's longtime enemy. The beginning of the Korean War in June 1950 had unexpected repercussions for West Germany. The fear that South Korea might fall to the Communist forces of the north led many Germans and Westerners to worry about the security of West Germany and led to calls for its rearmament. Although many people, concerned about a revival of German militarism, condemned this proposal, Cold War tensions were decisive. West Germany rearmed in 1955 and became a member of NATO.

Adenauer's chancellorship saw the resurrection of the West German economy, often referred to as the "economic miracle." It was largely guided by the minister of finance, Ludwig Erhard (LOOD-vik AYR-hart) (1897–1977), who pursued a policy of a new currency, free markets, low taxes, and elimination of controls, which, combined with American financial aid, led to rapid economic growth. Although West Germany had only 75 percent of the population and 52 percent of the territory of prewar Germany, by 1955 the West German gross national product exceeded that of prewar Germany. Real wages doubled between 1950 and 1965 even though work hours were cut by 20 percent. Unemployment fell from 8 percent in 1950 to 0.4 percent in 1965. To maintain its economic expansion, West Germany even imported hundreds of thousands of **guest workers**, primarily from Italy, Spain, Greece, Turkey, and Yugoslavia.

Throughout its postwar existence, West Germany was troubled by its Nazi past. The surviving major Nazi leaders had been tried and condemned as war criminals at war crimes trials held in Nuremberg in 1945 and 1946. As part of the denazification of Germany, the victorious Allies continued war crimes trials of lesser officials, but these diminished as the Cold War

brought about a shift in attitudes. By 1950, German courts had begun to take over the war crimes trials, and the German legal machine persisted in prosecuting cases. It was not until the 1960s, however, that Germans began to address the Nazi past more publicly by including the history of Nazism as part of the school curriculum (see the box on p. 883).

Adenauer resigned in 1963, after fourteen years of firmly guiding West Germany through its postwar recovery. Adenauer had wanted no grand experimentation at home or abroad; he was content to give Germany time to regain its equilibrium. Ludwig Erhard succeeded Adenauer and largely continued his policies. But an economic downturn in the mid-1960s opened the door to the rise of the Social Democrats, and in 1969, they became the leading party.

GREAT BRITAIN: THE WELFARE STATE The end of World War II left Britain with massive economic problems. In elections held immediately after the war, the Labour Party overwhelmingly defeated Churchill's Conservative Party. The Labour Party had promised far-reaching reforms, particularly in the area of social welfare, and in a country with a tremendous shortage of consumer goods and housing, its platform was quite appealing. The new Labour government, with Clement Attlee (1883–1967) as prime minister, proceeded to enact reforms that created a modern **welfare state**.

The establishment of the British welfare state began with the nationalization of the Bank of England, the coal and steel industries, public transportation, and public utilities, such as electricity and gas. In the area of social welfare, the new government enacted the National Insurance Act and the National Health Service Act in 1946. The insurance act established a

The British Welfare State: Free Milk at School. The creation of the welfare state was a prominent social development in postwar Europe. The desire to improve the health of children led to welfare programs that provided free food for young people. Pictured here are boys at a grammar school in England during a free milk break.

THE BURDEN OF GUILT

IN THE YEARS AFTER WORLD WAR II, West Germany focused primarily on rebuilding the country. Beginning in the 1960s, German educators started teaching Germany's Nazi past in schools. This selection is from *The Burden of Guilt: A Short History of Germany, 1914–1945*, published in 1961. The book was written by Hannah Vogt, a civil servant, and was widely used in secondary schools.

Hannah Vogt, The *Burden of Guilt*

A nation is made up of individuals whose ideas—right or wrong—determine their actions, their decisions, and their common life, and for this reason a nation, too, can look back at its history and learn from it. As Germans, we should not find it too difficult to understand the meaning of the fourteen years of the Weimar Republic and the twelve years of the Hitler regime. . . .

We have paid dearly once before for the folly of believing that democracy, being an ideal political arrangement, must function automatically while the citizens sit in their parlors berating it, or worrying about their money. Everybody must share in the responsibility and must be prepared to make sacrifices. . . .

Only if the citizens are thoroughly imbued with democratic attitudes can we put into practice those principles of political life which were achieved through centuries of experience. . . . The first such principle is the need for a continuous and vigilant control of power. For this, we need not only a free and courageous press but also some mechanism for shaping a vital political opinion in associations, parties, and other organizations. Equally necessary are clearly drawn lines of political responsibility, and a strong and respected political opposition. . . .

More than anything else we must base our concept of law on the idea of justice. We have had the sad experience that the principle "the law is the law" does not suffice, if the laws are being abused to cover up for crimes and to wrap injustices in a tissue of legality. Our actions must once again be guided by that idea which is the basis of a just life: no man must be used as a means to an end. . . .

Thus we are now faced with the difficult task of regaining, by peaceful means, the German unity that Hitler has gambled away. We must strive for it tirelessly, even though it may take decades. At the same time, we must establish a new relationship, based on trust, with the peoples of Europe and the nations of the world. . . .

We owe it to ourselves to examine our consciences sincerely and to face the naked truth, instead of minimizing it or glossing over it. This is also the only way we can regain respect in the world. Covering up or minimizing crimes will suggest that we secretly approve of them. Who will believe that we want to respect all that is human if we treat the death of nearly six million Jews as a "small error" to be forgotten after a few years?

 What does Vogt think is necessary for citizens to remain free? What lessons does she think Germans should learn from the Nazi era?

Source: From H. Vogt, *The Burden of Guilt*, trans. H. Strauss (Oxford: Oxford University Press, 1964), pp. 283–286.

comprehensive **social security** program and nationalized medical insurance, thereby enabling the state to subsidize the unemployed, the sick, and the aged. The health act created a system of **socialized medicine** that required doctors and dentists to work with state hospitals, although private practices could be maintained. This measure was especially costly for the state, but within a few years, 90 percent of medical practitioners were participating. The British welfare state became the model for most European states after the war.

The cost of building a welfare state at home forced the British to reduce expenses abroad. This meant the dismantling of the British Empire and the reduction of military aid to such countries as Greece and Turkey. It was not a belief in the morality of self-determination but economic necessity that brought an end to the British Empire.

Continuing economic problems, however, brought the Conservatives back into power from 1951 to 1964. Although they favored private enterprise, the Conservatives accepted the welfare state and even extended it when they undertook an ambitious construction program to improve British housing. Although the British economy had recovered from the war, it had done so at a slower rate than other European countries. Moreover, the slow rate of recovery masked a long-term economic decline caused by a variety of factors. The demands of British trade unions for wages that rose faster than productivity were a problem in the late 1950s and 1960s. As a result of the low productivity rates, British businesses were unwilling to invest in modern industrial machinery and to adopt new methods. British investment rates were the lowest of any West European country. Underlying the immediate problems, however, was a deeper issue. As a result of World War II, Britain had lost much of its prewar revenues from abroad but was left with a burden of debt from its many international commitments. Britain was no longer a world power.

ITALY: WEAK COALITION GOVERNMENT After the war, Italy faced a period of heavy reconstruction. Only Germany had sustained more physical destruction. The monarchy was abolished when 54 percent of Italian voters rejected the royal house, and in June 1946, Italy became a democratic republic.

In the first postwar parliamentary elections, held in April 1948, the Christian Democrats, still allied with the Catholic

Church, emerged as the leading political party. Alcide de Gasperi (ahl-SEE-day day GAHSS-pe-ree) (1881–1954) served as prime minister from 1948 to 1953, an unusually long span of time for an Italian government. Like pre-Fascist governments, postwar Italian coalitions, largely dominated by the Christian Democrats, were famous for their instability and short lives. Although the Italian Communist Party was one of Italy's three largest parties, it was largely excluded from all of these government coalitions. It did, however, manage to gain power in a number of provinces and municipalities in the 1960s. The Christian Democrats were able to maintain control by keeping the support of the upper and middle classes and the southern peasantry.

Italy, too, experienced an "economic miracle" after the war, although it was far less publicized than Germany's. The Marshall Plan helped stabilize the postwar Italian economy. Especially during the late 1950s and early 1960s, Italy made rapid strides in economic growth. The production of electrical appliances, cars, and office machinery made the most significant leap. As in other Western welfare states, the Italian economy combined private enterprise with government management, particularly of heavy industry. In 1965, for example, the government controlled 60 percent of Italy's steel production. The major economic problem continued to be the backwardness of southern Italy, a region that possessed 36 percent of the total population but generated only 25 percent of the national income. In the 1960s, millions of Italians from the south migrated to the more prosperous north.

Western Europe: The Move Toward Unity

As we have seen, the divisions created by the Cold War led the nations of Western Europe to form the North Atlantic Treaty Organization in 1949. But military unity was not the only kind of unity fostered in Europe after 1945. The destructiveness of two world wars caused many thoughtful Europeans to consider the need

CHRONOLOGY	Western Europe After the War	
Welfare state emerges in Great Britain		1946
Italy becomes a democratic republic		1946
Alcide de Gasperi becomes prime minister of Italy		1948
Konrad Adenauer becomes chancellor of West Germany		1949
Formation of European Coal and Steel Community		1951
West Germany joins NATO		1955
Suez Crisis		1956
Formation of EURATOM		1957
Formation of European Economic Community (Common Market)		1957
Charles de Gaulle assumes power in France		1958
Erhard becomes chancellor of Germany		1963

for some form of European unity. National feeling was still too powerful, however, for European nations to give up their political sovereignty. Consequently, the desire for a sense of solidarity focused primarily on the economic arena, not the political one.

In 1951, France, West Germany, the Benelux countries (Belgium, Netherlands, and Luxembourg), and Italy formed the European Coal and Steel Community (ECSC). Its purpose was to create a common market for coal and steel products among the six nations by eliminating tariffs and other trade barriers. Freer trade curtailed the power of monopolies and cartels and encouraged participating countries to concentrate on the production of goods in which they had a comparative advantage. The success of the ECSC encouraged its members to proceed further, and in 1957 they created the European Atomic Energy Community (EURATOM) to further European research on the peaceful uses of nuclear energy.

In the same year, these six nations signed the Rome Treaty, which created the European Economic Community (EEC), also known as the Common Market. The EEC eliminated customs barriers for the six member nations and created a large free-trade area protected from the rest of the world by a common external tariff. By promoting free trade, the EEC also encouraged cooperation and standardization in many aspects of the six nations' economies. All the member nations benefited economically. With a total population of 165 million, the EEC became the world's largest exporter and purchaser of raw materials. Only the United States surpassed the EEC in steel production.

European Economic Community, 1957

The United States and Canada: A New Era

 FOCUS QUESTION: What were the main political developments in North America between 1945 and 1965?

At the end of World War II, the United States was one of the world's two superpowers. As the Cold War with the Soviet Union intensified, the United States worked hard to prevent the spread of communism throughout the world. American domestic political life after 1945 was played out against a background of American military power abroad.

American Politics and Society in the 1950s

Between 1945 and 1970, the ideals of Franklin Roosevelt's New Deal largely determined the patterns of American domestic politics. The New Deal had brought basic changes to American society, including a dramatic increase in the role and power of the federal government, the rise of organized labor as a significant force in the economy and politics, the beginning of a welfare state, and a grudging realization of the need to deal fairly with the concerns of minorities.

The New Deal tradition was bolstered by the election of three Democratic presidents—Harry Truman in 1948, John Kennedy in 1960, and Lyndon Johnson in 1964. Even the election of a Republican president, Dwight Eisenhower, in 1952 and 1956 did not change the basic direction of American politics. Eisenhower stated that any political party that attempted to abolish Social Security and eliminate labor laws and farm programs would not be heard of "again in our political history."

The economic boom after World War II fueled confidence in the American way of life. A shortage of consumer goods during the war had left Americans with both extra income and a pent-up desire to buy these goods after the war. Then, too, the growth of labor unions brought higher wages that enabled more and more workers to buy consumer goods. Between 1945 and 1973, real wages grew 3 percent a year on average, the most prolonged advance in American history.

Prosperity was not the only characteristic of the early 1950s. Cold War confrontations abroad had repercussions at home. The takeover of China by Mao Zedong's Communist forces in 1949 and Communist North Korea's invasion of South Korea in 1950 led to a fear that Communists had infiltrated the United States. President Truman's attorney general warned that Communists "are everywhere—in factories, offices, butcher stores, on street corners, in private businesses." A demagogic senator from Wisconsin, Joseph R. McCarthy, helped intensify the "Red Scare" with his exposés of supposed Communists in high government positions. McCarthy went too far when he attacked alleged "Communist conspirators" in the U.S. Army and was censured by Congress in 1954. Very quickly, his anti-Communist crusade came to an end.

Decade of Upheaval: America in the 1960s

During the 1960s, the United States experienced a period of upheaval that brought to the fore problems that had been glossed over in the 1950s. The 1960s began on a youthful and optimistic note. At age forty-three, John F. Kennedy became the youngest elected president in the history of the United States. His own administration, cut short by an assassin's bullet on November 22, 1963, focused primarily on foreign affairs. Kennedy's successor, Lyndon B. Johnson (1908–1973), who won a new term as president in a landslide in 1964, used his stunning mandate to pursue what he called the Great Society, heir to the welfare state first begun in the New Deal. Johnson's programs included health care for the elderly, a "war on poverty" to be fought with food stamps and the new Job Corps, the new Department of Housing and Urban Development to deal with the problems of the cities, and federal assistance for education.

CIVIL RIGHTS MOVEMENT Johnson's other domestic passion was equal rights for African Americans. The civil rights movement had its beginnings in 1954 when the U.S. Supreme Court took the dramatic step of striking down the practice of racially segregating public schools. An eloquent Baptist minister named Martin Luther King Jr. (1929–1968) became the leader of a growing movement for racial equality, and by the early 1960s, a number of groups, including King's Southern Christian Leadership

The Civil Rights Movement. In the early 1960s, Martin Luther King Jr. and his Southern Christian Leadership Conference organized a variety of activities to pursue the goal of racial equality. He is shown here with his wife Coretta (right) and Rosa Parks and Ralph Abernathy (far left) leading a march against racial discrimination in 1965.

Bob Adelman/Magnum Photos

Conference (SCLC), were organizing sit-ins and demonstrations across the South to end racial segregation. In August 1963, King led the March on Washington for Jobs and Freedom to dramatize African Americans' desire for equal rights and opportunities. This march and King's impassioned plea for racial equality had an electrifying effect on the American people.

President Johnson took up the cause of civil rights. As a result of his initiative, Congress passed the Civil Rights Act of 1964, which created the machinery to end segregation and discrimination in the workplace and all public places. A voting rights act the following year made it easier for blacks to vote in southern states. But laws alone could not guarantee the Great Society, and Johnson soon faced bitter social unrest, both from African Americans and from the burgeoning movement opposing the Vietnam War.

In the North and the West, African Americans had had voting rights for many years, but local patterns of segregation led to higher unemployment rates for blacks than for whites and left African Americans segregated in huge urban ghettos. In these ghettos, the call for action by radical black leaders, such as Malcolm X (1925–1965) of the Black Muslims, attracted more attention than the nonviolent appeals of Martin Luther King. Malcolm X's advice was straightforward: "If someone puts a hand on you, send him to the cemetery."

In the summer of 1965, race riots broke out in the Watts district of Los Angeles. Thirty-four people died and more than one thousand buildings were destroyed. Cleveland, San Francisco, Chicago, Newark, and Detroit likewise exploded in the summers of 1966 and 1967. After the assassination of Martin Luther King in 1968, more than one hundred cities experienced riots. The combination of riots and extremist comments by radical black leaders led to a "white backlash" and a severe division of the American population.

The Development of Canada

Canada experienced many of the same developments as the United States in the postwar years. For twenty-five years after World War II, prosperous Canada set out on a new path of industrial development. Canada had always had a strong export economy based on its abundant natural resources. Now it also developed electronic, aircraft, nuclear, and chemical engineering industries on a large scale. Much of the Canadian growth, however, was financed by capital from the United States, which led to American ownership of Canadian businesses. Although many Canadians welcomed the economic growth, others feared American economic domination.

Canadians also worried about playing a secondary role politically and militarily to their neighboring superpower. Canada agreed to join NATO in 1949 and even sent military forces to fight in Korea the following year. At the same time, to avoid subordination to the United States, Canada actively supported the United Nations. Nevertheless, concerns about the United States did not keep Canada from maintaining a special relationship with its southern neighbor. The North American Air Defense Command (NORAD), formed in 1957, maintained close cooperation between the air forces of the two countries for the defense of North America against Soviet bombers.

After 1945, the Liberal Party continued to dominate Canadian politics until 1957, when John Diefenbaker (1895–1979) achieved a Conservative Party victory. But major economic problems returned the Liberals to power, and under Lester Pearson (1897–1972), they created Canada's welfare state by enacting a national social security system (the Canada Pension Plan) and a national health insurance program.

Postwar Society and Culture in the Western World

 FOCUS QUESTION: What major changes occurred in Western society and culture between 1945 and 1965?

During the postwar era, Western society and culture witnessed remarkably rapid change. Computers, television, jet planes, contraceptive devices, and new surgical techniques all dramatically and quickly altered the pace and nature of human life. The rapid changes in postwar society, fueled by scientific advances and rapid economic growth, led many to view it as a new society.

The Structure of European Society

The structure of European society was altered after 1945. Especially noticeable were the changes in the middle class. Such traditional middle-class groups as businesspeople and professionals in law, medicine, and the universities were greatly augmented by a new group of managers and technicians as large companies and government agencies employed increasing numbers of white-collar supervisory and administrative personnel. In both Eastern and Western Europe, the new managers and experts were very much alike. Everywhere their positions depended on specialized knowledge acquired from some form of higher education. Everywhere they focused on the effective administration of their organizations. Because their positions usually depended on their skills, they took steps to ensure that their own children would be educated.

A SOCIETY OF CONSUMERS Changes also occurred among the traditional lower classes. Especially noticeable was the dramatic shift of people from rural to urban areas. The number of people working in agriculture declined dramatically, yet the size of the industrial labor force remained the same. In West Germany, industrial workers made up 48 percent of the labor force throughout the 1950s and 1960s. Thereafter, the number of industrial workers began to dwindle as white-collar and service jobs increased. At the same time, a substantial increase in their real wages enabled the working classes to aspire to the consumption patterns of the middle class, leading to what some observers have called the **consumer society**. Buying on the installment plan, introduced in the 1920s, became widespread in the 1950s and gave workers a chance to imitate the middle class by buying such products as televisions, washing machines, refrigerators, vacuum cleaners, and stereos. Shopping for everyday commodities, such as food products, also became easier and cheaper with the introduction of supermarkets (see "Global Perspectives" on p. 887). But the most visible symbol of mass

The Rise of the Supermarket in West and East

FOR MORE THAN A DECADE AFTER World War II, many food products were still scarce in Europe. Consequently, food was much more expensive in Europe than in the United States. For American consumers, the introduction of standardized foodstuffs and self-service supermarkets had led to lower prices for basic staples, leaving families more money to spend on refrigerators, televisions, and automobiles. The Americanization of foodstuffs did not reach Europe until the mid-1950s, when supermarkets began to open in major European cities. The first photograph shows German shoppers looking at bins of produce at a new supermarket in Frankfurt in 1954. These early supermarkets were not an immediate success. Few Europeans had refrigerators or automobiles, making it difficult to store large food purchases. In time, however, as more women entered the workforce, both women and men began to appreciate the convenience of shopping at a supermarket. The photograph at the bottom shows shoppers looking at wrapped packages of meat in refrigerated cases, a new phenomenon. As families moved to the suburbs and acquired automobiles, supermarkets became more accessible.

The concept of the supermarket, with lower prices, self-service and a wide availability of goods, was adopted successfully in Japan during the 1950s. By the 1960s, many chain stores had opened throughout Tokyo, as shown in the last photograph of a Japanese supermarket in 1963. Notice the Western-style dress of the shoppers.

Charles Fenno Jacobs//Time Life Pictures/Getty Images

Popperfoto/Getty Images

ullstein bild/Getty Images

consumerism was the automobile. For the most part, only the European upper classes could afford cars before World War II. In 1948, there were 5 million cars in all of Europe, but by 1957, the number had tripled. By the 1960s, there were almost 45 million cars.

MASS LEISURE Rising incomes, combined with shorter working hours, created an even greater market for mass leisure activities. Between 1900 and 1960, the workweek was reduced from sixty hours to a little more than forty hours, and the number of paid holidays increased. In the 1960s, German and Italian workers received between thirty-two and thirty-five paid holidays a year. All aspects of popular culture—music, sports, media—became commercialized and offered opportunities for leisure activities, including concerts, sporting events, and television viewing.

Another visible symbol of mass leisure was the growth of mass tourism. Before World War II, mostly the upper and middle classes traveled for pleasure. After the war, the combination of more vacation time, increased prosperity, and the flexibility provided by package tours with their lower rates and less expensive lodgings enabled millions to expand their travel possibilities. By the mid-1960s, 100 million tourists were crossing European boundaries each year.

Creation of the Welfare State

One of the most noticeable social developments in postwar Europe was the creation of the welfare state. In one sense, the welfare state represented another extension of the power of the state over the lives of its citizens, a process that had increased dramatically as a result of the two world wars. Yet the goal of the welfare state was to make it possible for people to live better and more meaningful lives. Advocates of the welfare state believed that by eliminating poverty and homelessness, providing medical services for all, ensuring dignity for older people, and extending educational opportunities for all who wanted them, the state would satisfy people's material needs and thereby free them to achieve happiness.

Social welfare schemes were not new to Europe. Beginning in the late nineteenth century, some states had provided for the welfare of the working class by instituting old-age pensions, medical insurance, and unemployment compensation. But these efforts were piecemeal and were by no means based on a general belief that society had a responsibility to care for all of its citizens.

The new postwar social legislation greatly extended earlier benefits and created new ones as well. Of course, social welfare benefits differed considerably from country to country in quantity and quality as well as in how they were paid for and managed. Nevertheless, there were some common trends. In many countries, already existing benefits for sickness, accidents, unemployment, and old age were simply extended to cover more people and provide larger payments. Men were generally eligible for old-age pensions at age sixty-five and women at sixty.

Affordable health care for all people was another goal of the welfare state, although the methods of achieving this goal varied. In some countries, medical care was free to all people with some kind of insurance, but in others, people had to contribute toward the cost of their medical care. The amount ranged from 10 to 25 percent of the total cost.

Another feature of welfare states was the use of **family allowances**, which were instituted in some countries to provide a minimum level of material care for children. Most family allowance programs provided a fixed amount per child. Family allowances were also conceived in large part as a way to increase the population after the decline suffered during the war. The French, for example, increased the amount of aid for each new child after the first one.

Welfare states also sought to remove class barriers to opportunity by expanding the number of universities and providing scholarships to allow everyone to attend an institution of higher learning. Overall, European states moved toward free or only modest tuition for university attendance. These policies did not always achieve their goals, however. In the early 1960s, most students in Western European universities still came from privileged backgrounds. In Britain, 25 percent of university students came from working-class backgrounds; in France, the figure was only 17.6 percent.

The welfare state dramatically increased the amount of money states expended on social services. In 1967, such spending constituted 17 percent of the gross national product of the major European countries; by the 1980s, it absorbed 40 to 50 percent. To some critics, these figures proved that the welfare state had produced a new generation of citizens overly dependent on the state. But most people favored the benefits, and most leaders were well aware that it was political suicide to advocate curtailing or seriously lowering those benefits.

GENDER ISSUES IN THE WELFARE STATE Gender issues also influenced the form that the welfare state took in different countries. One general question dominated the debate: Should women be recognized in a special category as mothers, or should they be regarded as individuals? William Beveridge, the economist who drafted the report that formed the basis for the British welfare state, said that women had "vital work to do in ensuring the adequate continuance of the British race." "During marriage." he said, "most women will not be gainfully employed. The small minority of women who undertake paid employment or other gainful employment or other gainful occupations after marriage require special treatment differing from that of single women."[10] Accordingly, the British welfare system was based on the belief that women should stay home with their children: women received subsidies for children, but married women who worked were given few or no benefits. Employers were also encouraged to pay women lower wages to discourage them from joining the workforce. Thus, the British welfare system encouraged wives to be dependent on their husbands. So did the West German system. The West German government passed laws that discouraged women from working. In keeping its women at home, West Germany sought to differentiate itself from neighboring Communist countries in Eastern Europe and the Soviet Union, where women were encouraged to work outside the home. At the same time, to help working women raise families, Communist governments also provided day-care facilities, as well as family subsidies and maternity benefits.

France sought to maintain the individual rights of women in its welfare system. The French government recognized women as equal to men and thus entitled to the same welfare benefits as men for working outside the home. At the same time, wanting to encourage population growth, the government provided incentives for women to stay home and bear children as well as day-care and after-school programs to assist working mothers.

Women in the Postwar Western World

Despite their enormous contributions to the war effort, women were removed from the workforce at the end of World War II to provide jobs for the soldiers returning home. After the horrors of war, people seemed willing for a while to return to traditional family practices. Female participation in the workforce declined, and birthrates began to rise, creating a "baby boom." This increase in the birthrate did not last, however, and birthrates, and thus the size of families, began to decline by the end of the 1950s. Largely responsible for this decline was the widespread practice of birth control. Invented in the nineteenth century, the condom was already in wide use, but the development in the 1960s of oral contraceptives, known as birth control pills or simply "the pill," provided a reliable means of birth control that quickly spread to all Western countries.

WOMEN IN THE WORKFORCE The trend toward smaller families no doubt contributed to the change in the character of women's employment in both Europe and the United States, as women experienced considerably more years when they were not involved in rearing children. The most important development was the increased number of married women in the workforce. At the beginning of the twentieth century, even working-class wives tended to stay at home if they could afford to do so. In the postwar period, this was no longer the case. In the United States, for example, in 1900, married women made up about 15 percent of the female labor force; by 1970, their number had increased to 62 percent. The percentage of married women in the female labor force in Sweden increased from 47 to 66 percent between 1963 and 1975. Figures for the Soviet Union and its satellites were even higher. In 1970, fully 92.5 percent of all women in the Soviet Union held jobs, compared to around 50 percent in France and West Germany.

But the increased number of women in the workforce did not change some old patterns. Working-class women in particular still earned salaries lower than those of men for equal work. In the 1960s, women earned only 60 percent of men's wages in Britain, 50 percent in France, and 63 percent in West Germany. In addition, women still tended to enter traditionally female jobs. As one Swedish female guidance counselor remarked in 1975, "Every girl now thinks in terms of a job. This is progress. They want children, but they don't pin their hopes on marriage. They don't intend to be housewives for some future husband. But there has been no change in their vocational choices."[11] Many European women also still faced the double burden of earning income on the one hand and raising a family and maintaining the household on the other.

SUFFRAGE AND THE SEARCH FOR LIBERATION The participation of women in the two world wars helped them achieve one of the major aims of the nineteenth-century women's movement—the right to vote. Already after World War I, many governments acknowledged the contributions of women to the war effort by granting them suffrage. Sweden, Great Britain, Germany, Poland, Hungary, Austria, and Czechoslovakia did so in 1918, followed by the United States in 1920. Women in France and Italy did not obtain the right to vote until 1945. After World War II, European women tended to fall back into the traditional roles expected of them, and little was heard of feminist concerns.

A women's liberation movement would arise in the late 1960s (see Chapter 29), but much of the theoretical foundation for the postwar women's liberation movement was evident in the earlier work of Simone de Beauvoir (see-MUHN duh boh-VWAR) (1908–1986). Born into a Catholic middle-class family and educated at the Sorbonne in Paris, she supported herself as a teacher and later as a novelist and writer. She maintained a lifelong relationship (but not marriage) with Jean-Paul Sartre (ZHAHNH-POHL SAR-truh). Her involvement in the existentialist movement, the leading intellectual movement of the time (see "The Philosophical Dilemma: Existentialism" later in this chapter), led to her involvement in political causes. De Beauvoir believed that she lived a "liberated" life for a twentieth-century European woman, but for all her freedom, she still came to perceive that as a woman she faced limits that men did not. In 1949, she published her highly influential work *The Second Sex*, in which she argued that as a result of male-dominated societies, women had been defined by their differences from men and consequently received second-class status: "What peculiarly signalizes the situation of woman is that she—a free and autonomous being like all human creatures—nevertheless finds herself living in a world where men compel her to assume the status of the Other."[12] De Beauvoir played an active role in the French women's movement of the 1970s, and her book became a major influence on both sides of the Atlantic (see the box on p. 890).

Postwar Art and Literature

Many artists and writers struggled to understand the horrors of World War II. The German philosopher Theodor Adorno believed that "to write poetry after Auschwitz is barbaric."

ART Many artists and writers, particularly the Surrealists, fled to the United States during World War II to avoid persecution for their revolutionary ideas. Following the war, the United States dominated the art world, much as it did the world of popular culture (see "The Americanization of the World" later in this chapter). New York City replaced Paris as the artistic center of the West. The Guggenheim Museum, the Museum of Modern Art, and the Whitney Museum of American Art, together with New York's numerous art galleries, promoted modern art and helped determine artistic tastes throughout much of the world. One of the styles that became synonymous with the emergence of the New York art scene was **Abstract Expressionism**.

THE VOICE OF THE WOMEN'S LIBERATION MOVEMENT

SIMONE DE BEAUVOIR WAS AN IMPORTANT figure in the emergence of the postwar women's liberation movement. This excerpt is taken from her influential book *The Second Sex*, in which she argued that women have been forced into a position subordinate to men.

Simone de Beauvoir, *The Second Sex*

Now, woman has always been man's dependent, if not his slave; the two sexes have never shared the world in equality. And even today woman is heavily handicapped, though her situation is beginning to change. Almost nowhere is her legal status the same as man's and frequently it is much to her disadvantage. Even when her rights are legally recognized in the abstract, long-standing custom prevents their full expression in the mores. In the economic sphere men and women can almost be said to make up two castes; other things being equal, the former hold the better jobs, get higher wages, and have more opportunity for success than their new competitors. In industry and politics men have a great many more positions and they monopolize the most important posts. In addition to all this they enjoy a traditional prestige that the education of children tends in every way to support, for the present enshrines the past—and in the past all history has been made by men. At the present time, when women are beginning to take part in the affairs of the world, it is still a world that belongs to men—they have no doubt of it at all and women have scarcely any. To decline to be the Other, to refuse to be a party to a deal—this would be for women to renounce all the advantages conferred upon them by their alliance with the superior caste. Man-the-sovereign will provide woman-the-liege with material protection and will undertake the moral justification of her existence; thus she can evade at once both economic risk and the metaphysical risk of a liberty in which ends and aims must be contrived without assistance. Indeed, along with the ethical urge of each individual to affirm his subjective existence, there is also the temptation to forgo liberty and become a thing. This is an inauspicious road, for he who takes it—passive, lost, ruined—becomes henceforth the creature of another's will, frustrated in his transcendence and deprived of every value. But it is an easy road; on it one avoids the strain involved in undertaking an authentic existence. When man makes of woman the Other he may, then, expect her to manifest deep-seated tendencies toward complicity. Thus woman may fail to lay claim to the status of subject because she lacks definite resources, because she feels the necessary bond that ties her to man regardless of reciprocity, and because she is often very well pleased with her role as the *Other*.

Now, what peculiarly signalizes the situation of woman is that she—a free and autonomous being like all human creatures—nevertheless finds herself living in a world where men compel her to assume the status of the Other.

 What factors or values do you think informed de Beauvoir's implicit call for a new history of women? Why was she outraged by the neglect of women in the Western historical consciousness?

Source: Simone de Beauvoir, *The Second Sex*, trans. C. Borde and S. Malovany-Chevalller (New York: Knopf Doubleday Publishing, 2011).

Dubbed "action painting" by one critic, Abstract Expressionism was energetic and spontaneous, qualities evident in the enormous canvases of Jackson Pollock (1912–1956). In works such as *Convergence* (1952), paint seems to explode, enveloping the viewer with emotion and movement. Pollock's swirling forms and seemingly chaotic patterns broke all conventions of form and structure. His drip paintings, with their total abstraction, were extremely influential with other artists, and he eventually became a celebrity. Inspired by Native American sand painters, Pollock painted with the canvas on the floor. He explained, "On the floor I am more at ease. I feel nearer, more a part of the painting, since this way I can walk around in, work from four sides and be literally *in* the painting. When I am in the painting, I am not aware of what I am doing. There is pure harmony."

The 1950s and early 1960s saw the emergence of **Pop Art**, which took images of popular culture and transformed them into works of fine art. Several British art students, known as the Independent Group, incorporated science fiction and American advertising techniques into their exhibitions. Andy Warhol (1930–1987), who began as an advertising illustrator, became the most famous of the American Pop artists. Warhol adapted images from commercial art, such as Campbell's soup cans, and photographs of celebrities such as Marilyn Monroe. Derived from mass culture, these works were mass-produced and deliberately "of the moment," expressing the fleeting whims of popular culture. The detached style of Warhol's silk-screened prints put Pop Art at odds with the aggressive, painterly techniques of the Abstract Expressionists.

LITERATURE The most significant new trend in postwar literature was called the "Theater of the Absurd." This new convention in drama began in France in the 1950s, although its most famous proponent was the Irishman Samuel Beckett (1906–1990), who lived in France. In Beckett's *Waiting for Godot* (1952), the action on stage is not realistic. Two men wait incessantly for the appearance of someone, with whom they may or may not have an appointment. No background information on the two men is provided. During the course of the play, nothing seems to be happening. The audience is never told if what they are watching is real or not. Unlike traditional theater, suspense is maintained not by having the audience wonder what is going to happen next but by having them ask, what is happening now?

The Theater of the Absurd reflected its time. The postwar period was a time of disillusionment with ideological beliefs

in politics or religion. A sense of the world's meaninglessness underscored the desolate worldview of absurdist drama and literature. This can be seen in the novel *The Tin Drum* (1959) by Günter Grass (b. 1927), which reflected postwar Germany's preoccupation with the seeming incomprehensibility of Nazi Germany.

The Philosophical Dilemma: Existentialism

The sense of meaninglessness that inspired the Theater of the Absurd also underscored the philosophy of **existentialism**. It was born largely of the desperation caused by two world wars and the breakdown of traditional values. Existentialism reflected the anxieties of the twentieth century and became especially well known after World War II through the works of two Frenchmen, Jean-Paul Sartre (1905–1980) and Albert Camus (ahl-BAYR ka-MOO) (1913–1960).

The central point of the existentialism of Sartre and Camus was the absence of God in the universe. The death of God, though tragic, meant that humans had no preordained destiny and were utterly alone in the universe, with no future and no hope. As Camus expressed it:

> A world that can be explained even with bad reasons is a familiar world. But, on the other hand, in a universe suddenly divested of illusions and lights, man feels an alien, a stranger. His exile is without remedy since he is deprived of the

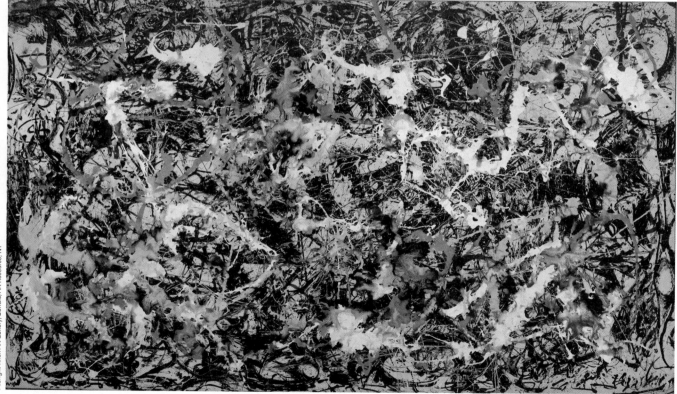

Jackson Pollock Painting. After World War II, Abstract Expressionism moved to the center of the artistic mainstream. One of its best-known practitioners was the American Jackson Pollock, who achieved his ideal of total abstraction in his drip paintings. He is shown here at work in his Long Island studio. Pollock found it easier to cover his large canvases with spontaneous patterns of color when he put them on the floor. Seen in the second photo is his *Convergence*, painted in 1952, just four years before his death.

memory of a lost home or the hope of a promised land. This divorce between man and his life, the actor and his setting, is properly the feeling of absurdity.[13]

According to Camus, then, the world was absurd and without meaning; humans, too, are without meaning and purpose. Reduced to despair and depression, humans have but one source of hope—themselves.

Though the world might be absurd, Camus argued, it could not be absurd unless people judged it to be so. People are unique in the world, and their kind of being is quite different from that of all others. In the words of Sartre, human "existence precedes essence." Humans are beings who first exist and then define themselves. They determine what they will be. According to Sartre, "Man is nothing else but what he makes of himself. Such is the first principle of existentialism." People, then, must take full responsibility for what they are. They create their values and give their lives meaning. And this can only be done by their involvement in life. Only through one's acts can one determine one's values.

Existentialism, therefore, involved an ethics of action, of involvement in life. But people could not define themselves without their involvement with others. Thus, existentialism's ethical message was just as important as its philosophy of being. Essentially, the message of existentialism was one of authenticity. Individuals true to themselves refused to be depersonalized by their society.

The Attempt to Revive Religion

Existentialism was one response to the despair generated by the apparent collapse of civilized values in the twentieth century. The attempt to revive religion was another. Ever since the Enlightenment of the eighteenth century, Christianity and religion had been on the defensive. But a number of religious thinkers and leaders attempted to bring new life to Christianity in the twentieth century.

One expression of this religious revival was the attempt by the Protestant theologian Karl Barth (BAHRT) (1886–1968) to infuse traditional Christian teachings with new life. In his numerous writings, Barth attempted to reinterpret the religious insights of the Reformation era for the modern world. To Barth, the sinful and hence imperfect nature of human beings meant that humans could know religious truth not through reason but only through the grace of God.

In the Catholic Church, an attempt at religious renewal also came from a charismatic pope. Pope John XXIII (1881–1963) reigned as pope for only a short time (1958–1963) but sparked a dramatic revival of Catholicism when he summoned the twenty-first ecumenical council of the Catholic Church. Known as Vatican II, the council liberalized a number of Catholic practices. For example, the liturgy of the Mass, the central feature of Catholic worship, was now to be spoken in the vernacular, not in Latin. New avenues of communication with other Christian faiths were also opened for the first time since the Reformation.

But these attempts to redefine Christianity were not necessarily successful at rekindling people's faith. Although many churches experienced an upswing in involvement in the late 1940s and early 1950s, no doubt as a response to the war, by the late 1950s and 1960s, attendance was declining at European churches. Even in Italy, regular attendance by members of the Catholic Church fell from 69 percent in 1956 to 48 percent in 1968.

The Explosion of Popular Culture

Since World War II, popular culture has played an increasingly important role in helping Western people define themselves. The history of popular culture is also the history of the economic system that supports it, for this system manufactures, distributes, and sells the images that people consume as popular culture. As popular culture and its economic support system have become increasingly intertwined, industries of leisure have emerged. As one historian of popular culture has argued, "Industrial societies turn the provision of leisure into a commercial activity, in which their citizens are sold entertainment, recreation, pleasure, and appearance as commodities that differ from the goods at the drugstore only in the way they are used."[14] Thus, modern popular culture is inextricably tied to the mass consumer society in which it has emerged.

THE AMERICANIZATION OF THE WORLD The United States has been the most influential force in shaping popular culture in the West and, to a lesser degree, the rest of the world. Through movies, music, advertising, and television, the United States has spread its particular form of consumerism and the American dream to millions around the world. Already in 1923, the New York *Morning Post* noted that "the film is to America what the flag was once to Britain. By its means Uncle Sam may hope some day . . . to Americanize the world."[15] In movies, television, and popular music, the impact of American popular culture on the Western world is pervasive.

Motion pictures were the primary vehicle for the diffusion of American popular culture in the years immediately following the war, and they continued to dominate both European and American markets in the next decades (40 percent of Hollywood's income in the 1960s came from the European market). Nevertheless, the existence of a profitable art-house circuit in America and Europe enabled European filmmakers to make films whose themes and avant-garde methods were quite different from those of Hollywood. Italy and Sweden, for example, developed a tradition of "national cinema" that reflected "specific cultural traits in a mode in which they could be successfully exported." The 1957 film *The Seventh Seal*, by the Swedish director Ingmar Bergman (1918–2007), was a good example of the successful European art film. Bergman's films caused him to be viewed as "an artist of comparable stature to a novelist or playwright."

Although developed in the 1930s, television did not become readily available until the late 1940s. By 1954, there were 32 million sets in the United States as television became the centerpiece of middle-class life. In the 1960s, as television spread around the world, American networks unloaded their products on Europe and the Third World at extraordinarily low prices. For instance, the British Broadcasting Corporation (BBC) could buy American programs for one-tenth the cost per viewer of producing its own. Only the establishment of quota systems prevented American television from completely inundating these countries.

The United States has dominated popular music since the end of World War II. Jazz, blues, rhythm and blues, and rock 'n' roll have been by far the most popular music forms in the Western world—and much of the non-Western world—during this time. All of them originated in the United States, and all are rooted in African American musical innovations. These forms later spread around the globe, inspiring local artists who then transformed the music in their own way. Often these transformed models then returned to the United States to inspire American artists. This was certainly the case with rock 'n' roll. Through the 1950s, American artists such as Chuck Berry, Little Richard, and Elvis Presley inspired the Beatles and other British performers, who then led an "invasion" of the United States in the 1960s, creating a sensation and in part sparking new rockers in America. The availability of cheap personal music players in the 1960s transformed the music industry, making albums more accessible to wider audiences instead of relying on radio broadcasts and concerts. Rock music itself developed in the 1950s. In 1952, white disc jockeys began playing rhythm and blues and traditional blues music performed by African Americans to young white audiences. The music was popular with this audience,

The Beatles. Although rock 'n' roll originated in the United States, it inspired musical groups around the world. This was certainly true of Britain's Beatles, who caused a sensation among young people when they came to the United States in the 1960s. Here the Beatles are shown during a performance on *The Ed Sullivan Show*.

and record companies began recording watered-down white "cover" versions of this music. It was not until performers such as Elvis Presley mixed white "folkabilly" with rhythm and blues that rock 'n' roll became popular with the larger white audience.

CHAPTER SUMMARY

At the end of a devastating world war, a new kind of conflict erupted in the Western world as two of the victors, the United States and the Soviet Union, emerged as superpowers and began to argue over the political organization of a Europe liberated from Nazi Germany. Europeans, whether they wanted to or not, were forced to become supporters of one  side or the other. The Western world was soon divided between supporters of a capitalistic West and adherents of a Communist East. In 1949, the North Atlantic Treaty Organization (NATO) was created by the United States,

Canada, and ten nations of Western Europe as a defensive alliance against Soviet aggression. In 1955, the Soviet Union formed a military alliance with seven Eastern European states, and Europe was once again divided into hostile alliance systems.

Western Europe emerged as a new community in the 1950s and the 1960s and staged a remarkable economic recovery. While the Western European economy boomed, Eastern Europe seemed to stagnate under the control of the Soviet Union. The economic integration of the Western European nations began in 1951 with the European Coal and Steel Community and continued in 1957 with the formation of the European Economic Community, also known as the Common Market. Eastern European states had made their

own efforts at economic cooperation when they formed the Council for Mutual Economic Assistance in 1949. Regardless of their economic differences, however, both Western and Eastern Europeans were well aware that their future still depended on the conflict between the two superpowers.

A new European society also emerged after World War II. White-collar workers increased in number, and installment plan buying helped create a consumer society. Rising incomes, combined with shorter working hours, created an ever-greater market for mass leisure activities. The welfare state provided both pensions and health care. Birth control led to smaller families, and more women joined the workforce.

In addition to the Cold War conflict, the postwar era was also characterized by decolonization. After World War II, the colonial empires of the European states were largely dissolved, and the liberated territories of Africa, Asia, and the Middle East emerged as sovereign states. All too soon, these newly independent nations often found themselves caught in the Cold War rivalry between the United States and the Soviet Union. After the United States fought in Korea to prevent the spread of communism, the ideological division that had begun in Europe quickly spread to the rest of the world.

CHAPTER TIMELINE

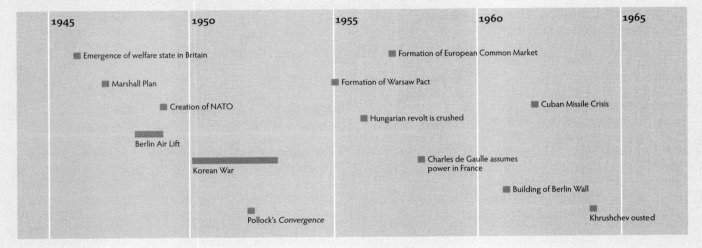

1945	1950	1955	1960	1965

■ Emergence of welfare state in Britain

■ Marshall Plan

■ Creation of NATO

■ Berlin Air Lift

■ Korean War

■ Formation of European Common Market

■ Formation of Warsaw Pact

■ Hungarian revolt is crushed

■ Cuban Missile Crisis

■ Charles de Gaulle assumes power in France

■ Building of Berlin Wall

■ Pollock's *Convergence*

■ Khrushchev ousted

CHAPTER REVIEW

Upon Reflection

Q What were the major turning points in the development of the Cold War through 1965?

Q How did Soviet policies affect the history of Eastern Europe between 1945 and 1965?

Q What role did popular culture play in the Western world between 1945 and 1965?

Key Terms

Truman Doctrine (p. 866)
Marshall Plan (p. 866)
containment (p. 866)
denazification (p. 866)
mutual deterrence (p. 867)
NATO (p. 867)
Warsaw Pact (p. 867)
rapprochement (p. 869)
decolonization (p. 871)
apartheid (p. 872)
de-Stalinization (p. 878)

Stalinization (p. 879)
nationalization (p. 881)
guest workers (p. 882)
welfare state (p. 882)
social security (p. 883)
socialized medicine (p. 883)
consumer society (p. 886)
family allowances (p. 888)
Abstract Expressionism (p. 889)
Pop Art (p. 890)
existentialism (p. 891)

Suggestions for Further Reading

GENERAL WORKS   For a well-written survey on Europe since 1945, see **T. Judt**, *Postwar: A History of Europe Since 1945* (New York, 2005). See also **W. I. Hitchcock**, *The Struggle for Europe: The Turbulent History of a Divided Continent, 1945–2002* (New York, 2003).

COLD WAR   There is a detailed literature on the Cold War. A good account is **J. L. Gaddis**, *The Cold War: A New History* (New York, 2005). See also **J. W. Langdon**, *A Hard and Bitter Peace: A Global History of the Cold War* (Englewood Cliffs, N.J., 1995). On the Berlin Wall and the Cold War in Germany, see **F. Taylor**, *The Berlin Wall: A World Divided, 1961–1989* (New York, 2006). For a good introduction to the arms race, see **E. M. Bottome**, *The Balance of Terror: A Guide to the Arms Race*, rev. ed. (Boston, 1986). On the Cuban Missile Crisis, see **D. Munton** and **D. A. Welch**, *The Real Thirteen Days: A Concise History of the Cuban Missile Crisis* (Oxford, 2006).

DECOLONIZATION   On decolonization after World War II, see **R. F. Betts**, *Decolonization*, 2nd ed. (London, 2004); **D. K. Fieldhouse**, *Western Imperialism in the Middle East 1914–1958* (Oxford, 2006); and **S. Smith**, *Ending Empire in the Middle East: Britain, the United States and Post-War Decolonization*

(London, 2012). To put the subject into a broader context, see **D. Newsom**, *Imperial Mantle: The United States, Decolonization and the Third World* (Bloomington, Ind., 2001).

SOVIET UNION AND EASTERN EUROPE   On the Khrushchev years, see **W. Taubman, *Khrushchev: The Man and His Era*** (New York, 2004). For a general study of the Soviet satellites in Eastern Europe, see **M. Pittaway**, *Brief Histories: Eastern Europe 1945–2000* (London, 2003).

POSTWAR WESTERN EUROPE   The rebuilding of postwar Europe is examined in **D. W. Ellwood**, *Rebuilding Europe: Western Europe, America, and Postwar Reconstruction* (London, 1992), and **M. A. Schoain, ed.**, *The Marshall Plan: Fifty Years After* (New York, 2001).

POSTWAR SOCIETY AND CULTURE   On women and the welfare state, see **R. Cleave et al.**, *Gender and the Welfare State* (New York, 2003). On Simone de Beauvoir, see **T. Keefe**, *Simone de Beauvoir* (New York, 1998). On existentialism, see **T. Flynn**, *Existentialism: A Very Short History*, 5th ed. (Oxford, 2006). On the arts, see **A. Marwick**, *Arts in the West Since 1945* (Oxford, 2002).

Notes

1. Quoted in J. M. Jones, *The Fifteen Weeks (February 21–June 5, 1947)*, 2nd ed. (New York, 1964), pp. 140–141.
2. Quoted in W. Laqueur, *Europe in Our Time* (New York, 1992), p. 111.
3. Quoted in W. Loth, *The Division of the World, 1941–1955* (New York, 1988), pp. 160–161.
4. Quoted in W. I. Hitchcock, *The Struggle for Europe: The Turbulent History of a Divided Continent, 1945–2002* (New York, 2003), p. 215.
5. Quoted in P. Lane, *Europe Since 1945: An Introduction* (Totowa, N.J., 1985), p. 248.
6. Quoted in Robert F. Kennedy, *Thirteen Days: A Memoir of the Cuban Missile Crisis* (New York, 1969), pp. 89–90.
7. Quoted in L. Collins and D. Lapierre, *Freedom at Midnight* (New York, 1975), p. 252.
8. R. Hilton, *Military Attaché in Moscow* (London, 1949), p. 41.
9. Nikita Khrushchev, *Khrushchev Remembers*, trans. S. Talbott (Boston, 1970), p. 77.
10. Quoted in B. G. Smith, *Changing Lives: Women in European History Since 1700* (Lexington, Mass., 1989), p. 513.
11. Quoted in H. Scott, *Sweden's "Right to Be Human": Sex-Role Equality—The Goal and the Reality* (London, 1982), p. 125.
12. Simone de Beauvoir, *The Second Sex*, trans. H. M. Parshley (New York, 1961), p. xxviii.
13. Quoted in H. Grosshans, *The Search for Modern Europe* (Boston, 1970), p. 421.
14. R. Maltby, ed., *Passing Parade: A History of Popular Culture in the Twentieth Century* (Oxford, 1989), p. 8.
15. Quoted in ibid., p. 11.

PROTEST AND STAGNATION: THE WESTERN WORLD, 1965–1985

The barricades go up in Paris in May 1968

Alain Nogues/Sygma/Corbis

CHAPTER OUTLINE AND FOCUS QUESTIONS

A Culture of Protest

Q What were the goals of the revolt in sexual mores, the youth protests and student revolts, the feminist movement, and the antiwar protests? To what extent were their goals achieved?

A Divided Western World

Q What were the major political developments in the Soviet Union, Eastern Europe, Western Europe, and the United States between 1965 and 1985?

The Cold War: The Move to Détente

Q What were the main events in the Cold War between 1965 and 1985, and how important was the role of détente in those events?

Society and Culture in the Western World

Q What were the major social and cultural developments in the Western world between 1965 and 1985?

Critical Thinking

Q *What are the similarities and differences between the feminist movement of the nineteenth century and the post–World War II feminist movement?*

Connections to Today

Q *During the 1960s, young people in the Western world protested against established political and social structures. What are the grievances of the young people protesting throughout Europe today?*

BETWEEN 1945 AND 1965, Europe not only overcame the devastating effects of World War II but actually experienced an economic recovery that seemed nothing less than miraculous to many people. Economic growth and virtually full employment continued so long that the first post–World War II recession in 1973 came as a shock to Western Europe.

In 1968, Europe had experienced a different kind of shock. May 1968 is now remembered as a historic month because of events in Paris. A student revolt erupted at the University of Nanterre outside Paris but soon spread to the Sorbonne, the main campus of the University of Paris, where about five hundred students gathered for demonstrations and demanded a greater voice in the administration of the university. The authorities decided to react with force and arrested a number of demonstrators, although one police officer said that they were not enthusiastic about it because "our interventions created more problems than they solved." Indeed, the students fought back, prying up paving stones from the streets to use as weapons. On May 3, eighty policemen and about three hundred students were hurt; almost six hundred students were arrested. Demonstrations then spread to other universities, which served to embolden the students in Paris. On the night of May 10, barricades, formed by overturned cars, went up in the streets of Paris. When police moved in to tear down the barricades, violence ensued. One eyewitness recounted: "A young girl came rushing out into the street practically naked and was manhandled from one cop to another; then beaten like the other wounded students." Students expanded the scale of their protests by inviting workers to support them. Half of the French workforce went on strike in May 1968. After de Gaulle's government instituted a hefty wage hike, the workers returned to work, and the police repressed the remaining student protesters.

The year 1968 saw widespread student protests around the world, and for a brief moment, students and radicals everywhere believed the time had come for a complete renovation of society and government. But the moment passed, and the Western world was left with the new order created in the twenty years after World War II. In Eastern Europe, the crushing of Czechoslovakia in 1968 by Soviet troops left Eastern Europeans with little choice but to remain as Soviet satellites. In Western Europe, democracies continued to evolve. But everywhere, resignation and stagnation seemed to prevail as the new order established in the Western world during the twenty years after World War II appeared to have become permanent: a prosperous, capitalistic West and an impoverished Communist East.

A Culture of Protest

 FOCUS QUESTIONS: What were the goals of the revolt in sexual mores, the youth protests and student revolts, the feminist movement, and the antiwar protests? To what extent were their goals achieved?

In the late 1960s, the Western world was rocked by a variety of protest movements relating to sexual mores, education, and women's rights as well as a strong antiwar movement against the Second Vietnam War (see "The Second Vietnam War" later in this chapter). Although many of the dreams of the protesters were not immediately realized, the forces they set in motion helped to transform Western society.

A Revolt in Sexual Mores

World War I had opened the first significant crack in the rigid code of manners and morals of the nineteenth century. The 1920s had witnessed experimentation with drugs, the appearance of pornography, and a new sexual freedom (police in Berlin, for example, issued cards that permitted female and male homosexual prostitutes to practice their trade). But these indications of a new attitude appeared mostly in major cities and touched only small numbers of people. After World War II, changes in manners and morals were far more extensive and far more noticeable, giving rise to what critics called the **permissive society**.

Sweden took the lead in the propagation of the so-called sexual revolution of the 1960s. Sex education in the schools and the decriminalization of homosexuality were but two aspects of Sweden's liberal legislation. The rest of Europe and the United States soon followed Sweden's example. A gay rights movement emerged in California in 1969 and had spread to France, Italy, and Britain by 1970.

The introduction of the birth control pill, which became widely available by the mid-1960s, gave people more freedom in sexual behavior. Meanwhile, sexually explicit movies, plays, and books broke new ground in the treatment of once-hidden subjects. Cities like Amsterdam, which allowed open prostitution and the public sale of pornography, attracted thousands of curious tourists.

The new standards were evident in the breakdown of the traditional family. Divorce rates increased dramatically, especially in the 1960s, and premarital and extramarital sexual experiences also rose substantially. A survey in the Netherlands in 1968 revealed that 78 percent of men and 86 percent of women had engaged in extramarital sex. The appearance of *Playboy* magazine in the 1950s had also already added a new dimension to the sexual revolution for adult males. Along with photographs of nude women, *Playboy* offered well-written articles on various aspects of masculinity. Its message was clear: men were encouraged to seek sexual gratification outside marriage.

Youth Protest and Student Revolt

The decade of the 1960s also saw the emergence of a drug culture, especially among young people. For most college and university students, marijuana was the recreational drug of choice. For young people more interested in mind expansion into higher levels of consciousness, Timothy Leary, who had done psychedelic research at Harvard on the effects of LSD (lysergic acid diethylamide), became the high priest of hallucinogenic experiences.

New attitudes toward sex and the use of drugs were only two manifestations of a growing youth movement in the 1960s that questioned authority and fostered rebellion against the older generation (see "Images of Everyday Life" on p. 898). Spurred on by the Second Vietnam War and a growing political consciousness, the youth rebellion became a youth protest movement by the second half of the 1960s (see the box on p. 899).

Before World War II, higher education had largely remained the preserve of Europe's wealthier classes. After the war, European states began to foster greater equality of opportunity in higher education by reducing or eliminating fees, and universities experienced an influx of students from the middle and lower classes. Enrollments grew dramatically; in France, 4.5 percent of young people attended a university in 1950. By 1965, the figure had increased to 14.5 percent.

But there were problems. Classrooms with too many students, professors who paid little attention to their students, and administrators who acted in an authoritarian fashion led to student resentment. In addition, despite changes in the curriculum, students often felt that the universities were not providing an education relevant to the realities of the modern age. This discontent led to an outburst of student revolts in the late 1960s (see the box on p. 900). In part, these protests were an extension of the spontaneous disruptions in American universities in the mid-1960s, which were often sparked by student opposition to the Second Vietnam War. Perhaps the most famous student revolt occurred in France in 1968, as we saw in the introduction to this chapter.

The French revolt spurred student protests elsewhere in Europe, although none of them succeeded in becoming mass

Youth Culture in the 1960s

PROTEST WAS AN INTEGRAL PART of the growing youth movement in the 1960s. Young people questioned authority and fostered rebellion in an attempt to change the social thinking of an older generation. The photograph at the bottom left shows a group of young protesters facing the bayonets of the National Guardsmen who had been called in by Governor Ronald Reagan to restore order on the Berkeley campus of the University of California during an antiwar rally. The "love-in" at the top left shows another facet of the youth movement. In the 1960s, a number of outdoor public festivals

for young people combined music, drugs, and sex. Flamboyant dress, face painting, free-form dancing, and drugs were vital ingredients in creating an atmosphere dedicated to "love and peace." A popular slogan was "Make Love, Not War." Shown here are dozens of hippies dancing around a decorated bus at a "love-in" during the Summer of Love, 1967. Many young people were excited about creating a new culture based on love and community. In the photograph at the right, a member of the Diggers, a communal group in San Francisco, is shown feeding a flower child.

Henry Diltz/Corbis

Ted Streshinsky/Corbis

Ted Streshinsky/Corbis

"THE TIMES THEY ARE A-CHANGIN'": THE MUSIC OF YOUTHFUL PROTEST

IN THE 1960S, THE LYRICS OF ROCK and folk music reflected the rebellious mood of many young people. Bob Dylan (b. 1941) expressed the feelings of the younger generation. His song "The Times They Are A-Changin'," released in 1964, has been called an "anthem for the protest movement."

Bob Dylan, "The Times They Are A-Changin'"

Come gather round people
Wherever you roam
And admit that the waters
Around you have grown
And accept it that soon
You'll be drenched to the bone
If your time to you
Is worth savin'
Then you better start swimmin'
Or you'll sink like a stone
For the times they are a-changin'

Come writers and critics
Who prophesize with your pen
And keep your eyes wide
The chance won't come again
And don't speak too soon
For the wheel's still in spin
And there's no tellin who
That it's namin'
For the loser now
Will be later to win
For the times they are a-changin'

Come senators, congressmen
please heed the call
Don't stand in the doorway
Don't block up the hall

For he that gets hurt
Will be he who has stalled
There's a battle outside
And it is ragin'
It'll soon shake your windows
And rattle your walls
For the times they are a-changin'

Come mothers and fathers
Throughout the land
And don't criticize
What you can't understand
Your sons and your daughters
Are beyond your command
Your old road
Is rapidly agin'
Please get out of the new one
If you can't lend your hand
For the times they are a-changin'

The line it is drawn
The curse it is cast
The slow one now
Will later be fast
As the present now
Will later be past
The order is
Rapidly fadin'
And the first one now
Will later be last
For the times they are a-changin'

 What caused the student campus revolts of the 1960s? What and whom does Dylan identify in this song as the problem?

movements. In West Berlin, university students led a protest against Axel Springer, leader of Germany's largest newspaper establishment. Many German students were motivated by a desire to destroy what they considered to be the corrupt old order and were especially influenced by the ideas of the German American social philosopher Herbert Marcuse (mar-KOO-zuh) (1898–1979). In *One-Dimensional Man*, published in 1964, Marcuse argued that capitalism had undermined the dissatisfaction of the oppressed masses by encouraging the consumption of material things. He proposed that a small cadre of unindoctrinated students could liberate the masses from the control of the capitalist ruling class. But the German students' attempt at revolutionary violence backfired as angry Berliners supported police repression of the students.

The student protest movement reached its high point in 1968, although scattered incidents lasted into the early 1970s. There were several reasons for the student radicalism. Some students were genuinely motivated by the desire to reform the university. Others were protesting the Second Vietnam War, which they viewed as a product of Western imperialism. They also attacked other aspects of Western society, such as its materialism, and expressed concern about becoming cogs in the large and impersonal bureaucratic jungles of the modern world. For many students, the calls for democratic decision making within the universities reflected their deeper concerns about the direction of Western society. Although the student revolts fizzled out in the 1970s, the larger issues they raised were increasingly revived in the 1990s and early 2000s.

1968: THE YEAR OF STUDENT REVOLTS

THE OUTBURST OF STUDENT UPHEAVALS in the late 1960s reached its high point in 1968. These two very different selections illustrate some of the issues that prompted university students to occupy campus buildings and demand reforms.

A Student Manifesto in Search of a Real and Human Educational Alternative, University of British Columbia, June 1968

Today we as students are witnessing a deepening crisis within our society. We are intensely aware, in a way perhaps not possible for the older generation, that humanity stands on the edge of a new era. Because we are young, we have insights into the present and visions of the future that our parents do not have. Tasks of an immense gravity wait solution in our generation. We have inherited these tasks from our parents. We do not blame them so much for that . . . but we do blame them for being unwilling to admit that there are problems or for saying that it is we who have visited these problems on ourselves because of our perversity, ungratefulness and unwillingness to listen to "reason."

Much of the burden of solving the problems of the new era rests on the university. We have been taught to look to it for leadership. While we know that part of the reason for the university is to render direct services to the community, we are alarmed at its servility to industry and government as to what and how it teaches. We are scandalized that the university fails to realize its role in renewing and vivifying those intellectual and moral energies necessary to create a new society—one in which a sense of personal dignity and human community can be preserved.

Source: G. F. McGuigan, *Student Protest* (London: Methuen & Co. Publishers, 1968).

Student Inscriptions on the Walls of Paris, May and June 1968

The dream is the reality.

May 1968. World revolution is the order of the day.

I decree a state of permanent happiness.

To be free in 1968 is to take part.

Take the trip every day of your life.

Make love, not war.

No exams.

The mind travels farther than the heart but it doesn't go as far.

Run, comrade, the old are behind you!

Don't make a revolution in the image of your confused and hide-bound university.

Exam = servility, social promotion, hierarchic society.

Love each other.

SEX. It's good, said Mao, but not too often.

Alcohol kills. Take LSD.

Are you consumers or participants?

Professors, you are as old as your culture; your modernism is only the modernization of the police.

Live in the present.

Revolution, I love you.

Long live direct democracy!

 Based on these selections, what do you believe were the key problems or causes that motivated the student protesters of this era? Did the student revolts resolve any of the issues raised, or are their complaints still relevant today?

The Feminist Movement

By the late 1960s, women began to assert their rights and speak as feminists. Along with the student upheavals of the late 1960s came renewed interest in **feminism**, or the women's liberation movement, as it was now called. Increasingly, women protested that the acquisition of political and legal equality had not brought true equality with men:

> We are economically oppressed: in jobs we do full work for half pay, in the home we do unpaid work full time. We are commercially exploited by advertisement, television, and the press; legally, we often have only the status of children. We are brought up to feel inadequate, educated to narrower horizons than men. This is our specific oppression as women. It is as women that we are, therefore, organizing.[1]

These were the words of a British Women's Liberation Workshop in 1969.

An important contributor to the growth of the women's movement in the 1960s was Betty Friedan (free-DAN) (1921–2006). A journalist and the mother of three children, Friedan grew increasingly uneasy with her attempt to fulfill the traditional role of the "ideal housewife and mother." In 1963, she published *The Feminine Mystique*, in which she analyzed the problems of middle-class American women in the 1950s and argued that women were being denied equality with men (see the box on p. 902). She wrote, "The problem that has no name—which is simply the fact that American women are kept from growing to their full human capacities—is taking a far greater toll on the physical and mental health of our country than any known disease."[2]

The Feminine Mystique became a best-seller and propelled Friedan into a newfound celebrity. In 1966, she founded the National Organization for Women (NOW), whose stated goal was to take "action to bring women into full participation in the mainstream of American society *now*, exercising all the

Women's Liberation Movement. In the late 1960s, as women began once again to assert their rights, a revived women's liberation movement emerged. Feminists in the movement maintained that women themselves must alter the conditions of their lives. During this women's liberation rally, some women climbed the statue of Admiral Farragut in Washington, D.C., to exhibit their signs.

privileges and responsibilities thereof in truly equal partnership with men." Friedan's voice was also prominent in calling for an amendment guaranteeing equal rights for women to be added to the U.S. Constitution.

Antiwar Protests

One of the major issues that mobilized youthful European protesters was the U.S. war in Vietnam, which they viewed as an act of aggression and imperialism. In 1968, demonstrations broke out in universities in Italy, France, and Britain. In London, 30,000 demonstrators took to the streets protesting America's war in Vietnam. But student protests in Europe also backfired by provoking a reaction from people who favored order over the lawlessness of privileged young people. As Pier Paolo Pasolini (PYER PAH-loh pah-SOH-lee-nee) (1922–1975), an Italian poet and intellectual, wrote: "Now all the journalists of the world are licking your arses . . . but not me, my dears. You have the faces of spoiled brats, and I hate you, like I hate your fathers. . . . When yesterday at Valle Giulia [in Rome] you beat up the police, I sympathized with the police because they are the sons of the poor."[3]

Antiwar protests also divided the American people after President Lyndon Johnson sent American troops to war in Vietnam. As the war dragged on and a military draft continued,

protests escalated. Teach-ins, sit-ins, and the occupation of buildings at universities alternated with more radical demonstrations that led to violence. The killing of four student protesters at Kent State University in 1970 by the Ohio National Guard caused a reaction, and the antiwar movement began to decline. By that time, however, antiwar demonstrations had worn down the willingness of many Americans to continue the war. The combination of antiwar demonstrations and ghetto riots in the cities also heightened the appeal of a call for "law and order," used by Richard Nixon, the Republican presidential candidate in 1968.

A Divided Western World

> **FOCUS QUESTION:** What were the major political developments in the Soviet Union, Eastern Europe, Western Europe, and the United States between 1965 and 1985?

Between 1945 and 1965, economic recovery had brought renewed growth to Europe. Nevertheless, the political divisions between Western and Eastern Europe remained; so did disparities in prosperity.

Stagnation in the Soviet Union

Between 1964 and 1982, significant change in the Soviet Union seemed highly unlikely. The man in charge, Leonid Brezhnev (1906–1982), lived by the slogan "No experimentation." Brezhnev had entered the ranks of the Party leadership under Stalin and, after the overthrow of Khrushchev in 1964, had become head of both the Communist Party and the state. He was optimistic, yet reluctant to reform. Overall, the Brezhnev years were relatively calm, although the **Brezhnev Doctrine**—the right of the Soviet Union to intervene if socialism was threatened in another socialist state—became an article of faith and led to the use of Soviet troops in Czechoslovakia in 1968.

THE BREZHNEV YEARS Brezhnev benefited from the more relaxed atmosphere associated with **détente** (day-TAHNT) (see "The Cold War: The Move to Détente" later in this chapter). The Soviets had reached a rough parity with the United States in nuclear arms and enjoyed a sense of external security that seemed to allow for a relaxation of authoritarian rule. The regime permitted more access to Western styles of music, dress, and art, although dissenters were still punished. Physicist Andrei Sakharov (ahn-DRAY SAH-kuh-rawf) (1921–1989), for example, who had played an important role in the development of the Soviet hydrogen bomb, was placed under house arrest for his defense of human rights.

In his economic policies, Brezhnev continued to emphasize heavy industry. Overall industrial growth declined, although the Soviet production of iron, steel, coal, and cement surpassed that of the United States. Two problems bedeviled the Soviet economy. The government's insistence on vigorous central planning led to a huge, complex bureaucracy that discouraged efficiency

BETTY FRIEDAN: THE PROBLEM THAT HAS NO NAME

BETTY FRIEDAN, AN AMERICAN JOURNALIST, published *The Feminine Mystique* in 1963. The book became a best-seller and made her an influential voice in the women's liberation movement. In this selection, Friedan discusses in detail what she called the "the problem that has no name."

Betty Friedan, *The Feminine Mystique*

The problem lay buried, unspoken, for many years in the minds of American women. It was a strange stirring, a sense of dissatisfaction, a yearning that women suffered in the middle of the twentieth century in the United States. Each suburban wife struggled with it alone. As she made the beds, shopped for groceries, matched slipcover material, ate peanut butter sandwiches with her children, chauffeured Cub Scouts and Brownies, lay beside her husband at night—she was afraid to ask even of herself the silent question—"Is this all?"

For over fifteen years there was no word of this yearning in the millions of words written about women, for women, in all the columns, books, and articles by experts telling women their role was to seek fulfillment as wives and mothers. Over and over women heard in voices of tradition and of Freudian sophistication that they could desire no greater destiny than to glory in their own femininity. . . . They were taught to pity the neurotic, unfeminine, unhappy women who wanted to be poets or physicists, or presidents. They learned that truly feminine women do not want careers, higher education, political rights—the independence and the opportunities that the old-fashioned feminists fought for. . . . All they had to do was devote their lives from earliest girlhood to finding a husband and bearing children. . . .

Gradually I came to realize that the problem that has no name was shared by countless women in America. . . . If I am right, the problem that has no name stirring in the minds of so many American women today is not a matter of loss of femininity or too much education, or the demands of domesticity. It is far more important than anyone recognizes. It is the key to these other new and old problems which have been torturing women and their husbands and children, and puzzling their doctors and educators for years. It may well be the key to our future as a nation and a culture. We can no longer ignore that voice within women that says: "I want something more than my husband and my children and my home."

 According to Friedan, what was the problem that had no name? Why is Friedan such a highly regarded figure in the women's movement?

Source: B. Friedan, *The Feminine Mystique* (New York: Dell, 1963), pp. 11, 14, 16, 27.

---

and reduced productivity. Moreover, the Soviet system, based on guaranteed employment and a lack of incentives, bred apathy, complacency, absenteeism, and drunkenness. Agricultural problems added to Soviet economic woes. Bad harvests in the mid-1970s, caused by a series of droughts, heavy rains, and early frosts, forced the Soviet government to buy grain from the West, particularly the United States. To their chagrin, the Soviets were increasingly dependent on capitalist countries.

By the 1970s, the Soviet Union had developed a ruling system that depended on patronage as a major avenue of advancement. Those who aspired to rise in the Communist Party and the state bureaucracy needed the support of successful Party leaders. At the same time, Party and state leaders—as well as leaders of the army and the secret police (KGB)—received awards and material privileges. Brezhnev was unwilling to tamper with the Party leadership and state bureaucracy despite the inefficiency and corruption that the system encouraged.

By 1980, the Soviet Union was ailing. A declining economy, a rise in infant mortality rates, a dramatic surge in alcoholism, and a deterioration in working conditions all gave impetus to a decline in morale and a growing perception that the system was foundering. Within the Party, a small group of reformers emerged who understood the real condition of the Soviet Union. One member of this group was Yuri Andropov (YOOR-ee ahn-DRAHP-awf) (1914–1985), head of the KGB and successor to Brezhnev after the latter's death in November 1982. But Andropov was in poor health when he came to power, and he was unable to make any substantive changes. His most significant move may have been his support for a young reformer, Mikhail Gorbachev (meek-HAYL GOR-buh-chawf) (b. 1931), who was climbing the rungs of the Party ladder. When Party leaders chose Gorbachev as Party secretary in March 1985, a new era began (see Chapter 30).

Conformity in Eastern Europe

As we saw in Chapter 28, the attempt of the Poles and Hungarians to gain their freedom from Soviet domination had been repressed in 1956. This year of discontent had consequences, however. Soviet leaders now recognized that Moscow could maintain control over its satellites in Eastern Europe only by granting them leeway to adopt domestic policies appropriate to local conditions. As a result, Eastern European Communist leaders now adopted reform programs to make socialism more acceptable to their subject populations.

In Poland, continued worker unrest led to the rise of the independent labor movement called Solidarity. Led by Lech Wałęsa (LEK vah-WENT-sah) (b. 1943), Solidarity represented 10 million of Poland's 35 million people. With the support of the workers, many intellectuals, and the Catholic Church, Solidarity was able to win a series of concessions. The Polish government seemed powerless to stop the flow of concessions until December 1981, when it arrested Wałęsa and other Solidarity leaders, outlawed the union, and imposed military rule.

Soviet Invasion of Czechoslovakia, 1968. The attempt of Alexander Dubček, the new first secretary of the Communist Party in Czechoslovakia, to liberalize Communist rule in that country failed when Soviet troops invaded and crushed the reform movement. This photograph, taken on August 21, shows Soviet tanks in Wenceslas Square while Prague residents look on.

The government of János Kádár in Hungary enacted the most far-reaching reforms in Eastern Europe. In the early 1960s, Kádár legalized small private enterprises, such as retail stores, restaurants, and artisan shops. His economic reforms were termed "Communism with a capitalist facelift." Under his leadership, Hungary moved slowly away from its strict adherence to Soviet dominance and even established fairly friendly relations with the West.

THE PRAGUE SPRING Czechoslovakia did not share in the thaw of the mid-1950s and remained under the rule of Antonín Novotný (AHN-toh-nyeen noh-VAHT-nee) (1904–1975), who had been placed in power by Stalin himself. By the late 1960s, however, Novotný had alienated many members of his own party and was particularly resented by Czechoslovakia's writers, such as the playwright Václav Havel (VAHT-slahf HAH-Vul) (1936–2011). A writers' rebellion late in 1967, in fact, led to Novotný's resignation. In January 1968, Alexander Dubček (DOOB-chek) (1921–1992) was elected first secretary of the Communist Party and soon introduced a number of reforms, including freedom of speech and the press, freedom to travel abroad, and a relaxation of secret police activities. Dubček hoped to create "communism with a human face." A period of euphoria erupted that came to be known as the "Prague Spring" (see "Opposing Viewpoints" on p. 904).

It proved short-lived. The euphoria had led many to call for more far-reaching reforms, including neutrality and withdrawal from the Soviet bloc. To forestall the spreading of this "spring" fever, the Red Army invaded Czechoslovakia in August 1968 and crushed the reform movement. Gustáv Husák (goo-STAHV HOO-sahk) (1913–1991), a committed nonreformist, replaced Dubček, abolished his reforms, and reestablished the old order.

Repression in East Germany and Romania

Elsewhere in Eastern Europe, Stalinist policies continued to hold sway. In the early 1950s, the ruling Communist government in East Germany, led by Walter Ulbricht, had consolidated its position and become a faithful Soviet satellite. Industry was nationalized and agriculture collectivized. After Soviet tanks crushed a workers' revolt in 1953, a steady flight of East Germans to West Germany ensued, primarily through the divided city of Berlin. This exodus of mostly skilled laborers created economic problems and led the East German government in 1961 to build the infamous Berlin Wall separating West from East Berlin, as well as equally fearsome barriers along the entire border with West Germany.

After building the wall, East Germany succeeded in developing the strongest economy among the Soviet Union's Eastern European satellites. In 1971, Ulbricht was succeeded by Erich Honecker (AY-rikh HOH-nek-uh) (1912–1992), a party hard-liner who made use of the Stasi (SHTAH-see), the secret police, to rule with an iron fist for the next eighteen years. By 1989, there was one Stasi officer for every 165 people in East Germany. Prosperity (by 1980, East Germany had the tenth-largest economy in the world) and repression were the two mainstays of East Germany's stability.

Repression was also an important part of Romania's postwar history. By 1948, with Soviet assistance, the Communist People's Democratic Front had assumed complete power in Romania. In 1965, leadership of the Communist government passed into the hands of Nicolae Ceauşescu (nee-koh-LY chow-SHES-koo) (1918–1989), who with his wife, Elena, established a rigid and dictatorial regime. Ceauşescu ruled Romania with an iron grip, using a secret police force—the Securitate—as his personal weapon against dissent.

Czechoslovakia, 1968: Two Faces of Communism

IN THE SUMMER OF 1968, a serious rupture began to appear in the Soviet-dominated Communist world. Under the guidance of Alexander Dubček, Czechoslovakia appeared poised to take a path that deviated from Soviet Communist ideals. The first selection is taken from a manifesto written by a group of Czech Communist intellectuals in June 1968. The manifesto became the symbol of the "Prague Spring." The second selection is taken from a letter written in July to the Communist Party of Czechoslovakia by Soviet leader Leonid Brezhnev to justify intervention in Czechoslovakia. In August military forces of several Soviet bloc nations entered Czechoslovakia and imposed a new government. The move was justified by the principle that came to be known as the Brezhnev Doctrine.

Two Thousand Words Manifesto

The first threat to our national life was from the war. Then came other evil days and events that endangered the nation's spiritual well being and character. Most of the nation welcomed the socialist program with high hopes. But it fell into the hands of the wrong people. . . .

After enjoying great popular confidence immediately after the war, the communist party by degrees bartered this confidence away for office, until it had all the offices and nothing else. We feel we must say this, it is familiar to those of us who are communists and who are as disappointed as the rest at the way things turned out. The leaders' mistaken policies transformed a political party and an alliance based on ideas into an organization for exerting power, one that proved highly attractive to power-hungry individuals eager to wield authority. . . . The influx of members such as these affected the character and behavior of the party, whose internal arrangements made it impossible, short of scandalous incidents, for honest members to gain influence and adapt it continuously to modern conditions. Many communists fought against this decline, but they did not manage to prevent what ensued.

We all bear responsibility for the present state of affairs. But those among us who are communists bear more than others, and those who acted as components or instruments of unchecked power bear the greatest responsibility of all. The power they wielded was that of a self-willed group spreading out through the party apparatus into every district and community. It was this apparatus that decided what might and might not be done. . . .

Since the beginning of this year we have been experiencing a regenerative process of democratization. It started inside the communist party, that much we must admit, even those communists among us who no longer had hopes that anything good could emerge from that quarter know this. It must also be added, of course, that the process could have started nowhere else. For after twenty years the communists were the only ones able to conduct some sort of political activity. It was only the opposition inside the communist party that had the privilege to voice antagonistic views. The effort and initiative now displayed by democratically minded communists are only then a partial repayment of the debt owed by the entire party

CHRONOLOGY	The Soviet Bloc	
Era of Brezhnev		1964–1982
Rule of Ceauşescu in Romania		1965–1989
Prague Spring		1968
Honecker succeeds Ulbricht in East Germany		1971
Emergence of Solidarity in Poland		1980
Gorbachev comes to power in the Soviet Union		1985

Western Europe: The Winds of Change

After two decades of incredible economic growth, Europe experienced severe economic recessions in 1973–1974 and 1979–1983. Full employment had given workers new bargaining rights, and in Italy, a 1969 labor contract increased wages by 16 percent, while in France, wages also grew dramatically between 1968 and 1973. This new prosperity had led to over-production and over-investment. A substantial increase in the price of oil in 1973, in addition to high wages, pushed the Western economy into a major downturn. Moreover, a worldwide recession had led to a decline in demand for European goods, and in Europe itself, the reconstruction of many European cities after their devastation in World War II had largely been completed. Both inflation and unemployment rose dramatically. Unemployment had remained between 2 and 4 percent between 1950 and 1973, although by 1975 unemployment stood at 12 percent. The economies of the Western European states recovered in the course of the 1980s, although problems remained.

WEST GERMANY After the Adenauer era, West German voters moved politically from the center-right politics of the Christian Democrats to center-left politics, and in 1969, the Social Democrats became the leading party. By forming a ruling coalition with the small Free Democratic Party (FPD), the Social Democrats remained in power until 1982. The first Social Democratic chancellor was Willy Brandt (VIL-ee BRAHNT) (1913–1992). Brandt was especially successful with his "opening toward the east"—known as *Ostpolitik* (OHST-paw-li-teek)—for which he received the Nobel Peace Prize in 1972. On March 19, 1971, Brandt met with Walter Ulbricht, the leader of East to the non-communists whom it had kept down in an unequal position. . . .

In this moment of hope, albeit hope still threatened, we appeal to you. It took several months before many of us believed it was safe to speak up; many of us still do not think it is safe. But speak up we did, exposing ourselves to the extent that we have no choice but to complete our plan to humanize the regime. If we did not, the old forces would exact cruel revenge. We appeal above all to those who so far have waited on the sidelines. The time now approaching will decide events for years to come.

A Letter to Czechoslovakia

To the Central Committee of the Communist Party of Czechoslovakia

Warsaw, July 15, 1968

Dear comrades!

On behalf of the Central Committees of the Communist and Workers' Parties of Bulgaria, Hungary, the German Democratic Republic, Poland, and the Soviet Union, we address ourselves to you with this letter, prompted by a feeling of sincere friendship based on the principles of Marxism-Leninism and proletarian internationalism and by the concern of our common affairs for strengthening the positions of socialism and the security of the socialist community of nations.

The development of events in your country evokes in us deep anxiety. It is our firm conviction that the offensive of the reactionary forces, backed by imperialists, against your Party and the foundations of the social system in the Czechoslovak Socialist Republic, threatens to push your country off the road

of socialism and that consequently it jeopardizes the interests of the entire socialist system. . . .

We neither had nor have any intention of interfering in such affairs as are strictly the internal business of your Party and your state, nor of violating the principles of respect, independence, and equality in the relations among the Communist Parties and socialist countries. . . .

At the same time we cannot agree to have hostile forces push your country from the road of socialism and create a threat of severing Czechoslovakia from the socialist community. . . . This is the common cause of our countries, which have joined in the Warsaw Treaty to ensure independence, peace, and security in Europe, and to set up an insurmountable barrier against aggression and revenge. . . . We shall never agree to have imperialism, using peaceful or nonpeaceful methods, making a gap from the inside or from the outside in the socialist system, and changing in imperialism's favor the correlation of forces in Europe. . . .

That is why we believe that a decisive rebuff of the anticommunist forces, and decisive efforts for the preservation of the socialist system in Czechoslovakia are not only your task but ours as well. . . .

We express the conviction that the Communist Party of Czechoslovakia, conscious of its responsibility, will take the necessary steps to block the path of reaction. In this struggle you can count on the solidarity and all-round assistance of the fraternal socialist countries.

 What Communist ideals are expressed in the manifesto? How do those ideals differ from those expressed by Leonid Brezhnev? How do you explain the differences?

Sources: Two Thousand Words Manifesto, in J. Navratil, *The Prague Spring 1968* (Budapest: Central European University Press, 1998); "A Letter to Czechoslovakia," *Moscow News*, supplement to no. 30917 (1968), pp. 3–6.

Germany, and worked out the details of a treaty that was signed in 1972. This agreement did not establish full diplomatic relations with East Germany but did call for "good neighborly" relations. As a result, it led to greater cultural, personal, and economic contacts between West and East Germany. Despite this success, the discovery of an East German spy among Brandt's advisers caused his resignation in 1974.

His successor, Helmut Schmidt (HEL-moot SHMIT) (1918–2015), was more of a technocrat than a reform-minded socialist and concentrated primarily on the economic problems largely brought about by high oil prices between 1973 and 1975. Schmidt was successful in eliminating a deficit of 10 billion marks in three years. In 1982, when the coalition of Schmidt's Social Democrats with the Free Democrats fell apart over the reduction of social welfare expenditures, the Free Democrats joined with the Christian Democratic Union of Helmut Kohl (HEL-moot KOHL) (b. 1930) to form a new government.

GREAT BRITAIN: THATCHER AND THATCHERISM Between 1964 and 1979, Britain's Conservative and Labour Parties alternated in power. Neither party could end the fighting between

Catholics and Protestants in Northern Ireland. Violence increased as the Irish Republican Army (IRA) staged a series of dramatic terrorist acts in response to the suspension of Northern Ireland's parliament in 1972 and the establishment of direct rule by London. Nor was either party able to deal with Britain's ailing economy. Failure to modernize had made British industry less and less competitive. Frequent labor strikes, many of them caused by conflicts between rival labor unions, also hampered the economy.

In 1979, after Britain's economic problems had seemed to worsen during five years of Labour government, the Conservatives returned to power under Margaret Thatcher (1925–2013). She became the first woman to serve as prime minister in British history. Thatcher pledged to lower taxes, reduce government bureaucracy, limit social welfare, restrict union power, and end inflation. The "Iron Lady," as she was called (see "Film & History" on p. 906), did break the power of the labor unions. Although she did not eliminate the basic components of the social welfare system, she instituted austerity measures to control inflation. "Thatcherism," as her economic policy was termed, improved the British economic situation,

but at a price (see the box on p. 907). The south of England, for example, prospered, but the old industrial areas of the Midlands and north declined and were beset by high unemployment, poverty, and sporadic violence. Cutbacks in education seriously undermined the quality of British education, long regarded as among the world's finest.

In the area of foreign policy, Thatcher, like Ronald Reagan in the United States, took a hardline approach toward communism. She oversaw a large military buildup aimed at replacing older technology and reestablishing Britain as a world police officer. In 1982, when Argentina attempted to take control of the Falkland Islands (one of Britain's few remaining colonial outposts; known to Argentines as the Malvinas) 300 miles off its coast, the British successfully rebuffed the Argentines, although

Margaret Thatcher. Great Britain's first female prime minister, Margaret Thatcher was a strong leader who dominated British politics in the 1980s. Thatcher is shown here with Soviet leader Mikhail Gorbachev at a press conference in Moscow in 1991.

at considerable economic cost and the loss of 255 lives. The Falklands War, however, did generate popular support for Thatcher, as many in Britain reveled in memories of the nation's glorious imperial past. In truth, however, in a world dominated by two superpowers—the United States and the Soviet Union—Britain was no longer a world power.

UNCERTAINTIES IN FRANCE The worsening of France's economic situation in the 1970s brought a shift to the left politically. By 1981, the Socialists had become the dominant party in the National Assembly, and the Socialist leader, François Mitterrand (frahnh-SWAH MEE-tayr-rahnh) (1916–1995), was elected president. His first priority was dealing with France's economic difficulties. In 1982, Mitterrand froze prices and wages in the hope of reducing the huge budget deficit and high inflation. He also passed a number of liberal measures to aid workers: an increased minimum wage, expanded social benefits, a mandatory fifth week of paid vacation for salaried workers, a thirty-nine-hour workweek, and higher taxes on the rich. Mitterrand's administrative reforms included both centralization (nationalization of banks and industry) and decentralization (granting local governments greater powers). The party's victory had convinced the Socialists that they could enact some of their more radical reforms. Consequently, the government nationalized the steel industry, major banks, the space and electronics industries, and important insurance firms.

The Socialist policies largely failed, however, and within three years, a decline in support for the Socialists caused the Mitterrand government to turn portions of the economy back over to private enterprise. Some economic improvement in the late 1980s enabled Mitterrand to win a second seven-year term in the 1988 presidential elections.

CONFUSION IN ITALY In the 1970s and 1980s, Italy continued to practice the politics of coalitions that had characterized much of its history. Italy witnessed the installation of its fiftieth postwar government in 1991, and its new prime minister, Giulio Andreotti (JOOL-yoh ahn-dray-AH-tee) (1919–2013), had already served six times in that office. Italian governments continued to consist of coalitions mostly led by the Christian Democrats.

In the 1980s, even the Communists had been included briefly in the government. The Italian Communists had become advocates of **Eurocommunism**, basically an attempt to broaden communism's support by dropping its Marxist ideology. Although its popularity declined in the 1980s, the Communist Party still garnered 26 percent of the vote in 1987. The Communists also won a number of local elections and took charge of municipal governments in several cities, including Rome and Naples, for a brief time.

In the 1970s, Italy suffered from a severe economic recession. The Italian economy, which depended on imported oil as its chief source of energy, was especially vulnerable to the steep increase in oil prices in 1973. The economic problems were accompanied by a host of political and social problems: student unrest, mass strikes, and terrorist attacks. Radical

MARGARET THATCHER: "THATCHERISM" AND THE FREE MARKET

DURING THE 1970S both Conservative and Labor governments had failed to maintain British prosperity. The British economy was stagnating while Britain failed to play a dominating role in global politics. In 1979, Margaret Thatcher won the election for the Conservative party and became Britain's first female prime minister. Thatcher enacted a series of economic policies dubbed "Thatcherism" based upon free-market ideals that would reduce the role of labor unions, privatize education and social services, and deregulate the economy. She expressed these views at Cambridge University on July 6, 1979, in a lecture entitled "The Renewal of Britain."

Margaret Thatcher, The Renewal of Britain

Experience has shown the practical failure of two fundamental Socialist arguments: that nationalization is justified because it makes economic power accountable to the people whose lives it affects; and that State planning can point to better ways forward than can be charted by free enterprise. The Socialists had grossly expanded State intervention in the economy. They were going so far as to claim that the State should have monopoly rights in the provision of health and education. . . .

Where Conservatives part company from Socialists is in the degree of confidence which we can place in the exclusive capacity of a Welfare State to relieve suffering and promote well-being. Charity is a personal quality—the supreme moral quality, according to St. Paul—and public compassion, State philanthropy and institutionalized charity can never be enough. There is no adequate substitute for genuine caring for one another on the part of families, friends and neighbors.

Heavy taxation had lowered fiscal morality. The malignant tumour of the so-called black economy was growing. We seemed to be losing our moral standards as well as our competence. . . . Then, partly as a result of high taxation, the idea of work well done had almost been forgotten. . . . Our industrial life seemed marked by petty labour disputes which were often both self destructive and humiliating. The time spent by works managers upon trade union matters of a non-productive nature might be half of their day's work. That was one reason for the failure of Britain both to gain and to fulfill export orders. . . .

At the heart of a new mood in the nation must be a recovery of our self-confidence and our self-respect. Nothing is beyond us. Decline is not inevitable. But nor is progress a law of nature. The ground gained by one generation may be lost by the next.

The foundation of this new confidence has to be individual responsibility. If people come to believe that the State, or their employer, or their union, owe them a living, and that, in turn, the world owes Britain a living, we shall have no confidence and no future. It must be quite clear that the responsibility is on each of us to make the full use of our talents and to care for our families. It must be clear, too, that we have a responsibility to our country to make Britain respected and successful in the world.

The economic counterpart of these personal and national responsibilities is the working of the market economy in a free society. I am sure that there is wide acceptance in Britain, going far beyond the supporters of our party, that production and distribution in our economy is best operated through free competition.

 Why did Margaret Thatcher oppose the socialist policies of the Labour party? What did she offer instead? How did she aim to achieve her goals? According to Thatcher, who should be responsible for charity?

Source: Margaret Thatcher, *The Revival of Britain: Speeches on Home and European Affairs 1975–1988* (London, Aurum Press: 1989), pp. 85–90.

---

groups occupied a Fiat factory in Milan and bombed the Piazza Fontana, killing sixteen people and wounding ninety others. In 1978, a former prime minister, Aldo Moro, was kidnapped and killed by the Red Brigades, a terrorist organization. Then, too, there was the all-pervasive and corrupting influence of the Mafia, which had always been an important factor in southern Italy but spread to northern Italy as well in the 1980s. Italy survived the crises of the 1970s and in the 1980s began to experience remarkable economic growth. But severe problems remained.

CHRONOLOGY	Western Europe, 1965–1985	
Willy Brandt becomes chancellor of West Germany		1969
Helmut Schmidt becomes chancellor of West Germany		1974
Margaret Thatcher becomes prime minister of Britain		1979
François Mitterrand becomes president of France		1981
Falklands War		1982
Helmut Kohl becomes chancellor of West Germany		1982

THE EUROPEAN COMMUNITY After 1970, Western European states continued to pursue the goal of integrating their economies. Beginning with six states in 1957, the European Economic Community expanded in 1973 when Great Britain, Ireland, and Denmark joined what its members now renamed the European Community (EC). Greece joined in 1981, followed by Spain and Portugal in 1986. The economic integration of the members of the EC led to cooperative efforts in international and political affairs as well. The foreign ministers of the twelve members consulted frequently and provided a common front in negotiations on important issues.

The United States: Turmoil and Tranquility

With the election of Richard Nixon (1913–1994) as president in 1968, American politics made a shift to the right. Nixon ended American involvement in Vietnam by 1973 by gradually withdrawing American troops. Politically, he pursued a "southern strategy," carefully calculating that "law and order" issues and a slowdown in racial desegregation would appeal to southern whites. The South, which had once been a Democratic stronghold, began to form a new allegiance to the Republican Party. The Republican strategy also gained support among white Democrats in northern cities, where court-mandated busing to achieve racial integration had led to a backlash among whites.

As president, Nixon was paranoid about conspiracies and began to use illegal methods to gather intelligence on his political opponents. One of the president's advisers explained that their intention was to "use the available federal machinery to screw our political enemies." Nixon's zeal led to the Watergate scandal—the attempted bugging of Democratic National Headquarters, located in the Watergate apartment and hotel complex in Washington, D.C. Although Nixon repeatedly lied to the American public about his involvement in the affair, secret tapes of his own conversations in the White House revealed the truth. On August 9, 1974, Nixon resigned the presidency rather than face possible impeachment and then trial by the U.S. Congress.

ECONOMIC PROBLEMS After Watergate, American domestic politics focused on economic issues. Vice President Gerald Ford (1913–2006) became president when Nixon resigned, only to lose in the 1976 election to the former governor of Georgia, Jimmy Carter (b. 1924). Both Ford and Carter faced severe economic problems. The period from 1973 to the mid-1980s was one of economic stagnation, which came to be known as **stagflation**—a combination of high inflation and high unemployment. In part, the economic downturn stemmed from a dramatic change in oil prices. Oil was considered a cheap and abundant source of energy in the 1950s, and Americans had grown dependent on imported oil from the Middle East. But an oil embargo and price increases by the Organization of Petroleum Exporting Countries (OPEC) as a result of the Arab-Israeli War in 1973 quadrupled oil prices. Additional price hikes increased oil prices twentyfold by the end of the 1970s, encouraging inflationary tendencies throughout the economy. American interest rates skyrocketed from 5.5 percent in 1977 to 13.4 percent by 1981, damaging the consumer economy.

By 1980, the Carter administration faced two devastating problems. High inflation and a noticeable decline in average weekly earnings were causing a drop in American living standards. At the same time, a crisis abroad had erupted when fifty-three Americans were taken hostage by the Iranian government of Ayatollah Khomeini (ah-yah-TUL-uh khoh-MAY-nee). Carter's inability to gain the release of the hostages led to perceptions at home that he was a weak president. His overwhelming loss to Ronald Reagan (1911–2004) in the election of 1980 enabled the chief exponent of right-wing Republican policies to assume the presidency and initiate a new political order.

THE REAGAN REVOLUTION The Reagan Revolution, as it has been called, consisted of a number of new policies. Reagan adhered to a new form of economic doctrine that promoted free-market economics; privatization of health care, pensions, insurance, and education; deregulation of industry and banking; and free trade. Reversing decades of increased spending on social welfare, Reagan cut back on the welfare state by reducing spending on food stamps, school lunch programs, and job programs. At the same time, his administration fostered the largest peacetime military buildup in American history. Total federal spending rose from $631 billion in 1981 to more than $1 trillion by 1986. But instead of raising taxes to pay for the new expenditures, which far outweighed the budget cuts in social areas, Reagan convinced Congress to rely on "supply-side economics." Massive tax cuts would supposedly stimulate rapid economic growth and produce new revenues. Much of the tax cut went to the wealthy. Reagan's policies seemed to work in the short run as the United States experienced an economic upturn that lasted until the end of the 1980s. The spending policies of the Reagan administration, however, also produced record government deficits, which loomed as an obstacle to long-term growth. In 1980, the total government debt was around $930 billion. By 1988, the total debt had almost tripled, reaching $2.6 trillion. In the long run, Reagan's deregulatory economic policies undermined the stability of the United States banking industry and resulted in the rise of a new financial system (see Chapter 30).

Canada

In 1963, during a major economic recession, the Liberals had been returned to power in Canada. The most prominent Liberal government was that of Pierre Trudeau (PYAYR troo-DOH) (1919–2000), who came to power in 1968. Although French Canadian in background, Trudeau was dedicated to Canada's federal union, and in 1968, his government passed the Official Languages Act that allowed both English and French to be used in the federal civil service. Although Trudeau's government vigorously pushed an industrialization program, high inflation and Trudeau's efforts to impose the will of the federal government on the powerful provincial governments alienated voters and weakened his government. Economic recession in the early 1980s brought Brian Mulroney (b. 1939), leader of the Progressive Conservative Party, to power in 1984.

The Cold War: The Move to Détente

 FOCUS QUESTION: What were the main events in the Cold War between 1965 and 1985, and how important was the role of détente in those events?

The Cuban Missile Crisis led to the lessening of tensions between the United States and the Soviet Union. But within another year the United States had been drawn into a confrontation that had an important impact on the Cold War—the Second Vietnam War.

The Second Vietnam War

After Vietnamese forces had defeated their French colonial masters in 1954, Vietnam had been divided. A strongly nationalistic regime in the north under Ho Chi Minh received Soviet aid, while American sponsors worked to establish a pro-Western regime in South Vietnam. President John F. Kennedy maintained Eisenhower's policy of providing military and financial aid to the regime of Ngo Dinh Diem (NGOH din DEE-em) (1901–1963), the autocratic ruler of South Vietnam. But the Kennedy administration grew increasingly disenchanted with the Diem regime, which was corrupt and seemed incapable of gaining support from the people. From the American point of view, this lack of support simply undermined the ability of the South Vietnamese government to deal with the Vietcong, the South Vietnamese Communist guerrillas backed by the North Vietnamese. In November 1963, the U.S. government supported a military coup that overthrew the Diem regime.

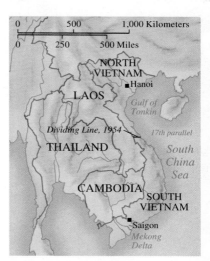

The Vietnam War

The new military government seemed even less able to govern the country, and by early 1965, the Vietcong, their ranks now swelled by military units infiltrating from North Vietnam, were on the verge of seizing control of the entire country. In desperation, President Lyndon Johnson decided to launch bombing raids on the north and to send U.S. combat troops to South Vietnam to prevent a total defeat of the anti-Communist government in Saigon and keep the Communist regime of the north from uniting the entire country under its control. Although nationalism played a powerful role in this conflict, American policy makers saw it in terms of a **domino theory** concerning the spread of communism. If the Communists succeeded in Vietnam, so the argument went, all the other countries in Asia freeing themselves from colonial domination would fall, like dominoes, to communism.

Despite their massive superiority in equipment and firepower, U.S. forces failed to prevail over the persistence of the North Vietnamese and especially the Vietcong. These guerrilla forces were extremely effective against American troops. Natives of Vietnam, they were able to live off the land, disappear among the people, and attack when least expected. Many South Vietnamese villagers were so opposed to their own government that they sheltered and supported the Vietcong.

The growing number of American troops sent to Vietnam soon produced a persistent antiwar movement in the United States, especially among college students of draft age. As described

The Second Vietnam War. Between 1965 and 1973, U.S. troops fought against Vietcong guerrillas and North Vietnamese regular forces until they were finally withdrawn as a result of the Paris Agreement reached in January 1973. Shown here are U.S. troops after a Vietcong attack. The helicopter that is arriving would soon remove the American wounded from the battlefield.

earlier, a similar movement also arose in Europe. Although Europeans had generally acquiesced in American leadership of the Cold War, some Europeans recognized the need for Europe to play its own role in foreign affairs. Under President Charles de Gaulle, France grew especially critical of U.S. involvement in Vietnam. De Gaulle believed that the Vietnamese should be allowed to live in their own unified country and in 1965 called the United States "the greatest danger in the world today to peace." After President Johnson escalated the American war effort, antiwar protests broke out all over France in 1966 and 1967 and soon spread throughout Europe.

The mounting destruction and increasing brutalization of the war, brought into American homes every evening on television, also turned American public opinion against the war. Finally, in 1973, President Richard Nixon reached an agreement with North Vietnam that allowed the United States to withdraw its forces. Within two years, Vietnam had been forcibly reunited by Communist armies from the North.

Despite the success of the North Vietnamese Communists, the domino theory proved unfounded. A noisy rupture between Communist China and the Soviet Union put an end to the idea of a monolithic communism directed by Moscow. Under President Nixon, American relations with China were resumed. New nations in Southeast Asia also managed to avoid Communist governments. Above all, Vietnam helped show the limitations of American power. By the end of the Second Vietnam War, a new era in American-Soviet relations, known as détente, had begun to emerge.

China and the Cold War

The Johnson administration had sent U.S. combat troops to South Vietnam in 1965 in an effort to prevent the expansion of communism in Southeast Asia. The primary concern of the United States, however, was not the Soviet Union but Communist China. By the mid-1960s, U.S. officials viewed the Soviet Union as an essentially conservative power, more concerned with protecting its vast empire than with expanding its borders. Mao Zedong's attempt to create a totally classless society had received much attention; now, despite his failures with the Great Leap Forward (see Chapter 28), he launched China on an even more dramatic forced march toward communism.

THE GREAT PROLETARIAN CULTURAL REVOLUTION Mao was convinced that only an atmosphere of constant revolutionary fervor would enable the Chinese to overcome the past and achieve the final stage of communism. Accordingly, in 1966 he unleashed the Red Guards, revolutionary units composed of unhappy Communist Party members and discontented young people who were urged to take to the streets to cleanse Chinese society of impure elements guilty of taking the capitalist road. Schools, universities, factories, and even government ministries were all subject to the scrutiny of the Red Guards. This so-called Great Proletarian Cultural Revolution (literally, the Chinese name translates as "great revolution to create a proletarian culture") lasted for ten years, from 1966 to 1976. Red Guards set out across the nation to eliminate the "four olds"—old ideas, old culture, old customs, and old habits (see the box on p. 911). They destroyed temples, books written by foreigners, and jazz records. They tore down street signs and replaced them with new ones carrying revolutionary names. Destruction of property was matched by vicious attacks on individuals who had supposedly deviated from Mao's thought. Those accused were humiliated at public meetings where they were forced to admit their "crimes." Many were brutally beaten, often to death.

Mao found, however, that it was not easy to maintain a constant mood of revolutionary enthusiasm. Key groups, including Party members, urban professionals, and many military officers, did not share Mao's desire for "permanent revolution."

The Great Proletarian Cultural Revolution. The Cultural Revolution, which began in 1966, was a massive effort by Mao Zedong and his radical supporters to eliminate rival elements within the Chinese Communist Party and achieve the final stage of communism—a classless society. Shown here in front of a picture of Chairman Mao Zedong is a group of Chinese children in uniform holding Mao's *Little Red Book* (a collection of Mao's thoughts that became a sort of bible for Chinese Communists) during the Cultural Revolution in 1968.

People began to turn against the movement, and in September 1976, when Mao died, a group of practical-minded reformers seized power from the radicals and adopted a more rational approach to China's problems.

U.S.-CHINA RELATIONS For years U.S. policy toward Communist China was determined by American fears of Communist expansion in Asia. Already in 1950, the Truman administration had adopted a new national policy that implied that the United States would take whatever steps were necessary to stem expansion of communism in the region, a policy that Truman invoked when he sent troops to Korea in 1950 (see "The Korean War" in Chapter 28). The Second Vietnam War raised additional concerns about Communist China's intentions.

President Richard Nixon, however, opened a new door in American relations when he visited China and met with Mao Zedong in 1972. Despite Nixon's reputation as a devout anti-Communist, the visit was a success, as the two leaders agreed to put aside their most bitter differences in an effort to reduce

THE FURY OF THE RED GUARDS

IN 1966, MAO ZEDONG UNLEASHED the fury of the Red Guards on all levels of society, exposing anti-Maoist elements, suspected "capitalists," and those identified with the previous ruling class. In this excerpt, Nien Cheng (nee-uhn CHUHNG), the widow of an official of Chiang Kai-shek's regime, describes a visit by Red Guards to her home during the height of the Cultural Revolution.

Nien Cheng, *Life and Death in Shanghai*

Suddenly the doorbell began to ring incessantly. At the same time, there was furious pounding of many fists on my front gate. . . . The cacophony told me that the time of waiting was over and that I must face the threat of the Red Guards and the destruction of my home. . . .

Outside, the sound of voices became louder. "Open the gate! Open the gate! Are you all dead? Why don't you open the gate?" Someone was swearing and kicking the wooden gate. . . .

I stood up to put the book on the shelf. A copy of the Constitution of the People's Republic caught my eye. Taking it in my hand and picking up the bunch of keys I had ready on my desk, I went downstairs.

At the same moment, the Red Guards pushed open the front door and entered the house. There were thirty or forty senior high school students, aged between fifteen and twenty, led by two men and one woman much older.

The leading Red Guard, a gangling youth with angry eyes, stepped forward and said to me, "We are the Red Guards. We have come to take revolutionary action against you!"

Though I knew it was futile, I held up the copy of the Constitution, and said calmly, "It's against the Constitution of the People's Republic of China to enter a private house without a search warrant."

Source: From N. Cheng, *Life and Death in Shanghai* (New York: Grove Press, 1986).

The young man snatched the document out of my hand and threw it on the floor. With his eyes blazing, he said, "The Constitution is abolished. It was a document written by the Revisionists within the Communist Party. We recognize only the teachings of our Great Leader Chairman Mao." . . .

Another young man used a stick to smash the mirror hanging over the blackwood chest facing the front door.

Mounting the stairs, I was astonished to see several Red Guards taking pieces of my porcelain collection out of their padded boxes. One young man had arranged a set of four wine cups . . . on the floor and was stepping on them. I was just in time to hear the crunch of delicate porcelain under the sole of his shoe. The sound pierced my heart. Impulsively I leapt forward and caught his leg just as he raised his foot to crush the next cup. He toppled. We fell in a heap together. . . . The other Red Guards . . . gathered around us, shouting at me for interfering in their revolutionary activities.

The young man whose revolutionary work of destruction I had interrupted said angrily, "You shut up! These things belong to the old culture. They are useless toys of the feudal emperors and the modern capitalist class and have no significance to us, the proletarian class. They cannot be compared to the cameras and binoculars, which are useful for our struggle in time of war. Our Great Leader Chairman Mao taught us, 'If we do not destroy, we cannot establish.' The old culture must be destroyed to make way for the new socialist culture."

 What were the tactics of the Red Guards? To what degree did they succeed in remaking the character of the Chinese people?

---

tensions in Asia. During the 1970s, Chinese-American relations continued to improve. In 1979, diplomatic ties were established between the two countries, and by the end of the 1970s, China and the United States had forged a "strategic relationship" in which they would cooperate against the threat of Soviet intervention in Asia.

The Practice of Détente

By the 1970s, American-Soviet relations had entered a new phase known as détente, marked by a reduction of tensions between the two superpowers. An appropriate symbol of détente was the Antiballistic Missile Treaty, signed in 1972, in which the two nations agreed to limit their systems for launching antiballistic missiles (ABMs). The U.S. objective in pursuing the treaty was to make it unlikely that either superpower could win a nuclear exchange by launching a preemptive strike against the other. U.S. officials believed that a policy of "equivalence," in which

there was roughly equal power on each side, was the best way to avoid a nuclear confrontation.

In 1975, the Helsinki Accords provided yet another example of reduced tensions between the superpowers. Signed by the United States, Canada, and all European nations, these accords recognized all borders that had been established in Europe since the end of World War II, thereby acknowledging the Soviet sphere of influence in Eastern Europe. The Helsinki Accords also committed the signatory powers to recognize and protect the human rights of their citizens.

The Limits of Détente

This protection of human rights became one of the major foreign policy goals of the next American president, Jimmy Carter. Although hopes ran high for the continuation of détente, the Soviet invasion of Afghanistan in 1979, undertaken to restore a pro-Soviet regime, hardened relations between the United

States and the Soviet Union. President Carter canceled American participation in the 1980 Olympic Games in Moscow and placed an embargo on the shipment of American grain to the Soviet Union.

The early administration of President Ronald Reagan witnessed a return to the harsh rhetoric, if not all of the harsh practices, of the Cold War. Calling the Soviet Union an "evil empire," Reagan began a military buildup that stimulated a renewed arms race. In 1982, the Reagan administration introduced the nuclear-tipped cruise missile, whose ability to fly at low altitudes made it difficult to detect. President Reagan also became an ardent proponent of the Strategic Defense Initiative (SDI), nicknamed "Star Wars." Its purpose was to create a space shield that could destroy incoming missiles.

By providing military support to the anti-Soviet insurgents in Afghanistan, the Reagan administration helped maintain a Vietnam-like war in Afghanistan that would embed the Soviet Union in its own quagmire. Like the Second Vietnam War, the conflict in Afghanistan resulted in heavy casualties and demonstrated that the influence of a superpower was limited in the face of strong nationalist, guerrilla-type opposition.

Society and Culture in the Western World

FOCUS QUESTION: What were the major social and cultural developments in the Western world between 1965 and 1985?

Dramatic social and cultural developments accompanied political and economic changes after 1965. Scientific and technological achievements revolutionized people's lives, while at the same time environmental problems were becoming increasingly apparent. Intellectually and culturally, the Western world after 1965 was notable for its diversity and innovation. New directions led some observers to speak of a Postmodern cultural world.

The World of Science and Technology

The sponsorship of research by governments and the military during World War II created a new scientific model (see Chapter 27). Science had become very complex, and only large organizations with teams of scientists, huge laboratories, and sophisticated equipment could undertake such large-scale projects. Only governments and large corporations could afford such expensive facilities.

There was no more stunning example of how the new scientific establishment operated than the space race of the 1960s. The Soviets' announcement in 1957 that they had sent the first space satellite, *Sputnik*, into orbit around the earth spurred the United States to launch a gigantic project to land a manned spacecraft on the moon within a decade. Massive government funds financed the

scientific research and technological advances that attained this goal in 1969, an achievement that was greeted by some with great expectations for the future of humanity. One *New York Times* editorialist wrote:

> It will take years, decades, perhaps centuries, for man to colonize even the moon, but that is the end inherent in Armstrong's first step on extraterrestrial soil. Serious and hard-headed scientists envision, even in the not remote future, lunar communities capable of growing into domed cities subsisting on hydroponically grown food, of developing the moon's resources, and eventually of acquiring a breathable atmosphere and a soil capable of being farmed. What with the dire threats of population explosion at best and nuclear explosion at worst, the human race, as Sir Bernard Lovell warns, may find itself sometime in the 21st century "having to consider how best to insure the survival of the species."[4]

THE COMPUTER The alliance of science and technology has led to an accelerated rate of change that has become a fact of life in Western society. One product of this alliance—the computer—may be the most revolutionary of all the technological inventions of the twentieth century. Early computers, which required thousands of vacuum tubes to function, were large and took up considerable space. An important figure in the development of the early computer was Grace Hopper (1906–1992), a career Navy officer. Hopper was instrumental in inventing COBOL, a computer language that enabled computers to respond to words as well as numbers.

The development of the transistor and then the silicon chip produced a revolutionary new approach to computers. In 1971, the invention of the microprocessor, a machine that combines the equivalent of thousands of transistors on a single, tiny silicon chip, opened the road for the development of the personal computer.

On the Moon. The first landing on the moon in 1969 was one of the great technological achievements of the twentieth century. This photograph shows astronaut James Irwin shortly after he raised the American flag during a moonwalk in 1971. The lunar module and lunar rover are also visible in the picture.

THE LIMITS OF MODERN TECHNOLOGY

ALTHOUGH SCIENCE AND TECHNOLOGY produced an amazing array of achievements in the postwar world, some voices were raised in criticism of their sometimes destructive aspects. In 1975, in his book *Small Is Beautiful*, the British economist E. F. Schumacher examined the effects modern industrial technology has had on the earth's resources.

E. F. Schumacher, *Small Is Beautiful*

Is it not evident that our current methods of production are already eating into the very substance of industrial man? To many people this is not at all evident. Now that we have solved the problem of production, they say, have we ever had it so good? Are we not better fed, better clothed, and better housed than ever before—and better educated? Of course we are: most, but by no means all, of us: in the rich countries. But this is not what I mean by "substance." The substance of man cannot be measured by Gross National Product. Perhaps it cannot be measured at all, except for certain symptoms of loss. However, this is not the place to go into the statistics of these symptoms, such as crime, drug addiction, vandalism, mental breakdown, rebellion, and so forth. Statistics never prove anything.

I started by saying that one of the most fateful errors of our age is the belief that the problem of production has been solved. This illusion, I suggested, is mainly due to our inability to recognize that the modern industrial system, with all its intellectual sophistication, consumes the very basis on which it has been erected. To use the language of the economist, it lives on irreplaceable capital which it cheerfully treats as income. I specified three categories of such capital: fossil fuels, the tolerance margins of nature, and the human substance. Even if some readers should refuse to accept all three parts of my argument, I suggest that any one of them suffices to make my case.

And what is my case? Simply that our most important task is to get off our present collision course. And who is there to tackle such a task? I think every one of us. . . . To talk about the future is useful only if it leads to action *now*. And what can we do now, while we are still in the position of "never having had it so good"? To say the least . . . we must thoroughly understand the problem and begin to see the possibility of evolving a new life-style, with new methods of production and new patterns of consumption: a life-style designed for permanence. To give only three preliminary examples: in agriculture and horticulture, we can interest ourselves in the perfection of production methods which are biologically sound, build up soil fertility, and produce health, beauty and permanence. Productivity will then look after itself. In industry, we can interest ourselves in the evolution of small-scale technology, relatively nonviolent technology, "technology with a human face," so that people have a chance to enjoy themselves while they are working, instead of working solely for their pay packet and hoping, usually forlornly, for enjoyment solely during their leisure time.

 What was Schumacher's critique of modern technology? To what extent has this critique been substantiated by developments since 1975?

Source: E. F. Schumacher, *Small Is Beautiful–From Small Is Beautiful: Economics as if People Mattered* (London: Blond-Briggs, 1973).

NEW CONCEPTION OF THE UNIVERSE After World War II, a number of physicists continued to explore the implications of Einstein's revolution in physics and raised fundamental questions about the nature of reality. To some physicists, quantum and relativity theory described a universe in which there were no isolated building blocks. Thus, the universe was not a "collection of physical objects" but a complicated web of relations between "various parts of a unified whole." Moreover, this web of relations also included the human observer. Human beings could not be objective observers of objects detached from themselves because the very act of observation made them participants in the process. These speculations implied that the old Newtonian conception of the universe as a machine was an outdated tool for understanding the nature of the universe.

DANGERS OF SCIENCE AND TECHNOLOGY Despite the marvels produced by the alliance of science and technology, some people came to question the underlying assumption of this alliance—that scientific knowledge gave human beings the ability to manipulate the environment for their benefit. They maintained that some technological advances had far-reaching side effects damaging to the environment. For example, the chemical fertilizers that were touted for producing larger crops wreaked havoc with the ecological balance of streams, rivers, and woodlands. *Small Is Beautiful*, written by the British economist E. F. Schumacher (1911–1977), was a fundamental critique of the dangers of the new science and technology (see the box above). The proliferation of fouled beaches and dying forests and lakes made environmentalism one of the important issues of the late twentieth century.

The Environment and the Green Movements

By the 1970s, serious ecological problems had become all too apparent. Air pollution, produced by nitrogen oxide and sulfur dioxide emissions from motor vehicles, power plants, and industrial factories, was causing respiratory illnesses and having corrosive effects on buildings and monuments. Many rivers, lakes, and seas had become so polluted that they posed serious health risks. Dying forests and disappearing wildlife alarmed more and more people. A nuclear power disaster at Chernobyl (chur-NOH-buhl) in the Ukrainian Soviet Socialist Republic in 1986 made Europeans even more aware of potential environmental hazards. The opening of Eastern Europe after the revolutions of 1989 (see Chapter 30) brought to the world's attention the incredible environmental destruction of that region caused by unfettered industrial pollution. Environmental concerns forced the major political parties in Europe to advocate new regulations for the protection of the environment.

Growing ecological awareness also gave rise to the Green movements and Green parties that emerged throughout Europe in the 1970s. The origins of these movements were by no means uniform. Some came from the antinuclear movement; others arose out of such causes as women's liberation and concerns for foreign workers. Most started at the local level and then gradually expanded to include activities at the national level, where they became formally organized as political parties. Green parties competed successfully in Sweden, Austria, and Switzerland. Most visible was the Green Party in Germany, which was officially organized in 1979 and by 1987 had elected forty-two delegates to the West German parliament.

Although the Green movements and parties played an important role in making people aware of ecological problems, they did not replace the traditional political parties, as some political analysts in the mid-1980s forecast. For one thing, the coalitions that made up the Greens found it difficult to agree on all issues and tended to splinter into different cliques. Moreover, traditional political parties co-opted the environmental issues of the Greens. More and more European governments began to sponsor projects to safeguard the environment and clean up the worst sources of pollution.

Postmodern Thought

The term *Postmodern* covers a variety of artistic and intellectual styles and ways of thinking that have been prominent since the 1970s. In the broadest sense, **Postmodernism** rejects the modern Western belief in an objective truth and instead focuses on the relative nature of reality and knowledge. Human knowledge is defined by a number of factors that must be constantly revised and tested by human experiences.

While existentialism wrestled with notions of meaning and existence, a group of French philosophers in the 1960s attempted to understand how meaning and knowledge operate through the study of language and signs. In the early twentieth century, the Swiss language scholar Ferdinand de Saussure (fayr-di-nawh duh soh-SOOR) (1857–1913) gave birth to structuralism by asserting that the very nature of signs is arbitrary and that language is a human construct. And though the external world has existed for ages, de Saussure believed that humans possessed no capacity for knowledge until language was devised. Language employs signs to denote meaning and, according to de Saussure, possesses two components: the *signifier*, the expression of a concept, and the *signified*, its meaning. For de Saussure, meaning seeks expression in language, although the reliance on language for knowledge suggested that such meaning is learned rather than preexisting.

Jacques Derrida (ZHAHK DEH-ree-duh) (1930–2004) drew on the ideas of de Saussure to demonstrate how dependent Western culture is on binary oppositions. In Western thought, one set of oppositions is generally favored over the other (in the case of de Saussure, speech was favored over writing), but Derrida showed that the privileged depends on the inferior. Rather than reversing the opposition and claiming that writing surpasses speech, for example, Derrida showed that spelling often altered pronunciation. This indebtedness to written language demonstrates that oral speech is not superior. **Poststructuralism,** or **deconstruction**, which Derrida formulated, believes that culture is created and can therefore be analyzed in a variety of ways, according to the manner in which people create their own meaning. Hence, there is no fixed truth or universal meaning.

Michel Foucault (mih-SHELL foo-KOH) (1926–1984) likewise drew upon de Saussure and Derrida to explore relationships of power. Believing that "power is exercised, rather than possessed," Foucault argued that the diffusion of power and oppression marks all relationships. For example, any act of teaching entails components of assertion and submission, as the student adopts the ideas of the one in power. Therefore, all norms are culturally produced and entail some degree of power struggle. In establishing laws of conduct, society not only creates ideal behavior from those who conform, but it also invents a subclass of individuals who do not conform. In *The History of Sexuality*, Foucault suggested that homosexuality was produced by cultures attempting to define and limit homosexual acts. Yet in seeking to control and delineate homosexuality, those in power established the grounds on which it could be defined and practiced. As such, power ultimately requires resistance for it to exist; otherwise, it loses all meaning.

Trends in Art, Literature, and Music

Beginning in the 1960s and continuing well into the 1980s, styles emerged that some have referred to as "Postmodern." Postmodernism tends to move away from the futurism or "cutting-edge" qualities of Modernism. Instead it favors "tradition," whether that means using earlier styles of painting or elevating traditional crafts to the level of fine art. Weavers, potters, glassmakers, metalsmiths, and furniture makers have gained respect as artists. Postmodern artists and architects frequently blur the distinction between the arts, creating works that include elements of film, performance, popular culture, sculpture, and architecture.

ART In the 1960s and 1970s, artists often rejected the notion of object-based artworks. Instead, performances and installations that were either too fleeting or too large to appear in the traditional context of a museum were produced. Allen Kaprow (1927–2006) suggested that "happenings," works of art rooted in performance, grew out of Jackson Pollock's process of action painting. Rather than producing abstract paintings, however, Kaprow created events that were not scripted but chance occurrences. These "happenings" often included audience participation. Kaprow's emphasis on the relationship of art to its surroundings was continued in the "land art" of the early 1970s. In one such example, *Spiral Jetty* (1970), Robert Smithson (1938–1973) used a bulldozer to move more than

Robert Smithson, *Spiral Jetty.* Built on an abandoned industrial site, *Spiral Jetty* disappears and reappears according to the rise and fall of the Great Salt Lake's water level. As seen in this 2002 photograph, the surface has become encrusted in salt as drought has lowered the lake level. Robert Smithson filmed the construction of *Spiral Jetty*, carefully noting the various geological formations included in his creation. Earthworks like *Spiral Jetty* increased in number as the welfare of the world's ecosystems became a growing concern in the 1960s and 1970s.

6,000 tons of earth into a 1,500-foot-long corkscrew in Utah's Great Salt Lake. Responding to the founding of the Environmental Protection Agency as well as to the cycles of nature, Smithson's artwork resembled a science-fiction wasteland while challenging notions of traditional fine art.

Postmodernism's eclectic mixing of past tradition with Modernist innovation became increasingly evident in architecture. Robert Venturi (b. 1925) argued that architects should look as much to the commercial strips of Las Vegas as to the historical styles of the past for inspiration. Venturi advocated an architecture of "complexity and contradiction" as appropriate for the diversity of experiences offered by contemporary life. One example is provided by Charles Moore (1929–1993). His *Piazza d'Italia* (1976–1980) in New Orleans is an outdoor plaza that combines Roman columns with stainless steel and neon lights. This blending of modern-day materials with historical reference distinguished the Postmodern architecture of the late 1970s and 1980s from the Modernist glass box.

Another Postmodern response to Modernism can be seen in a return to Realism in the arts, a movement called Photorealism. Some Photorealists paint or sculpt with such minute attention to detail that their paintings appear to be photographs and their sculptures living human beings. Their subjects are often ordinary individuals, stuck in ordinary lives, demonstrating the Postmodern emphasis on low culture and the commonplace rather than the ambitious nature of high art. These works were often pessimistic or cynical.

LITERATURE Postmodernism was also evident in literature. In the Western world, the best examples were found in Latin America, in a literary style called "magic realism," and in central and Eastern Europe. Magic realism combined realistic events with dreamlike or fantastic backgrounds. One of the finest examples of magic realism can be found in the novel *One Hundred Years of Solitude* by Gabriel García Márquez (gah-bree-EL gahr-SEE-ah MAHR-kes) (1928–2014), who won the Nobel Prize for Literature in 1982. The novel is the story of the fictional town of Macondo as seen by several generations of the Buendias, its founding family. The author slips back and forth between fact and fantasy. Villagers are not surprised when a local priest rises into the air and floats. Yet, when wandering Gypsies introduce these villagers to magnets, telescopes, and magnifying glasses, the villagers are dumbfounded by what they see as magic. According to the author, fantasy and fact depend on one's point of view.

The European center of Postmodernism is well represented by the work of the Czech writer Milan Kundera (MEE-lahn koon-DAYR-uh) (b. 1929). Like the magic realists of Latin America, Kundera also blended fantasy with realism. Unlike the magic realists, Kundera used fantasy to examine moral issues

Charles Moore, *Piazza d'Italia*. Dedicated to the Italian communities of New Orleans, *Piazza d'Italia* includes a schematic map of Italy on its pavement. The architect, Charles Moore, combined elements from Italy's rich cultural past, such as Roman columns and Renaissance Baroque colonnades, with modern materials like neon lighting and stainless steel to create an eclectic Postmodern plaza.

and remained optimistic about the human condition. Indeed, in his novel *The Unbearable Lightness of Being* (1984), Kundera does not despair because of the political repression in his native Czechoslovakia that he so aptly describes but allows his characters to use love as a way to a better life. The human spirit can be lessened but not destroyed.

MUSIC Like modern art, modern music has focused on variety and radical experimentation. Also like modern art, modern classical music witnessed a continuation of pre-war developments. Some composers, the neoclassicists, remained closely tied to nineteenth-century Romantic music, although they occasionally incorporated some twentieth-century developments, such as atonality and dissonance. Their style was strongly reminiscent of Stravinsky (see Chapter 24).

The major musical trend since the war, however, has been serialism. Inspired mostly by the twelve-tone music of Schönberg (see Chapter 26), serialism is a compositional procedure in which an order of succession is set for specific values: pitch (for tones of the tempered scale), loudness (for dynamic levels), and units of time (for rhythm). By predetermining the order of succession, the composer restricts his or her intuitive freedom as the work to some extent creates itself. Nevertheless, the mechanism the composer initially establishes could generate unanticipated musical events, thereby creating new and exciting compositions. Serialist composition diminishes the role of intuition and emotion in favor of intellect and mathematical precision. The first recognized serialist was the Frenchman Olivier Messiaen (oh-lee-VYAY meh-SYANH) (1908–1992). Significantly, Messiaen was influenced by, among other things, Indian and Greek music, plainchant, folk music, and birdsongs. Most critics have respected serialism, although the public has been largely indifferent, if not hostile, to it.

An offshoot of serialism that has won popular support, but not the same critical favor, is minimalism. Like serialism, this style uses repeated patterns and series and steady pulsation with gradual changes occurring over time. But whereas serialism is often atonal, minimalism is usually tonal and more harmonic. Perhaps the most successful minimalist composer is Philip Glass (b. 1937), who demonstrated in *Einstein on the Beach* that minimalist music could be adapted to full-scale opera. Like other modern American composers, Glass found no contradiction in moving between the worlds of classical music and popular music. His *Koyaanisqatsi* (koh-YAH-niss-kaht-si) was used as background music to a documentary film on the disintegrative forces in Western society.

Popular Culture: Image and Globalization

The period from 1967 to 1973 was probably the true golden age of rock. During this brief period, much experimentation in rock music took place, as it did in society in general. Straightforward rock 'n' roll competed with a new hybrid blues rock, created in part by British performers such as the Rolling Stones, who were in turn inspired by African American blues artists. Many musicians also experimented with non-Western musical sounds, such as Indian sitars. Some of the popular music of the 1960s also focused on social issues. It was against the Vietnam War and materialism and promoted "peace and love" as alternatives to the prevailing "establishment" culture.

The same migration of a musical form from the United States to Britain and back to the United States that characterized the golden age of rock also occurred when the early punk movement in New York spread to Britain in the mid-1970s after failing to make an immediate impact in the United States. The more influential British punk movement of 1976–1979 was also fueled by an economic crisis that had resulted in large numbers of unemployed and undereducated young people. Punk was not simply a proletarian movement, however. Many of its supporters, performers, and promoters were British art school graduates who applied avant-garde experimentation to the movement. Punk rockers such as Britain's Sex Pistols rejected most social conventions and preached anarchy and rebellion. They often wore tattered clothes and pins in their cheeks, symbolizing their rejection of a materialistic and degenerate culture. Pure punk was short-lived, partly because its intense energy quickly burned out (as did many of its performers) and partly because, as ex-punk Mick Hucknall said, "the biggest mistake of the punks was that they rejected music." Offshoots of punk proliferated through the 1980s, however, especially in Eastern Europe, with groups named Crisis, Sewage, and Dead Organism.

The introduction of the video music channel MTV in the early 1980s radically changed the music scene by making image as important as sound in selling records. Artists like Michael Jackson became superstars by treating the music video as an art form. Jackson's videos often were short films with elaborate staging, special effects and actors wearing costumes set to music. Technological advances helped shape the music of the 1980s with the advent of the synthesizer, an electronic piano that produced computerized sounds. Some performers replaced ensembles of guitar, bass, and drums with synthesizers, creating a futuristic and manufactured sound.

Paralleling the rise of the music video was the emergence of rap or hip-hop. Developed in New York City in the late 1970s and early 1980s, rap combined rhymed lyrics with disco beats and turntable manipulations. Early rap groups like Public Enemy and Grandmaster Flash and the Furious Five instilled social commentaries into their songs, using the popularity of hip-hop to raise awareness about social conditions in American cities.

The Growth of Mass Sports

Sports became a major product of both popular culture and the leisure industry. The development of satellite television and various electronic breakthroughs helped make sports a global phenomenon. The Olympic Games could now be broadcast around the globe from anywhere in the world. Sports were a cheap form of entertainment since fans did not have to leave their homes to enjoy athletic competitions. In fact, some sports organizations initially resisted television, fearing that it would hurt ticket sales. Soon, however, the tremendous revenues possible from television contracts overcame this hesitation. As sports television revenue escalated, many sports came to receive the bulk of their yearly revenue from television contracts. The Olympics, for example, are now funded primarily by American television. These contracts are paid for by advertising sponsors, mostly for products to be consumed while watching the sport: beer, soda, and snack foods.

Sports became big politics as well as big business. Football (soccer) remained the dominant world sport and more than ever became a vehicle for nationalist sentiment and expression. The World Cup is the most watched event on television. Although the sport can be a positive outlet for national and local pride, all too often it has been marred by violence as nationalistic energies have overcome rational behavior.

The most telling example of the potent mix of politics and sport continued to be the Olympic Games. When the Soviets entered Olympic competition in 1952, the Olympics began to take on Cold War implications and became known as the "war without weapons." The Soviets saw the Olympics as a way to stimulate nationalist spirit, as well as to promote the Communist system as the best path for social progress. The Soviets led the Olympics in terms of total medals won between 1956 and 1988. The nature of the Olympics, with their daily medal count by nation and elaborate ceremonies and rituals such as the playing of the national anthem of the winning athletes and the parade of nations, virtually ensured the politicization of the games originally intended to foster international cooperation through friendly competition.

The political nature of the games found expression in other ways as well. In 1956, six nations withdrew from the games to protest the Soviet crushing of the Hungarian uprising. In 1972, twenty-seven African nations threatened to pull out of the Munich Olympics because of apartheid in South Africa. Also at the Munich Games, the Palestinian terrorist group Black September seized eleven Israeli athletes as hostages, all of whom died in a confrontation at an airport. The United States led a boycott of the 1980 Moscow Games to protest the Soviet invasion of Afghanistan, and the Soviets responded by boycotting the Los Angeles Games in 1984.

POPULAR CULTURE: INCREASINGLY GLOBAL Media critic and theorist Marshall McLuhan (1911–1980) predicted in the 1960s that advances in mass communications technology, such as satellites and electronics, would eventually lead to a shrinking of the world, a lessening of cultural distinctions, and a breaking down of cultural barriers, all of which would in time transform the world into a single "global village." McLuhan was optimistic about these developments, and his ideas became quite popular at the time. Many critics have since argued that McLuhan was too utopian about the benefits of technological progress and maintain that the mass media created by these technological breakthroughs are still controlled by a small number of multinational corporations that "colonize the rest of the world, sometimes benignly, sometimes not." They argue that this has allowed Western popular culture to disrupt the traditional cultures of less developed countries and inculcate new patterns of behavior as well as new desires and new dissatisfactions. Cultural contacts, however, often move in two directions. While the world has been "Americanized" to a great extent, formerly unfamiliar ways of life and styles of music have also come into the world of the West (see Chapter 30).

The late 1960s experienced a rash of protest movements. The so-called sexual revolution of the 1960s led to a revolt in sexual mores, encouraged by the birth control pill as well as sexually explicit movies, plays, and books. A growing youth movement in the 1960s questioned authority and fostered rebellion against the older generation. Numerous groups of students and radicals protested the war in Vietnam and unsatisfactory university conditions. Women actively sought equality of rights with men. The women's movement gained momentum in the 1970s and 1980s, but the student upheavals were not a "turning point in the history of postwar Europe," as some people thought at the time, especially in 1968, when the student protest movement reached its height. In the 1970s and 1980s, student rebels became middle-class professionals, and revolutionary politics remained mostly a memory.

In the 1970s, the Cold War took a new direction known as détente as the Soviet Union and the United States moved, if ever fitfully, toward a lessening of tensions. With the Antiballistic Missile Treaty in 1972, the United States and the Soviet Union believed that they had reached a balance, or "equivalence," that would assure peace. The early 1980s, however, saw renewed tensions between the superpowers. The Soviet invasion of Afghanistan in 1979 and the introduction of the cruise missile and "Star Wars" by the American president Ronald Reagan brought a decline in détente. But as we shall see in the next chapter, a dramatic shift in Soviet leadership would soon bring an unexpected end to the Cold War.

Between 1965 and 1985, the Western world remained divided between a prosperous capitalistic and democratic West and a stagnant, politically repressed Eastern Europe. After two decades of incredible economic growth, Western European states experienced severe economic

recessions in 1973–1974 and 1979–1983, although their economies largely recovered in the course of the 1980s. In Eastern Europe, Soviet leaders continued to exercise control over their satellite states while recognizing the need to provide some leeway in adopting domestic policies appropriate to local conditions.

Dramatic social and cultural developments accompanied political and economic changes after 1965. Scientific and technological developments, especially the rapid advance of the personal computer, began to revolutionize

people's lives, while ecological problems became increasingly apparent and led to the Green movements and Green parties that emerged throughout Europe in the 1970s. Intellectually and culturally, the Western world after 1965 was notable for its diversity and innovation. New directions led some observers to speak of a Postmodern world in both literature and the arts.

CHAPTER TIMELINE

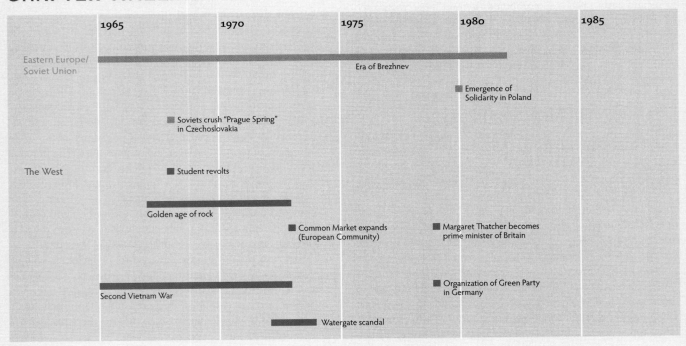

	1965	1970	1975	1980	1985

Eastern Europe/ Soviet Union

Era of Brezhnev

■ Emergence of Solidarity in Poland

■ Soviets crush "Prague Spring" in Czechoslovakia

The West

■ Student revolts

Golden age of rock

■ Common Market expands (European Community)

■ Margaret Thatcher becomes prime minister of Britain

■ Organization of Green Party in Germany

Second Vietnam War

Watergate scandal

CHAPTER REVIEW

Upon Reflection

Q What were the major turning points in the Cold War between 1965 and 1985?

Q What were the major successes and failures of the Western European democracies between 1965 and 1985, and

how did Soviet policies affect the Eastern European states during the same time period?

Q What role did popular culture play in the Western world between 1965 and 1985?

Key Terms

permissive society (p. 897)
feminism (p. 900)
Brezhnev Doctrine (p. 901)
détente (p. 901)
Eurocommunism (p. 906)

stagflation (p. 908)
domino theory (p. 909)
Postmodernism (p. 914)
poststructuralism, or **deconstruction** (p. 914)

Suggestions for Further Reading

GENERAL WORKS For a well-written survey on Europe between 1965 and 1985, see **T. Judt,** *Postwar: A History of Europe Since 1945* (New York, 2005), and **T. Buchanan,** *Europe's Troubled Peace, 1945–2000* (Oxford, 2006).

A CULTURE OF PROTEST On the sexual revolution of the 1960s, see **D. Allyn,** *Make Love, Not War: The Sexual Revolution— An Unfettered History* (New York, 2000). On the turbulent 1960s, see **A. Marwick,** *The Sixties: Social and Cultural Transformation in Britain, France, Italy, and the United States* (Oxford, 1999), and **J. Suri,** *The Global Revolutions of 1968* (New York, 2007). On the women's liberation movement, see **D. Meyer,** *The Rise of Women in America, Russia, Sweden, and Italy,* 2nd ed. (Middletown, Conn., 1989), and **K. C. Berkeley,** *The Women's Liberation Movement in America* (Westport, Conn., 1999).

SOVIET UNION AND EASTERN EUROPE On the Brezhnev era in the Soviet Union, see **E. Bacon, ed.,** *Brezhnev Remembered* (New York, 2003). On events in Eastern Europe, see the surveys listed in Chapter 28. On the Czech upheaval in 1968, see **G. Bischof, S. Karner,** and **P. Ruggenthaler eds.,** *The Prague Spring and the Warsaw Pact Invasion of Czechoslovakia in 1968* (Plymouth, U.K., 2010).

WESTERN EUROPE For general works on Western Europe and individual countries, see the works cited in Chapter 28.

More specific works dealing with the period 1965–1985 include **E. J. Evans,** *Thatcher and Thatcherism* (New York, 1997); **D. S. Bell,** *François Mitterrand* (Cambridge, 2005); and **R. J. Dalton,** *Politics in West Germany* (Glenview, Ill., 1989).

THE COLD WAR: THE MOVE TO DÉTENTE For general studies on the Cold War, see the works listed in Chapter 28. On the Second Vietnam War, see **M. Hall,** *The Vietnam War,* 2nd ed. (London, 2007). On China's cultural revolution, see **R. MacFarquhar** and **M. Schoenhals,** *Mao's Last Revolution* (Cambridge, Mass., 2006), and **T. Cheek,** *Mao Zedong and China's Revolutions: A Brief History* (Boston, 2002).

SOCIETY AND CULTURE On the development of the Green parties, see **M. O'Neill,** *Green Parties and Political Change in Contemporary Europe* (Aldershot, U.K., 1997). The space race is examined in **W. A. McDougall,** *The Heavens and the Earth: A Political History of the Space Age* (New York, 1987). For a general view of postwar thought and culture, see **J. A. Winders,** *European Culture Since 1848: From Modern to Postmodern and Beyond,* rev. ed. (New York, 2001). On Postmodernism, see **C. Butler,** *Postmodernism: A Very Short Introduction* (Oxford, 2002). The cultural impact of sports is examined in **T. Collins** and **W. Vamplew,** *Mud, Sweat and Beers: A Cultural History of Sport and Alcohol* (London, 2002).

Notes

1. Quoted in M. Rowe et al., *Spare Rib Reader* (Harmondsworth, U.K., 1982), p. 574.
2. B. Friedan, *The Feminine Mystique* (New York, 1963), p. 10.
3. Quoted in T. Judt, *Postwar: A History of Europe Since 1945* (New York, 2005), p. 390.
4. "To Walk the Moon," *New York Times,* July 20, 1969.

 **MindTap® is a fully online, highly personalized learning experience built upon Cengage Learning content. MindTap combines student learning tools—readings, multimedia, activities, and assessments—into a singular Learning Path that guides students through the course.**

AFTER THE FALL: THE WESTERN WORLD IN A GLOBAL AGE (SINCE 1985)

With clenched fist, Boris Yeltsin speaks out against an attempted right-wing coup

Pascal Le Segretain/Sygma/Corbis

CHAPTER OUTLINE AND FOCUS QUESTIONS

Toward a New Western Order

Q What reforms did Gorbachev institute in the Soviet Union, and what role did he play in the demise of the Soviet Union? What are the major political developments in Eastern Europe, Western Europe, and North America since 1985?

After the Cold War: New World Order or Age of Terrorism?

Q How and why did the Cold War end? What are the main issues in the struggle with terrorism?

New Directions and New Problems in Western Society

Q What are the major developments in the women's movement since 1985, and what problems have immigrants created for European society?

Western Culture Today

Q What major Western cultural trends have emerged since 1985?

Toward a Global Civilization: New Challenges and Hopes

Q What is globalization, and what are some of its important aspects in the twenty-first century?

Critical Thinking

Q *In what ways were the major social, economic, and political developments in the second half of the twentieth century similar to those in the first half of the century? In what ways were they different?*

Connections to Today

Q *More than twenty-five years ago, the destruction of the Berlin Wall brought forth great promise for a new Europe. What will be the challenges of the next twenty-five years for Western civilization?*

BY 1985, AFTER FOUR DECADES of the Cold War, Westerners had become accustomed to a new division of Europe between West and East that seemed to be permanent. A prosperous Western Europe allied with the United States stood opposed to a still-struggling Eastern Europe that remained largely subject to the Soviet Union. The division of Germany symbolized the new order, which seemed so well established. Yet within a few years, a revolutionary upheaval in the Soviet Union and Eastern Europe brought an end to the Cold War and to the division of postwar Europe. Even the Soviet Union ceased to exist as a nation.

On August 19, 1991, a group of Soviet leaders opposed to reform arrested Mikhail Gorbachev, the president of the Soviet Union, and tried to seize control of the government. Hundreds of thousands of Russians, led by Boris Yeltsin, poured into the streets of Moscow and Leningrad to resist the attempted coup. Some army units, sent out to enforce the wishes of the rebels, defected to Yeltsin's side, and within days, the rebels were forced to surrender. This failed attempt to seize power had unexpected results as Russia and many of the other Soviet republics declared their independence. By the end of 1991, the Soviet Union—one of the largest empires in world history—had come to an end, and a new era of cooperation between the successor states in the old Soviet Union and the nations of the West had begun.

As the world adjusted to the transformation from Cold War to post-Cold War sensibilities, other changes shaped the Western outlook. The demographic face of European countries changed as massive numbers of immigrants created more ethnically diverse populations. New artistic and intellectual currents, the continued advance of science and technology, the emergence of a Digital Age, the surge of the women's liberation movement—all spoke of a vibrant, ever-changing world. At the same time, a devastating terrorist attack on the World Trade Center in New York City and the Pentagon outside Washington, D.C., in 2001 made the Western world vividly aware of its vulnerability to international terrorism. Moreover, a financial collapse in 2008 threatened the economic security of the Western world as well as the entire global economy. But most important of all, Western nations, like all nations on the planet, have become aware of the political and economic interdependence of the world's nations and the global nature of our twenty-first-century problems.

Toward a New Western Order

 FOCUS QUESTIONS: What reforms did Gorbachev institute in the Soviet Union, and what role did he play in the demise of the Soviet Union? What are the major political developments in Eastern Europe, Western Europe, and North America since 1985?

Between 1945 and 1985, a new political order following the devastation of World War II had seemingly left the Western world divided permanently between a prosperous, capitalistic West and an impoverished, Communist East. But in the late 1980s and early 1990s, the Soviet Union and its Eastern European satellite states underwent a revolutionary upheaval that dramatically altered the European landscape (see Map 30.1) and left many Europeans with both new hopes and new fears.

The Revolutionary Era in the Soviet Union

By 1980, it was becoming apparent to a small number of reformers in the Communist Party that the Soviet Union was seriously ailing. When one of these young reformers, Mikhail Gorbachev, was chosen as Party secretary in March 1985, a new era began in the Soviet Union.

THE GORBACHEV ERA After receiving his law degree at the University of Moscow in 1955, Mikhail Gorbachev returned

to his native southern Russia, where he eventually became first secretary of the Party in the city of Stavropol (he had joined the Party in 1952). In 1980, Gorbachev became a full member of the ruling Politburo and secretary of the Central Committee. In March 1985, Party leaders elected him general secretary of the Party, and he became the new leader of the Soviet Union.

Educated during the years of reform under Khrushchev, Gorbachev seemed intent on taking earlier reforms to their logical conclusions. He had said to his wife on achieving power, "We cannot go on living like this."[1] By the 1980s, Soviet economic problems were obvious. Rigid, centralized planning had led to mismanagement and stifled innovation. Although the Soviets still excelled in space exploration, they had fallen behind the West in high technology, especially in the development and production of computers for private and public use. Most noticeable to the Soviet people was the decline in the standard of living. In February 1986, at the Twenty-Seventh Congress of the Communist Party, Gorbachev made clear the need for changes in Soviet society: "The practical actions of the Party and state agencies lag behind the demands of the times and of life itself. . . . Problems grow faster than they are solved. Sluggishness, ossification in the forms, and methods of management decrease the dynamism of work. . . . Stagnation begins to show up in the life of society."[2] Thus, from the start, Gorbachev preached the need for radical reforms.

The cornerstone of Gorbachev's radical reforms was **perestroika** (per-uh-STROI-kuh), or "restructuring" (see the box on p. 923). At first, this meant only a reordering of economic policy as Gorbachev called for the beginning of a market economy with limited free enterprise and some private property. Gorbachev soon perceived, however, that in the Soviet system, the economic sphere was intimately tied to the social and political spheres. Attempting to reform the economy without political or social reform would be doomed to failure. One of the most important instruments of perestroika was **glasnost** (GLAHZ-nohst), or "openness." Soviet citizens and officials were encouraged to discuss openly the strengths and weaknesses of the Soviet Union. *Pravda* (PRAHV-duh), the official newspaper of the Communist Party, began for the first time to include reports of official corruption, sloppy factory work, and protests against government policy.

Political reforms were equally revolutionary. At the Communist Party conference in 1988, Gorbachev called for the creation of a new Soviet parliament, the Congress of People's Deputies, whose members were to be chosen in competitive elections. It convened in 1989, the first such meeting in Russia since 1918. Early in 1990, Gorbachev legalized the formation of other political parties and struck Article 6, which had guaranteed the "leading role" of the Communist Party, from the Soviet constitution. At the same time, Gorbachev attempted to consolidate his power by creating a new state presidency. The new position was a consequence of the separation of the state from the Communist Party. Hitherto, the position of first secretary of the Party had been the most important post in the Soviet Union, but as the Communist Party became less closely associated with the state, the powers of this office diminished

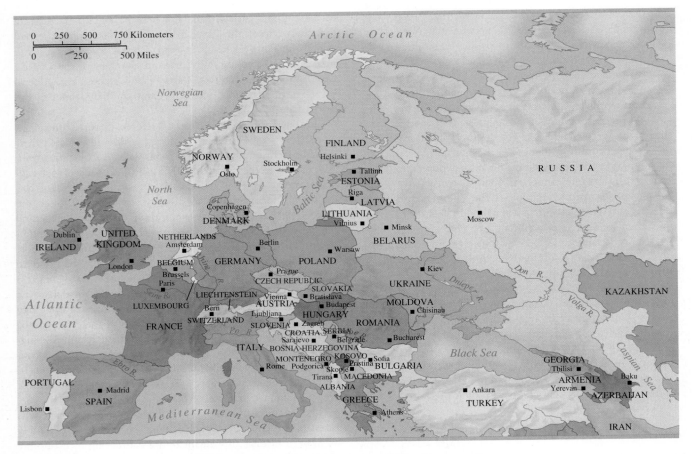

MAP 30.1 The New Europe. The combination of an inefficient economy and high military spending had led to stagnation in the Soviet Union by the early 1980s. Mikhail Gorbachev came to power in 1985, unleashing political, economic, and nationalist forces that led to independence for the former Soviet republics and also for Eastern Europe.

Q *Compare this map with Map 28.1. What new countries had emerged by the early twenty-first century?*

correspondingly. In March 1990, Gorbachev became the Soviet Union's first president.

One of Gorbachev's most serious problems stemmed from the nature of the nation he led. The Union of Soviet Socialist Republics was a truly multiethnic country, containing 92 nationalities and 112 recognized languages. Previously, the iron hand of the Communist Party, centered in Moscow, had kept a lid on the centuries-old ethnic tensions that had periodically erupted. As Gorbachev released this iron grip, tensions resurfaced, a by-product of *glasnost* that Gorbachev had not anticipated. Ethnic groups took advantage of the new openness to protest what they perceived as ethnically motivated slights. When violence erupted, the Soviet army, in disrepair since its ill-fated decade-long foray into Afghanistan, had difficulty controlling the situation.

The years 1988 to 1990 also witnessed the appearance of nationalist movements in the republics that made up the Soviet Union. Many were motivated by ethnic concerns, with calls for sovereignty and independence from Russian-based rule centered in Moscow. These movements sprang up first in Georgia in late 1988 and then in Latvia (LAT-vee-uh), Estonia

(ess-TOH-nee-uh), Moldova (mohl-DOH-vuh), Uzbekistan (ooz-BEK-i-stan), Azerbaijan (az-ur-by-JAHN), and Lithuania (li-thuh-WAY-nee-uh). On March 11, 1990, the Lithuanian Supreme Council proclaimed Lithuania an independent state.

THE END OF THE SOVIET UNION During 1990 and 1991, Gorbachev struggled to deal with Lithuania and the other problems unleashed by his reforms. On the one hand, he tried to appease conservatives who complained about the growing disorder within the Soviet Union. On the other hand, he tried to accommodate the liberal forces, especially those in the Soviet republics, who increasingly favored a new kind of decentralized Soviet federation. In particular, Gorbachev labored to cooperate more closely with Boris Yeltsin (YELT-sun) (1931–2007), who had been elected president of the Russian Republic in June 1991.

By 1991, the conservative leaders of the traditional Soviet institutions—the army, government, KGB, and military industries—had grown increasingly worried about the impending dissolution of the Soviet Union and its impact on their own fortunes. On August 19, 1991, a group of these discontented rightists arrested Gorbachev and attempted to seize power.

GORBACHEV AND *PERESTROIKA*

AFTER ASSUMING THE LEADERSHIP of the Soviet Union in 1985, Mikhail Gorbachev worked to liberalize and restructure the country. His policies opened the door to rapid changes in Eastern Europe and in Soviet-American relations at the end of the 1980s. In his book *Perestroika*, Gorbachev explained some of his "New Thinking."

Mikhail Gorbachev, *Perestroika*

The fundamental principle of the new political outlook is very simple: *nuclear war cannot be a means of achieving political, economic, ideological or any other goals.* This conclusion is truly revolutionary, for it means discarding the traditional notions of war and peace. It is the political function of war that has always been a justification for war, a "rational" explanation. Nuclear war is senseless; it is irrational. There would be neither winners nor losers in a global nuclear conflict: world Civilization would inevitably perish. . . .

But military technology has developed to such an extent that even a non-nuclear war would now be comparable with a nuclear war in its destructive effect. That is why it is logical to include in our category of nuclear wars this "variant" of an armed clash between major powers as well.

Thereby, an altogether different situation has emerged. A way of thinking and a way of acting, based on the use of force in world politics, have formed over centuries, even millennia. It seems they have taken root as something unshakable. Today, they have lost all reasonable grounds. . . . For the first time in history, basing international politics on moral and ethical norms that are common to all humankind, as well as humanizing interstate relations, has become a vital requirement. . . .

There is a great thirst for mutual understanding and mutual communication in the world. It is felt among politicians, it is gaining momentum among the intelligentsia, representatives of culture, and the public at large. And if the Russian word "perestroika" has easily entered the international lexicon, this is due to more than just interest in what is going on in the Soviet Union. Now the whole world needs restructuring, i.e., progressive development, a fundamental change.

People feel this and understand this. They have to find their bearings, to understand the problems besetting mankind, to realize how they should live in the future. The restructuring is a must for a world overflowing with nuclear weapons; for a world ridden with serious economic and ecological problems; for a world laden with poverty, backwardness and disease; for a human race now facing the urgent need of ensuring its own survival.

We are all students, and our teacher is life and time. I believe that more and more people will come to realize that through RESTRUCTURING in the broad sense of the word, the integrity of the world will be enhanced. Having earned good marks from our main teacher—life—we shall enter the twenty-first century well prepared and sure that there will be further progress.

 How revolutionary was Gorbachev's rejection of nuclear war? What impact did this idea of restructuring have on communism and the Soviet Union's ability to reform itself?

Source: Mikhail Gorbachev, *Perestroika* (New York: HarperCollins, 1987), pp. 140–141, 253–254.

Gorbachev's unwillingness to work with the conspirators and the brave resistance in Moscow of Yeltsin and thousands of Russians who had grown accustomed to their new liberties caused the coup to disintegrate rapidly. The actions of these right-wing plotters, however, served to accelerate the very process they had hoped to stop—the disintegration of the Soviet Union.

Despite desperate pleas by Gorbachev, the Soviet republics soon moved for complete independence. Ukraine voted for independence on December 1, 1991, and a week later, the leaders of Russia, Ukraine, and Belarus (bell-uh-ROOSS) announced that the Soviet Union had "ceased to exist" and would be replaced by the new and voluntary Commonwealth of Independent States. Gorbachev resigned on December 25, 1991, and turned over his responsibilities as commander in chief to Boris Yeltsin, the president of Russia. By the end of 1991, one of the largest empires in world history had evaporated, and a new era had begun in its lands.

HISTORIANS DEBATE **WHY DID THE SOVIET UNION COLLAPSE?** What caused the sudden collapse of the Soviet system? Some analysts in the United States argue that the ambitious defense policies adopted by the Reagan administration forced the Soviet Union into an arms race that it could not afford and that ultimately led to the collapse of the Soviet economy. Most observers, however, believe that the fall of the Soviet Union was primarily a consequence of conditions inherent in the system, some of which have been pointed out in this and the previous chapter. For years, Soviet leaders had denied or ignored the massive inefficiencies in the Soviet economy. Lack of investment in new technologies prevented innovation and development of new consumer goods. In the 1980s, time began to run out. The perceptive Mikhail Gorbachev tried to stem the decline with radical reforms, but by then it was too late.

One other factor should also be considered. One of the weakest aspects of the Soviet Union was its multiethnic character, with only a little more than half of the total population made up of ethnic Russians. As we have seen, many of the minority nationalities were demanding more autonomy or even independence for their regions. By the end of the 1980s, such demands brought about the final collapse of the Soviet system.

Yeltsin Resists a Right-Wing Coup. In August 1991, the attempt of right-wing plotters to overthrow Mikhail Gorbachev and seize power in the Soviet Union was thwarted by the efforts of Boris Yeltsin, president of the Russian Republic, and his supporters. Yeltsin (holding papers) is shown here atop a tank in front of the Russian parliament building in Moscow, urging the Russian people to resist the conspirators.

THE NEW RUSSIA A new power struggle soon ensued within Russia, by far the largest of the former Soviet republics. Yeltsin was committed to introducing a free market economy as quickly as possible, but the transition was not easy. Economic hardships and social disarray, made worse by a dramatic rise in the activities of organized crime mobs, led increasing numbers of Russians to support both former Communists and hardline nationalists, who criticized Russia's loss of prestige in world affairs.

During the mid-1990s, Yeltsin sought to implement reforms that would set Russia on a firm course toward a pluralistic political system and a market economy. But the new post-Communist Russia remained as fragile as ever. Growing economic inequality and rampant corruption aroused widespread criticism and shook the confidence of the Russian people in the superiority of the capitalist system over the one that had existed under Communist rule. A nagging war in the Caucasus—where the Muslim people of Chechnya (CHECH-nee-uh) sought national independence from Russia—drained the government's budget and exposed the decrepit state of the once vaunted Red Army. Yeltsin won reelection as president in 1996, although his precarious health raised serious questions about his ability to govern.

THE PUTIN ERA At the end of 1999, Yeltsin suddenly resigned and was replaced by Vladimir Putin (POO-tin) (b. 1952), a former member of the KGB. Putin vowed to strengthen the role of the central government in managing the affairs of state. During the succeeding months, the parliament approved his proposal to centralize power in the hands of the federal government in Moscow.

The new president also vowed to return the breakaway state of Chechnya to Russian authority and to adopt a more assertive role in international affairs. Fighting in Chechnya continued throughout 2000, nearly reducing the republic's capital city of Grozny (GRAWZ-nee) to ruins. In July 2001, Putin launched reforms, which included the unrestricted sale and purchase of land and tax cuts aimed at boosting economic growth and budget revenues. Although Russia soon experienced a budget surplus and a growing economy, serious problems remained.

Chechnya

Putin attempted to deal with the chronic problems in Russian society by centralizing his control over the system and by silencing critics—notably in the Russian media. Although he was criticized in the West for these moves, many Russians expressed sympathy with Putin's attempts to restore a sense of pride and discipline in Russian society.

In 2008, Dmitry Medvedev (di-MEE-tree mehd-VYEH-dehf) (b. 1965) became president of Russia when Putin could not run for reelection under Russia's constitution. Instead, Putin became prime minister, and the two men shared power. In 2012, however, despite public protests, Putin was again elected president to a six-year term.

In November 2013, protests erupted in the Ukraine following the sudden rejection of an agreement with the European Union, which would have aligned the Ukraine with the European Union and not its former ally, Russia. The protests grew violent and in February 2014, Putin responded by occupying Ukraine's southernmost region, the autonomous republic of the Crimea. Russian troops began taking over government buildings in the Crimea, while Crimean authorities scheduled an illegal referendum on Crimea's independence from the Ukraine. Approximately 99.67 percent voted in favor and the Crimean authorities signed an accession treaty with Russia on March 18, 2014. The UN General Assembly condemned the referendum and the annexation as illegal, and Western countries responded with diplomatic and economic sanctions against Russia.

Eastern Europe: The Revolutions of 1989 and the Collapse of the Communist Order

Stalin's postwar order had imposed Communist regimes throughout Eastern Europe. The process of sovietization seemed so complete that few people believed that the new order could be undone. But discontent with their Soviet-style regimes always simmered beneath the surface of these satellite states, and after Mikhail Gorbachev made it clear that his government would not intervene militarily, the Communist regimes fell quickly in the revolutions of 1989.

THE FALL Martial law had not solved Poland's problems after it had been imposed in 1981, and in 1988, new demonstrations led the Polish regime to agree to free parliamentary elections—the first free elections in Eastern Europe in forty years. Bowing to the inevitable, the military regime allowed the newly elected Solidarity coalition to form a new government, thus ending forty-five years of Communist rule. In December 1990, Lech Wałęsa, the head of Solidarity, was chosen as the new Polish president.

In Hungary, the economy had sagged by the late 1980s, and in 1989, the Communist regime, aware of growing dissatisfaction, began to undertake reforms. But they came too late as new political parties called for Hungary to become a democratic republic. After elections in March 1990, a new coalition government was formed that committed Hungary to democratic government.

Czechoslovakia, too, found a peaceful way to a new political system. Government attempts to suppress mass demonstrations in Prague and other cities in 1988 and 1989 only led to more and larger demonstrations. In December 1989, as demonstrations continued, the Communist government, lacking any real support, collapsed. President Gustáv Husák resigned and at the end of December was replaced by Václav Havel, a long-time dissident playwright who had played an important role in bringing down the Communist government. Havel set out on a goodwill tour to various Western countries where he proved to be an eloquent spokesman for Czech democracy and a new order in Europe (see the box on p. 926).

Czechoslovakia's revolutionary path was considerably less violent than Romania's, where opposition grew as the dictator Nicolae Ceauşescu rejected the reforms in Eastern Europe promoted by Gorbachev. Ceauşescu's extreme measures to reduce Romania's external debt led to economic difficulties and angered many Romanians. A small incident became the spark that ignited heretofore suppressed flames of discontent. The ruthless crushing of a demonstration in Timisoara in December 1989 led to other mass demonstrations. After the dictator was booed at a mass rally on December 21, the army refused to support any more repression. Ceauşescu and his wife were captured on December 22 and tried and executed on Christmas Day. Leadership now passed into the hands of the hastily formed National Salvation Front.

AFTER THE FALL The fall of Communist governments in Eastern Europe during the revolutions of 1989 brought a wave of euphoria to Europe. The new structures meant an end to a postwar European order that had been imposed on unwilling peoples by the victorious forces of the Soviet Union. In 1989 and 1990, new governments throughout Eastern Europe worked diligently to scrap the remnants of the old system and introduce the democratic procedures and market systems they believed would revitalize their scarred lands. But this process proved to be neither simple nor easy.

Most Eastern European countries had little or even no experience with democratic systems. Then, too, ethnic divisions,

A Romanian Revolutionary. The revolt against Communist rule in Eastern Europe in 1989 came last to Romania. It was also more violent, as the government at first tried to stem the revolt by massacring demonstrators. This picture shows a young Romanian rebel waving the national flag with the Communist emblem cut out of the center. He is on a balcony overlooking the tanks, soldiers, and citizens filling Palace Square in Bucharest.

VÁCLAV HAVEL: THE CALL FOR A NEW POLITICS

IN ATTEMPTING TO DEAL WITH the world's problems, some European leaders pointed to the need for a new perspective, especially a moral one, if people were to live in a sane world. These two excerpts are taken from speeches by Václav Havel, who was elected president of Czechoslovakia at the end of 1989. The first is from his inaugural address as president on January 1, 1990; the second is from a speech given to the U.S. Congress.

Václav Havel, Address to the People of Czechoslovakia, January 1, 1990

But all this is still not the main problem [the environmental devastation of the country by its Communist leaders]. The worst thing is that we live in a contaminated moral environment. We fell morally ill because we became used to saying something different from what we thought. We learned not to believe in anything, to ignore each other, to care only about ourselves. Concepts such as love, friendship, compassion, humility, or forgiveness lost their depth and dimensions, and for many of us they represented only psychological peculiarities, or they resembled gone-astray greetings from ancients, a little ridiculous in the era of computers and spaceships. Only a few of us were able to cry out loud that the powers that be should not be all-powerful, and that special farms, which produce ecologically pure and top-quality food just for them, should send their produce to schools, children's homes and hospitals if our agriculture was unable to offer them to all. The previous regime—armed with its arrogant and intolerant ideology—reduced man to a force of production and nature to a tool of production. In this it attacked both their very substance and their mutual relationship. It reduced gifted and autonomous people, skillfully working in their own country, to nuts and bolts of some monstrously huge, noisy, and stinking machine, whose real meaning is not clear to anyone.

Source: *Washington Post*, Feb. 22, 1990, p. 28d.

Václav Havel, Speech to Congress, February 21, 1990

For this reason, the salvation of this human world lies nowhere else than in the human heart, in the human power to reflect, in human meekness and in human responsibility.

Without a global revolution in the sphere of human consciousness, nothing will change for the better in the sphere of our being as humans, and the catastrophe toward which this world is headed—be it ecological, social, demographic or a general breakdown of civilization—will be unavoidable. . . .

We are still a long way from that "family of man." In fact, we seem to be receding from the ideal rather than growing closer to it. Interests of all kinds—personal, selfish, state, nation, group, and if you like, company interests—still considerably outweigh genuinely common and global interests. We are still under the sway of the destructive and vain belief that man is the pinnacle of creation and not just a part of it and that therefore everything is permitted. . . .

In other words, we still don't know how to put morality ahead of politics, science and economics. We are still incapable of understanding that the only genuine backbone of all our actions, if they are to be moral, is responsibility.

Responsibility to something higher than my family, my country, my company, my success—responsibility to the order of being where all our actions are indelibly recorded and where and only where they will be properly judged.

The interpreter or mediator between us and this higher authority is what is traditionally referred to as human conscience.

 How different is Havel's view of politics from the views of mainstream politicians? What broader forces working in modern European society do you believe shaped Havel's thinking? How can Havel's view of our common humanity and responsibility to conscience help revitalize Western civilization?

---

which had troubled these areas before World War II and had been forcibly submerged under Communist rule, reemerged with a vengeance. Finally, the rapid conversion to market economies also proved painful. Decades of lackluster investment in new technologies left most Eastern European countries ill-equipped to compete in a global market economy. The adoption of "shock-therapy" austerity measures led to much suffering. Unemployment, for example, climbed above 13 percent in Poland in 1992.

Nevertheless, by the beginning of the twenty-first century, many of these states, especially Poland and the Czech Republic, were making a successful transition to both free markets and democracy. In Poland, Aleksander Kwaśniewski (kwahsh-NYEF-skee) (b. 1954), although a former Communist, was elected president in November 1995 and pushed Poland toward an increasingly prosperous free market economy. His successor, Lech Kaczyński (LEK kuh-ZIN-skee) (1949–2010), emphasized the need to combine modernization with tradition. In July 2010, Bronisław Komorowski (brah-NEE-swahf koh-mor-RAHV-skee) (b. 1952) was elected president to succeed Kaczyński, who had died in a plane crash in April. In 2015, Komorowski lost the presidential election by a narrow margin to Andrezej Duda, who vows to reject the European Union's proposal of compulsory migrant quotas (see "Migration Crisis" later in this chapter). In Czechoslovakia, the shift to non-Communist rule was complicated by old problems, especially ethnic issues. Czechs and Slovaks disagreed over the makeup of the new state but were able to agree to a peaceful division of the country. On January 1, 1993, Czechoslovakia split into the Czech Republic and Slovakia. Václav Havel was elected the first president of the new

And the Wall Came Tumbling Down. The Berlin Wall, long a symbol of Europe's Cold War divisions, became the site of massive celebrations after the East German government opened its border with the West. On November 11, East German border guards demolished a section of the wall to create a new crossing point. As seen in this photograph, West Germans celebrated the opening of the new crossing point.

Czech Republic. In Romania Traian Băsescu (tri-YAHN buh-SES-koo) (b. 1951) was elected president of Romania in 2004 and remained in office until 2014 despite impeachment charges for political corruption. In 2014, a former physics teacher and mayor, Klaus Iohannis (b. 1959) was elected to office on the promise of ending corruption and adhering to pro-Western policies.

The revival of the post–Cold War Eastern European states is evident in their desire to join NATO and the European Union (EU), the two major Cold War institutions of Western European unity. In 1997, Poland, the Czech Republic, and Hungary became members of NATO. In 2004, ten nations—including Hungary, Poland, the Czech Republic, Slovenia, Estonia, Latvia, and Lithuania—joined the EU, Romania and Bulgaria joined in 2007, and Croatia joined in 2013.

Yet not all are convinced that inclusion in European integration is a good thing. Eastern Europeans fear that their countries will be dominated by investment from their prosperous neighbors, while their counterparts in Western Europe are concerned about a possible influx of low-wage workers from the new member countries. The global financial crisis that began in 2008 also added to the economic problems of Eastern European countries.

The Reunification of Germany

Perhaps the most dramatic events took place in East Germany, where a persistent economic slump and the ongoing oppressiveness of the regime of Erich Honecker led to a flight of refugees and mass demonstrations against the regime in the summer and fall of 1989. After more than half a million people flooded the streets of East Berlin on November 4, shouting, "The wall must go!" the German Communist government soon capitulated to popular pressure and on November 9 opened the entire border with the West. Hundreds of thousands of Germans swarmed across the border, mostly to visit and return. The Berlin Wall, long a symbol of the Cold War, became the site of massive celebrations as thousands of people used sledgehammers to tear it down. By December, new political parties had emerged, and on March 18, 1990, in East Germany's first free elections ever, the Christian Democrats won almost 50 percent of the vote. After months of political negotiations between West and East German officials as well as the original four postwar occupying powers (the United States, Great Britain, France, and the Soviet Union), political reunification was achieved on October 3, 1990. What had seemed almost impossible at the beginning of 1989 had become a reality by the end of 1990.

The Disintegration of Yugoslavia

From its beginning in 1919, Yugoslavia had been an artificial creation. The peace treaties at the end of World War I combined Serbs, Croats, and Slovenes into a new south Slav state called Yugoslavia (known until 1929 as the Kingdom of the Serbs, Croats, and Slovenes). After World War II, the dictatorial Marshal Tito had managed to hold the six republics and two autonomous provinces that constituted Yugoslavia together. After his

	1989
Collapse of Communist government in Czechoslovakia	December
Collapse of East German government	December
Execution of Ceauşescu in Romania	December 25
	1990
Lithuania declares independence	March 11
East German elections—victory of Christian Democrats	March 18
Reunification of Germany	October 3
Wałęsa becomes president of Poland	December
	1991
Yeltsin becomes president of Russia	June
Slovenia and Croatia declare independence	June
Right-wing coup in the Soviet Union	August 19
Dissolution of the Soviet Union	December

death in 1980, no strong leader emerged, and his responsibilities passed to a collective state presidency and the League of Communists of Yugoslavia. At the end of the 1980s, Yugoslavia was caught up in the reform movements sweeping through Eastern Europe. The League of Communists collapsed, and new parties quickly emerged.

In 1990, the republics of Slovenia, Croatia, Bosnia-Herzegovina, and Macedonia began to lobby for a new federal structure of Yugoslavia that would fulfill their separatist desires. Slobodan Milošević (sluh-BOH-dahn mi-LOH-suh-vich) (1941–2006), who had become the leader of the Serbian Communist Party in 1987 and had managed to stay in power by emphasizing his Serbian nationalism, rejected these efforts. He asserted that these republics could be independent only if new border arrangements were made to accommodate the Serb minorities in those republics who did not want to live outside the boundaries of a Greater Serbian state. Serbs constituted 11.6 percent of Croatia's population and 32 percent of Bosnia-Herzegovina's in 1991.

After negotiations among the six republics failed, Slovenia and Croatia declared their independence in June 1991. Milošević's government sent the Yugoslavian army, which it controlled, into Slovenia, without much success. In September 1991, it began a full assault against Croatia. Increasingly, the Yugoslavian army was becoming the Serbian army, while Serbian irregular forces played a growing role in military operations. Before a cease-fire was arranged, the Serbian forces had captured one-third of Croatia's territory in brutal and destructive fighting.

THE WAR IN BOSNIA The recognition of independent Bosnia-Herzegovina, Slovenia, and Croatia by many European states and the United States early in 1992 did not stop the Serbs from turning their guns on Bosnia. By mid-1993, Serbian forces had acquired 70 percent of Bosnian territory (see the box on p. 929). The Serbian policy of **ethnic cleansing**—killing or forcibly removing Bosnian Muslims from their lands—revived memories of Nazi atrocities during World War II. This account by one Muslim survivor from the town of Srebrenica (sreb-bruh-NEET-suh) is eerily reminiscent of the activities of the Nazi *Einsatzgruppen* (see Chapter 27):

> When the truck stopped, they told us to get off in groups of five. We immediately heard shooting next to the trucks. . . . About ten Serbs with automatic rifles told us to lie down on the ground face first. As we were getting down, they started to shoot, and I fell into a pile of corpses. I felt hot liquid running down my face. I realized that I was only grazed. As they continued to shoot more groups, I kept on squeezing myself in between dead bodies.[3]

Almost 8,000 men and boys were killed in the Serbian massacre at Srebrenica. Nevertheless, despite worldwide outrage, European governments failed to take a decisive and forceful stand against these Serbian activities. By 1995, some 250,000 Bosnians (mostly civilians) had been killed, and 2 million others were left homeless.

Renewed offensives by mostly Muslim Bosnian government army forces and by the Croatian army regained considerable territory that had been lost to Serbian forces. Air strikes by NATO bombers, strongly advocated by U.S. president Bill Clinton, were launched in retaliation for Serb attacks on civilians and weakened the Serb military positions. All sides were now encouraged by the United States to end the war and met in Dayton, Ohio, in November 1995 for negotiations. A formal peace treaty was signed in Paris on December 14 that split Bosnia into a loose union of a Serb republic (with 49 percent of the land) and a Muslim-Croat federation (with 51 percent of the land) (see Map 30.2).

THE WAR IN KOSOVO Peace in Bosnia, however, did not bring peace to the remnants of Yugoslavia. A new war erupted in 1999 over Kosovo, which had been made an autonomous province within Yugoslavia in 1974. Kosovo's inhabitants were mainly ethnic Albanians who were allowed to keep their Albanian language. But Kosovo also had a Serbian minority who considered Kosovo sacred territory because it contained the site where the Ottoman Turks had defeated Serbian forces in the fourteenth century in a battle that became a defining moment in Serbian history (see Chapter 12).

In 1989, Yugoslav president Milošević, who had become an ardent Serbian nationalist, stripped Kosovo of its autonomous status and outlawed any official use of the Albanian language. In 1993, some groups of ethnic Albanians founded the Kosovo Liberation Army (KLA) and began a campaign against Serbian rule in Kosovo. When Serb forces began to massacre ethnic Albanians in an effort to crush the KLA, the United States and its NATO allies sought to arrange a settlement. After months of negotiations, the Kosovo Albanians agreed to a peace plan that would have given the ethnic Albanians in Kosovo broad autonomy for a three-year interim period. When Milošević refused to sign the agreement, the United States and its NATO allies began

A CHILD'S ACCOUNT OF THE SHELLING OF SARAJEVO

WHEN BOSNIA DECLARED ITS INDEPENDENCE in March 1992, Serbian army units and groups of Bosnian Serbs went on the offensive and began to shell the capital city of Sarajevo. One of its residents was Zlata Filipović (ZLAH-tuh fil-ih-POH-vich), the ten-year-old daughter of a middle-class lawyer. Zlata was a fan of MTV and pizza, but when the Serbs began to shell Sarajevo from the hills above the city, her life changed dramatically, as is apparent in this excerpt from her diary.

Zlata Filipović, *Zlata's Diary: A Child's Life in Sarajevo*

April 3, 1992. Daddy came back . . . all upset. He says there are terrible crowds at the train and bus stations. People are leaving Sarajevo.

April 4, 1992. There aren't many people in the streets. I guess it's fear of the stories about Sarajevo being bombed. But there's no bombing. . . .

April 5, 1992. I'm trying hard to concentrate so I can do my homework (reading), but I simply can't. Something is going on in town. You can hear gunfire from the hills.

April 6, 1992. Now they're shooting from the Holiday Inn, killing people in front of the parliament. . . . Maybe we'll go to the cellar. . . .

April 9, 1992. I'm not going to school. All the schools in Sarajevo are closed. . . .

April 14, 1992. People are leaving Sarajevo. The airport, train and bus stations are packed. . . .

April 18, 1992. There's shooting, shells are falling. This really is WAR. Mommy and Daddy are worried, they sit up late at night, talking. They're wondering what to do, but it's hard to know. . . . Mommy can't make up her mind—she's constantly in tears. She tries to hide it from me, but I see everything.

April 21, 1992. It's horrible in Sarajevo today. Shells falling, people and children getting killed, shooting. We will probably spend the night in the cellar.

April 26, 1992. We spent Thursday night with the Bobars again. The next day we had no electricity. We had no bread, so for the first time in her life Mommy baked some.

April 28, 1992. SNIFFLE! Everybody has gone. I'm left with no friends.

April 29, 1992. I'd write to you much more about the war if only I could. But I simply don't want to remember all these horrible things.

 How do you think Zlata Filipović was able to deal with the new conditions in her life?

Source: Zlata Filipović, *Ziata's Diary: A Child's Life in Sarajevo* (1994), by Fixot et editions Robert Laffont.

---

a bombing campaign that forced the Yugoslavian government into compliance.

THE AFTERMATH By 2000, the Serbian people had finally tired of the violence and in the fall elections ousted Milošević from power. The new Serbian government under Vojislav Koštunica (VOY-slahv kawh-STOO-neet-suh) (b. 1944) moved quickly to cooperate with the international community and begin rebuilding the Serbian economy. On June 28, 2001, the Serbian government agreed to allow Milošević to be put on trial by an international tribunal for crimes against humanity for his ethnic cleansing policies throughout Yugoslavia's disintegration. He died in prison in 2006 before his trial could be completed.

The fate of Bosnia and Kosovo has not yet been finally determined. Troops from the European Union remain in Bosnia to keep the peace between the Serb republic and the Muslim-Croat federation. More than thirty international organizations are at work rebuilding schools, roads, and sewers, but only the presence of EU troops keeps old hatreds from erupting again.

In Kosovo, NATO military forces were brought in to maintain an uneasy peace, while United Nations officials worked to create democratic institutions and the European Union provided funds for rebuilding the region's infrastructure. These efforts are ongoing but are complicated by the festering hatred between Kosovo Albanians and the remaining Serbs.

The last political vestiges of Yugoslavia ceased to exist in 2004 when the Koštunica government officially renamed the truncated country Serbia and Montenegro. Two years later, Montenegrins voted in favor of independence, and in 2008, Kosovo declared its independence as well. Thus, ninety years after Yugoslavia was cobbled together, all six of its constituent republics (Slovenia, Croatia, Bosnia-Herzegovina, Serbia, Macedonia, and Montenegro) were once again independent nations, and a new one (Kosovo) had been born.

Western Europe and the Search for Unity

After the revolutions of 1989, Western Europe faced new political possibilities and challenges. Germany was once again united, delighting the Germans but frightening their neighbors. At the same time, new opportunities for thinking of all of Europe as a political entity also emerged. Eastern Europe was no longer cut off from Western Europe by the Iron Curtain of the Cold War.

GERMANY RESTORED With the end of the Cold War, West Germany faced a new challenge. Chancellor Helmut Kohl had benefited greatly from an economic boom in the mid-1980s. Gradually, however, discontent with the Christian Democrats increased, and by 1988, their political prospects seemed diminished. But unexpectedly, the 1989 revolution in East Germany led to the reunification of the two Germanies, leaving the

 MAP 30.2 **The Lands of the Former Yugoslavia, 1995.** By 1991, resurgent nationalism and the wave of independence sweeping across Europe overcame the forces that held Yugoslavia together. Declarations of independence by Slovenia, Croatia, and Bosnia-Herzegovina led to war with the Serbian-dominated rump Yugoslavia of Slobodan Milošević.

What aspects of Slovenia's location help explain why its war of liberation was briefer and less bloody than others in the former Yugoslavia?

new Germany, with its 79 million people, the leading power in Europe. Reunification, which was accomplished during Kohl's administration and owed much to his efforts, brought rich political dividends to the Christian Democrats.

But the excitement over reunification soon dissipated as new problems arose. All too soon, the realization set in that the revitalization of eastern Germany would take far more money than was originally thought, and Kohl's government was soon forced to face the politically undesirable task of raising taxes substantially. Moreover, the virtual collapse of the economy in eastern Germany led to extremely high levels of unemployment and severe discontent.

East Germans were also haunted by another memory from their recent past. The opening of the files of the secret police (the Stasi) showed that millions of East Germans had spied on their neighbors and colleagues, and even their spouses and parents, during the Communist era (see "Film & History" on this page). A few senior Stasi officials were put on trial for their past actions, but many Germans preferred simply to close the door on an unhappy period in their lives.

As the century neared its close, then, Germans struggled to cope with the challenge of building a new, united nation. In 1998, voters took out their frustrations at the ballot box. Helmut Kohl's conservative coalition was defeated in new elections, and a new prime minister, Social Democrat Gerhard Schröder (GAYR-hahrt SHRUR-duh) (b. 1944), came into office.

 FILM & HISTORY

Watch *Das Leben der Anderen* (The Lives of Others) (2006), a German film that recreates the depressing debilitation of East German society under its Communist regime and especially the Stasi, the secret police. The film chronicles the life of an East German writer who is spied on in an operation led by a police captain who over time becomes more sympathetic to the writer and hides the author's identity from the East German secret police (Stasi). The film brilliantly captures the stifling atmosphere of East Germany under Communist rule.

How does the film capture the drab environment of East Germany? Why do you think East Germans chose to forget the Stasi past?

But Schröder had little success at solving Germany's economic woes, and as a result of elections in 2005, Angela Merkel (AHNG-uh-luh MERK-uhl) (b. 1954), leader of the Christian Democrats, became the first female chancellor in German history. Merkel pursued health care reform and new energy policies at home while playing a leading role in the affairs of the

European Union. After new elections in 2009, she began a second term as Germany's chancellor and has led the EU nations in attempting to solve the financial problems of several EU members including Greece, Italy, Spain, and Portugal. Merkel came under heavy criticism for her acceptance of thousands of Syrian refugees as part of Europe's migration crisis (see "Migration Crisis" later in this chapter).

POST-THATCHER BRITAIN While Margaret Thatcher dominated British politics in the 1980s, the Labour Party, beset by divisions between its moderate and radical wings, offered little effective opposition. Only in 1990 did Labour's fortunes seem to revive when Thatcher's government attempted to replace local property taxes with a flat-rate tax that would enable the rich to pay the same rate as the poor. In 1990, after anti-tax riots broke out, Thatcher's once remarkable popularity fell to an all-time low. At the end of November, a revolt within her own party caused Thatcher to resign as Britain's longest-serving prime minister. She was replaced by John Major, whose Conservative Party won a narrow victory in the general elections held in April 1992. His government, however, failed to capture the imagination of most Britons.

In new elections on May 1, 1997, the Labour Party won a landslide victory. The new prime minister, Tony Blair (b. 1953), was a moderate whose youthful energy immediately instilled new vigor into the political scene. Adopting centrist policies, his party dominated the political arena into the new century. Blair was one of the prominent leaders in forming an international coalition against terrorism after the terrorist attack on the United States in 2001. Three years later, however, his support of the U.S. war in Iraq, when a majority of Britons opposed it, caused his popularity to plummet, although the failure of the Conservative Party to field a popular candidate kept him in power until the summer of 2007, when he stepped down and allowed the new Labour leader Gordon Brown (b. 1951) to become prime minister. Elections held in early May 2010 were inconclusive: the Conservatives won the largest number of seats in Parliament but were twenty short of a majority. When Brown resigned a few days after the elections, Conservative David Cameron (b. 1966) became prime minister on the basis of a coalition with the Liberal Democrats.

The Conservatives have passed several significant legislative acts since 2010, reforming Britain's welfare state by reducing the space allocated to those on public assistance and partially privatizing the National Health Services. Cameron has defied Conservatives by supporting same sex marriage in passing the Marriage (Same Sex Couples) Act in 2013. Cameron led the Conservatives to a second victory in 2015.

FRANCE: RIGHT AND LEFT Although François Mitterrand was able to win a second term as president in 1988, France's economic decline continued. In 1993, French unemployment stood at 10.6 percent, and in the elections in March of that year, the Socialists won only 28 percent of the vote as a coalition of conservative parties gained 80 percent of the seats in the National Assembly. The move to the right in France was strengthened when the conservative mayor of Paris, Jacques

Chirac (ZHAHK shee-RAK) (b. 1932), was elected president in 1995 and reelected in 2002.

By 1995, resentment against foreign-born residents had become a growing political reality. Spurred by rising rates of unemployment and large numbers of immigrants from North Africa (often identified in the public mind with terrorist actions committed by militant groups based in the Middle East), many French voters advocated restrictions on all new immigration. Chirac himself pursued a plan of sending illegal immigrants back to their home countries.

In the fall of 2005, however, anti-foreign sentiment provoked a backlash of its own, as young Muslims in the crowded suburbs of Paris rioted against dismal living conditions and the lack of employment opportunities for foreign residents in France. After the riots subsided, government officials promised to adopt measures to respond to the complaints, but tensions between the Muslim community and the remainder of the French population have become a chronic source of social unrest throughout the country—an unrest that Nicolas Sarkozy (nee-kohl-AH sar-koh-ZEE) (b. 1955), elected as president in 2007, promised to address but without much success. Sarkozy's administration passed tax cuts that favored the wealthy, increased the retirement age for state workers, and altered the thirty-five-hour work week by providing tax breaks to those who worked overtime. The unpopular measures led to mass strikes from the oil and railroad industries, causing transportation disruptions.

As France's economic troubles deepened, France elected Socialist Party leader François Hollande (frahn-SWAH oh-LAHN) (b. 1954) as president in 2012. Hollande promised to revoke Sarkozy's tax breaks for the wealthy, return the retirement age to sixty-five, create 60,000 more teaching positions, and raise taxes on corporations and banks. Hollande's support for the closure of failing factories led to workers' protests. Hollande's approval rating stood at 12 percent in late 2014, but his handling of two separate terrorist attacks in Paris in January and November of 2015 (see "Terrorism as Global War" later in this chapter) raised his approval to 40 percent.

CORRUPTION IN ITALY Corruption has continued to trouble Italian politics. In 1993, hundreds of politicians and business leaders were under investigation for their involvement in a widespread scheme to use political bribes to secure public contracts. Public disgust with political corruption became so intense that in April 1996, Italian voters took the unusual step of giving control of the government to a center-left coalition that included the Communists. In recent years, Silvio Berlusconi (SEEL-vee-oh bayr-loo-SKOH-nee) (b. 1936), owner of a media empire, has dominated Italian politics, even though he became a politician primarily in order to protect his own business interests. Although he lost to Socialist Romano Prodi (roh-MAH-noh PROH-dee) (b. 1939) in a close election in 2006, Berlusconi again became prime minister after new elections in 2008, only to resign in 2011. In the wake of the European economic crises, Italy faced severe economic shortfalls and chose an economist, Mario Monti (MAHR-yoh MAWN-tee) (b. 1943), to replace Berlusconi. Monti passed new legislation that raised the retirement age, increased property taxes, and simplified the

CHRONOLOGY	Western Europe Since 1985	
First all-German federal election		1990
Victory of Conservative Party under John Major in Britain		1992
Conservative victory in France		1993
Creation of European Union		1994
Jacques Chirac becomes president of France		1995
Election of Tony Blair in Britain		1997
Gerhard Schröder becomes chancellor of Germany		1998
Angela Merkel becomes chancellor of Germany		2005
Romano Prodi becomes prime minister of Italy		2006
Election of Nicolas Sarkozy in France		2007
David Cameron becomes prime minister of Britain		2010
Mario Monti becomes prime minister of Italy		2011
Election of François Hollande in France		2012
Matteo Renzi becomes prime minister of Italy		2014

tax code. His efforts at reform proved socially and politically unpopular, however, and he resigned as prime minister at the end of 2012. In 2014, Matteo Renzi (b. 1975), the leftist Democratic Party leader, became the youngest prime minister in Italian history. Renzi's government has acted quickly to change Italy's political corruption, while passing a series of economic reforms in an attempt to boost economic growth.

The Unification of Europe

With the addition of Austria, Finland, and Sweden in 1995, the European Community (EC) had grown to fifteen members. The EC was primarily an economic union, not a political one. By 2000, it contained 370 million people and constituted the world's largest single trading entity, transacting one-fourth of the world's commerce. In 1985, an agreement eliminated border checks for members and later created a common visa policy. In 1986, the EC had created the Single Europe Act, which had opened the door by 1992 to a truly united internal market, thereby eliminating all barriers to the exchange of people, goods, services, and capital. This was followed by a proposal for a monetary union and a common currency. The Treaty on European Union (also called the Maastricht Treaty after the city in the Netherlands where the agreement was reached) represented an attempt to create a true economic and monetary union of all EC members. On January 1, 1994, the EC renamed itself the European Union (EU). One of its first goals was to introduce a common currency, called the euro, adopted by twelve EU nations early in 1999. On June 1, 1999, a European Central Bank was created, and as of January 2013, the euro had officially replaced seventeen national currencies. The euro serves approximately 327 million people and has become the world's second largest reserve currency after the U.S. dollar.

A major crisis for the euro emerged in 2010 when the financial crises exposed the high public debt of Greece and other southern Eurozone countries. The uncertain consequences of a Greek default led other EU members, especially Germany, to put together a financial rescue plan (see "The End of Excess" later in this chapter). Subsequently, other countries in the eurozone, including Italy, Spain, Portugal, and Cyprus, also experienced financial problems.

GOALS In addition to having a single internal market for its members and a common currency, the European Union also established a common agricultural policy, under which subsidies are provided to farmers to enable them to sell their goods competitively on the world market. The policy also provides aid to the EU's poorest regions as well as subsidies for job training, education, and modernization. The end of national passports gave millions of Europeans greater flexibility in travel.

The EU has been less successful in setting common foreign policy goals, primarily because individual nations still see foreign policy as a national prerogative and are reluctant to give it up to an overriding institution. Nevertheless, the EU did create a military force of 60,000, to be used chiefly for humanitarian and peacekeeping purposes. Indeed, the focus of the EU is on peaceful conflict resolution, not making war.

In 2009, the EU ratified the Lisbon Treaty, which created a full-time presidential post and a new voting system that reflects the size of each country's population. It also provided more power for the European Parliament in an effort to promote the EU's foreign policy goals.

PROBLEMS As successful as the European Union has been, problems still exist. Europeans are often divided on the EU. Some oppose it because the official representatives of the EU are not democratically accountable to the people. Moreover, many Europeans do not regard themselves as "Europeans" but remain committed to a national identity. The European economic crisis has also exposed the weakness of the EU. The adoption of the euro removed trade barriers, but the countries that use the euro do not have a unified monetary policy. The European Central Bank does not serve all nations equally, as the Governing Council and the Executive Board make decisions communally, and members tend to vote in favor of national interests instead of pro-European interests. Europeans will need to unify politically to solve their economic problems. The Paris terrorist attacks in 2015 and the migration crisis have also led to disputes over the European Union's open border policy. A number of member countries introduced temporary border controls in 2016. Despite these problems, a majority—although not a large one—of the members remain committed to the EU.

TOWARD A UNITED EUROPE At the beginning of the twenty-first century, the EU established a new goal: to incorporate into the union the states of eastern and southeastern Europe. Many of these states are considerably poorer than the older members, which raised the possibility that adding these nations might weaken the EU itself. To lessen the danger, EU members

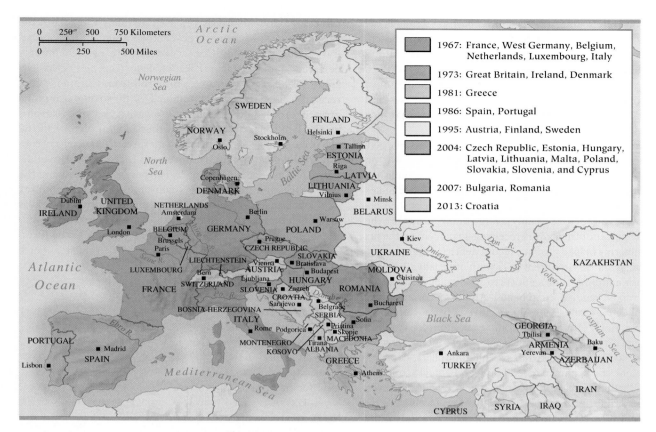

	1967: France, West Germany, Belgium, Netherlands, Luxembourg, Italy
	1973: Great Britain, Ireland, Denmark
	1981: Greece
	1986: Spain, Portugal
	1995: Austria, Finland, Sweden
	2004: Czech Republic, Estonia, Hungary, Latvia, Lithuania, Malta, Poland, Slovakia, Slovenia, and Cyprus
	2007: Bulgaria, Romania
	2013: Croatia

MAP 30.3 European Union, 2013. Beginning in 1967 as the European Economic Community, also known as the Common Market, the union of European states seeking to integrate their economies has gradually grown from six members to twenty-eight in 2013. By 2002, the European Union had achieved two major goals—the creation of a single internal market and a common currency—although it has been less successful at working toward common political and foreign policy goals.

 What additional nations do you think will eventually join the European Union?

established a set of qualifications that require a candidate for membership to demonstrate a commitment both to market capitalism and to democracy, including not only the rule of law but also respect for minorities and human rights. Hence, joining the EU might well add to the stability of these nations and transform the dream of a united Europe into a reality. In May 2004, the EU took the plunge and added ten new members: Cyprus, the Czech Republic, Estonia, Hungary, Latvia, Lithuania, Malta, Poland, Slovakia, and Slovenia. Their addition enlarged the population of the EU to 455 million people. In January 2007, the EU expanded again as Bulgaria and Romania joined the union, and in July 2013, Croatia joined (see Map 30.3).

The United States: Move to the Center

After twelve years of Republican administrations, the Democratic Party captured the U.S. presidency in the elections in November 1992. The inability of George H. W. Bush (b. 1924), Ronald Reagan's successor, to deal with the deficit problem, as

well as an economic downturn, enabled Democrat Bill Clinton (b. 1946) to become president. The new president was a southerner who claimed to be a "new Democrat"—one who favored fiscal responsibility and a more conservative social agenda—a clear indication that the rightward drift in American politics had not been reversed by his victory. During his first term in office, Clinton reduced the budget deficit and signed a bill turning the welfare program back to the states while pushing measures to provide job opportunities for those Americans removed from the welfare rolls. By seizing the center of the American political agenda, Clinton was able to win reelection in 1996, although the Republican Party now held a majority in both houses of Congress.

Clinton's political fortunes were helped considerably by a lengthy economic revival. At the same time, a steady reduction in the annual government budget deficit strengthened confidence in the performance of the national economy. Much of Clinton's second term, however, was overshadowed by charges of presidential misconduct stemming from the president's affair with a White House intern. After a bitter partisan struggle, the U.S. Senate acquitted the president on two articles of impeachment brought by the House of Representatives. But Clinton's problems helped the Republican candidate, George W. Bush (b. 1946), win the presidential election in 2000. Although Bush lost the popular vote to Al Gore, he narrowly won the electoral vote after a highly controversial victory in the state of Florida decided ultimately by the U.S. Supreme Court.

The first four years of Bush's administration were largely occupied with the war on terrorism and the U.S.-led war on Iraq. The Department of Homeland Security was established after the 2001 terrorist assaults to help protect the United States from future terrorist acts. At the same time, Bush pushed tax cuts through Congress that mainly favored the wealthy, with the richest one percent of taxpayers receiving 40 percent of the tax cuts. The tax cuts helped produce record deficits reminiscent of the Reagan years. Environmentalists were especially disturbed by the Bush administration's efforts to weaken environmental laws and impose regulations to benefit American corporations. In November 2004, after a highly negative political campaign, Bush was narrowly elected to a second term. From 2005 to 2007, Bush's popularity plummeted drastically as discontent grew. By 2005, the Iraq War had cost over 250 billion dollars, consuming 10 percent of the annual federal budget. High U.S. military casualties further enraged the public over the war. However, it was the administration's poor handling of relief efforts after Hurricane Katrina in 2005 that proved most devastating for the Bush administration.

The many failures of the Bush administration led to the lowest approval ratings for a modern president and opened the door for a dramatic change in American politics. The new and often inspiring voice of Barack Obama (b. 1961), who campaigned on a platform of change "we can believe in" and ending the war in Iraq, resulted in an overwhelming Democratic victory in the elections of 2008. The Democrats were also aided by the dramatic collapse of the American financial system in the fall of 2008. Obama moved quickly in 2009 to deal with the worst economic recession since the Great Depression. Obama also persuaded Congress to pass a sweeping health care bill to provide most Americans with medical insurance and to enact legislation aimed at regulating the financial institutions that caused the financial crisis. Obama initiated reforms on climate change and the education system. He was reelected for a second term in the fall of 2012, a term that began in the wake of a terrible gun tragedy—the massacre of twenty-six children and adults in Newtown, Connecticut. Deaths from gun violence had risen to 30,000 a year. Obama's first initiative during his second term was legislation banning assault weapons and expanding background checks, but the legislation was rejected by the Senate. During the next four years the United States faced a series of social crises from gun violence and police crimes against young African Americans.

Contemporary Canada

The government of Brian Mulroney, who came to power in 1984, sought greater privatization of Canada's state-run corporations and negotiated a free trade agreement with the United States. Bitterly resented by many Canadians, the agreement cost Mulroney's government much of its popularity. In 1993, the ruling Conservatives were overwhelmingly defeated, and the Liberal leader, Jean Chrétien (ZHAHNH kray-TEN) (b. 1934), became prime minister. Chrétien's conservative fiscal policies, combined with strong economic growth, enabled his government to have a budgetary surplus by the late 1990s and led to another Liberal victory in the elections of 1997. Charges of widespread financial corruption in the government, however, led to a Conservative victory early in 2006, and Stephen Harper (b. 1959) became the new prime minister. Harper's conservative policies and tax cuts left Canada with an increased deficit, although it was his unwillingness to communicate with the press that led to a resounding victory of the Liberal Party in 2015 led by Justin Trudeau (b. 1971), the son of former prime minister Pierre Trudeau.

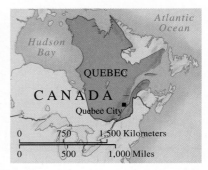

Mulroney's government had been unable to settle the ongoing crisis over the French-speaking province of Quebec. In the late 1960s, the Parti Québécois (par-TEE kay-bek-KWA), headed by René Lévesque (ruh-NAY luh-VEK), ran on a platform of Quebec's secession from

Quebec

the Canadian union. To pursue their dream of separation, some underground separatist groups even resorted to terrorist bombings. In 1976, the Parti Québécois won Quebec's provincial elections and in 1980 called for a referendum that would enable the provincial government to negotiate Quebec's independence from the rest of Canada. Quebec voters narrowly rejected the plan in 1995, however, and debate over the province's status continues to divide Canada.

After the Cold War: New World Order or Age of Terrorism?

 FOCUS QUESTIONS: How and why did the Cold War end? What are the main issues in the struggle with terrorism?

Even before the collapse of the Soviet Union, there had been tantalizing signs of a thaw in the Cold War. China and the United States had decided in 1979 to establish mutual diplomatic relations, a consequence of Beijing's decision to focus on domestic reform and stop supporting wars of national liberation in Asia. Six years later, the ascent of Mikhail Gorbachev to leadership, culminating in the demise of the Soviet Union in 1991, brought a final end to almost half a century of bitter rivalry between the world's two superpowers.

The End of the Cold War

The accession of Mikhail Gorbachev to power in the Soviet Union in 1985 eventually brought a dramatic end to the Cold War. Gorbachev was willing to rethink many of the fundamental assumptions underlying Soviet foreign policy, and his "New Thinking," as it was called, opened the door to a series of stunning changes. For one, Gorbachev initiated a plan for arms limitation that led in 1987 to an agreement with the United States to eliminate intermediate-range nuclear weapons (the INF Treaty). Both sides had incentives to dampen the expensive arms race. Gorbachev hoped to make extensive economic and internal reforms, and the United States had serious deficit problems. During the Reagan years, the United States had moved from being a creditor nation to being the world's biggest debtor nation. By 1990, both countries were becoming aware that their large military budgets made it difficult for them to solve their serious social problems.

The years 1989 and 1990 were a crucial period in the ending of the Cold War. As described earlier, the postwar settlements came unstuck as a mostly peaceful revolutionary upheaval swept through Eastern Europe. Gorbachev's policy of allowing greater autonomy for the Communist regimes of Eastern Europe meant that the Soviet Union would no longer militarily support Communist governments that faced internal revolt. The unwillingness of the Soviet regime to use force to maintain the status quo, as it had in Hungary in 1956 and in Czechoslovakia in 1968, opened the door to the overthrow of the Communist regimes. The reunification of Germany on October 3, 1990, marked the end of one of the most prominent legacies of the Cold War.

The Persian Gulf War provided the first major opportunity for testing the new relationship between the United States and the Soviet Union in the post–Cold War era. In early August 1990, Iraqi military forces suddenly occupied the small neighboring country of Kuwait, in the northeastern corner of the Arabian peninsula at the head of the Persian Gulf. The Iraqi invasion of Kuwait sparked an international outcry, and an international force led by the United States liberated Kuwait and destroyed a substantial part of Iraq's armed forces in the early months of 1991. The Gulf War was the first important military conflict in the post–Cold War period. Although Gorbachev tried to persuade Iraq to withdraw its forces from Kuwait before the war began, overall the Soviets played a minor role in the crisis and supported the American action. By the end of 1991, the Soviet Union had disintegrated, making any renewal of global rivalry between the superpowers impossible and leaving the United States as the world's leading military power. With the end of superpower rivalry and the collapse of the Soviet Union in 1991, attention focused on the new post–Cold War era. Many observers were optimistic. U.S. president George H. W. Bush looked forward to a new era of peace and international cooperation that he called the "new world order." Others predicted the beginning of a new "American century," characterized by the victory of liberal democratic values and free market capitalism.

But the voices of optimism began to fade as it became clear that forces were now being released that had long been held in check by the ideological rigidities of the Cold War. The age of conflict that had long characterized the twentieth century had not ended but was simply taking a different form.

This was soon apparent around the world. In Southeast Asia, even before the end of the Cold War, former allies in China, Vietnam, and Cambodia turned on each other in a conflict that joined

Reagan and Gorbachev. The willingness of Mikhail Gorbachev and Ronald Reagan to dampen the arms race was a significant factor in ending the Cold War confrontation between the United States and the Soviet Union. Reagan and Gorbachev are shown here standing before Saint Basil's Cathedral during Reagan's visit to Moscow in 1988.

AP Images/Ira Schwartz

territorial ambitions with deep-seated historical suspicions based on the memory of past conflicts. The pattern was repeated elsewhere: in Africa, where several nations erupted into civil war during the late 1980s and 1990s; in the Balkans, where Yugoslavia broke apart in a bitter conflict not yet completely resolved; and in the Middle East, where disputes in Palestine and the Persian Gulf have grown in strength and erupted into open war.

An Age of Terrorism?

Acts of terror by individuals and groups opposed to governments have become a frightening aspect of modern Western society and indeed of all the world. In 1996, President Clinton called terrorism "the enemy of our generation," and since the end of the Cold War, it has often seemed as though terrorism has replaced communism as the West's number one enemy. Already during the late 1970s and 1980s, concern about terrorism was often at the top of foreign policy agendas in the United States and many European countries. Small bands of terrorists used assassination, the taking of hostages, the hijacking of airplanes, and indiscriminate killing of civilians, especially by bombing, to draw attention to their demands or to destabilize governments in the hope of achieving their political goals. Terrorist acts garnered considerable media attention. When Palestinian terrorists kidnapped and killed eleven Israeli athletes at the Munich Olympic Games in 1972, hundreds of millions of people watched the drama unfold on television.

Motivations for terrorist acts varied considerably. Left- and right-wing terrorist groups flourished in the late 1970s and early 1980s. Left-wing groups, such as the Baader-Meinhof (BAH-durr-MYN-huff) gang (also known as the Red Army Faction) in Germany and the Red Brigades in Italy, consisted chiefly of affluent middle-class young people who denounced the injustices of capitalism and supported acts of revolutionary terrorism in an attempt to bring down the system. Right-wing terrorist groups, such as the New Order in Italy and the Charles Martel Club in France, used bombings to foment disorder and bring about authoritarian regimes. These groups received little or no public support, and authorities succeeded in crushing them fairly quickly.

But terrorist acts also stemmed from militant nationalists who wished to create separatist states. Because they received considerable support from local populations sympathetic to their cause, these terrorist groups could maintain their activities over a long period of time. Most prominent was the Irish Republican Army (IRA), which resorted to vicious attacks against the ruling government and innocent civilians in Northern Ireland. Over a period of twenty years, IRA terrorists were responsible for the deaths of two thousand people in Northern Ireland; three-fourths of the victims were civilians.

Although left- and right-wing terrorist activities declined in Europe in the 1980s, international terrorism remained commonplace. Angered by the loss of their territory to Israel in 1967, some militant Palestinians responded with terrorist attacks against Israel's supporters. Palestinian terrorists operated throughout European countries, attacking both Europeans and American tourists; Palestinian terrorists massacred vacationers at airports in Rome and Vienna in 1985. State-sponsored terrorism was often an integral part of international terrorism. Militant governments, especially in Iran, Libya, and Syria, assisted terrorist organizations that made attacks on Europeans and Americans. On December 21, 1988, Pan American flight 103 from Frankfurt to New York exploded over Lockerbie, Scotland, killing all 258 passengers and crew members. A massive investigation finally revealed that two Libyan terrorists who were connected to terrorist groups based in Iran and Syria planted the bomb responsible for the explosion.

Terrorist Attack on the United States

One of the most destructive acts of terrorism occurred on September 11, 2001, in the United States. Four groups of terrorists hijacked four commercial jet airplanes after takeoff from Boston, Newark, and Washington, D.C. The hijackers flew two of the airplanes directly into the towers of the World Trade Center in New York City, causing these buildings, as well as a number of surrounding buildings, to collapse. A third hijacked plane slammed into the Pentagon near Washington, D.C. The fourth plane, believed to be headed for Washington, crashed instead in an isolated area of Pennsylvania, apparently as the result of an attempt by a group of heroic passengers to overcome the hijackers. In total, nearly three thousand people were killed, including everyone aboard the four airliners.

These coordinated acts of terror were carried out by hijackers connected to an international terrorist organization known

Terrorist Attack on the World Trade Center in New York City. On September 11, 2001, hijackers flew two commercial jetliners into the twin towers of the World Trade Center. The photograph shows the second of the two jetliners about to hit one of the towers while smoke billows from the site of the first attack.

as al-Qaeda ("the Base"), run by Osama bin Laden (1957–2011). A native of Saudi Arabia, bin Laden used an inherited fortune to set up terrorist training camps in Afghanistan, under the protection of the nation's militant fundamentalist Islamic rulers known as the Taliban. Bin Laden recruited Islamic fighters from around the world to join his guerilla forces in Afghanistan. On May 2, 2011, U.S. Navy SEALS killed Bin Laden in the compound where he was living in Abbotabad, Pakistan.

WAR IN AFGHANISTAN U.S. president George W. Bush vowed to wage a lengthy war on terrorism and worked to create a coalition of nations to assist in ridding the world of al-Qaeda and other terrorist groups. In October 2001, United States and NATO air forces began bombing Taliban-controlled command centers, airfields, and al-Qaeda hiding places in Afghanistan. On the ground, Afghan forces opposed to the Taliban, assisted by U.S. special forces, pushed the Taliban out of the capital city of Kabul and seized control of nearly all of the country by the end of November. A multiethnic government was installed but faced problems as a result of renewed Taliban activity after the United States began to focus much of its military attention on the war in Iraq. In 2009, President Obama sent an additional 30,000 troops to deal with the deteriorating situation in Afghanistan. After the death of bin Laden, Obama announced that he would withdraw U.S. troops from Afghanistan beginning in the summer of 2011. By the autumn of 2012, the additional 30,000 troops sent earlier had returned home.

WAR IN IRAQ In 2002, President George W. Bush, charging that Iraqi dictator Saddam Hussein (1937–2006) had not only provided support to bin Laden's terrorist organization but also sought to develop weapons of mass destruction, threatened to invade Iraq and remove him from power. Both claims were widely doubted by other member states at the United Nations. As a result, the United States was forced to attack Iraq with little world support. Moreover, the plan to attack upset many Arab leaders and fanned anti-American sentiment throughout the Muslim world.

In March 2003, a largely American-led army invaded Iraq. The Iraqi army was quickly defeated, and in the months that followed, occupation forces sought to restore stability to the country while setting forth plans to lay the foundations of a future democratic society. But although Saddam Hussein was later captured by U.S. troops, Saddam's supporters, foreign terrorists, and Islamic militants continued to battle the American-led forces.

American efforts focused on training an Iraqi military force capable of defeating the insurgents and establishing an Iraqi government that could hold free elections and create a democracy. Establishing a new government was difficult, however, because of the differences among the three major groups in Iraqi society: Shi'ite Muslims, Sunni Muslims, and ethnic Kurds. Although a new Iraqi government came into being, it had great difficulty establishing a unified state. By 2006, violence had increased dramatically, and Iraq seemed to be descending into a widespread civil war, especially between the Shi'ites, who control southern Iraq, and the Sunnis, who control central Iraq. An increase in American troops in 2007 helped stabilize conditions within a year. The U.S. and Iraqi governments then agreed to a complete withdrawal of American troops by 2011, a goal that was achieved by the Obama administration in December 2011.

The West and Islam

One of the major sources of terrorist activity against the West, especially the United States, has come from some parts of the Muslim world. No doubt, the ongoing Israeli-Palestinian conflict, in which the United States has steadfastly supported Israel, helped give rise to anti-Western and especially anti-U.S. feeling among many Muslims. In 1979, a revolution in Iran that led to the overthrow of the shah and the creation of a new Islamic government led by Ayatollah Khomeini also fed anti-Western sentiment. In the eyes of the ayatollah and his followers, the United States was the "great Satan," the powerful protector of Israel, and the enemy of Muslim peoples everywhere. Furthermore, the United States was blamed for the corruption of Iranian society under the shah.

The involvement of the United States in the liberation of Kuwait in the Persian Gulf War in 1991 also had unexpected consequences in the relationship of Islam and the West. During that war, U.S. forces were stationed in Saudi Arabia, the location of many sacred Islamic sites. The presence of American forces was considered an affront to Islam by anti-Western Islamic groups, especially that of Osama bin Laden and his followers. These anti-Western attitudes came to be shared by a number of radical Islamic groups, as is evident in the 2003 bombing in Madrid and the 2005 bombing on subway trains in London.

The U.S. attack on Iraq in 2003 further inflamed some Islamic groups against the West. Although there was no evidence of a relationship between al-Qaeda terrorists and the regime of Saddam Hussein, the United States used this claim as one of the excuses to launch a preemptive war against Iraq. Although many Iraqis welcomed the overthrow of Saddam, the deaths of innocent civilians and the torturing of prisoners by American soldiers in prisons in Iraq served to deepen anti-American sentiment in the Muslim world (see the box on p. 938).

TERRORISM AS GLOBAL WAR During the 2003 Iraq War, many al-Qaeda fighters left Afghanistan to join in the fight against the U.S. led invasion. A group named al-Qaeda in Iraq (AQI) formed in 2004. After merging with other jihadist Islamic groups, it assumed the name Islamic State of Iraq (ISI). After taking control of territory in Syria in 2013, the group adopted the name Islamic State of Iraq and al-Sham or Syria (ISIS). The United States government and Western media outlets use the acronym ISIL, translating al-Sham as "the Levant," referring to the eastern Mediterranean region that includes Syria, Jordan, Israel, and Lebanon.

In 2014, the group renamed itself the Islamic State after separating from al-Qaeda in 2013 to pursue a more radical agenda. Adherents to this form of Islamic activism are engaged in a *jihad* (holy struggle) against Islam's enemies,

THE WEST AND ISLAM

THE RISE OF LARGE SCALE TERRORIST ACTS, such as the attack in New York on September 11, 2001, or the Paris attack of November 13, 2015, are indicative of a larger issue—the growth of religious extremism in the Muslim world. Religious extremism has long been a part of religious history. In this selection, Abbas Amanat, historian of Middle Eastern history, analyzes the roots of Islamic radicalism, focusing on the resentment many Muslims have against the West.

Abbas Amanat, Empowered Through Violence: The Reinvention of Islamic Extremism

The emergence of the construct we call Islamic extremism, with its penchant for . . . violence, has its roots in the history of the Muslim sense of decline and its unhappy encounter with the dominant West. It is sobering to remind ourselves how frequently the Middle East, as one part of the Muslim world, has been visited by waves of violence in its recent history. Since the end of the Second World War, the area extending from Egypt and Turkey in the west to Afghanistan in the northwest and Yemen in the south has suffered at least ten major wars. . . . Casualties have run into millions. Populations have been uprooted, societies torn up by their roots, political structures demolished—all on a massive scale. . . .

In the minds of many, Western powers shared the blame, both directly and indirectly. Whether based on historical reality or faulty perception, holding the Western powers responsible made special sense against the backdrop of a powerful West and a powerless Middle East. From the days of the European colonial powers in the 19th century to the more recent interventions of the superpowers, there has been a pattern of diplomatic, military and economic presence tying the fate of the Middle East and its resources to the West. . . .

Mistrust toward the West deepened as a result of the problematic way the Middle East improvised its own version of modernity. . . . It is grappling endlessly with failed centralized planning, high birthrates, lopsided distribution of wealth, high unemployment, widespread corruption, inefficient bureaucracies, and environmental and health problems. The frustration endemic among the young urban classes . . . is a response to these conundrums. . . .

In dealing with these restive multitudes, the governments of the Middle East and their associated ruling elites have little to offer. They are themselves part of the problem as they contribute to the public perception of powerlessness. In the period right after World War II, nationalist ideologies were highly effective in mobilizing the public against the European colonial presence. The army officers who came to power in Egypt, Syria, Iraq, and elsewhere . . . invested heavily in anti-Western rhetoric. Yet facing the erosion of their own legitimacy, they learned to pay a lip service to their rising Islamic sentiments in their societies, exploiting them as a cushion between the elite and the masses and to suppress individual freedoms. . . .

The decisive shift came not inside the Arab world but with the 1979 revolution in Iran. The establishment of an Islamic republic under the leadership of the uncompromising Ayatollah Khomeini evoked throughout the Muslim world the long-cherished desire for creating a genuine Islamic regime. . . .

The Iraq-Iran War of 1980–1988 further established the appeal of the paradigm of martyrdom that had long been deeply rooted in Shi'a Islam. That conflict was portrayed as an apocalyptic jihad between the forces of truth and falsehood . . . and the celebration of martyrdom found resonance far and wide. The . . . young Palestinians who eagerly volunteered for suicide bombing on behalf of the Hamas and Islamic Jihad saw martyrdom as a way of empowerment.

 How do Middle Easterners perceive Westerners? Why have their perceptions changed?

Source: Abbas Amanat, "Empowered Through Violence: The Reinvention of Islamic Extremism," in S. Talbott, *The Age of Terror* (New York: Basic Books, 2002).

including fellow Muslims who have abandoned what the extremists view as "true" Islam. ISIL and al-Qaeda are currently competing to be the dominant organization within the modern Islamic jihadist movement. ISIL has garnered worldwide condemnation for its acts of cruelty, mass killings, and enslavement of women.

In November 2015, ISIL carried out a series of coordinated terrorist attacks in Paris. Three suicide bombers attacked the soccer stadium while gunmen massacred patrons of cafés and restaurants before entering a music venue. The attackers targeted patrons of the 11th arrondissement, a highly diverse and young neighborhood. The terrorists killed 130 people while injuring another 368. In response, French president François Hollande issued a three-month state of emergency, banning public demonstrations and allowing police searches without warrants. ISIL struck again in Europe on March 22, 2016, when suicide bombers caused the death of 35 people at the airport and a metro station in Brussels, Belgium.

ISIL comprises fighters from at least 90 countries, including approximately 3,400 from the United States and Western Europe. It claims affiliates in countries such as Algeria, Libya, and Pakistan. The most notorious is the jihadist group Boko Haram in northern Nigeria, which pledged allegiance to ISIL in 2015. This group is responsible for the deaths of over 20,000 people and the displacement of over 2.3 million since 2009. Globalization and new technologies have enabled the growth of such extremist groups to carry out attacks far from their base of origin.

Paris Terrorist Attacks. United States president Barack Obama (right) pays tribute to the victims of the Paris attacks with French president François Hollande on November 30, 2015, outside the Bataclan music theatre, scene of terrorist attacks there on November 13, 2015.

PHILIPPE WOJAZER/AFP/Getty Images

New Directions and New Problems in Western Society

FOCUS QUESTION: What are the major developments in the women's movement since 1985, and what problems have immigrants created for European society?

Dramatic social developments have accompanied political and economic changes since 1985. New opportunities for women have emerged, and a reinvigorated women's movement has sought to bring new meaning to the principle of equality with men. New problems for Western society have also arisen with a growing reaction against foreign workers and immigrants.

Transformation in Women's Lives

It is estimated that parents need to average 2.1 children to ensure a natural replacement of a country's population. In many European countries, the population stopped growing in the 1960s, and the trend has continued since then. By the 1990s, birthrates were down drastically; among the nations of the European Union, the average number of children per mother was 1.4. Although the EU rate had risen somewhat to 1.59 by 2009, it remained well below the replacement rate. In 2011, Germany and Spain both had a rate of only 1.36.

At the same time, the number of women in the workforce continued to rise. In Britain, for example, women made up 44 percent of the labor force in 1990, up from 32 percent in 1970. By the twenty-first century, women constituted 48 percent of the labor force in the Scandinavian countries and 51 percent in the Eastern European countries. Moreover, women were entering new employment areas. Greater access to universities and professional schools enabled women to take jobs in law, medicine, government, business, and education. In the Soviet Union, about 70 percent of doctors and teachers had been women. Nevertheless, economic inequality still often prevailed; women received lower wages than men for comparable work and found fewer opportunities for advancement to management positions.

THE WOMEN'S MOVEMENT Feminists in the women's liberation movement came to believe that women themselves must transform the fundamental conditions of their lives. They did so in a variety of ways. First, they formed numerous "consciousness-raising" groups to heighten awareness of women's issues. Women got together to share their personal experiences and become aware of the many ways that male dominance affected their lives. This consciousness-raising helped many women become activists.

Women also sought and gained a measure of control over their own bodies by insisting that they had a right to both contraception and abortion. In the 1960s and 1970s, hundreds of thousands of European women worked, often successfully, to repeal the laws that outlawed contraception and abortion. In 1968, a French law permitted the sale of contraceptive devices, and in the 1970s, French feminists began to call for the legalization of abortion. One group of 343 prominent French women even signed a manifesto declaring that they had had abortions. In 1979, abortion became legal in France. Even in Catholic countries, where the church remained adamantly opposed to abortion, legislation allowing contraception and abortion was passed in the 1970s and 1980s.

As more women became activists, they also became involved in new issues. In the 1980s and 1990s, women faculty in universities concentrated on developing new cultural attitudes through the new academic field of women's studies. Courses in women's studies, which stressed the role and contributions of women in history, mushroomed in both American and European colleges and universities.

Other women began to try to affect the political environment by allying with the antinuclear movement. In 1982, a group of women protested American nuclear missiles in Britain by chaining themselves to the fence of an American military base. Thousands more joined in creating a peace camp around the military compound. Enthusiasm ran high; one participant said: "I'll never forget that feeling; it'll live with me forever. . . . We walked round, and we clasped hands. . . . It was for women; it was for peace; it was for the world."[4]

Some women joined the ecological movement. As one German writer who was concerned with environmental issues said, it is women "who must give birth to children, willingly or unwillingly, in this polluted world of ours." Especially prominent were the female members of the Green Party in Germany (see "The Environment and the Green Movements" in Chapter 29), which supported environmental issues and elected forty-two delegates to the West German parliament in 1987. Among the delegates was Petra Kelly (1947–2002), one of the founders of the German Green Party and a tireless campaigner for the preservation of the environment as well as human rights and equality.

Women in the West have also reached out through international conferences to work with women from the rest of the world in changing the conditions of their lives. Between 1975 and 1995, the United Nations held conferences in Mexico City, Copenhagen, Nairobi, and Beijing. These meetings made clear that women from Western and non-Western countries had different priorities. Whereas women from Western countries spoke about political, economic, cultural, and sexual rights, women from developing countries in Latin America, Africa, and Asia focused on bringing an end to the violence, hunger, and disease that haunt their lives. Despite these differences, the meetings were an indication of how women in both developed and developing nations were organizing to make people aware of women's issues.

Guest Workers and Immigrants

Despite an aging European population and declining birthrates, the total population of Europe has increased over the last decades due to mass migrations. As the economies of the Western European countries revived in the 1950s and 1960s and birthrates declined, a severe labor shortage encouraged them to rely on foreign workers. Government and businesses actively recruited so-called **guest workers** to staff essential jobs. Scores of Turks and eastern and southern Europeans came to Germany, North Africans to France, and people from the Caribbean, India, and Pakistan to Great Britain. With the collapse of the colonial system by the 1960s (see Chapter 28), millions of people from the former British, French, Dutch, and Portuguese colonies moved to Europe. Overall, there were probably 15 million guest workers in Europe in the 1980s, representing 5 to 6 percent of the population. They constituted 17 percent of the labor force in Switzerland and 10 percent in Germany.

Although these workers had been recruited for economic reasons, they often found themselves unwelcome socially and politically. Many foreign workers complained that they received lower wages and inferior social benefits. Moreover, their concentration in certain cities or certain sections of cities often created tensions with the local native populations. Foreign workers, many of them nonwhites, constituted almost one-fifth of the population in the German cities of Frankfurt, Munich, and Stuttgart. Having become settled in their new countries, many wanted to stay, even after the end of the postwar boom in the early 1970s led to mass unemployment. Moreover, as guest workers settled permanently in their host countries, additional family members migrated to join them. Although they had little success in getting guest workers already there to leave, some European countries passed legislation or took other measures to restrict new immigration.

In the 1980s, there was an influx of other refugees, especially to West Germany, which had liberal immigration laws that permitted people seeking asylum for political persecution to enter the country. During the 1970s and 1980s, West Germany absorbed more than a million refugees from Eastern Europe and East Germany. In 1986 alone, 200,000 political refugees from Pakistan, Bangladesh, and Sri Lanka entered the country. By 2005, 13 percent of Germany's residents were foreigners. Other parts of Europe saw a similar influx. Between 1992 and 2002, London and southeastern England received some 700,000 immigrants, primarily from Yugoslavia, Southeast Asia, the Middle East, and Africa. A survey in 1998 found that English was not the first language of one-third of inner-city children in London. Many other European countries experienced similar increases of immigrants during the 1990s and early 2000s. In 2000, Spain's immigrant population was 4.6 percent, but by 2006 it had grown to 10.8 percent.

The arrival of so many foreigners strained not only the social services of European countries but also the patience of many native residents who opposed making their countries ethnically diverse. Antiforeign sentiment, especially in a time of growing unemployment, increased and was encouraged by new right-wing political parties that catered to people's complaints. Thus, the National Front in France, organized by Jean-Marie Le Pen (ZHAHN-mah-REE luh PEHN) (b. 1928) and now led by his daughter Marine Le Pen (mah-REEN luh PEHN) (b. 1968), and the Republican Party in Germany, led by Franz Schönhuber (1923–2005), a former SS officer, advocated restricting all new immigration and limiting the assimilation of settled immigrants. Although these parties had only limited success in elections, even that modest accomplishment encouraged traditional conservative and even moderately conservative parties to adopt more nationalistic policies. Occasionally, an antiforeign party has been quite successful. Jorg Haider (YORG HY-dur) (1950–2008), whose Freedom Party received 27 percent of the vote in 1999, cushioned his rejection of foreigners by appealing to Austrian nationalism and attacking the European Union: "We Austrians should answer not to the European Union, not to Maastricht, not to some international idea or other, but to this our Homeland."[5] In 2012, Marine Le Pen won 17.9 percent of the vote in the French elections—the National Front's strongest showing. Even more frightening than the growth of these right-wing political parties were the organized campaigns of violence in the early 1990s, especially against African and Asian immigrants, by radical, right-wing groups.

Even nations that have traditionally been tolerant in opening their borders to immigrants and seekers of asylum are changing their policies. In the Netherlands, 19 percent of the residents have a foreign background, representing almost 180 nationalities. Two high-profile assassinations in the early 2000s, however, including the shooting of filmmaker Theodoor van Gogh, who had directed *Submission*, a film on the oppression of Muslim women in immigrant families, prompted the Dutch to alter their immigration policies. In 2004, the Dutch government

Migrant Crisis in Europe. In Budapest's main railway station, thousands of refugees who had come through Serbia are seen attempting to board trains in Budapest before authorities closed the railway station. Families were torn apart and refugees struggled to find provisions.

passed tough new immigration laws, including a requirement that newcomers pass a Dutch language and culture test before being admitted to the Netherlands.

Sometimes these policies have been aimed at religious practices. One of the effects of the influx of foreigners into Europe has been a dramatic increase in the Muslim population. Although Christians still constitute a majority (though many no longer practice their faith), the number of Muslims has mushroomed in France, Britain, Belgium, the Netherlands, and Germany. It has been estimated that at least 15 million Muslims were living in European Union nations in the first decade of the twenty-first century. In some nations, concern that Muslim immigration will result in an erosion of national values has led to attempts to restrict the display of Islamic symbols.

In 2004, France enacted a law prohibiting female students from wearing a headscarf (*hijab*) to school. Article 1 stated: "In public elementary, middle and high schools, the wearing of signs or clothing which conspicuously manifest students' religious affiliations is prohibited." The law further clarified "conspicuous" to mean "a large cross, a veil, or a skullcap."[6] Small religious symbols, such as small crosses or medallions, were not included. Critics of this law argue that it will exacerbate ethnic and religious tensions in France, while supporters maintain that it upholds the traditions of secularism and equality for women in France.

MIGRATION CRISIS European immigration has been at a relatively constant level since the end of World War II. In 2015, however, a sharp increase in migrants coming from the Middle East, especially from Syria, Iraq, and Afghanistan, entered Europe by the Mediterranean Sea to Greece before continuing through the Balkans to northern Europe. Europe accepted at least 1.2 million refugees in 2015. Germany alone accepted more than 800,000 refugees. German chancellor Angela Merkel called for a European Union-wide quota system, although many EU member states have rejected such a proposal. Eastern European countries, such as Hungary, Poland, Slovakia, and the Czech Republic, which are fairly homogenous after decades of ethnic

cleansing and have suffered during the financial crises, have been most vocal in defying obligatory quotas.

The New Urban Environment

In the postwar era, most Europeans were busy rebuilding their cities, while in the United States a mass exodus to suburbia began with the automobile and the construction of the U.S. highway system. By the twenty-first century, the process of deindustrialization as a result of globalization of trade and the mechanization of industry, as well as the rise of the service sector and high-tech industries changed the urban landscape of the United States and Europe. Former industrial cities, such as Detroit, Michigan, and Oberhausen, Germany, experienced sharp declines in population, while older cities such as New York, London, and Paris benefited from the new finance and high-tech economies. These new industries relied on a highly educated workforce and close proximity to other knowledge-based service sector people.

By 2010, the majority of Europeans and Americans were city dwellers, with 97 percent of the population in Belgium, 93 percent in Iceland, 90 percent in Britain, 88 percent in Germany, 86 percent in Denmark, and 83 percent in Sweden living in cities. While their eastern European counterparts in Warsaw, Budapest, and Prague experienced a slower return to urban dwelling, intensive investment in rehabilitation on behalf of the European Union during the early 2000s reinvigorated and transformed the major eastern European capitals.

Western Culture Today

 FOCUS QUESTION: What major Western cultural trends have emerged since 1985?

Western culture has expanded to most parts of the world, although some societies see it as a challenge to their own culture and national identity. At the same time, other societies are also strongly influencing Western cultural expressions, making recent Western culture a reflection of the evolving global response to the rapid changes in human society today.

Varieties of Religious Life

Despite the attempt to revive religion after World War II, church attendance in Europe and the United States declined dramatically in the 1960s and 1970s as a result of growing secular attitudes. Yet even though the numbers of regular churchgoers in established Protestant and Catholic churches continued to decline, the number of fundamentalist churches and churchgoers has been growing, especially in the United States.

Fundamentalism was originally a movement within Protestantism that arose early in the twentieth century. Its goal was to maintain a strict traditional interpretation of the Bible and the Christian faith, especially in opposition to the theory of Darwinian evolution and secularism. In the 1980s and 1990s, fundamentalists became involved in a struggle against so-called secular humanism, godless communism, legalized abortion, and homosexuality. Especially in the United States, fundamentalists organized politically to elect candidates who supported their views. This so-called Christian right played an influential role in electing both Ronald Reagan and George W. Bush to the presidency.

THE GROWTH OF ISLAM Fundamentalism, however, is not unique to Protestantism. In Islam, the term *fundamentalism* is used to refer to a return to traditional Islamic values, especially in opposition to a perceived weakening of moral values due to the corrupting influence of Western ideas and practices. After the Iranian Revolution of 1979, the term was also applied to militant Islamic movements, such as the Taliban in Afghanistan, who favored militant action against Western influence.

Despite the wariness of Islamic radicalism in the aftermath of the September 11, 2001, terrorist attacks on the United States, Islam is growing in both Europe and the United States, thanks primarily to the migration of people from Muslim countries. As Muslim communities became established in France, Germany, Britain, Italy, and Spain during the 1980s and 1990s, they built mosques for religious worship and religious education. In the United States, the states of California and New York each have more than two hundred mosques.

THE CATHOLIC CHURCH Although changes have also occurred in the Catholic Church, much of its history in the 1980s and 1990s was dominated by the charismatic Pope John Paul II (1920–2005). Karol Wojtyla (KAH-rul voy-TEE-wah), who had been the archbishop of Krakow in Poland before his elevation to the papacy in 1978, was the first non-Italian to be elected pope since the sixteenth century. Although he alienated a number of people by reasserting traditional Catholic teaching on such issues as birth control, women in the priesthood, and clerical celibacy, John Paul's numerous travels around the world helped strengthen the Catholic Church throughout the non-Western world. A strong believer in social justice, John Paul was a powerful figure in reminding Europeans of their spiritual heritage and the need to temper the pursuit of materialism with spiritual concerns. He also condemned nuclear weapons and constantly reminded leaders and laity of their obligations to prevent war.

The global nature of the Catholic Church became apparent on March 13, 2013, with the election of a new pope. Cardinal Jorge Mario Bergoglio (b. 1936), the archbishop of Buenos Aires, became the first Latin American as well as the first non-European since the eighth century to be elected pope. He chose to be called Pope Francis in honor of the humble Saint Francis of Assisi (see Chapter 10). In 2015, Pope Francis issued a papal encyclical, or letter, on the subject of climate change. Pope Francis called upon individuals and the international community to act upon climate change before it is too late and posed the question of climate change as a moral dilemma:

> When we ask ourselves what kind of world we want to leave behind, we think in the first place of its general direction, its meaning and its values. Unless we struggle with these deeper issues, I do not believe that our concern for ecology will produce significant results. But if these issues are courageously faced, we are led inexorably to ask other pointed questions: What is the purpose of our life in this world? Why are we here? What is the goal of our work and all our efforts? What need does the earth have of us? It is no longer enough, then, simply to state that we should be concerned for future generations. We need to see that what is at stake is our own dignity.[7]

The Digital Age

Since the invention of the microprocessor in 1971, the capabilities of computers have continued to grow, resulting in today's "Information" or "Digital Age." Beginning in the 1980s, companies like Apple and Microsoft competed to create more powerful computers and software. By the 1990s, the booming technology industry had made Microsoft founder Bill Gates the richest man in the world. Much of this success was due to several innovations that made computers essential for communication, information, and entertainment.

THE TECHNOLOGICAL WORLD The advent of electronic mail, or e-mail, in the mid-1990s transformed the way that people communicate. As the capacity of computers to transmit data increased, e-mail messages could carry document and image attachments, making them a workable and speedier alternative to "snail mail," as conventional postal mail came to be called. Perhaps even more transformative was the Internet, a network of smaller, interlinking Web pages with sites devoted to news, commerce, entertainment, and academic scholarship. At first, websites were limited to text-based documents, but as computer processors became more powerful, video and music were added.

By the early 2000s, the Internet had become a part of everyday life for the Western world. These new forms of communication have allowed for greater access to information and people in a short period. They have also changed how people receive information. In 1980, 40 percent of U.S. households watched the nightly news; by 2005 only 20 percent watched the news and over 100 million people confirmed that they receive their news from an online source. Advances in telecommunications led to cellular or mobile phones. Though cellular phones existed in the 1970s and 1980s, it was not until the digital components of these devices were reduced in size in the 1990s that cell phones became truly portable. In the early 2000s, smartphones were introduced to the market. Smartphones had advanced mobile operating systems and included GPS tracking systems. In 2007, Apple introduced the iPhone smartphone with a touch screen. By 2015, over 60 percent of the U.S. population owned a smartphone. The smartphone enabled social media companies such as Facebook, YouTube, Instagram, and Snapchat to facilitate handheld visual and text communication. Facebook's monthly active users totaled over 1.3 billion as of 2015, more than the entire population of China. The processing speed of new smartphones also transformed consumer patterns, with over 100 billion dollars of online sales in the United States in 2015; almost a third of online sales take place through the iPhone. Apple also introduced the iPod, a pocket-sized digital player, in 2001 that revolutionized the music industry, and the iPad in 2010, a small tablet computer with a touch screen.

Art in the Contemporary World

Over the past thirty years, the art world has been transformed by developments in technology and finance. Advances in computers have changed the ways in which art is produced and experienced, while the high stakes of the art market have impacted how galleries and museums operate. Many arts organizations, as well as artists themselves, adopted the techniques of marketing and advertising, while social media allows artists, curators, and critics to interact with audiences in new ways. The museum itself underwent transformation, with the construction of new buildings or renovation of existing structures that created dynamic landmarks that attracted visitors as much as the art itself. Ultimately, art became a key component of today's globalized society while retaining its capacity as a critical tool.

Postmodernism continued to impact the approaches of artists, with a pluralism of styles, mediums, and perspectives gaining currency throughout the previous decades. One movement rooted in postmodern ideas was Neo-Expressionism, which reached its zenith in the mid-1980s. After a period where Performance and Conceptual Art held sway in the art world, many returned to pictorial narrative and traditional mediums, incorporating historical references into large, gestural canvases. Neo-Expressionist artists such as Anselm Kiefer (AN-selm KEEF-uhr) became increasingly popular as the international art market soared. Born in Germany in 1945, Kiefer combines aspects of Abstract Expressionism, collage, and German Expressionism to create works that are stark and haunting. His paintings from the 1980s became a meditation on German history, especially the horrors of Nazism. Kiefer hoped that a portrayal of Germany's atrocities in such works as *Departure from Egypt* and *Nigredo* could free Germans from their past and bring some good out of evil.

Throughout the 1990s and early 2000s, artists continued to explore the politics of identity, creating works that questioned gender, ethnicity, and sexual orientation. Many artists utilized stereotypes to question our assumptions about other cultures. Shirin Neshat (b. 1957) rose to prominence during this time with large format photographs painted with *Farsi*, or Persian calligraphy, that covers her veiled, female subjects. Created after living in America during Iran's Islamic Revolution, Neshat's artworks

Bertrand Guay/AFP/Getty Images

Anselm Kiefer, *Athanor* (2007). In 2007, Kiefer painted a monumental work (30 feet by 15 feet) on the wall of a stairwell in the Louvre Museum in Paris. This textured painting is named after the athanor, a furnace that alchemists used in their efforts to transform base metals into gold. The painting shows a nude man on his back connected by a beam of light extending from his stomach to the heavens above. According to Kiefer, the man is not dead, but "in the universe." At the bottom of the painting Kiefer poured liquid lead onto a layer of soil from the area where he lives in southern France; higher up in the painting are silver and gold, symbolizing the stages of the alchemical process.

questioned the violence and gendered norms projected onto the Middle Eastern body.

Some artists engaged contemporary politics in their work while others participated in, and commented on, the global commercial art market. During the 2000s, prices for artwork increased as rapidly as housing prices, and with many equating merit with sales or economic value, galleries and artists increasingly relied on advertising strategies to gain attention. In order to accommodate the increase of consumer demand for artwork, the art world experienced an explosion of art fairs across the world. These events draw together international galleries to attract tourists and potential clients. In addition to these commercial trade fairs, cities increasingly host international exhibitions known as biennials. Staged every two or three years in cities as diverse as Dakar, Istanbul, Pittsburgh, Sydney,

Jeff Koons, *Balloon Dog* (1994–2006) on exhibition at the Palace of Versailles, France. In 2008, Jeff Koons became the first contemporary artist to have an exhibition at Versailles, the former Palace of Louis XIV. While some criticized his work as banal, others found the materialism and self-aggrandizement of Koons's artistic practice commensurate to that of the Sun King. The artist carefully selected which sculptures would be displayed in each room, as Koons sought a dialogue between his popular contemporary forms and the Baroque environment of the palace. The stainless steel *Balloon Dog* stands ten feet tall and weighs one ton, playfully altering the characteristics of its original reference.

and Venice, biennials present the latest contemporary art and promote a diplomatic exchange of culture. The expansion and location of these art fairs and biennials demonstrates the global appeal of contemporary art.

The high stakes and big money of contemporary art leads many institutions to seek blockbuster shows, and historic venues have followed this trend. In 2008, the Palace of Versailles in France hosted a solo exhibition of American artist Jeff

Koons (b. 1955), a controversial artist known for appropriating pre-existing objects and transforming them into monumental artworks. Koons selects his subjects from popular culture, producing new works in a high-tech studio that employs over one hundred artists. Organized like a Renaissance workshop, his studio produces enormous stainless steel sculptures and precision-made oil paintings. Koons claims to celebrate art among the commonplace, while others suggest the refined materials and exorbitant prices of his art reflect the materialism and vanity of contemporary society.

Like Neshat, many contemporary artists explore the interaction between the Western and non-Western world, particularly the **multiculturalism** generated by global migrations (see "The Social Challenges of Globalization" later in this chapter). For example, the art of Yinka Shonibare MBE (YEEN-kuh SHOW-nih-bar-eh) (b. 1962), who was born in London, raised in Nigeria, and now resides in England, creates works that investigate the notion of hybrid identity. This is evident in his sculpture *How to Blow Up Two Heads at Once (Gentlemen)* (2006), which depicts European Victorian figures dressed in Dutch wax cloth.

Shonibare works at the intersection of multiple mediums, including photography, film, sculpture, and installation. An installation is often a large, immersive environment created by an artist consisting of found and constructed objects, audio recordings, or video projections. Recently, critics have argued that installation is the most "contemporary" form of art because it exists as a real entity and requires the viewer's presence to fully experience the work. The Swiss American artist Christian Marclay (b. 1955) won the best artist award at the Venice Biennial in 2011 for his video installation *The Clock* (2010). This piece consists of a 24-hour long cinematic montage of scenes from movies where a character looks at his or her timepiece. Marclay synchronized the time on the watch or clock in each scene to real time, constructing a provocative

Yinka Shonibare MBE, *How to Blow Up Two Heads at Once (Gentlemen)* (2006). In this work, Yinka Shonibare MBE humorously re-creates a nineteenth-century European duel in which two headless figures wearing Victorian costumes are simultaneously aiming guns at each other's heads. His choice of Victorian figures and costumes reflect his interest in the history of Britain's colonial endeavors. The Dutch wax cloth used for the costumes symbolizes the complexity of modern African identity and globalization. The cloth was inspired by Indonesian batiks, produced in the Netherlands and Britain, and then sold in West Africa during the nineteenth century.

commentary on reality and the value of time. His use of editing technology reflects another major trend in contemporary art: time-based new media. Art no longer involves only painting, drawing, photography, or sculpture. Instead, many artists employ video cameras and computer software to generate photographs, films, web interfaces, and other technologically based artworks.

Music since 1985

In addition to film projects, Christian Marclay is known for manipulating technology to create sound collages and musical scores. Like the visual arts, music has changed dramatically over the past thirty years due to digital technology.

In the 1980s, many musicians experimented with synthesizers and electronic instruments, utilizing advancements in computers for popular hits. But as American musicians became increasingly disenchanted with the excesses of the Reagan era, they also began to question the consumerism that had seemingly homogenized popular culture. The emergence of "grunge" music in the early 1990s reflected this attitude as well as the influence of punk, as rock bands such as Nirvana, Sonic Youth, and Pearl Jam rejected the materialism of the previous decade. Employing distortion and amplified feedback in their music, grunge artists often sang of disillusion and angst. Rather than conforming to the mass-produced norms of the fashion industry, these musicians typically wore ripped jeans and weathered flannel attire to protest the excesses of capitalism.

In the early 1990s, hip-hop continued to gain popularity with rappers such as Dr. Dre and Snoop Doggy Dogg who created "gangsta rap," an offshoot of hip-hop with raw lyrics praising violence, drugs, and promiscuous sex. By the late 1990s, teen and preteen consumers had steered the music industry back to pop music, generating millions of dollars of sales in the process. Many pop acts became successful as music turned away from grunge and gangsta rap. Instead, musicians and audiences favored the lighthearted music that made Britney Spears, Justin Timberlake, and Ricky Martin famous. Drawing from rhythm and blues (R&B), Latin music, and hip-hop, these artists used catchy dance beats and extravagant music videos to market their work.

Throughout the early 2000s, hip-hop and R&B dominated the music charts. Mainstream hip-hop artists such as Outkast, Eminem, and Kanye West became internationally famous, while R&B singers including Lady Gaga, Destiny's Child with Beyoncé, and Adele had multiple hits over the past decade.

In a postmodern spirit, many musicians remix standards or classic songs, while traditional instruments, such as the fiddle or banjo, recently returned to prominence in rock music. The eclecticism of contemporary music has been shaped by the changing dynamics of the industry. With the advent of databases like iTunes and streaming radio stations such as Pandora, popular music is more fragmented yet accessible than ever. Rather than radio stations establishing the latest trends, listeners are directed to new music through recommendations generated by their previous purchases and stated tastes.

Toward a Global Civilization: New Challenges and Hopes

 FOCUS QUESTION: What is globalization, and what are some of its important aspects in the twenty-first century?

Multiculturalism in art reminds us that more and more people are becoming aware of the political, economic, and social interdependence of the world's nations and the global nature of our contemporary problems. We are coming to understand that destructive forces generated in one part of the world soon affect the entire world. Smokestack pollution in one nation can produce acid rain in another. Oil spills and dumping of wastes in the ocean have an impact on the shores of many nations. As crises of food, water, energy, and natural resources proliferate, one nation's solutions often become other nations' problems. The new globalism includes the recognition that the challenges that seem to threaten human existence today are global. In October 2001, in response to the terrorist attacks of September 11, British prime minister Tony Blair said, "We are realizing how fragile are our frontiers in the face of the world's new challenges. Today, conflict rarely stays within national boundaries."

As we saw in the discussion of the Digital Age, an important part of global awareness is the technological dimension. The growth of new technology has made possible levels of world communication that simply did not exist before. At the same time that Osama bin Laden and al-Qaeda were denouncing the forces of modernization, they were doing so by using advanced telecommunication systems that have only recently been developed. The technology revolution has tied peoples and nations closely together and contributed to **globalization**, the term that is frequently used today to describe the process by which peoples and nations have become more interdependent. Economically, globalization has taken the form of a **global economy**.

The Global Economy

Especially since the 1970s, the world has developed a global economy in which the production, distribution, and sale of goods are accomplished on a worldwide scale (see "Global Perspectives" on p. 946). Several international institutions have contributed to the rise of the global economy. Soon after the end of World War II, the United States and other nations established the World Bank and the International Monetary Fund (IMF). The World Bank (founded in 1945) is a group of five international organizations, largely controlled by developed countries, which provides grants, loans, and advice for economic development to developing countries. The goal of the IMF, which was also founded in 1945, is to oversee the global financial system by supervising exchange rates and offering financial and technical assistance to developing nations. Today, 188 countries are members of the IMF. Critics have argued that both the World Bank and the IMF push inappropriate Western economic practices on

The New Global Economy: Fast Fashion

AN EXAMPLE OF THE NEW GLOBAL company is Inditex, best known for Zara, its oldest brand. The owner of the company, Amancio Ortega Gaona, is one of the wealthiest people in the world. His company pioneered a new business model known as "fast fashion." It sells fashionable clothes for a fraction of the price of designer clothes in high-end retail stores, often located on some of the most fashionable shopping streets. Zara has capitalized on the new global economy of the late twentieth and early twenty-first centuries by using new technological, transportation, and communication systems to design and produce a garment

in less than three weeks. Zara makes 840 million garments a year and has around 5,900 stores in eighty-five countries. Seen on the left is the design area in the Zara factory in La Coruja, Spain, where a number of designers are working together. The photo below shows a shopper outside of a store in Beijing, China in 2015. The image at the right of Kate, the duchess of Cambridge, photographed in Zara clothing, is emblematic of Zara's appeal.

Q *How do you explain the success of "fast fashion"? What does it tell us about the contemporary world economy?*

Xurxo Lobato/Cover/Getty Images

Niki Nikolova/FilmMagic/Getty Images

Bloomberg/Getty Images

non-Western nations that only aggravate the poverty and debt of developing nations.

Another reflection of the new global economic order is the **multinational corporation** or **transnational corporation** (a company that has divisions in more than two countries). Prominent examples of multinational corporations include Siemens, General Electric, ExxonMobil, Mitsubishi, and the Sony Corporation. These companies are among the 200 largest multinational corporations, which are responsible for more than half of the world's industrial production. In 2000, 142 of the leading 200 multinational corporations were headquartered in three countries—the United States, Japan, and Germany. In addition, these super corporations dominate much of the world's investment capital, technology, and markets and control 75 percent of the world trade in manufactured goods. A recent comparison of corporate sales and national gross domestic product disclosed that only 49 of the world's largest economies are nations; the remaining 51 are corporations. For this reason, some observers believe that economic globalization is more appropriately labeled "corporate globalization."

Another important component of economic globalization is free trade. In 1947, talks led to the General Agreement on Tariffs and Trade (GATT), a global trade organization that was replaced in 1995 by the World Trade Organization (WTO). Made up of more than 150 member nations, the WTO arranges trade agreements and settles trade disputes. Yet many critics charge that the WTO has ignored environmental and health concerns, harmed small and developing countries, and created an ever-growing gap between rich and poor nations.

The relaxation of trade barriers created a boom in international trade in the last quarter of the twentieth century. In 1973, international trade was valued at $1.7 trillion; by 2000, it had increased to $5.8 trillion. At the same time, international financial transactions involving financial instruments such as bonds and equities were becoming an increasingly important component of the global economy. The value of financial transactions involving financial instruments rose to fifty times the value of world trade in goods. The global economy had entered a new era of finance, in which profits from financial transactions outpaced profits from manufactured goods, leading to catastrophic consequences in 2008.

THE END OF EXCESS The global economy began to experience worldwide financial troubles in 2007, following the collapse of the U.S. housing market. Spurred by low interest rates in the early 2000s, easily available mortgages drove up housing values in the United States. From 1945 to 1997, housing prices had kept pace with the overall rate of inflation; from 1997 to 2005, however, home prices increased by more than 45 percent after adjusting for inflation. At its peak in 2006, the wealth created by the housing bubble generated more than $1 trillion in annual demand. In response to the housing boom, investment banks began selling financial investments called collateralized debt obligations (CDOs), which were based on bundles of mortgages. Banks in New York sold CDOs to banks in Europe and elsewhere, spreading the wealth and the risk of investment. Many of the mortgages used as investments had been

sub-prime—issued to borrowers with low credit ratings and a high likelihood of default. As the low introductory rates on the mortgages expired beginning in 2006, default rates increased. By September 2008, a number of large financial institutions, insurance and mortgage companies, investment firms, and banks were approaching or had entered bankruptcy. The rapid collapse of CDO values and falling housing prices caused a precipitous decline in the U.S. stock market as stocks lost almost $8 trillion in value from mid-September to November.

In a globalized world economy, financial distress quickly spread as the inflated credit market burst, leaving many banks without enough capital (funds) to pay their depositors. Credit became largely unavailable in the last quarter of 2008, crippling industrial output. The IMF supplied rescue packages for many Eastern European countries, while Europe's stronger economies, primarily Germany and France, provided emergency funds to recapitalize their banks. In the United States, the government responded with an emergency program to recapitalize financial institutions and a stimulus package to support growth and reduce unemployment.

The greatest threat to the global economy, however, came from one of Europe's smallest nations. Despite its small size, Greece experienced an economic crisis that destroyed the country's economy, brought down the government, unleashed social unrest, and threatened the euro. Greece exemplified the European debt crisis—low interest rates, easily available bonds, and a strong euro had enabled the Greek government and people to run up large amounts of debt. By 2010, Greece had accumulated a national debt larger than its national economy. Unable to grow its way out of the problem because of its small economy, Greece faced the prospect of defaulting on its debt. It managed to avoid default only by agreeing to extreme austerity measures in return for a bailout of almost 240 billion euros from the European Union. The Greek government accepted the EU's plan for tax increases, spending cuts, and wage cuts, which sent the country into a deep recession. The Greek public responded with mass protests, and the social unrest, in turn, has led to the rise of far left and far right political parties.

Greece was not the only troubled nation in the European debt crisis, making recovery that much more difficult. Portugal, Ireland, Italy, Spain, and Cyprus also faced severe economic problems. Spanish unemployment rose to approximately 26 percent and exceeded 50 percent for young people. Property values plummeted by almost 15 percent in 2012, while 1.2 million houses remained empty, many due to foreclosures. The welfare state has been partially dismantled as pensions and health care services have been cut to provide funds to recapitalize the banks.

As of 2013, the United States and much of Europe had not recovered from the economic crisis. The austerity measures put into place have reduced pensions, wages, and health care services, leading to a wave of homelessness and hardship. Many of the severely affected European countries resent the policies imposed by the wealthier EU states, especially Germany. A growing mistrust of established governments has led to political upheaval. As the crisis deepens, Europeans will be forced to decide if they should move toward a more politically unified

A WARNING TO HUMANITY

AS HUMAN THREATS TO THE ENVIRONMENT grew, world scientists began to organize and respond to the crisis. One such group, founded in 1969, was the Union of Concerned Scientists, a nonprofit organization of professional scientists and private citizens, now with more than 200,000 members. In November 1992, the Union of Concerned Scientists published an appeal from 1,700 of the world's leading scientists. The first selection is taken from this "Warning to Humanity."

Earlier, in 1988, in response to the threat of global warming, the United Nations established an Intergovernmental Panel on Climate Change (IPCC) to study the most up-to-date scientific information on global warming and climate change. In 2013, thousands of scientists from more than 195 countries contributed to the group's most recent report, "Climate Change, 2013: The Fifth Assessment Report," released in September 2013. The second selection is taken from the IPCC report for policy makers that summarize the basic findings of the 2013 report.

World Scientists' Warning to Humanity, 1992

Human beings and the natural world are on a collision course. Human activities inflict harsh and often irreversible damage on the environment and on critical resources. If not checked, many of our current practices put at serious risk the future that we wish for human society and the plant and animal kingdoms, and may so alter the living world that it will be unable to sustain life in the manner that we know. Fundamental changes are urgent if we are to avoid the collision our present course will bring about. The environment is suffering critical stress:

The Atmosphere
Stratospheric ozone depletion threatens us with enhanced ultraviolet radiation at the earth's surface, which can be damaging or lethal to many life forms. Air pollution near ground level and acid precipitation are already causing widespread injury to humans, forests, and crops.

Water Resources
Heedless exploitation of depletable ground water supplies endangers food production and other essential human systems. Heavy demands on the world's surface waters have resulted in serious shortages in some 80 countries, containing 40% of the world's population. Pollution of rivers, lakes, and ground water further limits the supply.

Oceans
Destructive pressure on the oceans is severe, particularly in the coastal regions which produce most of the world's food fish. The total marine catch is now at or above the estimated maximum sustainable yield. Some fisheries have already shown signs of collapse.

Soil
Loss of soil productivity, which is causing extensive land abandonment, is a widespread by-product of current practices in agriculture and animal husbandry. Since 1945, 11% of the earth's vegetated surface has been degraded—an area larger than India and China combined—and per capita food production in many parts of the world is decreasing.

Forests
Tropical rain forests, as well as tropical and temperate dry forests, are being destroyed rapidly. At present rates, some critical forest types will be gone in a few years, and most of the tropical rain forest will be gone before the end of the next century. With them will go large numbers of plant and animal species.

Living Species
The irreversible loss of species, which by 2100 may reach one-third of all species now living, is especially serious. We are losing the potential they hold for providing medicinal and other benefits, and the contribution that genetic diversity of life forms gives to the robustness of the world's biological systems and to the astonishing beauty of the earth itself.

Europe or retreat into possible political chaos within the borders of their individual states.

Globalization and the Environmental Crisis

Taking a global perspective at the beginning of the twenty-first century has led many people to realize that everywhere on the planet human beings are interdependent in regard to the air they breathe, the water they drink, the food they consume, and the climate that affects their lives. At the same time, however, human activities are creating environmental challenges that threaten the very foundation of human existence on earth, especially evident in the Gulf of Mexico

oil spill in 2010—the worst oil spill in U.S. history (see the box above).

One problem is population growth. As of March 2016, the world population was estimated at more than 7.4 billion people, only twenty-eight years after passing the 5 billion mark. At its current rate of growth, the world population could reach 12.8 billion by 2050, according to the United Nations' long-range population projections. The result has been an increased demand for food and other resources that has put great pressure on the earth's ecosystems. At the same time, the failure to grow enough food for more and more people has created a severe problem, as an estimated 1 billion people worldwide today suffer from hunger. Every year, more

Much of this damage is irreversible on a scale of centuries, or permanent. Other processes appear to pose additional threats. Increasing levels of gases in the atmosphere from human activities, including carbon dioxide released from fossil fuel burning and from deforestation, may alter climate on a global scale.

Warning

We the undersigned, senior members of the world's scientific community, hereby warn all humanity of what lies ahead. A great change in our stewardship of the earth and the life on it is required, if vast human misery is to be avoided and our global home on this planet is not to be irretrievably mutilated.

Findings of the IPCC Fifth Assessment Report, 2013

Human Responsibility for Climate Change

The report finds that it is *"extremely likely* that human influence has been the dominant cause of the observed warming since the mid-20th century." This evidence has grown since the AR4 (the IPCC 2007 report).

Warming Is Unequivocal

The report concludes that warming of the climate system is "unequivocal," and "since the 1950s, many of observed changes are unprecedented over decades to millennia. The atmosphere and ocean have warmed, the amounts of snow and ice have diminished, sea level has risen, and the concentrations of greenhouse gasses have increased." Moreover, "each of the last three decades has been successively warmer at the Earth's surface than any preceding decade since 1850. In the Northern Hemisphere, 1983–2012 was likely the warmest 30-year period of the last 1400 years." The report also confirms that the current atmospheric concentrations of the greenhouse gases of carbon dioxide, methane, and nitrous oxide "have increased to levels unprecedented in at least the last 800,000 years." In 2011, the concentration of these gases . . . "exceeded the pre-industrial levels by about 40%, 150%, and 20% respectively."

Additional IPCC Findings on Recent Climate Change

Rising Temperatures

- By 2100, various climate change model simulations estimate that global surface temperatures could rise from 1.5°C to 4°C.
- Since about 1950, "it is very likely that the number of cold days and nights has decreased and the number of warm days and nights has increased on the global scale. It is likely that the frequency of heat waves has increased in large parts of Europe, Asia and Australia. There are likely more land regions where the number of heavy precipitation events has increased than where it has decreased."

Melting Glaciers and Snow

- The melting of ice glaciers has increased rapidly, "over the last two decades, the Greenland and Antarctic ice sheets have been losing mass, glaciers have continued to shrink almost worldwide, and the Artic sea ice and Northern Hemisphere spring snow cover have continued to decrease in extent."

Rising Sea Levels

- "The rate of sea level rise since the mid-19th century has been larger than the mean rate during the previous two millennia."

Increasingly Severe Weather (storms, precipitation, drought)

- "It is likely, that there will be increases in intensity and/or duration of drought, and increases in intense tropical cyclone (hurricane) activity."
- "It is very likely that heat waves will occur with a higher frequency and duration."
- Storms with heavy precipitation have increased in frequency over most land areas.
- "Air quality will continue to decrease due to high carbon emissions."

 What problems and challenges do these two reports present? What do these two reports have in common? How do they differ?

Source: IPCC, Fifth Assessment: http://www.climatechange2013.org/images/uploads/WGI_AR5_SPM_brochure.pdf.

than 8 million people die of hunger, many of them young children.

Another problem is the pattern of consumption, as the wealthy nations of the Northern Hemisphere consume vast quantities of the planet's natural resources. The United States, with just 6 percent of the planet's people, consumes 30 to 40 percent of its resources. The spread of these consumption patterns to other parts of the world raises serious questions about the ability of the planet to sustain itself and its population.

Yet another threat to the environment is **global warming**, which has the potential to create a global crisis. Virtually all of the world's scientists agree that the **greenhouse effect**, the warming of the earth because of the buildup of carbon dioxide in the atmosphere, is contributing to devastating droughts and storms, the melting of the polar ice caps, and rising sea levels that could inundate coastal regions in the second half of the twenty-first century. Scientists reported that 2015 was the hottest year on record in the United States. Also alarming is the potential loss of biodiversity. Seven out of ten biologists believe that the planet is now experiencing an alarming extinction of both plant and animal species.

In 2015, 195 nations agreed on the Paris Accord, a landmark climate change agreement that committed nearly every country to lower its carbon dioxide emissions. In 2009, leaders had failed to reach an agreement in Copenhagen. In 2014,

American president Barack Obama and Chinese president Xi Jinping announced that they would jointly pursue plans to cut greenhouse gas emissions. Their commitment led the way for other countries to join. Although the agreement is probably not enough to stave off the worst effects of climate change, it is a fundamental shift in global policy and offers hope for the preservation of planet Earth.

The Social Challenges of Globalization

Since 1945, tens of millions of people have migrated from one part of the world to another. These migrations have occurred for many reasons. Persecution for political reasons caused many people from Pakistan, Bangladesh, Sri Lanka, and Eastern Europe to seek refuge in Western European countries, while brutal civil wars in Asia, Africa, the Middle East, and Europe led millions of refugees to seek safety in neighboring countries. Most people who have migrated, however, have done so to find jobs. Latin Americans seeking a better life have migrated to the United States, while guest workers from Turkey, southern and eastern Europe, North Africa, India, and Pakistan have migrated to more prosperous Western European lands. In 2005, nearly 200 million people, about 3 percent of the world's population, lived outside the country where they were born.

As discussed earlier, the migration of millions of people has created a social backlash in many countries. Foreign workers often become scapegoats when countries face economic problems. Political parties in France and Norway have called for the removal of blacks and Arabs in order to protect the ethnic purity of their nations, while in Asian countries, there is animosity against other Asian ethnic groups. The problem of foreigners has also led to a more general attack on globalization itself as being responsible for a host of social ills that are undermining national sovereignty.

Another challenge of globalization is the wide gap between rich and poor nations. The rich nations, or **developed nations**, are located mainly in the Northern Hemisphere. They include countries such as the United States, Canada, Germany, and Japan, which have well-organized industrial and agricultural systems, advanced technologies, and effective educational systems. The poor nations, or **developing nations**, are located mainly in the Southern Hemisphere. They include many nations in Africa, Asia, and Latin America, which often have primarily agricultural economies with little technology. A serious problem in many developing nations is the explosive population growth, which has led to severe food shortages often caused by poor soil but also by economic factors. Growing crops for export to developed countries, for example, may lead to enormous profits for large landowners but leaves many small farmers with little land on which to grow food.

Civil wars have also created food shortages. War not only disrupts normal farming operations, but warring groups try to limit access to food to destroy their enemies. In the Sudan, 1.3 million people starved when combatants of a civil war in the 1980s prevented food from reaching them. As unrest continued during the early 2000s in Darfur, families were forced to leave their farms. As a result, an estimated 70,000 people starved by mid-2004.

New Global Movements and New Hopes

As the heirs of Western civilization have become aware that the problems humans face are not just national but global, they have responded to this challenge in different ways. One approach has been to develop grassroots social movements, including environmental, women's and men's liberation, human potential, appropriate-technology, and nonviolence movements. "Think globally, act locally" is frequently the slogan of these grassroots groups. Related to the emergence of these social movements is the growth of nongovernmental organizations (NGOs). According to one analyst, NGOs are an important instrument in the cultivation of global perspectives: "Since NGOs by definition are identified with interests that transcend national boundaries, we expect all NGOs to define problems in global terms, to take account of human interests and needs as they are found in all parts of the planet."[8] NGOs are often represented at the United Nations and include professional, business, and cooperative organizations; foundations; religious, peace, and disarmament groups; youth and women's organizations; environmental and human rights groups; and research institutes. The number of international NGOs has increased from 176 in 1910 to many thousands today.

And yet hopes for global approaches to global problems have also been hindered by political, ethnic, and religious disputes. Pollution of the Rhine River by factories along its banks provokes angry disputes among European nations, and the United States and Canada have argued about the effects of acid rain on Canadian forests. The collapse of the Soviet Union and its satellite system seemed to provide an enormous boost to the potential for international cooperation on global issues, but it has had almost the opposite effect. The bloody conflict in the former Yugoslavia indicates the dangers inherent in the rise of nationalist sentiment among various ethnic and religious groups in Eastern Europe. The widening gap between the wealthy nations in the Northern Hemisphere and the poor, developing nations in the Southern Hemisphere threatens global economic stability. Many conflicts begin with regional issues and then develop into international concerns. International terrorist groups seek to wreak havoc around the world.

Thus, even as the world becomes more global in culture and interdependent in its mutual relations, centrifugal forces are still at work attempting to redefine the political, cultural, and ethnic ways in which the world is divided. Such efforts are often disruptive and can sometimes work against measures to enhance our human destiny.

Many lessons can be learned from the history of Western civilization, but one of them is especially clear. Lack of involvement in the affairs of one's society can lead to a sense of powerlessness. In an age that is often crisis-laden and chaotic, an understanding of our Western heritage and its lessons can be instrumental in helping us create new models for the future. For we are all creators of history, and the future of Western and indeed world civilization depends on us.

When Mikhail Gorbachev came to power in the Soviet Union in 1985, he proposed radical reforms in both the economy and Soviet government. With these reforms, the pressure for more drastic change began to mount. In 1989, a wave of revolution swept through Eastern Europe as Communist regimes were overthrown and a new, mostly democratic order emerged, although serious divisions remained, especially in Yugoslavia. In 1991, the attempt of reactionary forces to undo the reforms of Gorbachev led instead to the complete disintegration of the Soviet Union and the emergence of a new Russia. The Cold War, which had begun at the end of World War II and had led to a Europe divided along ideological lines, was finally over.

Although many people were optimistic about a new world order after the collapse of communism, uncertainties still prevailed. Germany was successfully reunited, and the European Union became even stronger with the adoption of a common currency in the euro. Yugoslavia, however, disintegrated into warring states that eventually all became independent, and ethnic groups that had once been forced to live under distinct national banners began rebelling to form autonomous states. Although some were successful, others, such as the Chechnyans, were brutally repressed.

While the so-called new world order was fitfully developing, other challenges emerged. The arrival of many foreigners, especially in Western Europe, not only strained the social services of European countries but also led to antiforeign sentiment and right-wing political parties that encouraged it. Environmental abuses led to growing threats not only to Europeans but also all humans. Terrorism, especially that carried out by some parts of the Muslim world, emerged as a threat to many Western states. Since the end of the Cold War, terrorism seemed to have replaced communism as the number one enemy of the West.

At the beginning of the twenty-first century, a major realization has been the recognition that the problems afflicting the Western world have also become global problems. The nation-state, whose history dominated the nineteenth and twentieth centuries and which still plays an important role in contemporary affairs, nevertheless appears to be an outmoded structure if humankind is to resolve its many challenges. Nations and peoples have become more interdependent, and many Westerners recognize that a global perspective must also now become a part of the Western tradition.

CHAPTER TIMELINE

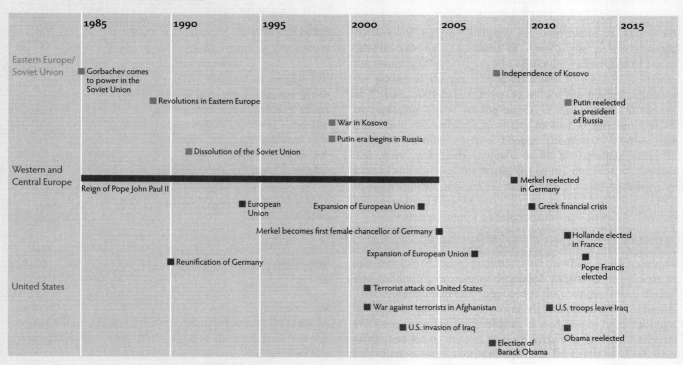

CHAPTER REVIEW

Upon Reflection

Q What roles did Mikhail Gorbachev and Ronald Reagan play in bringing an end to the Cold War? Which played a more important role? Why?

Q What directions did Eastern European nations take after they became free from Soviet control? Why did they react as they did?

Q What is globalization, and how does it relate to the technological and social concerns of our age?

Key Terms

perestroika (p. 921)
glasnost (p. 921)
ethnic cleansing (p. 928)
guest workers (p. 940)
multiculturalism (p. 944)
globalization (p. 945)
global economy (p. 945)

multinational corporation or **transnational corporation** (p. 947)
global warming (p. 949)
greenhouse effect (p. 949)
developed nations (p. 950)
developing nations (p. 950)

Suggestions for Further Reading

GENERAL WORKS For a well-written survey of Europe from 1985 to 2004, see **T. Judt,** *Postwar: A History of Europe Since 1945* (New York, 2005).

TOWARD A NEW WESTERN ORDER Aspects of the revolutionary upheaval in the Soviet Union and its aftermath are covered in **M. Kramer,** *Collapse of the Soviet Union* (Boulder, Colo., 2007), and **M. Garcelon,** *Revolutionary Passage: From Soviet to Post-Soviet Russia, 1985–2000* (Philadelphia, 2005).

AFTER THE COLD WAR On the end of the Cold War, see **S. Dockrill,** *The End of the Cold War Era* (London, 2005), and **J. L. Gaddis,** *The Cold War: A New History* (New York, 2005). On terrorism, see **W. Laqueur,** *History of Terrorism* (New York, 2001).

NEW DIRECTIONS AND NEW PROBLEMS IN WESTERN SOCIETY The changing role of women is examined in **R. Rosen,** *The World Split Open: How the Modern Women's Movement Changed America* (New York, 2001), and **J. W. Scott,** *The Politics of the Veil* (Princeton, N.J., 2009). The problems of

guest workers and immigrants are examined in **W. Laqueur,** *The Last Days of Europe: Epitaph for an Old Continent* (New York, 2007), and **R. Chin,** *Guest Worker Question in Germany* (Cambridge, 2007).

WESTERN CULTURE TODAY For a comprehensive examination of the Digital Age, see **M. Castells,** *The Information Age,* 3 vols. (Oxford, 1996–1998). On the role of the media in the Digital Age, see **R. Dominick,** *Dynamics of Mass Communication: Media in the Digital Age* (New York, 2006). On art, see **B. Wands,** *Art of the Digital Age* (London, 2007).

TOWARD A GLOBAL CIVILIZATION Useful books on different facets of the new global civilization include **M. B. Steger,** *Globalization: A Very Short Introduction* (New York, 2003); **J. H. Mittelman,** *The Globalization Syndrome* (Princeton, N.J., 2000); and **H. French,** *Vanishing Borders* (New York, 2000) on globalization and the environment. On the global financial crisis, see **N. Ferguson,** *The Ascent of Money: A Financial History of the World* (New York, 2008).

Notes

1. Quoted in T. Judt, *Postwar: A History of Europe Since 1945* (New York, 2005), p. 585.
2. Mikhail Gorbachev, "Report to the 27th Party Congress," February 25, 1986, in *Current Soviet Policies* 9 (1986): 10.
3. Quoted in W. I. Hitchcock, *The Struggle for Europe: The Turbulent History of a Divided Continent, 1945–2002* (New York, 2003), pp. 399–400.
4. Quoted in R. Bridenthal, "Women in the New Europe," in R. Bridenthal, S. Mosher Stuard, and M. E. Weisner, eds.,

Becoming Visible: Women in European History, 3rd ed. (Boston, 1998), pp. 564–565.
5. Quoted in Judt, *Postwar Europe,* p. 743.
6. Quoted in J. W. Scott, *The Politics of the Veil* (Princeton, N.J., 2009), p. 1.
7. Quoted in *Washington Post,* 10 Key Excerpts from Pope Francis's Encyclical on the Environment, June 18, 2015.
8. E. Boulding, *Women in the Twentieth-Century World* (New York, 1977), pp. 186–187.

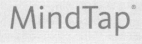 **MindTap®** is a fully online, highly personalized learning experience built upon Cengage Learning content. MindTap combines student learning tools—readings, multimedia, activities, and assessments—into a singular Learning Path that guides students through the course.

GLOSSARY

absolutism   form of government in which the sovereign power or ultimate authority rested in the hands of a monarch who claimed to rule by divine right and was therefore responsible only to God.

Abstract Expressionism   a post–World War II artistic movement that broke with all conventions of form and structure in favor of total abstraction.

abstract painting   an artistic movement that developed early in the twentieth century in which artists focused on color to avoid any references to visual reality.

Agricultural (Neolithic) Revolution   *see* **Neolithic Revolution**.

agricultural revolution   the application of new agricultural techniques that allowed for a large increase in productivity in the eighteenth century.

anarchism   a political theory that holds that all governments and existing social institutions are unnecessary and advocates a society based on voluntary cooperation.

anticlericalism   opposition to the power of the clergy, especially in political affairs.

anti-Semitism   hostility toward or discrimination against Jews.

apartheid   the system of racial segregation practiced in the Republic of South Africa until the 1990s, which involved political, legal, and economic discrimination against nonwhites.

appeasement   the policy, followed by the European nations in the 1930s, of accepting Hitler's annexation of Austria and Czechoslovakia in the belief that meeting his demands would assure peace and stability.

audiencias   advisory groups to viceroys in Spanish America.

Ausgleich   the "Compromise" of 1867 that created the Dual Monarchy of Austria-Hungary. Austria and Hungary each had its own capital, constitution, and legislative assembly but were united under one monarch.

authoritarian state   a state that has a dictatorial government and some other trappings of a totalitarian state but does not demand that the masses be actively involved in the regime's goals as totalitarian states do.

balance of power   a distribution of power among several states such that no single nation can dominate or interfere with the interests of another.

Baroque   an artistic movement of the seventeenth century in Europe that used dramatic effects to arouse the emotions and reflected the search for power that was a large part of the seventeenth-century ethos.

blitzkrieg   "lightning war." A war conducted with great speed and force, as in Germany's advance at the beginning of World War II.

Bolsheviks   a small faction of the Russian Social Democratic Party who were led by Lenin and dedicated to violent revolution. They seized power in Russia in 1917 and were subsequently renamed the Communists.

boyars   the Russian nobility.

Brezhnev Doctrine   the doctrine, enunciated by Leonid Brezhnev, that the Soviet Union had a right to intervene if socialism was threatened in another socialist state; used to justify moving Soviet troops into Czechoslovakia in 1968.

Burschenschaften   student societies in the German states dedicated to fostering the goal of a free, united Germany.

capital   material wealth used or available for use in the production of more wealth.

cartels   combinations of independent commercial enterprises that work together to control prices and limit competition.

Cartesian dualism   Descartes's principle of the separation of mind and matter (and mind and body) that enabled scientists to view matter as something separate from themselves that could be investigated by reason.

Catholic Reformation   the movement for the reform of the Catholic Church in the sixteenth century. It included a revived papacy; the regeneration of old religious orders and the founding of new ones, most notably the Jesuits; and the reaffirmation of traditional Catholic doctrine at the Council of Trent.

cholera   a serious and often deadly disease commonly spread by contaminated water; a major problem in nineteenth-century European cities before sewerage systems were installed.

Christian (northern Renaissance) humanism   an intellectual movement in northern Europe in the late fifteenth and early sixteenth centuries that combined the interest in the classics of the Italian Renaissance with an interest in the sources of early Christianity, including the New Testament and the writings of the church fathers.

civil disobedience   a policy of peaceful protest against laws or government policies in order to achieve political change.

Cold War   the ideological conflict between the Soviet Union and the United States after World War II.

Columbian Exchange   the reciprocal importation and exportation of plants and animals between Europe and the Americas.

confession   one of the seven sacraments of the Catholic Church. It provided for the forgiveness of one's sins.

conquistadors   "conquerors." Leaders in the Spanish conquests in the Americas, especially Mexico and Peru, in the sixteenth century.

conscription   a military draft.

conservatism an ideology based on tradition and social stability that favored the maintenance of established institutions, organized religion, and obedience to authority and resisted change, especially abrupt change.

consumer society a term applied to Western society after World War II as the working classes adopted the consumption patterns of the middle class and payment plans, credit cards, and easy credit made consumer goods such as appliances and automobiles affordable.

containment a policy adopted by the United States in the Cold War. Its goal was to use any means, short of all-out war, to limit Soviet expansion.

Continental System Napoleon's effort to bar British goods from the continent in the hope of weakening Britain's economy and destroying its capacity to wage war.

cosmopolitan the quality of being sophisticated and having wide international experience.

cottage industry a system of textile manufacturing in which spinners and weavers worked at home in their cottages using raw materials supplied to them by capitalist entrepreneurs.

Cubism an artistic style developed at the beginning of the twentieth century, especially by Pablo Picasso, that used geometric designs to re-create reality in the viewer's mind.

cultural relativism the belief that no culture is superior to another because culture is a matter of custom, not reason, and derives its meaning from the group holding it.

Dadaism an artistic movement in the 1920s and 1930s begun by artists who were revolted by the senseless slaughter of World War I and used their "anti-art" to express contempt for the Western tradition.

de-Christianization a policy, adopted in the radical phase of the French Revolution, aimed at creating a secular society by eliminating Christian forms and institutions from French society.

decolonization the process of becoming free of colonial status and achieving statehood. It occurred in most of the world's colonies between 1947 and 1962.

deconstruction *see* **poststructuralism**.

deism belief in God as the creator of the universe who, after setting it in motion, ceased to have any direct involvement in it and allowed it to run according to its own natural laws.

denazification after World War II, the Allied policy of rooting out any traces of Nazism in German society by bringing prominent Nazis to trial for war crimes and purging any known Nazis from political office.

depression a very severe, protracted economic downturn with high levels of unemployment.

de-Stalinization the policy of denouncing and undoing the most repressive aspects of Stalin's regime; begun by Nikita Khrushchev in 1956.

détente the relaxation of tension between the Soviet Union and the United States that occurred in the 1970s.

developed nations a term used to refer to rich nations, primarily in the Northern Hemisphere, that have well-organized industrial and agricultural systems, advanced technologies, and effective educational systems.

developing nations a term used to refer to poor nations, mainly in the Southern Hemisphere, that are primarily farming nations with little technology and serious population problems.

divine-right monarchy a monarchy based on the belief that monarchs receive their power directly from God and are responsible to no one except God.

domino theory the belief that if the Communists succeeded in Vietnam, other countries in Southeast and East Asia would also fall (like dominoes) to communism; cited as a justification for the U.S. intervention in Vietnam.

economic imperialism the process in which banks and corporations from developed nations invest in underdeveloped regions and establish a major presence there in the hope of making high profits; not necessarily the same as colonial expansion in that businesses invest where they can make a profit, which may not be in their own nation's colonies.

economic liberalism the idea that government should not interfere in the workings of the economy.

Einsatzgruppen in Nazi Germany, special strike forces in the SS that played an important role in rounding up and killing Jews.

empiricism the practice of relying on observation and experiment.

enclosure acts laws enacted in eighteenth-century Britain that allowed large landowners to enclose the old open fields, thereby combining many small holdings into larger units and forcing many small farmers to become tenant farmers or wage laborers on the large estates.

encomienda in Spanish America, a form of economic and social organization in which a Spaniard was given a royal grant that enabled the holder of the grant to collect tribute from the Indians and use them as laborers.

enlightened absolutism an absolute monarchy in which the ruler followed the principles of the Enlightenment by introducing reforms for the improvement of society, allowing freedom of speech and the press, permitting religious toleration, expanding education, and ruling in accordance with the laws.

Enlightenment an eighteenth-century intellectual movement, led by the philosophes, that stressed the application of reason and the scientific method to all aspects of life.

ethnic cleansing the policy of killing or forcibly removing people of another ethnic group; used by the Serbs against Bosnian Muslims in the 1990s.

Eurocommunism a form of communism that dropped its Marxist ideology. It was especially favored in Italy.

evolutionary socialism a socialist doctrine espoused by Eduard Bernstein who argued that socialists should stress cooperation and evolution to attain power by democratic means rather than by conflict and revolution.

existentialism a philosophical movement that arose after World War II that emphasized the meaninglessness of life, born of the desperation caused by two world wars.

family allowances one aspect of the welfare state whereby the state provides a minimum level of material assistance for children.

fascism an ideology or movement that exalts the nation above the individual and calls for a centralized government with a dictatorial leader, economic and social regimentation, and forcible suppression of opposition; in particular, the ideology of Mussolini's Fascist regime in Italy.

feminism the belief in the social, political, and economic equality of the sexes; also, organized activity to advance women's rights.

Final Solution the attempted physical extermination of the Jewish people by the Nazis during World War II.

Führerprinzip in Nazi Germany, a leadership principle based on the belief in a single-minded party (the Nazis) under one leader (Hitler).

functionalism the idea that the function of an object should determine its design and materials.

general strike a strike by all or most workers in an economy; espoused by Georges Sorel as the heroic action that could be used to inspire the workers to destroy capitalist society.

genocide the deliberate extermination of a people.

gentry well-to-do English landowners below the level of the nobility. They played an important role in the English Civil War of the seventeenth century.

geocentric conception the belief that the earth was at the center of the universe and that the sun and other celestial objects revolved around the earth.

Girondins a faction in the National Convention during the French Revolution that favored keeping the king alive; so-called because their leaders came from the Gironde in southwestern France.

glasnost "openness." Mikhail Gorbachev's policy of encouraging Soviet citizens to openly discuss the strengths and weaknesses of the Soviet Union.

global economy an interdependent economy in which the production, distribution, and sale of goods are accomplished on a worldwide scale.

global warming the increase in the temperature of the earth's atmosphere caused by the greenhouse effect.

globalization a term referring to the trend by which peoples and nations have become more interdependent; often used to refer to the development of a global economy and culture.

Gothic literature a form of literature used by Romantics to emphasize the bizarre and unusual, especially evident in horror stories.

greenhouse effect the warming of the earth caused by the buildup of carbon dioxide in the atmosphere as a result of human activity.

guest workers foreign workers working temporarily in European countries.

heliocentric conception the belief that the sun, not the earth, is at the center of the universe.

high culture the literary and artistic culture of the educated and wealthy ruling classes.

home rule in the United Kingdom, self-government by having a separate parliament but not complete independence.

Huguenots French Calvinists.

ideology a political philosophy such as conservatism or liberalism.

Impressionism an artistic movement that originated in France in the 1870s. Impressionists sought to capture their impressions of the changing effects of light on objects in nature.

individualism emphasis on and interest in the unique traits of each person.

infanticide the practice of killing infants.

intendants royal officials in seventeenth-century France who were sent into the provinces to execute the orders of the central government.

Janissaries an elite core of eight thousand troops personally loyal to the sultan of the Ottoman Empire.

joint-stock company a company or association that raises capital by selling shares to individuals who receive dividends on their investment while a board of directors runs the company.

joint-stock investment bank a bank created by selling shares of stock to investors. Such banks potentially have access to much more capital than private banks owned by one or a few individuals.

justification the primary doctrine of the Protestant Reformation, teaching that humans are saved not through good works but by the grace of God, bestowed freely through the sacrifice of Jesus.

Kulturkampf "culture conflict." The name given to Bismarck's attack on the Catholic Church in Germany; has come to refer to conflict between church and state anywhere.

laissez-faire "let (them) do (as they please)." An economic doctrine that holds that an economy is best served when the government does not interfere but allows the economy to self-regulate according to the forces of supply and demand.

Lebensraum "living space." The doctrine, adopted by Hitler, that a nation's power depends on the amount of land it occupies. Thus, a nation must expand to be strong.

liberalism an ideology based on the belief that people should be as free from restraint as possible. Economic liberalism is the idea that the government should not interfere in the workings of the economy. Political liberalism is the idea that there should be restraints on the exercise of power so that people can enjoy basic civil rights in a constitutional state with a representative assembly.

mandates   a system established after World War I whereby a nation officially administered a territory (mandate) on behalf of the League of Nations. Thus, France administered Lebanon and Syria as mandates, and Britain administered Iraq and Palestine.

Mannerism   a sixteenth-century artistic movement in Europe that deliberately broke down the High Renaissance principles of balance, harmony, and moderation.

Marshall Plan   the European Recovery Program, under which the United States provided financial aid to European countries to help them rebuild after World War II.

Marxism   the political, economic, and social theories of Karl Marx, which included the idea that history is the story of class struggle and that ultimately the proletariat will overthrow the bourgeoisie and establish a dictatorship en route to a classless society.

mass education   a state-run educational system, usually free and compulsory, that aims to ensure that all children in society have at least a basic education.

mass leisure   forms of leisure that appeal to large numbers of people in a society, including the working classes; emerged at the end of the nineteenth century to provide workers with amusements after work and on weekends; used during the twentieth century by totalitarian states to control their populations.

mass politics   a political order characterized by mass political parties and universal male and (eventually) female suffrage.

mass society   a society in which the concerns of the majority—the lower classes—play a prominent role; characterized by extension of voting rights, an improved standard of living for the lower classes, and mass education.

materialism   the belief that everything mental, spiritual, or ideal is an outgrowth of physical forces and that truth is found in concrete material existence, not through feeling or intuition.

mercantilism   an economic theory that held that a nation's prosperity depended on its supply of gold and silver and that the total volume of trade is unchangeable. Its adherents therefore advocated that the government play an active role in the economy by encouraging exports and discouraging imports, especially through the use of tariffs.

Middle Passage   the journey of slaves from Africa to the Americas as the middle leg of the triangular trade.

militarism   a policy of aggressive military preparedness; in particular, the large armies based on mass conscription and complex, inflexible plans for mobilization that most European nations had before World War I.

millenarianism   the belief that the end of the world is at hand and the kingdom of God is about to be established on earth.

ministerial responsibility   a tenet of nineteenth-century liberalism that held that ministers of the monarch should

be responsible to the legislative assembly rather than to the monarch.

mir   a peasant village commune in Russia.

mobilization   the organization of troops and supplies for service in time of war.

Modernism   the artistic and literary styles that emerged in the decades before 1914 as artists rebelled against traditional efforts to portray reality as accurately as possible (leading to Impressionism and Cubism) and writers explored new forms.

Mountain   a faction in the National Convention during the French Revolution that represented the interests of the city of Paris and favored the execution of the king.

multiculturalism   a term referring to the connection of several cultural or ethnic groups within a society.

multinational corporation   a company with divisions in two or more countries.

mutual deterrence   the belief that nuclear war could best be prevented if both the United States and the Soviet Union had sufficient nuclear weapons so that even if one nation launched a preemptive first strike, the other could respond and devastate the attacker.

nation in arms   the people's army raised by universal mobilization to repel the foreign enemies of the French Revolution.

nationalism   a sense of national consciousness based on awareness of being part of a community—a "nation"—that has common institutions, traditions, language, and customs and that becomes the focus of the individual's primary political loyalty.

nationalities problem   the dilemma faced by the Austro-Hungarian Empire in trying to unite a wide variety of ethnic groups (Austrians, Hungarians, Poles, Croats, Czechs, Serbs, Slovaks, and Slovenes, among others) in an era when nationalism and calls for self-determination were coming to the fore.

nationalization   the process of converting a business or industry from private ownership to government control and ownership.

NATO   the North Atlantic Treaty Organization, a military alliance formed in 1949 in which the signatories (Belgium, Canada, Denmark, France, Great Britain, Iceland, Italy, Luxembourg, the Netherlands, Norway, Portugal, and the United States) agreed to provide mutual assistance if any one of them was attacked; later expanded to include other nations.

natural laws   a body of laws or specific principles held to be derived from nature and binding on all human societies even in the absence of written laws governing such matters.

natural rights   certain inalienable rights to which all people are entitled, including the right to life, liberty, and property; freedom of speech and religion; and equality before the law.

natural selection   Darwin's idea that organisms that are most adaptable to their environment survive and pass on the variations that enabled them to survive, while less adaptable organisms become extinct; "survival of the fittest."

Nazi New Order the Nazis' plan for their conquered territories. It included the extermination of Jews and others considered inferior, ruthless exploitation of resources, German colonization in the east, and the use of Poles, Russians, and Ukrainians as slave labor.

neoclassicism a late-eighteenth-century artistic movement that emerged in France. It sought to recapture the dignity and simplicity of the classical style of ancient Greece and Rome.

New Economic Policy a modified version of the old capitalist system introduced in the Soviet Union by Lenin in 1921 to revive the economy after the ravages of the civil war and war communism.

new imperialism the revival of imperialism after 1880 in which European nations established colonies throughout much of Asia and Africa.

old order the political and social system of France in the eighteenth century before the Revolution.

organic evolution Darwin's principle that all plants and animals have evolved over a long period of time from earlier and simpler forms of life.

pantheism a doctrine that equates God with the universe and all that is in it.

panzer division in the German army under Hitler, a strike force of about three hundred tanks and accompanying forces and supplies.

parlements provincial law courts in France.

pasteurization a process developed by Louis Pasteur for heating a product to destroy the microorganisms that might cause spoilage.

patronage the practice of awarding titles and making appointments to government and other positions to gain political support.

perestroika "restructuring." A term applied to Mikhail Gorbachev's economic, political, and social reforms in the Soviet Union.

permissive society a term applied to Western society after World War II to reflect the new sexual freedom and the emergence of a drug culture.

phalanstery a self-sustaining cooperative community, as advocated by Charles Fourier in the early nineteenth century.

philosophes intellectuals of the eighteenth-century Enlightenment who believed in applying a spirit of rational criticism to all things, including religion and politics, and who focused on improving and enjoying this world, rather than on the afterlife.

Pietism a movement that arose in Germany in the seventeenth century whose goal was to foster a personal experience of God as the focus of true religious experience.

pig iron a type of iron produced by smelting iron ore with coke; of lower quality than wrought iron.

pluralism the practice of holding several church offices simultaneously; a problem of the late medieval church.

plutocrats members of the wealthy elite.

pogroms organized massacres of Jews.

political democracy a form of government characterized by universal suffrage and mass political parties.

politiques a group who emerged during the French Wars of Religion in the sixteenth century, placed politics above religion, and believed that no religious truth was worth the ravages of civil war.

Pop Art an artistic movement of the 1950s and 1960s in which artists took images of popular culture and transformed them into works of fine art. Andy Warhol's painting of Campbell's soup cans is one example.

popular culture as opposed to high culture, the unofficial written and unwritten culture of the masses, much of which was traditionally passed down orally and centered on public and group activities such as festivals. In the modern age, the term refers to the entertainment, recreation, and pleasures that people purchase as part of the mass consumer society.

populism a political philosophy or movement that supports the rights and power of ordinary people in their struggle against the privileged elite.

portolani charts of landmasses and coastlines made by navigators and mathematicians in the thirteenth and fourteenth centuries.

Post-Impressionism an artistic movement that began in France in the 1880s. Post-Impressionists sought to use color and line to express inner feelings and produce a personal statement of reality.

Postmodernism a term used to cover a variety of artistic and intellectual styles and ways of thinking prominent since the 1970s.

poststructuralism a system of thought, formulated by Jacques Derrida, that holds that culture is created in a variety of ways, according to the manner in which people create their own meaning. Hence, there is no fixed truth or universal meaning.

predestination the belief, associated with Calvinism, that God, as a consequence of his foreknowledge of all events, has predetermined those who will be saved (the elect) and those who will be damned.

prefects officials appointed by the central government to oversee all aspects of a local government during the reign of Napoleon.

price revolution the dramatic rise in prices (inflation) that occurred throughout Europe in the sixteenth and early seventeenth centuries.

primogeniture an inheritance practice in which the eldest son receives all or the largest share of the parents' estate.

principle of intervention the idea, after the Congress of Vienna, that the great powers of Europe had the right to send armies into countries experiencing revolution to restore legitimate monarchs to their thrones.

principle of legitimacy the idea that after the Napoleonic wars, peace could best be reestablished in Europe by restoring legitimate monarchs who would preserve traditional institutions; guided Metternich at the Congress of Vienna.

procurator the head of the Holy Synod, the chief decision-making body for the Russian Orthodox Church.

proletariat the industrial working class; in Marxism, the class that will ultimately overthrow the bourgeoisie.

propaganda a program of distorted information put out by an organization or government to spread its policy, cause, or doctrine.

psychoanalysis a method developed by Sigmund Freud to resolve a patient's psychic conflict.

Puritans English Protestants inspired by Calvinist theology who wished to remove all traces of Catholicism from the Church of England.

querelles des femmes "arguments about women." A centuries-old debate about the nature of women that continued during the Scientific Revolution as those who argued for the inferiority of women found additional support in the new anatomy and medicine.

rapprochement the rebuilding of harmonious relations between nations.

rationalism a system of thought based on the belief that human reason and experience are the chief sources of knowledge.

Realism a nineteenth-century school of painting that emphasized the everyday life of ordinary people, depicted with photographic accuracy.

Realpolitik "politics of reality." Politics based on practical concerns rather than theory or ethics.

reason of state the principle that a nation should act on the basis of its long-term interests and not merely to further the dynastic interests of its ruling family.

relativity theory Einstein's theory that, among other things, (1) space and time are not absolute but are relative to the observer and interwoven into a four-dimensional space-time continuum and (2) matter is a form of energy ($E = mc^2$).

reparations payments made by a defeated nation after a war to compensate another nation for damage sustained as a result of the war; required from Germany after World War I.

revisionism a socialist doctrine that rejected Marx's emphasis on class struggle and revolution and argued instead that workers should work through political parties to bring about gradual change.

revolution a fundamental change in the political and social organization of a state.

revolutionary socialism a socialist doctrine that violent action was the only way to achieve the goals of socialism.

risorgimento a movement in Italy in the nineteenth century aimed at the creation of a united Italian republica.

Rococo an eighteenth-century artistic movement that emphasized grace, gentility, lightness, and charm.

Romanticism a nineteenth-century intellectual and artistic movement that rejected the emphasis on reason of the Enlightenment. Instead, Romantics stressed the importance of intuition, feeling, emotion, and imagination as sources of knowing.

salons gatherings of philosophes and other notables to discuss the ideas of the Enlightenment; so called from the elegant drawing rooms (salons) where they met.

sans-culottes "without breeches." The common people, who did not wear the fine clothes of the upper classes and played an important role in the radical phase of the French Revolution.

scientific method a method of seeking knowledge through inductive principles, using experiments and observations to develop generalizations.

Scientific Revolution the transition from the medieval worldview to a largely secular, rational, and materialistic perspective that began in the seventeenth century and was popularized in the eighteenth.

self-determination the doctrine that the people of a given territory or a particular nationality should have the right to determine their own government and political future.

separation of powers a doctrine enunciated by Montesquieu in the eighteenth century that separate executive, legislative, and judicial powers serve to limit and control each other.

skepticism a doubtful or questioning attitude, especially about religion.

social Darwinism the application of Darwin's principle of organic evolution to the social order; led to the belief that progress comes from the struggle for survival as the fittest advance and the weak decline.

social security government programs that provide social welfare measures such as old-age pensions and sickness, accident, and disability insurance.

socialism an ideology that calls for collective or government ownership of the means of production and the distribution of goods.

socialized medicine health services for all citizens provided by government assistance.

soviets councils of workers' and soldiers' deputies formed throughout Russia in 1917 that played an important role in the Bolshevik Revolution.

squadristi in Italy in the 1920s, bands of armed Fascists used to create disorder by attacking Socialist offices and newspapers.

stagflation a combination of high inflation and high unemployment that was prevalent in the United States and elsewhere from 1973 to the mid-1980s.

Stalinization the adoption by Eastern European Communist countries of features of the economic, political, and military policies implemented by Stalin in the Soviet Union.

suffragists advocates of extending the right to vote to women.

Surrealism an artistic movement that arose between World War I and World War II. Surrealists portrayed recognizable objects in unrecognizable relationships in order to reveal the world of the unconscious.

tariffs duties (taxes) imposed on imported goods, usually to raise revenue and to discourage imports and protect domestic industries.

tithe a portion of one's harvest or income, paid by medieval peasants to the village church.

total war warfare in which all of a nation's resources, including civilians at home as well as soldiers in the field, are mobilized for the war effort.

totalitarian state a state characterized by government control over all aspects of economic, social, political, cultural, and intellectual life; the subordination of the individual to the state; and insistence that the masses be actively involved in the regime's goals.

trade unions associations of workers in the same trade formed to help members secure better wages, benefits, and working conditions.

transformism the theory that societies evolve gradually.

transnational corporation *see* **multinational corporation**.

transubstantiation a doctrine of the Roman Catholic Church that during the Eucharist, the substance of the bread and wine is miraculously transformed into the body and blood of Jesus.

trench warfare warfare in which the opposing forces attack and counterattack from a relatively permanent system of trenches protected by barbed wire; a characteristic of World War I.

triangular trade a pattern of trade in early modern Europe that connected Europe, Africa, and the Americas in an Atlantic economy.

Truman Doctrine the doctrine, enunciated by Harry Truman in 1947, that the United States would provide economic aid to countries that said they were threatened by Communist expansion.

ultraroyalists in nineteenth-century France, a group of aristocrats who sought to return to a monarchical system dominated by a landed aristocracy and the Catholic Church.

uncertainty principle a principle in quantum mechanics, posited by Heisenberg, that holds that one cannot determine the path of an electron because the very act of observing the electron would affect its location.

unconditional surrender complete, unqualified surrender of a belligerent nation.

utopian socialists intellectuals and theorists in the early nineteenth century who favored equality in social and economic conditions and wished to replace private property and competition with collective ownership and cooperation.

viceroy the administrative head of the provinces of New Spain and Peru in the Americas.

volkish thought the belief that German culture is superior and that the German people have a universal mission to save Western civilization from "inferior" races.

war communism Lenin's policy of nationalizing industrial and other facilities and requisitioning the peasants' produce during the civil war in Russia.

War Guilt Clause the clause in the Treaty of Versailles that declared that Germany (with Austria) was responsible for starting World War I and ordered Germany to pay reparations for the damage the Allies had suffered as a result of the war.

Warsaw Pact a military alliance, formed in 1955, in which Albania, Bulgaria, Czechoslovakia, East Germany, Hungary, Poland, Romania, and the Soviet Union agreed to provide mutual assistance.

welfare state a sociopolitical system in which the government assumes primary responsibility for the social welfare of its citizens by providing such things as social security, unemployment benefits, and health care.

world-machine Newton's conception of the universe as one huge, regulated, and uniform machine that operated according to natural laws in absolute time, space, and motion.

wrought iron a high-quality iron first produced during the eighteenth century in Britain; manufactured by puddling, a process developed by Henry Cort that involved using coke to burn away the impurities in pig iron.

zemstvos local assemblies established in Russia in 1864 by Tsar Alexander II.

Zionism an international movement that called for the establishment of a Jewish state or a refuge for Jews in Palestine.

Zollverein the customs union of all the German states except Austria, formed by Prussia in 1834.

INDEX

Italicized page numbers show the locations of illustrations and maps.

Abernathy, Ralph, *885*
Abolition of slavery, 580
Abortion, 704, 801, 813, 939
Abraham Lincoln Brigade, 816
Absolutism, 432, 469; in central Europe, 448–455, 628–629; in eastern Europe, 448–455; enlightened, 529, 536, 539, 556; in German States, *448*, 448–450, *449*; limits of, 455; in northern Europe, 448–455; philosophes on, 504–505; in Russia, 450–453, 716; in Sweden, 453, *453*; in western Europe, 440–447. *See also* Enlightened absolutism
Abstract Expressionism, 889–890
Abstract painting, 729, *730*, 820
Academy of Sciences, *501*
Acheson, Dean, 866
Acid rain, 945, 950
Act of Supremacy (England), 381, 395
Act of Union (1801), 712
Adams, John, 503, *562*
Addison, Joseph, 516–517
Address to the Nobility of the German Nation (Luther), 370
"Address to the People of Czechoslovakia" (Havel), 926
Address to the Reichstag (Bismarck), 715
Address to the Twentieth Party Congress (Khrushchev), 878
Adenauer, Konrad, 867, 882
Administration. *See* Government
Adrianople: Treaty of, 626
Adriatic Sea region, 752
Advertising, 712
Affonso of Congo (Bakongo), 414–415
Afghanistan, 751; Reagan and, 912; Russia and, 747; Soviets in, 922; U.S. war in, 937
Africa: in 1914, *744*; civil wars in (1980s and 1990s), 936; decolonization in, 871–872, *873*; imperialism in, 742–746, 749; independence and, 800–801, 871–872; Paris Peace Conference and, 786, 787; Portugal and, 745; slaves and, 421; slave trade and, 413, *413*; World War I and, 770;

after World War I, 800–801. *See also* specific locations
African Americans: civil rights movement and, 885–886; in World War II U.S., 852
African National Congress (ANC), 872
Afrika Korps, 840
Afrikaners (Boers), 744–745
Against the Robbing and Murdering Hordes of Peasants (Luther), 373, *374*
Age of Louis XIV, The (Voltaire), 441, 516
Agricultural revolution, 543, 546–548, 593
Agriculture: in 18th century, 533–534, *546*, 546–548; Columbian Exchange and, 423, 425–426, *426*; industrial economy and, 690; population growth and, 697; in Soviet Union, 812, 813, 814. *See also* Farms and farming; Land
Ahlwardt, Hermann, 734
Air force: in Spanish Civil War, 815, *817*; in World War II, 829, 835, 836, 853–854
Airplanes, 687–688; civilian travel on, 819; in World War I, 771–772; in World War II, 835, 852
Air pollution, 913
Aix-la-Chapelle: congress at, 623; treaty of, 540
Akbar (Mughal Empire), 418
Alaska, 747
Albania and Albanians, 360, 752; Communist Party and, 879; in Kosovo, 928, 929
Albert (England), 600–601, 669
Albuquerque, Afonso de, 403–404
Alcohol: in 18th century, 519–520
Aleshker, Lev, 697
Alexander I (Russia), 586, 629
Alexander I (Yugoslavia), 815
Alexander II (Russia), 658, 666–667, 669, 716
Alexander III (Russia), 669, 716
Alexander VI (Pope), 361–362
Alexandra (Russia), *739*, 778
Alexis (Russia), 778
al-Fatah, 875
Alfonso XII (Spain), 713

Alfonso XIII (Spain), 815
Algeria, 745, 872, 881
Alliances: of Bismarck, 751–752; in Cold War, 867, 868, 869; after Congress of Berlin, 752, *759*; defensive, 786, 789, 793; in Italy, 659; after Napoleonic wars, 621–622, *622*, 623–624; in Seven Years' War, 540–541; World War I and, 758; after World War I, 793–794; World War II and, 830. *See also* specific locations and pacts
Allied Reparations Commission, 794
Allies: World War I, 758, 770, 771, 783, 784, 785, 788; World War II (Grand Alliance), 837, 839, 842–843
All Quiet on the Western Front (Remarque), 767
All-Russian Congress of Soviets, 780
al-Qaeda, 937, 938
al-Qaeda in Iraq (AQI), 937
Alsace, 446, 664, 787
Alsace-Lorraine, Germany and, 751, 758
Alva, duke of, 393
Amalgamated Society of Engineers, 616
Amanat, Abbas, 938
Amazon region, 409
America(s): crops from, 543, 547; European empires in, 421–423; horses in, 410, 423; naming of, 406; plantation economy in, 421, 549; voyages to, *404*, 406–407; and War of the Austrian Succession, 540. *See also* New World; specific locations
American Federation of Labor, 740
American Indians. *See* Native Americans
Americanization: of culture, 917; after World War II, 892–893
American Medical Association: women in, 679
American Philosophical Society, 510
American Revolution, 560–563
American system, 603
Amiens, 586
Amish, 380
Amritsar Massacre (1919), 800
Amsterdam, *416*, 428, 456, 548
Amusement parks, 686
Anabaptists, 366, 379–380, 384
Anarchism, 696–697
Anatolia (Turkey). *See* Turkey

Anatomy, 484, 485, 488, 519
Ancient civilizations. *See* specific locations
Andersen, Hans Christian, 645
Andes Mountains, 625
Andreotti, Giulio, 906
Andropov, Yuri, 902
Anesthesia, 519, 678, 679
Angkor kingdom (Cambodia), 416
Anglican Church. *See* Church of England
Anglo-Dutch trade wars, 425–426
Anglo-German Naval Pact (1935), 830
Angola, 745
Animals: in Columbian Exchange, 425–426, *426*
Anjou, France, *356*
Annam, 747
Anne (England), 531
Anne of Austria, 441
Annotations (Erasmus), 367
Anticlericalism, 724
Anti-Comintern Pact, 830
Anti-Corn Law League, 636–637
Antiforeign parties, 940
Antinuclear movement: women in, 939–940
Anti-Semitism: in Austria, 734, 738; Dreyfus affair and, 737; in Germany, 734–735, 738, 810; of Hitler, 734, 806, 811, 843; Holocaust and, 845–848. *See also* Jews and Judaism
Antiwar protests: in Second Vietnam War, 897, 899, 901, 909
Anti-Western Islamic groups, *937*
Antwerp, 456
Apartheid, 872
Apothecaries, 519
Appeasement: Nazi Germany and, 830
Apple, *942, 943*
Apprentices: in 18th century, 554–555; pauper, 612
"April Theses" (Lenin), 779
Aqueducts, 408
Arab-Israeli disputes: in 1948, 873; in 1967, 875; in 1973, 908
Arab League, 873
Arabs and Arab world: Israel and, 873; trade and, 400–401, 403–404; World War I and, 788. *See also* Islam; Middle East
Arafat, Yasir, 875
Aragon: house of, *358, 358*
Architecture: of country houses, 552–554, *553*; functionalism in, 821–822, *822*; neo-Gothic, 645, *646*; Rococo, 513, *514*

Ardennes: in World War II, 836
Argentina, *624, 625*; Falkland Islands and, 906
Aristocracy. *See* Nobility
Aristotle: medieval learning and, 473; on motion, 480, 482
Arkwright, Richard, 549
Armada (Spain), *392, 396*
Armed forces. *See* Military; Navy; War(s) and warfare; specific wars and battles
Armenia, 782
Armenian people: genocide of, 784
Armistice (World War I), *764*, 784
Arms and armaments. *See* Weapons
Army Order No. 1 (Russia), 779
Arouet, François-Marie. *See* Voltaire
Art(s): Baroque, 464–465, *465*, 494; contemporary, 943–945; Dadaism in, 820, *821*; Dutch realism, 466, *466, 489*; French classicism in, 466–467, *467*; Mannerism in, 464, *464*; Modernism in, 725–731; Nazis and, 822; Postmodern, 914–915; Realism in, 680–682; in Renaissance, 356, 362–363; Rococo style in, 513, *513*; Romanticism in, 646–647, *647, 648*; scientific illustrations and, 485; Surrealism in, 820, *821*; after World War II, 889–891. *See also* specific arts
Art films: after World War II, 892
Articles of Confederation, 561
Art installation, 944
Artisans, 703; in 18th century, 546, 554–555; in 19th century, 611; British, 604
Artois, 447; count of, 573, 628
"Aryans," racist concept of, 724, 806, 808–809, 828, 844, 845–846, 848
Ashkenazic Jews, 522–523
Asia: in 1914, *748*; decolonization in, *876*; European involvement in, 747; events leading to World War II in, 833–835; imperialism in, 747–749; nationalism and communism in, 875–877; New Order in, 848–850; Portugal and, *403*, 403–404; trade with, 400–401; water route to, 406; World War II in, 838–839, *839*. *See also* Southeast Asia; specific locations
Asiento, 423
Assassinations, by anarchists, 697
Assembly line, 689
Assignats (paper money), 569, 582
Assimilation: of Jews, 734, 735, 737
Astell, Mary, 509–510
Astrolabe, 403

Astronomy: women in, 487–488. *See also* Universe
Atahualpa (Inca), 410
Atatürk. *See* Kemal, Mustafa
Athanor (Kiefer), *943*
Atheism, 507
Atlantic Ocean region: seaboard states in, 400, 427, 529–532; slave trade in, *413*; trade in, 550
Atmosphere: damage to, 948
Atomic bomb, 823, 851, 853, 854, *855*, 856
Atomic theory of universe, 720
Atomic weights, of elements, 676
Atonal music, 822
Auburn Prison, New York, 644–645
Audiencias, 410
Augsburg: Diet of, 376, 377; League of, 446; Peace of, 377 *375*, 396, 435
Augustinians, 369
Auschwitz-Birkenau, 846–847, *849*
Ausgleich (Compromise) of 1867, 666
Austerlitz, battle at, 586
Australia, 501, 518, 644, 747, 770, 771; World War II prisoner of war from, 850
Austria, 694, 815; alliances of, 752; Balkans and, 656, 751, 752–753; cities in, 607; Crimea War and, 657, 658; Denmark and, 662–663; France and, 573, 574; Germany and, 640, 661, 830–831; as great power, 529, *533*; Hitler in, 830–831, *831*; infanticide and, 545; Italy and, *449*, 449–450, 640, 659–660; Jews in, 523; military in, 532, 542; music in, 515–516; Napoleon and, 586; after Napoleonic wars, 621, *622*; nationalism in, 940; nationalities in, 640, 641, 666; Nazi Germany and, 830–831; Ottomans and, 360, 376, 449, *454*; Poland and, 534, 537, 537–538; Quadruple Alliance and, 621, 623–624; religious toleration in, 521; revolts in, 640, 650; rise of, 449, *449*; Rococo in, 513, *513*; in Triple Alliance, 752; and War of the Austrian Succession, 534, 540; after War of the Spanish Succession, 446; World War I and, 765, 785, 787. *See also* Austria-Hungary; Austrian Empire; Austrian Netherlands; World War II; specific rulers
Austria-Hungary, 785, 787; alliances of, 751; as dual monarchy, 666, 714–715; ethnic groups in, 666, *667*, 715, 738; Serbia and, 752–753, 759; World War I and, 760, 773

Austrian Empire: in 18th century, 515, *533*, 534–535; anti-Semitism in, 734; education in, 535; as multinational state, 629; Ottoman Empire and, 656, *657*; revolution of 1848 in, *638*, 640, 653, 666. *See also* Austria; Austria-Hungary

Austrian Netherlands, 540, 573, *576*, 621. *See also* Belgium; Spanish Netherlands

Austrian Peace Society, 734

Austro-Prussian War (1866), 660, 663–664, 666

Authoritarianism, 653, 664; in Iberian peninsula, 815–817; of Napoleon III, 664; World War I and, 772, 773

Authoritarian states: in eastern Europe, 814–815

Autobiography (Shibuzawa Eiichi), 610

Autocracy: in Austria, 666; in Russia, 716

Automobiles, 687

Auxiliary Service Law (Germany, 1916), 772

Avanti (Forward), 802

"Awakening," in Protestantism, 649, 650

Axis powers (World War II), 830, 839, 842

Ayacucho, battle at, 625

Azara, Félix de, 424

Azerbaijan, 782, 922

Aztec people, 408, *408*, 410–411, *412*

Baader-Meinhof gang (Germany), 936

Babeuf, Gracchus, 582

Babur (Mughal Empire), 418

Baby boom, 889

Babylonian Captivity of the Church (Luther), 371

Bach, Alexander von, 666

Bach, Johann Sebastian, 514

Bacon, Francis, 490–491

Bacon, John, and family, *545*

Bacteriology, 677–678

Baden-Powell, Agnes, 707

Baden-Powell, Robert, 706, 707

Baker, Josephine, 818

Bakongo, 403, 414

Bakunin, Michael, 697

Balaklava, Battle of, 657

Balance of power, 539, 654; in 18th century, 539; Bismarck and, 751; after Crimean War, 657, 658; after Napoleonic wars, 621–622, *622*

Balance of trade, 549

Balboa, Vasco Nuñez de, 406

Baldwin, Stanley, 798

Balkan League, 752

Balkan region, 656; by 1830, *627*; by 1878, *752*; in 1913, *753*; crises in (1908–1913), 752–753; crises in (1914), 759–760; Mussolini and, 836–837; Ottoman Empire in, 360, *360*, 751, 752; World War I and, 759–760, 787; in World War II, 836; Yugoslav breakup in, 936. *See also* specific locations

Ballet, 731

Balloon Dog (Koons), 944

Baltic region: Denmark and, 453, *453*; independence in, 922; Russia and, 781, 782; in Thirty Years' War, 436; before World War II, 833; in World War II, 843. *See also* specific locations

Banking, *602*; in Amsterdam, 428, 456; commercial capitalism and, 427–738; in England, 548; in Europe, 932; Fugger and, 428; in Germany, 688; industrialization and, 672–673; Jewish people in, 523

Banknotes, 548

Bank of England, 548, 565, 882

Baptism, 373, 379, 383

Bar (French province), 356

Barbados, 421, *421*

Barcelona: Orwell on, 816

Barclay family, 611

Baroque arts, 464–465, *465*, 494, 534

Barth, Karl, 892

Barton, Clara, 731

Baseball, 710

Băsecu, Traian, 927

Basel, 378

Bastille, fall of, 559, *559*, 566–567, 568, *569*

Bataan peninsula, 838

Batavia (Jakarta), 415–416, *416*

Batista, Fulgencio, 870

Battle of Britain, 836

Battles. *See* specific battles and wars

Bauhaus, 821–822, *822*

Bavaria and Bavarians, 435, 438, 714

Bayle, Pierre, 500–501

Bay of Pigs invasion, 870

BBC, 892

Beatles, 893, *893*

Beauvoir, Simone de. *See* De Beauvoir, Simone

Bebel, August, 694

Beccaria, Cesare, 518

Beckett, Samuel, 890

Beer Hall Putsch, 806, 807

Beethoven, Ludwig van, 648, 649

Beggars, 555, 556

Belarus: independence of, 923

Belgian Congo. *See* Congo; Zaire

Belgioioso, Cristina, 640

Belgium, 694, 787; Central Africa and, 745; Dutch Republic and, 621, 635; industrialization in, 601, *602*, 602–603, 605, 607; uprising in (1830), 635; World War I and, 760, 764, *764*; in World War II, 836. *See also* Austrian Netherlands; Low Countries

Belgrade, 454

Bell, Alexander Graham, 687

Bell, The (radical journal), 668

Bellarmine, Robert, 481–482

Belorussian people: Nazis and, 848

Belov, Max, 814

Benedict (Saint) and Benedictine monasticism, 387

Benelux countries, 884

Bengal, 418, 542

Benin, 423

Bergman, Ingmar, 892

Bergoglio, Jorge Mario. *See* Francis (Pope)

Bergson, Henri, 721

Berkeley, University of California at: antiwar rally at, *898*

Berlin, 554, 687, 785, *863*; blockade of, 866; Congress of (1878), 751–752; crisis over (1958), 869–870; police in, 643; Soviets in, 843

Berlin Academy, 487

Berlin Air Lift, 866, 867, *867*

Berlin Wall, 870, 903, 927

Berlioz, Hector, 648

Berlusconi, Silvio, 931

Bern, 378

Bernhardi, Friedrich von, 723–724

Bernini, Gian Lorenzo, 465, *465*, 480, *480*, 481

Bernstein, Eduard, 695, 696

Bessarabia, 656, 658

Bethmann-Hollweg, Theobald von, 760

Bible: higher criticism of, 724; Luther and, 372. *See also* New Testament

Bicameral legislature: in France, 627

Biennials: art exhibitions as, 943–944

Big Four, after World War I, 786

Big Three (World War I), 786

Big Three (World War II), 856; at Potsdam, 858–859; at Tehran, 856–857; at Yalta, 857, *857*

Bill of Rights: in England, 462; in United States, 561, 563, 630

Bin Laden, Osama, 937

Biodiversity, 949

Biology, 676

Birmingham, England, 627

Birth control, 801, 889, 939; in 18th century, 545–546; in 19th century, 704–705; Catholics on, 942; pill and, 889, 897

Birthrate: baby boom and, 889; decline in, 605, 704, 813, 939; in late 1800s, 697, 704; population growth and, 605; in United States, 604; after World War I, 784

Bishops and bishoprics, 458

Bismarck, Otto von, 654, 655, *662, 714*; alliance system of, 751–752; Austro-Prussian War and, 663–664; as chancellor, 714–715; Danish War and, 662–663; France and, 712; Franco-Prussian War and, 664–665; as Prussian prime minister, 662; William II (Germany) and, *714*, 715, 752

Black Hand (Serbian organization), 760

Black Hole of Calcutta, 418

Black Man's Burden, The (Morel), 743–744

Black Muslims, 886

Blacks. *See* Africa; African Americans

Black Sea region, 537, 656, 657, 747

Black September (Palestinian terrorists), 917

Blackshirts (Italy), 802, 803

Blackwell, Elizabeth, 679

Blair, Tony, 931, 945

Blanc, Louis, 638

"Blank check," 760

Blenheim, battle at, 446

Blitzkrieg, 830, 835

Blockades: of Berlin, 866; in World War I, 771, 772

Blocs of states: after World War II, 866

Blood circulation: Harvey on, 485–486

"Bloody Sunday" (Russia), 739, 740

Bloomsbury Circle, 823

Blues music, 893

Blum, Léon, 798

Board of Trade (Britain), 422

Bobbies (British police), 643, *643*

Bodichon, Barbara, 708

Bodin, Jean, 440

Boers, in South Africa, 412, 744–745, *745*

Boer War, 745

Bohemia: Austria and, 374, *448*, 449, 640, 666; Christianity in, 435; Nazis and, 831; Ottomans and, 360; Poland and, 359

Bohemian phase, of Thirty Years' War, 435–436

Boigne, Comtesse de, 531

Boko Haram, 938

Boleyn, Anne, 380, 381, 394

Bolívar, Simón, *624, 625, 626*

Bolivia, 615

Bolshevik Revolution (1917), 771, 779–781, *782*

Bolsheviks, *765*, 779, 780, 782, 783; Hitler on, 828. *See also* Red Army; Soviet Union

Bombs and bombings: suicide (ISIL), 938. *See also* Atomic bomb; specific battles and wars

Bonaparte family: Jerome, 586

Book of Common Prayer, 382, 396, 458

Books: Index of Forbidden Books and, 389, 489. *See also* Literature; specific books

Booth, William, 725

Borders: in EU, 932; Helsinki Accords and, 911; immigrants and, 940–941; Locarno Treaty and, 795

Bormann, Martin, 844

Borodino, battle at, 589

Bosnia, 360, 752; war in, *928*

Bosnia-Herzegovina, 928. *See also* Herzegovina

Bosnian Crisis (1908–1909), 752

Bosnian Muslims, 928

Bossuet, Jacques, 440

Bosworth Field, battle at, 357

Boulanger, Georges, 713

Boundaries. *See* Borders

Bourbon dynasty, 660; Habsburgs and, 446–447, 540; Huguenots and, 390; in Italy, 356; restoration of, *576*, 589, 621; in Spain, 423, 446–447, 538, 624; Thirty Years' War and, 435. *See also* specific rulers

Bourdonnaye, M. de la, 556

Bourgeois(ie): clergy in, 368; education and, 385; in France, 554, 564, 565, 571, 586; use of term, 610

Bourgeois monarchy, in France, 634–635

Boxer Rebellion (China), 749–750

Boyars (Russia), 450

Boyle, Robert, 486

Boys: education of, 708; in middle class, 707. *See also* Men

Boy Scouts, *707*, 708

Brahe, Tycho, 477, *477*

Brandenburg, *436*, 438, 446

Brandenburg-Prussia, 448, 448–449, 532, 543

Brandt, Willy, 904–905

Brazil, 413, *413*, 421, 423, 625

Breast-feeding, 543–544

Bremen, 436

Brest-Litovsk, Treaty of, *765*, 781

Brezhnev, Leonid, 878, 901–902

Brezhnev Doctrine, 901

Briand, Aristide, 795

Bristol, England, *549*, 550

Britain. *See* England (Britain)

Britain, Battle of, 836

British Broadcasting Corporation (BBC), 818

British Columbia, 741

British East India Company, 418–419, 541, *541*, 601, 604–605, 747

British Empire, *540*, 557, 593, 745; decolonization and, 870

British Museum, 492

British Soccer Cup Final, 710

British Women's Liberation Workshop, 900

Brittain, Vera, 777

"Broken Man, The" (Restif de la Bretonne), 518

Brothers Karamazov, The (Dostoevsky), 725

Brothers of the Common Life, 366

Brown, Gordon, 931

Broz, Josip. *See* Tito (Josip Broz)

Brüning, Heinrich, 808

Bucer, Martin, 378

Buda, 666

Budapest: Red Army in, 879

Bulganin, Nikolai, 869

Bulgaria, 694, 751, 752; authoritarianism in, 815; pro-Soviet regime in, 864; in World War I, 765, 770; in World War II, 836. *See also* Eastern Europe

Bullion, 428

Bundesrat, 664, 714

Burden of Guilt, The (Vogt), 883

Bureaucracy: in Austria-Hungary, 715; colonial, 749; in France, 585–586; in Prussia, 532, 533; in Scandinavia, 799; Soviet, 812, 813; in World War II U.S., 852

Burghers, 457, *457*, 467, 532. *See also* Bourgeois(ie)

Burgundy, duke of, 356

Burgundy and Burgundians, 356

Burke, Edmund, 622

Burma (Myanmar), 416, 418, 747, 842, 875; Japan and, 834, 848, 850

Burma-Thailand railway: forced labor for, 850

Burschenschaften, 628–629
Bush, George H. W., 933, 935
Bush, George W., 934; Afghanistan war and, 936; Iraq War and, 937–938
Business: small, 611; sports as, 917. *See also* Commercial capitalism; Industry
Business cycle, slumps in, 690
Butler, Josephine, 693
Byron, George Gordon (Lord), 646, 648
Byzantine Empire: end of, 359–360, *360*. *See also* Eastern Orthodoxy

Cabot, John, 406
Cabral, Pedro, 406
Cahiers de doléances, 566
Calas, Jean, Voltaire and, 505
Calcutta, 418, 542, *605*
Calendar: of Maya, 407; in revolutionary France, 579–580
Calicut, 403
Calonne, Charles de, 565
Calvin, John, and Calvinism, 366, *382*, 396–397; in 18th century, 521, 522; in German states, 435; Huguenots and, 396; in Netherlands, 393, 396, 457; Puritans and, 386, 395; rules of, 384; on salvation, 382–383
Cambodia, 747, 875
Cambridge University, 482, 485
Cameron, David, 931
Cameroons, 745
Camus, Albert, 891–892
Canada, 741, 886, 934; Dominion of, 672; economy in, 908; England and, 532, 540, *540*, 541–542, 560, 671–672; European migration to, 698, 735; France and, 422–423, 540, *540*, 541–542; French and Indian War and, 540, *540*, 541–542; Jewish migration to, 735; as New France, 671; after World War II, 886
Canals, 593, 603; Suez Canal, 745, 836, 873
Candide (Voltaire), 505
Cannons, 360, 402–403
Canton, China, 419
Cantons: in Switzerland, *377*, 377–378
Cape Colony, 744, 745
Cape of Good Hope, 403, 407, 412
Capitalism: commercial, 427–428; cottage industry and, 593; imperialism and, 742; industrial, 611; Russia and, 924
Capital punishment, 518, 644
Capuchins, 387
Caraffa, Gian Pietro, 389
Carbonari, 628

Caribbean region, 413; guest workers from, 940
Carinthia, 449
Carlstadt, Andreas, 373
Carlyle, Thomas, 645
Carmelite nuns, 386–387
Carnegie Steel Company, 739–740
Carniola, 449
Carnival (festival), 519, *520*
Carol II (Romania), 815
Caroline Islands: Japan and, 833
Cars. *See* Automobiles
Cartels, 688, 796
Carter, Jimmy, 908; human rights issues and, 911; Olympic Games and, 912
Cartesian dualism, 489
Cartier, Jacques, 422
Cartwright, Edmund, 595
Casa de Contractación, 473
Case of Labourers in Husbandry Stated and Considered, The (Davies), 547
Caspian Sea, 747
Castile, 358, *358*, 410, 538
Castro, Fidel, 870
Casualties. *See* specific battles and wars
Catalonia, 439
Catherine II the Great (Russia), *528*, 528–529, 535–537, 539
Catherine de' Medici, 390, *391*
Catherine of Aragon (England), 380, 381
Catholic Center Party (Germany), 805
Catholic Church, 942; in 18th century, 519, 521–524, *522*; by 1560, *387*; anticlericalism and, 724; in Asia, 389, 416, 420, 425; in Austria, 535, 629; in Austria-Hungary, 715; authority of, 361, 365; in colonies, 401, 423–424, 429; corruption in, 368; Council of Trent and, 389–390; divorce and, 731; doctrine of, 390; in England, 381–382, 461–462; Erasmus and, 366–367, *367*; exploration and, 402–403; in France, 390–392, 579, 584, 628, 724, 737; French Revolution and, 569; Galileo and, 475, 479–480, 493–494; in Germany, 714; Great Schism in, 361; Habsburgs and, 378; heresy and, 361; in Hungary, *359*; intolerance by, 505; in Ireland, 736; Italy and, 805, 883–884; in Japan, 389, 420, 425; Luther and, 369–371; Napoleon and, 584; Peace of Augsburg and, *375*, 377; Reformation and, 369–370; reforms of, 361, 369; in Renaissance, 361–362; revival of religious orders in, 644; Romantic movement and,

649; sacraments of, 390; saints, relics, and, 390; scripture interpreted by, 390; in Spain, 358, 538, 815; in Switzerland, *377*, 377–379; unity of, 374; after World War II, 892. *See also* Catholic Reformation; Christianity; Missions and missionaries; Monks and monasteries; Papacy; Protestant Reformation; specific church leaders and countries
Catholic League, of German states, 435, 436
Catholic Reformation, 386–387, *387*, 450
Cattle: in Americas, 423
Caucasus region, 782
Cavalier Parliament, 461
Cavendish, Margaret, 486, *486*–487
Cavour, Camillo di, 659–660
Ceaușescu, Nicolae and Elena, 903, 925
Cecil, William, 395
Celibacy, 381
Cellular (mobile) phones, 942–943
Censorship: in Enlightenment, 502; in World War I, 774
CENTO, 869
Central Africa: imperialism in, 745. *See also* Africa; specific locations
Central America, 406, 408; independence of, 625, *626*. *See also* Latin America; specific locations
Central Asia, 747. *See also* Asia; specific locations
Central Europe: 1936–1939, *832*; absolutism in, 532–538, *533*; Calvinism in, 383; Jews in, 523; repression in, 628–629. *See also* World War I; World War II; specific locations
Centralization: in European states, 529, 539; in World War I, 772–773
Central planning: Soviet, 901–902, 921
Central Powers (World War I), 770, 771, 777; peace treaties with, 787–788
Central Treaty Organization. *See* CENTO
Ceylon. *See* Sri Lanka (Ceylon)
Cézanne, Paul, *727*, 727–728
Chacabuco, Battle of, 625
Chadwick, Edwin, 609, 700
Chamberlain, Houston Stewart, 724
Chamberlain, Neville, 830, 831, 836; on Munich Conference, 833
Chamber of Deputies (France), 627, 635, 713
Chamber of Peers (France), 627
Champagne region, 766
Champaigne, Philippe de, 440, 494

Champlain, Samuel de, 422
Charity, 555
Charles I (England), 458
Charles II (England), 461 491
Charles II (Spain), 446
Charles III (Spain), 538
Charles V (Holy Roman Empire):
    Aztecs and, 409; Henry VIII and,
    380; Italy and, 376, 449; Lutheranism
    and, 374, *375, 376,* 376–377; Ottoman
    Empire and, *375,* 376–377
Charles VI (Austria), 540
Charles VII (France), *356*
Charles IX (France), 391
Charles X (France), 628, 634, *635*
Charles X (Sweden), 453
Charles XI (Sweden), 453
Charles XII (Sweden), 451–452, 453
Charles Albert (Piedmont), 640, 659
Charles the Bold (Burgundy), *356, 359*
Charleston (dance), 817, *818*
Charlotte (wife of Philip of Orléans),
    445
Charter of the Nobility (Russia), 537
Chartism, 616
Chateaubriand, François-René de, 649
Châtelet, marquise du, 505
Chechnya, 924, *924,* 951
Cheka, 783
Chemical fertilizers, 690
Chemical industry, 687
Chemistry, 486, 676, 690
Chennai, India. *See* Madras
Chernobyl: nuclear disaster at, 881,
    913–914
Chiang Kai-shek, 834, 875
Chicago School of architecture (1890s),
    821
Childe Harold's Pilgrimage (Byron), 646
Child labor, 612–613, *613,* 614, 615, 708
Children: in 18th century, 517–518, 543–
    545, *545;* in 19th century, 612–614,
    613, 617, 705, *706, 707;* day care for,
    888–889; in Fascist Italy, 804; middle
    class, 705, *706;* in Nazi Germany, 810;
    as workers, 546, 612–614, *613,* 617; in
    working class, 546, 707, 708. *See also*
    Child labor
Chile, 409, *624, 625*
China: civil war in, 569; Cold War and,
    867–869, 910; communism in, 875–
    877; Confucianism in, 501; England
    and, 418–419; Europeans and, 419;
    goods from, 549; imperialism in,
    747, 749–750; Japan and, 750, 770,
    833, 835; Jesuits in, 389, 425; Korean
    War and, 868–869; Nixon and, 910;

Portugal and, 419; Republic of,
    750; Russia and, 419; U.S. and, 885,
    910–911; Vietnam and, 869. *See also*
    specific locations and dynasties
Chloroform, 678
Chocolate, 425
Cholera, in cities, 609, 678
Chrétien, Jean, 934
Christian II (Denmark), 377
Christian III (Denmark), 377
Christian IV (Denmark), 436
Christian V (Denmark), 453
Christian, Frederick, *501*
Christian church. *See* Christianity;
    specific branches
Christian Democratic Union (West
    Germany), 905
Christian Democrats: in Germany,
    927; in Italy, 802, 883, 906; in West
    Germany, 882; after World War II,
    880
Christian humanism, 366–368, *367, 373,*
    378
Christianity: in 18th century, 521–522,
    522; attacks on, 724; division of, 377;
    Pascal on, 495; philosophes and,
    499–500; "philosophy of Christ" in,
    366–367, 369; response to attacks on,
    724–725; in Rome, 516; science and,
    494, 494–496; skepticism about, 499–
    500; in Spain, 358; warfare and, 432;
    in West, 942; after World War II, 892.
    See also Missions and missionaries;
    specific orders and groups
Christian right, 942
Christian Socialists (Austria), 734, 738
Christian Social Party (Germany), 734
Christina (Tuscany), 481
Christmas, 386
Church(es): in 18th century, 521–524,
    522; Christian, 724; in Germany,
    521; Protestant, 373–374, 377; in
    West, 942. *See also* Church and
    state; De-Christianization; Religion;
    specific religions
Church and state: in 18th century, 521–
    524; in France, 724, 737; separation
    of, 380
Churchill, John, duke of Marlborough,
    446
Churchill, Winston, *737,* 813; on British
    Empire, 870; on Europe after Second
    World War, 863; German bombings
    and, 854; "iron curtain" speech by,
    859; on Munich Conference, 833;
    World War II and, 836, 856. *See also*
    Big Three

Church of England, 366, 380–382, 395,
    458, 461, 521, 523–524
Cinema. *See* Movies
Circumnavigation of earth: by
    Magellan, 400
Cities and towns: in 18th century, 564;
    in 19th century, *602;* electricity in,
    687; in French Revolution, 564,
    566–567; growth of, 607–609,
    698–700, 738; housing in, 700, 701;
    industrialization and, 607, 607–609,
    608; lifestyle in, 607–608, *608,*
    700; majority of Europeans and
    Americans in, 941; pollution in, *608;*
    prostitution in, 693, 694; redesign of,
    700–702, 712; in Spanish colonies,
    410; in United States, 740; World
    War II destruction of, 853–854, *855,*
    856. *See also* Urban areas; Villages;
    specific locations
Citizens and citizenship: in France, 569;
    Jews and, 811
City councils: in Prussia, 588
Civil Code (Napoleon), 584–585, 627
Civil Constitution of the Clergy
    (France), 569, 571
Civil disobedience, Gandhi and, 800
Civilian Conservation Corps, 799
Civilians: in World War I, 784; in World
    War II, 853
Civilization: decline of European, 794;
    global, 945–950. *See also* Culture(s);
    specific civilizations
Civil liberties: in World War I, 774,
    790
Civil Rights Act (1964), 886
Civil rights movement (U.S.), 885,
    885–886
Civil service: in Prussia, 532–533. *See
    also* Bureaucracy
Civil war(s): in England, 458–459, *459;*
    food shortages and, 950; in Greece,
    864–866; in Nigeria, 872; in Russia,
    782, 782–783, 812; in Spain, 815–816;
    in United States, 671, *671,* 731, 762.
    See also specific locations
Clarendon, Lord (Edward Hyde),
    460
Class conflict, 776
Classes: in 18th century, 519–520,
    550–556, *555;* drinking habits of,
    519–520; in Enlightenment, 510;
    industrial middle class as, 609–611;
    in Prussia, 532–533, 661; World War
    I and, 775–776. *See also* Social orders;
    specific classes
Classical learning: in Renaissance, 366

Classicism: in arts, 514, 515; Romanticism and, 645. *See also* Art(s); Neoclassicism

Clemenceau, Georges, 773, 774, 785, 786, *788*; on peacemaking, 787

Clement VII (Pope), 376, 380

Clement XIV (Pope), 521

Clergy: in 18th century, 569; Catholic, 942; corruption of, 368; English, 381; as French First Estate, 563, *564*, 566, 577; French Revolution and, 571; Protestant, 373; salvation and, 369; in Spain, 358. *See also* specific religions

Climate change, 949; papal encyclical on, 942. *See also* Environment

Clinton, Bill, 933; Serbia and, 928; on terrorism, 936

Clive, Robert, 418–419, 541, *541*, 542

Clock, The (Marclay), 944

Clydebank (Scotland): bombing of, *855*

Coal and coal industry, 688, 738, 798; industrialization and, 596, *597*, *602*, 603, 672, 687; slump in, 796; working conditions in, 612, *613*, 617

Cobbett, William, 592

Cobden, Richard, 636–637

COBOL, 912

Cochin China, 747

Code Napoleon. *See* Civil Code (Napoleon)

Codes: military, 836, 856

Codes of law. *See* Law codes; specific codes

Codreanu, Corneliu, 815

Coffeehouses, 425, 517, *517*, 572

Coitus interruptus, 704

Coke (coal), 596, 603

Coke, Thomas, 554

Colbert, Jean-Baptiste, 443–444, *491*

Cold War, 801; China and, 867–869, 910; decolonization and, 877; détente in, 908–912; emergence of, 859; end of, 920–921, 935–936; escalation of, 869; globalization of, 867–870; new world order or terrorism after, 934–938; origins of, 864–867; socialism and, 880–881; U.S. and Soviet viewpoints on, 864–867; U.S. and, 885

Collateralized debt obligations (CDOs), 947

Collective bargaining, 774

Collective security, 828

Collectivization: in China, 876–877; in Soviet Union, 813, 814

Colleges. *See* Universities and colleges

Colombia, 625

Colonies and colonization: in Africa, 412, 742–746, *744*; British, *418*, 418–419, 421–422; Catholic Church in, 401, 423–424, 429; decolonization and, 870–875; Dutch, 412, *418*, 744; French, *418*, *418*, 422–423, 580–581, 745; guest workers from former, 940; India as, *418*, 418–419; mercantilist theory on, 549–550; missionaries in, 401, 410; in North America, 421–422, 540, *540*, 541–542; Portuguese, *403*, 404, 413, *413*, *418*, 521; Spanish, 408, 410, *413*, 415, 421, *421*, 425, 521, *561*; tourism in, 819; World War I and, 770–771, 787, 799. *See also* Decolonization; Imperialism; New imperialism

Columbian Exchange, 423, 425–426, *426*

Columbus, Christopher, 400, 406, *406*, 407

Combination Acts (Britain), 615

COMECON, 867

Commerce. *See* Mercantilism; Trade

Commercial capitalism, 427–428, 549

Committee of Public Safety, 575, 576–578, 581

Common Market, 884, *933*. *See also* European Economic Community

Common people: in French Revolution, 566–567

Commonwealth: of Australia, 747; in England, 459, 463

Commonwealth of Independent States, 923. *See also* Russia

Commune (France, 1871), 712–713. *See also* Paris Commune

Communication(s): revolution in, 687, 818; via Internet, 942

Communist League, 674

Communist Manifesto, The (Marx and Engels), 673, 674, 675

Communist Party: in Italy, 884, 906; Soviet, 902, 921. *See also* Communists and communism; specific locations

Communists and communism: in Asia, 875–877; in China, 868, 875–877; collapse of, 925–927; in Czechoslovakia, 904–905; day care and, 888–889; in eastern Europe, 879; Great Depression and, 797; in Indonesia, 877; McCarthy and, 885; Soviets and, 812; in Vietnam, 875; war communism, 783, 812; women and, 780; World War II resistance by, 845; after World War II, 866, 880.

See also Marx, Karl, and Marxism; specific locations

Compass, 403

Compendius History of the Cotton Manufacture, A (Guest), 595

Computers, 856, 912, 942

Comte, Auguste, 680

Concentration camps, 745, 808, 811

Conceptual Art, 943

Concert of Europe, 623–627, 658

Concordat, Napoleon and (1801), 584

Conditions of the Working Class in England, The (Engels), 674

Condoms, 889

Condorcet, Marie-Jean de, 507–508

Coney Island, 686, *686*

Confederate States of America, 670–671

Confederation of the Rhine, 586

Confession, Luther and, 369–370

Confucianism, 501

Congo, 745. *See also* Zaire

Congress (U.S.), 561, 642

Congress of Berlin (1878), 751–752

Congress of Vienna, 620, *620*, 621–622, *622*, 628, 635, 650, 657

Conquistadors (Spain), 401, 407–410, 429

Consciousness-raising groups: for women, 939

Conscription, 703; in France, 586; in Japan, 750; standing armies and, 438–439, 450, 542–543; World War I and, 759, 772

Conservatism, 622–623, 653–654; in 1840s, 637–642, 650; after Napoleonic wars, 621–630

Conservative Party: in Canada, 886, 934; in England, 461, 627, 670, 798, 882, 886, 905, 931

Conservatives, in Spain, 713

Consistory, in Geneva, 383

Conspiracy of Equals, 582

Constable, John, 647

Constables (Britain), 643

Constantine (Russia), 630

Constantinople (Istanbul), 751; siege and capture of (1204), 360, *360*; siege and capture of (1453), 360, 376, 453–454; trade in, *405*

Constituent Assembly: in Russia, 780

Constitution(s): in Austria-Hungary, 666, 715; in England, 459, 503, 504; in France, 566, 569, 571, 581, 639, 713, 881; of Frankfurt Assembly, 640; in Germany, 640, 713–714; in Prussia, 661; in Spain, 628, 713; in United States, 503, 561, 563, 641

Constitutional Democrats (Russia), 779

Constitutional monarchy, 653; in Belgium, 635; in England, 458, 459, 503; in France, 569, 571; in Prussia, 661; in Russia, 739

Consul: in France, 583, 585

Consumer(s): smartphone sales and, 942

Consumer goods, 428, 549, 688, 776

Consumer society, 886–888, 887

Consumption: global resources and, 949; mass, 689, 697, 711–712

Contagious Diseases Acts (England), 693, 694

Containment policy, 866

Contarini, Gasparo, 389

Continental Army, 560

Continental Europe: industrialization in, 672–673. See also specific locations

Continental System, of Napoleon, 587–588, 589

Contraception. See Birth control

Convention People's Party (Gold Coast), 871

Convents. See Nuns

Convergence (Pollock), 890, 891

Conversation in the Park (Gainsborough), 553

Conversion. See Missions and missionaries; specific religious groups

Cook, James, 501, 747

Cook, Thomas, 710

Cooperatives: farm, 690; Scandinavian, 799

Copernicus, Nicolaus, 475, 475–476, 479–480, 496

Corn, 423, 543, 547, 551

Corn Law (England), 627, 636–637

Cornwallis, Charles, 560

Coronation: of Napoleon, 585

Corporations: multinational/transnational, 947

Corregidor, 838

Corsica, 582

Cort, Henry, 596

Cortes (Spain), 628

Cortés, Hernán, 401, 409

Corvinus, Matthias (Hungary), 359

Cosimo II (Florence), 479

Cosmology: of Newton, 482–484, 483; Ptolemaic-Aristotelian, 474–475, 477, 493, 496

Cossacks, 537

Costa, Angelo, 555

Costa Rica, 625

Cottage industry, 548, 548–549, 593, 595, 598, 602–603

Cotton industry: in Britain, 549, 593, 594–595, 596, 613, 617, 672; on Continent, 602, 672; India and, 418, 549, 604–605; in U.S. South, 549; working conditions in, 592, 612. See also Textiles and textile industry

Council for Mutual Economic Assistance. See COMECON

Council of Elders, 581

Council of 500 (France), 581

Council of People's Commissars (Soviet Union), 780

Council of Troubles (Council of Blood, Netherlands), 394

Councils (Christian): of Constance, 361; of Trent, 389–390, 481

Counter-Reformation. See Catholic Reformation

Country houses, 552–554, 553

Coup d'état: in Bulgaria, 815; by Louis Napoleon, 655; by Napoleon, 582; in Romania, 858

Courbet, Gustave, 680, 680–682

Court (of law): hierarchy of, 518

Court (royal): in France, 445, 552; lifestyles in, 444–445, 552

Court Jews, 523

Court of Star Chamber (England), 357

Coventry, bombing of, 854

Craftspeople, 611

Cranmer, Thomas, 380–381

Creation, The (Haydn), 515

Credit, 604–605

Credit-Anstalt, 796

Creoles, 625

Crime: in 18th century, 518; poverty and, 643–644; property, 642. See also Punishment

Crimea, 656, 840, 925

Crime and Punishment (Dostoevsky), 725

Crimean War, 656–658, 657, 731; casualties in, 658

Crimes against humanity: by Milošević, 929

Croatia, 449, 656, 928

Croats, 641, 929

Crompton, Samuel, 595

Cromwell, Oliver, 458–461, 459

Cromwell, Thomas, 380–381

Crop(s): in 18th century, 543, 546–547; from Americas, 543, 547; in Americas, 423; fertilization of, 548; yields of, 547. See also Agriculture; specific crops

Cruz, Juana Inés de la, 425

Crystal Palace Exhibition, 599–601, 600

Cuba, 713

Cuban Missile Crisis, 870, 871

Cubism, 729, 730

Cultural relativism, 501

Cultural Revolution (China), 910, 910

Culture(s): avant-garde, 819–820; of Nazism, 822; postwar, 889–893; Romanticism and, 645–649; Western, 941–945; after World War I, 819–823; after World War II, 892–893; youth, 898. See also Art(s); Civilization; Nationalism; Popular culture; Renaissance; specific locations

Cummins, Nicholas, 606

Curie, Marie, 720, 721

Curie, Pierre, 720

Customs union, Zollverein as, 661

Cut with the Kitchen Knife... (Höch), 821

Cuzco, 408–409, 410

Cyprus, 393

Czechoslovakia, 785, 787; communism in, 904–905; after communism, 926–927; Communist collapse in, 925; democracy in, 815; Nazi Germany and, 830, 831; "Prague Spring" in, 903; Soviet invasion of, 903, 903. See also Eastern Europe

Czech people, 359, 640; Holy Roman Empire and, 361

Czech Republic, 926–927

Dada Dance (Höch), 820

Dadaism, 820

Da Gama, Vasco, 403, 405

Dahomey, 423

Daily Mail, 709

Daimler, Gottlieb, 687

Dali, Salvador, 820, 821

Dance: ballet, 731; in Roaring Twenties, 817–818, 818

Dance halls, 710

Danes. See Denmark

Danish phase, of Thirty Years' War, 436–437

Danish War (1864), 662–663

Danton, Georges, 573, 575

Danube River region, 360, 427, 454, 656, 672

Danzig, 832

Dardanelles, 656, 657

Darfur: starvation in, 950

Darwin, Charles, 493–494, 676, 677, 723, 724, 725

Das Kapital (Marx), 674

Das Leben der Anderen (movie), 930

Databases: music from, 945

David, Jacques-Louis, 514, *515*, 567, *585*
Davies, David, 547
Davison, Emily, 732, *733*
Dawes Plan, 795
Day care: in Communist countries, 888–889
Day in the Life of Ivan Denisovich, A (Solzhenitsyn), 878
Dayton meeting, 928
Death camps, 846–848
Death of Sardanapalus, The (Delacroix), 647, *648*
Death penalty, 518
Death rates: in 18th century, 543, 545, 555; in cities, 609; decline in, 543, 697; of infants, 545–546, 708; from Middle Passage, 414; from smallpox, 411
De Beauvoir, Simone, 889, 890
Debelleyme, Louis-Maurice, 643
Debt: Greek, 947; in U.S., 908, 935
Debt crisis, 947
Debussy, Claude, 730–731
De-Christianization: in French Revolution, 579–580
Declaration of Human Rights (Dutch Republic), 522
Declaration of Independence (U.S.), 529, 562, *562*; French Revolution and, 563, 568, 589
Declaration of Indulgence, 461, 462
Declaration of Pillnitz, 573
Declaration of the Rights of Man and the Citizen (France), 563, 567–568, 570, 589, 630
Declaration of the Rights of Woman and the Female Citizen (Gouges), 568, 571
Decline and Fall of the Roman Empire (Gibbon), 516
Decline of the West, The (Spengler), 793
Decolonization, 870–875; in Africa, 871–872, *873*; in Asia, 875, *876*; Cold War and, 877
Deconstruction, 914
Defence of the Realm Act (England), 773–774
Defensive alliance, after World War I, 786, 789, 793
Deffand, marquise du, 510
Deficits (financial): in U.S., 908, 933
Deflationary policy, classical liberal, 797
Defoe, Daniel, 594
De Gaulle, Charles, 845, 872, 881–882, 909
De Hooch, Pieter, *457*
Deism, 505, 507

Deities. *See* specific deities
Delacroix, Eugène, 647, *648*
Démar, Claire, 633
Demian (Hesse), 823
Demilitarized Rhineland, 830
Democracy: in eastern Europe, 815; participatory, 508; political, 712–713, 731, 793; in United States, 642; after World War I, 798–799, 801; after World War II, 880–882
Democratic Party (U.S.), 933
Demoiselles d'Avignon, Les (Picasso), 729, *730*
Denazification, 866, 882
Denikin, Anton, 782
Denmark, 799; in 18th century, 539; kingdom of, *436*, 453, *453*; Prussia and, 662–663; revolution in (1660), 453; Scandinavian unification under, 377; upheavals in, 440; World War II in, 836. *See also* Scandinavia
Department stores, 688, 689, 712
Departure from Egypt (Kiefer), 943
Depressions: of 1857–1858, 672; of 1873–1895, 690; Keynes on, 798. *See also* Great Depression
De Rerum Novarum (Leo XIII), 724
Derrida, Jacques, 914
De Saussure, Ferdinand, 914
Descartes, René, 489, *489*, 490, 491
Descent of Man, The (Darwin), 676, 677
Despotism, 502; in France, 586
De-Stalinization, 878
Détente: in Cold War, 908–912
Detroit: race riot in (1943), 852
Developed nations, 950
Developing nations, 950
Diaghilev, Sergei, 731
Dialogue on the Two Chief World Systems... (Galileo), 480
"Diary of a German Soldier," 841
Dias, Bartholomeu, 403
Díaz, Bernal, 411
Dickens, Charles, 609
Dictators and dictatorships: Fascist, in Italy, 803; Stalin as, 812. *See also* Totalitarian states
Diderot, Denis, 506–507, 509, 529; *Encyclopedia* of, 501; on hospitals, 519; on Jews, 523
Diefenbaker, John, 886
Diet (food): in 18th century, 543, 551; peasant, 551; in World War II, 850
Diet (legislative body): in Austria, 535; of Germanic Confederation, 662; in Poland, 359, 456
Diet of Augsburg, 376, 377

Diet of Worms, 371, 372
Dietrich, Marlene, 818
Diggers, 493
Digital Age, 921, 942–943
Diplomacy: in 18th century, 539–543; in England, 357; World War I and, 758, 795. *See also* Alliances
Directory (France), 581–582
Disarmament conferences, 795, 828
Disco music, 917
Discourse on Method (Descartes), 489, 490
Discourse on the Origins of the Inequality of Mankind (Rousseau), 508
Discovery. *See* Exploration
Disease: in 18th century, 543; in Crimean War, 658; decrease in, 605; European in New World, 410–412, *412*; germ theory of, 676, 677; in industrial cities, 609; medical advances and, 697; among prostitutes, 693, 694. *See also* Medicine
Displaced persons: after World War II, 856
Disraeli, Benjamin, 670, 734
Dissent: before World War I, 758–759. *See also* Protest(s); Revolts and rebellions; specific issues
Dissenters (England), 461, 462, 463
Diversity. *See* Minorities; Nationalities; specific groups
Divine-right monarchy, 440, 463, 629
Divorce, 731; in France, 585; in Soviet Union, 813
Dix, Otto, 820
Doctors. *See* Physicians
Does Germany Need Colonies? (Fabri), 746
Doll's House, A (Ibsen), 705
Domesticity: Dutch, 457, *457*; in late 1800s, 692, 703, 705–707
Domestic system, 547–548
Dominican Republic, 406
Dominicans, 387, 410, 424
Dominion of Canada. *See* Canada
Domino theory, 909, 910
Don Giovanni (Mozart), 516
Dopolavoro (Italy), 819
Doré, Gustave, *608*
Dostoevsky, Fyodor, 725, 726
Douhet, Giulio, 853
Draft (military). *See* Conscription
Drake, Francis, 395–396
Drama: in Elizabethan England, 467–468; in France, 468, 504; in Spain, 467–468
Dresden, bombing of, 854, *855*
Dreyfus, Alfred, 737

Dreyfus affair (France), 736, 737

Drinking. *See* Alcohol

Drogheda, battle at, 460

Drugs: student revolts and, 897

Dualism: Cartesian, 489

Dual Monarchy (Austria-Hungary), 666, 738. *See also* Austria-Hungary

Dubček, Alexander, 903, 904

Du Bois, W. E. B., 785, 801

Duda, Andreezej, 926

Dulce et Decorum Est (Owen), 768

Duma (Russia), 739, 779

Dunkirk, 836

Dürer, Albrecht, *356*, 373, 473

Dutch: in Africa, 744–745; Anabaptism and, 380; domestic life of, 457, *457*; France and, 446; immigration laws and, 940–941; independence from Spain, 394, 447; in Indonesia, 412–413, 423; in Japan, 420–421; North American colonies of, 421–422; painting of, *489*; in South Africa, 412, 744–745; World War II prisoners of war from, 850. *See also* Dutch Republic; Netherlands

Dutch East India Company, 412, 415–416, *416*, 428

Dutch East Indies, 415–416, 423, 838, 875; Japan and, 834, 848, 850

Dutch Empire, *540*

Dutch Republic: British industry and, 593; decline of, 532; exploration by, 418, 420–421; finance in, 548; France and, 574; golden age of, 456–457, *457*; as maritime power, 413, *416*, 543; religion in, *522*; Thirty Years' War and, 436, 447; upheavals in, 440

Dutch West India Company, 422

Duties of Man, The (Mazzini), 641

Dylan, Bob, 899

Dynasties. *See* specific dynasties and rulers

Eakins, Thomas, *678*

East Africa, 770

East Asia. *See* Asia; specific locations

East Berlin, 903; German reunification and, 927

Eastern Europe: absolutism in, 532–538, *533*; authoritarianism in, 814–815; Calvinism in, 383; Catholic Church in, 389; classes in, 551; COMECON in, 867; conformity in, 902–903; East-West disagreement over, 864; environmental damage in, 914; immigrants from, 698; Iron Curtain in, 879; Jews in, 523–524, 735;

kingdoms in, 359; migrants and, 941; monarchies in, 359; NATO, EU, and, 927; peasants in, 551; revolts in (1956), 879, 880; revolutions of 1989 and, 925; Soviets and, 878, 879; women in, 939; after World War I, 785, 787–788, 814–815, *815*; after World War II, 856, 857, 858. *See also* World War I; World War II; specific locations

Eastern Front: in World War I, 764–765, *765*

Eastern Orthodoxy: in 18th century, 521, *522*; Greece and, 656; Russia and, *537*, 656

Easter Rebellion (Ireland), 773

East Germany, 866, 867, 869; repression in, 903; reunification with West, 927, 929–930; West Germany and, 904–905. *See also* Eastern Europe; Germany; West Germany

East India Company. *See* British East India Company; Dutch East India Company

Eastman, George, 728

East-West divisions, 920–921

Eber, Nandor, 661

Ebert, Friedrich, 784, 785

EC. *See* European Community

Ecclesiastical Ordinances, 383

Eck, Johann, 370

Ecology, 423, 914; technology and, 913. *See also* Environment

Economic imperialism, 742

Economic liberalism, 507

Economics: supply-side, 507

Economic zones, European, 690

Economy: in 17th century, 428, 433; in 18th century, 548; in 19th century, 688; in Brandenburg-Prussia, 448; in Canada, 886; commercial capitalism in, 427–428; crisis after 2008, 947–948; in eastern Europe, 926; in eastern Germany, 930; in East Germany, 903; in England, 882–883, 905–906; in Europe, 932; financial crisis after 2008 and, 927; in France, 356, 548, 565–566, 656, 773, 881–882, 906; global, 691–692, 945–948; Great Depression and, 792–793, 796–797, 805; in Hungary, 903; industrial, 690; in Italy, 884, 907–908, 932; Nazi exploitation of, 845; recessions in (1973–1974, 1979–1983), 904; Second Industrial Revolution and, 689–692; Soviet, 877, 901–902, 921, 923; in U.S., 851, 885, 908, 933, 934; in West

Germany, 882; World War I and, 772–773; after World War I, 792; after World War II, 864–866. *See also* Mercantilism; Trade; specific locations

Ecstasy of Saint Theresa, The (Bernini), *465*

Ecuador, 409

Edict of Fontainebleau, 443

Edict of Nantes, 392, 443, 469

Edict of Restitution, 437

Edict of Worms, 371

Edison, Thomas, 687

Education: in 18th century, 517–518, 535; in Austria, 535; compulsory, 693, 708; in European civilization, 366; in Fascist Italy, 803–804; in India, 750; Luther on, 385; mass, 708–709, 720; for middle class, 707; primary, 520–521; in Reformation, 385–386; in Renaissance, 362; in Soviet Union, 814; student protests and, 897–899; for women, 386–387, 632, 708, *709*, 731. *See also* Schools; Universities and colleges

Education Act (England, 1870), 670

Edward VI (England), 382, 395

Ego, 722, 823

Egypt: Britain and, 745; independence for, 872; Nasser and, 873–874, 875; Suez Canal and, 745, 873; in World War I, 770; in World War II, 836, 840. *See also* specific locations and rulers

Eiffel Tower, 719, *719*

Eight-hour workday, 819

Einsatzgruppen, 846, 847

Einstein, Albert, 720–721, 823

Einstein on the Beach (Glass), 916

Eisenhower, Dwight D., 842, 869, 885, 909

El Alamein, 840

Elba: Napoleon at, 589, 622

Elections. *See* Voting and voting rights; specific locations and political parties

Electricity, 676, 687, 689

Electric light, 687

"Electro-Dynamics of Moving Bodies, The" (Einstein), 720

Elementary schools, 708

Elements of universe, 475

El Greco, 464, *464*

Elites: in India, 751; as industrial entrepreneurs, 593, 610–611; in Latin America, 625; in mass society, 702; science and, 474, 493. *See also* Classes; Nobility

Elizabeth (movie), 396

Elizabeth (Russia), 541

Elizabeth I (England), 381, 382, *394*, 396, 467

El Salvador, 625

e-mail, 942

Emancipation: of Jews, 734, 735; of serfs, in Austria, 666; of serfs, in Russia, *666*, 666–667, 668; of slaves, in U.S., 668, 671

Emancipation Proclamation (Lincoln), 668, 671

Emigration: European between 1876–1910, *699*; of Irish, 606–607; of Jews, 735, 846; from Nazi Germany, 811, 846. *See also* Immigration; Migration; specific groups

Émile (Rousseau), 508, 509, 511, 544

Emperor. *See* specific emperors

Empires. *See* Imperialism; Seven Years' War; specific empires and emperors

Employment. *See* Labor; Unemployment; Workers

Empowerered Through Violence: The Reinvention of Islamic Extremism (Amanat), 938

Enabling Act (Germany), 808

Enclosure acts (England), 547

Encomienda system, 410

Encyclopedia (Diderot), 501, 506–507, 510

Energy (power), 687. *See also* specific types

Engels, Friedrich, 673, 674, 675

Engine: internal combustion, 687–688; steam, 672, 676

Engineering: electrical, 690

England (Britain): in 18th century, 547–548, 550–551, 552; in Africa, 800, 801; agriculture in, 547–548; alliances of, 541, 586, 621, 623–624; American colonies of, 421, *421*, 422, *561*; Canada and, 671–672; China and, 418–419, 747; cities in, 607–609, *608*; civil wars in, *356–357*, 458–459, *459*, 493; conservatism in, 627; Conservative Party in, 461, 627, 670, 798, 905; Crimean War and, 656–658, *657*; decolonization and, *876*; economy in, *356*, 548, 669; France and, 574, 753; Germany and, 690; Glorious Revolution in, 462; government of, 458, 459, 461, 616–617, 712, 772–773, 798; grand tour and, 554; Great Depression in, 796, 798; as great power, 529, *533*; Hundred Years' War and, 356; illegitimacy in, 545; immigrants in,

940; imperialism of, 741, 745, 746, 747; India and, *418*, 418–419, *605*, 747, 800, 875; Industrial Revolution in, 593–601, *597*, 603, 605, 617; Ireland and, 459, 460, 712; liberalism in, 670, 735–736; magazines in, 516–517; mandates of, 873; middle class in, 669–670; Middle East and, 788; mobilization in World War II, 850; monarchy in, 356–357, 381, 394–395, *461*, 461–463, 502–503; Monroe Doctrine and, 625; Napoleon and, 586, 587–588, 589; navy of, 543, 587, 625; Nazi Germany and, 829–830, 830–831; peasants in, 551; police in, 643, *643*; population of, *433*, 543, 605; Protestant revivalism in, *523*, 523–524; punk movement and, 917; Quadruple Alliance and, 621, 623–624; Reformation in, 380–382; reform in, 609, 616–617, 635–637, 644–645, 669–670, 693, 700, 712, 735–736; religion in, 380–381, *523*, 523–524; restoration in, *461*, 461–463; Rome and, 380–381; sciences in, 482, 485–486, 490–491; in Seven Years' War, *540*, 540–542; Shakespeare and, 468; ships and, *549*, 549–550; Spain and, 382, 396; Spanish Armada and, *392*, 396; suffragists in, 731–732, *733*; textile industry in, 550, 593, 595–596, *598*, 603; Thatcher and Thatcherism in, 905–906; after Thatcher, 931; trade unions in, 695; Triple Entente and, 752; Victorian Age in, 669–670; after War of the Spanish Succession, 447; welfare state in, *882*, 882–883; women in, 679, 774, 888; World War I and, 757, 760–761, 764, 770, 772–773, *773*, 773–774; after World War I, 798; before World War II, 832, 833; in World War II, 836; World War II prisoners of war from, 850. *See also* Stuart dynasty; Tudor dynasty; World War I; World War II; specific rulers

English Football Association, 710, *710*

English Royal Society. *See* Royal Society (England)

Enlightened absolutism, 529, 536, 539, 556

Enlightenment: arts in, *513*, 513–516, *514*, *515*; culture and society in, 510–521; in Europe, *503*; families and, 509; Jews and Muslims in, *522*, 522–523; later period in, 507–508, *508*; philosophes in, 499–500, 502–510,

525; politics and, 516; science in, 500, *501*; social status and, 508, 509; travel literature in, 501; women in, 509–510. *See also* Scientific Revolution

Entertainment: in 1920s, 817–818; at Versailles, 445

Entrepreneurs: industrial, 593, 610–611

Environment, 697; crisis in, 948–950; scientists' warning about, 948–949; urban, 941; U.S. and, 934; women and, 940. *See also* Climate; Pollution

Environmental movement, 913–914

Epicycles: of planetary bodies, 476

Epidemics, 408, 410–411, 412, *605*. *See also* Disease

Epistles (Paul): to the Romans, 369

Equality: of Jews, 734; in Soviet Union, 813; of women, 774, 813

Erasmus, Desiderius, 366–367, *367*, 373, 389

Eroica symphony (Beethoven), 648

Essay Concerning Human Understanding (Locke), 502

Essay on the Principles of Population (Malthus), 630

Estates (social orders), 550–551; in France, 563–565, *564*, 566–567

Estates-General: in France, 356, 565–566; in Prussia, 448

Estonia, 452, 787, 833, 922

Ethics Demonstrated in the Geometrical Manner (Spinoza), 494

Ethiopia, 745, 746, 751; Italian invasion of, 830; Italy and, 745, 746, 830

Ethnic cleansing, 928

Ethnic groups: in eastern Europe, 925–926. *See also* Ethnic cleansing; Minorities; Nationalities; specific groups and locations

EU. *See* European Union (EU)

Eucharist (Lord's Supper), 373, 378, 380

EURATOM (European Atomic Energy Community), 884

Euripides, 468

Euro, 932

Eurocommunism, 906

Europa, Europa (movie), 846

Europe: in 15th century, *387*; in 1763, *533*; in 1871, *665*; in 1914, *759*; in 1919, *789*; in Africa, 742, 744, 746; American empires of, 407–410, 421–423; in Asia, 418–421, 747; coalition against French Revolution, 573; after Congress of Vienna (1815), 621–622, *622* 628, 635, 650; debt crisis in, 947; decolonization and, 870–875; devastation after World War II, 863–864; economic zones in, 690; emigration from, 698, 699; English industrialization in, 594, 601; events leading to World War II in, 830–833; great powers in, 529, 533; Holocaust in, 845; industrialization in, 601–603, 602; industrial regions (late 19th century), 691; New (1980s), 922; population growth in (1820–1900), 698; population of cities in, 941; populations from 1851–1911, 697; postwar society in, 886–889; recovery and renewal after World War II, 877–884; Renaissance monarchies in, 356–360, 357; resistance to Nazis in, 845; unification of, 932–933; women in, 939; world economy and, 690–691; World War II in, 837. See also specific locations

European Central Bank, 932

European Coal and Steel Community (ECSC), 884

European Community (EC), 907; membership in, 932. See also European Union (EU)

European Economic Community (EEC), 907, 933. See also Common Market

European Parliament, 932

European Recovery Program. See Marshall Plan

European Union (EU), 932–933; in 2013, 933; eastern European states in, 927; problems of, 932; Treaty on, 932; troops in Bosnia and, 929

Eurozone, 932

Evangelicalism, 599, 649, 725; of Lutheranism, 372–373, 377; of Zwingli, 378

Evil empire: Reagan on, 912

Evolution, Darwin on, 676, 677, 724

Evolutionary socialism, 695, 696

Evolutionary Socialism (Bernstein), 695, 696

Exchange Bank of Amsterdam, 428

Excommunication, 371, 383

Execrabulis (papal bull), 361

Executions: in 18th century, 518; in Reign of Terror, 576–578

Existentialism, 889, 891–892

Expansion: economy and, 400–401; during French Revolution, 574–576, 576; impact of European, 423–427, 426; by Russia, 537, 537–538. See

also Colonies and colonization; Exploration; Imperialism; New Imperialism; specific locations

Exploration: in 15th and 16th centuries, 404, 406–407, 421–422; of New World, 404, 406–407, 421–422; Portuguese, 399, 399–400, 403, 403–405, 404, 406; Spanish, 401, 404, 406, 406–407. See also Colonies and colonization

Exports, 549

Expressionism, 943; German, 830

Extermination camps. See Death camps

Extremists, 937–938

Eylau, battle at, 586

Fabian Socialists, 735

Fabri, Friedrich, 746

Facing Mount Kenya (Kenyatta), 801

Factories: child labor in, 612–614; discipline in, 598–599; electricity and, 687; growth of, 689; industrialization and, 598, 598–599, 673; in Japan, 692; labor in, 603–604, 612–614; in Russia, 738; in United States, 603–604; women in, 603, 775; working conditions in, 592, 612–614; World War II women in, 850, 851

Factory acts: in England, 613, 617

Fairy tales, 645

Faith. See Justification by faith alone

Falange, 816–817

Falkland Islands: England and, 906

Families: in 18th century, 509, 543–546; economy and, 546; as factory workers, 603–604, 613; in Italy, 804, 805; middle-class, 705–707, 706; Protestantism and, 374, 383–385; size of, 704, 708; working-class, 707–708. See also Children

Family allowances, 888

Family of Henry VIII, The, 381

Family planning, 704–705. See also Birth control

Famine: disappearance of, 605; Great Famine in Ireland, 605, 606; in Soviet Union, 812, 813. See also Starvation

"Famine in Skibbereen, The" (Cummins), 606

Fanon, Frantz, 874

Fantasy literature: expansion and, 400

Faraday, Michael, 676

Farm cooperatives, 690

Farms and farming: collective, 813, 814; overproduction by, 796. See also Agriculture; Crop(s)

Farouk (Egypt), 872

Farsi (Neshat), 943

Fascio di Combattimento (League of Combat), 802

Fascism, 797; in Italy, 801, 802–805. See also Nazi Germany

Fashion: Zara and, 946

Fawcett, Millicent, 731

Federalists (U.S.), 641–642

Federal Republic of Germany. See West Germany

Female Association for the Care of the Poor and Sick, 731

Female Medical College of Pennsylvania, 679

Female Spectator, The (periodical), 517

Feminine Mystique, The (Friedan), 900, 902

Feminism, 510, 731, 900–901; in Europe, 939; after World War II, 889. See also Women; Women's liberation movement; Women's rights

Ferdinand, duke of Modena, 535

Ferdinand I (Austria), 640

Ferdinand I (Holy Roman Empire), 375, 377

Ferdinand I (Naples and Sicily), 624

Ferdinand II (Holy Roman Empire), 435–437

Ferdinand VII (Spain), 624, 628

Ferdinand of Aragon, 358, 358, 359, 375, 406

Fertilizers: ecology and, 913

Festivals: in 18th century, 519; in France, 579

Fichte, Johann Gottlieb, 588

Fielden, Joshua, 611

Fielding, Henry, 516

Fifth Republic (France), 881

Filipinos. See Philippines

Filipović, Zlata, 929

Films. See Movies; specific movies

Final Solution, 846, 847, 848

Finances. See Economy; specific locations

Financial crisis (2008), 927, 934

"Findings of the IPCC Fifth Assessment Report" (2013), 949

Finland, 732, 781, 787, 799

Firebird, The (Stravinsky), 731

Fireworks Music (Handel), 514

First Balkan War, 752

First Estate: in France, 563, 564, 566; Swedish nobility as, 453

First International, 674

First Vietnam War, 869

First World War. See World War I

First Zionist Congress, 735
Five-year plans: in Soviet Union, 812, *813*
"Flappers," 818
Flaubert, Gustav, 680, 681
Fleury (Cardinal), 530
Florence: arts in, 465; Carnival in, *520*
Florida, 542
Flying shuttle, 549, 595
Foch, Ferdinand, 783
Fontenelle, Bernard de, 500
Food(s): in 18th century, 543, 547–548; in 19th century, 609, 690; demand for, 948; population growth and, 543, 548, 630, 697; shortages of, 950; World War I and, 772, 773. *See also* Diet (food); Famine
Food and drug act: in England, 609
Football (soccer), 710, 711, 819
Forced labor: in 18th century, 518; Japanese, 850; Nazi, 845; Soviet, 813
Ford, Gerald, 908
Ford, Henry, 687
Foreign Affairs (magazine), 866
Foreigners: French resentment against residents, 931; in Germany, 940; social backlash against, 950
Foreign policy: in EU, 932; of Thatcher, 906. *See also* specific locations
Forests: damage to, 948
Formosa (Taiwan), 876; Japan and, 833
Fort William. *See* Calcutta
Foucault, Michel, 914
Foundations of the Nineteenth Century, The (Chamberlain), 724
Foundling homes, 545
Fourier, Charles, 632
Fourteen Points, 785
Fourth Republic (France), 881
Fragonard, Jean-Honoré, 513, *514*
France: in 17th century, 446, *446*; absolutism in, 440–441; administrative restructuring of, 441–443, 571; African colonies of, 745; Algerian independence and, 872; alliances of, 541, 623, 752, 753, 793–794; American colonies of, 421, *421*, 422–423, 561, 580–581; American Revolution and, 560; anti-Semitism in, 737; Austria and, 573; bourgeoisie in, 554, 564, 565, 571, 586; British industry and, 593; bureaucracy in, 585–586; Calvinism in, 383, 390; Canada and, 422–423, 540, *540*, 541–542, 671; Catholic Church in, 569; cities in, 607; Classicism in arts and, 468, 514; clergy in, 563, *564*,

566, 577; constitutions in, 566, 569, 571, 581, 639; Crimean War and, 656–658, *657*; decolonization and, *876*; de Gaulle and, 845, 872, 881–882; domestic policy in, 656; drama in, 468, 503; economy in, 356, 548, 565–566, 656, 906; Enlightenment and, 502, 517; Estates-General in, 356; in European Coal and Steel Community, 884; feminists in, 939; First Vietnam War and, 869; foreign policy of, 656; Germany and, 789, 794–795; government-in-exile of, 836; government of, 441–443, 565–566, 570, 583, 585–586; in Great Depression, 798; as great power, 529, *533*; Holy Roman Empire and, *375*, 376–377; Hundred Years' War and, 356; illegitimacy in, 545; India and, 418, 418–419; Indochina and, 416, 747–748; industrialization in, 601, *602*, 602–603, 605, 656, 737; Italy and, 659–660; Jesuits and, 521; Jews in, 734; mandates of, 873; in Middle East, 788; military in, 532, 574, *575*, 759; monarchs in, 530; after Napoleonic wars, *622*, 627–628; National Assembly in, 566, 567, 568, 569, 572; nationalization of industries in, 881–882; Nazi Germany and, 829; nobility in, 390, 440, 441, 503, 563–564, *564*, 565, 566, 577, 586; North Africa and, 840; old regime in, 563–565, 567–573; Paris Commune and, 712–713; at Paris Peace Conference, 785, 786, 788; peasants in, *564*, 564–565, 566, 577; police in, 643; political banquets in, 638; population of, 433, 543, 605, 606; poverty in, 555, 556; reforms in, 566, 569, 644–645; religion in, 389, 724; republics in, 574, 654, 712–713, 737; restoration in, 627–628; revolts in, 439, 504–505; revolutionary army in, *575*–576; revolution of 1830 in, 634–635, *635*; revolution of 1848 in, 637–639, *638*; right and left wings in, 931; salons in, 499, 510, *512*, 563, 566; sciences and, 486, 491, *491*; Second Empire in, 654–656, 664; secularism in, 569; socialist parties in, 694; socialists in, 880; Spain and, 447; student revolt in, 896–897; after Thirty Years' War, 438; trade unions in, 585, 695–696; Triple Entente and, 752; Vietnam and, 869; War of the Austrian Succession and, 540,

541; War of the Spanish Succession and, *446*, 446–447; Wars of Religion in, 390–392, *391*; welfare in, 888; witchcraft trial in, 434; women in, 707, 774; workshops in, 638, 639; World War I and, 757, 760, 764, *764*, 770, 773; after World War I, 793, 798; before World War II, 832, 833; in World War II, 835–836. *See also* French Revolution; Government; Huguenots; Monarchs and monarchies; World War I; World War II; specific rulers
Franche-Comté, 359, 446
Francis (Pope), 942
Francis I (Austrian Empire), 620, 640
Francis I (France), *376*, 376–377, 382
Franciscans, 387, 424
Francis Ferdinand (Austria), 758, 760, 790
Francis Joseph I (Austria), 666, 715, 738
Francis of Assisi (Saint), 387
Franco, Francisco, 815, 816–817, 830
Franco-Prussian War, 656, 660, 664, 751
Franco-Swedish phase, of Thirty Years' War, 437–438
Frankenstein (Mary Shelley), 645, 646
Frankfurt Assembly, 640, 650, 661
Franklin, Benjamin, 503, *562*
Frederick I (Denmark), 377
Frederick I (Prussia), 448–449, 532
Frederick II (Holy Roman Empire), 477
Frederick II the Great (Prussia), 529, 533–534, *535*, 539, 540, 557; on government, 539
Frederick III (Holy Roman Empire), 359
Frederick IV (Elector of Palatinate), 435
Frederick V (Elector of Palatinate), 435
Frederick the Wise (Saxony), 368
Frederick William (Great Elector), 448, *448*
Frederick William I (Prussia), 532, 534
Frederick William II (Prussia), 573
Frederick William III (Prussia), 628
Frederick William IV (Prussia), 640, 661
Free Corps (Germany), 785
Free Democratic Party (West Germany), 882, 904, 905
Freedom(s). *See* Liberty; Rights
Freedom Party (Austria), 940
Free-market economies, 772, 908
Freemasons. *See* Masons
Free trade, 688, 947; U.S.-Canada agreement and, 934
French and Indian War, *540*, 541–542, 560
French Canadians, 423, 671

French Empire, *540*; of Napoleon I, 586, *587*

French Guiana, 645

French language, 554

French Popular Movement, 881

French Revolution: destruction of old order in, 559–560, 567–573; European concerns about, 573, 592; expansion during, 574–576, *576*; military in, 574–576, *575*; radical revolution in, 573–581; uprisings leading to, 566–567. *See also* Reign of Terror

French Royal Academy of Sciences. *See* Royal Academy of Sciences (France)

Frequens (decree), 361

Freud, Sigmund, 722, *722*, 723, 823

Friedan, Betty, 900, 902

Friedland, battle at, 586

Friedrich, Caspar David, 646–647, *647*

Friends of the Blacks, 580

Frith, William P., *706*

Fronde, 441

Fugger, Jacob, 428

Führerprinzip, 807

Functionalism, in architecture, 821–822, *822*

Fundamentalism: Islamic, 937; religious, 724; use of term, 942

Futurism, 914

Gagern, Heinrich von, 629

Gainsborough, Thomas, *553*

Galen (physician), 473, 484, 485, 519

Galicia, *449*, 537, *538*, 666, 765

Galilei, Galileo, 473, 478–482, *480*, 493, 496

Gallipoli campaign, 770

Games: in 19th century, 707. *See also* Olympic games

Gamond, Zoé Gatti de, 632–633

Gandhi, Mohandas (Mahatma), 800, *800*, 875

Gangsta rap, 945

Gapon, Gregory, 740

Garcia Márquez, Gabriel, 915

Garibaldi, Giuseppe, 660, 661

Garret, Elizabeth, 679

Garvey, Marcus, 801

Gas chambers, 847–848

Gasperi, Alcide de, 884

Gaudry, Suzanne: trial of, 434

Gay rights movement, 897

Gays and lesbians. *See* Homosexuals and homosexuality

Gender and gender issues: Enlightenment, 509; industrialization and, 703, 704–705; role reversal in Great Depression, 797; in sports, 711; in welfare state, 888–889; World War I roles for women, 774–775, 801. *See also* Men; Women

General Agreement on Tariffs and Trade (GATT), 947

General Confederation of Labor (France), 696

General Directory (Prussia), 532

General strike: in England, 1926, 798; Sorel on, 722

General Theory of Employment, Interest, and Money (Keynes), 798

General War Commissariat (Prussia), 448

Generation of 1898 (Spain), 713

Geneva Conference (1954), 869

Geneva summit (1955), 869

Genghis Khan, 418

Genius of Christianity (Chateaubriand), 649

Genoa, 538–539

Genocide: against Armenians, 784. *See also* Holocaust

Gentile, Giovanni, 804

Gentileschi, Artemisia, 465, *466*

Gentry: in England, 458, 531; in Russia, 535, 537

Geocentric conception of universe, *474*, 474–475

Geoffrin, Marie-Thérèse de, 499, *499*, 510, *512*

Geography (Ptolemy), *402*

George I (England), 531

George II (England), 531

George III (England), 419, 532

Georgia, 782, 922

Georgian style houses, 552

German Democratic Republic. *See* East Germany

German Democrats, 805

German Empire, *653*, 787

German Federal Republic. *See* West Germany

German Girls Association, 810

Germanic Confederation, 628–629, *638*, 640, 661, 662

German language, 535

German people: in Austria-Hungary, 666, 715, 738

German Social Democratic Party (SPD). *See* Social Democrats, in Germany

German Workers' Party. *See* National Socialist German Workers' Party

Germany: African imperialism by, 745; alliances of, 751, 752; anti-Semitism in, 734–735, 738; Balkans and, 753; Bismarck in, 714–715; bombings of, in World War II, 854, *855*; cartels in, 688; Catholic Church in, 389; cities in, 607; colonies of, 745, 746, 770–771, 787; Communist Party in, 784–785, 795; denazification and partitioning of, 866–867; economy in, 772; emigration from, 606–607; foreigners in, 940; French coercion policy and, 794–795; government of, 713–714, 772, 795; Great Depression in, 796, 797, 805, 807; Green Party in, 914; guest workers in, 882, 940; Holy Roman Empire and, 376–377; illegitimacy in, 545; industrialization in, 601, *602*, 602–603, 689, 737–738; industrial leadership in, 687, 690; in late 1800s, 713–715; Lutheranism in, 372–373, 378; military in, 759; mobilization in World War I, 760, 761; mobilization in World War II, 852; nationalism in, 588, 628, 636; Nazis in, 795, 806–807; November Revolution in (1918), 784–785; Paris Peace Conference and, 785, 786; passive resistance policy of, 794–795; peasants in, 551; Peasants' War in, 373, 374; Pietism in, 523, 649; police force in, 643; politics in, 737–738; population of, 606, 607; postwar occupation of, 857; Reformation in, 369–377; religion in, 369–377; reparations and, 786–787, 794–795; republic in, 784, 785, 805; reunification of, 927, 929–930, 935; revolution of 1848 in, 636, 640; student protests in, 899; Syrian independence and, 873; Syrian refugees in, 931; after Thirty Years' War, 438; trade unions in, 696; in Triple Alliance, 752; unification of, 653, 654, 661–665, *663*; universities in, 628–629; U.S. loans to, 796; Versailles Treaty and, 786–787, 789, 793; volkish thought in, 724; World War I and, 758, 760–761, 763–764, *764*, 764–765, *765*, 770, 781, 783–784; after World War II, 856. *See also* Berlin; East Germany; Nazi Germany; Prussia; Weimar Republic; West Germany; World War I; World War II

Germ theory, 676, 677

Ghana, independence of, 872

Ghent, 394

Ghettos: for Jews, 847

Ghirlandaio, Ridolfo, *406*
Gibbon, Edward, 516
Gibbs, Philip, 757
Gin, 519
Giolitti, Giovanni, 737, 802
Girl by the Window (Morisot), 726, *728*
Girls: education for, 708; in middle class, 707; in working class, 707. *See also* Gender and gender issues; Women
Girondins, 573, 576
Gladstone, William, 670, 712
Glasnost, 921
Glass, Philip, 916
Gleaners, The (Millet), *682*
Gleichschaltung, 808
Global civilization, 945–950
Global economy, 549–550, 945–948; financial crisis in, 947–948
Globalization, 938, 941, 945; of Cold War, 867–870; East-West European division and, 920–921; environment and, 948–950; of popular culture, 917; shared problems in, 950; social challenges of, 950
Global movements, 950
Global warming, 949–950
Globe theater, 467
Glorious Revolution (England), 462
Goa, Portugal and, *403*, 404
Goebbels, Joseph, 818
Goethe, Johann Wolfgang von, 645
Golan Heights, 875
Gold: in Africa, 403, 412; for trade, 403, 412, 425, 428
Gold Coast, 403, 871, 872. *See also* Ghana
Gömbös, Julius, 815
Gomez, Franco, *624*
Gomulka, Wladyslaw, 879
Goodbye to All That (Graves), 763
Gorbachev, Mikhail, 902, *906*, 951; end of Cold War and, 920–921, 934, 935, *935*; Soviet Union under, 921–923
Gore, Al, 934
Göring, Hermann, 808
Gothic architecture, 645
Gothic literature, 645
Gottwald, Klement, 879
Gouges, Olympe de, 568, 570–571, 576
Government: of cities, 700; economic involvement by, 507, 630, 797; of EU, 932; of France, 441–443, 565–566, 570, 583, 585–586, 654–656, 713, 773, 931; Germanic, 640; of Germany, 713–714, 772, 795, 930–931; in Great Depression, 797, 798; of Hungary, 925; industrialization and, 593,

601–602, 672–673; of Italy, 931–932; mass society and, 687; Montesquieu on, 502–503, 504; Ottoman, 454; of Prussia, 661; of Russia, 450, 667–668; of Spain, 713; of Spanish America, 410; of United States, 561–562, 641; World War I and, 772–774. *See also* Monarchs and monarchies; specific locations and forms
Goya, Francisco, *588*
Graff, Anton, *535*
Grain, 690
Grammar schools, 517
Granada, 357, 358
Grand Alliance (World War II), 839; Italian invasion by, *837*. *See also* Allies, World War II; Big Three
Grand Army (Napoleon), *587*, 589
Grand Empire (Napoleon), 586–587, *587*
Grandeur and Misery of Victory (Clemenceau), 786, *787*
Grand National Consolidated Trades Union, 616
Grand tour, 554
Grand viziers (Ottoman), 454
Grant, Ulysses S., 671
Grass, Günter, 891
Graves, Robert, 763
Gravity: Newton on, 483–484
Gray, Thomas, 519, 554
Great Britain. *See* England (Britain)
Great Depression, 792–793, 796, 796–797, 798, 799, 801
Great East Asia Co-Prosperity Sphere, *839*, 848
Great Exhibition (1851), 599–601, *600*, 617
Great Famine (Ireland), 605, 606
Great Fear: in French Revolution, 567
Great Instauration, The (Bacon), 490
Great Lakes region, 541–542, 603
Great Leap Forward, 876
Great Northern War, 451–452
Great Patriotic War: in Soviet Union, 850
Great powers, 529, *533*, 624; before 1914, 751; Crimean War and, 658; World War I and, 761. *See also* specific countries
Great Proletarian Cultural Revolution (China), 910, *910*
"Great Retreat," by Napoleon, 589
Great Salt Lake: Spiral Jetty and, 915, *915*
Great Schism (Catholic Church), 361
Great Society, 885
Great Trek (South Africa), 744–745, *745*

Great War. *See* World War I
Great War for Empire, 541
Greece: authoritarianism in, 815; Balkan wars and, 752; civil war in, 864–866; economic crisis in, 947; European Union and, 932; independence of, 656; Italian attack on, 837; Nazi attack on, 837; revolt in, 625–627, *627*, 656; Truman Doctrine and, 864–866
Greek Orthodoxy. *See* Eastern Orthodoxy
Greenhouse effect, 949, 950
Greenland, 426
Green movement, 913–914
Green Party, 914, 940
Greenwich, England: Royal Observatory at, 492
Grieg, Edvard, 729–730
Grimm brothers, 645
Gropius, Walter, 821, 822, *822*
Gros, Antoine-Jean (Baron), *583*
Gross Clinic, The (Eakins), *678*
Grossdeutsch state, 640
Gross national product (GNP): in West Germany, 882; in World War II U.S., 852
Grosz, George, 820
Groza, Petra, 858
Grozny, Chechnya, 924
Grunge music, 945
Guadeloupe, 421, *421*
Guam, 749
Guatemala, 625
Guernica, 815, *817*
Guernica (Picasso), *817*
Guest, Richard, 595
Guest workers, 882; globalization and, 950; immigrants and, 940–941
Guggenheim Museum (New York), 889
Guilds: in 18th century, 554–555; industrialization and, 601, 611; Renaissance artists and, 466
Guillotine, *574*, 577, 581
Guindorf, Reine, 633
Guise family (France), 390–392
Guizot, François, 635, 638
Gulf of Aqaba, 875
Gulf War. *See* Persian Gulf War
Gunpowder, 493
Gun violence: in U.S., 934
Gustavus III (Sweden), 539
Gustavus Adolphus (Sweden), 437–438, 453
Gustavus Vasa. *See* Vasa, Gustavus
Guzman, Gaspar de. *See* Olivares (Count)

Gymnasium, 386, 517, 628
Gypsies, in death camps, 848

Habsburg dynasty, *375*, 666, 715; in 17th century, 449, *449*; in 18th century, 520–521, *533*, 534–535, 538; Bourbon dynasty and, 446–447; conservatism in, 628–629, 640; economy and, 428; Italy and, 538; reforms in, 551; success of, 358–359; Thirty Years' War and, 435–438, *436*; and War of the Austrian Succession, 534, 540
Habsburg-Valois Wars, 376–377
Haider, Jorg, 940
Haiti, 406, 580–581
Hall of Mirrors (Versailles), *444*, *653*, 654, 664
Hals, Frans, *489*
Hamburg, 436, *555*; bombing in World War II, 853, 854
Hamilton, Alexander, 503, 641–642
Hancock, John, *562*
Handbook of the Christian Knight (Erasmus), 366
Handel, George Frederick, 514–515
Hankou, 834
Hanoverian dynasty (England), 531, 552
Happenings: works of performance art as, 914
Hardenberg, Karl August von, 588, 628
Hargreaves, James, 595
Harkis (Muslim Algerians), 872
Harpers Ferry arsenal, 603
Harris, Arthur, 854
Harvey, William, 485–486
Hauser, Heinrich, 797
Haushofer, Karl, 828
Haussmann (Baron), Paris and, 656
Havel, Václav, 903, 925, 926–927
Hawaii, 748–749; Japanese attack in, 838, *839*
Hay, John, 747
Haydn, Franz Joseph, 515, 648, 649
Haywood, Eliza, 517
Headscarves *(hijabs)*: in France, 941
Healing. *See* Medicine
Health and health care: improvements in, 700; revolution in, 677–679. *See also* Medicine
Hegel, Georg Wilhelm Friedrich, 674
Heisenberg, Werner, 824
Heliocentric conception of universe, *475*, 475–476, 477
Helsinki Accords (1975), 911
Henrietta Marie (England), 458
Henry II (France), 377, 390
Henry III (France), 391

Henry IV (France), 391–392
Henry VII (England), 357, 406
Henry VIII (England), 367, 368, 380–382, *381*, 394, 395
Henry the Navigator (Portugal), 401, 403, *404*
Herculaneum, 514
Heresy: in England, 361, 382; in Renaissance, 361. *See also* specific types
Hermeticism, 474, 477
Herz, Henriette, *512*
Herzegovina, 752. *See also* Bosnia-Herzegovina
Herzen, Alexander, 668–669
Herzl, Theodor, 735, 736, 737
Hesse, Hermann, 823
Hevelius, Johannes, *480*
Heydrich, Reinhard, 846, 847
High culture: of 18th century, 516–518, 554
Hijabs. *See* Headscarves (hijabs)
Hill, Octavia, 700, 701
Himmler, Heinrich, 810, 844, 849
Hindenburg, Paul von, 764, 772, *773*, 783, 805, 807
Hindus, in India, 875
Hip-hop, 917, 945
Hippolytus (Euripides), 468
Hirado, 420
Hiroshima: atomic bombing of, 853, 854, *855*
Hispaniola, 406, 407, 410, 411, *421*, 580–581
History and historians: Enlightenment writing and, 516; Romantic interest in, 645; on totalitarianism, 801–802. *See also* specific historians
History of a Collective Farm, The (Belov), 814
History of Sexuality, The (Foucault), 914
History of the Rebellion and Civil Wars in England, The (Clarendon), 460
History of Tom Jones, The... (Fielding), 516
Hitler, Adolf, 784, 785, 787, 805–807, *807*, 810; anti-Semitism of, 734, 806, 811, 843; diplomatic revolution of, 828–830; foreign policy goals of, 829, 830–833; goals of, 808–809; on modern art, 822; Nazi seizure of power and, 808; New Order of, 844; plots against, 845; Poland and, 831–832; radio and movie use by, 818; suicide by, 843; in Vienna, *831*; war declared by (1939), *834*; before World

War II, 828–833. *See also* Holocaust; Nazi Germany; World War II
Hitler Youth, 810, 847
Hobbes, Thomas, 463
Ho Chi Minh, 869, 875, 877, 909
Hoffman, E. T. A., 648, 649
Hohenzollern dynasty, 448, 664
Holbach, Paul d' (Baron), 507, 517
Holbein, Ambrosius, *386*
Holbein, Hans, the Younger, *367*
Holidays, 386
Holland. *See* Dutch; Netherlands
Hollande, François, 931
Holocaust, 845–848, *847*, *848*, *849*; Israel and, 873
Holstein, 662, 663
Holtzendorff, Henning von, 771
Holy Land. *See* Jerusalem
Holy League, 391
Holy Office. *See* Roman Inquisition
Holy Roman Empire: Bohemia in, 361, 374; Catholic Church and, 374; Charles V and, 374, *375*, 376–377; France and, 446; German city-states and, 376; Habsburgs and, 358–359, 374; independence of states in, 438; sovereign states in, 374; Thirty Years' War and, 435–438, *436*
Homage to Catalonia (Orwell), 816
Home front: in World War I, 771, 772–776; in World War II, 850–854
Home Guard (England), 850
Homeland Security, Department of, 934
Homelessness: in Great Depression, 793, 796, 797; after World War II, 864
Home rule, for Ireland, 712, 736
Homes of the London Poor (Hill), 701
Homosexuals and homosexuality: Foucault on, 914; gay rights movement and, 897; Nazis and, 848; Soviets and, 813. *See also* Same sex marriage
Hondius, Henricus, *427*
Honduras, 625
Honecker, Erich, 903, 927
Hong Kong, 747
Hoover, Herbert, 793
"Hoovervilles," *792*, 793
Hopkins, Harry, 856–857
Horthy, Miklós, 815
Höss, Rudolf, on death camps, 847
Hot-line communication system (Soviet-U.S.), 870
Hötzendorf, Franz Conrad von, 760
Households: in Amsterdam, 457, *457*; industrial, 614; middle class, 707. *See also* Families

House of Commons (England), 458, 459, *530, 532*, 627, 712, 735, 736

House of Lords (England), 459, 461, *530, 531*, 736

House of Medici. *See* Medici family

House of Representatives (U.S.), 561

Housing: architecture of, 821; in cities, 700; falling prices and mortgages in, 947; in United States, 603–604; of workers, 603–604, 607–609, *608*, 700, 701

Housing and Urban Development, Department of, 885

Howard, Catherine, 382

How to Blow Up Two Heads at Once (Gentlemen) (Shonibare), 944, *944*

Huayna Inca, 409

Huber, V. A., 700

Hubertusburg, Peace of, 541

Hucknall, Mick, 916

Hudson, Henry, 421

Hudson's Bay Territory, 447

Hugo, Victor, 597

Huguenots, 390–392, *391*, 396, 440, 443, 521

Huizinga, Johan, 794

Humanism: Christian, 366–368, *367, 373*; education and, 385; in Renaissance Italy, 362; sciences and, 486

Human rights: Helsinki Accords and, 911; Soviet Union and, 911–912

Hume, David, 507

Hundred Years' War: effects of, 356, 382

Hungarian people, in Austrian Empire, 360, 640, 666

Hungary, 694, 815; 1956 protests in, 879; Austria and, 374, 449, *449*, 640, 641, 666, 714–715; Magyars in, 715–716, 738; nationalities in, 641; Ottomans and, 360, 376, 454, 656; Poland and, 359; pro-Soviet regime in, 864; reforms in, 903; revolts in, 640; revolution in, 869, 879, 880; Roman Catholicism in, 359; World War I and, 785, 787; in World War II, 836. *See also* Austria-Hungary; Eastern Europe; specific leaders

Hunger, 948–949

Hunt, Harriet, 678–679

Hus, John, and Hussites, 361

Husák, Gustáv, 903, 925

Husbands. *See* Families; Men; specific groups

Hussein, Saddam, 937

Hussite wars, 359

Hyde, Edward (first earl of Clarendon), 460

Hydroelectric power, 687

Hygiene, 543, 678, 697

Iberian peninsula, *358*, 815–816. *See also* Portugal; Spain

Ibsen, Henrik, 705, 730

Id, 722, 823

Ideal Marriage . . . (van de Velde), 820

Identity politics: in arts, 943

Ideology, 622, 630–634. *See also* specific ideologies

Ignatius of Loyola. *See* Loyola, Ignatius of

Ignorant Philosopher, The (Voltaire), 505

Illegitimacy, 545, 703

Illiteracy, 385, 520–521, 708–709, 751

Illness. *See* Disease; Medicine

Imitation Game, The (movie), 856

Imitation of Christ, The (Thomas à Kempis), 369

Immigration: to Canada, 741; to England, 940; to Europe, 940; to Germany, 940; guest workers and, 940–941; to Netherlands, 940–941; United States and, 604. *See also* Emigration; Migrant crisis

Immunological science, 677

Impeachment: of Clinton, 934; Nixon and, 908

Imperial Decree, on emancipation of serfs (Russia), 668

Imperialism: in 19th century, 741–751; economic, 742; responses to, 749–751. *See also* New imperialism

Imperialism, the Highest Stage of World Capitalism (Lenin), 742

Imports, 549, 691; in 18th century, 428, 549; of American silver, 433. *See also* specific products and countries

Impression, Sunrise (Monet), 726, *727*

Impressionism, 725–726, *727, 728*

Inca Empire, *408*, 408–410, 411

Income, national, 688

Independence: of Yugoslavian republics, 928. *See also* specific locations

Independence movements: decolonization and, 870–875; in Soviet Union, 922

Independent Group (art students), 890

Independent Social Democratic Party (Germany), 784

Index of Forbidden Books, 389, 489

India: Britain and, 750–751; England and, *418*, 418–419, 747, 800; France and, *418*, 418–419; Gandhi in, 800; goods from, 601; guest workers from, 940; independence of, 875; industrialization and, 604–605, 751; Jesuits in, 389; Mughal Empire in, 418, *418*; Nehru in, 877; new imperialism in, 747, 750–751; Portugal and, *403*, 403–404; in Seven Years' War, 540, *540*, 541; and War of the Austrian Succession, 540; World War I and, 770; World War II and, 842

Indian music, 916

Indian National Congress, 751, 875

Indians. *See* Native Americans

Individualism: Romanticism and, 645

Indochina, 875; France and, 747–748; Japan and, 834. *See also* Cambodia; Laos; Vietnam

Indonesia, 415–416, 423, 875; Communist Party in, 877

Induction, 490–491

Indulgences, 368–369

Industrial economy, 690

Industrialization: in Austria, 666, 738; of Continental Europe, 601–603, *602*, 672–673; factories and, 689; in France, 656, 737; government and, 593, 601–602; Latin America and, 625; Marxism and, 674; mass education and, 708; middle class and, 609–611, 627, 630; in nonindustrialized world, 604–605; poor people and, 613–614; Romantics and, 646; in Soviet Union, 812–813; spread of, 690–691; and technology, 594–599, *597, 598*, 603, 687–688; in United States, 603–604, 689, 739–740. *See also* Entrepreneurs; Industrial Revolution; specific locations

Industrial Revolution: in England, 593–601, *597*, 617, 672; Second, 686, 687–697, *688*; social impact of, 605–617; spread of, 601–605; transportation revolution and, 596–598, *597*. *See also* Industrialization

Industry: in England, 798; entrepreneurial class in, 593, 610–611; European, 548–550, *602*, 602–603, *691*; land and, 611; mechanized, 605; in Nazi Germany, 810; population in, 593, 605–607; Soviet, 812, 901; in U.S. during World War II, 851–852; in World War I, 774, 776; after World War II, 864. *See also* specific locations and industries

Inequality: economic, for women, 939

Infanticide, 704, 751; in 18th century, 545. *See also* Children

Infant mortality, 545–546, 708

Inflation: in 16th century, 393, 427; in 1970s, 904; in Germany, 794–795, *795*, 805; U.S. economy and, 908; in World War I, 776, 802. *See also* Economy

Inquisition, 366; Galileo and, 479–480; Roman, 389, 479–480, 493; Spanish, 358, 410, 538

Institutes of the Christian Religion (Calvin), 382

Instrument of Government (England), 459

Intellectual thought: in 17th century, 494, *494*–496; Greece and, 484; on irrational, 721–722; medieval universities and, 484; Postmodern, 914; pre-World War I sciences and, 720–721; in Renaissance Italy, 362; women and, *486*, 486–488. *See also* Enlightenment; Humanism; Philosophy; Renaissance; Scientific Revolution

Intendants, 441, 585

Interchangeable parts, 603, 689

Intercontinental ballistic missile (ICBM), 869

Intermarriage: in Latin America, 423. *See also* Marriage

Internal combustion engine, 687–688

International Monetary Fund (IMF), 945–947

Internationals, Marx and, 674

International tribunal for crimes against humanity, 929

International women's conferences, 940

International Women's Day, 778

International Working Men's Association, 674

Internet, 942

Internment: of Japanese Americans, 852

Interpretation of Dreams, The (Freud), 722

Intervention principle, 624, 628

In the Shadow of Tomorrow (Huizinga), 794

Invalides (armory), 566–567

Inventions: electric, 687. *See also* specific inventions

Investment: industrialization and, 597, 672–673; mortgages as, 947; U.S., in Europe, 795, 796

iPad, 943

iPhone, 943

iPod, 943

Iran: independence of, 872; Revolution of 1979 in, 937, 942; terrorism and, 936. *See also* Persia; Persian Empire

Iran crisis (1980s), 908

Iraq, 788; Pan-Arabism and, 874; in Persian Gulf War, 935. *See also* Mesopotamia

Iraq War (2003–2011), 931, 934, 937–938

Ireland: emigration from, 606–607; England and, 459, 460, 712, 736; Great Famine in, 605, 606; Northern, 736, 905, 936; potato in, 547, 606; in World War I, 773

Irish Land League, 712

Irish Republican Army (IRA), 936

Irish Republican Brotherhood, 773

Iron and iron industry: in Britain, 596, 672; on Continent, 603, 672; industrialization and, 596, *602*, 603, 672; steel and, 687

Iron Curtain, 879

Iron curtain speech (Churchill), 859

"Iron Lady": Thatcher as, 905

Iron Lady, The (movie), 906

Irrationality, 721–722

Isabella II (Spain), 664

Isabella of Castile, *358*, *358*, 359, *375*, 406, 410

ISIL, 937–938

Islam: fundamentalist, 937; growth of, 942; in Turkey, 800; West and, 937–938. *See also* Muslims

Islamic State, 937–938

Islamic State of Iraq (ISI), 937

Islamic State of Iraq and al-Sham or Syria (ISIS), 937

Isolationism: in U.S., 828

Israel: Arab-Israeli disputes and, 873, 874–875; creation of, 873; Egypt and, 873–874. *See also* Arab-Israeli disputes

Istanbul. *See* Constantinople (Istanbul)

Isthmus of Panama, 406

Italy, 713; in 1815, *628*; in 1970s and 1980s, 906–907; Allied invasion of, *837*; Austria and, 449, *449*–450, 538, 659–660; Baroque in, 464–465, 513; coalition government in, 883–884; corruption in, 931–932; Dopolavoro in, 819; economy in, 433; emigration from, 698; Ethiopia and, 745, 746, 830; in European Coal and Steel Community, 884; fascism in, 801, 802–805; France and, 659–660; Holy Roman Empire and, *375*, 376; liberalism in, 640, 641, 737; Mafia in, 907; mannerism in, 464, *464*;

Napoleon and, 586; nationalism in, 640, 641; Nazi Germany and, 829–830; papacy and, 628; at Paris Peace Conference, 786; revolts in, 623–624; Spain and, 392, 449–450, 538, 815; states in, 628, *628*; in Triple Alliance, 752; unification of, 653, *659*, 659–660; uprising in (1830), 635; World War I and, 765, 770, 771, 773, 802, *802*; in World War II, 842. *See also* Renaissance; Roman Empire; World War I; World War II

iTunes, 945

Ivan III (Russia), 359

Ivan IV the Terrible (Russia), 450

Jackson, Andrew, 642

Jacob, Aletta, 704

Jacobins, 572, 573, 581

Jacob's Room (Woolf), 823

Jacquard, Joseph-Marie, 603

Jadwiga (Poland), 455

Jagiello dynasty (Poland), 455

Jahn, Friedrich Ludwig, 628

Jakarta. *See* Batavia (Jakarta)

Jamaica, 421, *421*

James I (England), 458

James II (England), 461–462

Jamestown, 422

Janissaries, 454–455

Japan: Allied colonies and, 870; atomic bombing of, 853, 854; Catholic Church in, 389; China and, 750, *835*; Europeans and, 420–421, *421*; expansion by, 750, *750*; imperialism and, 747, 750, 751; industrialization in, 610, 690–691, *692*; Jesuits in, 389, 420, 425; at Midway, 841–842; mobilization in World War II, 852–853; modernization of, 750, *750*; Nazi Germany and, 834; New Order in Asia and, 848–850; Pearl Harbor attack by, 838; Russo-Japanese War and, 739, 747, 750; Southeast Asia and, 834, 839–840; textile factory in, 692, *692*; World War I and, 770, 787; before World War II, 833–835; World War II and, 838, *839*; after World War II and, 854–855

Japanese Americans: World War II racism against, 852

Japanese Empire, 833

Jaurès, Jean, 694

Java, 415–416

Jazz, 818

Jefferson, Thomas, 503, *562*, 642

Jena, battles at, 586
Jerrold, Blanchard, *608*
Jerusalem: Arab meeting in, 874–875
Jesuits, 387–389, *389*, 420, 424, 425, 521, 538
Jet planes, 856
Jewish State, The (Herzl), 735, 736
Jews and Judaism: banking, commerce, and, 523; in eastern Europe, 522–523, 735; Enlightenment and, *512*; Holocaust and, 845–848, 849, *849*; migration by, 698, 735; Nazis and, 808, 810, 811; Palestine and, 873; in Prussia, 533; in Spain, 358, 523; toleration and, 522–523; Zionism and, 735, 736. *See also* Anti-Semitism; Holocaust; Israel (modern)
Jex-Blake, Sophia, 679
Jihad, 937–938
Job Corps, 885
Jobs, for women, 692–693, *693*, 774–775, *776*, 810–811
Joffre, Joseph, 764
John XXIII (pope), 892
John of Leiden, 380
John Paul II (pope), 942
Johns Hopkins University School of Medicine, 678
Johnson, Lyndon B., 885; Vietnam and, 901, 909
Johnson, Samuel, 554
Joint-stock company, 428, 597
Joint-stock investment banks, 672–673
Jordan, 799; independence of, 872, 873
Joseph II (Austria), 521, 523, 529, 535, *535*, 539, 556
Josephine de Beauharnais (France), 583
Journal des Savants, 493
Journalism: mass, 720. *See also* Newspapers
Joyce, James, 822
Judaism. *See* Jews and Judaism
Judith Beheading Holofernes (Gentileschi), 465, *466*
Julius Excluded from Heaven (Erasmus), 367
Julius II (Pope), 361, 367
July Revolution (France, 1830), 634–635, *635*
Jung, Carl, 823
Jünger, Ernest, 822
Junkers, 448, 532, 714
Justification by faith alone, 369–370, 382–383, 396
Jutland, Battle of, 771

Kabul, Afghanistan, 937
Kaczyński, Lech, 926

Kádár, János, 879, 903
Kandinsky, Wassily, 729, *730*
Kangxi (China), 419, *442*
Kant, Immanuel, 500, *503*
Kaprow, Allen, 914
Karelia, 452
Karlowitz, Treaty of, 449
Karlsbad Decrees, 629
Kaunitz, Wenzel von, 540
Kay-Shuttleworth, James, 609
Kellogg, Frank B., 795
Kellogg-Briand pact, 795
Kelly, Petra, 940
Kemal, Mustafa (Atatürk), 799–800
Kennan, George, 865, 866
Kennedy, John F., 870, 885, 909
Kent State University, protesters at, 901
Kenya, 801, 871–872
Kenya African National Union, 871
Kenyatta, Jomo, 801, 871
Kepler, Johannes, 477–478, 496
Kerensky, Alexander, 779
Keynes, John Maynard, 798
KGB, 902
Khomeini, Ayatollah, 908, 937
Khrushchev, Nikita, 869, 870, 901; on Cuban Missile Crisis, 871; Soviet Union under, 877–878
Khubilai Khan, 400
Kiefer, Anselm, 943, *943*
Kiel mutiny, 784
Kikuyu people, Mau Mau movement of, 871–872
King, Coretta, *885*
King, Martin Luther, Jr., *885*, 885–886
Kingdom of the Two Sicilies, 660, 661
Kings and kingdoms. *See* Monarchs and monarchies; specific rulers and locations
Kipling, Rudyard, 743
Kirch, Gottfried, 487
Kitchener (Lord), 751
Kivshenko, Alexei, 666
Kleindeutsch state, 640
Knowledge, theory of, 502
Knox, John, 383
Koch, Robert, 677–678
Kohl, Helmut, 905, 930
Kolchak, Alexander, 782
Kollontai, Alexandra, 780
Komorowski, Bronislaw, 926
Königgrätz (Sadowa), battle at, 663
Koons, Jeff, *944*
Korea, 739, 747, 750; Japan and, 833, 850
Korean War, 867–869, *869*; China and, 910; West Germany and, 882
Kornilov, Lavr, 779

Kosovo: Albanians in, 928, 929; Battle of (1389), 360; war in, 928–929
Kosovo Liberation Army (KLA), 928
Kossuth, Louis, 640, 666
Koštunica, Vojislav, 929
Koyaanisqatsi (Glass), 916
Kraft durch Freude (Strength Through Joy), 819
Kristallnacht, 811, *811*
Krupp armaments, 744
Kuchuk-Kainarji, Treaty of, 537
Kulaks, 813
Kulturkampf, 714
Kundera, Milan, 915–916
Kurds, 937
Kurile Islands, 857
Kuroda Seiki, 728, *728*
Kursk, Battle of, 842
Kuwait, 935, 937
Kwaśniewski, Aleksander, 926
Kyoto, Japan, *520*
Kyushu, 420, 425

La belle époque era, 690
Labor: agricultural, 611; in factories, 598–599; in France, 882; Nazi, 845; slave, 411–412; in Soviet Union, 812–813, 877; in United States, 603–604; women as, 692–693, 810–811; World War I and, 770, 774. *See also* Child labor; Forced labor; Slavery; Trade unions; Workers; Working class
Labor Front (Germany), 808, 810
Labor unions: in U.S., 799. *See also* Strikes; Trade unions
Labour Party (England), 735, 798, 882, 931
La Bruyère, Jean de, 488
Ladies' Football Club, *710*, 711
Lafayette, marquis de, 563, 569
Laibach: congress at, 624
Laissez-faire doctrine, 507, 581, 630, 797
Lake Texcoco, 408
Land: economic theories on, 507. *See also* Agriculture; Forests
Land and Freedom (Russia), 668, 669
Landed estates, 551
Landlords, 547, 552
Language(s): in Austria-Hungary, 715; Bible available in, 366, 372; in Russia, 716; vernacular, 366, 367. *See also* specific languages
Laocoön (El Greco), 464
Laos, 747, 875
Las Casas, Bartolomé de, 411
Lateran Accords (1929), 805
Later Middle Ages, 484

Latin America: in early 19th century, *626*; European colonies in, 423; independence and, 580–581, *626*; Monroe Doctrine and, 625; revolts in, 580–581, *624*, 624–625. *See also* Colonies and colonization; specific locations

Latin Christianity. *See* Catholic Church

Latin language: New Testament in, 367

Latin music, 945

La Tour, Maurice-Quentin de, *504, 508*

Latvia, 787, 833, 922

Laud, William, 458

Launay, marquis de, 559

Laurier, Wilfred, 741

Lavasseur, E., 689

Lavoisier, Antoine and Marie-Anne, 486

Law(s). *See* Law codes; Scientific laws; specific laws

Law, John, 548

Law codes: Napoleonic, 584–585

Law of 14 Frimaire, 581

Law of the General Maximum, 578

Lawrence, T. E. (Lawrence of Arabia), 770

Lay Down Your Arms (Suttner), 734

Lazar (Serbia), 360

League of Communists of Yugoslavia, 928

League of Nations, 786, 792, 793, 794, 828; Germany and, 795; mandates and, 788

League of Strasbourg, War of the, 446

Learning. *See* Education; Intellectual thought

Leary, Timothy, 897

Lebanon, 788, 799, 872

Lebensraum, 806, 828

Le Bon Marché, 689, 712

Lee, Robert E., 671

Leeds Woolen Workers' Petition, The, 550

Left wing: in France, 931; terrorism by, 936

Legal issues. *See* Law codes; specific laws

Legion of the Archangel Michael (Romania), 815

Legislation. *See* specific laws

Legislative Assembly (France), 569, 571, 572–573

Legislative Corps (France), 656

Legislature. *See* specific bodies

Legitimacy principle, Metternich and, 621

Leiden, University of, 519

Leighton, Roland, 777

Leipzig Debate, 370–371

Leisure, 686, 703, 705, 709–711, 888; after World War I, 819

Lend-Lease, 858

Lenin, V. I., 742, 779–780, *780*, 790; economic policy of, 812; war communism and, 812

Leningrad: Nazi attack on, 837; siege of, 843

Leo X (Pope), 362, *362*, 370

Leo XIII (Pope), 724

Leonardo da Vinci, 474

Leopold I (Holy Roman Emperor), 449

Leopold II (Belgium), 745

Leopold II (Holy Roman Emperor), *535*, 573

Leopold of Hohenzollern-Sigmaringen, 664

Leopold of Saxe-Coburg, 635

Lepanto, Battle of, 393, 454

Le Pen, Jean-Marie, 940

Le Pen, Marine, 940

Lerma, duke of (Spain), 447

Lesbians. *See* Homosexuals and homosexuality

Lesseps, Ferdinand de, *673*

"Letter from a Peasant to the Bolshevik Leaders," 781

"Letter from a Soldier in Leningrad to Lenin," 781

Letters: Louis XIV and King of Tonkin, 417

Letters from a Lost Generation (Brittain), 777

"Letter to Czechoslovakia, A," 905

"Letter to Paolo Foscarini" (Bellarmine), 481–482

Lettow-Vorbeck, Paul von, 770

Levellers, 459, 493

Lévesque, René, 934

Leviathan (Hobbes), 463

Ley, Robert, 810

Leyster, Judith, 466, *466*

Liberal arts, 385

Liberal Democrats (England), 931

Liberalization, in France, 589

Liberal Party: in Canada, 886, 934; in England, 670, 735–736, 798; in Italy, 802

Liberals, in Spain, 713

Liberals and liberalism, 653; economic, 630; nationalism and, 621, 629, 650; political, 630–633; in World War I, 773. *See also* specific locations

Liberia, 746

Liberty: Locke on, 562; Mill on, 630

Libya: Italy and, 737; terrorism and, 936; Tripoli as, 745; in World War II, 840

Liebknecht, Karl, 784, 785

Liebknecht, Wilhelm, 693–694

Life and Death in Shanghai (Nien Cheng), 911

Lifestyle, 554; in 18th century, 425; of 19th-century workers, 598–599, 607–609, *608*; in cities, 700; Columbian Exchange and, 425; in country houses, 552–554, *553*; of Dutch, 457, *457*; in Industrial Revolution, 607–609, *608*, 614–615; of middle class, 703; in United States, 950; of urban poor, 555–556; in World War I trenches, 766–770, *769*

Lightning war, 830, 835

Lima, Pizarro in, 410

Limited monarchies, 455–463

Limmer, Walter, letter to his parents, 763

Lincoln, Abraham, 668

Linen Cupboard, The (de Hooch), *457*

Lisbon, Portugal, 538, 550, 554

Lisbon Treaty (2009), 932

List, Friedrich, 602

Lister, Joseph, 678

Liszt, Franz, 682–683

Literacy, 385, 520–521, 708–709

Literature: Elizabethan, 467; in France, 468; for masses, 709; Modernism in, 725; Naturalism in, 725; Postmodernism in, 915–916; Realism in, 680, 681; Romantic, 645–646; in Spain, 467–468; stream-of-consciousness technique in, 822–823; Symbolism in, 725; travel, 501; unconscious in, 822–823; on World War I, 763, 767, 777; after World War II, 890–891. *See also* specific writers and works

Lithuania, 380, 455, 787, 922

Little Entente, 793–794, *794*

"Little ice age," 433, 546

Little Pretty Pocket-Book, 544

Little Red Book (Mao Zedong), *910*

Liturgy: of Mass, 892

"Live and let live" system: in trench warfare, 768

Liverpool-Manchester railroad, 596–597, *597*

Living space. *See* Lebensraum

Living species: damage to, 948

Livingston, Robert, *562*

Livingstone, David, 745

Livonia, 452

Li Zicheng (China), 419

Lloyd George, David, 735–736, *737*, 773, 776, 798; at Paris Peace Conference, 785, 786, *788*

Lo Bengula, 746
Locarno, Treaty of, 795
Locke, John, 463, 502, 562
Lockerbie, Scotland: Pan Am plane explosion over, 936
Lollardy, 361
Lombardy, 621, 628, 640, 660
London: bombing in World War II, 853, 854; finance in, 548; immigrants in, 940; living conditions in, 607, 608, 609; police in, 643; population of, 554, 607
London: A Pilgrimage (Jerrold), 608
London Conference, after Balkan wars, 752–753
London Mechanics' Institute, 644
London School of Medicine for Women, 679
London Working Men's Association, 616
Long Parliament, 458
Long Telegram, The (Kennan), 865
Looms, 549, 595, 603, 672
Lope de Vega, Félix, 468
Lord Protector (England), 459
Lords. *See* Nobility
Lord's Supper. *See* Eucharist
Lorenzo de' Medici (the Magnificent): Medici family, 362
Lorraine, 445, 446, 664, 787. *See also* Alsace-Lorraine
Los Alamos: atomic bomb and, 854
Los Angeles: race riot in, 886
"Lost generation," 784, 793
Loughnan, Naomi, 775
Louis XI ("Spider" king, France), 356
Louis XIII (France), 437, 440, 441, 458
Louis XIV (France), 432, 432–433, 442; absolutism of, 440–441, 565; correspondence with king of Tonkin, 417; parlements and, 441, 443; reign of, 441–447; religious minorities and, 443, 521; Royal Academy of Sciences and, 491, 491, 495; Versailles court of, 441, 443, 444, 552; wars of, 446, 446–447
Louis XV (France), 530, 563–564
Louis XVI (France), 530, 531, 562; escape of, 572; execution of, 574, 574; French Revolution and, 559, 567, 568–569; National Assembly and, 566, 569
Louis XVIII (France), 589, 621, 628
Louisbourg, 540, 541
Louisiana Purchase, 561
Louis of Hungary, 376
Louis-Philippe (France), 634, 635, 638, 639

Louvois, marquis de (François-Michel Le Tellier), 446
"Love-in," 898
Low Countries, 359, 374, 376–377, 547, 551, 601. *See also* Belgium; Netherlands
Lower Austria, 449
Lower Canada (Quebec), 671
Lower classes, 686, 693, 703. *See also* Classes
Loyalists: in American Revolution, 560
Loyola, Ignatius of (Saint), 387–388, 389
LSD, 897
Lübeck, 436
Lublin Poles, 857
Luddites, 616
Ludendorff, Erich, 764–765, 772, 773, 783, 784
Ludlow, Edmund, 460
Lueger, Karl, 734
Luftwaffe, 830, 836, 838, 853–854
Lumiére brothers, 818
Lusitania (ship), 771
Luther (movie), 372
Luther, Martin, 365, 365, 476; on education, 385; marriage of, 370, 374; Ninety-Five Theses of, 370, 371, 396, 629; Peasants' War and, 373, 374; Reformation and, 369–377; Zwingli and, 378, 379
Lutheranism: in 18th century, 521; in Scandinavia, 377, 453, 521; spread of, 372–373
Lützen, Battle of, 437
Luxembourg, 359; in World War II, 836
Luxemburg, Rosa, 784, 785
Luxury goods, 443, 603
Lyons, 574, 576–577, 603

Maastricht Treaty, 932
MacArthur, Douglas: in Korea, 868; in Philippines, 842
Macartney (Lord), China trade and, 419–420
Macaulay, Thomas Babington, 636
MacDonald, Ramsay, 798
Macedonia, 752, 928
Machine gun, 746, 766, 766
Machinery, 549, 550, 603; agricultural, 690
Madame Bovary (Flaubert), 680, 681
Madison, James, 503, 642
Madras (Chennai), 418, 540, 541
Madrid, 815, 816; population of, 554
Madrigals, 355–356
Mafia: in Italy, 907
Magazines, 516–517, 709, 768

Magdeburg, 439
Magellan, Ferdinand, 399–400, 406, 415
Magenta, battle at, 659
Magic, 474
Magic Flute, The (Mozart), 516
Magic realism, 915
Maginot Line, 836
Magyar(s), 666, 738
Magyar language (Hungary), 716
Maine, France, 356
Main River region, 664
Mainz, 555
Maistre, Joseph de, 622
Maize. *See* Corn
Major, John, 931
Malacca, 389, 404, 415
Malaya, 838; Japan and, 833, 850
Malay States, 747
Malay world, 418
Malcolm X, 886
Mallarmé, Stéphane, 730
Malnutrition, 751
Malthus, Thomas, 630, 676
Malvinas, 906
Manchester: factory in, 592; Peterloo in, 627
Manchu dynasty (China), 419, 419, 747, 750
Manchukuo, 834
Manchuria, 747; Japan and, 833, 834
Mandates, 788, 788, 799, 873
Mandela, Nelson, 872
Manhattan Project, 851
Manitoba, 741
Mannerism, 464, 464
Mantua, 449
Manufacturing: on Continent, 602–603; in France, 443–444; in Germany, 690; handicraft, 546. *See also* Industry; specific locations
Many Happy Returns of the Day (Frith), 706
Mao Zedong, 868, 875–877, 885, 910, 910
Maps, 402, 402, 426, 427
Marburg Colloquy, 378, 379
March on Washington for Jobs and Freedom (1963), 886
March Revolution (Russia), 778, 778–779
Marclay, Christian, 944–945
Marconi, Guglielmo, 687, 818
Marco Polo Bridge, 834
Marcuse, Herbert, 899
Mariana Islands: Japan and, 833
Maria Theresa (Austria), 534–535, 535, 540
Marie Antoinette (France), 530, 535, 576

Marie Antoinette (movie), 530

Market economy, 796

Markets: in 18th century, *555*; for British products, 593–594; commercial capitalism and, 427; industrial production and, 593–594, 672, 688–689; transportation and, 593–594

Marlborough, duke of (Charles Spencer-Churchill), 702

Marne: First Battle of, 764, *764*; Second Battle of, 783

Marriage, 681; in 18th century, 545–546, 551; in 19th century, 703; intermarriage and, 423; Luther and, *370*, 374; in New World, 423, 425; nuclear, 545; Protestantism and, 383–385; in upper classes, 702; welfare system and, 888

Marriage (Same Sex Couples) Act (England, 2013), 931

Marriage of Figaro, The (Mozart), 516

Married Love (Stopes), 820

Married women: in workforce, 889

"Marseillaise," 573

Marseilles, 520, 574, 576, 607

Marshall, George C., 866

Marshall, John, 593, 642

Marshall Islands: Japan and, 833

Marshall Plan, 866

Martin V (Pope), 361

Marx, Karl, and Marxism, 673, 673–674, 675, 694, 695, 779; Great Depression and, 797; on imperialism, 742

Marxist Social Democratic Labor Party (Russia), 694, 738, 779

Mary (Virgin), 523

Mary, queen of Scots, 395

Mary (Burgundy), marriage of, *375*

Mary I (England), 382

Mary II (England), 462–463

Masaryk, Thomas, 815

Masons, 510

Mass (Catholic Church), 378, 523

Massachusetts Bay Colony, 422

Mass communication, revolution in, 818, 917

Mass culture: expansion of, 819–823; popular audience for, 822

Mass education, 708–709, 720

Massive retaliation policy, 869

Mass leisure, 686, 703, 705, 709–711, 819, 888

Mass marketing, 688, 689

Mass meetings, in Nazi Germany, 809, *810*, 818, 819

Mass politics: in late 1800s, 712, 731; after World War I, 801

Mass production, 687

Mass society, 686–687, 697–712; classes in, 702–703; education in, 708–709

Mass sports, 917

Mass tourism, growth of, 710

Mästlin, Michael, 477

Masurian Lakes, Battle of, 764

Materialism, 676, 680

Mathematical Principles of Natural Philosophy (Newton). *See Principia* (Newton)

Mathematics, 482, 680; Scientific Revolution and, 474, 482

Mau Mau movement, 871–872

Mauryan Empire (India), 418

Maximilian (Bavaria), 435

Maximilian I (Holy Roman Empire), 359, 374, *375*

Maximilian of Austria, in Mexico, 656

Maya, 407–408, *408*

May Day, 694–695

Mayhew, Henry, 694

Mazarin, Jules (Cardinal), 441

Mazzini, Giuseppe, 640, 641, 660

McCarthy, Joseph R., 885

McKinley, William, 749

McLuhan, Marshall, 917

Meat Inspection Act (U.S.), 740–741

Mechanics: motion and, 480, 482–483, 493

Mechanization, 604, 616, 672

Media. *See* specific media

Medical schools, 518–519, 678–679

Medici family: Catherine de', 390, 391; Cosimo II, 479; Lorenzo the Magnificent, 362

Medicine: in 18th century, 518–519; death rate decline and, 697; in Middle Ages, 519; scientific basis for, 676; in Scientific Revolution, 484–486, *485*; women in, 678–679, 734. *See also* Disease; Health and health care

Mediterranean region, 656, 657, 751; in 18th century, 538–539; after World War II, 864–865; in World War II, 836. *See also* specific locations

Medvedev, Dmitry, 924

Mehmet II (Ottomans), 360

Meiji restoration (Japan), 750

Mein Kampf (Hitler), 806–807, 828

Melanchthon, Philip, 373, 385, 476

Melchiorites, 380

Memoirs (Comtesse de Boigne), 531

Memoirs (Ludlow), 460

Memoirs (Metternich), 623

Memoirs (Saint-Simon), 445

Men: consumer culture and, 712; in Great Depression, 797; roles of, 384; sports and, 711. *See also* Boys; Gender and gender issues

Mendeleyev, Dmitri, 676

Mennonites, 380

Mensheviks, 779, 780

Mercantilism, 428, 443–444, 448, 549–550

Mercator, Gerardus, 426

Mercenaries, 543

Merchants: in Asia, 416; mercantilism and, 443–444, 448. *See also* Trade

Merian, Maria Sibylla, 487

Merkel, Angela, 930–931, 941

Mesoamerica, 407–408

Mesopotamia, 770

Messiaen, Olivier, 916

Messiah (Handel), 515

Mestizos, 423

Metallurgy, 428, 493, 603

Metals, 427, 428. *See also* Gold; Silver

Metamorphosis of the Insects of Surinam (Merian), *487*

Metaxas, John, 815

Methodism, *523*, 523–524, 599, 649

Metternich, Klemens von, 621, 623, 628, 629, 635, 640

Metz, 438

Mexico, 425; France and, 656; Spanish conquests in, 403, 408

Mexico City, 410

Michel, Louise, 713

Microcosm, man as, 485

Microprocessor, 912

Microsoft, 942

Middle class(es): in Africa, 749; British, 610, 631, 669; in cities, 554; families of, 705–707, *706*; French, 564–565; German, 807; industrial, 609–611, 627, 630; in Industrial Revolution, 607–609; in Italy, 801–802; in late 1800s, 687, 702–703; Prussian, 533, 661; in Russia, 739; television and, 892–893; women in, 693, 707; World War I and, 762, 776

Middle East: in 1919, *788*; conflicts in, 936; decolonization and conflict in, 872–875, *875*; Ottomans in, *875*; World War I and, 770, 788; between World Wars, 799–800. *See also* Arabs and Arab world; specific locations

Middle Passage, 413

Midway, Battle of, 841–842

Midwives, 488, 519

"Mighty Fortress Is Our God, A" (Luther), 372

Migrant crisis: in Europe, 941, *941*. *See also* Immigration; Migration

Migration: crisis over, 931; globalization and, 950; of Jews, 735; into Poland, 926. *See also* Emigration; Immigration; specific groups

Milan: Austria and, 447, 449–450; duchy of, 538

Militarism: Prussian, *533*; before World War I, 759

Military: in 18th century, 532–533, 542–543; in Austria, 532, 542; in France, 532, 574–576, *575*, 737; in Germany, 714, 787, 808; Japanese, 750, 848–849; of Nazi Germany, 828, 830; nobility and, 532–533, 542–543, 551–552; Ottoman, 454–455; in Prussia, 532–533, 534, 542–543, 588, 662, 664; Russian, 532, 542–543, 777, 779, 781; Soviet, 922; in Spain, 358; after Thirty Years' War, 438–439; in U.S., 908; in Vietnam, 909; before World War I, 759; in World War II, 835. *See also* Mercenaries; Navy; specific leaders, battles, and wars

Military alliances: after World War II, 867

Milk, pasteurization of, 678, 697

Mill, John Stuart, 631–632

Millenarianism, 380, 493

Millet, Jean-François, 682, *682*

Milligen, J. G., 577

Mills, 593

Milošević Slobodan, 928

Minerals, 593

Mines and mining, 596, *602*, 603, 612, *613*, 615, 798

Ming dynasty (China), 419

Minimalism, in music, 916

Ministerial responsibility, 628, 631

Ministry of Munitions (England), 773

Minorities: in Austria-Hungary, 666, 697, 738; World War I and, 758, 788. *See also* Nationalities; specific groups

Mir (village commune), 667

Missiles, 869, 870

Mission, The (movie), 424

Missions and missionaries: in Asia, 389, 416, 417, 420, 425; in colonies, 423–425; English, 524; evangelical, 725; imperialism and, 423–425; in Japan, 389, 420, 425; Jesuit, 389, 420, *424*; Methodist, *523*, 523–524, 649. *See also* specific orders

Mississippi River region, 541, 603

Mitterrand, François, 906

Mobilization: in World War I, 760, 761, 772, 773; in World War II, 850–853

Model T Ford, 687

Modena, 660

Modern Devotion, 369

Modernism (arts), 725–731; in music, 916; Postmodernism and, 914, 915

Modernism (religious movement), 724

Mohács, Battle of, 376

Moldavia, 626, 656, 657, 658

Moldova, 922

Molière, Jean-Baptiste, 468

Molotov, Vyacheslav, 859, 865

Moluccas (Spice Islands), 389, 404, 415

Monarchists, in France, 639, 712, 713

Monarchs and monarchies: in 17th century, 439; in 18th century, 529, 556; Austrian, 358–359, 449; Carolingian, 440; centralized power of, 356, 359, 363; constitutional, 458, 459, 503, 569, 571, 635; Declaration of Pillnitz and, 573; divine right and, 440, 463; in Dutch Republic, 394, 456; in eastern Europe, 359; in England, 356–357, 381, 394–395, 458–463, *461*, 502–503; in France, 356, 390–392, 440, 530, 565, 634–635; in Germany, 373; limited, 455–463; Napoleon on, 586–587; in Poland, 359, 455–456, *456*; in Renaissance, 356, 363; in Spain, 357–358, 374, *375*, 392–393, 410; in Sweden, 453. *See also* Absolutism; Limited monarchies; specific rulers and locations

Monasticism. *See* Monks and monasteries

Monet, Claude, 726, *727*

Monetary union: in Europe, 932

Money: medieval trade and, 507. *See also* Inflation

Mongols, 359

Monism. *See* Pantheism

Monks and monasteries: criticism of, 368; wealth of, 521. *See also* specific orders and monasteries

Monogenesis, 501

Monopolies: in spice trade, 403

Monroe, James, 625

Monroe Doctrine, 625

Montcalm, Louis-Joseph, 541–542

Montecino, Antón, 410

Montenegro, 751, 752, 929

Montesquieu, baron de (Charles de Secondat), 502–503

Montessori, Maria, 734

Monti, Mario, 931

Mont Sainte-Victoire (Cézanne), *727*, 727–728

Moon, U.S. landing on, 912, *912*

Moore, Charles, 915, 916

Moravia: Nazis and, 831

Moravian Brethren, 523

More, Hannah, 521

More, Thomas, 367–368, 381

Morel, Edward, 743

Morisot, Berthe, 726

Moro, Aldo, 907

Morocco, 745, 872

Mortality. *See* Death rates

Mortgages, 947

Moscow, 554, 589; in World War II, 837–838

Mosques: in United States, 942

Mother, The (de Hooch), *457*

Mothers: in Fascist Italy, 805; in Nazi Germany, 810; in Soviet Union, 813. *See also* Families; Women

Motion, 480, 482–483

Mountain, the (France), 573

Mountains. *See* specific mountains

Movies, 818; Americanization through, 892. *See also* specific movies

Mozambique, 745

Mozart, Wolfgang Amadeus, 515–516, 648, 649

Mrs. Dalloway (Woolf), 823

MTV, 917

Mughal Empire, 418, *418*

Mühlberg, Battle of, 377

Mulattoes, 423

Multiculturalism, 944

Multiethnicity: in Soviet Union, 922, 923

Multinational corporation, 947

Multinational states: Austria as, 629; nationalism and, 632

Multiracial society, in Latin America, 423

Mumbai (Bombay), 404

Munich: Hitler in, 795, 831

Munich Conference (1938), 831, 833

Munich Olympics, 917; Palestinian terrorists at, 936

"Munition Work" (Loughnan), 775

Münster, Anabaptists in, 380

Müntzer, Thomas, 373

Murad (Ottoman Turks), 360

Museums: art, 889

Music: in 1960s, 893; since 1985, 945; atonal, 822; in Enlightenment, 514–515; instrumental, 649; jazz, 818; Modernism in, 729–731, 916; New German School of, 682–683; primitivism in, 731; program,

648; protest, 899; in Renaissance, 355–356; Romanticism in, 648, 649, 682–683. *See also* specific composers and types

Music halls, 709–710

Music industry, 893

Muslim League, 875

Muslims: in Algeria, 872; immigration restrictions on, 941; in India, 875; in Pakistan, 875; Palestine and, 873; in Paris, 931; in Spain, 358. *See also* Islam

Mussolini, Benito, 801, 802–805, *803*; on Balkan region, 836–837; Ethiopia and, 830; France and, 836; in World War II, 842

Mutsuhito (Japan), 750

Mutual assistance treaty: after World War II, 867

Mutual deterrence policy, 867

Myanmar. *See* Burma (Myanmar)

My Own Story (Emmeline Pankhurst), 732

Mysticism, 369, 386–387, 489, 495, 523, 524

Nagasaki, 420–421, *421*; atomic bombing of, 854, *855*

Nagy, Imry, 879

Nanjing, Japan and, 834, 850

Nanterre, University of, 896

Nantes, in French Revolution, 567

Naples, 660; Austria and, 447, 449, 538; kingdom of, 374, 628, 660; market square in, *555*; population of, 554; revolt in, 439

Napoleon I Bonaparte (France), *583*, *585*, 622; calendar of, 579–580; Civil Code of, 584–585, 627; Congress of Vienna and, 620, *620*, 621–622; defeat of, 589; Grand Empire of, 586–587, *587*; military career of, 583; on monarchs, 586–587; rise of, 582–583, 584, 625

Napoleon III (France), 639, *654*, 654–656, 657, 659–660, 663, 664, 702, 712

Narva, Battle of, 451

Naseby, battle at, 460

Nashoba, Tennessee, 632

Nasser, Gamal Abdel, 873–874, 875

National Assembly (France), 566, 567, 568, 569, 572, 639, 654, 712, 906

National Convention (France), 573, *574*, 574–575, 576–578, 581, 583

National debt, 548

National Front, 940

National Government (England), 798

National Guard (France), 569, 572

National Guard (U.S.): at Kent State, 901

National Health Services (England), 931

National Insurance Act (England): of 1911, 735; of 1946, 882

Nationalism, 653, 654; in Africa, 749, 800–801; in Asia, 875–877; in Austria, 667, 734, 940; dangers of, 950; Darwin's ideas and, 723–724; German, 588, 661, 738; of Hitler, 805–806; imperialism and, 741; in Italy, 640, 641, 660, 661; liberalism and, 621, 628, 632, 650; Napoleon and, 588; in Prussia, 588, 664; racism and, 724; revolutions of 1830 and, 634–635, *635*; Serbian, 928; socialism and, 695; Spanish, 588; terrorism and, 936; World War I and, 758, 762, 793; in Yugoslavia, 928

Nationalist Association of Italy, 724

Nationalist China, 834, 876

Nationalists (Spain), 815

Nationalities: in Austria-Hungary, 738, 785. *See also* Minorities; specific groups

Nationalities problem (Austria-Hungary), 715

Nationalization: in England, 882; in France, 881–882; in Russia, 783, 812; in World War I, 772

National Labor Relations Act (1935, U.S.), 799

National Liberation Front (Algeria), 872

National Organization for Women (NOW), 900

National Service Act (England, 1946), 882

National Socialist German Workers' Party, 806, 828. *See also* Nazi Germany; Nazi Party

National System of Political Economy (List), 602

Nation building, 654, 665

Nation in arms, 575, 581, 588

Native Americans: in French and Indian War, *540*, 541–542; Spanish treatment of, 410, 411–412, 423

Native peoples. *See* Decolonization; Native Americans

NATO, 867; Canada in, 886; eastern European states in, 927; in former Yugoslavia, 929; in Serbia, 928

Nattier, Jean Marc, *452*

Naturalism, in literature, 725

Natural law, 484, 502, 507; of economics, 507; natural rights and, 529. *See also* specific scientists and philosophers

Natural man, 501

Natural philosophers, 473, 480, 484, 493, 499

Natural rights, 529, 563, 570–571

Natural selection, 676

Nature: Romanticism and, 646, 647, *647*; state of, 463, 508

Navarre, 357, 390, 391

Navigational aids, 402–403; astrolabe as, 403; compass as, 403

Navy, 439; in 19th century, 687; British, 541, 771, 830; Dutch, 543; French, 541; Japanese, 739, 750, 834; Russian, 739; in World War I, 771. *See also* Armada (Spain); Military

Nazi Germany, 808–811, 827–838; aftermath of World War II and, 854–856, *855*; anti-Semitism in, 810; appeasement of, 830; Austrian annexation by, 830–831; culture of, 822; Czechoslovakia and, 831; development of total state, 808–811; empire of, 843–848; events leading to World War II and, 830–833; German teaching about, 883; Holocaust in, 845–848; Japan and, 834; mass leisure in, 819; mass meetings in, 809, *810*, 818, 819; navy of, 830; Poland and, 831–832; propaganda in, 809; rearmament of, 829–830; resistance in, 845; Rhineland occupied by, 830; Soviet Union and, 833, 836–838, *838*, 850; Spanish Civil War and, 815; women in, 810–811. *See also* Germany; Holocaust; World War II

Nazi Party, 795, 806, 807, 808

Near East. *See* Middle East; specific locations

Necker, Suzanne, *512*

Nehru, Jawaharlal, 877

Neoclassicism, 468, *514*, *515*

Neo-Gothic architecture, 645, *646*

Nepotism, 361

Neshat, Shirin, 943

Netherlands, 621, 694; Calvinism in, 383, 386, 393; foreigners in, 940; France and, 586; in World War II, 836. *See also* Austrian Netherlands; Dutch; Dutch Republic; Low Countries; Spanish Netherlands

Neumann, Balthasar, 513, *514*

Neumann, Solomon, 700

Neutrality: in India, 877; in World War II, 843

New Brunswick, 741

New Caledonia, 713
New Deal, 799
New Economic Policy (NEP), 812
New Europe (1980s), *922*
Newfoundland, 447
New France, 671. *See also* Canada
New German School, music and, 682–683
New Guinea, 771; in World War II, 842
New Harmony, Indiana, 632
New imperialism, 741–742; in Africa, 742–746, 749; in Asia, 747–749, 749–751; results of, 751; by United States, 748–749. *See also* Imperialism; specific locations
New Jerusalem, John of Leiden and, 380
New Lanark, Scotland, 632, *634*
New Model Army (England), 458–459, *459*
New monarchies, in Renaissance, 356
New Netherland, 421–422
New Order: in Asia, 848–850; Nazi, 843–848
New Spain, 410
Newspapers, 517, 586, 658, 709
New Testament, 366, 372. *See also* Bible
Newton, Isaac, 482–484, *483*, 496, 500, 502, 505, 720
"New woman," 734
New World: Dutch and, 413, *413*, *421*; England and, 413, *413*, 421, *421*, 518; European diseases in, 410–412, *412*; exploration of, *404*, 406–407, 421–422; France and, 413, *413*, 421, *421*; Monroe Doctrine and, 625; Portugal and, *404*, 407, 413, *413*, 421; Spain and, *404*, 407–410, *408*, 413, *413*, 421, *421*; voyages to, *399*, *404*, 406–407. *See also* America(s); specific locations
New world order: after Cold War, 935
New York City: World Trade Center destruction in, 936
New Zealand, 501, 747, 770, 771
Ngo Dinh Diem (Vietnam), 909
NGOs. *See* Nongovernmental organizations
Nicaragua, 625
Nice, 660
Nicholas I (Russia), 630, 640, 658
Nicholas II (Russia), 716, 738, 739, *739*, 777; capture and murder of, 782; communications with William II, 761; World War I and, 760, 778
Nien Cheng, 911
Nietzsche, Friedrich, 721
Nigeria, 800, 872; Boko Haram in, 938

Nightingale, Florence, 658, *658*, 731
Nightwatch, The (Rembrandt), *467*
Nigredo (Kiefer), *943*
Niña (ship), 406
Nineteenth Amendment (U.S.), 775
Ninety-Five Theses (Luther), 370, 371, 629
Nixon, Richard, 901, 908; China and, 910–911; resignation of, 908; Vietnam War and, 909
Nkrumah, Kwame, 871, 872
Nobility: in 18th century, 516, 521, 551–554, *553*; in England, 669, 702, 736; in France, 390, 440, 441, 503, 563–564, *564*, 565, 566, 577, 586; grand tour and, 554; in Poland, 456; in Prussia, 532–533, 534, 542–543, 551–552; in Russia, 450, 537; in Scandinavia, 453; as social estate, 453; in Sweden, 453. *See also* specific locations
"Noble savage" idea, 501
Nonaggression pact: Nazi-Soviet, 833, 834
Non-Aryans, Nazis and, 811
Nongovernmental organizations (NGOs), 950
Nonintervention agreement (1936): for Spanish Civil War, 815
Nonviolent resistance, Gandhi and, 800
Nördlingen, Battle of, 437
Normandy, 603; World War II invasion of, 842
North Africa: decolonization in, 872; France and, 745, 840; Ottomans and, 376; World War II in, 836, *837*, 840
North Africans: as guest workers, 940
North America: 1700–1803, *561*; British in, 421–422, 540, *540*, 541–542, 560; Dutch in, 421–422; European migration to, 698; French in, 422–423, 540, *540*, 541–542; in Seven Years' War, 540, *540*, 541–542; Spain and, *540*, 542; in War of the Spanish Succession, 446–447. *See also* specific locations
North American Air Defense Command (NORAD), 886
North Atlantic, Battle of the, 840
North Atlantic Treaty Organization. *See* NATO
Northern Hemisphere: wealthy nations in, 950
Northern Ireland, 736, 905, 936. *See also* Ireland
Northern Renaissance humanism, 366–368, *367*
Northern Union (Russia), 630
North German Confederation, 664

North Korea, 868. *See also* Korea; Korean War
North Vietnam. *See* Vietnam; Vietnam War
Norway, 732, 799; kingdom of, *436*; Scandinavian unification and, 377; World War II in, 836. *See also* Scandinavia
Notes from Underground (Dostoevsky), 726
Notre-Dame Cathedral (Paris): as Temple of Reason, 579, *580*
Novalis, Friedrich, 646
Nova Scotia, 447, 741
Novels, 516, 645. *See also* Literature; specific works
November Revolution (Germany), 784–785
Novikov, Nikolai, 865
NOW. *See* National Organization for Women
Nuclear family, 545
Nuclear power: Chernobyl disaster and, 881, 913–914; in France, 881
Nuclear weapons: arms race and, 867; in France, 881; women's protests about, 939–940
Nuns, 425
Nuremberg: Nazi rallies in, 809, 818, 819
Nuremberg laws, 811
Nuremberg trials: after World War II, 882
Nursing, 658, 693, 731
Nutrition, 697
Nystadt, Peace of, 452, *453*

Oath of the Horatii (David), 514, *515*
Obama, Barack: Afghanistan and, 937; greenhouse gas emissions and, 950
Observations upon Experimental Philosophy... (Cavendish), 486–487
Observatories, *503*
Occupation: Nazi, of Soviet Union, 851; of Rhineland, 830, *832*; zones in Germany, 857, 866–867
Oceans: damage to, 948
October Manifesto (Russia), 739
Oedipus complex, 722, 823
Office of Scientific Research and Development (U.S.), 852
Ohio River region, 541
Oil and oil industry: Italy and, 906; Middle East and, 874; U.S. and, 908
Old-age pensions, 714–715, 799
Old Bolsheviks, 812, 813

Old order (regime, France), 563–565, 567–573, 574, 586
Oligarchy: in Dutch Republic, 532
Olivares (Count), 447
Olson, Culbert, 852
Olympic Games: in Berlin (1936), 819; global broadcast of, 917; mass sports and, 917; in Moscow (1980), 911; Palestinian terrorists at, 936; Soviets and, 917
Omdurman, Battle of, 746
On Anatomical Procedures (Galen), 485
On Crimes and Punishments (Beccaria), 518
One-Dimensional Man (Marcuse), 899
One Hundred Years of Solitude (Garcia Márquez), 915
On Parisian Department Stores (Lavasseur), 689
Ontario, 671, 741
On the Fabric of the Human Body (Vesalius), 485
On the Motion of the Heart and Blood (Harvey), 485–486
On the Origin of Species by Means of Natural Selection (Darwin), 676, 725
On the Revolutions of the Heavenly Spheres (Copernicus), *475*, 475–476
On the Subjection of Women (Mill and Taylor), 631
OPEC. *See* Organization of Petroleum Exporting Countries
Open border policy: in EU, 932
Open door policy, in China, 747
Open-field system, 546
Opera, 514, 515–516, 683; minimalist, 916
Oppenheimer, J. Robert, 854, 856
Orange, house of, 456, 462, 532
Orange Free State, 745
Orbits, of planets, 475, 477, 496
Order of Preachers. *See* Dominicans
Orders of Friars Minor. *See* Franciscans
Organic chemistry, 690
Organic evolution, 676, 677
Organization of Petroleum Exporting Countries (OPEC), 908
Origin and Development of Psychoanalysis, The (Freud), 723
Orléans, duke of, 530
Orthodox Christianity. *See* Eastern Orthodoxy
Orwell, George, 816
Ostpolitik, 904
Ottoman Empire, *540*, 787; in 16th and 17th centuries, *449*, *449*, 453–455, *454*; Balkan wars and, 359–360, *360*,

751, 752, *753*; Charles V and, *375*, 376–377; Crimean War and, 656–658, *657*; decline of, *657*; Greek revolt and, 625–627, *627*, 656; Middle East and, *875*; Palestine in, 656, 735; regimes after, 799–800; Russian expansion and, 537, 626, 656, 747; in World War I, 770
Ottoman Turks. *See* Ottoman Empire
Overpopulation, 606, 630, 698
Overproduction, 796
Overseas trade, 428, 565
OVRA (Italian secret police), 803
Owen, Robert, 615–616, *616*, 632, *634*
Owen, Wilfred, 768
Oxenstierna, Axel, 453
Oxford University (England), 502

Pachakuti (Inca), 409
Pacification of Ghent, 394
Pacific Ocean region, 787; American imperialism in, 748–749; World War I and, 770–771; World War II and, 833, 838–839, *839*, 841–842
Padua: medical school in, 519
Painting: abstract, 729, *730*, 820; Abstract Expressionist, 889–890, *891*; Baroque, 464–465, *465*; Cubist, 729, *730*; German Expressionist, 820; Impressionist, 725–726, *727*, *728*; Modernist, 725–729; perspective and proportion in, *356*; Post-Impressionist, 726–728, *727*, *729*; Realism in, 680–682; Rococo, 513, *513*; Romanticist, 646–647, *647*, *648*; Surrealist, 820, *821*; text, *356*; after World War II, 889–890, *891*
Pakistan, 875; guest workers from, 940
Palaces, *503*, 513, *514*, 534
Palatinate, 435
Paleologus dynasty, 360
Palermo, 554; Garibaldi in, 661
Palestine, 656; conflicts in, 936; division of, 873; independence and, 873; Israel and, 873, 875; terrorists from, 917, 936; after World War I, 788, 799; Zionism and, 735, *735*. *See also* Arab-Israeli disputes; Israel
Palestine Liberation Organization (PLO), 875
Palmerston, Lord (Henry John Temple), 669–670
Pan-African Congress, 786, 787
Pan American flight 103, 936
Pan-Arabism, 874
Pan-German League, 738

Pankhurst family: Christabel, 731; Emmeline, 731, 732, *733*; Sylvia, 731
Pantheism, 494, 646
Panzer divisions, 830, 835, 836, 838
Papacy: authority of, 370, 381; in Catholic Reformation, 366, 389; decline in, 521; France and, 584; Italy and, 361, 628; in Renaissance, 361–362, 367. *See also* specific popes
Papal bulls, 388
Papal encyclical: on climate change, 942
Papal States: Italy and, 660
Paper money, 794–795
Paracelsus, 484–485, 493
Paraguay, 424, 521, 625
Paris: in Enlightenment, 502; fall of Bastille in, 559, *559*, 566–567, 568, *569*; foundling homes in, 545; Franco-Prussian War in, 664; French Revolution and, 566–567, 572; Fronde in, 441; Muslims in, 931; peace treaty in (1995), 928; population of, 554, 607; reconstruction of, 656, 701, *702*; salons in, 499, 510, *512*, 563, 566, 586; student inscriptions on walls of (1968), 900; student revolt in (1968), 896; terrorism in, 931, *939*; in World War II, 842
Paris, Treaty of: of 1763, 541, 542, 671; of 1783, 560; of 1856, 658
Paris Accord (2015), 949
Paris Commune: in 1871, 712–713; in French Revolution, 573, 574, 578, 581
Paris Peace Conference, 785–789
Parks, Rosa, *885*
Parlement of Paris, 566
Parlements (France), 441, 443, 565
Parliament: in Austria-Hungary, 738; in Germany, 640, 714; in Italy, 802; in Prussia, 662. *See also* Parliament (England)
Parliament (England), 381, 395, 422, 547, 669, 679; Cavalier Parliament and, 461; English civil war and, 458–459; monarchy and, 357, 458, 461, 463, 530, 530–532; reform of, 459; structure of, 627. *See also* specific monarchs
Parliamentary governments: in eastern Europe, 815
Parma, 660
Parma, duke of, 394
Parnell, Charles, 712
Parr, Catherine, 382
Parti Québécois (Canada), 934

Partitions: of Germany, 866–867; of India, 875

Party of Movement (France), 635

Party of Resistance (France), 635

Pascal, Blaise, *494*, 494–496

Pasolini, Pier Paolo, 901

Pasteur, Louis, 676, 677

Pasteurization, 677, 678, 697

Patch (General), *842*

Paths of Glory (novel and film), 768

Patricians, *555*

Patriotism, 741, 770, 772; in Japan, 833

Patriots: in American Revolution, 560; in Dutch Republic, 532; women in France as, *579*

Patronage: in England, 531; in Enlightenment, 514; in Italian Renaissance, 362; of scientists, 490, *491*, 492, 493

Paul III (Pope), 389, 389–390

Paul IV (Pope), 389

Paul of Tarsus (Saint), 369

Paulus, Friedrich, 841

Pauper apprentices, 612

Peace: after Napoleonic wars, 621–622, *622*; women's efforts for, 732–734, 939–940; World War I and, 773. *See also* specific settlements and treaties

Peace of Augsburg, *375*, 377, 396

Peace of the Pyrenees, 438

Peace settlement (World War I), 785–789

Pearl Harbor, 748; Japanese attack on, 838, *839*

Pearson, Karl, 741–742

Pearson, Lester, 886

Peasants: in 16th century, 428; in 18th century, 520, 551; in China, 876; in England, 551; in France, 564, 567, 577; landless, 564; landowning, 703; in military, 759; in Prussia, 533; revolts by, 373, 374, 380, 439, 567; in Russia, 450, 780, 781; in Soviet Union, 813; World War I and, 776. *See also* Serfs and serfdom

Peasants' War, 373, 374, 380

Peel, Robert, 613, 637, 643, *643*

Peer Gynt Suite (Grieg), 730

Penny, Edward, *541*

Pensées (Pascal), *495*, 496

Pentonville (Britain), 645

People's Budget (England), *737*

People's Charter, 616

People's Liberation Army (China), 875, 876

People's Republic of Korea. *See* North Korea

People's Will, 669

Perel, Salomon, 846

Perestroika, 921, 923

Performance art, 914, 943

Periodic law, 676

Perkin, William Henry, 690

Permissive society, 897

Perry, Matthew, 747

Persia: Russia and, 747. *See also* Persian Empire

Persian Empire, 799. *See also* Persia

Persian Gulf War, 935, 937

Persian Letters (Montesquieu), 502

Persistence of Memory, The (Dali), 820, *821*

Personal computers, 942

Peru, 410, *425*, 624, 625

Pétain, Henri, 836

Peterloo Massacre (1819), *627*

Peter the Great (Russia), 450–453, *452*, *453*, 469, 537

Petite Roquette (France), 645

Petition of Right (England), 458

Petrograd. *See* Saint Petersburg, Russia

Petrograd soviet, 779

Petrushka (Stravinsky), 731

Phalanstery, 632

Phèdre (Racine), 468

Philip, Landgrave of Hesse, 378

Philip II (Spain), *393*, 447, 449–450; Elizabeth I (England) and, 382; French Wars of Religion and, 391–392; revolt of Netherlands and, 393–394; Spanish power under, *392*

Philip III (Spain), 447

Philip IV (Spain), 447

Philip V (Spain), 446, 538

Philip of Burgundy, marriage of, 359

Philip of Orléans, 445

Philippines, 400, 415, 713, 749, 838; independence of, 875; Japan and, 848

Philosophes, 499–500, 502–510; French Revolution and, 565; as historians, 516; natural rights and, 529, 563; on punishment, 518; social environment of, 510; on war, 539. *See also* specific individuals

"Philosophical and Physical Opinions, The" (Cavendish), 487

Philosophical Transactions (Royal Society), 493

Philosophic Letters on the English (Voltaire), 504, 505

Philosophy: existentialism and, 889, 891–892; after World War II, 889. *See also* specific philosophers

"Philosophy of Christ," 366–367, 369

"Phony war" (World War II), 836

Photography, 728

Photorealism, 915

Physicians: in 18th century, 518–519; in Middle Ages, 484. *See also* Medicine

Physics, 676, 720–721, 823–824; uncertainty principle and, 824

Physiocrats, 507

Piazza d'Italia (Moore), 915, *916*

Picasso, Pablo, 729, *730*, 817

Piedmont, 621, 628, 640, 659, 660

Pietism, 523, 649

Pig iron, 596

Pill, the, 889, 897

Pilsudski, Joseph, 815

Pinta (ship), 406

Pirates, 395–396, 426

Piscator, Erwin, 822

Pissarro, Camille, 725–726

Pitt, William: the Elder, 532, 539, 541; the Younger, *530*, 532

Pius II (Pope), 361

Pius VII (Pope), 584

Pius IX (Pope), 640, 724

Plains of Abraham, 541

Planck, Max, 720, 823

Planetary motion, 477

Planets, 474, 475, 476, 477, 478, 480

Planned economies, 772

Plantation economy, 421

Plantations, *604*

Plassey, Battle of, 418, 542

Plato, 473

Pleasure principle, 722

PLO. *See* Palestine Liberation Organization

Pluralism, 368

Plurality of Worlds (Fontenelle), 500

Plutocrats, 702

Pocket boroughs (England), 531, 627

Poe, Edgar Allan, 645

Poets and poetry: Romantic, 645–646; Symbolists and, 730; on World War I, 768. *See also* Literature; specific poets

Pogroms, 735

Poison gas, in World War I, 768, 769

Poland, 694; in 17th century, 456, *456*; 1956 protests in, 879; Anabaptists in, 380; authoritarianism in, 815; Christianity in, 389; Communist collapse in, *925*; emigration from, 698; Jews in, 522–523; monarchy in, *359*, 455–456, *456*, 537; after Napoleonic wars, 621, *622*; Nazis and, 831–833, *834*, 844; Ottomans and, 360; partitions of, 534, 537–538,

538; pro-Soviet regime in, 864; revolt in, 663; Russia and, 359, *537*, 537–538, 781; Solidarity movement in, 902; uprising in (1830), 635; after World War I, 785, 787, 815; World War II and, 831–833, 835; after World War II, 856, 857, 858. *See also* Eastern Europe

Poland-Lithuania, 380, 455

Police forces, 642–644. *See also* Secret police

Polish people: Nazis and, 848

Politburo (Soviet Union), 812

"Political and Social Doctrine of Fascism, The" (Mussolini), 804

Political clubs: in France, 571–572

Political democracy, 712–713, 731, 793. *See also* Democracy

Political parties: in France, 881; in West Germany, 881–882. *See also* specific parties

Politics: between 1894 and 1914, 731–741; of Anabaptists, 380; in arts, 943–944; in Canada, 886; in England, 798; Enlightenment and, 516; French Wars of Religion and, 391–392; in Germany, 713–715, 930–931; in Great Depression, 798, 801; in Italy, 737, 883–884, 931–932; mass, 712; mass education and, 708; Olympic Games and, 917; Soviet, 921–922; in United States, 933–934; in U.S. (1950s), 885; in western Europe, 880–882; women and, 633

Politics Drawn from the Very Words of Holy Scripture (Bossuet), 440

Politiques, 390

Pollock, Jackson, 890, *891*, 914

Pollution, 913–914; global, 945

Polo, Marco, 400, 401

Poltava, Battle of, 452

Polygenesis, 501

Pombal, marquis of, 538

Pompadour, Madame de, 530

Pompeii, 514

Poor Law (England, 1834), 613–614, 636

Poor Law Commission (Britain), 609

Poor people. *See* Poverty

Pop Art, 890

Pope. *See* Papacy; specific popes

Popolari (Christian Democrats), 802

Popular culture: in 18th century, 516, 519–521, 554; global nature of, 917; rock music in, 916–917; after World War II, 892–893

Popular Front: in France, 798, 819; in Spain, 815, 816

Population: in 17th century, 433, 438; in 18th century, 543, 548; of Amsterdam, 456; in cities, 700, 740; in Europe, 605–607; in France, 433, 543, *564*, 565; growth of, 543, 548, 564, 565, 593, 605–607, 697, *698*, 948–949; in India, 751; in Industrial Revolution, 593, 605–607; Jews in, 734; in Latin America, 410–411, 423; in Mesoamerica, 408

Populism, in Russia, 669

Port Arthur, Russo-Japanese War in, 739

Portolani (charts), 402

Portugal: in 18th century, 538, 574; Africa and, 745; Americas and, 413, *413*, 421, 423, *625*, *626*; Asia and, *403*, 403–404; Brazil and, 413, 421, 423, *625*, *626*; China and, 419; dictatorship in, 817; empire of, *403*, 403–404; exploration by, *399*, 399–400, *403*, 403–405, *404*, 406; India and, *403*, 403–404, 418, *418*; Japan and, 420–421, *421*; Jesuits and, 521; Latin America and, 413, 421, 423; New World and, 413, 421, 423; slavery and, 403, 412–413; Spain and, 357, *358*, *404*, 407; sphere of influence of, 407

Portuguese Empire, *403*, 403–404, 413, 429, *540*

Post-Impressionism, 726–728, *727*, *729*

Postmodernism, 914–915, 943; in literature, 915–916

Poststructuralism (deconstruction), 914

Potatoes, 423, 425, 543, 547, 551, 606

Potsdam Conference, 858–859

Pottery works: child labor in, 612–613

Poverty: in 18th century, 519–520, 551, 555–556; in cities, 555–556; crime and, 643–644; in France, 555, 556, 565; of peasants, 551; rural, 606; in working classes, 613–614

Power (energy). *See* Energy

Power (political): between World War I and World War II, 828

Power loom, 595–596, 672

Praecepter Germaniae, 385?

Pragmatic Sanction, 540

Prague, 435, 640

Prague Spring, 903, 904

Praise of Folly, The (Erasmus), 367, 368

Pravda, 921

Predestination, Calvin on, 383

Prefects (France), 585

Prelude to the Afternoon of a Faun (Debussy), 730–731

Presbyterians, 459

Presbyters, 458

Presley, Elvis, 893

Prester John, kingdom of, 400

Price revolution, 427

Primary education, 520–521, 535, 708

Primitivism: in music, 731

Primo de Rivera, José Antonio (Spain), 816–817

Primo de Rivera, Miguel (Spain), 815

Primogeniture, 544

Princess, The (Tennyson), 703

Principia (Newton), 482, 483, 500, 505

Principle of intervention, 624, 628

Principle of legitimacy, 621

Principles of Political Economy (Ricardo), 630

Printing, 473, 485, 639

Prisoners of war: in World War II, 850; after World War II, 864

Prisons, reform of, 644–645

Private schools: Protestant, 386. *See also* Schools

Privatization: in Canada, 934; in U.S., 908

Proclamation to the French Troops in Italy (Napoleon I), 584

Proclamation to the People (Napoleon III, 1851), 655

Procurator (Russia), 450–451

Prodi, Romano, 931

Production: industrial, 672, 688–689, 796; mass, 687; in Soviet Union, 877

Professionalism: in policing, 643; in sports, 710; in surgery, 678

Professions: women and, 731

Progress: in late 1800s, *688*, 716; before World War I, 720, 726

Progressive Era (United States), 740–741

Progress of the Human Mind, The (Condorcet), 507–508

Proletariat, 666, 674; industrial, 673

Prometheus Unbound (Shelley), 646

Propaganda: in Fascist Italy, 803; in Nazi Germany, 809, 818; radio, movies, and, 818; in Soviet Union, 813; totalitarianism and, 801; World War I and, 774, *774*, 793

Property: women and, 731

Prosperity: in 1800s, 686; in 1950s, 885; after World War I, 795, 796. *See also* Economy; specific locations

Prostitution: in 19th century, *693*, 694; lower-class women in, 555

Protective tariffs, 428, 688, 738

Protectorates, 656, 745, 747

Protest(s): in 1960s, 897–901; in Africa, 800–801; in eastern Europe (1956),

879; in Italy, 906–907; music of, 899; in Romania, 925; student (1968), 896–899; in Ukraine, 924; against Vietnam War, 897, 899, 901, 909

Protestantism: by 1560, *387*; in 18th century, 521–524, *522*; aid to working classes and, 644; church organization in, 373–374; education and, 385–386; fundamentalism in, 724; in Ireland, 736; Peace of Augsburg and, *375*, 377; Pietism and, 523, 649; Puritans and, 386; revivalism in, *523*, 523–524; Romantic movement and, 649; spread of, 377–379; women and, 384–385. *See also* Huguenots; specific leaders and countries

Protestant Reformation, 369–377, 377–383, 383–386, *387*, 396

Protestant Union, 435

Provence, France, 356

Provisional government: in Russia, 779, 780

Prudhomme, Louis-Marie, 572

Prussia, 714; in 18th century, 532–534, *533*, 552, 574; agriculture in, 533–534; Austria and, 660, 663–664; Dutch Republic and, 532; Franco-Prussian War and, 664; German unification and, 661–665; as great power, 529, *533*; Italy and, 660; military in, 532–533, 534, 542–543, 588, 662; Napoleon and, 586, 588, 589; after Napoleonic wars, 621, *622*; nobility in, 532–533, 551–552; Poland and, *537*, 537–538, 787; Quadruple Alliance and, 621, 623–624; reforms in, 588; rise of, *448*, 448–450; serfs in, 448, 532, 534, 588, 628. *See also* Brandenburg-Prussia; Silesia

Psychoanalysis, 722

Psychology, unconscious in, 823

Ptolemaic-Aristotelian cosmology, 474–475, 477, 493, 496

Ptolemy, Claudius, *402*, 473, 476

Public education. *See* Education

Public health, 609, 678, 700

Public Health Act (1875, Britain), 700

Public opinion, in World War I, 773–774

Public order, in World War I, 773

Public parks, 700

Public schools, 385–386, 517; British, 710

Public works: in Nazi Germany, 810; in New Deal, 799

Publishing, 516. *See also* Books; Printing

Puddling, in iron industry, 603

Puerto Rico, 749

Pugachev, Emelyan, 537, *537*

Pulp fiction, 709

Punishment: in Austria, 535; in Calvinism, 383

Punk movement, 917

Punk music, 945

Pure Food and Drug Act (U.S.), 740–741

Purgatory, 368–369

Purges: in Soviet Union, 813, 877

Puritans, 386, 395, 458–459, 493

Putin, Vladimir, 924

Putting-out system, 547–548

Pym, John, 458

Pyrenees, Peace of the, 447

Qianlong (China), 419, 420

Qing Empire (China), 419, *419*

Quadruple Alliance, 621, 623

Quakers, 415, 611

Quantum theory, 720

Quebec, 422, 541, 671, 741, *934*; secession and, 934

Queens. *See* specific rulers

Querelles des femmes, 488

Quesnay, François, 507

Quotas: on immigrants, 941

Race and racism: classification of, 501; in Germany, 811; of Hitler, 811; in India, 751; against Japanese Americans, 852; nationalism and, 724; Nazi, 844; new imperialism and, 741–742; before World War II, 828

Race riots: in 1965, 886; in Detroit (1943), 852

Racine, Jean-Baptiste, 468

Radar, 856

Radiation, 720

Radicals (political party), in France, 798

Radicals and radicalism: in French Revolution, 573–581

Radio, 687, 818

Railroads, 596–598, *597*, *602*, 663, 673; commuter, 701–702; electric, 687; industrialization on Continent and, 672; in Russia, 739; in United States, 603

Rain, Steam, and Speed—The Great Western Railway (Turner), *647*

Ranters, 493

Rap groups, 917

Rapprochement, 869

Rasputin, 778

Rastatt, Peace of, 446

Rathenau, Walter, 772

Rationalism, 489, 502, 721, 722. *See also* Reason

Rationing: in World War I, 772, 773, *774*

Raw materials, 541, 593, 625, 772; in Japan, 833–834; Nazis and, 845

Reading. *See* Literacy

Reagan, Ronald, 898, 906, 908, 933, *935*; on Soviet Union, 912

Reagan Revolution, 908

Realism, 725; in arts, 680–682, 915; in literature, 680; magic, 915

Realpolitik, 653, 655, 662

Realschule (Germany), 517–518

Real wages, 669, 688, 813

Rearmament: of Germany, 829–830, 882

Reason: in Enlightenment, 500, 507; before World War I, 720, 721. *See also* Irrationality; Rationalism

Reason of state, 539

Rebellions. *See* Revolts and rebellions

Recessions: in 17th century, 433; in 19th century, 688; in 1866–1867, 672; in 1973–1974, 896, 904; in 1973–1974, 904; in 1979–1983, 904; in Canada, 908; in Italy, 907–908; in United States, 934

Reconstruction: after World War II, 864–865

Recovery: after World War II, 877–884

Red Army, 782, *782*, 783; in eastern Europe, *858*; in Hungary, 879; in World War II, 851, 857; after World War II, 864

Red Army Faction (Germany), 936

Red Brigades (Italy), 907, 936

Red Guards (China), 910, 911

Redistribution Act (England), 712

Red Scare: in 1950s, 885

Red Shirts, 660, 661

Red Terror (Russia), 783

Reflections on the Revolution in France (Burke), 622

Reform(s): of Catholic Church, 361, 386–387; Christian humanism and, 366–368, *367*; in England, 609, 616–617, 635–636, 669–670, 693, 700, 712, 735–736; in France, 565, 566, 569, 586–587; in Hungary, 903; in Italy, 931–932; Napoleonic, 586–587; in Poland and Hungary, 879; in Prussia, 588; in Russia, 629–630, 666, 666–669; in Soviet Union, 921; in Sweden, 539; urban, 609, 700. *See also* Reformation

Reform Acts (England): of 1832, 635–636, 637, 669, 670; of 1867, 670, *670*, 712; of 1884, *670*, 712

Reformation, 366. *See also* Catholic Reformation; Protestant Reformation

Refugees: from East Germany, 927; to Europe, 940; Syrian, 931

Regency: in England, 382

Regensburg Colloquy, 389

Reichsrat (Austria), 666

Reichstag (Germany), 359, 371, 664, 694, 714, 738, 808

Reign of Terror (French Revolution), 576–578, 581, 590

Reinsurance Treaty, 752

Relativism. *See* Cultural relativism

Relativity theory, 720–721

Relics (Catholic Church), 368

Religion: in 18th century, 521–524, *522*, 525; in France, 579–580, 584; in Germany, 369–377; immigration restrictions and, 941; new imperialism and, 742; in Romantic age, 649; skepticism about, 500–501; Thirty Years' War and, 435; Voltaire on, 505; in West, 942; witchcraft craze and, 433; working class and, 644; after World War II, 892. *See also* Reformation; specific religions and religious orders

Religious orders, 366, 387, 644. *See also* Monks and monasteries; specific orders

Religious toleration: in 18th century, 501, 502, 505, 521–523, 533; by Joseph II (Austria), 521, 523, 535; Voltaire on, 505

Remarque, Erich Maria, 767

Rembrandt van Rijn, 466, *467*

Renaissance: arts in, 349–356, *356*, 485; Catholic Church in, 361–362; music in, 355–356; papacy in, 361–362, 367, 368; printing in, 485; state in, 356–360, *357, 358*

Renan, Ernst, 724

Renzi, Matteo, 932

Reparations: Dawes Plan and, 795; after World War I, 786–787, 794–795; after World War II, 866

Report on the Condition of the Labouring Population of Great Britain (Chadwick), 609

Representative assembly, 560

Repression: in East Germany, 903; political and military, 810; psychological, 722, 723, 823; in Romania, 903

Republic. *See* specific republics

Republican Party (Germany), 940

Republican Party (U.S.), 641–642, 908, 933

Republicans: in France, 639, 712, 713, 737; in Spain, 815–816

Republic of Korea. *See* South Korea

Republic of Virtue, in France, 578, 581

Resistance movements, against Nazis, 845

Resorts, mass leisure and, 686

Restif de la Bretonne, Nicolas, 518

Restoration: in England, 461, 461–463; in France, 589, 627–628; in Spain, 538, 628

Return from Cythera (Watteau), 513, *513*

Reunification, of Germany, 927, 935

Revisionism, 695

Revisionist historians: on Cold War, 864

Revivalism, Protestant, *523*, 523–524

Revolts and rebellions: in Canada, 672; in China, *569*; in cities, 439–440; in eastern Europe, 879, 880; in England, 459; in France, 439, 441, 566–582; in Greece, 656; in Italy, 623–624; in Latin America, 580–581, *624*, 624–625; Luther and, *373*; in Paris (1968), 896–897; in Russia, 439–440, 451, 537, *537*, 666; in Spain, 439, 623–624, 713; student, 896–899, 900; Thirty Years' War and, 439–440

Revolution(s): 1830–1850, *638*; of 1848–1849, 637–642, *638*, 650, 653, 666; of 1989, 925; in France, 637–639, *638*. *See also* Revolts and rebellions; specific locations

Revolutionaries, anarchist, 697

Revolutionary socialism, 721–722, 780

Revolutionary Tribunal, 576

Revolutionary Tribunal, The (Milligen), 577

Révolutions de Paris (Prudhomme), 572

Rhineland, 573, 603, 663, 672, 770; Nazi occupation of, 830

Rhine River region, 427, 621, 787; in World War II, 842, *842*

Rhodes, 376

Rhodes, Cecil, 745

Rhodesia, 745

Rhythm and blues (R&B), 893, 945

Ricardo, David, 630

Ricci, Matteo, 389, 425

Richard II (Shakespeare), 468

Richard III (England), *357*

Richardson, Samuel, 516

Richelieu (Cardinal), 437, *440*, 440–441

Riefenstahl, Leni, 819

Rigaud, Hyacinthe, *442*

Rights: in 18th century, 532, 539, 552; in England, 462; in France, 392; of nobility, 552; in Prussia, 532; of women, 939–940

Right wing: antiforeign sentiment and, 940; in France, 798, 931; terrorism in, 936

Riksdag (Sweden), 453

Ring of the Nibelung, The (Wagner), 683

Risorgimento, 640, 641

Rite of Spring, The (Stravinsky), 731

Rivals, The (Sheridan), 544

Rivers. *See* specific river regions

Roads and highways: in Industrial Revolution, 593, 603

Roaring Twenties, 817–818

Robespierre, Maximilien, 576, 578, 579, 581, *581*

Rochefoucauld-Liancourt, duc de la, 559

Rocket (railroad engine), 596–597

Rockets, 856

Rock 'n' roll, 893, 916–917

Rococo style, 513, *513*

Rocroi, Battle of, 437–438

Röhm, Ernst, 808

Rolling Stones, 916

Roman Catholic Church. *See* Catholic Church

Roman Empire: Christianity in, 516. *See also* Byzantine Empire; specific rulers

Romania, 360, 694, 751, 752, 785, 787; Băsecu in, 927; Communist collapse in, 925; coup d'état in, 858; fascist movement in, 815; pro-Soviet regime in, 864; repression in, 903; revolt in, 925, *925*; secret police in, 903; in World War II, 836. *See also* Eastern Europe

Roman Inquisition, 389, 479–480, 493

Roman law. *See* Law codes

Romanov dynasty, 450, 621

Romanticism, 680; in art, 646–647, *647*, *648*; in music, 648, 649, 682–683; in poetry, 645–646; religion and, 649, 650; Rousseau and, 509

Rome (city): Fascist Blackshirts in, 803; Italian annexation of, 660; population of, 554; sack of (1527), 376, 380

Rome-Berlin Axis, 830

Rommel, Erwin, 840

Roosevelt, Franklin D.: death of, 858; Great Depression and, 799; in World War II, 838. *See also* Big Three

Rossbach, Battle of, 541

Rotten boroughs (England), 531, 627

Rotterdam, 836

Rougon-Macquart (Zola), 725

Rousseau, Jean-Jacques, *508*, 508–509, 511, 544, 565, 578, 707

Royal Academy of Sciences (France), 491, *491*, 495, 500

Royal Botanical Garden, 492

Royal College of Physicians (England), 492, 519

Royal College of Surgeons (England), 519

Royal Council (Britain), 422

Royalists: in England, 459

Royal Society (England), 482, 491, 492, 493

Rubens, Peter Paul, 465, *465*

Rudolf II (Holy Roman Empire), 477

Rugby Football Union (England), 710

Ruhr region, 603, 698; French occupation of, 794, 795

Rules: of Jesuits, 388

"Rules of Reasoning in Philosophy" (Newton), 483

Rump Parliament, 459

Russia: in 18th century, 535–537, 552; alliances of, 541, 751, 752, 753; Asian expansion by, 747; Balkans and, 751, 752, 753, 758, 759–760; China and, 419; civil war in, *782*, 782–783; Communist Party in, 780–781; Crimean War and, 656–658, *657*, 666; development of, *452*; emancipation of serfs in, 666, 666–667; government of, 450, 779; as great power, 529, *533*; independence of, 923; industrialization in, 604, 690, 738; Japan and, 833; Jews and, 735; in late 1800s, 716; literature in, 725, 726; military in, 450, 759; Mongols in, 359; Napoleon and, 586, 589; after Napoleonic wars, 621, *622*, 629–630; Ottoman Empire and, 537, 626; Peter the Great and, 450–453, *452*; Poland and, 359, 534, *537*, 537–538; population of, 543; Putin in, 924–925; Quadruple Alliance and, 621, 623–624; reforms in, 666–669; revolts in, 439–440, 537, *537*; socialist party in, 694; after Soviet Union, 924; Triple Entente and, 752; Ukraine and, 924–925; westernization of, 450, 451, 452–453; women in, 451, 778, *778*; World War I and, 757, 760, 761, 764–765, *765*, 771, 773, 777–778, 781. *See also* Commonwealth of Independent States; Soviet Union;

World War I; World War II; specific leaders

Russian Empire, 537, *540*, 541, *561*, 656, 787

Russian Orthodox Church, 450, 656. *See also* Eastern Orthodoxy

Russian Republic, 922

Russian Revolutions: of 1905, 738–739, 740, 777, 778; Bolshevik Revolution (1917) and, 771, 779–781, *782*; Hitler and, 828; of March, 1917, 778, 778–779, *782*

Russian-Turkish war, 626

Russification policy, 716

Russo-Japanese War, 739, 747, 750, 752

Rutherford, Ernest, 823

Ryswick, Treaty of, 446, *446*

SA. *See* Storm Troops (SA)

Sacks of cities. *See* specific cities

Sacraments: Calvin on, 383

Sacrosancta (decree), 361

Saddam Hussein, 937

Saigon, 747, 869

Sailors and sailing: Portuguese, 403. *See also* Ships and shipping

Saint(s): in Catholic Church, 523; Protestantism and, 386. *See also* specific saints

Saint Bartholomew's Day Massacre, 390–391, *391*

Saint-Domingue, 421, *421*, 580–581. *See also* Haiti

Saint Helena, Napoleon on, 589

Saint-Just, Louis, 577–578

Saint Lawrence River region, 540, 541–542

St. Peter's Basilica (Rome), 362, 465, *465*

St. Petersburg, Russia, 451, 452, 469, 739, 778; in 18th century, 545, 554; foundling home in, 545

"Saints," Anabaptists as, 380

Saint-Simon, comte de (socialist), 633

Saint-Simon, duc de (Louis de Rouvroy), 433, 445

Saint Vincent de Paul: religious order of, 555

Sakhalin Island, 857

Sakharov, Andrei, 901

Salazar, Antonio, 817

Salieri, Antonio, *515*

Salons, 499, 510, *512*, 563, 566, 586

Salt, Titus, *607*

Saltaire, England, *607*

Salvation: Calvin on, 382–383; Christian, 369–370; clergy and, 369; Luther and, 369–370, 373;

before Reformation, 366; search for, 368–369

Salvation Army, 725

Same sex marriage: in England, 931. *See also* Homosexuals and homosexuality

Samurai (Japan), 750

Samurai revolt (1867), 750

Sanford, Elizabeth Poole, 704

Sanger, Margaret, 820

Sanitation: in cities, 607–609, *608*, 700

San Martín, José de, *624*, 625, *626*

Sans-culottes, 573, 576, 577

San Stefano, Treaty of, 751, 752

Santa María (ship), 406

Santo Domingo, 410

Sarajevo, 929; Francis Ferdinand in, 758

Sardinia: Austria and, 449, 538, 621, *622*

Sarkozy, Nicolas, 931

Sartre, Jean-Paul, 889, 891

Sasson, Siegfried, 768

Satellites (countries): in eastern Europe, 878, 879

Satellites (space): *Sputnik* as, 869, 877, 912

Satellite television, 917

Sati, 751

Saudi Arabia: independence of, 872; Pan-Arabism and, 874

Savoy, 538, 660

Saxony, 368, 541, 621

Scandinavia: in 18th century, 539; Great Depression in, 799; Lutheranism in, 377; women in, *939*. *See also* specific locations

Schleswig, 662, 663

Schleswig-Holstein, 663

Schlieffen, Alfred von, 760

Schlieffen Plan, 760, 763–764, *764*

Schmalkaldic League, 376

Schmidt, Helmut, 905

Scholarship. *See* Intellectual thought

Schönberg, Arnold, 822

Schönborn prince-bishop (Würzburg): palace of, 513

Schönhuber, Franz, 940

Schools: in 18th century, 517–518, 535; for girls, 385–386, 518; humanist, 385; Jesuit, 388; in mass society, 708; medical, 678–679; private, 386; Protestant, 385–386; student protests and, 897. *See also* Education; Universities and colleges

Schröder, Gerhard, 930

Schumacher, E. F., 913

Schurz, Carl, 636, 637

Schuschnigg, Kurt von, 830
Schutzmannschaft (German police), 643
Schutzstaffeln (SS), 810, 811
Science: in 19th century, 675–676; dangers of, 913; in Enlightenment, 500, *501*; religion and, 493–496, *494*, 724; Romantics and, 646; society and, 493, 680; technology and, 690; women in, 486, 486–488; before World War I, 720–721. *See also* Medicine; Scientific Revolution; specific sciences
Science of man: Diderot on, 507
Scientific laws: of Kepler, 477; of Newton, 482–484
Scientific method, 490–491, 500, 676
Scientific research, 492–493
Scientific Revolution, 675; astronomy in, *474*, 474–484, *475*, 487–488; background to, 473–474; medicine and chemistry in, 484–486
Scientific societies, 491, 491–493, *501*
Scotland: bombing of, in World War II, *855*; Calvinism in, 383, 395; England and, 459; Knox in, 383; Mary, queen of Scots, in, 395; and plane explosion over Lockerbie, 936; Presbyterian Church in, 458, 459
Scott, Walter, 645
Scout, The, 706, 707
Scripture, 390. *See also* Catholic Church; Protestantism
Sculpture: Baroque, 465, *465. See also* specific sculptors and works
Sea routes: in Renaissance, 400, *404*
Seasons, The (Haydn), 515
SEATO, 869
Secession: of Quebec, 934
Secondary education, 517, 708, 803
Second Balkan War, 752
Second Continental Congress, 560, 562, *562*
Second Empire (France), 654–656, 664, 712
Second Estate: in France, 563–564, *564*, 566
Second front: in World War II, 842
Second German Empire, 664
Second Industrial Revolution, 686, 687–697, *688*, 708
Second International, 694–695
Second Republic (France), 639
Second Sex, The (de Beauvoir), 889, 890
Second Vietnam War, 908, 909–910; bombings in, 909; protests against, 897, 899, 901
Second World War. *See* World War II

Secret Book (Hitler), 829
"Secret Conversations" (Hitler), 844
Secret police: in East Germany, 903; in Italy, 803; in Nazi Germany, 810; in Romania, 903; in Russia, 630, 716; in Soviet Union, 783, 902; Stalinist, 879
Secret societies: in Enlightenment, 510; in Italy, 628; in Russia, 630
Secularism, 432, 500–501, 516, 525; France and, 569
Secularization: in 19th century, 676
Securitate (secret police), 903
Sedan, battle at, 664
Seed drills, *546, 547*
Seeman, Enoch, *483*
Segregation: in colonies, 749
Ségur Law, 564
Seigneurial system, 567
Sejm (Polish diet), 359, 456
Select Society of Edinburgh, Scotland, 510
Self-determination: for eastern Europe, 632, 787–788; World War I and, 785, 788; after World War II, 857
Self-government: in India, 800; in towns, 585
Self-Help (Smiles), 610
Self-Portrait (Dürer), *356*
Senate: in France, 713; in United States, 561, 789
Senegal: troops from, *771*
Separation of church and state, 380
Separation of powers, Montesquieu on, 503, 504
Separatist movement(s): in Austria-Hungary, 738; in Yugoslavia, 928
Sephardic Jews, 524
Sepoys, 542, 747
September 11, 2001, terrorist attacks, 936, *936*
Serbia, 360, 656, 751, 752–753, 787; rebuilding of, 929; World War I and, 759–760
Serbian Communist Party, 928
Serbs, 641, 927; ethnic cleansing by, 928; in Kosovo, 928
Serfs and serfdom: in Austria, 535, 666; in eastern Europe, 541; peasants and, 551; in Prussia, 448, 532, 534, 588, 628; in Russia, 536, 537, 541, *666*, 666–667. *See also* Peasants
Serialism, in music, 916
Serious Proposal to the Ladies, A (Astell), 509
Servants, 611; as urban workers, 555, 611–612; women as, 612

Sevastopol, siege of, 658
Seventh Seal (movie), 892
Seven Years' War: battlefields of, *540*; colonies and, 418, 423, 530, 532; French Canada and, 423, 532, 540, *540*, 541–542, *561*; India and, 418, 532, 540, *540*, 541; Prussia in, *540*, 540–542
Sewage and sewer systems, *608*, 678, 700
Sex and sexuality: Christianity and, 383; Freud on, 722; in marriage, 820; movies and, 818; prostitution in 19th century, 693, 694; revolt in mores and, 897; witchcraft and, 433–435. *See also* Gender and gender issues
Seymour, Jane, 381
Seyss-Inquart, Arthur, *831*
Shah of Iran, 937
Shakespeare, William, 467, 468
Shanghai, *835*, 876
Shelley, Mary, 645, 646
Shelley, Percy Bysshe, 645–646
Sheridan, Richard, 544
Sherman, Roger, *562*
Shibuzawa Eiichi, 610
Shi'ite Muslims, 937
Shikoku, 425
Ship money (English tax), 458
Ships and shipping, 697; British, *549*, 549–550, *605*; Dutch *fluyt*, 456; exploration and, 402–403; slave trade and, 549; trade and, 413, 427–428. *See also* Navy; Steamboats
Shock therapy: in eastern Europe, 926
Shogun (Japan), 420, 750
Shonibare, Yinka, 944, *944*
Siam. *See* Thailand (Siam)
Siberia, 747, 782, 813; prison camps in, 878
Sicily, 660; Bourbons in, 538; Kingdom of, 628; Naples and, 628; revolts in, 439, 640; in World War II, 842
Sieveking, Amalie, 731
Sieyès, Abbé, 566
Sigismund (Holy Roman Empire), 361
Sigismund III (Sweden and Poland), 455–456
Signing of the Declaration, The (Trumbull), *562*
Silesia, 449, 534, 540, 557
Silicon chip, 912
Silk and silk industry, 603, *692*
Silver: Spanish, 393; for trade, 410, 411–412, 425, 428
Simons, Menno, 380
Sinai peninsula, 874, 875

Single Europe Act (1986), 932
Sisters of Charity, 555
Sitar, 916
Six Day War (1967), 867
Sixtus IV (Pope), 361
Skepticism, 500–501
Skilled workers: mass education for, 708; in World War I, 776
Skyscrapers, 821
Slater, Samuel, 603
Slave labor: Slavs as, 828
Slavery: African, 421, 549; in French Revolution, 580–581; in Haiti, 421, 580–581; in United States, 668, 670–671, *671*
Slave trade, 403, *413*, 414–415, *415*
Slavic peoples, 747; in Austria-Hungry, 666, 715; in Balkans, 752; eastern, 359; Nazis and, 844, 848; racist views of, 848
Slavs. *See* Slavic peoples
Sloane, Hans, 492, *492*
"Slop work," 692
Slovakia, 926–927; Nazis and, 831
Slovenes, 641, 929
Slovenia, 449, 656, 928
Slums, in England, 700
Small Is Beautiful (Schumacher), 913
Smallpox, 543; Aztecs and, 408, 410–411, *412*; Inca and, 410, 411
Smartphones, 943
Smiles, Samuel, 610
Smith, Adam, 507
Smithson, Robert, 914–915, *915*
Soccer. *See* Football (soccer)
Social classes. *See* Classes
Social contract: Rousseau on, 508, 509
Social Contract, The (Rousseau), 508, 509
Social Darwinism, 722–723, 806; imperialism and, 741–742
Social Democrats: in Austria, 738; in Germany, 693–694, 714, 715, 738, 762, 784–785, 805, 808, 882, 904, 905; in Russia, 694, 738, 779; in Scandinavia, 799; after World War II, 880
Social engineering: Nazi, 844
Socialism, 632, 673; Bismarck and, 714–715; evolutionary, 695, 696; Marx and, 674; Marxist, 724, 798; nationalism and, 695; revolutionary, 721–722, 780; utopian, 632; World War I and, 759, 762, 773; after World War II, 880
Socialist Party, 693–695; in France, 694, 798, 906; in Italy, 802

Socialist Revolutionaries (Russia), 780, 782
Socialized medicine, 883
Social orders: in 18th century, 550–556, *555*. *See also* Estates (social orders); specific groups
Social Revolutionaries (Russia), 738
Social sciences: in Enlightenment, 507, 516
Social security, 883; in United States, 799
Social services: in Scandinavia, 799
Social Statics (Spencer), 723
Social welfare: in Canada, 886; in England, 735–736; in Germany, 714–715; in Italy, 737; in Scandinavia, 799; in United States, 799, 885. *See also* Welfare state
Society: classless, Marx and Engels on, 675; European, 886–889; popular culture and, 916–917; revolts in 1960s, 897–901; in U.S., 885–886; welfare state and, 888; in West, 912–917; World War I and, 774–776; in World War II U.S., 851–852. *See also* Lifestyle; Mass society; specific groups and countries
Society for Revolutionary Republican Women, 578
Society for the Diffusion of Useful Knowledge in the Field of Natural Sciences, Technical Science, and Political Economy, 644
Society of Friends. *See* Quakers
Society of Harmonious Fists (China), 749
Society of Jesus. *See* Jesuits
Society of Thirty, 563, 566
Sociology, Comte and, 680
Soil: damage to, 948
Solar system. *See* Universe
Soldiers. *See* Military; specific battles and wars
Solferino, battle at, 659
Solidarity movement, 902, 925
Solzhenitsyn, Alexander, 878
Some Reflections upon Marriage (Astell), 509
Somme, Battle of, *757*, *757*, 766
Sophia (Austria), 760
Sorbonne: revolt in, 896
Sorel, Georges, 721–722
Sorrows of the Young Werther, The (Goethe), 645
Soto, Hernando de, 423
South Africa, 744–745; independence in, 800, 872

South African Republic, 745
South America: Spain and, 421, 625, *626*. *See also* Latin America; specific locations
Southeast Asia: Dutch in, 415–416, 423; Japan and, 834, 839–840; new imperialism in, 747–748; western involvement in, 415–418, *416*. *See also* specific locations
Southeast Asia Treaty Organization. *See* SEATO
Southern Christian Leadership Conference (SCLC), *885*, 885–886
Southern Europe: emigration from, 698. *See also* specific locations
Southern Hemisphere: wealthy nations in, 950
South Korea, 868. *See also* Korea; Korean War
South Slav state, 927
South Vietnam, 909. *See also* Vietnam; Vietnam War
South-West Africa, 745
Soviets, in Russia, 779
Soviet Union, 801; breakup of, 921; coexistence with, 795–796; Cold War and, 864–870; Czechoslovakia invaded by, 903; détente and, 911–912; eastern Europe and, 879, 902–903; economy in, 812; end of, 922–923; under Gorbachev, 921–923; industry in, 812–813; under Khrushchev, 877–878; mobilization in World War II, 850–851; multiethnic nature of, 922; Nazi attack on, 836–838, *837*, *838*; Nazi treaty with, 833; Olympics and, 917; reasons for collapse, 923; reforms in, 921; Reagan and, 912; Second Vietnam War and, 908, 909–910; Spanish Civil War and, 815–816; stagnation in, 901–902; under Stalin, 812–814; Stalingrad battle in, *840*, 840–841; totalitarianism in, 801; U.S. differences with, 857–859; Vietnam and, 909; women in, 813, 939; in World War II, 842–843; after World War II, 856, 877–879. *See also* Cold War; Commonwealth of Independent States; Russia; World War II; specific leaders
Soviet Union (former), 924
Space exploration: *Sputnik I* and, 869, 877, 912
Spain: in 18th century, 538, 551, 552, 574; African possession of, 745; in Americas, 407–410, *408*, *413*,

421, *421*; in Asia, 415; Aztecs and, 408, 409; Bourbons in, 423, 538, 628; Catholic Church in, 358, 713; colonies of, 415, 625, *626*; decline of, 447; dictatorship in, 815, 816–817; economy in, *433*, 538; England and, 382, *392*, 395–396; exploration by, 401, *404*, 406, 406–407; France and, 446, 574; Franco in, 830; French and Indian War and, *540*, 540–541; government of, 713; Habsburg emperors and, 374, *375*, 376–377, 435, 538; Inca Empire and, 410; Italy and, 392, 449–450; Jesuits and, 424, 538; Jews expelled from, 358, 523; Latin America and, 407–410, *408*; monarchs in, *375*, *622*; Napoleon and, 586, 588, *588*; Netherlands and, 393–394; New World and, 407–410, *408*; Ottoman Turks and, 454; Popular Front in, 815; population of, 543, 606; Portugal and, 357, *358*, *404*, 407; railroads in, 673; republic in, 815; revolts and, 439, 623–624, 664; slavery and, 413, 423; Southeast Asia and, 415; sphere of influence of, 407; Thirty Years' War and, 435, 437–438, 447; unification of, 357–358, *358*; War of the Spanish Succession and, 446, 449, 450. *See also* Spanish Civil War
Spanish-American War, 713, 749
Spanish Armada, *392*, 396
Spanish Civil War, 815–816, 830; casualties in, 816, *817*
Spanish Empire, *404*, 407–410, 468, *540*
Spanish Netherlands, 392, 393–394, 446, 447, 449
Spectator (periodical), 516–517
Spectator sports, 710
Speech at Fulton, Missouri (Churchill), 859
Speech at the Nuremberg Party Rally (Hitler, 1936), 809
Speeches (Wilson), 786
Speech to Congress (Havel), 926
Speech to SS Leaders (Himmler), 849
Speech to the German Reichstag (Bismarck, 1888), 655
Speech to the House of Commons (Chamberlain), 833
Speech to the House of Commons (Churchill), 833
Speech to the Prussian Reichstag (Bismarck, 1862), 655
Spencer, Herbert, 722–723
Spengler, Lazarus, 373
Spengler, Oswald, 793

Speransky, Michael, 629–630
Spheres of influence: in Asia, 747; in China, 747, 750; German and Soviet, 833; Spanish and Portuguese, *404*, 407; of women, 488. *See also* specific locations
Spice Islands. *See* Moluccas (Spice Islands)
Spices and spice trade: Arab traders and, 400–401, 404–405, *405*; Dutch and, 418; Portugal and, 403, 404–405
Spinning frame, 595
Spinning jenny, 595
Spinoza, Benedict de, 494
Spiral Jetty (Smithson), 914–915, *915*
Spirit of the Laws, The (Montesquieu), 502
Spiritual Exercises (Loyola), 388
Sports: mass, 917; mass leisure and, 710–711, 819; team, 710–711
Sputnik I, 869, 877, 912
Squadristi, 802
Square with White Border (Kandinsky), 729, *730*
Srebrenica: massacre in, 928
Sri Lanka (Ceylon), 405, 415, 875
SS (Nazi Germany), 844. *See also* *Einsatzgruppen*
Stadholder, 456
Staël, Germaine de, 586
Stagflation, 908
Stakhanov, Alexei, 813
Stalin, Joseph, 812–814, *813*; on Churchill speech, 859; economic policy of, 812–813; Khrushchev's denunciation of, 877–878; Tito and, 879; in World War II, 851; after World War II, 877. *See also* Big Three
Stalingrad, Battle of, *840*, 840–841
Stalinization: in eastern Europe, 879
Standard of living. *See* Lifestyle
Standard Oil Company, 741
Standing army, 438–439, 448, 542–543, 588
Stanley, Henry M., 745
Starry Messenger, The (Galileo), 478–479
Starry Night, The (van Gogh), 728, *729*
Starvation, 950; after World War II, 856. *See also* Famine
Stasi (East Germany), 903, 930
State (nation): in 18th century, 521, 672; centralization of, 772–773; in late 1800s, 687; World War I and, 758. *See also* Church and state; Government; specific locations
State of nature: Hobbes on, 463, 508
States General (Netherlands), 456

Statues. *See* Sculpture; specific statues
Status. *See* Classes
Stauffenberg, Claus von, 845
Steamboats, 603, *604*
Steam engine, 595–596, *596*, 603, 607, 672, 676
Steele, Richard, 516–517
Steel industry, 687, 688, 738, 739–740, 812; EEC and, 884; in Italy, 884
Stein, Heinrich von, 588, 628
Stephenson, George, 596–597, 673
Steppenwolf (Hesse), 823
Stöcker, Adolf, 734
Stock exchanges, 456
Stock market (U.S.), 796, 947
Stolypin, Peter, 739
Stonebreakers, The (Courbet), *680*
Stopes, Marie, 820
Storm of Steel, The (Jünger), 822
Storm Troops (SA), 806, 808
Strait of Magellan, 399
Strasbourg: occupation of, 446; Sturm school in, 385–386
Strategic Defense Initiative (SDI, Star Wars), 912
Stravinsky, Igor, 731, 822
Streaming, 945
Stream-of-consciousness, in literature, 822–823
Streetcars, 687, 701–702
Streltsy rebellion, Peter the Great and, 451
Stresemann, Gustav, 795
Strikes (labor): in England, 615–616, 735, 798; in France, 737, 882, 896–897; general, 722; in Italy, 802; trade unions and, 615–616, 696; in World War I, 773, 778
Struensee, John Frederick, 539
Strutt, Jedediah, 611, 613
Stuart dynasty (England), 458, 461, 461–463, 469, 531
Student(s): inscriptions on walls of Paris (1968), 900; protests by (1968), 896; revolts by, 897–899, 900. *See also* Universities and colleges
Student Manifesto in Search of a Real and Human Educational Alternative, A, 900
Student societies (German), 628–629
Styria, 449
Submarines, 771; in World War II, 840
Submission (movie), 941
Subways, 687
Sudan, 745, 746
Sudetenland, 831, 856
Suez Canal, *673*, 745, 873; in World War II, 836

Suffrage. *See* Voting and voting rights
Suffragette (film), 734
Suffragists, 731–732, *733*, 734
Sugar and sugar industry, 411–412, 413, 421, *422*, 748
Suharto (Indonesia), 877
Suicide bombings: by ISIL, 938
Suicide in the Trenches (Sasson), 768
Sukarno (Indonesia), 877
Suleiman I the Magnificent (Ottoman Empire), 376, 454
Sullivan, Louis H., 821
Sultans: in Ottoman Empire, 454. *See also* specific individuals
Sumatra, 415–416
Summer of Love (1967), *898*
Sunni Muslims, 937
Sun Yat-sen (China), 750
Superego, 722
Supermarkets, 886, *887*
Superpowers: United States as, 884; after World War II, 864–870. *See also* Cold War; Soviet Union; United States
Supplement to the Voyage of Bougainville (Diderot), 506
Supply-side economics, 507, 908
Supreme Court (U.S.), 561, 642
Surat, India, 418
Surgeons and surgery, 519, 678, 679
Surrealism, 820, *821*
Suttner, Bertha von, 734
Swan, Joseph, 687
Sweated industries, 692
Sweatshops, 692
Sweden, 799; in 17th century, 437, 453, *453*; in 18th century, 539; kingdom of, *436*, 453, *453*; population in, 606; religion in, 377; Russian attack on, 451–452; Scandinavian unification and, 377; sexual revolution in, 896; upheavals in, 440. *See also* Scandinavia
Swedish Lutheran National Church, 377
Swedish phase, of Thirty Years' War, 437
Swiss Brethren, 380
Swiss Confederation, *377*, 377–378
Swiss Republic: France and, 586
Switzerland, 377, 377–378
Syllabus of Errors (Pius IX), 724
Symbolism, in literature, 725
Symphonic poem (Liszt), 683
Symphonie Fantastique (Berlioz), 648
Synthesizers, 917
Syria, 788, 799; independence of, 872, 873; Israel and, 875; Pan-Arabism

and, 874; refugees from, 931; terrorism and, 936
System of Nature (Holbach), 507
System of Positive Philosophy (Comte), 680

Taaffe, Edward von, 715
Table of Ranks (Russia), 450
Tabula rasa, Locke on, 502
Tahiti, 501
Taille (French tax), 356, 441, 556, 563, 564
Taiping Rebellion, 569
Taiwan. *See* Formosa (Taiwan)
Taliban, 937, 942
Tanganyika, 745
Tanks, 772, 830, 842
Tannenberg, Battle of, 764
Tariffs, 428, 507, 601–602, 688, 690, 738, 797
Tartuffe (Molière), 468
Taverns, 519–520
Taxation: of American colonies, 560; British, in India, 418; in England, 458, 736; in France, 572, 585, 931; in Prussia, 664; in Scandinavia, 799; by Spain, 393, 394; in U.S., 741, 908, 934
Taylor, Harriet, 632
Tea, 425
Teaching, 693, 708, 731, 734
Team sports, 710–711
Tears of the Indians, The (Las Casas), 411
Technology, 912–913; computers and, 856, 912, 942; dangers of, 913; in digital age, 942–943; in East Germany, 866; industrial, 676; leisure and, 709; limits of, 913; in metallurgy, 428, 493; music and, 917; revolution in, 473–474; science and, 690; Scientific Revolution and, 473–474; totalitarianism and, 801; since World War II, 856
Tehran conference, 856–857
Telecommunications, 942
Telegraph, 658
Telephone, 687, *693*; cellular (mobile), 942–943
Telescope, 473, 478, *480*
Television, 892–893; satellite, 917
Temple of Reason, Notre-Dame as, 579, 580
Tenant farmers, 547
Ten Hours Act (1847), 617
Tennis Court Oath, 566, *567*
Tennyson, Alfred (Lord), 703
Tenochtitlán, 408, 409, 410–411
Teresa of Avila (Saint), 386–387

Terror, the. *See* Reign of Terror
Terrorism: by anarchists, 697; as global war, 937–938; in Ireland, 712; Islamic, 942; in Italy, 802, 906, 907; Middle Easterners and, 931; at Munich Olympics, 917; in Nazi Germany, 810; in Paris, 931, *939*; in Russia, 738; on September 11, 2001, 921, 936, *936*
Test Act (England), 461
Tetzel, Johann, 370
Texcoco, Lake, 408
Textiles and textile industry, 692; in Britain, 550, 593, 595–596, *598*; child labor in, 612–614; on Continent, *602*, 602–603; as cottage industry, 547–548, *548*, 593, 598; India and, 418, 549, 604–605; mechanization in, 672; in Netherlands, 393; in United States, 603–604. *See also* Industrial Revolution
Text painting, 356
Thackeray, William, 680
Thailand (Siam), 416, 748, 751, 850
Thatcher, Margaret, and Thatcherism, 905–906, *906*, 907
Theater. *See* Drama
Theater of the Absurd, 890–891
Theatines, 387
Theology. *See also* specific religions
Thermidorean Reaction, 581
Thermodynamics, 676
Thiers, Adolphe, 635, 638
Third Coalition, 586
Third Estate (France), 564, 564–565, 566, *567*; as National Assembly, 566. *See also* Peasants
Third Man, The (movie), 866
Third of May 1808, The (Goya), *588*
Third Republic (France), 712–713, 737
Third Section (Russia), 630
Thirty-Nine Articles, 395
Thirty Years' War, 435–438, *436*, *437*, 447, 453
Thomas (apostle): community in India and, 400
Thomas à Kempis, 369
Three Emperors' League, 751, 752
Threepenny Opera, The (Weill), 822
Throne of Saint Peter (Bernini), 465
Tilly (Count), 436
Tilsit, Treaties of, 586
Time of Troubles (Russia), 450
"Times They Are A-Changin', The" (Dylan), 899
Timisoara, Romania, 925
Tin Drum, The (Grass), 891

Tisza, Istvàn, 738
Tithes, 551, 567
Titian, *376*, *393*
Tito (Josip Broz), 845, 879, 927–928
Tobruk, 840
Togoland, 745, 770
Tokugawa Ieyasu (Japan), 420, 425
Tokyo. *See* Japan
Toleration. *See* Religious toleration
Toleration Act (England, 1689), 463
Toleration Patent (Austria), 521
Tolstoy, Leo, 725
Tonkin, 747
Tonkin, king of: Louis XIV
    correspondence with, 417
Tools: precision, 689
Topa Inca, 409
Topography. *See* Geography
Tordesillas, Treaty of, *404*, 407
Tories (England), 461, 627, 670
Torture, 518, 937
Totalitarian states, 801–802, 803
Total war: World War I as, 772–776;
    World War II as, 828
Toul, 438
Tourism, 710, 819, 888
Toussaint L'Ouverture, 580–581
Towns. *See* Cities and towns; Villages
Toynbee, Arnold, 758
Toys, in 19th century, 707
Trade: in 18th century, 549–550;
    balance of, 549; boom in, 947; with
    China, 747; commercial capitalism
    and, 427–428; globalization and,
    549–550; Great Depression and, 796;
    industrialization and, 672; overseas,
    428; triangular, 413, *413*; worldwide,
    549–550. *See also* Mercantilism; Slave
    trade; specific locations
Trade barriers: in EU, 932; relaxation
    of, 947
Trade fairs: art, 943
Trade routes: overland, 400
Trade unions, 673, 693; in Britain, 615–
    616, *616*, 695, 735, 798; in World War
    I, 774. *See also* Labor unions
Trading companies: Dutch East India
    Company, 412, 415–416, *416*
Trading empires: of Portugal, *403*,
    403–404
Trafalgar, Battle of, 587
Trains. *See* Railroads
Transformism, 737
Transistor, 912
Transnational corporation, 947
Transportation: in cities, 687; expansion
    in, 596–598, *597*; improvements in,

697; mass leisure and, 686, 710; in
    United States, 603. *See also* Airplanes;
    Automobiles; Railroads; Roads and
    highways
Transport Ministry (Germany), 847
Trans-Siberian Railroad, 738
Transubstantiation, Luther on, 373
Transvaal, 745
Transylvania, 449, 656
Travel, 819
Travels (Cook), 501
Travels (Polo), 400, 401
Travels of John Mandeville, The, 400
Treaties. *See* specific treaties
Treatise on Human Nature (Hume), 507
Treatise on Toleration (Voltaire), 505–506
Treaty on European Union. *See*
    Maastricht Treaty
Trench warfare, in World War I, 764,
    764, 765–770, *769*
Trent, Council of, 389–390, 450, 481
Trevithick, Richard, 596
Trials: for witchcraft, 433–435; for
    World War II war crimes, 882
Triangular trade, 413, *413*
Triennial Act (England), 458
Trieste, 802
Triple Alliance, 446, 720, 752
Triple Entente, 720, 752
Tripoli: as Libya, 745
Tristan, Flora, 633–634
Triumph of the Will, The (movie), 818,
    819
Troppau: congress at, 623–624
Trotsky, Leon, 780, *780*, 782, 812
Trudeau, Justin, 934
Trudeau, Pierre, 908
Truman, Harry, 864, 866, 885; at
    Potsdam, 858–859
Truman Doctrine, 864–866
Trumbull, John, *562*
Tsar (Russia). *See* specific tsars
Tsushima, in Russo-Japanese War, 739
Tuberculosis, 677
Tudor dynasty (England), 357, *381*, 458.
    See also specific rulers
Tull, Jethro, *546*, 547
Tunisia, 745, 872
Turing, Alan, 856
Turkestan, 747
Turkey: Armenian genocide by, 784;
    independence of, 872; Truman
    Doctrine and, 864–866; after World
    War I, 799–800
Turks, *359*, *393*; as guest workers, 940.
    See also Ottoman Empire
Turner, J. M. W., 647, *647*

Turnips, 546–547
Turnpikes, 596
Tuscany, 660
Twentieth Congress of the Communist
    Party, Khrushchev at, 877, 878
Two Thousand Words Manifesto, 904
Two Treatises of Government (Locke),
    463
Two Women Teach a Child to Walk (de
    Hooch), *457*
Tyrol, 449, 802
Tzara, Tristan, 820

UAR. *See* United Arab Republic (UAR)
Uhuru (freedom), 871
Ukraine, 781, 782; anti-Jewish pogroms
    in, 735; Chernobyl disaster in, 913–
    914; Crimea and, 925; famine in, 813;
    independence of, 923; Nazis and,
    837, 848; Russia and, 924–925
Ulbricht, Walter, 870, 903, 904–905
Ulianov, Vladimir. *See* Lenin, V. I.
Ulm, Battle of, 586
Ultra-Catholics, 390, 391
Ultra intelligence operation, 836
Ultraroyalists (France), 628
Ulysses (Joyce), 822
Unbearable Lightness of Being, The
    (Kundera), 916
Uncertainty principle, 824
Unconditional surrender: in World War
    II, 839, 857
Unconscious, 722, 822–823
Under the Trees (Kuroda Seiki), *728*
Unemployment, 644, 904; debt
    crisis and, 947; in England, 798;
    in Germany, 810, 882; in Great
    Depression, 796, 797, 799, 805, 807;
    Keynes on, 798; of women, after
    World War I, 775. *See also* Economy;
    specific locations
Unification: of Europe, 932–933; of
    Germany, 653, 654, 661–665, *663*; of
    Italy, 653, *659*, 659–660
Union for the Liberation of the
    Working Class, 779
Union of Arras, 394
Union of Concerned Scientists: on
    environment, 948–949
Union of French Indochina, 747
Union of Kalmar, 377
Union of South Africa, 745
Union of Soviet Socialist Republics
    (USSR). *See* Soviet Union
Union of Utrecht, 394, 522
Unions. *See* Labor unions; Trade unions
United Arab Republic (UAR), 874

United Kingdom, 531. *See also* England (Britain)

United Nations, 857; on Crimea annexation, 925; Iraq War and, 937; Korean War and, 868–869

United Netherlands. *See* Dutch Republic

United Provinces. *See* Dutch Republic

United States: architecture in, 821; China and, 910–911; city dwellers in, 941; Civil War in, 671, 731, 762; Cold War and, 864–870; conferences on women, 940; creation of, 560–561, *563*; decolonization and, *876*; economy in, 799; financial decline in (2008), 934, 947; Great Depression in, *792*, 793, 796, 799; immigration to, 606–607, 698, 735; imperialism of, 748–749; industrialization of, 601, 603–604, 617, 689, 739–740; Japan and, 747, 824, 835; labor in, 603–604; Latin America and, 625; League of Nations and, 793; medicine in, 678–679; mobilization in World War II, 851–852; Nazi declaration of war on, 839; Nixon and, 908; Philippines and, 875; politics in, 933–934; Progressive Era in, 740–741; Reagan Revolution in, 908; resource consumption in, 949; slavery and, 415, 668, 670–671, *671*; society in (1960s), 885–886; Soviet differences with, 857–859; transportation in, 603, *604*; Versailles Treaty and, 789; voting rights in, 732, 755; War of 1812 and, 642; welfare state in, 799, 885; World War I and, 771, *771*, 783; in World War II, 851–852; after World War II, 884–886. *See also* Cold War; World War I; World War II; specific presidents and wars

Universal male suffrage: in France, 655, 656; in Prussia, 661

Universe: geocentric view of, 474–475, 496; heliocentric view of, *475*, 496; Kepler on, 477; mechanistic, 500; medieval conception of, *474*, 496; Scientific Revolution and, *474*, 474–484, *475*. *See also* Astronomy

Universities and colleges, 708; in 18th century, *503*, 517–518; *Burschenschaften* in, 628–629; student protests and, 897–899; women and, 708, *709*. *See also* Education; Students; specific schools

University of California: at Berkeley, *898*

Unskilled workers, 776

Upper Austria, 449

Upper Canada (Ontario), 671

Upper classes: in 18th century, 516–518, 520, 521, *545*; in late 1800s, 702; Renaissance artists and, *363*; women and, 702. *See also* Classes

Upper Italy, kingdom of, 659

Urban areas: in 18th century, 554–555, 564; in 19th century, 607–609, *608*; environment of, 941. *See also* Cities and towns; Ghettos

Urbanization, 698–700, 740

Ursulines, 387

Uruguay, 625

USSR. *See* Soviet Union

Utopia (More), 367

Utopian socialists, 632

Utrecht: Treaty (Peace) of (1713), 423, 446–447, 538

Uzbekistan, 922

Vacations, mass leisure and, *706*, 710, 819, 888

Vaccinations, 677

Valéry, Paul, 820

Valley of Mexico, 408. *See also* Mexico

Valois dynasty (France), 376–377, 390

Vanderbilt, Consuelo, 702

Van de Velde, Theodore, 820

Van Gogh, Theodoor, 940

Van Gogh, Vincent, 728, *729*

Vanity Fair... (Thackeray), 680

Vasa, Gustavus, 377

Vassy, Huguenot massacre at, 390–391, *391*

Vatican City, 805

Vendée revolt, *574*, *574*, 576–577

Venereal disease (VD), 693

Venetia, 621, 628, 640, 660, 664

Venezuela, 625

Venice: in 18th century, *517*, 538–539

Venturi, Robert, 915

Verdun, 438; battle at, 766

Vernacular languages: Bible in, 366, 367; Catholic Mass in, 892

Verona: congress at, 624

Versailles, 441, *653*, 654, 664; architecture and, *443*, 444, 513; Estates-General at, 566; Koons exhibit in, 944, *944*; lifestyle at, 444–445, 530, 552; Treaty of, 786–787, 789, 793, 830; women's march to, 568–569, *570*

Vesalius, Andreas, 485, *485*, 488

Vespucci, Amerigo, 406

Veterans: of World War I, 793

Viceroy, 410

Vichy France, 836

Victor Emmanuel II (Italy), 659, 660

Victor Emmanuel III (Italy), 803

Victoria (England), 600, *600*, 669, *669*, 688, 746, 747

Victorian England, 669–670, 705

Video: in art, 944–945; MTV and, 917

Vienna, 534, 666; Congress of, 620, *620*, 621–622, *622*, 628, 635, 650, 657; Hitler in, *831*; Jews in, 734; medical school at, 519; Ottomans and, 376–377, 449, 454, 455; population of, 554, 607; re-design of, 701; revolution of 1848 in, 640

Vierzehnheiligen, church of, *514*

Vietcong, 909

Vietminh, 869, 875

Vietnam, 416, 417, 835; division of, 875; Japan and, 848

Vietnam War: First, 869; Second, 897, 899, 908, 909–910; U.S. and, 908

Villages, 547, 551

Vindication of the Rights of Woman (Wollstonecraft), 510, 511

Violence: anarchists and, 697; antiforeign, in colonies, 749–750; fascism and, 802; revolutionary socialism and, 721–722; in Russia, 669. *See also* specific types and locations

Virchow, Rudolf, 700

Virgin Mary, 523

Vodka, 519

Vogt, Hannah, 883

Voilquin, Suzanne, 633

Volga River region, 537

Volkish thought, 724

Volkschulen (Austrian Empire), 520

Voltaire (François-Marie Arouet), 441, 503–506, *504*, 528, 533; on gender equality, 509; on writing of history, 516

Von Bora, Katherina, *370*, 374

Voting and voting rights: in England, 531, 627, 635–636, 670, *670*, 712; in France, 638, 641, 654; mass education and, 708; political liberalism and, 631; revolutions of 1848 and, 635–636, 638, 640, 641; in United States, 642, 732; women and, 712, 731–732, 775, 798, 889

Voyages of exploration, *404*, 406–407

Vulgate Bible: Erasmus and, 367

Wafd (Egyptian political party), 872

Wages, 797, 798; industrialization and, 614, 813; women *vs.* men, 615, 774; for workers, 612, 614, 669

Wagner, Richard, 683

Waiting for Godot (Beckett), 890

Wałęsa, Lech, 902, 925

Wallachia, 360, 454, 626, 656, 657, 658

Wallenstein, Albrecht von, 436, 437

Walnut Street Prison, Philadelphia, 645

Walsingham, Francis, 395

War, The (Dix), 820

War and Peace (Tolstoy), 725

War(s) and warfare: in 18th century, 539–543, 542–543, 544; over colonies, 540, 540–542; Dutch and, 543; ideological, 543; limited objectives in, 543; submarine, 771; trench warfare, 764, 764, 765–770, 769. *See also* specific battles, wars, and leaders

War communism, in Russia, 783, 812

War crimes: in World War II, 882

War for Independence. *See* American Revolution

War Guilt Clause, 786

Warhol, Andy, 890

"Warning to Humanity" (world scientists), 948–949

War of 1812, 642

War of the Austrian Succession, 534, 540, 541, 557

War of the Spanish Succession, 446, 446–447, 450

War of the Three Henries (France), 391

War on terrorism, 934; Bush, George W., and, 937

War Raw Materials Board, 772

Warsaw, 586; Soviets in, 843

Warsaw Pact, 867; Poland in, 879

Wars of Religion, 391, 391–392

Wartburg Castle: Luther at, 371

Washington, George, 560, 562, 563

Wastewater treatment, 700

Water: clean, 697, 700; damage to, 948

Water frame, 549, 595

Watergate scandal, 908

Waterloo, battle at, 589

Water pollution, 608

Watt, James, 595, 596

Watteau, Antoine, 513, 513

Watts: race riot in, 886

Wealth: Catholic Church and, 521; in England, 736; in late 1800s, 702; in U.S., 604, 740; World War I and, 776

Wealth gap: dangers of, 950

Wealth of Nations, The (Smith), 507

Weapons: in Austro-Prussian War, 663; Portuguese, 405; in Thirty Years' War, 438–439; in World War I, 766, 766, 768, 769. *See also* Atomic bomb; Nuclear weapons; specific weapons

Weapons of mass destruction, 937

Weather. *See* Climate

Weaving: in Industrial Revolution, 595–596

Web pages, 942

Wedgwood, Josiah, 549

Weill, Kurt, 822

Weimar Republic, 805, 806, 821, 822

Welfare state: in Canada, 886; creation of, 888; in Great Britain, 736, 882, 882–883; in Scandinavia, 799; in U.S., 799, 885, 908; women in, 888–889. *See also* Social welfare

Wellington, duke of, 589

Wesley, John, 523, 523–524

West, the. *See* Western world

West Africa, 423, 745, 770

West Bank (Jordan River), 875

West Berlin, 866, 866–867, 867, 869–870, 903. *See also* Berlin

Western Europe: democracy in, 712–713, 880–882; NATO in, 867; recession in 1973, 896; unity in, 884, 929–932. *See also* World War I; World War II; specific locations

Western Front, in World War I, 763–764, 764, 771

Westernization: of Russia, 450, 451, 452–453; of Turkey, 799–800

Western world: contemporary culture of, 941–945; Islam and, 937–938; women in, 939–940. *See also* Western Europe; specific locations

West Germany, 866–867, 904–905; Berlin Wall and, 903; denazification of, 882; in European Coal and Steel Community, 884; Green Party in, 914; political parties in, 882; refugees in, 940; reunification with East, 927, 929–930; teaching of Nazi past, 883; women in, 888. *See also* East Germany; specific leaders

West Indies, 421, 421, 422, 580–581

Westphalia, 586, 621; Peace of, 438, 447, 448, 456

West Prussia, 537

Wet nurses, 543–544

Wheat: price of, 690

Whewell, William, 601

Whigs (Britain), 461, 627, 670

White blacklash: in U.S., 886

White-collar workers, 692–693, 703, 886

White forces, in Russia, 782, 782, 783

White Man's Burden, The (Kipling), 743

"White man's burden," 742, 742, 743, 746

White Mountain, Battle of, 436

William I (Belgium), 621

William I (Germany), 654, 661–662, 664, 665

William II (Germany), 737, 738, 752, 758, 760, 773, 784; Bismarck and, 714, 715, 752; communications with Nicholas II, 761; submarine warfare and, 771

William III (Orange), 456, 462

William and Mary (England), 462–463

William of Nassau. *See* William of Orange (the Silent)

William of Orange. *See* William and Mary (England)

William of Orange (the Silent), 456

Wilson, Richard, 553

Wilson, Woodrow, 741, 793, 798; Fourteen Points of, 785; mandate system and, 788; at Paris Peace Conference, 785, 786, 788; speeches of, 786; on World War I, 772

Windischgrätz, Alfred, 640

Winds, knowledge of, 402–403

Winkelmann, Maria, 487–488

Winter Palace (Russia), 739

Witchcraft, 433–435, 520, 523

"With Germany's Unemployed" (Hauser), 797

Witte, Sergei, 738

Wittenberg, Luther in, 369, 372

Wolfe, James, 541

Wollstonecraft, Mary, 510, 511

Wolsey, Thomas (Cardinal), 380

Woman in Her Social and Domestic Character (Sanford), 704

Women: as artists, 465–466, 466; childbearing and, 545–546; Christianity and, 366; Dadaism and, 820; debates on nature of, 488; de Beauvoir and, 889, 890; Diderot on, 509; education and, 384–385, 632, 708, 709; in Enlightenment, 509–510, 517, 525; in factories, 592, 603, 612–613; feminism and, 900–901; as flappers, 818; in France, 558–569, 570, 571, 578–579, 585; in Great Depression, 797; Impressionist paintings by, 726; in India, 751; Italian, 640; Italian Fascists and, 804–805; in late 1800s, 703–708; literature and, 516; magazines for, 517; medical schools and, 678–679; middle class, 693, 707; Mill and Taylor on, 632;

missionary nunneries and, 425; in Nazi Germany, 810–811; "new woman" and, 734; Paris Commune and, 578–579, 712–713; politics and, 633; in postwar West, 889; property of, 731; prostitution and, 693, 694; Protestant, 384–385; in resistance, World War II, 845; role in society, 703–708; Rousseau on, 509, 511; in Russia, 451, 778, *778*, 780; salons and, 499, 510, *512*, 563, 586; in sciences, 486, *486*–488, 720; soccer and, *710*, 711; Soviet, 813, 850–851, 877; as teachers, 708, 731; UN conferences about, 940; utopian socialists and, 632–633; voting by, 712, 731–732, 775, 798; in welfare state, 888–889; in Western society, 939–940; witchcraft and, 433–435; as workers, 612–614, *613*, 692–693, *693*, 774–775, *775*; in workforce, 889; World War I and, 774–775, *775*; in World War II, *851*. *See also* Birth control; Gender and gender issues; Sex and sexuality; Women's rights; specific women and countries

Women's liberation movement, 633–634, 889, *901*, 921

Women's march, to Versailles, 568–569, *570*

Women's March in Petrograd, *778*

Women's movement, 939–940

Women's rights: in France, 568–569, 571; Mill on, 632; movements for, 633–634, 731–734; Wollstonecraft on, 510, 511

Women's Social and Political Union (England), 731

Women's suffrage movement, 731–732, *733*

Woolf, Virginia, 822–823

Wordsworth, William, 646

Workers: in 18th century, 554–555; children as, 546, 612–614, *613*; Christianity and, 724; education of, 708; in factories, 598–599, 611–614, 689; foreign, 950; in France (1968), 896–897; in French Revolution, 564; industrialization and, 598–600, 611–616, *613*, 673, 690–691; lifestyle of, 598–599, 607–609, *608*, 703, 819; Luddites and, 616; in Nazi Germany, 810–811, 845; skilled, *616*; unskilled, 604; women as, 603, 692–693, *693*, 774–775, *776*; after World War II,

886. *See also* Labor; Labor unions; Trade unions; Working classes

Worker's Union (Tristan), 633–634

Workforce: women in, 889, 939

Workhouses, 614, 636, 644

Working classes: applied sciences and, 644; in England, 735; factory conditions and, 592; families of, 546, 707–708; in France, 634–635, 656, 712–713, 737; housing of, 700; industrial, 611–616, 634–635, 673; lifestyle of, 819; Marx, Engels, and, 674, 675; organizing, 693–697; religion and, 725; in Russia, 738, 739, 778; urban, 607–609, *608*, 634–635, 703; women in, 693, 707–708, 778. *See also* Workers

Workplace, 612. *See also* Industrialization

Workshops: in France, 638, 639

Works Progress Administration, 799

World Bank, 945–947

World Cup, 819

World economy, 691–692. *See also* Global economy

World-machine: of Newton, 484, 505

World of Yesterday, The (Zweig), 763

World's Fair (Paris), 719, *719*

World Trade Center: terrorist attack on, 921, 936, *936*

World Trade Organization (WTO), 947

Worldview: scientific, 484

World War I, *757*, 757–758; in 1914–1915, 762–765; in 1916–1917, 765–770; in 1918, 783–784; airplanes in, 771–772; Balkan region and, 752–753; casualties in, 757, 765, 766, 771, 772, 776, 777, 784, 802; Eastern Front in, 764–765, *765*; enthusiasm for, *762*, 762–763; events leading to, 758–761; as global conflict, 770–771, *771*; home front in, 771, 772–776; international rivalry before, 758; mobilization in, 760, 772, 773; peace settlement after, 785–789; Russia and, 777–781; social impact of, 774–776, 793; socialism and, 695; submarine warfare in, 771; tanks in, 772; treaties for, 785–789; trench warfare in, 764, *764*, 765–770, *769*; United States in, 771, 783; Western Front in, 763–764, *764*, 771; woman suffrage after, 889. *See also* specific locations

World War II, 758, 799; aftermath of, 854–859; alliances in, 830; Allied

conferences in, 856–859; in Asia, 833–835, 838–839, *839*; bombings in, 853–854; casualties in, 856; costs of, 856; course of, 835–843; in Europe, 830–833, *837*; events leading to, 830–833; Hitler and prelude to, 828–833; Hitler's declaration of, *834*; home front in, 850–854; Japanese Americans in, 852; last years of, 842–843; mobilization in, 850–853; North Africa in, *837*, 840; opening of, 833; in Pacific, *839*; Soviet Union in, 850–851; tanks in, 772; technology in and after, 856; territorial changes after, *858*; turning point of, 839–842; United States in, 838, 851–852; women in, 850–851, *851*; women after, 889

Worms: Diet of, 371, 372

Wretched of the Earth, The (Fanon), 874

Wright, Frances, 632

Wright, Frank Lloyd, 821

Wright, Wilbur and Orville, 687–688

Wrought iron, 596

Würzburg, 435, 513

Wyclif, John, 361

Xavier, Francis (Saint), 389, 420

Xhosa peoples, 745

Xi Jinping: greenhouse gas emissions and, 950

Ximenes, Cardinal (Spain), 358, 369

Yalta conference, 857, *857*

Yellow press, 709

Yeltsin, Boris, 920, 922, 923, 924

Yorktown, battle at, 560

Young Fascists (Italy), 804

Young Italy movement, 641, 660

Young people, 710; in Fascist Italy, 804; Nazis and, 807, 810

Young Victoria, The (movie), 669

Youth culture: in 1960s, 898. *See also* Student(s)

Ypres, battle at, 766

Yucatán peninsula, 407

Yugoslavia, 785, 787, 815; breakup of, *936*; communism in, 879; disintegration of, 927–929; Nazi attack on, *837*; resistance movement in, 845; royal dictatorship in, 815

Zaire, independence of, 872

Zaire (Congo) River, 403

Zanzibar. *See* Tanganyika

Zara, 946

Zasulich, Vera, 669
Zell, Katherine, 385
Zemsky Sobor (national assembly), 450
Zemstvos (assemblies), 667–668, 716, 739
Zeppelin airship, 687, 772
Zhenotdel (women's bureau), 780

Zinzendorf, Nikolaus von (Count), 523
Zionism, 735, *735*, 736; Palestine and, 873
Zlata's Diary: A Child's Life in Sarajevo, 929
Zola, Émile, 703, 725
Zollverein (customs union), 661

Zones of occupation. *See* Occupation
Zulu peoples, 745
Zürich, Protestants in, 378
Zweig, Stefan, 763
Zwickau, 384–385
Zwingli, Ulrich, 366, 377–379
Zyklon B (hydrogen cyanide), 847